Adolescence

TENTH EDITION

John W. Santrock
University of Texas at Dallas

Boston   Burr Ridge, IL   Dubuque, IA   Madison, WI   New York   San Francisco   St. Louis
Bangkok   Bogotá   Caracas   Kuala Lumpur   Lisbon   London   Madrid   Mexico City
Milan   Montreal   New Delhi   Santiago   Seoul   Singapore   Sydney   Taipei   Toronto

The McGraw-Hill Companies

Higher Education

ADOLESCENCE, TENTH EDITION

Published by McGraw-Hill, a business unit of The McGraw-Hill Companies, Inc., 1221 Avenue of the Americas, New York, NY, 10020. Copyright © 2005, 2003, 2001, 1998 by The McGraw-Hill Companies, Inc. All rights reserved. No part of this publication may be reproduced or distributed in any form or by any means, or stored in a database or retrieval system, without the prior written consent of The McGraw-Hill Companies, Inc., including, but not limited to, in any network or other electronic storage or transmission, or broadcast for distance learning.

Some ancillaries, including electronic and print components, may not be available to customers outside the United States.

This book is printed on acid-free paper.

1 2 3 4 5 6 7 8 9 0 QPD/QPD 0 9 8 7 6 5 4

ISBN 0–07–290015–6

Publisher: *Stephen Rutter*
Director of development: *Judith Kromm*
Senior developmental editor: *Elsa Peterson*
Marketing manager: *Melissa S. Caughlin*
Media technology producer: *Ginger Bunn*
Project manager: *Rick Hecker*
Production supervisor: *Carol Bielski*
Designer: *Cassandra J. Chu*
Lead supplement producer: *Marc Mattson*
Photo research coordinator: *Alexandra Ambrose*
Art manager: *Robin K. Mouat*
Photo researcher: *LouAnn Wilson*
Permissions editor: *Marty Granahan*
Cover design: *Bill Stanton*
Interior design: *Kay Fulton*
Typeface: *9.5/12 Meridian*
Compositor: *GAC Indianapolis*
Printer: *Quebecor World Dubuque Inc.*

The credit section for this book begins on page C-1 and is considered an extension of the copyright page.

Library of Congress Cataloging-in-Publication Data

Santrock, John W.
    Adolescence / John W. Santrock.— 10th ed.
      p. cm.
    Includes bibliographical references and index.
    ISBN 0-07-290015-6 (alk. paper)
    1. Adolescence. 2. Adolescent psychology. I. Title.
HQ796.S26 2005
305.235—dc22

                                                            200306603

The Internet addresses listed in the text were accurate at the time of publication. The inclusion of a website does not indicate an endorsement by the authors or McGraw-Hill, and McGraw-Hill does not guarantee the accuracy of the information presented at these sites.

www.mhhe.com

To Tracy and Jennifer, who, as they have matured, have helped me appreciate the marvels of adolescent development

About the Author

John W. Santrock

received his Ph.D. from the University of Minnesota in 1973. He taught at the University of Charleston and the University of Georgia before joining the psychology department at the University of Texas at Dallas. He has been a member of the editorial boards of *Developmental Psychology* and *Child Development.* His research on father custody is widely cited and used in expert witness testimony to promote flexibility and alternative considerations in custody disputes. John has also authored these exceptional McGraw-Hill texts: *Child Development,* Tenth Edition, *Life-Span Development,* Ninth Edition, *Children,* Eighth Edition, *Psychology,* Seventh Edition, and *Educational Psychology,* Second Edition.

John Santrock has been teaching an undergraduate course on adolescent development every year since 1981 and continues to teach this course and a range of other undergraduate courses at the University of Texas at Dallas.

Brief Contents

Contents

SECTION 2 Biological and Cognitive Development 79

SECTION 4 ## The Contexts of Adolescent Development 305

CHAPTER 10

Peers 349

CHAPTER 11

Schools 385

CHAPTER 12

Achievement, Work, and Careers 427

Preface

More undergraduate students in the world continue to learn about the field of adolescent development from this text than from any other. The 10th edition appears some 23 years after the first edition, signaling its status in development as an emerging adult. As with human development, there have been major changes and transitions across these 10 editions. Through these many changes, though, a basic core of topics and content continues to serve as the foundation for our study of adolescent development.

MAIN CHANGES IN THE 10TH EDITION

The main changes in the 10th edition involve: (1) a reorganization of the sequence of main sections and chapters, (2) an extensive updating of research, and (3) a revised and improved learning system.

Reorganization of the Sequence of Main Sections and Chapters

A number of adopters and reviewers recommended that I change the sequencing of main sections and chapters in the book. Thus, in the new 10th edition, the "Social, Emotional, and Personality Development" section now precedes "The Contexts of Adolescent Development" section. In the previous edition these main sections were reversed. The chapter "Achievement, Work, and Careers" also was moved to the "Contexts of Adolescent Development" section and now follows Chapter 11, "Schools." The chapter "Culture" now follows "Achievement, Work, and Careers" as the last chapter in "The Contexts of Adolescent Development" section.

Why make these sequence changes in main sections and chapters? With the new organization, main sections 2 and 3 now focus on individual development while section 4 emphasizes the contexts of development. Also, following the section on biological and cognitive development with the section on social, emotional, and personality development makes sense because the latter section is conceptually rooted in cognitive development. In addition, much of the material on achievement, work, and careers involves the contexts of adolescent development. Lastly, placing the "Schools" chapter just before the "Achievement, Work, and Careers" chapter provides a better connection between the material on schools and achievement.

Extensive Research Updating

Above all else, the field of adolescent development is based on a solid foundation of research. We are fortunate that more and more researchers are studying adolescent development and this is leading to a better understanding of how adolescents develop.

Contemporary Research As an indication of the breadth of updating in the 10th edition of this book, it includes more than 800 twenty-first-century citations, many of which are from 2002 and 2003. You will find substantial research updating in each of the 14 chapters of Adolescence, 10th edition.

Expanded Research Emphasis Among the main topics given greater emphasis in the 10th edition are: Culture, college and emerging adulthood, and health and well-being.

Culture Beginning with the first edition of *Adolescence*, culture has been an important theme in this book. *Adolescence*, 10th edition, has an entire chapter (chapter 13) devoted to culture; other discussions of culture are also embedded in every chapter. We especially expanded and updated the research on cross-cultural comparisons of adolescents. Here are some of the locations where the updated and expanded discussions of culture can be found:

Chapter 1: Introduction
- Major new section: "The Global Perspective," which describes cross-cultural comparisons (Brown & Larson, 2002)
- New material on cultural variations in adolescent health and well-being (World Health Organization, 2002)
- New discussion of culture and gender, and cross-cultural variations in families and peers (Booth, 2002)
- Inclusion of recent data on the increase in Latino and Asian American adolescents and projections through 2100, including new figures 1.1 and 1.2 (U.S. Bureau of the Census, 2002)

Chapter 2: The Science of Adolescent Development
- New photographs that dramatically illustrate how the outcome of a research study might be very different if the participants are all non-Latino White males or male and female adolescents from diverse ethnic backgrounds

Chapter 5: The Self, Identity, Emotions, and Personality
- Much expanded, updated coverage of immigration and ethnic identity development (Phinney, 2003)

Chapter 6: Gender
- Updated and expanded material on gender and culture, including a UNICEF (2000) analysis of gender and education in different regions of the world
- New discussion of areas of the world where gender equity is beginning to appear (Brown & Larson, 2002)

Chapter 8: Moral Development, Values, and Religion
- New description of research on prosocial and caring behavior of adolescents living in an impoverished inner-city area

Chapter 9: Families
- Expanded, updated coverage of cross-cultural comparisons of families (Booth, 2002; Brown & Larson, 2002)
- New discussion of family duty and obligation in different ethnic groups (Fulgini & Pedersen, 2002)

Chapter 10: Peers
- Much expanded discussion of peers and culture (Nsame-nang, 2002; Welti, 2002)
- New section on gender, culture, and romantic relationships

Chapter 11: Schools
- New comparisons of the United States with other countries on the transition from school to work (Kerckhoff, 2002)
- New section on culture and schooling, including recent cross-cultural comparisons (Brown & Larson, 2002)

Chapter 12: Achievement, Work, and Careers
- New discussion of recent cross-cultural comparisons of the science and math literacy of 14- and 15-year olds, including new figure 12.4.
- New figure 12.5 to illustrate Harold Stevenson's research on the reasons Asian and American parents give for the children's level of math achievement
- New section: "Work Profiles of Adolescents Around the World"

Chapter 13: Culture
- New section on how adolescents around the world spend their time, including new figure 13.1 (Larson, 2001)
- New section on immigration and recent research on the degree of acculturation and adolescent problems (Gonzales & others, in press)
- Updated and revised discussion of socioeconomic differences in parenting (Hoff, Laursen, & Tardif, 2002)
- Expanded, updated coverage of technology and sociocultural diversity, including new figure 13.8 on daily computer use by adolescents from three different socioeconomic groups (Roberts & others, 1999)

Chapter 14: Adolescent Problems
- New discussion of ethnic variations in being overweight in youth, including new figure 14.13 (National Center for Health Statistics, 2002)
- Added recent cross-cultural comparisons in being overweight in adolescence (Wang & others, 2002)

College and Emerging Adulthood There is increased interest in the developmental transition from adolescence to adulthood, as evidenced by reviewers who requested more information about this transition. This book has always included considerable information on the transition from childhood to adolescence, and in the 9th edition more emphasis was given to emerging adulthood.

In the 10th edition, the discussion of changes during the college years and emerging adulthood has been expanded further. The increased coverage of college and emerging adulthood includes:

Chapter 1: Introduction
- Expanded discussion of emerging adulthood, including new figure 1.5 on data pertaining to self-perceptions of adult status

Chapter 5: The Self, Identity, Emotions, and Personality
- New discussion of research on developmental changes in identity in emerging and early adulthood (Pukkinen & Kokko, 2000)
- New longitudinal research study on stability and change in personality from age 18 to age 26 (Roberts, Caspi, & Moffitt, 2001)
- New coverage of temperament in childhood, personality in adulthood, and intervening contexts, including new figure 5.7

Chapter 9: Families
- New research in figure 9.7 on changes in attitudes regarding respect for family from adolescence into emerging adulthood for individuals from different ethnic groups (Fulgini & Pedersen, 2002)

Chapter 11: Schools
- New coverage of the transition from college to work (Mortimer & Larson, 2002)
- New discussion of cross-cultural comparisons of colleges (U.S. Department of Education, 1999; Welti, 2002)

Chapter 12: Achievement, Work, and Careers
- New section: "Working While Going to College," including new figure 12.8 on the link between the number of hours worked during college and grades
- New section on work/career-based learning in college

Chapter 14: Adolescent Problems
- Inclusion of recent research on drinking patterns in college students (Wechsler & others, 2002), including new figure 14.5 on binge drinking from adolescence into early adulthood

Health and Well-Being The health and well-being of adolescents continues to be a major concern, and research in areas related to this topic has expanded considerably in recent years. Here are some of the areas where there is substantial research updating related to the health and well-being of adolescents in the 10th edition:

Chapter 3: Puberty, Health, and Biological Foundations
- New material on the decline in physical activity in African American and non-Latino White girls (Marcell & others, 2002)
- New discussion of neurotransmitter changes in adolescence and possible links to increased risk-taking behavior (Spear, 2002)
- Updated coverage of the causes of death in adolescence, including new figure 3.13
- New discussion of stress and resilience from an evolutionary perspective

Chapter 4: Cognitive Development
- New coverage of recent intervention study to improve the practical intelligence of adolescents toward school through better metacognitive skills (Williams & others, 2002)

Chapter 5: The Self, Identity, Emotions, and Personality
- New discussion of emotional competence emphasizing Carolyn Saarni's (1999) ideas

Chapter 6: Gender
- New material on the problems of adolescent boys in school (DeZolt & Hull, 2001)
- New coverage of William Pollack's (1999) view of the national crisis for boys involving their inability to reveal their emotions and other problems

Chapter 7: Sexuality
- Updated and revised material on suicide in gay and lesbian adolescents (Savin-Williams, 2001)
- Updated coverage of AIDS
- New discussion of genital warts
- Much expanded coverage of date, or acquaintance, rape, including Fisher, Cullen, and Turner's research on the sexual victimization of college women; new figure 7.8 shows completed and attempted rape of college women according to victim-offender relationship

Chapter 9: Families
- New research in figure 9.6 on divorce and children's emotional problems (Hetherington & Kelly, 2002)

Chapter 11: Schools
- Updated, recent data on school dropouts, including new figure 11.3
- Expanded, updated coverage of bullying, including new figure 11.5 (Nansel & others, 2001)

Chapter 13: Culture
- Updated, expanded discussion of why parents need to be concerned if their adolescents' Internet use is not monitored

Chapter 14: Adolescent Problems
- Extensive updating of adolescent drug use based on recent national research (Johnston, O'Malley, & Bachman, 2003)
- Substantial updating of cigarette smoking by youth
- Updating of adolescent use of ecstasy and other drugs
- Recent research from the Pittsburgh Youth Study on developmental pathways to delinquency (Stoutheimer-Loeber & others, 2002)
- Added new predictors/antecedents of delinquency
- Updated coverage of suicide in adolescence
- New discussion of *Fast Track*, a program that seeks to prevent adolescent problems and its research evaluation
- New coverage of findings of the National Longitudinal Study on Adolescent Health (Resnick & others, 2001) that shows which factors are most likely to protect adolescents from developing problems

Substantial Increase in Research Figures Reviewers recommended that I include more graphs to show how researchers visually present their data. I took this recommendation to heart. There are more than 50 new figures of research data in *Adolescence*, 10th edition. Special care was taken to ensure that these illustrations are designed clearly so that students can interpret and understand them.

Expert Consultants Adolescence has become such an enormous, complex field that no single author can possibly be an ex-

pert in all its areas. Recognizing this challenge, I have sought the input of some of the world's leading experts in different areas of adolescent development. These experts provided me with detailed recommendations on new research to include in every chapter. The expert consultants for the 10th edition of *Adolescence* were the following:

Elizabeth Susman	*Pennsylvania State U.*	Chapter 3: Puberty, Health, and Biological Foundations
Daniel Keating	*U. of Toronto*	Chapter 4: Cognitive Development
Catherine Cooper	*U. of California–Santa Cruz*	Chapter 5: The Self, Identity, Emotions, and Personality
Jerome Dusek	*Syracuse University*	Chapter 5: The Self, Identity, Emotions, and Personality
Nancy Galambos	*U. of Alberta*	Chapter 6: Gender, and Gender throughout the book
Shirley Feldman	*Stanford University*	Chapter 7: Sexuality
Constance Flanagan	*Pennsylvania State U.*	Chapter 8: Moral Development
Christy Buchanan	*Wake Forest University*	Chapter 9: Families
Duane Buhrmester	*U. of Texas at Dallas*	Chapter 10: Peers
Brett Laursen	*Florida Atlantic U.*	Chapter 10: Peers
Kathryn Wentzel	*U. of Maryland*	Chapter 11: Schools
Allan Wigfield	*U. of Maryland*	Chapter 12: Achievement, Work, and Careers
Fred Vondracek	*Pennsylvania State U.*	Chapter 12: Achievement, Work, and Careers
Reed Larson	*U. of Illinois Urbana–Champaign*	Chapter 13: Culture
Peter Benson	*Search Institute*	Chapter 14: Adolescent Problems

Their photographs and biographies appear on pages xxx thru xxiv of the preface.

Revised and Improved Learning System

I strongly believe that students should be not only challenged to study hard and think more deeply and productively about adolescent development but also provided with an effective learning system. Instructors and students alike continue to comment about how student-friendly this text is. However, I strive to keep making the learning system better, and I am truly excited about the improvements for this edition.

Now more than ever, students struggle to find the main ideas in their courses, especially in courses like adolescence, which includes so much material. The new learning headings and learning system centers on learning goals that, together with the main text headings, keep the key ideas in front of the reader from the beginning to the end of a chapter. Each chapter has no more than six main headings and corresponding learning goals, which are presented side by side on the chapter-opening spread. At the end of each main section of a chapter, the learning goal is repeated in a new feature called "Review and Reflect," which prompts students to review the key topics in the section and poses a question to encourage them to think critically about what they have read. At the end of the chapter, "Reach Your Learning Goals" guides students through a bulleted chapter review.

In addition to the verbal tools just described, maps that link up with the learning goals are presented at the beginning of each major section in the chapter. At the end of each chapter, the section maps are assembled into a complete map of the chapter that provides a visual review guide. The complete learning system, which includes many more features than are mentioned here, is presented later in the preface section titled "To the Student."

As important as it is to provide students with an effective learning system, it is imperative to present them with theories and research at a level they can understand and that motivates them to learn. In each edition of the book, I have carefully rewritten much of the material to make sure it strikes the right balance between challenging students and being accessible. I also continually seek better examples of concepts and material that will interest students.

BALANCE OF RESEARCH AND APPLICATIONS

While the 10th edition of *Adolescence* has a strong research emphasis, the book also continues to include substantial material on the application of information to the real lives of adolescents with the goal of improving their opportunities for success in negotiating the path from childhood to adulthood. As in past editions, these applications have been integrated within each chapter.

In addition to applications content woven throughout the book, each chapter includes one or more "Careers in Adolescent Development" inserts that profile a number of actual people in a wide variety of careers in adolescent development. The career profiles provide information about the person's education, the nature of his/her work, and a photograph of the individual at work. Further information on careers is found in the "Careers in Adolescent Development" appendix following chapter 1. Here students can read about the nature of careers in these areas of adolescent development: education/research; clinical/counseling/medical; and families/relationships.

A new applications addition to the text's Online Learning Center (OLC) is "Self-Assessment," which consists of one or more interactive exercises for each chapter giving students an opportunity to evaluate themselves on topics related to the chapter's contents. For example, chapter 5, "The Self, Identity, Emotions, and Personality" has four self-assessments: (1) My Self-Esteem, (2) Exploring My Identity, (3) Loneliness, and (4) Am I Extraverted or Introverted?

Other new applications additions to the text's OLC are the health and well-being, parenting, and education scenarios, which help students to practice their decision-making skills in various areas of adolescent development.

CONTENT CHANGES IN INDIVIDUAL CHAPTERS

As mentioned earlier, substantial changes and updating of content occurred in every chapter of the book. Here are some of the main content changes in each chapter.

CHAPTER 1
Introduction

- Major new section, "The Global Perspective," focusing on cross-cultural comparisons of adolescents around the world (Brown & Larson, 2002)
- New material on cultural variations in adolescent health and well-being (Call & others, 2002; World Health Organization, 2002)
- New discussion of culture and gender, and cross-cultural variations in families and peers (Booth, 2002; Brown & Larson, 2002; Larson & others, 2002)
- Inclusion of recent data on the increase in Latino and Asian American adolescents and projections of the percentage and number of adolescents from different ethnic groups through 2100 (U.S. Census Bureau, 2002). Includes new figures 1.1 and 1.2.
- Expanded, updated coverage of emerging adulthood, including new figure 1.5 on data pertaining to self-perceptions of adult status
- New section, "History Matters," in the discussion of "What Matters in Understanding Adolescence"
- Addition of material on pubertal changes in the section "Biological Processes Matter" (Archibald, Graber, & Brooks-Gunn, 2003; Susman, Dorn, & Schiefelbein, 2003)

CHAPTER 2
The Science of Adolescent Development

- Substantially revised presentation of Vygotsky's theory for improved student understanding
- Extensive reworking of section on research methods
- Reorganization of main section on types of research into descriptive, correlational, and experimental
- New example of naturalistic observation research involving parents' explanatory talk at a science museum to sons and daughters (Tannenbaum & others, 2001), including new research in figure 2.8
- New section on the experience sampling method (ESM) and new figure 2.9 on data collected using the ESM that focuses on differences in the emotional extremes of adolescents and their parents
- Fascinating new example of a case study involving Michael Rehbein and the removal of his brain's left hemisphere; includes new figure 2.10 of brain scans showing the reorganization of his right hemisphere to illustrate the brain's plasticity in adolescence
- New figure 2.13 that compares the cross-sectional and longitudinal research designs
- Expanded and updated coverage of ethics
- New photographs to dramatically emphasize how the outcomes of a research study might be different if all of the adolescent participants were non-Latino White males compared with adolescent males and females from diverse ethnic backgrounds

CHAPTER 3
Puberty, Health, and Biological Foundations

- Updating of section on puberty (Susman & Rogol, 2004)
- Inclusion of experimental research on the effects of testosterone and estrogen on adolescent development (Finkelstein & others, 1997; Liben & others, 2002; Susman & others, 1998)
- Expanded, updated coverage of the brain's development in adolescence (Walker, 2002)
- New discussion of neurotransmitter changes involving an increase in dopamine and its link to risk-taking behavior in adolescence (Spear, 2002)
- New section on environmental experience and the brain's plasticity with discussions of deprived and enriched environments, whether new brain cells can be generated in adolescence, and whether an adolescent's brain can recover from injury (Anderton, 2002; Nottebohm, 2002; Slomine & others, 2002)

- New section on the development of the brain and education
- New material on the decline in physical activity in African American and non-Latino White girls during adolescence (Marcell & others, 2002)
- Updated coverage of the causes of death in adolescence, including new figure 3.14 on recent statistics (National Center for Health Statistics, 2003)
- New main section on evolution, heredity, and environment
- New discussion of developmental evolutionary psychology, an increasingly popular view (Bjorklund & Pellegrini, 2002)
- New figure 3.14 on the brain sizes of various primates and humans in relation to the length of the juvenile period
- New discussion of stress and resilience in adolescence from an evolutionary perspective
- New sections on heredity and heredity-environment interaction
- New section on the epigenetic model, including new figure 3.18 (Gottlieb, 2002)

CHAPTER 4
Cognitive Development

- Addition of sociocultural contexts to figure 4.5 on comparison of Piaget's and Vygotsky's theories
- Updated, expanded coverage of adult changes in cognition and whether there is a postformal stage (Commons & Richards, 2003; Sinnott, 2003)
- New figure 4.6 showing developmental changes in memory span
- New figure 4.8 illustrating Baddeley's working memory model
- New description of research study showing a link between working memory and children's and adolescents' reading comprehension, including new research in figure 4.9
- Expanded coverage of decision making to include links to personality traits and more information about the kinds of changes in decision making that take place in adolescence (Klaczynski, Byrnes, & Jacobs, 2001)
- Reorganization of material on the psychometric/intelligence view. The information about intelligence testing is now grouped together under the heading "Intelligence Tests" (with subheadings of "The Binet Test," "The Wechsler Scales," "Ethnicity and Culture," and "The Use and Misuse of Intelligence Tests").
- New coverage of recent intervention study by Williams, Blythe, Li, Gardner, & Sternberg (2002) to help students improve their practical intelligence about school through better metacognitive skills
- New figure 4.14 that compares Sternberg's, Gardner's, and Salovey/Mayer/Goleman's views

- New section, "Do Adolescents Have a General Intelligence?," that includes information about the ability of general intelligence to predict job success and John Carroll's research
- New coverage of the concept of heritability
- New discussion of gender and intelligence
- New coverage of the concept of stereotype threat and performance on intelligence tests

CHAPTER 5
The Self, Identity, Emotions, and Personality

- New location for chapter, now following cognitive development chapter; in the previous edition, this chapter followed the chapter on culture and was much later in the book
- New chapter title. Title in previous edition was "The Self and Identity." In this new edition, new main sections on emotion and personality have been added so the new chapter title that reflects these new topics is "The Self, Identity, Emotions, and Personality."
- New section, "Does Self-Esteem Change During Adolescence?," including new research in figure 5.2 showing data from a recent life-span study of changes in self-esteem (Robins & others, 2002)
- New figure 5.3 showing correlations between domains of competence and global self-esteem in adolescents from the United States and other countries (Harter, 1999)
- New subsection, "Social Contexts of Self-Esteem," including new material on self-esteem and transitions in schooling
- New discussion of research on developmental changes in identity after adolescence, including refining and enhancing identity choices well into early adulthood, and increased identity commitment from 27 to 36 years of age (Pukkinen & Kokko, 2000)
- Much expanded, updated coverage of immigration and ethnic identity development, including Jean Phinney's (2003) latest ideas
- New main section on emotional development
- New discussion of the emotions of adolescence, including very recent views of developmental changes (Rosenblum & Lewis, 2003)
- New section on hormones, experience, and emotions
- New section on emotional competence with an emphasis on Carolyn Saarni's (1999) views
- Main new section on personality development, including connection of personality to the three main topics discussed so far in the chapter: the self, identity, and emotions
- New section on personality traits with the main focus on the "big five" personality traits, including new figure 5.6
- Discussion of longitudinal study on stability and change in personality from age 18 through 26 (Roberts, Caspi, & Moffitt, 2001)

- New section on temperament with discussions of temperament categories and the roles of development and contexts in understanding temperament; new figure 5.7 on temperament in childhood, personality in adulthood, and intervening contexts (Wachs, 2000)
- New discussion of recently completed longitudinal study of temperament from infancy through adolescence (Guerin & others, 2003)

CHAPTER 6
Gender

- New chapter opening "Images of Adolescent Development: The Changing Gender Worlds of Adolescents." Quotes from two adolescents reveal the confusion many adolescents have regarding what is appropriate gender behavior (Pollack, 1998; Zager & Rubenstein, 2002).
- Completely revised and updated coverage of school and teacher influences with increased material on the problems male adolescents have in school (DeZolt & Hull, 2001)
- Expanded, updated material on gender and the brain (Halpern, 2001; Swaab & others, 2001)
- New coverage of gender and relational aggression (Crick & others, 2002; Underwood, 2002)
- Updated and expanded coverage of gender and culture, including a UNICEF (2000) analysis of gender and education in different regions of the world
- New discussion of areas of the world where evidence of gender equity is beginning to appear (Brown & Larson, 2002)
- New figure 6.4 showing the four different classification categories of gender roles
- New discussion of William Pollack's (1999) view of the national crisis for boys involving their inability to reveal their emotions and other problems
- Updated research on gender and the media, including recent research on body image (Anderson & others, 2001; Polce-Lynch & others, 2001)
- New section on sibling influences on gender

CHAPTER 7
Sexuality

- New quotes from adolescents added in "Images of Adolescent Development" to better reflect the chapter's themes
- Expanded description of the link between gender and sexuality (Peplau, 2002)
- New section on developmental pathways in gay and lesbian youth (Diamond, 2003)

- Updated, revised, and expanded discussion of suicide in gay and lesbian adolescents with revised conclusions about the incidence of suicide in these adolescents because of methodological flaws in many studies (Savin Williams, 2001)
- Inclusion of recent research on condom availability in high schools and its link with sexual activity (Blake & others, 2003)
- Extensively expanded coverage of cross-cultural comparisons of adolescent pregnancy, including new research in figure 7.5. New emphasis is given to four main reasons for the high adolescent pregnancy rate in the United States (Alan Guttmacher Institute, 2002).
- New figure 7.6 on births to married and unmarried 15- to 19-year-old girls from 1950 through 2000 (National Vital Statistics Report, 2001)
- New longitudinal data on the lower achievement of children born to adolescent mothers compared with adult mothers (Hofferth & Reid, 2002)
- New section on abortion in adolescence, including recent research and issues (Adler, Ozer, & Tschann, 2003)
- New label, "sexually transmitted infections (STI)," used as a replacement for "sexually transmitted diseases (STD)" in keeping with the new use of the term in the field of human sexuality (Alan Guttmacher Institute, 2002)
- Updated coverage of AIDS and movement of AIDS discussion to the beginning of the section on sexually transmitted infections
- New discussion of genital warts
- Much expanded coverage of date, or acquaintance, rape including discussion of Fisher, Cullen, & Turner's (2000) research on the sexual victimization of college women. New figure 7.8 shows completed and attempted rape of college women according to victim-offender relationship.

CHAPTER 8
Moral Development, Values, and Religion

- Reorganization of chapter with first main heading now being "Domains of Moral Development" and second main heading, "Contexts of Moral Development"
- New figure 8.2 showing examples of responses to Kohlberg's Heinz and the Druggist story at each of Kohlberg's stages
- New figure 8.3 showing research data from longitudinal study of Kohlberg's theory
- New discussion of Bandura's (2002) recent social cognitive views on moral development, including new material on how social cognitive theory explains terrorists' moral justifications of their actions
- Substantial revision of material on gender and the care perspective that includes a meta-analysis (Hyde & Jaffee, 2000) and important new research on gender-role classification

and moral reasoning (Eisenberg, Zhou, & Koller, 2001; Skoe & others, 2002)
- Detailed discussion of research by Eisenberg & others (1999) on the continuity between positive moral acts in childhood and emerging adulthood
- New coverage of gender differences in prosocial behavior and volunteering (Eisenberg & Morris, 2004)
- New description of research on prosocial and caring behavior in adolescents who live in a highly impoverished inner-city area
- Recent research on the link between maternal warmth, children's empathy, and the mother's positive expression of emotions (Zhou & others, 2002)
- Updated coverage of national study of college freshman attitudes and values (Sax & others, 2002)
- Discussion of new research on the link between adolescents' involvement in school and community groups and higher levels of social trust and altruism (Flanagan & Faison, 2001)
- Discussion of recent research on adolescent values (Steen, Kachorek, & Peterson, 2003)
- Reorganization of section on religion and adolescents, including new material on parenting/attachment and religious interest in adolescents (Ream & Savin-Williams, 2003)
- New section on the positive role of religion in adolescents' lives

CHAPTER 9
Families

- New section title, "Reciprocal Socialization and the Family as a System, with new discussion of the link between marital relationships and parenting (Grych, 2002) and new figure 9.1 on direct and indirect parenting effects
- New research in figure 9.2 on the link between pubertal change and parenting
- Expanded, updated coverage of the importance of viewing competent parents as managers (Mortimer & Larson, 2002; Youniss & Ruth, 2002)
- New discussion of why authoritative parenting is the most effective parenting style with adolescents (Steinberg & Silk, 2002)
- Evaluating whether authoritative parenting is the most effective parenting style across different ethnic groups, social strata, and diverse family households (Steinberg & Silk, 2002)
- New coverage of recent study on adolescent sibling relationships (Tucker, McHale, & Crouter, 2003)
- New coverage of coparenting (McHale & others, 2002)
- New material on historical changes in the U.S. divorce rate and a comparison of the U.S. divorce rate with Japan's

divorce rate (Ministry of Health, Education, and Welfare, 2002)

- New research in figure 9.6: Divorce and Children's Emotional Problems based on Hetherington and Kelly's (2002) analysis
- Recent research added on relocation and divorce (Braver, Ellman, & Frabicus, 2003)
- Recent review of custody research described (Bauserman, 2003)
- New section on gay and lesbian parenting, including new coverage of the diversity in lesbian mothers, gay fathers, and their adolescents, as well as the effects on adolescents of having lesbian mothers and gay fathers (Patterson, 2002)
- Expanded, updated coverage of cross-cultural comparisons of families (Booth, 2002; Brown & Larson, 2002)
- New discussion of family duty and obligation in different ethnic groups and material from a recent research study, including new research in figure 9.7 on changes in attitudes regarding respect for family from adolescence into emerging adulthood for individuals from different ethnic groups (Fulgini & Pedersen, 2002)

CHAPTER 10
Peers

- New research in figure 10.1 on developmental changes in conformity to peers
- Updated, improved, revised coverage of parent and peer relationships in adolescence, including Smetana's (2003) recent views
- Updated and expanded coverage of social skills training in adolescence
- New research in figure 10.2 on developmental changes in self-disclosing conversations
- New section on the peer group, gender, and culture
- New material on gender differences in group size and interaction in same-sex groups in adolescence (Maccoby, 2002)
- New discussion of the importance of a friend's character in the section on friendship
- Much expanded coverage of the peer group and culture (Booth, 2002; Brown & Larson, 2002; Nsamenang, 2002; Weiti, 2002)
- New section on romantic relationships in sexual minority youth (Diamond, 2003; Diamond & Savin-Williams, 2003)
- New section on gender, culture, and romantic relationships

CHAPTER 11
Schools

- New location for this chapter now allows the material on schools to come just before the chapter on "Achievement,

Work, and Careers," which allows for a better connection of the material on schools and achievement

- Reorganization of section on approaches to education with deletion of two topics: cross-cultural comparisons and changing social developmental contexts; those topics have been moved to later in the chapter where the culture and schooling and the social contexts of schooling discussions have been expanded
- Updating of education of adolescents with material from *Turning Points 2000*
- Inclusion of recent research on extracurricular activities and school success (Valentine & others, 2002)
- New section on the American high school and recommendations for changes in U.S. high schools in the twenty-first century (National Commission on the High School Senior Year, 2001)
- Updated, recent data on school dropouts, including new figure 11.3 on trends in dropout rates from 1972 through 2000 for different ethnic groups
- Updated coverage of the transition from school to work and comparison of the U.S. with other countries in this aspect of development (Kerckhoff, 2002)
- New section "Transition from College to Work," that highlights the benefits of a college education and the difficulties in the transition from college to work (Mortimer & Larson, 2002)
- New main section titled "The Social Contexts of Schools"
- New section on peers and schooling that includes the link between the structure of middle schools and peer experiences (Wentzel, 2003), peer statuses and academic success, new section on bullying (previously in peers chapter), including new research in figure 11.5 based on a national study of bullying behaviors by U.S. youth (Nansel & others, 2001); new discussions on friendship and schooling, and on peer crowds and schooling, are also included
- New section on culture and schooling, including recent cross-cultural comparisons (Brown & Larson, 2002)
- New discussion of cross-cultural comparisons of colleges (U.S. Department of Education, 1999; Welti, 2002)

CHAPTER 12
Achievement, Work, and Careers

- New figure 12.3 on behaviors that suggest helplessness (Stipek, 2002)
- New discussion of recent cross-cultural comparisons of math and science literacy in 14- and 15-year olds, including new figure 12.4
- New figure 12.5 to illustrate Harold Stevenson's research on the reasons Asian and American parents give for their children's level of math achievement

- Inclusion of recent research on the motivational factors involved in improving young adolescents' math achievement (Blackwell, Trzesniewski, & Dweck, 2003)
- New section on identity development and career development, including new discussion of study on developmental changes in different domains of identity with vocational identity emerging as a key identity domain; also includes new figure 12.8
- Expanded coverage of the roles of parents and peers in career development (Vondracek, 2003)
- New section "Work Profiles of Adolescents Around the World"
- New section, Working While Going to College, including new figure 12.8 on the link between the number of hours worked during college and grades
- New section on work/career-based learning in college with a focus on cooperative education and internship programs

CHAPTER 13
Culture

- Reorganization of chapter at the request of reviewers and adopters with the section "Ethnicity" now following the opening section "Culture and Adolescence," and then the section "Socioeconomic Status and Poverty" following "Ethnicity"
- New section on how adolescents around the world spend their time, including new figure 13.1 that summarizes daily time use patterns of adolescents in different regions of the world (Larson, 2001; Larson & Varma, 1999)
- New section on immigration and recent research on the degree of acculturation and adolescent problems (Gonzales & others, in press; Epstein, Botvin, & Diaz, 1998)
- Updated and revised description of socioeconomic differences in parenting (Hoff, Laursen, & Tardif, 2002)
- Extensively revised and updated main section on the media and technology with new section head, "The Media and Technology"
- Inclusion of recent national data on U.S. adolescents' use of different media, including new figure 13.4 (Roberts & Foehr, 2003)
- New figure 13.5 showing the link between viewing educational TV programs in early childhood and grades in high school for boys (Anderson & others, 2001)
- Updated, expanded coverage of television and sex, including recent national data on sexual content and adolescent TV watching (Kaiser Family Foundation, 2002b)
- New discussion of rap music (Strasburger & Wilson, 2002)
- New figure 13.6 on the percentage of substance-abuse references in different types of music (Roberts, Henrikson, & Christensen, 1999)
- New discussion of the link between adolescents' playing of violent electronic games and their aggression

- Updated, expanded discussion of technology, computers, and the Internet
- New discussion of national survey on the importance of having a computer with Internet access to U.S. adolescents (Roberts & others, 1999)
- Much expanded, updated coverage of the Internet and adolescent development (Anderson, 2002; Donnerstein, 2002) with recent dramatic increases in use. Also information about how adolescents learned to use the Internet (Kaiser Family Foundation, 2002a). Included is new figure 13.7 on the percentage of U.S. 15- to 17-year-olds engaging in different Internet activities (Kaiser Family Foundation, 2001).
- Expanded, updated material on why parents should be concerned about their adolescents' unmonitored use of the Internet
- Expanded, updated discussion of technology and sociocultural diversity, including new figure 13.8 on daily computer use by adolescents from three different socioeconomic groups (Roberts & others, 1999)
- Inclusion of new information about the National Educational Technology Standards (NETS) (International Society for Technology in Education, 2000, 2001)

CHAPTER 14
Adolescent Problems

- Extensive updating of adolescent drug use data based on recent national research by Johnston, O'Malley, and Bachman (2003); this is especially important because the most recent data reported (2002) showed a rather significant downturn in use of a number of different drugs by adolescents
- New discussion of the reasons for the very recent downturn in drug use by adolescents
- Recent research on drinking patterns in college students (Wechsler & others, 2002)
- Expanded coverage of substance use in emerging adulthood, including new figure 14.5 on binge drinking in the transition from adolescence through early adulthood
- Updating of adolescent use of LSD and marijuana, cocaine and amphetamines, and barbiturates, tranquilizers, and steroids (Johnston, O'Malley, & Bachman, 2003)
- Substantial updating of material on adolescent cigarette smoking, including new figure 14.7 on trends in smoking cigarettes by U.S. adolescents (Johnston, O'Malley, & Bachman, 2003)
- Updating of adolescent use of Ecstasy and new figure 14.8 showing an MRI image of an adolescent's brain while under the influence of Ecstasy
- Added recent research from the Pittsburgh Youth Study on the developmental pathways to delinquency (Stoutheimer-Loeber & others, 2002)

- New research showing a link between early aggression problems in childhood and delinquency in adolescence for boys but not girls (Broidy & others, 2003)
- Added new predictors/antecedents of delinquency: authority conflict, covert acts such as lying, and overt acts such as aggression followed by fighting (based on the Pittsburgh Youth Study), as well as cognitive distortions and sibling relations to figure 14.10, The Antecedent of Juvenile Delinquency
- Updated coverage of suicide in adolescence, including Savin-Williams' (2001) findings that suicide attempts have been overestimated in gay and lesbian adolescents because of methodological flaws in most studies
- New discussion of ethnic variations in being overweight in U.S. adolescent boys and girls, including new figure 14.13 (National Center for Health Statistics, 2002)
- Added recent research on cross-cultural comparisons and trends in being overweight in adolescence (Wang & others, 2002)
- Added discussion of recent study on factors related to bulimia nervosa (Stice, 2002)
- New discussion of *Fast Track,* a program that seeks to prevent adolescent problems, and its research evaluation
- New coverage of findings from the National Longitudinal Study on Adolescent Health (Resnick & others, 2001) that shows which factors are most likely to protect adolescents from developing problems

SUPPLEMENTS

The supplements listed here may accompany Santrock, *Adolescence,* 10th edition. Please contact your McGraw-Hill representative for details concerning policies, prices, and availability as some restrictions may apply.

FOR THE INSTRUCTOR

Instructor's Manual

Jessica L. Miller
Mesa State College

Each chapter of the *Instructor's Manual* contains a Total Teaching Package Outline, a fully integrated tool to help instructors better use the many resources for the course. This outline shows instructors which supplementary materials can be used in the teaching of a particular chapter topic. In addition, there is a summary of each chapter, suggested lecture topics, classroom discussion topics and activities, critical thinking exercises, scenarios appropriate for discussion or assignments, abstracts of current research articles, suggested student research projects, essay questions, and exercises tied to video clips found on the LifeMap CD.

Test Bank and Dual Platform Computerized Test Bank on CD-ROM

Jane P. Sheldon
University of Michigan–Dearborn

This comprehensive test bank includes approximately 1700 multiple-choice questions, of which more than 25% are conceptual, more than 25% applied, and the remainder factual; in addition, each chapter offers 5 or more essay questions. Every question indicates the correct answer and is identified by type of question (conceptual, applied, or factual), refers to the chapter topic it addresses, and indicates the page number in the text where the corresponding material can be found.

Available on the Instructor's Resource CD-ROM, the test bank is compatible for both Macintosh and Windows platforms. The CD-ROM provides an editing feature that enables instructors to integrate their own questions, scramble items, and modify questions. McGraw-Hill's Computerized Testing is the most flexible and easy-to-use electronic testing program available in higher education. It allows you to create a print version, an online version (to be delivered to a computer lab), or an Internet version of each test.

The program allows instructors to create tests from book specific test banks. It accommodates a wide range of question types and instructors may add their own questions. Multiple versions of the test can be created. The program is available for Windows, Macintosh, and Linux environments.

The CD-ROM also offers an instructor the option of implementing the following features unique to this program: Online Testing Program, Internet Testing, and Grade Management.

PowerPoint Slide Presentations

This resource offers the instructor an array of 30 to 40 PowerPoint slides per chapter, organized to follow the chapter organization of *Adolescence.* They include lecture landmarks highlighting the main section headings of each chapter, lists of key concepts, and line art figures from the text.

Instructor's Resource CD-ROM (IRCD)

This CD-ROM offers instructors a convenient tool for customizing the McGraw-Hill materials to prepare for and create their lecture presentations. Among the resources included on the IRCD are the Instructor's Manual, Test Bank, and PowerPoint slides.

Multimedia Courseware for Child Development

Charlotte J. Patterson
University of Virginia

This interactive CD-ROM includes video footage of classic and contemporary experiments, detailed viewing guides, challenging preview, follow up and interactive feedback, graphics, graduated developmental charts, a variety of hands on projects, related websites. and navigation aids. The CD-ROM is programmed in a modular format. Its content focuses on integrating digital media to better explain physical, cognitive, social and emotional development throughout childhood and adolescence. It is compatible with both Mac and PCs.

Taking Sides: Clashing Views on Controversial Issues in Childhood and Society

Taking Sides is a debate-style reader designed to introduce students to controversial viewpoints on some of the most critical issues in the field. Each issue is framed for the student, and the pro and con essays represent the arguments of leading scholars and commentators in their fields. An Instructor's Guide containing testing materials is available.

Annual Editions: Child Growth and Development

Published by Dushkin/McGraw-Hill, this is a collection of articles on topics related to the latest research and thinking in child development. These editions are updated annually and contain useful features, including a topic guide, an annotated table of contents, unit overviews, and a topical index. An Instructor's Guide, containing testing materials, is also available.

Online Learning Center

This extensive website, designed specifically to accompany this edition of *Adolescence,* offers a wide variety of resources for both instructors and students. The password-protected instructor's side of the site includes the Instructor's Manual, PowerPoint lecture slides, images, interactive links, and an Internet guide. These resources and more can be found by logging on to the website: www.mhhe.com/santrocka10

McGraw-Hill's Developmental Supersite

This comprehensive web page provides a superstructure that organizes and houses all of our developmental text websites. The Developmental Tree serves as a portal through which instructors and students can access each text-specific online learning center as well as many universally useful teaching and study tools. Visit us at http://www.mhhe.com/developmental.

The Critical Thinker

Richard Mayer and Fiona Goodchild of the University of California, Santa Barbara, use excerpts from introductory psychology textbooks to show how to think critically about psychology.

FOR THE STUDENT

Study Guide

Daniel D. Houlihan
Minnesota State University–Mankato

This comprehensive study guide integrates the Learning Goals system found in the textbook. Designed to promote active learning, it is written in question form, including short answer, multiple choice, and matching exercises. Each chapter of the *Study Guide* includes section reviews and a comprehensive review for each chapter, key terms and key people, and an answer key. The *Study Guide* also promotes independent critical thinking through self-reflection exercises such as Cognitive Challenge, Adolescence in Research, Adolescence in Books, and Adolescence in Movies, Videos, and DVD.

LifeMap CD-ROM

This user-friendly CD-ROM gives students an opportunity to explore the course material in greater depth. Created specifically for this edition of *Adolescence,* the CD includes concept maps for each chapter; multiple-choice self-quiz questions; and selected video segments with commentary, pre- and post-test questions, and web links to related sites. Also included are a Guide to Electronic Research, Internet Primer, Resources, and McGraw-Hill's unique Learning Styles Assessment tool.

Online Learning Center (OLC)

This extensive website, created specifically to accompany this edition of *Adolescence,* offers a wide variety of resources for both instructors and students. The student side of the website includes Learning Goals which are expanded from the Learning Goals review questions found in the book's Review & Reflect boxes, averaging 75 entries per chapter. In addition, it offers "Who Am I?" exercises for key people and Flashcards for key terms, multiple choice quizzes, and interactive Health and Wellness Scenarios. These resources and more can be found by logging on to the website: www.mhhe.com/santrocka10

McGraw-Hill's Developmental Supersite

This useful web page provides a superstructure that organizes and houses all of our developmental text websites. The Developmental Tree serves as a portal through which instructors and students can access each text-specific online learning center as well as many universally useful teaching and study tools. Visit us at http://www.mhhe.com/developmental.

ACKNOWLEDGEMENTS

I very much appreciate the support and guidance provided to me by many people at McGraw-Hill. Steve Debow, President, and Thalia Dorwick, Editor-in-Chief, have been truly outstanding in their administration of the social sciences area at McGraw-Hill. Steve Rutter, Publisher, has brought a wealth of publishing knowledge and vision to bear on improving this book. Judith Kromm, Senior Developmental Editor, has done a remarkable job of coordinating and managing the editorial and production phases of this project. The new edition has considerably benefited from the enthusiasm and competence of Betty Morgan and Elsa Peterson, Developmental Editors; and Kate Russillo, Editorial Coordinator. Melissa Caughlin, Marketing Manager, has contributed in numerous creative ways to this book. Rick Hecker was a superb project manager and Bea Sussman did outstanding work in copyediting the book.

Thanks go to the many reviewers of both the 10th and earlier editions of this text. Their extensive contributions have made this a far better book.

Peer Reviewers of *Adolescence,* 10th edition

Sandy Arntz, *Northern Illinois University*
James I. Byrd, *University of Wisconsin at Stout*
Mark Chapell, *Rowan University*
Gary Creasey, *Illinois State University*
Nancy Defrates-Densch, *Northern Illinois University*
Imma Destefanis, *Boston College*
Jerome Dusek, *Syracuse University*
Steve Ellyson, *Youngstown State University*
Leslie Fisher, *Cleveland State University*
Marguerite D. Kermis, *Canisius College*
Heidi Legg-Burross, *University of Arizona*
Jessica Miller, *Mesa State College*
Shana Pack, *Western Kentucky University*
Ian Payton, *Bethune-Cookman College*
Richard Pisacreta, *Ferris State University*

Expert Consultants for *Adolescence,* 10th edition

Elizabeth J. Susman, *Pennsylvania State University*
Daniel P. Keating, *University of Toronto*
Nancy L. Galambos, *University of Alberta in Edmonton*
Reed W. Larson, *University of Illinois at Urbana–Champaign*
Catherine R. Cooper, *University of California at Santa Cruz*
Peter Benson, *Search Institute, Minneapolis*
Shirley Feldman, *Stanford University*
Jerome Dusek, *Syracuse University*
Kathryn Wentzel, *University of Maryland, College Park*
Duane Buhrmester, *University of Texas at Dallas*
Christy M. Buchanan, *Wake Forest University*
Allan Wigfield, *University of Maryland, College Park*
Constance Flanagan, *Pennsylvania State University*
Brett Laursen, *Florida Atlantic University*
Fred W. Vondracek, *Pennsylvania State University*

The following expert consultants also gave valuable feedback on previous editions of the book.

Joseph Allen, *University of Virginia*
Carole Beale, *University of Massachusetts*
Nancy Busch-Rossnagel, *Fordham University*
James Byrnes, *University of Maryland*
P. Lindsay Chase-Lansdale, *University of Chicago*
Joy Dryfoos, *Hastings-on-Hudson, New York*
Carol Dweck, *Columbia University*
Glen Elder, *University of North Carolina*
Wyndol Furman, *University of Denver*
Harold Grotevant, *University of Minnesota*
Daniel Keating, *University of Toronto*
Daniel Lapsley, *Brandon University*
Nancy Leffert, *Search Institute, Minneapolis*
Beth Manke, *University of Houston*
James Marcia, *Simon Fraser University*
Daniel Offer, *University of Michigan*
James Rest, *University of Minnesota*
Elizabeth Susman, *Pennsylvania State University*
Ruby Takanishi, *Foundation for Child Development*
Lawrence Walker, *University of British Columbia*
Allan Wigfield, *University of Maryland*

In addition, I thank the following peer reviewers for their evaluations of previous editions:

Alice Alexander, *Old Dominion University*
Frank Ascione, *Utah State University*
Luciane A. Berg, *Southern Utah University*
David K. Bernhardt, *Carleton University*
Fredda Blanchard-Fields, *Louisiana State University*
Belinda Blevins-Knabe, *University of Arkansas*
Robert Bornstein, *Miami University*
Geraldine Brookins, *University of Minnesota*
Deborah Brown, *Friends University*
Christy Buchanan, *Wake Forest University*
Duane Buhrmester, *University of Texas at Dallas*
William Bukowski, *Concordia University*
James Byrnes, *University of Maryland*
Cheryl A. Camenzuli, *Hofstra University*
Elaine Cassel, *Marymount University*
Mark S. Chapell, *Rowan University*
Stephanie M. Clancy, *Southern Illinois University at Carbondale*
Ronald K. Craig, *Cincinnati State College*
Rita M. Curl, *Minot State University*
Peggy A. DeCooke, *Northern Illinois University*
R. Daniel DiSalvi, *Kean College*
James A. Doyle, *Roane State Community College*
Mark W. Durm, *Athens State University*
Laura Duvall, *Heartland Community College*
Celina Echols, *Southern Louisiana State University*
Richard M. Ehlenz, *Lakewood Community College*
Gene Elliott, *Glassboro State College*
Robert Enright, *University of Wisconsin at Madison*
Jennifer Fager, *Western Michigan University*
Douglas Fife, *Plymouth State College*
Urminda Firlan, *Michigan State University*

Martin E. Ford, *Stanford University*
Gregory T. Fouts, *University of Calgary*
Mary Fraser, *San Jose State University*
Charles Fry, *University of Virginia*
Nancy Galambos, *University of Victoria*
Anne R. Gayles-Felton, *Florida A&M University*
Margaret J. Gill, *Kutztown University*
Sam Givhan, *Mississippi State University*
William Gnagey, *Illinois State University*
Sandra Graham, *UCLA*
B. Jo Hailey, *University of Southern Mississippi*
Dick E. Hammond, *Southwest Texas State University*
Frances Harnick, *University of New Mexico, Indian Children's Program, and Lovelace-Bataan Pediatric Clinic*
Algea Harrison, *Oakland University*
Susan Harter, *University of Denver*
Dan Houlihan, *Minnesota State University*
June V. Irving, *Ball State University*
Beverly Jennings, *University of Colorado at Denver*
Joline Jones, *Worcester State College*
Alfred L. Karlson, *University of Massachusetts at Amherst*
Lynn F. Katz, *University of Pittsburgh*
Roger Kobak, *University of Delaware*
Tara Kuther, *Western Connecticut State University*
Emmett C. Lampkin, *Scott Community College*
Royal Louis Lange, *Ellsworth Community College*
Philip Langer, *University of Colorado*
Bonnie Leadbeater, *University of Victoria*
Heidi Legg-Burross, *University of Arizona*
Neal E. Lipsitz, *Boston College*
Nancy Lobb, *Alvin Community College*
Daniel Lynch, *University of Wisconsin at Oshkosh*
Beth Manke, *University of Houston*
Joseph G. Marrone, *Siena College*
Ann McCabe, *University of Windsor*
Susan McCammon, *East Carolina University*
Sherri McCarthy-Tucker, *Northern Arizona University*
E. L. McGarry, *California State University at Fullerton*

Jessica Miller, *Mesa State College*
John J. Mirich, *Metropolitan State College*
John J. Mitchell, *University of Alberta*
Suzanne F. Morrow, *Old Dominion University*
Lloyd D. Noppe, *University of Wisconsin at Green Bay*
Michelle Paludi, *Michelle Paludi & Associates*
Joycelyn G. Parish, *Kansas State University*
Peggy G. Perkins, *University of Nevada, Las Vegas*
James D. Reid, *Washington University*
Anne Robertson, *University of Wisconsin at Milwaukee*
Tonie E. Santmire, *University of Nebraska*
Douglas Sawin, *University of Texas*
Jane Sheldon, *University of Michigan at Dearborn*
Kim Shifren, *Towson University*
Susan Shonk, *State University of New York*
Dale Shunk, *Purdue University*
Vern Tyler, *Western Washington University*
Rhoda Unger, *Montclair State College*
Elizabeth Vozzola, *Saint Joseph's College*
Barry Wagner, *Catholic University of America*
Lawrence Walker, *University of British Columbia*
Rob Weisskirch, *California State University at Fullerton*
Wanda Willard, *State University of New York at Oswego*
Carolyn L. Williams, *University of Minnesota*
Shelli Wynants, *California State University*

A final note of thanks goes to my family. My wife, Mary Jo Santrock, has lived through ten editions of *Adolescence*. I sincerely appreciate the support and encouragement she has given to my writing. My two daughters, Tracy and Jennifer, provided me with firsthand experience of watching adolescents develop. Through the years, they have helped me to render a treatment of adolescence that captures its complexity, its subtlety, and its humanity. I am also fortunate once again to experience the marvels of adolescence—this time through my granddaughter, Jordan, who began making the transition to early adolescence at the time I wrote this new edition of the book.

Expert Consultants

Elizabeth Susman

Elizabeth Susman is one of the world's leading experts on puberty. She is the Jean Phillips Shibley Professor of Biobehavioral Health in the Department of Biobehavioral Health, Pennsylvania State University. Dr. Susman received a Ph.D. in Human Development and postdoctoral training in Developmental Psychology. She did a postdoctoral fellowship at the National Institute of Mental Health and the National Cancer Institute. Her research program combines biology, behavioral endocrinology, and developmental psychology. The research is based on theories that integrate biological, psychological, and contextual aspects of psychological and physical development during childhood and adolescence. An important component of the research is considering the dynamic interaction of experience, behavior, and developing neurobiological systems. Her studies have focused on the important issue of how changes in emotions and antisocial behavior parallel changes in hormones of adrenal and gonadal origin at puberty in boys and girls.

Dr. Susman's research is published in biomedical and psychological journals. Her research has been funded by the National Institute of Child Health and Human Development, National Institute of Mental Health, John D. and Catherine T. MacArthur Foundation, National Institute of Justice, and the William T. Grant Foundation. Dr. Susman has served on multiple research and health policy-related national committees that include a National Institutes of Health (NIH) Consensus Development Conference on Glucocorticoids and Fetal Maturation, NIH Expert Priority Panel on Health on Youth, Institute of Medicine Panel on Innovations in Mental Health and Puberty, Steering Committee for Health Futures II, a Bureau of Maternal and Child Health initiative that planned an agenda for research and health policy for youth in the 21st century, and the NIMH Task Force on Externalizing Behaviors.

She has been co-editor of the *Journal of Research on Adolescence,* is a consulting editor for numerous scientific journals, and is a member of National Institute of Health review groups. Dr. Susman is the President-elect for the Society for Research on Adolescence.

Daniel Keating

Daniel Keating is one of the world's leading experts on adolescent cognitive development. He is the Atkinson Professor in Human Development and Applied Psychology at the Ontario Institute for Studies in Education, University of Toronto. He is also a Fellow of the Canadian Institute for Advanced Research (CIAR). Dr. Keating has written extensively on human development, adolescent development, developmental health, and education, focusing on the developmental sources of human diversity, and on the prospects for human development in a learning society. A conceptual framework that synthesizes much of this work has been summarized in his book, *Developmental Health and the Wealth of Nations* (with Clyde Hertzman and the CIAR Human Development Program).

Nancy Galambos

Nancy Galambos is one of the world's leading experts on gender and adolescent development. She currently is Professor of Psychology at the University of Alberta in Edmonton. She received her Ph.D. from Pennsylvania State University in human development, worked at the Institute for Psychology at the Technical University of Berlin, Germany, and was on the faculty at the University of Victoria in Canada for many years. Now at the University of Alberta, she is continuing her research on antecedents and consequences of adolescent risk and health behavior, the importance of the family context in shaping adolescent behavior, and the nature and definition of psychosocial maturity in adolescence and emerging adulthood. Her interests in gender roles have led to publications on gender differences in risk behaviors, depression, and nonverbal behaviors in young people. Recent publications have included an examination of the impact of parenting on change over time in adolescents' externalizing problems, cultural perspectives on the markers of adulthood, and the identification of biological, cognitive, and contextual determinants of psychosocial maturity in adolescence. Dr. Galambos is currently Assistant Editor for the *Journal of Adolescence,* has served on numerous editorial boards for journals in the field of adolescence, and was co-editor for 10 years of the *Research Monographs in Adolescence* series.

Reed Larson

Reed Larson is one of the world's leading experts on contexts and community influences in adolescent development. He is the Pampered Chef Ltd Endowed Chair in Family Resiliency and a professor in the Departments of Human and Community Development, Psychology, Leisure Studies, and Educational Psychology at the University of Illinois at Urbana-Champaign. His research focuses on the daily experience of adolescents and their parents. He is author of *Divergent Realities: The Emotional Lives of Mothers, Fathers, and Adolescents* (with Maryse Richards), which examines the organization of time and emotions within the daily lives of families and how emotions are transmitted between family members. He is also the author of *Being Adolescent: Conflict and Growth in the Teenage Years* (with Mihaly Csikszentmihalyi), which deals with the daily experience of high school students. He has conducted research on adolescents' media use, time alone, experience with friends, and school experience. He recently completed a study of middle socioeconomic status adolescents in India, and was the chair of the Study Group on Adolescence in the 21st Century, sponsored by the Society for Research on Adolescence. His current area of interest is adolescents' experience in extra-curricular activities, community-based programs, and other structured, voluntary activities in the after-school hours. He holds a B.A. degree in psychology from the University of Minnesota and a Ph.D. in Human Development from the University of Chicago.

Catherine Cooper

Catherine Cooper is one of the world's leading experts on families, ethnic influences, and identity development in adolescence. She is Professor of Psychology and Education at the University of California, Santa Cruz. She received her Ph.D. in Developmental Psychology from the University of Minnesota. Dr. Cooper focuses on how youth forge identities in school, career, and family roles by coordinating their cultural and family traditions with their schools, communities, and work. She developed the Bridging Multiple Worlds Theory to trace how youth connect their worlds in ways that reflect individuality and connectedness in identities, relationships, and achievements. With colleagues and students, she is continuing to test this theory across cultural communities, working with youth of African, Chinese, Filipino, Latino, Native American, European, Japanese, and Vietnamese descent as well as Japanese youth. To benefit youth, families, schools, and community programs and advance science, policy, and practice, her team builds university-community partnerships to strengthen diversity along the academic pipeline from kindergarten to adulthood. She is a member of the MacArthur Research Network on Successful Pathways through Middle Childhood and Director of the Program on Families, Schools, Peers, and Communities of the Center for Research on Education, Diversity and Excellence (CREDE) of the U.S. Department of Education. She serves as Faculty Associate to the Vice President for Educational Outreach in the University of California Office of the President. Her most recent book, *Bridging Multiple Worlds: Culture, Youth Identity, and Pathways to College,* is in preparation with Oxford University Press.

Peter Benson

Peter Benson is one of the world's most influential experts on ways to improve the health and well-being of adolescents. He is president of Search Institute, Minneapolis, a national non-profit research organization dedicated to promoting the well-being of children and adolescents. In this role since 1985, Dr. Benson oversees the work of 70 social scientists, educators, and writers. As lecturer, author, researcher, and consultant, he focuses his work on strengthening communities, social institutions, and public policy on behalf of America's youth. He sits on many national boards, including America's Promise, the Center for the Victims of Torture, the John Templeton Foundation, and the Youth, Education and Family Institute at the National League of Cities. He has taught at Yale University, the University of Minnesota, and the University of Denver, is an adjunct professor in the Department of Education Policy and Administration at the University of Minnesota, and serves as the first Visiting Scholar at The William T. Grant Foundation in New York City. In 1991 Dr. Benson received the William James Award for career contributions to the psychology of religion from the American Psychological Association. In 2002 he was named International Fellow in Applied Developmental Science by Tufts University for "career achievements in positive youth development." He is the author of twelve books on children, adolescents, and the community forces that shape their lives.

Shirley Feldman

Shirley Feldman is one of the world's leading experts on adolescent sexuality. She is an Australian who has spent the last 37 years at Stanford University. Dr. Feldman joined the faculty of Human Biology in the first year of its existence and for the last fifteen years has been a Senior Research Scientist in the Division of Child Psychiatry. Her research in developmental psychology focuses on family influences across the life span. In recent years, she has especially focused on adolescence and has conducted several longitudinal studies including one on the transition into adolescence and another on the transition out of adolescence into young adulthood. She studies both normal processes such as autonomy, sexual development, moral development, coping, and defense mechanisms; as well as on problem outcomes such as misconduct, post traumatic stress disorder, and unsafe sexual practices. She has edited and written a number of books, including the influential volume *At the Threshold: The Developing Adolescent*, and has published more than 100 research papers and monographs.

Chuck Painter/
Stanford News
Service

Jerome Dusek

Jerome Dusek is one of the world's leading experts on the development of the self in adolescence. He is Professor of Psychology at Syracuse University. He received his B.A. degree from the University of Michigan and his M.A. and Ph.D. degrees from the University of Illinois-Urbana. He has been Director of the Developmental Psychology Graduate Training Program at Syracuse University. He teaches courses in child development and adolescent development. His research interests lie in the areas of adolescent identity and self-esteem development, gender roles, coping with stress, test anxiety, and romantic relationships. He has published numerous papers in these areas and has contributed invited chapters to a number of edited books. His research has received funding from the Council on Basic Research in Education and the National Institutes of Health, and he acts as a reviewer for research publications submitted to various funding agencies. He is a member of the Editorial Boards of the *Journal of Early Adolescence* and the *Journal of Adolescent Research*, and is a regular reviewer of articles submitted for publication in a number of other national and international outlets. He authored *Adolescent Development and Behavior*, co-authored *Child Psychology*, and edited the definitive book *Teacher Expectancies*.

Kathryn Wentzel

Kathryn Wentzel is one of the world's leading experts on adolescent motivation and adjustment to school. She obtained her Ph.D. from Stanford University and is currently a Professor of Human Development in the Department of Human Development/Institute for Child Study in the College of Education at the University of Maryland, College Park. Dr. Wentzel is Vice President of Division E, Counseling and Human Development, of the American Educational Research Association, and has also held positions in the American Psychological Association, Division 15, as well as the Society for Research on Child Development. Her research focuses on connections between young adolescents', as well as relationships with parents, peers, and teachers and their motivation and adjustment to middle school.

Duane Buhrmester

Duane Buhrmester is one of the world's leading experts on adolescent peer relations. He has been studying and publishing in the area of child and adolescent interpersonal development since the early 1980s. Professor Buhrmester earned his Ph.D. in Developmental Psychology from the University of Denver and is currently the Psychology Program Head and Associate Dean for Undergraduate Education at the University of Texas at Dallas, where he has been since 1989. Dr. Buhrmester is best known for his research that explores the implications of Sullivan's theory of interpersonal development. He has published a number of influential papers in collaboration with Professor Wyndol Furman on developmental changes in the social provisions provided by different social network members. He is especially interested in intimate friendships during adolescence and the social skills that friendships foster. He also has written about the changing qualities and significance of sibling relationships and about the peer relationships of children diagnosed with ADHD. He has served on the editorial boards of the field's leading journals, including *Child Development*, *Developmental Psychology*, and the *Journal of Research on Adolescence*.

Christy Buchanan

Christy Buchanan is one of the world's leading experts on family processes in adolescence. She is a professor in the Department of Psychology at Wake Forest University. She received her doctorate in Developmental Psychology from the University of Michigan. She conducts research on adolescent development in the family, examining how adolescent-parent relationships, parenting practices, and adolescents' well-being are influenced by factors such as pubertal development, family structure, marital conflict, and parents' and children's beliefs and expectations about adolescence. She is co-author with Eleanor Maccoby and Sanford Dornbusch of *Adolescents after Divorce*, published by Harvard University Press.

Allan Wigfield

Allan Wigfield is one of the world's leading experts on the roles of schools and motivation in adolescent development. He is Professor of Human Development and Distinguished Scholar-Teacher at the University of Maryland, College Park. His research focuses on the development of children's motivation in different areas, including reading. He has authored more than 80 peer-reviewed journal articles and book chapters on children's motivation. He is Associate Editor of *Child Development*. He is a Fellow of Division 15 of the American Psychological Association. Dr. Wigfield currently is collaborating with John Guthrie on a National Science Foundation-funded study of how two reading programs, Concept Oriented Reading Instruction and Strategy Instruction, influence elementary school-aged children's reading motivation and comprehension.

Constance Flanagan

Constance Flanagan is one of the world's leading experts on adolescent civic and political development. She earned her Ph.D. in developmental psychology at the University of Michigan and is currently a professor of youth civic development in the Department of Agricultural and Extension Education at Pennsylvania State University. Her program of work, "Adolescents and the social contract," focuses on the ways that young people interpret the rights and obligations individuals and societies owe one another. She directed a seven-nation study on this topic as well as a study of inter-group relations and beliefs about justice among youth from different racial/ethnic backgrounds in the United States. Two new projects include: a longitudinal study of peer loyalty and social responsibility as it relates to teens' views about health as a public or private issue and a study on the developmental correlates of social trust.

Dr. Flanagan is a William T. Grant Faculty Scholar, a member of the MacArthur Network on the Transition to Adulthood and Public Policy, and a fellow in the Society for the Psychological Study of Social Issues (SPSSI), Division 9 of the American Psychological Association. She is on the editorial board of five journals and has served as a consultant or advisor to CIRCLE (the Center for Information and Research on Civic Learning and Engagement), the Annenberg Center's Student Voices project, the Social Science Research Council's Youth and Globalization project, Health Rocks!, City Year, and the Inter-American Foundation. She also has chaired the Society for Research in Child Development's Committee on Public Policy and Public Information.

Brett Laursen

Brett Laursen is one of the world's leading experts on family processes in adolescence. He is a Professor of Psychology at Florida Atlantic University. He received his Ph.D. in Child Psychology from the Institute of Child Development at the University of Minnesota. A Fellow in the American Psychological Association (Division 7, Developmental), Dr. Laursen has served as Co-Chair of the biennial meetings of the Society for Research in Child Development and as Treasurer and Membership Secretary of the International Society for the Study of Behavioral Development. With funding from the National Institute of Child Health and Human Development, the National Institute of Mental Health, and the Johann Jacobs Foundation, Dr. Laursen's research addresses close relationships with parents and peers and their influence on adolescent adaptation. Much of this work focuses on developmental changes in interpersonal conflict and closeness. His edited works include *Close Friendship During Adolescence, Social Exchange in Development* (with W. G. Graziano), and *Relationships as Developmental Contexts* (with W. A. Collins). Professor Laursen is a consulting editor for *Child Development, International Journal of Behavioral Development, Journal of Research on Adolescence,* and *Merrill-Palmer Quarterly.*

Fred Vondracek

Fred Vondracek is one of the world's leading experts on career development. He currently serves as Associate Dean for Undergraduate Programs and Outreach in Pennsylvania State University's College of Health and Human Development, where he has been since 1969. After stepping down as Director of the Division of Individual and Family Studies, Dr. Vondracek has collaborated with Richard Lerner and John Schulenberg on a number of influential articles and a book, entitled *Career Development: A Life-Span Developmental Approach*. He also has collaborated with his students and with colleagues from Germany and from Japan in empirical research on career decision making and the processes of vocational identity development. He has served on the editorial boards of *The Career Development Quarterly,* the *International Journal of Behavioral Development,* the *Journal of Adolescent Research,* and the *Journal of Vocational Behavior.*

A Visual Tour for Students

This book provides you with important study tools to help you learn about adolescence more effectively. Especially important is the learning goals system that is integrated throughout each chapter. In the following visual walk-through of features, pay special attention to how the learning goals system works.

THE LEARNING GOALS SYSTEM

Using the learning goals system will help you to learn the material more easily. Key aspects of the learning goals system are the learning goals, chapter maps, Review and Reflect, and Reach Your Learning Goals Sections, which are all linked together.

At the beginning of each chapter, you will see a page that includes both a chapter outline and three to six learning goals that preview the chapter's main themes and underscore the most important ideas in the chapter. Then, at the beginning of each major section of a chapter, you will see a mini-chapter map that provides you with a visual organization of the key topics you are about to read in the section. At the end of each section is Review and Reflect, in which the learning goal for the section is restated; a series of review questions related to the mini-chapter map are asked, and a question that encourages you to think critically about a topic related to the section appears. At the end of the chapter, you will come to a section titled "Reach Your Learning Goals." This includes an overall chapter map that visually organizes all of the main headings, a restatement of the chapter's learning goals, and a summary of the chapter's content that is directly linked to the chapter outline at the beginning of the chapter and the questions asked in the Review part of Review and Reflect within the chapter. The summary essentially answers the questions asked in the within-chapter Review sections.

THE LEARNING GOALS SYSTEM

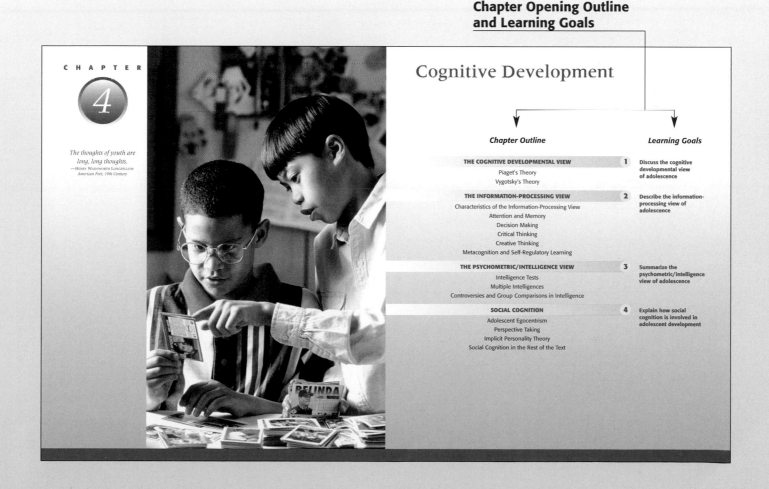

Chapter Opening Outline and Learning Goals

CHAPTER

4

The thoughts of youth are long, long thoughts.
—HENRY WADSWORTH LONGFELLOW
American Poet, 19th Century

Cognitive Development

Chapter Outline

THE COGNITIVE DEVELOPMENTAL VIEW
Piaget's Theory
Vygotsky's Theory

THE INFORMATION-PROCESSING VIEW
Characteristics of the Information-Processing View
Attention and Memory
Decision Making
Critical Thinking
Creative Thinking
Metacognition and Self-Regulatory Learning

THE PSYCHOMETRIC/INTELLIGENCE VIEW
Intelligence Tests
Multiple Intelligences
Controversies and Group Comparisons in Intelligence

SOCIAL COGNITION
Adolescent Egocentrism
Perspective Taking
Implicit Personality Theory
Social Cognition in the Rest of the Text

Learning Goals

1 Discuss the cognitive developmental view of adolescence

2 Describe the information-processing view of adolescence

3 Summarize the psychometric/intelligence view of adolescence

4 Explain how social cognition is involved in adolescent development

Mini-chapter Map

Review and Reflect

Reach Your Learning Goals

Cognitive Development

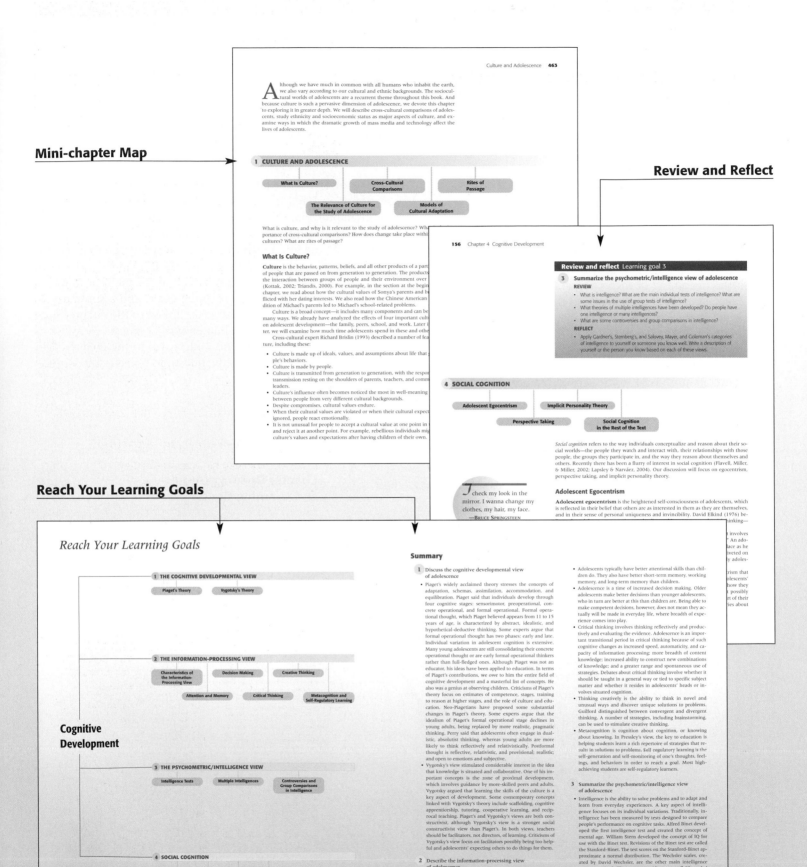

Although we have much in common with all humans who inhabit the earth, we also vary according to our cultural and ethnic backgrounds. The sociocultural worlds of adolescents are a recurrent theme throughout this book. And because culture is such a pervasive dimension of adolescence, we devote this chapter to exploring it in greater depth. We will describe cross-cultural comparisons of adolescents, study ethnicity and socioeconomic status as major aspects of culture, and examine ways in which the dramatic growth of mass media and technology affect the lives of adolescents.

1 CULTURE AND ADOLESCENCE

What Is Culture?

Cross-Cultural Comparisons

Rites of Passage

The Relevance of Culture for the Study of Adolescence

Models of Cultural Adaptation

What is culture, and why is it relevant to the study of adolescence? Wh... portance of cross-cultural comparisons? How does change take place withi... cultures? What are rites of passage?

What Is Culture?

Culture is the behavior, patterns, beliefs, and all other products of a part... of people that are passed on from generation to generation. The products... the interaction between groups of people and their environment over... (Kottak, 2002; Triandis, 2000). For example, in the section at the begin... chapter, we read about how the cultural values of Sonya's parents and b... flicted with her dating interests. We also read how the Chinese American... dition of Michael's parents led to Michael's school-related problems.

Culture is a broad concept—it includes many components and can be... many ways. We already have analyzed the effects of four important cult... on adolescent development—the family, peers, school, and work. Later i... ter, we will examine how much time adolescents spend in these and othe...

Cross-cultural expert Richard Brislin (1993) described a number of fea... ture, including these:

- Culture is made up of ideals, values, and assumptions about life that ... ple's behaviors.
- Culture is made by people.
- Culture is transmitted from generation to generation, with the respon... transmission resting on the shoulders of parents, teachers, and comm... leaders.
- Culture's influence often becomes noticed the most in well-meaning ... between people from very different cultural backgrounds.
- Despite compromises, cultural values endure.
- When their cultural values are violated or when their cultural expect... ignored, people react emotionally.
- It is not unusual for people to accept a cultural value at one point in ... and reject it at another point. For example, rebellious individuals mi... culture's values and expectations after having children of their own.

Review and reflect Learning goal 3

3 Summarize the psychometric/intelligence view of adolescence

REVIEW

- What is intelligence? What are the main individual tests of intelligence? What are some issues in the use of group tests of intelligence?
- What theories of multiple intelligences have been developed? Do people have one intelligence or many intelligences?
- What are some controversies and group comparisons in intelligence?

REFLECT

- Apply Gardner's, Sternberg's, and Salovey, Mayer, and Coleman's categories of intelligence to yourself or someone you know well. Write a description of yourself or the person you know based on each of these views.

4 SOCIAL COGNITION

Adolescent Egocentrism

Implicit Personality Theory

Perspective Taking

Social Cognition in the Rest of the Text

Social cognition refers to the way individuals conceptualize and reason about their social worlds—the people they watch and interact with, their relationships with those people, the groups they participate in, and the way they reason about themselves and others. Recently there has been a flurry of interest in social cognition (Flavell, Miller, & Miller, 2002; Lapsley & Narváez, 2004). Our discussion will focus on egocentrism, perspective taking, and implicit personality theory.

I check my look in the mirror. I wanna change my clothes, my hair, my face.
—BRUCE SPRINGSTEEN

Adolescent Egocentrism

Adolescent egocentrism is the heightened self-consciousness of adolescents, which is reflected in their belief that others are as interested in them as they are themselves, and in their sense of personal uniqueness and invincibility. David Elkind (1976) be...

Reach Your Learning Goals

1 THE COGNITIVE DEVELOPMENTAL VIEW

Piaget's Theory

Vygotsky's Theory

2 THE INFORMATION-PROCESSING VIEW

Characteristics of the Information-Processing View

Decision Making

Creative Thinking

Attention and Memory

Critical Thinking

Metacognition and Self-Regulatory Learning

3 THE PSYCHOMETRIC/INTELLIGENCE VIEW

Intelligence Tests

Multiple Intelligences

Controversies and Group Comparisons in Intelligence

4 SOCIAL COGNITION

Adolescent Egocentrism

Implicit Personality Theory

Perspective Taking

Social Cognition in the Rest of the Text

Summary

1 Discuss the cognitive developmental view of adolescence

- Piaget's widely acclaimed theory stresses the concepts of adaptation, schemas, assimilation, accommodation, and equilibration. Piaget said that individuals develop through four cognitive stages: sensorimotor, preoperational, concrete operational, and formal operational. Formal operational thought, which Piaget believed appears from 11 to 15 years of age, is characterized by abstract, idealistic, and hypothetical-deductive thinking. Some experts argue that formal operational thought has two phases: early and late. Individual variation in adolescent cognition is extensive. Many young adolescents are still consolidating their concrete operational thought or are early formal operational thinkers rather than full-fledged ones. Although Piaget was not an educator, his ideas have been applied to education. In terms of Piaget's contributions, we owe to him the entire field of cognitive development and a masterful list of concepts. He also was a genius at observing children. Criticisms of Piaget's theory focus on estimates of competence, stages, training to reason at higher stages, and the role of culture and education. Neo-Piagetians have proposed some substantial changes in Piaget's theory. Some experts argue that the idealism of Piaget's formal operational stage declines in young adults, being replaced by more realistic, pragmatic thinking. Perry said that adolescents often engage in dualistic, absolutist thinking, whereas young adults are more likely to think reflectively and relativistically. Postformal thought is reflective, relativistic, and provisional; realistic; and open to emotions and subjective.
- Vygotsky's view stimulated considerable interest in the idea that knowledge is situated and collaborative. One of his important concepts is the zone of proximal development, which involves guidance by more-skilled peers and adults. Vygotsky argued that learning the skills of the culture is a key aspect of development. Some contemporary concepts linked with Vygotsky's theory include scaffolding, cognitive apprenticeship, tutoring, cooperative learning, and reciprocal teaching. Piaget's and Vygotsky's views are both constructivist, although Vygotsky's view is a stronger social constructivist view than Piaget's. In both views, teachers should be facilitators, not directors, of learning. Criticisms of Vygotsky's view focus on facilitators possibly being too helpful and adolescents' expecting others to do things for them.

2 Describe the information-processing view of adolescence

- Siegler states that the information-processing view emphasizes thinking, change mechanisms (encoding, automaticity, strategy construction, and generalization), and self-modification.

- Adolescents typically have better attentional skills than children do. They also have better short-term memory, working memory, and long-term memory than children.
- Adolescence is a time of increased decision making. Older adolescents make better decisions than younger adolescents, who in turn are better at this than children are. Being able to make competent decisions, however, does not mean they actually will be made in everyday life, where breadth of experience comes into play.
- Critical thinking involves thinking reflectively and productively and evaluating the evidence. Adolescence is an important transitional period in critical thinking because of such cognitive changes as increased speed, automaticity, and capacity of information processing; more breadth of content knowledge; increased ability to construct new combinations of knowledge; and a greater range and spontaneous use of strategies. Debates about critical thinking involve whether it should be taught in a general way or tied to specific subject matter and whether it resides in adolescents' heads or involves situated cognition.
- Thinking creatively is the ability to think in novel and unusual ways and discover unique solutions to problems. Guilford distinguished between convergent and divergent thinking. A number of strategies, including brainstorming, can be used to stimulate creative thinking.
- Metacognition is cognition about cognition, or knowing about knowing. In Pressley's view, the key to education is helping students learn a rich repertoire of strategies that results in solutions to problems. Self-regulatory learning is the self-generation and self-monitoring of one's thoughts, feelings, and behaviors in order to reach a goal. Most high-achieving students are self-regulatory learners.

3 Summarize the psychometric/intelligence view of adolescence

- Intelligence is the ability to solve problems and to adapt and learn from everyday experiences. A key aspect of intelligence focuses on its individual variations. Traditionally, intelligence has been measured by tests designed to compare people's performance on cognitive tasks. Alfred Binet developed the first intelligence test and created the concept of mental age. William Stern developed the concept of IQ for use with the Binet test. Revisions of the Binet test are called the Stanford-Binet. The test scores on the Stanford-Binet approximate a normal distribution. The Wechsler scales, created by David Wechsler, are the other main intelligence assessment tool. These tests provide an overall IQ, verbal and performance IQs, and information about 11 subtests. Group intelligence tests are convenient and economical, but they do not allow an examiner to monitor the testing closely. When used by a judicious examiner, tests can be

OTHER LEARNING SYSTEM FEATURES

Images of Adolescent Development

Each chapter opens with a high-interest story that is linked to the chapter's content.

Images of Adolescent Development

The Youths of Jeffrey Dahmer and Alice Walker

Jeffrey Dahmer's senior portrait in high school.

Alice Walker

J effrey Dahmer had a troubled childhood and adolescence. His parents constantly bickered before they divorced. His mother had emotional problems and doted on his younger brother. He felt that his father neglected him, and he had been sexually abused by another boy when he was 8 years old. But the vast majority of people who suffered through a painful childhood and adolescence do not become serial killers as Dahmer did. Dahmer murdered his first victim in 1978 with a barbell and went on to kill 16 other individuals before being caught and sentenced to 15 life terms in prison.

A decade before Dahmer's first murder, Alice Walker, who would later win a Pulitzer Prize for her book *The Color Purple*, spent her days battling racism in Mississippi. Born the eighth child of Georgia sharecroppers, Walker knew the brutal effects of poverty. Despite the counts against her, she went on to become an award-winning novelist. Walker writes about people who, as she puts it, "make it, who come out of nothing. People who triumph."

What leads one adolescent, so full of promise, to commit brutal acts of violence and another to turn poverty and trauma into a rich literary harvest? How can we attempt to explain how one adolescent can pick up the pieces of a life shattered by tragedy, such as a loved one's death, whereas another one seems to come unhinged by life's minor hassles? Why is it that some adolescents are whirlwinds—successful in school, involved in a network of friends, and full of energy—while others hang out on the sidelines, mere spectators of life? If you have ever wondered what makes adolescents tick, you have asked yourself the central question we explore in this book.

Appendix *Careers in Adolescent Development*

Some of you may be quite sure about what you plan to make your life's work. Others of you may not have decided on a major yet and are uncertain about which career path you want to follow. Each of us wants to find a rewarding career and enjoy the work we do. The field of adolescent development offers an amazing breadth of career options that can provide extremely satisfying work.

If you decide to pursue a career in adolescent development, what career options are available to you? There are many. College and university professors teach courses in adolescent development, education, family development, and medicine. Middle school and high school teachers impart knowledge, understanding, and skills to adolescents. Counselors, clinical psychologists, and physicians help adolescents to cope more effectively with the unique challenges of adolescence. And various professionals work with families of adolescents to improve the adolescent's development.

By choosing one of these career options, you can guide youth in improving their lives, help others to understand them better, or even advance the state of knowledge in the field. You can have an enjoyable time while you are doing these things. Although an advanced degree is not absolutely necessary in some areas of adolescent development, you usually can expand your opportunities (and income) considerably by obtaining a graduate degree. Many careers in adolescent development pay reasonably well. For example, psychologists earn well above the median salary in the United States.

If you are considering a career in adolescent development, as you go through this term, try to spend some time with adolescents of different ages. Observe their behavior; talk with them about their lives. Think about whether you would like to work with youth in your life's work.

Another worthwhile activity is to talk with people who work with adolescents. For example, if you have some interest in becoming a school counselor, call a school, ask to speak with a counselor, and set up an appointment to discuss the counselor's career path and work. Be prepared with a list of questions to ask and take notes if you wish.

Working in one or more jobs related to your career interests while you are in college can also benefit you. Many colleges and universities offer internships or work experiences for students who major in fields such as development. In some instances, these opportunities are for course credit or pay; in others, they are strictly on a volunteer basis. Take advantage of these opportunities. They can provide you with valuable experiences to help you decide if this is the right career area for you, and they can help you get into graduate school, if you decide you want to go.

In the following sections, we profile careers in three areas: education/research; clinical/counseling/medical; and families/relationships. These are not the only career options in the field of adolescent development, but they should provide you with an idea of the range of opportunities available and information about some of the main career avenues you might pursue. In profiling these careers, we address the amount of education required, the nature of the training, and a description of the work.

38

Careers in Adolescent Development Appendix

A Career in Adolescent Development appendix that describes a number of careers appears following chapter 1.

Careers in Adolescent Development

These inserts appear one or more times in each chapter and provide a description of an individual who works in the field of adolescent development.

Puberty **93**

Gulotta). Have the effects of puberty been exaggerated? Puberty affects some adolescents more strongly than others, and some behaviors more strongly than others. Body image, interest in dating, and sexual behavior are quite clearly affected by pubertal change. In one study, early-maturing boys and girls reported more sexual activity and delinquency than late maturers (Flannery, Rowe, & Gulley, 1993). Yet, if we look at overall development and adjustment over the human life span, puberty and its variations have less dramatic effects than is commonly thought for most individuals. For some young adolescents, the path through puberty is stormy, but for most it is not. Each period of the human life span has its stresses and puberty is no different. While it poses new challenges, the vast majority of adolescents weather the stresses effectively. Besides the biological influences on adolescent development, cognitive and social or environmental influences also shape who we become (Sarigiani & Petersen, 2000; Susman & Rogol, 2004). Singling out biological changes as the dominant influence during adolescence may not be wise.

Although extremely early and late maturation may be risk factors in development, we have seen that the overall effects of early or late maturation often are not great. Not all early maturers will date, smoke, and drink, and not all late maturers will have difficulty in peer relations. In some instances, the effects of an adolescent's grade in school are stronger than maturational timing (Petersen & Crockett, 1985). Because the adolescent's social world is organized by grade rather than physical development, this finding is not surprising. However, that does not mean that age of maturation has no influence on development. Rather, we need to evaluate puberty's effects within the larger framework of interacting biological, cognitive, and socioemotional contexts (Brooks-Gunn, 1992; Sarigiani & Petersen, 2000).

Pubertal Timing and Health Care

What can be done to identify early and late maturers who are at risk for health problems? Adolescents whose development is extremely early or late, such as a boy who has not had a growth spurt by age 16 or a girl who has not menstruated by age 15, are likely to come to the attention of a physician. Girls and boys who are early or late maturers, but are still well within the normal range, are less likely to be seen by a physician. Nonetheless, these boys and girls may have doubts and fears about being normal that they will not raise unless a physician, counselor, or other health-care provider does. A brief discussion of the usual sequence and timing of events, and the large individual variations in them, may be all that is required to reassure many adolescents who are maturing very early or very late.

Health-care providers may want to discuss an adolescent's early or late development with parents as well. Information about peer pressures can be helpful, especially the peer pressures to date on early-maturing girls and engage in

Careers in Adolescent Development

Anne Petersen
Researcher and Administrator

A nne Petersen has had a distinguished career as a researcher and administrator with a main focus on adolescent development. Anne obtained three degrees (B.A., M.A., and Ph.D.) from the University of Chicago in math and statistics. Her first job after she obtained her Ph.D. was as a research associate/professor involving statistical consultation, and it was on this job that she was introduced to the field of adolescent development, which became the focus of her subsequent work.

Anne moved from the University of Chicago to Pennsylvania State University, where she became a leading researcher in adolescent development. Her research included a focus on puberty and gender. Anne also has held numerous administrative positions. In the mid-1990s, Anne became Deputy Director of the National Science Foundation and since 1996 has been Senior Vice-President for programs at the W. K. Kellogg Foundation.

Anne says that what inspired her to enter the field of adolescent development and take her current position at the Kellogg Foundation was her desire to make a difference for people, especially youth. In her position at Kellogg, Anne is responsible for all programming and services provided by the foundation for adolescents. Her goal is to make a difference for youth in this country and around the world. She believes that too often adolescents have been neglected.

Anne Petersen, interacting with adolescents.

Key Terms and Glossary

Key terms appear in boldface. Their definitions appear in the margin near where they are introduced.

Evolution, Heredity, and Environment 111

- **Active (niche-picking) genotype-environment correlations** occur when children seek out environments that they find compatible and stimulating. *Niche-picking* refers to finding a setting that is suited to one's abilities. Adolescents select from their surrounding environment some aspect that they respond to, learn about, or ignore. Their active selections of environments are related to their particular genotype. For example, attractive adolescents tend to seek out attractive peers. Adolescents who are musically inclined are likely to select musical environments in which they can successfully perform their skills.

Scarr believes that the relative importance of the three genotype-environment correlations changes as children develop from infancy through adolescence. In infancy, much of the environment that children experience is provided by adults. Thus, passive genotype-environment correlations are more common in the lives of infants and young children than they are for older children and adolescents who can extend their experiences beyond the family's influence and create their environments to a greater degree.

Critics argue that the concept of heredity-environment correlation gives heredity too much influence in determining development (Gottlieb, 2002). Heredity-environment correlation stresses that heredity determines the types of environments children experience. Next, we examine a view that emphasizes the importance of the nonshared environment of siblings and their heredity as important influences on their development.

Shared and Nonshared Environmental Experiences Behavior geneticists believe that another way of analyzing the environment's role in heredity-environment interaction is to consider experiences that adolescents share in common with other adolescents living in the same home, as well as experiences that are not shared (Feinberg & Hetherington, 2001; Plomin, Ashbury, & Dunn, 2001).

Shared environmental experiences are siblings' common experiences, such as their parents' personalities or intellectual orientation, the family's socioeconomic status, and the neighborhood in which they live. By contrast, **nonshared environmental experiences** are an adolescent's unique experiences, both within the family and outside the family; these are not shared with a sibling. Even experiences occurring within the family can be part of the "nonshared environment." For example, parents often interact differently with each sibling, and siblings interact differently with parents (Hetherington, Reiss, & Plomin, 1994; Reiss & others, 2000). Siblings often have different peer groups, different friends, and different teachers at school.

Behavior geneticist Robert Plomin (1993) has found that common rearing, or shared environment, accounts for little of the variation in adolescents' personality or interests. In other words, even though two adolescents live under the same roof with the same parents, their personalities are often very different. Further, behavior geneticists argue that heredity influences the nonshared environments of siblings in the manner we described earlier in the concept of heredity-environment correlations (Plomin & others, 2001). For example, an adolescent who has inherited a genetic tendency to be athletic is likely to spend more time in environments related to sports while an adolescent who has inherited a tendency to be musically inclined is more likely to spend time in environments related to music.

The Epigenetic View The heredity-environment correlation view emphasizes how heredity directs the kind of environmental experiences individuals have. However, earlier we described how DNA is collaborative, not determining an individual's traits

active (niche-picking) genotype-environment correlations Correlations that occur when children seek out environments that they find compatible and stimulating.

shared environmental experiences Siblings' common experiences such as their parents' personalities and intellectual orientation, the family's social class, and the neighborhood in which they live.

nonshared environmental experiences The adolescent's own unique experiences, both within a family and outside the family, that are not shared by another sibling.

116 Chapter 3 Puberty, Health, and Biological Foundations

psychology is the view that adaptation, reproduction, and "survival of the fittest" are important in explaining behavior. Evolutionary developmental psychology has promoted a number of ideas, including the view that an extended "juvenile" period is needed to develop a large brain and learn the complexity of human social communities. Critics argue that the evolutionary perspective does not give adequate attention to experience and humans as a culture-making species.

- The nucleus of each human cell contains 46 chromosomes, which are composed of DNA. Genes are short segments of DNA that direct cells to reproduce and manufacture proteins that maintain life. DNA does not act independently to produce a trait or behavior. Rather, it acts collaboratively. Genotype refers to the unique configuration of genes, while phenotype involves observed and measurable characteristics.
- Behavior genetics is the field concerned with the degree and nature of behavior's hereditary basis. Methods used by behavior geneticists include twin studies and adoption studies. In Scarr's heredity-environment correlations view, heredity directs the types of environments that children experience. She describes three genotype-environment correlations: passive, evocative, and active (niche-picking). Scarr be-

lieves that the relative importanc… environment correlations chan… Shared environmental experience… experiences, such as their parents'… tual orientation, the family's soci… neighborhood in which they live. … experiences involve the adolesc… both within a family and outsi… shared with a sibling. Many b… that differences in the develop… to nonshared environmental ex… rather than shared environmen… genetic view emphasizes that de… an ongoing, bidirectional intercha… environment.

- Many complex behaviors have s… gives people a propensity for a pa… jectory. However, actual developm… ronment and that environment is… of heredity and environment is e… be discovered about the specific w… vironment interact to influence d…

Key Terms

puberty 83
hormones 83
androgens 84
estrogens 84
menarche 86
spermarche 86
neurons 94
basal metabolism rate (BMR) 99
evolutionary psychology 105
chromosomes 107
DNA 107
genes 107
genotype 109
phenotype 109
behavior genetics 109
twin study 109
adoption study 110
passive genotype-environment correlations 110
evocative genotype-environment correlations 110
active (niche-picking) genotype-environment correlations 111
shared … ences 111
nonshared environmental experiences 111
epigenetic view 112

Key terms also are listed and page-referenced at the end of each chapter.

Key People

Roberta Simmons and Dale Blyth 92
Mary Carskadon 102
David Buss 105
Mihalyi Csikszentmihalyi and Jennifer Schmidt 106
Albert Bandura 106
David Moore 108
Sandra Scarr 110
Robert Plomin 111

Resources for Improving the Lives of Adolescents

Journal of Adolescent Health Care

This journal includes articles about a wide range of health-related and medical issues, including reducing smoking, improving nutrition, health promotion, and physicians' and nurses' roles in reducing health-compromising behaviors of adolescents.

The Society for Adolescent Medicine

10727 White Oak Avenue
Granada Hills, CA 91344

This organization is a valuable source of information about competent physicians who specialize in treating adolescents. It maintains a list of recommended adolescent specialists across the United States.

…y

…stment to new

…ange that results … contact between …ups.

active (niche-picking) genotype-environment correlations correlations that occur when children seek out environments that they find compatible and stimulating.

adolescence the developmental period of transition from childhood to early adulthood; it involves biological, cognitive, and socioemotional changes.

adolescent egocentrism the heightened self-consciousness of adolescents, which is reflected in their belief that others are as interested in them as they themselves are, and in their sense of personal uniqueness.

adolescent generalization gap Adelson's concept of generalizations about adolescents based on information about a limited, highly visible group of adolescents.

adolescents who are gifted adolescents who have above-average intelligence (usually defined as an IQ of 130 or higher) and/or superior talent in some domain, such as art, music, or mathematics.

adoption study a study in which investigators seek to discover whether the behavior and psychological characteristics of adopted children are more like their adoptive parents, who have provided a home environment, or more like those of their biological parents, who have contributed their heredity. Another form of adoption study involves comparing adoptive and biological siblings.

affectionate love also called companionate love, this love occurs when an individual desires to have another person near and has a deep, caring affection for that person.

AIDS acquired immune deficiency syndrome, a primarily sexually transmitted infection caused by the HIV virus, which destroys the body's immune system.

alternation model this model assumes that it is possible for an individual to know and understand two different cultures. It also assumes that individuals can alter their behavior to fit a particular social context.

altruism unselfish interest in helping another person.

anabolic steroids drugs derived from the male sex hormone, testosterone. They promote muscle growth and lean body mass.

androgens the main class of male sex hormones.

androgyny the presence of a high degree of desirable feminine and masculine characteristics in the same individual.

anorexia nervosa an eating disorder that involves the relentless pursuit of thinness through starvation.

anxiety a vague, highly unpleasant feeling of fear and apprehension.

assimilation the absorption of ethnic minority groups into the dominant group, which often means the loss of some or virtually all of the behavior and values of the ethnic minority group.

assimilation the incorporation of new information into existing knowledge.

attention deficit hyperactivity disorder (ADHD) children and adolescents with ADHD show one or more of the following characteristics over a period of time: inattention, hyperactivity, and impulsivity.

attribution theory the concept that individuals are motivated to discover the underlying causes of their own behavior or performance in their effort to make sense of it.

authoritarian parenting this is a restrictive, punitive style in which the parent exhorts the adolescent to follow the parent's directions and to respect work and effort. Firm limits and controls are placed on the adolescent, and little verbal exchange is allowed. This style is associated with adolescents' socially incompetent behavior.

authoritarian strategy of classroom management this teaching strategy is restrictive and punitive. The focus is mainly on keeping order in the classroom rather than on instruction and learning.

authoritative parenting this style encourages adolescents to be independent but still places limits and controls on their actions. Extensive verbal give-and-take is allowed, and parents are warm and nurturant toward the adolescent. This style is associated with adolescents' socially competent behavior.

authoritative strategy of classroom management this teaching strategy encourages students to be independent thinkers and doers but still involves effective monitoring. Authoritative teachers engage students in considerable verbal give-and-take and show a caring attitude toward them. However, they still declare limits when necessary.

autonomous morality the second stage of moral development in Piaget's theory, displayed by older children (about 10 years of age and older). The child becomes aware that rules and laws are created by people and that, in judging an action, one should consider the actor's intentions as well as the consequences.

B

back-to-basics movement this philosophy stresses that the function of schools should be the rigorous training of intellectual skills through such subjects as English, mathematics, and science.

basal metabolism rate (BMR) the minimum amount of energy an individual uses in a resting state.

behavior genetics the field that seeks to discover the influence of heredity and environment on individual differences in human traits and development.

G-1

Key terms are alphabetically listed, defined, and page-referenced in a glossary at the end of the book.

Quotations

These appear occasionally in the margins to stimulate further thought about a topic.

334 Chapter 9 Families

As marriage has become a more optional, less permanent institution in contemporary America, children and adolescents are encountering stresses and adaptive challenges associated with their parents' marital transitions.

—E. Mavis Hetherington
Contemporary Psychologist, University of Virginia

www.mhhe.com/santrocka10

For Adolescents: Dealing with Parents' Divorce
Divorce Resources
Single Fathers

What roles do noncustodial parents play in the lives of children and adolescents in divorced families? Most nonresidential fathers have a friendly, companionable relationship with their children and adolescents rather than a traditional parental relationship (Munsch, Woodward, & Darling, 1995). They want their visits to be pleasant and entertaining, so they are reluctant to assume the role of a disciplinarian or teacher. They are less likely than nondivorced fathers to criticize, control, and monitor the child's or adolescent's behavior or to help them with such tasks as homework (Bray & Berger, 1993). Frequency of contact with noncustodial fathers and adjustment of children and adolescents are usually found to be unrelated (Amato & Keith, 1991). The quality of the contact matters more. Under conditions of low conflict, when noncustodial fathers participate in a variety of activities with their offspring and engage in authoritative parenting, children and adolescents, especially boys, benefit (Lindner-Gunnoe, 1993). We know less about noncustodial mothers than fathers, but research suggests that these mothers are less adept than custodial mothers at controlling and monitoring their child's or adolescent's behavior (Furstenberg & Nord, 1987). Noncustodial mothers' warmth, support, and monitoring can improve children's and adolescents' adjustment (Lindner-Gunnoe, 1993).

What Factors Are Involved in the Adolescent's Individual Risk Vulnerability in a Divorced Family? Among the factors involved in individual risk vulnerability are the adolescent's adjustment prior to the divorce, personality and temperament, developmental status, gender, and custody. Children and adolescents whose parents later divorce show poorer adjustment before the breakup (Amato & Booth, 1996). When antecedent levels of problem behaviors are controlled, differences in the adjustment of children and adolescents in divorced and nondivorced families are reduced (Cherlin & others, 1991).

Personality and temperament also play a role in adolescent adjustment in divorced families. Adolescents who are socially mature and responsible, who show few behavioral problems, and who have an easy temperament are better able to cope with their parents' divorce. Children and adolescents with a difficult temperament often have problems coping with their parents' divorce (Hetherington & Stanley-Hagan, 2002).

Focusing on the developmental status of the child or adolescent involves taking into account the age of onset of the divorce and the time when the child's or adolescent's adjustment is assessed. In most studies, these factors are confounded with length of time since the divorce occurred. Some researchers have found that preschool children whose parents divorce are at greater risk for long-term problems than are older children (Zill, Morrison, & Coiro, 1993). The explanation for this focuses on their inability to realistically appraise the causes and consequences of divorce, their anxiety about the possibility of abandonment, their self-blame for the divorce, and their inability to use extrafamilial protective resources. However, problems in adjustment can emerge or increase during adolescence, even if the divorce occurred much earlier.

Earlier studies reported gender differences in response to divorce, with divorce being more negative for boys than for girls in mother-custody families. However, more-recent studies have shown that gender differences are less pronounced and consistent than was previously believed. Some of the inconsistency could be due to the increase in father-custody and joint-custody families and increased involvement of noncustodial fathers, especially in their sons' lives. Female adolescents in divorced families are more likely to drop out of high school and college than are their male counterparts. Male and female adolescents from divorced families are similarly affected in the likelihood of becoming teenage parents, but single parenthood affects girls more adversely (McLanahan & Sandefur, 1994).

In recent decades, an increasing number of children and adolescents have lived in father-custody and joint-custody families. What is their adjustment like, compared with the adjustment of children and adolescents in mother-custody families?

232 Chapter 7 Sexuality

We are born twice over; the first time for existence, the second for life; Once as human beings and later as men or as women.

—Jean-Jacques Rousseau
Swiss-Born French Philosopher, 18th Century

In chapter 5, we described sexual identity as one of the dimensions of personal identity (Russell & Troung, 2002). Intimacy with another is an important aspect of the dyadic nature of adolescent sexuality.

In chapter 6, we examined the physical and biological differences between females and males. We also saw that according to the gender intensification hypothesis, pubertal changes can lead boys and girls to conform to traditional masculine and feminine behavior, respectively. Further, when college students are asked to rate the strength of their sex drive, men report higher levels of sexual desire than women. The adolescent developmental transition, then, may be seen as a bridge between the asexuality of childhood and the fully developed sexual identity of adulthood.

Four chapters in the remainder of the book also include discussions that are important for understanding adolescent sexuality. In chapter 9, we will learn that intense, prolonged conflict with parents is associated with adolescent sexual problems as is a lack of parental monitoring. Better relationships with parents are correlated with postponing sexual intercourse, less frequent intercourse, and fewer partners in adolescence (Miller, Benson, & Galbraith, 2001). Later in this chapter, we will see that adolescents receive very little sex education from parents and that parents and adolescents rarely discuss sex.

In chapter 10, we will read about how same-sex siblings, peers, and friends often discuss sexuality (Caruthers & Ward, 2002). We will also learn that early dating is associated with a number of adolescent problems and that romantic love is important (especially for girls) in adolescence.

In chapter 11, we will study how schools are playing an increasingly important role in adolescent sexuality. And as we will see later in this chapter, most parents now recognize that sex education in schools is an important aspect of education.

In chapter 13, we will describe the vast cultural variations in sexuality. In some cultures sexuality is extremely repressed; other cultures have far more liberal standards for sexuality. The media often present sexuality to adolescents in an unrealistic way (Kim, 2002). An increasing concern is adolescents' access to sexual material on the Internet.

As you can see, sexuality has ties to virtually all areas of adolescent development that we discuss in this book. Let's now explore the sexual culture American adolescents are exposed to.

Sex is virtually everywhere in the American culture and is used to sell just about everything. *Is it surprising, then, that adolescents are so curious about sex and tempted to experiment with sex?*

Critical Thinking and Content Questions in Photograph Captions

Most photographs have a caption that ends with a critical thinking or knowledge question in italics to stimulate further thought about a topic.

172 Chapter 5 The Self, Identity, Emotions, and Personality

self-descriptions as they attempt to construct a general theory of self, an integrated sense of identity.

Because the adolescent creates multiple self-concepts, the task of integrating these varying self-conceptions becomes problematic. At the same time that adolescents are feeling pressure to differentiate the self into multiple roles, the emergence of formal operational thought presses them for *integration* and the development of a consistent, coherent theory of self. At first, their budding formal operational skills represent a liability, allowing adolescents to detect inconsistencies in the self across varying roles. Only later do these skills provide the cognitive capacity to *integrate* such apparent contradictions. In the excerpt that opened this chapter, the 15-year-old girl wondered how she could move so quickly from being cheerful to being depressed and then to being sarcastic. "Which is the real me?" she asked. Researchers have found that 14- to 15-year-olds not only detect these inconsistencies across various roles (with parents, friends, and romantic partners, for example) but also are much more troubled by these contradictions than younger (11- to 12-year-old) and older (17- to 18-year-old) adolescents (Damon & Hart, 1988).

Conclusions As we have seen, the development of self-understanding in adolescence is complex, involving a number of aspects of the self. The rapid changes that occur during the transition from childhood to adolescence produce a heightened self-awareness and self-consciousness, which in turn can produce doubt about who the self is and which facets of the self are "real" (Hart, 1996).

James Marcia (1996) believes that changes in the self during adolescence can best be understood by dividing them into early ("deconstruction"), middle ("reconstruction"), and late ("consolidation") phases. That is, in the early phase the adolescent confronts contradictory self-descriptions. In the middle phase, the adolescent attempts to resolve these contradictions. Finally in the late phase the adolescent develops a more integrated self-theory (identity).

Self-Understanding and Sociocultural Contexts We have seen that the adolescent's self-understanding can vary across relationships and social roles. Researchers have found that adolescents' portraits of themselves can differ depending on whether they describe themselves when they are with their mother, father, close friend, romantic partner, or peer. They also can differ depending on whether they describe themselves in the role of student, athlete, or employee. Similarly, adolescents might create different selves depending on their ethnic and cultural background and experiences (Lalonde & Chandler, 2004).

The multiple selves of ethnically diverse youth reflect their experiences in navigating their multiple worlds of family, peers, school, and community (Cooper & others, 2002). Research with U.S. youth of African, Chinese, Filipino, Latino, European, Japanese, and Vietnamese descent, as well as with Japanese youth, shows that as these youth move from one culture to another, they can encounter barriers related to language, racism, gender, immigration, and poverty. In each of their different worlds, however, they also can find resources—in institutions, in other people, and in themselves. Youth who find it too difficult to move between worlds can become alienated from their school, family, or peers. However, youth who can navigate effectively between different worlds can develop bicultural or multicultural selves and become "culture brokers" for others.

Hazel Markus and her colleagues (Markus & Kitayama, 1994; Markus, Mullally, & Kitayama, 1999) believe understanding how multiple selves emerge through participation in cultural practices is important. They argue that all selves are culture-specific that emerge as individuals adapt to their cultural environments. In North American contexts (especially middle-SES contexts), the culture promotes and maintains individuality. When given the opportunity to describe themselves, North Americans often provide not only current portraits but notions of their future selves as well. They frequently show a need for multiple selves that are stable and consistent. In Japan,

www.mhhe.com/santrocka10

Hazel Markus Talks About Selfways

The Internet

Web icons appear a number of times in each chapter. They signal you to go to the book's website where you will find connecting links that provide additional information on the topic discussed in the text. The labels under the Web icon appear as web links at the Santrock *Adolescence, 10th ed.* website, under that chapter for easy access.

Key People

The most important theorists and researchers in each chapter are listed and page-referenced at the end of that chapter.

---

adopt their parents' religious beliefs. Links have been found between adolescent sexuality and religiousness.

• Cults have been defined in various ways, ranging from dangerous institutions to fringe, often new, religious movements. Many people who join cults are in a transitional phase in their lives, and cults promise to fulfill their needs. The potential for the worst abuse is when a cult is physically and socially isolated from the outside community.

Key Terms

moral development 273
heteronomous morality 274
autonomous morality 274
immanent justice 274
cognitive disequilibrium theory 274
internalization 275

preconventional reasoning 275
conventional reasoning 276
postconventional reasoning 276
justice perspective 280
care perspective 280
social cognitive theory of moral development 283

altruism 284
forgiveness 284
ego ideal 285
conscience 285
empathy 286
love withdrawal 288
power assertion 288

induction 288
hidden curriculum 289
character education 289
values clarification 289
cognitive moral education 290
service learning 290
values 292

Key People

Jean Piaget 274
Martin Hoffman 274
Lawrence Kohlberg 275
James Rest 279

Richard Shweder 280
Carol Gilligan 280
Hugh Hartshorne and Mark May 283

Albert Bandura 283
Sigmund Freud 285
Erik Erikson 286
Nancy Eisenberg 288

John Dewey 289
James Fowler 295

Resources for Improving the Lives of Adolescents

Cults

(1999) by Marc Galanter
New York: Oxford University Press

This book explores many aspects of cults, including their social psychological characteristics.

Education in the Moral Domain

(2001) by Larry Nucci
New York: Cambridge University Press.

Larry Nucci, who has made important contributions to the field of moral development, provides concrete recommendations for creating a moral classroom climate.

Invitation to the Psychology of Religion

(2000, 3rd ed.) by Raymond Paloutzian
Needham Heights, MA: Allyn & Bacon

This book provides a broad overview of topics in the psychology of religion, including religious development, conversion, religious experience, attitudes and behavior, and mental health.

Meeting at the Crossroads

(1992) by Lyn Mikel Brown and Carol Gilligan
Cambridge, MA: Harvard University Press

This book provides a vivid portrayal of how adolescent girls are often ignored and misunderstood as they make their passage through adolescence.

Moral Development and Reality

(2003) by John Gibbs
Thousand Oaks, CA: Sage

Leading researcher John Gibbs provides an insightful, contemporary examination of many aspects of moral development, including treatment programs for antisocial youth.

National Helpers Network, Inc.

245 Fifth Avenue, Suite 1705
New York, NY 10016-8728
212-679-7461

This network developed the Early Adolescent Helper Program, an approach to service learning.

Service Learning

(1997) by Alan Waterman (Ed.)
Mahwah, NJ: Erlbaum

A number of leading experts discuss many aspects of service learning.

E-Learning Resources

This feature appears at the end of each chapter and consists of three parts: *Taking It to the Net,* which involves Internet problem-solving exercises; *Self-Assessment,* which consists of one or more self-evaluations; and *Health and Well-Being, Parenting and Education* scenarios, which provide an opportunity to practice decision-making skills. By going to the Online Learning Center for this book, you can complete these valuable and enjoyable exercises for this book, where you will find many learning activities to improve your knowledge and understanding of the chapter.

E-Learning Tools

To help you master the material in this chapter, you will find a number of valuable study tools on the student CD-ROM that accompanies this book. In addition, visit the Online Learning Center for *Adolescence, 10th Edition,* where you will find helpful resources for chapter 6, "Gender."

Taking It to the Net

http://www.mhhe.com/santrocka10

1. Gender roles influence how we perceive ourselves and others, our desires and goals, and our personalities. But they also impact on the everyday lives of adults in very basic and fundamental ways. What might the issues of balancing home and career be and how are they similar and different for males and females?

2. Great changes have occurred in gender roles since the 1970s, particularly in the lives of women. But have these changes impacted on the nature and quality of married life? How do you view the relation between gender roles and marriage? How might your spouse view that relationship?

3. Gender differences in humans in part reflect physical/biological differences. How might other disciplines such as biology inform your understanding of how these physical differences came into play?

Connect to **http://www.mhhe.com/santrocka10** to research the answers and complete these exercises. In some cases, you'll also find further instructions on this site.

Self-Assessment

To evaluate yourself, complete this self-assessment: My Attitudes Toward Women.

Health and Well-Being, Parenting, and Education

To practice your decision-making skills, complete the health and well-being, parenting, and education scenarios.

Adolescence

The Nature of Adolescent Development

In no order of things is adolescence the simple time of life.
—JEAN ERSKINE STEWART
American Writer, 20th Century

Adolescence is a transitional period in the human life span, linking childhood and adulthood. Understanding the meaning of adolescence is important because adolescents are the future of any society. This first section contains two chapters: chapter 1, "Introduction," and chapter 2, "The Science of Adolescent Development."

CHAPTER

1

A few years ago, it occurred to me that, when I was a teenager, in the early Depression years, there were no teenagers! Teenagers have sneaked up on us in our own lifetime, and yet it seems they always have been with us. . . . The teenager had not yet been invented, though, and there did not yet exist a special class of beings, bounded in a certain way— not quite children and certainly not adults.

—P. MUSGROVE
American Writer, 20th Century

Introduction

Chapter Outline	***Learning Goals***

THE HISTORICAL PERSPECTIVE   **1**   Describe the historical perspective of adolescence

Early History

The Twentieth Century

Stereotyping of Adolescents

A Positive View of Adolescence

TODAY'S ADOLESCENTS IN THE UNITED STATES   **2**   Discuss today's U.S. adolescents and social policy issues involving adolescents

The Current Status of U.S. Adolescents

Social Contexts

Social Policy and Adolescents' Development

THE GLOBAL PERSPECTIVE   **3**   Characterize the current global perspective on adolescence

Youth Around the World

Global Traditions and Changes in Adolescence

THE NATURE OF DEVELOPMENT   **4**   Summarize the developmental processes, periods, transitions, and issues related to adolescence

Processes and Periods

Developmental Transitions

Developmental Issues

UNDERSTANDING ADOLESCENCE: WHAT MATTERS   **5**   Explain what matters in understanding adolescence

History Matters

Science Matters

Biological Processes Matter

Cognitive Processes Matter

Social and Personality Development Matter

Contexts Matter

Problems Matter

Reflective and Critical Thinking Matter

Images of Adolescent Development

The Youths of Jeffrey Dahmer and Alice Walker

Jeffrey Dahmer's senior portrait in high school.

Alice Walker

Jeffrey Dahmer had a troubled childhood and adolescence. His parents constantly bickered before they divorced. His mother had emotional problems and doted on his younger brother. He felt that his father neglected him, and he had been sexually abused by another boy when he was 8 years old. But the vast majority of people who suffered through a painful childhood and adolescence do not become serial killers as Dahmer did. Dahmer murdered his first victim in 1978 with a barbell and went on to kill 16 other individuals before being caught and sentenced to 15 life terms in prison.

A decade before Dahmer's first murder, Alice Walker, who would later win a Pulitzer Prize for her book *The Color Purple,* spent her days battling racism in Mississippi. Born the eighth child of Georgia sharecroppers, Walker knew the brutal effects of poverty. Despite the counts against her, she went on to become an award-winning novelist. Walker writes about people who, as she puts it, "make it, who come out of nothing. People who triumph."

What leads one adolescent, so full of promise, to commit brutal acts of violence and another to turn poverty and trauma into a rich literary harvest? How can we attempt to explain how one adolescent can pick up the pieces of a life shattered by tragedy, such as a loved one's death, whereas another one seems to come unhinged by life's minor hassles? Why is it that some adolescents are whirlwinds—successful in school, involved in a network of friends, and full of energy—while others hang out on the sidelines, mere spectators of life? If you have ever wondered what makes adolescents tick, you have asked yourself the central question we explore in this book.

*A*dolescence, 10th ed., is a window into the nature of adolescent development—your own and that of every other adolescent. In this first chapter, you will read about the history of the field; the characteristics of today's adolescents, both in the United States and the rest of the world; the way in which adolescents develop; and what matters in seeking an understanding of adolescence.

1 THE HISTORICAL PERSPECTIVE

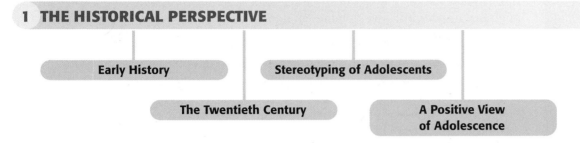

What have the portraits of adolescence been like at different points in history? When did the scientific study of adolescence begin?

Early History

In early Greece, the philosophers Plato and Aristotle both commented about the nature of youth. According to Plato (fourth century B.C.), reasoning doesn't belong to childhood, but rather first appears in adolescence. Plato thought that children should spend their time in sports and music while adolescents should study science and mathematics.

Aristotle (fourth century B.C.) argued that the most important aspect of adolescence is the ability to choose, and that self-determination is a hallmark of maturity. Aristotle's emphasis on the development of self-determination is not unlike some contemporary views that see independence, identity, and career choice as the key themes of adolescence. Aristotle also recognized adolescents' egocentrism, commenting once that adolescents think they know everything and are quite sure about it.

In the Middle Ages, children and adolescents were viewed as miniature adults and were subjected to harsh discipline. In the eighteenth century, French philosopher Jean-Jacques Rousseau offered a more enlightened view of adolescence, restoring the belief that being a child or an adolescent is not the same as being an adult. Like Plato, Rousseau thought that reasoning develops in adolescence. He said that curiosity should especially be encouraged in the education of 12- to 15-year-olds. From 15 to 20 years of age, Rousseau believed individuals mature emotionally, and their selfishness is replaced by an interest in others. Thus, Rousseau revived the belief that development has distinct phases. But his ideas were speculative; not until the beginning of the twentieth century did the scientific exploration of adolescence begin.

The Twentieth Century

The end of the nineteenth century and the early part of the twentieth century saw the invention of the concept we now call adolescence. Between 1890 and 1920, a number of psychologists, urban reformers, educators, youth workers, and counselors began to mold the concept. At this time, young people, especially boys, were increasingly seen as being passive and vulnerable—qualities previously associated only with the adolescent female. When G. Stanley Hall's book on adolescence was published in 1904 (see the next section), it played a major role in restructuring thinking about adolescence. Hall wrote that although many adolescents appear to be passive, they are experiencing considerable turmoil within.

When educators, counselors, and psychologists began to develop behavior norms for adolescents, Hall's view substantially influenced those norms. As a result, in the

G. Stanley Hall, father of the scientific study of adolescence

Anthropologist Margaret Mead (*left*) with a Samoan adolescent girl. Mead found that adolescence in Samoa was relatively stress-free, although recently her findings have been criticized. *How does Mead's view of adolescence contrast with Hall's view?*

---

storm-and-stress view G. Stanley Hall's concept that adolescence is a turbulent time charged with conflict and mood swings.

1900 to 1920 period, adults tried to impose conformity and passivity on adolescents. Examples of this conformity included the encouragement of school spirit, loyalty, and hero worship on athletic teams. In the following sections, we will explore Hall's view, as well as two other prominent viewpoints of the twentieth century.

G. Stanley Hall's Storm and Stress View

Historians have described G. Stanley Hall (1844–1924) as the father of the scientific study of adolescence. In 1904, Hall published his ideas in a two-volume set: *Adolescence.*

Hall was strongly influenced by Charles Darwin, the famous evolutionary theorist. Applying Darwin's view to the study of adolescent development, he proposed that all development is controlled by genetically determined physiological factors. The environment, he thought, plays a minimal role in development, especially during infancy and childhood. Hall did acknowledge that environment accounts for more developmental change in adolescence than in earlier periods, however. At least with regard to adolescence, then, Hall believed—as we do today—that heredity interacts with environmental influences to determine an individual's development.

According to Hall (1904), adolescence is the period from 12 to 23 years of age and it is characterized by considerable upheaval. The **storm-and-stress view** is Hall's concept that adolescence is a turbulent time charged with conflict and mood swings. Hall borrowed the label *storm and stress* from the *Sturm und Drang* descriptions of German writers, such as Goethe and Schiller, who wrote novels full of idealism, passion, and feeling. Hall sensed a parallel between the themes of the German authors and the psychological development of adolescents. In his view, adolescents' thoughts, feelings, and actions oscillate between conceit and humility, good intentions and temptation, happiness and sadness. An adolescent might be nasty to a peer one moment and kind the next moment; in need of privacy one moment, but seconds later want companionship.

Hall was a giant in the field of adolescence. He began the theorizing, systematizing, and questioning that went beyond mere speculation and philosophizing. Indeed, we owe the beginnings of the scientific study of adolescence to Hall.

Margaret Mead's Sociocultural View of Adolescence

Anthropologist Margaret Mead (1928) studied adolescents on the South Sea island of Samoa. She concluded that the basic nature of adolescence is not biological, as Hall envisioned, but rather sociocultural. In cultures that provide a smooth, gradual transition from childhood to adulthood, which is the way adolescence is handled in Samoa, she found little storm and stress associated with the period. Mead's observations of Samoan adolescents revealed instead that their lives were relatively free of turmoil. Mead concluded that cultures that allow adolescents to observe sexual relations, see babies born, regard death as natural, do important work, engage in sex play, and know clearly what their adult roles will be tend to promote a relatively stress-free adolescence. However, in cultures like the United States, in which children are considered very different from adults and adolescence is not characterized by the same experiences, the period is more likely to be stressful.

More than half a century after Mead's Samoan findings, her work was criticized as biased and error-prone (Freeman, 1983). Current criticism states that Samoan adolescence is more stressful than Mead suggested and that delinquency appears among Samoan adolescents just as it does among Western adolescents. Despite the controversy over Mead's findings, some researchers have defended Mead's work (Holmes, 1987).

The Inventionist View

Although adolescence has a biological base, as G. Stanley Hall believed, it also has a sociocultural base, as Margaret Mead believed. Indeed, sociohistorical conditions contributed to the emergence of the concept of adolescence. In the quotation that opens this chapter, P. Musgrove notes that at a point in history not too long ago, the idea of the teenager had not yet been invented. According to the

inventionist view, adolescence is a sociohistorical creation. Especially important in this view of adolescence are the sociohistorical circumstances at the beginning of the twentieth century, a time when legislation was enacted that ensured the dependency of youth and made their move into the economic sphere more manageable. These sociohistorical circumstances included a decline in apprenticeship; increased mechanization during the Industrial Revolution, which raised the level of skill required of laborers and necessitated a specialized division of labor; the separation of work and home; age-graded schools; urbanization; the appearance of youth groups, such as the YMCA and the Boy Scouts; and the writings of G. Stanley Hall.

Schools, work, and economics are important dimensions of the inventionist view of adolescence (Elder, 1975; Fasick, 1994; Lapsley, Enright, & Serlin, 1985). Some scholars argue that the concept of adolescence was invented mainly as a by-product of the movement to create a system of compulsory public education. In this view, the function of secondary schools is to transmit intellectual skills to youth. However, other scholars argue that the primary purpose of secondary schools is to deploy youth within the economic sphere, and to serve as a cog in the authority structure (Lapsley, Enright, & Serlin, 1985). In this view, American society conferred the status of adolescence on youth through child-saving legislation. By developing special laws for youth, adults restricted their options, encouraged their dependency, and made their move into the world of work more manageable.

Historians now call the period between 1890 and 1920 the "age of adolescence." In this period, lawmakers enacted a great deal of compulsory legislation aimed at youth. In virtually every state, they passed laws that excluded youth from most employment and required them to attend secondary school. Much of this legislation included extensive enforcement provisions.

Two clear changes resulted from this legislation: decreased employment and increased school attendance among youth. From 1910 to 1930, the number of 10- to 15-year-olds who were gainfully employed dropped about 75 percent. In addition, between 1900 and 1930 the number of high school graduates increased substantially. Approximately 600 percent more individuals graduated from high school in 1930 than in 1900.

An analysis of the content of the oldest continuing journal in developmental psychology, the *Journal of Genetic Psychology* (formerly called the *Pedagogical Seminary*) provides further evidence of history's role in the creation of adolescence (Enright & others, 1987). Four historical periods—the depressions of the 1890s and 1930s and the two world wars—produced quite different appraisals of the capacities of youths. During the depression periods, scholars wrote about the psychological immaturity of youth and their educational needs. In contrast, during the world wars, scholars did not describe youths as immature, but rather underscored their importance as draftees and factory workers. Let's take a closer look at how popular conceptions of adolescence changed with the changing times of the twentieth century.

Further Changes in the Twentieth Century   In the three decades from 1920 to 1950, adolescents gained a more prominent status in society as they went through a number of complex changes. Adolescents' lives took a turn for the better in the 1920s, but they moved through difficult times in the 1930s and 1940s. In the Roaring Twenties, passivity and conformity to adult leadership were replaced by increased autonomy and conformity to peer values. Adults began to model the styles of youth rather than vice versa. If a new dance came into vogue, the adolescent girl tried it first, and her mother learned it from her. Though prohibition was the law of the time, many adolescents drank heavily. More permissive attitudes toward the other sex developed; kissing parties and short skirts became standard fare. Soon the YMCA was campaigning against such "abnormal" behavior.

Just when adolescence was getting to be fun, the Great Depression arrived, followed by World War II. Serious economic and political concerns replaced the hedonistic values of the 1920s. Radical protest groups that were critical of the government

inventionist view The view that adolescence is a sociohistorical creation. Especially important in this view are the sociohistorical circumstances at the beginning of the twentieth century, a time when legislation was enacted that ensured the dependency of youth and made their move into the economic sphere more manageable.

(*a*) The Roaring Twenties was a time when adolescents began to behave more permissively. Adults began to model the styles of youth. Adolescent drinking increased dramatically. (*b*) In the 1940s, many youth served in World War II. Military service exposed many youth to life-threatening circumstances and allowed them to see firsthand the way people in other countries live. (*c*) In the 1950s, many youth developed a stronger orientation toward education. Television was piped into many homes for the first time. One of the fads of the 1950s, shown here, was seeing how many people could squeeze into a phone booth. (*d*) In the late 1960s, many youth protested U.S. participation in the Vietnam War. Parents became more concerned about adolescent drug use as well. (*e*) Since the 1970s much of the radical protest of youth quieted down. Today's adolescents are achievement oriented, more likely to be working at a job, experiencing adult roles earlier, showing more interest in equality of the sexes, and heavily influenced by the media.

increased in number starting in the 1930s, and World War II was a serious life-threatening event for adolescents. On the other hand, military service provided travel and exposure to youth from other regions of the United States, promoting a broader perspective on life and a greater sense of independence.

By 1950, the developmental period we refer to as adolescence had come of age. It possessed not only physical and social identities, but a legal identity as well, for every state had developed special laws for youths between the ages of 16 and 18 to 20. Adolescents of the 1950s have been described as the silent generation. For them, life was much better than it had been in the 1930s and 1940s. Television was beginning to invade their homes and the government was paying for veterans' college educations through the GI Bill. Getting a college degree—the key to a good job—was on the minds of many adolescents during the 1950s, as was getting married, having a family, and settling down to the life of luxury displayed in television commercials.

While adolescents' pursuit of higher education continued into the 1960s, many African American adolescents not only were denied a college education but received an inferior secondary education as well. Ethnic conflicts in the form of riots and sit-ins became pervasive, and college-age adolescents were among the most vocal participants.

The political protests reached a peak in the late 1960s and early 1970s, when millions of adolescents reacted violently to what they saw as the United States' immoral participation in the Vietnam War. As parents watched the 1968 Democratic National Convention on television, they saw not only political speeches in support of the candidates but demonstrations in which adolescents fought with the police and yelled obscenities at adults who supported the war. At the same time, parents became concerned about the teenage increase in drug use. Sexual permissiveness in the form of premarital sex, cohabitation, and previously prohibited sexual conduct also increased.

By the mid-1970s, the radical protests of adolescents began to abate along with U.S. involvement in Vietnam. They were replaced by increased concern for upward mobility through achievement in high school, college, or vocational training. Material interests began to dominate adolescents' motives again, while ideological challenges to social institutions began to recede.

In the 1970s, the women's movement changed both the description and the study of adolescence. In earlier years, descriptions of adolescence had pertained more to males than to females. The dual family and career objectives that female adolescents have today were largely unknown to female adolescents of the 1890s and early 1900s. And for many years, barriers had prevented most females and ethnic minorities from entering the field of adolescent development. Those dedicated individuals who did obtain doctoral degrees had to overcome considerable bias. One pioneer was Leta Hollingworth, who conducted important research on adolescent development, mental retardation, and gifted children. Pioneering African American psychologists included Kenneth and Mamie Clark, who conducted research on the self-esteem of African American children (Clark & Clark, 1939). And in 1932, George Sanchez documented cultural bias in intelligence tests for children and adolescents.

We have described the important sociohistorical circumstances surrounding the development of the concept of adolescence, and we have evaluated how society viewed adolescents at different points in history. Next we will explore why we need to exercise caution in generalizing about the adolescents of any era.

Women have often been overlooked in the history of psychology. In the field of adolescence, one such overlooked individual is Leta Hollingworth (*above*). She was the first individual to use the term *gifted* to describe youth who scored exceptionally high on intelligence tests (Hollingworth, 1916). She also played an important role in criticizing theories of her time that promoted the idea that males were superior to females (Hollingworth, 1914). For example, she conducted a research study refuting the myth that phases of the menstrual cycle are associated with a decline in performance in females.

Stereotyping of Adolescents

A **stereotype** is a generalization that reflects our impressions and beliefs about a broad category of people. All stereotypes carry an image of what the typical member of a particular group is like. We live in a complex world. Stereotyping is one way we simplify this complexity. We simply assign a label to a group of people. For example, we say that youths are promiscuous. Then we have much less to consider when we

stereotype A generalization that reflects our impressions and beliefs about a broad group of people. All stereotypes refer to an image of what the typical member of a particular group is like.

Have adolescents been stereotyped too negatively? Explain.

think about this group of people. Once we assign a stereotype, it is difficult to abandon it, even in the face of contradictory evidence.

Stereotypes of adolescents are plentiful: "They say they want a job, but when they get one, they don't want to work"; "They are all lazy"; "They are all sex fiends"; "They are all into drugs, every last one of them"; "Kids today don't have the moral fiber of my generation"; "The problem with adolescents today is that they all have it too easy"; "They are a bunch of egotistical smart alecks."

Indeed, during most of the twentieth century, adolescents have been portrayed as abnormal and deviant rather than normal and nondeviant. Consider Hall's image of storm and stress. Consider, too, media portrayals of adolescents as rebellious, conflicted, faddish, delinquent, and self-centered—*Rebel Without a Cause* in the late 1950s and *Easy Rider* in the 1960s. Consider the image of the stressed and disturbed adolescent—*Sixteen Candles* and *The Breakfast Club* in the 1980s, *Boyz N the Hood* in the 1990s. In one recent analysis of local television coverage, the most frequently reported topics involving youth were crime victimization, accidents, and violent juvenile crime, which accounted for nearly half (46%) of all coverage of youths (Gilliam & Bales, 2001). Especially distressing is that when given evidence of youths' positive accomplishments—that a majority of adolescents participate in community service, for example—many adults either deny the facts or say that they must be exceptions (Gilliam & Bales, 2001; Youniss & Ruth, 2002).

Stereotyping of adolescents is so widespread that adolescence researcher Joseph Adelson (1979) coined the term **adolescent generalization gap,** which refers to generalizations that are based on information about a limited, often highly visible group of adolescents.

A Positive View of Adolescence

The negative stereotyping of adolescents is overdrawn (Damon, 2003; Howe & Strauss, 2000; Perkins & Borden, 2003; Stepp, 2000). In a cross-cultural study, Daniel Offer and his colleagues (1988) found no support for such a negative view. The researchers assessed the self-images of adolescents around the world—in the United States, Australia, Bangladesh, Hungary, Israel, Italy, Japan, Taiwan, Turkey, and West Germany—and discovered that at least 73 percent of the adolescents had a positive self-image. The adolescents were self-confident and optimistic about their future. Although there were some exceptions, as a group, the adolescents were happy most of the time, enjoyed life, perceived themselves as capable of exercising self-control, valued work and school, expressed confidence in their sexuality, showed positive feelings toward their families, and felt they had the capacity to cope with life's stresses—not exactly a storm-and-stress portrayal of adolescence.

Old Centuries and New Centuries For much of the last century in the United States and other Western cultures, adolescence was perceived as a problematic period of the human life span akin to G. Stanley Hall's (1904) storm-and-stress portrayal. But as the research study just described indicates, a large majority of adolescents are not nearly as disturbed and troubled as the popular stereotype suggests.

The end of an old century and the beginning of the next has a way of stimulating reflection on what was as well as visions of what could and should be. In the field of psychology in general, as in its subfield of adolescent development, psychologists have looked back at a century in which the discipline became too negative (Larson, 2000; Santrock, 2003; Seligman & Csikszentmihalyi, 2000; Snyder & Lopez, 2002). Psychology had became an overly grim science in which people were too often characterized

Practical Resources and Research Adolescence Directory On-Line (ADOL) Children, Youth, and Family Consortium American Youth Policy Forum

adolescent generalization gap Adelson's concept of generalizations about adolescents based on information about a limited, highly visible group of adolescents.

as being passive victims. Psychologists are now calling for a focus on the positive side of human experience and greater emphasis on hope, optimism, positive individual traits, creativity, and positive group and civic values, such as responsibility, nurturance, civility, and tolerance (Flanagan, 2004; Flay, 2003; Hunter & Csikszentmihalyi, 2003; Lerner, Jacobs, & Wertlieb, 2003; Perkins & Borden, 2003; Rich, 2003; Youniss & Silbereisen, 2003).

Generational Perceptions and Misperceptions Adults' perceptions of adolescents emerge from a combination of personal experience and media portrayals, neither of which produces an objective picture of how typical adolescents develop (Feldman & Elliott, 1990). Some of the readiness to assume the worst about adolescents likely involves the short memories of adults. Adults often portray today's adolescents as more troubled, less respectful, more self-centered, more assertive, and more adventurous than they were.

However, in matters of taste and manners, the youths of every generation have seemed radical, unnerving, and different from adults—different in how they look, how they behave, the music they enjoy, their hairstyles, and the clothing they choose. It is an enormous error to confuse adolescents' enthusiasm for trying on new identities and indulging in occasional episodes of outrageous behavior with hostility toward parental and societal standards. Acting out and boundary testing are time-honored ways in which adolescents move toward accepting, rather than rejecting, parental values.

> *In case you're worried about what's going to become of the younger generation, it's going to grow up and start worrying about the younger generation.*
> —ROGER ALLEN
> *Contemporary American Writer*

Review and reflect Learning goal 1

1 Describe the historical perspective of adolescence

REVIEW

- What was the early history of interest in adolescence?
- What characterized adolescence in the twentieth century?
- How extensively are adolescents stereotyped?
- Why is a more positive view of adolescence needed?

REFLECT

- You likely experienced some instances of stereotyping as an adolescent. What are some examples of circumstances in which you think you were stereotyped as an adolescent?

2 TODAY'S ADOLESCENTS IN THE UNITED STATES

| The Current Status of U.S. Adolescents | Social Contexts | Social Policy and Adolescents' Development |

You should now have a good sense of the historical aspects of adolescence. With this background in mind, what is the current status of adolescents in the United States?

The Current Status of U.S. Adolescents

In many ways, today is both the best of times and the worst of times for adolescents in the United States. They possess longer life expectancies and luxuries inconceivable less than a century ago—television, computers satellites, air travel. However, the temptations and hazards of the adult world descend on them so early that too often they are not cognitively and emotionally ready to handle them effectively.

Crack, for example, is far more addictive than marijuana, the drug of an earlier generation. And the media present a bizarre version of reality. Talk-show hosts offer sensationalized accounts of exotic drugs and serial murders. Strange fragments of sex and violence flash across television and movie screens and lodge in the minds of youthful viewers. The messages are powerful and contradictory. Rock videos suggest orgiastic sex; public health officials counsel safe sex.

Every stable society transmits values from one generation to the next; that is civilization's work. Today, there is special concern about the values being communicated to American adolescents. Only half a century ago, two of three families in the United States consisted of a breadwinner father, a stay-at-home mother, and the children and adolescents they were raising. Today, fewer than one in five families fits that description. Terms such as *quality time* have found their way into the American vocabulary. Absence is a motif in the lives of many adolescents—absence of authority, absence of limits, absence of emotional commitment (Morrow, 1988).

In many ways, today's adolescents inhabit an environment that is less stable than that of adolescents several decades ago (Weissberg & Greenberg, 1998). High divorce rates, high adolescent pregnancy rates, and increased geographic mobility of families contribute to this lack of stability. The rate of adolescent drug use in the United States is the highest in the industrialized world.

Yet growing up has never been easy. In many ways, the developmental tasks today's adolescents face are no different from those of adolescents 50 years ago. For a large majority of youth, adolescence is not a time of rebellion, crisis, pathology, and deviance. Rather it is a time of evaluation, decision making, commitment, and finding a place in the world.

Our discussion underscores an important point about adolescents: they are not a homogeneous group (Cohen & others, 2003). Most adolescents successfully negotiate the lengthy path to adult maturity, but a large minority do not. Socioeconomic, ethnic, cultural, gender, age, and lifestyle differences influence the developmental trajectory of every adolescent.

Social Contexts

Of special interest to researchers is how social contexts influence adolescent development (Bronfenbrenner, 2000; Compas, 2004; Eccles, 2002; Lerner, 2000; McAdoo & Martin, 2003). **Contexts** are the settings in which development occurs; they are influenced by historical, economic, social, and cultural factors. To understand how important contexts are in adolescent development, consider the task of a researcher who wants to discover whether today's adolescents are more racially tolerant than those of a decade or two ago. Without reference to the historical, economic, social, and cultural aspects of race relations, adolescents' racial tolerance cannot be fully evaluated. Each adolescent's development occurs against a cultural backdrop of contexts that includes family, peers, school, church, neighborhood, community, region, and nation, each with its cultural legacies (Chun, Organista, & Marin, 2003; McLoyd, 1998, 2000).

The cultural context for U.S. adolescents is changing with the dramatic increase in the number of adolescents immigrating from Latino and Asian countries. Figure 1.1 shows the projected percentage increase for White, non-Latino, Latino, African American, and Asian American adolescents through 2100. Notice that Asian Americans are expected to be the fastest-growing ethnic group of adolescents with a growth rate of more than 600 percent growth by 2100. Latino adolescents are projected to increase almost 400 percent by 2100. Figure 1.2 shows the actual numbers of adolescents in different ethnic groups in the year 2000, as well as the projected numbers projected through 2100. Notice that by 2100, Latino adolescents are expected to outnumber non-Latino, White adolescents.

These changing social contexts will receive special attention in this book. All of section 4 is devoted to contexts, with separate chapters on families, peers, schools, and culture. As we will see next, some experts argue that the social policy of the United

contexts The settings in which development occurs. These settings are influenced by historical, economic, social, and cultural factors.

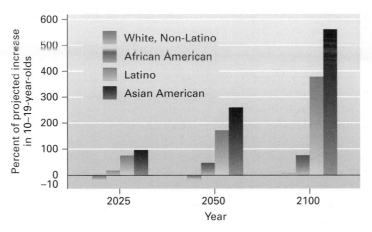

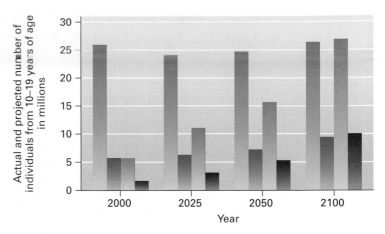

FIGURE 1.1 Projected Percentage Increase in Adolescents Aged 10–19, 2025–2100

An actual decrease in the percentage of non-Latino White adolescents from 10 to 19 years of age is projected through 2050. By contrast, dramatic percentage increases are projected for Asian American (233% in 2050 and 530% in 2100) and Latino (175% in 2050 and 371% in 2100) adolescents.

FIGURE 1.2 Actual and Projected Number of U.S. Adolescents Aged 10–19, 2000–2100

In 2000, there were more than 25 million White, non-Latino adolescents aged 10–19 years of age in the United States, while the numbers for ethnic minority groups were substantially lower. However, projections for 2025 through 2100 reveal dramatic increases in the number of Latino and Asian American adolescents to the point at which in 2100 it is projected that there will be more Latino than White non-Latino adolescents in the United States and more Asian American than African American adolescents.

States should place stronger emphasis on improving the contexts in which adolescents live.

Social Policy and Adolescents' Development

Social policy is the course of action designed by the national government to influence the welfare of its citizens. Currently, many researchers in adolescent development are attempting to design studies whose results will lead to wise and effective social policy decision making (Bogenschneider, 2002; Carlson & McLanahan, 2002; Edelman, 1997; Ferber, 2002; Pittman & Diversi, 2003; Pittman & others, 2003; Wertlieb, Jacobs, & Lerner, 2003).

Marian Wright Edelman, president of the Children's Defense Fund, has been a tireless advocate for children's rights. Especially troublesome to Edelman (1997) are the indicators of social neglect that place the United States at or near the bottom of the list of industrialized nations in the treatment of children and adolescents. Edelman believes that parenting and nurturing the next generation of children and youth is our society's most important function, and that we need to take it more seriously than we have in the past. She points out that while we hear a lot from politicians these days about "family values," when we examine our nation's policies for families, they do not reflect the politicians' words. We need a better health-care system for families, safer schools and neighborhoods, better parent education, and improved family support programs, Edelman says.

At the same time that U.S. adolescents have been suffering from governmental neglect, older generations have been benefiting from social policy. **Generational inequity,** in which older adults receive inequitably large allocations of resources, such as Social Security and Medicare benefits, at the expense of younger generations, raises questions about whether the young should have to pay for the old. Older adults enjoy publicly provided pensions, health care, food stamps, housing subsidies, tax breaks, and other benefits that younger groups do not. While the trend toward greater services for the elderly has been developing, the percentage of children and adolescents

Children's Defense Fund

social policy A national government's course of action designed to influence the welfare of its citizens.

generational inequity The unfair treatment of younger members of an aging society in which older adults pile up advantages by receiving inequitably large allocations of resources, such as Social Security and Medicare.

Through the Eyes of Adolescents

Land of Diminished Dreams

The year is two-thousand fifty-four,
The world is full of curses.
People walk the streets no more,
No women carry purses.

The name of the game is survival now—
Safety is far in the past.
Families are huge, with tons of kids
In hopes that one will last.

Drugs are no longer looked down on,
They are a way of life.
They help us escape the wrenching stress
Of our fast world's endless strife . . .

I wake up now—it was only a dream,
But the message was terribly clear.
We'd better think hard about the future
Before our goals and our dreams disappear.

—*Jessica Inglis, Age 16*

www.mhhe.com/santrocka10

The Search Institute

living in poverty has been rising. Adolescents have been especially underserved by the government.

Bernice Neugarten (1988) says the problem should not be viewed as one of generational inequity, but rather as a major shortcoming of our nation's economic and social policy. She believes we should develop a spirit of support for people of all ages. It is important to keep in mind that children will one day become older adults and be supported by the efforts of their children. If there were no Social Security system, many adult children would have to support their aging parents, which would reduce resources available to their children (Schaie, 2000).

The well-being of adolescents should be one of America's foremost concerns (Pittman & Diversi, 2003; Pittman, Yohalem, & Irby, 2003; Pittman & others, 2003). The future of our youth is the future of our society. Adolescents who do not reach their full potential, who make fewer contributions to society than it needs, and who do not take their place in society as productive adults diminish our society's future.

In a recent effort to define what is needed for more positive youth development, Reed Larson (2000) and his colleagues (Dworkin, Larson, & Hansen, 2003) have argued that adolescents need more opportunities to develop their capacity for initiative—to become self-motivated and expend effort to reach challenging goals. Too often adolescents find themselves bored with life (Hunter & Csikszentmihalyi, 2003). To counter their boredom and help them develop more initiative, Larson recommends structured voluntary activities, such as sports, arts, and participation in organizations.

Careers in Adolescent Development

Peter Benson
Director, Search Institute

Peter Benson has been the Director of the Search Institute in Minneapolis since 1985. The Search Institute is an independent, nonprofit organization whose mission is to advance the well-being of adolescents. The Institute conducts applied scientific research, provides information about many aspects of improving adolescents' lives, gives support to communities, and trains people to work with youth.

Peter obtained his undergraduate degree in psychology from Augustana College, master's degree in the psychology of religion from Yale University, and Ph.D. in social psychology from the University of Denver. Peter directs a staff of 80 individuals at the Search Institute, lectures widely about youth, and consults with a number of communities and organizations on adolescent issues.

Under Peter's direction, the Search Institute has determined through research that a number of assets (such as family support

and good schools) serve as a buffer to prevent adolescents from developing problems and increase the likelihood that adolescents will competently make the transition from adolescence to adulthood. We further discuss these assets in chapter 14, "Adolescent Problems."

Peter Benson, talking with adolescents.

Review and reflect Learning goal 2

2   Discuss today's U.S. adolescents and social policy issues involving adolescents

REVIEW
- What is the current status of today's adolescents?
- What is social policy? What are some important social policy issues concerning today's adolescents?

REFLECT
- How are today's adolescents similar to or different from the adolescents of 20 to 30 years ago?

3 THE GLOBAL PERSPECTIVE

Youth Around the World

Global Traditions and Changes in Adolescence

What are the world's youth like? What traditions remain for adolescents around the globe? What circumstances are changing adolescents' lives?

Youth Around the World

The way we present adolescence in this text is based largely on the writing and research of scholars in the Western world, especially Europe and North America. In fact, some experts argue that adolescence is typically thought of in a "Eurocentric" way (Nsamenang, 2002). Others note that advances in transportation and telecommunication are spawning a global youth culture in which adolescents everywhere wear the same type of clothing and have similar hairstyles, listen to the same music, and use similar slang expressions (Schegel, 2000). But cultural differences among adolescents have by no means disappeared (Larson & Wilson, 2004).

Consider some of the variations of adolescence around the world (Brown & Larson, 2002):

- Two-thirds of Asian Indian adolescents accept their parents' choice of a marital partner for them (Verma & Saraswathi, 2002).
- In the Philippines, many female adolescents sacrifice their own futures by migrating to the city to earn money that they can send home to their families.
- Street youth in Kenya and other parts of the world learn to survive under highly stressful circumstances. In some cases abandoned by their parents, they may engage in delinquency or prostitution to provide for their economic needs.
- In the Middle East, many adolescents are not allowed to interact with the other sex, even in school (Booth, 2002).
- Even though individuals in the United States are marrying later than in past generations, youth in Russia are marrying earlier to legitimize sexual activity (Stetsenko, 2002).

Thus, depending on the culture being observed, adolescence may involve many different experiences (Larson & Wilson, 2004).

Global Traditions and Changes in Adolescence

Rapid global change is altering the experience of adolescence, presenting new opportunities and challenges to young people's health and well-being. Around the world,

Muslim school in Middle East with boys only

Asian Indian adolescents in a marriage ceremony

Street youth in Rio De Janeiro

adolescents' experiences may differ depending on their gender, families, schools, and peers (Brown & Larson, 2002; Larson & Wilson, 2004). However, some adolescent traditions remain the same in various cultures.

Health and Well-Being   Adolescent health and well-being has improved in some areas but not in others. Overall, fewer adolescents around the world die from infectious diseases and malnutrition now than in the past (Call & others, 2002; World Health Organization, 2002). However, a number of behaviors that compromise adolescent health (especially illicit drug use and unprotected sex) are increasing in frequency (Blum & Nelson-Mmari, 2004). Dramatic increases in the rates of HIV in adolescents have occurred in many sub-Saharan countries (World Health Organization, 2002).

Gender   Around the world, the experiences of male and female adolescents continue to be quite different (Brown & Larson, 2002; Larson & Wilson, 2004). Except for Japan, the Philippines, and Western countries, males have far greater access to educational opportunities than females. In many countries, adolescent females have less freedom to pursue a variety of careers and engage in various leisure acts than males. Gender differences in sexual expression are widespread, especially in India, Southeast Asia, Latin America, and Arab countries where there are far more restrictions on the sexual activity of adolescent females than males.

These gender differences do appear to be narrowing over time, however. In some countries, educational and career opportunities for women are expanding and in some parts of the world control over adolescent girls' romantic and sexual relationships is weakening.

Family   In some countries, adolescents grow up in closely knit families with extensive extended kin networks, which tend to reinforce traditional ways of life. For example, in Arab countries, adolescents are socialized to observe strict codes of family conduct and loyalty. However, in Western countries such as the United States, adolescents are growing up in much larger numbers in divorced families and stepfamilies. Parenting in Western countries is less authoritarian than in the past.

Some of the trends that are occurring in many countries around the world include increased family mobility; increased migration to urban areas or to distant cities or countries; decreased family size; fewer extended family connections; and increased maternal employment (Larson & others, 2002). Unfortunately, many of these changes may reduce the ability of families to provide time and resources for adolescents (Brown & Larson, 2002).

School In general, the number of adolescents in school in developing countries is increasing. However, schools in many parts of the world—especially Africa, South Asia, and Latin America—still do not provide education to all adolescents. Indeed, there has been a decline in recent years in the percentage of Latin American adolescents who have access to secondary and higher education (Welti, 2002). Furthermore, many schools do not provide students with the skills they need to be successful in adult work.

Peers Some cultures give peers a stronger role in adolescence than others (Brown, 2004; Brown & Larson, 2002). In most Western nations, peers figure prominently in adolescents' lives, in some cases taking on responsibilities that are otherwise assumed by parents. Among street youth in South America, the peer network serves as a surrogate family that supports survival in dangerous and stressful settings. In other regions of the world, such as in Arab countries, peers have a very restrictive role, especially for girls (Booth, 2002).

In sum, adolescents' lives are characterized by a combination of change and tradition. Researchers have found both similarities and differences in the experiences of adolescents in different countries (Larson & Wilson, 2004). In chapter 13, "Culture," we will discuss these cross-cultural comparisons further.

Review and reflect Learning goal 3

3 Characterize the current global perspective on adolescence

REVIEW

- How is adolescence changing for youth around the globe?
- What traditions still characterize adolescents around the world? How are adolescents' experiences changing in terms of health and well-being, gender, families, schools, and peers?

REFLECT

- To what extent have you spent time with adolescents from other countries around the world? how was your experience of adolescence similar to or different from theirs? If you have not spent any time with adolescents from other cultures, how might such an experience influence your view of adolescence?

---

4 THE NATURE OF DEVELOPMENT

| Processes and Periods | Developmental Transitions | Developmental Issues |

In certain ways, each of us develops like all other individuals; in other ways, like no other individuals. Most of the time, our attention focuses on our individual uniqueness, but researchers who study development are drawn to our shared as well as our unique characteristics. As humans, we travel some common paths. Each of us— Leonardo da Vinci, Joan of Arc, George Washington, Martin Luther King, Jr., you, and I—walked at about the age of 1, talked at about the age of 2, engaged in fantasy play as a young child, and became more independent as a youth.

What do we mean when we speak of an individual's development? **Development** is the pattern of change that begins at conception and continues through the life span. Most development involves growth, although it also includes decay (as in death and dying). The pattern is complex because it is the product of several processes.

Processes and Periods

Human development is determined by biological, cognitive, and socioemotional processes. It is often described in terms of periods.

Biological, Cognitive, and Socioemotional Processes

Biological processes involve physical changes in an individual's body. Genes inherited from parents, the development of the brain, height and weight gains, advances in motor skills, and the hormonal changes of puberty all reflect biological processes. These biological processes are discussed extensively in chapter 3.

Cognitive processes involve changes in an individual's thinking and intelligence. Memorizing a poem, solving a math problem, and imagining what being a movie star would be like all reflect cognitive processes. Chapter 4 discusses cognitive processes in detail.

Socioemotional processes involve changes in an individual's emotions, personality, relationships with others, and social contexts. Talking back to parents, aggression toward peers, assertiveness, enjoyment of social events such as an adolescent's senior prom, and gender-role orientation all reflect the role of socioemotional processes. Sections 3 and 4 focus on socioemotional processes in adolescent development.

Biological, cognitive, and socioemotional processes are intricately interwoven. Socioemotional processes shape cognitive processes; cognitive processes advance or restrict socioemotional processes; and biological processes influence cognitive processes. Although you will read about these processes in separate sections of the book, keep in mind that you are studying about the development of an integrated human being who has only one interdependent mind and body (see figure 1.3).

Periods of Development

Human development is commonly described in terms of periods. We will consider developmental periods that occur in childhood, adolescence, and adulthood. Approximate age ranges are given for the periods to provide a general idea of when they begin and end.

Childhood

Childhood includes the prenatal period, infancy, early childhood, and middle and late childhood.

The **prenatal period** is the time from conception to birth—approximately 9 months. It is a time of tremendous growth—from a single cell to an organism complete with a brain and behavioral capabilities.

Infancy is the developmental period that extends from birth to 18 or 24 months of age. Infancy is a time of extreme dependency on adults. Many psychological activities—for example, language, symbolic thought, sensorimotor coordination, social learning, and parent-child relationships—begin in this period.

Early childhood is the developmental period that extends from the end of infancy to about 5 or 6 years of age, sometimes called the preschool years. During this time, young children learn to become more self-sufficient and to care for themselves. They develop school readiness (following instructions, identifying letters) and spend many hours in play and with peers. First grade typically marks the end of early childhood.

Middle and late childhood is the developmental period that extends from the age of about 6 to 10 or 11 years of age. In this period, sometimes called the elementary school years, children master the fundamental skills of reading, writing, and arith-

---

development The pattern of change that begins at conception and continues throughout the life span. Most development involves growth, although it also includes decay (as in death and dying).

biological processes Physical changes in an individual's body.

cognitive processes Changes in an individual's thinking and intelligence.

socioemotional processes Changes in an individual's relationships with other people, emotions, personality, and social contexts.

prenatal period The time from conception to birth.

infancy The developmental period that extends from birth to 18 or 24 months.

early childhood The developmental period extending from the end of infancy to about 5 or 6 years of age; sometimes called the preschool years.

middle and late childhood The developmental period extending from about 6 to about 10 or 11 years of age; sometimes called the elementary school years.

metic, and they are formally exposed to the larger world and its culture. Achievement becomes a central theme of the child's development and self-control increases. For example, notice how this theme is evident in the expressions of Laura (age 10) and Jared (age 8) by watching the video on "Self-perception at 10 Years & 8 Years of Age."

Adolescence As our developmental timetable suggests, considerable development and experience have occurred before an individual reaches adolescence. No girl or boy enters adolescence as a blank slate, with only a genetic code to determine thoughts, feelings, and behaviors. Rather, the combination of heredity, childhood experiences, and adolescent experiences determines the course of adolescent development. As you read through this book, keep in mind this continuity of development between childhood and adolescence.

A definition of adolescence requires a consideration not only of age but also of sociohistorical influences: recall our discussion of the inventionist view of adolescence. With the sociohistorical context in mind, we define **adolescence** as the period of transition between childhood and adulthood that involves biological, cognitive, and socioemotional changes. A key task of adolescence is preparation for adulthood. Indeed, the future of any culture hinges on how effective this preparation is (Larson & others, 2002).

Although the age range of adolescence can vary with cultural and historical circumstances, in the United States and most other cultures today, adolescence begins at approximately 10 to 13 years of age and ends between the ages of about 18 and 22. The biological, cognitive, and socioemotional changes of adolescence range from the development of sexual functions to abstract thinking processes to independence.

Increasingly, developmentalists describe adolescence in terms of early and late periods. **Early adolescence** corresponds roughly to the middle school or junior high school years and includes most pubertal change. **Late adolescence** refers approximately to the latter half of the second decade of life. Career interests, dating, and identity exploration are often more pronounced in late adolescence than in early adolescence. Researchers often specify whether their results generalize to all of adolescence or specifically to early or late adolescence.

The old view of adolescence was that it is a singular, uniform period of transition resulting in entry to the adult world. Current approaches emphasize a variety of transitions and events that define the period, as well as their timing and sequence (Larson & others, 2002; Sarigiani & Petersen, 2000). For instance, puberty and school events are seen as key transitions that signal entry into adolescence; completing school or taking one's first full-time job are key transitional events that signal an exit from adolescence and entry into adulthood.

Today, developmentalists do not believe that change ends with adolescence (Baltes, 2000; Demick & Andreoletti, 2003; Overton, 2003; Santrock, 2004). Remember that development is defined as a lifelong process. Adolescence is part of the life course and as such is not an isolated period of development. Though it has some unique characteristics, what takes place during adolescence is connected with development and experiences in both childhood and adulthood. Figure 1.4 summarizes the developmental periods in the human life span and their approximate age ranges.

Adulthood Like childhood and adolescence, adulthood is not a homogeneous period of development. Developmentalists often describe three periods of adult development: early adulthood, middle adulthood, and late adulthood. **Early adulthood** usually begins in the late teens or early twenties and lasts through the thirties. It is a time of establishing personal and economic independence, and career development intensifies.

Middle adulthood begins at approximately 35 to 45 years of age and ends at some point between approximately 55 and 65 years of age. This period is especially important in the lives of adolescents whose parents are either in or about to enter this adult period. Middle adulthood is a time of increasing interest in transmitting values

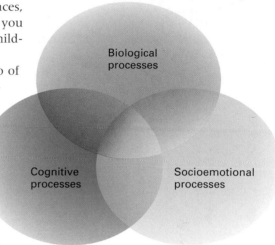

FIGURE 1.3 Developmental Changes Are the Result of Biological, Cognitive, and Socioemotional Processes
These processes interact as individuals develop.

adolescence The developmental period of transition from childhood to early adulthood; it involves biological, cognitive, and socioemotional changes.

early adolescence The developmental period that corresponds roughly to the middle school or junior high school years and includes most pubertal change.

late adolescence Approximately the latter half of the second decade of life. Career interests, dating, and identity exploration are often more pronounced in late adolescence than in early adolescence.

early adulthood The developmental period beginning in the late teens or early twenties and lasting into the thirties.

middle adulthood The developmental period that is entered at about 35 to 45 years and exited at about 55 to 65 years of age.

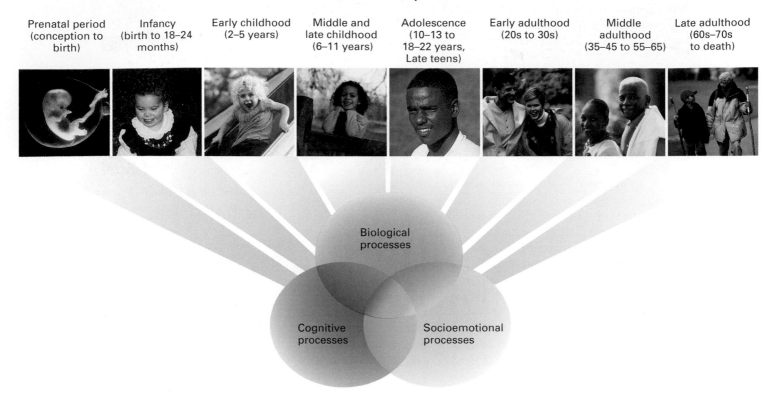

Periods of Development

FIGURE 1.4 Processes and Periods of Development
The unfolding of life's periods of development is influenced by the interaction of biological, cognitive, and socioemotional processes.

to the next generation, increased reflection about the meaning of life, and enhanced concern about one's body. In chapter 9, we will see how the maturation of both adolescents and parents contributes to the parent-adolescent relationship.

Eventually, the rhythm and meaning of the human life span wend their way to **late adulthood,** the developmental period that lasts from approximately 60 or 70 years of age until death. This is a time of adjustment to decreasing strength and health, and to retirement and reduced income. Reviewing one's life and adapting to changing social roles also characterize late adulthood, as do lessened responsibility and increased freedom.

Developmental Transitions

Developmental transitions are often important junctures in people's lives. Such transitions include moving from the prenatal period to birth and infancy, from infancy to early childhood, and from early childhood to middle and late childhood. For our purposes, two important transitions are from childhood to adolescence and from adolescence to adulthood. Let's explore these transitions.

Childhood to Adolescence   The transition from childhood to adolescence involves a number of biological, cognitive, and socioemotional changes. Among the biological changes are the growth spurt, hormonal changes, and sexual maturation that come with puberty. In early adolescence, changes take place in the brain that allow for more advanced thinking. Also at this time, adolescents begin to stay up later and sleep later in the morning.

Among the cognitive changes that occur during the transition from childhood to adolescence are increases in abstract, idealistic, and logical thinking. As they make this

late adulthood The developmental period that lasts from about 60 to 70 years of age until death.

Developmental transitions from childhood to adolescence involve biological, cognitive, and socioemotional changes. *What are some of these changes?*

transition, adolescents begin to think in more egocentric ways, often sensing that they are onstage, unique, and invulnerable. In response to these changes, parents place more responsibility for decision making on the young adolescents' shoulders.

Among the socioemotional changes adolescents undergo are a quest for independence, conflict with parents, and a desire to spend more time with peers. Conversations with friends become more intimate and include more self-disclosure. As children enter adolescence, they attend schools that are larger and more impersonal than their neighborhood grade schools. Achievement becomes more serious business, and academic challenges increase. Also at this time, increased sexual maturation produces a much greater interest in romantic relationships. Young adolescents also experience greater mood swings than they did when they were children.

In sum, the transition from childhood to adolescence is complex and multidimensional, involving change in many different aspects of an individual's life. Negotiating this transition successfully requires considerable adaptation and thoughtful, sensitive support from caring adults.

Adolescence to Adulthood   Another important transition occurs from adolescence to adulthood (Gutman, 2002; Jozefowicz, 2002; Montgomery & Cote, 2003; Raymore, Barber, & Eccles, 2001). It has been said that adolescence begins in biology and ends in culture. That is, the transition from childhood to adolescence begins with the onset of pubertal maturation, while the transition from adolescence to adulthood is determined by cultural standards and experiences. Around the world, youth are increasingly expected to delay their entry into adulthood, in large part because the information society in which we now live requires that they obtain more education

Copyright © 1986, Washington Post Writers Group. Reprinted with permission.

than their parents' generation (Mortimer & Larson, 2002). Thus, the transition between adolescence and adulthood can be a long one as adolescents develop more effective skills to become full members.

Do individuals enter adulthood abruptly? That is unlikely. Sociologist Kenneth Kenniston (1970) proposed that the transition between adolescence and adulthood can last two to eight years, or even longer. **Youth** is Kenniston's term for the transitional period between adolescence and adulthood, which is a time of economic and personal temporariness. Facing a complex world of work that requires specialized career preparation, many individuals choose to spend an extended period in a technical institute, college, or graduate/professional school. During this transition, their income is often low and sporadic, and they may frequently change their residences. Marriage and a family may be delayed.

Emerging Adulthood   More recently, the transition from adolescence to adulthood has been referred to as **emerging adulthood** (Arnett, 2000). Like youth, the age range for emerging adulthood is approximately 18 to 25 years of age. Experimentation and exploration characterize the emerging adult. At this point in their development, many individuals are still exploring which career path they want to follow, what they want their identity to be, and which lifestyle they want to adopt (for example, single, cohabiting, or married).

Determining just when an individual becomes an adult is difficult. The most widely recognized marker of entry into adulthood is when an individual takes a more or less permanent, full-time job, which usually happens when an individual finishes school—high school for some, college for others, graduate or professional school for still others (Graber & Brooks-Gunn, 1996). However, other criteria are far from clear. Economic independence is considered one marker of adult status, but developing it is often a long, drawn-out process. Increasingly, college graduates are returning to live with their parents as they seek to get their feet on the ground financially. About 40 percent of individuals in their late teens to early twenties move back into their parents' home at least once (Goldscheider & Goldscheider, 1999).

Self-responsibility and independent decision making are other possible markers of adulthood. Indeed, in one study, adolescents cited taking responsibility for themselves and making independent decisions as the markers of entry into adulthood (Scheer & Unger, 1994). In another study, more than 70 percent of college students said that being an adult means accepting responsibility for the consequences of one's actions; deciding on one's own beliefs and values; and establishing a relationship equal with parents (Arnett, 1995).

Is there a specific age at which individuals become an adult? One study examined emerging adults' perception of whether they were adults (Arnett, 2000). The majority of the 18- to 25-year-olds responded neither "yes" nor "no," but "in some respects yes, in some respects no" (see figure 1.5). In this study, not until the late twenties and early thirties did a clear majority of respondents agree that they had reached adulthood. Thus, these emerging adults saw themselves as being in an in-between period—not adolescents, but not full-fledged adults either.

In another study, however, 21-year-olds said that they had reached adult status when they were 18 to 19 years old (Scheer, 1996). In this study, both social status factors (financial status and graduation/education) and cognitive factors (being responsible and making independent decisions) were cited as markers for reaching adulthood. Clearly, reaching adulthood involves more than just attaining a specific chronological age (Cohen & others, 2003).

At some point in the late teens through the early twenties, then, individuals reach adulthood. In becoming an adult, they accept responsibility for themselves, become capable of making independent decisions, and gain financial independence from their parents (Arnett, 2000).

What we have said so far about the determinants of adult status mainly addresses individuals in industrialized societies, especially the United States (Nelson, Badger, & Wu, 2004). In developing countries, marriage is often a more significant marker for

youth Kenniston's term for the transitional period between adolescence and adulthood, which is a time of economic and personal temporariness.

emerging adulthood Occurring from approximately 18 to 25 years of age, this transitional period between adolescence and adulthood is characterized by experimentation and exploration.

entry into adulthood than in the United States, and it usually occurs much earlier than in the United States (Arnett, 2000; Davis & Davis, 1989).

Personal and Social Assets   Certain personal and social assets are linked to well-being in adolescence and emerging adulthood. Jacquelynne Eccles (Eccles, 2002; Eccles & Goodman, 2002; Eccles & others, 2003) recently examined research and concluded that three types of assets are especially important: intellectual, psychological, and social.

- *Intellectual Assets*. Researchers have found positive links between life skills, school academic success, planfulness, and good decision-making skills and positive outcomes in both adolescence and emerging adulthood. These positive outcomes include mental health, school completion, adult level of educational and occupational attainment, positive moral values, positive parent-child relationships, and avoidance of problem behaviors (Cairns & Cairns, 1994; Scales & Leffert, 1999).
- *Psychological Assets*. Researchers have found that positive mental health, optimism, self-regulatory skills, mastery motivation, and confidence in one's competence in those domains valued most by the individual are related to a wide variety of indicators of well-being in both adolescence and emerging adulthood (Bandura, 2001; Connell & others, 1995; Eccles, Wigfield, & Schiefele, 1998; Scales & Leffert, 1999). Although fewer studies have focused on the relation of identity, moral development, values, spirituality, and community contributions to well-being in adolescence and emerging adulthood, results indicate that these assets are also important (Ream & Savin-Williams, 2003; Youniss, McLellan, & Yates, 1997; Youniss & others, 2003).
- *Social Assets*. Strong research evidence suggests the importance of connectedness, integration, and feelings of belongingness to well-being in both adolescence and emerging adulthood (Eccles & Goodman, 2002; Scales & Leffert, 1999). The indicators of well-being include success in secondary school, mastery of a wide variety of life skills, adult educational and occupational attainment, positive mental health, optimism, and good self-regulation skills. Social assets also predict more effective transitions into key adult roles such as partner, spouse, parent, worker, and active community member (Werner & Smith, 1982). More now than ever, individuals who are entering adulthood need to be connected to kin or nonkin who can help with education, employment, housing, and health care (Larson & others, 2002).

Throughout this book, we will highlight these intellectual, psychological, and social assets that are so important to well-being in adolescence and emerging adulthood. So far in our coverage of the nature of development, we have focused on processes and periods in development, as well as developmental transitions. Next, we will explore some important issues in development.

Developmental Issues

Is development due more to nature (heredity) or to nurture (environment)? Is it more continuous and smooth or discontinuous and stagelike? Is it due more to early

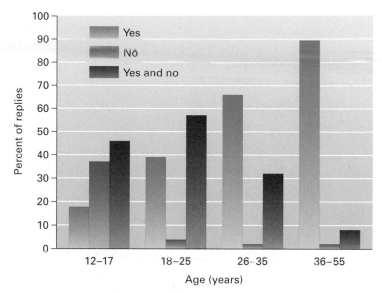

FIGURE 1.5 Self-Perceptions of Adult Status
In one study, individuals were asked, "Do you feel that you have reached adult status?" and were given a choice of answering "yes," "no," or "in some respects yes, in some respects no" (Arnett, 2000). As indicated in the graph, the majority of the emerging adults (18 to 25) responded "in some respects yes, in some respects no."

What are some of the intellectual, psychological, and social assets that are linked to success and well-being in adolescence and emerging adulthood?

FIGURE 1.6 Continuity and Discontinuity in Development

Is human development like a seedling gradually growing into a giant oak? Or is it more like a caterpillar suddenly becoming a butterfly?

Continuity and Discontinuity

nature-nurture issue Involves the debate about whether development is primarily influenced by nature or nurture. Nature refers to an organism's biological inheritance, nurture to its environmental experiences.

continuity-discontinuity issue The issue regarding whether development involves gradual, cumulative change (continuity) or distinct stages (discontinuity).

experience or to later experience? These are three important issues raised in the study of adolescent development.

Nature and Nurture   The **nature-nurture issue** involves the debate about whether development is primarily influenced by nature or nurture. *Nature* refers to an organism's biological inheritance, nurture to its environmental experiences. "Nature" proponents claim that the most important influence on development is biological inheritance. "Nurture" proponents claim that environmental experiences are the most important influence.

According to the nature advocates, just as a sunflower grows in an orderly way—unless flattened by an unfriendly environment—so does the human grow in an orderly way. The range of environments can be vast, but the nature approach argues that the genetic blueprint produces commonalities in growth and development. We walk before we talk, speak one word before two words, grow rapidly in infancy and less so in early childhood, experience a rush of sexual hormones in puberty, reach the peak of our physical strength in late adolescence and early adulthood, and then physically decline. The nature proponents acknowledge that extreme environments—those that are psychologically barren or hostile—can depress development. However, they believe that basic growth tendencies are genetically wired into humans.

By contrast, other psychologists emphasize the importance of *nurture,* or environmental experiences, in development. Experiences run the gamut from the individual's biological environment—nutrition, medical care, drugs, and physical accidents—to the social environment—family, peers, schools, community, media, and culture.

Some adolescent development researchers believe that, historically, too much emphasis has been placed on the biological changes of puberty as determinants of adolescent psychological development (Montemayor & Flannery, 1991). They recognize that biological change is an important dimension of the transition from childhood to adolescence, one that is found in all primate species and in all cultures throughout the world. However, they believe that social contexts (nurture) play important roles in adolescent psychological development as well, roles that until recently have not been given adequate attention.

Continuity and Discontinuity   Think for a moment about your development. Was your growth into the person you are today gradual, like the slow, cumulative growth of a seedling into a giant oak? Or did you experience sudden, distinct changes in your growth, like the remarkable change from a caterpillar into a butterfly (see figure 1.6)? The **continuity-discontinuity issue** focuses on the extent to which development involves gradual, cumulative change (continuity) or distinct stages (discontinuity). For the most part, developmentalists who emphasize experience have described development as a gradual, continuous process; those who emphasize nature have described development as a series of distinct stages.

In terms of continuity, a child's first word, while seemingly an abrupt, discontinuous event, is actually the result of weeks and months of growth and practice. Similarly, puberty, while also seeming to be abrupt and discontinuous, is actually a gradual process that occurs over several years.

In terms of discontinuity, each person is described as passing through a sequence of stages in which change is qualitatively, rather than quantitatively, different. As the oak moves from seedling to giant tree, it becomes more oak—its development is continuous. As a caterpillar changes into a butterfly, it does not become more caterpillar; it becomes a different kind of organism—its development is discontinuous. For example, at some point a child moves from not being able to think abstractly about the world to being able to. This is a qualitative, discontinuous change in development, not a quantitative, continuous change.

Early and Later Experience   Another important debate is the **early-later experience issue,** which focuses on the degree to which early experiences (especially early in childhood) or later experiences are the key determinants of development. That is, if infants or young children experience negative, stressful circumstances in their lives, can those experiences be overcome by later, more positive experiences in adolescence? Or are the early experiences so critical, possibly because they are the infant's first, prototypical experiences, that they cannot be overridden by a later, more enriched environment in childhood or adolescence?

The early-later experience issue has a long history, and developmentalists continue to debate it. Some believe that unless infants experience warm, nurturant caregiving in the first year or so of life, their development will never be optimal (Bowlby, 1989; Main, 2000; Sroufe, 2001). Plato was sure that infants who were rocked frequently became better athletes. Nineteenth-century New England ministers told parents in Sunday sermons that the way they handled their infants would determine their children's future character. The emphasis on the importance of early experience rests on the belief that each life is an unbroken trail on which a psychological quality can be traced back to its origin.

The early-experience doctrine contrasts with the later-experience view that, rather than achieving statuelike permanence after change in infancy, our development continues to be like the ebb and flow of a river. The later-experience advocates argue that children and adolescents are malleable throughout development and that later sensitive caregiving is just as important as earlier sensitive caregiving. A number of life-span developmentalists, who focus on the entire life span rather than only on child development, stress that too little attention has been given to later experiences in development (Baltes, 1987, 2000). They accept that early experiences are important contributors to development, but no more important than later experiences. Jerome Kagan (1992, 2000) points out that even children who show the qualities of an inhibited temperament, which is linked to heredity, have the capacity to change their behavior. In his research, almost one-third of a group of children who had an inhibited temperament at 2 years of age were not unusually shy or fearful when they were 4 years of age (Kagan & Snidman, 1991).

People in Western cultures, especially those steeped in the Freudian belief that the key experiences in development are children's relationships with their parents in the first five years of life, have tended to support the idea that early experiences are more important than later experiences (Chan, 1963). In contrast, the majority of people in the world do not share this belief. For example, people in many Asian countries believe that experiences occurring after about 6 to 7 years of age are more important aspects of development than earlier experiences are. This stance stems from the long-standing belief in Eastern cultures that children's reasoning skills begin to develop in important ways in the middle childhood years.

Evaluating the Developmental Issues   As we consider further these three salient developmental issues—nature and nurture, continuity and discontinuity, and early and later experience—it is important to realize that most developmentalists recognize that it is unwise to take an extreme position on these issues. Development is not all nature or all nurture, not all continuity or discontinuity, and not all early experience or all later experience. Nature and nurture, continuity and discontinuity, and early and later experience all affect our development throughout the human life span. For example, in considering the nature-nurture issue, the key to development is the interaction of nature and nurture rather than either factor alone (Coll, Bearer, & Lerner, 2004; Gottlieb, 2004; Loehlin, 1995, 2000). An individual's cognitive development, for instance, is the result of heredity-environment interaction, not heredity or environment alone. Much more about the role of heredity-environment interaction appears in chapter 3.

Consider also the behavior of adolescent males and females (Feldman & Elliott, 1990). Nature factors continue to influence differences between adolescent boys and

early-later experience issue This issue focuses on the degree to which early experiences (especially early in childhood) or later experiences are the key determinants of development.

girls in such areas as height, weight, and age at pubertal onset. On the average, girls are shorter and lighter than boys and enter puberty earlier. However, some previously well-established differences between adolescent females and males are diminishing, suggesting an important role for nurture. For example, adolescent females are pursuing careers in math and science in far greater numbers than in the past, and they are seeking autonomy in a much stronger fashion. Unfortunately, adolescent females also are increasing their use of drugs and cigarette smoking compared with adolescent females in earlier eras. The shifting patterns of gender similarities and differences underscore the belief that simplistic explanations based only on biological or only on environmental causes are unwise.

Although most developmentalists do not take extreme positions on the developmental issues we have discussed, this consensus has not meant the absence of spirited debate about how strongly development is determined by these factors. Continuing with our example of the behavior of female and male adolescents, are girls less likely to do well in math because of their "feminine" nature or because of society's masculine bias? Consider also adolescents who, as children, experienced poverty, parental neglect, and poor schooling. Could enriched experiences in adolescence overcome the "deficits" they encountered earlier in development? The answers developmentalists give to such questions reflect their stance on the issues of nature and nurture, continuity and discontinuity, and early and later experiences. The answers also influence public policy about adolescents and how each of us lives throughout the human life span.

Review and reflect Learning goal 4

4 **Summarize the developmental processes, periods, transitions, and issues related to adolescence**

REVIEW

- What are the key processes involved in adolescent development? What are the main childhood, adolescence, and adult periods of development?
- What is the transition from childhood to adolescence like? What is the transition from adolescence to adulthood like?
- What are three important developmental issues?

REFLECT

- As you go through this course, ask yourself questions about how you experienced particular aspects of adolescence. Be curious. Ask your friends and classmates about their experiences in adolescence and compare them with yours. For example, ask them how they experienced the transition from childhood to adolescence. Also ask them how they experienced or are experiencing the transition from adolescence to adulthood.

5 UNDERSTANDING ADOLESCENCE: WHAT MATTERS

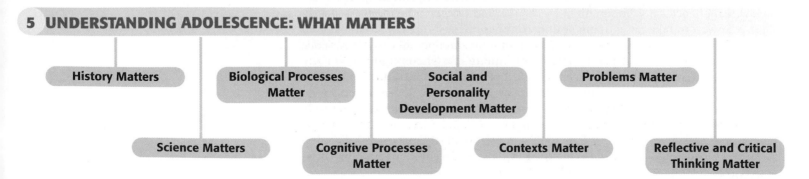

History Matters

Biological Processes Matter

Social and Personality Development Matter

Problems Matter

Science Matters

Cognitive Processes Matter

Contexts Matter

Reflective and Critical Thinking Matter

What matters in adolescence? What factors are at work when adolescents make a healthy journey from childhood to adulthood? What goes wrong when they fall off course and fail to reach their full potential? Earlier, we described some of the intellectual, psychological, and social assets that are linked to well-being in adolescence and emerging adulthood (Eccles, 2002; Eccles & Goodman, 2002). In thinking further about what really matters in adolescence, let's examine some of the main themes of this book and explore contemporary thinking about these themes. To understand adolescence, these things matter: history, science, biological processes, cognitive processes, social and personality development, contexts, and problems. Thinking reflectively and critically about these matters can substantially improve your understanding of adolescent development.

History Matters

As you have seen in this chapter, adolescence is influenced by historical events and times. Major social changes and political conflicts can significantly alter the lives of adolescents. Wars, legislation, economic upheavals, and advances in technology have modified how many adolescents experience their lives. Such historical changes can be negative, as in the case of war when the education of youth may be short-circuited and many youth die. Historical changes can also be positive as in the current trend toward adolescent females gaining greater access to education around the world.

Science Matters

You have probably heard it said that experience is the most important teacher. However, much of the personal knowledge we get from experience is based on our individual observations and interpretations. How do we know if these are accurate? Sometimes we make errors in watching, listening, and interpreting (Best & Kahn, 2003; McMillan & Wergin, 2002). In recent decades, an increasing number of researchers have studied adolescents, and the result is a dramatic improvement in our knowledge of how they develop (Lerner & Steinberg, 2004). Although we have much left to discover and there are many controversies about adolescent development, scientists are making considerable progress in improving our understanding of adolescence. An emphasis on research appears throughout this book, and in chapter 2 we will especially examine the scientific aspects of adolescent development in greater detail.

Biological Processes Matter

Earlier in the chapter, we examined the nature-nurture issue. Recall that this issue raises the question of how strongly adolescents' biological makeup (nature) influences their behavior and development. Controversy swirls about this topic. To Hall and Freud, biology was dominant. Today, experts also believe that biology plays a key role in adolescent development, but they emphasize the interaction of heredity and environment.

A current trend is to examine the role of evolution in adolescent development (Bjorklund & Pelligrini, 2002; Buss, 1998, 2000, 2004; Csikszentmihalyi & Schmidt, 1998). The field of evolutionary psychology—the most recent major theoretical view in psychology—seeks to examine how adaptation, reproduction, and "survival of the fittest" can help to explain behavior and development. We will evaluate evolution's role in depth in chapter 3, "Puberty, Health, and Biological Foundations," and chapter 6, "Gender."

There is also considerable interest today in studying how heredity is involved in behavior and development (Lewis, 2003; Rogers & Bard, 2003). Scientists are making considerable progress in charting the role of genes in various diseases and disorders (Hartwell & others, 2004; Nester & others, 2004). We will explore heredity more extensively in chapter 3.

A central aspect of biological processes in adolescence is puberty. Researchers want to know how early and late maturation influence development, the extent to which hormones and experience influence an adolescent's behavior, and similarities and differences in the ways boys and girls experience puberty (Archibald, Graber, & Brooks-Gunn, 2003; Susman, Dorn, & Schiefelbein, 2003; Susman & Rogol, 2004). We will extensively examine puberty in chapter 3.

The health of today's adolescents is a special concern. Far too many adolescents engage in health-compromising behaviors, such as smoking, excessive drinking, and risk-taking adventures (Blum, 2003; Blum & Nelson-Mmari, 2004; Polivy & others, 2003; Windle & Windle, 2003). We will examine adolescents' health throughout the book, but especially focus on it in chapter 3.

Cognitive Processes Matter

How important is the adolescent's mind in what she or he does? Adolescents are not only biological beings, they are mental beings. Considerable changes take place in cognition during adolescence (Byrnes, 2001, 2003; Eccles, Wigfield, & Byrnes, 2003; Keating, 2004; Kuhn, 2000). Although adolescents have more sophisticated thinking skills than children, there are considerable individual variations from one adolescent to another. But in general, advances in adolescent cognition not only help them solve difficult academic problems in areas such as mathematics but also change the way they think about their social lives.

Increasingly, developmentalists are concentrating on adolescents' decision making and asking how it can be improved (Jacobs & Kalczynski, 2002). They are also trying to find ways to help adolescents think more critically and deeply about various problems and issues. Another contemporary interest is determining what the components of intelligence are and creating educational programs that address these components (Sternberg, 2003; Torff, 2000). We will study cognitive processes in much greater detail in chapter 4, "Cognitive Development."

Social and Personality Development Matter

Many important aspects of adolescents' lives involve their social and personality development. A key aspect of adolescents' development, especially for older adolescents, is their search for identity (Adams, Abraham, & Markstrom, 2000; Comas-Díaz, 2001; Kroger, 2003). Researchers are interested in determining the contextual and developmental factors that promote healthy or unhealthy identity development (Kroger, 2003; Phinney, 2003; Rodriquez & Quinlan, 2002). We will examine these and many other aspects of the self and identity in chapter 5.

Gender is a pervasive aspect of adolescent development. Researchers are motivated to find out how contexts influence gender development (Galambos, 2004; Larson & Wilson, 2004). They are also interested in the role that sexuality plays in gender development during adolescence, how adolescence might be a critical juncture in gender development (especially for girls), gender similarities and differences, and adolescent male and female issues (Bumpas, Crouter, & McHale, 2001; Eagly, 2001; Koch, 2003). We will examine these and many other aspects of gender in chapter 6.

Sexuality has long been described as a key dimension of adolescent development. In adolescence, boys and girls take the journey to becoming men and women. It is a complex journey filled with mysteries and curiosities. An important point is that sexuality is a normal aspect of adolescent development. Developmentalists are motivated to discover adolescents' heterosexual and homosexual attitudes and behaviors, why the United States has the highest adolescent pregnancy rate in the industrialized world and what can be done about it, and strategies for reducing sex-

Through the Eyes of Adolescents

Wanting to Be Treated as an Asset

Many times teenagers are thought of as a problem that no one really wants to deal with. People are sometimes intimidated and become hostile when teenagers are willing to challenge their authority. It is looked at as being disrespectful. Teenagers are, many times, not treated like an asset and as innovative thinkers who will be the leaders of tomorrow. Adults have the power to teach the younger generation about the world and allow them to feel they have a voice in it."

—*Zula, Age 16*
Brooklyn, New York

ually transmitted diseases (Basen-Enquist & others, 2001; DiClemente & Crosby, 2003; Ford, Sohn, & Lepkowski, 2001; Savin-Williams & Diamond, 2004). We will discuss these topics and many others involving sexuality in chapter 7.

Moral development is another important aspect of adolescents' lives. Researchers seek to discover the roles of thoughts, feelings, and contexts in adolescents' moral development (Bandura, 2002; Damon, 2000; Eisenberg & Morris, 2004; Lapsley & Narváez, 2004; Smetana & Turiel, 2003). They want to know how important parents and peers are in adolescents' moral development. There also is considerable interest in the best way to morally educate adolescents, what adolescents' values are, the benefits of service learning, and developmental changes in the way they think about religion (Flanagan, 2004; Pritchard & Whitehead, 2004; Ream & Savin-Williams, 2003; Youniss & others, 2003). We will explore these and many other aspects of moral development in chapter 8.

Contexts Matter

Earlier we described the increasing trend of examining contexts or settings to better understand adolescent development. Especially important contexts in adolescents' lives are their family, peer, school, and cultural contexts (Compas, 2004; Eccles, 2002; Harkness & Super, 2002; Larson & others, 2002; Parke, 2004). Families have a powerful influence on adolescent development, and today large numbers of researchers are charting many aspects of family life, such as conflict, attachment, and divorce, to determine how they affect adolescent outcomes (Collins & Laursen, 2004; Granic & Dishion, 2003; Harvey & Fine, 2004; Hetherington & Stanley-Hagan, 2002; Rutter, 2002). We will explore these and many other aspects of families in chapter 9.

Like families, peers play powerful roles in adolescents' lives. Researchers are studying how peer status (such as being isolated, rejected, or popular), friends, cliques,

Teens Only!
Three Teenagers
Children, Youth, and Family Consortium
Trends in the Well-Being of
America's Youth
KidLink

Why do contexts matter in understanding adolescent development?

Careers in Adolescent Development

Luis Vargas
Child Clinical Psychologist

Luis Vargas is Director of the Clinical Child Psychology Internship Program and a professor in the Department of Psychiatry at the University of New Mexico Health Sciences Center. He also is Director of Psychology at the University of New Mexico Children's Psychiatric Hospital.

Luis got an undergraduate degree in psychology from St. Edwards University in Texas, a master's degree in psychology from Trinity University in Texas, and his Ph.D. in clinical psychology from the University of Nebraska–Lincoln.

His main interests are cultural issues and the assessment and treatment of children, adolescents, and families. He is motivated to find better ways to provide culturally responsive mental health services. One of his special interests is the treatment of Latino youth for delinquency and substance abuse. He recently co-authored (with Joan Koss-Chioino) *Working with Latino Youth* (Koss-Chioino & Vargas, 1999), which spells out effective strategies for improving the lives of at-risk Latino youth.

Luis Vargas, counseling an adolescent girl.

and dating and romantic relationships are involved in the adolescent's development (Brown, 2002, 2003, 2004). We will examine these and other aspects of peer relations in chapter 10.

Schools are another important context in adolescents' lives (Eccles, 2002, 2004; Eccles & Wigfield, 2000; Sadker & Sadker, 2003). Currently there is a great deal of concern about the quality of secondary education for adolescents. There also is controversy about the best way to teach adolescents (Pressley & others, 2003). A current trend is for teachers to act as guides in providing adolescents with learning opportunities in which they can actively construct their understanding of a topic or issue (Cobb, 2000). We will examine such concerns and trends in chapter 11, "Schools."

In adolescence, achievement becomes a more serious matter. Researchers are interested in determining how such factors as being internally motivated, planning, setting goals, self-monitoring, and having a mastery motivation are involved in the adolescent's motivation to achieve (Elliott & McGregor, 2001; Stipek, 2002). They also want to better understand the role of work in adolescent development and how adolescents think about careers (Shanahan, Mortimer, & Kruger, 2003; Spokane, 2000; Vondracek & Porfeli, 2003). We will examine these and other aspects of achievement in chapter 12.

The culture in which adolescents live is another important context in their development (Greenfield, 2000, 2002; Larson, Brown, & Mortimer, 2003; Triandis, 2000). Many researchers are comparing how adolescents in the United States are similar to or different from adolescents in other countries. In addition, they are seeking to discover how to improve relationships between people from different cultural worlds (Larson & others, 2002). A special concern also is that far too many American adolescents are growing up in poverty (Fuligni & Yoshikawa, 2003; Magnuson & Duncan, 2002; McLoyd, 2000). In recent years, there also has been a considerable increase in studying the role of ethnicity in adolescent development (Wong & Rowley, 2001). Another important aspect of culture today is technology (Calvert, 1999; Murray, 2000; Larson, Brown, & Mortimer, 2003; Van Evra, 2004). We will examine these and many other aspects of culture in chapter 13, "Culture."

Problems Matter

Far too many adolescents have problems that restrict their ability to optimally reach adulthood (Flannery & others, 2003; Seroczynski, Jacquez, & Cole, 2003). Researchers study such problems as drug use and abuse, delinquency, depression and suicide, and eating disorders (Farrington, 2004; Graber, 2004; Polivy & others, 2003; Windle & Windle, 2003). They want to know what causes adolescents to develop these problems and what the best ways are to prevent them in the first place and intervene in them when they do develop. A current trend is the understanding that many at-risk adolescents have more than one problem and that intervention programs need to take this into account. We will examine these and other aspects of problems in chapter 14.

Reflective and Critical Thinking Matter

Are you a reflective and critical thinker? What does it mean to be a reflective and critical thinker? Reflective and critical thinkers think deeply and productively and evaluate evidence. Thinking reflectively and critically means asking yourself how you know something. Too often we have a tendency to recite, define, describe, state, and list rather than analyze, infer, connect, synthesize, criticize, create, evaluate, think, and rethink (Brooks & Brooks, 1993, 2001). Reflective and critical thinkers are open-minded and intellectually curious, look for multiple determinants of behavior, and often think like a scientist (Halpern, 1996). Thinking scientifically involves keeping in mind that personal experiences and interpretations are error-prone and that it is important to examine the evidence about a topic or issue in adolescent development.

As you study adolescent development in this course, take a critical thinking stance. To encourage your reflective and critical thinking, many questions appear throughout this text; "Reflect" questions in the "Review and Reflect" feature at the end of each major section of a chapter challenge you to think critically. And at the end of each chapter "Taking It to the Net" exercises encourage you to reflect and think critically about problems and issues that you can explore on the Internet.

www.mhhe.com/santrocka10

Critical Thinking

Review and reflect Learning goal 5

5   **Explain what matters in understanding adolescence**

REVIEW

- Why does history matter in understanding adolescence?
- Why does science matter in understanding adolescence?
- Why do biological processes matter in understanding adolescence?
- Why do cognitive processes matter in understanding adolescence?
- Why does social and personality development matter in understanding adolescence?
- Why do contexts matter in understanding adolescence?
- Why do problems matter in understanding adolescence?
- Why do reflective and critical thinking matter in understanding adolescence?

REFLECT

- Imagine what your development as an adolescent would have been like in a culture that offered few choices compared with the Western world—Communist China during the Cultural Revolution. Young people could not choose their jobs or their mates in rural China. They also were not given the choice of migrating to the city in search of a better life. Now imagine another cultural context, this one in a blighted, inner-city neighborhood in the United States. What would your life as an adolescent have been like if you had grown up in an area where most services had been discontinued, schools were inferior, poverty was extreme, and crime was common? Unfortunately, some of you did grow up in these circumstances.

In this chapter, we have introduced the field of adolescent development. In exploring what matters in understanding adolescence, we emphasized that science matters. In the next chapter, we will examine this topic in much greater depth.

Reach Your Learning Goals

Introduction

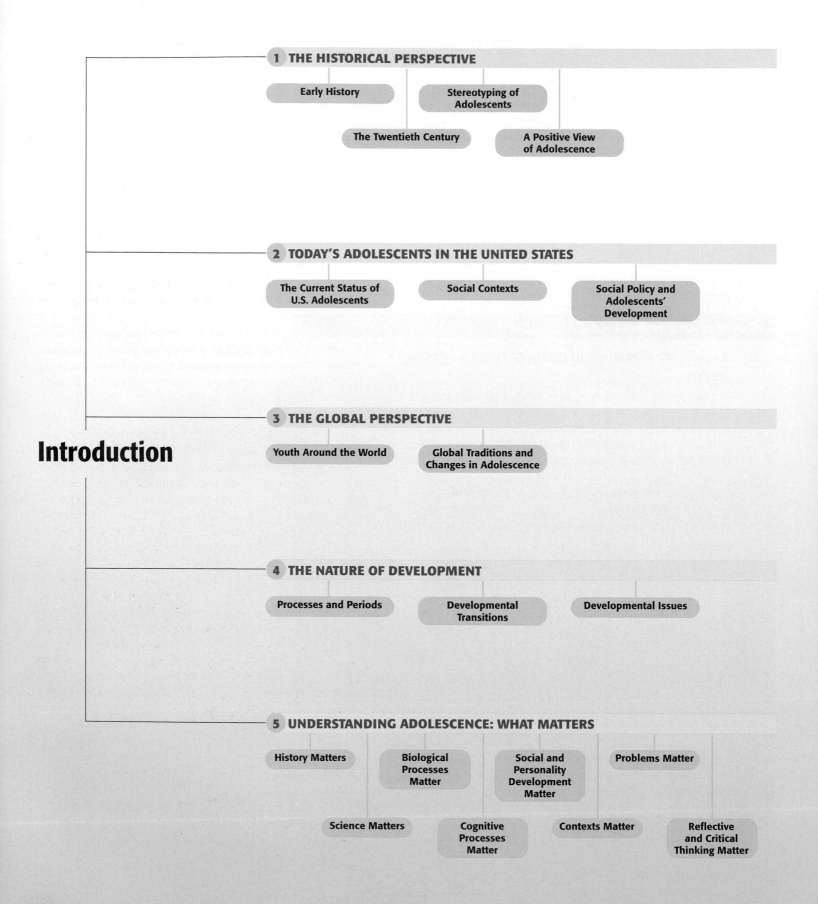

1 THE HISTORICAL PERSPECTIVE

- Early History
- Stereotyping of Adolescents
- The Twentieth Century
- A Positive View of Adolescence

2 TODAY'S ADOLESCENTS IN THE UNITED STATES

- The Current Status of U.S. Adolescents
- Social Contexts
- Social Policy and Adolescents' Development

3 THE GLOBAL PERSPECTIVE

- Youth Around the World
- Global Traditions and Changes in Adolescence

4 THE NATURE OF DEVELOPMENT

- Processes and Periods
- Developmental Transitions
- Developmental Issues

5 UNDERSTANDING ADOLESCENCE: WHAT MATTERS

- History Matters
- Biological Processes Matter
- Social and Personality Development Matter
- Problems Matter
- Science Matters
- Cognitive Processes Matter
- Contexts Matter
- Reflective and Critical Thinking Matter

Summary

1 Describe the historical perspective of adolescence

- Plato said that reasoning first develops in adolescence and Aristotle argued that self-determination is the hallmark of adolescence. In the Middle Ages, knowledge about adolescence moved a step backward: children were viewed as miniature adults and developmental transformations in adolescence were ignored. Rousseau provided a more enlightened view of adolescence, including an emphasis on different phases of development.
- Between 1890 and 1920, a cadre of psychologists, urban reformers, and others began to mold the concept of adolescence. G. Stanley Hall is the father of the scientific study of adolescence. In 1904, he proposed the storm-and-stress view of adolescence, which has strong biological foundations. In contrast to Hall's biological view, Margaret Mead argued for a sociocultural interpretation of adolescence. In the inventionist view, adolescence is a sociohistorical invention. Legislation was enacted early in the twentieth century that ensured the dependency of adolescents and delayed their entry into the workforce. From 1900 to 1930, there was a 600 percent increase in the number of high school graduates in the United States. Adolescents gained a more prominent place in society from 1920 to 1950. By 1950, every state had developed special laws for adolescents. Barriers prevented many ethnic minority individuals and females from entering the field of studying adolescent development in the early and middle part of the twentieth century. Leta Hollingworth was a pioneering female, and Kenneth and Mamie Clark and George Sanchez were pioneering ethnic minority individuals in studying adolescents.
- Negative stereotyping of adolescents in any historical era has been common. Joseph Adelson described the concept of the "adolescent generalization gap," which states that generalizations are often based on a limited set of highly visible adolescents.
- For too long, adolescents have been viewed in negative ways. Research shows that a considerable majority of adolescents around the world have positive self-esteem. The majority of adolescents are not highly conflicted but rather are searching for an identity.

2 Discuss today's U.S. adolescents and social policy issues involving adolescents

- Adolescents are heterogeneous. Although a majority of adolescents successfully make the transition from childhood to adulthood, too large a percentage do not and are not provided with adequate opportunities and support. Different portraits of adolescents emerge depending on the particular set of adolescents being described. Contexts, the settings in which development occurs, play important roles in adolescent development. These contexts include families, peers, schools, and culture.
- Social policy is a national government's course of action designed to influence the welfare of its citizens. The U.S. social policy on adolescents needs revision to provide more services for youth. Some experts argue that adolescents as an age group have been underserved by the government and that a generational inequity has evolved with a much greater percentage of government support going to older adults.

3 Characterize the current global perspective on adolescence

- There are both similarities and differences in adolescents across different countries. Much of what has been written and researched about adolescence comes from American and European scholars. With technological advances, a youth culture with similar characteristics may be emerging. However, there still are many variations in adolescents across cultures.
- In some countries, traditions are being continued in the socialization of adolescence, whereas in others, substantial changes in the experiences of adolescents are taking place. These traditions and changes involve health and well-being, gender, families, schools, and peers.

4 Summarize the developmental processes, periods, transitions, and issues related to adolescence

- Development is the pattern of movement or change that occurs throughout the life span. Biological processes involve physical changes in the individual's body. Cognitive processes consist of changes in thinking and intelligence. Socioemotional changes focus on changes in relationships with people, in emotion, in personality, and in social contexts. Development is commonly divided into these periods: prenatal, infancy, early childhood, middle and late childhood, adolescence, early adulthood, middle adulthood, and late adulthood. Adolescence is the developmental period of transition between childhood and adulthood that involves biological, cognitive, and socioemotional changes. In most cultures, adolescence begins at approximately 10 to 13 years of age and ends at about 18 to 22 years of age. Developmentalists increasingly distinguish between early adolescence and late adolescence.
- Two important transitions in development are from childhood to adolescence and adolescence to adulthood. In the transition from childhood to adolescence, pubertal change is prominent, although cognitive and socioemotional changes occur as well. It sometimes has been said that adolescence begins in biology and ends in culture. The concepts of youth and emerging adulthood have been proposed to describe the transition from adolescence to adulthood. Among the criteria for determining adulthood are self-responsibility, independent decision making, and economic independence. A

number of intellectual, psychological, and social assets are linked to well-being in both adolescence and emerging adulthood.

- Three important issues in development are (1) the nature-nurture issue (is development mainly due to heredity [nature] or environment [nurture]?), (2) the continuity-discontinuity issue (is development more gradual, cumulative [continuity] or more abrupt and sequential [discontinuity]?), (3) the early-later experience issue (is development due more to early experiences, especially in infancy and early childhood, or to later [more recent and current] experiences)? Most developmentalists do not take extreme positions on these issues although they are extensively debated.

5 Explain what matters in understanding adolescence

- In terms of history, historical changes can be negative (war, for example) or positive (increased education opportunities for adolescent females around the world, for example).

- In terms of science, scientific studies help us to correct our individual observations and personal interpretations of adolescence.
- In terms of biological processes, there is considerable interest in the roles of heredity and environment, evolution, puberty, and health in adolescent development.
- In terms of cognitive processes, we need to understand changes in thinking skills and decision making. Also important is charting the nature of intelligence in adolescence.
- In terms of social and personality development, there is considerable interest in the self and identity, gender, sexuality, moral development, and achievement.
- In terms of contexts, key contexts or settings for adolescent development are families, peers, schools, and culture.
- In terms of problems, researchers study such problems as substance abuse, juvenile delinquency, depression and suicide, and eating disorders.
- In terms of reflective and critical thinking, to better understand adolescence it is important to think deeply and productively about this topic.

Key Terms

storm-and-stress view 8
inventionist view 9
stereotype 11
adolescent generalization gap 12
contexts 14
social policy 15

generational inequity 15
development 20
biological processes 20
cognitive processes 20
socioemotional processes 20
prenatal period 20
infancy 20

early childhood 20
middle and late childhood 20
adolescence 21
early adolescence 21
late adolescence 21
early adulthood 21
middle adulthood 21

late adulthood 22
youth 24
emerging adulthood 24
nature-nurture issue 26
continuity-discontinuity issue 26
early-later experience issue 27

Key People

G. Stanley Hall 8
Margaret Mead 8
Leta Hollingworth 11

Kenneth and Mamie Clark 11
George Sanchez 11
Daniel Offer 12

Marian Wright Edelman 15
Bernice Neugarten 16
Reed Larson 16

Kenneth Kenniston 24

Resources for Improving the Lives of Adolescents

Children's Defense Fund

25 E. Street, NW
Washington, DC 20001
202–628–8787
http://www.childrensdefense.org/

The Children's Defense Fund, headed by Marian Wright Edelman, exists to provide a strong and effective voice for children and adolescents who cannot vote, lobby, or speak for themselves.

Great Transitions

(1995) by the Carnegie Council on Adolescent Development
New York: Carnegie Corporation. Available on the Internet at:
http://www.carnegie.org/sub/pubs/reports/great_transitions/gr_exec.html

This report by the Carnegie Council on Adolescent Development covers a wide range of topics, including reengaging families with their adolescents, educating adolescents, promoting adolescent health, strengthening communities, and redirecting the pervasive power of the media.

The Search Institute

Thresher Square West
700 South Third Street, Suite 210
Minneapolis, MN 55415
612–376–8955
http://www.search-institute.org/

The Search Institute has available a large number of resources for improving the lives of adolescents. The brochures and books available address school improvement, adolescent literacy, parent education, program planning, and adolescent health and include resource lists. A free quarterly newsletter is available.

Securing the Future

(2000) by Sheldon Danziger and Jane Waldfogel (Eds.)
New York: Russell Sage Foundation

This book includes articles from scholars in a number of different disciplines (such as economics, psychology, and sociology) to explore effective ways to improve social policy for children and youth.

E-Learning Tools

http://www.mhhe.com/santrocka10
To help you master the material in this chapter, you will find a number of valuable study tools in the Student CD-ROM that accompanies this book. In addition, visit the Online Learning Center for *Adolescence, 10th Edition,* where you will find helpful resources for chapter 1, "Introduction."

Taking It to the Net

1. About a century ago, G. S. Hall wrote that adolescence was an especially stressful period of time, a stereotype that continues today as evidenced in media representations of adolescence as well as in literary works. Adolescents often are portrayed as interested only in drugs, as engaging in promiscuous and risky sex, and as alcohol abusers. What is the evidence about the percentages of adolescents in these categories that you can cite to refute the stereotype?

2. You are a student teacher for Ms. Masterson, who teaches tenth-grade English. She is trying to capitalize on the vast store of information on the Web by helping students integrate Web resources into their papers. Knowing that it is important to think critically when gleaning information from the Web, Ms. Masterson asks you to help her formulate guidelines students can use to evaluate websites. What clues will you suggest Ms. Masterson provide her classes to help the students evaluate website information?

3. Our version of adolescence evolved because of a variety of social reforms, including child labor laws that limit adolescent involvement in the workforce. When you took your first job, you likely were limited in the kind of work you could do because of these laws. Do you think they are fair? How would you argue for a more individual case-by-case application of these laws?

Connect to **http://www.mhhe.com/santrocka10** to research the answers and complete these exercises. In some cases, you'll also find further instructions on this site.

Self-Assessment

Use the self-assessment, *Evaluating My Interest in a Career in Adolescent Development,* to explore whether any of the many careers interest you.

Health and Well-Being, Parenting, and Education

To practice your decision-making skills, complete the health and well-being, parenting, and education scenarios.

Appendix *Careers in* *Adolescent Development*

**On-Line Psychology Center
Jobs with an Undergraduate Degree
in Psychology**

Some of you may be quite sure about what you plan to make your life's work. Others of you may not have decided on a major yet and are uncertain about which career path you want to follow. Each of us wants to find a rewarding career and enjoy the work we do. The field of adolescent development offers an amazing breadth of career options that can provide extremely satisfying work.

If you decide to pursue a career in adolescent development, what career options are available to you? There are many. College and university professors teach courses in adolescent development, education, family development, and medicine. Middle school and high school teachers impart knowledge, understanding, and skills to adolescents. Counselors, clinical psychologists, and physicians help adolescents to cope more effectively with the unique challenges of adolescence. And various professionals work with families of adolescents to improve the adolescent's development.

By choosing one of these career options, you can guide youth in improving their lives, help others to understand them better, or even advance the state of knowledge in the field. You can have an enjoyable time while you are doing these things. Although an advanced degree is not absolutely necessary in some areas of adolescent development, you usually can expand your opportunities (and income) considerably by obtaining a graduate degree. Many careers in adolescent development pay reasonably well. For example, psychologists earn well above the median salary in the United States.

If you are considering a career in adolescent development, as you go through this term, try to spend some time with adolescents of different ages. Observe their behavior; talk with them about their lives. Think about whether you would like to work with youth in your life's work.

Another worthwhile activity is to talk with people who work with adolescents. For example, if you have some interest in becoming a school counselor, call a school, ask to speak with a counselor, and set up an appointment to discuss the counselor's career path and work. Be prepared with a list of questions to ask and take notes if you wish.

Working in one or more jobs related to your career interests while you are in college can also benefit you. Many colleges and universities offer internships or work experiences for students who major in fields such as development. In some instances, these opportunities are for course credit or pay; in others, they are strictly on a volunteer basis. Take advantage of these opportunities. They can provide you with valuable experiences to help you decide if this is the right career area for you, and they can help you get into graduate school, if you decide you want to go.

In the following sections, we profile careers in three areas: education/research; clinical/counseling/medical; and families/relationships. These are not the only career options in the field of adolescent development, but they should provide you with an idea of the range of opportunities available and information about some of the main career avenues you might pursue. In profiling these careers, we address the amount of education required, the nature of the training, and a description of the work.

EDUCATION/RESEARCH

Education and research offer a wide range of career opportunities to work with adolescents. These range from being a college professor to secondary school teacher to school psychologist.

College/University Professor

Courses in adolescent development are taught in different programs and schools in college and universities, including psychology, education, child and family studies, social work, and medicine. They are taught at research universities that offer one or more master's or Ph.D. programs in development; at four-year colleges with no graduate programs; or at community colleges. The work college professors do includes teaching courses either at the undergraduate or graduate level (or both); conducting research in a specific area; advising students and/or directing their research; and serving on college or university committees. Some college instructors do not conduct research but instead focus mainly on teaching. Research is most likely to be part of the job description at universities with master's and Ph.D. programs.

A Ph.D. or master's degree almost always is required to teach in some area of adolescent development in a college or university. Obtaining a doctoral degree usually takes four to six years of graduate work. A master's degree requires approximately two years of graduate work. The training involves taking graduate courses, learning to conduct research, and attending and presenting papers at professional meetings. Many graduate students work as teaching or research assistants to professors, an apprenticeship relationship that helps them to develop their teaching and research skills.

If you are interested in becoming a college or university professor, you might want to make an appointment with your instructor to learn more about the profession and what his or her career/work is like.

Researcher

In most instances, individuals who work in research positions will have either a master's degree or Ph.D. in some area of adolescent development. They might work at a university, perhaps in a research program; in government at agencies such as the National Institute of Mental Health; or in private industry. Those who have full-time research positions generate innovative research ideas, plan studies, and carry out research by collecting data, analyzing the data, and then interpreting it. Some spend much of their time in a laboratory, while others work outside the lab in schools, hospitals, and other settings. Researchers usually attempt to publish their research in a scientific journal. They often work in collaboration with other researchers and may present their work at scientific meetings, where they learn about other research.

Secondary School Teacher

Secondary school teachers teach one or more subjects, prepare the curriculum, give tests, assign grades, monitor students' progress, conduct parent-teacher conferences, and attend in-service workshops. At minimum, becoming a secondary school teacher requires an undergraduate degree. The training involves taking a wide range of courses, with a major or concentration in education, as well as completion of a supervised practice-teaching internship.

Exceptional Children (Special Education) Teacher

Teachers of exceptional children concentrate their efforts on individual children who either have a disability or are gifted. Among the children they might work with are children with learning disabilities, ADHD (attention deficit hyperactivity disorder), mental retardation, or a physical disability such as cerebral palsy. Some of their work is done outside of the regular classroom, some of it in the regular classroom. The exceptional children teacher works closely with both the regular classroom teacher and parents to create the best educational program for each student. Becoming a teacher of exceptional children requires a minimum of an undergraduate degree. The training consists of taking a wide range of courses in education with a concentration of courses in educating children with disabilities or children who are gifted. Teachers of exceptional children often continue their education after obtaining their undergraduate degree and many attain a master's degree in special education.

Family and Consumer Science Educator

Family and consumer science educators may specialize in early childhood education or instruct middle and high school students about matters such as nutrition, interpersonal relationships, human sexuality, parenting, and human development. Hundreds of colleges and universities throughout the United States offer two- and four-year degree programs in family and consumer science. These programs usually include an internship requirement. Additional education courses may be needed to obtain a teaching certificate. Some family and consumer science educators go on to graduate school for further training, which provides preparation for jobs in college teaching or research.

Educational Psychologist

Most educational psychologists teach in a college or university setting and conduct research on learning, motivation, classroom management, or assessment. These professors help to train students to enter the fields of educational psychology, school psychology, and teaching. Many educational psychologists have a doctorate in education, which requires four to six years of graduate work

School Psychologist

School psychologists focus on improving the psychological and intellectual well-being of elementary and secondary school students. They may work in a school district's centralized office or in one or more schools where they give psychological tests, interview students and their parents, consult with teachers, and provide counseling to students and their families. School psychologists usually have a master's or doctoral degree in school psychology. In graduate school, they take courses in counseling, assessment, learning, and other areas of education and psychology.

CLINICAL/COUNSELING/MEDICAL

A wide variety of clinical, counseling, and medical professionals work with adolescents, from clinical psychologists to adolescent drug counselors and adolescent medicine specialists.

Clinical Psychologist

Clinical psychologists seek to help people with their psychological problems. They work in a variety of settings, including colleges and universities, clinics, medical schools, and private practice. Most clinical psychologists conduct psychotherapy; some perform psychological assessment as well; and some do research.

Clinical psychologists must obtain either a Ph.D, which involves clinical and research training, or a Psy.D. degree, which involves only clinical training. This graduate training, which usually takes five to seven years, includes courses in clinical psychology and a one-year supervised internship in an accredited setting. In most cases, candidates for these degrees must pass a test to become licensed to practice and to call themselves clinical psychologists.

Psychiatrist

Like clinical psychologists, psychiatrists might specialize in working with adolescents. They might work in medical schools, both as teachers and researchers, in medical clinics, and in private practice. Unlike psychologists, however, psychiatrists can administer psychiatric drugs to clients. Psychiatrists must first obtain a medical degree and then do a residency in psychiatry. Medical school takes approximately four years to complete and the psychiatric residency another three to four years.

Psychiatric Nurse

Psychiatric nurses work closely with psychiatrists to improve adolescents' mental health. This career path requires two to five years of education in a certified nursing program. Psychiatric nursing students take courses in the biological sciences, nursing care, and psychology and receive supervised clinical training in a psychiatric setting. Designation as a clinical specialist in adolescent nursing requires a master's degree or higher in nursing.

Counseling Psychologist

Counseling psychologists go through much the same training as clinical psychologists and work in the same settings. They may do psychotherapy, teach, or conduct research, but they normally do not treat individuals with severe mental disorders, such as schizophrenia. Counseling psychologists must have either a master's degree or a doctoral degree, as well as a license to practice their profession. One type of master's degree in counseling leads to the designation of licensed professional counselor.

School Counselor

School counselors help students to identify their abilities and interests, and then guide them in developing academic plans and exploring career options. High school counselors advise students on choosing a major, meeting the admissions requirements for college, taking entrance exams, applying for financial aid, and obtaining vocational and technical training. School counselors may also help students to cope with adjustment problems, working with them individually, in small groups, or even in the classroom. They often consult with parents, teachers, and school administrators when trying to help students with their problems. School counselors usually have a master's degree in counseling.

Career Counselor

Career counselors help individuals to identify their career options and guide them in applying for jobs. They may work in private industry or at a college or university, where they usually interview individuals to identify careers that fit their interests and abilities. Sometimes career counselors help individuals to create professional résumés, or they conduct mock interviews to help them prepare for a job interview. They may also create and promote job fairs or other recruiting events to help individuals obtain jobs.

Social Worker

Social workers are often involved in helping people with their social or economic problems. They may investigate, evaluate, and attempt to rectify reported cases of abuse, neglect, endangerment, or domestic disputes. They can intervene in families if necessary and provide counseling and referral services to individuals and families. They often work for publicly funded agencies at the city, state, or national level, although increasingly they work in the private sector in areas such as drug rehabilitation and family counseling. In some cases, social workers specialize in certain types of work. For example, family-care social workers often work with families in which a child, adolescent, or older adult needs support services. Social workers must have at least an undergraduate degree from a school of social work, including course work in various areas of sociology and psychology. Some social workers also have a master's or doctoral degree.

Drug Counselor

Drug counselors provide counseling to individuals with drug-abuse problems, either on an individual basis or in group therapy sessions. They may work in private practice, with a state or federal agency, for a company, or in a hospital setting. Some specialize in working with adolescents. At a minimum, drug counselors must have an associate degree or certificate. Many have an undergraduate degree in substance-abuse counseling, and some have master's and doctoral degrees. In most states, drug counselors must fulfill a certification procedure to obtain a license to practice.

Health Psychologist

Health psychologists work with many different health-care professionals, including physicians, nurses, clinical psychologists, psychiatrists, and social workers, in an effort to improve the health of adolescents. They may conduct research, perform clinical assessments, or give treatment. Many health psychologists focus on prevention through research and clinical interventions designed to foster health and reduce the risk of disease. More than half of all health psychologists provide clinical services. Among the settings in which health psychologists work are primary care programs, inpatient medical units, and specialized care programs in areas such as women's health, drug treatment, and smoking cessation.

Health psychologists typically have a doctoral degree (Ph.D. or Psy.D.) in psychology. Some receive training in clinical psychology as part of their graduate work. Others have obtained their doctoral degree in some area other than health psychology and then pursue a postdoctoral degree in health psychology. A postdoctoral degree usually takes about two additional years of graduate study. Many doctoral programs in clinical, counseling, social, and experimental psychology have specialized tracks in health psychology.

Adolescent Medicine Specialist

Adolescent medicine specialists evaluate the medical and behavioral problems that are common among adolescents, including growth disorders (such as delayed puberty), acne, eating disorders, substance abuse, depression, anxiety, sexually transmitted diseases, contraception and pregnancy, and sexual identity concerns. They may work in private practice, in a medical clinic, in a hospital, or in a medical school. As a medical doctor, they can administer drugs and may counsel parents and adolescents on ways to improve the adolescent's health. Many adolescent medicine specialists on the faculty of medical schools also teach and conduct research on adolescents' health and diseases.

Adolescent medicine specialists must complete medical school and then obtain further training in their specialty, which usually involves at least three more years of schooling. They must become board certified in either pediatrics or internal medicine.

FAMILIES/RELATIONSHIPS

Adolescents sometimes benefit from help that is provided to the entire family. One career that involves working with adolescents and their families is marriage and family therapy.

Marriage and Family Therapist

Many individuals who have psychological problems benefit when psychotherapy is provided within the context of a marital or family relationship. Marriage and family therapists may provide marital therapy, couple therapy to those individuals who are not married, and family therapy to two or more members of a family.

Marriage and family therapists must have a master's or doctoral degree. Their training is similar to that of a clinical psychologist but with a focus on marital and family relationships. In most states, professionals must go through a licensing procedure to practice marital and family therapy.

WEBSITE CONNECTIONS FOR CAREERS IN ADOLESCENT DEVELOPMENT

The website for this book offers more detailed information about the careers in adolescent development described in this appendix. Go to the website connections in the Career Appendix section, where you will find a description of the relevant websites. Then click on a title that interests you and you will be linked directly to the website. Choose from the following website connections.

Education/Research

Careers in Psychology
Elementary and Secondary School Teaching
Exceptional Children Teachers
Educational Psychology
School Psychology

Clinical/Counseling/Medical

Clinical Psychology
Psychiatry
Counseling Psychology
School Counseling
Social Work
Drug Counseling
Health Psychology
Pediatrics
Adolescent Medicine

Families/Relationships

Marriage and Family Therapist

*Science refines
everyday thinking.*
—ALBERT EINSTEIN
*German-Born American Physicist,
20th Century*

The Science of
Adolescent Development

Images of Adolescent Development

The Youths of Erikson and Piaget

Two important developmental theorists, whose views are described later in this chapter, are Erik Erikson and Jean Piaget. Let's examine their experiences as youth to discover how those might have contributed to the theories they developed.

Erik Homberger Erikson (1902–1994) was born near Frankfurt, Germany, to Danish parents. Before he was born, his parents separated, and his mother left Denmark to live in Germany. When Erik became ill at age 3, his mother took him to a pediatrician named Homberger. She fell in love with the man, married him, and renamed Erik after his new stepfather.

Erik attended primary school from ages 6 to 10 and then the gymnasium (high school) from ages 11 to 18. There he studied art and a number of languages rather than sciences such as biology and chemistry. Erik's dislike for formal schooling was reflected in his grades. Rather than go to college, at age 18 he began wandering around Europe, recording his experiences in a diary. After a year of travel, he returned to Germany and enrolled in art school but became dissatisfied and enrolled in another.

Jean Piaget (1896–1980) was born in Neuchtel, Switzerland. His father was an intellectual who taught him to think systematically. Jean's mother, whom he described as prone to frequent neurotic outbursts, was also very bright. His father maintained an air of detachment from his mother.

At the age of 22, Piaget went to work in the psychology laboratory at the University of Zurich. There he was exposed to the insights of Alfred Binet, who developed the first intelligence test. By the time Piaget was 25, his experience in various disciplines had helped him to discover the links between philosophy, psychology, and biology.

These excerpts from Erikson's and Piaget's lives illustrate how personal experiences can influence the development of a theory. Erikson's wanderings and search for self contributed to his theory of identity development. Piaget's schooling and intellectual discussions with his parents contributed to his theory on cognitive development.

Some individuals have difficulty thinking of adolescent development as being a science in the same way that physics, chemistry, and biology are sciences. Can a discipline that studies pubertal change, parent-adolescent relationships, and adolescent thinking be equated with disciplines that investigate how gravity works and the molecular structure of compounds? The answer is yes because a science is not defined by *what* it investigates but by *how* it investigates. Whether you are studying photosynthesis, Saturn's moons, or adolescent development, it is the way you study the subject that matters. In this chapter we will examine the major theories of adolescent development, see how research is conducted, and consider the challenges of evaluating research.

1 THEORIES OF DEVELOPMENT

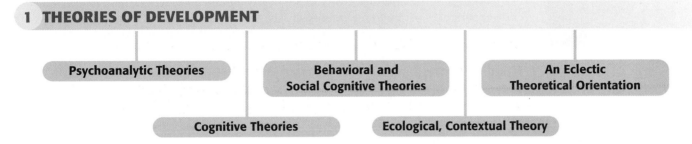

All scientific knowledge stems from a rigorous, systematic method of investigation. The *scientific method* is essentially a four-step process:

1. Conceptualize the process or problem to be studied.
2. Collect research information (data).
3. Analyze the data.
4. Draw conclusions.

In step 1, when researchers are formulating a problem to study, they often draw on *theories* and develop *hypotheses*. A **theory** is an interrelated, coherent set of ideas that helps to explain observations and make predictions. **Hypotheses** are specific assumptions and predictions that can be tested to determine their accuracy. For example, a theory on mentoring might predict and explain why sustained support, guidance, and concrete experience make a difference in the lives of adolescents who come from impoverished backgrounds. The theory might focus on adolescents' opportunities to model mentors' behavior and strategies, or it might emphasize the effects of individual attention, which might have been missing in the lives of impoverished adolescents.

The diversity of theories makes understanding adolescent development a challenging undertaking. Just when you think one theory offers the correct explanation of adolescent development, another theory crops up and makes you rethink your earlier conclusion. To keep from getting frustrated, remember that adolescent development is a complex, multifaceted topic. No single theory has yet been able to account for all aspects of it. Rather, each theory contributes an important piece to the adolescent development puzzle. Although the theorists sometimes disagree about certain aspects of adolescent development, much of their thinking is complementary rather than contradictory. Together their theories let us see the total landscape of adolescent development in all its richness.

In this section we will briefly explore four major theoretical perspectives on human development: psychoanalytic, cognitive, behavioral and social cognitive, and ecological, contextual. Recall that in chapter 1 we described the three major processes in adolescent development: biological, cognitive, and socioemotional. The theoretical approaches described in this section reflect these processes. Biological processes are important in Freud's psychoanalytic theory; cognitive processes in Piaget's cognitive developmental theory, Vygotsky's sociocultural cognitive theory, information-processing theory, and social cognitive theory; and emotional processes are important

theory An interrelated, coherent set of ideas that helps to explain observations and make predictions.

hypotheses Specific assumptions and predictions that can be tested to determine their accuracy.

Sigmund Freud, the architect of psychoanalytic theory.

in Freud's and Erikson's psychoanalytic theories, in Vygotsky's sociocultural cognitive theory, in behavioral and social cognitive theories, and in ecological, contextual theory. You will read more about these theories and processes at different points in later chapters.

Psychoanalytic Theories

Psychoanalytic theory describes human development as primarily unconscious—that is, beyond awareness—and heavily colored by emotion. Psychoanalytic theorists believe that behavior is merely a surface characteristic and that, to truly understand development, we have to analyze the symbolic meanings of behavior and the deep inner workings of the mind (Bornstein, 2003). Psychoanalytic theorists also stress that early experiences with parents extensively shape our development. These characteristics are highlighted in the main psychoanalytic theory, that of Sigmund Freud.

Freud's Theory   Freud (1856–1939) developed psychoanalytic theory out of his work with mental patients. A medical doctor who specialized in neurology, Freud spent most of his life in Vienna, moving to London near the end of his career to escape the Nazis' anti-Semitism.

Personality Structure   Freud (1917) divided personality into three structures: the id, the ego, and the superego. The *id* consists of instincts, which are an individual's reservoir of psychic energy. In Freud's view, the id is totally unconscious; it has no contact with reality. As children experience the demands and constraints of reality, a new structure of personality emerges—the *ego*, which deals with the demands of reality. The ego is called the "executive branch" of personality because it makes rational decisions. The id and the ego have no morality—they do not take into account whether something is right or wrong. The *superego* is the moral branch of personality. The superego takes into account whether something is right or wrong. Think of the superego as what we often refer to as our "conscience." You probably are beginning to sense that both the id and the superego make life rough for the ego. Your ego might say, "I will have sex only occasionally and be sure to take the proper precautions because I don't want a child to interfere with the development of my career." However, your id is saying, "I want to be satisfied; sex is pleasurable." Your superego is at work too: "I feel guilty about having sex."

Freud considered personality to be like an iceberg. Most of personality exists below our level of awareness, just as the massive part of an iceberg is beneath water's surface.

Freud believed that adolescents' lives are filled with tension and conflict. To reduce the tension, he thought adolescents bury their conflicts in their unconscious mind. Freud believed that even trivial behaviors can become significant when the unconscious forces behind them are revealed. A twitch, a doodle, a joke, a smile—each might betray unconscious conflict. For example, 17-year-old Barbara, while kissing and hugging Tom, exclaims, "Oh, *Jeff*, I love you so much." Repelled, Tom explodes: "Why did you call me Jeff? I thought you didn't think about him anymore. We need to have a talk!" You probably can remember times when a Freudian slip revealed your own unconscious motives.

Defense Mechanisms   The ego resolves conflict between its reality demands, the id's wishes, and the superego's constraints through *defense mechanisms*. These are unconscious methods of distorting reality the ego uses to protect itself from the anxiety produced by the conflicting demands of the three personality structures. When the ego senses that the id's demands may cause harm, anxiety develops, alerting the ego to resolve the conflict by means of defense mechanisms.

psychoanalytic theory Describes development as primarily unconscious and heavily colored by emotion. Behavior is merely a surface characteristic and the symbolic workings of the mind have to be analyzed to understand behavior. Early experiences with parents are emphasized.

According to Freud, *repression* is the most powerful and pervasive defense mechanism. It pushes unacceptable id impulses out of awareness and back into the unconscious mind. Repression is the foundation on which all other defense mechanisms rest since the goal of every defense mechanism is to repress, or push, threatening impulses out of awareness. Freud thought that early childhood experiences, many of which he believed are sexually laden, are too threatening and stressful for people to deal with consciously, so they repress them.

However, Peter Blos (1989), a British psychoanalyst, and Anna Freud (1966), Sigmund Freud's daughter, believe that defense mechanisms provide considerable insight into adolescent development. Blos states that regression during adolescence is actually not defensive at all, but rather an integral, normal, inevitable, and universal aspect of puberty. The nature of regression may vary from one adolescent to the next. It may involve compliance, and cleanliness, or it may involve a sudden return to the passiveness that characterized the adolescent's behavior during childhood.

Anna Freud (1966) developed the idea that defense mechanisms are the key to understanding adolescent adjustment. She believed that the problems of adolescence are not rooted in the id, or instinctual forces, but in the "love objects" in the adolescent's past. Attachment to these love objects, usually parents, is carried forward from the infant years and merely toned down or inhibited during the childhood years, she argued. During adolescence, these urges might be reawakened, or, worse, newly acquired urges might combine with them.

Bear in mind that defense mechanisms are unconscious; adolescents are not aware they are using them to protect their egos and reduce anxiety. When used temporarily and in moderation, defense mechanisms are not necessarily unhealthy. However, defense mechanisms should not be allowed to dominate an individual's behavior and prevent a person from facing reality.

Anna Freud, Sigmund Freud's daughter. *How did her view differ from her father's?*

Psychosexual Stages   As Freud listened to, probed, and analyzed his patients, he became convinced that their problems were the result of early life experiences. He theorized that humans go through five stages of psychosexual development, and that at each stage of development individuals experience pleasure in one part of the body more than in others (see figure 2.1):

- ***Oral stage.*** The *oral stage* is the first Freudian stage of development, occurring during the first 18 months of life, in which the infant's pleasure centers around the mouth. Chewing, sucking, and biting are the chief sources of pleasure. These actions reduce tension in the infant.
- ***Anal stage.*** The *anal stage* is the second Freudian stage of development, occurring between 1½ and 3 years of age, in which the child's greatest pleasure involves the anus or the eliminative functions associated with it. In Freud's view, the exercise of anal muscles reduces tension.
- ***Phallic stage.*** The *phallic stage* is the third Freudian stage of development, which occurs between the ages of 3 and 6; its name comes from the Latin word *phallus*,

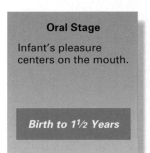

Oral Stage

Infant's pleasure centers on the mouth.

Birth to 1½ Years

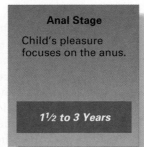

Anal Stage

Child's pleasure focuses on the anus.

1½ to 3 Years

Phallic Stage

Child's pleasure focuses on the genitals.

3 to 6 Years

Latency Stage

Child represses sexual interest and develops social and intellectual skills.

6 Years to Puberty

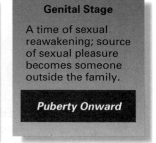

Genital Stage

A time of sexual reawakening; source of sexual pleasure becomes someone outside the family.

Puberty Onward

FIGURE 2.1 Freudian Stages

Karen Horney   Nancy Chodorow

FIGURE 2.2 Feminist-Based Criticisms of Freud's Theory
The first feminist-based criticism of Freud's theory was proposed by psychoanalytic theorist Karen Horney (1967). She developed a model of women with positive feminine qualities and self-evaluation. Her critique of Freud's theory included reference to a male-dominant society and culture. Rectification of the male bias in psychoanalytic theory continues today. For example, Nancy Chodorow (1978, 1989) emphasizes that many more women than men define themselves in terms of their relationships and connections to others. Her feminist revision of psychoanalytic theory also stresses the meaningfulness of emotions for women, as well as the belief that many men use the defense mechanism of denial in self-other connections.

Freud's Theory
Horney's Theory
Erikson's Theory

which means "penis." During the phallic stage, pleasure focuses on the genitals as the child discovers that self-manipulation is enjoyable.

In Freud's view, the phallic stage has a special importance in personality development because it is during this period that the Oedipus complex appears. This name comes from Greek mythology, in which Oedipus, the son of the King of Thebes, unwittingly kills his father and marries his mother. The *Oedipus complex,* in Freudian theory, is the young child's intense desire to replace the parent of the same sex and enjoy the affections of the opposite-sex parent. Freud's concept of the Oedipus complex has been criticized by some psychoanalysts and writers.

How is the Oedipus complex resolved? At about 5 to 6 years of age, children recognize that their same-sex parent might punish them for their incestuous wishes. To reduce this conflict between fear and desire, the child identifies with the same-sex parent, striving to be like him or her. If the conflict is not resolved, Freud believed the individual can become fixated at the phallic stage.

• *Latency stage.* The *latency stage* is the fourth Freudian stage of development, which occurs between approximately 6 years of age and puberty; the child represses all interest in sexuality and develops social and intellectual skills. This activity channels much of the child's energy into emotionally safe areas and helps the child forget the highly stressful conflicts of the phallic stage.

• *Genital stage.* The *genital stage* is the fifth and final Freudian stage of development, occurring from puberty on. The genital stage is a time of sexual reawakening; the source of sexual pleasure now becomes someone outside of the family. Freud believed that unresolved conflicts with parents reemerge during adolescence. When these are resolved, the individual is capable of developing a mature love relationship and functioning independently as an adult.

Revisions of Freud's Theory
Freud's theory has undergone significant revisions by a number of psychoanalytic theorists (Bornstein, 2003; Luborsky, 2000). Many contemporary psychoanalytic theorists place less emphasis than Freud on sexual instincts and more on cultural experiences as determinants of development. Unconscious thought remains a central theme, but most contemporary psychoanalysts believe that conscious thought makes up more of the iceberg than Freud envisioned. Feminist criticisms of Freud's theory have also been made (see figure 2.2). Next, we explore the ideas of an important revisionist of Freud's ideas—Erik Erikson.

Erikson's Theory
Erik Erikson (1902–1994) recognized Freud's contributions but believed that he misjudged some important dimensions of human development. In contrast to Freud's *psychosexual stages,* Erikson (1950, 1968) proposed a series of *psychosocial stages.* Whereas for Freud, the primary motivation for human behavior was sexual, for Erikson it was social, reflecting a desire to affiliate with other people. Erikson also emphasized developmental change throughout the life span, whereas Freud argued that a person's basic personality is shaped in the first five years of life. According to **Erikson's theory,** humans progress through eight stages of development over the course of the life span (see figure 2.3). In each stage, a unique developmental task confronts the individual with a crisis that must be faced. This crisis is not a catastrophe but a turning point of increased vulnerability and enhanced potential. The more successfully an individual resolves the crises, the healthier that person's development will be (Hopkins, 2000).

Trust versus mistrust is Erikson's first psychosocial stage, which occurs in the first year of life. A sense of trust requires a feeling of physical comfort and a minimal amount of fear and apprehension about the future. Trust in infancy sets the stage for a lifelong expectation that the world will be a good and pleasant place in which to live.

Autonomy versus shame and doubt is Erikson's second stage of development, occurring in late infancy and toddlerhood (ages 1 to 3). After gaining trust in their caregivers, infants begin to discover that their behavior is their own. Soon they start to assert their sense of independence or autonomy. If toddlers are restrained too much or punished too harshly, they are likely to develop a sense of shame and doubt.

Initiative versus guilt is Erikson's third stage of development, occurring during the preschool years. As preschool children encounter a widening social world, they are challenged more than when they were infants. Active, purposeful behavior is needed to cope with these challenges. In this stage, children are asked to assume responsibility for their bodies, their behavior, their toys, and their pets. Developing a sense of responsibility increases initiative. Uncomfortable guilt feelings may arise, though, in children who are irresponsible and are made to feel too anxious. Erikson has a positive outlook on this stage. He believes that most guilt is quickly compensated for by a sense of accomplishment.

Industry versus inferiority is Erikson's fourth developmental stage, occurring approximately in the elementary school years. Children's initiative brings them in contact with a wealth of new experiences. As they move into middle and late childhood, they direct their energy toward mastering knowledge and intellectual skills. At no other time is the child more enthusiastic about learning than at the end of early childhood's period of expansive imagination. The danger in the elementary school years is the development of a sense of inferiority—of feeling incompetent and unproductive. Erikson believes that teachers have a special responsibility for children's development of industry. Teachers should "mildly but firmly coerce children into the adventure of

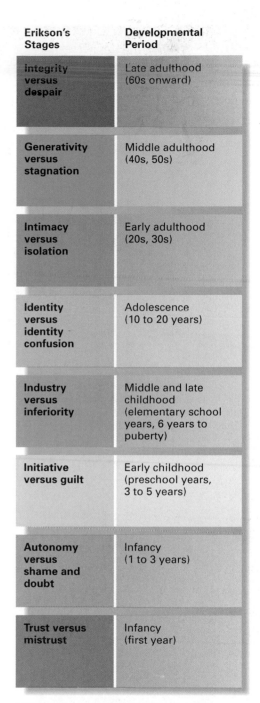

FIGURE 2.3 Erikson's Eight Life-Span Stages

Erikson's Stages	Developmental Period
Integrity versus despair	Late adulthood (60s onward)
Generativity versus stagnation	Middle adulthood (40s, 50s)
Intimacy versus isolation	Early adulthood (20s, 30s)
Identity versus identity confusion	Adolescence (10 to 20 years)
Industry versus inferiority	Middle and late childhood (elementary school years, 6 years to puberty)
Initiative versus guilt	Early childhood (preschool years, 3 to 5 years)
Autonomy versus shame and doubt	Infancy (1 to 3 years)
Trust versus mistrust	Infancy (first year)

Erikson's theory Includes eight stages of human development. Each stage consists of a unique developmental task that confronts individuals with a crisis that must be faced.

Erik Erikson with his wife, Joan, an artist. Erikson generated one of the most important developmental theories of the twentieth century.

finding out that one can learn to accomplish things which one would never have thought of by oneself" (Erikson, 1968, p. 127).

Identity versus identity confusion is Erikson's fifth developmental stage, which occurs during the adolescent years. At this time individuals seek to find out who they are, what they are all about, and where they are going in life. Adolescents are confronted with new roles and statuses—vocational and romantic, for example. Parents need to allow them to explore many different roles, as well as different paths within a particular role. If the adolescent explores such roles in a healthy manner and arrives at a positive path to follow in life, then a positive identity will be achieved. If an identity is pushed on the adolescent by parents, if the adolescent does not adequately explore many roles, and if a positive future path is not defined, then identity confusion reigns.

Intimacy versus isolation is Erikson's sixth developmental stage, which individuals experience during the early adulthood years. At this time, individuals face the developmental task of forming intimate relationships with others. Erikson describes intimacy as finding oneself yet losing oneself in another. If the young adult forms healthy friendships and an intimate close relationship with another individual, intimacy will be achieved; if not, isolation will result.

Generativity versus stagnation is Erikson's seventh developmental stage, which individuals experience during middle adulthood. A chief concern in this stage involves assisting the younger generation in developing and leading useful lives—a task Erikson called generativity. The feeling of having done nothing to help the next generation is called stagnation.

Integrity versus despair is Erikson's eighth and final developmental stage, which individuals experience during late adulthood. Older adults look back and evaluate what they have done with their lives. Through many different routes, the older person may have developed a positive outlook in most or all of the previous developmental stages. If so, the retrospective glances reveal a life well spent, and the person feels a sense of satisfaction—integrity is achieved. If the older adult resolved many of the earlier developmental stages negatively, the retrospective glances likely will yield doubt or gloom—the despair Erikson talks about.

Erikson did not believe that the proper solution to a stage crisis must be completely positive. Exposure to the negative side of a stage is sometimes inevitable—you cannot trust all people under all circumstances, for example. Nonetheless, positive resolutions to stage crises should outweigh negative resolutions for optimal development (Hopkins, 2000).

Evaluating the Psychoanalytic Theories   The contributions of psychoanalytic theories include their emphases on these factors:

- Early experiences play an important part in development.
- Family relationships are a central aspect of development.
- Personality can be better understood if it is examined developmentally.
- The mind is not all conscious; unconscious aspects of the mind are significant.
- Changes take place in adulthood as well as childhood (Erikson).

These are some of the criticisms of psychoanalytic theories:

- The main concepts of psychoanalytic theories have been difficult to test scientifically.
- Much of the data used to support psychoanalytic theories come from individuals' reconstruction of the past—often the distant past—and are of unknown accuracy.
- The sexual underpinnings of development are overemphasized (especially in Freud's theory).
- The unconscious mind is given too much credit for influencing development.
- Psychoanalytic theories present an image of humans that is too negative (especially Freud).

Sensorimotor Stage	**Preoperational Stage**	**Concrete Operational Stage**	**Formal Operational Stage**
The infant constructs an understanding of the world by coordinating sensory experiences with physical actions. An infant progresses from reflexive, instinctual action at birth to the beginning of symbolic thought toward the end of the stage.	The child begins to represent the world with words and images. These words and images reflect increased symbolic thinking and go beyond the connection of sensory information and physical action.	The child can now reason logically about concrete events and classify objects into different sets.	The adolescent reasons in more abstract, idealistic, and logical ways.
Birth to 2 Years of Age	*2 to 7 Years of Age*	*7 to 11 Years of Age*	*11 Years of Age through Adulthood*

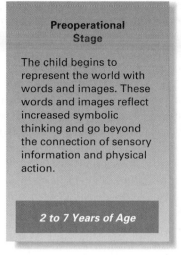

FIGURE 2.4 **Piaget's Four Stages of Cognitive Development**

Cognitive Theories

Whereas psychoanalytic theories stress the importance of adolescents' unconscious thoughts, cognitive theories emphasize their conscious thoughts. Three important cognitive theories are Piaget's cognitive developmental theory, Vygotsky's sociocultural cognitive theory, and information-processing theory.

Piaget's Cognitive Developmental Theory   The famous Swiss psychologist Jean Piaget (1896–1980) proposed an important theory of cognitive development. **Piaget's theory** states that individuals actively construct their understanding of the world as they go through four stages of cognitive development. Two processes—organization and adaptation—underlie this cognitive construction of the world. To make sense of our world, we *organize* our experiences. For example, we separate important ideas from less important ideas or we connect one idea to another. We also *adapt* our thinking to include new ideas because additional information furthers our understanding.

Piaget (1954) theorized that people progress through four stages in developing their understanding of the world (see figure 2.4). Each of these age-related stages consists of distinct ways of thinking. In Piaget's theory, it is the *different* way of understanding the world that makes one stage more advanced than another; simply knowing *more* information does not make a person's thinking more advanced. Thus, Piaget said that a child's cognition is *qualitatively* different from one stage to another.

What are Piaget's four stages of cognitive development? The *sensorimotor stage,* which lasts from birth to about 2 years, is the first Piagetian stage. In this stage, infants construct an understanding of the world by coordinating sensory experiences (such as seeing and hearing) with physical, motoric actions—hence the term *sensorimotor.* At the beginning of this stage, newborns display little more than reflexive patterns. By the end of the stage, 2-year-olds have developed complex sensorimotor patterns and are beginning to use primitive symbols.

The *preoperational stage,* which lasts approximately from 2 to 7 years of age, is the second Piagetian stage. In this stage, children begin to represent the world with words, images, and drawings. Symbolic thought goes beyond simple connections of sensory information and physical action. However, although preschool children can symbolically represent the world, according to Piaget, they still lack the ability to perform *operations,* the Piagetian term for internalized mental actions that allow children to do mentally what they previously did physically.

The *concrete operational stage,* which lasts from approximately 7 to 11 years of age, is the third Piagetian stage. In this stage, children can perform operations, and logical

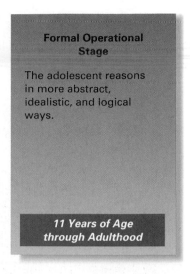

Jean Piaget, the famous Swiss developmental psychologist, changed the way we think about the development of children's minds. *What are some key ideas in Piaget's theory?*

Piaget's theory States that children actively construct their understanding of the world and go through four stages of cognitive development.

There is considerable interest today in Lev Vygotsky's sociocultural cognitive theory of child development.

Piaget's Theory
Vygotsky's Theory

reasoning replaces intuitive thought as long as reasoning can be applied to specific or concrete examples. For instance, concrete operational thinkers cannot imagine the steps necessary to complete an algebraic equation, which is too abstract for thinking at this stage of development.

The *formal operational stage,* which occurs between the ages of 11 and 15, is the fourth and final Piagetian stage. In this stage, individuals move beyond concrete experiences and think in abstract and more logical terms. As part of thinking more abstractly, adolescents develop images of ideal circumstances. They might think about what an ideal parent is like and compare their parents with this ideal standard. They begin to entertain possibilities for the future and are fascinated with what they can be. In solving problems, formal operational thinkers are more systematic, developing hypotheses about why something is happening the way it is, then testing these hypotheses in a deductive fashion. We will have much more to say about Piaget's theory in chapter 4, "Cognitive Development."

Vygotsky's Sociocultural Cognitive Theory   The Russian developmentalist Lev Vygotsky (1896–1934) was born the same year as Piaget, but he died much earlier, at the age of 37. Vygotsky believed that individuals actively construct their knowledge of the world. However, he gave far more importance to social interaction and culture than Piaget. Both Piaget's and Vygotsky's ideas remained virtually unknown to American scholars until the 1960s. In the past several decades, American psychologists and educators have shown increased interest in Vygotsky's (1962) views.

Vygotksy's theory is a sociocultural cognitive theory that emphasizes how culture and social interaction guide cognitive development. Vygotsky portrayed development as inseparable from social and cultural activities (John-Steiner & Mahn, 2003). He believed that the development of memory, attention, and reasoning involves learning to use the inventions of society, such as language, mathematical systems, and memory strategies. In one culture, this might consist of learning to count with the help of a computer. In another, it might consist of counting on one's fingers or using beads.

Vygotsky's theory has stimulated considerable interest in the view that knowledge is *collaborative* (John-Steiner & Mann, 2003; Kozulin, 2000; Rogoff, 2001). In this view, knowledge is not generated from within the individual but rather is constructed through interaction with others and with objects in the culture, such as books. Thus, knowledge can best be advanced through interaction with others in cooperative activities, according to Vygotksy. Specifically, he believed that social interaction with more skilled adults and peers is indispensable in advancing cognitive development. Through this interaction, less-skilled members of the culture learn to use the tools that will help them adapt and be successful.

Vygotsky articulated unique and influential ideas about cognitive development. In chapter 4, "Cognitive Development," we will explore Vygotsky's contributions further.

Information-Processing Theory   **Information-processing theory** emphasizes that individuals manipulate information, monitor it, and strategize about it. Central to this theory are the processes of memory and thinking. According to information-processing theory, adolescents develop a gradually larger capacity for processing information, which allows them to acquire increasingly complex knowledge and skills (Feldman, 2003; Siegler, 2001). Unlike Piaget's cognitive developmental theory, information-processing theory does not describe development as stagelike.

Although a number of factors stimulated the growth of information-processing theory, none was more important than the advent of the computer, which demonstrated that a machine could perform logical operations. Psychologists began to wonder if the logical operations carried out by computers might tell us something about how the human mind works. To explain the relation between cognition or thinking and the brain, they drew analogies to computers and the brain, comparing the human brain to the computer's hardware and cognition to its software. Although hardware and software are not a perfect analogy for the brain and cognitive activity, the

Vygotsky's theory A sociocultural cognitive theory that emphasizes how culture and social interaction guide cognitive development.

information-processing theory Emphasizes that individuals manipulate information, monitor it, and strategize about it. Central to this approach are the processes of memory and thinking.

comparison contributed to our thinking about the mind as an active information-processing system.

Robert Siegler (1998), a leading expert on information processing, believes that thinking is information processing. He says that when individuals perceive, encode, represent, store, and retrieve information, they are thinking. Siegler especially believes that an important aspect of development is to learn good strategies for processing information. For example, becoming a better reader might involve learning to monitor the key themes of the material being read. We will further explore information-processing theory in chapter 4, "Cognitive Development."

Evaluating the Cognitive Theories   The contributions of the cognitive theories include:

- Cognitive theories present a positive view of development, emphasizing conscious thinking.
- Cognitive theories (especially Piaget's and Vygotsky's) emphasize the active construction of understanding.
- Piaget's and Vygotsky's theories underscore the importance of examining developmental changes in thinking.
- Information-processing theory offers detailed descriptions of cognitive processes.

The criticisms of the cognitive theories include:

- Cognitive development is not as stagelike as Piaget's theory states.
- The cognitive theories do not give adequate attention to individual variations in cognitive development.
- Information-processing theory does not provide an adequate description of developmental changes in cognition.
- Psychoanalytic theorists argue that the cognitive theories do not give enough emphasis to unconscious thought.

Through the Eyes of Adolescents

The Cobwebs of Memory

I think the point of having memories is to share them, especially with close friends or family. If you don't share them, they are just sitting inside your brain getting cobwebs. If you have a great memory of Christmas and no one to share it with, what's the point of memories?

Seventh-Grade Student
West Middle School
Ypsilanti, Michigan

Behavioral and Social Cognitive Theories

Seventeen-year-old Tom is going steady with 16-year-old Ann. Both have warm, friendly personalities, and they enjoy being together. Psychoanalytic theorists would say that their warm, friendly personalities are derived from long-standing relationships with their parents, especially during their early years. These theorists would also argue that the reason for the couple's attraction is unconscious; they are unaware of how their biological heritage and early life experiences have been carried forward to influence their adolescent behavior.

Behaviorists and social cognitive theorists would observe Tom and Ann and see something quite different. These theorists would examine Tom and Ann's experiences, especially their most recent ones, to understand the reason for their attraction to each other. Tom would be described as rewarding Ann's behavior, and vice versa. No reference would be made to unconscious thoughts, the Oedipus complex, stages of development, or defense mechanisms. The *behavioral and social cognitive theories* emphasize the importance of environmental experiences and observable behavior in understanding adolescent development. Social cognitive theorists also emphasize person/cognitive factors in development.

Skinner's Behaviorism   *Behaviorism* emphasizes the scientific study of observable behavioral responses and their environmental determinants. In the behaviorism of

Albert Bandura (*above*) and Walter Mischel are the architects of contemporary social cognitive theory.

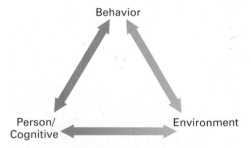

FIGURE 2.5 Bandura's Social Cognitive Theory

Bandura's social cognitive theory emphasizes reciprocal influences of behavior, environment, and person/cognitive factors.

www.mhhe.com/santrocka10

Skinner's View
Albert Bandura

social cognitive theory The view of psychologists who emphasize behavior, environment, and cognition as the key factors in development.

B. F. Skinner (1904–1990), the mind, conscious or unconscious, is not needed to explain behavior and development. For him, development is behavior. For example, observations of Sam reveal that his behavior is shy, achievement oriented, and caring. Why is Sam's behavior this way? For Skinner (1938), rewards and punishments in Sam's environment have shaped him into a shy, achievement-oriented, and caring person. Because of interactions with family members, friends, teachers, and others, Sam has *learned* to behave in this fashion.

Since behaviorists believe that development is learned and often changes according to environmental experiences, it follows that rearranging experiences can change development (Adams, 2000; Staats, 2003). For behaviorists, shy behavior can be transformed into outgoing behavior; aggressive behavior can be shaped into docile behavior; lethargic, boring behavior can be turned into enthusiastic, interesting behavior.

Social Cognitive Theory Some psychologists believe that the behaviorists are basically right when they say that personality is learned and is strongly influenced by environmental factors. But they think Skinner went too far in declaring that characteristics of the person or cognitive factors are unimportant in understanding development (Epstein, 2003). **Social cognitive theory** states that behavior, environment, and person/cognitive factors are important in understanding development.

Albert Bandura (1986, 1997, 2000, 2001) and Walter Mischel (1973, 1995, 2004) are the architects of the contemporary version of social cognitive theory, which initially was labeled *cognitive social learning theory* by Mischel (1973). As shown in figure 2.5, Bandura says that behavior, environment, and person/cognitive factors, such as beliefs, plans, and thinking, can interact in a reciprocal manner. Thus, in Bandura's view, the environment can determine a person's behavior (which matches up with Skinner's view), but there is much more to consider. The person can act to change the environment. Person/cognitive factors can influence a person's behavior and vice versa. Person/cognitive factors include self-efficacy (a belief that one can master a situation and produce positive outcomes), plans, and thinking skills. We will have much more to say about self-efficacy in chapter 12, "Achievement, Careers, and Work."

Bandura believes that observational learning is a key aspect of how we learn. Through observational learning, we form ideas about the behavior of others and then possibly adopt this behavior ourselves (Zimmerman & Schunk, 2002). For example, a boy might observe his father's aggressive outbursts and hostile exchanges with people; when the boy is with his peers, he interacts in a highly aggressive way, showing the same characteristics as his father's behavior.

Like Skinner's behavioral approach, the social cognitive approach emphasizes the importance of empirical research in studying development. This research focuses on the processes that explain development—the socioemotional and cognitive factors that influence what we are like as people.

Evaluating the Behavioral and Social Cognitive Theories These are some of the contributions of the behavioral and social cognitive theories:

- An emphasis on the importance of scientific research
- A focus on the environmental determinants of behavior
- An underscoring of the importance of observational learning (Bandura)
- An emphasis on person and cognitive factors (social cognitive theory)

These are some of the criticisms of the behavioral and social cognitive theories:

- Too little emphasis on cognition (Skinner)
- Too much emphasis on environmental determinants
- Inadequate attention to developmental changes
- Too little emphasis on human spontaneity and creativity

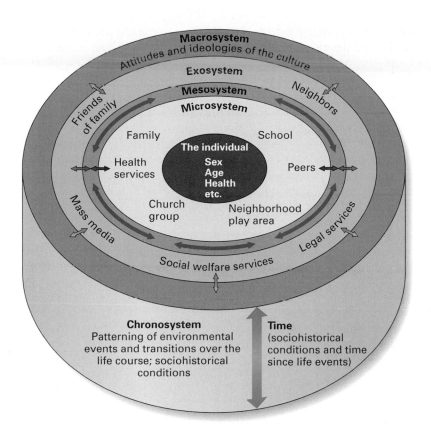

FIGURE 2.6 **Bronfenbrenner's Ecological Theory of Development**
Bronfenbrenner's ecological theory consists of five environmental systems: microsystem, mesosystem, exosystem, macrosystem, and chronosystem.

Ecological, Contextual Theory

Another approach that underscores the importance of environmental influences on development is Urie Bronfenbrenner's (1917–) **ecological, contextual theory,** which is receiving increased attention. It consists of five environmental systems, ranging from the direct interactions with social agents to the broad-based inputs of culture. The five systems in Bronfenbrenner's ecological theory are the microsystem, mesosystem, exosystem, macrosystem, and chronosystem (Bronfenbrenner, 1986, 1995, 2000; Bronfenbrenner & Morris, 1998; see figure 2.6):

- *Microsystem:* The setting in which the adolescent lives. These contexts include the adolescent's family, peers, school, and neighborhood. It is in the microsystem that an adolescent's most direct interactions with social agents take place—with parents, peers, and teachers, for example. The adolescent is viewed not as a passive recipient of experiences in these settings, but as someone who helps to construct them.
- *Mesosystem:* Involves relations between two or more microsystems. Examples are the connections between family experiences and school experiences, school experiences and church experiences, and family experiences and peer experiences. For example, children and adolescents whose parents have rejected them may have difficulty developing positive relations with their teachers.
- *Exosystem:* Social settings in which the adolescent does not have an active role but which influence the adolescent's experiences. For example, a woman's work experiences can affect her relationship with her husband and their adolescent. She might receive a promotion that requires her to travel more, which could increase marital conflict with her husband and change her relationship with her adolescent. Another example of an exosystem is city government, which is responsible for the quality of parks, recreation centers, and library facilities for children and adolescents.
- *Macrosystem:* The culture in which the adolescent lives. *Culture* refers to the behavior patterns, beliefs, and all other products of a group of people that are

Urie Bronfenbrenner developed ecological theory, a perspective that is receiving increased attention. His theory emphasizes the importance of both micro and macro dimensions of the environment in which the child lives.

ecological, contextual theory
Bronfenbrenner's environmental systems theory that focuses on five environmental systems: microsystem, mesosystem, exosystem, macrosystem, and chronosystem.

Bronfenbrenner's Theory
Bronfenbrenner and a
Multicultural Framework

passed on from generation to generation. *Cross-cultural studies*—the comparison of one culture with one or more other cultures—provide information about the generality of development.

- *Chronosystem:* The pattern of environmental events and transitions over the life course, as well as sociohistorical circumstances. For example, in studying the effects of divorce on children, researchers have found that the negative effects often peak in the first year after the divorce. The effects also are more negative for sons than for daughters (Hetherington, 1993). By two years after the divorce, family interaction is less chaotic and more stable. With regard to sociocultural circumstances, adolescent girls today are much more likely to be encouraged to pursue a career than they were 20 or 30 years ago.

Bronfenbrenner (1995; Bronfenbrenner & Morris, 1998) has added biological influences to his theory and now terms it *bioecological theory*. Nonetheless, ecological, environmental contexts still predominate in his theory (Ceci, 2000).

The contributions of ecological, contextual theory include:

- A systematic examination of both macro and micro dimensions of environmental systems
- Attention to connections between environmental settings (mesosystem)
- Consideration of sociohistorical influences on development (chronosystem)

The criticisms of ecological, contextual theory include:

- Even with the recent addition of biological influences in recent years, too little attention given to biological foundations of development
- Inadequate attention to cognitive processes

An Eclectic Theoretical Orientation

Those who adopt an **eclectic theoretical orientation** do not favor any one theoretical approach, but rather select and use whatever they consider the best in each theory. In this view, no single theory described in this chapter is infallible or capable of explaining entirely the rich complexity of adolescent development. Rather, each has made an important contribution to our understanding of adolescent development, but none provides a complete description and explanation.

For this reason, the four major approaches to adolescent development are presented in this text in an unbiased fashion so that you can view the field of adolescent development as it actually exists—with different theorists drawing different conclusions. Many other theories of adolescent development, not discussed in this chapter, arc woven through the discussion of adolescent development in the remainder of the book. For example, chapter 5 examines the humanistic approach, which emphasizes the adolescent's development of self, and chapter 12 discusses attribution theory, which focuses on adolescents' motivation for understanding the causes of their own and others' behavior.

Many "local" theories or mini-models also guide research in specific areas of development (Kuhn, 1998). For example, in chapter 9, "Families," you will read about the new look in theorizing about parent-adolescent relationships. In chapter 11, "Schools," you will read about some models for improving adolescents' education. Throughout this book you will read about these local theories that focus on specific aspects of adolescent development. Together, the grand theories and micro approaches give us a more complete portrait of how the journey of adolescent development unfolds.

eclectic theoretical orientation An orientation that does not follow any one theoretical approach, but rather, selects from each theory whatever is considered the best in it.

Review and reflect Learning goal 1

1 **Describe the major theories of development**

REVIEW

- What is the relationship between a theory and hypotheses? What are some theories that involved the psychoanalytic revision of Freud's theory? What is Erikson's theory? What are some strengths and weaknesses of the psycho-analytic theories?
- What are three main cognitive theories? What are some strengths and weak-nesses of the cognitive theories?
- What are the two main behavioral and social cognitive theories? What are some strengths and weaknesses of the behavioral and social cognitive theories?
- What is the nature of ecological, contextual theory? What are some strengths and weaknesses of the theory?
- What is an eclectic theoretical orientation?

REFLECT

- Which of the theories do you think best explains your own development? Why?

2 RESEARCH IN ADOLESCENT DEVELOPMENT

Types of Research	**Time Span of Research**	**The Field of Adolescent Development Research**

Generally, research in adolescent development is designed to test hypotheses, which in some cases are derived from the theories just described. Through research, theories are modified to reflect new data, and occasionally new theories arise. What types of research are conducted in adolescent development? If researchers want to study children and adolescents of different ages, what research designs can they use? These are the questions that we will examine next.

Types of Research

This section describes the major methods used to gather data about adolescent development. For this purpose, there are three basic types of research: descriptive, correlational, and experimental. Each has strengths and weaknesses.

Descriptive Research **Descriptive research** has the purpose of observing and recording behavior. For example, a psychologist might observe the extent to which adolescents are considerate or aggressive toward each other. By itself, descriptive research cannot prove what causes a phenomenon, but it can reveal important information about adolescent development. Descriptive research methods include: observation, surveys and interviews, standardized tests, experience sampling, physiological measures, and case studies.

Observation Scientific observation requires an important set of skills (McMillan & Wergin, 2002). Unless we are trained in and practice those skills regularly, we might not know what to look for, remember what we saw, or even realize that what we are looking for is changing from one moment to the next. Moreover, we might not communicate our observations effectively.

For our observations to be effective, they must be systematic (Elmes, Kantowitz, & Roedinger, 2003). We need to know whom we are observing, when and where we

*T*ruth is arrived at by the painstaking process of eliminating the untrue.

—Arthur Conan Doyle
British Physician and Detective-Story Writer, 20th Century

descriptive research Has the purpose of observing and recording behavior.

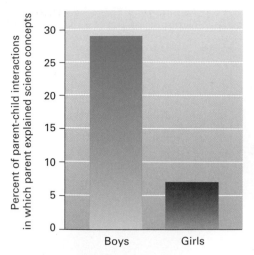

FIGURE 2.7 Parents' Explanations of Science to Sons and Daughters at a Science Museum

In a naturalistic observation study at a children's science museum, parents were three times more likely to explain science to boys than to girls (Crowley & others, 2001). The gender difference occurred regardless of whether the father, the mother, or both parents were with the child, although the gender difference was greatest for fathers' science explanations to sons and daughters.

"Would you say Attila is doing an excellent job, a good job, a fair job, or a poor job?"

© The New Yorker Collection, 1982. Charles Addams from cartoonbank.com. All rights reserved.

laboratory A controlled setting in which many of the complex factors of the "real world" are removed.

naturalistic observation Observing behavior in real-world settings.

will observe, and how we will make the observations. We can record our observations in writing or on audio- or videotape.

In deciding where we should make our observations, we have two choices: the laboratory and the everyday world. When we observe scientifically, we may need to control certain factors that determine behavior but are not the focus of our inquiry (Crano & Brewer, 2002; Hoyle & Judd, 2002). For this reason, some research adolescent development is conducted in a **laboratory,** a controlled setting that removes many of the complex factors present in the "real world."

An experiment conducted by Albert Bandura (1965) found that children behaved more aggressively after observing an adult model being rewarded for aggression. Bandura conducted his study in a laboratory with adults the children did not know. Thus, he controlled when the children witnessed aggression, how much aggression they saw, and what form the aggression took. Bandura would not have had as much control over the experiment, or as much confidence in the results, if he had conducted it in the children's homes and if familiar people, such as parents, siblings, or the children's friends had been present.

Laboratory research does have some drawbacks. First, it is almost impossible to conduct research without the participants' knowing they are being studied. Second, the laboratory setting is unnatural, so it can cause the participants to behave unnaturally. A third drawback is that people who are willing to come to a university laboratory may not be representative of the general population. People who are unfamiliar with university settings, or with the idea of "advancing science," may be too intimidated by the setting to agree to participate in an experiment. Finally, some aspects of adolescent development are difficult if not impossible to examine in the laboratory. Laboratory studies of certain types of stress may even be unethical.

Another method, **naturalistic observation,** involves observing behavior in real-world settings and makes no effort to manipulate or control the situation. Researchers conduct naturalistic observation in homes and schools, at sporting events and malls, and in other settings adolescents frequent.

In one study, researchers used naturalistic observation to study parent-child interaction in a children's science museum (Crowley & others, 2001). They found that parents were three times as likely to engage boys in explanatory talk, suggesting a gender bias that encourages boys more than girls in science (see figure 2.7). In another study conducted at a science museum, researchers found that Mexican American parents who had completed high school used more explanations with their children than Mexican American parents who had not completed high school (Tenenbaum & others, 2002).

Surveys and Interviews   Sometimes the best and quickest way to get information about adolescents is to ask them for it. One technique is to *interview* them directly. A related method that is especially useful when researchers need information from many people is the *survey.* Sometimes referred to as a questionnaire, a survey consists of a standard set of questions used to obtain participants' self-reported attitudes or beliefs about a particular topic. In a good survey, the questions are clear and unbiased, allowing respondents to answer unambiguously (Gallup, 1987; Tourangeau, 2004).

Some survey and interview questions are unstructured and open-ended, such as "What do you think could be done to improve schools for teenagers?" They allow for unique responses from each person surveyed. Other questions are more structured and specific. For example, in one national poll on what needs to be done to improve U.S. schools, adults were asked: "Of the following four possibilities, which one do you think offers the most promise for improving public schools in the community: a qualified, competent teacher in every classroom; free choice for parents among a number of private, church-related, and public schools; rigorous academic standards; the elimination of social promotion; or don't know?" (Rose & Gallup, 2000). More than half

When conducting surveys or interviews with adolescents, what are some strategies that need to be exercised?

the respondents to this question said that the most promising way to improve schools is to staff every classroom with a qualified, competent teacher.

One problem with surveys and interviews is the tendency of participants to answer in a way they think is socially acceptable or desirable rather than saying what they truly think or feel (Best & Kahn, 2003). For example, on a survey of risk-taking behavior, some adolescents might reply that they do not take drugs or engage in sexual intercourse, even though they do.

Standardized Tests   A **standardized test** is a test that offers uniform procedures for administration and scoring so that a person's performance can be compared with that of other individuals (Aiken, 2003; Cohen & Swerdlik, 2002). Scores on standardized tests are often stated in percentiles. Suppose you were in the 92nd percentile on the SAT when you were in high school. Your score would mean that 92 percent of a large group of individuals who took the test in the past scored lower than you did.

One widely used standardized test in psychology is the Stanford-Binet intelligence test, which is described in chapter 4, "Cognitive Development." The most widely used standardized test of personality is the Minnesota Multiphasic Personality Inventory (MMPI) (Butcher, 2000). The MMPI-A (the A stands for Adolescent) is a downward extension of the MMPI intended to assess the personality of adolescents in clinical and research settings (Butcher & others, 1992). The test includes several scales not found in the MMPI for adults, such as Alienation, Conduct Problems, Low Aspirations, School Problems, Immaturity, Alcohol/Drug Problems Proneness, and Alcohol/Drug Problems Acknowledgment (Holmbeck & Shapera, 1999). The MMPI-A also includes a number of validity scales that can be used to detect whether an adolescent is being truthful or responding in a socially desirable way (Baer & others, 1997). In chapter 5, "The Self, Identity, Emotions, and Personality" we will explore assessment of self-worth and self-esteem, which are central dimensions of personality.

The main advantage of standardized tests is that they provide information about individual differences among people. One problem is that they do not always predict behavior in nontest situations. Another problem is that they are based on the expectation that an adolescent's behavior will be consistent and stable, yet personality and intelligence—two primary targets of standardized testing—can vary with the situation. For example, an adolescent might perform poorly on a standardized intelligence test in a school psychologist's office but score much higher at home, where he or she is less anxious.

This criticism is especially relevant for members of minority groups, some of whom have been inaccurately classified as mentally retarded on the basis of their

standardized test A test with uniform procedures for administration and scoring. Many standardized tests allow a person's performance to be compared with the performance of other individuals.

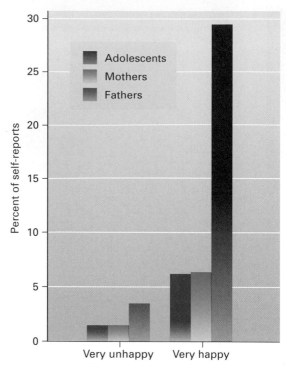

FIGURE 2.8 Self-Reported Extremes of Emotion by Adolescents, Mothers, and Fathers Using the Experience Sampling Method

In the study by Reed Larson and Maryse Richards (1994), adolescents and their mothers and fathers were beeped at random times by researchers using the experience sampling method. The researchers found that adolescents were more likely to report more emotional extremes than their parents.

scores on intelligence tests (Valencia & Suzuki, 2001). In addition, cross-cultural psychologists caution that many psychological tests developed in Western cultures may not be appropriate in other cultures (Cushner, McLelland, & Safford, 2003). People in those cultures may have had experiences that cause them to interpret and respond to the questions much differently from the people on whom the test was standardized.

Experience Sampling In the **experience sampling method (ESM),** participants in a study are given electronic pagers. Then, researchers "beep" them at random times. When they are beeped, the participants report on various aspects of their immediate situation, including where they are, what they are doing, who they are with, and how they are feeling.

The ESM has been used in a number of studies to determine the settings in which adolescents are most likely to spend their time, the extent to which they spend time with parents and peers, and the nature of their emotions. Using this method, Reed Larson and Maryse Richards (1994) found that across the thousands of times they reported their feelings, adolescents experienced emotions that were more extreme and more fleeting than their parents. For example, adolescents were five times more likely than their parents to report being "very happy" when they were beeped, and three times more likely to feel "very unhappy" (see figure 2.8).

Physiological Measures Researchers are increasingly using physiological measures when they study adolescent development. One type of physiological measure involves an assessment of the hormones in an adolescent's bloodstream. As puberty unfolds, glandular secretions in the blood increase, raising the blood levels of hormone samples. To determine the nature of these hormonal changes, researchers take blood samples from willing adolescents (Susman, 1997; Susman, Dorn, & Schiefelbein, 2003).

The body composition of adolescents also is a focus of physiological assessment. There is a special interest in the increase in fat content in the body during pubertal development.

Until recently, little research had focused on the brain activity of adolescents. However, the development of neuroimaging techniques has led to a flurry of research studies (Thompson & others, 2000). One technique that is being used in a number of them is *magnetic resonance imaging (MRI)*, in which radio waves are used to construct images of a person's brain tissue and biochemical activity (Bauer, Bowers, & Leritz, 2003). We will have much more to say about these physiological measures in chapter 3, "Puberty, Health, and Biological Foundations."

Case Studies A **case study** is an in-depth look at a single individual. Case studies are performed mainly by mental health professionals, when for practical or ethical reasons, the unique aspects of an individual's life cannot be duplicated and tested in other individuals (Dattilio, 2001). A case study provides information about one person's fears, hopes, fantasies, traumatic experiences, upbringing, family relationships, health, or anything else that helps the psychologist to understand the person's mind and behavior (Beins, 2004).

Consider the case study of Michael Rehbein, which illustrates the flexibility and resilience of the developing brain. At age 7, Michael began to experience uncontrollable seizures—as many as 400 a day. Doctors said that the only solution was to remove the left hemisphere of his brain where the seizures were occurring. Though Michael's recovery was slow, eventually his right hemisphere began to reorganize and take over functions that normally reside in the brain's left hemisphere, such as speech. The neuroimage in figure 2.9 shows this reorganization of Michael's brain vividly.

Although case histories provide dramatic, in-depth portrayals of people's lives, we must be cautious in generalizing from them. The subject of a case study is unique,

experience sampling method (ESM)
Involves providing participants with electronic pagers and then beeping them at random times, at which time they are asked to report on various aspects of their lives.

case study An in-depth look at a single individual.

(a)

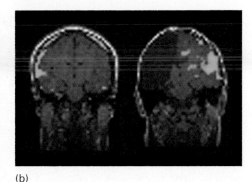

(b)

FIGURE 2.9 Plasticity in the Brain's Hemispheres

(*a*) Michael Rehbein at 14 years of age. (*b*) Michael's right hemisphere (*near left*) has reorganized to take over the language functions normally carried out by corresponding areas in the left hemisphere of an intact brain (*far left*). However, the right hemisphere is not as efficient as the left, and more areas of the brain are recruited to process speech.

with a genetic makeup and personal history that no one else shares. In addition, case studies involve judgments of unknown reliability. Psychologists who conduct a case study rarely check to see whether other psychologists agree with their observations.

Correlational Research   In **correlational research,** the goal is to describe the strength of the relationship between two or more events or characteristics. The more strongly the two events are correlated (related or associated), the more effectively we can predict one event from the other (Whitley, 2002). For example, if researchers find that low-involved, permissive parenting is correlated with an adolescents' lack of self-control, then low-involved, permissive parenting might be one source of the lack of self-control. This form of research is a key method of data analysis, the third step in the scientific method.

A caution is in order, however. Correlation does not mean causation. The correlational finding just mentioned does not mean that permissive parenting necessarily causes low self-control in adolescents. It could mean that, but it could also mean that adolescents' lack of self-control causes parents to simply throw up their arms in despair and give up trying to control their adolescents. It could also mean that other factors, such as heredity or poverty, underlie the correlation between permissive parenting and low self-control. Figure 2.10 illustrates these possible interpretations. Throughout this book you will read about numerous correlational research studies. Keep in mind how easy it is to assume causality when two events or characteristics merely are correlated.

Researchers use a *correlation coefficient,* a number based on statistical analysis that is used to describe the degree of association between two variables. The correlation coefficient ranges from +1.00 to −1.00. A negative coefficient indicates an inverse relationship. For example, researchers often find a *negative* correlation between permissive parenting and adolescents' self-control. In contrast, they often find

correlational research The goal is to describe the strength of the relationship between two or more events or characteristics.

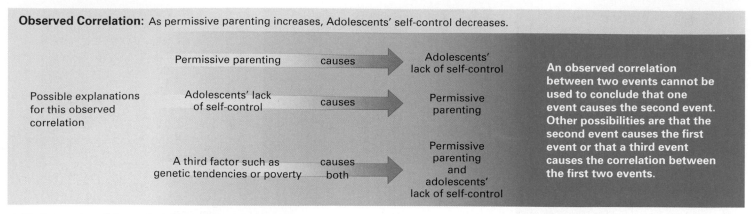

Observed Correlation: As permissive parenting increases, Adolescents' self-control decreases.

Possible explanations for this observed correlation

Permissive parenting — causes → Adolescents' lack of self-control

Adolescents' lack of self-control — causes → Permissive parenting

A third factor such as genetic tendencies or poverty — causes both → Permissive parenting and adolescents' lack of self-control

An observed correlation between two events cannot be used to conclude that one event causes the second event. Other possibilities are that the second event causes the first event or that a third event causes the correlation between the first two events.

FIGURE 2.10 Possible Explanations of Correlational Data

**Correlational Research
Experimental Research**

a *positive* correlation between parental monitoring of adolescents and adolescents' self-control. The higher the correlation coefficient, whether positive or negative, the stronger the association between the two variables. A correlation of −.40, then, is stronger than a correlation of +.20 because we disregard whether the correlation is positive or negative in determining the strength of the correlation. A correlation of 0 means there is no association between the variables.

Experimental Research Unlike correlational research, **experimental research** allows us to determine the causes of behavior. We accomplish this task by performing an *experiment,* a carefully regulated procedure in which we manipulate one or more of the factors we believe to influence the behavior we are studying while we hold all other factors constant. If the behavior we are studying changes when we manipulate the chosen factor, we can say that factor causes change. The "cause" is the factor or event being manipulated; the "effect" is the behavior that changes because of the manipulation. Experimental research is the only reliable method of establishing cause and effect. Because correlational research does not involve the manipulation of factors, it is not a dependable way to establish a cause (Leary, 2004).

Independent and Dependent Variables All experiments involve at least one independent variable and one dependent variable. The **independent variable** is the factor that is manipulated. The term *independent* indicates that this variable can be manipulated independently of all other factors. For example, suppose we want to design an experiment to establish the effects of peer tutoring on adolescents' achievement. In this example, the amount and type of peer tutoring could be the independent variable. The **dependent variable** is the factor that is measured; it can change as the independent variable is manipulated. The term *dependent* indicates that this variable depends on what happens as the independent variable is manipulated. In the peer tutoring study, adolescents' achievement would be the dependent variable. It might be assessed in a number of ways, perhaps by scores on a nationally standardized achievement test.

Experimental and Control Groups In an experiment, researchers manipulate the independent variable by giving different experiences to one or more experimental groups and one or more control groups. An *experimental group* is a group whose experience is manipulated. A *control group* is a group that is treated like the experimental group in every other way except for the manipulated factor. The control group serves as a baseline against which the effects on the manipulated group can be compared. In the peer tutoring study, we would need to have one group of adolescents that got peer tutoring (experimental group) and one that didn't (control group).

experimental research Research that involves an experiment, a carefully regulated procedure in which one or more of the factors believed to influence the behavior being studied are manipulated while all other factors are held constant.

independent variable The factor that is manipulated in experimental research.

dependent variable The factor that is measured in experimental research.

An important principle of experimental research is *random assignment*—assigning participants to experimental and control groups by chance (Christensen, 2004). This practice reduces the likelihood that the results of the experiment will be affected by preexisting differences between the groups. In our study of peer tutoring, random assignment would greatly reduce the probability that the two groups differed in age, family background, initial achievement, intelligence, personality, or health.

To summarize, in our study of peer tutoring and adolescent achievement, we would assign participants randomly to two groups. One (the experimental group) would be given peer tutoring and the other (the control group) would not. The different experiences that the experimental and control groups receive would be the independent variable. After the peer tutoring had been completed, the adolescents would be given a nationally standardized achievement test (the dependent variable). Figure 2.11 applies the experimental research method applied to a different problem: whether a time management program can improve adolescents' grades.

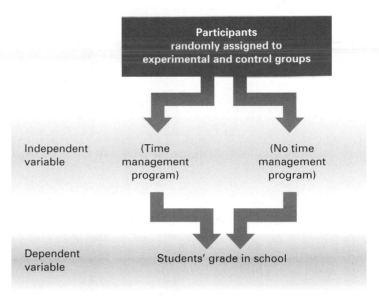

FIGURE 2.11 Random Assignment and Experimental Design

Time Span of Research

A special concern of developmentalists is the time span of a research investigation. Studies that focus on the relation of age to some other variable are common. Researchers have two options: They can study different individuals of different ages and compare them; or they can study the same individuals as they age over time.

Cross-Sectional Research   **Cross-sectional research** involves studying people all at one time. For example, a researcher might study the self-esteem of 10-, 15-, and 20-year-olds. In a cross-sectional study, all participants' self-esteem would be assessed at one time.

The main advantage of a cross-sectional study is that researchers do not have to wait for the individuals to grow older. Despite its time efficiency, however, the cross-sectional approach has its drawbacks. It gives no information about how individuals change or about the stability of their characteristics. The increases and decreases of development—the hills and valleys of growth and development—can become obscured in the cross-sectional approach. For example, in a cross-sectional study of self-esteem, average increases and decreases might be revealed. But the study would not show how the life satisfaction of individual children waxed and waned over the years. It also would not tell us whether younger children who had high or low self-esteem as young adults continued to have high or low self-esteem, respectively, when they became older.

Longitudinal Research   **Longitudinal research** involves studying the same individuals over a period of time, usually several years or more. In a longitudinal study of self-esteem, the researcher might examine the self-esteem of a group of 10-year-olds, then assess their self-esteem again when they are 15, and then again when they are 20. Figure 2.12 compares the cross-sectional and longitudinal approaches.

Although longitudinal studies provide a wealth of information about such important issues as stability and change in development and the importance of early experience for later development, they are not without their problems (Raudenbush, 2001). They are expensive and time-consuming. The longer the study lasts, the more participants drop out—they move, get sick, lose interest, and so forth. Participants can bias the outcome of a study, because those who remain may be dissimilar to those who drop out. Those individuals who remain in a longitudinal study over a number of

cross-sectional research A research strategy in which individuals of different ages are compared at one time.

longitudinal research A research strategy in which the same individuals are studied over a period of time, usually several years or more.

Cross-sectional approach

Year of testing: 2000

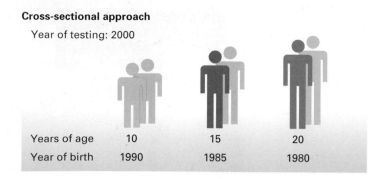

Years of age	10	15	20
Year of birth	1990	1985	1980

Longitudinal approach

Participants' year
of birth: 1980

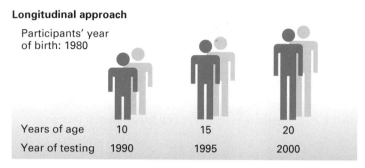

Years of age	10	15	20
Year of testing	1990	1995	2000

FIGURE 2.12 A Comparison of Cross-Sectional and Longitudinal Approaches

years may be more compulsive and conformity-oriented, for example, or they might have more stable lives.

The Field of Adolescent Development Research

Knowledge in the field of adolescence rests heavily on the development of a broad, competent research base. When I wrote the first edition of *Adolescence* in the late 1970s, only a small number of scholars were studying adolescent development. Researchers were studying adults and children, but not adolescents. Over the last two decades—especially the last decade—the research base of adolescence has grown enormously as an increasing number of investigators have become intrigued by issues and questions that involve the developmental period between childhood and adulthood. The growth of research on adolescent development is reflected in the increasing number of research journals and scholars from different disciplines devoted to advancing scientific knowledge about adolescence (Lerner & Steinberg, 2004).

Why were researchers so neglectful of adolescence until recently? For most of the twentieth century, experiences in childhood, especially the early childhood years, were thought to be so critical that later experiences, such as those occurring in adolescence, were believed to have little impact on development (Bruer, 1999). But beginning in the 1980s, developmentalists seriously challenged the early-experience doctrine, concluding that later experiences were more important in development than had been commonly believed (Brim & Kagan, 1980). The increased research interest in adolescence also has resulted from observations that extensive changes take place between childhood and adulthood (Dornbusch, Petersen, & Hetherington, 1991).

The main outlets for the vast amount of research being conducted on adolescence are journals and papers presented at scientific meetings. Whether or not you pursue a career in adolescent development, psychology, or a related scientific field, you can benefit by learning about the journal process. Possibly as a student you will be required to look up original research in journals as part of writing a term paper. As a parent, teacher, or nurse you might want to consult journals to obtain information that will help you understand and work more effectively with adolescents. As an inquiring person, you might look up information in journals after you have heard or read something that piqued your curiosity.

A journal publishes scholarly and academic information, usually in a specific domain—like physics, math, sociology, or, in the case of our interest, adolescence. Scholars in these fields publish most of their research in journals, which are the core sources of information in virtually every academic discipline. In psychology and the field of adolescence, most journal articles are reports of original research. Many journals also include review articles that present an overview of different studies on a particular topic—such as adolescent depression, attachment in adolescence, or adolescent decision making.

Journal articles are usually written for other professionals in the field of the journal's focus—such as geology, anthropology, or, again in our case, adolescence. They often contain technical language and specialized terms related to a specific discipline that are difficult for nonprofessionals to understand. Most of you have already had one or more courses in psychology, and you will be learning a great deal more about the specialized field of adolescent development in this course. This should improve your ability to understand journal articles in this field.

An increasing number of journals publish information about adolescence. Some are devoted exclusively to adolescence; others include information about other periods of the human life span as well. Journals devoted exclusively to adolescence include *Journal of Research on Adolescence, Journal of Early Adolescence, Journal of Youth and Adolescence, Adolescence,* and *Journal of Adolescent Health Care.* Journals that include research on adolescence but also research on other age ranges include *Child Development, Developmental Psychology,* and *Human Development.* Also, a number of journals that do not focus on development include articles on adolescence, such as *Journal of Educational Psychology, Sex Roles, Journal of Marriage and the Family,* and *Journal of Consulting and Clinical Psychology.*

Many journals are selective about what they publish. Every journal has an editorial board of experts that evaluate the articles submitted for publication. Each submitted paper is carefully examined by one or more of the experts, who accept or reject it based on such factors as its contribution to the field, theoretical soundness, methodological excellence, and clarity of writing. Some of the most prestigious journals reject as many as 80 to 90 percent of the articles that are submitted because they fail to meet the journal's standards.

Where do you find journals? Your college or university library likely has one or more of the journals just listed. Some public libraries also carry journals. I encourage you to look up one or more of the journals that include material on adolescence.

To help you understand the journals, let's examine the format followed by many of them. Their organization often takes this course: abstract, introduction, method, results, discussion, and references.

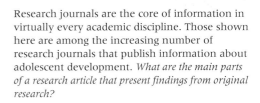

The *abstract* is a brief summary that appears at the beginning of the article. The abstract lets readers quickly determine whether the article is relevant to their interests and whether they want to read the entire article. The *introduction,* as its title suggests, introduces the problem or issue that is being studied. It includes a concise review of research relevant to the topic, theoretical ties, and one or more hypotheses to be tested. The *method* section consists of a clear description of the participants evaluated in the study, the measures used, and the procedures that were followed. The method section should be sufficiently clear and detailed so that by reading it another researcher could repeat, or replicate, the study. The *results* section reports the analysis of the data collected. In most cases, the results section includes statistical analyses that are difficult for nonprofessionals to understand. The *discussion* section presents the author's conclusions, inferences, and interpretation of what was found. Statements are usually made about whether the hypotheses presented in the introduction were supported, limitations of the study, and suggestions for future research. The *references* section is the last part of the journal article and gives a bibliographic listing for every source cited in the article. The references section is often a good source for finding other articles relevant to the topic you are interested in.

Research journals are the core of information in virtually every academic discipline. Those shown here are among the increasing number of research journals that publish information about adolescent development. *What are the main parts of a research article that present findings from original research?*

Adolescence Research Journals

www.mhhe.com/santrocka10

Review and reflect Learning goal 2

2 **Explain how research on adolescent development is conducted**

REVIEW

- How is research on adolescent development conducted?
- What are some ways that researchers study the time span of people's lives?
- What is the field of adolescent development research like? What are the main sections of a research journal article?

REFLECT

- You have learned that correlation does not mean causation. Develop an example of two variables (two sets of observations) that are correlated but almost certainly do not have a causal relationship.

3 FACING UP TO RESEARCH CHALLENGES

| Conducting Ethical Research | Minimizing Bias | Being a Wise Consumer of Information About Adolescence |

The scientific foundation of research in adolescent development helps to minimize the effect of individual researchers' biases and to maximize the objectivity of the results. Still, some subtle challenges remain. One is to ensure that research is conducted in an ethical way; another is to recognize, and try to overcome, researchers' deeply buried personal biases. Yet another challenge is to become a wise consumer of information about research on adolescent development.

Conducting Ethical Research

Ethics is an important part of your understanding of the science of adolescent development. Ethics in research may affect you personally if you serve at some point as a participant in a study. In that event, you need to know about your rights as a participant and about the responsibilities researchers have in ensuring that these rights are safeguarded. The failure to consider participants' well-being can have life-altering consequences for them. For example, one investigation of young dating couples asked them to complete a questionnaire that coincidentally stimulated some of the participants to think about potentially troublesome issues (Rubin & Mitchell, 1976). One year later, when the researchers followed up with the original sample, 9 of 10 participants said they had discussed their answers with their dating partner. In most instances, the discussions helped to strengthen the relationships. In some cases, though, the participants used the questionnaire as a springboard to discuss previously hidden problems or concerns. One participant said, "The study definitely played a role in ending my relationship with Larry." In this case, the couple had different views about how long they expected to be together. She was thinking of a short-term dating relationship only, while he was thinking in terms of a lifetime. Their answers to the questions brought the disparity in their views to the surface and led to the end of their relationship. Researchers have a responsibility to anticipate the personal problems their study might cause and to at least inform the participants of the possible fallout.

If you ever become a researcher in adolescent development yourself, you will need an even deeper understanding of ethics. You may never become a researcher in the field of adolescent development, but you may conduct one or more studies in this or other courses. Even smart, conscientious students frequently do not consider the rights of the participants who serve in their experiments. A student might think, "I volunteer in a home several hours per week for adolescents who are mentally retarded. I can use the residents of the home in my study to see if a particular treatment helps improve their memory for everyday tasks." However, without proper permissions the most well-meaning, kind, and considerate studies still violate the rights of the participants.

Today colleges and universities have review boards that evaluate the ethics of research conducted at their institutions. Research proposals must pass the scrutiny of a research ethics committee before the research can be initiated.

In addition, the American Psychological Association (APA) has developed ethics guidelines for its members. The APA's code of ethics instructs psychologists to protect their participants from mental and physical harm and to keep their best interests uppermost in their minds (Rosnow, 1995). Specifically, the APA guidelines address four issues:

- *Informed consent.* All participants, 7 years or older, must give their consent to participate. If participants are not old enough to consent, their parents' or guardians' consent must be obtained. Informed consent means that the participants (and/or their parents or legal guardians) have been told what their participation will entail and any risks that might be involved. For example, if researchers want to study the effects of conflict in divorced families on adolescents' self-esteem, the participants should be informed that in some instances discussion of a family's experiences may improve family relationships, but in other cases might raise unwanted stress. After informed consent is given, participants have the right to withdraw at any time.

- *Confidentiality.* Researchers are responsible for keeping all of the data they gather on individuals completely confidential and, when possible, completely anonymous.
- *Debriefing.* After the study has been completed, participants should be informed of its purpose and the methods that were used. In most cases, the experimenter also can inform participants in a general manner beforehand about the purpose of the research without leading participants to behave in a way they think that the experimenter is expecting. When preliminary information about the study is likely to affect the results, participants can at least be debriefed after the study has been completed.
- *Deception.* This is an ethical issue that psychologists debate extensively (Hoyle & Judd, 2002; Whitley, 2002). In some circumstances, telling the participant beforehand what the research study is about substantially alters the participant's behavior and invalidates the researcher's data. In all cases of deception, however, the researcher must ensure that the deception will not harm the participant and that the participant will be told the complete nature of the study (debriefed) as soon as possible after the study is completed. To examine the role of deception in research and find out how it might raise ethical questions, watch the Discovery video segment entitled "Obedience to Authority."

Ethical Principles

LifeMAP

Minimizing Bias

Studies of adolescent development are most useful when they are conducted without bias or prejudice toward any particular group of people. Of special concern is bias based on gender and bias based on culture or ethnicity.

Gender Bias Society continues to have a gender bias, a preconceived notion about the abilities of females and males that prevents individuals from pursuing their own interests and achieving their potential. But gender bias also has had a less obvious effect within the field of adolescent development (Etaugh & Bridges, 2001; Koch, 2003; Shields & Eyssell, 2001). For example, too often researchers have drawn conclusions about females' attitudes and behaviors from research conducted with males as the only participants.

When gender differences are found, they sometimes are unduly magnified (Denmark & others, 1988). For example, a researcher might report in a study that 74 percent of the boys had high achievement expectations versus only 67 percent of the girls and go on to talk about the differences in some detail. In reality, this might be a rather small difference. It also might disappear if the study were repeated or the study might have methodological problems that don't allow such strong interpretations.

Researchers who are concerned about giving females equal rights in research have raised some new questions (Tetreault, 1997):

- How might gender bias influence the choice of hypotheses, participants, and research design? The most widely known theory of moral development was proposed by a male (Lawrence Kohlberg) in a male-dominant society (the United States), and for many years, males were the main participants in research used to support his theory. What would have been the outcome if females had been included?
- How might research on topics of primary interest to females, such as relationships, feelings, and empathy, challenge existing theory? In the study of moral

Pam Reid
Educational and Developmental Psychologist

As a child, Pam Reid played with chemistry sets, and at the university she was majoring in chemistry, planning on becoming a medical doctor. Because some of her friends signed up for a psychology course as an elective, she decided to join them. She was so intrigued by learning more about how people think, behave, and develop that she changed her major to psychology. She says, "I fell in love with psychology." Pam went on to obtain her Ph.D. in educational psychology.

Today, Pam is a professor of education and psychology at the University of Michigan. She is also a research scientist for the University of Michigan Institute for Research on Women and Gender. Her main interest is how children and adolescents develop social skills, and especially how gender, socioeconomic status, and ethnicity are involved in development. Because many psychological findings have been based on research with middle-socioeconomic status and non-Latino White populations, Pam believes it is important to study people from different ethnic groups. She stresses that by understanding the expectations, attitudes, and behavior of diverse groups, we enrich the theory and practice of psychology. Currently Pam is working with her graduate students on a project involving middle school girls. She is interested in why girls, more often than boys, stop taking classes in mathematics.

Pam Reid (*back row, center*) with graduate students she is mentoring at the University of Michigan.

ethnic gloss Using an ethnic label such as African American or Latino in a superficial way that portrays an ethnic group as being more homogeneous than it really is.

development just mentioned, the highest level of development has often been portrayed as being based on a principle of "justice for the individual" (Kohlberg, 1976). However, more recent theorizing notes individuality and autonomy tend to be male concerns and suggests that a principle based on relationships and connections with others be added to our thinking about high-level moral development (Gilligan, 1982, 1996).

- How has research that has exaggerated gender differences influenced the way the people think about females? Some researchers believe that gender differences in mathematics have been exaggerated and have been fueled by societal bias against females (Hyde & Mezulis, 2001; Hyde & Plant, 1995). The exaggeration of differences can lead to negative expectations for females' math performance.

Cultural and Ethnic Bias   At the same time researchers have been struggling with gender bias, the realization that research needs to include more people from diverse ethnic groups has also been building (Chun, Organista, & Marin, 2003: Graham, 1992). Historically, members of ethnic minority groups (African American, Latino, Asian American, and Native American) have been discounted from most research in the United States and simply thought of as variations from the norm or average. Because their scores don't always fit neatly into measures of central tendency (such as a mean score to reflect the average performance of group of participants), minority individuals have been viewed as confounds or "noise" in data. Consequently, researchers have deliberately excluded them from the samples they have selected (Ryan-Finn, Cauce, & Grove, 1995). Given the fact that individuals from diverse ethnic groups were excluded from research on adolescent development for so long, we might reasonably conclude that children's real lives are perhaps more varied than research data have indicated in the past (Ponterotto & others, 2001; Stevenson, 1995).

Researchers also have tended to overgeneralize about ethnic groups (Trimble, 1989). **Ethnic gloss** is using an ethnic label such as African American or Latino in a superficial way that portrays an ethnic group as being more homogeneous than it really is. For example, a researcher might describe a research sample like this: "The participants were 20 Latinos and 20 Anglo-Americans." A more complete description of the Latino group might be something like this: "The 20 Latino participants were Mexican Americans from low-income neighborhoods in the southwestern area of Los Angeles. Twelve were from homes in which Spanish is the dominant language spoken, 8 from homes in which English is the main language spoken. Ten were born in the United States, 10 in Mexico. Ten described themselves as Mexican American, 5 as Mexican, 3 as American, 2 as Chicano, and 1 as Latino." Ethnic gloss can cause researchers to obtain samples of ethnic groups that

Look at the two photographs above, one of all White males, the other of a diverse group of females and males from different ethnic groups, including some White individuals. Consider a topic in psychology, such as parenting, love, or cultural values. *If you were conducting research on this topic, might the results of the study be different depending on whether the participants in your study were the individuals in the photograph on the left or those on the right?*

are not representative of the group's diversity, which can lead to overgeneralization and stereotyping.

Being a Wise Consumer of Information About Adolescence

We live in a society that generates a vast amount of information about adolescents in various media that range from research journals to newspaper and television accounts. The information varies greatly in quality. How can we evaluate it? Six guidelines follow.

Be Cautious of What Is Reported in the Popular Media   Television, radio, newspapers, and magazines frequently report the results of research on adolescent development. Many researchers regularly supply the media with information about adolescents and most colleges have media relations departments that publicize faculty research. In some cases, this research has been published in professional journals or presented at national meetings and then is picked up by the popular media.

However, not all research on adolescents that appears in the media comes from reputable professionals. Journalists, television reporters, and other media personnel are not scientifically trained, so it is no easy task for them to sort through the avalanche of material they receive and decide which information to report.

Unfortunately, when the media do report on research, they tend to focus on sensational, dramatic findings. Even if the information they gather from research journals is not sensational, they may embellish or sensationalize it, distorting the researcher's intentions.

Another problem with research that is reported in the media is a lack of time or space to discuss important details of a study. Reporters often get only get a few lines or moments to summarize complex findings as best they can. Too often the result is overgeneralized and stereotyped.

Avoid Assuming Individual Needs on the Basis of Group Research   Most research on adolescents is conducted at the level of the group. Such studies are termed *nomothetic research*. Individual variations in the way adolescents behave are not a focus

of this type of research. For example, if researchers are interested in the effects of divorce on adolescents' school achievement, they might conduct a study of 50 adolescents from divorced families and 50 adolescents from intact, never-divorced families. They might find that as a group adolescents from divorced families had lower achievement in school than adolescents from intact families. This type of nomothetic finding that applies to adolescents from divorced families as a group is commonly reported in the media and in research journals. What goes unsaid is that in this particular study, some of the adolescents from divorced families probably had higher school achievement than some of the adolescents from intact families. Indeed, it is entirely possible that of the 100 adolescents in the study, the 2 or 3 adolescents who had the highest school achievement came from divorced families. But that information would not typically be reported in the media or a research journal.

Nomothetic research provides valuable information about the characteristics of a group of adolescents, revealing strengths and weaknesses of the group. However, in many instances, parents, teachers, and others want to know about how to help one particular adolescent cope and learn more effectively. *Idiographic needs* are needs of the individual, not of the group. Unfortunately, although nomothetic research can point up problems for certain groups of adolescents, its findings do not always hold for an individual adolescent.

Recognize the Tendency to Overgeneralize About a Small or Clinical Sample

There often isn't space or time in media presentations to go into details about the nature of the sample of adolescents on which the study is based. In many cases, samples are too small to let us generalize to a larger population. For example, if a study of adolescents from divorced families is based on only 10 or 20 adolescents, what is found in the study cannot be generalized to all adolescents from divorced families. Perhaps the sample was drawn from families who have substantial economic resources, are Anglo-American, live in a small southern town, and are undergoing therapy. From this study, we clearly would be making unwarranted generalizations if we thought the findings also characterize adolescents who are from low- to moderate-income families, are from other ethnic backgrounds, live in a different geographic region, and are not undergoing therapy.

Be Aware That a Single Study Is Usually Not the Defining Word

The media might identify an interesting research study and claim that it is something phenomenal with far-reaching implications. As a competent consumer of information, be aware that it is extremely rare for a single study to have earth-shattering, conclusive answers that apply to all adolescents. In fact, where large numbers of studies focus on a particular issue, it is not unusual to find conflicting results from one study to the next. Reliable answers about adolescent development usually emerge only after many researchers have conducted similar studies and drawn similar conclusions. In our example of divorce, if one study reports that a counseling program for adolescents from divorced families improved their achievement, we cannot conclude that the counseling program will work as effectively with all adolescents from divorced families until many more studies have been conducted.

Remember That Causal Conclusions Cannot Be Drawn from Correlational Studies

Drawing causal conclusions from correlational studies is one of the most common mistakes made by the media. In a nonexperimental study (one in which the participants are not randomly assigned to treatments or experiences), two factors might be related to each other. However, we cannot say that one factor causes the other. A headline might read: "Divorce causes adolescents to have low achievement." We read the story and find out that the information is based on the results of a research study. Because we obviously cannot, for ethical and practical reasons, randomly assign adolescents to families that will become divorced or remain intact, this headline is based on a correlational study and the causal statements are unproven. It could well be, for example, that both adolescents' poor school performance and parents' divorce are typically due to some other factor, such as family conflict or economic problems.

Consider the Source of the Information and Evaluate Its Credibility   Studies are not automatically accepted by the research community. As we saw earlier in this chapter, researchers usually submit their findings to a research journal where they are reviewed by experts, who decide whether or not to publish the research. The quality of research that is published in journals is far from uniform, but in most cases it has undergone far more scrutiny and careful consideration of its quality than research that has not gone through the journal process. And within the mass media, we can distinguish between respected newspapers, such as the *New York Times* and *Washington Post*, as well as creditable magazines such as *Time* and *Newsweek*, and much less respected tabloids, such as the *National Inquirer* and *Star*.

Review and reflect   Learning goal 3

3   **Discuss three research challenges in adolescent development**

REVIEW

- What are researchers' ethical responsibilities to the people they study?
- How can gender, cultural, and ethnic bias affect the outcome of a research study?
- How can you be a wise consumer of information about adolescence?

REFLECT

- Imagine that you are conducting a research study on adolescents' sexual attitudes and behaviors. What ethical safeguards should you use in conducting the study?

Reach Your Learning Goals

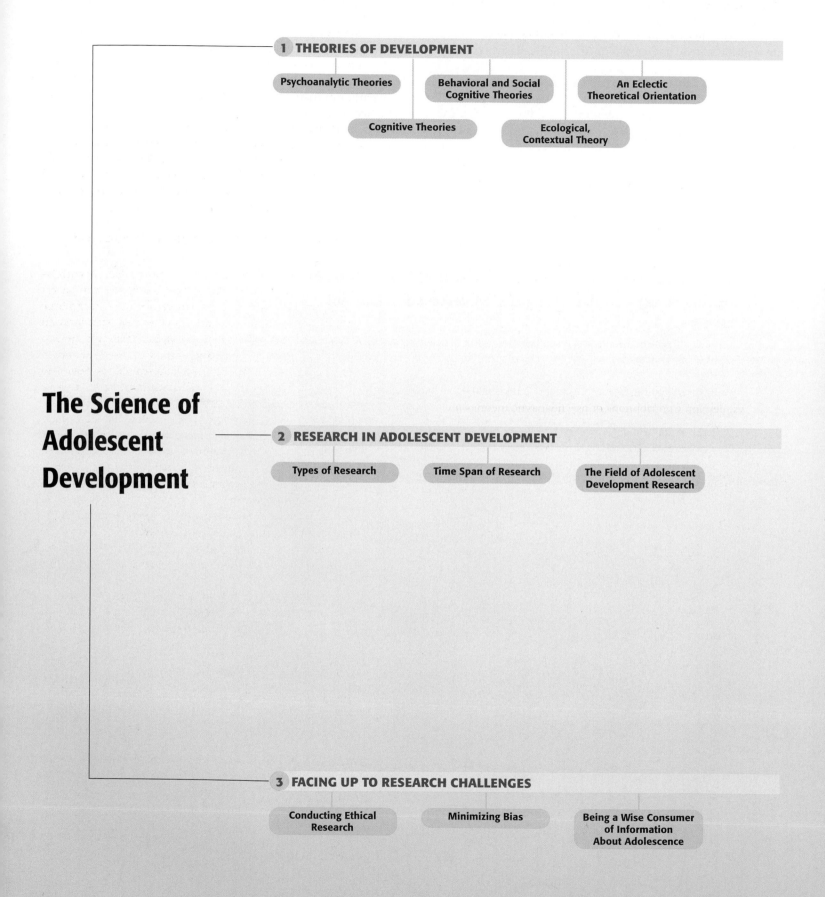

The Science of Adolescent Development

1 THEORIES OF DEVELOPMENT

- Psychoanalytic Theories
- Cognitive Theories
- Behavioral and Social Cognitive Theories
- Ecological, Contextual Theory
- An Eclectic Theoretical Orientation

2 RESEARCH IN ADOLESCENT DEVELOPMENT

- Types of Research
- Time Span of Research
- The Field of Adolescent Development Research

3 FACING UP TO RESEARCH CHALLENGES

- Conducting Ethical Research
- Minimizing Bias
- Being a Wise Consumer of Information About Adolescence

Summary

1 Describe the major theories of development

- The scientific method has four main steps: (1) conceptualize a problem, (2) collect data, (3) analyze data, and (4) draw conclusions. Theory is often involved in conceptualizing a problem. A theory is an interrelated, coherent set of ideas that helps to explain and to make predictions. Hypotheses are specific assumptions and predictions, often derived from theory, that can be tested to determine their accuracy.

- Psychoanalytic theory describes development as primarily unconscious and as heavily colored by emotion. Psychoanalytic theorists believe that behavior is merely a surface characteristic and that early experiences with parents shape development. Freud said that personality is made up of three structures—id, ego, and superego. The conflicting demands of these structures produce anxiety. Freud also believed that individuals go through five psychosexual stages—oral, anal, phallic, latency, and genital. A number of psychoanalytic revisions of Freud's theory have been made, including femininist-based revisions. Erikson's theory emphasizes these eight psychosocial stages of development: trust vs. mistrust, autonomy vs. shame and doubt, initiative vs. guilt, industry vs. inferiority, identity vs. identity confusion, intimacy vs. isolation, generativity vs. stagnation, and integrity vs. despair. Contributions of psychoanaytic theories include an emphasis on a developmental framework. One criticism is that they often lack scientific support.

- Cognitive theories emphasize conscious thoughts. Piaget proposed a cognitive developmental theory that involves the processes of organization and adaptation to understand the world. In Piaget's theory, children go through four cognitive stages: sensorimotor, preoperational, concrete operational, and formal operational. Vygotsky's sociocultural cognitive theory emphasizes how culture and social interaction guide cognitive development. Information-processing theory emphasizes that individuals manipulate information, monitor it, and strategize about it. Contributions of cognitive theories include an emphasis on the active construction of understanding. One criticism is that they give too little attention to individual variations.

- The behavioral and social cognitive theories include Skinner's behaviorism and Bandura's social cognitive theory. In Skinner's operant conditioning, the consequences of a behavior produce changes in the probability of the behavior's occurrence. In Bandura's social cognitve theory, observational learning is a key aspect of development. Bandura emphasizes reciprocal interactions among the person (cognition), behavior, and environment. Contributions of the behavioral and social cognitive theories include an emphasis on scientific research. One criticism is that they give inadequate attention to developmental changes.

- Ecological, contextual theory is Bronfenbrenner's environmental systems view of development. It consists of five environmental systems: microsystem, mesosystem, exosystem, macrosystem, and chronosystem. Contributions of the theory include a systematic examination of macro and micro dimensions of environmental systems. One criticism is that it gives inadequate attention to biological and cognitive factors.

- An eclectic theoretical orientation does not follow any one theoretical approach, but rather, selects from each theory whatever is considered the best in it. Research is not only guided by grand theories, such as Piaget's, but also by local or micro theories that focus on a specific aspect or time frame of development.

2 Explain how research on adolescent development is conducted

- Three main types of research are: (1) descriptive, (2) correlational, and (3) experimental. Six types of descriptive research are observation (in a laboratory or a naturalistic setting), survey (questionnaire) or interview, standardized test, experience sampling, physiological measures (which can assess hormones, body composition, and/or brain activity), and case study. In correlational research, the goal is to describe the strength of the relationship between two or more events or characteristics. Experimental research involves conducting an experiment, which can determine cause and effect. An independent variable is the manipulated, influential, experimental factor. A dependent variable is a factor that can change in an experiment in response to changes in the independent variable. Experiments can involve one or more experimental groups and control groups. In random assignment, researchers assign participants to experimental and control groups by chance.

- When researchers decide about the time span of their research, they can conduct cross-sectional or longitudinal studies.

- The field of adolescent development research is growing. The main outlets for this research are journals and papers presented at professional meetings. Research journals follow this format: abstract, introduction, method, results, and discussion.

3 Discuss three research challenges in adolescent development

- Researchers' ethical responsibilities include seeking participants' informed consent, ensuring their confidentiality, debriefing them about the purpose and potential personal consequences of participating, and avoiding unnecessary deception of participants.

- Researchers need to guard against gender, cultural, and ethnic bias in research.

- Being a wise consumer of information about adolescent development includes being cautious about accepting what is reported in the media; avoiding an interpretation of group research in terms of an individual's needs; not overgeneralizing about a small or clinical sample; not taking a single study as the defining word; not accepting causal interpretations of correlational studies; and considering the source of information and evaluating its credibility.

Key Terms

theory 47
hypotheses 47
psychoanalytic theory 48
Erikson's theory 51
Piaget's theory 53
Vygotsky's theory 54
information-processing
  theory 54

social cognitive theory 56
ecological, contextual
  theory 57
eclectic theoretical
  orientation 58
descriptive research 59
laboratory 60
naturalistic observation 60

standardized test 61
experience sampling method
  (ESM) 62
case study 62
correlational research 63
experimental research 64
independent variable 64
dependent variable 64

cross-sectional research 65
longitudinal research 65
ethnic gloss 70

Key People

Sigmund Freud 48
Peter Blos 49
Anna Freud 49
Karen Horney 50

Nancy Chodorow 50
Erik Erikson 52
Jean Piaget 53
Lev Vygotsky 54

Robert Siegler 55
B. F. Skinner 55
Albert Bandura 56
Walter Mischel 56

Urie Bronfenbrenner 57
Reed Larson and
  Maryse Richards 62

Resources for Improving the Lives of Adolescents

Identity: Youth and Crisis

(1968) by Erik H. Erikson
New York: W. W. Norton

Erik Erikson is one of the leading theorists in the field of life-span development. In *Identity: Youth and Crisis,* he outlines his eight stages of life-span development and provides numerous examples from his clinical practice to illustrate the stages. Special attention is given to the fifth stage in Erikson's theory, identity versus identity confusion.

Observational Strategies of Child Study

(1980) by D. M. Irwin and M. M. Bushnell
Fort Worth, TX: Harcourt Brace

Being a good observer can help you help children and adolescents reach their full potential. Observational skills can be learned. This practical book gives you a rich set of observational strategies that will make you a more sensitive observer of adolescent behavior.

Youth Policy
Youth Policy Institute

Cardinal Station
Washington, DC 20064
202–755–8078

A monthly publication issued by a cooperative venture of national organizations, foundations, and academic institutions interested in the future of adolescents. It provides information about federal and nonfederal programs for youth, and it includes a six-month calendar of events and conferences involving or concerned with youth.

E-Learning Tools

To help you master the material in this chapter, you will find a number of valuable study tools in the student CD-ROM that accompanies this book. In addition, visit the Online Learning Center for *Adolescence, 10th Edition,* where you will find helpful resources for chapter 2, "The Science of Adolescent Development."

Taking It to the Net

http://www.mhhe.com/santrocka10

1. Child neglect is a serious problem. It affects children and adolescents and has implications for how they will rear their own future children. How might you use Bronfenbrenner's theory to organize information about the factors underlying child neglect in a paper or class presentation?

2. Drinking and other drug use by college students is a serious concern on most college campuses. Suppose a representative of the Dean of Students office came into your classroom and distributed a survey of drinking and drug use, asking you to complete it anonymously. Are any of your rights as a human participant being violated?

3. A requirement for your methods course is to design and carry out an original research project. Among the many decisions you must make is what type of data you will collect. You decide to research adapting to college life. Your instructor asks if you will use an interview or a survey. Which will you use, what is the distinction between an interview and a survey, and what are the benefits and difficulties of each?

Connect to **http://www.mhhe.com/santrocka10** to research the answers and complete these exercises. In some cases, you'll also find further instructions on this site.

Self-Assessment

To examine the importance of observational learning, complete the self-assessment: Models and Mentors in My Life.

Health and Well-Being, Parenting, and Education

To practice your decision-making skills, complete the health and well-being, parenting, and education scenarios.

Biological and Cognitive Development

I think that what is happening to me is so wonderful and not only what can be seen on my body, but all that is taking place inside. I never discuss myself with anybody; that is why I have to talk to myself about them.
—ANNE FRANK
German Jewish Diarist, 20th Century

Adolescence, the transition from childhood to adulthood, involves biological, cognitive, and socio-emotional development. These strands of development are interwoven in the adolescent's life. This first section focuses on adolescents' biological and cognitive development and consists of two chapters: chapter 3, "Puberty, Health, and Biological Foundations," and chapter 4, "Cognitive Development."

In youth, we clothe ourselves with rainbows and go brave as the zodiac.
—RALPH WALDO EMERSON
American Poet and Essayist, 19th Century

Puberty, Health, and Biological Foundations

Chapter Outline

Learning Goals

PUBERTY

Determinants of Puberty

Growth Spurt

Sexual Maturation

Secular Trends in Puberty

Psychological Dimensions

Pubertal Timing and Health Care

1 Discuss the determinants, characteristics, and timing of puberty

THE BRAIN

Neurons

Brain Structure

Experience and Plasticity

2 Describe the developmental changes in the brain during adolescence

ADOLESCENT HEALTH

Adolescence: A Critical Juncture in Health

Nutrition

Exercise and Sports

Sleep

Health Services

Leading Causes of Death

3 Characterize the health of adolescents

EVOLUTION, HEREDITY, AND ENVIRONMENT

The Evolutionary Perspective

The Genetic Process

Heredity-Environment Interaction

4 Explain the contributions of evolution, heredity, and environment to adolescent development

Images of Adolescent Development

Puberty's Mysteries and Curiosities

I am pretty confused. I wonder whether I am weird or normal. My body is starting to change, but I sure don't look like a lot of my friends. I still look like a kid for the most part. My best friend is only 13, but he looks like he is 16 or 17. I get nervous in the locker room during PE class because when I go to take a shower, I'm afraid somebody is going to make fun of me since I'm not as physically developed as some of the others.

—Robert, age 12

I don't like my breasts. They are too small, and they look funny. I'm afraid guys won't like me if they don't get bigger.

—Angie, age 13

I can't stand the way I look. I have zits all over my face. My hair is dull and stringy. It never stays in place. My nose is too big. My lips are too small. My legs are too short. I have four warts on my left hand, and people get grossed out by them. So do I. My body is a disaster!

—Ann, age 14

I'm short and I can't stand it. My father is 6 feet tall, and here I am only five foot four. I'm 14 already. I look like a kid, and I get teased a lot, especially by other guys. I'm always the last one picked for sides in basketball because I'm so short. Girls don't seem to be interested in me either because most of them are taller than I am.

—Jim, age 14

The comments of these four adolescents in the midst of pubertal change underscore the dramatic upheaval in their bodies following the calm, consistent growth of middle and late childhood. Young adolescents develop an acute concern about their bodies.

Puberty's changes are perplexing to adolescents. Although these changes bring forth doubts, fears, and anxieties, most adolescents eventually overcome them. We will explore many aspects of pubertal change in this chapter, from growth spurts and sexual maturation to the psychological aspects of puberty. We will also examine other topics related to adolescent physical development, including the development of the brain, adolescent health, and the roles of evolution, heredity, and environment in adolescent development.

1 PUBERTY

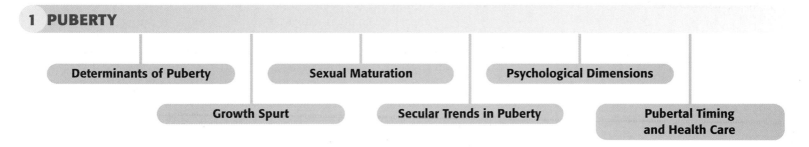

Puberty can be distinguished from adolescence. For virtually everyone, puberty ends long before adolescence is exited. Puberty is often thought of as the most important marker for the beginning of adolescence. **Puberty** is a period of rapid physical maturation involving hormonal and bodily changes that take place primarily in early adolescence.

Determinants of Puberty

Puberty is triggered by a number of complex factors, among the most important of which are heredity; hormones; the endocrine system; and weight, body fat, and leptin.

Heredity   Puberty is not an environmental accident. Programmed into the genes of every human being is the timing for the emergence of puberty (Adair, 2001). Puberty does not take place at 2 or 3 years of age and it does not occur in the twenties. In the future, molecular genetic studies may identify specific genes that are linked to the onset and progression of puberty. Nonetheless, as we will see later in our discussion of puberty, which takes place between about 9 and 16 years of age, environmental factors can also influence its onset and duration.

Hormones   Behind the first whisker in boys and the widening of hips in girls is a flood of **hormones,** powerful chemical substances secreted by the endocrine glands and carried throughout the body by the bloodstream. Two classes of hormones

puberty A period of rapid physical maturation involving hormonal and bodily changes that take place primarily in early adolescence.

hormones Powerful chemicals secreted by the endocrine glands and carried through the body by the bloodstream.

From *Penguin Dreams and Stranger Things* by Berkeley Breathed. Copyright © 1985 by The Washington Post Company/Berkeley Breathed. Reprinted by permission of Little, Brown and Company, (Inc.) and International Creative Management, Inc.

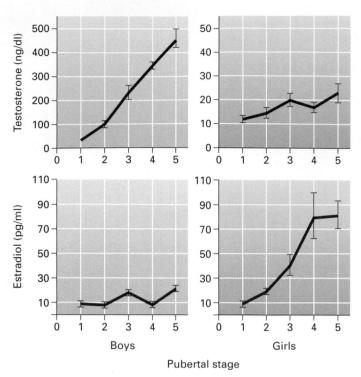

FIGURE 3.1 Hormone Levels by Sex and Pubertal Stage for Testosterone and Estradiol

The five stages range from the early beginning of puberty (stage 1) to the most advanced stage of puberty (stage 5). Notice the significant increase in testosterone in boys and the significant increase in estradiol in girls.

www.mhhe.com/santrocka10

Biological Changes

androgens The main class of male sex hormones.

estrogens The main class of female sex hormones.

have significantly different concentrations in males and females: **androgens,** the main class of male sex hormones, and **estrogens,** the main class of female hormones. Note that although these hormones function more strongly in one sex or the other, they are produced by both males and females.

Testosterone is an androgen that plays an important role in male pubertal development. Throughout puberty, rising testosterone levels are associated with a number of physical changes in boys, including the development of external genitals, an increase in height, and voice changes (Hiort, 2002). *Estradiol* is an estrogen that plays an important role in female pubertal development. As estradiol levels rise, breast development, uterine development, and skeletal changes occur. Both boys and girls experience an increase in both hormones during puberty. In one study, testosterone levels increased 18-fold in boys but only 2-fold in girls during puberty; estradiol levels increased 8-fold in girls but only 2-fold in boys during puberty (Nottelman & others, 1987) (see figure 3.1).

The Endocrine System The endocrine system's role in puberty involves the interaction of the hypothalamus, the pituitary gland, and the gonads (sex glands) (see figure 3.2). The *hypothalamus* is a structure in the higher portion of the brain that monitors eating, drinking, and sex. The *pituitary gland* is the endocrine gland that controls growth and regulates other glands. The *gonads* are the sex glands—the testes in males, the ovaries in females.

How does the endocrine system work? The pituitary gland sends a signal via gonadotropins (hormones that stimulate sex glands) to the testes or ovaries to manufacture the hormone. Then, through interaction with the hypothalamus, the pituitary gland detects when the optimal level of hormones has been reached and maintains it with additional gonadotropin secretions.

Levels of sex hormones are regulated by two hormones secreted by the pituitary gland: *FSH* (follicle-stimulating hormone) and *LH* (luteinizing hormone). FSH stimulates follicle development in females and sperm production in males. LH regulates estrogen secretion and ovum development in females and testosterone production in males (Hyde & DeLamater, 2003; Welt & others, 2003). In addition, the hypothalamus secretes a substance called *GnRh* (gonadotropin-releasing hormone) (Tauber & others, 2003).

These hormones are regulated by a *negative feedback system*. If the level of sex hormones rises too high, the hypothalamus and pituitary gland reduce their stimulation of the gonads, decreasing the production of sex hormones. If the level of sex hormones falls too low, the hypothalamus and pituitary gland increase their production of the sex hormones.

Figure 3.3 shows how the feedback system works. In males, the pituitary gland's production of LH stimulates the testes to produce testosterone. When testosterone levels rise too high, the hypothalamus decreases its production of GnRH, which reduces the pituitary's production of LH. When the level of testosterone falls as a result, the hypothalamus produces more GnRH and the cycle starts again. The negative feedback system operates in a similar way in females, except that LH and GnRH regulate the ovaries and the production of estrogen.

This negative feedback system in the endocrine system can be compared to a thermostat and furnace. If a room becomes cold, the thermostat signals the furnace to turn on. The action of the furnace warms the air in the room, which eventually triggers the thermostat to turn off the furnace. The room temperature gradually begins to fall again until the thermostat once again signals the furnace to turn on, repeating the

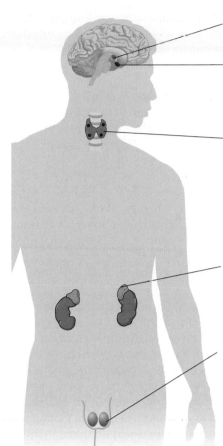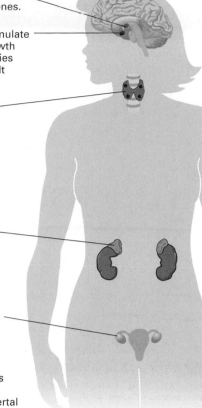

Hypothalamus: A structure in the brain that interacts with the pituitary gland to monitor the bodily regulation of hormones.

Pituitary: This master gland produces hormones that stimulate other glands. It also influences growth by producing growth hormones; it sends gonadotropins to the testes and ovaries and a thyroid-stimulating hormone to the thyroid gland. It sends a hormone to the adrenal gland as well.

Thyroid gland: It interacts with the pituitary gland to influence growth.

Adrenal gland: It interacts with the pituitary gland and likely plays a role in pubertal development, but less is known about its function than about sex glands. Recent research, however, suggests it may be involved in adolescent behavior, particularly for boys.

The gonads, or sex glands: These consist of the testes in males and the ovaries in females. The sex glands are strongly involved in the appearance of secondary sex characteristics, such as facial hair in males and breast development in females. The general class of hormones called estrogens is dominant in females, while androgens are dominant in males. More specifically, testosterone in males and estradiol in females are key hormones in pubertal development.

FIGURE 3.2 The Major Endocrine Glands Involved in Pubertal Change

cycle. This type of system is called a *negative* feedback loop because a *rise* in temperature turns *off* the furnace, while a *decrease* in temperature turns *on* the furnace.

The level of sex hormones is low in childhood but increases in puberty. It is as if the thermostat is set at 50°F in childhood and now becomes set at 80°F in puberty. At the higher setting, the gonads have to produce more sex hormones, and that is what happens during puberty.

Growth Hormones We have seen that the pituitary gland releases gonadotropins that stimulate the testes and ovaries. In addition, through interaction with the hypothalamus, the pituitary gland also secretes hormones that lead to growth and skeletal maturation either directly or through interaction with the *thyroid gland*, located in the neck region (see figure 3.2).

At the beginning of puberty, growth hormone is secreted at night. Later in puberty, it also is secreted during the day, although daytime levels are usually very low (Susman, Dorn, & Schiefelbein, 2003). Cortisol, a hormone that is secreted by the adrenal cortex, also influences growth as do testosterone and estrogen (Guercio & others, 2003).

Adrenarche and Gonadarche Two phases of puberty are linked with hormonal changes: adrenarche and gonadarche (Susman, Dorn, & Schiefelbein, 2003; Susman & Rogol, 2004). *Adrenarche* involves hormonal changes in the adrenal glands, located just above the kidneys. These changes occur surprisingly early, from about 6 to 9 years

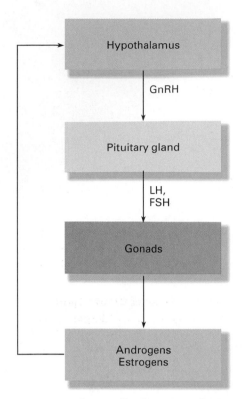

FIGURE 3.3 The Feedback System of Sex Hormones

of age, before what is generally considered the beginning of puberty. During adrenarche and continuing through puberty, the adrenal glands secrete adrenal androgens.

Gonadarche, which follows adrenarche by about two years, is the period most people think of as puberty (Archibald, Graber, & Brooks-Gunn, 2003). Gonadarche involves sexual maturation and the development of reproductive maturity. In the United States, this period begins at approximately 9 to 10 years of age in non-Latino White girls, and 8 to 9 years in African American girls (Grumach & Styne, 1992). In boys, gonadarche begins at about 10 to 11 years of age. The culmination of gonadarche in girls is **menarche,** the first menstrual period, and in boys it is **spermarche,** a boy's first ejaculation of semen.

Weight, Body Fat, and Leptin Some researchers believe that a child must reach a critical body mass before puberty, especially *menarche,* emerges (Weise, Eisenhofer, & Merke, 2002). One recent study found that higher weight was strongly associated with having reached menarche (Anderson, Dallal, & Must, 2003). Some have even proposed that a body weight of 106 ±3 pounds triggers menarche and the end of the pubertal growth spurt (Friesch, 1984). However, this specific weight target is not well documented (Susman, 2001).

Other scientists have hypothesized that the onset of menarche is influenced by the percentage of body fat in relation to total body weight. For menarche to occur, they say that a minimum of 17 percent of a girl's body weight must be comprised of body fat. As with the weight target, this percentage has not been consistently verified. However, both anorexic adolescents whose weight drops dramatically and females who participate in certain sports (such as gymnastics and swimming) may not menstruate (Fujii & Demura, 2003; Phillips, 2003). In boys, undernutrition may delay puberty (Susman, Dorn, and Schiefelbein, 2003).

The hormone *leptin* may signal the beginning and progression of puberty (Apter & Hermanson, 2002; Mantzoros, 2000; Rogol, Roemmich & Clark, 2002; Susman & Rogol, 2004). Leptin concentrations, which are higher in girls than in boys, are related to the amounts of fat in girls and androgen in boys (Roemmich & others, 1999). Thus, a rise in leptin may indicate adequate fat stores for reproduction and the maintenance

menarche A girl's first menstrual period.

spermarche A boy's first ejaculation of semen.

What are some of the differences in the ways girls and boys experience pubertal growth?

of pregnancy (Kiess & others, 1999). Changes in leptin levels have not yet been studied in relation to adolescent behavior, however.

We have seen that the determinants of puberty include heredity and hormones. Next, we turn our attention to the growth spurt that characterizes puberty.

Growth Spurt

Growth slows throughout childhood, so puberty brings forth the most rapid increases in growth since infancy. Figure 3.4 shows that the growth spurt associated with puberty occurs approximately two years earlier for girls than for boys. For girls, the mean beginning of the growth spurt is 9 years of age; for boys, it is 11 years of age. The peak of pubertal change occurs at 11.5 years for girls and 13.5 years for boys. During their growth spurt, girls increase in height about 3½ inches per year; boys, about 4 inches.

Boys and girls who are shorter or taller than their peers before adolescence are likely to remain so during adolescence. At the beginning of adolescence, girls tend to be as tall as or taller than boys of their age, but by the end of the middle school years most boys have caught up with them, or in many cases even surpassed them in height. Though height in elementary school is a good predictor of height later in adolescence, as much as 30 percent of an individual's height in late adolescence is unexplained by the child's height in elementary school.

The rate at which adolescents gain weight follows approximately the same developmental timetable as the rate at which they gain height. Marked weight gains coincide with the onset of puberty (Susman & Rogol, 2004). Fifty percent of adult body weight is gained during adolescence (Rogol, Roemmich, & Clark, 1998). At the peak of this weight gain, girls gain an average of 18 pounds in one year at roughly 12 years of age (approximately six months after their peak height increase). Boys' peak weight gain per year (20 pounds) occurs at about the same time as their peak increase in height, about 13 to 14 years of age. During early adolescence, girls tend to outweigh boys, but just as with height, by about 14 years of age, boys begin to surpass girls in weight.

In addition to increases in height and weight, puberty brings changes in hip and shoulder width. Girls experience a spurt in hip width, while boys undergo an increase in shoulder width. In girls, increased hip width is linked with an increase in estrogen. In boys, increased shoulder width is associated with an increase in testosterone (Susman & Rogol, 2004).

Finally, the later growth spurt of boys produces a greater leg length in boys than in girls. In many cases, boys' facial structure becomes more angular during puberty, while girls' facial structure becomes rounder and softer.

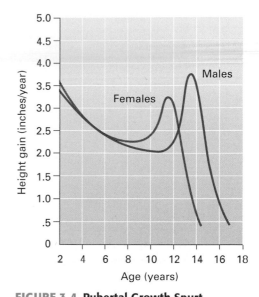

FIGURE 3.4 Pubertal Growth Spurt

On the average, the peak of the growth spurt that characterizes pubertal change occurs two years earlier for girls (11½) than for boys (13½).

© ZITS Partnership. Reprinted with special permission of King Features Syndicate.

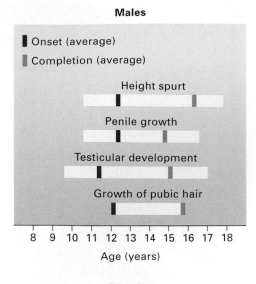

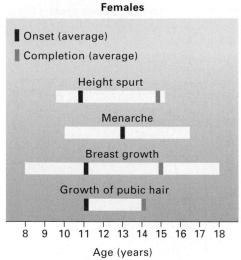

FIGURE 3.5 Normal Range and Average Development of Sexual Characteristics in Males and Females

Sexual Maturation

Think back to the onset of your puberty. Of the striking changes that were taking place in your body, what was the first that occurred? Researchers have found that male pubertal characteristics develop in this order: increased penis and testicle size; appearance of straight pubic hair; minor voice change; first ejaculation (spermarche—this usually occurs through masturbation or a wet dream); appearance of kinky pubic hair; onset of maximum growth; growth of hair in armpits; more detectable voice changes; and growth of facial hair. Three of the most noticeable signs of sexual maturation in boys are penis elongation, testes development, and growth of facial hair. The normal range and average age of development for these sexual characteristics, along with height spurt, are shown in figure 3.5. Figure 3.6 illustrates the typical course of male sexual development during puberty.

What is the order of appearance of physical changes in females? First, either the breasts enlarge or pubic hair appears. Later, hair appears in the armpits. As these changes occur, the female grows in height, and her hips become wider than her shoulders. Her first menstruation (menarche) occurs rather late in the pubertal cycle. Initially, her menstrual cycles may be highly irregular and for the first several years, she might not ovulate every cycle. In some instances, a female does not become fertile until two years after her period begins. No voice changes occur that are comparable to those in pubertal males. By the end of puberty, the female's breasts have become more fully rounded. Two of the most noticeable aspects of female pubertal change are pubic hair and breast development. Figure 3.5 shows the normal range and average development for two of the most noticeable female sexual characteristics—pubic hair and breast development. The figure also provides information about menarche and height gain. Figure 3.6 illustrates the typical course of female sexual development during puberty.

Note that there may be wide individual variations in the onset and progression of puberty. For boys, the pubertal sequence may begin as early as 10 years of age or as late as 13½. It may end as early as 13 years or as late as 17. The normal range is wide enough that given two boys of the same chronological age, one might complete the pubertal sequence before the other one has begun it. For girls, the normal age range for menarche is even wider, between 9 and 15 years of age.

Secular Trends in Puberty

Imagine a toddler displaying all the features of puberty—a 3-year-old girl with fully developed breasts, or a boy just slightly older, with a deep male voice. That is what we would see by the year 2250 if the age at which puberty arrives continued to drop at the rate at which it occurred for much of the twentieth century. However, we are unlikely to ever see pubescent toddlers because of genetic limits on how early puberty can occur.

The term *secular trends* refers to patterns seen over time, especially across generations. For example, in Norway, menarche now occurs at just over 13 years of age, compared with 17 years of age in the 1840s (de Munich Keizer & Mul, 2001; Petersen, 1979). In the United States, where children mature physically up to a year earlier than in European countries, menarche now occurs at about 12½ years of age compared with over 14 years of age a century ago (see figure 3.7).

The earlier onset of puberty in the twentieth century was likely due to improved health and nutrition. An increase in obesity may also be implicated. For example, in one recent study, the more sexually developed girls were, the greater their body mass was (Kaplowitz & others, 2001). We will have more to say about obesity in adolescence later in this chapter and in chapter 14, "Adolescent Problems."

So far we have been concerned mainly with the physical dimensions of puberty. As we see next, the psychological dimensions of puberty are also important.

MALE SEXUAL DEVELOPMENT

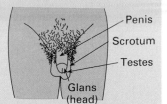

1.
No pubic hair. The testes, scrotum, and penis are about the same size and shape as those of a child.

2.
A little soft, long, lightly colored hair, mostly at the base of the penis. This hair may be straight or a little curly. The testes and scrotum have enlarged, and the skin of the scrotum has changed. The scrotum, the sack holding the testes, has lowered a bit. The penis has grown only a little.

3.
The hair is darker coarser, and more curled. It has spread to thinly cover a somewhat larger area. The penis has grown mainly in length. The testes and scrotum have grown and dropped lower than in stage 2.

4.
The hair is now as dark, curly, and coarse as that of an adult male. However, the area that the hair covers is not as large as that of an adult male; it has not spread to the thighs. The penis has grown even larger and wider. The glans (the head of the penis) is bigger. The scrotum is darker and bigger because the testes have gotten bigger.

5.
The hair has spread to the thighs and is now like that of an adult male. The penis, scrotum, and testes are the size and shape of those of an adult male.

FEMALE SEXUAL DEVELOPMENT

1.
The nipple is raised just a little. The rest of the breast is still flat.

2.
The breast bud stage. The nipple is raised more than in stage 1. The breast is a small mound, and the areola is larger than in stage 1.

3.
The areola and the breast are both larger than in stage 2. The areola does not stick out from the breast.

4.
The areola and the nipple make up a mound that sticks up above the shape of the breast. (Note: This may not happen at all for some girls; some develop from stage 3 to stage 5, with no stage 4.)

5.
The mature adult stage. The breasts are fully developed. Only the nipple sticks out. The areola has moved back to the general shape of the breast.

FIGURE 3.6 The Five Pubertal Stages of Male and Female Sexual Development

Psychological Dimensions

A host of psychological changes accompanies an adolescent's pubertal development (Sarigiani & Petersen, 2000; Susman & Rogol, 2004). Try to remember when you were entering puberty. Not only did you think of yourself differently, but your parents and peers also began treating you differently. Maybe you were proud of your changing

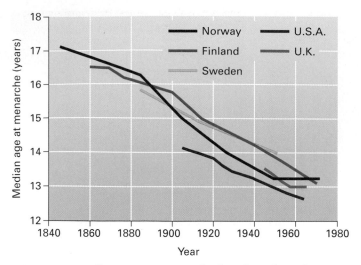

FIGURE 3.7 Median Ages at Menarche in Selected Northern European Countries and the United States from 1845 to 1969
Notice the steep decline in the age at which girls experienced menarche in five different countries. Recently the age at which girls experience menarche has been leveling off.

Through the Eyes of Adolescents

Attractive Blond Females and Tall Muscular Males

When columnist Bob Greene (1988) called Connections in Chicago, a chatline for teenagers, to find out what young adolescents were saying to each other, the first things the boys and girls asked for—after first names—were physical descriptions. The idealism of the callers was apparent. Most of the girls described themselves as having long blond hair, being 5 feet 5 inches tall, and weighing 110 pounds. Most of the boys said that they had brown hair, lifted weights, were 6 feet tall, and weighed 170 pounds.

body, even though it perplexed you. Perhaps your parents felt they could no longer sit in bed and watch television with you or even kiss you goodnight.

Far less research has been conducted on the psychosocial aspects of male pubertal transitions than on female pubertal transitions, possibly because of the difficulty in detecting when the male transitions occur. Wet dreams are one marker, yet there has been little research on the topic (Susman & others, 1995).

Body Image One psychological aspect of puberty is certain for both boys and girls: Adolescents are preoccupied with their bodies (McCabe & Ricciardelli, 2003). In puberty, adolescents develop individual images of their bodies. Perhaps you looked in the mirror on a daily—and sometimes even hourly—basis to see if you could detect anything different in your changing body. Preoccupation with one's body image is strong throughout adolescence, but it is especially acute during puberty.

Gender differences characterize adolescents' perceptions of their bodies. In general, girls are less happy with their bodies and have more negative body images than boys throughout puberty (Brooks-Gunn & Paikoff, 1997; Henderson & Zivian, 1995; Phillips, 2003). As pubertal change proceeds, girls often become more dissatisfied with their bodies, probably because their body fat increases. In contrast, boys become more satisfied as they move through puberty, probably because their muscle mass increases (Phillips, 2003; Seiffge-Krenke, 1998).

Currently, a major concern is adolescent girls' motivation to be very thin. In fact, many adolescent girls believe they cannot be too thin. This has been fueled by the media's equation of extremely thin with beautiful. We will have much more to say about this topic in chapter 14, "Adolescent Problems," where we will discuss eating disorders.

Hormones and Behavior Are concentrations of hormones linked to adolescent behavior? Hormonal factors are thought to account for at least part of the increase in negative and variable emotions that characterize adolescents (Archibald, Graber, & Brooks-Gunn, 2003; Dorn, Williamson, & Ryan, 2002). Researchers have found that in boys higher levels of androgens are associated with violence and acting-out problems (van Goozen & others, 1998; Susman & others, 1987). And in an experimental study, delayed pubertal boys and girls were administered doses of testosterone or estrogen (Finkelstein & others, 1997; Liben & others, 2002; Susman & others, 1998). Significant increases in aggression against peers and adults were observed in boys but only at the middle dose of testosterone. In contrast, in girls, significant increases in aggression toward peers and adults occurred at the low and middle doses of estrogen but not the high dose. There is also some indication that increased estrogen levels are linked to depression in adolescent girls (Angold & others, 1999). Further, high levels of adrenal androgens are associated with negative affect in girls (Susman & Rogol, 2004). One recent study found that early-maturing girls with high levels of adrenal androgens had higher emotional arousal and depressive affect than other girls (Graber, Brooks-Gunn, & Warren, in press).

In any event, hormonal factors alone are not responsible for adolescent behavior (Ge & Brody, 2002; Susman & Rogol, 2004; Susman, Schiefelbein, & Heaton, 2002). For example, one study found that social factors accounted for two to four times as

Adolescents show a strong preoccupation with their changing bodies and develop images of what their bodies are like. *Why might adolescent males have more positive body images than adolescent females?*

much variance as hormonal factors in young adolescent girls' depression and anger (Brooks-Gunn & Warren, 1989). Another study found little direct connection between adolescent male and females' testosterone levels and risk behavior or depression (Booth & others, 2003). In contrast, a link with risk behavior depended on the quality of parent-adolescent relations. When relationship quality decreased, testosterone-linked risk-taking behavior and symptoms of depression increased. Thus, the hormones do not function independently with hormonal activity being influenced by many environmental factors, including parent adolescent relationships. Stress, eating patterns, sexual activity, and depression can also activate or suppress various aspects of the hormone system (Archibald, Graber, & Brooks-Gunn, 2003).

Menarche and the Menstrual Cycle In most historical accounts of adolescence, the onset of puberty and menarche have been treated as a "main event" (Erikson, 1968; Freud, 1917/1958; Hall, 1904). Basically, the idea is that pubertal changes and events such as menarche produce a different body that requires considerable change in one's self-conception, possibly resulting in an identity crisis. Only recently has empirical research been directed at understanding the female adolescent's adaptation to menarche and the menstrual cycle (Brooks-Gunn, Graber, & Paikoff, 1994).

One study of 639 girls revealed a wide range of reactions to menarche (Brooks-Gunn & Ruble, 1982). Most were quite mild: Girls described their first period as a little upsetting, a little surprising, or a little exciting. In this study, 120 fifth- and sixth-grade girls were telephoned to obtain personal, detailed information about their experience with menarche. The most frequent theme of the responses was positive—namely, that menarche was an index of their maturity. Other positive reports indicated that the girls could now have children, were experiencing something that made them more like adult women, and now were more like their friends. The most frequently reported negatives were the hassle of having to carry around supplies and messiness. A minority of the girls reported physical discomfort, behavioral limitations, and emotional changes.

The researchers asked questions about the extent to which the girls communicated with others about their menarche; the extent to which they were prepared for it; and its relation to early or late maturation. Virtually all the girls told their mothers immediately, but most did not tell anyone else; only one in five informed a friend. After two or three periods, most girls had talked with their girlfriends about menstruation, however. Girls who were not prepared for menarche reported more negative feelings than those who were more prepared for it. In addition, girls who matured early had more negative reactions than average- or late-maturing girls. In sum, menarche may be disruptive at first, especially for unprepared and early-maturing girls, but it typically does not provoke the tumultuous, conflicting reactions described by some early theoreticians.

For many girls, menarche occurs on time, but for others it can come early or late. Next, we will examine the effects of early and late maturation on both boys and girls.

Early and Late Maturation Some of you entered puberty early, others late; yet others entered on time. When adolescents mature earlier or later than their peers, do they perceive themselves differently? In the Berkeley Longitudinal Study conducted in the middle of the twentieth century, early-maturing boys perceived themselves more positively and had more successful peer relations than their late-maturing counterparts (Jones, 1965). For early-maturing girls, the findings were similar but not as strong as for boys. When the late-maturing boys were studied in their thirties, however, they had developed a stronger sense of identity than the early-maturing boys (Peskin, 1967). Late-maturing boys may have had more time to explore a wide variety of options. They may have focused on how career development and achievement would serve them better in life than the emphasis on physical status by their early-maturing counterparts.

More recent research confirms that at least during adolescence, though, it is advantageous to be an early-maturing rather than a late-maturing boy (Petersen, 1987). Roberta Simmons and Dale Blyth (1987) studied more than 450 adolescents for five years, beginning in the sixth grade and continuing through the tenth grade, in Milwaukee, Wisconsin. They interviewed students and obtained their achievement test scores and grade point averages. The presence or absence of menstruation and the relative onset of menses were used to classify girls as early, middle, or late maturers. The peak of growth in height was used to classify boys in the same categories.

In the Milwaukee study, more mixed and complex findings emerged for girls (Simmons & Blyth, 1987). Early-maturing girls had more problems in school, were more independent, and were more popular with boys than late-maturing girls were. The time at which maturation was assessed also was a factor. In the sixth grade, early-maturing girls were more satisfied with their body image than late-maturing girls were, but by the tenth grade, late-maturing girls were more satisfied (see figure 3.8). Why? Because by late adolescence, early-maturing girls are shorter and stockier, while late-maturing girls are taller and thinner. The late-maturing girls in late adolescence have body images that more closely approximate the current American ideal of feminine beauty—tall and thin.

In the last decade an increasing number of studies have found that early maturation increases girls' vulnerability to a number of problems (Ge, Conger, & Elder, 2001; Sarigiani & Petersen, 2000; Stattin & Magnusson, 1990; Wiesner & Ittel, 2002). Early-maturing girls are more likely than others to smoke, drink, become depressed, develop an eating disorder, seek independence from their parents earlier, and choose older friends; and their physical development likely leads to earlier dating and earlier sexual experiences. In one study, early-maturing girls were found to have lower educational and occupational attainment than others as adults (Stattin & Magnusson, 1990). Apparently their social and cognitive immaturity, combined with their early physical development, can lure early-maturing girls into problem behaviors that can have long-term effects on their development (Ge & others, 2002; Petersen, 1993).

Are Puberty's Effects Exaggerated? Some researchers have begun to question whether puberty's effects are as strong as was once believed (Montemayor, Adams, &

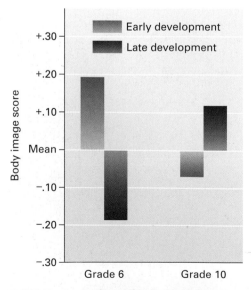

FIGURE 3.8 Early- and Late-Maturing Adolescent Girls' Perceptions of Body Image in Early and Late Adolescence

Gulotta). Have the effects of puberty been exaggerated? Puberty affects some adolescents more strongly than others, and some behaviors more strongly than others. Body image, interest in dating, and sexual behavior are quite clearly affected by pubertal change. In one study, early-maturing boys and girls reported more sexual activity and delinquency than late maturers (Flannery, Rowe, & Gulley, 1993). Yet, if we look at overall development and adjustment over the human life span, puberty and its variations have less dramatic effects than is commonly thought for most individuals. For some young adolescents, the path through puberty is stormy, but for most it is not. Each period of the human life span has its stresses and puberty is no different. While it poses new challenges, the vast majority of adolescents weather the stresses effectively. Besides the biological influences on adolescent development, cognitive and social or environmental influences also shape who we become (Sarigiani & Petersen, 2000; Susman & Rogol, 2004). Singling out biological changes as the dominant influence during adolescence may not be wise.

Although extremely early and late maturation may be risk factors in development, we have seen that the overall effects of early or late maturation often are not great. Not all early maturers will date, smoke, and drink, and not all late maturers will have difficulty in peer relations. In some instances, the effects of an adolescent's grade in school are stronger than maturational timing (Petersen & Crockett, 1985). Because the adolescent's social world is organized by grade rather than physical development, this finding is not surprising. However, that does not mean that age of maturation has no influence on development. Rather, we need to evaluate puberty's effects within the larger framework of interacting biological, cognitive, and socioemotional contexts (Brooks-Gunn, 1992; Sarigiani & Petersen, 2000).

Pubertal Timing and Health Care

What can be done to identify early and late maturers who are at risk for health problems? Adolescents whose development is extremely early or late, such as a boy who has not had a growth spurt by age 16 or a girl who has not menstruated by age 15, are likely to come to the attention of a physician. Girls and boys who are early or late maturers, but are still well within the normal range, are less likely to be seen by a physician. Nonetheless, these boys and girls may have doubts and fears about being normal that they will not raise unless a physician, counselor, or other health-care provider does. A brief discussion of the usual sequence and timing of events, and the large individual variations in them, may be all that is required to reassure many adolescents who are maturing very early or late.

Health-care providers may want to discuss an adolescent's early or late development with parents as well. Information about peer pressures can be helpful, especially the peer pressures to date on early-maturing girls and engage in

Careers in Adolescent Development

Anne Petersen
Researcher and Administrator

Anne Petersen has had a distinguished career as a researcher and administrator with a main focus on adolescent development. Anne obtained three degrees (B.A., M.A., and Ph.D.) from the University of Chicago in math and statistics. Her first job after she obtained her Ph.D. was as a research associate/professor involving statistical consultation, and it was on this job that she was introduced to the field of adolescent development, which became the focus of her subsequent work.

Anne moved from the University of Chicago to Pennsylvania State University, where she became a leading researcher in adolescent development. Her research included a focus on puberty and gender. Anne also has held numerous administrative positions. In the mid-1990s, Anne became Deputy Director of the National Science Foundation and since 1996 has been Senior Vice-President for programs at the W. K. Kellogg Foundation.

Anne says that what inspired her to enter the field of adolescent development and take her current position at the Kellogg Foundation was her desire to make a difference for people, especially youth. In her position at Kellogg, Anne is responsible for all programming and services provided by the foundation for adolescents. Her goal is to make a difference for youth in this country and around the world. She believes that too often adolescents have been neglected.

Anne Petersen, interacting with adolescents.

adultlike behavior. For girls and boys who are in the midst of puberty, the transition to middle school, junior high school, or high school may be more stressful (Brooks-Gunn, 1988).

If pubertal development is extremely late, a physician may recommend hormonal treatment. This approach may or may not be helpful (Lee, 2003; Yanovski & others, 2003). In one study of extended pubertal delay in boys, hormonal treatment helped to increase height, dating interest, and peer relations in several boys but brought little or no improvement in other boys (Lewis, Money, & Bobrow, 1977).

In sum, most early- and late-maturing individuals manage to weather puberty's challenges and stresses. For those who do not, discussions with sensitive and knowledgeable health-care providers and parents can improve the adolescent's coping abilities (Phillips, 2003).

Review and reflect   Learning goal 1

1   Discuss the determinants, characteristics, and timing of puberty

REVIEW

- What are puberty's main determinants?
- What characterizes the growth spurt in puberty?
- How does sexual maturation develop in puberty?
- What are some secular trends in puberty?
- How are psychological dimensions linked to pubertal change?
- What are some aspects of pubertal timing and health care?

REFLECT

- Did you experience puberty early, late, or on time? How do you think the timing of puberty affected your development?

2 THE BRAIN

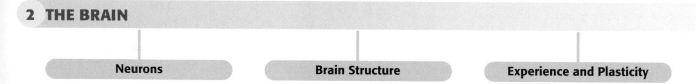

| Neurons | Brain Structure | Experience and Plasticity |

Until recently, little research has been conducted on developmental changes in the brain during adolescence. While research in this area is still in its infancy, an increasing number of studies are under way (Walker, 2002). Scientists now believe that the adolescent's brain is different from the child's brain, and that in adolescence the brain is still growing (Crews, 2001; Keating, 2004).

Neurons

Neurons, or nerve cells, are the nervous system's basic units. A neuron has three basic parts: the cell body, dendrites, and axon (see figure 3.9). The *dendrite* is the receiving part of the neuron, while the *axon* carries information away from the cell body to other cells. A *myelin sheath,* or a layer of fat cells, encases most axons. The sheath helps to insulate the axon and speeds up the transmission of nerve impulses.

Interestingly, researchers have found that cell bodies and dendrites do not change much during adolescence, but that axons continue to develop (Pfefferbaum & others, 1994; Rajapakse & others, 1996). The growth of axons is likely due to increased myelination (Giedd, 1998). Researchers have found that dendritic growth can continue even in older adults, however, so further research may show more growth in dendrites during adolescence than these early studies suggest (Coleman, 1986).

neurons Nerve cells, which are the nervous system's basic units.

In addition to dendritic spreading and the encasement of axons through myelination, another important aspect of the brain's development is the dramatic increase in connections between neurons, a process that is called *synaptogenesis* (Ramey & Ramey, 2000). *Synapses* are gaps between neurons, where connections between the axon and dendrites take place. Synaptogenesis begins in infancy and continues through adolescence.

Researchers have discovered that nearly twice as many synaptic connections are made than will ever be used (Huttenlocher & others, 1991; Huttenlocher & Dabholkar, 1997). The connections that are used are strengthened and survive, while the unused ones are replaced by other pathways or disappear. That is, in the language of neuroscience, these connections will be "pruned." Figure 3.10 vividly illustrates the dramatic growth and later pruning of synapses in the visual, auditory, and prefrontal cortex of the brain (Huttenlacher & Dabholkar, 1997). These areas are critical for higher-order cognitive functioning such as learning, memory, and reasoning.

As shown in figure 3.10, the time course for synaptic "blooming and pruning" varies considerably by brain region. In the visual cortex, the peak of synaptic overproduction takes place at about the fourth postnatal month, followed by a gradual reduction until the middle to end of the preschool years (Huttenlocher & Dabholkar, 1997). In the auditory and prefrontal cortex, which are involved in hearing and language, synaptic production follows a similar although somewhat later course. In the prefrontal cortex (where higher-level thinking and self-regulation occur), the peak of overproduction takes place at about 1 year of age. Not until middle to late adolescence does this area reach its adult density of synapses.

What determines the timing and course of synaptic "blooming" and "pruning"? Both heredity and experience are thought to be influential (Greenough, 2000; Greenough & Black, 1992). For instance, the amount of visual and auditory stimulation a child receives could speed up or delay the process.

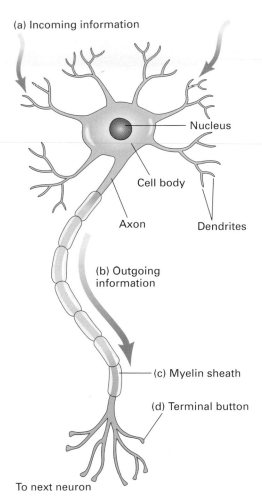

(a) Incoming information

Nucleus

Cell body

Axon   Dendrites

(b) Outgoing information

(c) Myelin sheath

(d) Terminal button

To next neuron

FIGURE 3.9 The Neuron

(*a*) The dendrites of the cell body receive information from other neurons, muscles, or glands. (*b*) An axon transmits information away from the cell body. (*c*) A myelin sheath covers most axons and speeds information transmission. (*d*) As the axon ends, it branches out into terminal buttons.

www.mhhe.com/santrocka10

Neural Processes
Neuroimaging
Internet Neuroscience Resources

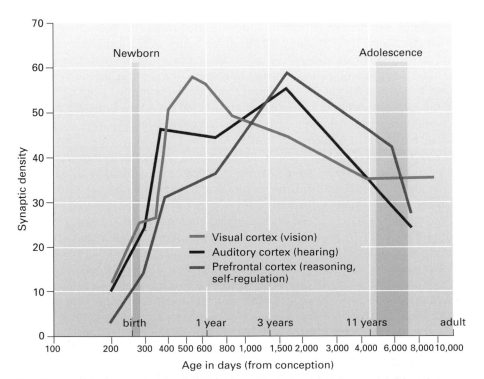

FIGURE 3.10 Synaptic Density in the Human Brain from Infancy to Adulthood
The graph shows the dramatic increase and then pruning in synaptic density for three regions of the brain: visual cortex, auditory cortex, and prefrontal cortex. Synaptic density is believed to be an important indication of the extent of connectivity between neurons.

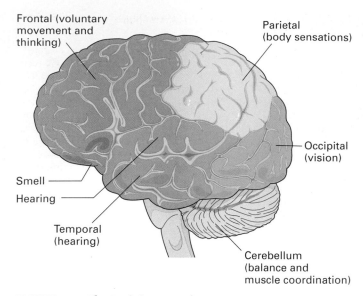

Frontal (voluntary movement and thinking)

Parietal (body sensations)

Occipital (vision)

Smell

Hearing

Temporal (hearing)

Cerebellum (balance and muscle coordination)

FIGURE 3.11 The Brain's Four Lobes
Shown here are the locations of the brain's four lobes: frontal, occipital, temporal, and parietal.

With the onset of puberty, the levels of *neurotransmitters*—chemicals that carry information across the synaptic gap between one neuron and the next—change. For example, an increase in the neurotransmitter dopamine occurs in both the prefrontal cortex and the limbic system (Lewis, 1997). Increases in dopamine have been linked to increased risk taking and the use of addictive drugs (Spear, 2000). Increases in dopamine may also be related to an increase in the onset of schizophrenia, one of the most debilitating mental disorders, during adolescence (Walker, 2002).

Brain Structure

Neurons do not simply float in the brain. Connected in precise ways, they form the various structures in the brain. Among brain structures that have recently been the focus of research in adolescent development are the four lobes in the highest part of the brain—the cerebral cortex (see figure 3.11). The *occipital lobe* is involved in visual functioning, the *temporal lobe* in hearing, the *parietal lobe* in the perception of bodily sensations, and the *frontal lobe* in reasoning and personality. Another structure of the brain that has been studied during adolescents is the *amygdala*, which is involved in emotion.

One of the main reasons scientists only recently have begun to study brain development in adolescence has been a lack of technology to do so. However, the creation of sophisticated brain scanning devices, such as magnetic resonance imaging (MRI), is allowing better detection of changes in the brain during adolescence (Blumenthal & others, 1999; Sowell & others, 2001, 2002). Magnetic resonance imaging consists of creating a magnetic field around a person's body and bombarding the brain with radio waves. The result is a computerized image of the brain's tissues and biochemical activities.

Using MRIs, scientists have recently discovered that children's and adolescents' brains undergo significant anatomical changes between 3 and 15 years of age (Thompson & others, 2000). By repeatedly scanning the brains of the same individuals over as many as four years, they identified rapid, distinct spurts of growth. The amount of material in some areas of the brain nearly doubled within as little as one year of time, followed by a drastic loss of tissue as unneeded cells were purged and the brain continued to reorganize itself. In this research, the overall size of the brain did not change from 3 to 15 years of age. However, what did change dramatically were local patterns within the brain.

Researchers found that the location of the growth spurts changed over time. From 3 to 6 years of age, the most rapid growth occurred in the frontal lobe, which is involved in planning and organizing new actions, and in maintaining attention to tasks. From age 6 through puberty, the most growth took place in the temporal and parietal lobes, especially the area of those lobes involved in language and spatial relations.

In another study, researchers used MRIs to discover if brain activity during the processing of emotional information differed in adolescents (10 to 18 years of age) and adults (20 to 40 years of age) (Baird & others, 1999). In this study, participants were asked to view pictures of faces displaying fearful expressions while they underwent an MRI. When adolescents (especially younger ones) processed the emotional information, their brain activity was more pronounced in the amygdala than in the frontal lobe. The reverse occurred in the adults. As we saw earlier, the amygdala is involved in emotion, while the frontal lobes are involved in higher-level reasoning and thinking. The researchers interpreted their findings to mean that adolescents tend to respond with "gut" reactions to emotional stimuli while adults are more likely to respond in rational, reasoned ways. The researchers also concluded that these changes are linked to growth in the frontal lobe of the brain from adolescence to adulthood. However, more research is needed to clarify these findings on possible developmental changes in brain activity during the processing of emotional stimuli (Dahl, 2001;

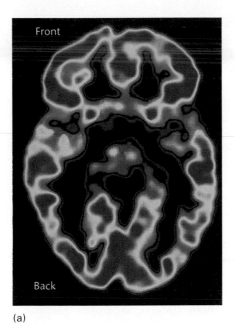

(a)

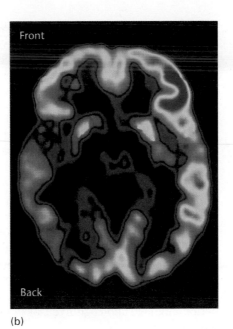

(b)

FIGURE 3.12 Early Deprivation and Brain Activity

These two photographs are PET (positron emission tomography) (which use radioactive tracers to image and analyze blood flow and metabolic activity in the body's organs) scans of the brains of (*a*) a normal child and (*b*) an institutionalized Romanian orphan who experienced substantial deprivation since birth. In PET scans, the highest to lowest brain activity is reflected in the colors of red, yellow, green, blue, and black, respectively. As can be seen, red and yellow show up to a much greater degree in the PET scan of the normal child than the deprived Romanian orphan.

DeBellis & others, 2001; Spear, 2000). Other researchers have found that the amygdala and hippocampus, both limbic system structures involved in emotion, increase in volume during adolescence (Giedd & others, 1999; Sowell & Jernigan, 1998).

Leading researcher Charles Nelson (2003) points out that while adolescents are capable of very strong emotions their prefrontal cortex hasn't adequately developed to the point at which they can control these passions. It is as if their brain doesn't have the brakes to slow down their emotions. But what about the brain of a young genius—does it process information differently than the brains of other adolescents? Watch the Discovery video segment entitled "The Adolescent Brain" to learn what some researchers have discovered.

Experience and Plasticity

Scientists are especially interested in the extent to which environmental experiences influence the brain's development. They also want to know how much plasticity the brain retains as individuals progress through their childhood, adolescent, and adult years.

Deprived and Enriched Environments Until the middle of the twentieth century, scientists believed that the brain's development was determined almost exclusively by genetic factors. Then, researcher Mark Rosenzweig (1969) conducted a classic study. He was curious about whether early experiences can change the brain's development. He randomly assigned rats and other animals to grow up in different environments. Some lived in an enriched early environment with stimulating features, such as wheels to rotate, steps to climb, levers to press, and toys to manipulate. In contrast, others lived in standard cages or in barren, isolated environments. The results were stunning. The brains of the animals from "enriched" environments weighed more and had thicker layers, more neural connections, and higher levels of neurochemical activity than the brains of the "deprived" animals. Similar findings occurred when older animals were reared in vastly different environments, although the results were not as strong as for younger animals.

Researchers have also found depressed activity in children who grow up in unresponsive and unstimulating environments. As figure 3.12 shows , a child who grew up in a impoverished Romanian orphanage had brain activity that was considerably depressed compared with that of a normal child.

Can New Brain Cells Be Generated in Adolescence?   Until close to the end of the twentieth century, scientists believed that the brain generated no new cells (neurons) after the early child years. However, researchers have recently discovered that people can generate new brain cells throughout their lives (Gould & others, 1999; Nelson, 2003; Nottebohm, 2002). Furthermore, evidence now shows that exercise and enriched experiences can produce new brain cells (Churchill & others, 2002; Cotman & Berchtold, 2002).

Can the Adolescent's Brain Recover from Injury?   In adolescence and even through late adulthood, the brain has a remarkable ability to repair itself (Anderton, 2002). In chapter 2, you read about Michael Rehbein, whose left hemisphere was removed because of brain seizures. The plasticity of the human brain was apparent as his right hemisphere reorganized itself to take over functions, such as speech, that normally take place in the left hemisphere.

One recent study examined 68 children from 7 to 15 years of age and found that the later their brain injuries occurred, the less effective their performance was on a number of language and cognitive tasks (Slomine & others, 2002).

While the brain retains considerable plasticity in adolescence, the earlier a brain injury occurs, the more likelihood of a successful recovery (Bhutta & Anand, 2002). One recent study examined 68 children from 7 to 15 years of age and found that the later their brain injuries occurred, the less effective their performance was on a number of language and cognitive tasks (Slomine & others, 2002).

Brain Development and Education   Numerous claims have been made that elementary and secondary education should be brain-based. Some journalists have even suggested that educators should look to neuroscientists for answers about how best to teach children and adolescents. Unfortunately, such bold statements are speculative at best and far removed from what neuroscientists actually know about the brain (Breur, 1999). We don't need to look any further than the oversimplified hype about logical "left-brained" individuals and creative "right-brained" individuals to see how easily the relevance of neuroscience to education has been exaggerated (Sousa, 1995).

One common misapplication of neuroscience to education is the idea of a critical or sensitive period—a biological window of opportunity—when learning is easy, effective, and readily retained. However, there is no neuroscience evidence to support this belief (Breur, 1999). One leading neuroscientist even told educators that although children acquire a great deal of information during the early years, most learning likely takes place after synaptic formation stabilizes, which is after the age of 10 (Goldman-Rakic, 1996).

Keep in mind that we still know very little about brain development in adolescence. In the next decade, we are likely to see many more research studies on brain development in adolescence.

Review and reflect Learning goal 2

 2   Describe the developmental changes in the brain during adolescence

REVIEW

- What are neurons? How do the brain's neurons change in adolescence?
- What changes in brain structure occur in adolescence?
- How much plasticity does the brain have in adolescence?

REFLECT

- Find an article on brain-based education in a magazine or on the Internet. Use your critical thinking skills to evaluate the article's credibility. Does the author present research evidence to support the link between neuroscience and the brain-based method being recommended? Explain.

So far in this chapter we have studied puberty and the brain. Next, we explore another very important topic in adolescence: health.

3 ADOLESCENT HEALTH

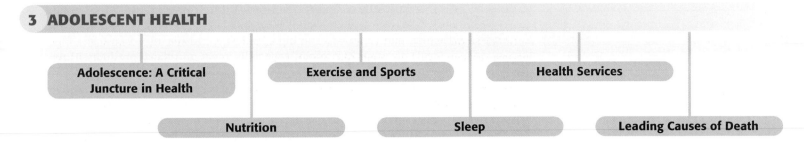

We begin our discussion of adolescent health by evaluating why adolescence is a critical juncture in the health of many individuals. Other topics we examine include nutrition, exercise and sports, sleep, and the leading causes of death in adolescence.

Adolescence: A Critical Juncture in Health

Adolescence is a critical juncture in the adoption of behaviors that are relevant to health (Blum & Nelson-Mmari, 2004; Maggs, Schulenberg, & Hurrelmann, 1997; Roth & Brooks-Gunn, 2000). Many of the behaviors that are linked to poor health habits and early death in adults begin during adolescence. Conversely, the early formation of healthy behavior patterns, such as regular exercise and a preference for foods low in fat and cholesterol not only has immediate health benefits but helps in adulthood to delay or prevent disability and mortality from heart disease, stroke, diabetes, and cancer (Barakat, Kunin-Batson, & Kaszak, 2003; Phillips, 2003).

Unfortunately, even though the United States has become a health-conscious nation, many adults and adolescents still smoke, have poor nutritional habits, and spend too much of their lives as couch potatoes. Why is this so?

In adolescence, many individuals reach a level of health, strength, and energy that they will never match during the remainder of their lives. They also have a sense of uniqueness and invulnerability that convinces them that they will never suffer from poor health, or if they do, they will quickly recover. Given this combination of physical strength and cognitive deception, it is not surprising that many adolescents develop poor health habits.

Many health experts believe that improving adolescents' health involves far more than taking them to the doctor's office when they are sick. Increasingly, experts recognize that whether or not adolescents develop health problems depends primarily on their behavior (Phillips, 2003; Tinsley, 2003). These experts' goals are to (1) reduce adolescents' *health-compromising behaviors,* such as drug abuse, violence, unprotected sexual intercourse, and dangerous driving; and (2) increase adolescents' *health-enhancing behaviors,* such as exercising, eating nutritiously, wearing seat belts, and getting adequate sleep.

Nutrition

The recommended range of energy intake for adolescents takes into account the needs of different adolescents, their growth rate and level of exercise, and their age and gender. Males have higher energy needs than females. Some adolescents' bodies simply burn energy faster than others. **Basal metabolism rate (BMR)** is the minimum amount of energy an individual uses in a resting state. As figure 3.13 shows, BMR declines gradually from the beginning of adolescence through the end of adolescence.

Concern is often expressed over adolescents' tendency to eat between meals. However, their choice of foods is much more important than the time or place of eating. Fresh vegetables and fruits as well as whole-grain products are needed to complement the foods adolescents commonly choose, which tend to be high in protein and energy value.

basal metabolism rate (BMR) The minimum amount of energy an individual uses in a resting state.

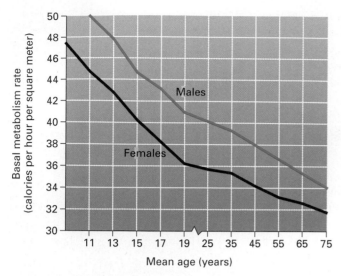

FIGURE 3.13 Basal Metabolic Rates (BMRs) for Females and Males, 11 to 25 Years of Age

A special concern in American culture is the amount of fat in our diet. Many of today's adolescents virtually live on fast-food meals, which contributes to the high fat levels in their diet. Most fast-food meals are high in protein, especially meat and dairy products. However, the average American adolescent does not need to worry about getting enough protein. What should be of concern is the vast number of adolescents who consume large quantities of fast foods that are not only high in protein but high in fat (Lissau & others, 2004).

Medical personnel and psychologists are becoming increasingly concerned with the health hazards associated with obesity (Corsica & Perri, 2003; Schimmer, Burwinkle, & Varni, 2003). Eating patterns established in childhood and adolescence are closely associated with obesity in adulthood: 80 percent of obese adolescents become obese adults. Currently, an estimated 25 percent of American adolescents are obese. We will explore adolescent obesity further in chapter 14, "Adolescent Problems." In that chapter, we will also discuss two disorders that have increasingly characterized adolescent females—anorexia nervosa and bulimia.

Through the Eyes of Adolescents

Body Preoccupation and Concerns

After locking the bathroom door, 12-year-old Anya carefully examines her still shower-damp body. She pokes disgustedly at her stomach. A year ago she wasn't as concerned about her body and it felt more familiar. Now the body she looks at in the mirror has new curves and hair she is not sure she likes. She feels as though she is too heavy and thinks, "Maybe I should try that diet that Becky told me about." Sighing, she pulls on her oversize sweatshirt and wonders what to do (Lerner & Olson, 1995).

Exercise and Sports

Do American adolescents get enough exercise? How extensive is the role of sports in their lives? The answers to these questions have an impact on their health.

Exercise Three recent national studies clearly showed that adolescents are not getting enough exercise. The first study compared adolescents' exercise patterns in 1987 and 2001 (American Sports Data, 2001). The results: In 1987, 31 percent of 12- to 17-year-olds said they exercised frequently, compared with only 18 percent in 2001. In the second study, physical activity declined from early to late adolescence (National Center for Health Statistics, 2000a). That is, adolescents in grade 9 were more likely to participate in moderate or vigorous physical activity than their counterparts in grades 10 through 12. Males were far more likely to exercise than females were. In the third study, few adolescents participated in physical education (PE) classes (Gordon-Larsen, McMurray, & Popkin, 2000). Only about 20 percent took a PE class one or more days per week. Participation in PE classes was especially low for African American and Latino adolescents.

The ethnic differences in participation rates is noteworthy (Frenn & others, 2003; Saxena, Borzekowski, & Rickert, 2002). In one recent study, the activity habits of more than 1,000 African American and more than 1,000 non-Latino White girls were examined annually from 9–10 years of age to 18–19 years of age (Kimm & others, 2002). (The study did not include boys because it was designed to determine why more African American women than non-Latino White women become obese.) At 9–10 years of age, most girls reported they were engaging in some physical activity outside of school. However, by 16–17 years of age, 56 percent of African American girls and 31 percent of non-Latino White girls were not engaging in any regular physical activity in their spare time. By 18–19 years of age, the figures were 70 percent and 29 percent, respectively. In sum, physical activity declines substantially in girls during adolescence and more in African American than non-Latino White girls (Kimm & Obarzanek, 2002).

Do U.S. adolescents exercise less than their counterparts in other countries? A recent comparison of adolescents in 28 countries found that U.S. adolescents exercised less and ate more junk food than adolescents in most of the other countries (World Health Organization, 2000). Just two-thirds of U.S. adolescents exercised at least twice a week compared with 80 percent or more of adolescents in Ireland, Austria, Germany, and the Slovak Republic. U.S. adolescents were more likely to eat fried food and less likely to eat fruits and vegetables than adolescents in most other countries studied. U.S. adolescents' eating choices were similar to those of adolescents in England.

Some health experts blame television for the poor physical condition of American adolescents. In one investigation, adolescents who watched little television were much more physically fit than those who watched heavily (Tucker, 1987). The more television adolescents watch, the more likely they are to be overweight. No one is sure whether their obesity results from spending their leisure time in front of a television set or from eating the junk food they see advertised on television. It may be that less physically fit youth simply find physical activity less reinforcing than watching television.

Some of the blame for the poor physical condition of U.S. children and adolescents falls on U.S. schools, many of which fail to provide physical education class on a daily basis. One extensive investigation of physical education classes at four different schools revealed how little vigorous exercise takes place in these classes (Parcel & others, 1987). Boys and girls moved through space only 50 percent of the time they were in the classes, and moved continuously an average of only 2.2 minutes. In sum, not only does the adolescent's school week include inadequate physical education, but the majority of adolescents do not exercise vigorously even when they are in physical education. Furthermore, while much is made of the exercise revolution among adults, most children and adolescents report that their parents are poor role models when it comes to vigorous physical exercise (Feist & Brannon, 1989).

How much exercise do adolescents get? What can schools do to improve adolescents' physical fitness?

Does pushing children and adolescents to exercise more vigorously in school make a difference? One investigation provided an affirmative answer to this question (Tuckman & Hinkle, 1988). One hundred fifty-four boys and girls were randomly assigned either to three 30-minute running programs per week or to regular attendance in physical education classes. Although the results sometimes varied by sex, for the most part those in the running program showed increased cardiovascular health and creativity. For example, boys in the running program had less body fat, and girls in the running program were more creatively involved in their classrooms.

An exciting possibility is that physical exercise might act as a buffer against the stress adolescents experience. In one investigation of 364 girls in grades 7 through 11, the negative impact of stressful events on girls' health declined as their exercise levels rose (Brown & Siegel, 1988). In another investigation, adolescents who exercised regularly coped more effectively with stress and had more positive identities than adolescents who engaged in little exercise (Grimes & Mattimore, 1989). And in one recent study, high school seniors who exercised frequently had higher grade point averages, used drugs less frequently, were less depressed, and got along better with their parents than those who rarely exercised (Field, Diego, & Sanders, 2001).

In the fourth century B.C., Aristotle commented that the quality of life is determined by its activities. Today, we know that exercise is one of the principal activities that improves the quality of life, both in adolescence and adulthood (Malina, 2001).

Sports   Sports play an important role in the lives of many adolescents (Danish, 2003; Kuchenbecker, 2000). Some estimates indicate that as many as 40 to 70 percent of American youths participate in various organized sports (Ferguson, 1999).

Sports can have both positive and negative influences on adolescent development. Many sports activities can improve adolescents' physical health and well-being, self-confidence, motivation to excel, and ability to work with others (Cornock, Bowker, & Gadbois, 2001). In some cases, adolescents who spend considerable time in sports are less likely than others to engage in drugs and delinquency.

In one recent study of sports participation and health-related behaviors in more than 14,000 U.S. high school students, approximately 70 percent of the males and

53 percent of the females said they had participated in one or more sports teams in school or nonschool settings (Pate & others, 2000). Male sports participants were more likely than nonparticipants to say they had eaten fruit and vegetables the previous day, and less likely to report cigarette smoking, cocaine and other illegal drug use, and attempts to lose weight. Compared with female nonparticipants, female sports participants were more likely to say they had eaten vegetables on the previous day, and less likely to report having sexual intercourse over the past three months.

The downside of the extensive participation in sports by American adolescents includes pressure by parents and coaches to win at all costs (Kuchenbecker, 2000). Researchers have found that adolescents' participation in competitive sports is linked with competition anxiety and self-centeredness (Bredemeier & Shields, 1996; Smith & Smoll, 1997). Furthermore, some adolescents spend so much time in sports that their academic skills suffer. Increasingly, adolescents are pushing their bodies beyond their capabilities, stretching the duration, intensity, and frequency of their training to the point that they cause overuse injuries (Hellmich, 2000).

Some of the problems adolescents experience in sports involve their coaches. Many youth coaches create a performance-oriented motivational climate that is focused on winning, public recognition, and performance relative to others. But other coaches place more emphasis on mastery motivation that focuses adolescents' attention on the development of their skills and self-determined standards of success. Researchers have found that athletes who have a mastery focus are more likely than others to see the benefits of practice, to persist in the face of difficulty, and to show significant skill development over the course of a season (Roberts, Treasure, & Kavussanu, 1997).

Sleep

Recently there has been a surge of interest in adolescent sleep patterns (Carskdadon, 2002; Giannotti, & others, 2002; Park & others, 2002; Pollack & Bright, 2003). This interest focuses on the belief that many adolescents are not getting enough sleep and that their desire to stay up later at night and sleep longer in the morning has physiological underpinnings. These findings have implications for the hours during which adolescents learn most effectively in school (Dahl & Lewin, 2002; Fukuda & Ishihara, 2001).

In one recent study, researchers examined the sleep patterns of children in the second, fourth, and sixth grades (Sadeh, Raviv, & Gruber, 2000). They monitored the children's activity levels, and the children and their parents completed sleep questionnaires and daily reports. Sixth-grade children went to sleep at night about one hour later (just after 10:30 P.M. versus just after 9:30 P.M.) and reported more daytime sleepiness than the second-grade children. Girls spent more time in sleep than boys. Also, family stress was linked with poor sleep, such as nightly wakings, in children.

Mary Carskadon and her colleagues (Acebo & Carskadon, 2002; Carskadon, Acebo, & Seifer, 2001; Carskadon & others, 1998, 1999) have conducted a number of research studies on adolescent sleep patterns. They found that when given the opportunity adolescents will sleep an average of 9 hours and 25 minutes a night. Most get considerably less than 9 hours of sleep, especially during the week. This shortfall creates a sleep deficit, which adolescents often attempt to make up on the weekend. The researchers also found that older adolescents tend to be more sleepy during the day than younger adolescents. They theorized that this sleepiness was not due to academic work or social pressures. Rather, their research suggests that adolescents' biological clocks undergo a shift as they get older, delaying their period of wakefulness by about one hour. A delay in the nightly release of the sleep-inducing hormone melatonin, which is produced in the brain's pineal gland, seems to underlie this shift. Melatonin is secreted at about 9:30 P.M. in younger adolescents and approximately an hour later in older adolescents.

Carskadon has suggested that early school starting times may cause grogginess, inattention in class, and poor performance on tests. Based on her research, school

How might changing sleep patterns in adolescents affect their school performance?

officials in Edina, Minnesota, decided to start classes at 8:30 A.M. rather than the usual 7:25 A.M. Since then there have been fewer referrals for discipline problems and the number of students who report being ill or depressed has decreased. The school system reports that test scores have improved for high school students, but not for middle school students. This finding supports Carskadon's suspicion that early start times are likely to be more stressful for older than for younger adolescents. For another perspective on an early adolescent's need for sleep, watch the video segment entitled "Overscheduling our Adolescents," in which Dr. Ronald Dahl calls for a healthy balance between teenage activity and "down time."

Health Services

Though adolescents suffer from a greater number of acute health conditions than adults, they see private physicians less often than any other age group (Edelman, 1996). Adolescents also underutilize other health-care systems (Drotar, 2000; Klein & others, 2001; Seiffge-Krenke, 1998). Health services are especially unlikely to meet the needs of younger adolescents, ethnic minority adolescents, and adolescents living in poverty.

In the National Longitudinal Study of Adolescent Health, more than 12,000 adolescents were interviewed about the extent to which they needed but did not receive health care (Ford, Bearman, & Moody, 1999). Approximately 19 percent of those interviewed reported forgoing health care in the preceding year. Among those who especially needed health care but did not seek it were adolescents who smoked cigarettes on a daily basis, drank alcohol frequently, and engaged in sexual intercourse.

Of special concern is the decrease in use of health services by older adolescent males. One recent national study in the United States found that 16- to 20-year-old males have significantly less contact with health-care services than 11- to 15-year-old males (Marcell & others, 2002). In contrast, 16- to 20-year-old females have more contact with health-care services than younger females.

Among the chief barriers to better health care for adolescents are cost, poor organization and availability of health services, and lack of confidentiality. Few health-care providers receive any special training in working with adolescents. Many say they feel unprepared to provide services such as contraceptive counseling or to evaluate what constitutes abnormal behavior in adolescents (Irwin, 1993). Health-care providers may transmit to their patients their discomfort in discussing topics such as sexuality and drugs, causing adolescents to avoid discussing sensitive issues with them (Marcell & Millstein, 2001).

www.mhhe.com/santrocka10

Adolescent Health
National Longitudinal Study
of Adolescent Health
Health Risks for Adolescents

Leading Causes of Death

Medical improvements have increased the life expectancy of today's adolescents compared with their counterparts in the early twentieth century. Still, life-threatening factors do exist in adolescents' lives.

The three leading causes of death in adolescence are accidents, homicide, and suicide (National Center for Health Statistics, 2000b) (see figure 3.14). More than half of all deaths from 15 to 24 years of age are due to accidents, approximately three-fourths of them involving motor vehicles. Risky driving habits, such as speeding, tailgating, and driving under the influence of alcohol or other drugs, may be more important contributors to these accidents than lack of driving experience. In about 50 percent of motor vehicle fatalities involving adolescents, the driver has a blood alcohol level of 0.10 percent—twice the level needed to be designated as "under the influence" in some states. A high rate of intoxication is also found in adolescents who die as pedestrians, or while using recreational vehicles.

Homicide also is another leading cause of death in adolescence, especially among African American male adolescents who are three times more likely to

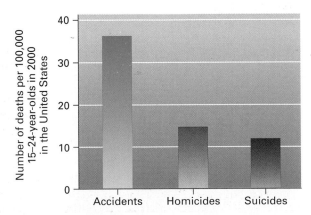

FIGURE 3.14 Leading Causes of Death in Adolescents and Emerging Adults

be killed by guns than by natural causes (Simons, Finlay, & Yang, 1991). Suicide is the third leading cause of death in adolescence. Since the 1950s the adolescent suicide rate has tripled. We will discuss suicide further in chapter 14, "Adolescent Problems."

In this chapter we have discussed some important aspects of adolescent health. In later chapters, we will explore many of them further. For example, in chapter 7, we will examine many aspects of adolescent sexuality, such as unprotected sexual intercourse and sexually transmitted infections. In chapter 14, we will discuss drug abuse, violence, smoking, and eating disorders.

Review and reflect Learning goal 3

3 Characterize the health of adolescents

REVIEW

- Why is adolescence a critical juncture in the health of many individuals?
- How does basal metabolism change in adolescence? Why are health-care professionals concerned about adolescents' eating habits?
- How can exercise improve the lives of adolescents?
- How extensively do adolescents use health services?
- What are the leading causes of death in adolescence?

REFLECT

- To what extent did you practice good health habits during adolescence? If you engaged in any bad health habits in adolescence, have you since dropped them? Explain.

---

4 EVOLUTION, HEREDITY, AND ENVIRONMENT

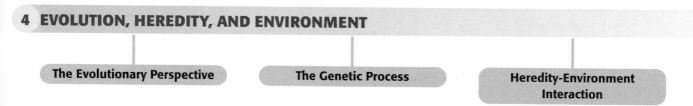

| The Evolutionary Perspective | The Genetic Process | Heredity-Environment Interaction |

What roles do evolution and heredity play in adolescent development? What conclusions can we reach about the interaction of heredity and environment?

The Evolutionary Perspective

In terms of evolutionary time, humans are relative newcomers to the earth. If we think of the broad expanse of time as a calendar year, then humans arrived on Earth in the last moments of December (Sagan, 1977). As our earliest ancestors left the forest to feed on the savannahs, and finally to form hunting societies on the open plains, their minds and behaviors changed. How did this evolution come about?

Natural Selection and Adaptive Behavior *Natural selection* is the evolutionary process that favors those individuals of a species who are best adapted to survive and reproduce. To understand natural selection, let's return to the middle of the nineteenth century, when the British naturalist Charles Darwin was traveling the world, observing many different species of animals in their natural habitats. In his groundbreaking book, *On the Origin of Species* (1859), Darwin noted that most species reproduce at rates that would cause enormous increases in their population and yet populations remained nearly constant. He reasoned that an intense struggle for food, water, and resources must occur among the many young born in each generation, because many of them do not survive. Darwin believed that those who do survive to reproduce and pass on their genes to the next generation are probably superior to others in a number of ways. In other words, the survivors are better adapted to their world than the nonsurvivors (Mader, 2004; Raven & others, 2002). Over the course of many generations, Darwin reasoned, organisms with the characteristics needed for survival would compose a larger and larger percentage of the population, producing a gradual modification of the species. If environmental conditions changed, however, other characteristics might be favored by natural selection, moving the evolutionary process in a different direction.

To understand the role of evolution in behavior, we need to understand the concept of adaptive behavior (Lewis & others, 2004). In evolutionary conceptions of psychology, *adaptive behavior* is a modification of behavior that promotes an organism's survival in the natural habitat (Cosmides & others, 2003). All organisms must adapt to particular places, climates, food sources, and ways of life in order to survive. In humans, attachment ensures an infant's closeness to the caregiver for feeding and protection from danger. This behavioral characteristic promotes survival just as an eagle's claw, which facilitates predation, ensures the eagle's survival.

Evolutionary Psychology   Although Darwin introduced the theory of evolution by natural selection in 1859, his ideas only recently have been used to explain behavior. The field of **evolutionary psychology** emphasizes the importance of adaptation, reproduction, and "survival of the fittest" in explaining behavior. Because evolution favors organisms that are best adapted to survive and reproduce in a particular environment, evolutionary psychology focuses on the conditions that allow individuals to survive or perish. In this view, the process of natural selection favors those behaviors that increase organisms' reproductive success and their ability to pass their genes on to the next generation (Bjorklund & Pellegrini, 2002; Caporael, 2001; Cosmides & others, 2003; Crawford & Salmon, 2004).

David Buss's (1995, 1999, 2000, 2004; Larsen & Buss, 2002) ideas on evolutionary psychology have produced a wave of interest in how evolution can explain human behavior. Buss believes that just as evolution shapes our physical features, such as our body shape and height, it also influences our decision making, our aggressive behavior, our fears, and our mating patterns.

Evolutionary Developmental Psychology   Much of the thinking in evolutionary psychology has not had a developmental focus. Recently, however, considerable interest has been generated in applying evolutionary principles to the changes that take place as humans develop. Evolutionary developmental psychologists have proposed the following views (Bjorklund & Pellegrini, 2002):

- *Humans need an extended "juvenile" period to develop a large brain and learn to cope with their complex social communities.* Humans take longer to mature reproductively than any other mammal. The benefits of this extended juvenile period can be seen in the development of a large brain and the experiences required for mastering the complexities of human society (see figure 3.15).
- *Many aspects of childhood function as a preparation for adulthood and the struggle for survival.* Through their play, children learn much about their physical and social worlds that can help them to adapt and survive as adults. Sex differences in childhood play are especially significant in this regard. Beginning in the preschool years, boys in all cultures engage in more rough-and-tumble play than girls. The evolutionary function of this play may have been to prepare boys for their adulthood role as fighters and hunters. In contrast, girls engage in more parenting play (such as doll play) and less physical dominance than boys, a

evolutionary psychology An approach that emphasizes the importance of adaptation, reproduction, and "survival of the fittest" in explaining behavior.

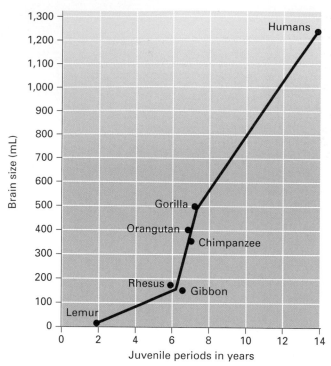

FIGURE 3.15 The Brain Sizes of Various Primates and Humans in Relation to the Length of the Juvenile Period

difference that evolutionary psychologists believe evolved to support the development of the female role as caregiver.

- *Many evolved psychological mechanisms are domain-specific.* A basic theme of evolutionary psychology is that specific types of information processing have evolved to help people deal with recurring problems faced by their ancestors. In this view, the mind is not a general-purpose device that can be applied equally well to a vast array of problems. Rather, it consists of a set of modules specialized for tasks such as mathematics and language. Thus, infants enter the world prepared to learn some types of information more readily than others. This predisposition serves as a foundation for their social and cognitive development across the childhood and adolescent years. In chapter 4, "Cognitive Development," we will examine the issue of whether intelligence is a general ability or consists of a number of specific intelligences.

- *Evolved behaviors are not necessarily adaptive in contemporary society.* Some behaviors that were adaptive for our prehistoric ancestors may not serve us well today. For example, being physically dominant and aggressive was necessary for survival among prehistoric males but it is not necessary or even helpful today. This characteristic might be "natural" in an evolutionary sense but that does not mean its expression is inevitable or morally acceptable today.

Mihalyi Csikszentmihalyi and Jennifer Schmidt (1998) have examined stress and resilience in adolescence from an evolutionary perspective. They argue that evolution has programmed humans to act in predictable ways from puberty into early adulthood. For example, through natural selection, males have become physically aggressive, adventurous, and independent, while females have become sociable and nurturant in nature. However, changing cultural conditions over the last 2,000 years—especially in the last two centuries—no longer allow the expression of these traits in either gender during adolescence; thus, the stress and anxiety that is characteristic of this age period.

From a biological perspective, adolescence should be the best period in life. Many physical and psychological functions—such as speed, strength, and possibly some information-processing skills—reach peak efficiency in adolescence and emerging adulthood. Adolescents also have a built-in resilience to turn negative conditions into positive ones. As we saw in chapter 2, for example, negative emotions don't persist nearly as long in adolescents as they do in adults (Larson & Richards, 1994). Nonetheless, this potential for positive experiences often runs afoul of the limitations of our complex social systems, which results in stress for many adolescents. Societal limitations on adolescents include restrictions on their physical movement and freedom, an absence of responsibility, problems with sexuality and intimacy, isolation from adult role models, and a lack of power and control.

Csikszentmihalyi and Schmidt (1998) emphasize that when adolescents become depressed and rebellious, or engage in other maladaptive behaviors, we might ask the following questions: Is the adolescent being physically stifled? Does the adolescent have appropriate responsibilities and meaningful challenges? Is the adolescent being adequately integrated into the adult world? How much control over life does the adolescent have?

Evaluating Evolutionary Psychology Albert Bandura (1998), whose social cognitive theory was described in chapter 2, has complained of the "biologizing" of psychology. Bandura acknowledges the influence of evolution on human adaptation and

THE WIZARD OF ID

By permission of Johnny L. Hart FLP, and Creators Syndicate, Inc.

change. However, he rejects what he calls "one-sided evolutionism," in which social behavior is seen as the product of evolved biology. Bandura believes that evolutionary pressures favored biological adaptations that encouraged the use of tools, allowing humans to manipulate, alter, and construct new environmental conditions. In time, humans' increasingly complex environmental innovations produced new pressures that favored the evolution of specialized brain systems to support consciousness, thought, and language.

In other words, evolution gave us our body structures and biological potentialities, not behavioral dictates. Having evolved our advanced biological capacities, we can use them to produce diverse cultures—aggressive or pacific, egalitarian or autocratic. As American scientist Stephen Jay Gould (1981) concluded, in most domains, human biology allows a broad range of cultural possibilities. The sheer pace of social change, Bandura (1998) notes, underscores the range of possibilities biology permits.

The Genetic Process

Every species has a mechanism for transmitting characteristics from one generation to the next. This mechanism is explained by the principles of genetics. Each of us carries a "genetic code" that we inherited from our parents, and it is a distinctly human code. Because it carries this human code, a fertilized human egg cannot grow into an egret, eagle, or elephant.

Each of us began life as a single cell weighing about one twenty-millionth of an ounce! This tiny piece of matter housed our entire genetic code—instructions that orchestrated growth from that single cell to a person made of trillions of cells, each containing a perfect replica of the original genetic code. That code is carried by our genes. What are they and what do they do?

DNA: The Collaborative Gene   The nucleus of each human cell contains 46 **chromosomes,** which are threadlike structures that contain the remarkable substance deoxyribonucleic acid, or DNA. **DNA** is a complex molecule that contains genetic information. It has a double helix shape, like a spiral staircase. **Genes,** the units of hereditary information, are short segments composed of DNA, as you can see in figure 3.16. They direct cells to reproduce themselves and to assemble proteins. Proteins, in turn, are the building blocks of cells and direct the body's processes.

Each gene has its own function, and each gene has its own location, its own designated place on a particular chromosome. Today, there is a great deal of enthusiasm about efforts to discover the specific locations of genes that are linked to certain

www.mhhe.com/santrocka10

**Behavior Genetics
Human Genome Project**

chromosomes Threadlike structures that contain deoxyribonucleic acid or DNA.

DNA A complex molecule that contains genetic information.

genes The units of hereditary information, which are short segments composed of DNA.

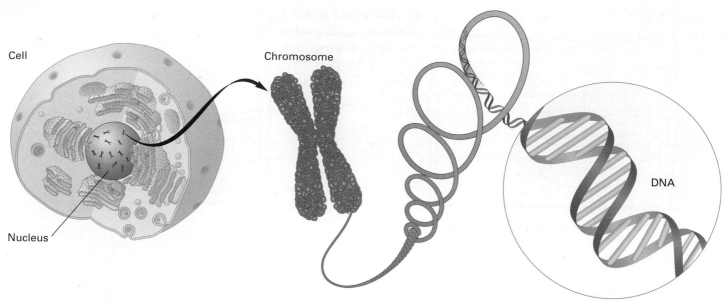

FIGURE 3.16 Cells, Chromosomes, Genes, and DNA

(*Left*) The body contains trillions of cells, which are the basic structural units of life. Each cell contains a central structure, the nucleus. (*Middle*) Chromosomes and genes are located in the nucleus of the cell. Chromosomes are made up of threadlike structures composed of DNA molecules. (*Right*) A gene, a segment of DNA that contains the hereditary code. The structure of DNA is a spiraled double chain.

functions (Nester & others, 2004; Venter, 2003). An important step in this direction was accomplished when the Human Genome Project and the Celera Corporation completed a preliminary map of the human *genome*—the complete set of instructions for making an organism (U.S. Department of Energy, 2001).

One of the big surprises of the Human Genome Project was the finding that humans have only about 30,000 genes (U.S. Department of Energy, 2001). They had thought that humans had as many as 100,000 or more genes. They had also believed that each gene programmed just one protein. In fact, humans appear to have far more proteins than they have genes, so there cannot be a one-to-one correspondence between them (Commoner, 2002; Moore, 2001). Each segment of DNA is not translated, in automation-like fashion, into one and only one protein. It does not act independently, as developmental psychologist David Moore (2001) emphasized by titling his recent book *The Dependent Gene.*

Instead, the DNA gene acts only in collaboration with many other molecules and processes in the cell. The collaboration operates at many points. Small pieces of DNA are mixed, matched, and linked by the cellular machinery. That machinery is sensitive to its context; that is, it is influenced by what is going on around it. Whether a gene is turned "on," working to assemble proteins, is also a matter of collaboration. The activity of genes (*genetic expression*) is affected by their environment (Gottlieb, 1998, 2002, 2004). For example, hormones that circulate in the blood make their way into the cell where they can turn genes "on" and "off." And the flow of hormones can be affected by environmental conditions, such as light, day length, nutrition, and behavior. Numerous studies have shown that external events outside of the cell and the person, and internal events inside of the cell, can excite or inhibit gene expression (Gottlieb, Wahlsten, & Lickliter, 1998; Mauro & others, 1994; Rusak & others, 1990).

In short, no single gene is the source of the protein's genetic information, much less of an inherited trait (Gottlieb, 2002, 2004; Moore, 2001). Rather than being an independent gene, DNA is a collaborative gene.

Genotype and Phenotype   No one possesses all the characteristics that his or her genetic structure makes possible. A person's genetic heritage—the actual genetic material—is called a **genotype.** Not all of this genetic material is apparent in our observed and measurable characteristics. The way an individual's genotype is expressed in observed and measurable characteristics is called a **phenotype.** Phenotypes include physical traits, such as height, weight, eye color, and skin pigmentation, as well as psychological characteristics, such as intelligence, creativity, personality, and social tendencies.

For each genotype, a range of phenotypes can be expressed. Imagine that we could identify all the genes that would make an adolescent introverted or extraverted. Could we predict measured introversion or extraversion in a particular person from our knowledge of those genes? The answer is no, because even if our genetic model was adequate, introversion and extraversion are characteristics that are shaped by experience throughout life. For example, a parent might push an introverted child into social situations, encouraging the child to become more gregarious. Or the parent might support the child's preference for solitary play.

Heredity-Environment Interaction

So far, we have described genes and how they work, and one theme is apparent: Heredity and environment interact to produce development (Hartwell & others, 2004). Whether we are studying how genes produce proteins or their influence on how tall a person is, we end up discussing heredity-environment interactions. Is it possible, though, to untangle the influence of heredity from that of environment and discover the role of each in producing individual differences in development? When heredity and environment interact, how does heredity influence the environment, and vice versa?

Behavior Genetics   **Behavior genetics** is the field that seeks to discover the influence of heredity and environment on individual differences in human traits and development (Maxson, 2003; Rodgers & Bard, 2003). If you think about all of the people you know, you have probably realized that people differ in terms of their level of introversion/extraversion. What behavior geneticists try to do is to figure out what is responsible for those differences—that is, to what extent do people differ because of differences in genes, environment, or a combination of these?

To study the influence of heredity on behavior, behavior geneticists often use either twins or adoption situations. In the most common **twin study,** the behavioral similarity of identical twins is compared with the behavioral similarity of fraternal twins. *Identical twins* (called monozygotic twins) develop from a single fertilized egg that splits into two genetically identical replicas, each of which becomes a person. *Fraternal twins* (called dizygotic twins) develop from separate eggs and separate sperm, making them genetically no more similar than ordinary siblings. Although fraternal twins share the same womb, they are no more alike genetically than are nontwin brothers and sisters, and they may be of different sexes.

By comparing groups of identical and fraternal twins, behavior geneticists capitalize on the basic knowledge that identical twins are more similar genetically than are fraternal twins (Jacob & others, 2001). In one twin study, the extraversion and neuroticism (psychological instability) of 7,000 pairs of Finnish identical and fraternal twins were compared (Rose & others, 1988). On both of these personality traits, the identical twins were much more similar than the fraternal twins were, suggesting an important role for heredity in both traits. However, several issues complicate interpretation of twin studies. For example, perhaps the environments of identical twins are more similar than the environments of fraternal twins. Adults might stress the similarities of identical twins more than those of fraternal twins, and identical twins might perceive themselves as a "set" and play together more than fraternal twins do. If so,

> *C*he frightening part about heredity and environment is that we parents provide both.
> —NOTEBOOK OF A PRINTER

What is the nature of the twin study method?

genotype A person's genetic heritage; the actual genetic material.

phenotype The way an individual's genotype is expressed in observed and measurable characteristics.

behavior genetics The field that seeks to discover the influence of heredity and environment on individual differences in human traits and development.

twin study A study in which the behavioral similarity of identical twins is compared with the behavioral similarity of fraternal twins.

Heredity-Environment Correlation	Description	Examples
Passive	Children inherit genetic tendencies from their parents and parents also provide an environment that matches their own genetic tendencies.	Musically inclined parents usually have musically inclined children and they are likely to provide an environment rich in music for their children.
Evocative	The child's genetic tendencies elicit stimulation from the environment that supports a particular trait. Thus genes evoke environmental support.	A happy, outgoing child elicits smiles and friendly responses from others.
Active (niche-picking)	Children actively seek out "niches" in their environment that reflect their own interests and talents and are thus in accord with their genotype.	Libraries, sports fields, and a store with musical instruments are examples of environmental niches children might seek out if they have intellectual interests in books, talent in sports, or musical talents, respectively.

FIGURE 3.17 Exploring Heredity-Environment Correlations

Twin Research

adoption study A study in which investigators seek to discover whether the behavior and psychological characteristics of adopted children are more like their adoptive parents, who have provided a home environment, or more like those of their biological parents, who have contributed their heredity. Another form of adoption study involves comparing adoptive and biological siblings.

passive genotype-environment correlations Correlations that occur because biological parents, who are genetically related to the child, provide a rearing environment for the child.

evocative genotype-environment correlations Correlations that occur when an adolescent's genetically shaped characteristics elicit certain types of physical and social environments.

observed similarities in identical twins could be more strongly influenced by the environment than the results suggested.

In an **adoption study,** investigators seek to discover whether the behavior and psychological characteristics of adopted children are more like those of their adoptive parents, who have provided a home environment, or more like those of their biological parents, who have contributed their heredity (Abrahamson, Baker, & Caspi, 2002; Wadsworth & others, 2003). Another form of the adoption study involves comparing adoptive and biological siblings.

Heredity-Environment Correlations The difficulties that researchers encounter when they interpret the results of twin studies and adoption studies reflect the complexities of heredity-environment interaction. Some of these interactions are *heredity-environment correlations,* which means that individuals' genes influence the types of environments to which they are exposed. In a sense, individuals "inherit" environments that are related or linked to genetic propensities (Plomin & McGuffin, 2002). Behavior geneticist Sandra Scarr (1993) described three ways that heredity and environment are correlated (see figure 3.17):

- **Passive genotype-environment correlations** occur because biological parents, who are genetically related to the child, provide a rearing environment for the child. For example, the parents might have a genetic predisposition to be intelligent and read skillfully. Because they read well and enjoy reading, they provide their children with books to read. The likely outcome is that their children, given their own inherited predispositions from their parents, will become skilled readers.
- **Evocative genotype-environment correlations** occur because an adolescent's genetically shaped characteristics elicit certain types of physical and social environments. For example, active, smiling children receive more social stimulation than passive, quiet children do. Cooperative, attentive adolescents evoke more pleasant and instructional responses from the adults around them than uncooperative, distractible adolescents do. Athletically inclined youth tend to elicit encouragement to engage in school sports. As a consequence, these adolescents tend to be the ones who try out for sport teams and go on to participate in athletically oriented activities.

- **Active (niche-picking) genotype-environment correlations** occur when children seek out environments that they find compatible and stimulating. *Niche-picking* refers to finding a setting that is suited to one's abilities. Adolescents select from their surrounding environment some aspect that they respond to, learn about, or ignore. Their active selections of environments are related to their particular genotype. For example, attractive adolescents tend to seek out attractive peers. Adolescents who are musically inclined are likely to select musical environments in which they can successfully perform their skills.

Scarr believes that the relative importance of the three genotype-environment correlations changes as children develop from infancy through adolescence. In infancy, much of the environment that children experience is provided by adults. Thus, passive genotype-environment correlations are more common in the lives of infants and young children than they are for older children and adolescents who can extend their experiences beyond the family's influence and create their environments to a greater degree.

Critics argue that the concept of heredity-environment correlation gives heredity too much influence in determining development (Gottlieb, 2002). Heredity-environment correlation stresses that heredity determines the types of environments children experience. Next, we examine a view that emphasizes the importance of the nonshared environment of siblings and their heredity as important influences on their development.

Shared and Nonshared Environmental Experiences   Behavior geneticists believe that another way of analyzing the environment's role in heredity-environment interaction is to consider experiences that adolescents share in common with other adolescents living in the same home, as well as experiences that are not shared (Feinberg & Hetherington, 2001; Plomin, Ashbury, & Dunn, 2001).

Shared environmental experiences are siblings' common experiences, such as their parents' personalities or intellectual orientation, the family's socioeconomic status, and the neighborhood in which they live. By contrast, **nonshared environmental experiences** are an adolescent's unique experiences, both within the family and outside the family; these are not shared with a sibling. Even experiences occurring within the family can be part of the "nonshared environment." For example, parents often interact differently with each sibling, and siblings interact differently with parents (Hetherington, Reiss, & Plomin, 1994; Reiss & others, 2000). Siblings often have different peer groups, different friends, and different teachers at school.

Behavior geneticist Robert Plomin (1993) has found that common rearing, or shared environment, accounts for little of the variation in adolescents' personality or interests. In other words, even though two adolescents live under the same roof with the same parents, their personalities are often very different. Further, behavior geneticists argue that heredity influences the nonshared environments of siblings in the manner we described earlier in the concept of heredity-environment correlations (Plomin & others, 2001). For example, an adolescent who has inherited a genetic tendency to be athletic is likely to spend more time in environments related to sports while an adolescent who has inherited a tendency to be musically inclined is more likely to spend time in environments related to music.

The Epigenetic View   The heredity-environment correlation view emphasizes how heredity directs the kind of environmental experiences individuals have. However, earlier we described how DNA is collaborative, not determining an individual's traits

active (niche-picking) genotype-environment correlations Correlations that occur when children seek out environments that they find compatible and stimulating.

shared environmental experiences Siblings' common experiences such as their parents' personalities and intellectual orientation, the family's social class, and the neighborhood in which they live.

nonshared environmental experiences The adolescent's own unique experiences, both within a family and outside the family, that are not shared by another sibling.

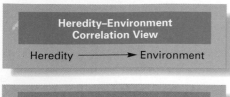

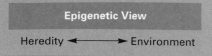

FIGURE 3.18 Comparison of the Heredity-Environment Correlation and Epigenetic Views

"The interaction of heredity and environment is so extensive that to ask which is more important, nature or nurture, is like asking which is more important to a rectangle, height or width."

—WILLIAM GREENOUGH,
*Contemporary Psychologist,
University of Illinois*

**Genes and Parenting
Heredity Resources**

epigenetic view Emphasizes that development is the result of an ongoing bidirectional interchange between heredity and environment.

in an independent matter, but rather in an interactive manner with the environment. In line with the concept of a collaborative gene, the **epigenetic view** emphasizes that development is the result of an ongoing, bidirectional interchange between heredity and the environment (Gottlieb, 1998, 2002, 2004). Figure 3.18 compares the heredity-environment correlation and epigenetic views of development.

Conclusions About Heredity-Environment Interaction Heredity and environment operate together—or cooperate—to produce a person's intelligence, temperament, height, weight, ability to pitch a baseball, ability to read, and so on (Gottlieb, 2002, 2004; Gottlieb, Wahlsten, & Lickliter, 1998). If an attractive, popular, intelligent girl is elected president of her senior class in high school, is her success due to heredity or to environment? Of course, the answer is both.

The relative contributions of heredity and environment are not additive. That is, we can't say that such-and-such a percentage of nature and such-and-such a percentage of experience make us who we are. Nor is it accurate to say that full genetic expression happens once, around conception or birth, after which we carry our genetic legacy into the world to see how far it takes us. Genes produce proteins throughout the life span, in many different environments. Or they don't produce these proteins, depending in part on how harsh or nourishing those environments are.

The emerging view is that many complex behaviors likely have some *genetic loading* that gives people a propensity for a particular developmental trajectory (Plomin & others, 2001). However, the actual development requires more: an environment. And that environment is complex, just like the mixture of genes we inherit (Coll, Bearer, & Lerner, 2004; Overton, 2004; Sternberg & Grigorenko, 2001). Environmental influences range from the things we lump together under "nurture" (such as parenting, family dynamics, schooling, and neighborhood quality) to biological encounters (such as viruses, birth complications, and even biological events in cells) (Greenough, 1997, 1999; Greenough & others, 2001).

Imagine for a moment that there is a cluster of genes somehow associated with youth violence (this example is hypothetical because we don't know of any such combination). The adolescent who carries this genetic mixture might experience a world of loving parents, regular nutritious meals, lots of books, and a series of masterful teachers. Or the adolescent's world might include parental neglect, a neighborhood in which gunshots and crime are everyday occurrences, and inadequate schooling. In which of these environments are the adolescent's genes likely to manufacture the biological underpinnings of criminality?

The most recent nature-nurture controversy erupted when Judith Harris (1998) published *The Nurture Assumption*. In this provocative book, she argued that what parents do does not make a difference in their children's and adolescents' behavior. Yell at them. Hug them. Read to them. Ignore them. Harris says it won't influence how they turn out. She argues that genes and peers are far more important than parents in children's and adolescents' development.

Genes and peers do matter, but Harris' descriptions of peer influences do not take into account the complexity of peer contexts and developmental trajectories (Hartup, 1999). In addition, Harris is wrong in saying that parents don't matter. For example, in the early child years parents play an important role in selecting children's peers and indirectly influencing children's development (Baumrind, 1999). A huge parenting literature with many research studies documents the importance of parents in children's and adolescents' development (Bradley & Corwyn, 2004; Collins & others, 2000, 2001; Collins & Laursen, 2004; Maccoby, 2002; Parke, 2004). We will discuss parents' important roles throughout this book.

Review and reflect Learning goal 4

4 **Explain the contributions of evolution, heredity, and environment to adolescent development**

REVIEW

- What role has evolution played in adolescent development? How do the fields of evolutionary psychology and evolutionary developmental psychology describe evolution's contribution to understanding adolescence?
- What is the genetic process?
- What is the nature of heredity-environment interaction?

REFLECT

- Someone tells you that he or she has analyzed his or her genetic background and environmental experiences and reached the conclusion that environment definitely has had little influence on his or her intelligence. What would you say to this person about his or her ability to make this self-diagnosis?

Reach Your Learning Goals

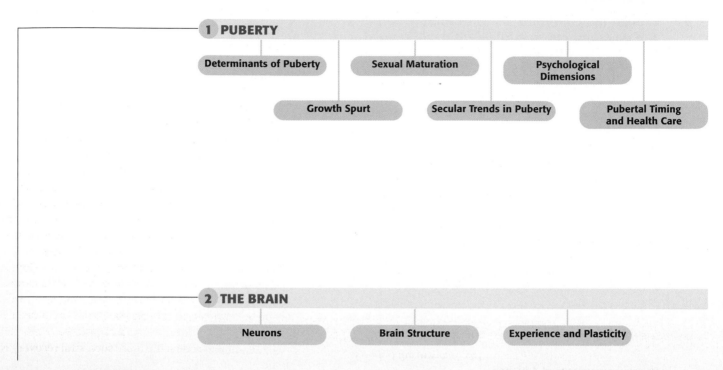

1 PUBERTY

- Determinants of Puberty
- Sexual Maturation
- Psychological Dimensions
- Growth Spurt
- Secular Trends in Puberty
- Pubertal Timing and Health Care

2 THE BRAIN

- Neurons
- Brain Structure
- Experience and Plasticity

Puberty, Health, and Biological Foundations

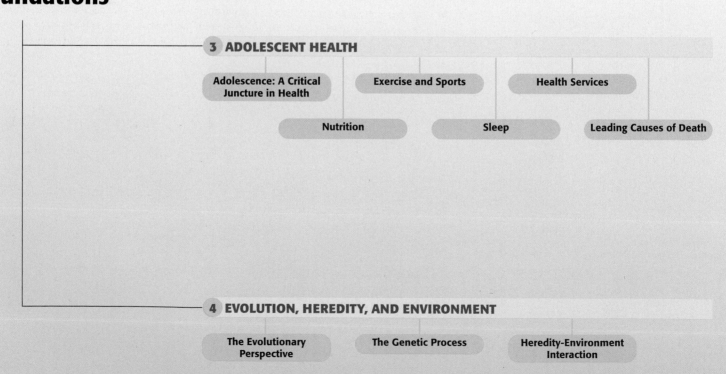

3 ADOLESCENT HEALTH

- Adolescence: A Critical Juncture in Health
- Exercise and Sports
- Health Services
- Nutrition
- Sleep
- Leading Causes of Death

4 EVOLUTION, HEREDITY, AND ENVIRONMENT

- The Evolutionary Perspective
- The Genetic Process
- Heredity-Environment Interaction

Summary

1 **Discuss the determinants, characteristics, and timing of puberty**

- Puberty is a period of rapid physical maturation involving hormonal and bodily changes that take place primarily in early adolescence. Puberty's determinants include heredity, hormones, and possibly weight, percentage of body fat, and leptin. Two classes of hormones that are involved in pubertal change and have significantly different concentrations in males and females are androgens and estrogens. The endocrine system's role in puberty involves the interaction of the hypothalamus, pituitary gland, and gonads. FSH and LH, which are secreted by the pituitary gland, are important aspects of this system. So is GnRH, which is produced by the hypothalamus. The sex hormone system is a negative feedback system. Growth hormone also contributes to pubertal change. Puberty has two phases: adrenarche and gonadarche. The culmination of gonadarche in boys is spermarche; in girls, it is menarche.

- The onset of pubertal growth occurs on the average at 9 years of age for girls and 11 years for boys. The peak of pubertal change for girls is 11.5 years; for boys it is 13.5 years. Girls grow an average of 3½ inches per year during puberty; boys grow an average of 4 inches.

- Sexual maturation is a key feature of pubertal change. Individual variation in puberty is extensive and is considered to be normal within a wide age range.

- Secular trends in puberty took place in the twentieth century with puberty coming earlier. Recently, there has been a slowdown in how early puberty occurs.

- Adolescents show heightened interest in their bodies and body images. Younger adolescents are more preoccupied with these images than older adolescents. Adolescent girls often a have more negative body image than adolescent boys. Researchers have found connections between pubertal change and behavior but environmental influences need to be taken into account. Menarche and the menstrual cycle produce a wide range of reactions in girls. Early maturation often favors boys, at least during early adolescence, but as adults, late-maturing boys have a more positive identity than early-maturing boys. Early-maturing girls are at risk for a number of developmental problems. Some scholars doubt that puberty's effects on development are as strong as once envisioned. Most early- and late-maturing adolescents weather the challenges of puberty successfully.

- For those who do not adapt well to pubertal changes, discussions with knowledgeable health-care providers and parents can improve the coping abilities of off-time adolescents.

2 **Describe the developmental changes in the brain during adolescence**

- Neurons are the basic units of the nervous system and are made up of a cell body, dendrites, and an axon. So far, researchers have found that greater increases in the axon (probably because of increased myelination) take place in adolescence than in the cell body or dendrites. Synaptogenesis in the prefrontal cortex, where reasoning and self-regulation occur, continues through adolescence.

- Using magnetic resonance imaging (MRI), scientists found in one study that between 3 and 15 years of age, rapid, distinct spurts of growth in the brain occur. In this study, from age 6 through puberty, the most growth took place in the temporal and parietal lobes, especially in areas that involve language and spatial relations. Other researchers have found that during adolescence, brain activity is more pronounced in the amygdala, which is involved in emotion, while in young adults, greater brain activity occurs in the frontal lobes, where higher reasoning takes place. Research on the development of the brain is in its infancy, and the next decade is likely to see an increasing number of studies as technology in investigating the brain advances.

- Experience plays an important role in development of the brain in childhood and adolescence. While early experiences are very important in the development of the brain, the brain retains considerable plasticity in adolescence. New brain cells may be generated during adolescence. The earlier brain injury occurs, the more successful recovery is likely to be.

3 **Characterize the health of adolescents**

- Adolescence is a critical juncture in the adoption of positive health behaviors. Many health-compromising behaviors, such as drug abuse and unprotected sexual intercourse, begin in the adolescent years.

- A lower basal metabolism in adolescence means adolescents have to burn up more calories to maintain a healthy weight. There is concern about the eating habits of adolescents and obesity.

- Many adolescents do not get adequate exercise. Television, parents, and schools are possible contributors to the low exercise levels of adolescents. There are both positive and negative aspects of adolescents' participation in organized sports.

- Adolescents like to go to bed later and sleep later than children do. This may be linked with developmental changes in the brain. A special concern is the extent to which these changes in sleep patterns in adolescence affect academic behavior.

- Adolescents use health services far less than any other age group. From 16 to 20 years of age, males are especially low users of health services. There are a number of barriers to providing better health services for adolescents.

- The leading causes of death in adolescence are (1) accidents, (2) homicide, and (3) suicide.

4 **Explain the contributions of evolution, heredity, and environment to adolescent development**

- Natural selection—the process that favors the individuals of a species that are best adapted to survive and reproduce—is a key aspect of the evolutionary perspective. Evolutionary psychology is the view that adaptation, reproduction, and "survival of the fittest" are important in explaining behavior. Evolutionary developmental psychology has promoted a number of ideas, including the view that an extended "juvenile" period is needed to develop a large brain and learn the complexity of human social communities. Critics argue that the evolutionary perspective does not give adequate attention to experience and humans as a culture-making species.

- The nucleus of each human cell contains 46 chromosomes, which are composed of DNA. Genes are short segments of DNA that direct cells to reproduce and manufacture proteins that maintain life. DNA does not act independently to produce a trait or behavior. Rather, it acts collaboratively. Genotype refers to the unique configuration of genes, while phenotype involves observed and measurable characteristics.

- Behavior genetics is the field concerned with the degree and nature of behavior's hereditary basis. Methods used by behavior geneticists include twin studies and adoption studies. In Scarr's heredity-environment correlations view, heredity directs the types of environments that children experience. She describes three genotype-environment correlations: passive, evocative, and active (niche-picking). Scarr be-

lieves that the relative importance of these three genotype-environment correlations changes as children develop. Shared environmental experiences refer to siblings' common experiences, such as their parents' personalities and intellectual orientation, the family's socioeconomic status, and the neighborhood in which they live. Nonshared environmental experiences involve the adolescent's unique experiences, both within a family and outside a family, that are not shared with a sibling. Many behavior geneticists argue that differences in the development of siblings are due to nonshared environmental experiences (and heredity) rather than shared environmental experiences. The epigenetic view emphasizes that development is the result of an ongoing, bidirectional interchange between heredity and environment.

- Many complex behaviors have some genetic loading that gives people a propensity for a particular developmental trajectory. However, actual development also requires an environment and that environment is complex. The interaction of heredity and environment is extensive. Much remains to be discovered about the specific ways that heredity and environment interact to influence development.

Key Terms

puberty 83	basal metabolism rate	behavior genetics 109	active (niche-picking)
hormones 83	(BMR) 99	twin study 109	genotype-environment
androgens 84	evolutionary psychology 105	adoption study 110	correlations 111
estrogens 84	chromosomes 107	passive genotype-environment	shared environmental
menarche 86	DNA 107	correlations 110	experiences 111
spermarche 86	genes 107	evocative genotype-	nonshared environmental
neurons 94	genotype 109	environment	experiences 111
	phenotype 109	correlations 110	epigenetic view 112

Key People

Roberta Simmons and	David Buss 105	Albert Bandura 106	Robert Plomin 111
Dale Blyth 92	Mihalyi Csikszentmihalyi and	David Moore 108	
Mary Carskadon 102	Jennifer Schmidt 106	Sandra Scarr 110	

Resources for Improving the Lives of Adolescents

Journal of Adolescent Health Care

This journal includes articles about a wide range of health-related and medical issues, including reducing smoking, improving nutrition, health promotion, and physicians' and nurses' roles in reducing health-compromising behaviors of adolescents.

The Society for Adolescent Medicine

10727 White Oak Avenue
Granada Hills, CA 91344

This organization is a valuable source of information about competent physicians who specialize in treating adolescents. It maintains a list of recommended adolescent specialists across the United States.

E-Learning Tools

To help you master the material in this chapter, you will find a number of valuable study tools in the student CD-ROM that accompanies this book. In addition, visit the Online Learning Center for *Adolescence, 10th Edition,* where you will find helpful resources for chapter 3, "Puberty, Health, and Biological Foundations."

Taking It to the Net

http://www.mhhe.com/santrocka10

1. The growth spurt is accompanied by weight increases. Those whose weight increases too much are at an increased risk for negative health outcomes, including obesity, hypertension, and other health risks. One's body mass index (BMI) is a measure of the "fit" of one's weight to one's height. Is your BMI in the "healthy" range or are you at risk for future health problems? How does your BMI relate to diet, exercise, and other measures of healthiness?

2. Your instructor assigns a brief paper in which you are, first, to define the term "body image," including positive and negative aspects of it and, second, to devise procedures to improve an adolescent's negative body image, focusing on male body image as opposed to the more commonly researched and discussed female body image. What procedures would you suggest to enhance a negative male body image?

3. A major health concern during the adolescent years centers on the adolescent's diet. Keep track of everything you eat and drink for the next three days. What is your daily caloric intake? Is it in the appropriate quantities recommended in the food pyramid? Are you eating healthfully?

Connect to **http://www.mhhe.com/santrocka10** to research the answers and complete these exercises. In some cases, you'll also find further instructions on this site.

Self-Assessment

To evaluate your genetic background, sleep patterns, and health, complete these self-assessments: (1) My Family Tree, (2) Do I Get Enough Sleep, (3) Is My Lifestyle Good for My Health?, and (4) My Health Habits.

Health and Well-Being, Parenting, and Education

To practice your decision-making skills, complete the health and well-being, parenting, and education scenarios.

CHAPTER 4

The thoughts of youth are long, long thoughts.
—HENRY WADSWORTH LONGFELLOW
American Poet, 19th Century

Cognitive Development

Learning Goals

1 Discuss the cognitive developmental view of adolescence

2 Describe the information-processing view of adolescence

3 Summarize the psychometric/intelligence view of adolescence

4 Explain how social cognition is involved in adolescent development

Images of Adolescent Development

The Developing Thoughts of Adolescents

One of my most vivid memories of my oldest daughter, Tracy, is from when she was 12 years of age. I had accompanied her and her younger sister, Jennifer (10 at the time), to a tennis tournament. As we walked into a restaurant to have lunch, Tracy bolted for the restroom. Jennifer and I looked at each other, wondering what was wrong. Five minutes later Tracy emerged, looking calmer. I asked what had happened. Her response: "This one hair was out of place and every person in here was looking at me!"

Consider another adolescent—Margaret. During a conversation with her girlfriend, 16-year-old Margaret says, "Did you hear about Catherine? She's pregnant. Do you think I would ever let that happen to me? Never."

Also think about 13-year-old Adam as he describes himself: "No one understands me, especially my parents. They have no idea of what I am feeling. They have never experienced the pain I'm going through."

Comments like Tracy's, Margaret's, and Adam's reflect the emergence of egocentric thought during adolescence. When we think about thinking, we usually consider it in terms of school subjects like math and English, or solving intellectual problems. But people's thoughts about social circumstances are also important. Later in the chapter we will further explore adolescents' social thoughts.

When we think about adolescence, we often focus on the biological changes of puberty or on socioemotional changes, such as the motivation for independence, relations with parents and peers, and problems such as drug abuse and delinquency. We will see in this chapter, however, that adolescents also undergo some impressive cognitive changes. To begin, we will study three different views of cognitive development: cognitive developmental, information processing, and psychometric. The chapter closes by examining social cognition, including the emergence of adolescent egocentrism.

1 THE COGNITIVE DEVELOPMENTAL VIEW

Piaget's Theory   **Vygotsky's Theory**

When you were a young adolescent, were your thinking skills as good as they are now? Could you solve difficult abstract problems and reason logically about complex topics? Or did those skills improve in your high school years? Can you describe any ways in which your thinking skills are better now than they were in high school?

In chapter 2, "The Science of Adolescent Development," we briefly examined Jean Piaget's theory of cognitive development. Piaget was intrigued by the changes in thinking that take place through childhood and adolescence. In this section, we will further explore his ideas about adolescent cognition, as well as the increasingly popular sociocultural cognitive theory of Lev Vygotsky.

Piaget's Theory

We begin our coverage of Piaget's theory by describing the main processes he believed are responsible for cognitive changes in development. Then we turn to his cognitive stages, giving special attention to concrete operational and formal operational thought.

Cognitive Processes   Piaget's theory is the best-known, most widely discussed theory of adolescent cognitive development. According to his theory, adolescents are motivated to understand their world because doing so is biologically adaptive. Adolescents actively construct their own cognitive worlds; information doesn't just pour into their minds from the environment. To make sense out of the world, adolescents organize their experiences, separating important ideas from less important ones and connecting one idea to another. They also adapt their thinking to include new ideas, because the additional information furthers their understanding.

In actively constructing their world, adolescents use schemas. A **schema** is a mental concept or framework that is useful in organizing and interpreting information. Piaget was especially interested in how children and adolescents use schemas to organize and make sense out of their current experiences.

He found that children and adolescents use and adapt their schemas through two processes: assimilation and accommodation (Piaget, 1952). **Assimilation** is the incorporation of new information into existing knowledge. In assimilation, the schema does not change. **Accommodation** is the adjustment of a schema to new information. In accommodation, the schema changes.

Suppose, for example, that a 16-year-old girl wants to learn how to use a computer. Her parents buy her a computer for her birthday. Although she has never had the opportunity to use one, from her experience and observation, she realizes that she needs to press a switch to turn the computer on and insert a CD-ROM into a slot. These behaviors fit into an existing conceptual framework (assimilation). But as she strikes several keys, she makes some errors. Soon she realizes that she needs help in

*W*e are born capable of learning.
—JEAN-JACQUES ROUSSEAU
Swiss-Born French Philosopher, 18th Century

schema A mental concept or framework that is useful in organizing and interpreting information.

assimilation The incorporation of new information into existing knowledge.

accommodation An adjustment to new information.

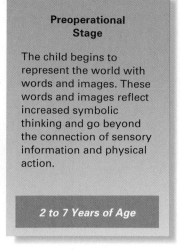

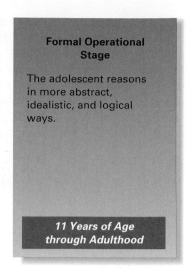

FIGURE 4.1 Piaget's Four Stages of Cognitive Development

equilibration A mechanism in Piaget's theory that explains how children or adolescents shift from one state of thought to the next. The shift occurs as they experience cognitive conflict or a disequilibrium in trying to understand the world. Eventually, the child or adolescent resolves the conflict and reaches a balance, or equilibrium.

sensorimotor stage Piaget's first stage of development, lasting from birth to about 2 years of age. In this stage, infants construct an understanding of the world by coordinating sensory experiences with physical, motoric actions.

preoperational stage Piaget's second stage, which lasts approximately from 2 to 7 years of age. In this stage, children begin to represent their world with words, images, and drawings.

concrete operational stage Piaget's third stage, which lasts approximately from 7 to 11 years of age. In this stage, children can perform operations. Logical reasoning replaces intuitive thought as long as the reasoning can be applied to specific or concrete examples.

learning how to use the computer either from a friend or from a teacher. This adjustment in her approach shows her awareness of the need to alter her conceptual framework (accommodation).

Equilibration, another process Piaget identified, is a shift in thought from one state to another. At times adolescents experience cognitive conflict or a sense of disequilibrium in their attempt to understand the world. Eventually they resolve the conflict and reach a balance, or equilibrium, of thought. Piaget believed that they move back and forth between states of cognitive equilibrium and disequilibrium. For example, if a child believes that the amount of a liquid increases when it is poured into a container of a different shape, she might wonder where the "extra" liquid came from or whether there really is more liquid in the second container. Eventually the child will resolve these puzzles as her thought becomes more advanced. In the everyday world, children constantly face such cognitive inconsistencies.

Stages of Cognitive Development Piaget theorized that individuals develop through four cognitive stages: sensorimotor, preoperational, concrete operational, and formal operational (see figure 4.1). Each of these age-related stages consists of distinct ways of thinking. This *different* way of understanding the world is what makes one stage more advanced than another; simply knowing more information does not make an adolescent's thinking more advanced. Thus, in Piaget's theory, a person's cognition is *qualitatively* different in one stage compared with another.

Sensorimotor and Preoperational Thought The **sensorimotor stage,** which lasts from birth to about 2 years of age, is the first Piagetian stage. In this stage, infants construct an understanding of the world by coordinating sensory experiences (such as seeing and hearing) with physical, motoric actions—hence the term sensorimotor. At the beginning of this stage, newborns have little more than reflexive patterns with which to work. By the end of the stage, 2-year-olds have complex sensorimotor patterns and are beginning to operate with primitive symbols.

The **preoperational stage,** which lasts approximately from 2 to 7 years of age, is the second Piagetian stage. In this stage, children begin to represent the world with words, images, and drawings. Symbolic thought goes beyond simple connections of information and action.

Concrete Operational Thought The **concrete operational stage,** which lasts approximately from 7 to 11 years of age, is the third Piagetian stage. Logical reasoning replaces intuitive thought as long as the reasoning can be applied to specific or

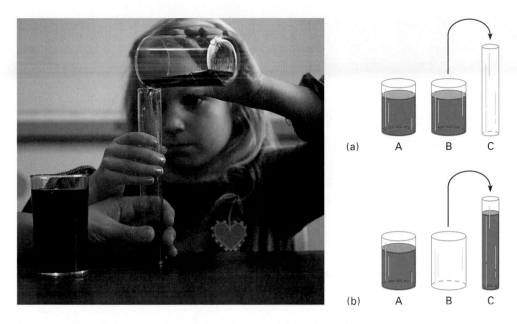

FIGURE 4.2 Piaget's Conservation Task
The beaker test is a well-known Piagetian test to determine whether the child can think operationally—that is, can mentally reverse actions and show conservation of the substance. (*a*) Two identical beakers are presented to the child. Then the experimenter pours the liquid from B into C, which is taller and thinner than A or B. (*b*) The child is now asked if these beakers (A and C) have the same amount of liquid. The preoperational child says no. When asked to point to the beaker that has more liquid, the preoperational child points to the tall, thin beaker.

concrete examples. According to Piaget, concrete operational thought involves *operations*—mental actions that allow an individual to do mentally what was done before physically.

In Piaget's most famous task, a child is presented with two identical beakers, each filled with the same amount of liquid (see figure 4.2). Children are asked if these beakers have the same amount of liquid, and they usually say yes. Then, the liquid from one beaker is poured into a third beaker, which is taller and thinner than the first two (see figure 4.2). Children are then asked if the amount of liquid in the tall, thin beaker is equal to that which remains in one of the original beakers. Concrete operational thinkers answer yes and justify their answers appropriately. Preoperational thinkers (usually children under the age of 7) often answer no and justify their answer in terms of the differing height and width of the beakers. This example reveals the ability of the concrete operational thinker to decenter and coordinate several characteristics (such as height and width), rather than focusing on a single property of an object (such as height). Concrete operational thinkers can also reverse operations mentally. For example, they can mentally reverse the transfer of liquid from one beaker to another and conclude that the volume is the same, even though the beakers differ in height and width.

Piaget used the term *conservation* to refer to an individual's ability to recognize that the length, number, mass, quantity, area, weight, and volume of objects and substances do not change through transformations that alter their appearance.

Another characteristic of concrete operational thought is *classification*, or class inclusion reasoning. Children who engage in classification can systematically organize objects into hierarchies of classes and subclasses.

Although concrete operational thought is more advanced than preoperational thought, it has its limitations. Logical reasoning replaces intuitive thought as long as the principles can be applied to specific, *concrete* examples. For example, the concrete operational child cannot imagine the steps necessary to complete an algebraic equation, an abstract statement with no connection to the concrete world. A summary of the characteristics of concrete operational thought is shown in figure 4.3.

Formal Operational Thought

The **formal operational stage** is Piaget's fourth and final stage of cognitive development. Piaget believed that this stage emerges at 11 to 15 years of age. Adolescents' developing power of thought opens up new cognitive and social horizons. What are the characteristics of formal operational thought, which

formal operational stage Piaget's fourth and final stage of cognitive development, which he believed emerges at 11 to 15 years of age. It is characterized by abstract, idealistic, and logical thought.

Can use operations, mentally reversing action; shows conservation skills

Logical reasoning replaces intuitive reasoning, but only in concrete circumstances

Not abstract (can't imagine steps in algebraic equation, for example)

Classification skills—can divide things into sets and subsets and reason about their interrelations

FIGURE 4.3 Characteristics of Concrete Operational Thought

"and give me good abstract-reasoning ability, interpersonal skills, cultural perspective, linguistic comprehension, and a high sociodynamic potential."

hypothetical-deductive reasoning Piaget's term for adolescents' ability, in the formal operational stage, to develop hypotheses, or best guesses, about ways to solve problems; they then systematically deduce, or conclude, the best path to follow in solving the problem.

Piaget believed develops in adolescence? Most significantly, formal operational thought is more abstract than concrete operational thought. Adolescents are no longer limited to actual, concrete experiences as anchors for thought. They can conjure up make-believe situations—events that are purely hypothetical possibilities or strictly abstract propositions—and try to reason logically about them.

The abstract quality of the adolescent's thought at the formal operational level is evident in the adolescent's verbal problem-solving ability. While the concrete operational thinker would need to see the concrete elements A, B, and C to be able to make the logical inference that if A = B and B = C, then A = C, the formal operational thinker can solve this problem merely through verbal representation.

Another indication of the abstract quality of adolescents' thought is their increased tendency to think about thought itself. As one adolescent commented, "I began thinking about why I was thinking what I was. Then I began thinking about why I was thinking about why I was thinking about what I was." If this statement sounds abstract, it is, and it characterizes the adolescent's enhanced focus on thought and its abstract qualities. Later in this chapter we will return to the topic of thinking about thinking, which is called *metacognition*.

Besides being abstract, formal operational thought is full of idealism and possibilities. While children frequently think in concrete ways about what is real and limited, adolescents begin to engage in extended speculation about ideal characteristics—qualities they desire in themselves and others. Such thoughts often lead adolescents to compare themselves and others in regard to such ideal standards. And during adolescence, the thoughts of individuals are often fantasy flights into future possibilities. It is not unusual for the adolescent to become impatient with these newfound ideal standards and perplexed over which of many ideals to adopt.

At the same time adolescents think more abstractly and idealistically, they also think more logically. Adolescents begin to reason more as a scientist does, devising ways to solve problems and test solutions systematically. Piaget gave this type of problem solving an imposing name, **hypothetical-deductive reasoning,** which means the ability to develop hypotheses, or best guesses, about how to solve problems, such as algebraic equations. Having developed a hypothesis, the formal operational thinker then systematically deduces, or concludes, the best path to follow in solving the problem. In contrast, children are more likely to solve problems by trial and error.

Might adolescents' ability to reason hypothetically and to evaluate what is ideal versus what is real lead them to engage in demonstrations, such as this protest related to better ethnic relations? What other causes might be attractive to adolescents' newfound cognitive abilities of hypothetical-deductive reasoning and idealistic thinking?

One example of hypothetical-deductive reasoning involves a version of the familiar game "Twenty Questions." Individuals are shown a set of 42 color pictures displayed in a rectangular array of six rows of seven pictures each. They are asked to determine which picture the experimenter has in mind (that is, which is "correct") by asking questions to which the experimenter can answer only yes or no. The object of the game is to select the correct picture by asking as few questions as possible.

Adolescents who are deductive hypothesis testers will formulate a plan and test a series of hypotheses that considerably narrows the field of choices. The most effective plan is a "halving" strategy (Question: Is the picture in the right half of the array? Answer: No. Question: OK. Is it in the top half? And so on). An efficient halving strategy guarantees the answer to this problem in seven questions or less. In contrast, the concrete operational thinker might persist with questions that continue to test some of the same possibilities that previous questions could have eliminated. For example, after asking whether the correct picture is in row 1 and being told that it is not, the concrete operational thinker might later ask whether the picture is x, which is in row 1.

Thus, formal operational thinkers test their hypotheses with judiciously chosen questions and tests. Concrete operational thinkers, on the other hand, often fail to understand the relation between a hypothesis and a well-chosen test of it, stubbornly clinging to ideas that already have been discounted.

Piaget believed that formal operational thought is the best description of how adolescents think. A summary of formal operational thought's characteristics is shown in figure 4.4. Formal operational thought is not a homogeneous stage of development, however. Not all adolescents are full-fledged formal operational thinkers. Instead, some developmentalists believe that formal operational thought consists of two subperiods (Broughton, 1983):

- *Early Formal Operational Thought.* Adolescents' newfound ability to think in hypothetical ways produces unconstrained thoughts with unlimited possibilities. In this early period, flights of fantasy may submerge reality and the world is perceived too subjectively and idealistically. Assimilation is the dominant process in this subperiod.
- *Late Formal Operational Thought.* As adolescents test their reasoning against experience, intellectual balance is restored. Through accommodation, adolescents begin to adjust to the upheaval they have experienced. Late formal thought may appear in the middle adolescent years.

www.mhhe.com/santrocka10

Piaget's Theory

Abstract	Idealistic	Logical
Adolescents think more abstractly than children. Formal operational thinkers can solve abstract algebraic equations, for example.	Adolescents often think about what is possible. They think about ideal characteristics of themselves, others, and the world.	Adolescents begin to think more like scientists, devising plans to solve problems and systematically testing solutions. Piaget called this type of logical thinking hypothetical-deductive reasoning.

FIGURE 4.4 Characteristics of Formal Operational Thought
Adolescents begin to think more as scientists think, devising plans to solve problems and systematically testing solutions. Piaget gave this type of thinking the imposing name of hypothetical-deductive reasoning.

In any consideration of adolescent cognition it is important to recognize the wide variation in performance among them.
—DANIEL KEATING,
University of Toronto

In this view, assimilation characterizes early formal operational thought; accommodation characterizes late formal operational thought (Lapsley, 1990).

In his early writings, Piaget (1952) indicated that both the onset and consolidation of formal operational thought are completed during early adolescence, from about 11 to 15 years of age. Later, Piaget (1972) revised his view and concluded that formal operational thought is not completely achieved until later in adolescence, between approximately 15 and 20 years of age.

Still, his theory does not adequately account for the individual differences that characterize the cognitive development of adolescents, which have been documented in a number of investigations (Neimark, 1982; Overton & Byrnes 1991). Some young adolescents are formal operational thinkers; others are not. For instance, a review of formal operational thought investigations revealed that only about one out of every three eighth-grade students is a formal operational thinker (Strahan, 1983). Some investigators found that formal operational thought increased with age in adolescence; others did not. In fact, many college students and adults do not think in formal operational ways either. Investigators have found that from 17 to 67 percent of college students think on the formal operational level (Elkind, 1961; Tomlinson-Keasey, 1972).

At the same time that many young adolescents are just beginning to think in a formal operational manner, others are at the point of consolidating their concrete operational thought, using it more consistently than they did in childhood. By late adolescence, many youths are beginning to consolidate their formal operational thought, using it more consistently. And there often is variation across the content areas of formal operational thought, just as there is in concrete operational thought in childhood. A 14-year-old adolescent might reason at the formal operational level when analyzing algebraic equations but not do so with verbal problem solving or when reasoning about interpersonal relations.

Adolescents are more likely to use formal operational thought in areas in which adolescents have the most experience and knowledge. Children and adolescents gradually build up elaborate knowledge through extensive experience and practice in various sports, games, hobbies, and school subjects, such as math, English, and science. The development of expertise in different domains may make possible high-level, developmentally mature-looking thought. In some instances, the sophisticated reasoning of formal operational thought might be responsible. In other instances, however, the thought might be largely due to the accumulation of knowledge that allows more automatic, memory-based processes to function. Some developmentalists wonder if the acquisition of knowledge could account for all cognitive growth. Most, however, argue that both cognitive changes in such areas as concrete and formal operational thought and the development of expertise through experience are at work in understanding the adolescent's cognitive world.

Educational Implications of Piaget's Theory   Piaget's theory has been widely applied to education, more extensively with children than with adolescents. Piaget was not an educator and never pretended to be, but he did provide a sound conceptual framework from which to view educational problems (Elkind, 1976).

In Piaget's theory, the adolescent's mind is not a blank slate. Adolescents come to school with their own ideas about space, time, causality, quantity, and number. Educators need to comprehend what adolescents are saying and respond to their ideas. Second, adolescents are by nature knowing beings. The best way to nurture their motivation to learn is to allow them to interact with the environment in a spontaneous way. Educators need to ensure that they do not dull adolescents' eagerness to know by providing an overly rigid curriculum that disrupts adolescents' rhythm and pace of learning.

Why have applications of Piaget's theory to adolescent education lagged behind its applications to children's education? One reason is that adolescents who are formal operational thinkers are at a level similar to that of their teachers and their textbook authors. Thus, it is no longer necessary to pay attention to qualitative changes in their cognition. The structure of education also changes considerably between the elementary and secondary levels. For children, the basic focus of education is the classroom where they might be involved at most with several teachers during the day. For adolescents, the focus shifts to subject-matter divisions in the curriculum. Students see each teacher for 45 to 60 minutes a day in connection with a single content area—English, history, math. Thus, both teachers and texts tend to be more focused on the development of curriculum than on students' developmental characteristics. When secondary school teachers become concerned about their students' development, they pay more attention to social-personality dimensions than to cognitive dimensions.

One implication that has emerged from the educational application of Piaget's theory is that the instruction of adolescents may too often be at the formal operational level, even though the majority of adolescents are not full-fledged formal operational thinkers. That is, instruction might be too formal and too abstract from a developmental point of view. Researchers have found that adolescents construct a view of the world based on their observations and experiences. The implication is that educators should take this into account when developing a curriculum for adolescents (Linn, 1991).

Evaluating Piaget's Theory   What were Piaget's main contributions? Has his theory withstood the test of time? In this section, we examine both Piaget's contributions and criticisms of his work.

Piaget, shown sitting on a bench, was a genius at observing children. By carefully observing and interviewing children, Piaget constructed his comprehensive theory of children's cognitive development. *What are some other contributions, as well as criticisms, of Piaget's theory?*

Contributions Piaget has been a giant in the field of developmental psychology. We owe to him the present field of cognitive development as well as a long list of masterful concepts of enduring power and fascination: assimilation, accommodation, conservation, and hypothetical-deductive reasoning, among others. We also owe to Piaget the current vision of children as active, constructive thinkers (Vidal, 2000).

Piaget was a genius when it came to observing children. His careful observations documented inventive new ways to discover how children act on and adapt to their world. Piaget showed us some important things to look for in cognitive development, such as the shift from pre-operational to concrete operational thinking. He also pointed out that children need to make their experiences fit their schemas, or cognitive frameworks, yet can simultaneously adapt their schemas to experience. He also revealed that cognitive change is likely to occur if the context is structured to allow gradual movement to the next-higher level. We owe to Piaget the current belief that a concept does not emerge all of a sudden, full blown, but develops instead through a series of partial accomplishments that lead to an increasingly comprehensive understanding (Haith & Benson, 1998).

Criticisms Piaget's theory has not gone unchallenged (Keating, 2004). Questions are raised about the timing of development, the four stages he identified, the usefulness of training in reasoning, and the effects of culture on cognitive development areas. Let's consider each of these criticisms in turn.

In terms of timing, some cognitive abilities have been found to emerge earlier than Piaget had thought. For example, some aspects of object permanence emerge earlier in infancy than he believed. Even 2-year-olds are nonegocentric in some contexts. When they realize that another person cannot see an object, they investigate whether the person is blindfolded or looking in a different direction. Similarly, conservation of number has been demonstrated as early as age 3; Piaget thought it did not emerge until 7. The fact is, young children are not as uniformly preoperational as Piaget thought. Other cognitive abilities can emerge later than Piaget indicated. Many adolescents still think in concrete operational ways or are just beginning to master formal operations. Even as adults, many individuals are not formal operational thinkers. In sum, recent theoretical revisions highlight the cognitive competencies of infants and young children and the cognitive shortcomings of adolescents and adults (Flavell, Miller, & Miller, 2002; Wertsch, 2000).

Another criticism of Piaget's theory concerns the stages he identified. Piaget conceived of stages as unitary levels of thought. Thus, his theory assumes developmental synchrony: various aspects of a developmental stage should emerge at the same time. However, some concrete operational concepts do not appear in synchrony. For example, children do not learn to conserve at the same time they learn to cross-classify. Thus, most contemporary developmentalists agree that children's cognitive development is not as stagelike as Piaget thought (Brainerd, 2002; Kuhn, 2000).

Another topic of controversy has been the usefulness of training children to reason at a higher level. Some children who are in one cognitive stage (such as preoperational) can be trained to reason at a higher cognitive stage (such as concrete operational). This fact poses a problem for Piaget's theory. Piaget saw such training as only superficial and ineffective, unless the child is at a transition point between stages (Gelman & Williams, 1998).

Finally, culture exerts stronger influence on development than Piaget envisioned. For example, the age at which individuals acquire conservation skills is associated to some extent with the degree to which their culture provides relevant educational practice (Cole, 1997). In many developing countries, educational opportunities are limited and formal operational thought is rare. You will read shortly about Lev Vygotsky's theory of cognitive development in which culture is given a more prominent role than in Piaget's theory.

One group of cognitive developmentalists believe that Piaget's theory needs to be modified. These **neo-Piagetians** place more emphasis on how children use attention, memory, and cognitive strategies to process information, and on more precise explanations of cognitive changes. They especially believe that a more accurate vision of children's and adolescents' thinking requires more knowledge of the strategies they use, how fast and automatically they process information, the particular cognitive tasks involved in processing information, and the division of cognitive problems into smaller, more precise steps.

The leading proponent of the neo-Piagetian view has been Canadian developmental psychologist Robbie Case (1992, 1998, 2000). Case accepts Piaget's four stages of cognitive development but believes that a more precise description of changes within each stage is needed. He believes that children's and adolescents' growing ability to process information efficiently is linked to their brain growth and memory development. In particular, Case cites the increasing ability to hold information in working memory (a workbench for memory similar to short-term memory) and manipulate it more effectively as critical to understanding cognitive development.

Cognitive Changes in Adulthood   As we indicated earlier, according to Piaget, adults and adolescents use the same type of reasoning. Adolescents and adults think in *qualitatively* the same way. Piaget did acknowledge that adults can be *quantitatively* more advanced in their knowledge. What are some ways that adults might be more advanced in their thinking than adolescents?

Realistic and Pragmatic Thinking   Some developmentalists have proposed that as young adults move into the world of work, their way of thinking does change. One idea is that as they face the constraints of reality, which work promotes, their idealism decreases (Labouvie-Vief, 1986).

A related change in thinking was proposed by K. Warner Schaie (1977). He concluded that it is unlikely that adults go beyond the powerful methods of scientific thinking characteristic of the formal operational stage. However, Schaie argued that adults do progress beyond adolescents in their use of intellect. For example, in early adulthood individuals often switch from acquiring knowledge to applying knowledge as they pursue success in their work.

Reflective and Relativistic Thinking   William Perry (1970) also described changes in cognition that take place in early adulthood. He said that adolescents often view the world in terms of polarities—right/wrong, we/they, or good/bad. As youth age into adulthood, they gradually move away from this type of absolutist thinking as they become aware of the diverse opinions and multiple perspectives of others. Thus, in Perry's view, the absolutist, dualistic thinking of adolescence gives way to the reflective, relativistic thinking of adulthood. Other developmentalists also believe that reflective thinking is an important indicator of cognitive change in young adults (Fischer & Pruyne, 2003).

Is There a Fifth, Postformal Stage?   Some theorists have pieced together these descriptions of adult thinking and proposed that young adults move into a new qualitative stage of cognitive development, postformal thought (Sinnott, 2003). **Postformal thought** is

- *Reflective, relativistic, and contextual.* As young adults engage in solving problems, they might think deeply about many aspects of work, politics, relationships, and other areas of life (Labouvie-Vief, 1996). They find that what might be the best

neo-Piagetians Theorists who argue that Piaget got some things right but that his theory needs considerable revision. In their revision, they give more emphasis to information processing that involves attention, memory, and strategies; they also seek to provide more precise explanations of cognitive changes.

postformal thought Thought that is reflective, relativistic, and provisional; realistic; and open to emotions and subjective.

Upper limit

Level of additional responsibility child or adolescent can accept with assistance of an able instructor

Zone of proximal development (ZPD)

Lower limit

Tasks too difficult for child or adolescent to master alone; level of problem solving reached on these tasks by child or adolescent working alone

FIGURE 4.5 Vygotsky's Zone of Proximal Development (ZPD)

Vygotsky's zone of proximal development has a lower limit and an upper limit. Tasks in the ZPD are too difficult for the child or adolescent to perform alone. They require assistance from an adult or a more-skilled youth. As children and adolescents experience the verbal instruction or demonstration, they organize the information in their existing mental structures so they can eventually perform the skill or task alone.

zone of proximal development (ZPD)

Vygotsky's concept that refers to the range of tasks that are too difficult for an individual to master alone, but that can be mastered with the guidance or assistance of adults or more-skilled peers.

solution to a problem at work (with a boss or co-worker) might not be the best solution at home (with a romantic partner). Thus, postformal thought holds that the correct answer to a problem requires reflective thinking and may vary from one situation to another.

- *Provisional.* Many young adults also become more skeptical about the truth and unwilling to accept an answer as final. Thus, they come to see the search for truth as an ongoing and perhaps never-ending process.
- *Realistic.* Young adults understand that thinking can't always be abstract. In many instances it must be realistic and pragmatic.
- *Open to emotions and subjective.* Many young adults accept that emotion and subjective factors can influence thinking (Kitchener & King, 1981; Kramer, Kahlbaugh, & Goldston, 1992). For example, as young adults, they understand that a person thinks more clearly in a calm rather than an angry state.

How strong is the evidence for a fifth, postformal stage of cognitive development? Researchers have found that young adults are more likely to engage in this postformal thinking than adolescents are (Commons & Richards, 2003; Commons & others, 1989). But critics argue that research has yet to document that postformal thought is a qualitatively more advanced stage than formal operational thought.

Vygotsky's Theory

Lev Vygotsky's (1962) theory was introduced in chapter 2, "The Science of Adolescent Development." This theory has stimulated considerable interest in the view that knowledge is *situated* and *collaborative* (Greeno, Collins, & Resnick, 1996; John-Steiner & Mahn, 2003; Pontecorvo, 2004; Rogoff, 1998, 2003). That is, knowledge is distributed among people and their environments, which include objects, artifacts, tools, books, and the communities in which people live. This distribution suggests that knowing can best be advanced through interaction with others in cooperative activities (Glassman, 2001; Kozulin, 2000; Tudge & Scrimsher, 2002).

One of Vygotsky's most important concepts is the **zone of proximal development (ZPD),** which refers to the range of tasks that are too difficult for an individual to master alone, but that can be mastered with the guidance and assistance of adults or more-skilled peers. Thus, the lower level of the ZPD is the level of problem solving reached by an adolescent working independently. The upper limit is the level of thinking the adolescent can accept with the assistance of an able instructor (see figure 4.5). Vygotsky's emphasis on the ZPD underscored his belief in the importance of social influences on cognitive development.

In Vygotsky's approach, formal schooling is but one of the cultural agents that determines an adolescent's growth (Keating, 1990; Rowe & Wertsch, 2002; Tudge & Scrimsher, 2003). Parents, peers, the community, and the culture's technological orientation of the culture also influence adolescents' thinking. For example, parents' and peers' attitudes toward intellectual competence affect their motivation to acquire knowledge. So do the attitudes of teachers and other adults in the community. Today, media influences, especially television and the computer, play an increasingly important role in the cognitive socialization of adolescents. Some critics charge that television trains adolescents to become passive learners, detracting from their intellectual pursuits. We will consider television's role in adolescent development in chapter 13, "Culture."

Another implication of Vygotsky's theory is that cognitive development can be encouraged through stimulating environments and attention to the role of social factors in cognitive growth (Brown, Metz, & Campione, 1996; Perret-Clermont & others, 2004; Tudge, 2004). Approaches that take into account adolescents' self-confidence, expectations for achievement, and sense of purpose are likely to be just as effective as, or even more effective than, narrower approaches to shaping adolescents' cognitive growth. A knowledge of physics, for example, could be of limited use to an inner-city youth whose prospects of employment are severely limited (Keating, 1990).

www.mhhe.com/santrocka10

Vygotsky Links

Exploring Some Contemporary Concepts   A number of contemporary concepts are compatible with Vygotsky's theory. They include the concepts of scaffolding, cognitive apprenticeship, tutoring, cooperative learning, and reciprocal teaching.

Scaffolding   *Scaffolding* is changing the level of support over the course of a teaching session: a more-skilled person (teacher or more-advanced peer of the adolescent) adjusts the amount of guidance to fit the adolescent's current level of performance. When the task the adolescent is learning is new, direct instruction might be used. As the adolescent's competence increases, less guidance is provided. Think of scaffolding in learning as like the scaffolding used to build a bridge—it is used for support when needed but is adjusted or removed as the project unfolds.

Cognitive Apprenticeship   Barbara Rogoff (1990, 1998, 2003) believes that an important aspect of learning is *cognitive apprenticeship*, in which an expert stretches and supports the novice's understanding of and use of the culture's skills. The term *apprenticeship* underscores the importance of activity in learning and highlights the situated nature of learning. In a cognitive apprenticeship, adults often model strategies for adolescents, then support their efforts at doing the task. Finally, they encourage adolescents to work independently.

A key aspect of a cognitive apprenticeship is the expert's evaluation of when the learner is ready to take the next step with support from the expert. In one study of secondary school science and math students, experts used the timing of the students' participation in discourse to infer student understanding of the points of the lesson; the experts provided pauses to allow students to take responsibility for an idea by anticipating or completing the experts' ideas (Fox, 1993). Experts also used information regarding the length of each response opportunity students passed up and what the students were doing during the passed-up opportunity (such as calculating or

What is a cognitive apprenticeship? When teachers think of their relationship with students as a cognitive apprenticeship, how is teaching likely to proceed?

expressing a blank stare). When students passed up two or three opportunities, experts continued with an explanation. If no evidence of understanding occurred during the explanation, the expert repeated or reformulated it. The experts also used "hint" questions to get students unstuck and observed the looks on their faces and how they responded to questions for discerning their understanding.

Tutoring   *Tutoring* involves a cognitive apprenticeship between an expert and a novice. Tutoring can take place between an adult and an adolescent or between a more-skilled adolescent and a less-skilled adolescent. Fellow students can be effective tutors. Cross-age tutoring usually works better than same-age tutoring. Researchers have found that peer tutoring often benefits students' achievement (Mathes & others, 1998). And tutoring can benefit the tutor as well as the tutee, especially when the older tutor is a low-achieving student. Teaching something to someone else is one of the best ways to learn.

Cooperative Learning   *Cooperative learning* involves students working in small groups to help each other learn. Cooperative learning groups vary in size, although a typical group will have about four students. Researchers have found that cooperative learning can be an effective strategy for improving achievement, especially when these two conditions are met (Slavin, 1995): (1) group rewards are generated (these help group members see that it is in their best interest to help each other learn), and (2) individuals are held accountable (that is, some method of evaluating an individual's contribution, such as an individual quiz, is used). Cooperative learning helps promote interdependence and connection with other students (Slavin, Hurley, & Chamberlin, 2003). In chapter 11, "Schools," we will further examine the concept of cooperative learning.

Scaffolding
Peer Tutoring
Cooperative Learning
Schools for Thought

Reciprocal Teaching   *Reciprocal teaching* involves students taking turns leading a small-group discussion. Reciprocal teaching also can involve an adult and an adolescent. As in scaffolding, the teacher gradually assumes a less active role, letting the student assume more initiative. This technique has been widely used to help students learn to read more effectively. For example, Ann Brown and Annemarie Palincsar (1984) used reciprocal teaching to improve students' abilities to enact certain strategies to improve their reading comprehension. In this teacher-scaffolded instruction, teachers worked with students to help them *generate questions* about the text they had read, *clarify* what they did not understand, *summarize* the text, and *make predictions*.

Ann Brown's most recent efforts focused on transforming schools into communities of thinking and learning. Her ideas have much in common with Vygotsky's emphasis on learning as a collaborative process.

Evaluating Vygotsky's Theory   Even though their theories were proposed at about the same time, most of the world learned about Vygotsky's theory later than they learned about Piaget's theory, so Vygotsky's theory has not yet been evaluated as thoroughly. Vygotsky's view of the importance of sociocultural influences on children's development fits with the current belief that it is important to evaluate the contextual factors in learning (Kozulin, 2000).

Although both theories are constructivist, Vygotsky's is a **social constructivist approach,** which emphasizes the social contexts of learning and the construction of knowledge through social interaction. In moving from Piaget to Vygotsky, the conceptual shift is from the individual to collaboration, social interaction, and sociocultural activity (Rogoff, 1998, 2003). The endpoint of cognitive development for Piaget is formal operational thought. For Vygotsky, the endpoint can differ depending on which skills are considered to be the most important in a particular culture. For Piaget, children construct knowledge by transforming, organizing, and reorganizing previous knowledge. For Vygotsky, children construct knowledge through social interaction

social constructivist approach Emphasizes the social contexts of learning and the construction of knowledge through social interaction.

	Vygotsky	Piaget
Sociocultural Context	Strong Emphasis	Little Emphasis
Constructivism	Social constructivist	Cognitive constructivist
Stages	No general stages of development proposed	Strong emphasis on stages (sensorimotor, preoperational, concrete operational, and formal operational)
Key Processes	Zone of proximal development, language, dialogue, tools of the culture	Schema, assimilation, accommodation, operations, conservation, classification, hypothetical-deductive reasoning
Role of Language	A major role; language plays a powerful role in shaping thought	Language has a minimal role; cognition primarily directs language
View on Education	Education plays a central role, helping children learn the tools of the culture.	Education merely refines the child's cognitive skills that have already emerged.
Teaching Implications	Teacher is a facilitator and guide, not a director; establish many opportunities for children to learn with the teacher and more skilled peers	Also views teacher as a facilitator and guide, not a director; provide support for children to explore their world and discover knowledge

FIGURE 4.6 **Comparison of Vygotsky's and Piaget's Theories**

(Hogan & Tudge, 1999; Tudge, 2004). The implication of Piaget's theory for teaching is that children need support to explore their world and discover knowledge. The main implication of Vygotsky's theory for teaching is that students need many opportunities to learn with the teacher and more-skilled peers (Scrimsher & Tudge, 2003). In both Piaget's and Vygotsky's theories, teachers serve as facilitators and guides, rather than as directors and molders of learning. Figure 4.6 compares Vygotsky's and Piaget's theories.

Criticisms of Vygotsky's theory also have surfaced. Some critics say his emphasis on collaboration and guidance has potential pitfalls. Might facilitators be too helpful in some cases, as when a parent becomes too overbearing and controlling? Further, some adolescents might become lazy and expect help when they might have done something on their own.

Review and reflect   Learning goal 1

1   Describe the cognitive developmental view of adolescence

REVIEW

- What is Piaget's view of adolescence?
- What is Vygotsky's view of adolescence?

REFLECT

- Suppose an 8-year-old and a 16-year-old are watching a political convention on television. In terms of Piaget's stages of cognitive development, how would their perceptions of the proceedings be likely to differ? What would the 8-year-old "see" and comprehend? What would the 16-year-old "see" and comprehend? What Piagetian concepts would these differences in cognition reflect?

Characteristics of the Information-Processing View		Decision Making		Creative Thinking

| | Attention and Memory | | Critical Thinking | | Metacognition and Self-Regulatory Learning |

Chapter 2, "The Science of Adolescent Development," briefly described the information-processing view. We saw that information processing includes how information gets into adolescents' minds, how it is stored, and how adolescents retrieve information to think about and solve problems.

Information processing is both a framework for thinking about adolescent development and a facet of that development. As a framework, the information-processing view includes certain ideas about how adolescents' minds work and how best to study those workings (Logan, 2000). As a facet of development, information processing changes as children make the transition from adolescence to adulthood. Changes in attention and memory, for example, are essentially changes in the way individuals process information (Mayer, 2003). In our exploration of information processing, we will discuss developmental changes in attention and memory, as well as other cognitive processes, but first let's examine some basic characteristics of the information-processing view.

Characteristics of the Information-Processing View

Robert Siegler (1998) described three main characteristics of the information-processing view. The first is an emphasis on thinking as information processing. When adolescents perceive, encode, represent, and store information from the world, Siegler says, they are engaging in thinking. Siegler believes that thinking is highly flexible, allowing individuals to adapt and adjust to many changes in their circumstances, task requirements, and goals. However, the human's remarkable thinking abilities do have some limitations. Individuals can attend to only a limited amount of information at one point in time, and they are constrained by how fast they can process it.

The second characteristic of the information-processing view is an emphasis on mechanisms of change. In this regard, Siegler believes that four mechanisms—encoding, automaticity, strategy construction, and generalization—work together to create changes in children's and adolescents' cognitive skills.

Encoding is the process by which information gets into memory. A key to solving problems is encoding relevant information and ignoring what is irrelevant.

Automaticity refers to the ability to process information with little or no effort. With age and experience, information processing becomes increasingly automatic, allowing children and adolescents to detect connections among ideas and events that they otherwise would miss. An able 12-year-old zips through a list of multiplication problems with little conscious effort; a 16-year-old picks up the newspaper and quickly scans the entertainment section to learn the location and time of a movie. In both cases, information processing is more automatic and less effortful than it is for children.

Earlier in this chapter we described Robbie Case's neo-Piagetian view. Case's view emphasizes changes in the way adolescents process information differently than children,

Through the Eyes of Adolescents

We Think More Than Adults Think We Do

"I don't think adults understand how much kids think today. We just don't take something at face value. We want to understand why things are the way they are and the reasons behind things. We want it to be a better world and we are thinking all of the time how to make it that way. When we get to be adults, we will make the world better."

—*Jason, Age 15*
Dallas, Texas

including automaticity. In Case's (1992, 1998, 2000) view, adolescents have more cognitive resources available to them because of automaticity, increased information-processing capacity, and greater familiarity with a range of content knowledge. These advances in information processing reduce the load on the cognitive system, allowing the adolescent to hold in mind several dimensions of a topic or problem simultaneously. In contrast, children are more prone to focus on only one dimension of a topic.

Let's examine the third and fourth change mechanisms proposed by Siegler: strategy construction and generalization. *Strategy construction* is the discovery of a new procedure for processing information. Siegler says to solve a problem, adolescents need to encode key information about it and then find a way to coordinate that information with relevant prior knowledge. To fully benefit from a newly constructed strategy, adolescents then need to *generalize* it, or apply it to other problems.

The third characteristic of the information-processing view is an emphasis on *self-modification*. Advocates of the contemporary version of the information-processing view argue, as does Piaget's theory, that adolescents play an active role in their development. They use the knowledge and strategies they have learned to adapt their responses to new learning situations. In this manner, adolescents construct more sophisticated responses from prior knowledge and strategies.

www.mhhe.com/santrocka10

Strategies

Attention and Memory

Although the bulk of research on information processing has been conducted with children and adults, the information-processing view is still important in understanding adolescent cognition. Especially important in this view are the processes of attention and memory.

Attention   *Pay attention* is a phrase children and adolescents hear all the time. Just what is *attention*? *Attention* is the concentration and focusing of mental effort. Attention is both selective and shifting. For example, when adolescents take a test, they must be able to focus their mental effort on certain stimuli (the test questions) while excluding other stimuli. This important aspect of attention is called *selectivity*. When

What changes in attention characterize adolescence?

selective attention fails adolescents, they have difficulty ignoring irrelevant information. For example, if a television set is blaring while an adolescent is studying, the adolescent might have difficulty concentrating.

Not only is attention selective; it is also *shiftable*. If a teacher asks students to pay attention to a certain question and they do so, their behavior indicates that they can shift the focus of their mental effort from one stimulus to another. If the telephone rings while the adolescent is studying, the adolescent may shift attention from studying to the telephone. An external stimulus is not necessary to cause a shift in attention, however. At any moment, adolescents can shift their attention from one topic to another, virtually at will. They might think about the last time they went to a play, then shift their thoughts to an upcoming musical recital, and so on.

In one investigation, 12-year-olds were markedly better than 8-year-olds, and slightly worse than 20-year-olds, at allocating their attention between two tasks (Manis, Keating, & Morrison, 1980). Adolescents may have more resources available to them than children (through increased processing speed, capacity, and automaticity), or they may be more skilled at directing the resources.

Memory Links

Memory   There are few moments when adolescents' lives are not steeped in memory. Memory is at work with each step adolescents take, each thought they think, and each word they utter. *Memory* is the retention of information over time. It is central to mental life and to information processing. To successfully learn and reason, adolescents need to hold onto information and retrieve it when necessary. Three important memory systems, short-term memory, working memory, and long-term memory, are involved in adolescents' learning.

Short-Term Memory   *Short-term memory* is a limited-capacity memory system in which information is retained for as long as 30 seconds, unless the information is rehearsed, in which case it can be retained longer. A common way to assess short-term memory is to present a list of items to remember, which is often referred to as a memory span task. If you have taken an IQ test, you probably were asked to remember a string of numbers or words. You simply hear a short list of stimuli—usually digits—presented at a rapid pace (one per second, for example). Then you are asked to repeat the digits back. Using the memory span task, researchers have found that short-term memory increases extensively in early childhood and continues to increase in older children and adolescents, but at a slower pace. For example, in one investigation, memory span increased by 1½ digits between the ages of 7 and 13 (Dempster, 1981) (see figure 4.7). Keep in mind, though, memory span's individual differences, which is why IQ and various aptitude tests are used.

How might short-term memory be used in problem solving? In a series of experiments, Robert Sternberg and his colleagues (Sternberg, 1977; Sternberg & Nigro, 1980; Sternberg & Rifkin, 1979) attempted to answer this question by giving third-grade, sixth-grade, ninth-grade, and college students analogies to solve. The main differences occurred between the younger (third- and sixth-grade) and older (ninth-grade and college) students. The older students were more likely to complete the information processing required to solve the analogy task. The children, by contrast, often stopped their processing of information before they had considered all of the necessary steps required to solve the problems. Sternberg believes that information processing was incomplete because the children's short-term memory was overloaded. Solving problems such as analogies requires individuals to make continued comparisons between newly encoded information and previously coded information. Sternberg argues that adolescents probably have more storage space in short-term memory, which results in fewer errors on problems like analogies.

In addition to more storage space, are there other reasons adolescents might perform better on memory span tasks and in solving analogies? Though many other factors could be involved, information-processing

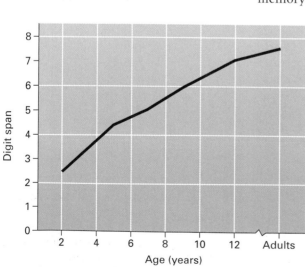

FIGURE 4.7 Developmental Changes in Memory Span

In one study, memory span increased about 3 digits from 2 years of age to 5 digits at 7 years of age (Dempster, 1981). By 12 years of age, memory span had increased on average another 1½ digits.

psychologists believe that changes in the speed and efficiency of information processing are important—especially the speed with which information is identified.

Working Memory Short-term memory is like a passive storehouse with shelves to store information until it is moved to long-term memory. *Working memory* is a kind of mental "workbench" where individuals manipulate and assemble information when they make decisions, solve problems, and comprehend written and spoken language (Baddeley, 1992, 2000) (see figure 4.8). Many psychologists prefer the term working memory over short-term memory to describe how memory works. Working memory is described as more active and powerful in modifying information than short-term memory.

Working memory is linked to children's and adolescents' reading comprehension (Bjorklund, 2001). It is important to retain information in working memory as long as possible so that each newly read word in a passage can be interpreted with the words and concepts that just preceded it. Children and adolescents who are competent at reading have a larger working memory capacity than children and adolescents who have problems in reading. In one study, 7- to 13-year-olds who were either normal readers or had reading problems were given a series of incomplete sentences that required them to supply the final word of each sentence (Siegel & Ryan, 1989). Examples of sentences were: "In the summer it is very _____." With dinner, we sometimes eat bread and _____." After being presented with a series of such sentences, participants were asked to repeat the final word that they had generated for each sentence earlier. As shown in figure 4.9, as children got older, working memory capacity improved for both the normal and the problem readers, but the problem readers had lower working memory capacity (shorter memory spans) than the normal readers at each age level.

In another study, the performances of individuals from 6 to 57 years of age were examined on both verbal and visuospatial working memory tasks (Swanson, 1999). The two verbal tasks were auditory digit sequence (the ability to remember numerical information embedded in a short sentence, such as "Now suppose somebody wanted to go to the supermarket at 8651 Elm Street") and semantic association (the ability to organize words into abstract categories). In the semantic association task, the participant was presented with a series of words (such as shirt, saw, pants, hammer, shoes, and nails) and then asked to remember how they go together. The two visuospatial tasks involved mapping/directions and a visual matrix. In the mapping/directions task, the participant was shown a street map illustrating the route a bicycle (child/young adolescent) or car (adult) would follow to go through a city. After briefly looking at the map, participants were asked to redraw the route on a blank map. In the visual matrix task, participants were asked to study a matrix showing a series of dots. After looking at the matrix for five seconds, they were asked to answer questions about the location of the dots.

As shown in figure 4.10, working memory increased substantially from 8 through 24 years of age no matter what the task. Thus, the adolescent years are likely to be an important developmental period for improvement in working memory. Note that working memory continues to improve through the transition to adulthood and beyond. Watch the Discovery video entitled "Mnemonic Strategies in Memory" to learn more about other studies in working memory and memory techniques.

Long-Term Memory *Long-term memory* is a relatively permanent memory system that holds huge amounts of information for a long period of time. Long-term memory increases substantially in the middle and late childhood years and likely continues to improve during adolescence, although this has not been well documented by researchers. If anything at all is known about long-term memory, it is that it depends on

Working Memory

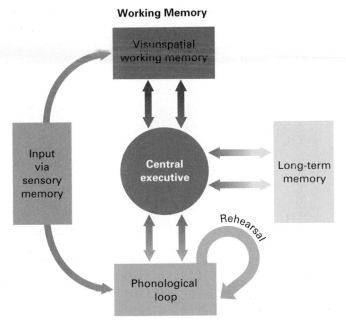

FIGURE 4.8 Working Memory

In Baddeley's working memory model, working memory is like a mental workbench where a great deal of information processing is carried out. Working memory consists of three main components: The phonological loop and visuospatial working memory serve as assistants, helping the central executive do its work. Input from sensory memory goes to the phonological loop, where information about speech is stored and rehearsal takes place, and visuospatial working memory, where visual and spatial information, including imagery, are stored. Working memory is a limited-capacity system, and information is stored there for only a brief time. Working memory interacts with long-term memory, using information from long-term memory in its work and transmitting information to long-term memory for longer storage.

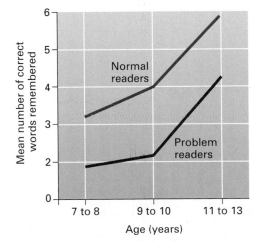

FIGURE 4.9 Working Memory Capacity in Normal and Problem Readers

As they increased in age, the working memory capacity of both normal readers and problem readers improved (Siegel & Ryan, 1989). However, problem readers had a lower working memory capacity than normal readers at each age level.

		Task			
		Verbal		*Visuospatial*	
		Semantic Association	Digit/ Sentence	Mapping/ Directions	Visual Matrix
Age	8	1.33	1.75	3.13	1.67
	10	1.70	2.34	3.60	2.06
	13	1.86	2.94	4.09	2.51
	16	2.24	2.98	3.92	2.68
	24	2.60	3.71	4.64	3.47
	Highest Working Memory Performance				
		3.02 (age 45)	3.97 (age 35)	4.90 (age 35)	3.47 (age 24)

the learning activities engaged in when learning and remembering information (Pressley & Schneider, 1997; Siegler, 1996). Most learning activities fit under the category of *strategies*, activities under the learner's conscious control. There are many such activities, but one of the most important is organization, the tendency to group or arrange items into categories. We will have more to say about strategies shortly.

Attention and memory are important dimensions of information processing, but other dimensions also are important. Once adolescents attend to information and retain it, they can use the information to engage in a number of cognitive activities, such as making decisions, thinking critically, and thinking creatively. Let's begin our exploration of these cognitive activities by examining what is involved in decision making.

Decision Making

Adolescence is a time of increased decision making—which friends to choose, which person to date, whether to have sex, buy a car, go to college, and so on (Byrnes, 1998, 2003; Galotti & Kozberg, 1996; Parker & Fischhoff, 2002). How competent are adolescents at making decisions? In some reviews, older adolescents are described as more competent than younger adolescents, who in turn are more competent than children (Keating, 1990). Compared with children, young adolescents are more likely to generate different options, examine a situation from a variety of perspectives, anticipate the consequences of decisions, and consider the credibility of sources.

One study documents that older adolescents are better at decision making than younger adolescents are (Lewis, 1981). Eighth-, tenth-, and twelfth-grade students were presented with dilemmas involving the choice of a medical procedure. The oldest students were most likely to spontaneously mention a variety of risks, to recommend consultation with an outside specialist, and to anticipate future consequences. For example, when asked a question about whether to have cosmetic surgery, a twelfth-grader said that different aspects of the situation need to be examined along with its effects on the individual's future, especially relationships with other people. In contrast, an eighth-grader presented a more limited view, commenting on the surgery's effects on getting turned down for a date, the money involved, and being teased by peers.

In sum, older adolescents often make better decisions than younger adolescents, who in turn, make better decisions than children. The ability to regulate one's emotions during decision making, to remember prior decisions and their consequences, and to adapt subsequent decision making on the basis of those consequences appear to improve with age at least through the early adulthood years (Klaczynski, Byrnes, & Jacobs, 2001).

However, older adolescents' decision-making skills are far from perfect, as are adults' (Jacobs & Klaczynski, 2002; Keating, 2004; Klaczynski, 1997; Klaczynski, Byrnes, & Jacobs, 2001). Indeed, some researchers have found that adolescents and adults do not differ in their decision-making skills (Quadrel, Fischoff, & Davis, 1993). Furthermore, researchers have found that adolescent decision making is linked to some personality traits. Adolescents who are impulsive and seek sensation are often not very effective decision makers, for example (Byrnes, 1998).

Being able to make competent decisions does not guarantee that one will make them in everyday life, where breadth of experience often comes into play (Jacobs & Potenza, 1990; Keating, 1990). For example, driver-training courses improve adolescents' cognitive and motor skills to levels equal to, or sometimes superior to, those of adults. However, driver training has not been effective in reducing adolescents' high rate of traffic accidents (Potvin, Champagne, & Labcrgc-Nadeau, 1988). An important research agenda is to study the ways adolescents make decisions in practical situations.

Adolescents need more opportunities to practice and discuss realistic decision making (Jones, Rasmussen, & Moffitt, 1997). Many real-world decisions on matters such as sex, drugs, and daredevil driving occur in an atmosphere of stress that includes time constraints and emotional involvement. One strategy for improving adolescent decision making in such circumstances is to provide more opportunities for them to engage in role playing and group problem solving.

Another strategy is for parents to involve adolescents in appropriate decision-making activities. In one study of more than 900 young adolescents and a subsample of their parents, adolescents were more likely to participate in family decision making when they perceived themselves as in control of what happens to them and if they thought that their input would have some bearing on the outcome of the decision-making process (Liprie, 1993).

Critical Thinking

Making competent decisions is closely related to critical thinking, currently a buzzword in education and psychology (Brooks & Brooks, 2001; Halonen, 1995). **Critical thinking** is thinking reflectively and productively and evaluating evidence. In one study of fifth-, eighth-, and eleventh-graders, critical thinking increased with age, but still occurred only in 43 percent of eleventh-graders (Klaczynski & Narasimham, 1998). Many adolescents showed self-serving biases in their reasoning.

Adolescence is an important transitional period in the development of critical thinking (Keating, 1990). Among the cognitive changes that allow improved critical thinking during this period are the following:

- Increased speed, automaticity, and capacity of information processing, which free cognitive resources for other purposes
- Greater breadth of content knowledge in a variety of domains
- Increased ability to construct new combinations of knowledge
- A greater range and more spontaneous use of strategies and procedures for obtaining and applying knowledge, such as planning, considering the alternatives, and cognitive monitoring

Although adolescence is an important period in the development of critical-thinking skills, if an individual has not developed a solid basis of fundamental skills (such as literacy and math skills) during childhood, critical-thinking skills are unlikely to mature in adolescence. For the subset of adolescents who lack such fundamental skills, potential gains in adolescent thinking are not likely.

Considerable interest has recently developed in teaching critical thinking in schools. Cognitive psychologist Robert J. Sternberg (1985) believes that most school programs that teach critical thinking are flawed. He thinks that schools focus too much

www.mhhe.com/santrocka10

**Exploring Critical Thinking
Critical-Thinking Resources
Odyssey of the Mind
The Jasper Project**

critical thinking Thinking reflectively and productively and evaluating the evidence.

Laura Bickford
Secondary School Teacher

Laura Bickford teaches English and journalism in grades 9 to 12 and she is Chair of the English Department at Nordhoff High School in Ojai, California.

Laura especially believes it is important to encourage students to think. Indeed, she says that "the call to teach is the call to teach students how to think." She believes teachers need to show students the value in asking their own questions, in having discussions, and in engaging in stimulating intellectual conversations. Laura says that she also encourages students to engage in metacognitive strategies (knowing about knowing). For example, she asks students to comment on their learning after particular pieces of projects have been completed. She requires students to keep reading logs so they can observe their own thinking as it happens.

Laura Bickford, working with students writing papers.

on formal reasoning tasks and not enough on the critical-thinking skills needed in everyday life. Among the critical-thinking skills that Sternberg believes adolescents need in everyday life are these: recognizing that problems exist, defining problems more clearly, handling problems with no single right answer or any clear criteria for the point at which the problem is solved (such as selecting a rewarding career), making decisions on issues of personal relevance (such as deciding to have a risky operation), obtaining information, thinking in groups, and developing long-term approaches to long-term problems.

One educational program that embodies Sternberg's recommendations for increased critical thinking in schools is the *Jasper Project*, 12 videodisc-based adventures that focus on solving real-world math problems. The Jasper Project is the brainchild of the Cognition and Technology Group at Vanderbilt (1997). Figure 4.11 shows one of the Jasper adventures. For students in grades 5 and up, Jasper helps them make connections with other disciplines, including science, history, and social studies. Jasper's creators think that students need to be exposed to authentic, real-world problems that occur in everyday life. As students work together over several class periods, they have numerous opportunities to communicate about math, share their problem-solving strategies, and get feedback from others that refines their thinking. Jasper videodiscs for science also have been created.

For many years, a major debate in teaching critical thinking has been whether critical-thinking skills should be taught as general entities or in the context of specific subject matter (math, English, or science, for example). This debate continues. Another debate focuses on the source or location of critical thinking. Traditionalists see critical thinking as a set of mental competencies that reside in adolescents' heads, while advocates of situated cognition contend that intellectual skills are exercised and shared within a social community (Resnick & Nelson-Gall, 1997; Rogoff, 1998). This ongoing debate has yet to be resolved.

Creative Thinking

creativity The ability to think in novel and unusual ways and discover unique solutions to problems.

convergent thinking A pattern of thinking in which individuals produce one correct answer; characteristic of the items on conventional intelligence tests; coined by Guilford.

divergent thinking A pattern of thinking in which individuals produce many answers to the same question; more characteristic of creativity than convergent thinking; coined by Guilford.

Creativity is the ability to think in novel ways and discover unique solutions to problems. Thus, intelligence, which we will discuss shortly, and creativity are not the same thing. J. P. Guilford (1967) first made this distinction by contrasting **convergent thinking,** which produces one correct answer and is characteristic of the kind of thinking required on a conventional intelligence test, and **divergent thinking,** which produces many answers to the same question and is more characteristic of creativity. For example, a typical item on a conventional intelligence test is "How many quarters will you get in return for 60 dimes?" This question has only one correct answer. In contrast, the following questions have many possible answers: "What image comes to mind when you hear the phrase *sitting alone in a dark room?*" or "Can you think of some unique uses for a paper clip?"

Are intelligence and creativity related? Although most creative adolescents are quite intelligent, the reverse is not necessarily true (Lubart, 2003). Many highly intelligent adolescents are not very creative.

"Blueprint for Success"   **Christina and Marcus,** two students from Trenton, visit an architectural firm on Career Day. While learning about the work of architects, Christina and Marcus hear about a vacant lot being donated in their neighborhood for a playground. This is exciting news because there is no place in their downtown neighborhood for children to play. Recently, several students have been hurt playing in the street. The challenge is for students to help Christina and Marcus design a playground and ballfield for the lot.

FIGURE 4.11 A Problem-Solving Adventure in the Jasper Project

An important goal of education is to help adolescents become more creative (Csikszentmihalyi, 2000; Runco, 2004). Here are some good strategies for accomplishing this goal:

- *Encourage adolescents to engage in brainstorming and generate as many meaningful ideas as possible. Brainstorming* is a group technique in which individuals are encouraged to play off each other's ideas, saying practically whatever comes to mind about a particular topic. Even on an individual basis, a good strategy for increasing creativity is to generate as many new ideas as possible. The famous twentieth-century Spanish artist Pablo Picasso produced more than 20,000 works of art, not all of which were masterpieces. The more ideas adolescents produce, the better are their chances of creating something unique.

- *Provide adolescents with environments that stimulate creativity.* Some settings nourish adolescents' natural curiosity and creativity, while others depress it. Science and discovery museums offer rich opportunities to stimulate adolescents' creative thinking.

- *Don't overcontrol.* Telling adolescents exactly how to accomplish a task leaves them feeling that originality is a mistake and exploration is a waste of time (Amabile, 1993). Letting adolescents select their interests and supporting their inclinations is less likely to destroy their natural curiosity than dictating which activities they should pursue (Conti & Amabile, 1999; Runco, 2000).

- *Encourage internal motivation.* Excessive use of prizes, such as money, can stifle creativity by undermining the intrinsic pleasure adolescents derive from creative activities. Creative adolescents' motivation is the satisfaction generated by the work itself.

- *Foster flexible and playful thinking.* Creative thinkers are flexible and like to play with ideas and problems. Paradoxically, while creativity takes effort, the effort goes more smoothly if adolescents take the process lightly. In a way, humor can grease the wheels of creativity (Goleman, Kaufmann, & Ray, 1993). When adolescents are joking around, they are more likely to consider unusual solutions to problems (O'Quin & Dirks, 1999).

- *Introduce adolescents to creative people.* Poet Richard Lewis (1997) visits classrooms in New York City. He brings with him only a prism that reflects a rainbow of colors. He lifts it above his head so that every student can see its colored charm, asking "Who can see something playing inside?" Then he asks students to write about what they see. One middle school student named Snigdha wrote that she

"What do you mean 'What is it?' It's the spontaneous, unfettered expression of a young mind not yet bound by the restraints of narrative or pictorial representation."

Copyright © 2000 Sidney Harris. Reprinted with permission.

www.mhhe.com/santrocka10

Teresa Amabile's Research Harvard Project Zero

sees the rainbow rising and the sun sleeping with the stars. She also sees the rain dropping on the ground, stems breaking, apples falling from trees, and the wind blowing the leaves.

- *Talk with adolescents about creative people or assign readings about them*. Mihaly Csikszentmihalyi (pronounced ME-high CHICK-sent-me-high-ee) (1995) interviewed 90 leading figures in the sciences, government, business, and education about their creativity. Mark Strand, a U.S. poet laureate, said that his most creative moments come when he loses his sense of time and becomes totally absorbed in what he is doing. He commented that the absorbed state comes and goes; he can't stay in it for an entire day. When Strand gets an intriguing idea, he focuses intensely on it and transforms it into a visual image.

Metacognition and Self-Regulatory Learning

We have discussed some important ways in which adolescents process information. In this section, we explore how they monitor their information processing and regulate their learning strategies.

What Is Metacognition?   Earlier in this chapter in discussing Piaget's theory, we learned that adolescents increase their thinking about thinking. Cognitive psychologists call this kind of thought **metacognition**—that is, cognition about cognition, or "knowing about knowing" (Flavell, 1999; Flavell, Miller, & Miller, 2002; McCormick, 2003).

Metacognitive skills have been taught to students to help them solve math problems (Cardelle-Elawar, 1992). In each of 30 daily lessons involving verbal math problems, a teacher guided low-achieving students in learning to recognize when they did not know the meaning of a word, did not have all the necessary information to solve a problem, did not know how to subdivide a problem into specific steps, or did not know how to carry out a computation. After completing these lessons, the students who had received the metacognitive training had better math achievement and better attitudes toward math.

Strategies and Self-Regulation   In the view of Michael Pressley (1983, 2003; McCormick & Pressley, 1997; Pressley & Roehrig, 2002; Pressley & others, 2003), the key to education is helping students to learn a rich repertoire of strategies for solving problems. Good thinkers routinely use strategies and effective planning to solve problems. They also know when and where to use strategies (that is, they have metacognitive knowledge about strategies). An understanding of when and where to use strategies often results from the learner's monitoring of the learning situation. But Pressley thinks this skill can be taught. When students are given instruction about strategies that are new to them, they can often apply those strategies on their own.

Pressley emphasizes that students benefit when the teacher models the appropriate strategy and verbalizes the steps in the strategy. Then students should practice the strategy, guided and supported by the teacher's feedback until they can execute it autonomously. In instructing students about a strategy, it also is a good idea to explain how using the strategy will benefit them.

Practicing a new strategy usually is not enough to persuade students to continue to use it and transfer it to new situations. Learners also need to be motivated to use new strategies. To encourage maintenance and transfer of a strategy, teachers should encourage students to monitor the effectiveness of the new strategy relative to old strategies by comparing their performance on tests and other assessments. It is not enough to say, "Try it, you will like it," Pressley says. Teachers need to say "Try it and compare."

Learning how to use strategies effectively usually takes time and requires guidance and support from the teacher. With practice, students will execute strategies faster and more competently. "Practice" means using the effective strategy over and

metacognition Cognition about cognition, or "knowing about knowing."

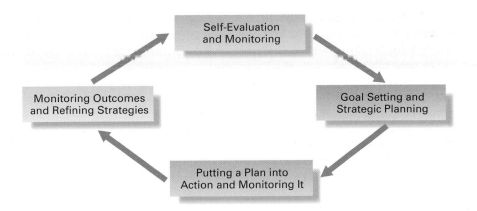

FIGURE 4.12 A Model of Self-Regulatory Learning

over again until it becomes automatic. To execute strategies effectively, learners must hold them in long-term memory, and extensive practice makes that retention possible.

Do children and adolescents use one strategy or multiple strategies in memory and problem solving? They often use more than one strategy (Schneider & Bjorklund, 1998; Siegler, 1998). Most children and adolescents benefit from generating a variety of alternative strategies and experimenting with different approaches to a problem, discovering what works well, when, and where (Schneider & Bjorklund, 1998).

Self-Regulatory Learning **Self-regulatory learning** is the self-generation and self-monitoring of one's thoughts, feelings, and behaviors in order to reach a goal. Those goals might be academic (improving reading comprehension, becoming a better organized writer, learning how to multiply, asking relevant questions) or they might be socioemotional (controlling one's anger, getting along better with peers). What are some of the characteristics of self-regulated learners? Self-regulatory learners (Winne, 1995, 1997; Winne & Perry, 2000) do the following:

- Set goals for extending their knowledge and sustaining their motivation
- Are aware of their emotional makeup and follow strategies for managing their emotions
- Periodically monitor their progress toward a goal
- Fine-tune or revise their strategies based on the progress they have made
- Evaluate obstacles that arise and make the necessary adaptations

Researchers have found that most high-achieving students are self-regulatory learners (Paris & Paris, 2001; Pressley, 1995; Pressley & others, 2003; Rudolph & others, 2001; Schunk, 2004; Schunk & Zimmerman, 2003; Zimmerman, 2000, 2002). For example, compared with low-achieving students, high-achieving students set more specific learning goals, use more learning strategies, self-monitor their learning more, and evaluate their progress toward a goal more systematically (Schunk & Ertmer, 2000).

Teachers, tutors, mentors, counselors, and parents can help students to become self-regulatory learners. Barry Zimmerman, Sebastian Bonner, and Robert Kovach (1996) developed a model for turning low-self-regulatory students into students who engage in these multistep strategies: (1) self-evaluation and monitoring, (2) goal setting and strategic planning, (3) implementing a plan and monitoring its execution, and (4) monitoring the outcomes and refining strategies (see figure 4.12). They describe a seventh-grade student who is doing poorly in history and apply their model to her situation. In step 1, the student self-evaluates her studying and test preparation by keeping a detailed record. (The teacher gives her some guidelines for keeping the records.) After several weeks, the student turns in the record and traces her poor test performance to low comprehension of difficult reading material.

In step 2, the student sets a goal—in this case, improving reading comprehension—and plans how to achieve it. The teacher assists her in breaking down the goal into parts, such as locating main ideas and setting specific objectives for understanding

self-regulatory learning The self-generation and self-monitoring of one's thoughts, feelings, and behaviors in order to reach a goal.

a series of paragraphs in her textbook. The teacher also provides the student with strategies, such as focusing on the first sentence of each paragraph and then scanning the others to identify main ideas. Another support the teacher might offer the student is adult or peer tutoring in reading comprehension, if available.

In step 3, the student puts the plan into action and begins to monitor her progress. At first she might need help from the teacher or tutor in identifying the main ideas in the textbook. Such feedback can help her to monitor her reading comprehension more effectively on her own.

In step 4, the student monitors her improvement in reading comprehension by evaluating whether it has had an impact on her learning outcomes. Has her improvement in reading comprehension led to better performance on history tests? The answer should be yes.

Review and reflect Learning goal 2

2 Describe the information-processing view of adolescence

REVIEW

- What are the main characteristics of the information-processing view?
- What developmental changes characterize attention and memory in adolescence?
- How can adolescent decision making best be described?
- What is critical thinking? What is the nature of critical thinking in adolescence?
- What is metacognition? How does it change developmentally? What is self-regulatory learning? What are some strategies for self-regulatory learning?

REFLECT

- How might metacognition be involved in the improved study skills of adolescents and emerging adults?

---

3 THE PSYCHOMETRIC/INTELLIGENCE VIEW

| **Intelligence Tests** | **Multiple Intelligences** | **Controversies and Group Comparisons in Intelligence** |

The two views of adolescent cognition that we have discussed so far—cognitive developmental and information processing—do not emphasize individual variations in intelligence. The **psychometric/intelligence view** does emphasize the importance of individual differences in intelligence; many advocates of this view favor the use of intelligence tests. An increasing issue in the field of intelligence involves pinning down what the components of intelligence really are (Embretson & McCollom, 2000).

Twentieth-century English novelist Aldous Huxley said that children are remarkable for their curiosity and intelligence. What did Huxley mean when he used the word *intelligence?* Intelligence is one of our most prized possessions, yet even the most intelligent people have not been able to agree on what intelligence is. Unlike height, weight, and age, intelligence cannot be directly measured. You can't peer into a student's head and observe the intelligence going on inside. We only can evaluate a student's intelligence indirectly by studying the intelligent acts that it generates. For the most part, psychologists have relied on written intelligence tests to provide an estimate of a student's intelligence (Aiken, 2003; Kaufman, 2000a).

Some experts think intelligence includes verbal ability and problem-solving skills. Others describe it as the ability to adapt to and learn from life's everyday experiences.

psychometric/intelligence view A view that emphasizes the importance of individual differences in intelligence; many advocates of this view also argue that intelligence should be assessed with intelligence tests.

Combining these ideas we can arrive at a fairly traditional definition of **intelligence** as the ability to solve problems and adapt to and learn from everyday experiences. Even this broad definition doesn't satisfy everyone, however. As we will see shortly, some theorists propose that musical skills should be considered a part of intelligence. And a definition of intelligence based on Vygotsky's theory would have to include the ability to use the tools of a culture, with help from more skilled individuals. Because intelligence is such an abstract, broad concept, it is not surprising that it has many different definitions.

Intelligence Tests

Robert J. Sternberg recalls being terrified of taking IQ tests as a child. He literally froze, he says, when the time came to take such tests. Even as an adult, Sternberg is stung by humiliation when he recalls in the sixth grade being asked to take an IQ test with fifth-graders. Sternberg eventually overcame his anxieties about IQ tests. Not only did he begin to perform better on them, but at age 13 he devised his own IQ test and began using it to assess his classmates—that is, until the school principal found out and scolded him. Sternberg became so fascinated by intelligence that he made its study one of his lifelong pursuits. Later in this chapter we will discuss his theory of intelligence. To begin, though, let's step back in time to examine the first valid intelligence test.

The Binet Tests In 1904 the French Ministry of Education asked psychologist Alfred Binet to devise a method to determine which students would not profit from typical school instruction. Binet and his student Theophile Simon developed an intelligence test to meet this request. The test consisted of 30 items ranging from the ability to touch one's nose or ear when asked to the ability to draw designs from memory and to define abstract concepts.

The Binet tests represented a major advance over earlier efforts to measure intelligence. Binet stressed that the core of intelligence consists of complex cognitive processes, such as memory, imagery, comprehension, and judgment. In addition, he believed that a developmental approach was crucial for understanding intelligence. He proposed that a child's intellectual ability increases with age. Therefore, he tested potential items and determined that age at which a typical child could answer them correctly. Thus, Binet developed the concept of **mental age (MA),** which is an individual's level of mental development relative to others. For an average child, mental age (MA) scores correspond to *chronological age (CA)*, which is age from birth. A bright child has an MA considerably above CA; a dull child has an MA considerably below CA.

The Binet test has been revised many times to incorporate advances in the understanding of intelligence and intelligence testing. Many revisions were carried out by Lewis Terman, who developed extensive norms and provided detailed, clear instructions for each problem on the test. Terman also applied a concept introduced by William Stern. In 1812, Stern coined the term **intelligence quotient (IQ)** to refer to an individual's mental age divided by chronological age multiplied by 100:

$$IQ = \frac{MA}{CA} \times 100$$

If an adolescent's mental age, as measured by the Binet test, was the same as the adolescent's chronological age, then the adolescent's IQ score would be 100. If the measured mental age was above chronological age, then the IQ score was more than 100. If mental age was below chronological age, the IQ score was less than 100. Although this scoring system is no longer used, the term *IQ* is often still used to refer to a score on a standardized intelligence test.

In 1985, the test, now called the Stanford-Binet (Stanford University is where the revisions were done), was revised to analyze an individual's responses in four content areas: verbal reasoning, quantitative reasoning, abstract/visual reasoning, and

www.mhhe.com/santrocka10

Mental Measurements Yearbook
Alfred Binet

intelligence The ability to solve problems and to adapt to and learn from everyday experiences; not everyone agrees on what constitutes intelligence.

mental age (MA) An individual's level of mental development relative to others; a concept developed by Binet.

intelligence quotient (IQ) A person's tested mental age divided by chronological age, multiplied by 100.

FIGURE 4.13 **The Normal Curve and Stanford-Binet IQ Scores**
The distribution of IQ scores approximates a normal curve. Most of the population falls in the middle range of scores, between 84 and 116. Notice that extremely high and extremely low scores are rare. Only about 1 in 50 individuals has an IQ of more than 132 or less than 68.

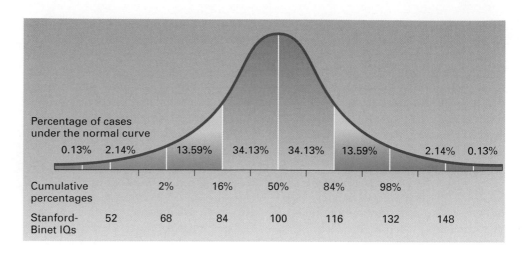

short-term memory. A general composite score also is obtained. Today the test is scored by comparing how the test-taker performs compared with other people of the same age. The average score is set at 100.

The current Stanford-Binet is given to individuals from the age of 2 through adulthood. It includes a wide variety of items, some requiring verbal responses, others nonverbal responses (Kamphaus & Kronke, 2004). For example, a 6-year-old is expected to complete the verbal task of defining at least six words, such as *orange* and *envelope,* and the nonverbal task of tracing a path through a maze. An adult with average intelligence is expected to define such words as *disproportionate* and *regard,* explain a proverb, and compare the concepts of idleness and laziness.

Over the years, the Binet test has been given to thousands of children, adolescents, and adults of different ages. By administering the test to large numbers of individuals selected at random from different parts of the United States, it has been found that the scores approximate a normal distribution (see figure 4.13). A **normal distribution** is a symmetrical, bell-shaped curve with a majority of the cases falling in the middle of the range of possible scores and few scores appearing toward the extremes of the range. The Stanford-Binet continues to be one of the most widely used individual tests of intelligence.

The Wechsler Scales Besides the Stanford-Binet, the other most widely used intelligence tests are the Wechsler scales, developed by David Wechsler. In 1939, Wechsler introduced the first of his scales, designed for use with adults (Wechsler, 1939). Now in its third edition, the Wechsler Adult Intelligence Scale-III (WAIS-III), was followed by the Wechsler Intelligence Scale for Children-III (WISC-III) for children between the ages of 6 and 16, and the Wechsler Preschool and Primary Scale of Intelligence (WPPSI) for children from the ages of 4 to 6½.

The Wechsler scales not only provide an overall IQ score but also scores on six verbal and five nonverbal measures. This allows the examiner to separate verbal and nonverbal IQ scores and to see quickly the areas in which the individual is below average, average, or above average (Kaufman, 2000b; Zhu & others, 2004). The inclusion of a number of nonverbal subscales makes the Wechsler test more representative of verbal and nonverbal intelligence; the Binet test includes some nonverbal items, but not as many as the Wechsler scales. Two of the Wechsler subscales are shown in figure 4.14.

The Use and Misuse of Intelligence Tests Psychological tests are tools. Like all tools, their effectiveness depends on the knowledge, skill, and integrity of the user. A hammer can be used to build a beautiful kitchen cabinet or it can be used as a weapon of assault. Like a hammer, psychological tests can be used for positive purposes or they can be abused.

normal distribution A symmetrical distribution of values or scores, with a majority of scores falling in the middle of the possible range of scores and few scores appearing toward the extremes of the range; a distribution that yields what is called a "bell-shaped curve."

Verbal Subscales

Similarities

An individual must think logically and abstractly to answer a number of questions about how things might be similar.

Example: "In what way are an hour and a week alike?"

Performance Subscales

Block Design

An individual must assemble a set of multicolored blocks to match designs that the examiner shows. Visual-motor coordination, perceptual organization, and the ability to visualize spatially are assessed.

Example: "Use the four blocks on the left to make the pattern on the right."

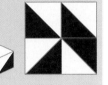

Remember that the Wechsler includes 11 subscales, 6 verbal and 5 nonverbal. Two of the subscales are shown here.

FIGURE 4.14 Sample Subscales of the Wechsler Adult Intelligence Scale-Revised

Remember that the Wechsler includes 11 subscales, 6 verbal and 5 nonverbal. Two of the subscales are shown here.

Simulated items similar to those in the Wechsler Adult Intelligence Scale-Revised. Copyright © 1949, 1955, 1974 by The Psychological Corporation. Reproduced by permission. All rights reserved. "Wechsler Adult Intelligence Scale" and "WAIS-R" are trademarks of Harcourt Assessment, Inc., formerly known as The Psychological Corporation, registered in the United States of America and/or other jurisdictions.

Intelligence tests have real-world applications as predictors of school and job success (Brody, 2000). For example, scores on tests of general intelligence are substantially correlated with school grades and achievement test performance, both at the time of the test and years later (Brody, 2000). IQ in the sixth grade correlates about .60 with the number of years of education the individual will eventually obtain.

Intelligence tests are moderately correlated with work performance (Lubinski, 2000). Individuals with higher scores on tests designed to measure general intelligence tend to get higher-paying, more prestigious jobs (Wagner, 1997). However, general IQ tests predict only about one-fourth of the variation in job success with the majority of job success due to factors such as motivation, education, and other factors (Wagner & Sternberg, 1986). Further, the correlations between IQ and achievement decrease the longer people work at a job, presumably because as they gain more job experience they perform better (Hunt, 1995).

Despite its links with academic achievement and occupational success, it is important to keep in mind that many other factors contribute to success in school and work. These include the motivation to succeed, physical and mental health, and social skills (Sternberg, 2003).

The single number provided by many IQ tests can easily lead to false expectations about an individual (Rosenthal, 2000). Sweeping generalizations are too often made on the basis of an IQ score. For example, imagine that you are a teacher in the teacher's lounge the day after school has started in the fall. You mention a student— Johnny Jones—and a fellow teacher remarks that she had Johnny in class last year; she comments that he was a real dunce and points out that his IQ is 78. You cannot help but remember this information, and it might lead to thoughts that Johnny Jones is not very bright so it is useless to spend much time teaching him. In this way, IQ scores are misused and can become self-fulfilling prophecies (Rosenthal & Jacobsen, 1968).

Intelligence tests can help teachers group children who function at roughly the same level in such subject areas as math or reading so they can be taught the same concepts together. However, extreme caution is necessary when test scores are used to place children in tracks, such as "advanced," "intermediate," and "low." Periodic assessment is required. Intelligence tests measure *current* performance, and maturational changes or enriched experiences may advance a child's intelligence, indicating that he or she should be moved to a higher-level group.

Even though they have limitations, tests of intelligence are among psychology's most widely used tools. To be effective, they should be used in conjunction with other information about an individual. For example, an intelligence test alone should not determine whether a child or adolescent is placed in a special education or gifted class. The individual's developmental history, medical background, performance in school, social competencies, and family experiences should be taken into account, too.

Despite their limitations, when used judiciously, intelligence tests provide valuable information. There are not many alternatives to these tests. Subjective judgments about individuals simply reintroduce the bias that the tests were designed to eliminate.

Multiple Intelligences

Multiple-Intelligences Links

The use of a single score to describe how people perform on intelligence tests suggests intelligence is a general ability, a single trait. The Wechsler scales provide scores for a number of intellectual skills, as well as an overall score. Do people have some general mental ability that determines how they perform on all of these tests? Or is intelligence a label for a combination of several distinct abilities? And do conventional intelligence tests measure everything that should be considered part of intelligence? Psychologists disagree about the answers to these questions.

Wechsler was not the first psychologist to break down intelligence into a number of abilities. Nor was he the last. A number of contemporary psychologists continue to search for specific components that make up intelligence. Some do not rely on traditional intelligence tests in their conceptualization of intelligence. Let's explore several key alternative conceptions of intelligence, beginning with Wechsler's predecessor, Charles Spearman.

Factor Approaches   Some time before Wechsler analyzed intelligence in terms of general and specific abilities, Charles Spearman (1927) proposed that intelligence has two factors. *Two-factor theory* is Spearman's theory that individuals have both general intelligence, which he called *g,* and a number of specific abilities, or *s.* Spearman believed that these two factors account for a person's performance on an intelligence test. Spearman developed his theory by applying a technique called *factor analysis* to a number of intelligence tests. Factor analysis is a statistical procedure that correlates test scores to identify underlying clusters, or factors.

L. L. Thurstone (1938) also used factor analysis in analyzing a number of intelligence tests, but he concluded that the tests measure only a number of specific factors, and not general intelligence. *Multiple-factor theory* is Thurstone's theory that intelligence consists of seven primary mental abilities: verbal comprehension, number ability, word fluency, spatial visualization, associative memory, reasoning, and perceptual speed.

Gardner's Theory of Multiple Intelligences   Both Spearman and Thurstone relied on traditional types of intelligence tests in their attempts to clarify the nature of intelligence. In contrast, Howard Gardner argues that these tests are far too narrow. Imagine someone who has great musical skills but does not do well in math or English. The famous composer, Ludwig van Beethoven, was just such a person. Would you call Beethoven "unintelligent"? Unlikely!

According to Gardner, people have multiple intelligences and IQ tests measure only a few of these. These intelligences are independent of one another. For evidence of the existence of multiple intelligences, Gardner uses information about the ways in which certain cognitive abilities survive particular types of brain damage. He also points to child prodigies and to some individuals who are retarded or autistic with an extraordinary skill in a particular domain.

Gardner (1983, 1993, 2001, 2002) has proposed eight types of intelligence. They are described in the following list along with examples of the occupations in which they are reflected as strengths (Campbell, Campbell, & Dickinson, 2004):

- *Verbal Skills:* The ability to think in words and use language to express meaning
  Occupations: Authors, journalists, speakers

- *Mathematical Skills:* The ability to carry out mathematical operations
  Occupations: Scientists, engineers, accountants
- *Spatial Skills:* The ability to think three-dimensionally
  Occupations: Architects, artists, sailors
- *Bodily-Kinesthetic Skills*: The ability to manipulate objects and be physically adept
  Occupations: Surgeons, craftspeople, dancers, athletes
- *Musical Skills*: A sensitivity to pitch, melody, rhythm, and tone
  Occupations: Composers, musicians, and sensitive listeners
- *Interpersonal Skills*: The ability to understand and effectively interact with others
  Occupations: Successful teachers, mental health professionals
- *Intrapersonal Skills*: The ability to understand oneself
  Occupations: Theologians, psychologists
- *Naturalist Skills:* The ability to observe patterns in nature and understand natural and human-made systems
  Occupations: Farmers, botanists, ecologists, landscapers

According to Gardner, everyone has all of the preceding intelligences but to varying degrees. As a result, we prefer to learn and process information in different ways. People learn best when they can apply their strong intelligences to the task.

Gardner believes that each of the eight intelligences can be destroyed by brain damage, that each involves unique cognitive skills, and that each shows up in exaggerated fashion in both the gifted and individuals who have mental retardation or autism (a psychological disorder marked by deficits in social interaction and interests). Dustin Hoffman portrayed an individual with autism who had a remarkable computing ability in the movie *Rain Man*. In one scene, Hoffman's character helped his brother successfully gamble in Las Vegas by keeping track of all the cards that had been played.

Sternberg's Triarchic Theory   Like Gardner, Robert J. Sternberg (1986, 1999, 2002, 2003) believes that traditional IQ tests fail to measure some important dimensions of intelligence. Sternberg proposes that there are three main types of intelligence: analytical, creative, and practical. To understand what analytical, creative, and practical intelligence mean, let's look at examples of people who reflect the three types of intelligence that compose Sternberg's **triarchic theory of intelligence**:

- Consider Latisha, who scores high on traditional intelligence tests such as the Stanford-Binet and is a star analytical thinker. Sternberg calls Latisha's analytical thinking and abstract reasoning *analytical intelligence*. It is the closest to what has traditionally been called intelligence and what is commonly assessed by intelligence tests. In Sternberg's view of analytical intelligence, the basic unit of analytical intelligence is a *component*, which is a basic unit of information processing. Sternberg's components include the ability to acquire or store information; to retain or retrieve information; to transfer information; to plan, make decisions, and solve problems; and to translate thoughts into performance.
- Todd does not have the best test scores but has an insightful and creative mind. The type of thinking at which Todd excels is called *creative intelligence* by Sternberg. According to Sternberg, creative people like Todd have the ability to solve new problems quickly, but they also learn how to solve familiar problems in an automatic way so their minds are free to handle other problems that require insight and creativity.
- Finally, consider Emanuel, a person whose scores on traditional IQ tests are low but who quickly grasps real-life problems. He easily picks up knowledge about how the world works. Emanuel's "street smarts" and practical know-how indicate that he has what Sternberg calls *practical intelligence*. Practical intelligence includes the ability to get out of trouble and a knack for getting along with people. Sternberg describes practical intelligence as all of the important information about getting along in the world that you are not taught in school.

triarchic theory of intelligence Sternberg's view that intelligence comes in three main forms: analytical, creative, and practical.

"You're wise, but you lack tree smarts."

Sternberg's Theory

emotional intelligence The ability to perceive and express emotion accurately and adaptively, to understand emotion and emotional knowledge, to use feelings to facilitate thought, and to manage emotions in oneself and others.

Assessing Triarchic Intelligence   Sternberg (1993) developed the Sternberg Triarchic Abilities Test (STAT) that assesses analytical, creative, and practical intelligence. The three kinds of abilities are examined in four different ways: (1) verbal, (2) quantitative, (3) figural multiple-choice items, and (4) essays. The goal is to obtain a more complete assessment of intelligence than is possible with a conventional test.

The memory-analytical section is much like a conventional test, with individuals required to provide the meanings of words, complete number series, and complete matrices. The creative and practical sections are much different from conventional tests. For example, in the creative section, individuals are required to write an essay on designing an ideal school. The practical section requires individuals to solve practical everyday problems that involve such matters as planning routes and purchasing tickets to an event.

An increasing number of studies are investigating the effectives of the STAT in predicting such important aspects of life as success in school. For example, in one recent study of 800 college students, scores on the STAT were effective in predicting college grade point average (Sternberg & others, 2001a). However, more research is needed to determine the validity and reliability of the STAT.

Triarchic Theory in the Classroom   Sternberg (1997) says that students with different triarchic patterns look different in school. Students with high analytic ability tend to be favored in conventional schools. They often do well in classes in which the teacher lectures and gives objective tests. They often are considered smart students, typically get good grades, do well on traditional IQ tests and the SAT, and later gain admission to competitive colleges.

Students who are high in creative intelligence often are not in the top rung of their class. Creatively intelligent students might not conform to the expectations that teachers have about how assignments should be done. They give unique answers, for which they might get reprimanded or marked down.

Like students high in creative intelligence, students who are practically intelligent often do not relate well to the demands of school. However, these students frequently do well outside the classroom's walls. Their social skills and common sense may allow them to become successful managers, entrepreneurs, or politicians, despite undistinguished school records.

Sternberg (1999) believes that few tasks are purely analytic, creative, or practical. Most tasks require some combination of these skills. For example, when students write a book report, they might (1) analyze the book's main themes, (2) generate new ideas about how the book could have been written better, and (3) think about how the book's themes can be applied to people's lives. Sternberg argues that it is important for classroom instruction to give students opportunities to learn through all three types of intelligence.

Emotional Intelligence   Both Gardner's and Sternberg's theories include one or more categories related to social intelligence. In Gardner's theory, the categories are interpersonal intelligence and intrapersonal intelligence; in Sternberg's theory, practical intelligence. Another theory that emphasizes interpersonal, intrapersonal, and practical aspects of intelligence is called **emotional intelligence,** which has been popularized by Daniel Goleman (1995) in his book *Emotional Intelligence.* The concept of emotional intelligence was initially developed by Peter Salovey and John Mayer (1990), who define it as the ability to perceive and express emotion accurately and adaptively (such as taking the perspective of others), to understand emotion and emotional knowledge (such as understanding the roles that emotions play in friendship and marriage), to use feelings to facilitate thought (such as being in a positive mood, which is linked to creative thinking), and to manage emotions in oneself and others (such as being able to control one's anger).

Recently, the Mayer-Salovey-Caruso Emotional Intelligence Test (MSCEIT) was developed to measure the four aspects of emotional intelligence just described: perceiving emotions, understanding emotions, facilitating thought, and managing emotions (Mayer, Salovey, & Caruso, 2002). The test consists of 141 items, can be given to individuals 17 years of age and older, and takes about 30–45 minutes to administer. Because the MSCEIT has only been available since 2001, few studies have been conducted to examine its ability to predict outcomes (Salovey & Pizarro, 2003). One recent study that used the MSCEIT found that youths with higher emotional intelligence were less likely to have smoked cigarettes or to have used alcohol (Trinidad & Johnson, 2002).

Sternberg	Gardner	Salovey/Mayer/Goleman
Analytical	Verbal Mathematical	
Creative	Spatial Movement Musical	
Practical	Interpersonal Intrapersonal	Emotional
	Naturalistic	

FIGURE 4.15 Comparison of Sternberg's, Gardner's, and Mayer/Salovey/Goleman's Views

Do People Have One Intelligence or Many Intelligences? Figure 4.15 provides a comparison of Sternberg's, Gardner's, and Mayer/Salovey/Goleman's views. Notice that Gardner includes a number of types of intelligence that are not addressed by the other views and that Sternberg is unique in emphasizing creative intelligence. These theories of multiple intelligence have much to offer. They have stimulated us to think more broadly about what makes up people's intelligence and competence. And they have motivated educators to develop programs that instruct students in different domains.

Theories of multiple intelligences also have many critics. Many argue that the research base to support these theories has not yet developed. In particular, some critics say that Gardner's classification seems arbitrary. For example, if musical skills represent a type of intelligence, why don't we also refer to chess intelligence, prizefighter intelligence, and so on?

A number of psychologists still support Spearman's concept of *g* (general intelligence). For example, one expert on intelligence, Nathan Brody (2000) argues that people who excel at one type of intellectual task are likely to excel in other intellectual tasks. Thus, individuals who do well at memorizing lists of digits are also likely to be good at solving verbal problems and spatial layout problems. This general intelligence includes abstract reasoning or thinking, the capacity to acquire knowledge, and problem-solving ability (Brody, 2000; Carroll, 1993).

Some experts who argue for the existence of general intelligence believe that individuals also have specific intellectual abilities (Brody, 2000). In one study, John Carroll (1993) conducted an extensive examination of intellectual abilities and concluded that all intellectual abilities are related to one another, which supports the concept of general intelligence, but that there are many specialized abilities as well. Some of these specialized abilities, such as spatial abilities and mechanical abilities, are not adequately reflected in the curriculum of most schools.

Controversies and Group Comparisons in Intelligence

We have seen that intelligence is a slippery concept with competing definitions, tests, and theories. It is not surprising, therefore, that attempts to understand the concept of intelligence is filled with controversy. In some cases, the controversies involve comparisons of the intelligence of different groups, such as people from different cultures or ethnic groups.

The Influence of Heredity and Environment One of the hottest areas in the study of intelligence centers on the extent to which intelligence is influenced by genetics and the extent to which it is influenced by environment (Petrill, 2003). In chapter 3, we indicated how difficult it is to tease apart these influences, but that has not kept psychologists from trying to unravel them.

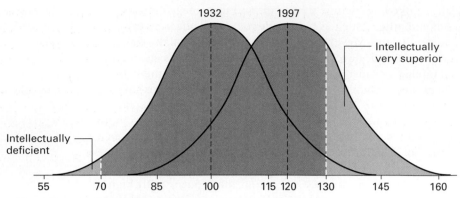

FIGURE 4.16 The Increase in IQ Scores from 1932 to 1997

As measured by the Stanford-Binet intelligence test, American children seem to be getting smarter. Scores of a group tested in 1932 fell along a bell-shaped curve with half below 100 and half above. Studies show that if children took that same test today, half would score above 120 on the 1932 scale. Very few of them would score in the "intellectually deficient" end, on the left side, and about one-fourth would rank in the "very superior" range.

Heredity   How strong is the effect of heredity on intelligence? The concept of heritability attempts to tease apart the effects of heredity and environment in a population. **Heritability** is the fraction of the variance in a population that is attributed to genetics. The heritability index is computed using correlational techniques. Thus, the highest degree of heritability is 1.00 and correlations of .70 and above suggest a strong genetic influence. A committee of respected researchers convened by the American Psychological Association concluded that by late adolescence, the heritability of intelligence is about .75, which reflects a strong genetic influence (Neisser & others, 1996).

An important point to keep in mind about heritability is that it refers to a specific group (population), *not* to individuals (Okagaki, 2000). Researchers use the concept of heritability to try to describe why people differ. Heritability says nothing about why a single individual, like yourself, has a certain intelligence; nor does it say anything about differences *between* groups.

The heritability index has several flaws (Dickens & Flynn, 2001). It is only as good as the data that are entered into its analysis and the interpretations made from it. The data are virtually all from traditional IQ tests, which some experts believe are not always the best indicator of intelligence (Gardner, 2002; Sternberg, 2002). Also, the heritability index assumes that we can treat genetic and environmental influences as factors that can be separated, with each part contributing a distinct amount of influence. As we discussed in chapter 2, genes and the environment always work together. Genes always exist in an environment, and the environment shapes their activity. Further, most research on heredity and environment does not include environments that differ radically. Thus, it is not surprising that many genetic studies show environment to be a fairly weak influence on intelligence (Fraser, 1995).

Environment   One of the strongest arguments for the influence of environment on intelligence involves the rapidly increasing IQ test scores around the world (Flynn, 1999). IQ scores have been increasing so fast that a high percentage of people regarded as having average intelligence at the turn of the century would be considered below average in intelligence today (Howard, 2001) (see figure 4.16). If a representative sample of people today took the Stanford-Binet test used in 1932, about one-fourth would be defined as having very superior intelligence, a label usually accorded to fewer than 3 percent of the population. Because the increase has taken place in a relatively short time, it can't be due to heredity, but rather may be due to increasing

heritability The fraction of the variance in a population that is attributed to genetics.

levels of education attained by a much greater percentage of the world's population or to other environmental factors such as the explosion of information to which people are exposed. The worldwide increase in intelligence test scores that has occurred over a short time frame has been called the *Flynn effect,* after the researcher who discovered it—James Flynn.

Keep in mind that environmental influences are complex (Neisser & others, 1996; Sternberg, 2003). Growing up with all the "advantages," for example, does not guarantee success. Children and adolescents from wealthy families may have easy access to excellent schools, books, travel, and tutoring, but they may take such opportunities for granted and fail to develop the motivation to learn and to achieve. In the same way, "poor" or "disadvantaged" does not automatically equal "doomed."

Group Comparisons and Issues   Among the ways that group comparisons in intelligence can be made involve cultures, ethnic groups, and males and females.

Cross-Cultural Comparisons   Cultures vary in the way they describe what it means to be intelligent (Benson, 2003). People in Western cultures tend to view intelligence in terms of reasoning and thinking skills while people in Eastern cultures see intelligence as a way for members of a community to successfully engage in social roles (Nisbett, 2003). One study found that Taiwanese-Chinese conceptions of intelligence emphasize understanding and relating to others, including when to show and when not to show one's intelligence (Yang & Sternberg, 1997).

Robert Serpell (1974, 1982, 2000) has studied concepts of intelligence in rural African communities since the 1970s. He has found that people in rural African communities, especially those in which Western schooling is not common, tend to blur the distinction between being intelligent and being socially competent. In rural Zambia, for example, the concept of intelligence involves being both clever and responsible. Elena Grigorenko and her colleagues (2001) have also studied the concept of intelligence among rural Africans. They found that people in the Luo culture of rural Kenya view intelligence as consisting of four domains: (1) academic intelligence, (2) social qualities such as respect, responsibility, and consideration, (3) practical thinking, and (4) comprehension. In another study in the same culture, children who scored highly on a test of knowledge about medicinal herbs—a measure of practical intelligence— tended to score poorly on tests of academic intelligence (Sternberg & others, 2001b). These results indicated that practical and academic intelligence can develop independently and may even conflict with each other. They also suggest that the values of a culture may influence the direction in which a child develops. In a cross-cultural context, then, intelligence depends a great deal on environment.

Cultural Bias in Testing   Many of the early intelligence tests were culturally biased, favoring people who were from urban rather than rural environments, middle-socioeconomic status rather than low-socioeconomic status, and White rather than African American (Miller-Jones, 1989; Nell, 2004; Provenzo, 2002; Watras, 2002). For example, one question on an early test asked what you should do if you find a 3-year-old child in the street. The correct answer was "call the police." But children from inner-city families who perceive the police as adversaries are unlikely to choose this answer. Similarly, children from rural areas might not choose this answer if there is no police force nearby. Such questions clearly do not measure the knowledge necessary to adapt to one's environment or to be "intelligent" in an inner-city neighborhood or in rural America (Scarr, 1984). Also, members of minority groups who do not speak English or who speak nonstandard English are at a disadvantage in trying to understand questions framed in standard English (Gibbs & Huang, 1989).

A specific case illustrating how cultural bias in intelligence tests can affect people is that of Gregory Ochoa. When Gregory was a high school student, he and his classmates took an IQ test. Gregory understood only a few words on the test because

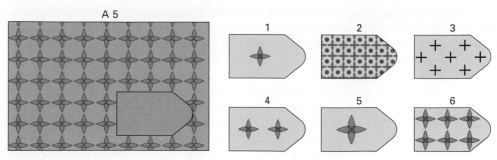

FIGURE 4.17 Sample Item from the Raven Progressive Matrices Test
Individuals are presented with a matrix arrangement of symbols, such as the one to the left of this figure, and must then complete the matrix by selecting the appropriate missing symbol from a group of symbols.

he did not speak English very well and spoke Spanish at home. Several weeks later, Gregory was placed in a special class for mentally retarded students. Many of the students in the class, it turns out, had last names such as Ramirez and Gonzales. Gregory lost interest in school, dropped out, and eventually joined the navy. In the navy, Gregory took high school courses and earned enough credits to attend college later. He graduated from San Jose City College as an honor student, continued his education, and became a professor of social work at the University of Washington in Seattle.

As a result of cases like Gregory Ochoa's, researchers have developed **culture-fair tests,** which are intelligence tests that are intended not to be culturally biased. Two types of culture-fair tests have been developed. The first includes questions that are familiar to people from all socioeconomic and ethnic backgrounds. For example, a child might be asked how a bird and a dog are different, on the assumption that virtually all children are familiar with birds and dogs. The second type of culture-fair test contains no verbal questions. Figure 4.17 shows a sample question from the Raven Progressive Matrices Test. Even though tests such as the Raven Progressive Matrices are designed to be culture-fair, people with more education still score higher than those with less education do (Greenfield, 2003).

Why is it so hard to create culture-fair tests? Most tests tend to reflect what the dominant culture thinks is important (Aiken, 2003; Greenfield & others, 2003; Hambleton, Merenda, & Spielberger, 2004). If tests have time limits, that will bias the test against groups not concerned with time. If languages differ, the same words might have different meanings for different language groups (Merenda, 2004; Sireci, 2004). Even pictures can produce bias because some cultures have less experience with drawings and photographs (Anastasi & Urbina, 1996). Within the same culture, different groups could have different attitudes, values, and motivation, and this could affect their performance on intelligence tests. Items that ask why buildings should be made of brick are biased against children who have little or no experience with brick houses. Questions about railroads, furnaces, seasons of the year, distances between cities, and so on can be biased against groups who have less experience than others with these contexts.

Ethnic Comparisons In the United States, children from African American and Latino families score below children from White families on standardized intelligence tests. On the average, African American schoolchildren score 10 to 15 points lower on standardized intelligence tests than White American schoolchildren do (Brody, 2000; Lynn, 1996). These are *average scores,* however. About 15 to 25 percent of African American schoolchildren score higher than half of White schoolchildren do, and many Whites score lower than most African Americans. The reason is that the distribution of scores for African Americans and Whites overlap.

A controversy erupted in response to the book *The Bell Curve: Intelligence and Class Structure in American Life* (1994) by Richard Herrnstein and Charles Murray. Recall that

culture-fair tests Tests of intelligence that are intended to be free of cultural bias.

the bell curve is the shape of a normal distribution graph, which represents large numbers of people who are sorted according to some shared characteristic, such as weight, taste in clothes, or IQ. Herrnstein and Murray note that predictions about any individual based exclusively on the person's IQ are virtually useless. Weak correlations between IQ and job success have predictive value only when they are applied to large groups of people. But within large groups, say Herrnstein and Murray, the pervasive influence of IQ on human society becomes apparent The authors argued that America is developing a huge underclass of intellectually deprived individuals whose cognitive abilities will never match the future needs of most employers. They believe that this underclass, a large proportion of which is African American, may be doomed by their shortcomings to welfare dependency, poverty, and crime.

Significant criticisms have been leveled at *The Bell Curve*. The average score of African Americans is lower than the average score of Whites on IQ tests. However, as we have discussed, many experts raise serious questions about the ability of IQ tests to accurately measure a person's intelligence.

As African Americans have gained social, economic, and educational opportunities, the gap between African Americans and Whites on standardized intelligence tests has begun to narrow (Ogbu & Stern, 2001; Onwuegbuzi & Daley, 2001). This gap especially narrows in college, where African American and White students often experience more similar environments than in the elementary and high school years (Myerson & others, 1998). Also, when children from disadvantaged African American families are adopted into more-advantaged middle-socioeconomic-status families, their scores on intelligence tests more closely resemble national averages for middle-socioeconomic-status children than for lower-socioeconomic-status children (Scarr & Weinberg, 1983).

One potential influence on intelligence test performance is *stereotype threat*, the anxiety that one's behavior might confirm a negative stereotype about one's group. For example, when African Americans take an intelligence test, they may experience anxiety about confirming the old stereotype that Blacks are "intellectually inferior." In one study, the verbal part of the GRE was given individually to African American and White students at Stanford University (Steele & Aronson, 1995). Half the students of each ethnic group were told that the researchers were interested in assessing their intellectual ability. The other half were told that the researchers were trying to develop a test and that it might not be reliable and valid (therefore, it would not mean anything in relation to their intellectual ability). The White students did equally well on the test in both conditions. However, the African American students did more poorly when they thought the test was assessing their intellectual ability; when they thought the test was just in the development stage and might not be reliable or valid, they performed as well as the White students.

Other studies have confirmed the existence of stereotype threat. African American students do more poorly on standardized tests if they believe they are being evaluated. If they believe the test doesn't count, they perform as well as White students (Aronson, 2002; Aronson & others, 1999; Aronson, Fried, & Good, 2002). However, some critics believe the extent to which stereotype threat explains the testing gap has been exaggerated (Sackett, 2003).

Gender Comparisons   The average scores of males and females do not differ on intelligence tests, but variability in their scores does differ (Brody, 2000). For example, males are more likely than females to have extremely high or extremely low scores.

There also are gender differences in specific intellectual abilities (Brody, 2000). Males score better than females in some nonverbal areas, such as spatial reasoning, and females score better than males in some verbal areas, such as the ability to find synonyms for words. However, there often is extensive overlap in the scores of females and males in these areas, and there is debate about how strong the differences are (Hyde & Mezulis, 2001).

Review and reflect Learning goal 3

3 **Summarize the psychometric/intelligence view of adolescence**

REVIEW

- What is intelligence? What are the main individual tests of intelligence? What are some issues in the use of group tests of intelligence?
- What theories of multiple intelligences have been developed? Do people have one intelligence or many intelligences?
- What are some controversies and group comparisons in intelligence?

REFLECT

- Apply Gardner's, Sternberg's, and Salovey, Mayer, and Goleman's categories of intelligence to yourself or someone you know well. Write a description of yourself or the person you know based on each of these views.

4 SOCIAL COGNITION

Adolescent Egocentrism

Implicit Personality Theory

Perspective Taking

Social Cognition
in the Rest of the Text

Social cognition refers to the way individuals conceptualize and reason about their social worlds—the people they watch and interact with, their relationships with those people, the groups they participate in, and the way they reason about themselves and others. Recently there has been a flurry of interest in social cognition (Flavell, Miller, & Miller, 2002; Lapsley & Narváez, 2004). Our discussion will focus on egocentrism, perspective taking, and implicit personality theory.

Adolescent Egocentrism

Adolescent egocentrism is the heightened self-consciousness of adolescents, which is reflected in their belief that others are as interested in them as they are themselves, and in their sense of personal uniqueness and invincibility. David Elkind (1976) believes that adolescent egocentrism can be dissected into two types of social thinking—imaginary audience and personal fable.

The *imaginary audience* refers to the aspect of adolescent egocentrism that involves attention-getting behavior—the attempt to be noticed, visible, and "onstage." An adolescent might think that others are as aware of a few hairs that are out of place as he is. An adolescent girl walks into her classroom and thinks that all eyes are riveted on her complexion. Adolescents especially sense that they are onstage in early adolescence, believing they are the main actors and all others are the audience.

According to Elkind, the *personal fable* is the part of adolescent egocentrism that involves an adolescent's sense of personal uniqueness and invincibility. Adolescents' sense of personal uniqueness makes them feel that no one can understand how they really feel. For example, an adolescent girl thinks that her mother cannot possibly sense the hurt she feels because her boyfriend has broken up with her. As part of their effort to retain a sense of personal uniqueness, adolescents might craft stories about

I check my look in the mirror. I wanna change my clothes, my hair, my face.

—BRUCE SPRINGSTEEN
Contemporary American Rock Star

adolescent egocentrism The heightened self-consciousness of adolescents, which is reflected in their belief that others are as interested in them as they themselves are, and in their sense of personal uniqueness.

themselves that are filled with fantasy, immersing themselves in a world that is far removed from reality. Personal fables frequently show up in adolescent diaries.

Adolescents also often show a sense of invincibility—feeling that although others might be vulnerable to tragedies, such as a terrible car wreck, these things won't happen to them. Some developmentalists believe that the sense of uniqueness and invincibility that egocentrism generates is responsible for some of the seemingly reckless behavior of adolescents, including drag racing, drug use, suicide, and failure to use contraceptives during intercourse (Dolcini & others, 1989). For example, one study found that eleventh- and twelfth-grade females who were high in adolescent egocentrism were more likely to say they would not get pregnant from engaging in sex without contraception than were their counterparts who were low in adolescent egocentrism (Arnett, 1990).

Perspective Taking

Researchers have found that changes in *perspective taking*, the ability to assume another person's perspective and understand his or her thoughts and feelings, are likely involved in the development of adolescent egocentrism (Lapsley & Murphy, 1985). The link be-

What is adolescent egocentrism?

tween perspective taking and adolescent egocentrism likely occurs because advances in perspective taking cause young adolescents to be acutely concerned about what others think.

Perspective taking can increase adolescents' self-understanding, and it also can improve their peer group status and the quality of their friendships (Selman & Adalbjarnardottir, 2000; Selman & Schultz, 1999). For example, in one investigation, the most popular children in the third and eighth grades had competent perspective-taking skills (Kurdek & Krile, 1982). Adolescents who are competent at perspective

What role does perspective taking play in adolescence?

taking are better at understanding the needs of their companions so that they likely can communicate more effectively with them. Further, in one study, competence in social perspective coordination was an important influence on adolescent friendship formation following residential relocation (Vernberg & others, 1994).

The relation between the self and another individual is complex. Most major developmental theorists believe that development changes in self-other relationships are characterized by movement from egocentrism to perspectivism, but the considerable overlap in the age range at which various levels of perspective taking emerge make generalizations about clear-cut stages difficult. Next, we turn our attention to another aspect of social cognition that changes during adolescence—implicit personality theory.

Implicit Personality Theory

Implicit personality theory is the layperson's conception of personality. Do adolescents conceptualize an individual's personality differently than children do? Adolescents are more likely to interpret an individual's personality in the way that many personality theorists in psychology do than children are (Barenboim, 1981). Adolescents interpret personality differently than children in three ways. First, when adolescents are given information about another person, they are more likely to consider both previously acquired information and current information, rather than relying only on the concrete information at hand, as children do. Second, adolescents are more likely to detect the situational or contextual variability in personality, rather than thinking that personality is always stable. Third, rather than merely accepting surface traits as a valid description of someone's personality, adolescents are more likely than children to look for deeper, more complex, even hidden causes of personality.

In these comments obtained in one developmental investigation of how individuals perceive others, we can see how the development of an implicit personality theory proceeds (Livesley & Bromley, 1973):

> Max sits next to me, his eyes are hazel and he is tall. He hasn't got a very big head, he's got a big pointed nose. (p. 213; age 7 years, 6 months)

> He smells very much and is very nasty. He has no sense of humor and is very dull. He is always fighting and he is cruel. He does silly things and is very stupid. He has brown hair and cruel eyes. He is sulky and eleven years old and has lots of sisters. I think he is the most horrible boy in the class. He has a croaky voice and always chews his pencil and picks his teeth and I think he is disgusting. (p. 217; age 9 years, 11 months)

> Andy is very modest. He is even shyer than I am when near strangers and yet is very talkative with people he knows and likes. He always seems good tempered and I have never seen him in a bad temper. He tends to degrade other people's achievements, and yet never praises his own. He does not seem to voice his opinions to anyone. He easily gets nervous. (p. 221; age 15 years, 8 months)

> . . . she is curious about people but naive, and this leads her to ask too many questions so that people become irritated with her and withhold information, although she is not sensitive enough to notice it. (p. 225; young adult)

Social Cognition in the Rest of the Text

Interest in social cognition has blossomed, and the approach has infiltrated many aspects of the study of adolescent development. In the overview of the self and identity in chapter 5, social cognition's role in understanding the self and identity is explored. In the evaluation of moral development in chapter 8, considerable time is devoted to discussing Kohlberg's theory, which is a prominent aspect of the study of social cogni-

*S*ocial cognition has as its objects humans and human affairs; it means cognition and knowledge about people and their doings.

—JOHN FLAVELL
Contemporary Psychologist, Stanford University

implicit personality theory The layperson's conception of personality.

tion in adolescence. Further, in the discussion of families in chapter 9, the emerging cognitive abilities of the adolescent are evaluated in concert with parent-adolescent conflict and parenting strategies. Also, in the description of peer relations in chapter 10, the importance of social knowledge and social information processing in peer relations is highlighted.

Review and reflect Learning goal 4

4   Explain how social cognition is involved in adolescent development

REVIEW

- What characterizes adolescent egocentrism?
- How does perspective taking change during adolescence?
- What is implicit personality theory? How does it develop in adolescence?
- How is social cognition related to other topics discussed in this text?

REFLECT

- Does adolescent egocentrism ever disappear? Is it maladaptive in your late teens or early twenties to act as if all eyes are riveted on you, to have a strong desire to be noticed, visible, "onstage," and to feel as most others are as interested in you as you are? How can you draw the line between self-interest that is adaptive, protective, and appropriate and self-interest that is maladaptive, selfish, and inappropriate? One good strategy is to consider the extent to which egocentrism overwhelms and dominates the person's life.

In this chapter, we have examined cognitive development in adolescence. In the next chapter, the first chapter in Section 3, "Social, Emotional, and Personality Development," we will explore the development of the self and identity in adolescence. You will see that changes in cognitive development described in this chapter serve as foundations for some of the changes that take place in the self and identity during adolescence.

Reach Your Learning Goals

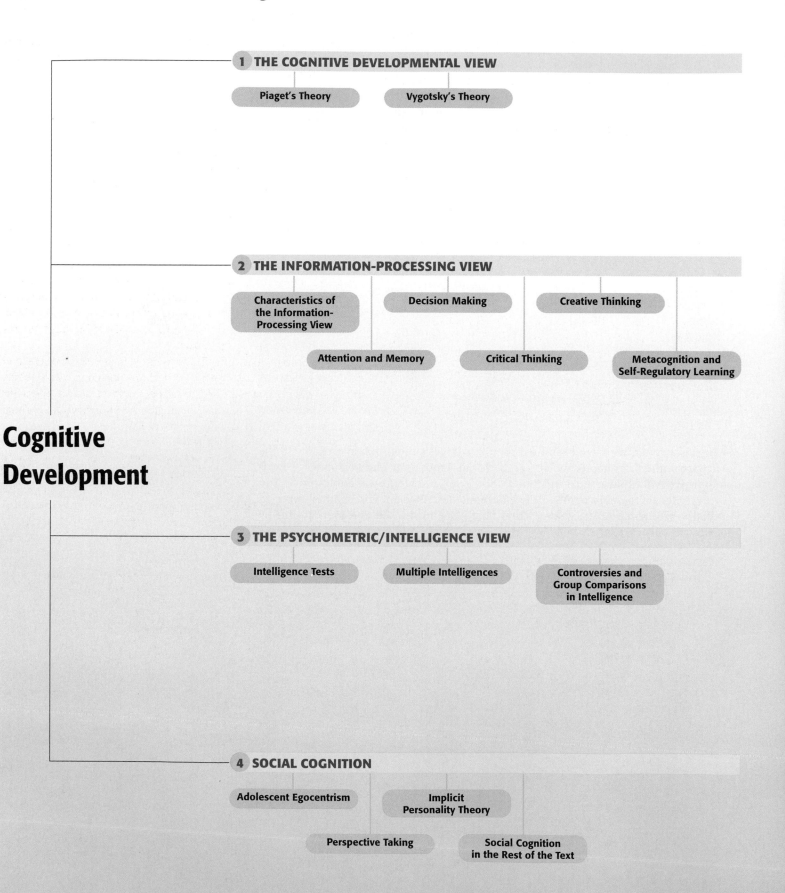

Cognitive Development

1 THE COGNITIVE DEVELOPMENTAL VIEW

- Piaget's Theory
- Vygotsky's Theory

2 THE INFORMATION-PROCESSING VIEW

- Characteristics of the Information-Processing View
- Attention and Memory
- Decision Making
- Critical Thinking
- Creative Thinking
- Metacognition and Self-Regulatory Learning

3 THE PSYCHOMETRIC/INTELLIGENCE VIEW

- Intelligence Tests
- Multiple Intelligences
- Controversies and Group Comparisons in Intelligence

4 SOCIAL COGNITION

- Adolescent Egocentrism
- Perspective Taking
- Implicit Personality Theory
- Social Cognition in the Rest of the Text

Summary

1 Discuss the cognitive developmental view of adolescence

- Piaget's widely acclaimed theory stresses the concepts of adaptation, schemas, assimilation, accommodation, and equilibrium. Piaget said that individuals develop through four cognitive stages: sensorimotor, preoperational, concrete operational, and formal operational. Formal operational thought, which Piaget believed appears from 11 to 15 years of age, is characterized by abstract, idealistic, and hypothetical-deductive thinking. Some experts argue that formal operational thought has two phases: early and late. Individual variation in adolescent cognition is extensive. Many young adolescents are still consolidating their concrete operational thought or are early formal operational thinkers rather than full-fledged ones. Although Piaget was not an educator, his ideas have been applied to education. In terms of Piaget's contributions, we owe to him the entire field of cognitive development and a masterful list of concepts. He also was a genius at observing children. Criticisms of Piaget's theory focus on estimates of competence, stages, training to reason at higher stages, and the role of culture and education. Neo-Piagetians have proposed some substantial changes in Piaget's theory. Some experts argue that the idealism of Piaget's formal operational stage declines in young adults, being replaced by more realistic, pragmatic thinking. Perry said that adolescents often engage in dualistic, absolutist thinking, whereas young adults are more likely to think reflectively and relativistically. Postformal thought is reflective, relativistic, and provisional; realistic; and open to emotions and subjective.
- Vygotsky's view stimulated considerable interest in the idea that knowledge is situated and collaborative. One of his important concepts is the zone of proximal development, which involves guidance by more-skilled peers and adults. Vygotsky argued that learning the skills of the culture is a key aspect of development. Some contemporary concepts linked with Vygotsky's theory include scaffolding, cognitive apprenticeship, tutoring, cooperative learning, and reciprocal teaching. Piaget's and Vygotsky's views are both constructivist, although Vygotsky's view is a stronger social constructivist view than Piaget's. In both views, teachers should be facilitators, not directors, of learning. Criticisms of Vygotsky's view focus on facilitators possibly being too helpful and adolescents' expecting others to do things for them.

2 Describe the information-processing view of adolescence

- Siegler states that the information-processing view emphasizes thinking, change mechanisms (encoding, automaticity, strategy construction, and generalization), and self-modification.

- Adolescents typically have better attentional skills than children do. They also have better short-term memory, working memory, and long-term memory than children.
- Adolescence is a time of increased decision making. Older adolescents make better decisions than younger adolescents, who in turn are better at this than children are. Being able to make competent decisions, however, does not mean they actually will be made in everyday life, where breadth of experience comes into play.
- Critical thinking involves thinking reflectively and productively and evaluating the evidence. Adolescence is an important transitional period in critical thinking because of such cognitive changes as increased speed, automaticity, and capacity of information processing; more breadth of content knowledge; increased ability to construct new combinations of knowledge; and a greater range and spontaneous use of strategies. Debates about critical thinking involve whether it should be taught in a general way or tied to specific subject matter and whether it resides in adolescents' heads or involves situated cognition.
- Thinking creatively is the ability to think in novel and unusual ways and discover unique solutions to problems. Guilford distinguished between convergent and divergent thinking. A number of strategies, including brainstorming, can be used to stimulate creative thinking.
- Metacognition is cognition about cognition, or knowing about knowing. In Pressley's view, the key to education is helping students learn a rich repertoire of strategies that results in solutions to problems. Self-regulatory learning is the self-generation and self-monitoring of one's thoughts, feelings, and behaviors in order to reach a goal. Most high-achieving students are self-regulatory learners.

3 Summarize the psychometric/intelligence view of adolescence

- Intelligence is the ability to solve problems and to adapt and learn from everyday experiences. A key aspect of intelligence focuses on its individual variations. Traditionally, intelligence has been measured by tests designed to compare people's performance on cognitive tasks. Alfred Binet developed the first intelligence test and created the concept of mental age. William Stern developed the concept of IQ for use with the Binet test. Revisions of the Binet test are called the Stanford-Binet. The test scores on the Stanford-Binet approximate a normal distribution. The Wechsler scales, created by David Wechsler, are the other main intelligence assessment tool. These tests provide an overall IQ, verbal and performance IQs, and information about 11 subtests. Group intelligence tests are convenient and economical, but they do not allow an examiner to monitor the testing closely. When used by a judicious examiner, tests can be valuable tools for determining individual differences in intelligence. Test scores should be only one type of information used to evaluate an individual. IQ scores can produce unfortunate stereotypes and expectations. Ability tests can help divide children into homogeneous groups but periodic testing should be done to ensure that the groupings are appropriate.

- Factor analysis is a statistical procedure that compares various items or measures and identifies underlying factors that are correlated with each other. Spearman (two-factor theory of *g* and *s*) and Thurstone (multiple-factor theory) used factor analysis in developing their views of intelligence. Gardner believes there are eight types of intelligence: verbal skills, mathematical skills, spatial skills, bodily-kinesthetic skills, musical skills, interpersonal skills, intrapersonal skills, and naturalist skills. Sternberg's triarchic theory states that there are three main types of intelligence: analytical, creative, and practical. Sternberg created the Sternberg Triarchic Abilities Test to assess these three types of intelligence and has described applications of triarchic theory to children's education. Emotional intelligence is the ability to perceive and express emotion accurately and adaptively, to understand emotion and emotional knowledge, to use feelings to facilitate thought, and to manage emotions in oneself and others. The multiple intelligences approaches have broadened the definition of intelligence and motivated educators to develop programs that instruct students in different domains. Critics maintain that the multiple intelligence theories include factors that really aren't part of intelligence, such as musical skills and creativity. Critics also say that there isn't enough research to support the concept of multiple intelligences.
- Genetic similarity might explain why identical twins show stronger correlations on intelligence tests than fraternal twins do. Some studies indicate that the IQs of adopted children are more similar to the IQs of their biological parents than to those of their adoptive parents. Many studies show that intelligence has a reasonably strong heritability component. Criticisms of the heritability concept have been made. Intelligence test scores have risen considerably around the world in recent decades—called the Flynn effect—and this supports the role of environment in intelligence. Cultures vary in the way they define intelligence. Early intelligence tests favored White, middle-socioeconomic-status urban individuals. Tests may be biased against certain groups because they are not familiar with a standard form of English, with the content tested, or with the testing situation. Tests are likely to reflect the values and experience of the dominant culture. In the United States, children and adolescents from African American and Latino families score below children and adolescents from White families on standardized intelligence tests. Males are more likely than females to have extremely high or extremely low IQ scores. There also are gender differences in specific intellectual abilities.

4 Explain how social cognition is involved in adolescent development

- Social cognition refers to how people conceptualize and reason about their social world, including the relation of the self to others. Elkind proposed that adolescents, especially young adolescents, develop an egocentrism that consists of an imaginary audience and a personal fable. Critics argue that perspective taking rather than formal operational thought is the main factor in the development of adolescent egocentrism.
- Perspective taking is the ability to take another person's perspective and understand his or her thoughts and feelings. Adolescents are better at perspective taking than children are, but there is considerable overlap in the ages at which the higher states of perspective taking occur.
- Implicit personality theory is the public's or layperson's conception of personality. Adolescents' implicit personality theory is closer to that of scientists who study personality than is the implicit personality of children. Compared with children, adolescents describe personality as having more past-present connections, as more contextual, and as more unconscious.
- We will study social cognition throughout this text, especially in chapters on the self and identity, moral development, peers, and families.

Key Terms

schema 121
assimilation 121
accommodation 121
equilibration 122
sensorimotor stage 122
preoperational stage 122
concrete operational stage 122
formal operational stage 123
hypothetical-deductive
  reasoning 124
neo-Piagetians 129
postformal thought 129
zone of proximal development
  (ZPD) 130
social constructivist
  approach 132
critical thinking 139
creativity 140
convergent thinking 140
divergent thinking 140
metacognition 142
self-regulatory learning 143
psychometric/intelligence
  view 144
intelligence 145
mental age (MA) 145
intelligence quotient (IQ) 145
normal distribution 146
triarchic theory of
  intelligence 149
emotional intelligence 150
heritability 152
culture-fair tests 154
adolescent egocentrism 156
implicit personality
  theory 158

Key People

Resources for Improving the Lives of Adolescents

Children's Thinking

(1998, 3rd ed.) by Robert Siegler
Upper Saddle River, NJ: Prentice Hall

In-depth coverage of information processing by one of the field's leading experts.

Encyclopedia of Creativity

(1999, Vols. 1 & 2) by Mark Runco & Steven Pritzker (Eds.)
San Diego: Academic Press

A wealth of information about virtually every imaginable aspect of creativity, written by leading experts.

How People Learn

(1999) by the Committee on Developments in the Science of Learning
Washington, DC: National Academy Press

A prestigious panel headed by John Bransford and Ann Brown describes the current state of knowledge about how children and youth think and learn.

Models of Intelligence

(2003) edited by Robert J. Sternberg, Jacques Lautrey, and Todd Lubart.
Washington, DC: American Psychological Association.

A wide variety of views on intelligence are presented by leading experts, including Sternberg and Gardner.

Teaching and Learning Through Multiple Intelligences

(2004, 3rd ed.) by Linda Campbell, Bruce Campbell, and Dee Dickinson
Boston: Allyn & Bacon

Provides applications of Gardner's eight intelligences to classrooms.

E-Learning Tools

To help you master the material in this chapter, you will find a number of valuable study tools in the student CD-ROM that accompanies this book. In addition, visit the Online Learning Center for *Adolescence, 10th Edition*, where you will find helpful resources for chapter 4, "Cognitive Development."

Taking It to the Net

http://www.mhhe.com/santrocka10

1. Your psychology instructor notes that in surfing the Web one can find a large number of sites with IQ tests, including tests for emotional IQ, sports IQ, trivia IQ, social IQ, musical IQ, as well as tests for IQs in a variety of other areas. As an extra credit assignment the instructor challenges the class to write a two-page paper indicating whose theoretical stance about intelligence could encompass such IQ concepts and how it would do so. What would you write?

2. Suppose your roommate complains that there is just too much material to learn in his or her classes and that he or she has a lot of trouble getting all the information into memory. You recognize this as a metamemory (thinking about memory) problem. What means would you suggest your roommate use to improve getting information into memory?

3. As a dual major in biology and psychology, you realize that fundamental psychological processes such as memory, problem solving, and information processing must ultimately be tied to components of biological development. You decide to write your term paper on the links between neuroscience and cognitive development. What themes will you write about?

Connect to **http://www.mhhe.com/santrocka10** to research the answers and complete these exercises. In some cases, you'll also find further instructions on this site.

Self-Assessment

Complete the following self-assessments to explore your cognitive development and processes: (1) Exploring Changes in My Thinking from Adolescence to Adulthood, (2) My Study Skills, (3) Examining My Creative Thinking, (4) Evaluating Myself on Gardner's Eight Types of Intelligence, and (5) How Emotionally Intelligent Am I?

Health and Well-Being, Parenting, and Education

To practice your decision-making skills, complete the health and well-being, parenting, and education scenarios.

Social, Emotional, and Personality Development

He who would learn to fly one day must learn to stand and walk and climb and dance: one cannot fly into flying.

—Friedrich Nietzsche
German Philosopher, 19th Century

So far, we have studied the adolescent's biological and cognitive development. In this section, we will examine the adolescent's social, emotional, and personality development. Section 3 consists of four chapters: chapter 5, "The Self, Identity, Emotions, and Personality"; chapter 6, "Gender"; chapter 7, "Sexuality"; and chapter 8, "Moral Development, Values, and Religion."

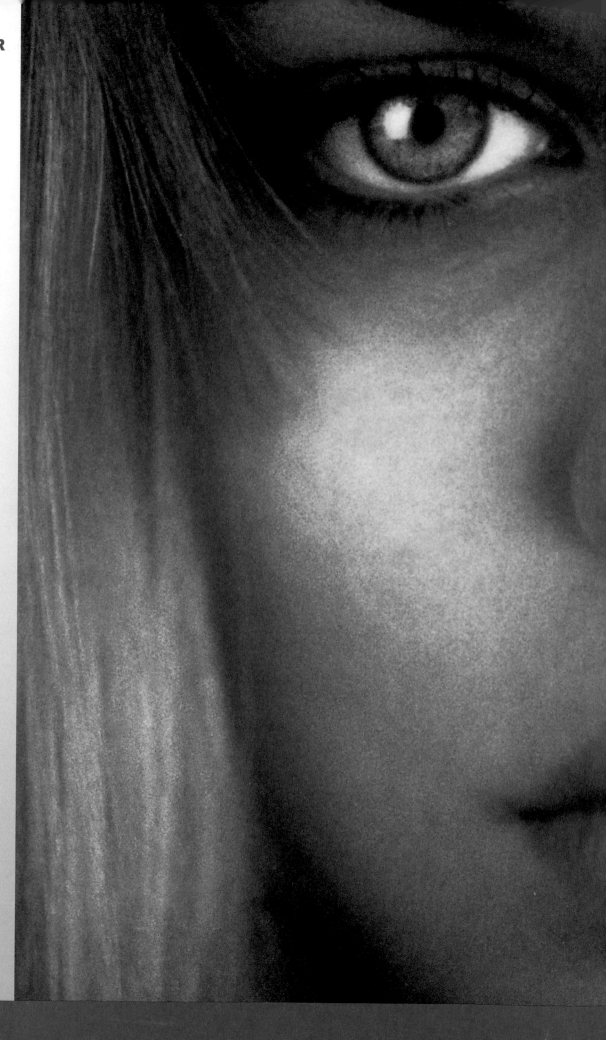

"Who are you?" said the Caterpillar. Alice replied, rather shyly, "I—I hardly know, Sir, just at present— at least I know who I was when I got up this morning, but I must have changed several times since then."
—LEWIS CARROLL
English Writer, 19th Century

The Self, Identity, Emotions, and Personality

Learning Goals

1 Describe the development of the self in adolescence

2 Explain the many facets of identity development

3 Discuss the emotional development of adolescents

4 Characterize the personality development of adolescents

Images of Adolescent Development

A 15-Year-Old Girl's Self-Description

How do adolescents describe themselves? How would you have described yourself when you were 15 years old? What features would you have emphasized? The following is a self-portrait of one 15-year-old girl:

What am I like as a person? Complicated! I'm sensitive, friendly, outgoing, popular, and tolerant, though I can also be shy, self-conscious, and even obnoxious. Obnoxious! I'd like to be friendly and tolerant all of the time. That's the kind of person I want to be, and I'm disappointed when I'm not. I'm responsible, even studious now and then, but on the other hand, I'm a goof-off, too, because if you're too studious, you won't be popular. I don't usually do that well at school. I'm a pretty cheerful person, especially with my friends, where I can even get rowdy. At home I'm more likely to be anxious around my parents. They expect me to get all A's. It's not fair! I worry about how I probably should get better grades. But I'd be mortified in the eyes of my friends. So I'm usually pretty stressed-out at home, or sarcastic, since my parents are always on my case. But I really don't understand how I can switch so fast. I mean, how can I be cheerful one minute, anxious the next, and then be sarcastic? Which one is the real me? Sometimes, I feel phony, especially around boys. Say I think some guy might be interested in asking me out. I try to act different, like Madonna. I'll be flirtatious and fun-loving. And then everybody, I mean everybody else is looking at me like they think I'm totally weird. Then I get self-conscious and embarrassed and become radically introverted, and I don't know who I really am! Am I just trying to impress them or what? But I don't really care what they think anyway. I don't want to care, that is. I just want to know what my close friends think. I can be my true self with my close friends. I can't be my real self with my parents. They don't understand me. What do they know about what it's like to be a teenager? They still treat me like I'm still a kid. At least at school people treat you more like you're an adult. That gets confusing, though. I mean, which am I, a kid or an adult? It's scary, too, because I don't have any idea what I want to be when I grow up. I mean, I have lots of ideas. My friend Sheryl and I talk about whether we'll be flight attendants, or teachers, or nurses, veterinarians, maybe mothers, or actresses. I know I don't want to be a waitress or a secretary. But how do you decide all of this? I really don't know. I mean, I think about it a lot, but I can't resolve it. There are days when I wish I could just become immune to myself. (Harter, 1990b, pp. 352–353)

This excerpt illustrates the increased self-understanding, identity exploration, and emotional changes that are among the hallmarks of adolescent development. Far more than as children, adolescents seek to know who they are, what they are all about, and where they are going in life. In the first two sections of this chapter, we will explore the self and identity, which are often considered to be central aspects of personality development in adolescence. Next, we will turn our attention to the emotional landscape of adolescence and then conclude the chapter by examining the personality traits and temperament of adolescents.

1 THE SELF

Self-Understanding   **Self-Esteem and Self-Concept**

Adolescents carry with them a sense of who they are and what makes them different from everyone else. Consider one adolescent male's self-description: "I am male, bright, an athlete, a political liberal, an extravert, and a compassionate individual." He takes comfort in his uniqueness: "No one else is quite like me. I am 5 feet 11 inches tall and weigh 160 pounds. I live in a suburb and plan to attend the state university. I want to be a sports journalist. I am an expert at building canoes. When I am not going to school and studying, I write short stories about sports figures, which I hope to publish someday." Real or imagined, an adolescent's developing sense of self and uniqueness is a motivating force in life. Our exploration of the self begins with information about adolescents' self-understanding and then turns to their self-esteem and self-concept.

Self-Understanding

Though individuals become more introspective in adolescence, this self-understanding is not completely internal; rather, self-understanding is a social-cognitive construction (Bergman, 2004; Bosma & Kunnen, 2001; Harre, 2004; Tesser, Fleeson, & Suls, 2000). That is, adolescents' developing cognitive capacities interact with their sociocultural experiences to influence their self-understanding. These are among the questions we will examine in this section: What is self-understanding? What are some important dimensions of adolescents' self-understanding?

What Is Self-Understanding? **Self-understanding** is the adolescent's cognitive representation of the self, the substance and content of the adolescent's self-conceptions. For example, a 12-year-old boy understands that he is a student, a football player, a family member, and a video game lover. A 14-year-old girl understands that she is a cheerleader, a student council member, a movie fan, and a rock music fan. An adolescent's self-understanding is based, in part, on the various roles and membership categories that define who adolescents are (Harter, 1990a). Though self-understanding provides the rational underpinnings, it is not the whole of personal identity.

Dimensions of Adolescents' Self-Understanding The development of self-understanding in adolescence is complex and involves a number of aspects of the self (Harter, 1998, 1999). Let's examine how the adolescent's self-understanding differs from the child's.

Abstraction and Idealism Remember from our discussion of Piaget's theory of cognitive development in chapters 2 and 4 that many adolescents begin to think in more *abstract and idealistic* ways. When asked to describe themselves, adolescents are more

self-understanding The adolescent's cognitive representation of the self; the substance and content of the adolescent's self-conceptions.

The contemporary perspective on the self emphasizes the construction of multiple self-representations across different relational contexts.

—SUSAN HARTER
*Contemporary Psychologist,
University of Denver*

likely than children to use abstract and idealistic terms. Consider 14-year-old Laurie's abstract description of herself: "I am a human being. I am indecisive. I don't know who I am." Also consider her idealistic description of herself: "I am a naturally sensitive person who really cares about people's feelings. I think I'm pretty good-looking." Not all adolescents describe themselves in idealistic ways, but most adolescents distinguish between the real self and the ideal self.

Differentiation   Over time, an adolescent's self-understanding becomes increasingly *differentiated*. Adolescents are more likely than children to note contextual or situational variations in describing themselves (Harter, Waters, & Whitesell, 1996). For example, a 15-year-old girl might describe herself by using one set of characteristics in connection with her family and another set of characteristics in connection with her peers and friends. Yet another set of characteristics might appear in her self-description of her romantic relationship. In sum, adolescents are more likely than children to understand that they possess several different selves, each one depending on a particular role or context.

The Fluctuating Self   Given the contradictory nature of the self in adolescence, it is not surprising that the self fluctuates across situations and across time (Harter, 1990a; Harter & Whitesell, 2002). The 15-year-old girl who was quoted at the beginning of this chapter remarked that she could not understand how she could switch from being cheerful one moment, to being anxious the next, and then sarcastic a short time later. One researcher has referred to the fluctuating adolescent's self as "the barometric self" (Rosenberg, 1979). In most cases, the self continues to be characterized by instability until late adolescence or even early adulthood, when a more unified theory of self is constructed. We will have more to say about fluctuations in adolescents' emotions later in the chapter.

Contradictions Within the Self   As adolescents begin to differentiate their concept of the self into multiple roles in different relationship contexts, they sense potential contradictions between their differentiated selves. In one study, Susan Harter (1986) asked seventh-, ninth-, and eleventh-graders to describe themselves. She found that the number of contradictory self-descriptions they mentioned (moody *and* understanding, ugly *and* attractive, bored *and* inquisitive, caring *and* uncaring, introverted *and* fun-loving) increased dramatically between the seventh and ninth grades. Though the number of contradictory self-descriptions students mentioned declined in the eleventh grade, they still outnumbered those noted in the seventh grade. Adolescents develop the cognitive ability to detect these inconsistencies as they strive to construct a general theory of the self (Harter & Monsour, 1992).

Real Versus Ideal, True Versus False Selves   Adolescents' emerging ability to construct ideal selves can be perplexing to them. While the capacity to recognize a discrepancy between the *real* and *ideal* selves represents a cognitive advance, the humanistic theorist Carl Rogers (1950) believed that a strong discrepancy between the real and ideal selves is a sign of maladjustment. Too great a discrepancy between one's actual self and one's ideal self—the person one wants to be—can produce a sense of failure and self-criticism and can even trigger depression.

   Although some theorists consider a strong discrepancy between the ideal and real selves maladaptive, others argue that it need not always be, especially in adolescence. In one view, an important aspect of the ideal or imagined self is the **possible self**: what individuals might become, what they would like to become, and what they are afraid of becoming (Cota-Robles, Neiss, & Hunt, 2000; Markus & Nurius, 1986). Thus, adolescents' possible selves include both what they hope to be as well as what they dread they could become (Martin, 1997). In this view, the presence of both hoped-for and dreaded ideal selves is psychologically healthy, lending balance to an adolescent's perspective and motivation. That is, the attributes of the future positive self—getting

possible self What individuals might become, what they would like to become, and what they are afraid of becoming.

into a good college, being admired, having a successful career—can direct an adolescent's positive actions, while the attributes of the future negative self—being unemployed, being lonely, not getting into a good college—can identify behaviors to be avoided.

Can adolescents distinguish between their *true* and *false* selves? In one research study, they could (Harter & Lee, 1989). Adolescents are most likely to show their false selves with classmates and in romantic or dating situations; they are least likely to show their false selves with close friends. Adolescents may display a false self to impress others or to try out new behaviors or roles. They may feel that others do not understand their true selves or that others force them to behave in false ways. Some adolescents report that they do not like their false-self behavior, but others say that it does not bother them. Harter, Stocker, and Robinson (1996) found that experienced authenticity of the self is highest among adolescents who say they receive support from their parents.

Social Comparison   Some developmentalists believe that adolescents are more likely than children to use *social comparison* in evaluating themselves (Ruble & others, 1980). However, adolescents' willingness to *admit* that they engage in social comparison for this purpose declines during adolescence because they view social comparison as socially undesirable. That is, they think that acknowledging their social comparison motives will endanger their popularity.

Relying on social comparison information can be confusing to adolescents because of the large number of reference groups available to them. Should adolescents compare themselves to classmates in general? To friends of their own gender? To popular adolescents, good-looking adolescents, athletic adolescents? Considering all of these social comparison groups simultaneously can be perplexing for adolescents.

Self-Consciousness   Adolescents are more likely than children to be *self-conscious* about and preoccupied with their self-understanding. Although adolescents become more introspective, they do not always develop their self-understanding in social isolation. Adolescents turn to their friends for support and self-clarification, including their friends' opinions in their emerging self-definitions. As one researcher on self-development commented, adolescents' friends are often the main source of reflected self-appraisals, the social mirror into which adolescents anxiously stare (Rosenberg, 1979). This self-consciousness and self-preoccupation reflect adolescent egocentrism, which we discussed in chapter 4.

Self-Protection   In adolescence, the sense of confusion and conflict that is stimulated by the efforts to understand oneself is accompanied by a need to *protect the self*. In an attempt to protect the self, adolescents are prone to deny their negative characteristics. For example, in Harter's investigation of self-understanding, adolescents were more likely than not to see positive self-descriptions such as *attractive, fun-loving, sensitive, affectionate,* and *inquisitive* as central, important aspects of the self, and to see negative self-descriptions such as *ugly, mediocre, depressed, selfish,* and *nervous* as peripheral, less important aspects of the self (Harter, 1986). This tendency is consistent with adolescents' tendency to describe the self in idealistic ways.

The Unconscious Self   In adolescence, self-understanding involves greater recognition that the self includes *unconscious* as well as conscious components. This recognition is not likely to occur until late adolescence, however (Selman, 1980). That is, older adolescents are more likely than younger adolescents to believe that certain aspects of their mental experience are beyond their awareness or control.

Self-Integration   Especially in late adolescence and emerging adulthood, self-understanding becomes more *integrative,* with the disparate parts of the self pieced together more systematically. Older youth may detect inconsistencies in their earlier self-descriptions as they attempt to construct a general theory of self, an integrated sense of identity.

Because the adolescent creates multiple self-concepts, the task of integrating these varying self-conceptions becomes problematic. At the same time that adolescents are feeling pressure to differentiate the self into multiple roles, the emergence of formal operational thought presses them for *integration* and the development of a consistent, coherent theory of self. At first, their budding formal operational skills represent a liability, allowing adolescents to detect inconsistencies in the self across varying roles. Only later do these skills provide the cognitive capacity to *integrate* such apparent contradictions. In the excerpt that opened this chapter, the 15-year-old girl wondered how she could move so quickly from being cheerful to being depressed and then to being sarcastic. "Which is the real me?" she asked. Researchers have found that 14- to 15-year-olds not only detect these inconsistencies across various roles (with parents, friends, and romantic partners, for example) but also are much more troubled by these contradictions than younger (11- to 12-year-old) and older (17- to 18-year-old) adolescents (Damon & Hart, 1988).

Conclusions As we have seen, the development of self-understanding in adolescence is complex, involving a number of aspects of the self. The rapid changes that occur during the transition from childhood to adolescence produce a heightened self-awareness and self-consciousness, which in turn can produce doubt about who the self is and which facets of the self are "real" (Hart, 1996).

James Marcia (1996) believes that changes in the self during adolescence can best be understood by dividing them into early ("deconstruction"), middle ("reconstruction"), and late ("consolidation") phases. That is, in the early phase the adolescent confronts contradictory self-descriptions. In the middle phase, the adolescent attempts to resolve these contradictions. Finally in the late phase the adolescent develops a more integrated self-theory (identity).

Self-Understanding and Sociocultural Contexts We have seen that the adolescent's self-understanding can vary across relationships and social roles. Researchers have found that adolescents' portraits of themselves can differ depending on whether they describe themselves when they are with their mother, father, close friend, romantic partner, or peer. They also can differ depending on whether they describe themselves in the role of student, athlete, or employee. Similarly, adolescents might create different selves depending on their ethnic and cultural background and experiences (Lalonde & Chandler, 2004).

The multiple selves of ethnically diverse youth reflect their experiences in navigating their multiple worlds of family, peers, school, and community (Cooper & others, 2002). Research with U.S. youth of African, Chinese, Filipino, Latino, European, Japanese, and Vietnamese descent, as well as with Japanese youth, shows that as these youth move from one culture to another, they can encounter barriers related to language, racism, gender, immigration, and poverty. In each of their different worlds, however, they also can find resources—in institutions, in other people, and in themselves. Youth who find it too difficult to move between worlds can become alienated from their school, family, or peers. However, youth who can navigate effectively between different worlds can develop bicultural or multicultural selves and become "culture brokers" for others.

Hazel Markus and her colleagues (Markus & Kitayama, 1994; Markus, Mullally, & Kitayama, 1999) believe understanding how multiple selves emerge through participation in cultural practices is important. They argue that all selves are culture-specific that emerge as individuals adapt to their cultural environments. In North American contexts (especially middle-SES contexts), the culture promotes and maintains individuality. When given the opportunity to describe themselves, North Americans often provide not only current portraits but notions of their future selves as well. They frequently show a need for multiple selves that are stable and consistent. In Japan,

Hazel Markus Talks About Selfways

multiple selves are often described in terms of relatedness to others (Dedikdes & Brewer, 2001). For many Japanese, self-improvement is also an important aspect of these multiple selves. Markus and her colleagues recognize that cultural groups are characterized by diversity but conclude that placing the dominant aspects of multiple selves in a culture is helpful.

At this point we have discussed many aspects of self-understanding. Recall, however, that the self involves not only self-understanding but also self-esteem and self-concept. That is, adolescents not only try to define and describe the attributes of the self (self-understanding), they also evaluate those attributes (self-concept and self-esteem).

Self-Esteem and Self-Concept

What are self-esteem and self-concept? How are they measured? Are some domains more salient to the adolescent's self-esteem than others? How do relationships with parents and peers influence adolescents' self-esteem? What are the consequences of low self-esteem in adolescents and how can their self-esteem be raised?

What Are Self-Esteem and Self-Concept?   **Self-esteem,** also referred to as *self-worth* or *self-image,* is the global evaluative dimension of the self. For example, an adolescent might perceive that she is not merely a person, but a good person. Of course, not all adolescents have an overall positive image of themselves. **Self-concept** refers to domain-specific evaluations of the self. Adolescents make self-evaluations in many domains—academic, athletic, physical appearance, and so on. In sum, self-esteem refers to global self-evaluations, self-concept to domain-specific evaluations.

Investigators have not always made a clear distinction between self-esteem and self-concept, sometimes using the terms interchangeably or not precisely defining them (Dusek & McIntyre, 2003). As you read the remaining discussion of self-esteem and self-concept, the distinction between self-esteem as global self-evaluation and self-concept as domain-specific self-evaluation should help you to keep the terms straight.

Measuring Self-Esteem and Self-Concept   Measuring self-esteem and self-concept hasn't always been easy, especially in assessing adolescents (Dusek & McIntyre, 2003; Owens, Stryker, & Goodman, 2001; Wylie, 1979). For many years, such measures were designed primarily for children or for adults, with little attention paid to adolescents. Then, Susan Harter (1989) developed a separate measure for adolescents: the Self-Perception Profile for Adolescents. It assesses eight domains—scholastic competence, athletic competence, social acceptance, physical appearance, behavioral conduct, close friendship, romantic appeal, and job competence—plus global self-worth. The adolescent measure has three skill domains not present in the measure she developed for children: job competence, romantic appeal, and close friendship.

Some assessment experts argue that a combination of several methods should be used in measuring self-esteem. In addition to self-reporting, rating of an adolescent's self-esteem by others and observations of the adolescent's behavior in various settings could provide a more complete and more accurate self-esteem picture. Peers, teachers, parents, and even others who do not know the adolescent can be asked to rate the adolescent's self-esteem. Adolescents' facial expressions and the extent to which they congratulate or condemn themselves are also good indicators of how they view themselves. For example, adolescents who rarely smile or rarely act happy are revealing something about their self-esteem. One investigation that used behavioral observations in the assessment of self-esteem shows some of the positive as well as negative behaviors that can provide clues to the adolescent's self-esteem (see figure 5.1) (Savin-Williams & Demo, 1983). By using a variety of methods (such as self-report and behavioral observations) and obtaining information from various sources (such as the adolescent, parents, friends, and teachers), investigators probably can construct a more accurate picture of the adolescent's self-esteem. To learn more about how there is a need in

www.mhhe.com/santrocka10

An Adolescent Talks About Self-Esteem

self-esteem The global evaluative dimension of the self; also referred to as self-worth or self-image.

self-concept Domain-specific evaluations of the self.

Positive Indicators	Negative Indicators
1. Gives others directives or commands	1. Puts down others by teasing, name-calling, or gossiping
2. Uses voice quality appropriate for situation	2. Uses gestures that are dramatic or out of context
3. Expresses opinions	3. Engages in inappropriate touching or avoids physical contact
4. Sits with others during social activities	4. Gives excuses for failures
5. Works cooperatively in a group	5. Brags excessively about achievements, skills, appearance
6. Faces others when speaking or being spoken to	6. Verbally puts self down; self-deprecation
7. Maintains eye contact during conversation	7. Speaks too loudly, abruptly, or in a dogmatic tone
8. Initiates friendly contact with others	
9. Maintains comfortable space between self and others	
10. Has little hesitation in speech, speaks fluently	

FIGURE 5.1 Behavioral Indicators of Self-Esteem

adolescence for multiple selves, watch the video "Adolescent Self Esteem." Also, see for yourself how self-esteem fluctuates for three girls as they discusss different factors contributing to their self-perceptions in the video "Adolescent Self Concept at Age 16."

Does Self-Esteem Change During Adolescence? The extent to which self-esteem changes during adolescence, and the question of whether there are gender differences in adolescent self-esteem, are still the subject of controversy. Although an increasing number of studies have found that self-esteem declines in early adolescence, more so for girls than for boys, critics argue that more research needs to be conducted before firm conclusions can be drawn. They note that when developmental changes and gender differences do occur, they are often small (Harter, 2002; Kling & others, 1999).

Researchers have found that self-esteem often decreases when children make the transition from elementary school to middle or junior high school (Hawkins & Berndt, 1985; Simmons & Blyth, 1987; Twenge & Campbell, 2001). Indeed, during and just after many life transitions, individuals' self-esteem often decreases. This decrease in self-esteem may occur during the transition from middle or junior high school to high school, and from high school to college.

Self-esteem does seem to fluctuate across the life span. One recent cross-sectional study assessed the self-esteem of a very large, diverse sample of 326,641 individuals from 9 to 90 years of age (Robins & others, 2002). About two-thirds of the participants were from the United States. The individuals were asked to respond to the item, "I have high self-esteem" on a five-point scale in which 1 stood for "strongly agree" and 5 stood for "strongly disagree." Self-esteem decreased in adolescence, increased in the twenties, leveled off in the thirties, rose in the fifties and sixties, and then dropped in the seventies and eighties (see figure 5.2). At most ages, males reported higher self-esteem than females.

Some researchers argue that while there may be a decrease in self-esteem during adolescence, the drop is actually very slight and not nearly as pronounced as presented in the media (Harter, 2002; Kling & others, 1999). Also note in figure 5.2 that despite the drop in self-esteem among adolescent girls, their average score (3.3) was still slightly higher than the neutral point on the scale (3.0).

Recent research based on data collected in the Family Health Study found that self-esteem declined among female adolescents from 12 to 17 years of age (Baldwin & Hoffman, 2002). In contrast, self-esteem rose among males from 12 to 14 years of age, then decreased until approximately 16 years of age, when it began to rise again. Keep

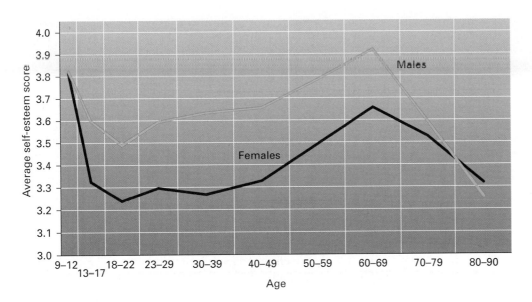

FIGURE 5.2 Self-Esteem Across the Life Span

One large-scale study asked more than 300,000 individuals to rate the extent to which they have high self-esteem on a 5-point scale, 5 being "Strongly Agree" and 1 being "Strongly Disagree." Self-esteem dropped in adolescence and late adulthood. Self-esteem of females was lower than self-esteem of males through most of the life span.

in mind, however, that in the view of some researchers, developmental changes and gender differences in self-esteem are often small (Harter, 2002; Kling & others, 1999). In this study, fluctuations in self-esteem during adolescence were related to life events and family cohesiveness (Baldwin & Hoffman, 2002).

One explanation for the decline in the self-esteem among females during early adolescence focuses on girls' more negative body images during pubertal change compared with boys. Another explanation involves the greater interest young adolescent girls take in social relationships and society's failure to reward that interest.

Might adolescents' self-esteem be influenced by cohort effects? (*Cohort effects* are effects that are due to a person's time of birth or generation but not to actual age.) A recent analysis of studies conducted from the 1960s into the 1990s found that the self-esteem of college students was higher in the 1990s than it was in the 1960s (Twenge & Campbell, 2001). The explanation given for this increase in self-esteem involves the self-esteem movement and the active encouragement of self-esteem in schools.

Are Some Domains More Closely Linked to Self-Esteem Than Others? Physical appearance is an especially powerful contributor to self-esteem in adolescence. In Harter's research, for example, global self-esteem was correlated most strongly with physical appearance, a link that has been found in both the United States and other countries (Fox & others, 1994; Harter, 1999; Maeda, 1999) (see figure 5.3). In another study, adolescents' concept of their physical attractiveness was the strongest predictor of their overall self-esteem (Lord & Eccles, 1994). This strong association between perceived appearance and general self-worth is not confined to adolescence, but holds across the life span, from early childhood through middle age (Harter, 1999).

Social Contexts and Self-Esteem Social contexts such as the family, peers, and schools contribute to the development of an adolescent's self-esteem (Dusek & McIntyre, 2003). One recent study found that as family cohesiveness increased, adolescents' self-esteem increased over time (Baldwin & Hoffman, 2002). In this study, family cohesion was based on the amount of time the family spent together, the quality of their communication, and the extent to which the adolescent was involved in family decision making.

Domain	Harter's U.S. Samples	Other Countries
Physical Appearance	.65	.62
Scholastic Competence	.48	.41
Social Acceptance	.46	.40
Behavioral Conduct	.45	.45
Athletic Competence	.33	.30

FIGURE 5.3 Correlations Between Global Self-Esteem and Domains of Competence

Note: The correlations shown are the average correlations computed across a number of studies. The other countries in this evaluation were England, Ireland, Australia, Canada, Germany, Italy, Greece, the Netherlands, and Japan. Recall from chapter 2 that correlation coefficients can range from −1.00 to +1.00. The correlations between physical appearance and global self-esteem (.65 and .62) are moderately high.

In another investigation of self-esteem and parent-child relationships, a measure of self-esteem was administered to boys, and the boys and their mothers were interviewed about family relationships (Coopersmith, 1967). Based on these assessments, the following parenting attributes were associated with boys' high self-esteem:

- Expression of affection
- Concern about the boys' problems
- Harmony in the home
- Participation in joint family activities
- Availability to give competent, organized help when the boys needed it
- Setting clear and fair rules
- Abiding by the rules
- Allowing the boys freedom within well-prescribed limits

Remember that because these findings are correlational, researchers cannot say that these parenting attributes *cause* children's high self-esteem. Expressing affection and allowing children freedom within well-prescribed limits probably do contribute to children's self-esteem, but researchers must still say that they are *related* to rather than *cause* children's self-esteem, based on the available research data.

Peer judgments gain increasing importance in adolescence. The correlation between peer approval and self-worth increases during adolescence (Harter, 1990b). However, support from the general peer group (classmates, peers in organizations) is more strongly related to self-worth than is support from close friends (Harter, 1999). Although peer approval is linked with self-worth, parental approval continues to be related to adolescents' self-worth through adolescence and this correlation does not decline until emerging adulthood (Harter, 1999).

The transition from elementary school to middle or junior high school is associated with lowered self-esteem. Researchers have found that self-esteem is higher in the last year of elementary school than in middle or junior high school, especially in the first year after the transition (Hawkins & Berndt, 1985; Simmons & Blyth, 1987). We will have much more to say about the transition from elementary to middle or junior high school in chapter 11, "Schools."

Consequences of Low Self-Esteem   For most adolescents, the emotional discomfort of low self-esteem is only temporary. But in some, low self-esteem can develop into other problems (Usher & others, 2000; Zimmerman, Copeland, & Shope, 1997). Low self-esteem has been implicated in depression, suicide, anorexia nervosa, delinquency, and other adjustment problems (Fenzel, 1994). The seriousness of the problem depends not only on the nature of the adolescent's low self-esteem, but on other conditions as well. When low self-esteem is compounded by difficult school transitions, a troubled family life, or other stressful events, an adolescent's problems can intensify.

Increasing Adolescents' Self-Esteem   Given the potential consequences of low self-esteem, how can adults help to improve adolescents' self-esteem? Four ways to improve adolescents' self-esteem are (1) identify the causes of low self-esteem and the domains of competence important to the self, (2) provide emotional support and social approval, (3) foster achievement, and (4) help adolescents to cope (see figure 5.4).

Identifying an adolescent's sources of self-esteem—that is, the domains that are important to the self—is critical to improving self-esteem. Self-esteem theorist and researcher Susan Harter (1990b) points out that the self-esteem enhancement programs of the 1960s, in which self-esteem itself was the target and individuals were encouraged to simply feel good about themselves, were ineffective. Rather, Harter (1998) believes that intervention must occur at the level of the *causes* of self-esteem if an adolescent's self-esteem is to improve significantly. Adolescents have the highest self-esteem when they perform competently in domains important to the self. Therefore, adolescents should be encouraged to identify and value their domains of competence.

FIGURE 5.4 Four Main Ways to Improve Self-Esteem

Identifying the causes of low self-esteem and which domains of competence are important to the self

Emotional support and social approval

Achievement

Coping

Emotional support and social approval in the form of confirmation from others can also powerfully influence an adolescent's self-esteem (Harter, 1990b). Some youth with low self-esteem come from conflicted families or conditions in which they experienced abuse or neglect—situations in which support is unavailable. In some cases, alternative sources of support can be implemented, either informally through the encouragement of a teacher, a coach, or another significant adult, or more formally, through programs such as Big Brothers and Big Sisters. While peer approval becomes increasingly important during adolescence, both adult and peer support are important influences on the adolescent's self-esteem. In one recent study, both parental and peer support were related to the adolescent's general self-worth (Robinson, 1995).

Achievement can also improve adolescents' self-esteem (Bednar, Wells, & Peterson, 1995). For example, the straightforward teaching of real skills to adolescents often results in increased achievement and, thus, in enhanced self-esteem. Adolescents develop higher self-esteem because they know what tasks are important for achieving goals, and they have experienced performing them or similar behaviors. The emphasis on the importance of achievement in improving self-esteem has much in common with Albert Bandura's (2000, 2002) social cognitive concept of *self-efficacy*, which refers to individuals' beliefs that they can master a situation and produce positive outcomes.

Self-esteem often increases when adolescents face a problem and try to cope with it rather than avoid it (Lazarus, 1991). Facing problems realistically, honestly, and nondefensively produces favorable self-evaluative thoughts, which lead to the self-generated approval that raises self-esteem. The converse is true of avoidant behavior. Denial, deception, and avoidance of that which has already been glimpsed as true trigger unfavorable self-evaluations.

Review and reflect Learning goal 1

1 **Describe the development of the self in adolescence**

REVIEW

- What is self-understanding? What are the key dimensions of self-understanding in adolescence?
- What are self-esteem and self-concept? How can they be measured? Are some domains more salient than others to adolescents' self-esteem? How are social contexts linked with adolescents' self-esteem? What are the consequences of low self-esteem? How can adolescents' self-esteem be increased?

REFLECT

- Think about what your future selves might be. What do you envision will make you the happiest about the future selves you aspire to become? What prospective selves hold negative possibilities?

2 IDENTITY

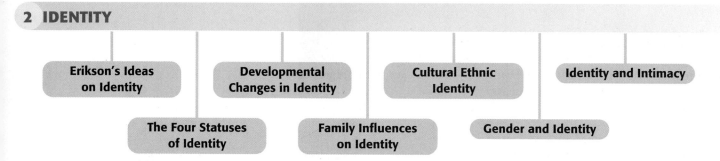

An important characteristic of self-understanding that was described earlier in this chapter was self-integration, or the piecing together of different aspects of the self. Self-integration is exemplified in the development of an identity. By far the most comprehensive and provocative theory of identity development is that of Erik Erikson. In fact, some experts on adolescence consider Erikson's ideas to be the single most influential theory of adolescent development. Erikson's theory was introduced in chapter 2; we will expand on that introduction, beginning with an analysis of his ideas on identity.

Erikson's Ideas on Identity

Who am I? What am I all about? What am I going to do with my life? What is different about me? How can I make it on my own? These questions, not usually considered in childhood, surface as a common, virtually universal concern during adolescence. Adolescents clamor for solutions to questions of identity. Erik Erikson (1950, 1968) was the first to realize how central such questions are to understanding adolescent development. That today identity is believed to be a key concept in adolescent development results directly from Erikson's masterful thinking and analysis.

Revisiting Erikson's Views on Identity Identity versus identity confusion, Erikson's fifth developmental stage, occurs during the adolescent years. At this time, adolescents are faced with deciding who they are, what they are all about, and where they are going in life. They confront many new roles, from vocational to romantic. As part of their identity exploration, adolescents experience a **psychosocial moratorium,** Erikson's term for the gap between childhood security and adult autonomy. In the course of exploring and searching their culture's identity files, they often experiment with different roles. Youth who successfully cope with these

identity versus identity confusion
Erikson's fifth developmental stage, which occurs during adolescence. At this time, individuals are faced with deciding who they are, what they are all about, and where they are going in life.

psychosocial moratorium Erikson's term for the gap between childhood security and adult autonomy that adolescents experience as part of their identity exploration.

conflicting roles and identities emerge with a new sense of self that is both refreshing and acceptable. But adolescents who do not successfully resolve the identity crisis suffer what Erikson calls identity confusion. Either they withdraw, isolating themselves from peers and family, or they immerse themselves in the world of peers and lose their identity in the crowd.

Erikson's ideas about adolescent identity development reveal rich insights into adolescents' thoughts and feelings. Reading one or more of his original books is worthwhile. A good starting point is *Identity: Youth and Crisis* (1968). Other works that deal with identity development are *Young Man Luther* (1962) and *Gandhi's Truth* (1969), which won a Pulitzer Prize.

One of Erik Erikson's strategies for explaining the nature of identity development was to analyze the lives of famous individuals. One such individual was Mahatma Gandhi (*center*), the spiritual leader of India in the mid–twentieth century, about whom Erikson (1969) wrote in *Gandhi's Truth.*

Personality and Role Experimentation   Two core ingredients in Erikson's theory of identity development are personality and role experimentation. As we have seen, Erikson believed that adolescents face an overwhelming number of choices and at some point during their youth enter a period of psychological moratorium (Hopkins, 2000). During this moratorium and before they reach a stable sense of self, they try out different roles and personalities. They might be argumentative one moment, cooperative the next. They might dress neatly one day and sloppily the next day. One week they might like a particular friend, the next week they might despise the friend. This personality experimentation is a deliberate effort on the part of adolescents to find their place in the world.

As adolescents gradually come to realize that they will soon be responsible for themselves and their lives, they search for what those lives are going to be. Many parents and other adults, accustomed to having children go along with what they say, may be bewildered or incensed by the wisecracks, rebelliousness, and rapid mood changes that accompany adolescence. But it is important for these adults to give adolescents the time and opportunity to explore different roles and personalities. In turn, most adolescents eventually discard undesirable roles.

There are literally hundreds of roles for adolescents to try out, and probably just as many ways to pursue each role. Erikson believed that by late adolescence, vocational roles become central to identity development, especially in a highly technological society like that of the United States. Youth who have been well trained to enter a workforce that offers the potential of reasonably high self-esteem will experience the least stress during this phase of identity development. Some youth may reject jobs offering good pay and traditionally high social status, choosing instead work that allows them to be more genuinely helpful to others, perhaps in the Peace Corps, a mental health clinic, or a school for children in a low-income neighborhood. Some youth may prefer unemployment to the prospect of work they feel they could not perform well or would make them feel useless. To Erikson, such choices reflect the desire to achieve a meaningful identity by being true to oneself, rather than by burying one's identity in the larger society.

According to Erikson, identity is a self-portrait that is composed of many pieces:

- The career and work path a person wants to follow (vocational/career identity)
- Whether a person is politically conservative, liberal, or middle of the road (political identity)
- A person's spiritual beliefs (religious identity)
- Whether a person is single, married, divorced, or cohabiting (relationship identity)
- The extent to which a person is motivated to achieve and is intellectual (achievement, intellectual identity)
- Whether a person is heterosexual, homosexual, or bisexual (sexual identity)

Exploring Identity
The Society for Research on Identity Development

- Which part of the world or country a person is from and how intensely the person identifies with his or her cultural heritage (cultural/ethnic identity)
- The things a person likes to do, including sports, music, and hobbies (interest)
- An individual's personality characteristics (introverted or extraverted, anxious or calm, friendly or hostile, and so on) (personality)
- A person's body image (physical identity)

Some Contemporary Thoughts on Identity Contemporary views of identity development suggest that it is a lengthy process, in many instances more gradual and less cataclysmic than Erikson's term crisis implies (Baumeister, 1991). Today's theorists believe this extraordinarily complex process neither begins nor ends with adolescence (Marcia, 1989). It begins in infancy with the appearance of attachment, the development of a sense of self, and the emergence of independence. It ends with a life review and integration in old age. What is important about identity development in adolescence—especially late adolescence—is that for the first time, physical, cognitive, and socioemotional development advance to the point at which the individual can sort through and synthesize childhood identities and identifications to construct a viable path toward adult maturity (Marcia & Carpendale, 2004). Resolution of the identity issue during adolescence does not mean that identity will be stable through the remainder of one's life. An individual who develops a healthy identity is flexible and adaptive, open to changes in society, in relationships, and in careers (Adams, Gulotta, & Montemayor, 1992). This openness assures numerous reorganizations of identity throughout the individual's life.

Just as researchers increasingly describe the adolescent's self-understanding in terms of multiple selves, there also is a trend in characterizing the adolescent's identity in terms of multiple identities (Brooks-Gunn & Graber, 1999). While adolescent identities are preceded by childhood identities, central questions such as "Who am I?" come up more frequently in the adolescent years. During adolescence, identities are characterized more strongly by the search for balance between the needs for autonomy and for connectedness.

Identity formation neither happens neatly, nor is it usually cataclysmic. At the bare minimum, it involves commitment to a vocational direction, an ideological stance, and a sexual orientation. Synthesizing the components of identity can be a long, drawn-out process, with many negations and affirmations of various roles. Identity development gets done in bits and pieces. Decisions are not made once and for all, but must be made again and again. While the decisions might seem trivial at the time—whom to date, whether or not to have intercourse, to break up, to take drugs; whether to go to college or get a job, to study or play, to be politically active or not—over the years, they begin to form the core of what an individual is all about.

The Four Statuses of Identity

James Marcia (1980, 1994) believes that Erikson's theory of identity development implies four identity statuses, or ways of resolving the identity crisis: identity diffusion, identity foreclosure, identity moratorium, and identity achievement. That is, Marcia uses the extent of an adolescent's crisis and commitment to classify individuals according to these four identity statuses. He defines the term **crisis** as a period of identity development during which the adolescent is choosing among meaningful alternatives. (Most researchers use the term *exploration*.) By **commitment,** he means a personal investment in what an individual is going to do.

Let's examine each of Marcia's four identity statuses:

- **Identity diffusion** is Marcia's term for the state adolescents are in when they have not yet experienced an identity crisis (that is, have not yet explored meaningful alternatives) and have not made any commitments. Not only are adolescents in this status undecided about occupational and ideological choices, they usually show little interest in such matters.

www.mhhe.com/santrocka10

Concepts of Person and Self
Recent and Forthcoming Books
on the Self
International Society for Self
and Identity

crisis A period of identity development during which the adolescent is choosing among meaningful alternatives.

commitment The part of identity development in which adolescents show a personal investment in what they are going to do.

identity diffusion Marcia's term for the state adolescents are in when they have not yet experienced a crisis or made any commitments.

- **Identity foreclosure** is Marcia's term for the state adolescents are in when they have made a commitment but have not experienced an identity crisis. This status occurs most often when parents hand down commitments to their adolescents, usually in an authoritarian way. Thus, adolescents with this status have not had adequate opportunities to explore different approaches, ideologies, and vocations on their own.
- **Identity moratorium** is Marcia's term for the state of adolescents who are in the midst of an identity crisis, but who have not made a clear commitment to an identity.
- **Identity achievement** is Marcia's term for the status of adolescents who have undergone an identity crisis and made a commitment. Figure 5.5 summarizes Marcia's four statuses of identity development.

		Has the person made a commitment?	
		Yes	No
Has the person explored meaningful alternatives regarding some identity question?	Yes	Identity Achievement	Identity Moratorium
	No	Identity Foreclosure	Identity Diffusion

FIGURE 5.5 Marcia's Four Statuses of Identity

Let's explore some specific examples of Marcia's identity statuses. A 13-year-old adolescent has neither begun to explore her identity in a meaningful way nor made an identity commitment; she is *identity diffused.* An 18-year-old boy's parents want him to be a doctor, so he is planning on majoring in premedicine in college and has not adequately explored any other options; he is *identity foreclosed.* Nineteen-year-old Sasha is not quite sure what life path she wants to follow, but she recently went to the counseling center at her college to find out about different careers; she is in an *identity moratorium.* Twenty-one-year-old Marcelo extensively explored a number of different career options in college, eventually got his degree in science education, and is looking forward to his first year of teaching high school; he is *identity achieved.* While these examples of identity statuses focus on careers, remember that the whole of identity has multiple dimensions.

Marcia's approach has been sharply criticized by some researchers and theoreticians (Blasi, 1988; Bosma & Kunnen, 2001; Cote & Levine, 1988; Goosens, 1995; Kroger, 2003; Lapsley & Power, 1988; Van Hoof, 1999), who believe that it distorts and trivializes Erikson's concepts of crisis and commitment. Erikson emphasized that youth question the perceptions and expectations of their culture and the development of an autonomous position with regard to one's society. In Marcia's approach, these complex questions are reduced to whether a youth has thought about certain issues and considered the alternatives. Similarly, in Marcia's approach, Erikson's idea of commitment loses its meaning of investing oneself in certain lifelong projects and is interpreted simply as having made a firm decision. Other researchers still believe that Marcia's approach is a valuable contribution to understanding identity (Archer, 1989; Berzonsky & Adams, 1999; Waterman, 1989, 1999).

Developmental Changes in Identity

During early adolescence, most youth are primarily in the identity statuses of diffusion, foreclosure, or moratorium. According to Marcia (1987, 1996), at least three aspects of the young adolescent's development are important to identity formation. Young adolescents must be confident that they have parental support, must have an established sense of industry, and must be able to take a self-reflective stance toward the future.

Some researchers believe the most important identity changes take place in emerging adulthood rather than in adolescence. For example, Alan Waterman (1985, 1989, 1992, 1999) has found that from the years preceding high school through the last few years of college, the number of individuals who are identity achieved increases, while the number who are identity diffused decreases. College upperclassmen are more likely to be identity achieved than college freshmen or high school students. Many young adolescents, on the other hand, are identity diffused. These developmental changes are especially true for vocational choice. In terms of religious

identity foreclosure Marcia's term for the state adolescents are in when they have made a commitment but have not experienced a crisis.

identity moratorium Marcia's term for the state of adolescents who are in the midst of a crisis but who have not made a clear commitment to an identity.

identity achievement Marcia's term for an adolescent who has undergone a crisis and made a commitment.

beliefs and political ideology, fewer college students reach the identity-achieved status; a substantial number are characterized by foreclosure and diffusion. Thus, the timing of identity development may depend on the particular dimension involved (Arehart & Smith, 1990; Harter, 1990b).

Researchers have shown that identity consolidation—the process of refining and enhancing the identity choices that are made in emerging adulthood—continues well into early adulthood and possibly the early part of middle adulthood (Pals, 1999). One research study found that women and men continued to show identity development from 27 through 36 years of age with the main changes in the direction of greater commitment (Pulkkinen & Kokko, 2000). In this study, adults more often moved into achieved and foreclosed identities than into moratorium or diffused identities. Further, as individuals move from early to middle adulthood they become more certain about their identity. For example, a longitudinal study of Smith college women found that identity certainty increased from the thirties through the fifties (Stewart, Ostrove, & Helson, 2001; Zucker, Ostrove, & Stewart, 2002).

Some researchers believe that a common pattern of individuals who develop positive identities is what is called the "MAMA" cycle: *moratorium–achievement–moratorium–achievement* (Archer, 1989). Individuals may repeat this cycle throughout their lives as personal, family, and societal changes require them to explore new alternatives and develop new commitments (Francis, Fraser, & Marcia, 1989). Indeed, Marcia (1996) believes that the first identity an individual commits to is just that—it is not, and should not be expected to be, the final product.

Family Influences on Identity

Parents are influential figures in an adolescent's search for identity. In studies that relate identity development to parenting style, democratic parents who encourage adolescents to participate in family decision making have been found to foster identity achievement. In contrast, autocratic parents, who control adolescents' behavior and do not give them an opportunity to express their opinions, encourage identity foreclosure. Permissive parents who provide little guidance and allow adolescents to make their own decisions promote identity diffusion (Enright & others, 1980).

In addition to parenting style, researchers have examined the role of individuality and connectedness in the development of identity. Catherine Cooper and her colleagues (Carlson, Cooper, & Hsu, 1990; Cooper & Grotevant, 1989; Grotevant & Cooper, 1985, 1998) believe a family atmosphere that promotes both individuality and connectedness is important to an adolescent's identity development. Cooper and her colleagues define these terms as follows:

- **Individuality** has two dimensions: self-assertion, or the ability to have and communicate a point of view; and separateness, or the use of communication patterns to express how one is different from others.
- **Connectedness** also has two dimensions: mutuality, or sensitivity to and respect for others' views; and permeability, or openness to others' views.

In general, Cooper's research findings reveal that identity formation is enhanced by family relationships that are both individuated, encouraging adolescents to develop their own point of view, and connected, providing a secure base from which to explore the social world. However, when connectedness is strong and individuation is weak, adolescents may move into identity foreclosure; when connectedness is weak, adolescents often reveal identity confusion (Archer & Waterman, 1994). Also, cultural conditions vary as to how individuality and connectedness are expressed. For example, in many cultural traditions, daughters and sons may express their ideas to their fathers only indirectly through a third person rather than tell them directly (Cooper & others, 1993).

Stuart Hauser and his colleagues (Hauser & Bowlds, 1990; Hauser & others, 1984) have identified other family processes that promote adolescent identity development. Parents who engage in *enabling* behaviors (such as explaining, accepting, and giving empathy) facilitate the adolescent's identity development more than parents who en-

individuality An important element in adolescent identity development. It consists of two dimensions: self-assertion, the ability to have and communicate a point of view; and separateness, the use of communication patterns to express how one is different from others.

connectedness An important element in adolescent identity development. It consists of two dimensions: mutuality, or sensitivity to and respect for others' views; and permeability, openness to others' views.

gage in *constraining* behaviors (such as judging and devaluing). In sum, family interaction styles that give adolescents the right to question and to be different within a context of support and mutuality foster healthy patterns of identity development (Harter, 1990b).

Cultural and Ethnic Identity

Erikson was especially sensitive to the role of culture in identity development. Throughout the world, he noted, ethnic minority groups have struggled to maintain their cultural identities while blending in with the dominant culture (Erikson, 1968). Erikson thought this struggle for an inclusive identity, or separate identity within the larger culture, has been the driving force in the founding of churches, empires, and revolutions throughout history.

For ethnic minority individuals, adolescence is often a special juncture in their development (Bat-Chava & others, 1997; Kurtz, Cantu, & Phinney, 1996; Quintana, 2004; Spencer & Dornbusch, 1990). Although children are aware of some ethnic and cultural differences, individuals consciously confront their ethnicity for the first time in adolescence. Unlike children, adolescents have the ability to interpret ethnic and cultural information, to reflect on the past, and to speculate about the future (Wong, 1997). What is ethnic identity, and why is it a special part of identity development?

Defining and Exploring Ethnic Identity   Jean Phinney (1996) defined **ethnic identity** as an enduring, basic aspect of the self that includes a sense of membership in an ethnic group, along with the attitudes and feelings related to that membership. Thus, for adolescents from ethnic minority groups, the process of identity formation has an added dimension: the choice between two or more sources of identification—their own ethnic group and the mainstream, or dominant culture (Phinney, 2000, 2003). Many adolescents resolve this choice by developing a *bicultural identity.* That is, they identify in some ways with their ethnic group and in other ways with the majority culture (Kuperminc & others, 2002; Phinney, 2003; Sidhu, 2000). For example, watch the video segment entitled "Ethnic and Racial Identity in Adolescence" and notice how two teenager girls describe their being "black" as being a mixture of many different cultures.

The indicators of identity change often differ for each succeeding generation (Phinney, 2003). First-generation immigrants are likely to be secure in their identities and unlikely to change much; they may or may not develop a new identity. The degree to which they begin to feel "American" appears to be related to whether or not they learn English, develop social networks beyond their ethnic group, and become culturally competent in their new country. Second-generation immigrants are more likely to think of themselves as "American" possibly because citizenship is granted at birth. Their ethnic identity is likely to be linked to retention of their ethnic language and social networks. In the third and later generations, the issues become more complex. Historical, contextual, and political factors that are unrelated to acculturation may affect the extent to which members of this generation retain their ethnic identities. For non-European ethnic groups, racism and discrimination influence whether ethnic identity is retained.

Researchers have found that ethnic identity increases with age, and that higher levels of ethnic identity are linked to more positive attitudes, not only toward one's own ethnic group but also toward members of other ethnic groups (Phinney, Ferguson, & Tate, 1997). Ethnic identity is also stronger among members of minority groups than among members of mainstream groups. In one investigation, researchers found that ethnic identity exploration was higher among ethnic minority college students than among White non-Latino college students (Phinney & Alipuria, 1990). Minority students who had thought about and resolved issues involving their ethnicity had higher self-esteem than minority students who had not. In another investigation, the

"Do you have any idea who I am?"

www.mhhe.com/santrocka10

Exploring Ethnic Identities
Ethnic Identity
Ethnic Identity Research

LifeMAP

"*M*any ethnic minority youth must bridge 'multiple worlds' in constructing their identities."

—CATHERINE COOPER
Contemporary Developmental Psychologist, University of California-Santa Cruz

ethnic identity   An enduring, basic aspect of the self that includes a sense of membership in an ethnic group and the attitudes and feelings related to that membership.

Through the Eyes of Adolescents

Identity Exploring

Michelle Chin, age 16: "Parents do not understand that teenagers need to find out who they are, which means a lot of experimenting, a lot of mood swings, a lot of emotions and awkwardness. Like any teenager, I am facing an identity crisis. I am still trying to figure out whether I am a Chinese American or an American with Asian eyes."

Michelle Chin

ethnic identity development of Asian American, African American, Latino, and White non-Latino tenth-grade students in Los Angeles was studied (Phinney, 1989). Adolescents in all three ethnic minority groups faced a need to deal with ethnicity in a predominantly White non-Latino culture. But in some instances, the adolescents from the three ethnic minority groups perceived different issues to be important in the resolution of their ethnic identity. For Asian American adolescents, pressures to achieve academically and concerns about quotas that make it difficult to get into good colleges were salient issues. Many African American adolescent females discussed their realization that White American standards of beauty (especially hair and skin color) did not apply to them; African American adolescent males were concerned with possible job discrimination and the need to distinguish themselves from a negative societal image of African American male adolescents. For Latino adolescents, prejudice was a recurrent theme, as was the conflict in values between their Latino culture heritage and the majority culture.

Researchers are also increasingly finding that positive ratings of ethnic identity are related to more positive school engagement and fewer problem behaviors in African American and Latino adolescents (Fridrich & Flannery, 1995). For example, one recent study revealed that ethnic identity was linked with higher school engagement and lower aggression (Van Buren & Graham, 2003).

Helms' Model of Ethnic Identity Development Janet Helms (1990, 1996) has proposed a model of ethnic identity development that consists of four stages. In *stage 1, pre-encounter,* ethnic minority individuals prefer the dominant society's cultural values to those of their own culture. They draw their role models, lifestyles, and value systems from the dominant group, viewing the physical and/or cultural characteristics that single them out as ethnic minorities as a source of pain and stress. For example, African Americans may perceive their physical features as undesirable, and their cultural values as an impediment to success.

The move to *stage 2, encounter* is usually a gradual one. Individuals may reach this stage after an event that makes them realize they will never belong to the mainstream. Either a monumental event, such as the assassination of Martin Luther King, Jr., or a more personal "identity-shattering" event may serve as the trigger. In this stage, minority individuals begin to break through their denial. For example, Latinos who feel ashamed of their cultural upbringing may speak with Latinos who are proud of their cultural heritage. Gradually, they become aware that not all cultural values of the dominant group are beneficial to them. Conflicting attitudes about the self, minority group culture, and the dominant culture characterize this stage. Helms proposes that minority individuals want to identify with their ethnic group but do not know how. The recognition that an ethnic identity must be developed rather than found leads to the third stage, immersion/emersion.

At the beginning of *stage 3, immersion/emersion,* ethnic minority individuals immerse themselves completely in the minority culture and reject the dominant society. Movement into this stage likely occurs when individuals begin to resolve some of the conflicts from the previous stage and develop a better understanding of societal forces such as racism and discrimination. They begin to ask themselves, "Why should I feel ashamed of who I am?" The answer, at this point, often elicits both guilt and anger—guilt at having "sold out" in the past, and anger at having been "brainwashed" by the dominant group.

Later in this stage, individuals experience discontent and discomfort with their rigid attitudes they developed at the beginning of the stage. Gradually, they develop a sense of autonomy. *Emersion*—that is, emergence—allows them to vent the anger they developed at the beginning of the stage, through rap groups, cultural explorations, discussions of racial/ethnic issues, and so on. With education and the expulsion of hostile feelings, individuals' emotions begin to level off, so that they can think more clearly and adaptively. No longer do they find it necessary to reject everything from the dominant culture and accept everything from their own culture. They now have the autonomy to evaluate the strengths and weaknesses of both their subculture and the mainstream culture, and to decide which parts of it will become part of their own identity.

In *stage 4, internalization/commitment,* individuals experience a sense of fulfillment that arises from the integration of their personal and cultural identities. They have resolved the conflicts and discomforts of the immersion/emersion stage and attained greater self-control and flexibility. They can also examine the cultural values of other ethnic groups, both minority and majority, more objectively. At this stage, individuals want to eliminate all forms of discrimination. The term *commitment* in the name for this stage refers to the enactment of the individual's newly realized identity. Individuals in this stage take action to eliminate discrimination, whether through large-scale political or social activism or through small, everyday activities that are consistent with their ethnic identities.

Contexts and Ethnic Identity   The contexts in which ethnic minority youth live influence their identity development (Cuéllar & others, 2004; Hecht, Jackson, & Ribeau, 2002; Spencer, 1999, 2000; Spencer & others, 2001). In the United States, many ethnic minority youth live in low-SES urban settings where support for developing a positive identity is lacking. Many of these youth live in pockets of poverty; are exposed to drugs, gangs, and criminal activities; and interact with youth and adults who have dropped out of school or are unemployed. In such settings, support organizations and programs for youth can make an important contribution to their identity development.

Shirley Heath and Milbrey McLaughlin (1993) studied 60 youth organizations that involved 24,000 adolescents over a period of five years. They found these organizations were especially good at building a sense of ethnic pride in inner-city youth. Heath and McLaughlin believe that many inner-city youth have too much time on their hands, too little to do, and too few places to go. Inner-city youth want to participate in organizations that nurture them and respond positively to their needs and interests. Organizations that perceive youth as fearful, vulnerable, and lonely but also frame them as capable, worthy, and eager to have a healthy and productive life contribute in positive ways to the identity development of ethnic minority youth.

Gender and Identity

Erikson's (1968) classic presentation of identity development reflected the traditional division of labor between the sexes that was common at the time. Erikson wrote that males were mainly oriented toward career and ideological commitments, while females were mainly oriented toward marriage and childbearing. In the 1960s and 1970s researchers found support for this assertion of gender differences in identity. For example, they found that vocational concerns were more central to male identity, while affiliative concerns were more central to female identity (La Voie, 1976). In the last several decades, however, as females have developed stronger vocational interests, these gender differences have begun to disappear (Madison & Foster-Clark, 1996; Waterman, 1985).

Identity and Intimacy

What is intimacy and why is it important? How did Erikson conceptualize intimacy? In this section we examine intimacy, as well as social isolation and loneliness.

Erikson's Stage of Intimacy Versus Isolation   Erikson (1968) believed that intimacy should develop after individuals are well on their way to establishing a stable and successful identity. **Intimacy versus isolation** is Erikson's sixth developmental stage, which individuals experience during early adulthood. At this time, individuals face the task of forming intimate relationships with others. Erikson describes intimacy as finding oneself, yet losing oneself in another. If young adults form healthy friendships and an intimate relationship with another individual, intimacy will be achieved; if not, isolation will result.

In one study of unmarried college students 18 to 23 years of age, a strong sense of self, expressed through identity achievement and an instrumental orientation, was an important factor in forming intimate connections, for both males and females (Madison & Foster-Clark, 1996). However, insecurity and a defensive posture in relationships were expressed differently in males' and females' relationships, with males displaying greater superficiality and females more dependency.

An inability to develop meaningful relationships with others can harm an individual's personality. It may lead individuals to repudiate, ignore, or attack those who frustrate them. Such circumstances account for the shallow, almost pathetic attempts of youth to merge themselves with a leader. Many youths want to be apprentices or disciples of leaders and adults who will shelter them from the harm of the "out-group" world. If this fails, and Erikson believes that it must, sooner or later the individuals retreat to search themselves to discover where they went wrong. This introspection sometimes leads to painful depression and isolation and can contribute to a mistrust of others and restrict the youths' willingness to act on their own initiative.

Styles of Intimate Interaction   Adolescents and young adults show different styles of intimate interaction. Jacob Orlofsky (1976) developed one classification with five styles: intimate, preintimate, stereotyped, pseudointimate, and isolated (Orlofsky, Marcia, & Lesser, 1973):

- **Intimate style:** The individual forms and maintains one or more deep and long-lasting love relationships.
- **Preintimate style:** The individual shows mixed emotions about commitment, an ambivalence reflected in the strategy of offering love without obligations or long-lasting bonds.
- **Stereotyped style:** The individual has superficial relationships that tend to be dominated by friendship ties with same-sex rather than opposite-sex individuals.
- **Pseudointimate style:** The individual maintains a long-lasting sexual attachment with little or no depth or closeness.
- **Isolated style:** The individual withdraws from social encounters and has little or no attachment to same- or opposite-sex individuals. Occasionally, the isolate shows signs of developing close interpersonal relationships, but usually the interactions are stressful.

In one investigation, intimate and preintimate individuals were more sensitive to their partners' needs and were more open in their friendships than individuals in the other three intimacy statuses were (Orlofsky, Marcia, & Lesser, 1973).

Loneliness and the Need for Intimacy   Though we often think of older adults as the loneliest individuals, surveys have found that the highest levels of loneliness often appear during late adolescence and emerging adulthood (Cutrona, 1982). Some young people feel lonely because they have strong needs for intimacy but have not yet developed the social skills or relationship maturity to satisfy these needs. They might feel isolated and sense that they do not have anyone they can turn to for intimacy. In one study, teenage loneliness appeared to be part of a depressive complex for girls while signaling poor scholastic functioning for boys (Koenig & Faigeles, 1995). Society's contemporary emphasis on self-fulfillment and achievement, the importance attached to commitment in relationships, and the decline in stable, close relationships are among the reasons feelings of loneliness are common today.

intimacy versus isolation Erikson's sixth developmental stage, which individuals experience during the early adulthood years. At this time, individuals face the developmental task of forming intimate relationships with others.

intimate style The individual forms and maintains one or more deep and long-lasting love relationships.

preintimate style The individual shows mixed emotions about commitment, an ambivalence reflected in the strategy of offering love without obligations.

stereotyped style The individual has superficial relationships that tend to be dominated by friendship ties with same-sex rather than opposite-sex individuals.

pseudointimate style The individual maintains a long-lasting sexual attachment with little or no depth or closeness.

isolated style The individual withdraws from social encounters and has little or no attachment to same- or opposite-sex individuals.

Loneliness is associated with numerous factors, including time spent with females, attachment history, self-esteem, and social skills. A lack of time spent with females, on the part of both males and females, is associated with loneliness. Lonely adolescents are not adequately integrated into the peer system and might not have close friends (Hicks & Connolly, 1995). Also, individuals who are lonely often have a poor relationship with their parents. Early experiences of rejection and loss (as when a parent dies) can cause a lasting effect of feeling alone. Lonely individuals often have low self-esteem and tend to blame themselves more than they deserve for their inadequacies. Lonely individuals also are often deficient in social skills. For example, they show inappropriate self-disclosure, self-attention at the expense of attention to a partner, or an inability to develop comfortable intimacy.

The social transition to college is a time when loneliness might develop, as individuals leave behind the familiar world of hometown and family. Many college freshmen feel anxious about meeting new people and developing a new social life. As one student commented:

> My first year here at the university has been pretty lonely. I wasn't lonely at all in high school. I lived in a fairly small town—I knew everyone and everyone knew me. I was a member of several clubs and played on the basketball team. It's not that way at the university. It is a big place, and I've felt like a stranger on so many occasions. I'm starting to get used to my life here, and the last few months I've been making myself meet people and get to know them, but it has not been easy.

As reflected in the comments of this college freshman, individuals usually cannot bring their popularity and social standing from high school into the college environment. There might be a dozen high school basketball stars, National Merit scholars, and former student council presidents on a single dormitory floor. Especially if students attend college away from home, they face the task of forming completely new social relationships.

In one investigation that was conducted two weeks after the school year began, 75 percent of the 354 college freshmen said that they had felt lonely at least part of the time since arriving on campus (Cutrona, 1982). More than 40 percent said their loneliness was moderate to severe in intensity. Students who were the most optimistic and had the highest self-esteem were more likely to overcome their loneliness by the end of the freshman year. Loneliness is not reserved only for college freshmen, though. It is not uncommon to find a number of upperclassmen who are also lonely.

Researchers have developed measures of loneliness in which individuals are asked to respond to statements such as these:

"I don't feel in tune with the people around me."
"I can't find companionship when I want it."

Individuals who consistently respond that they never or rarely feel in tune with the people around them and rarely or never can find companionship when they want to are likely to be moderately or intensely lonely.

According to Robert Weiss (1973), loneliness is virtually always a response to the absence of a particular type of relationship. Weiss distinguished two forms of loneliness, *emotional isolation* and *social isolation:*

- **Emotional isolation** arises when a person lacks an intimate relationship; single, divorced, and widowed adults often experience this type of loneliness.
- **Social isolation** occurs when a person lacks a sense of integrated involvement. Without participation in a group or community that offers companionship, shared interests, organized activities, and meaningful roles, a person can become alienated, bored, and uneasy. Married couples often experience social isolation when they relocate and leave their old friends and community.

It is common for adolescents to experience both types of loneliness. Being left out of a clique can give rise to painful feelings of social isolation. Not having an intimate dating or romantic partner can give rise to emotional isolation.

**Intimacy
Loneliness
Shyness**

emotional isolation A type of loneliness that arises when a person lacks an intimate attachment relationship; single, divorced, and widowed adults often experience this type of loneliness.

social isolation A type of loneliness that occurs when a person lacks a sense of integrated involvement. Being deprived of participation in a group or community involving companionship, shared interests, organized activities, and meaningful roles causes a person to feel alienated, bored, and uneasy.

Individuals can reduce their loneliness by changing either their social relationships or their social needs and desires (Peplau & Perlman, 1982). Probably the most direct and satisfying choice is to form new social relationships by using their existing social network more competently, or by creating surrogate relationships with pets, television personalities, and the like. Another way to reduce loneliness is to reduce one's desire for social contact. Over the short run, individuals can do so by selecting activities they can enjoy alone rather than in others' company. In the long run, however, an effort should be made to form new relationships. A maladaptive coping strategy is to distract oneself from the painful feelings of loneliness by consuming alcohol or other drugs or by becoming a workaholic. Some of the negative health consequences of loneliness may be the product of such maladaptive coping strategies. If you perceive yourself to be lonely, you might consider contacting the counseling center at your college for advice on how to reduce your loneliness and improve your relationship skills.

Review and reflect   Learning goal 2

2 Explain the many facets of identity development

REVIEW

- What is Erikson's view of identity development?
- What are the four statuses of identity development?
- What developmental changes characterize identity?
- How do family processes influence identity development?
- What roles do culture and ethnicity play in identity development?
- How is gender involved in identity development?
- What is Erikson's view on identity and intimacy? What are five styles of intimate interaction?
- What characterizes loneliness in adolescence?

REFLECT

- How would you describe your current identity ? Which of Marcia's identity statuses best describes you?

In our discussion of loneliness, we described emotional isolation as one type of loneliness. We examine emotional development more extensively in the next section.

3 EMOTIONAL DEVELOPMENT

The Emotions of Adolescence   **Hormones, Experience, and Emotions**   **Emotional Competence**

So far in this chapter, we have focused on the development of the self and identity. How are these concepts linked to emotion? **Emotion** is feeling or affect that involves physiological arousal (a rapid heartbeat, for example), behavioral expression (a smile or grimace, for example), and sometimes conscious experience (thinking about a romantic experience, for example). Emotion is closely connected to self-esteem. Negative emotions, such as sadness, are associated with low self-esteem, while positive emotions, such as joy, are linked to high self-esteem. Some psychologists argue that emotions are the "glue" that connects our life events (Haviland & others, 1994). The emotional experiences involved in events, such as emerging sexual experiences,

emotion Feeling or affect that involves physiological arousal, behavioral expression, and sometimes conscious experience.

dating and romantic encounters, and driving a car, contribute to the adolescent's developing identity (Rosenblum & Lewis, 2003).

Indeed, emotions are involved in many aspects of adolescence, from the hormonal fluctuations of puberty to the sadness of adolescent depression. In this section, we examine the extent to which adolescents' emotions are linked to both their hormones and their experience. We also explore what it means to be emotionally competent in adolescence. First, though, we need to survey the adolescent's emotional landscape.

The Emotions of Adolescence

Adolescence has long been described as a time of emotional turmoil (Hall, 1904). In its extreme form, this view is too stereotypical because adolescents are not constantly in a state of "storm and stress." Nonetheless, early adolescence is a time when emotional highs and lows occur more frequently (Rosenblum & Lewis, 2003). Young adolescents can be on top of the world one moment and down in the dumps the next. In many instances, the intensity of their emotions seems out of proportion to the events that elicit them (Steinberg & Levine, 1997). Young adolescents may sulk a lot, not knowing how to express their feelings adequately. With little or no provocation, they may blow up at their parents or siblings, projecting their unpleasant feelings onto another person.

As we saw in chapter 2, Reed Larson and Maryse Richards (1994) found that adolescents reported more extreme emotions and more fleeting emotions than their parents. For example, adolescents were five times more likely than their parents to report being "very happy" and three times more likely to report being "very sad." These findings lend support to the perception that adolescents are moody and changeable (Rosenblum & Lewis, 2003). Researchers have also found that from the fifth through the ninth grades, both boys and girls experience a 50 percent decrease in the state of being "very happy" (Larson & Lampman-Petraitis, 1989). In this study, adolescents were more likely than preadolescents to report mildly negative mood states.

It is important for adults to recognize that moodiness is a *normal* aspect of early adolescence, and that most adolescents eventually emerge from these moody times and become competent adults. Nonetheless, for some adolescents, intensely negative emotions can reflect serious problems. For example, rates of depressed moods become more frequent in girls during adolescence (Nolen-Hoeksema, 2004). We will have much more to say about depression in adolescence in chapter 14, "Adolescent Problems."

Hormones, Experience, and Emotions

As we saw in chapter 3, significant hormonal changes occur during puberty. The emotional fluctuations of early adolescence may be related to variability in hormone levels during this period. As adolescents move into adulthood, their moods become less extreme, perhaps due to their adaptation to hormone levels over time (Rosenblum & Lewis, 2003).

Researchers have discovered that pubertal change is associated with an increase in negative emotions (Archibald, Graber, & Brooks-Gunn, 2003; Brooks-Gunn, Graber, & Paikoff, 1994; Dorn, Williamson, & Ryan, 2002). However, most researchers conclude that such hormonal influences are small and are usually associated with other factors, such as stress, eating patterns, sexual activity, and social relationships (Rosenblum & Lewis, 2003; Susman, Dorn, & Schiefelbein, 2003; Susman & Rogol, 2004). Indeed, environmental experiences may contribute more to the emotions of adolescence than hormonal changes. Recall from chapter 3 that in one study, social factors accounted for two to four times as much variance as hormonal factors in young adolescent girls' depression and anger (Brooks-Gunn & Warren, 1989).

Among the stressful experiences that might contribute to changes in emotion during adolescence are the transition to middle or junior high school and the onset of sexual experiences and romantic relationships. For many boys and girls, moving to the less protected, less personal, and more achievement-oriented context of middle school or junior high is stressful and can be expected to increase negative emotions. We will explore this school transition further in chapter 11. Moreover, the vulnerability and confusion involved in emerging sexual and romantic relationships can be expected to fuel emotional changes in adolescence. In one study, real and fantasized sexual/romantic relationships were responsible for more than one-third of ninth- to twelfth-graders' strong emotions (Wilson-Shockley, 1995). We will examine sexuality and romantic relationships in greater detail in chapters 7 and 10.

In sum, both hormonal changes and environmental experiences are involved in the changing emotions of adolescence. So is the young person's ability to manage his or her emotions. In chapter 4, we studied the concept of emotional intelligence. Now let's examine a closely related concept, emotional competence.

Emotional Competence

In adolescence, individuals are more likely to become aware of their emotional cycles, such as feeling guilty about being angry. This new awareness may improve their ability to cope with their emotions. Adolescents also become more skillful at presenting their emotions to others. For example, they become aware of the importance of covering up their anger in social relationships. And they are more likely to understand the importance of being able to communicate their emotions constructively to improve the quality of a relationship (Saarni, 1999).

Although the increased cognitive abilities and awareness of adolescents prepare them to cope more effectively with stress and emotional fluctuations, many adolescents do not effectively manage their emotions. As a result, they may become prone to depression, anger, and poor emotional regulation, which in turn can trigger problems such as drug abuse, juvenile delinquency, or eating disorders.

The emotional competencies that are important for adolescents to develop include the following (Saarni, 1999):

Emotional Competence	Example
Being aware that the expression of emotions plays a major role in relationships.	Knowing that expressing anger toward a friend on a regular basis can harm the friendship.
Adaptively coping with negative emotions by using self-regulatory strategies that reduce the intensity and duration of such emotional states.	Reducing anger by walking away from a negative situation and engaging in an activity that takes one's mind off it.
Understanding that inner emotional states do not have to correspond to outer expressions. As adolescents become more mature, they begin to understand how their emotionally expressive behavior may impact others, and they take that understanding into account in the way they present themselves.	Recognizing that one can feel angry yet manage one's emotional expression so that it appears more neutral.
Being aware of one's emotional states without becoming overwhelmed by them.	Differentiating between sadness and anxiousness, and focusing on coping rather than becoming overwhelmed by these feelings.
Being able to discern others' emotions.	Perceiving that another person is sad rather than afraid.

Review and reflect Learning goal 3

3 Discuss the emotional development of adolescents

REVIEW

- How would you characterize adolescents' emotions?
- How extensively are adolescents' emotions linked to their hormones and experiences?
- What does it take to be emotionally competent in adolescence?

REFLECT

- How would you describe your emotions in early adolescence? Did you experience more extremes of emotion when you were in middle or junior high school than you do today? Have you learned how to control your emotions better now than you did in early adolescence? Explain.

4 PERSONALITY DEVELOPMENT

Personality Traits   **Temperament**

So far in this chapter, we have discussed the development of the self, identity, and emotion in adolescence. How are these concepts linked with personality? In many views, the self is the central aspect of personality. During adolescence, through self-understanding, individuals develop an integrated sense of identity. In terms of personality traits, identity development can lead to both stability (the achievement of an identity) and change (the exploration of new identities and modification of personality traits) (Roberts & Caspi, 2003). The description of an individual's personality traits and temperament often involves emotions. For example, an adolescent may be described in terms of emotional stability/instability and positive/negative affectivity. How are such traits manifested in adolescence? Which traits are most important?

Personality Traits

The search for the core personality traits that characterize people has a long history (Galambos & Costigan, 2003). In recent years, researchers have focused on the **big five factors of personality:** openness to experience, conscientiousness, extraversion, agreeableness, and neuroticism (emotional instability) (see figure 5.6). If you create an acronym from these trait names, you get the word OCEAN.

Much of the research on the big five factors has used adults as the participants in studies (Costa & McRae, 1998; McCrae & Costa, 2003). In one study, the mothers of 12- to 13-year-old African American and non-Latino White boys rated the sons' personalities (John & others, 1994). The researchers found that the ratings reflected the big five factors, but that two additional factors described the boys: (1) irritability ("whines," "feelings are easily hurt") and (2) positive activity ("energetic," "physically active"). Researchers do not completely agree on the core personality traits that typify adolescents (or children and adults for that matter). Two other traits that have appeared in some studies are excellent/ordinary and evil/decent (Almagor, Tellegen, & Waller, 1995).

How stable are personality traits in adolescence? Some researchers have found that personality is not as stable in adolescence as in adulthood (Roberts & Caspi, 2003). Researchers have also have found that personality becomes more stable after 50 years of age (Roberts & DelVecchio, 2000). The greater degree of change in

big five factors of personality Five core traits of personality: openness to experience, conscientiousness, extraversion, agreeableness, and neuroticism (emotional instability).

Openness	**C**onscientiousness	**E**xtraversion	**A**greeableness	**N**euroticism (emotional stability)
• Imaginative or practical	• Organized or disorganized	• Sociable or retiring	• Softhearted or ruthless	• Calm or anxious
• Interested in variety or routine	• Careful or careless	• Fun-loving or somber	• Trusting or suspicious	• Secure or insecure
• Independent or conforming	• Disciplined or impulsive	• Affectionate or reserved	• Helpful or uncooperative	• Self-satisfied or self-pitying

FIGURE 5.6 The Big Five Factors of Personality
Each of the broad supertraits encompasses more narrow traits and characteristics. Use the acronym OCEAN to remember the big five personality factors (*o*penness, *c*onscientiousness, and so on).

personality during adolescence may be linked to the exploration of new identities (Roberts & Caspi, 2003).

But while personality changes more in adolescence than during adulthood, it still shows some stability (Hair & Graziano, 2003). In one longitudinal study, individual personalities were assessed at three points in their development: junior high school, senior high school, and 30 to 40 years of age (Block, 1993). There was both stability and change in the personality traits of the individuals over time. Some researchers have concluded that aggression, dominance, dependency, sociability, and shyness tend to remain stable from middle and late childhood through adolescence and adulthood (Caspi & Bem, 1990).

One longitudinal study examined stability and change in personality from 18 through 26 years of age (Roberts, Caspi, & Moffitt, 2001). Using the Multidimensional Personality Questionnaire (Tellegen, 1982), more stability than change was found. The personality changes that did occur from adolescence to adulthood reflected growth in the direction of greater maturity, with many adolescents becoming more controlled, socially more confident, and less angry as adults.

Many psychologists argue that it is better to view personality not only in terms of traits, but also in terms of contexts and situations (Mischel, 1968, 2004). They believe that the trait approach ignores environmental factors and places too much emphasis on stability and lack of change. This criticism was first leveled by social cognitive theorist Walter Mischel (1968), who argued that personality varies according to the situation. Thus, adolescents might behave quite differently when they are in a library than when they are at a party.

Today, most psychologists are interactionists, believing that both traits and situations need to be taken into account in understanding personality (Block, 2002; Mischel, 2004; Mischel, Shoda, & Mendoza-Denton, 2002; Roberts & Robins, 2004). Let's again consider the situations of being in a library or at a party and focus on two adolescents, Jane who is an introvert, and Sandra who is an extravert. Jane, who is an introvert, is more likely to enjoy being in the library while Sandra, the extravert, is more likely to enjoy herself at the party.

Temperament

temperament An individual's behavioral style and characteristic way of responding.

While the study of personality has focused mainly on adults, the study of temperament has been primarily confined to infants and children (Galambos & Costigan, 2003). **Temperament** can be defined as an individual's behavioral style and characteristic way of responding. Many psychologists believe that temperament forms the foundation of personality (Galambos & Costigan, 2003). Through increasing capacities and interactions with the environment, temperament evolves or becomes elaborated across childhood and adolescence into a set of personality traits (Caspi, 1998; Putnam, Sanson, & Rothbart, 2002).

The close link between temperament and personality is supported by research that connects some of the Big Five personality factors to temperament categories (Caspi, 1998). For example, the temperament category of positive emotionality is related to the personality trait of extraversion, negative emotionality maps onto neuroticism (emotional stability), and effortful control is linked to conscientiousness (Putnam, Sanson, & Rothbart, 2002).

Temperament Categories   Just as with personality, researchers are interested in discovering what the key dimensions of temperament are. Psychiatrists Alexander Chess and Stella Thomas (Chess & Thomas, 1977; Thomas & Chess, 1991) followed a group of infants into adulthood and concluded that there are three basic types, or clusters, of temperament:

- **Easy child:** This child is generally in a positive mood, quickly establishes regular routines, and adapts easily to new experiences.
- **Difficult child:** This child reacts negatively to many situations and is slow to accept new experiences.
- **Slow-to-warm-up child:** This child has a low activity level, is somewhat negative, and displays a low intensity of mood.

New classifications of temperament continue to be forged (Rothbart & Putnam, 2002; Wachs & Kohnstamm, 2001). In a review of temperament research, Mary Rothbart and John Bates (1998) concluded that the best framework for classifying temperament involves a revision of Chess and Thomas' categories of easy, difficult, and slow to warm up. The general classification of temperament now focuses more on:

- *Positive affect and approach:* This category is much like the personality trait of extraversion/introversion.
- *Negative affectivity:* This involves being easily distressed. Children with a temperament that involves negative affectivity may fret and cry often. Negative affectivity is closely related to the personality traits of introversion and neuroticism (emotional instability).
- *Effortful control (self-regulation):* This involves the ability to control one's emotions. Thus, adolescents who are high on effortful control show an ability to keep their arousal from getting too high and have strategies for soothing themselves. By contrast, adolescents who are low on effortful control often show an inability to control their arousal, and they become easily agitated and intensely emotional (Eisenberg & others, 2002).

Developmental Connections and Contexts   How stable is temperament from childhood to adulthood? Do young adults show the same behavioral style and characteristic emotional responses that they did when they were infants or young children? For instance, activity level is an important dimension of temperament. Are children's activity levels linked to their personality in emerging and early adulthood? In one longitudinal study, children who were highly active at age 4 were likely to be very outgoing at age 23, which reflects continuity (Franz, 1996). Yet in other ways temperament may change. From adolescence into early adulthood, most individuals show fewer emotional mood swings, become more responsible, and engage in less risk-taking behavior, reflecting discontinuity of temperament (Caspi, 1998).

Is temperament in childhood linked to adjustment in adolescence and adulthood? Here is what we know based on the few longitudinal studies that have been conducted on this topic (Caspi, 1998).

easy child This child is generally in a positive mood, quickly establishes regular routines, and adapts easily to new experiences.

difficult child This child reacts negatively to many situations and is slow to accept new experiences.

slow-to-warm-up child This child has a low activity level, is somewhat negative, and displays a low intensity of mood.

A longitudinal study using Chess and Thomas' categories found a link between temperament assessed at 1 year of age and adjustment at 17 years of age (Guerin & other, 2003). Those with easier temperaments as infants showed more optimal development across behavioral and intellectual domains in late adolescence. The individuals with easier temperaments experienced a family environment that was more stimulating and cohesive and had more positive relationships with their parents during adolescence than their counterparts with more difficult temperaments. When the participants were characterized by a difficult temperament in combination with a family environment that was high in conflict, an increase in externalizing behavior problems (conduct problems, delinquency) occurred.

With regard to a link between temperament in childhood and adjustment in adulthood, in one longitudinal study, children who had an easy temperament at 3 to 5 years of age were likely to be well adjusted as young adults (Chess & Thomas, 1977). In contrast, many children who had a difficult temperament at 3 to 5 years of age were not well adjusted as young adults. Other researchers have found that boys who have a difficult temperament in childhood are less likely than others to continue their formal education as adults; girls with a difficult temperament in childhood are more likely to experience marital conflict as adults (Wachs, 2000).

In sum, across a number of longitudinal studies, an easy temperament in childhood is linked with more optimal development and adjustment in adolescence and adulthood. When the contexts in which individuals live are problematic, such as living in a family environment high in conflict, the long-term outcomes of having a difficult temperament are exacerbated.

Inhibition is another temperament characteristic that has been studied extensively (Kagan, 2002). Researchers have found that individuals with an inhibited temperament in childhood are less likely as adults to be assertive or experience social support, and more likely to delay entering a stable job track (Wachs, 2000).

Yet another aspect of temperament is emotionality and the ability to control one's emotions. In one longitudinal study, individuals who as 3-year-old children showed good control of their emotions and were resilient in the face of stress were likely to continue to handle their emotions effectively as adults (Block, 1993). In contrast, individuals who as 3-year-olds had low emotional control and were not very resilient were likely to show the same problems as young adults.

In sum, these studies reveal some continuity between certain aspects of temperament in childhood and adjustment in early adulthood. Keep in mind, however, that these connections between childhood temperament and adult adjustment are based on only a small number of studies; more research is needed to verify the links. Indeed, Theodore Wachs (1994, 2000) has proposed ways that the links between childhood temperament and adult personality might vary depending on the intervening contexts an individual experiences (see figure 5.7).

The match between an individual's temperament and the environmental demands the individual must cope with, called **goodness of fit,** can be important to an adolescent's adjustment (Matheny & Phillips, 2001). In one study of seventh-graders and their parents, two dimensions were examined: adaptability and activity level (Galambos & Turner, 1999). Mother-son conflict was highest between mothers who were low in adaptability and sons with low activity levels. In keeping with gender stereotypes, the less adaptable mothers may have interpreted their sons' low activity levels negatively. In mother-daughter dyads, conflict was highest when mothers were low in adaptability and daughters were high in activity. Again, less adaptable mothers may have had more difficulty with their high-activity daughters because such activity runs counter to gender stereotypes.

goodness of fit The match between an individual's temperament style and the environmental demands the individual must cope with.

Summary

1 Describe the development of the self in adolescence

- Self-understanding is the adolescent's cognitive representation of the self, the substance and content of the adolescent's self-conceptions. Dimensions of the adolescent's self-understanding include abstract and idealistic; differentiated, contradictions within the self; real and ideal, true and false selves, social comparison; self-conscious; unconscious; and self-integrative. The increasing number of selves in adolescence can vary across relationships with people, social roles, and sociocultural contexts.
- Self-esteem is the global, evaluative dimension of the self, and also is referred to as self-worth or self-image. According to Harter, self-concept involves domain-specific self-evaluations. For too long, little attention was given to developing measures of self-esteem and self-concept specifically tailored to adolescents. Harter's Self-Perception Profile is one adolescent measure. Controversy characterizes the extent to which self-esteem changes during adolescence and whether there are gender differences in self-esteem. Researchers have found that self-esteem often drops during and just after developmental transitions, such as going from elementary school to middle or junior high school. Some researchers have found that the self-esteem of girls declines in adolescence, especially during early adolescence, although other researchers argue that this decline has been exaggerated and actually is only modest in nature. Perceived physical appearance is an especially strong contributor to global self-esteem. Peer acceptance also is linked to global self-esteem in adolescence. In Coopersmith's study, children's self-esteem was associated with such parenting practices as affection and allowing children freedom within well-prescribed limits. Peer and friendship relations also are linked with self-esteem. Self-esteem is higher in elementary school than in middle or junior high school. For most adolescents, low self-esteem results in only temporary emotional discomfort. However, for others, especially when low self-esteem persists, it is linked with depression, suicide, anorexia nervosa, and delinquency. Four ways to increase adolescents' self-esteem are (1) identify the causes of low self-esteem and which domains of competence are important to the adolescent, (2) provide emotional support and social approval, (3) help the adolescent to achieve, and (4) improve the adolescent's coping skills.

2 Explain the many facets of identity development

- Identity versus identity confusion is Erikson's fifth developmental stage, which individuals experience during adolescence. As adolescents are confronted with new roles, they enter a psychosocial moratorium. Personality and role experimentation are two key ingredients of Erikson's view. In technological societies like the United States, the vocational role is especially important. Identity development is extraordinarily complex and is done in bits and pieces.
- Marcia proposed four identity statuses: diffused, foreclosed, moratorium, and achieved. A combination of crisis (exploration) and commitment yields one of the statuses. Some critics argue that Marcia's four identity statuses oversimplify identity development.
- Some experts believe that the main identity changes take place in late adolescence or youth, rather than in early adolescence. College upperclassmen are more likely to be identity achieved than are freshmen or high school students, although many college students are still wrestling with ideological commitments. Individuals often follow "moratorium-achievement-moratorium-achievement" cycles.
- Parents are important figures in adolescents' identity development. Researchers have found that democratic parenting, individuality, connectedness, and enabling behaviors are linked with positive aspects of identity.
- Erikson was especially sensitive to the role of culture in identity development, underscoring the fact that throughout the world ethnic minority groups have struggled to maintain their cultural identities while blending into majority culture. Adolescence is often a special juncture in the identity development of ethnic minority individuals because for the first time they consciously confront their ethnic identity. Many ethnic minority adolescents have a bicultural identity. Helms proposed a model of ethnic identity development. Contexts influence ethnic identity development.
- Erikson believed that adolescent males have a stronger vocational identity, female adolescents a stronger social identity. However, researchers are finding that these gender differences are disappearing.
- Intimacy versus isolation is Erikson's sixth stage of human development, which individuals experience during early adulthood. Orlofsky described five styles of intimate interaction: intimate, preintimate, stereotyped, pseudointimate, and isolated. Surveys often find that the highest levels of loneliness occur during late adolescence and youth. The social transition to college is a time when loneliness is often present. Weiss distinguished between emotional isolation and social isolation.

3 Discuss the emotional development of adolescents

- Emotion is feeling or affect that involves physiological arousal, behavioral expression, and sometimes conscious experience. Adolescents report more extreme and fleeting emotions than their parents, and as individuals go through early adolescence they are less likely to report being very happy. However, it is important to view moodiness as a normal aspect of early adolescence.
- Although pubertal change is associated with an increase in negative emotions, hormonal influences are often small and environmental experiences may contribute more to the emotions of adolescence than hormonal changes.
- Adolescents' increased cognitive abilities and awareness provide them with the opportunity to cope more effectively

with stress and emotional fluctuations. However, the emotional burdens of adolescence can be overwhelming for some adolescents. Among the emotional competencies that are important for adolescents to develop are being aware that the expression of emotions plays a major role in relationships, adaptively coping with negative emotions by using self-regulatory strategies, understanding how emotionally expressive behavior influences others, being aware of one's emotional states without being overwhelmed by them, and being able to discern others' emotions.

4 Characterize the personality development of adolescents

- There has been a long history of interest in discovering the core traits of personality, and recently that search has focused on the big five factors of personality: openness to experience, conscientiousness, extraversion, agreeableness, and neuroticism (emotional instability). Much of the research on the "big five" has focused on adults but some evi-

dence for their presence in adolescents has been found. However, researchers continue to debate what the core characteristics of personality are. Critics of the trait approach argue that it places too much emphasis on stability and not enough on change and situational influences. Today, many psychologists believe that personality is best described in terms of both traits and situational influences.

- Many psychologists believe that temperament forms the foundation for personality. Chess and Thomas described three basis types of temperament: easy child, difficult child, and slow-to-warm-up child. New classifications of temperament include: positive affect and approach, negative affectivity, and effortful control (self-regulation). Connections between the temperament of individuals from childhood to adulthood have been found, although these links may vary according to the contexts of people's lives. Goodness of fit refers to the match between an individual's temperament and the environmental demands of individuals.

Key Terms

self-understanding 169
possible self 170
self-esteem 173
self-concept 173
identity versus identity confusion 178
psychosocial moratorium 178
crisis 180

commitment 180
identity diffusion 180
identity foreclosure 181
identity moratorium 181
identity achievement 181
individuality 182
connectedness 182
ethnic identity 183

intimacy versus isolation 186
intimate style 186
preintimate style 186
stereotyped style 186
pseudointimate style 186
isolated style 186
emotional isolation 187
social isolation 187

emotion 188
big five factors of personality 191
temperament 192
easy child 193
difficult child 193
slow-to-warm-up child 193
goodness of fit 194

Key People

Susan Harter 170
Erik Erikson 178
James Marcia 180
Alan Waterman 181

Catherine Cooper 182
Stuart Hauser 182
Jean Phinney 183
Janet Helms 184

Jacob Orlofsky 186
Robert Weiss 187
Reed Larson and Maryse Richards 189

Walter Mischel 192
Alexander Chess and Stella Thomas 193

Resources for Improving the Lives of Adolescents

Adolescent Psychological Development: Rationality, Morality, and Identity

(1999) by David Moshman
Mahwah, NJ: Erlbaum

A contemporary analysis of several important dimensions of adolescent development, including identity.

The Construction of the Self

(1999) by Susan Harter
New York: Guilford

A leading self theorist and researcher, Susan Harter provides an in-depth analysis of how children and adolescents see themselves.

Ghandi's Truth

(1969) by Erik Erikson
New York: W. W. Norton

This Pulitzer Prize–winning book by Erik Erikson, who developed the concept of identity as a central aspect of adolescent development, analyzes the life of Mahatma Gandhi, the spiritual leader of India in the middle of the twentieth century.

Identity Development in Adolescence

by Jane Kroger (2003). In G. Adams & M. Berzonsky (Eds.), *Blackwell handbook of adolescence*. Malden, MA: Blackwell.

One of the leading experts on adolescence, Jane Kroger, provides a contemporary analysis of identity development research.

Self-Esteem and Self-Concept

(2003) by Jerome Dusek and J.G. McIntyre. In G. Adams and M. Berzonsky (Eds.), *Blackwell handbook of adolescence*. Malden, MA: Blackwell.

An excellent chapter on the current state of theory and research related to self-esteem and self-concept.

E-Learning Tools

To help you master the material in this chapter, you will find a number of valuable study tools on the student CD-ROM that accompanies this book. In addition, visit the Online Learning Center for *Adolescence, 10th Edition,* where you will find helpful resources for chapter 5, "The Self, Identity, Emotions, and Personality."

Taking It to the Net

http://www.mhhe.com/santrocka10

1. Your roommate returns from the computer lab and announces he took a self-esteem test on the Web and scored really high. Knowing something about test reliability and validity, you are really skeptical about such tests. What will you advise your roommate about the reliability and validity of online self-esteem tests?
2. Your sister returns home from her first few weeks at college and seems to be not as confident and self-assured as she was when she left. She complains about her friends at school tugging her in different directions, about feeling awkward in various social situations, and of having lost control of her attention and concentration. Is it possible that she is undergoing a change in identity?
3. In Erikson's theory, the quality of resolution of earlier crises impacts on the quality of resolution of later crises. What might be some of the outcomes of a less desirable resolution of the identity crisis on the resolution of the intimacy crisis that follows it?

Connect to **http://www.mhhe.com/santrocka10** to research the answers and complete these exercises. In some cases, you'll also find further instructions on this site.

Self-Assessment

To evaluate your self, identity, and personality complete these self-assessments: (1) My Self-Esteem, (2) Exploring My Identity, and (3) Am I Extraverted or Introverted?

Health and Well-Being, Parenting, and Education

To practice your decision-making skills, complete the health and well-being, parenting, and education scenarios.

CHAPTER

6

It is fatal to be man or woman pure and simple; one must be woman-manly or man-womanly.

—Virginia Woolf
English Novelist, 20th Century

Gender

Images of Adolescent Development

The Changing Gender Worlds of Adolescents

You know it seems like girls are more emotionally sensitive than guys, especially teenage guys. We don't know all the reasons, but we have some ideas about why this might be true. Once a girl reaches 12 or so and begins to mature physically, it seems as though nature is preparing her to be sensitive to others the way a mother might be to her baby, to feel what others feel so she can provide love and support to her children. Our culture tells boys different things. They are expected to be "tough" and not get carried away with their feelings. . . . In spite of this, don't think that girls cannot be assertive and boys cannot be sensitive. In fact, boys do feel emotions but many of them simply don't know how to express their feelings or fear that they will be teased.

—Zoe, age 13 (Zager & Rubenstein, 2002, pp. 21–22)

With all the feminist ideas in the country and the equality, I think guys sometimes get put on the spot. Guys might do something that I think or they think might not be wrong at all, but they still get shot down for it. If you're not nice to a girl, she thinks you don't care. But if you are nice, she thinks you are treating her too much like a lady. Girls don't understand guys, and guys don't understand girls very well.

—Toby, age 17 (Pollack, 1998, p. 164)

The comments of these two adolescents—one female, one male—reflect the confusion that many adolescents feel about how to act as a female or a male. Nowhere in adolescents' socioemotional development have more sweeping changes occurred in recent years than in the area of gender, and these changes have led to the confusion about gender behavior just described.

What exactly is meant by *gender?* Whereas the term *sex* refers to the biological dimension of being male or female, **gender** refers to the psychological and sociocultural dimensions of being male or female. Few aspects of adolescents' development are more central to their identity and to their social relationships than gender. One aspect of gender bears special mention: A **gender role** is a set of expectations that prescribes how females or males should think, act, and feel. For example, should males be more assertive than females, and should females be more sensitive than males to others' feelings?

gender The sociocultural and psychological dimensions of being male or female.

gender role A set of expectations that prescribes how females and males should think, act, and feel.

Though individuals become aware of gender early in childhood, a new dimension is added to their understanding with the onset of puberty and the sexual maturation it brings. This chapter begins with a discussion of the biological as well as the social and cognitive influences on gender. We will distinguish gender stereotypes from actual differences between the sexes. We will also examine the range of gender roles, both traditional and nontraditional, that adolescents can adopt. The chapter closes by exploring the developmental changes in gender that characterize adolescence.

1 BIOLOGICAL, SOCIAL, AND COGNITIVE INFLUENCES ON GENDER

Biological Influences on Gender	Social Influences on Gender	Cognitive Influences on Gender

How strong is biology's influence on gender? How extensively does experience shape children's and adolescents' gender development? Do cognitive factors influence gender development? We will address each of these questions in the following sections.

Biological Influences on Gender

Pubertal change is clearly a biological influence on gender behavior in adolescence. Freud and Erikson also believed that the physical characteristics of males and females influence their behavior. And evolutionary psychologists emphasize the role of gender in the survival of the fittest.

Pubertal Change and Sexuality   Puberty brings an increased incorporation of sexuality into adolescents' gender attitudes and behavior (Galambos, 2004). As their bodies flood with hormones, girls may behave in traditionally feminine ways, males in traditionally masculine ways. The increased incorporation of sexuality into adolescents' gender behavior may heighten stereotypical male and female behavior especially when they interact with the other sex. Thus, girls might behave in a sensitive, charming, and soft-spoken manner with a boy they would like to date while boys might behave in an assertive, cocky, and forceful way, perceiving that such behaviors enhance their sexuality. Later in the chapter, we will further evaluate the hypothesis that young adolescents may behave in more gender stereotypic ways than children.

There have been few attempts to relate puberty's sexual changes to gender behavior. Researchers have found that sexual behavior is related to hormonal changes during puberty, at least for boys. For example, in one study, Robert Udry (1990) found that rising androgen levels were related to boys' increased sexual activity. For adolescent girls, androgen levels and sexual activity were associated, but girls' sexual activity was more strongly influenced by the type of friends they had than by their hormone levels. In the same study, Udry investigated whether hormone increases in puberty were related to gender behaviors, such as being affectionate, charming, assertive, or cynical, but found no significant association.

In sum, pubertal changes may result in masculinity and femininity being renegotiated during adolescence. And much of the renegotiation likely involves sexuality.

Freud and Erikson—Anatomy Is Destiny   Both Sigmund Freud and Erik Erikson argued that an individual's genitals influence his or her gender behavior and, therefore, that anatomy is destiny. One of Freud's basic assumptions was that human behavior is directly related to reproductive processes. From this assumption arose his belief that gender and sexual behavior are essentially unlearned and instinctual. Erikson (1968) extended Freud's argument, claiming that the psychological differences between males and females stem from their anatomical differences. Erikson argued that,

As the man beholds
the woman
As the woman sees
the man,
Curiously they note
each other,
As each other they only can.

—BRYAN PROCTER
English Poet, 19th Century

"It's a guy thing."

© The New Yorker Collection 1995 Donald Reilly from cartoonbank.com. All Rights Reserved.

because of genital structure, males are more intrusive and aggressive, females more inclusive and passive. Critics of the anatomy-is-destiny view believe that experience is not given enough credit. The critics say that females and males are more free to choose their gender roles than Freud and Erikson allow. In response to the critics, Erikson modified his view, saying that females in today's world are transcending their biological heritage and correcting society's overemphasis on male intrusiveness.

Evolutionary Psychology and Gender   In chapter 3 we described the approach of evolutionary psychology, which emphasizes that adaptation during the evolution of humans produced psychological differences between males and females (Buss, 1995, 2000, 2001, 2004). Evolutionary psychologists argue that primarily because of their differing roles in reproduction, males and females faced different pressures in primeval environments when the human species was evolving. In particular, because having multiple sexual liaisons improves the likelihood that males will pass on their genes, natural selection favored males who adopted short-term mating strategies. These males competed with other males to acquire more resources in order to access females. Therefore, say evolutionary psychologists, males evolved dispositions that favor violence, competition, and risk taking (Thornhill & Palmer, 2004).

In contrast, according to evolutionary psychologists, females' contributions to the gene pool were improved by securing resources for their offspring, which was promoted by obtaining long-term mates who could support a family. As a consequence, natural selection favored females who devoted effort to parenting and chose mates who could provide their offspring with resources and protection. Females developed preferences for successful, ambitious men who could provide these resources.

This evolutionary unfolding, according to some evolutionary psychologists, explains key gender differences in sexual attitudes and sexual behavior. For example, in one study, men said that ideally they would like to have more than 18 sexual partners in their lifetime, whereas women stated that ideally they would like to have only 4 or 5 (Buss & Schmitt, 1993). In another study, 75 percent of the men but none of the women approached by an attractive stranger of the opposite sex consented to a request for sex (Clark & Hatfield, 1989).

Such gender differences, says David Buss (2001, 2004), are exactly the type predicted by evolutionary psychology. Buss argues that men and women differ psychologically in those domains in which they have faced different adaptive problems during evolutionary history. In all other domains, predicts Buss, the sexes will be psychologically similar.

Critics of evolutionary psychology argue that its hypotheses are backed by speculations about prehistory, not evidence, and that in any event people are not locked into behavior that was adaptive in the evolutionary past. Critics also claim that the evolutionary view pays little attention to cultural and individual variations in gender differences (Unger & Crawford, 2004).

Social Influences on Gender

Many social scientists do not locate the cause of psychological gender differences in biological dispositions. Rather, they argue that these differences are due to social experiences. Alice Eagly (2000, 2001) proposed **social role theory,** which states that gender differences result from the contrasting roles of females and males. In most cultures around the world, females have less power and status than males have, and they control fewer resources (Wood, 2001). Compared with men, women perform more domestic work, spend fewer hours in paid employment, receive lower pay, and are more thinly represented in the highest levels of organizations. In Eagly's view, as women adapted to roles with less power and less status in society, they showed more cooperative, less dominant profiles than men. Thus, the social hierarchy and division of labor are important causes of gender differences in power, assertiveness, and nurture (Eagly & Diekman, 2003).

www.mhhe.com/santrocka10

Gender Resources
Alice Eagly's Research

social role theory States that gender differences result from the contrasting roles of females and males with females having less power and status than males have and they control fewer resources.

Parental Influences   Parents, by action and example, influence their children's and adolescents' gender development (Maccoby, 2003; McHale, Crouter, & Whiteman, 2003). During the transition from childhood to adolescence, parents allow boys more independence than girls, and concern about girls' sexual vulnerability may cause parents to monitor their behavior more closely and ensure that they are chaperoned. Families with young adolescent daughters indicate that they experience more intense conflict about sex, choice of friends, and curfews than do families with young adolescent sons (Papini & Sebby, 1988).

Parents may also have different achievement expectations for their adolescent sons and daughters, especially in academic areas such as math and science. For example, many parents believe that math is more important to their sons' futures than their daughters'. These beliefs influence the value that adolescents place on math achievement (Eccles, 1987). We will have more to say about gender and achievement later in this chapter.

Social cognitive theory has been especially important in understanding social influences on gender (Bussey & Bandura, 1999). The **social cognitive theory of gender** emphasizes that children's and adolescents' gender development is influenced by their observation and imitation of others' gender behavior, as well as by the rewards and punishments they experience for gender-appropriate and -inappropriate behavior. By observing parents and other adults, as well as peers, at home, at school, in the neighborhood, and in the media, adolescents are exposed to a myriad of models who display masculine and feminine behavior. And parents often use rewards and punishments to teach their daughters to be feminine ("Karen, that dress you are wearing makes you look so pretty.") and their sons to be masculine ("Bobby, you were so aggressive in that game. Way to go!").

One major change in the gender-role models adolescents have been exposed to in recent years is the increasing number of working mothers. Most adolescents today have a mother who is employed at least part-time. Although maternal employment is not specific to adolescence, it does influence gender-role development, and its influence likely depends on the age of the child or adolescent involved. Young adolescents may be especially attuned to understanding adult roles, so their mothers' role choices may be important influences on their concepts and attitudes about women's roles (Huston & Alvarez, 1990). Adolescents with working mothers have less-stereotyped concepts of female roles (and sometimes male roles as well) than do adolescents whose mothers are full-time homemakers. They also have more positive attitudes about nontraditional roles for women. Daughters of employed mothers have higher educational and occupational aspirations than do daughters of homemakers (Hoffman, 1989, 2000). Thus, working mothers often serve as models who combine traditional feminine home roles with less traditional activities away from home.

Siblings   Siblings also play a role in gender socialization (Galambos, 2004). One study revealed that over a two-year time frame in early adolescence, siblings became more similar to their older siblings in terms of gender-role and leisure activity (McHale & others, 2001). For example, if a younger sibling had an older sibling who was masculine and engaged in masculine leisure activities, over the two years the younger sibling became more masculine and participated in more masculine leisure activities. In contrast, older siblings became less like their younger siblings over the two-year period.

Peers   Parents provide the first models of gender behavior, but before long, peers also are responding to and modeling masculine and feminine behavior. In middle and late childhood, children show a clear preference for being with and liking same-sex peers (Maccoby, 1996, 1998, 2002). After extensive observations of elementary school playgrounds, two researchers characterized the play settings as "gender school," pointing out that boys teach one another the required masculine behavior and reinforce it, and that girls also teach one another the required feminine behavior and reinforce it (Luria & Herzog, 1985).

social cognitive theory of gender This theory emphasizes that children's and adolescents' gender development occurs through observation and imitation of gender behavior, and through rewards and punishments they experience for gender-appropriate and -inappropriate behavior.

Adolescents spend increasing amounts of time with peers. In adolescence, peer approval or disapproval is a powerful influence on gender attitudes and behavior. Peers can socialize gender behavior partly by accepting or rejecting others on the basis of their gender-related attributes. Deviance from sex-typed norms often leads to low peer acceptance, but within a broad range of normal behavior it is not clear that conformity to sex-typed personality attributes is a good predictor of peer acceptance (Huston & Alvarez, 1990).

Schools and Teachers There are concerns that schools and teachers have biases against both boys and girls (Koch, 2003). What evidence exists that the classroom is biased against boys? Here are some factors to consider (DeZolt & Hull, 2001):

- Compliance, following rules, and being neat and orderly are valued and reinforced in many classrooms. These are behaviors that are typically associated with girls rather than boys.
- A large majority of teachers are females, especially in the elementary school. This may make it more difficult for boys than girls to identify with their teachers and model their teachers' behavior.
- Boys are more likely than girls to be identified as having learning problems.
- Boys are more likely than girls to be criticized.
- School personnel tend to ignore that many boys are clearly having academic problems, especially in the language arts.
- School personnel tend to stereotype boys' behavior as problematic.

What evidence is there that the classroom is biased against girls? Consider the following (Sadker & Sadker, 2003):

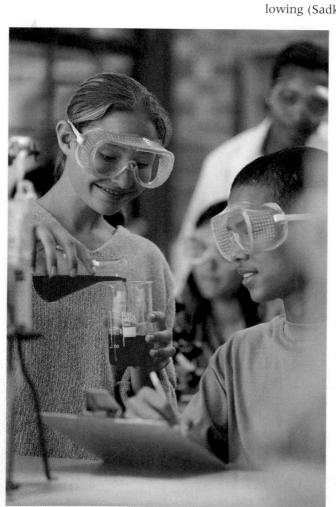

How are gender and schools linked during adolescence?

- In a typical classroom, girls tend to be more compliant, boys more rambunctious. Boys demand more attention, girls are more likely to quietly wait their turn. Teachers are more likely to scold and reprimand boys, as well as send boys to school authorities for disciplinary action. Educators worry that girls' tendency to be compliant and quiet comes at a cost: diminished assertiveness.
- In many classrooms, teachers spend more time watching and interacting with boys while girls work and play quietly on their own. Most teachers don't intentionally favor boys by spending more time with them, yet somehow the classroom frequently ends up with this type of gendered profile.
- Boys get more instruction than girls and more help when they have trouble with a question. Teachers often give boys more time to answer a question, more hints at the correct answer, and further tries if they give the wrong answer.
- Boys are more likely than girls to get lower grades and to be grade repeaters, yet girls are less likely to believe that they will be successful in college work.
- Girls and boys enter first grade with roughly equal levels of self-esteem. Yet by the middle school years, girls' self-esteem is significantly lower than boys' (American Association of University Women, 1992).
- When elementary school children are asked to list what they want to do when they grow up, boys describe more career options than girls do.

A special concern is that most middle and junior high schools consist of independent, masculine learning environments, which appear better suited to the learning style of the average adolescent boy than to that of the average adolescent girl (Huston & Alvarez, 1990). Compared with elementary schools, middle and junior high schools provide a more impersonal environment, which meshes better with the autonomous orientation of male adolescents than with the relationship, connectedness orientation of female adolescents.

Concern has been raised about gender equity not only in secondary schools, but in colleges and universities as well (Paludi, 2002). In some colleges, male students dominate class discussions. In one study, numerous hours of videotape supplied by 24 professors at Harvard University were analyzed (Krupnick, 1985). Males usually dominated the discussions, especially in classes in which the instructor and the majority of the students were male. In contrast, at one state university, female and male students participated virtually equally in class discussion (Crawford & MacLeod, 1990). Reports from all-female institutions (such as Smith and Wellesley) suggest that females there are often assertive in the classroom (Matlin, 1993).

Too often, girls who are interested in the sciences hear the message that they don't fit in this area not only from society but also sometimes from professors themselves. Another group of females who are vulnerable to the "don't fit in" message are women of color. In one study, female and male Latino students who were enrolled at two Ivy League colleges were interviewed (Ethier & Deaux, 1990). Some of the Latina students especially felt uncomfortable, tense, and aware of being different at the predominantly Anglo institutions. Other Latina students perceived little discomfort or prejudicial treatment, reflecting individual variations in these ethnic minority females.

In sum, there is evidence of gender bias against both males and females in schools (DeZolt & Hull, 2001; Koch, 2003; Sadker & Sadker, 2003). Unfortunately, many school personnel are not aware of their gender-biased attitudes, which are deeply entrenched in and supported by the general culture. Increasing awareness of gender bias in schools is clearly an important strategy in reducing such bias.

Females are often portrayed in sexually provocative ways on MTV and in rock videos.

Mass Media Influences   As already described, adolescents encounter gender roles in their everyday interactions with parents, peers, and teachers. The messages about gender roles carried by the mass media also are important influences on adolescents' gender development (Galambos, 2004; Huston & Alvarez, 1990).

Television shows directed at adolescents are extremely stereotyped in their portrayal of the sexes, especially teenage girls (Beal, 1994). One study found that teenage girls were portrayed as being concerned primarily with dating, shopping, and their appearance (Campbell, 1988). They rarely were shown as being interested in school or career plans. Attractive girls were often typed as "airheads" and intelligent girls as unattractive.

Another highly stereotyped form of programming that specifically targets teenage viewers is music videos. What adolescents see on MTV and some other TV shows is highly stereotyped and slanted toward a male audience. Females are twice as likely to be dressed provocatively in music videos as they are in prime-time programming. MTV has been described as a teenage boy's "dreamworld," filled with beautiful, aroused women who outnumber men, seek out and even assault them to have sex, and always mean yes, even when they say no (Jhally, 1990).

Early adolescence may be a period of heightened sensitivity to television messages about gender roles. Increasingly, young adolescents view programs designed for adults that include messages about gender-appropriate behavior, especially in heterosexual relationships. Cognitively, adolescents engage in more idealistic thoughts than children do, and television certainly has its share of idealized characters with whom adolescents can identify and imitate—highly appealing models who are young, glamorous, and successful.

The world of television is highly gender-stereotyped and conveys clear messages about the relative power and importance of women and men (Calvert, 1999; Huston & Alvarez, 1990). Males are overrepresented and females are underrepresented: On virtually every type of program, males outnumber females by approximately two or three to one (Williams & others, 1986). Moreover, male and female TV characters tend to engage in sex-typed occupational and family roles. In the 1970s, female characters appeared more often than males in the contexts of the home, romance, and physical appearance, males more frequently than females in the contexts of work, cars, and sports. By the mid-1980s, when females were portrayed outside the home, their roles were almost as likely to be nontraditional (for example, police officer or attorney) as traditional (for example, secretary or nurse). Men continued to be shown almost entirely in traditional male occupations. Such portrayals are even more frequent on music videos. Male characters are portrayed more often than female characters as aggressive, dominant, competent, autonomous, and active, while female characters are more often portrayed as passive. In one analysis, women were shown as sexual objects (that is, in scanty clothing or engaged in sexually provocative behavior) in 35 percent of the commercial television programs in 1985 (Williams & others, 1986).

Researchers have studied how early adolescent television viewing influences gender attitudes and behavior (Morgan, 1984, 1987). The researchers adopt the assumption that television carries sexist messages and that the more the adolescent is exposed, the greater the number of stereotyped messages the adolescent likely receives. In one investigation of eighth-grade boys and girls, heavy television viewing predicted an increased tendency to endorse traditional gender-role divisions of labor with respect to household chores (Morgan, 1987).

The media influence adolescents' body images, and some studies reveal gender differences in this area. For example, one study of 10- to 17-year-olds found that girls more so than boys perceived that the media influence their body images (Polce-Lynch & others, 2001). However, another study revealed that the more adolescent girls and boys watched entertainment television, the more negative their body images were (Anderson & others, 2001).

If television can communicate sexist messages that influence adolescents' gender behavior, could nonstereotyped gender messages reduce sexist behavior? One major effort to reduce gender stereotyping was the television series *Freestyle,* a series designed to counteract career stereotypes in 9- to 12-year-olds (Johnston, Etteman, & Davidson, 1980). After watching *Freestyle* both girls and boys were more open to nontraditional career possibilities. The benefits of the series were greatest for students who viewed it in the classroom and participated in discussion groups led by their teacher. Classroom discussion was especially helpful in altering boys' beliefs, which were initially more stereotyped than girls'.

However, in one study of young adolescents 12 to 13 years of age, the strategy of nonstereotyped television programming backfired (Durkin & Hutchins, 1984). The adolescents watched sketches about people who held nontraditional jobs, such as a male secretary, a male nurse, and a female plumber. After viewing the series, the adolescents still held traditional views about careers, and in some cases were even more disapproving of alternative careers than they had been before watching the series. Once stereotypes are strongly entrenched, they are difficult to modify.

Cognitive Influences on Gender

Observation, imitation, rewards and punishment—these are the mechanisms by which gender develops according to social cognitive theory. Interactions between the adolescent and the social environment are the main keys to gender development in this view. Some critics argue that this explanation pays too little attention to the adolescent's own mind and understanding and portrays the child as passively acquiring gender roles (Martin, Ruble, & Szkrybalo, 2002). Two cognitive theories—cognitive developmental theory and gender schema theory—stress that individuals actively construct their gender world:

cognitive developmental theory of gender
In this view, children's gender-typing occurs after they have developed a concept of gender. Once they begin to consistently conceive of themselves as male or female, children often organize their world on the basis of gender.

- The **cognitive developmental theory of gender** states that gender-typing occurs *after* children think of themselves as boys and girls. Once they consistently conceive of themselves as male or female, children prefer activities, objects, and attitudes consistent with this label.

- **Gender schema theory** states that gender-typing emerges as individuals gradually develop gender schemas of what is gender-appropriate and gender-inappropriate in their culture. A **schema** is a cognitive structure, a network of associations that guide an individual's perceptions. A **gender schema** organizes the world in terms of female and male. Individuals are internally motivated to perceive the world and to act in accordance with their developing schemas.

Initially proposed by Lawrence Kohlberg (1966), the cognitive developmental theory of gender holds that gender development depends on cognition, and it applies the ideas of Piaget that we discussed in chapter 4. As young children develop the conservation and categorization skills described by Piaget, said Kohlberg, they develop a concept of gender. What's more, they come to see that they will always be male or female. As a result, they begin to select models of their own sex to imitate. The little girl acts as if she is thinking, "I'm a girl, so I want to do girl things. Therefore, the opportunity to do girl things is rewarding."

Notice that in this view gender-typed behavior occurs only after children develop *gender constancy,* which is the understanding that sex remains the same, even though activities, clothing, and hairstyle might change (Ruble, 2000). However, researchers have found that children do not develop gender constancy until they are about 6 or 7 years old. Before this time, most little girls prefer girlish toys and clothes and games, and most little boys prefer boyish toys and games. Thus, contrary to Kohlberg's description of cognitive developmental theory, gender-typing does not appear to depend on gender constancy.

Do the cognitive developmental changes that occur in adolescence influence gender behavior? The abstract, idealized, logical characteristics of formal operational thought mean that adolescents have the cognitive capacity to analyze themselves and decide what they want their gender identity to be. Adolescence is the developmental period when individuals begin to focus their attention on vocational and lifestyle choices. With their increased cognitive skills, adolescents become more aware of the gender-based nature of vocational and lifestyle choices. As they pursue an identity—"Who am I, what am I all about, where am I going in life?"—they have choices to make about gender roles. Recall the discussion of gender and identity in the last chapter. In recent years, as females have developed stronger vocational interests, sex differences are now turning into similarities. Even so, adolescent females still show greater interest in relationships and emotional bonds than males. In sum, both the changes ushered in by formal operational thought and increased interest in identity concerns lead adolescents to examine and redefine their gender attitudes and behavior.

Unlike cognitive developmental theory, gender schema theory does not require children to perceive gender constancy before they begin gender-typing. Instead, gender schema theory states that gender-typing occurs when children are ready to encode and organize information along the lines of what is considered appropriate for females and males in their society (Martin & Dinella, 2001; Martin & Halverson, 1981). Bit by bit, children pick up what is gender-appropriate and gender-inappropriate in their culture and develop gender schemas that shape how they perceive the world and what they remember. Children are motivated to act in ways that conform with these gender schemas. Thus, gender schemas fuel gender-typing.

For a real-life example of gender schemas and their influence on adolescents, consider a 17-year-old high school student deciding which hobby to try from among many available possibilities. The student could ask how expensive each possibility is, whether it can be done in cold weather, whether it will interfere with studying, and so on. But the adolescent is also likely to look at the hobby through the lens of gender, asking, "What sex is the hobby? What sex am I? Do the sexes match? If they do, I will consider the hobby further. If not, I will reject it." This student may not be consciously aware of the gender schema's influence on the decision. Indeed, in many of our everyday encounters, we are not consciously aware of how gender schemas affect our behavior.

gender schema theory According to this theory, an individual's attention and behavior are guided by an internal motivation to conform to gender-based sociocultural standards and stereotypes.

schema A concept or framework that exists in the individual's mind to organize and interpret information.

gender schema A cognitive structure that organizes the world in terms of male and female.

In sum, cognitive factors contribute to the way adolescents think and act as males and females. Through biological, social, and cognitive processes, children develop their gender attitudes and behaviors.

Review and reflect   Learning goal 1

1   Describe the biological, social, and cognitive influences on gender

REVIEW

- How can gender and gender roles be defined? What are some important biological influences on gender?
- What are some important social influences on gender?
- What are some important cognitive influences on gender?

REFLECT

- Which theory of gender development do you like the best? What might an eclectic view of gender development be like? (You might want to review the discussion of an eclectic theoretical orientation in chapter 2.)

Regardless of the factors that influence gender behavior, the consequences of gender have become the subject of intense focus and research over the last several decades. Next, we explore the myths and realities of how females and males do or do not differ.

2   GENDER STEREOTYPES, SIMILARITIES, AND DIFFERENCES

| Gender Stereotyping | Gender Similarities and Differences | Gender in Context |

How pervasive is gender stereotyping? What are the real differences between boys and girls, and why is this issue such a controversial one? In this section, we try not just to answer these questions but to put gender behavior in context.

Gender Stereotyping

Gender stereotypes are broad categories that reflect our impressions and beliefs about females and males. All stereotypes, whether they are based on gender, ethnicity, or other groupings, carry an image of what the typical member of a particular social category is like. These oversimplifications help us to deal with an extremely complex world. Every day we are confronted with thousands of different stimuli. If we assign a label (such as *feminine* or *masculine*) to someone, we will have much less to consider when we think about that individual. However, once such labels have been assigned they are remarkably difficult to abandon, even in the face of contradictory evidence.

Many stereotypes are so general they are ambiguous. Consider the stereotypes for masculine and feminine behaviors. Each stereotype includes diverse behaviors, such as scoring a touchdown or growing facial hair for "masculine" and playing with dolls or wearing lipstick for "feminine." Stereotypes may also be modified in the face of cultural change. At one point in history, masculinity may be thought of in terms of muscular development; at another point, it may be associated with a more slender physique. The behaviors that are popularly agreed on as reflecting a stereotype may

gender stereotypes Broad categories that reflect our impressions and beliefs about females and males.

also vary according to socioeconomic circumstances. For example, lower socioeconomic groups may be more likely than higher socioeconomic groups to include "rough and tough" as part of a masculine stereotype.

Even though the behaviors that are supposed to fit the stereotype often do not, the label itself can have significant consequences for an individual. Labeling a male "feminine" and a female "masculine" can produce significant social reactions to those individuals in terms of their status and acceptance in groups, for example (Best, 2001; Galliano, 2003; Kite, 2001).

How widespread is gender stereotyping? According to a far-ranging study of college students in 30 countries, stereotyping of females and males is pervasive (Williams & Best, 1982). Across cultures, males were widely believed to be dominant, independent, aggressive, achievement oriented, and enduring, while females were widely believed to be nurturant, affiliative, less esteemed, and more helpful in times of distress.

In another investigation, women and men who lived in more highly developed countries perceived themselves as being more similar than women and men who lived in less-developed countries (Williams & Best, 1989). This finding makes sense, since women in the more highly developed countries were more likely to attend college and be gainfully employed. Thus, as sexual equality increases, gender stereotypes, along with actual behavioral differences between the sexes, may diminish. In this investigation, women were more likely than men to perceive similarities between the sexes (Williams & Best, 1989). Respondents in Christian societies were more likely to perceive similarities than respondents in Muslim societies.

Because stereotypes are often negative, they sometimes produce prejudice and discrimination. **Sexism** is prejudice and discrimination against an individual on the basis of her or his sex. A person who says that women cannot become competent lawyers is expressing sexism; so is a person who says that men cannot become competent nursery school teachers. Prejudice and discrimination against women have a long history. Consider the story of Ann Hopkins, one of the first female accountants employed by the huge public accounting firm Price Waterhouse (Fiske & others, 1991). Hopkins had performed admirably at Price Waterhouse. She had accumulated more billable hours than any of her 87 male co-workers and had brought in $25 million in new business. However, when a partnership in the firm opened up, Hopkins was not chosen. Executives at Price Waterhouse claimed that she had weak interpersonal skills, needed a "charm school" course, and was too "macho." Hopkins sued the firm. After a lengthy trial, the U.S. Supreme Court ruled in her favor, stating that gender-based stereotyping had played a significant role in the firm denying her a partnership.

Sexism can be obvious, as when a chemistry professor tells a female premed student that women belong in the home, or can be more subtle, as when a supervisor refers to a mature woman as a *girl* (Matlin, 1993). In one analysis, an attempt was made to distinguish between old-fashioned and modern sexism (Swim & others, 1995). *Old-fashioned sexism* is characterized by endorsement of traditional gender roles, differential treatment for men and women, and a stereotype that females are less competent than males. Like modern racism, *modern sexism* is characterized by the denial that there is still discrimination, antagonism toward women's demands, and lack of support for policies designed to help women (for example, in education and work). Figure 6.1 shows the types of items that were developed to measure old-fashioned and modern sexism.

Gender Similarities and Differences

What is the reality behind gender stereotypes? Let's now examine some of the differences between the sexes, keeping the following in mind:

- The differences are average and do apply to all females or all males.
- Even when gender differences occur, there often is considerable overlap between males and females.

If you are going to generalize about women, you will find yourself up to here in exceptions.
—**Dolores Hitchens**
American Mystery Writer, 20th Century

www.mhhe.com/santrocka10

**Positive Expectations for Girls
Girls and Technology
Telementoring for Girls**

sexism Prejudice and discrimination against an individual because of her or his sex.

FIGURE 6.1 Types of Items Developed to Measure Old-Fashioned and Modern Sexism

Old-Fashioned Sexism

Women are generally not as smart as men.

I would not be as comfortable having a woman for a boss as I would be having a man for a boss.

It is more important to encourage boys than to encourage girls to participate in athletics.

Women are not as capable as men of thinking logically.

When both parents are employed and their child gets sick at school, the school should call the mother rather than the father.

Modern Sexism

Discrimination against women is no longer a problem in the United States.

Women rarely miss out on good jobs because of sexist discrimination.

It is rare to see women treated in a sexist manner on television.

On the average, people in our society treat husbands and wives equally.

Society has reached the point where women and men have equal opportunities for achievement.

It is not easy to understand why women's groups are still concerned about societal limitations on women's opportunities.

It is not easy to understand the anger of women's groups in America.

Over the past few years, the government and news media have been showing more concern about the treatment of women than is warranted by women's actual experiences.

Note: Endorsement of the above items reflects old-fashioned sexism and modern sexism, respectively. The wording of the items has been changed from the original research for ease of understanding.

- The differences may be due primarily to biological factors, sociocultural factors, or both.

First, we will examine physical differences, and then we will turn to cognitive and socioemotional differences.

Physical Similarities and Differences   We could devote pages to describing physical differences between the average man and woman. For example, women have about twice the body fat of men, most concentrated around breasts and hips. In males, fat is more likely to go to the abdomen. On the average, males grow to be 10 percent taller than females. Androgens (the "male" hormones) promote the growth of long bones; estrogens (the "female" hormones) stop such growth at puberty.

Many physical differences between men and women are tied to health. From conception on, females have a longer life expectancy than males, and females are less likely than males to develop physical or mental disorders. Females are more resistant to infection and their blood vessels are more elastic than males'. Males have higher levels of stress hormones, which cause faster clotting and higher blood pressure.

Does gender matter when it comes to brain structure and activity? Human brains are much alike, whether the brain belongs to a male or a female (Halpern, 2001). However, researchers have found some differences (Goldstein & others, 2001; Kimura, 2000). Among the differences that have been discovered are the following:

- One part of the hypothalamus involved in sexual behavior tends to be larger in men than women (Swaab & others, 2001).

- Portions of the corpus callosum—the band of tissues through which the brains' two hemispheres communicate—tend to be larger in females than males (Le Vay, 1994).
- An area of the parietal lobe that functions in visuospatial skills tends to be larger in males than females (Frederikse & others, 2000).
- The areas of the brain involved in emotional expression tend to show more metabolic activity in females than males (Gur & others, 1995).

Similarities and differences in the brains of males and females could be due to evolution and heredity, as well as social experiences.

"So according to the stereotype, you can put two and two together, but I can read the handwriting on the wall."

Cognitive Similarities and Differences   Many years ago, Eleanor Maccoby and Carol Jacklin (1974) concluded that males have better math and visuospatial skills (the kinds of skills an architect needs to design a building's angles and dimensions) than females, whereas females have better verbal abilities than males. Subsequently, Maccoby (1987) concluded that the verbal differences between females and males had virtually disappeared but that the math and visuospatial differences persisted. Today, some experts in gender, such as Janet Shibley Hyde (1993, 2004; Hyde & Mezulis, 2001), believe that the cognitive differences between females and males have been exaggerated. For example, Hyde points out that there is considerable overlap in the distributions of female and male scores on math and visuospatial tasks (see figure 6.2).

When researchers examine how children perform in school or on standardized tests, some differences between U.S. boys and girls persist. In a national study by the U.S. Department of Education (2000), boys did slightly better than girls at math and science. Overall, though, girls were far superior students, earning better grades, and they were significantly better than boys in reading. In another recent national study, females had higher reading achievement and better writing skills than males in grades 4, 8, and 12 with the gap widening as students progressed through school (Coley, 2001). Males are more likely than females to be assigned to special/remedial education classes. Females are more likely to be engaged with academic material, be attentive in class, put forth more academic effort, and participate more in class than boys (DeZolt & Hull, 2001).

Keep in mind, though, that measures of achievement in school or scores on standardized tests may reflect many factors besides cognitive ability. For example, some test scores may reflect stereotype threat (as discussed in chapter 4). Performance in school may in part reflect attempts to conform to gender roles or differences in motivation, self-regulation, or other socioemotional characteristics.

Socioemotional Similarities and Differences   Are "men from Mars" and "women from Venus"? Perhaps the gender differences that most fascinate people are those in how males and females relate to each other as people. For just about every imaginable socioemotional characteristic, researchers have examined whether there are differences between males and females. Here we will examine three: aggression, communication in relationships, and self-regulation of emotion and behavior.

Aggression   One of the most consistent gender differences is that boys are more physically aggressive than girls. The difference occurs in all cultures and appears very early in children's development (White, 2001). The difference in physical aggression is especially pronounced when children are provoked. Although boys are consistently more physically aggressive than girls, might girls be just as aggressive or even more aggressive than boys in other ways? The answer appears to be yes when two other types of aggression are considered. First, when researchers have examined verbal aggression, such as yelling, females are often as aggressive or even more aggressive than males (Eagly & Steffen, 1986). Second, girls are more likely than boys to engage in *relational aggression,* which involves such behaviors

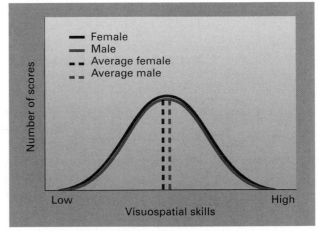

FIGURE 6.2 Visuospatial Skills of Males and Females

Notice that, although an average male's visuospatial skills are higher than an average female's, scores for the two sexes almost entirely overlap. Not all males have better visuospatial skills than all females—the overlap indicates that, although the average male score is higher, many females outperform most males on such tasks.

*W*hat are little boys
made of?
Frogs and snails
and puppy dogs' tails.
What are little girls made of?
Sugar and spice
And all that's nice
—J.O. HALLIWELL
English Author, 19th Century

as spreading malicious rumors in order to get others to dislike a child or ignoring someone when angry at him or her (Crick & others, 2001; Underwood, 2002, 2003).

Communication in Relationships Sociolinguist Deborah Tannen (1990) distinguishes between rapport talk and report talk:

- **Rapport talk** is the language of conversation and a way of establishing connections and negotiating relationships. Females enjoy rapport talk and conversation that is relationship oriented more than boys do.
- **Report talk** is talk that gives information. Public speaking is an example of report talk. Males hold center stage through report talk with such verbal performances as storytelling, joking, and lecturing with information.

Tannen says that boys and girls grow up in different worlds of talk—parents, siblings, peers, teachers, and others talk to boys and girls differently. The play of boys and girls is also different. Boys tend to play in large groups that are hierarchically structured, and their groups usually have a leader who tells the others what to do and how to do it. Boys' games have winners and losers and often are the subject of arguments. And boys often boast of their skill and argue about who is best at what. In contrast, girls are more likely to play in small groups or pairs and at the center of a girl's world is often a best friend. In girls' friendships and peer groups, intimacy is pervasive. Turn taking is more characteristic of girls' games than of boys' games. And much of the time, girls simply like to sit and talk with each other, concerned more about being liked by others than jockeying for status in some obvious way.

In sum, Tannen, like other gender experts such as Carol Gilligan, whose ideas you will read about later in this chapter and in chapter 8, "Moral Development, Values, and Religion," believes that girls are more relationship oriented than boys—and that this relationship orientation should be prized as a skill in our culture more than it currently is.

Self-Regulation of Emotion and Behavior Males usually show less self-regulation of emotions and behavior than females, and this low self-control can translate into behavioral problems (Eisenberg, & others, 2001, 2003). In one study, children's low self-regulation was linked with greater aggression, teasing, overreaction to frustration, low cooperation, and inability to delay gratification (Block & Block, 1980).

Are psychological differences between males and females large or small? Alice Eagly (2001) argues that a belief that the differences are small arose from a feminist commitment to similarity between the sexes as a route to political equality, and from piecemeal and inadequate interpretations of research. Many feminists fear that differences between females and males will be interpreted as deficiencies in females and as biologically based, which could promote the old stereotypes that women are inferior to men (Unger & Crawford, 2004). According to Eagly, contemporary psychology has produced a large body of research that reveals that behavior varies with gender and that the differences are socially induced. Recall, however, that evolutionary psychologist David Buss (2000, 2004) argues that there are substantial gender differences, but, unlike Eagly, he emphasizes that they are evolutionary based. In sum, controversy continues over whether sex differences are rare and small or common and large, in part because gender is a political issue.

Gender in Context

In thinking about gender, it is important to consider the context of behavior (Galambos, 2004; Matlin, 2004), as gender behavior often varies across contexts. Consider helping behavior. Males are more likely to help in contexts in which a perceived danger is present and they feel competent to help (Eagly & Crowley, 1986). For example, males are more likely than females to help a person who is stranded by the roadside with a flat tire; automobile problems are an area about which many males feel competent. In contrast, when the context involves volunteering time to help a child with a personal problem, females are more likely to help than males are, because there is

rapport talk The language of conversation, establishing connections, and negotiating relationships.

report talk Talk that gives information; public speaking is an example.

little danger present and females feel more competent at nurturing. In many cultures, girls show more caregiving behavior than boys do. However, in the few cultures where they both care for younger siblings on a regular basis, girls and boys are similar in their tendencies to nurture (Whiting, 1989).

Context is also relevant to gender differences in the display of emotions (Shields, 1991). Consider anger. Males are more likely to show anger toward strangers, especially other males, when they think they have been challenged. Males also are more likely than females to turn their anger into aggressive action, especially when the culture endorses such action (Tavris & Wade, 1984).

We find contextual variations regarding gender in specific situations not only within a particular culture but also across cultures (Nadien & Denmark, 1999). In many cultures around the world, traditional gender roles guide the behavior of males and females. In China and Iran, for instance, it is still widely accepted for males to engage in dominant behavior and females to behave in subordinate ways. Many Western cultures, such as the United States, have become more flexible about gender behavior.

> *There is more difference within the sexes than between them.*
>
> —IVY COMPTON-BURNETT
> *English Novelist, 20th Century*

Review and reflect Learning goal 2

2 Discuss gender stereotyping, similarities, and differences

REVIEW

- How extensive is gender stereotyping?
- How similar or different are adolescent males and females in their physical, cognitive, and socioemotional development?
- How extensively is gender development influenced by contexts?

REFLECT

- Several decades ago, the word *dependency* was used to describe the relational orientation of femininity. Dependency took on a negative connotation for females—for instances, that females can't take care of themselves while males can. Today, the term *dependency* is being replaced by the term *relational abilities*, which has more positive connotations (Caplan & Caplan, 1999). Rather than being thought of as dependent, women are now more often described as skilled in forming and maintaining relationships. Make up a list of words that you associate with masculinity and femininity. Do these words have any negative connotations for males and females? For the words that do have negative connotations, are there words that could be used to replace them?

3 GENDER-ROLE CLASSIFICATION

Masculinity, Femininity, and Androgyny	Androgyny and Education	Gender-Role Transcendence
Context, Culture, and Gender Roles	Traditional Masculinity and Problem Behaviors in Adolescent Males	

Not very long ago, it was accepted that boys should grow up to be masculine and girls to be feminine, that boys are made of "frogs and snails" and girls are made of "sugar and spice and all that's nice." Let's further explore such gender classifications of boys and girls as "masculine" and "feminine."

FIGURE 6.3 The Bem Sex-Role Inventory

Scoring: The items are scored on independent dimensions of masculinity and femininity as well as androgyny and undifferentiated classifications.

The following items are from the Bem Sex-Role Inventory. When taking the BSRI, a person is asked to indicate on a 7-point scale how well each of the 60 characteristics describes herself or himself. The scale ranges from 1 (never or almost never true) to 7 (always or almost always true).

EXAMPLES OF MASCULINE ITEMS	EXAMPLES OF FEMININE ITEMS
Defends open beliefs	Does not use harsh language
Forceful	Affectionate
Willing to take risks	Loves children
Dominant	Understanding
Aggressive	Gentle

Scoring: The items are scored on independent dimensions of masculinity and feminity as well as androgyny and undifferentiated classifications.

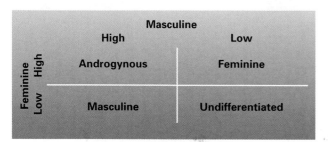

FIGURE 6.4 Gender-Role Classification

Masculinity, Femininity, and Androgyny

In the past, a well-adjusted boy was supposed to be independent, aggressive, and powerful. A well-adjusted girl was supposed to be dependent, nurturant, and uninterested in power. The masculine characteristics were considered to be healthy and good by society; the feminine characteristics were considered undesirable.

In the 1970s, as both males and females became dissatisfied with the burdens imposed by their stereotyped roles, alternatives to "masculinity" and "femininity" were explored. Instead of thinking of masculinity and femininity as a continuum, with more of one meaning less of the other, it was proposed that individuals could show both expressive and instrumental traits. This thinking led to the development of the concept of **androgyny,** the presence of a high degree of masculine and feminine characteristics in the same individual (Bem, 1977; Spence & Helmreich, 1978). The androgynous individual might be a male who is assertive (masculine) and sensitive to others' feelings (feminine), or a female who is dominant (masculine) and caring (feminine).

Measures have been developed to assess androgyny. One of the most widely used gender measures, the *Bem Sex-Role Inventory,* was constructed by a leading early proponent of androgyny, Sandra Bem (1974). Figure 6.3 shows examples of masculine and feminine items on the Bem Sex-Role Inventory. Based on their responses to the items in this inventory, individuals are classified as having one of four gender-role orientations—masculine, feminine, androgynous, or undifferentiated (see figure 6.4):

- The androgynous individual is simply a female or a male who has a high degree of both feminine (expressive) and masculine (instrumental) traits. No new characteristics are used to describe the androgynous individual.
- A feminine individual is high on feminine (expressive) traits and low on masculine (instrumental) traits.
- A masculine individual is high on instrumental traits and low on expressive traits.
- An undifferentiated person is low on both feminine and masculine traits.

Androgynous women and men, according to Bem, are more flexible and more mentally healthy than either masculine or feminine individuals; undifferentiated individuals are the least competent. One recent study found that androgyny was linked to well-being and lower levels of stress (Stake, 2000). Another recent study with emerging adults revealed that androgynous individuals reported better health practices (such as safety belt use, less smoking) than masculine, feminine, or undifferentiated individuals (Shifren, Furnham, & Bauserman, 2003).

androgyny The presence of a high degree of desirable feminine and masculine characteristics in the same individual.

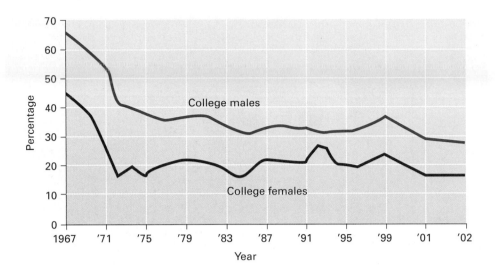

FIGURE 6.5 Changing Attitudes About Gender Roles

Note: Data show the percentage of first-year college students agreeing with the statement, "The activities of married women are best confined to home and family" from 1967 through 2002.

Context, Culture, and Gender Roles

The concept of gender-role classification involves a personality-trait-like categorization of a person. However, it is important to think of personality in terms of both traits and contexts rather than personality traits alone. In close relationships, a feminine or androgynous gender role may be more desirable because of the expressive nature of close relationships. However, a masculine or androgynous gender role may be more desirable in academic and work settings because of their demands for action and assertiveness.

The importance of considering gender in context is nowhere more apparent than when examining what is culturally prescribed behavior for females and males in different countries around the world (Gibbons, 2000). Increasing numbers of children and adolescents in the United States and other modernized countries such as Sweden are being raised to behave in androgynous ways. In the last 30 to 40 years in the United States, a decline in the adoption of traditional gender roles has occurred. For example, in recent years U.S. female college students have shown a propensity for turning in their aprons for careers. In 1967, more than 40 percent of college females and more than 60 percent of college males agreed with the statement, "The activities of married women are best confined to home and family." In 2002, those percentages had dropped to 16 percent for college females and 28 percent for college males (Sax & others, 2002). As shown in figure 6.5, the greatest change in these attitudes occurred in the 1960s and early 1970s.

But traditional gender roles continue to dominate the cultures of many countries around the world today. For example, in countries where the Islamic religion dominates, the man's duty is to provide for his family, the woman's duty to care for her family and household (Dickersheid & others, 1988). Any deviations from this traditional gender-role orientation are severely disapproved of.

Though girls' access to education has improved around the world, they still lag behind boys. According to recent UNICEF (2000) analysis of education worldwide, by age 18, girls have received an average of 4.4 years less education than boys. Their abbreviated schooling reduces their chances of developing to their full potential. Noticeable exceptions to this generalization are found in Western nations, Japan, and the Philippines (Brown & Larson, 2002). In most countries, however, males receive more advanced training and advanced degrees than females (Fussell & Greene, 2002).

Despite these gender gaps, evidence of increasing gender equality is appearing (Brown & Larson, 2002). For example, among upper-socioeconomic-status families in India and Japan, fathers are assuming more child-rearing responsibilities (Stevenson

Adolescent girls in Iran. *How might gender-role socialization for girls in Iran compare with that in the United States?*

Gender Around the World

& Zusko, 2002; Verma & Saraswathi, 2002). Rates of employment and career opportunities are expanding in many countries for women. Control over adolescent girls' social relationships, especially sexual and romantic relationships, is decreasing in some countries.

Androgyny and Education

Can and should androgyny be taught to students? In general, it is easier to teach androgyny to girls than to boys and easier to teach it before the middle school grades. For example, in one study, a gender curriculum was put in place for one year in the kindergarten, fifth, and ninth grades (Guttentag & Bray, 1976). It involved books, discussion materials, and classroom exercises with an androgynous bent. The program was most successful with the fifth-graders, least successful with the ninth-graders. The ninth-graders, especially the boys, showed a boomerang effect, in which they had more traditional gender-role attitudes after the year of androgynous instruction than before it.

Despite such mixed findings, the advocates of androgyny programs believe that traditional sex-typing is harmful for all students and especially has prevented many girls from experiencing equal opportunity. The detractors argue that androgynous educational programs are too value-laden and ignore the diversity of gender roles in our society.

Traditional Masculinity and Problem Behaviors in Adolescent Males

In our discussion of masculinity so far, we have discussed how the masculine role has been accorded a prominent status in the United States, as well as in most other cultures. However, might there be a negative side to traditional masculinity, especially in adolescence? An increasing number of gender theorists and researchers believe there is (Levant, 1999).

Concern about the ways boys have been brought up in traditional ways has been called a "national crisis of boyhood" by William Pollack (1999) in his book *Real Boys*. He says that although there has been considerable talk about the "sensitive male," little has been done to change what he calls the "boy code."

Pollack argues that this code tells boys they should show little if any emotion as they are growing up. Too often boys are socialized to not show their feelings and act tough, says Pollack. Boys learn the boy code in many different contexts—sandboxes, playgrounds, schoolrooms, camps, hangouts—and are taught the code by parents, peers, coaches, teachers, and other adults. Pollack, as well as many others, believes that boys would benefit from being socialized to express their anxieties and concerns rather than keep them bottled up as well as to learn how to better regulate their aggression.

There also is a special concern about boys who adopt a strong masculine role in adolescence, because this is increasingly being found to be associated with problem behaviors. Joseph Pleck (1995) believes that what defines traditional masculinity in many Western cultures includes behaviors that do not have social approval but nonetheless validate the adolescent boy's masculinity. That is, in the male adolescent culture, male adolescents perceive that they will be thought of as more masculine if they engage in premarital sex, drink alcohol and take drugs, and participate in illegal delinquent activities.

Gender-Role Transcendence

Some critics of androgyny say enough is enough and that there is too much talk about gender. They believe that androgyny is less of a panacea than originally envisioned (Paludi, 2002). An alternative is **gender-role transcendence,** the view that when an individual's competence is at issue, it should be conceptualized on a person basis rather than on the basis of masculinity, femininity, or androgyny (Pleck, 1983). That is, we should think about ourselves as people, not as masculine, feminine, or androgynous. Parents should rear their children to be competent boys and girls, not masculine, feminine, or androgynous, say the gender-role critics. They believe such gender-role classification leads to too much stereotyping.

Psychological Study of Men and Masculinity
Male Issues
Men's Movement Organizations

Review and reflect   Learning goal 3

3   **Characterize the variations in gender-role classification**

REVIEW

- How can traditional gender roles be described? What is androgyny? How is androgyny related to social competence?
- How do context and culture influence gender roles?
- How effectively can androgyny be taught in schools?
- How is traditional masculinity linked with the behavior of adolescent males?
- What is gender-role transcendence?

REFLECT

- How would you describe your gender-role classification today? How satisfied are you with your gender-role classification? What factors contributed to your classification?

gender-role transcendence The belief that, when an individual's competence is at issue, it should be conceptualized not on the basis of masculinity, femininity, or androgyny but, rather, on a person basis.

4 DEVELOPMENTAL CHANGES AND JUNCTURES

Early Adolescence and Gender Intensification	Is Early Adolescence a Critical Juncture for Females?

What changes take place during early adolescence that might affect gender roles? Is early adolescence a critical juncture in female development?

Early Adolescence and Gender Intensification

Toward the beginning of this chapter, we described how pubertal changes might be linked to gender roles. Here we briefly review and then expand on the earlier discussion. As females and males experience the many physical and social changes of early adolescence, they have to come to terms with new definitions of their gender roles (Belansky & Clements, 1992; Feiring, 1999; Huston & Alvarez, 1990). During early adolescence, individuals develop the adult, physical aspects of their sex. Some theorists and researchers have proposed that, with the onset of puberty, girls and boys experience an intensification in gender-related expectations. The **gender intensification hypothesis** states that psychological and behavioral differences between boys and girls become greater during early adolescence because of increased socialization pressures to conform to traditional masculine and feminine gender roles (Hill & Lynch, 1983; Lynch, 1991). Puberty may signal to socializing others—parents, peers, and teachers—that an adolescent is approaching adulthood and should begin to act in stereotypical male or female ways. In one study, sex differences in gender-role attitudes increased across the early adolescent years. Gender-role attitudes were measured by the Attitudes Toward Women Scale (Galambos & others, 1985), which

The gender intensification hypothesis states that psychological and behavioral differences between boys and girls become greater during early adolescence because of increased socialization pressures to conform to traditional masculine and feminine gender roles. Puberty's role in gender intensification may involve a signaling to socializing others—parents, peers, and teachers, for example—that the adolescent is beginning to approach adulthood and, therefore, should begin to act in ways that resemble the stereotypical female or male adult. The jury is still out on the validity of the gender intensification hypothesis.

gender intensification hypothesis This hypothesis states that psychological and behavioral differences between boys and girls become greater during early adolescence because of increased socialization pressures to conform to masculine and feminine gender roles.

assesses the extent to which adolescents approve of gender-based division of roles. For example, the adolescent is asked such questions as whether girls should have the same freedom as boys. Other researchers also have reported evidence of gender intensification in early adolescence (Hill & Lynch, 1983). However, not every female and male shows gender intensification during puberty, and the family context influences how strongly gender intensification occurs (Crouter, Manke, & McHale, 1995). Some experts argue that the jury is not yet in on the validity of the gender intensification hypothesis (Galambos, 2004).

As adolescent boys and girls grow older, they tend to show less stereotypic gender behavior. In one study of eighth- and eleventh-graders, the eleventh-graders were more similar to each other on both masculine and feminine traits than were the eighth-graders (Karniol & others, 1998). Irrespective of gender, the eleventh-graders showed less masculinity than the eighth-graders. The eleventh-grade girls were also lower on femininity than the eighth-grade girls, and the eleventh-grade boys higher on femininity than the eighth-grade boys. Indeed, no eighth-grade boys fell into the low-masculinity/high-femininity category. Watch the video clip entitled "Girls and Body Image" in which two mature 14-year-old girls discuss how magazines and members of their peer group seem to define femininity as attaining a specific body type and maintaining an anti-intellectual—or "ditzy"—behavior.

LifeMAP

Is Early Adolescence a Critical Juncture for Females?

Carol Gilligan has conducted extensive interviews with girls from 6 to 18 years of age (Gilligan, 1996; Gilligan, Brown, & Rogers, 1990). She and her colleagues have reported that girls consistently reveal detailed knowledge of human relationships that is based on their experiences with others. According to Gilligan, girls are sensitive to different rhythms and emotions in relationships. Gilligan believes that girls experience life differently from boys; in her words, girls have a "different voice."

Gilligan also believes that adolescence is a critical juncture in girls' development. In early adolescence (usually around 11 to 12 years of age), she says, girls become aware the male-dominated culture does not value their intense interest in intimacy, even though society values women's caring and altruism. The dilemma, says Gilligan, is that girls are presented with a choice that makes them appear either selfish (if they become independent and self-sufficient) or selfless (if they remain responsive to others). As young adolescent girls struggle with this dilemma, Gilligan states, they begin to "silence" their "different voice," becoming less confident and more tentative in offering their opinions. This reticence often persists into adulthood. Some researchers believe that the self-doubt and ambivalence girls experience in early adolescence translate into depression and eating disorders.

Contextual variations influence the degree to which adolescent girls silence their "voice." In one study, Susan Harter and her colleagues (Harter, Waters, & Whitesell, 1996) found that feminine girls reported lower levels of voice in public contexts (at school with teachers and classmates) but not in more private interpersonal relationships (with close friends and parents). However, androgynous girls reported a strong voice in all contexts. Harter and her colleagues found that adolescent girls who buy into societal messages that females should be seen and not heard are at the greatest risk in their development. The greatest liabilities occurred for females who not only lacked a "voice" but who emphasized the importance of appearance. In focusing on their outer selves, these girls faced formidable challenges in meeting the punishing cultural standards of attractiveness.

Some critics argue that Gilligan and her colleagues overemphasize differences in gender. One of those critics is developmentalist Eleanor Maccoby, who says that Gilligan exaggerates the differences in intimacy and connectedness between males and females. Other critics fault Gilligan's research strategy, which rarely includes a comparison group of boys or statistical analysis. Instead, Gilligan conducts extensive

Careers in Adolescent Development

Carol Gilligan
Professor and Chair of Gender Studies Program

Carol Gilligan obtained an undergraduate degree from Swarthmore College, a master's degree in clinical psychology from Radcliffe College, and a Ph.D. in social psychology from Harvard University. Her teaching career at Harvard began in 1967, when she co-taught a developmental psychology class with Erik Erikson. In 1997, Carol was appointed to the first position at Harvard in Gender Studies and is now the Chair of the gender studies program.

Carol Gilligan's work has expanded the understanding of gender development. Her research has shown that the inclusion of girls' voices can make an important difference in development, especially in the domains of gender and morality.

Carol's ideas especially became well known with the publication of *In a Different Voice* (1982). In another book, *Between Voice and Silence: Women and Girls, Race and Relationship* (with J. McLean Taylor and A. Sullivan) (1996), she studied girls from low-income families and their struggles to be heard and taken seriously. Her recent work includes the Harvard Project on Women's Psychology and Girls' Development, as well as a prevention project, Strengthening Healthy Resistance and Courage in Girls. Carol also is currently writing a new book, *The Birth of Pleasure*.

Carol Gilligan (right, in maroon dress) with some of the females she has interviewed about their relationships with others.

interviews with girls and then provides excerpts from the girls' narratives to buttress her ideas. Other critics fear that Gilligan's findings reinforce stereotypes—females as nurturing and sacrificing, for example—that might undermine females' struggle for equality. These critics say that Gilligan's "different voice" perhaps should be called "the voice of the victim." What we should be stressing, say these critics, is more opportunities for females to reach higher levels of achievement and self-determination.

In reply, revisionists such as Gilligan say that their work provides a way to liberate females and transform a society that has far too long discriminated against females. They also say that if females' approach to life is acknowledged as authentic, women will no longer have to act like men. The revisionists argue that females' sensitivity in relationships is a special gift in our culture (Brown, Way, & Duff, 1999). Influenced by Gilligan's and other feminists' thinking, some schools are beginning to incorporate the feminine voice into their curriculum. For example, at the Emma Willard School in Troy, New York, the entire curriculum has been revamped to emphasize cooperation rather than competition, and to encourage girls to analyze and express ideas from their own perspective rather than responding in stereotyped or conformist ways.

Whether you believe the connectionist arguments of Gilligan or the achievement/self-determination arguments of her critics, there is increasing evidence that adolescence is a critical juncture in the psychological development of females. In chapter 5, "The Self, Identity, Emotions, and Personality," we described a recent large-scale national study that revealed a decrease in the self-esteem of boys and girls during adolescence, but a more substantial decrease for adolescent girls than boys (Robins & others, 2002). In another national survey that was conducted by the American Association of University Women (1993), girls revealed a significantly greater drop in self-esteem during adolescence than boys did. In yet another study, the self-esteem of girls declined during adolescence (Rosner & Rierdan, 1994). At ages 8 and 9, 60 percent of the girls were confident and assertive and felt positive about themselves, compared with 67 percent of the boys. However, over the next eight years, the girls' self-esteem fell 31 percentage points—only 29 percent of high school girls felt positive about themselves. Across the same age range, boys' self-esteem dropped 21 points—leaving 46 percent of the high school boys with high self-esteem, which makes for a gender gap of 17 percentage points. Keep in mind, though, as we indicated in chapter 5, that some psychologists believe that gender differences in self-esteem during adolescence are quite small (Harter, 2002).

Review and reflect Learning goal 4

4 **Summarize developmental changes in gender**

REVIEW

- How might early adolescence influence gender development?
- Is early adolescence a critical juncture for females?

REFLECT

- Did your gender behavior change as you went through early adolescence? Explain.

In this chapter we have examined many aspects of gender. We saw that sexuality influences gender in adolescence more than in childhood. In chapter 7, we will explore adolescent sexuality more extensively.

Reach Your Learning Goals

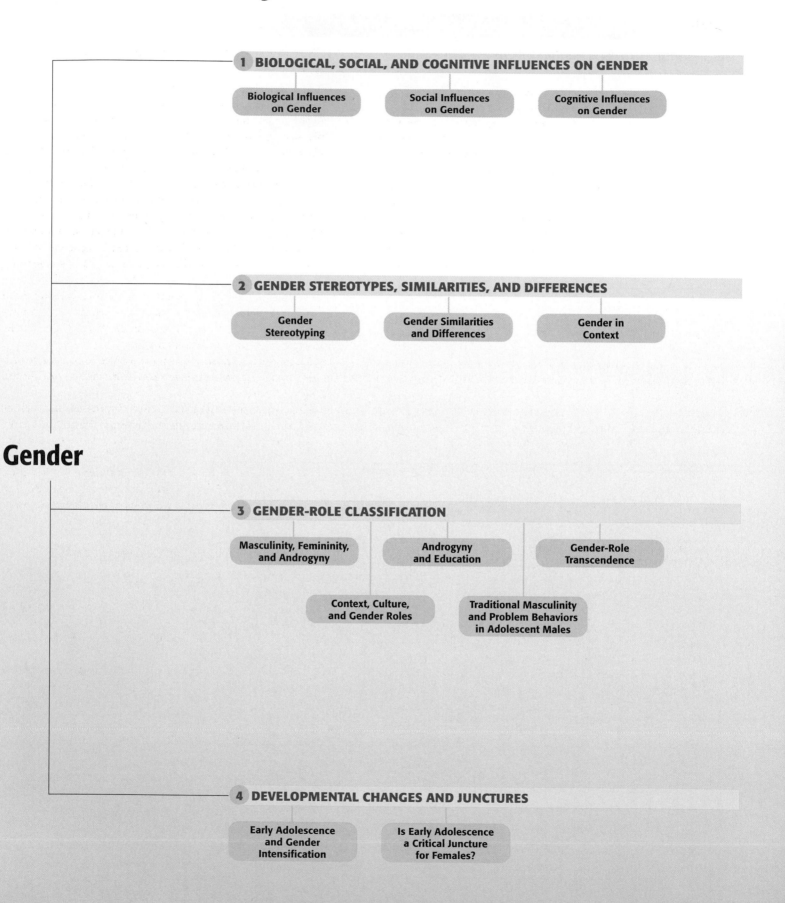

Gender

1 BIOLOGICAL, SOCIAL, AND COGNITIVE INFLUENCES ON GENDER

- Biological Influences on Gender
- Social Influences on Gender
- Cognitive Influences on Gender

2 GENDER STEREOTYPES, SIMILARITIES, AND DIFFERENCES

- Gender Stereotyping
- Gender Similarities and Differences
- Gender in Context

3 GENDER-ROLE CLASSIFICATION

- Masculinity, Femininity, and Androgyny
- Androgyny and Education
- Gender-Role Transcendence
- Context, Culture, and Gender Roles
- Traditional Masculinity and Problem Behaviors in Adolescent Males

4 DEVELOPMENTAL CHANGES AND JUNCTURES

- Early Adolescence and Gender Intensification
- Is Early Adolescence a Critical Juncture for Females?

224

Summary

1 Describe biological, social, and cognitive influences on gender

- Gender involves the psychological and sociocultural dimensions of being male or female. A gender role is a set of expectations that prescribes how females or males should think, act, and feel. Because of pubertal change, sexuality plays a more important role in gender development for adolescents than for children. Freud's and Erikson's ideas promote the idea that anatomy is destiny. Today's developmentalists are interactionists when biological and environmental influences on gender are at issue. In the evolutionary psychology view, evolutionary adaptations produced psychological sex differences especially in the area of mate selection. Criticisms of the evolutionary psychology view have been made.
- In the social roles view, women have less power and status than men do and control fewer resources. In this view, gender hierarchy and sexual division of labor are important causes of sex-differentiated behavior. The social cognitive theory of gender emphasizes that adolescents' gender development is influenced by their observation and imitation of others' gender behavior, as well as by rewards and punishments of gender-appropriate and gender-inappropriate behavior. Parents and siblings influence adolescents' gender roles. Peers are especially adept at rewarding gender-appropriate behavior. There is still concern about gender inequity in education. Despite improvements, TV still portrays males as more competent than females.
- Kohlberg proposed a cognitive developmental theory of gender development. Gender schema theory states that individuals develop a schema for gender influenced by sociocultural standards and stereotypes of gender.

2 Discuss gender stereotypes, similarities, and differences

- Gender stereotypes are general impressions and beliefs about males and females. Gender stereotypes are widespread.
- There are a number of physical differences in males and females. Gender differences in verbal skills are often small or nonexistent. However, girls significantly outperform boys in reading skills and get better grades in school. Socioemotional differences include: males are more physically aggressive and active; females show a stronger interest in relationships and are better at self-regulation of behavior and emotion.
- Gender in context is an important concept.

3 Characterize the variations in gender-role classification

- In the past, the well-adjusted male was supposed to show instrumental traits, the well-adjusted female expressive traits. In the 1970s, alternatives to traditional gender roles were introduced. It was proposed that competent individuals could show both masculine and feminine traits. This thinking led to the development of the concept of androgyny, the presence of desirable masculine and feminine traits in one individual. Gender-role measures often categorize individuals as masculine, feminine, androgynous, or undifferentiated. Most androgynous individuals are flexible and mentally healthy, although the particular context and the individual's culture also determine the adaptiveness of a gender-role orientation.
- In thinking about gender, it is important to keep in mind the context in which gender behavior is displayed. In many countries around the world, such as Egypt and China, traditional gender roles are still dominant.
- Androgyny education programs have been more successful with females than males and more successful with children than adolescents.
- A special concern is that boys raised in a traditional manner are socialized to conceal their emotions. Researchers have found that problem behaviors often characterize highly masculine adolescents.
- One alternative to androgyny states that there has been too much emphasis on gender and that a better strategy is to think about competence in terms of people rather than gender.

4 Summarize developmental changes in gender

- The gender intensification hypothesis states that psychological and behavioral differences between boys and girls become greater during adolescence because of increased socialization pressures to conform to traditional gender roles. The jury is still out on the validity of the gender intensification hypothesis.
- Gilligan believes that girls come to a critical juncture in their development during early adolescence. Girls become aware that their intense interest in intimacy is not prized by the male-dominant society. Some critics say that Gilligan exaggerates gender differences in intimacy.

Key Terms

gender 202
gender role 202
social role theory 204
social cognitive theory
    of gender 205

cognitive developmental
    theory of gender 208
gender schema theory 209
schema 209
gender schema 209

gender stereotypes 210
sexism 211
rapport talk 214
report talk 214
androgyny 216

gender-role transcendence 219
gender intensification
    hypothesis 220

Key People

Sigmund Freud 203
Erik Erikson 203
Alice Eagly 204

Lawrence Kohlberg 209
Eleanor Maccoby 213
Carol Jacklin 213

Janet Shibley Hyde 213
Deborah Tannen 214
David Buss 214

Sandra Bem 216
Joseph Pleck 219
Carol Gilligan 221

Resources for Improving the Lives of Adolescents

Beyond Appearance

(1999) by Norine Johnson, Michael Roberts, and Judith Worrell (Eds.). Washington, DC: American Psychological Association

A number of experts discuss the gender development of adolescent girls, including gender-role prescriptions, stereotypes, relationships with family and peers, and experiences at school.

Gender and Gender Role Development in Adolescence

(2004) by Nancy Galambos. In R. Lerner & L. Steinberg (Eds.), *Handbook of Adolescence*. New York: Wiley.

An expert on gender development in adolescence, Nancy Galambos, evaluates many different research areas.

Real Boys

(1999) by William Pollack
New York: Owl Books.

Pollack examines the ways boys have been reared and concludes that there needs to be a major change in this rearing.

The Two Sexes

(1998) by Eleanor Maccoby
Cambridge, MA: Harvard University Press

In this book you can explore how gender differences emerge in children's groups.

YMCA

101 North Wacker Drive
Chicago, IL 60606

The YMCA provides a number of programs for teenage boys. A number of personal health and sports programs are available.

You Just Don't Understand!

(1990) by Deborah Tannen
New York: Ballantine

This is a book about how women and men communicate—or, all too often, miscommunicate—with each other.

YWCA

726 Broadway
New York, NY 10003

The YWCA promotes health, sports participation, and fitness for women and girls. Its programs include instruction in health, teen pregnancy prevention, family life education, self-esteem enhancement, parenting, and nutrition.

E-Learning Tools

To help you master the material in this chapter, you will find a number of valuable study tools on the student CD-ROM that accompanies this book. In addition, visit the Online Learning Center for *Adolescence, 10th Edition,* where you will find helpful resources for chapter 6, "Gender."

Taking It to the Net

http://www.mhhe.com/santrocka10

1. Gender roles influence how we perceive ourselves and others, our desires and goals, and our personalities. But they also impact on the everyday lives of adults in very basic and fundamental ways. What might the issues of balancing home and career be and how are they similar and different for males and females?

2. Great changes have occurred in gender roles since the 1970s, particularly in the lives of women. But have these changes impacted on the nature and quality of married life? How do you view the relation between gender roles and marriage? How might your spouse view that relationship?

3. Gender differences in humans in part reflect physical/biological differences. How might other disciplines such as biology inform your understanding of how these physical differences came into play?

Connect to **http://www.mhhe.com/santrocka10** to research the answers and complete these exercises. In some cases, you'll also find further instructions on this site.

Self-Assessment

To evaluate yourself, complete this self-assessment: My Attitudes Toward Women.

Health and Well-Being, Parenting, and Education

To practice your decision-making skills, complete the health and well-being, parenting, and education scenarios.

CHAPTER 7

If we listen to boys and girls at the very moment they seem most pimply, awkward, and disagreeable, we can penetrate a mystery most of us once felt heavily within us, and have now forgotten. This mystery is the very process of creation of man and woman.

—COLIN MCINNES
Contemporary Scottish Author

Sexuality

Learning Goals

1 Discuss sexuality as a normal aspect of adolescence and summarize the nature of adolescent sexual attitudes and behavior

2 Describe the main sexual problems that can emerge in adolescence

3 Characterize the sexual literacy of adolescents and sex education

4 Explain what is needed for well-being and social policy in adolescent sexuality

Images of Adolescent Development

The Mysteries and Curiosities of Adolescent Sexuality

I guess when you give a girl a sexy kiss you're supposed to open your lips and put your tongue in her mouth. That doesn't seem very sexy to me. I can't imagine how a girl would like that. What if she has braces on her teeth and your tongue gets scratched? And how are you supposed to breathe? Sometimes I wish I had an older brother I could ask stuff like this.

—Frank, age 12

I can't believe I'm so much in love! I just met him last week but I know this is the real thing. He is much more mature than the boys who have liked me before. He's a senior and has his own car. When he brought me home last night, we got so hot I thought we were going to have sex. I'm sure it will happen the next time we go out. It goes against everything I've been taught—but I can't see how it can be wrong when I'm so much in love and he makes me feel so fantastic!

—Amy, age 15

Ken and I went on a camping trip last weekend and now I'm sure that I'm gay. For a long time I've known I've been attracted to other guys, like in the locker room at school it would sometimes be embarrassing. Ken and I are great friends and lots of times we would mess around wrestling or whatever. I guessed that he felt the way I did. Now I know. Sooner or later, I'll have to come out, as they say, but I know that is going to cause a lot of tension with my parents and for me.

—Tom, age 15

I'm lucky because I have a good figure and I'm popular. I've had boyfriends since middle school and I know how to take care of myself. It's fun when you're out with a guy and you can be intimate. The only thing is, Dan and I had sex a few weeks ago and I'm wondering if I'm pregnant. He used a contraceptive, but maybe it didn't work. Or maybe I'm just late. Anyway, if I have a baby, I could deal with it. My aunt wasn't married when she got pregnant with my cousin, and it turned out okay.

—Claire, age 16

About a month ago my mom's friend's daughter tested positive for HIV. Until then my mom and stepfather never talked about sex with me, but now they're taking turns lecturing me on the theme of "don't have sex until you're married." Give me a break! Nicole and I have been together for a year and a half. What do they think we do when we go out, play tiddlywinks? Besides, my real father never remarried and has girlfriends all the time. All my life I've been seeing movies and TV shows where unmarried people sleep together and the worst that happens is maybe a broken heart. I don't know that woman's daughter, but she must have been mixed up with some pretty bad characters. Me, I always use a condom.

—Sean, age 17

During adolescence, the lives of males and females become wrapped in sexuality. Adolescence is a time of sexual exploration and incorporating sexuality into one's identity. In chapter 3, we studied the biological basis of sexual maturation, including the timing of these changes and the hormones involved. This chapter focuses on the sexual experiences, attitudes, and behaviors of adolescents. We will begin with an overview of sexuality in adolescent development and then examine some problems involving sexual activity such as adolescent pregnancy, sexually transmitted infections, and forcible sex. Next, we will explore the ways in which adolescents learn about sex. The chapter concludes with a discussion of how social policy relates to adolescent sexuality and sexual well-being.

1 EXPLORING ADOLESCENT SEXUALITY

A Normal Aspect of Adolescent Development

Sexual Attitudes and Behavior

Adolescents have an almost insatiable curiosity about the mysteries of sex. They wonder whether they are sexually attractive, how to behave sexually, and what the future holds for their sexual lives. Most adolescents eventually manage to develop a mature sexual identity, even though, as adults can attest, there are always times of vulnerability and confusion along life's sexual journey.

A Normal Aspect of Adolescent Development

Much of what we hear about adolescent sexuality involves problems, such as adolescent pregnancy and sexually transmitted infections. While these are significant concerns, it is important not to lose sight of the fact that sexuality is a normal part of adolescence (Nichols & Good, 2004; Senanayake & Faulkner, 2003).

A Bridge Between the Asexual Child and the Sexual Adult An important theme of adolescence that we have underscored in this book is that too often adolescents are negatively stereotyped. The themes of negative stereotyping and adolescent problems also apply to the topic of adolescent sexuality. Although we will discuss a number of problems that can occur in the area of adolescent sexuality, we must keep in mind that the majority of adolescents have healthy sexual attitudes and engage in sexual behaviors that will not compromise their journey to adulthood (Crockett, Raffaelli, & Moilanen, 2003).

Every society pays some attention to adolescent sexuality (Feldman, 1999). In some societies, adults chaperone adolescent females to protect them from males; others promote very early marriage. Still other societies, such as the United States, allow some sexual experimentation, although there is a wide range of opinions about just how far this experimentation should be allowed to go.

Four previous chapters introduced topics that are a backdrop for understanding sexual attitudes and behavior in adolescence. In chapter 3, we saw that an important aspect of pubertal change involves sexual maturation and a dramatic increase in androgens in males and estrogens in females. Puberty is coming earlier today than in previous generations, which can lead to early dating and early sexual activity.

In chapter 4, we indicated that young adolescents tend to exhibit a form of egocentrism—they perceive themselves as unique and invulnerable. This can lead them to take sexual risks. In emotional moments like those involved in sexual experimentation, adolescents' sexual urges can overwhelm their ability to make competent decisions.

Sexual arousal emerges as a new phenomenon in adolescence and it is important to view sexuality as a normal aspect of adolescent development.

—SHIRLEY FELDMAN,
Contemporary Psychologist, Stanford University

$\mathcal{W}$e are born twice over;
the first time for existence,
the second for life; Once as
human beings and later as
men or as women.

—JEAN-JACQUES ROUSSEAU
*Swiss-Born French Philosopher,
18th Century*

In chapter 5, we described sexual identity as one of the dimensions of personal identity (Russell & Troung, 2002). Intimacy with another is an important aspect of the dyadic nature of adolescent sexuality.

In chapter 6, we examined the physical and biological differences between females and males. We also saw that according to the gender intensification hypothesis, pubertal changes can lead boys and girls to conform to traditional masculine and feminine behavior, respectively. Further, when college students are asked to rate the strength of their sex drive, men report higher levels of sexual desire than women. The adolescent developmental transition, then, may be seen as a bridge between the asexuality of childhood and the fully developed sexual identity of adulthood.

Four chapters in the remainder of the book also include discussions that are important for understanding adolescent sexuality. In chapter 9, we will learn that intense, prolonged conflict with parents is associated with adolescent sexual problems as is a lack of parental monitoring. Better relationships with parents are correlated with postponing sexual intercourse, less frequent intercourse, and fewer partners in adolescence (Miller, Benson, & Galbraith, 2001). Later in this chapter, we will see that adolescents receive very little sex education from parents and that parents and adolescents rarely discuss sex.

In chapter 10, we will read about how same-sex siblings, peers, and friends often discuss sexuality (Caruthers & Ward, 2002). We will also learn that early dating is associated with a number of adolescent problems and that romantic love is important (especially for girls) in adolescence.

In chapter 11, we will study how schools are playing an increasingly important role in adolescent sexuality. And as we will see later in this chapter, most parents now recognize that sex education in schools is an important aspect of education.

In chapter 13, we will describe the vast cultural variations in sexuality. In some cultures sexuality is extremely repressed; other cultures have far more liberal standards for sexuality. The media often present sexuality to adolescents in an unrealistic way (Kim, 2002). An increasing concern is adolescents' access to sexual material on the Internet.

As you can see, sexuality has ties to virtually all areas of adolescent development that we discuss in this book. Let's now explore the sexual culture American adolescents are exposed to.

Sex is virtually everywhere in the American culture and is used to sell just about everything. *Is it surprising, then, that adolescents are so curious about sex and tempted to experiment with sex?*

The Sexual Culture It is important to put adolescent sexuality into the broader context of sexuality in the American culture (Crockett, Raffaelli, & Moilanen, 2003). Whereas fifty years ago sex was reserved for married couples, today adult sex is openly acknowledged among divorcées, with extramarital partners, and so on. There has been an enormous increase in the incidence of pregnancy in unmarried women who are adults. Sex among unmarried teenagers is an extension of this general trend toward greater sexual permissiveness in the adult culture.

Many Americans are ambivalent about sex. Advertisers use sex to sell just about everything, from cars to detergents. Sex is explicitly portrayed in movies, TV shows, videos, lyrics of popular music, MTV, and Internet websites (Pettit, 2003; Roberts & others, 2004; Ward, 2003). Why, then, should we be so surprised that adolescents are so curious and want to experiment with sex?

Sexuality often involves more tension between parents and adolescents in the United States than in most cultures. In one cross-cultural analysis, it was concluded that parent-adolescent tension about sex is greater in the United States than in Japan because U.S. adolescents engage in more sexual activity and because sexual activity is imbued with certain social meanings, such as high status for males (Rothbaum & others, 2000).

Developing a Sexual Identity Mastering emerging sexual feelings and forming a sense of sexual identity is multifaceted (Brooks-Gunn & Paikoff, 1997; Graber & Brooks-Gunn, 2002). This lengthy process involves learning to manage sexual feelings, such as sexual arousal and attraction, developing new forms of intimacy, and learning the skills to regulate sexual behavior to avoid undesirable consequences. Developing a sexual identity also involves more than just sexual behavior. Sexual identities emerge in the context of physical factors, social factors, and cultural factors, with most societies placing constraints on the sexual behavior of adolescents.

An adolescent's sexual identity involves an indication of sexual orientation (homosexual, heterosexual, bisexual), and it also involves activities, interests, and styles of behavior. A study of 470 tenth- to twelfth-grade Australian youth characterized an adolescent's sexual identity as following one of five different styles (Buzwell & Rosenthal, 1996):

- *Sexually naïve.* This group had low sexual self-esteem, suggesting a lack of confidence and some discontent regarding their sexuality and physical characteristics. They also had high anxiety about sex and were lower than any other group on sexual arousal and exploration. This group consisted primarily of tenth-grade girls, the vast majority of whom were virgins.
- *Sexually unassured.* This group reported especially low sexual self-esteem and high anxiety about sex. They felt sexually unattractive, were dissatisfied with their sexual behavior, and perceived their bodies as underdeveloped and unappealing. This group was predominantly male, and most were virgins.
- *Sexually competent.* This group had high sexual self-esteem, appearing confident of their sexual appeal and body and comfortable about their sexual behavior. They had a moderate level of sexual commitment and were only somewhat anxious about sex. This group was composed mainly of twelfth-graders, with slightly more girls than boys. A majority of them were sexually experienced.
- *Sexually adventurous.* This group had high sexual self-esteem, low sexual anxiety, low sexual commitment, and high interest in exploring sexual options. This group included substantially more girls than boys, and most were nonvirgins.
- *Sexually driven.* These adolescents had high sexual self-esteem, felt sexually attractive, and were confident in their ability to manage sexual situations. They had the lowest score of all groups on sexual commitment. This group was almost entirely male and had the largest number of sexually experienced adolescents.

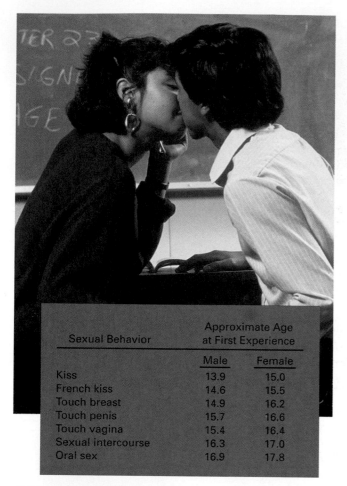

Sexual Behavior	Approximate Age at First Experience	
	Male	Female
Kiss	13.9	15.0
French kiss	14.6	15.5
Touch breast	14.9	16.2
Touch penis	15.7	16.6
Touch vagina	15.4	16.4
Sexual intercourse	16.3	17.0
Oral sex	16.9	17.8

FIGURE 7.1 Age at First Experience of Various Sexual Behaviors

The Kinsey Institute Sexuality Research Information Service

Obtaining Information About Adolescent Sexuality Assessing sexual attitudes and behavior is not always a straightforward affair (Kelly, 2004). Consider how you would respond if someone asked you, "How often do you have intercourse?" or "How many different sexual partners have you had?" The people most likely to respond to sexual surveys are those with liberal sexual attitudes who engage in liberal sexual behaviors. Thus, research is limited by the reluctance of individuals to answer questions about extremely personal matters candidly and by researchers' inability to get any answer, candid or otherwise, from individuals who simply refuse to talk to strangers about sex (Halonen & Santrock, 1999). In addition, when asked about their sexual activity, individuals may respond truthfully or they may give socially desirable answers. For example, a ninth-grade boy might report that he has had sexual intercourse, even if he has not, because he is afraid someone will find out that he is sexually inexperienced.

Researchers have been developing methods to increase the validity of sexual self-report information. In one study, each adolescent spoke individually with a same-sex interviewer who asked questions of increasing sexual involvement until the respondent reported that he or she had not engaged in a behavior, at which point the interview was ended (Paikoff & others, 1997). This strategy might be preferable to a checklist, which can lead to over- or underreporting and embarrassment. Some researchers also have presented adolescents with audiotaped questions to reduce any embarrassment about reporting sexual behaviors to an interviewer.

Sexual Attitudes and Behavior

Let's now explore adolescents' sexual attitudes and behavior. First, we study heterosexual attitudes and behavior, and then homosexual attitudes and behavior.

Heterosexual Attitudes and Behavior What is the progression of adolescent sexual behaviors? How extensively have heterosexual attitudes and behaviors changed in the twentieth century? What sexual scripts do adolescents follow? Are some adolescents more vulnerable than others to irresponsible sexual behavior? We will examine each of these questions.

The Progression of Adolescent Sexual Behaviors Adolescents typically engage in a rather consistent progression of sexual behaviors. In one study, 452 18- to 25-year-olds were asked about their own past sexual experiences (Feldman, Turner, & Araujo, 1999). The following progression of sexual behaviors occurred: kissing preceded petting, which preceded sexual intercourse and oral sex. Figure 7.1 shows the approximate ages at which males and females typically first engaged in a variety of sexual behaviors. Notice that male adolescents reported engaging in these sexual behaviors approximately one year earlier than female adolescents.

Adolescent Heterosexual Behavior—Trends and Incidence Had you been a college student in 1940, you probably would have had a different attitude about many aspects of sexuality than you do today. A review of college students' sexual practices in the twentieth century reveals two important trends (Darling, Kallen, & VanDusen, 1984). First, the percentage of youth who say they have had sexual intercourse has increased dramatically. Second, the proportion of female college students who report that they have had sexual intercourse has increased more rapidly than that of males, although the initial base for males was greater.

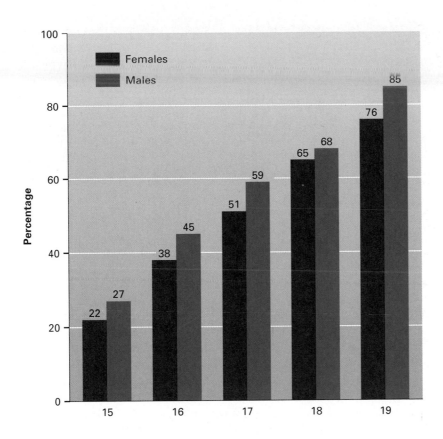

What is the current profile of sexual activity of adolescents? Based on a national survey of adolescents, sexual intercourse is uncommon in early adolescence but becomes more common in the high school and college years (see figure 7.2) (Alan Guttmacher Institute, 1995, 1998; Centers for Disease Control and Prevention, 2000). These are some of the findings:

- Eight in 10 girls and 7 in 10 boys are virgins at age 15.
- The probability that adolescents will have sexual intercourse increases steadily with age, but 1 in 5 individuals have not yet had sexual intercourse by age 19.
- Initial sexual intercourse occurs in the mid- to late-adolescent years for a majority of teenagers, about eight years before they marry; more than one-half of 17-year-olds have had sexual intercourse.

Most studies find that adolescent males are more likely than adolescent females to say that they have had sexual intercourse and are sexually active (Feldman, Turner, & Araujo, 1999; Hayes, 1987). Adolescent males are also more likely than their female counterparts to describe sexual intercourse as an enjoyable experience. And African Americans are more likely to have a less restrictive timetable for sexual behaviors than other groups, whereas Asian Americans are more likely to have a more restrictive one (Feldman, Turner, & Araujo, 1999) (see figure 7.3).

The percentages of sexually active young adolescents may vary with location, being higher in inner cities. In one area of Baltimore, 81 percent of the males at age 14 said that they already had engaged in sexual intercourse. Other surveys in inner-city, low-SES areas also reveal a high incidence of early sexual intercourse (Clark, Zabin, & Hardy, 1984).

Some reports of an increase in oral sex among adolescents have recently appeared (Remez, 2000; Schuster, 2000). Possible reasons for the increase in oral sex include preventing pregnancy and a belief that oral sex is safe from disease, although as we will see later oral sex is not always disease-free.

How is it that, in the human body, reproduction is the only function to be performed by an organ of which an individual carries only one half so that he has to spend an enormous amount of time and energy to find another half?

—FRANCOIS JACOB
French Biologist, 20th Century

FIGURE 7.3 Sexual Timetables of White, African American, Latino, and Asian American Adolescents

Sexual timetable	White	African American	Latino	Asian American
Kiss	14.3	13.9	14.5	15.7
French kiss	15.0	14.0	15.3	16.2
Touch breast	15.6	14.5	15.5	16.9
Touch penis	16.1	15.0	16.2	17.8
Touch vagina	16.1	14.6	15.9	17.1
Sexual intercourse	16.9	15.5	16.5	18.0
Oral sex	17.1	16.9	17.1	18.3

In sum, in the United States the majority of individuals have had sexual intercourse by the end of adolescence. Male, African American, and inner-city adolescents report being the most sexually active. Though sexual intercourse can be a meaningful experience for older, mature adolescents, many adolescents are not emotionally prepared to handle sexual experiences, especially in early adolescence. In one study, early sexual activity was associated with adjustment problems (Bingham & Crockett, 1996).

The timing of teenage sexual initiation varies widely by country and gender. In one recent study, among females, the proportion having first intercourse by age 17 ranged from 72 percent in Mali to 47 percent in the United States, and 45 percent in Tanzania (Singh & others, 2000). The proportion of males who had their first intercourse by age 17 ranged from 76 percent in Jamaica to 64 percent in the United States and 63 percent in Brazil. Not all countries were represented in this study, and it is generally agreed that in some Asian countries, such as China and Japan, first intercourse occurs much later than in the United States.

Sexual activity patterns for 15- to 19-year-olds follow very different patterns for males and females in almost every geographic region of the world (Singh & others, 2000). The vast majority of sexually experienced males in this age group are unmarried, while two-thirds or more of the sexually experienced females at these ages are married in developing countries. However, in the United States and in other developed nations such as the Netherlands, Sweden, and Australia, the overwhelming majority of 15- to 19-year-old females are unmarried.

Adolescent Female and Male Sexual Scripts As adolescents explore their sexual identities, they are guided by sexual scripts. A **sexual script** is a stereotyped pattern of role prescriptions for how individuals should behave sexually. By the time individuals reach adolescence, females and males have been socialized to follow different sexual scripts. Differences in female and male sexual scripting can cause problems and confusions for adolescents as they work out their sexual identities. Female adolescents learn to link sexual intercourse with love (Michael & others, 1994). They often rationalize their sexual behavior by telling themselves that they were swept away by the passion of the moment. A number of studies have found that adolescent females are more likely than their male counterparts to report being in love as the main reason they are sexually active (Hyde & DeLamater, 2003). Other reasons that females give for being sexually active include giving in to male pressure, gambling that sex is a way to get a boyfriend, curiosity, and sexual desire unrelated to loving and caring. Note the different perspectives on love and sex that three adolescent girls present in the video clip "Sex Among Teens at Age 15."

The majority of adolescent sexual experiences involve the male making sexual advances, and it is up to the female to set the limits on the male's sexual overtures (Goodchilds & Zellman, 1984). Adolescent boys experience considerable peer pressure to have sexual intercourse. As one adolescent remarked, "I feel a lot of pressure from my buddies to go for the score." I myself vividly remember the raunchy conversation that filled our basketball locker room when I was in junior high school. By the end of

LifeMAP

sexual script A stereotyped pattern of role prescriptions for how individuals should sexually behave. Females and males have been socialized to follow different sexual scripts.

What is the nature of adolescent sexual scripts?

the ninth grade, I was sure that I was the only virgin left on the 15-member team, but I wasn't about to acknowledge that to my teammates.

In one study, adolescent boys reported they expected sex and put pressure on girls to have sex with them, but said that they do not force girls to have sex (Crump & others, 1996). And in a national survey, 12- to 18-year-olds said the following are "often a reason" teenagers have sex (Kaiser Family Foundation, 1996):

- A boy or girl is pressuring them (61 percent of girls, 23 percent of boys)
- They think they are ready (59 percent of boys, 51 percent of girls)
- They want to be loved (45 percent of girls, 28 percent of boys)
- They don't want people to tease them for being a virgin (43 percent of boys, 38 percent of girls)

Risk Factors and Sexual Problems Most adolescents become sexually active at some point during adolescence, but many adolescents are at risk for sexual problems and other problems when they have sexual intercourse before 16 years of age. Adolescents who have sex before they are 16 years old are often ineffective users of contraceptives, which puts them at risk for adolescent pregnancy and sexually transmitted infections. Early sexual activity is also linked with other at-risk behaviors such as excessive drinking, drug use, delinquency, and school-related problems (Rosenbaum & Kandel, 1990).

In one recent longitudinal study, sexual involvement by girls in early adolescence was linked with lower self-esteem, more depression, more sexual activity, and lower grades in the high school years (Buhrmester, 2001). For boys, early sexual involvement was related to more substance abuse and sexual activity in the high school years.

Through the Eyes of Adolescents

Struggling with a Sexual Decision

Elizabeth is an adolescent girl who is reflecting on her struggle with whether to have sex with a guy she is in love with. She says it is not a question of whether she loves him or not. She does love him, but she still doesn't know if it is right or wrong to have sex with him. He wants her to have sex, but she knows her parents don't. With her friends, some say yes, others say no. So Elizabeth is confused. After a few days of contemplation, in a moment of honesty, she admits that she is not his special love. This finally tilts the answer to not having sex with him. She realizes that if the relationship falls through, she will look back and regret it if she does have sex. In the end, Elizabeth decided not to have sex with him.

Elizabeth's reflections reveal her struggle to understand what is right and what is wrong, whether to have sex or not. In her circumstance, the fact that in a moment of honesty she admitted that she was not his special love made a big difference in her decision.

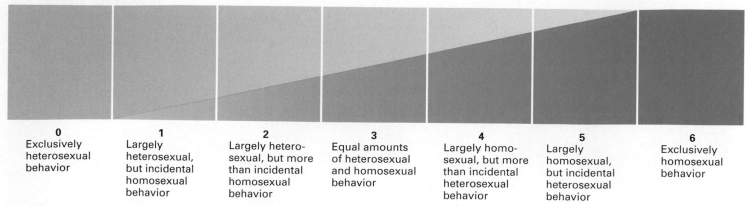

0	1	2	3	4	5	6
Exclusively heterosexual behavior	Largely heterosexual, but incidental homosexual behavior	Largely heterosexual, but more than incidental homosexual behavior	Equal amounts of heterosexual and homosexual behavior	Largely homosexual, but more than incidental heterosexual behavior	Largely homosexual, but incidental heterosexual behavior	Exclusively homosexual behavior

FIGURE 7.4 The Continuum of Sexual Orientation

The continuum ranges from exclusive heterosexuality, which Kinsey and associates (1948) labeled 0, to exclusive homosexuality, 6. People who are about equally attracted to both sexes, 2 to 4, are bisexual.

Risk factors for sexual problems in adolescence include contextual factors such as socioeconomic status (SES) and family/parenting circumstances (Huebner & others, 2003). In one recent review, living in a dangerous and/or a low-income neighborhood were at-risk factors for adolescent pregnancy (Miller, Benson, & Galbraith, 2001). Also in this review, these aspects of parenting were linked with reduced risk of adolescent pregnancy: parent/adolescent closeness or connectedness, parental supervision or regulation of adolescents' activities, and parental values against intercourse or unprotected intercourse in adolescence (Miller, Benson, and Galbraith, 2001). Other researchers have found that an attachment style in which adolescents and parents avoid each other is associated with early sexual activity (Williams & Schmidt, 2003). Further, having older sexually active siblings or pregnant/parenting teenage sisters places adolescents at an elevated risk of adolescent pregnancy (Miller, Benson, & Galbraith, 2001).

Another important factor in sexual risk-taking is *self-regulation*—the ability to regulate one's emotions and behavior. One longitudinal study found that a lower level of self-regulation at 12 to 13 years of age was linked with a higher level of sexual risk-taking four years later (Rafaelli & Crockett, 2003). Other researchers have also found a relation between low self-regulation and high sexual risk-taking (Kahn & others, 2002).

Now that we have considered a number of ideas about heterosexual attitudes and behaviors in adolescence, we turn our attention to homosexual attitudes and behaviors.

Homosexual Attitudes and Behavior   On the surface one might think that heterosexual behavior and homosexual behavior are distinct patterns that can be easily defined. In fact, however, preference for a sexual partner of the same or opposite sex is not always a fixed decision, made once in life and adhered to forever. For example, it is not unusual for an individual, especially a male, to engage in homosexual experimentation in adolescence, but not engage in homosexual behavior as an adult. For others, the opposite progression applies.

A Continuum of Heterosexuality and Homosexuality   Until the middle of the twentieth century, it was generally believed that people were either heterosexual or homosexual. Today, sexual orientation is seen as a continuum from exclusive heterosexuality to exclusive homosexuality. Pioneering this view were Alfred Kinsey and his associates (1948), who represented sexual orientation on a seven-point scale, with 0 signifying exclusive heterosexuality and 6 indicating exclusive homosexuality (see figure 7.4). Some individuals are **bisexual,** being sexually attracted to people of both sexes. In Kinsey's research, the vast majority of individuals were heterosexual. Approximately 1 percent of individuals reported being bisexual (1.2 percent of males

bisexual A person who is attracted to people of both sexes.

and 0.7 percent of females) and between 2 and 5 percent of individuals reported being homosexual (4.7 percent of males and 1.8 percent of females). In more recent national surveys, the percentage of individuals who reported being active homosexuals was even lower (2.3 to 2.7 percent of males and 1.1 to 1.3 percent of females) (Alan Guttmacher Institute, 1995; Michael & others, 1994).

Causes of Homosexuality   Why are some individuals homosexual and others heterosexual? Speculation about this question has been extensive, but no firm answers are available. Homosexual and heterosexual males and females have similar physiological responses during sexual arousal and seem to be aroused by the same types of tactile stimulation. Investigators find no differences between homosexuals and heterosexuals for a wide range of attitudes, behaviors, and adjustments (Bell, Weinberg, & Mammersmith, 1981; Savin-Williams, 1995). In the 1970s, both the American Psychiatric Association and the American Psychological Association recognized that homosexuality is not a form of mental illness and discontinued classification of homosexuality as a disorder.

Recently researchers have explored the possible biological basis of homosexuality (D'Augelli, 2000; Herek, 2000; Quinsey, 2003; Swaab & others, 2003). In this regard, we will evaluate hormone, brain, and twin studies regarding homosexual orientation. The results of hormone studies have been inconsistent. Indeed, if male homosexuals are given male sexual hormones (androgens), their sexual orientation does not change; their sexual desire merely increases. A very early critical period might influence sexual orientation. In the second to fifth months after conception, exposure of the fetus to hormone levels characteristic of females might cause the individual (female or male) to become attracted to males (Ellis & Ames, 1987). If this critical-period hypothesis turns out to be correct, it would explain why clinicians have found that sexual orientation is difficult, if not impossible, to modify (Meyer-Bahlburg & others, 1995).

With regard to anatomical structures, neuroscientist Simon LeVay (1991) found that a tiny area of the hypothalamus that governs sexual behavior is twice as large in heterosexual men as in homosexual men. The area is about the same size in homosexual men as in heterosexual women. Critics of LeVay's work point out that many of the homosexuals in the study had AIDS, which could have altered their brains.

One study investigated homosexual orientation in pairs of twins (Whitman, Diamond, & Martin, 1993). The researchers began with a group of homosexuals, each of whom had a twin sibling, and investigated the sexual orientation of the siblings. Almost two-thirds of the siblings who were an identical twin of a homosexual had a homosexual orientation. Less than one-third of the siblings who were a fraternal twin of a homosexual had a homosexual orientation. The authors interpret their results as supporting a biological interpretation of homosexuality since identical twins are more genetically similar than fraternal twins. However, not all of the identical twins had a homosexual orientation, so clearly environmental factors were involved in at least those cases.

Most experts on homosexuality believe that no one factor alone causes homosexuality and that the relative weight of each factor may vary from one individual to the next. An individual's sexual orientation—heterosexual, homosexual, or bisexual—is most likely determined by a combination of genetic, hormonal, cognitive, and environmental factors (Mustanski, Chivers, & Bailey, 2003; Strickland, 1995). In effect, no one knows exactly what causes an individual to be homosexual. Having investigated and rejected a variety of hypotheses, scientists have a clearer picture of what does *not* cause homosexuality. For example, children raised by gay or lesbian parents or couples are no more likely to be homosexual than are children raised by heterosexual parents (Patterson, 2000, 2002). There also is no evidence to support the once popular theories that male homosexuality is caused by a dominant mother or a weak father, or that female homosexuality is caused by girls' choosing male role models.

Developmental Pathways   It is commonly believed that most gay and lesbian individuals quietly struggle with same-sex attractions in childhood, do not engage in

Through the Eyes of Adolescents

Not Interested in the "Oogling" That My Friends Engaged In

"In middle school I was very involved with the drama club. My singing voice is a cross between Elvis and Roger Rabbit, but I was always on stage in the school musicals. I was an attention 'addict.' . . . I was very charismatic and self-confident until the subject of sex was brought up. I just couldn't participate in the 'oogling' that my friends engaged in. I didn't find Danissa and her chest as inviting as everyone else did. John's conquest of Cindy wasn't the least bit interesting to me, particularly because I didn't have the sex drive to engage in these behaviors myself. When I did develop this drive, I guess in the eighth grade, I found myself equally disinterested in Danissa and her chest. Instead, I found myself very interested in Tony and his sharp features and muscular build."

—*Gay Adolescent Male*

The International Lesbian and Gay Association National Gay and Lesbian Task Force Supporting Gay and Lesbian Rights

LifeMAP

heterosexual dating, and gradually recognize that they are gay or lesbian in mid to late adolescence (Diamond, 2003; Savin-Williams & Diamond, 2004). Many youths do follow this developmental pathway, but others do not. For example, many youths have no recollection of same-sex attractions and experience a more abrupt sense of their same-sex attraction in late adolescence (Savin-Williams, 2001a). Researchers also have found that the majority of adolescents with same-sex attractions also experience some degree of other-sex attractions (Garofalo & others, 1999). And although some adolescents who are attracted to same-sex individuals fall in love with these individuals, others claim that their same-sex attractions are purely physical (Savin-Williams, 2001a).

In sum, sexual minority youth have diverse patterns of initial attraction, often have bisexual attractions, and may have physical or emotional attraction to same-sex individuals but do not always fall in love with them (Diamond, 2003). We will have more to say about romantic development and dating in sexual minority youth in chapter 10, "Peers."

Gay or Lesbian Identity in Adolescence Although the development of gay or lesbian identity has been widely studied in adults, few researchers have investigated the gay or lesbian identity (often referred to as the coming-out process) in adolescents (Flowers & Buston, 2001). In one study of gay male adolescents, coming out was conceptualized in three stages: sensitization; awareness with confusion, denial, guilt, and shame; and acceptance (Newman & Muzzonigro, 1993). The majority of the gay adolescents said they felt different from other boys as children. The average age at having their first crush on another boy was 12.7 years, and the average age at realizing they were gay was 12.5 years. Most of the boys said they felt confused when they first became aware that they were gay. About half of the boys said they initially tried to deny their identity as a gay.

Reactions to homosexual self-recognition range from relief and happiness ("Now I understand and I feel better") to anxiety, depression, and suicidal thoughts ("I can't let anybody know; I've got to kill myself"). Gay adolescents often develop a number of defenses against self-recognition and labeling. The defenses include these (Savin-Williams & Rodriguez, 1993):

"I guess I was drunk."
"It was just a phase I was going through."
"I've heard that all guys do it once."
"I just love her and not all girls."
"I was lonely."
"I was just curious."

Such defenses might be temporary, or they might be lifelong. They might have some positive outcomes (such as redirecting sexual energies into successful academic pursuits) or destructive outcomes (such as marrying a person whom one does not find erotically or emotionally attractive). However, as Dr. Savin-Williams of Cornell University has found, changes in social norms today have allowed many GLBT youth to feel more secure in their sexual identities (learn more about Dr. Savin-Williams' research in the video clip entitled "Sexual Minority Youth").

Disclosure Based on empirical research, these conclusions can be reached about adolescents who disclose their gay or lesbian identity (Savin-Williams, 1998, 2001a):

Why are some individuals homosexual and others heterosexual? How do adolescents disclose their gay, lesbian, or bisexual identity to family members?

- Parents are seldom the first person an adolescent tells about his or her same-sex attractions.
- Mothers are usually told before fathers, possibly because adolescents have more distant relationships with fathers.
- Mothers are more likely than fathers to know about their adolescent's (son's or daughter's) same-sex attractions.
- Approximately 50 to 60 percent of lesbian, gay, and bisexual adolescents have disclosed to at least one sibling, but siblings are still seldom the first person to whom a sexual minority youth discloses.
- The first person to whom adolescents may disclose their homosexual or bisexual identity is likely to be a friend.

Discrimination and Bias   Having irrational negative feelings against homosexuals is called *homophobia*. In its more extreme forms, homophobia can lead individuals to ridicule, physically assault, or even murder people they believe to be homosexual. More typically homophobia is associated with avoidance of homosexuals, faulty beliefs about the homosexual lifestyle (such as believing the falsehood that most child molesters are homosexuals), and subtle or overt discrimination in housing, employment, and other areas of life (Meyer, 2003).

One of the harmful aspects of the stigmatization of homosexuality is the self-devaluation engaged in by gay individuals (Patterson, 2002; Savin-Williams & Diamond, 2004; Savin-Williams & Rodriguez, 1993). One common form of self-devaluation is called *passing*, the process of hiding one's real social identity. Passing strategies include giving out information that hides one's homosexual identity. Passing behaviors include lying to others, saying, "I'm straight and attracted to opposite-sex individuals." Such defenses against self-recognition are heavily entrenched in our society. Without adequate support, and with fear of stigmatization, many gay and lesbian youth retreat to the closet and then emerge at a safer time later, often in college. A special concern is the lack of support gay adolescents receive from parents, teachers, and counselors (Savin-Williams, 2001a).

Last, another concern is a possible link between suicide risk and sexual orientation (Morrison & L'Heureux, 2001; Rose & Rogers, 2000). In one study of 12,000 adolescents, approximately 15 percent of gay and lesbian youth said that they had attempted suicide compared with 7 percent of heterosexual youth (Russell & Joyner, 2001). However, a leading researcher on gay and lesbian adolescents, Richard Savin-Williams (2001b) argues that only slightly more homosexual than heterosexual

In the last decade, an increasing number of youths have disclosed their gay, lesbian, or bisexual attraction to their parents.

—Richard Savin-Williams,
*Contemporary Psychologist,
Cornell University*

adolescents attempt suicide. In his view, many studies likely exaggerate the suicide rates for gay adolescents because they only surveyed the most disturbed youth who were attending support groups or hanging out at shelters for gay youth.

Now that we have explored adolescent heterosexual and homosexual attitudes and behavior, let's examine another dimension of adolescent sexuality: self-stimulation.

Self-Stimulation   Regardless of whether adolescents have a heterosexual or homosexual orientation, they must equally confront increasing feelings of sexual arousal. One way in which many youths who are not dating or who consciously choose not to engage in sexual intercourse or sexual explorations deal with these insistent feelings of sexual arousal is through masturbation or self-stimulation.

As indicated earlier, a heterosexual continuum of kissing, petting, and intercourse or oral sex characterizes many adolescents' sexual experiences. Substantial numbers of adolescents, though, have sexual experience outside of this heterosexual continuum through masturbation or same-sex behavior. Most boys have an ejaculation for the first time at about 12 to 13 years of age. Masturbation, genital contact with a same-sex or other-sex partner, or a wet dream during sleep are common circumstances for ejaculation.

Masturbation is the most frequent sexual outlet for many adolescents (Gates & Sonnenstein, 2000). Adolescents today do not feel as guilty about masturbation as they once did, although they still may feel embarrassed or defensive about it. In past eras, masturbation was denounced as causing everything from warts to insanity. Today, as few as 15 percent of adolescents attach any stigma to masturbation (Hyde & DeLamater, 2003).

In one study, the masturbation practices of female and male college students were studied (Leitenberg, Detzer, & Srebnik, 1993). Almost twice as many males as females said they had masturbated (81 percent versus 45 percent), and the males who masturbated did so three times more frequently during early adolescence and early adulthood than did the females who masturbated during the same age periods. No association was found between the quality of sexual adjustment in adulthood and a history of engaging in masturbation during preadolescence and/or early adolescence.

Contraceptive Use   Sexual activity, while a healthy behavior necessary for procreation, carries with it considerable risks if appropriate safeguards are not taken (Zimmer-Gembeck, Doyle, & Daniels, 2001). Youth encounter two kinds of risks: unintended unwanted pregnancy and sexually transmitted infections. Both of these risks can be reduced significantly if contraception is used. While gay and lesbian youth are spared the risk of pregnancy, like their heterosexual peers, they still face the risk of sexually transmitted infections.

The good news is that adolescents are increasing their use of contraceptives (Child Trends, 2000). Adolescent girls' contraceptive use at first intercourse rose from 48 percent to 65 percent during the 1980s (Forrest & Singh, 1990). By 1995, use at first intercourse reached 78 percent, with two-thirds of that figure involving condom use. A sexually active adolescent who does not use contraception has a 90 percent chance of pregnancy within one year (Alan Guttmacher Institute, 1998). The method adolescent girls use most frequently is the pill (44 percent), followed by the condom (38 percent). About 10 percent rely on an injectable contraceptive, 4 percent on withdrawal, and 3 percent on an implant (Alan Guttmacher Institute, 1998). Approximately one-third of adolescent girls who rely on condoms also take the pill or practice withdrawal.

Although adolescent contraceptive use is increasing, many sexually active adolescents still do not use contraceptives, or they use them inconsistently (Alan Guttmacher Institute, 2003; Ford, Sohn, & Lepkowski, 2001). Sexually active younger adolescents are less likely to take contraceptive precautions than older adolescents. Those who do are more likely to use a condom or withdrawal, whereas older adolescents are more likely to use the pill or a diaphragm. In one study, adolescent females reported changing their behavior in the direction of safer-sex practices more than did adolescent males (Rimberg & Lewis, 1994).

In thinking about contraceptive use in adolescence, it is important to consider the interpersonal context of adolescents' lives (Rimsza, 2003). For example, one reason adolescent girls have sex without condoms is that they don't want to risk losing their partners. In the eyes of the adolescent girl, then, the risk of pregnancy or sexually transmitted infection is not as threatening as the risk of losing a partner.

The issue of contraception is more difficult for adolescents than adults because of differing patterns of sexual activity (Feldman, 1999). Whereas many adults, especially married adults, have sex on a regular and predictable schedule, and typically with one partner (or relatively few partners), adolescents' sexual activity often reflects a pattern of feast or famine, occurring unpredictably and intermittently (Creighton & Miller, 2003). Thus, some forms of contraception that are most effective and widely used by adults (such as the pill and IUD) are not as well suited for adolescents' patterns of sexual activity. Also, married couples often discuss and mutually agree on the form of contraception that they plan to use; such discussions are far less likely to occur among adolescent partners and unmarried young adults. This means that adolescents frequently resort to the use of condoms, which are not completely reliable. The good news, though, is that condoms (unlike the pill or IUD) help protect against sexually transmitted infections.

What factors are related to unsuccessful contraceptive use? Being from a low-SES family is one of the best predictors of adolescents' failure to use contraceptives. Younger adolescents are less likely to use contraceptives than older adolescents (Hofferth, 1990). Not being involved in a steady, committed dating relationship is also associated with a lack of contraceptive use (Chilman, 1979). Condom use is inhibited by concerns about embarrassment and reduced sexual pleasure. In addition, adolescents with poor coping skills, lack of a future orientation, high anxiety, poor social adjustment, and a negative attitude toward contraceptives are not as likely to use them.

Conversely, degree of personal concern about AIDS and the perception that a partner would appreciate condom use are associated with more consistent use of condoms by male adolescents (Pleck, Sonenstein, & Ku, 1991). Educational efforts that include information about AIDS and pregnancy prevention may promote more consistent use of condoms by adolescent males.

Although American adolescents' use of contraceptives has increased in the last two decades, adolescents in Canada, Great Britain, France, Sweden, and the Netherlands are still more likely to use contraceptives than are adolescents in the United States (Child Trends, 2000). U.S. adolescents are especially less likely to use effective contraceptives like the pill than their counterparts in other developed countries.

Researchers have found that interventions which provide training in assertiveness and sexual communication skills help to encourage safer sex (Dittman, 2003). One intervention involves adolescents being shown an interactive video and given three options after each scenario (Downs, 2003) (see figure 7.5). For example, in one scenario, two adolescents are discussing whether to have intercourse and these are the three options: "I want to, but not today," "We can't do this," or "How long will your parents be gone?" When the adolescent selects a low-risk behavior for the girl in the video (refraining from sex or using a condom), the video then shows the boy trying to pressure her while the girl remains assertive about her decision. When a high-risk option is chosen, no reinforcement is provided. All adolescents are eventually directed to a section of the video in which the girl chooses to bring a condom with her and refuses to have sex without it.

Adolescents are increasing their use of contraceptives, although large numbers of sexually active adolescents still do not use contraceptives, especially at first intercourse.

www.mhhe.com/santrocka10

The Alan Guttmacher Institute

FIGURE 7.5 Interactive Video DVD That Provides Training in Assertiveness and Sexual Communication Skills

An adolescent participates in an interactive video session developed by Julie Downs and her colleagues at the Department of Social and Decision Making Sciences at Carnegie Mellon University. The videos help adolescents evaluate their responses and decisions in high-risk sexual contexts.

Review and reflect Learning goal 1

1 **Discuss sexuality as a normal aspect of adolescence and summarize the nature of adolescent sexual attitudes and behavior**

REVIEW

- How is sexuality related to other aspects of adolescent development? What is the sexual culture like that adolescents experience? How do adolescents develop a sexual identity? What caution needs to be exercised about obtaining information about adolescents?
- What are adolescent heterosexual attitudes and behaviors like? How would you characterize adolescent homosexual behavior and attitudes?

REFLECT

- In our discussion of developing a sexual identity, we described these five styles that characterize adolescents: sexually naïve, sexually unassured, sexually competent, sexually adventurous, and sexually driven. Read the descriptions of these styles again. Which style best characterizes your sexual identity as an adolescent? Has your style changed since you were in high school?

2 ADOLESCENT SEXUAL PROBLEMS

Adolescent Pregnancy	Sexually Transmitted Infections	Forcible Sexual Behavior and Sexual Harassment

Sexual problems in adolescence include adolescent pregnancy, sexually transmitted infections, and forcible sexual behavior and sexual harassment. Let's begin by exploring adolescent pregnancy and its prevalence in the United States and around the world.

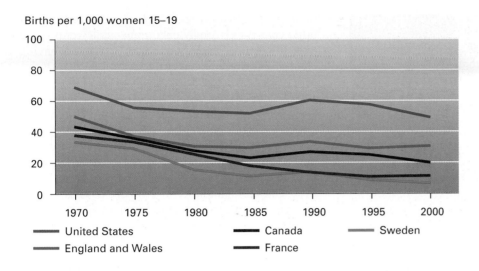

Births per 1,000 women 15–19

FIGURE 7.6 Cross-Cultural Comparisons of Adolescent Pregnancy Rates

— United States   — Canada   — Sweden
— England and Wales   — France

Adolescent Pregnancy

Angela is 15 years old. She reflects, "I'm three months pregnant. This could ruin my whole life. I've made all of these plans for the future, and now they are down the drain. I don't have anybody to talk with about my problem. I can't talk to my parents. There is no way they can understand." Pregnant adolescents were once virtually invisible and unmentionable, shuttled off to homes for unwed mothers where relinquishment of the baby for adoption was their only option, or subjected to unsafe and illegal abortions. But yesterday's secret has become today's dilemma. Our exploration of adolescent pregnancy focuses on its incidence and nature, its consequences, cognitive factors that may be involved, adolescents as parents, and ways in which adolescent pregnancy rates can be reduced.

Incidence of Adolescent Pregnancy in the United States and Other Countries   Adolescent girls who become pregnant are from different ethnic groups and from different places, but their circumstances have the same stressfulness. To many adults, they represent a flaw in America's social fabric. More than 200,000 females in the United States have a child before their eighteenth birthday. Like Angela, far too many become pregnant in their early or middle adolescent years. As one 17-year-old Los Angeles mother of a 1-year-old son said, "We are children having children."

Cross-Cultural Comparisons   In recent cross-cultural comparisons, the United States continued to have one of the highest rates of adolescent pregnancy and childbearing in the developed world, despite a considerable decline in the 1990s (Alan Guttmacher Institute, 2003a; Centers for Disease Control and Prevention, 2001a). U.S. adolescent pregnancy rates are similar to those of Russia and several Eastern European countries, such as Bulgaria; nearly twice those of Canada and Great Britain; and at least four times the rates in France, Sweden, Germany, and Japan (see figure 7.6). While U.S. adolescents are no more sexually active than their counterparts in countries such as France and Sweden, their adolescent pregnancy rate is much higher.

Why are U.S. adolescent pregnancy rates so high? Three reasons based on cross-cultural studies are as follows (Alan Guttmacher Institute, 2002):

Adolescent Pregnancy

- *Childbearing not regarded as adult activity.* European countries, as well as Canada, give a strong consensus that childbearing belongs in adulthood when young people have completed their education, are employed, and are living independently from their parents in stable relationships. In the United States, this belief is not as strong and varies across groups and areas of the country.

Through the Eyes of Adolescents

Kids Having Kids

Here are some comments by adolescents and adults about adolescent pregnancy.

Having children too young is not fair to the child or yourself. Love is not enough. I was 16 and unmarried when I had my first child, I dropped out of school and had the baby in a different state. My mother made arrangements to put the child up for adoption. How I suffered, cried, and worried all alone in a room far from home. I wanted to die, then wanted to live to see the child I was carrying. I saw him briefly after he was born, and then many years later I contacted him. He could not forgive me.

—*Hope, an adult reflecting on her youth*

Create a comfortable atmosphere where teenagers can ask questions. Then more teenagers will want to get condoms and birth control pills.

—*Sarah, 17 years old*

We should be asking "Why are so many parents so negligent?" instead of "Why do so many teens end up pregnant?"

—*Susan, American teenager*

High school programs should show teens what life is like with a baby. Experience, even simulated, is the best method of learning.

—*Russell, who became a father when he was 17 years old*

- *No clear messages about sexual behavior.* Although adults in other countries strongly encourage adolescents to wait until they have established themselves before having children, they are usually more accepting than American adults of adolescents having sex. In France and Sweden, for example, adolescent sexual expression is viewed as normal and positive but there are widespread expectations that the sex will take place within a committed relationship. Indeed, U.S. adolescents tend to have more sporadic and short-lived sexual relationships than their counterparts in European countries. The expectation that adolescents who are having sex will take precautions to protect themselves and their partners from pregnancy and sexually transmitted infections is also stronger in Europe than in the United States. In keeping with this view, schools in Great Britain, France, Sweden, and most of Canada have sex education programs that provide more comprehensive information about prevention than U.S. schools. In addition, these countries use the media more often in government-sponsored campaigns for promoting responsible sexual behavior. The United States is the only country with formal policies directing state and federal funds toward educational programs that have as their sole purpose the promotion of abstinence. More than one-third (35 percent) of all local U.S. school districts that have policies on sex education require that abstinence be taught as the only appropriate option for unmarried individuals, and that contraception either be presented as ineffective in preventing pregnancy or not be covered at all. Among school districts in the South—where birthrates to adolescent mothers are substantially higher than the national average—that figure rises to 55 percent.

- *Less access to family planning services.* In countries with a more accepting attitude toward adolescent sexual relationships, adolescents have easier access not only to information and contraception, but also to reproductive health services. For example, in Canada, France, Great Britain, and Sweden, contraceptive services are integrated into other types of primary health care and are available free or at a low cost for adolescents. Generally, adolescents in these countries know where to obtain such services and are confident that they will receive competent, confidential, nonjudgmental care. In the United States, where attitudes about adolescent sexual relationships are more conflicted, adolescents have a more difficult time obtaining contraceptive services. Many do not have health insurance and cannot get birth control as part of their basic health care.

Decreasing U.S. Adolescent Pregnancy Rates Despite the negative comparisons of the United States with many other developed countries, there are encouraging trends in U.S. adolescent pregnancy rates (Alan Guttmacher Institute, 2003a). In 2000, births to adolescent girls fell to a record low (Centers for Disease Control & Prevention, 2001a). For every 1,000 girls 15 to 19 years of age, there were 49 births—the lowest rate in the six decades this statistic has been kept. The rate of births to adolescent girls has dropped 22 percent since 1991. Reasons for the decline include increased contraceptive use and fear of sexually transmitted infections such as AIDS.

The greatest drop in the U.S. adolescent pregnancy rate in the 1990s was for 15- to 17-year-old African American girls. Fear of sexually transmitted infections, especially AIDS; school/community health classes; and a greater hope for the future are the likely reasons for the decrease in U.S. adolescent pregnancy rates in the 1990s.

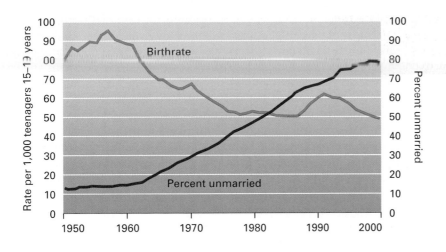

FIGURE 7.7 Births to Married and Unmarried 15- to 19-Year-Old Girls from 1950 through 2000

Latino adolescents are more likely than African American and non-Latino White adolescents to become pregnant (Child Trends, 2001). Latino and African American adolescent girls who have a child are more likely to have a second child than are non-Latino White adolescent girls.

Even though adolescent childbearing overall has declined steeply over the last half century, the proportion of adolescent births that are nonmarital has increased in equally dramatic fashion, from 13 percent in 1950 to 79 percent in 2000 (see figure 7.7). Two factors are responsible for this trend. First, marriage in adolescence has now become quite rare (the average age of first marriage in the United States is now 26 for women and 28 for men). Second, pregnancy is no longer seen as a reason for marriage. In contrast to the days of the "shotgun marriage" (when a male was forced to marry an adolescent girl if he made her pregnant), very few adolescents who become pregnant now marry before their baby is born. To learn more on the theories behind the decline of teen-pregnancy in the U.S., watch the video entitled "Teen Pregnancy Prevention," in which Dr. Jeanne Brooks-Gunn of Columbia University discusses the circumstances of teen pregnancy and the new goals of prevention efforts.

Abortion   Impassioned debate characterizes abortion in the United States today, and this debate is likely to continue in the foreseeable future (Maradiegue, 2003). The experiences of U.S. adolescents who want to have an abortion vary by state and region. In 2003, thirty-two states restricted adolescents' access to abortion. Urban adolescents in New York or California, where parental consent is not required and public and private providers are available, have far greater access to abortion services than their counterparts in North Dakota or Mississippi, which require consent of both parents, or who live in a rural area where there are no providers.

Abortion is easier to obtain in some countries, most notably the Scandinavian countries, than in the United States, where abortion and adolescent sexual activity are more stigmatized. In many developing countries, such as Nigeria, abortion is far more unsafe than in the United States (Murphy, 2003).

In the United States, 19 percent of abortions are performed on 15- to 19-year-old girls while less than 1 percent are carried out with those less than 15 years of age (Alan Guttmacher Institute, 2003b). Adolescent girls are more likely than older women to delay having an abortion until after 15 weeks of pregnancy, when medical risks associated with abortion increase significantly (Alan Guttmacher Institute, 2003b).

Legislation mandating parental consent for an adolescent girl's abortion has been justified by several assumptions, including high risk of harm from abortion, adolescents' inability to make an adequately informed decision, and benefits of parental involvement. Research related to each of these assumptions was the focus of a recent review (Adler, Ozer, & Tschann, 2003).

Researchers have found that legal abortion in the United States itself carries few medical risks if performed in the first trimester of pregnancy, especially compared with the risks of childbearing, for adolescent girls (Centers for Disease Control and Prevention, 1997). In terms of psychological risks, one study evaluated 360 adolescent girls over two years after they had been interviewed when seeking a pregnancy test (Zabin, Hirsch, & Emerson, 1989). Some had a negative test, some were pregnant and carried to term, and some were pregnant and had an abortion. The adolescent girls who had an abortion showed a drop in anxiety and an increase in self-esteem from the beginning of the study to two years later. Further, they appeared to be functioning as well as the girls who had a negative pregnancy test or who had carried until term. They also were more likely than the other two groups to be in school or to have graduated from high school and less likely to have a subsequent pregnancy. Other researchers have found that adolescents are not psychologically harmed by their abortion experience (Pope, Adler, & Tschann, 2001; Quinton, Major, & Richards, 2001).

A second rationale for restrictive abortion laws for adolescents is that they are not capable of making an adequately informed choice. As we saw in chapter 4, some researchers have found that older adolescents are better at decision making than younger adolescents, while other researchers have discovered that adolescents and adults do not differ in their decision-making skills (Quadrel, Fischoff, & Davis, 1993). Several studies revealed that adolescents as young as 13 years of age do not differ from adults in their decision making about having an abortion (Ambuel & Rappaport, 1992; Lewis, 1980). The focus of these studies is on such matters as the general quality of reasoning, awareness of the consequences of the decision, and the types of considerations expressed regarding the decision.

A third rationale for restrictive abortion laws is that parents need to be involved in their daughter's decision making and care. Thus, parental involvement laws seek to promote family communication and functioning. However, little research has been conducted about whether such laws actually do so.

Regardless of research outcomes, pro-life and pro-choice advocates are convinced of the rightness of their positions (Hyde & DeLamater, 2003). Their conflict has a foundation in religious beliefs, political convictions, and certainty about what is morally right and wrong, and this conflict has no easy solutions.

Consequences of Adolescent Pregnancy   The consequences of America's high adolescent pregnancy rate are cause for great concern (Kalil & Kunz, 2000; Lindberg, 2003; McNulty & Burnette, 2004). Adolescent pregnancy creates health risks for both the baby and the mother. Infants born to adolescent mothers are more likely to have low birth weights—a prominent factor in infant mortality—as well as neurological problems and childhood illness (Dryfoos, 1990). Adolescent mothers often drop out of school. Although many adolescent mothers resume their education later in life, they generally do not catch up economically with women who postpone childbearing until their twenties. One longitudinal study found that the children of women had who their first birth during their teens had lower achievement test scores and more behavioral problems than did children whose mothers had their first birth as adults (Hofferth & Reid, 2002).

Though the consequences of America's high adolescent pregnancy rate are cause for great concern, it often is not pregnancy alone that leads to negative consequences for an adolescent mother and her offspring (Brooks-Gunn & Paikoff, 1997; Feldman, 1999; Pittman, 2000). Adolescent mothers are more likely to come from low-SES backgrounds (Fessler, 2003; Hoffman, Foster, & Furstenberg, 1993). Many adolescent mothers also were not good students before they became pregnant. However, not every adolescent female who bears a child lives a life of poverty and low achievement. Thus, although adolescent pregnancy is a high-risk circumstance and adolescents who do not become pregnant generally fare better than those who do, some adolescent mothers do well in school and have positive outcomes (Ahn, 1994; Leadbetter & Way, 2000).

Cognitive Factors in Adolescent Pregnancy   Cognitive changes have intriguing implications for adolescents' sex education (Lipsitz, 1980). With their developing

What are some changes that have taken place in adolescent pregnancy since the 1950s and 1960s?

idealism and ability to think in more abstract and hypothetical ways, young adolescents may become immersed in a mental world far removed from reality. They may see themselves as omnipotent and indestructible and believe that bad things cannot or will not happen to them, characteristics of adolescent egocentrism we discussed in chapter 4. Consider the personal fable aspect of adolescent egocentrism reflected in this 14-year-old's words: "Hey, it won't happen to me."

Informing adolescents about contraceptives is not enough—what seems to predict whether or not they will use contraceptives is their acceptance of themselves and their sexuality. This acceptance requires not only emotional maturity but cognitive maturity.

Most discussions of adolescent pregnancy and its prevention assume that adolescents have the ability to anticipate consequences, to weigh the probable outcome of behavior, and to project into the future what will happen if they engage in certain acts, such as sexual intercourse. That is, prevention is based on the belief that adolescents have the cognitive ability to approach problem solving in a planned, organized, and analytical manner. However, while many adolescents 16 years of age and older have these capacities, it does not mean they use them, especially in emotionally charged situations, such as when they are sexually aroused or are being pressured by a partner.

Indeed, young adolescents (10 to 15 years of age) seem to experience sex in a de-personalized way that is filled with anxiety and denial. This depersonalized orientation toward sex is not likely to lead to preventive behavior. Middle adolescents (15 to 17 years of age) often romanticize sexuality. Late adolescents (18 to 19 years of age) are to some degree realistic and future oriented about sexual experiences, just as they are about careers and marriage. For a personal perspective on this topic, watch the video "Coping as Teen Parents," in which Andrea and Joel describe how they deal with high school, living arrangements, babysitting, and the stigma of having a child as teenagers.

LifeMAP

Adolescents as Parents   Children of adolescent parents face problems even before they are born. Only one of every five pregnant adolescent girls receives any prenatal care at all during the important first three months of pregnancy. Pregnant adolescents are more likely to have anemia and complications related to prematurity than are mothers aged 20 to 24. The problems of adolescent pregnancy double the normal risk of delivering a low birth weight baby (one that weighs under 5.5 pounds), a category that places that infant at risk for physical and mental deficits (Dryfoos, 1990). In some cases, infant problems may be due to poverty rather than the mother's age.

Infants who escape the medical hazards of having an adolescent mother might not escape the psychological and social perils (Brooks-Gunn & Chase-Lansdale, 1995; Luster & others, 1995). Children born to adolescent mothers do not perform as well on intelligence tests and have more behavioral problems than children born to mothers in their twenties (Silver, 1988). Adolescent mothers are less competent at child rearing and have less realistic expectations for their infants' development than do older mothers (Osofsky, 1990). Said one 18-year-old mother, "Not long after he was born, I began to resent him. I wouldn't play with him the first year. He didn't talk until he was two—he would just grunt. I'm sure some of his slow development is my fault. Now I want to make up for it and try to give him extra attention, but he still is behind his age." Other adolescent mothers might get excited about having "this little adorable thing" and anticipate that their world with their child will be marvelous. But as the infant demands more and more of their attention and they have to take care of the infant instead of going out on dates, their positive expectations turn sour.

So far, we have talked exclusively about adolescent mothers. Although some adolescent fathers are involved with their children, the majority are not. In one study, only one-fourth of adolescent mothers with a 3-year-old child said the father had a close relationship with them (Leadbetter, Way, & Raden, 1994). Another study showed that in the last two decades there was a dramatic decline in father involvement with the children of adolescent mothers (Leadbetter, 1994).

Adolescent fathers have lower incomes, less education, and more children than do men who delay having children until their twenties. One reason for these difficulties is that the adolescent father compounds his problem of getting his girlfriend pregnant by dropping out of school (Resnick, Wattenberg, & Brewer, 1992). As soon as he leaves school, the adolescent father moves directly into a low-paying job. Adolescent fathers are saying to themselves, "You need to be a good father. The least you can do is get a job and provide some support," but this short-term view ignores the importance of education as preparation for eventual success in a career.

Many young fathers have little idea of what a father is supposed to do. They may love their baby but not know how to behave. American society has given them few guidelines and few supports. Programs designed to help adolescent fathers are still relatively rare, but they are increasing. Terry, who is now 21, has a 17-month-old child and is himself the child of adolescent parents. After receiving support from the Teenage Pregnancy and Parenting Project in San Francisco, he is now a counselor there. He reports, "My father was a parent when he was an adolescent. So was my grandfather. I know it will stop with my son" (Stengel, 1985).

Reducing Adolescent Pregnancy Serious, extensive efforts are needed to help pregnant adolescents and young mothers enhance their educational and occupational opportunities. Adolescent mothers also need extensive help in obtaining competent child care and in planning for the future (Klaw & Saunders, 1994). John Conger (1988) offered the following four recommendations for reducing the high rate of adolescent pregnancy: (1) sex education and family planning, (2) access to contraceptive methods, (3) the life options approach, and (4) broad community involvement and support, each of which we consider in turn.

Age-appropriate family-life education benefits adolescents (Weyman, 2003). Much more about sex education appears later in this chapter.

In addition to age-appropriate family-life and sex education, sexually active adolescents need access to contraceptive methods (Paukku & others, 2003). These needs often can be handled through adolescent clinics that provide comprehensive, high-quality health services. In the 1980s when teen pregnancy rates were very high, four of the nation's oldest adolescent clinics, in St. Paul, Minnesota, managed to drop the overall annual rate of first-time pregnancies from 80 per 1,000 to 29 per 1,000 (Schorr, 1989). These clinics offer everything from immunizations to sports physicals to treatment for sexually transmitted infections. Significantly, they also advise adolescents on contraception and dispense prescriptions for birth control (provided parents have agreed beforehand to allow their adolescents to visit the clinic). An important aspect of the clinics is the presence of individuals trained to understand the special needs and confusions of the adolescent age group.

Better sex education, family planning, and access to contraceptive methods alone will not remedy the adolescent pregnancy crisis, especially for high-risk adolescents. Adolescents have to become *motivated* to reduce their pregnancy risk. This motivation will come only when adolescents look to the future and see that they have an opportunity to become self-sufficient and successful. Adolescents need opportunities to improve their academic and career-related skills, job opportunities, life-planning consultation, and extensive mental health services.

Finally, for adolescent pregnancy prevention to ultimately succeed, we need broad community involvement and support (Duckett, 1997). This support is a major reason for the success of pregnancy prevention efforts in other developed nations where rates of adolescent pregnancy, abortion, and childbearing are much lower than in America despite similar levels of sexual activity. In the Netherlands, as well as other European countries such as Sweden, sex does not carry the mystery and conflict it does in American society. The Netherlands does not have a mandated sex education program, but adolescents can obtain contraceptive counseling at government-sponsored clinics for a small fee. The Dutch media also have played an important role in educating the public about sex through frequent broadcasts focused on birth control, abortion, and related matters. Perhaps as a result, Dutch adolescents are unlikely to have sex without contraception.

One strategy for reducing adolescent pregnancy, called the Teen Outreach Program (TOP), focuses on engaging adolescents in volunteer community service and stimulates discussions that help adolescents appreciate the lessons they learn through volunteerism. In one study, 695 adolescents in grades 9 to 12 were randomly assigned to either a Teen Outreach group or a control group (Allen & others, 1997). They were assessed at both program entry and at program exit nine months later. The rate of pregnancy was substantially lower for the Teen Outreach adolescents. These adolescents also had a lower rate of school failure and academic suspension.

Girls, Inc., has four programs that are intended to increase adolescent girls' motivation to avoid pregnancy until they are mature enough to make responsible decisions about motherhood (Roth & others, 1998). Growing Together, a series of five 2-hour workshops for mothers and adolescents, and Will Power/Won't Power, a series of six 2-hour sessions that focus on assertiveness training, are for 12- to 14-year-old girls. For older adolescent girls, Taking Care of Business provides nine sessions that emphasize career planning as well as information about sexuality, reproduction, and contraception. Health Bridge coordinates health and education services—girls can participate in this program as one of their club activities. Research on girls' participation in these programs revealed a significant drop in their likelihood of getting pregnant, compared with girls who did not participate (Girls, Inc., 1991).

So far, we have discussed four ways to reduce adolescent pregnancy: sex education and family planning, access to contraceptive methods, life options, and broad community involvement and support. A fifth consideration, which is especially

Careers in Adolescent Development

Lynn Blankenship
Family and Consumer Science Educator

Lynn Blankenship is a family and consumer science educator. She has an undergraduate degree in this area from the University of Arizona. She has taught for more than 20 years, the last 14 at Tucson High Magnet School.

Lynn was awarded the Tucson Federation of Teachers Educator of the Year Award for 1999–2000 and the Arizona Association of Family and Consumer Science Teacher of the Year in 1999.

Lynn especially enjoys teaching life skills to adolescents. One of her favorite activities is having students care for an automated baby that imitates the needs of real babies. Lynn says that this program has a profound impact on students because the baby must be cared for around the clock for the duration of the assignment. Lynn also coordinates real-world work experiences and training for students in several child care facilities in the Tucson area.

Lynn Blankenship with students carrying their automated babies.

These are not adolescent mothers, but rather adolescents who are participating in the Teen Outreach Program (TOP) which engages adolescents in volunteer community service. These adolescent girls are serving as volunteers in a daycare center for crack babies. Researchers have found that such volunteer experiences can reduce the rate of adolescent pregnancy.

important for young adolescents, is abstinence. As we mentioned previously, abstinence is increasingly being included as a theme in sex education classes (Darroch, Landry, & Singh, 2000).

Sexually Transmitted Infections

Tammy, age 15, just finished listening to an expert lecture in her health class. We overhear her talking to one of her girlfriends as she walks down the school corridor: "That was a disgusting lecture. I can't believe all the infections you can get by having sex. I think she was probably trying to scare us. She spent a lot of time talking about AIDS, which I have heard that normal people do not get. Right? I've heard that only homosexuals and drug addicts get AIDS. And I've also heard that gonorrhea and most other sexual infections can be cured, so what is the big deal if you get something like that?" Tammy's view of sexually transmitted infections—that they always happen to someone else, that they can be easily cured without any harm done, that they are too disgusting for a nice young person to hear about, let alone get—is common among adolescents. Tammy's view is wrong. Adolescents who are having sex run the risk of getting sexually transmitted infections.

Sexually transmitted infections (STIs) are infections that are contracted primarily through sexual contact. This contact is not limited to vaginal intercourse but includes oral-genital and anal-genital contact as well. STIs are an increasing health problem. Approximately 25 percent of sexually active adolescents are estimated to become infected with an STI each year (Alan Guttmacher Institute, 1998).

Among the main STIs adolescents can get are three STIs caused by viruses—AIDS (acquired immune deficiency syndrome), genital herpes, and genital warts—and three STIs caused by bacterial infections—gonorrhea, syphilis, and chlamydia.

The Body: An AIDS and HIV Information Resource Center for AIDS Prevention Studies

sexually transmitted infections (STIs)
Diseases that are contracted primarily through sexual contact. This contact is not limited to vaginal intercourse but includes oral-genital contact and anal-genital contact as well.

AIDS Acquired immune deficiency syndrome, a primarily sexually transmitted infection caused by the HIV virus, which destroys the body's immune system.

AIDS No single STI has had a greater impact on sexual behavior, or created more public fear in the last two decades, than AIDS. We explore its nature and incidence, how it is transmitted, stages of the disease, and prevention.

AIDS is a sexually transmitted infection that is caused by a virus, the human immunodeficiency virus (HIV), that destroys the body's immune system. Following exposure to HIV, an individual is vulnerable to germs that a normal immune system could destroy.

Through December 2001, there were 4,428 cases of AIDS in 13- to 19-year-olds in the United States (Centers for Disease Control and Prevention, 2001b). Among those 20 to 24 years of age, more than 28,665 AIDS cases had been reported. The long incubation period between infection with the HIV virus and AIDS diagnosis is an indication that most of the 20- to 24-year-olds were infected during adolescence.

Worldwide, the greatest concern about AIDS is in sub-Saharan Africa, where it has reached epidemic proportions (Pisani, 2000; UNICEF, 2002; World Health Organization, 2000). Adolescent girls in many African countries are especially vulnerable to infection with the HIV virus by adult men. Approximately six times as many adolescent girls as boys have AIDS in these countries. In Kenya, 25 percent of the 15- to 19-year-old girls are HIV positive, compared with only 4 percent of this age group of boys. In Botswana, more than 30 percent of the adolescent girls who are pregnant are infected with the HIV virus.

In the United States, more adolescent boys than adolescent girls are infected with the HIV virus (Centers for Disease Control and Prevention, 2002). The Africa and U.S. gender difference is likely due to the much higher transmission of the HIV virus to adolescent girls by adult men in sub-Saharan Africa and the higher transmission in homosexual males than heterosexual individuals in the United States.

There continues to be great concern about AIDS in many parts of the world, not just sub-Saharan Africa (Carey & Venable, 2003; Ford, Odallo, & Chorlton, 2003; Obregon, 2003). In the United States, prevention is especially targeted at groups that show the highest incidence of AIDS. These include drug users, individuals with other STIs, young homosexual males, individuals living in low-income circumstances, Latinos, and African Americans (Centers for Disease Control and Prevention, 2002). Also, in recent years, there has been increased heterosexual transmission of the HIV virus in the United States.

There are some differences in AIDS cases in U.S. adolescents, compared with AIDS cases in U.S. adults:

- A higher percentage of adolescent AIDS cases are acquired by heterosexual transmission.
- A higher percentage of adolescents are asymptomatic individuals (but will become symptomatic in adulthood).
- A higher percentage of African American and Latino cases occur in adolescence.
- A special set of ethical and legal issues are involved in testing and informing partners and parents of adolescents.
- Adolescents have less access to contraceptives and are less likely to use them than are adults.

In one study, condom use among U.S. adolescents who are at the greatest risk of contracting AIDS—for example, intravenous drug users—was significantly below average (Sonenstein, Pleck, & Ku, 1989). Only 21 percent of the adolescents who had used intravenous drugs or whose partners had used intravenous drugs used condoms. Among adolescents who reported having sex with prostitutes, only 17 percent said they used condoms. And among adolescents who reported having sex with five or more partners in the last year, only 37 percent reported using condoms. Adolescents who reported homosexual intercourse reported the highest condom use—66 percent.

Experts say that AIDS can be transmitted only by sexual contact, the sharing of needles, or blood transfusion (which in recent years has been tightly monitored) (Kelly, 2000). Although 90 percent of AIDS cases in the United States continue to occur among homosexual males and intravenous drug users, a disproportionate increase among females who are heterosexual partners of bisexual males or of intravenous drug users has been recently noted. This increase suggests that the risk of AIDS may be increasing among heterosexual individuals who have multiple sex partners. Figure 7.8 describes what's risky and what's not, regarding AIDS.

Merely asking a date about his or her sexual behavior, of course, does not guarantee protection from AIDS or other STIs. For example, in one investigation, 655 college students were asked to answer questions about lying and sexual behavior (Cochran & Mays, 1990). Of the 422 respondents who said they were sexually active,

The AIDS virus is not transmitted like colds or the flu, but by an exchange of infected blood, semen, or vaginal fluids. This usually occurs during sexual intercourse, in sharing drug needles, or to babies infected before or during birth.

You Won't Get AIDS From:

Everyday contact with individuals around you in school or the workplace, at parties, child-care centers, or stores

Swimming in a pool, even if someone in the pool has the AIDS virus

A mosquito bite, or from bedbugs, lice, flies, or other insects

Saliva, sweat, tears, urine, or feces

A kiss

Clothes, telephones, or toilet seats

Using a glass or eating utensils that someone else has used

Being on a bus, train, or crowded elevator with an individual who is infected with the virus or who has AIDS

Blood Donations and Transfusions:

You will not come into contact with the AIDS virus by donating blood at a blood bank.

The risk of getting AIDS from a blood transfusion has been greatly reduced. Donors are screened for risk factors, and donated blood is tested for HIV antibodies.

Risky Behavior:

Your chances of coming into contact with the virus increase if you:

Have more than one sex partner

Share drug needles and syringes

Engage in anal, vaginal, or oral sex without a condom

Perform vaginal or oral sex with someone who shoots drugs

Engage in sex with someone you don't know well or with someone who has several sex partners

Engage in unprotected sex (without a condom) with an infected individual

Safe Behavior:

Not having sex

Having sex that does not involve fluid exchange (rubbing, holding, massage)

Sex with one mutually faithful, uninfected partner

Sex with proper protection

Not shooting drugs

Source: *America Responds to AIDS*. U.S. Government educational pamphlet, 1988.

FIGURE 7.8 Understanding AIDS: What's Risky, What's Not

34 percent of the men and 10 percent of the women said they had lied so their partner would have sex with them. Much higher percentages—47 percent of the men and 60 percent of the women—said they had been lied to by a potential sexual partner. When asked what aspects of their past they would be most likely to lie about, more than 40 percent of the men and women said they would understate the number of their sexual partners. Twenty percent of the men, but only 4 percent of the women, said they would lie about their results from an AIDS blood test.

Because it is possible, and even probable among high-risk groups, to have more than one STI at a time, efforts to prevent one infection help reduce the prevalence of other infections. Efforts to prevent AIDS can also help prevent adolescent pregnancy and other sexually related problems. Because of the high rate of sexually transmitted infections, it is crucial that both adolescents and adults understand these diseases (Johnston & others, 2003).

One study evaluated 37 AIDS prevention projects with children and adolescents (Janz & others, 1996). Small-group discussions, outreach to populations engaged in high-risk behaviors, and training of peers and volunteers were the activities rated the most effective. Small-group discussions, with an emphasis on open communication and repetition of messages, are excellent opportunities for adolescents to learn and share information about AIDS. The best outreach programs are culturally tailored and include incentives to participate. Outreach workers who are familiar and respected might be able to break through the barriers of fear and mistrust to ensure that appropriate messages are heard and heeded. For incentives to work, they also must be tailored for specific populations. School-age children might be attracted by academic credit or a stipend. For injection drug users, food, shelter, and a safe place to congregate might attract participants. For working women, child care and an opportunity to spend time with other adults might draw participants. The use of peer educators is often an effective strategy. As role models, peers can mirror healthy lifestyles for the target population as well as provide reinforcement and shape group norms in support of behavioral change. Peer educators often are effective at getting adolescents involved in AIDS prevention projects.

Genital Herpes Genital herpes is a sexually transmitted infection caused by a large family of viruses with many different strains, some of which produce other, non–sexually transmitted diseases such as cold sores, chicken pox, and mononucleosis. Three to five days after contact, itching and tingling can occur, followed by an eruption of painful sores and blisters. The attacks can last up to three weeks and can recur as frequently as every few weeks or as infrequently as every few years. It is direct contact with the sores that transmits the virus to a partner; the virus can also pass through nonlatex condoms as well as contraceptive foams and creams.

Although drugs such as acyclovir can alleviate symptoms, there is no known cure for herpes. Therefore, people infected with herpes often experience severe emotional distress in addition to the considerable physical discomfort. They may feel conflicted or reluctant about sex, angry about the unpredictability of the infection, and fearful that they won't be able to cope with the pain of the next attack. For these reasons, many communities have established support groups for victims of herpes.

Genital Warts Genital warts are caused by the human papillomavirus (HPV), which is difficult to test for and does not always produce symptoms but is very contagious nonetheless. Genital warts usually appear as small, hard, painless bumps on the penis, in the vaginal area, or around the anus. There are about 5.5 million new cases of genital warts each year in the United States, making this the most common STI in the United States. Treatment involves the use of a topical drug, freezing, or surgery. Unfortunately genital warts may return despite treatment, and in some cases they are linked to cervical cancer and other genital cancers. Condoms afford some protection against HPV infection.

We now turn to three STIs—gonorrhea, syphilis, and chlamydia—caused by bacteria.

Gonorrhea Gonorrhea is a sexually transmitted infection that is commonly called the "drip" or the "clap." It is caused by a bacterium called *Neisseria gonorrhoeae*, which thrives in the moist mucous membranes lining the mouth, throat, vagina, cervix, urethra, and anal tract. The bacterium is spread by contact between the infected moist membranes of one individual and the membranes of another.

Early symptoms of gonorrhea are more likely to appear in males, who are likely to have a discharge from the penis and burning during urination. The early sign of gonorrhea in females, often undetectable, is a mild, sometimes irritating vaginal discharge. Complications of gonorrhea in males include prostate, bladder, and kidney problems, as well as sterility. In females, gonorrhea may lead to infertility due to the abdominal adhesions or pelvic inflammatory disease (PID) that it can cause (Crooks & Bauer, 2002).

Gonorrhea can be successfully treated in its early stages with penicillin or other antibiotics. Although the incidence of gonorrhea has declined, more than 500,000 cases are still reported annually, and the highest rates among women and second highest among men are in adolescence (Centers for Disease Control, 2000).

Syphilis Syphilis is a STI caused by the bacterium *Treponema pallidum*, a member of the spirochete family. The spirochete needs a warm, moist environment to survive, and it is transmitted by penile-vaginal, oral-genital, or anal contact. It can also be transmitted from a pregnant woman to her fetus after the fourth month of pregnancy;

**CDC National Prevention Network
American Social Health Association
Adolescents' STD Knowledge
Preventing STDs in Adolescents
Syphilis
Chlamydia
Genital Herpes**

genital herpes A sexually transmitted infection caused by a large family of viruses of different strains. These strains produce other, non–sexually transmitted diseases such as chicken pox and mononucleosis.

genital warts Caused by the human papillomavirus, and the most common STI in the United States, genital warts are very contagious.

gonorrhea Reported to be one of the most common STIs in the United States, this sexually transmitted infection is caused by a bacterium called *Neisseria gonorrhoeae*, which thrives in the moist mucous membranes lining the mouth, throat, vagina, cervix, urethra, and anal tract. This disease is commonly called the "drip" or the "clap."

syphilis A sexually transmitted infection caused by the bacterium *Treponema pallidum*, a spirochete.

if she is treated before this time with penicillin, the syphilis will not be transmitted to the fetus.

If untreated, syphilis may progress through four phases: primary (chancre sores appear), secondary (general skin rash occurs), latent (can last for several years in which no overt symptoms are present), and tertiary (cardiovascular disease, blindness, paralysis, skin ulcers, liver damage, and mental problems may occur) (Crooks & Bauer, 2002). In its early phases, syphilis can be effectively treated with penicillin. Approximately 100,000 cases of syphilis are reported in the United States each year.

Chlamydia Chlamydia, one of most common of all STIs, is named for *Chlamydia trachomatis,* an organism that spreads by sexual contact and infects the genital organs of both sexes. Although fewer individuals have heard of chlamydia than have heard of gonorrhea and syphilis, its incidence is much higher. About 4 million Americans are infected with chlamydia each year. About 10 percent of all college students have chlamydia. This STI is highly infectious; women run a 70 percent risk of contracting it in a single sexual encounter with an infected partner. The male risk is estimated at between 25 and 50 percent.

Many females with chlamydia have few or no symptoms. When symptoms do appear, they include disrupted menstrual periods, pelvic pain, elevated temperature, nausea, vomiting, and headache. Possible symptoms of chlamydia in males are a discharge from the penis and burning during urination.

Because many females with chlamydia are asymptomatic, the infection often goes untreated and the chlamydia spreads to the upper reproductive tract where it can cause pelvic inflammatory disease (PID). The resultant scarring of tissue in the fallopian tubes can result in infertility or in ectopic pregnancies (tubal pregnancies), or a pregnancy in which the fertilized egg is implanted outside the uterus. One-quarter of females who have PID become infertile; multiple cases of PID increase the rate of infertility to half. Some researchers suggest that chlamydia is the number one preventable cause of female infertility.

Although they can occur without sexual contact and are therefore not classified as STIs, urinary tract or bladder infections and vaginal yeast infections (also called *thrush*) are common in sexually active females, especially those who have an intense "honeymoon" lovemaking experience. Both of these infections clear up quickly with medication, but their symptoms (urinary urgency and burning in urinary tract infections; itching, irritation, and whitish vaginal discharge in yeast infections) may be frightening, especially to adolescents who may already have considerable anxiety about sex. We mention them because one of the non-STIs may be what brings an adolescent girl to a doctor, nurse practitioner, or family planning clinic, providing an opportunity for her to receive sex education and contraception.

So far we have discussed these problems that involve adolescent sexuality: adolescent pregnancy and sexually transmitted infections. Next, we explore these adolescent sexuality problems: forcible sexual behavior and sexual harassment.

Forcible Sexual Behavior and Sexual Harassment

Most people choose to engage in sexual intercourse or other sexual activities, but, unfortunately, some people force others to engage in sex. Too many adolescent girls and young women report that they believe they don't have adequate sexual rights (East & Adams, 2002). These include the right to not have sexual intercourse when they don't wish to, the right to tell a partner that he is being too rough, or the right to use any form of birth control during intercourse. One recent study found that almost 20 percent of 904 sexually active 14- to 26-year-old females believed that they never have the right to make decisions about contraception, to tell their partner that they don't want to have intercourse without birth control, that they want to make love differently or that their partner is being too rough, and to stop foreplay at any time, including at the point of intercourse (Rickert, Sanghvi, & Wiemann, 2002). In this study,

chlamydia One of most common sexually transmitted infections, named for *Chlamydia trachomatis,* an organism that spreads by sexual contact and infects the genital organs of both sexes.

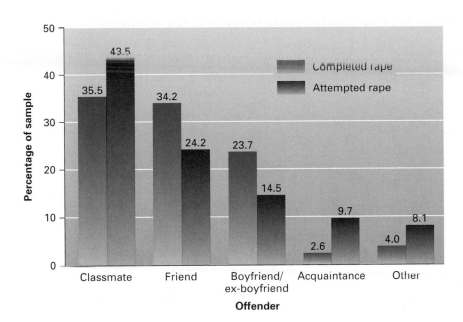

FIGURE 7.9 Completed Rape and Attempted Rape of College Women According to Victim-Offender Relationship

poor grades in school and sexual inexperience were linked to a lack of sexual assertiveness in females.

Forcible Sexual Behavior   **Rape** is forcible sexual intercourse with a person who does not give consent. Legal definitions of rape vary from state to state. In some states, for example, the law allows husbands to force their wives to have sex. Because of the difficulties involved in reporting rape, the actual incidence is not easily determined (Erlick Robinson, 2003; Watts & Zimmerman, 2002). It appears that rape occurs most often in large cities, where it has been reported that 8 of every 10,000 women 12 years old and older are raped each year. Nearly 200,000 rapes are reported each year in the United States. Although we tend to assume that all rapists are men, in fact, only 95 percent of rapes are committed by men.

Why is rape so pervasive in the American culture? Feminist writers assert that males are socialized to be sexually aggressive, to regard females as inferior beings, and to view their own pleasure as the most important objective. Researchers have found the following characteristics common among rapists: Aggression enhances their sense of power or masculinity; they are angry at females generally; and they want to hurt their victims.

A form of rape that went unacknowledged until recent decades is **date, or acquaintance, rape,** which is coercive sexual activity directed at someone whom the perpetrator knows. Acquaintance rape is an increasing problem in high schools and on college campuses (Christopher & Kisler, 2004).

A major study that focused on campus sexual assault involved a phone survey of 4,446 women attending two- or four-year colleges (Fisher, Cullen, & Turner, 2000). In this study, slightly less than 3 percent said that they either had experienced a rape or an attempted rape during the academic year. About 1 of 10 college women said that they had experienced rape in their lifetime. Unwanted or uninvited sexual contacts were widespread with more than one-third of the college women reporting such incidents. As shown in figure 7.9, in this study, most women (about 9 of 10) knew the person who sexually victimized them. Most of the women attempted to take protective actions against their assailants but were then reluctant to report the victimization to the police. Several factors were associated with sexual victimization: living on campus, being unmarried, getting drunk frequently, and having been sexually victimized on a prior occasion.

rape Forcible sexual intercourse with a person who does not give consent.

date, or acquaintance, rape Coercive sexual activity directed at someone whom the perpetrator knows.

In another study, about two-thirds of the sexual victimization incidents were perpetrated by a romantic acquaintance (Flanagan, 1996). In yet another study, approximately 2,000 ninth- through twelfth-grade females were asked about the extent to which they had experienced physical and sexual violence (Silverman & others, 2001). About 20 percent of the females said they had been physically or sexually abused by a dating partner. Further, the physical and sexual abuse was linked with substance use.

Rape is a traumatic experience for the victim and those close to her or him (Frazier, 2003; Thompson & others, 2003). The rape victim initially feels shock and numbness and often is acutely disorganized. Some women show their distress through words and tears, others show more internalized suffering. As victims strive to get their lives back to normal, they might experience depression, fear, and anxiety for months or years. Sexual dysfunctions, such as reduced sexual desire and the inability to reach orgasm, occur in 50 percent of rape victims. Many rape victims make lifestyle changes, moving to a new apartment or refusing to go out at night. About one-fifth of rape victims have made a suicide attempt—a rate eight times higher than that of women who have not been raped.

A female's recovery depends on both her coping abilities and psychological adjustment prior to the assault (Mein & others, 2003). Social support from parents, partner, and others close to her are also important factors in recovery, as is the availability of professional counseling, sometimes obtained through a rape crisis center (Koss, 1993). Many rape victims become empowered by reporting their rape to the police and assisting in the prosecution of the rapist if caught. However, women who take a legal approach are especially encouraged to use supportive counselors to aid them throughout the legal ordeal. Each female must be allowed to make her own, individual decision about whether to report the rape or not.

Although most victims of rape are female, rape of men does occur. Men in prisons are especially vulnerable to rape, usually by heterosexuals who are using homosexual rape to establish their domination and power within the prison (Robertson, 2003). Though it might seem impossible for a man to be raped by a woman, a man's erection is not completely under his voluntary control, and some cases of male rape by women have been reported (Sarrel & Masters, 1982).

Sexual Harassment Females encounter sexual harassment in many different forms—ranging from sexist remarks and covert physical contact (patting, brushing against bodies) to blatant propositions and sexual assaults (Fitzgerald, 2000; Kern & Alessi, 2003; Paludi, 2002). Literally millions of females experience such sexual harassment each year in educational and work settings. In one study, 85 percent of eighth- to eleventh-grade girls reported that they were often sexually harassed (American Association of University Women, 1993). A surprisingly large percentage (75 percent) of boys also said they often were sexually harassed. Sexual comments, jokes, gestures, and looks were the most common forms of harassment. Students also reported other objectionable behavior, ranging from being the subject of sexual rumors to being forced to do something sexual.

The Office for Civil Rights in the U.S. Department of Education published a 40-page policy guide on sexual harassment. In this guide, a distinction is made between quid pro quo and hostile environment sexual harassment (Chmieleski, 1997):

- **Quid pro quo sexual harassment** occurs when a school employee threatens to base an educational decision (such as a grade) on a student's submission to unwelcome sexual conduct. For example, a teacher gives a student an A for allowing the teacher's sexual advances, or the teacher gives the student an F for resisting the teacher's approaches.
- **Hostile environment sexual harassment** occurs when students are subjected to unwelcome sexual conduct that is so severe, persistent, or pervasive that it limits the students' ability to benefit from their education. Such a hostile environment is usually created by a series of incidents, such as repeated sexual overtures.

Sexual Assault
Sexual Harassment

quid pro quo sexual harassment Sexual harassment in which a school employee threatens to base an educational decision (such as a grade) on a student's submission to unwelcome conduct.

hostile environment sexual harassment Sexual harassment in which students are subjected to unwelcome sexual conduct that is so severe, persistent, or pervasive that it limits the students' ability to benefit from their education.

Quid pro quo and hostile environment sexual harassment are illegal in the workplace as well as in educational settings, but potential victims are often not given access to a clear reporting and investigation mechanism where they can make a complaint.

Sexual harassment is a form of power and dominance of one person over another, which can result in harmful consequences for the victim. Sexual harassment can be especially damaging when the perpetrators are teachers, employers, and other adults who have considerable power and authority over students (Lee & others, 1995). As a society, we need to be less tolerant of sexual harassment (Bonner, Peretz, & Ehrenfeld, 2003; Firpo-Triplett, 1997; Shrier, 2003).

Review and reflect Learning goal 2

2   Describe the main sexual problems that can emerge in adolescence

REVIEW

- How would you characterize adolescent pregnancy?
- What are the main sexually transmitted infections in adolescence?
- What is the nature of forcible sexual behavior and sexual harassment in adolescence?

REFLECT

- Caroline contracted genital herpes from her boyfriend whom she had been dating for the past three years. After breaking off the relationship and spending some time on her own, she began dating Charles. Should Caroline tell Charles about her sexually transmitted infection? If so, how and when?

3 SEXUAL LITERACY AND SEX EDUCATION

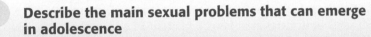

| Sexual Literacy | Sources of Sex Information | Sex Education in Schools |

Given the high rate of STIs, a special concern is the knowledge that both adolescents and adults have about these infections and about other aspects of sexuality. How sexually literate are Americans? What are adolescents' sources of sex education? What is the role of schools in sex education?

Sexual Literacy

According to June Reinisch (1990), director of the Kinsey Institute for Sex, Gender, and Reproduction, U.S. citizens know more about how their automobiles function than about how their bodies function sexually. American adolescents and adults are not sheltered from sexual messages; indeed, Reinisch says, adolescents too often are inundated with sexual messages, but not sexual facts. Sexual information is abundant, but much of it is misinformation. In some cases, even sex education teachers display sexual ignorance. One high school sex education teacher referred to erogenous zones as "erroneous zones," causing students to wonder if their sexually sensitive zones were in error!

Most adolescents do not know at what stage of the menstrual cycle females are most likely to get pregnant (Loewen & Leigh, 1986; Zelnick & Kantner, 1977). In one study, 12 percent of more than 8,000 students thought that birth control pills provide some protection against AIDS, and 23 percent believed they could tell by just looking at a potential sexual partner whether he or she was infected with HIV (Hechinger,

1992). In a national survey of more than 1,500 adolescents 12 to 18 years old, the respondents said that they have enough information to understand pregnancy but not enough about how to obtain and use birth control (Kaiser Family Foundation, 1996).

Sources of Sex Information

One 14-year-old was asked where he learned about sex. He responded, "In the streets." Asked if this was the only place, he said, "Well, I learned some more from *Playboy* and the other sex magazines." What about school, he was asked. He responded, "No, they talk about hygiene, but not much that could help you out." When asked about his parents' contributions, he replied, "They haven't told me one thing."

Parents are an important missing ingredient in the fight against adolescent pregnancy and STIs (Brock & Jennings, 1993; Jaccard, Dodge, & Dittus, 2002; Kirby & Miller, 2002). Surveys indicate that about 17 percent of adolescents' sex education comes from mothers and only about 2 percent from fathers (Thornburg, 1981). A large majority of adolescents say that they cannot talk freely with their parents about sexual matters, but those who can talk with their parents openly and freely about sex are less likely to be sexually active. Contraceptive use by female adolescents also increases when adolescents report that they can communicate about sex with their parents (Fisher, 1987).

Adolescents are far more likely to have conversations about sex with their mothers than with their fathers (Kirkman, Rosenthal, & Feldman, 2002). This is true of both female and male adolescents, although female adolescents report having more frequent conversations about sex with their mothers than their male counterparts do (Feldman & Rosenthal, 1999, 2002; Lefkowitz & others, 1999). In one study that involved videotaped conversations about sexual matters between mothers and adolescents, adolescent girls were more responsive and enthusiastic than adolescent boys were (Lefkowitz & others, 1999).

In a survey of all 1,152 students at a midwestern high school, students were asked where they learned about various aspects of sex (Thornburg, 1981). As in other investigations, the most common source of sex information was peers, followed by literature, mothers, schools, and experience. Though adults usually think of schools as a main source of sex education, only 15 percent of the adolescents' information about sex came from school instruction. In one study, college students said that they got more sex education from reading than from any other source (Andre, Frevert, & Schuchmann, 1989).

Sex Education in Schools

One survey found that 93 percent of Americans support the teaching of sex education in high schools and 84 percent support its teaching in middle/junior high schools (SIECUS, 1999). The dramatic increase in HIV/AIDS and other STIs is the main reason that Americans have increasingly supported sex education in schools in recent years. This survey also found that more than 8 of 10 Americans think that adolescents should be given information to protect themselves from unwanted pregnancies and STIs, as well as about abstinence. And more than 8 of 10 Americans rejected the idea that providing such sex education encourages sexual activity.

The nature of sex education in schools is changing. In one study, trends in sex education in American public schools from 1988 through 1999 were examined (Darroch, Landy, & Singh, 2000). Among the results of the survey:

• Some topics—how HIV is transmitted, STIs, abstinence, how to resist peer pressure to have intercourse, and the correct way to use a condom—were taught in earlier grades in 1999 than in 1988.
• In 1999, 23 percent of secondary school sex education teachers taught abstinence as the only way of preventing pregnancy and STIs, compared with only

The AIDS epidemic has led to an increased awareness of the importance of sex education in adolescence.

2 percent in 1988. Teachers surveyed in 1999 also were more likely than those in 1988 to cite abstinence as the most important message they wished to convey (41 percent versus 25 percent).

- Steep declines occurred between 1988 and 1999 in the percentage of teachers who supported teaching about birth control, abortion, and sexual orientation.

In sum, sex education in U.S. schools today is increasingly focused on abstinence and is less likely to present students with comprehensive teaching that includes information about birth control, abortion, and sexual orientation (Alan Guttmacher Institute, 2003).

In another study, 1,789 fifth- and sixth-grade U.S. teachers were asked about the nature of their sex education instruction in 1999 (Landry, Singh, & Darroch, 2000). The results included:

- Seventy-two percent said that sex education is taught in their schools at either the fifth grade, sixth grade, or both.
- More than 75 percent of teachers who include sex education in their instruction cover these topics: puberty, HIV and AIDS transmission, alcohol and drug use, and how to stick to a decision. However, many fifth- and sixth-grade teachers do not teach sex education at all. It was estimated that overall these topics are taught in about half of fifth- and sixth-grade classrooms.
- More than half of the teachers include the topic of abstinence in the sex education instruction.

Sex education programs in schools might not by themselves prevent adolescent pregnancy and STIs. Researchers have found that sex education classes do improve adolescents' knowledge about human sexuality but do not always change their sexual behavior. When sex education programs are combined with contraceptive availability, the pregnancy rates of adolescents are more likely to drop (Wallis, 1985). This has led to the development of *school-linked* rather than school-based approaches to sex education and pregnancy prevention (Kirby & others, 1993). In one program pioneered by some Baltimore public schools in cooperation with Johns Hopkins University, family-planning clinics are located adjacent to the schools (Zabin, 1986). The clinics send a nurse and social worker into the schools, where they make formal presentations about the services available from the clinics and about sexuality. They also are available to the students several hours each day for counseling. The same health personnel also conduct after-school sessions at the clinics. These sessions involve further counseling, films, and family-planning information. The results have been very positive. Students who participated in the programs delayed their first intercourse longer than did students in a control group. After 28 months, the pregnancy rate had declined by 30 percent in the program schools, while it rose 60 percent in the control-group schools. This program demonstrates that a key dimension of pregnancy prevention is the link between information and support services (Kenney, 1987).

However, some critics charge that school-linked health clinics promote premarital sex and encourage abortion for pregnant adolescents. These critics believe that more effort should be devoted to promoting adolescents' abstention from sex. Supporters of the school-linked clinics argue that sexual activity in adolescence has become a normative behavior and, therefore, interventions should focus on teaching responsible sexual behavior and providing access to contraception (Dryfoos, 1995). In one recent study, the effects of a schoolwide program called "Safer Choices," which discussed pregnancy prevention and condom use, was effective in increasing condom use and in decreasing the number of sex partners (Basen-Enquist & others, 2001). And in another recent study, students in high schools where condoms were available were more likely to receive condom use instruction and less likely to report lifetime or recent sexual intercourse than their counterparts in schools where condoms were not available (Blake & others, 2003). Sexually active adolescents in schools where condoms were available were twice as likely to use condoms, but less likely to use other contraceptive methods, in their most recent sexual encounter. In most cases, the condoms were available from the school nurse or from other school personnel, such as a gym teacher.

SIECUS
Does Sex Education Work?

In the United States, the media entice adolescents with stories of romantic love and portrayals of sex. Parents encourage boy-girl contact but are often reluctant to discuss sex openly; are unwilling to make contraceptives, including condoms, available to adolescents; and fail to offer alternatives other than abstinence (Crockett, Raffaelli, & Moilanen, 2003).

U.S. sex education typically has focused on the hazards of sex and the need to protect adolescent females from male predators (Fine, 1988). The contrast between the United States and other Western nations is remarkable. For example, the Swedish State Commission on Sex Education recommends that students gain knowledge to help them to experience sexual life as a source of happiness and fellowship with others. Swedish adolescents are sexually active at an earlier age than are American adolescents, and they are exposed to even more explicit sex on television. However, the Swedish National Board of Education has developed a curriculum to give every child, beginning at age 7, a thorough grounding in reproductive biology and, by the age of 10 or 12, information about various forms of contraception. Teachers handle the subject of sex whenever it becomes relevant, regardless of the subject they are teaching. The idea is to de-dramatize and demystify sex so that familiarity will make students less vulnerable to unwanted pregnancy and STIs. Despite a relatively early onset of sexual activity, the adolescent pregnancy rate in Sweden is one of the lowest in the world.

Sex is more demystified and less dramatized in Sweden than in the United States. Adolescent pregnancy rates are much lower in Sweden than in the United States.

Review and reflect Learning goal 3

3 **Characterize the sexual literacy of adolescents and sex education**

REVIEW

- How sexually literate are U.S. adolescents?
- What are adolescents' sources of sexual information?
- How would you describe sex education in schools?

REFLECT

- Think about how you learned the "facts of life." Did most of your information come from well-informed sources? Were you able to talk freely and openly with your parents about what to expect sexually? Did you acquire some false beliefs through trial-and-error efforts? As you grew older, did you discover that some of what you thought you knew about sex was inaccurate? Think also about the sex education you received in school. How adequate was it? What do you wish the schools you attended would have done differently in regard to sex education?

4 SEXUAL WELL-BEING, SOCIAL POLICY, AND ADOLESCENTS

Sexual Well-Being and Developmental Transitions

Social Policy and Adolescent Sexuality

Earlier in the chapter, we discussed some of the things that can go wrong in adolescent sexuality, such as unintended pregnancy, sexually transmitted infections, forcible sexual behavior, and sexual harassment. It is important to remember that in general sexual interest and activity are a normal—not an abnormal—aspect of adolescent development. However, as we mentioned earlier in the chapter, American society dispenses mixed messages. We expect children to be asexual but normal adults to be sexually responsive (in the context of marriage). Yet we provide no clear agreements about how this transition from the asexual child to the sexual adult should take place. This is one of life's most important transitions, and it deserves more attention. Let's now explore some links between developmental transitions in adolescence and sexual well-being.

Sexual Well-Being and Developmental Transitions

All societies have mechanisms for regulating adolescent sexuality, and some are more successful than others (Brooks-Gunn & Paikoff, 1997). Variations in parental control, peer group influence, societal norms, and neighborhood settings occur within and across societies. Historical changes also affect how much a culture's subgroups adhere to societal norms. In traditional societies, adolescents often marry soon after they reach sexual maturity (Paige & Paige, 1985). But in more industrialized societies, which require more formal educational skills, first marriages are delayed until early adulthood. The trends of an earlier occurrence of puberty and a later age of marriage have increased the time period between onset of reproductive maturity and marriage. In 1890, the interval was just over 7 years; today it is about 12 years—an interminable wait for an adolescent or emerging adult experiencing sexual arousal.

No matter how much some adults might like to ignore the fact, sex has great meaning in adolescents' lives. Adolescents form their sexual identity, engage in sexual exploration (whether kissing, intercourse, or just dreaming about sex), and negotiate autonomy and intimacy in sexual contexts.

Over the past 30 to 40 years dramatic changes have taken place in our society in adolescents' entry into sexuality, marriage, and parenting. Changes in links between sexual activity and marriage began to erode with increased options for contraception, changes in society's norms, and opening up of economic opportunities for women.

—JEANNE BROOKS-GUNN, *Contemporary Psychologist, Columbia University*

Adolescents should be encouraged to do community service in child care centers. This can help them to see firsthand what is required to raise children.

An important social policy agenda is to educate adolescents about parenthood.

Most research on adolescent sexuality has focused on understanding sexual intercourse and the use of contraception rather than examining its multifaceted, contextual dimensions. The study of adolescent sexuality can be broadened by exploring adolescents' feelings about puberty and their bodies, sexual arousal and desire, sexual behavior as more than intercourse, and safe sex as being more than the use of condoms (Graber, Brooks-Gunn, & Galen, 1999). According to Jeanne Brooks-Gunn and Roberta Paikoff (1997), five developmental issues need to be examined more thoroughly in the study of adolescent sexuality:

- *Timing of sexual maturation.* Being an early-maturing girl is associated with having sexual intercourse. Indeed, maturing early sometimes results in a cascade of events, such as early dating, having older friends, being pursued by older males, demanding more autonomy from parents, and spending more time in activities that are not supervised by adults. Thus, early-maturing girls are in special need of skills and supervision to limit their participation in high-risk sexual activities (Graber, Britto, & Brooks-Gunn, 1999).
- *Co-occurrence of behaviors detrimental to health.* Early maturation is linked not only with sexual intercourse but also with early drinking and smoking. Many high-risk youth don't have just a single problem; they have multiple problems. The confluence of such problems as unprotected sexual intercourse, drug abuse, delinquency, and school-related difficulties places adolescents on a precarious developmental trajectory, especially when these behaviors appear in early adolescence.
- *The contexts of sexual behavior.* Sexual behavior in adolescence is influenced by contextual factors, such as poverty and how long it persists, neighborhood quality, school characteristics, and peer group norms (Brooks-Gunn & others, 1993). At many different points in this chapter, we have seen that the incidences of sexual intercourse and adolescent pregnancy differ across and within cultures.
- *The timing of sexual experiences.* Young adolescents should not have sexual intercourse. They are less likely to engage in protected intercourse than older adolescents, increasing the probability of pregnancy and STIs. Cognitively and emotionally, young adolescents have difficulty handling sexuality's intense, varied feelings and understanding sexuality's complex meanings. The question of when an adolescent is mature enough to have sex is an individual one and its answer depends on many factors.
- *Gender and sexuality.* The sexual experiences of many young adolescent girls are involuntary or at the very least occur in settings in which male dominance plays a role. Further, as we saw earlier in the chapter, sexual scripts are often different for females and males.

The study of adolescent sexuality can be reframed to take into account behaviors and feelings, to promote a more multidimensional approach, and to explore sexual transitions beyond first intercourse and first contraceptive use. Healthy sexual pathways include (Brooks-Gunn & Paikoff, 1997):

- Practicing sexual abstinence but having positive feelings about one's body
- Engaging in sexual exploration without the expectation that it will lead to sexual intercourse
- Engaging in sexual intercourse with another individual in the context of a committed relationship in late adolescence or early adulthood and using safe sex practices

Social Policy and Adolescent Sexuality

Adolescents should learn about human sexuality and reproduction early, *before* they become sexually active. Programs that promote sexual health should not begin any later than early adolescence and should include information about preventing transmission of AIDS. For example, many young adolescents do not know that the AIDS incubation period can be 10 or more years or that a pregnant female can transmit HIV to her fetus. Interventions should identify the sexually oriented encounters that adolescents are likely to experience and provide life skills training on ways to avoid such situations or manage them more effectively. Schools, families, and the media can contribute to this effort.

Adolescent pregnancy is also an important target of social policy initiatives (Dannhausen-Brun, Shalowitz, & Berry, 1997). Most adolescent pregnancies are unintended. Any sound educational approach needs to make it very clear that becoming a parent at the right time—after adolescence—is critical to optimal development, for both the parent and the offspring.

The Carnegie Foundation's report *Starting Points: Meeting the Needs of Our Youngest Children* (1994) emphasized the importance of preparing adolescents for responsible parenthood. One way to do this is to encourage adolescents to do community service in child care centers, enabling them to experience and understand what is required to raise young children. Families are an important source of what it takes to be a parent, but so are schools, places of worship, and community organizations.

What policy recommendations could help adolescents who, despite advice to the contrary, become parents? Four such recommendations are these (Chase-Lansdale & Brooks-Gunn, 1994): First, the life-course diversity of adolescent mothers suggests that no single service delivery program is universally applicable. Rather, different types of programs should be developed for different types of adolescent mothers. For example, those who have dropped out of school and receive welfare need different services than those who graduate from high school and are employed. Second, services should be expanded to include the elementary-age children of mothers who became pregnant in adolescence. Despite the fact that most studies show more negative consequences for older rather than younger children, most child-oriented services target infants and preschool children.

Two other policy implications involve the coordination of services and family systems. Better coordination of services for mothers and children is needed. Historically, programs have targeted either mothers (emphasizing work training) or children (emphasizing early enrichment) but have not linked the lives of adolescent mothers and their children. Also, a family systems perspective is missing from policy perspectives. Grandmothers are often significant members of teenage mothers' families, and service programs that take this into account are nonexistent in most locales. In addition, policymakers need to recognize that, depending on its resources, the family system might help or hinder the young mother's efforts to be an effective parent or to achieve economic security.

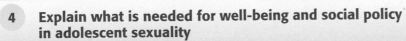

Review and reflect   Learning goal 4

4   Explain what is needed for well-being and social policy in adolescent sexuality

REVIEW

- What issues need to be explored to better understand and improve the well-being of adolescents' sexuality?
- What can be done to improve social policy related to adolescent sexuality?

REFLECT

- What do you think should be the main focus of social policy regarding adolescent sexuality?

Reach Your Learning Goals

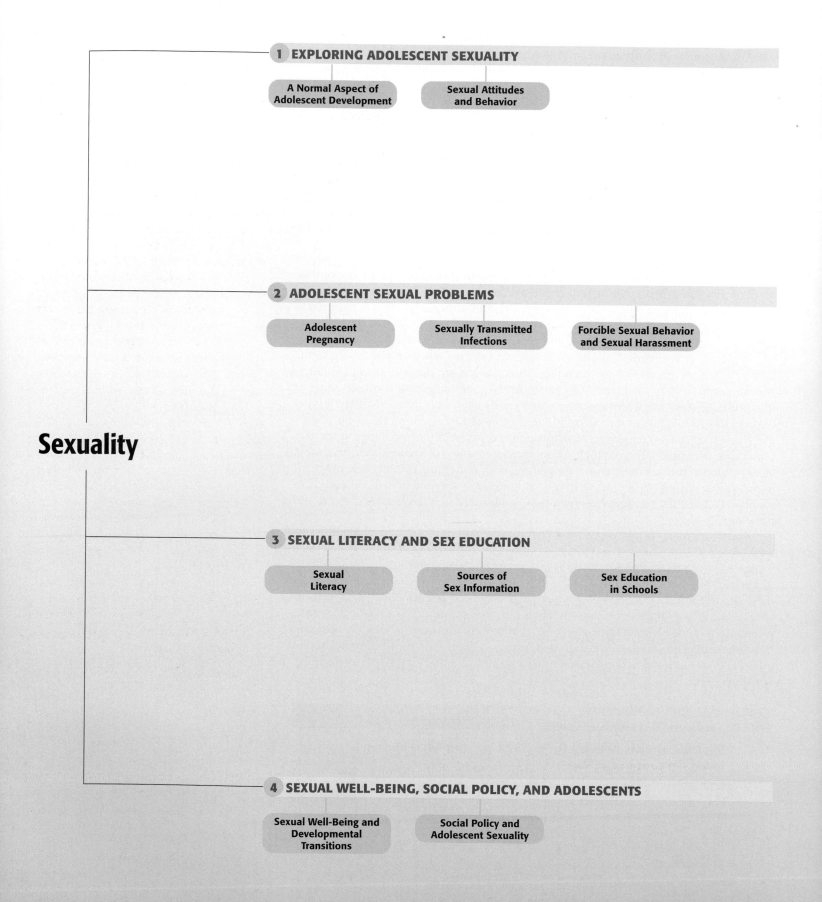

Sexuality

1 EXPLORING ADOLESCENT SEXUALITY

- A Normal Aspect of Adolescent Development
- Sexual Attitudes and Behavior

2 ADOLESCENT SEXUAL PROBLEMS

- Adolescent Pregnancy
- Sexually Transmitted Infections
- Forcible Sexual Behavior and Sexual Harassment

3 SEXUAL LITERACY AND SEX EDUCATION

- Sexual Literacy
- Sources of Sex Information
- Sex Education in Schools

4 SEXUAL WELL-BEING, SOCIAL POLICY, AND ADOLESCENTS

- Sexual Well-Being and Developmental Transitions
- Social Policy and Adolescent Sexuality

Summary

1 Discuss sexuality as a normal aspect of adolescence and summarize the nature of adolescent sexual attitudes and behavior

- Too often the problems adolescents encounter with sexuality are emphasized rather than the fact that sexuality is a normal aspect of adolescent development. Adolescence is a bridge between the asexual child and the sexual adult. Adolescent sexuality is related to many other aspects of adolescent development, including physical development and puberty, cognitive development, the self and identity, gender, families, peers, schools, and culture. Increased permissiveness in adolescent sexuality is linked to increased permissiveness in the larger culture. Developing a sexual identity is multifaceted. An adolescent's sexual identity involves an indication of sexual orientation, interests, and styles of behavior. One study identified five sexual styles in adolescence: naïve, unassured, competent, adventurous, and driven. Obtaining valid information about adolescent sexuality is not easy. Much of the data are based on interviews and questionnaires, which can involve untruthful or socially desirable responses.
- The progression of sexual behaviors is typically necking, petting, sexual intercourse, or, in some cases, oral sex. The number of adolescents reporting having had sexual intercourse increased significantly in the twentieth century. The proportion of females engaging in intercourse increased more rapidly than for males. National data indicate that slightly more than half of all adolescents today have had sexual intercourse by age 17, although the percentage varies by sex, ethnicity, and context. Male, African American, and inner-city adolescents report the highest sexual activity. A common adolescent sexual script involves the male making sexual advances, and it is left up to the female to set limits on the male's sexual overtures. Adolescent females' sexual scripts link sex with love more than adolescent males' sexual scripts do. Risk factors for sexual problems include early sexual activity, having a number of sexual partners, not using contraception, engaging in other at-risk behaviors such as drinking and delinquency, living in a low-SES neighborhood, and ethnicity. Today, it is widely accepted that sexual orientation should be viewed as a continuum from exclusive heterosexuality to exclusive homosexuality. An individual's sexual orientation—whether bisexual, heterosexual, or homosexual—is likely caused by a mix of genetic, hormonal, cognitive, and environmental factors. Developmental pathways for sexual minority youth are often diverse, may involve bisexual attractions, and do not always involve falling in love with a same-sex individual. Recent research has focused on adolescents' disclosure of same-sex attractions and the struggle they often go through in doing this. Discrimination and bias against homosexuality produces considerable stress for adolescents with a homosexual interest. Self-stimulation is part of the sexual activity of virtually all adolescents and one of their most frequent sexual outlets. Adolescents are increasing their use of contraceptives, but large numbers of sexually active adolescents still do not use them. Young adolescents and those from low-SES backgrounds are less likely to use contraceptives than their older, middle-SES counterparts.

2 Describe the main sexual problems that can emerge in adolescence

- The U.S. adolescent pregnancy rate is one of the highest in the Western world. Fortunately, the U.S. adolescent pregnancy rate has recently started to decline. A complex, impassioned issue involving an unintended pregnancy is the decision of whether to have an abortion. Adolescent pregnancy increases health risks for the mother and the offspring. Adolescent mothers are more likely to drop out of school and have lower paying jobs than their adolescent counterparts who do not bear children. It is important to remember, though, that it often is not pregnancy alone that places adolescents at risk. Adolescent mothers often come from low-income families and were not doing well in school prior to their pregnancy. Cognitive factors, such as egocentric and immature thought, may be involved in adolescent pregnancy. The infants of adolescent parents are at risk both medically and psychologically. Adolescent parents are less effective in rearing their children than older parents are. Many adolescent fathers do not have a close relationship with their baby and the adolescent mother. Recommendations for reducing adolescent pregnancy include sex education and family planning, access to contraception, life options, community involvement and support, and abstinence. In one study, volunteer community service was linked with a lower incidence of adolescent pregnancy.
- Sexually transmitted infections (STIs) are contracted primarily through sexual contact with an infected partner. The contact is not limited to vaginal intercourse but includes oral-genital and anal-genital contact as well. AIDS (acquired immune deficiency syndrome) is caused by the HIV virus, which destroys the body's immune system. Currently, the rate of AIDS in U.S. adolescents is relatively low, but it has reached epidemic proportions in sub-Saharan Africa, especially in adolescent girls. Because of the long incubation period, many 20- to 24-year-olds who are diagnosed with AIDS were infected during adolescence. AIDS can be transmitted through sexual contact, sharing needles, and blood transfusions. A number of projects are focusing on AIDS prevention. Genital herpes is caused by a family of viruses with different strains. Genital warts, caused by a virus, is the most common STI. Commonly called the "drip" or "clap," gonorrhea is another common STI. Syphilis is caused by the bacterium *Treponema pallidum*, a spirochete. Chlamydia is one of the most common STIs.

- Some individuals force others to have sex with them. Rape is forcible sexual intercourse with a person who does not give consent. About 95 percent of rapes are committed by males. An increasing concern is date, or acquaintance, rape. Sexual harassment is a form of power of one person over another. Sexual harassment of adolescents is widespread. Two forms are quid pro quo and hostile environment sexual harassment.

3 Characterize the sexual literacy of adolescents and sex education

- American adolescents and adults are not very knowledgeable about sex. Sex information is abundant but too often it is misinformation.
- Adolescents get most of their information about sex from peers, followed by literature, mothers, schools, and experience.

- A majority of American parents support sex education in schools and this support has increased in concert with increases in STIs, especially AIDS. Some experts believe that school-linked sex education that ties in with community health centers is a promising strategy.

4 Explain what is needed for well-being and social policy in adolescent sexuality

- We need to examine five issues more thoroughly: the timing of behaviors associated with adolescent sexuality, the co-occurrence of sexual behaviors and other health-related behaviors, the contexts of sexual behavior, the age at which transitions take place, and gender.
- We also need improved and expanded initiatives to reduce adolescent pregnancy and educate adolescents about the responsibilities of parenting.

Key Terms

sexual script 236	AIDS 252	syphilis 255	quid pro quo sexual
bisexual 238	genital herpes 255	chlamydia 256	harassment 258
sexually transmitted infections	genital warts 255	rape 257	hostile environment sexual
(STIs) 252	gonorrhea 255	date, or acquaintance, rape 257	harassment 258

Key People

Alfred Kinsey 238	Richard Savin-Williams 241	Jeanne Brooks-Gunn 264
Simon LeVay 239	June Reinisch 259	

Resources for Improving the Lives of Adolescents

AIDS Hotline

National AIDS Information Clearinghouse
P.O. Box 6003
Rockville, MD 20850
800–342–AIDS; 800–344–SIDA (Spanish); 800–AIDS–TTY (Deaf)

The people answering the hotline will respond to any questions children, youth, or adults have about HIV infection or AIDS. Pamphlets and other materials on AIDS are available.

Alan Guttmacher Institute

111 Fifth Avenue
New York, NY 10003
212–254–5656

The Alan Guttmacher Institute is an especially good resource for information about adolescent sexuality. The Institute publishes a well-respected journal, *Perspectives on Sexual and Reproductive Health* (renamed in 2003, formerly *Family Planning Perspectives*), which includes articles on many dimensions of sexuality, such as adolescent pregnancy, statistics on sexual behavior and attitudes, and sexually transmitted infections.

Boys and Sex

(1991) by Wardell Pomeroy
New York: Delacorte Press

This book was written for adolescent boys and stresses the responsibility that comes with sexual maturity.

Girls and Sex

(1991) by Wardell Pomeroy
New York: Delacorte Press

The author poses a number of questions that young girls often ask about sex and then answers them. Many myths that young girls hear about sex are also demystified.

Mom, Dad, I'm Gay

(2001) by Richard Savin-Williams
Washington, DC: American Psychological Association

As a leading researcher on adolescent homosexual relationships, Richard Savin-Williams examines how gay and lesbian adolescents develop their sexual identity.

National Sexually Transmitted Diseases Hotline

800–227–8922

This hotline provides information about a wide variety of sexually transmitted infections.

Sex Information and Education Council of the United States (SIECUS)

130 West 42nd Street
New York, NY 10036
212–819–9770

This organization serves as an information clearinghouse about sex education. The group's objective is to promote the concept of human sexuality as an integration of physical, intellectual, emotional, and social dimensions.

E-Learning Tools

To help you master the material in this chapter, you will find a number of valuable study tools on the student CD-ROM that accompanies this book. In addition, visit the Online Learning Center for *Adolescence, 10th Edition*, where you will find helpful resources for chapter 7, "Sexuality."

Taking It to the Net

http://www.mhhe.com/santrocka10

1. Adolescence is a time when we not only are learning about sexuality but also are dealing with emerging sexuality and learning sexual scripts. Your instructor assigns a paper in which you are to evaluate the importance of sexual scripts in the change, or not, of gender roles. What information will you include?

2. While home for vacation you notice that your younger sister says that she wants to break up with her boyfriend but she fears he will hurt himself or someone else. She seems to feel guilty about wanting to break up because she seems to be the only person who loves and understands him. You begin to wonder if she might be in an abusive relationship. What are the signs of an abusive dating relationship?

3. Do you or any of your friends know a teenage father? How does he cope with being a father? What special needs might he have in becoming a responsible father?

Connect to **http://www.mhhe.com/santrocka10** to research the answers and complete these exercises. In some cases, you'll also find further instructions on this site.

Self-Assessment

To evaluate yourself, complete these self-assessments: (1) My Knowledge of Sexual Myths and Realities, and (2) How Much Do I Know About STIs?

Health and Well-Being, Parenting, and Education

To practice your decision-making skills, complete the health and well-being, parenting, and education scenarios.

It is one of the beautiful compensations of this life that no one can sincerely try to help another without helping himself.
—CHARLES DUDLEY WARNER
American Essayist, 19th Century

Moral Development, Values, and Religion

Chapter Outline		*Learning Goals*

DOMAINS OF MORAL DEVELOPMENT　　**1**　　Discuss theories and research on moral thought, behavior, and feeling

    Moral Thought

    Moral Behavior

    Moral Feeling

CONTEXTS OF MORAL DEVELOPMENT　　**2**　　Describe how the contexts of parenting and schools can influence moral development

    Parenting

    Schools

VALUES, RELIGION, AND CULTS　　**3**　　Explain the roles of values, religion, and cults in adolescents' lives

    Values

    Religion

    Cults

Images of Adolescent Development

The Morals of a High School Newspaper

What moral dilemmas might crop up for adolescents who are responsible for the school newspaper?

Fred, a senior in high school, wanted to publish a mimeographed newspaper for students so that he could express many of his opinions. He wanted to speak out against some of the school's rules, like the rule forbidding students from wearing certain types of T-shirts.

Before Fred started his newspaper, he asked his principal for permission. The principal said that it would be all right if, before every publication, Fred would turn over all of his articles for the principal's approval. Fred agreed and turned in several articles for approval. The principal approved all of them, and Fred published two issues of the paper in the next two weeks.

But the principal had not expected Fred's newspaper to receive so much attention. Students were so excited about the paper that they began to organize protests against the T-shirt regulation and other school rules. Angry parents objected to Fred's opinions. They phoned the principal, telling him that the newspaper was unpatriotic and should not be published. As a result of the rising excitement, the principal ordered Fred to stop publishing on the grounds that Fred's activities were disruptive to the operation of the school. (Rest, 1986, p. 194)

The preceding story about Fred and his newspaper raises a number of questions related to adolescents' moral development:

- Was it right for the principal to have stopped the newspaper?
- When the welfare of the school is threatened, does the principal have the right to give orders to students?
- Does the principal have the freedom of speech to say no in this case?
- When the principal stopped the newspaper, was he preventing full discussion of an important problem?
- Is Fred actually being loyal to his school and patriotic to his country?
- What effect would stopping the newspaper have on the students' education in critical thinking and judgments?
- Was Fred in any way violating the rights of others in publishing his own opinions?

Moral development is one of the oldest topics of interest to those who are curious about human nature. Most people have strong opinions about acceptable and unacceptable behavior, ethical and unethical behavior, and ways in which acceptable and ethical behaviors are to be fostered in adolescents. This chapter is about moral development, values, and religion in adolescence. These topics involve the distinction between right and wrong, what matters to people, and what people should do in their interactions with others. We begin by describing the three domains of moral development: moral thoughts, behavior, and feeling. Next, we will explore the context in which moral development takes place, focusing on families and schools. The chapter concludes with an examination of adolescent values and the influence of religion and cults on adolescent development.

1 DOMAINS OF MORAL DEVELOPMENT

Moral Thought	Moral Behavior	Moral Feeling

Moral development involves thoughts, behaviors, and feelings regarding standards of right and wrong. Moral development has an intrapersonal dimension (a person's basic values and sense of self) and an interpersonal dimension (a focus on what people should do in their interactions with other people) (Gibbs, 2003; Walker & Pitts, 1998). The intrapersonal dimension regulates a person's activities when she or he is not engaged in social interaction. The interpersonal dimension regulates people's social interactions and arbitrates conflict. Let's now further explore some basic ideas about moral thoughts, feelings, and behaviors.

First, how do adolescents *reason* or think about rules for ethical conduct? For example, we might present an adolescent with a story in which someone has a conflict about whether or not to cheat in a particular situation, such as taking an exam in school. The adolescent is asked to decide what is appropriate for the character to do and why. This was the strategy used in the section regarding Fred's newspaper. The focus is placed on the reasoning adolescents use to justify their moral decisions.

Second, how do adolescents actually *behave* in moral circumstances? For example, with regard to cheating, we might observe adolescents' cheating and the environmental circumstances that produced and maintain the cheating. This could be done through a one-way mirror as adolescents are taking an exam. The observer might note whether they take out "cheat" notes, look at another student's answers, and so on.

Third, how do adolescents *feel* about moral matters? In the example of cheating, do the adolescents feel enough guilt to resist temptation? If adolescents do cheat, do feelings of guilt after the transgression keep them from cheating the next time they face temptation?

The remainder of this discussion of moral development focuses on these three facets—thought, behavior, and feelings. Keep in mind that although we have separated moral development into three components—thought, behavior, and feelings—the components often are interrelated. For example, if the focus is on the individual's behavior, it is still important to evaluate the person's intentions (moral thought). Similarly, emotions accompany, and can distort, moral reasoning.

Moral Thought

How do adolescents think about standards of right and wrong? Piaget had some thoughts about this question. So did Lawrence Kohlberg.

moral development Thoughts, behaviors, and feelings regarding standards of right and wrong.

Piaget's Theory and Cognitive Disequilibrium Theory Interest in how children and adolescents think about moral issues was stimulated by Piaget (1932), who extensively observed and interviewed children from the ages of 4 to 12. Piaget watched children play marbles to learn how they used and thought about the game's rules. He also asked children questions about ethical issues—theft, lies, punishment, and justice, for example. Piaget concluded that children think in two distinct ways about morality, depending on their developmental maturity:

- **Heteronomous morality** is the first stage of moral development in Piaget's theory, occurring at 4 to 7 years of age. Justice and rules are conceived of as unchangeable properties of the world, removed from the control of people.
- **Autonomous morality,** the second stage of moral development in Piaget's theory, is displayed by older children (about 10 years of age and older). The child becomes aware that rules and laws are created by people, and that, in judging an action, one should consider the actor's intentions as well as the consequences. Children 7 to 10 years of age are in a transition between the two stages, evidencing some features of both.

A heteronomous thinker judges the rightness or goodness of behavior by considering the consequences of the behavior, not the intentions of the actor. For example, the heteronomous thinker says that breaking twelve cups accidentally while trying to steal a cookie is worse than breaking one cup intentionally. For the moral autonomist, the reverse is true. The actor's intentions assume paramount importance. The heteronomous thinker also believes that rules are unchangeable and are handed down by all-powerful authorities. When Piaget suggested to a group of young children that new rules be introduced into the game of marbles, they resisted. By contrast, older children—moral autonomists—accept change and recognize that rules are merely convenient, socially agreed-upon conventions, subject to change by consensus.

According to Piaget, the heteronomous thinker also believes in **immanent justice**, the idea that, if a rule is broken, punishment will be meted out immediately. The young child believes that the violation is somehow connected automatically to the punishment. Thus, young children often look around worriedly after committing a transgression, expecting inevitable punishment. Immanent justice also implies that if something unfortunate happens to someone, it must be because the person had transgressed earlier. Older children, who are moral autonomists, recognize that punishment is socially mediated and occurs only if a relevant person witnesses the wrongdoing and that, even then, punishment is not inevitable.

Piaget argued that, as children develop, they become more sophisticated in thinking about social matters, especially about the possibilities and conditions of cooperation. Piaget believed that this social understanding comes about through the mutual give-and-take of peer relations. In the peer group, where others have power and status similar to the child's, plans are negotiated and coordinated, and disagreements are reasoned about and eventually settled. Parent-child relations, in which parents have the power and children do not, are less likely to advance moral reasoning, because rules are often handed down in an authoritarian way.

As we have discussed in earlier chapters, Piaget believed that adolescents usually become formal operational thinkers. They no longer are tied to immediate and concrete phenomena but are more logical, abstract, and deductive reasoners. Formal operational thinkers frequently compare the real to the ideal; create contrary-to-fact propositions; are cognitively capable of relating the distant past to the present; understand their roles in society, in history, and in the universe; and can conceptualize their own thoughts and think about their mental constructs as objects. For example, around age 11 or 12, boys and girls spontaneously introduce concepts of belief, intelligence, and faith into their definitions of their religious identities.

Stimulated by Piaget's ideas, Martin Hoffman (1980) developed **cognitive disequilibrium theory,** which states that adolescence is an important period in

heteronomous morality The first stage of moral development in Piaget's theory, occurring at 4 to 7 years of age. Justice and rules are conceived of as unchangeable properties of the world, removed from the control of people.

autonomous morality The second stage of moral development in Piaget's theory, displayed by older children (about 10 years of age and older). The child becomes aware that rules and laws are created by people and that, in judging an action, one should consider the actor's intentions as well as the consequences.

immanent justice Piaget's concept that if a rule is broken, punishment will be meted out immediately.

cognitive disequilibrium theory Hoffman's theory that adolescence is an important period in moral development, in which, because of broader experiences associated with the move to high school or college, individuals recognize that their set of beliefs is but one of many and that there is considerable debate about what is right and wrong.

moral development, especially as individuals move from the relatively homogeneous grade school to the more heterogeneous high school and college environments, where they are faced with contradictions between the moral concepts they have accepted and experiences outside their family and neighborhood. At this point adolescents come to recognize that their set of beliefs is but one of many and that there is considerable debate about what is right and what is wrong. Thus adolescents and emerging adults start to question their former beliefs and, in the process, develop their own moral system.

Kohlberg's Theory   One of the most provocative views of moral development was crafted by Lawrence Kohlberg (1958, 1976, 1986), who believed that moral development is based primarily on moral reasoning and unfolds in a series of stages.

Kohlberg's Stages   Kohlberg arrived at his view after about 20 years of research involving unique interviews with individuals of different ages. In the interviews, individuals were presented with a series of stories in which characters face moral dilemmas. The following is the most popular of the Kohlberg dilemmas:

Lawrence Kohlberg

> In Europe, a woman was near death from a special kind of cancer. There was one drug that the doctors thought might save her. It was a form of radium that a druggist in the same town had recently discovered. The drug was expensive to make, but the druggist was charging ten times what the drug cost him to make. He paid $200 for the radium and charged $2,000 for a small dose of the drug. The sick woman's husband, Heinz, went to everyone he knew to borrow the money, but he could only get together $1,000, which is half of what it cost. He told the druggist that his wife was dying and asked him to sell it cheaper or let him pay later. But the druggist said, "No, I discovered the drug, and I am going to make money from it." So Heinz got desperate and broke into the man's store to steal the drug for his wife. (Kohlberg, 1969, p. 379)

This story is one of eleven that Kohlberg devised to investigate the nature of moral thought. After reading the story, interviewees are asked a series of questions about the moral dilemma: Should Heinz have stolen the drug? Was stealing it right or wrong? Why? Is it a husband's duty to steal the drug for his wife if he can get it no other way? Would a good husband steal it? Did the druggist have the right to charge that much when there was no law setting a limit on the price? Why?

From the answers interviewees gave for this and other moral dilemmas, Kohlberg hypothesized three levels of moral development, each of which is characterized by two stages. A key concept in understanding moral development is **internalization,** the developmental change from behavior that is externally controlled to behavior that is controlled by internal standards and principles. As children and adolescents develop, their moral thoughts become more internalized. Let's look further at Kohlberg's three levels of moral development (see figure 8.1).

Kohlberg's Level 1: Preconventional Reasoning   **Preconventional reasoning** is the lowest level in Kohlberg's theory of moral development. At this level, the individual shows no internalization of moral values—moral reasoning is controlled by external rewards and punishments. Its two stages are heteronomous morality and individualism, instrumental purpose, and exchange.

- Stage 1. *Heteronomous morality* is the first stage in Kohlberg's theory. At this stage, moral thinking is often tied to punishment. For example, children and adolescents obey adults because adults tell them to obey.
- Stage 2. *Individualism, instrumental purpose, and exchange* is the second Kohlberg stage of moral development. At this stage, individuals pursue their own interests but also let others do the same. Thus, what is right involves an equal exchange. People are nice to others so that they will be nice to them in return.

internalization The developmental change from behavior that is externally controlled to behavior that is controlled by internal standards and principles.

preconventional reasoning The lowest level in Kohlberg's theory of moral development. The individual shows no internalization of moral values—moral reasoning is controlled by external rewards and punishment.

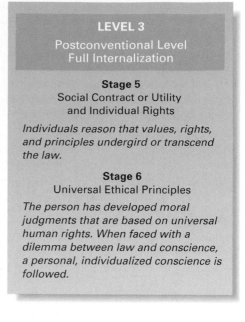

FIGURE 8.1 **Kohlberg's Three Levels and Six Stages of Moral Development**

Kohlberg's Level 2: Conventional Reasoning **Conventional reasoning** is the second, or intermediate, level in Kohlberg's theory of moral development. At this level, internalization is intermediate. Individuals abide by certain standards (internal), but they are the standards of others (external), such as parents or the laws of society. The conventional reasoning level consists of two stages: mutual interpersonal expectations, relationships and interpersonal conformity, and social systems morality.

- Stage 3. *Mutual interpersonal expectations, relationships, and interpersonal conformity* is Kohlberg's third stage of moral development. At this stage, individuals value trust, caring, and loyalty to others as a basis of moral judgments. Children and adolescents often adopt their parents' moral standards at this stage, seeking to be thought of by their parents as a "good girl" or a "good boy."
- Stage 4. *Social systems morality* is the fourth stage in Kohlberg's theory of moral development. At this stage, moral judgments are based on understanding the social order, law, justice, and duty. For example, adolescents may say that, for a community to work effectively, it needs to be protected by laws that are adhered to by its members.

Kohlberg's Level 3: Postconventional Reasoning **Postconventional reasoning** is the highest level in Kohlberg's theory of moral development. At this level, morality is completely internalized and is not based on others' standards. The individual recognizes alternative moral courses, explores the options, and then decides on a personal moral code. The postconventional level of morality consists of two stages: social contract or utility and individual rights, and universal ethical principles.

- Stage 5. *Social contract or utility and individual rights* is the fifth Kohlberg stage. At this stage, individuals reason that values, rights, and principles undergird or transcend the law. A person evaluates the validity of actual laws and examines social systems in terms of the degree to which they preserve and protect fundamental human rights and values.
- Stage 6. *Universal ethical principles* is the sixth and highest stage in Kohlberg's theory of moral development. At this stage, the person has developed a moral standard based on universal human rights. When faced with a conflict between law

conventional reasoning The second, or intermediate, level in Kohlberg's theory of moral development. Internalization is intermediate. Individuals abide by certain standards (internal), but they are the standards of others (external), such as parents or the laws of society.

postconventional reasoning The highest level in Kohlberg's theory of moral development. Morality is completely internalized.

Stage Description	Examples of Moral Reasoning That Support Heinz's Theft of the Drug	Examples of Moral Reasoning That Indicate That Heinz Should Not Steal the Drug
Preconventional reasoning		
Stage 1: Heteronomous morality	Heinz should not let his wife die; if he does, he will be in big trouble.	Heinz might get caught and sent to jail.
Stage 2: Individualism, purpose, and exchange	If Heinz gets caught, he could give the drug back and maybe they would not give him a long jail sentence.	The druggist is a businessman and needs to make money.
Conventional reasoning		
Stage 3: Mutual interpersonal expectations, relationships, and interpersonal conformity	Heinz was only doing something that a good husband would do; it shows how much he loves his wife.	If his wife dies, he can't be blamed for it; it is the druggist's fault. The druggist is the selfish one.
Stage 4: Social systems morality	If you did nothing, you would be letting your wife die; it is your responsibility if she dies. You have to steal it with the idea of paying the druggist later.	It is always wrong to steal; Heinz will always feel guilty if he steals the drug.
Postconventional reasoning		
Stage 5: Social contract or utility and individual rights	The law was not set up for these circumstances; taking the drug is not really right, but Heinz is justified in doing it.	You can't really blame someone for stealing, but extreme circumstances don't really justify taking the law into your own hands. You might lose respect for yourself if you let your emotions take over; you have to think about the long term.
Stage 6: Universal ethical principles	By stealing the drug, you would have lived up to society's rules, but you would have let down your conscience.	Heinz is faced with the decision of whether to consider other people who need the drug as badly as his wife. He needs to act by considering the value of all the lives involved.

FIGURE 8.2 Moral Reasoning at Kohlberg's Stages in Response to the "Heinz and the Druggist" Story

and conscience, the person will follow conscience, even though the decision might involve personal risk.

How might individuals at each of the six Kohlberg stages respond to the "Heinz and the druggist" moral dilemma described earlier? Figure 8.2 provides some examples of these responses.

Kohlberg believed that these levels and stages occur in a sequence and are age related: Before age 9, most children reason about moral dilemmas in a preconventional way; by early adolescence, they reason in more conventional ways. Most adolescents reason at stage 3, with some signs of stages 2 and 4. By early adulthood, a small number of individuals reason in postconventional ways. In a 20-year longitudinal investigation, the uses of stages 1 and 2 decreased (Colby & others, 1983) (see figure 8.3). Stage 4, which did not appear at all in the moral reasoning of 10-year-olds, was reflected in 62 percent of the moral thinking of 36-year-olds. Stage 5 did not appear until age 20 to 22 and never characterized more than 10 percent of the individuals. Thus, the moral stages appeared somewhat later than Kohlberg initially envisioned, and the higher stages, especially stage 6, were extremely elusive. Recently, stage 6 was removed from the Kohlberg moral judgment scoring manual, but it still is considered to be theoretically important in the Kohlberg scheme of moral development. A review of data from 45 studies in 27 diverse world cultures provided support for the universality of Kohlberg's first four stages but suggested that stages 5 and 6 tend to vary across cultures (Snarey, 1987).

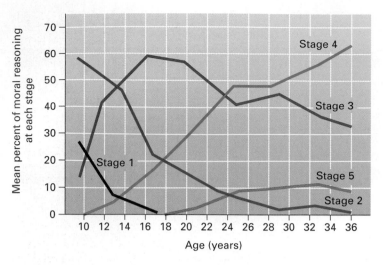

FIGURE 8.3 Age and the Percentage of Individuals at Each Kohlberg Stage

In one longitudinal study of males from 10 to 36 years of age, at age 10 most moral reasoning was at stage 2 (Colby & others, 1983). At 16 to 18 years of age, stage 3 became the most frequent type of moral reasoning and it was not until the mid-20s that stage 4 became the most frequent. Stage 5 did not appear until 20 to 22 years of age and it never characterized more than 10 percent of the individuals. In this study, the moral stages appeared somewhat later than Kohlberg envisioned and stage 6 was absent.

www.mhhe.com/santrocka10

**Kohlberg's Theory of Moral Development
Kohlberg's Moral Dilemmas
Kohlberg's Moral Stages**

Any change in moral reasoning between late adolescence and early adulthood appears to be relatively gradual (Eisenberg & Morris, 2004). One study found that when 16- to 19-year-olds and 18- to 25-year-olds were asked to reason about real-life moral dilemmas and coded using Kohlberg stages, there was no significant difference in their moral reasoning (Walker & others, 1995).

Influences on the Kohlberg Stages Kohlberg believed that the individual's moral orientation unfolds as a consequence of cognitive development. Children and adolescents construct their moral thoughts as they pass from one stage to the next, rather than passively accepting a cultural norm of morality (Brabeck, 2000). Investigators have sought to understand factors that influence movement through the moral stages, among them modeling, cognitive conflict, peer relations, and role-taking opportunities.

Modeling and Cognitive Conflict Several investigators have attempted to advance individuals' levels of moral development by having a model present arguments that reflect moral thinking one stage above the individuals' established levels. These studies are based on the cognitive developmental concepts of equilibrium and conflict (Walker & Taylor, 1991). By presenting moral information slightly beyond the individual's cognitive level, a disequilibrium is created that motivates a restructuring of moral thought. The resolution of the disequilibrium and conflict should be toward increased competence. In one study, participants did prefer stages higher than their own more than stages lower than their own (Walker, deVries, & Trevethan, 1987). In sum, moral thought can be moved to a higher level through exposure to models or discussion that is more advanced than the adolescent's level.

Peer Relations and Role-Taking Opportunities Like Piaget, Kohlberg believed that peer interaction is a critical part of the social stimulation that challenges individuals to change their moral orientation. Whereas adults characteristically impose rules and regulations on children, the mutual give-and-take in peer interaction provides the child with an opportunity to take the role of another person and to generate rules democratically. Kohlberg stressed that role-taking opportunities can, in principle, be engendered by any peer group encounter. Researchers have found that more advanced moral reasoning takes place when peers engage in challenging, even moderately conflicting, conversation (Berkowitz & Gibbs, 1983; Walker, Hennig, & Krettenauer, 2000). In another study, having a greater number of close friends and being perceived as a leader with high peer acceptance was associated with higher levels of moral reasoning (Schonert-Reichl, 1999).

Kohlberg did believe that certain types of parent-child experiences can induce the child and adolescent to think at more advanced levels of moral thinking. In particular, parents who allow or encourage conversation about value-laden issues promote more advanced moral thought in their children and adolescents. Unfortunately, many parents do not systematically provide their children and adolescents with such role-taking opportunities. Nonetheless, in one study, children's moral development was related to their parents' discussion style, which involved questioning and supportive interaction (Walker & Taylor, 1991). In recent years, there has been increasing emphasis on the role of parenting in moral development (Eisenberg & Morris, 2004).

Why Is Kohlberg's Theory Important for Understanding Moral Development in Adolescence? Kohlberg's theory is essentially a description of the progressive conceptions people use to understand social cooperation. In short, it tells the developmental story of people trying to understand things like society, rules and roles, and institutions and relationships. Such basic conceptions are fundamental to adolescents, for whom ideology becomes important in guiding their lives and making life decisions.

Kohlberg's Critics Kohlberg's provocative theory of moral development has not gone unchallenged (Eisenberg & Morris, 2004; Gilligan, 1982, 1996; Lapsley, 1996; Lapsley & Narváez, 2004; Rest & others, 1999; Smetana & Turiel, 2003). The criticisms involve the link between moral thought and moral behavior, the quality of the research, inadequate consideration of culture's role in moral development, and underestimation of the care perspective.

Moral Thought and Moral Behavior Kohlberg's theory has been criticized for placing too much emphasis on moral thought and not enough emphasis on moral behavior. Moral reasons can always be a shelter for immoral behavior. Bank embezzlers, presidents, and religious figures endorse the loftiest of moral virtues when commenting about moral dilemmas, but their own behavior may be immoral. No one wants a nation of cheaters and thieves who can reason at the postconventional level. The cheaters and thieves may know what is right and wrong, yet still do what is wrong.

In evaluating the relation between moral thought and moral behavior, consider the corrupting power of rationalizations and other defenses that disengage us from self-blame; these include interpreting a situation in our favor and attributing blame to authorities, circumstances, or victims (Bandura, 1991). One area in which a link between moral judgment and behavior has been found is where higher Kohlberg-stage reasoning acts as a buffer against criminal activity (Taylor & Walker, 1997).

Given the terrorist attacks of September 11, 2001, and the continuing war on terrorism, it is intriguing to explore how heinous actions can be cloaked in a mantle of moral virtue and why that is especially dangerous. Social cognitive theorist Albert Bandura (1999, 2002) argues that people usually don't engage in harmful conduct until they have justified the morality of their actions to themselves. In this process of moral justification, immoral conduct is made personally and socially acceptable by portraying it as serving socially worthy or moral purposes. In many instances throughout history, perpetrators have twisted theology so that they see themselves as doing God's will. Bandura provides the example of Islamic extremists who mount their jihad (holy war) as self-defense against tyrannical, decadent people who they see as seeking to enslave the Islamic world.

Assessment of Moral Reasoning Some developmentalists fault the quality of Kohlberg's research and believe that more attention should be paid to the way moral development is assessed (Boyes, Giordano, & Galperyn, 1993). For example, James Rest (1986) argued that alternative methods should be used to collect information about moral thinking instead of relying on a single method that requires individuals to reason about hypothetical moral dilemmas. Rest also said that Kohlberg's stories are extremely difficult to score. To help remedy this problem, Rest developed his own measure of moral development, called the Defining Issues Test (DIT).

The DIT attempts to determine which moral issues individuals feel are more critical in a given situation by presenting them with a series of dilemmas and a list of definitions of the major issues involved (Kohlberg's procedure does not make use of such a list). In the dilemma of Heinz and the druggist, individuals might be asked whether a community's laws should be upheld or whether Heinz should be willing to risk being injured or caught as a burglar. They might also be asked to list the most important values that govern human interaction. They are given six stories and asked to rate the importance of each issue involved in deciding what ought to be done. Then they are asked to list what they believe are the four most important issues. Rest argued that this method provides a more valid and reliable way to assess moral thinking than Kohlberg's method.

What are some effective strategies to help children cope with traumatic events, such as the terrorist attacks on the United States on 9/11/2001?

Story subject	Grade		
	7	9	12
	Percentage		
Alcohol	2	0	5
Civil rights	0	6	7
Drugs	7	10	5
Interpersonal relations	38	24	35
Physical safety	22	8	3
Sexual relations	2	20	10
Smoking	7	2	0
Stealing	9	2	0
Working	2	2	15
Other	1	26	20

FIGURE 8.4 Actual Moral Dilemmas Generated by Adolescents

Researchers also have found that the hypothetical moral dilemmas posed in Kohlberg's stories do not match the moral dilemmas many children and adults face in their everyday lives (Walker, deVries, & Trevethan, 1987; Yussen, 1977). Most of Kohlberg's stories focus on the family and authority. However, when one researcher invited adolescents to write stories about their own moral dilemmas, the adolescents generated dilemmas that were broader in scope, focusing on friends, acquaintances, and other issues, as well as family and authority (Yussen, 1977). The adolescents' moral dilemmas also were analyzed in terms of their content. As shown in figure 8.4, the moral issue that concerned adolescents more than any other was interpersonal relationships.

Some moral development researchers believe that a valuable method is to have research participants recall and discuss real-life dilemmas from their own experience (Walker, deVries, & Trevethan, 1987). This strategy can provide a valid assessment not only of individuals' moral stage but also of how they interpret moral situations that are relevant to them.

Culture and Moral Development   Another criticism of Kohlberg's view is that it is culturally biased (Glassman, 1997; Miller, 1995). A review of research on moral development in 27 countries concluded that moral reasoning is more culture-specific than Kohlberg envisioned and that Kohlberg's scoring system does not recognize higher-level moral reasoning in certain cultural groups (Snarey, 1987). Examples of higher-level moral reasoning that would not be scored as such by Kohlberg's system include values related to communal equity and collective happiness in Israel, the unity and sacredness of all life-forms in India, and the relation of the individual to the community in New Guinea. These examples of moral reasoning would not be scored at the highest level in Kohlberg's system because they do not emphasize the individual's rights and abstract principles of justice. One study assessed the moral development of 20 adolescent male Buddhist monks in Nepal (Huebner & Garrod, 1993). The issue of justice, a basic theme in Kohlberg's theory, was not of paramount importance in the monks' moral views, and their concerns about prevention of suffering and the role of compassion are not captured by Kohlberg's theory.

According to moral development theorist and researcher William Damon (1988), where culturally specific practices take on profound moral and religious significance, as in India, the moral development of children focuses extensively on their adherence to custom and convention. In contrast, Western moral doctrine tends to elevate abstract principles, such as justice and welfare, to a higher moral status than customs or conventions. As in India, socialization practices in many third world countries actively instill in children a great respect for their culture's traditional codes and practices.

In Richard Shweder's (1991) view of culture and moral development, three ethical orientations or worldviews appear: (1) an ethic of autonomy (dominant in Western cultures), (2) an ethic of community (prominent in cultures that emphasize communitarian values and tradition), and (3) an ethic of divinity (characteristic of cultures in which morality is mainly derived from religious prescriptions).

In sum, although Kohlberg's approach does capture much of the moral reasoning voiced in various cultures around the world, as we have just seen, there are some important moral concepts in particular cultures that his approach misses or misconstrues (Walker, 1996).

Gender and the Care Perspective   Carol Gilligan (1982, 1992, 1996; Gilligan & others, 2003) argues that Kohlberg's theory of moral development does not adequately reflect relationships and concern for others. A **justice perspective** is a moral perspective that focuses on the rights of the individual; individuals stand alone and independently make moral decisions. Kohlberg's theory is a justice perspective. By contrast, a **care perspective** is a moral perspective that views people in terms of their connectedness with others and emphasizes interpersonal communication, relation-

justice perspective A moral perspective that focuses on the rights of the individual; individuals independently make moral decisions.

care perspective The moral perspective of Carol Gilligan, which views people in terms of their connectedness with others and emphasizes interpersonal communication, relationships with others, and concern for others.

ships with others, and concern for others. Gilligan's theory is a care perspective. According to Gilligan, Kohlberg greatly underplayed the care perspective in moral development. She believes that this may be because he was a male, because most of his research was with males rather than females, and because he used male responses as a model for his theory.

In extensive interviews with girls from 6 to 18 years of age, Gilligan and her colleagues found that girls consistently interpret moral dilemmas in terms of human relationships and base these interpretations on listening and watching other people (Gilligan, 1992, 1996). According to Gilligan, girls are sensitive to different rhythms in relationships and often are able to follow the pathways of feelings. Gilligan believes that girls reach a critical juncture in their development when they reach adolescence.

A meta-analysis (a statistical analysis that combines the results of many different studies) casts doubt on Gilligan's claim of substantial gender differences in moral judgment (Jaffee & Hyde, 2000). In this study, overall, only a small sex difference in care-based reasoning favored females, but this sex difference was greater in adolescence than childhood. When differences occurred, they were better explained by the nature of the dilemma than by gender (for example, both males and females tended to use care-based reasoning to deal with interpersonal dilemmas and justice reasoning to handle societal dilemmas).

Researchers have found that females report feeling more guilty about interpersonal transgressions and generate more interpersonal real-life conflicts than males do (Skoe & others, 1996; Williams & Bybee, 1994). One study also found that young adolescent girls used more care-based reasoning about dating dilemmas than boys (Weisz & Black, 2002). These findings suggest that females consider care-oriented, relational moral dilemmas to be more salient or moral than males do (Wark & Krebs, 1996). In support of this idea, one recent study found that females rated prosocial dilemmas as more significant than males did (Wark & Krebs, in press).

The possibility has recently been raised that the obtained differences between males and females in regard to caring and prosocial behavior are more a function of gender-role classification than biological sex. As we saw in chapter 6, "Gender," the femininity dimension of gender-role classification is defined in terms of relations and connections to people more than the masculine dimension. In line with this possibility, in one study, feminine gender-role classification rather than sex per se was linked with the empathy of the participants (Karniol & others, 1998). In a study of Brazilian adolescents, femininity but not sex was related to prosocial behavior (Eisenberg, Zhou, & Koller, 2001). Further, one recent study asked college students about the importance of real-life moral dilemmas that were care-related, justice-related, or mixed (both care- and justice-related) (Skoe & others, 2002). The gender-role classification of the college students also was assessed. Women and feminine persons viewed moral conflicts as more important than men and masculine persons. On the mixed dilemmas, women scored higher than men on care reasoning while men scored higher than women on justice reasoning. Regardless of sex or gender role, relational real-life dilemmas elicited ratings of higher importance and care reasoning scores than did nonrelational ones. Women and persons high in femininity showed more empathic concern for other people. Masculine persons scored lower on personal distress while androgynous individuals reported more helpful behaviors than all others. In sum, researchers recently have found stronger links between gender-role classification and moral reasoning than between biological sex and moral reasoning.

Reasoning in Different Social Cognitive Domains An increasing number of theorists and researchers believe it is important to make distinctions about different

This 14-year-old boy in Nepal is thought to be the sixth holiest Buddhist in the world. In one study of 20 adolescent male Buddhist monks in Nepal, the issue of justice, a basic theme in Kohlberg's theory, was not a central focus in the monks' moral views. Also, the monks' concerns about prevention of suffering and the importance of compassion are not captured in Kohlberg's theory.

www.mhhe.com/santrocka10

**In a Different Voice
Exploring Girls' Voices**

domains when considering adolescents' reasoning about various sociocognitive issues (Killen, 1991; Nucci, 1996, 2001; Smetana & Turiel, 2003; Turiel, 1998, 2003). The three domains that have been given the most attention are moral, social, and personal:

- The *moral domain* involves issues about justice, such as fairness, the welfare of others, and rights. Moral concepts are believed to be generalized and unchangeable (Ardila-Rey & Killen, in press). For example, research studies of children in a number of countries consistently view acts of harm as wrong in any context (Killen, McGlotlin, & Lee-Kim, in press).
- The *social-conventional domain* pertains to regularities designed to ensure the smooth functioning of social groups, such as customs and etiquette. Thus, not eating with one's fingers and raising one's hand in class before asking a question are social-conventional concepts. Social-conventional concepts are believed to be context specific and changeable. Both moral and social-conventional concepts are viewed as issues that are regulated by adults.
- The *personal domain* reflects decisions that are based on personal choice, such as choice of friends and choice of activities. The personal domain often involves issues of individual autonomy, personal prerogatives, and personal goals. For example, conflict sometimes occurs between parents and adolescents because parents and adolescents may interpret the events as belonging to different domains. Thus, an adolescent may regard smoking as an issue of personal choice while his parents view it as a moral issue. Adolescents typically view concepts in the personal domain as involving decision making that is not regulated by adults (Nucci, 1996).

Moral Behavior

We saw that one of the criticisms of Kohlberg's theory is that it does not give adequate attention to the link between moral thought and moral behavior. In our exploration of moral behavior, we will focus on these questions: What are the basic processes that behaviorists believe are responsible for adolescents' moral behavior? How do social cognitive theorists view adolescents' moral development? What is the nature of prosocial behavior?

Basic Processes   Behavioral views emphasize the moral behavior of adolescents. The familiar processes of reinforcement, punishment, and imitation have been invoked to explain how and why adolescents learn certain moral behaviors and why their behaviors differ from one another. The general conclusions to be drawn are the same as for other domains of social behavior. When adolescents are positively reinforced for behavior that is consistent with laws and social conventions, they are likely to repeat that behavior. When models who behave morally are provided, adolescents are likely to adopt their behavior. And when adolescents are punished for immoral or unacceptable behavior, those behaviors can be eliminated, but at the expense of sanctioning punishment by its very use and of causing emotional side effects for the adolescent.

To these general conclusions, we can add several qualifiers. The effectiveness of reinforcement and punishment depends on how consistently they are administered and the schedule that is adopted. The effectiveness of modeling depends on the characteristics of the model (power, warmth, uniqueness, and so on) and the presence of cognitive processes, such as symbolic codes and imagery, to enhance retention of the modeled behavior.

What kind of adult moral models are adolescents being exposed to in American society? Do such models usually do what they say? Adolescents are especially alert to adult hypocrisy, and evidence indicates that they are right to believe that many adults display a double standard, their moral actions not always corresponding to their moral thoughts or pronouncements. A poll of 24,000 adults presented detailed scenarios of everyday moral problems to test moral decision making on a wide variety of issues. Consider the example of whether the adult would knowingly buy a stolen television set. More than 20 percent said that they would, even though 87 percent said that this act is probably morally wrong. And approximately 31 percent of the adults said that they would be more likely to buy the stolen television if they knew they would not get caught. While moral thought is an important dimension of moral development, these data glaringly underscore that what adults believe about right and wrong does not always correspond with how they will act in moral situations.

In addition to emphasizing the role of environmental determinants and the gap between moral thought and moral action, behaviorists also emphasize that moral behavior is situationally dependent. That is, they say that adolescents are not likely to display consistent moral behavior in diverse social settings. In a classic investigation of moral behavior—one of the most extensive ever conducted—Hugh Hartshorne and Mark May (1928–1930) observed the moral responses of 11,000 children and adolescents who were given the opportunity to lie, cheat, and steal in a variety of circumstances—at home, at school, at social events, and in athletics. A completely honest or a completely dishonest child or adolescent was difficult to find. Situation-specific moral behavior was the rule. Adolescents were more likely to cheat when their friends pressured them to do so and when the chance of being caught was slim. Other analyses suggest that some adolescents are more likely to lie, cheat, and steal than others, indicating more consistency of moral behavior in some adolescents than in others (Burton, 1984).

Social Cognitive Theory of Moral Development The **social cognitive theory of moral development** emphasizes a distinction between adolescents' moral competence—the ability to produce moral behaviors—and moral performance—the enactment of those behaviors in specific situations (Mischel & Mischel, 1975). Competence, or acquisition, is primarily the outgrowth of cognitive-sensory processes. Competencies include what adolescents are capable of doing, what they know, their skills, their awareness of moral rules and regulations, and their cognitive ability to construct behaviors. In contrast, adolescents' moral performance, or behavior, is determined by their motivation and the rewards and incentives to act in a specific moral way. Albert Bandura (1991, 2002) also believes that moral development is best understood by considering a combination of social and cognitive factors, especially those involving self-control.

Bandura (2002) proposes that in developing a moral self, individuals adopt standards of right and wrong that serve as guides and deterrents for conduct. In this self-regulatory process, people monitor their conduct and the conditions under which it occurs, judge it in relation to moral standards, and regulate their actions by the consequences they apply to themselves. They do things that provide them satisfaction and a sense of self-worth. They often refrain from engaging in ways that violate their moral standards in order to avoid self-condemnation. Thus, self-sanctions keep conduct in line with internal standards. In Bandura's view, morality is rooted in self-regulation rather than abstract reasoning.

Not surprisingly, social cognitive theorists have been critical of Kohlberg's emphasis on abstract reasoning, as well as his lack of emphasis on moral behavior and the situational determinants of morality. However, although Kohlberg argued that moral judgment is an important determinant of moral behavior, he, like the Mischels, stressed that an individual's interpretation of both the moral and the factual aspects of a situation leads to a moral decision (Kohlberg & Candee, 1979). For example, Kohlberg mentioned that "extra-moral" factors, such as the desire to avoid embarrassment, may cause children to fail to do what they believe to be morally right. In sum, according to both the Mischels and Kohlberg, moral action is influenced by complex factors.

Overall, the findings are mixed with regard to the association of moral thought and behavior (Arnold, 1989), although in one investigation with college students,

social cognitive theory of moral development The theory that distinguishes between moral competence (the ability to produce moral behaviors) and moral performance (performing those behaviors in specific situations).

individuals with both highly principled moral reasoning and high ego strength were less likely to cheat in a resistance-to-temptation situation than were their low-principled and low-ego-strength counterparts (Hess, Lonky, & Roodin, 1985).

Moral behavior includes both negative aspects of behavior—cheating, lying, and stealing, for example—and positive aspects of behavior—such as being considerate to others and giving to a worthy cause. Let's now explore the positive side of moral behavior—*prosocial behavior*.

Prosocial Behavior Many prosocial acts involve **altruism,** an unselfish interest in helping another person. Although adolescents have often been described as egocentric and selfish, adolescent acts of altruism are, nevertheless, plentiful (Eisenberg & Morris, 2004; Eisenberg & Wang, 2003; Puka, 2004). We see examples daily in the hard-working adolescent who places a one-dollar bill in the church offering plate each week; the adolescent-sponsored car washes, bake sales, and concerts organized to make money to feed the hungry and help children who are mentally retarded; and the adolescent who takes in and cares for a wounded cat. How do psychologists account for such altruistic acts?

Reciprocity and exchange are involved in altruism (Brown, 1986). Reciprocity is found throughout the human world and is the highest moral principle in Christianity, Buddhism, Hinduism, Islam, and Judaism. Reciprocity encourages adolescents to do unto others as they would have others do unto them. In one study, adolescents showed more helping behavior around the house when mothers were involved with and spent time helping the adolescent (Eberly & Montemayor, 1996).

Not all adolescent prosocial behavior is motivated by reciprocity and exchange, but self-other interactions and relationships help us to understand altruism's nature (Eisenberg & Morris, 2004). The circumstances most likely to involve altruism by adolescents are empathetic or sympathetic emotion for an individual in need or a close relationship between the benefactor and the recipient (Clark & others, 1987). Prosocial behavior occurs more often in adolescence than in childhood, although examples of caring for others and comforting someone in distress occur even during the preschool years (Eisenberg & Fabes, 1998; Eisenberg & Morris, 2004).

Are there gender differences in prosocial behavior during adolescence? Adolescent females view themselves as more prosocial and empathic, and also engage in more prosocial behavior than males (Eisenberg & Morris, 2004). For example, a review of research found that across childhood and adolescence, females engaged in more prosocial behavior (Eisenberg & Fabes, 1998). The biggest gender difference occurred for kind and considerate behavior with a smaller difference in sharing.

Forgiveness is an aspect of prosocial behavior that occurs when the injured person releases the injurer from possible behavioral retaliation. In one investigation, individuals from the fourth grade through college and adulthood were asked questions about forgiveness (Enright, Santos, & Al-Mabuk, 1989). The adolescents were especially swayed by peer pressure in their willingness to forgive others.

Despite some changes in altruism in adolescence, there is continuity between engaging in positive moral acts in childhood and the extent of such behavior in emerging adulthood. For example, Nancy Eisenberg and her colleagues (1999) conducted a longitudinal study of 32 individuals from the time they were 4 to 5 years of age to when they were in their early twenties. They were assessed on eleven occasions with a variety of measures, including observations, interviews, parents' reports, and friends' reports.

Following is a brief description of some of the main measures the researchers used. Observations of prosocial behavior when the children were in preschool focused on behaviors of sharing, helping, and offering comfort. In elementary school, the experimenter gave each child money (eight nickels) and an opportunity to donate it anonymously to a charity for needy children. Children's helping behavior was also assessed in such tasks as giving them an opportunity to help the experimenter pick up dropped paper clips. In the later elementary school years, adolescence, and in their

altruism Unselfish interest in helping another person.

forgiveness This is an aspect of prosocial behavior that occurs when an injured person releases the injurer from possible behavioral retaliation.

early twenties, the individuals filled out a self-report scale of items that focused on altruism.

The results indicated that the observed prosocial behaviors in preschool (sharing, helping, and offering comfort) were related to the children's prosocial behaviors in the elementary school years and in the early twenties. These findings support the view that prosocial behavior is rather stable from the early childhood years into at least the first part of early adulthood.

One study examined prosocial behavior and caring in adolescents who lived in a highly impoverished area of Camden, New Jersey (Hart & Fegley, 1995). Participants were African American and Latino adolescents who had been nominated by community leaders for demonstrating unusual commitments to care for others or the community. The highly caring adolescents were compared with a comparison group of adolescents who had not been singled out for their caring. The caring adolescents were more likely to (1) describe themselves in terms of moral personality traits and goals, and (2) think of themselves as incorporating their ideals and parental images.

The nineteenth-century U.S. poet and essayist Ralph Waldo Emerson once said, "The meaning of good and bad, better and worse, is simply helping or hurting." By developing adolescents' capacity for empathy and altruism, the United States can become a nation of people who help rather than hurt. Later in the chapter in our coverage of moral education, we will explore adolescent helping in the context of service learning.

So far we have examined two of the three main domains of moral development: thought and behavior. Next, we explore the third main domain: moral feeling.

Moral Feeling

Among the ideas formulated about the development of moral feelings are concepts central to psychoanalytic theory, the nature of empathy, and the role of emotions in moral development.

Psychoanalytic Theory   As we discussed in chapter 2, Sigmund Freud's psychoanalytic theory describes the *superego* as one of the three main structures of personality (the id and the ego being the other two). In Freud's classical psychoanalytic theory, an individual's superego—the moral branch of personality—develops in early childhood when the child resolves the Oedipus conflict and identifies with the same-sex parent. According to Freud, one reason why children resolve the Oedipus conflict is to alleviate the fear of losing their parents' love and of being punished for their unacceptable sexual wishes toward the opposite-sex parent. To reduce anxiety, avoid punishment, and maintain parental affection, children form a superego by identifying with the same-sex parent. In Freud's view, through this identification, children internalize the parents' standards of right and wrong that reflect societal prohibitions. At the same time, children turn inward the hostility that was previously aimed at the same-sex parent. This inwardly directed hostility is then experienced self-punitively (and unconsciously) as guilt. In the psychoanalytic account of moral development, self-punitiveness of guilt keeps children and, later on, adolescents from committing transgressions. That is, children and adolescents conform to societal standards to avoid guilt.

In Freud's view, the superego consists of two main components—the ego ideal and the conscience—which promote children's and adolescents' development of moral feelings. The **ego ideal** is the component of the superego that involves ideal standards approved by parents, whereas the **conscience** is the component of the superego that involves behaviors not approved of by parents. An individual's ego ideal rewards the individual by conveying a sense of pride and personal value when the individual acts according to moral standards. The conscience punishes the individual for acting immorally by making the individual feel guilty and worthless. In this way, self-control replaces parental control.

ego ideal The component of the superego that involves ideal standards approved by parents.

conscience The component of the superego that involves behaviors disapproved of by parents.

Erik Erikson (1970) outlined three stages of moral development: specific moral learning in childhood, ideological concerns in adolescence, and ethical consolidation in adulthood. According to Erikson, during adolescence, individuals search for an identity. If adolescents become disillusioned with the moral and religious beliefs they acquired during childhood, they are likely to lose, at least temporarily, their sense of purpose and feel that their lives are empty. This may lead to adolescents' search for an ideology that will give some purpose to their lives. For the ideology to be acceptable, it must both fit the evidence and mesh with adolescents' logical reasoning abilities. If others share this ideology, a sense of community is felt. For Erikson, ideology surfaces as the guardian of identity during adolescence because it provides a sense of purpose, assists in tying the present to the future, and contributes meaning to the behavior (Hoffman, 1988).

Empathy Positive feelings, such as empathy, contribute to adolescents' moral development. Feeling **empathy** means reacting to another's feelings with an emotional response that is similar to that person's feelings. Although empathy is experienced as an emotional state, it often has a cognitive component—the ability to discern another's inner psychological states, or what we have previously called perspective taking.

At about 10 to 12 years of age, individuals develop an empathy for people who live in unfortunate circumstances (Damon, 1988). Children's concerns are no longer limited to the feelings of particular persons in situations they directly observe. Instead, 10- to 12-year-olds expand their concerns to the general problems of people in unfortunate circumstances—the poor, the handicapped, the socially outcast, and so forth. This newfound sensitivity may lead older children to behave altruistically, and later may give a humanitarian flavor to adolescents' development of ideological and political views.

Although every adolescent may be capable of responding with empathy, not everyone does so. Adolescents' empathic behavior varies considerably. For example, in older children and adolescents, empathic dysfunctions can contribute to antisocial behavior. Some delinquents convicted of violent crimes show a lack of feeling for their victims' distress. A 13-year-old boy convicted of violently mugging a number of older adults, when asked about the pain he had caused one blind woman, said, "What do I care? I'm not her" (Damon, 1988).

The Contemporary Perspective We have seen that classical psychoanalytic theory emphasizes the power of unconscious guilt in moral development but that other theories, such as that of Damon, emphasize the role of empathy. Today, many developmentalists believe that both positive feelings, such as empathy, sympathy, admiration, and self-esteem, and negative feelings, such as anger, outrage, shame, and guilt, contribute to adolescents' moral development (Damon, 1988, 1995; Eisenberg & Fabes, 1998). When strongly experienced, these emotions influence adolescents to act in accord with standards of right and wrong. Such emotions as empathy, shame, guilt, and anxiety over other people's violations of standards are present early in development and undergo developmental change throughout childhood and adolescence. These emotions provide a natural base for adolescents' acquisition of moral values, both orienting adolescents toward moral events and motivating them to pay close attention to such events. However, moral emotions do not operate in a vacuum to build adolescents' moral awareness, and they are not sufficient in themselves to generate moral responsivity. They do not give the "substance" of moral regulation—the rules, values, and standards of behavior that adolescents need to understand and act on. Moral emotions are inextricably interwoven with the cognitive and social aspects of adolescents' development.

In one study of fifth-, eighth-, and eleventh-graders, parents were the individuals most likely to evoke guilt (Williams & Bybee, 1994). With development, guilt evoked by members of the extended family and siblings was less prevalent, but guilt engendered by girlfriends or boyfriends was more frequent. At the higher grade levels, the

www.mhhe.com/santrocka10

Developing Empathy in Children and Youth
Exploring Emotions and Emotional Intelligence
International Society for Research on Emotions

empathy Reacting to another's feelings with an emotional response that is similar to the other's response.

percentage of students reporting guilt over aggressive, externalizing behavior declined, whereas those mentioning guilt over internal thoughts and inconsiderateness increased. Males were more likely to report guilt over externalizing behaviors, whereas females reported more guilt over violating norms of compassion and trust.

Review and reflect   Learning goal 1

1 **Discuss theories and research on moral thought, behavior and feeling**

REVIEW

- What is moral development? What are the main points of Piaget's and Kohlberg's theories of moral development? How has Kohlberg's theory been criticized? How is reasoning different in the moral, social-conventional, and personal domains?
- What are some basic processes in the behavioral view of moral development? What is the social cognitive view of moral development? What is the nature of prosocial behavior?
- What is the psychoanalytic view of moral development? What role does empathy play in moral development? What is the contemporary perspective on moral feeling?

REFLECT

- What do you think about the following circumstances?
  —A man who had been sentenced to serve ten years for selling a small amount of marijuana walked away from a prison camp after serving only six months of his sentence. Twenty-five years later he was caught. He is now in his fifties and is a model citizen. Should he be sent back to prison? Why or why not? At which Kohlberg stage should your response be placed?
  —A young woman who had been in a tragic accident is "brain dead" and has been kept on life support systems for four years without ever regaining consciousness. Should the life support systems be removed? Explain your response. At which Kohlberg stage should your response be placed?

---

2 CONTEXTS OF MORAL DEVELOPMENT

Parenting   Schools

Earlier in the chapter, we saw that both Piaget and Kohlberg believed that peer relations are an important context for moral development. Adolescents' experiences in families and schools also are important contexts for moral development.

Parenting

Both Piaget and Kohlberg held that parents do not provide any unique or essential inputs to children's moral development. They do believe that parents are responsible for providing general role-taking opportunities and cognitive conflict, but they reserve the primary role in moral development for peers. Researchers have revealed how both parents and peers contribute to the development of moral maturity (Walker, Hennig, & Krettenauer, 2000). In one study, a general Socratic style of eliciting the other's opinion and checking for understanding was effective in advancing moral maturity in both parent and peer contexts (Walker, Hennig, & Krettenauer, 2000). In general, higher-level moral reasoning in adolescence is linked with parenting that is supportive and encourages adolescents to question and expand on their moral reasoning (Eisenberg & Morris, 2004). Next, we focus on parental discipline and its role in moral development and then draw some conclusions about parenting and moral development.

Parental Discipline In Freud's psychoanalytic theory, the aspects of child rearing that encourage moral development are practices that instill the fears of punishment and of losing parental love. Child developmentalists who have studied child-rearing techniques and moral development have focused on parents' discipline techniques. These include love withdrawal, power assertion, and induction (Hoffman, 1970):

- **Love withdrawal** comes closest to the psychoanalytic emphasis on fear of punishment and of losing parental love. It is a discipline technique in which a parent withholds attention or love from the adolescent, as when the parent refuses to talk to the adolescent or states a dislike for the child.
- **Power assertion** is a discipline technique in which a parent attempts to gain control over the adolescent or the adolescent's resources. Examples include spanking, threatening, or removing privileges.
- **Induction** is the discipline technique in which a parent uses reason and explanation of the consequences for others of the adolescent's actions. Examples of induction include, "Don't hit him. He was only trying to help" and "Why are you yelling at her? She didn't mean to hurt your feelings."

Moral development theorist and researcher Martin Hoffman (1970) believes that any discipline produces arousal on the adolescent's part. Love withdrawal and power assertion are likely to evoke a very high level of arousal, with love withdrawal generating considerable anxiety and power assertion considerable hostility. Induction is more likely to produce a moderate level of arousal in adolescents, a level that permits them to attend to the cognitive rationales parents offer. When a parent uses power assertion or love withdrawal, the adolescent may be so aroused that, even if the parent gives accompanying explanations about the consequences for others of the adolescent's actions, the adolescent might not attend to them. Power assertion presents parents as weak models of self-control—as individuals who cannot control their feelings. Accordingly, adolescents may imitate this model of poor self-control when they face stressful circumstances. The use of induction, however, focuses the adolescent's attention on the action's consequences for others, not on the adolescent's own shortcomings. For these reasons, Hoffman (1988) believes that parents should use induction to encourage adolescents' moral development. In research on parenting techniques, induction is more positively related to moral development than is love withdrawal or power assertion, although the findings vary according to developmental level and socioeconomic status. For example, induction works better with adolescents and older children than with preschool children (Brody & Shaffer, 1982) and better with middle-SES than with lower-SES children (Hoffman, 1970). Older children and adolescents are generally better able to understand the reasons given to them and better at perspective taking than younger children. Some theorists believe the reason that internalization of society's moral standards is more likely among middle-SES than among lower-SES individuals is that internalization is more rewarding in the middle-SES culture (Kohn, 1977).

Parenting Moral Children and Adolescents Parental discipline does contribute to children's moral development, but there are other aspects of parenting that also play an important role, such as providing opportunities for perspective taking and modeling moral behavior and thinking. Nancy Eisenberg and her colleagues (Eisenberg & Morris, 2004; Eisenberg & Murphy, 1995; Eisenberg & Valiente, 2002) summarized the findings from the research literature on ways in which parenting can

love withdrawal A discipline technique in which a parent removes attention or love from a child.

power assertion A discipline technique in which a parent attempts to gain control over a child or a child's resources.

induction A discipline technique in which a parent uses reason and explanation of the consequences for others of a child's actions.

influence children's and adolescents' moral development. They concluded that, in general, moral children and adolescents tend to have parents who:

- Are warm and supportive rather than punitive. One recent study found that maternal warmth was linked with children's empathy through the mother's positive expression of emotions (Zhou & others, 2002).
- Use inductive discipline.
- Provide opportunities for their children and adolescents to learn about others' perspectives and feelings.
- Involve children and adolescents in family decision making and in the process of thinking about moral decisions.
- Model moral behaviors and thinking themselves and provide opportunities for their children and adolescents to model such moral behaviors and thinking.
- Stimulate adolescents to question and expand their moral reasoning.

Parents who show this configuration of behaviors likely foster the development of concern and caring about others, and they create a positive parent-adolescent relationship. These parents also provide information about what behaviors are expected of the adolescent and why, and they promote an internal rather than an external sense of morality. To learn more about the different combinations of parents' and adolescents' emotional behavior, how they differ and how they can clash, watch the video segment entitled "Adolescent and Parent Emotions."

Schools

Schools are an important context for moral development. Moral education is hotly debated in educational circles. We first study one of the earliest analyses of moral education and then turn to some contemporary views on moral education.

The Hidden Curriculum   More than 60 years ago, educator John Dewey (1933) recognized that even when schools do not have specific programs in moral education, they provide moral education through a "hidden curriculum." The **hidden curriculum** is conveyed by the moral atmosphere that is a part of every school.

The moral atmosphere is created by school and classroom rules, the moral orientation of teachers and school administrators, and text materials. Teachers serve as models of ethical or unethical behavior. Classroom rules and peer relations at school transmit attitudes about cheating, lying, stealing, and consideration for others. And through its rules and regulations, the school administration infuses the school with a value system.

Character Education   **Character education** is a direct approach that involves teaching students a basic moral literacy to prevent them from engaging in immoral behavior and doing harm to themselves and others. According to the character education advocates, such behaviors as lying, stealing, and cheating are wrong and students should be taught this throughout their education (Williams & others, 2003). Every school should have an explicit moral code that is clearly communicated to students, and any violations of the code should be met with sanctions (Bennett, 1993). Instruction in specified moral concepts, like honesty, can take the form of example and definition, class discussions and role-playing, or rewarding students for proper behavior.

Some character education movements are the Character Education Partnership, the Character Education Network, the Aspen Declaration on Character Education, and the publicity campaign "Character Counts." Books designed to promote character education include William Bennett's (1993) *Book of Virtues* and William Damon's (1995) *Greater Expectations.*

Values Clarification   **Values clarification** means helping people to clarify what is important to them, what is worth working for, and what purpose their lives are

National Service-Learning Clearinghouse

hidden curriculum The pervasive moral atmosphere that characterizes schools.

character education A direct moral education approach that involves teaching students a basic moral literacy to prevent them from engaging in immoral behavior or doing harm to themselves or others.

values clarification An educational approach that focuses on helping people clarify what is important to them, what is worth working for, and what purpose their lives are to serve. Students are encouraged to define their own values and understand others' values.

to serve. In this approach, students are encouraged to define their own values and understand the values of others (Williams & others, 2003). Values clarification differs from character education in that it does not tell students what their values should be.

In the following values clarification example, students are asked to select from among ten people the six who will be admitted to a safe shelter because a third world war has broken out (Johnson, 1990).

> You work for a government agency in Washington, D.C., and your group has to decide which six of the following ten people will be admitted to a small fallout shelter. Your group has only 20 minutes to make the decision. These are your choices:
>
> - A 30-year-old male bookkeeper
> - The bookkeeper's wife, who is 6 months pregnant
> - A second-year African American male medical student who is a political activist
> - A 42-year-old male who is a famous historian-author
> - A Hollywood actress who is a singer and dancer
> - A female biochemist
> - A 54-year-old male rabbi
> - A male Olympic athlete who is good in all sports
> - A female college student
> - A policeman with a gun

In this type of values clarification exercise, there are no right or wrong answers. The clarification of values is left up to the individual student. Advocates of values clarification say it is value-free. However, critics argue that its controversial content offends community standards. They also say that because of its relativistic nature, values clarification undermines accepted values and fails to stress distinctions between right and wrong behavior.

Cognitive Moral Education **Cognitive moral education** is a concept based on the belief that students should learn to value things like democracy and justice as their moral reasoning develops. Kohlberg's theory has been the basis for a number of cognitive moral education programs. In a typical program, high school students meet in a semester-long course to discuss a number of moral issues. The instructor acts as a facilitator rather than as a director of the class. Cognitive moral education aims to encourage students to develop more advanced notions of such concepts as cooperation, trust, responsibility, and community. Toward the end of his career, Kohlberg (1986) recognized that the moral atmosphere of the school is more important than he initially envisioned. For example, in one study, a semester-long moral education class based on Kohlberg's theory was successful in advancing moral thinking in three democratic schools but not in three authoritarian schools (Higgins, Power, & Kohlberg, 1983).

In our coverage of moral education, we have examined John Dewey's concept of the hidden curriculum, character education, values clarification, and cognitive moral education. As we see next, there is increasing interest in including service learning in education, especially at the secondary school level.

Service Learning **Service learning** is a form of education that promotes social responsibility and service to the community. In service learning, adolescents engage in activities such as tutoring, helping older adults, working in a hospital, assisting at a child-care center, or cleaning up a vacant lot to make a play area. An important goal of service learning is for adolescents to become less self-centered and more strongly motivated to help others (Pritchard & Whitehead, 2004; Waterman, 1997).

Service learning takes education out into the community (Flanagan, 2004; Flanagan & Faison, 2001; Levesque & Prosser, 1996; Youniss, 2002; Youniss & others, 2003). One eleventh-grade student worked as a reading tutor for students from low-income backgrounds with reading skills well below their grade levels. She commented that until she did the tutoring she did not realize how many students had not experienced

www.mhhe.com/santrocka10

Exploring Character Education
The Center for the Fourth and Fifth RS
Exploring Values Education
Variations in Moral Education
Association for Moral Education
Moral Education in Japan
Volunteer Matching Online

cognitive moral education An approach based on the belief that students should learn to value things like democracy and justice as their moral reasoning develops; Kohlberg's theory has been the basis for many of the cognitive moral education approaches.

service learning A form of education that promotes social responsibility and service to the community.

the same opportunities that she had when she was growing up. An especially rewarding moment was when one young girl told her, "I want to learn to read like you so I can go to college when I grow up." Thus, a key feature of service learning is that it not only benefits adolescents but also the recipients of their help.

Adolescent volunteers tend to share certain characteristics, such as extraversion, a commitment to others, and a high degree of self-understanding (Eisenberg & Morris, 2004). Also, adolescent girls are more likely to volunteer to engage in service learning than adolescent boys (Eisenberg & Morris, 2004).

Researchers have found that service learning benefits adolescents in a number of ways:

- Their grades improve, they become more motivated, and they set more goals (Johnson & others, 1998; Search Institute, 1995; Serow, Ciechalski, & Daye, 1990).
- Their self-esteem improves (Hamburg, 1997; Johnson & others, 1998).
- They have an improved sense of being able to make a difference for others (Search Institute, 1995).
- They become less alienated (Calabrase & Schumer, 1986).
- They increasingly reflect on society's political organization and moral order (Yates, 1995).

Even though required community service has increased in high schools, in one survey of 40,000 adolescents, two-thirds said that they had never done any volunteer work to help other people (Benson, 1993). In another survey, only 15 percent of the nation's largest school districts had such a requirement (National Community Service Coalition, 1995). The benefits of service learning, both for the volunteer and the recipient, suggest that more adolescents should be required to participate in such programs.

Review and reflect Learning goal 2

2 **Describe how the contexts of parenting and schools can influence moral development**

REVIEW

- How does parental discipline affect moral development? What are some effective parenting strategies for advancing children's and adolescents' moral development?
- What is the hidden curriculum? What are some contemporary approaches to moral education used in schools?

REFLECT

- What type of discipline did your parents use with you? What effect do you think this has had on your moral development?

Through the Eyes of Adolescents

Finding a Way to Get a Playground

Twelve-year-old Katie Bell more than just about anything else wanted a playground in her New Jersey town. She knew that other kids also wanted one so she put together a group, which generated fund-raising ideas for the playground. They presented their ideas to the town council. Her group got more youth involved. They helped raise money by selling candy and sandwiches door-to-door. Katie says, "We learned to work as a community. This will be an important place for people to go and have picnics and make new friends." Katie's advice, "You won't get anywhere if you don't try."

Katie Bell (*front*) and some of her volunteers.

3 VALUES, RELIGION, AND CULTS

Values	Religion	Cults

What are adolescents' values like today? How powerful is religion in adolescents' lives? Why do some adolescents become involved in cults? We will consider each of these questions in turn.

Values of American College Freshmen

Values

Adolescents carry with them a set of values that influences their thoughts, feelings, and actions. **Values** are beliefs and attitudes about the way things should be. They involve what is important to us. We attach values to all sorts of things: politics, religion, money, sex, education, helping others, family, friends, career, cheating, self-respect, and so on.

Over the past two decades, adolescents have shown an increased concern for personal well-being and a decreased concern for the well-being of others, especially for the disadvantaged (Sax & others, 2002). As shown in figure 8.5, today's college freshmen are more strongly motivated to be well off financially and less motivated to develop a meaningful philosophy of life than were their counterparts of 20 years ago. Student commitment to becoming very well off financially as a "very important" reason for attending college was at a high level in the 2002 survey (73 percent), compared with the 1970s (50 percent in 1971).

However, two aspects of values that increased during the 1960s continue to characterize many of today's youth: self-fulfillment and self-expression (Conger, 1981, 1988). As part of their motivation for self-fulfillment, many adolescents show great

values Beliefs and attitudes about the way things should be.

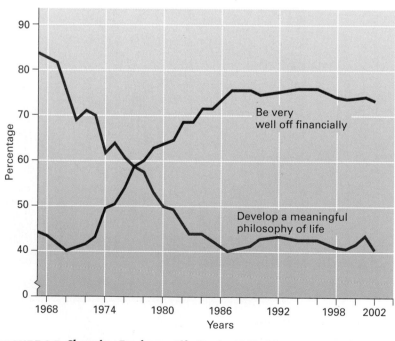

FIGURE 8.5 Changing Freshmen Life Goals, 1968–2002
In the last three decades, a significant change has occurred in freshmen students' life goals. A far greater percentage of today's college freshmen state that a "very important" life goal is to be well off financially, and far fewer state that developing a meaningful philosophy of life is a "very important" life goal.

interest in their physical health and well-being. Greater self-fulfillment and self-expression can be laudable goals, but if they become the only goals, self-destruction, loneliness, or alienation can result. Young people also need to develop a corresponding sense of commitment to others' welfare. Encouraging adolescents to have a strong commitment to others, in concert with an interest in self fulfillment, is an important task for the United States at the beginning of the twenty-first century.

But there are some signs that today's college students are shifting toward a stronger interest in the welfare of society. For example, the percentage of college freshman who said they would very likely participate in volunteer or community service work in the coming year increased from 17 percent in 1990 to 25 percent in 2002 (Sax & others, 2002).

Research on adolescents in seven different countries revealed that family values of compassion and social responsibility were the values that were most consistently linked with adolescent participation in community service, commitment to serving their country, and empathy for disenfranchised groups (Flanagan, 2004; Flanagan & Faison, 2001; Flanagan, Gill, & Galley, 1998). In one recent analysis, it was revealed that middle school civics textbooks are far more likely to discuss an individual's rights rather than social responsibility (Simmons & Avery, in press). Thus, adolescents may benefit from a stronger emphasis on social responsibility in both family and school contexts.

Other research on values has found that adolescents who are involved in groups that connect themselves to others in school, their communities, or faith-based institutions report higher levels of social trust, altruism, commitments to the common good of people, and endorsements of the rights of immigrants for full inclusion in society (Flanagan & Faison, 2001). In this research, adolescents who were uninvolved in such groups were more likely to endorse self-interest and materialistic values.

One recent study of 459 students from 20 different high school classrooms participated in focus group discussions about the most important values they perceived that youth could possess (Steen, Kachorek, & Peterson, 2003). The students especially endorsed the character strengths of leadership, practical intelligence, wisdom, love of learning, spirituality, and the capacity to love and be loved. The students believed that these positive traits are mainly learned rather than innate and that these strengths develop through ongoing real-world experiences rather than through formal instruction.

Careers in Adolescent Development

Constance Flanagan
Professor of Youth Civic Development

Constance (Connie) Flanagan is a professor of youth civic development in the College of Agricultural Sciences at Pennsylvania State University. Her research focuses on youths' views about justice and the factors in families, schools, and communities that promote civic values, connections, and skills in youth (Flanagan, 2002).

Connie obtained her undergraduate degree in psychology from Duquesne University, her master's degree in education from the University of Iowa, and her Ph.D. from the University of Michigan. She has a special interest in improving the U.S. social policy for adolescents and serves as co-chair of the Committee on Child Development. In addition to teaching undergraduate and graduate classes, conducting research, and serving on various committees, Connie also evaluates research for potential publication as a member of the editorial board of *Journal of Adolescent Research* and *Journal of Research on Adolescence*. She also presents her ideas and research at numerous national and international meetings.

Connie Flanagan with adolescents.

Religion

Religious issues are important to adolescents (Paloutzian & Santrock, 2000). In one survey, 95 percent of 13- to 18-year-olds said that they believe in God or a universal spirit (Gallup & Bezilla, 1992). Almost three-fourths of adolescents said that they pray, and about one-half indicated that they had attended religious services within the past week. Almost one-half of the youth said that it is very important for a young person to learn religious faith.

*R*eligion enlightens, terrifies, subdues; it gives faith, inflicts remorse, inspires resolutions, and inflames devotion.

—HENRY NEWMAN
English Churchman and Writer, 19th Century

**Exploring the Psychology of Religion
Psychology of Religion Resources
Psychology of Religion Journals**

The Positive Role of Religion in Adolescents' Lives   Researchers have found that various aspects of religion are linked with positive outcomes for adolescents. For example, in one recent study of 9,700 adolescents, going to church was linked with better grades for students from low-income backgrounds (Regnerus, 2001). Church-going may benefit students because religious communities encourage socially accept-able behavior, which includes doing well in school. Churchgoing may also benefit students because churches often offer positive role models for students.

Many religious adolescents also internalize their religion's message about caring and concern for others (Ream & Savin-Williams, 2003). For example, in one survey, religious youth were almost three times as likely to engage in community service as nonreligious youth (Youniss, McLellan, & Yates, 1999).

Religion is often an asset to the communities in which adolescents live (Ream & Savin-Williams, 2003). In some instances, religious institutions are the only organiza-tion that initiates efforts to work with adolescents in inner cities. For inner-city youth, as well as other youth, religion offers possible answers to questions about meaning, purpose, and direction in life (Trulear, 2000).

Developmental Changes   Adolescence can be an especially important juncture in religious development. Even if children have been indoctrinated into a religion by their parents, because of advances in their cognitive development they may begin to question what their own religious beliefs truly are.

Erikson's Theory and Identity   During adolescence, especially in late adolescence and the college years, identity development becomes a central focus (Erikson, 1968). Adolescents want to know answers to questions like these: "Who am I?" "What am I all about as a person?" "What kind of life do I want to lead?" As part of their search for identity, adolescents begin to grapple in more sophisticated, logical ways with such questions as "Why am I on this planet?" "Is there really a God or higher spiritual be-ing, or have I just been believing what my parents and the church imprinted in my mind?" "What really are my religious views?"

Applying Piaget's Theory to Religious Development   The cognitive developmental theory of Jean Piaget (1952) provides a theoretical backdrop for understanding reli-gious development in children and adolescents. For example, in one study children were asked about their understanding of certain religious pictures and Bible stories (Goldman, 1964). The children's responses fell into three stages closely related to Pi-aget's theory.

In the first stage (up until 7 or 8 years of age)—*preoperational intuitive religious thought*—children's religious thoughts were unsystematic and fragmented. The chil-dren often either did not fully understand the material in the stories or did not con-sider all of the evidence. For example, one child's response to the question "Why was Moses afraid to look at God?" (Exodus 3:6) was "Because God had a funny face!"

In the second stage (from 7 or 8 to 13 or 14 years of age)—*concrete operational reli-gious thought*—children focused on particular details of pictures and stories. For exam-ple, in response to the question about why Moses was afraid to look at God, one child said, "Because it was a ball of fire. He thought he might burn him." Another child voiced, "It was a bright light and to look at it might blind him."

In the third stage (age 14 through the remainder of adolescence)—*formal opera-tional religious thought*—adolescents revealed a more abstract, hypothetical religious un-derstanding. For example, one adolescent said that Moses was afraid to look at God because "God is holy and the world is sinful." Another youth responded, "The awe-someness and almightiness of God would make Moses feel like a worm in comparison."

Other researchers have found similar developmental changes in children and ado-lescents. For example, in one study, at about 17 or 18 years of age adolescents in-creasingly commented about freedom, meaning, and hope—abstract concepts—when making religious judgments (Oser & Gmünder, 1991).

How do religious thought and behavior change as children and adolescents develop? How are children's and adolescents' religious conceptions influenced by their cognitive development?

Fowler's Life-Span Developmental Theory James Fowler (1981, 1996) proposed a theory of religious development that focuses on the motivation to discover meaning in life, either within or outside of organized religion. Fowler proposed six stages of religious development that are related to Erikson's, Piaget's, and Kohlberg's theories of development (Torney-Purta, 1993):

Stage 1. Intuitive-projective faith (early childhood). After infants learn to trust their caregiver (Erikson's formulation), they invent their own intuitive images of what good and evil are. As children move into Piaget's preoperational stage, their cognitive worlds open up a variety of new possibilities. Fantasy and reality are taken as the same thing. Right and wrong are seen in terms of consequences to the self. Children readily believe in angels and spirits.

Stage 2. Mythical-literal faith (middle and late childhood). As children move into Piaget's concrete operational stage, they begin to reason in a more logical, concrete, but not abstract way. They see the world as more orderly. Grade-school-age children interpret religious stories literally, and they perceive God as being much like a parent figure who rewards the good and punishes the bad. What is right is often perceived as fair exchange.

Stage 3. Synthetic-conventional faith (transition between childhood and adolescence, early adolescence). Adolescents now start to develop formal operational thought (Piaget's highest stage) and begin to integrate what they have learned about religion into a coherent belief system. According to Fowler, although the synthetic-conventional faith stage is more abstract than the previous two stages, young adolescents still mainly conform to the religious beliefs of others (as in Kohlberg's conventional level of morality) and have not yet adequately analyzed alternative religious ideologies. Someone's behavior that involves a question of right and wrong is seen in terms of the harm it does to a relationship or what others might say. Fowler believes that most adults become locked into this stage and never move on to higher stages of religious development. The faith of adolescents often involves a personal relationship with God. God is thought of as "always there for me."

Stage 4. Individuative-reflective faith (transition between adolescence and adulthood, early adulthood). Fowler believes that, at this stage, individuals are capable for the first time of taking full responsibility for their religious beliefs. Often precipitated by the *leaving-home* experience, young people begin to take responsibility for their lives. Young adults now start to realize that they can choose the course of their lives and that they must expend effort to follow a particular life course. Individuals come face-to-face with such decisions as these: "Should I consider myself first, or should I consider the welfare of others first?" "Are the religious doctrines that were taught to me when I was growing up absolute, or are they more relative than I was led to believe?" Fowler believes that both formal operational thought and the intellectual challenges to an individual's values and religious ideologies that often develop in college are essential to developing individuative-reflective faith.

Stage 5. Conjunctive faith (middle adulthood). Fowler believes that only a small number of adults ever move on to this stage, which involves being more open to paradox and opposing viewpoints. This openness stems from people's awareness of their finiteness and limitations. One woman Fowler placed at this stage revealed the following complex religious understanding: "Whether you call it God or Jesus or Cosmic Flow or Reality or Love, it doesn't matter what you call it, it is there" (Fowler, 1981, p. 192).

Stage 6. Universalizing faith (middle adulthood or late adulthood). Fowler says that the highest stage in religious development involves transcending specific belief systems to achieve a sense of oneness with all being and a commitment to breaking down the barriers that are divisive to people on this planet. Conflictual events are no longer seen as paradoxes. Fowler argues that very, very few people ever achieve this elusive, highest stage of religious development. Three who have, he says, are Mahatma Gandhi, Martin Luther King, Jr., and Mother Teresa.

Figure 8.6 provides an overview of Fowler's theory. Although Fowler's theory has received considerable attention, a research base has not been developed in regard to this theory.

Religious Indoctrination and Parenting Religious institutions created by adults are designed to introduce certain beliefs to children and thereby ensure that they will carry on a religious tradition. Various societies utilize Sunday schools, parochial education, tribal transmission of religious traditions, and parental teaching of children at home to further this aim.

Does this indoctrination work? In many cases it does (Paloutzian, 2000). In general, adults tend to adopt the religious teachings of their upbringing. For instance, individuals who are Catholics by the time they are 25 years of age, and who were raised as Catholics, likely will continue to be Catholics throughout their adult years. If a religious change or reawakening occurs, it is most likely to take place during adolescence.

However, it is important to consider the quality of the parent-adolescent relationship (Ream & Savin-Williams, 2003). Adolescents who have a positive relationship with their parents and/or are securely attached to them are likely to adopt the religious orientation of their parents. Adolescents who have a negative relationship with their parents and/or are insecurely attached to them may disaffiliate from religion or seek religion-based attachments that are missing in their family system (Streib, 1999).

STAGE 6
Universalizing Faith
(Middle and Late Adulthood)

- Transcending belief systems to achieve a sense of oneness with all being
- Conflictual events are no longer viewed as paradoxes

STAGE 5
Conjunctive Faith
(Middle Adulthood)

- Becoming more open to paradox and opposing viewpoints
- Stems from awareness of one's finiteness and limitations

STAGE 4
Individuative-Reflective Faith
(Late Adolescence, Early Adulthood)

- For the first time, individuals are capable of taking full responsibility for their religious beliefs
- In-depth exploration of one's values and religious beliefs is carried out

STAGE 3
Synthetic-Conventional Faith
(Early Adolescence)

- More abstract thought
- Conformity to religious beliefs of others

STAGE 2
Mythical-Literal Faith
(Middle/Late Childhood)

- More logical, concrete thought
- Literal interpretation of religious stories; God is like a parent figure

STAGE 1
Intuitive-Projective Faith
(Early Childhood)

- Intuitive images of good and evil
- Fantasy and reality are the same

FIGURE 8.6 Fowler's Stage Theory of Religious Development

Many children and adolescents show an interest in religion, and many religious institutions created by adults (such as this Muslim school in Malaysia) are designed to introduce them to religious beliefs and ensure that they will carry on a religious tradition.

Religiousness and Sexuality in Adolescence   One area of religion's influence on adolescent development involves sexual activity. Although variability and change in church teachings make it difficult to generalize about religious doctrines, most churches discourage premarital sex. Thus, the degree of adolescent participation in religious organizations may be more important than affiliation with a particular religion as a determinant of premarital sexual attitudes and behavior. Adolescents who frequently attend religious services are likely to hear messages about abstaining from sex. Involvement of adolescents in religious organizations also enhances the probability that they will become friends with adolescents who have restrictive attitudes toward premarital sex.

One recent national study of 3,356 adolescent girls (mean age = 16 years) focused on four aspects of religiousness: (1) attendance at religious events ("In the past 12 months, how often did you attend religious services?" and "Many churches, synagogues, and other places of worship have special activities for teenagers, such as youth groups, Bible classes, or choir. In the past 12 months, how often did you attend such youth activities?"), (2) personal conservatism ("Do you agree or disagree that the sacred scriptures of your religion are the word of God and are completely without any mistakes?" and "Do you think of yourself as a born-again Christian?"), (3) personal devotion ("How often do you pray?" and "How important is religion to you?"), and (4) religious denomination (Miller & Gur, 2002). The results indicated a link between personal devotion and fewer sexual partners outside a romantic relationship. Frequent attendance at religious events was related to a greater perception of risk of contracting HIV or pregnancy from unprotected intercourse and a responsible and planned use of birth control. Personal conservativism was linked with unprotected sex. Another study similarly found links between religion and sexuality (Fehring & others, 1998). In college students, guilt, prayer, organized religious activity, and religious well-being were associated with fewer sexual encounters.

As we have seen, religion is a pervasive influence throughout the world. Next, we focus on cults, which in some cases have been described as fringe religions.

Cults

Cults have been defined in various ways, ranging from "dangerous institutions that cause severe emotional harm" to "marginal and deviant groups" to "fringe, often new, religious movements." Cults have been described as being controlled by a charismatic leader, as fostering the idea that there is only one correct set of beliefs and practices, as demanding unquestionable loyalty and obedience, as using mind-control techniques, as using deception and deceit in recruiting and interacting with the outside world, and as exploiting members' labor and finances (Galanter, 1999, 2000).

What is the difference between a cult and a church, a service club, or groups like Alcoholics Anonymous? There are many differences, but a major one involves the ultimate goal of the group (Cialdini & Rhoad, 1999). Established religions and altruistic movements focus outward, attempting to better the lives of members as well as nonmembers. Cults direct their energies inward rather than outward, serving their own purposes and those of the cult's leader. Religions and altruistic movements usually do not involve overbearing authoritarian control by a leader, the use of deception in recruiting members, coercive influence techniques, or the replacement of a recruit's identity with a new identity that would not have been freely chosen by the individual before joining the group.

Who joins cults? For the most part, normal, average people. Approximately two-thirds of cult members are psychologically healthy individuals who come from normal families (Cialdini & Rhoad, 1999). The remaining one-third often have depressive symptoms, in many cases linked with personal loss such as a death in the family, a failed romantic relationship, or career problems. Only about 5 percent of cult members have major psychological problems before joining the cult. Cults prefer intelligent, productive individuals who can contribute money and talent to "the cause," whatever that might be.

It is possible that timing rather than personality is the determining factor in vulnerability to cults. Many individuals who become cult members are in a transitional phase of life. They have moved to a new city, lost a job, dropped out of school, or given up traditional religion as personally irrelevant. Potential cult members might find their work boring or stressful, their education meaningless, their social life not going well, their family remote or dysfunctional, their friends too busy to spend time with them, or their trust in government lost. Cults promise to fulfill most of a person's individual needs and to make his or her life safe, healthy, caring, and predictable. Cult leaders offer followers simple or predictable paths to happiness.

Some cult leaders have total authority over their disciples in both spiritual and material matters (Saliba, 1996). These leaders might portray themselves as inspired by, and receiving special revelations from, God. Some cults are based on writings by a cult leader that are believed to be revealed or inspired, as in the case of the late L. Ron Hubbard, founder of the Church of Scientology.

One all-powerful cult leader was Marshall Herff Applewhite, who recruited followers to the Heaven's Gate cult, a blend of New Age occultism and science-fiction fantasy. In 1997, 39 cult members died when they swallowed pudding laced with barbiturates and washed it down with vodka. After swallowing the lethal concoction, they reclined on their beds so their spirits could ascend to the "Level Above Human," as Applewhite called it. He had convinced the followers that a UFO was in the Hale-Bopp comet's slipstream and that the comet's appearance was a sign that it was time to go home.

Clearly, any cult that persuades its disciples to kill themselves is very dangerous, but cults pose many other dangers, some less obvious to outsiders. Philip Zimbardo (1997) points out that the dangers posed depend to some degree on the kind of cult,

www.mhhe.com/santrocka10

Cults 101
Cults and Mind Control
Social Psychological Aspects of Cults
The Heaven's Gate Website
Why Do People Join Cults?

since they come in so many sizes, purposes, and disguises. At last count there were more than 2,500 cults in the United States. Some cults are in the business of power and money, needing members to give money, work for free, beg, and recruit new members. Some cults require members to turn over exorbitant amounts of money or property, some require exhausting labor. Most demand that members sever ties with former friends and family (which creates total dependence on the cult for one's identity), and many cults seek to destroy the individual's freedom of thought. The potential for abuse is highest in cults that are physically and socially isolated from the outside community.

Review and reflect Learning goal 3

3 Explain the roles of values, religion, and cults in adolescents' lives

REVIEW

- What are values? What are some of today's college students' values and how have they changed over the last several decades?
- How does religion develop in adolescents' lives? How are religion and sexuality linked in adolescence?
- What is a cult and how does it differ from a religion? Why are some adolescents attracted to cults? How do cults influence adolescents?

REFLECT

- What were your values and religious interest in middle school and high school? Have they changed since then? If so, how?

Reach Your Learning Goals

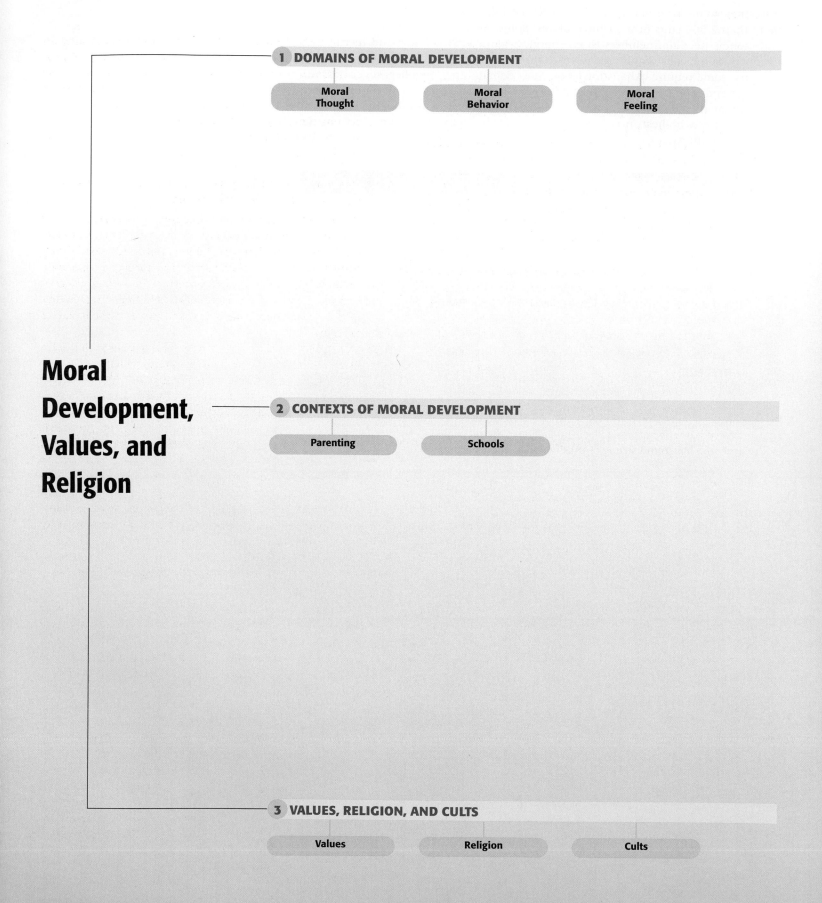

CHAPTER 8

Moral Development, Values, and Religion

1 DOMAINS OF MORAL DEVELOPMENT

- Moral Thought
- Moral Behavior
- Moral Feeling

2 CONTEXTS OF MORAL DEVELOPMENT

- Parenting
- Schools

3 VALUES, RELIGION, AND CULTS

- Values
- Religion
- Cults

Summary

1 Discuss theories and research on moral thought, behavior, and feeling

- Moral development involves thoughts, feelings, and behaviors regarding standards of right and wrong. Moral development consists of intrapersonal and interpersonal dimensions. Piaget distinguished between the heteronomous morality of younger children and the autonomous morality of older children. Formal operational thought might undergird changes in adolescents' moral reasoning. Hoffman proposed cognitive disequilibrium theory, which describes individuals as moving from a relatively homogeneous grade school to the more heterogeneous secondary school and college environments, where individuals often experience contradictions regarding their moral stance.

- Kohlberg developed a provocative theory of moral reasoning. He argued that moral development consists of three levels—preconventional, conventional, and postconventional—and six stages (two at each level). Increased internalization characterizes movement to levels 2 and 3. Influences on the stages include cognitive development, imitation and cognitive conflict, peer relations, and perspective taking. Kohlberg's critics say that he gave inadequate attention to moral behavior, did not adequately assess moral development, underestimated cultural influences, and underestimated the care perspective (Gilligan's theory). Recent research has found stronger links between gender-role classification and moral reasoning than between biological sex and moral reasoning. Distinctions are made between these social cognitive domains: (1) moral, (2) social-conventional, and (3) personal.

- Behaviorists argue that moral behavior is determined by the processes of reinforcement, punishment, and imitation. Situational variability in moral behavior is stressed by behaviorists. Hartshorne and May's classic study found considerable variation in moral behavior across situations. The social cognitive theory of moral development emphasizes a distinction between moral competence (the ability to produce moral behaviors) and moral performance (performing those behaviors in specific situations). Social cognitive theorists believe Kohlberg gave inadequate attention to moral behavior and situational variations. Prosocial behavior has especially been studied in the realm of altruism. Adolescents engage in more prosocial behavior than children, and adolescent girls engage in prosocial behavior more than adolescent boys.

- In Freud's theory, the superego—the moral branch of personality—is one of personality's three main structures. Freud also believed that through identification children internalize a parent's standards of right and wrong. Children may conform to moral standards in order to avoid guilt, in the Freudian view. The two main components of the superego are the ego ideal and conscience. Feeling empathy means reacting to another's feelings with an emotional response that is similar to that person's feelings. Empathy involves perspective taking as a cognitive component. Empathy changes developmentally. The contemporary perspective on emotions and moral development is that both positive feelings (such as empathy) and negative feelings (such as guilt) contribute to moral development. Emotions are interwoven with the cognitive and social dimensions of moral development.

2 Describe how the contexts of parenting and schools can influence moral development

- Discipline can involve love withdrawal, power assertion, or induction. Induction has been the most effective technique, especially with middle-SES children. Children's moral development is advanced when parents are warm and supportive rather than punitive, provide opportunities for their children to learn about others' perspectives and feelings, involve children in family decision making, and model moral behavior and thinking.

- The hidden curriculum concept was proposed by John Dewey to refer to the moral atmosphere of a school. Character education is a direct education approach that advocates teaching adolescents a basic moral literacy. Values clarification focuses on helping people clarify what is important to them, what is worth working for, and what purpose their lives are to serve. Cognitive moral education, based on Kohlberg's theory, stresses that adolescents should learn to value things like democracy and justice as their moral reasoning develops. Service learning is a form of education that promotes social responsibility and service to the community. Participation in service learning is linked with a number of positive aspects of adolescent development.

3 Explain the roles of values, religion, and cults in adolescents' lives

- Values are the beliefs and attitudes about the way things should be. Over the last two decades, adolescents have shown an increased concern for personal well-being and a decreased interest in the welfare of others. Recently, adolescents have shown an increased interest in community values and societal issues.

- Many children and adolescents show an interest in religion, and religious institutions are designed to introduce them to religious beliefs. Adolescence may be a special juncture in religious development for many individuals. Various aspects of religion are linked with positive outcomes in adolescent development. Erikson's ideas on identity can be applied to understanding the increased interest in religion during adolescence. Piaget's theory provides a theoretical foundation for understanding developmental changes in religion. Fowler proposed a six-stage, life-span developmental view of religion. When adolescents have a positive relationship with parents and/or are securely attached to them they often adopt their parents' religious beliefs. Links have been found between adolescent sexuality and religiousness.

- Cults have been defined in various ways, ranging from dangerous institutions to fringe, often new, religious move-

ments. Many people who join cults are in a transitional phase in their lives, and cults promise to fulfill their needs. The potential for the worst abuse is when a cult is physically and socially isolated from the outside community.

Key Terms

moral development 273
heteronomous morality 274
autonomous morality 274
immanent justice 274
cognitive disequilibrium
    theory 274
internalization 275

preconventional reasoning 275
conventional reasoning 276
postconventional reasoning 276
justice perspective 280
care perspective 280
social cognitive theory of
    moral development 283

altruism 284
forgiveness 284
ego ideal 285
conscience 285
empathy 286
love withdrawal 288
power assertion 288

induction 288
hidden curriculum 289
character education 289
values clarification 289
cognitive moral education 290
service learning 290
values 292

Key People

Jean Piaget 274
Martin Hoffman 274
Lawrence Kohlberg 275
James Rest 279

Richard Shweder 280
Carol Gilligan 280
Hugh Hartshorne and
    Mark May 283

Albert Bandura 283
Sigmund Freud 285
Erik Erikson 286
Nancy Eisenberg 288

John Dewey 289
James Fowler 295

Resources for Improving the Lives of Adolescents

Cults

(1999) by Marc Galanter
New York: Oxford University Press

This book explores many aspects of cults, including their social psychological characteristics.

Education in the Moral Domain

(2001) by Larry Nucci
New York: Cambridge University Press.

Larry Nucci, who has made important contributions to the field of moral development, provides concrete recommendations for creating a moral classroom climate.

Invitation to the Psychology of Religion

(2000, 3rd ed.) by Raymond Paloutzian
Needham Heights, MA: Allyn & Bacon

This book provides a broad overview of topics in the psychology of religion, including religious development, conversion, religious experience, attitudes and behavior, and mental health.

Meeting at the Crossroads

(1992) by Lyn Mikel Brown and Carol Gilligan
Cambridge, MA: Harvard University Press

This book provides a vivid portrayal of how adolescent girls are often ignored and misunderstood as they make their passage through adolescence.

Moral Development and Reality

(2003) by John Gibbs
Thousand Oaks, CA: Sage

Leading researcher John Gibbs provides an insightful, contemporary examination of many aspects of moral development, including treatment programs for antisocial youth.

National Helpers Network, Inc.

245 Fifth Avenue, Suite 1705
New York, NY 10016-8728
212–679–7461

This network developed the Early Adolescent Helper Program, an approach to service learning.

Service Learning

(1997) by Alan Waterman (Ed.)
Mahwah, NJ: Erlbaum

A number of leading experts discuss many aspects of service learning.

E-Learning Tools

To help you master the material in this chapter, you will find a number of valuable study tools on the student CD-ROM that accompanies this book. In addition, visit the Online Learning Center for *Adolescence, 10th Edition*, where you will find helpful resources for chapter 8, "Moral Development, Values, and Religion."

Taking It to the Net

http://www.mhhe.com/santrocka10

1. Young children do what they think is right and do not do what they think is wrong in order to avoid punishment. The reasons for doing "right" change as we grow into and through the adolescent years. As a future parent, what can you do to foster this aspect of moral development in your children?

2. You are discussing issues of right and wrong, punishment, and moral reasoning in your philosophy class. Your instructor has broken the class into groups, and your group is assigned to evaluate arguments, pro and con, concerning the death penalty and to classify them according to Kohlberg's stages of moral reasoning. What are some of the arguments pro and con and how did your group classify them?

3. The nature and content of sex education instruction in public schools often is a lightning rod, attracting large numbers of parents to school board meetings. In trying to explain why, your adolescent psychology professor mentions issues of moral education, the hidden curriculum, and character education. How do these concerns relate to the large parental turnout at school board meetings?

Connect to **http://www.mhhe.com/santrocka10** to research the answers and complete these exercises. In some cases, you'll also find further instructions on this site.

Self-Assessment

To evaluate yourself in regard to your values and religion, complete the self-assessment: My Spiritual Well-Being.

Health and Well-Being, Parenting, and Education

To practice your decision-making skills, complete the health and well-being, parenting, and education scenarios.

The Contexts of Adolescent Development

Man is a knot, a web, a mesh into which relationships are tied.
—ANTOINE DE SAINT-EXUPERY
French Novelist and Aviator, 20th Century

Adolescent development takes place in social contexts, which provide the setting and sociohistorical, cultural backdrop for physical, cognitive, and socioemotional growth. This fourth section consists of five chapters: chapter 9, "Families"; chapter 10, "Peers"; chapter 11, "Schools"; chapter 12, "Achievement, Careers, and Work"; and chapter 13, "Culture."

It is not enough for parents to understand children. They must accord children the privilege of understanding them.
—MILTON SAPERSTEIN
American Author, 20th Century

Families

Chapter Outline		*Learning Goals*
FAMILY PROCESSES	**1**	Discuss the nature of family processes in adolescence
Reciprocal Socialization and the Family as a System		
The Developmental Construction of Relationships		
Maturation		
Sociocultural and Historical Changes		
PARENT-ADOLESCENT RELATIONSHIPS	**2**	Describe parent-adolescent relationships
Parents as Managers		
Parenting Styles		
Gender, Parenting, and Coparenting		
Parent-Adolescent Conflict		
Autonomy and Attachment		
SIBLING RELATIONSHIPS	**3**	Characterize sibling relationships in adolescence
Sibling Roles		
Developmental Changes		
Birth Order		
THE CHANGING FAMILY IN A CHANGING SOCIETY	**4**	Describe the changing family in a changing society
Divorced Families		
Stepfamilies		
Working Parents		
Gay and Lesbian Parents		
Culture and Ethnicity		
SOCIAL POLICY, ADOLESCENTS, AND FAMILIES	**5**	Explain what is needed for improved social policy involving adolescents and their families

Images of Adolescent Development

Variations in Adolescents' Perceptions of Parents

My mother and I depend on each other. However, if something separated us, I think I could still get along O.K. I know that my mother continues to have an important influence on me. Sometimes she gets on my nerves, but I still basically like her, and respect her, a lot. We have our arguments, and I don't always get my way, but she is willing to listen to me.

—Amy, age 16

You go from a point at which your parents are responsible for you to a point at which you want a lot more independence. Finally, you are more independent, and you feel like you have to be more responsible for yourself; otherwise you are not going to do very well in this world. It's important for parents to still be there to support you, but at some point, you've got to look in the mirror and say, "I can do it myself."

—John, age 18

I don't get along very well with my parents. They try to dictate how I dress, who I date, how much I study, what I do on weekends, and how much time I spend talking on the phone. They are big intruders in my life. Why won't they let me make my own decisions? I'm mature enough to handle these things. When they jump down my throat at every little thing I do, it makes me mad and I say things to them I probably shouldn't. They just don't understand me very well.

—Ed, age 17

My father never seems to have any time to spend with me. He is gone a lot on business, and when he comes home, he is either too tired to do anything or plops down and watches TV and doesn't want to be bothered. He thinks I don't work hard enough and don't have values that were as solid as his generation. It is a very distant relationship. I actually spend more time talking to my mom than to him. I guess I should work a little harder in school than I do, but I still don't think he has the right to say such negative things to me. I like my mom a lot better because I think she is a much nicer person.

—Tom, age 14

We have our arguments and our differences, and there are moments when I get very angry with my parents, but most of the time they are like heated discussions. I have to say what I think because I don't think they are always right. Most of the time when there is an argument, we can discuss the problem and eventually find a course that we all can live with. Not every time, though, because there are some occasions when things just remain unresolved. Even when we have an unresolved conflict, I still would have to say that I get along pretty good with my parents.

—Ann, age 16

Although parent-adolescent relationships can vary considerably, researchers are finding that for the most part, the relationships are both (1) very important aspects of development, and (2) more positive than once believed. This chapter examines families as a context for adolescent development. We will begin by exploring family processes, then discuss parent-adolescent relationships followed by sibling relationships. Next, an exploration of the changes experienced by families in today's changing society precedes a discussion of social policy recommendations for the well-being of adolescents and their families.

1 FAMILY PROCESSES

- Reciprocal Socialization and the Family as a System
- Maturation
- The Developmental Construction of Relationships
- Sociocultural and Historical Changes

We begin our exploration of family processes by focusing on how family members interact with one another.

Reciprocal Socialization and the Family as a System

For many years, socialization between parents and children/adolescents was considered to be a one-way process: Children and adolescents were seen as the products of their parents' socialization techniques. As we see next, however, today parent-adolescent interaction is viewed as a reciprocal process.

Reciprocal Socialization **Reciprocal socialization** is the process by which children and adolescents socialize parents just as parents socialize them (Patterson & Fisher, 2002). To get a better feel for how reciprocal socialization works, consider two situations: the first emphasizing the impact of growing up in a single-parent home (parental influences), the second presenting the dilemma of a talented teenage ice skater (adolescent influences). In the first situation, the speaker is 14-year-old Robert:

> I never have seen my father. He never married my mother, and she had to quit school to help support us. Maybe my mother and I are better off that he didn't marry her because he apparently didn't love her . . . but sometimes I get very depressed about not having a father, especially when I see a lot of my friends with their fathers at ball games and such. My father still lives around here, but he has gotten married, and I guess he wants to forget about me and my mother. . . . A lot of times I wish my mother would get married and I could at least have a stepfather to talk with about things and do things with me.

In the second situation, the first speaker is 13-year-old Kathy:

> "Mother, my skating coach says that I have a lot of talent, but it is going to take a lot of lessons and travel to fully develop it." Her mother responds, "Kathy, I just don't know. We will have to talk with your father about it tonight when he gets home from work." That evening, Kathy's father tells his wife, "Look, to do that for Kathy, I will have to get a second job, or you will have to get a job. There is no way we can afford what she wants with what I make."

reciprocal socialization The process by which children and adolescents socialize parents, just as parents socialize them.

As developmentalists probe the nature of reciprocal socialization, they are impressed with the importance of synchrony in parent-child and parent-adolescent relationships. **Synchrony** refers to the carefully coordinated interaction between the parent and the child or adolescent, in which, often unknowingly, they are attuned to each other's behavior. The turn-taking that occurs in parent-adolescent negotiation reflects the reciprocal, synchronous nature of parent-adolescent relationships. The interactions of parents and adolescents in synchronous relationships can be conceptualized as a dance or a dialogue in which successive actions of the partners are closely coordinated. This coordinated dance or dialogue can assume the form of mutual synchrony (each individual's behavior depends on the partner's previous behavior), or it can be reciprocal in a more precise sense: The actions of the partners can be matched, as when one partner imitates the other or there is mutual smiling.

Family as a System   As a social system, the family can be thought of as a constellation of subsystems defined in terms of generation, gender, and role. Divisions of labor among family members define particular subunits, and attachments define others. Each family member is a participant in several subsystems—some dyadic (involving two people), some polyadic (involving more than two people) (Minuchin, 2002). The father and adolescent represent one dyadic subsystem, the mother and father another; the mother-father-adolescent represent one polyadic subsystem, the mother and two siblings another (Piotrowski, 1997).

An organizational scheme that highlights the reciprocal influences of family members and family subsystems is shown in figure 9.1 (Belsky, 1981). As the arrows in the figure show, marital relations, parenting, and adolescent behavior can have both direct and indirect effects on each other. An example of a direct effect is the influence of the parent's behavior on the adolescent. An example of an indirect effect is how the relationship between the spouses mediates the way a parent acts toward the adolescent (Emery & Tuer, 1993). For example, marital conflict might reduce the efficiency of parenting, in which case marital conflict would have an indirect effect on the adolescent's behavior (Wilson & Gottman, 1995).

Interaction between individuals in a family can change, depending on who is present. In one investigation, 44 adolescents were observed either separately with their mother and father (dyadic settings) or in the presence of both parents (triadic setting) (Gjerde, 1986). The presence of the father improved mother-son relationships, but the presence of the mother decreased the quality of father-son relations. This may have occurred because the father takes the strain off the mother by controlling the adolescent, or because the mother's presence reduces father-son interaction, which may not be high in many instances. Indeed, in one recent investigation, sons directed more negative behavior toward their mothers than toward their fathers in dyadic situations (Buhrmester & others, in press). However, in a triadic context of adolescent-mother-father, fathers helped "rescue" mothers by attempting to control the sons' negative behavior. In one recent study that focused on adolescents in middle-socioeconomic-status African American families, both mothers' and fathers' communication was more positive in dyadic than triadic interactions (Smetana, Abernethy, & Harris, 2000).

Marital Relationships and Parenting   As researchers have broadened their focus in families beyond just studying the parent-adolescent relationship, an increasingly studied aspect of the family system involves the link between marital relationships and parenting. The most consistent findings are that happily married parents are more sensitive, responsive, warm, and affectionate toward their children and adolescents (Grych, 2002). Researchers have also found that marital satisfaction is often related to good parenting. The marital relationship is an important support for parenting. When parents report more intimacy and better communication in their marriage, they are more affectionate to their children and adolescents (Grych, 2002). Thus, an important, if unintended, benefit of marriage enhancement programs is the improvement of

synchrony The carefully coordinated interaction between the parent and the child or adolescent in which, often unknowingly, they are attuned to each other's behavior.

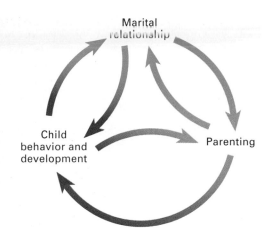

FIGURE 9.1 Interaction Between Adolescents and Their Parents: Direct and Indirect Effects

parenting, and consequently healthier children and adolescents. Programs that focus on parenting skills might also benefit from including attention to the participants' marriages.

The Developmental Construction of Relationships

Developmentalists have shown an increased interest in understanding how we construct relationships as we grow up (Collins & Madsen, 2002). Psychoanalytic theorists have always been interested in how this process works in families. However, the current explanations of how relationships are constructed is virtually stripped of Freud's psychosexual stage terminology and also is not always confined to the first five years of life, as has been the case in classical psychoanalytic theory. Today's **developmental construction** views share the belief that as individuals grow up, they acquire modes of relating to others. There are two main variations within this view, one of which emphasizes continuity and stability in relationships throughout the life span; the other emphasizes discontinuity and change in relationships throughout the life span (Conger, Lorenz, & Wickrama, 2004; Scarmella & Conger, 2004).

The Continuity View   The **continuity view** emphasizes the role that early parent-child relationships play in constructing a basic way of relating to people throughout the life span. These early parent-child relationships are carried forward to later points in development to influence all subsequent relationships (with peers, with friends, with teachers, and with romantic partners, for example) (Ainsworth, 1979; Bowlby, 1989; Sroufe, 2002). In its extreme form, this view states that the basic components of social relationships are laid down and shaped by the security or insecurity of parent-infant attachment relationships in the first year or two of the infant's life. More about the importance of secure attachment in the adolescent's development appears later in the chapter when we discuss autonomy and attachment.

Close relationships with parents also are important in the adolescent's development because these relationships function as models or templates that are carried forward over time to influence the construction of new relationships. Clearly, close relationships do not repeat themselves in an endless fashion over the course of the child's and adolescent's development. And the quality of any relationship depends to some degree on the specific individual with whom the relationship is formed. However, the nature of earlier relationships that are developed over many years often can be detected in later relationships, both with those same individuals and in the formation of relationships with others at a later point in time (Gjerde, Block, & Block,

developmental construction views Views sharing the belief that as individuals grow up, they acquire modes of relating to others. There are two main variations of this view. One emphasizes continuity and stability in relationships throughout the life span; the other emphasizes discontinuity and changes in relationships throughout the life span.

continuity view A developmental view that emphasizes the role of early parent-child relationships in constructing a basic way of relating to people throughout the life span.

To what extent is an adolescent's development likely to be influenced by early experiences with parents?

1991). Thus, the nature of parent-adolescent relationships does not depend only on what happens in the relationship during adolescence. Relationships with parents over the long course of childhood are carried forward to influence, at least to some degree, the nature of parent-adolescent relationships. And the long course of parent-child relationships also could be expected to influence, again at least to some degree, the fabric of the adolescent's peer relationships, friendships, and dating relationships.

In the research of Alan Sroufe and his colleagues, evidence for continuity is being found (Sroufe, 2002; Sroufe, Egeland, & Carson, 1999). Attachment history and early care were related to peer competence in adolescence, up to 15 years after the infant assessments. In interviews with adolescents, those who formed couple relationships during camp retreats had been securely attached in infancy. Also, ratings of videotaped behavior revealed that those with secure attachment histories were more socially competent, which included having confidence in social situations and showing leadership skills. For most children, there was a cascading effect in which early family relationships provided the necessary support for effectively engaging in the peer world, which in turn provided the foundation for more extensive, complex peer relationships.

How childhood experiences with parents are carried forward and influence the nature of the adolescent's development is important, but the nature of intergenerational relationships is significant as well. As the life-span perspective has taken on greater acceptance among developmental psychologists, researchers have become interested in the transmission of close relationships across generations (Elder, 2000; Kandel & Wu, 1995).

The middle generation in three generations is especially important in the socialization process. For example, the parents of adolescents can be studied in terms of their relationships with their own parents, when they were children and currently, and in terms of their relationships with their own adolescents, both when the adolescents were children and currently. Life-span theorists point out that the middle-aged parents of adolescents may have to give more help than they receive. Their adolescents probably are reaching the point where they need considerable financial support for education, and their aging parents, whose generation is living longer than past generations, may also require financial support, as well as more comfort and affection than earlier in the life span.

The Discontinuity View   The **discontinuity view** emphasizes change and growth in relationships over time. As people grow up, they develop many different types of relationships (with parents, peers, teachers, and romantic partners, for example). Each of these relationships is structurally different. With each new type of relationship, individuals encounter new modes of relating (Buhrmester & Furman, 1987; Furman & Wehner, 1997; Piaget, 1932; Sullivan, 1953; Youniss, 1980). For example, Piaget (1932) argued that parent-child relationships are strikingly different from children's peer relationships. Parent-child relationships, he said, are more likely to consist of parents having unilateral authority over children. By contrast, peer relationships are more likely to consist of participants who relate to each other on a much more equal basis. In parent-child relationships, since parents have greater knowledge and authority, children often must learn how to conform to rules and regulations laid down by parents. In this view, we use the parental-child mode when relating to authority figures (such as with teachers and experts) and when we act as authority figures (by becoming parents, teachers, and experts).

In contrast, relationships with peers have a different structure and require a different mode of relating to others. This more egalitarian mode is later called upon in relationships with romantic partners, friends, and co-workers. Because two peers possess relatively equal knowledge and authority (their relationship is reciprocal and symmetrical), children learn a democratic mode of relating that is based on mutual influence. With peers, children learn to formulate and assert their own opinions, appreciate the perspective of peers, cooperatively negotiate solutions to disagreements, and evolve standards for conduct that are mutually acceptable. Because peer relationships are voluntary (rather than obligatory, as in the family), children and adolescents who fail to become skillful in the symmetrical, mutual, egalitarian, reciprocal mode of relating have difficulty being accepted by peers.

Although the discontinuity view does not deny that prior close relationships (such as with parents) are carried forward to influence later relationships, it does stress that each new type of relationship that children and adolescents encounter (such as with peers, with friends, and with romantic partners) requires the construction of different and even more sophisticated modes of relating to others. Further, in the change/growth version, each period of development uniquely contributes to the construction of relationship knowledge; development across the life span is not solely determined by a sensitive or critical period during infancy.

Evidence for the discontinuity view of relationships was found in the longitudinal study conducted by Andrew Collins and his colleagues (Collins, Hennighausen, & Sroufe, 1998). Quality of friendship interaction (based on observations of coordinated behavior, such as turn-taking, sharing, eye contact, and touching, and their duration) in middle childhood was related to security with dating, and disclosure and intimacy with a dating partner, at age 16.

Maturation

Nineteenth- and twentieth-century American author Mark Twain once remarked that when he was 14 his father was so ignorant he could hardly stand to have the man around him, but when Mark got to be 21, he was astonished at how much his father had learned in those seven years! Mark Twain's comments suggest that maturation is an important theme of parent-adolescent relationships. Adolescents change as they make the transition from childhood to adulthood, but their parents also change during their adult years (Grotevant, 1998).

Adolescent Changes   Among the changes in the adolescent that can influence parent-adolescent relationships are puberty, expanded logical reasoning, increased idealistic thought, violated expectations, changes in schooling, peers, friendships, dating, and movement toward independence. Several investigations have shown that conflict between parents and adolescents, especially between mothers and sons, is the most

discontinuity view A developmental view that emphasizes change and growth in relationships over time.

stressful during the apex of pubertal growth (Steinberg, 1988). For example, mothers were less satisfied with their sons' participation in family activities during the apex of pubertal growth (Hill & others, 1985). Further, early-maturing sons and daughters experience more conflict with parents than adolescents who mature on time, presumably because parents don't agree with their adolescents that physical maturation is a sufficient reason for granting more autonomy (Collins & Laursen, 2004).

In terms of cognitive changes, the adolescent can now reason in more logical ways with parents than in childhood. During childhood, parents may be able to get by with saying, "O.K. That is it. We do it my way or else," and the child conforms. But with increased cognitive skills, adolescents no longer are likely to accept such a statement as a reason for conforming to parental dictates. Adolescents want to know, often in fine detail, why they are being disciplined. Even when parents give what seem to be logical reasons for discipline, adolescents' cognitive sophistication may call attention to deficiencies in the reasoning.

In addition, the adolescent's increasing idealistic thought comes into play in parent-adolescent relationships. Parents are now evaluated vis-à-vis what an ideal parent is like. The very real interactions with parents, which inevitably involve some negative interchanges and flaws, are placed next to the adolescent's schema of an ideal parent. And, as part of their egocentrism, adolescents' concerns with how others view them are likely to produce overreactions to parents' comments. A mother may comment to her adolescent daughter that she needs a new blouse. The daughter might respond, "What's the matter? You don't think I have good taste? You think I look gross, don't you? Well, you are the one who is gross!" The same comment made to the daughter several years earlier in late childhood probably would have elicited a less intense response.

Another dimension of the adolescent's changing cognitive world related to parent-adolescent relations is the expectations parents and adolescents have for each other (Collins & Laursen, 2004; Collins & Luebker, 1994; Zimmer-Gembeck & Collins, 2003). Preadolescent children are often compliant and easy to manage. As they enter puberty, children begin to question or seek rationales for parental demands (Maccoby, 1984). Parents might perceive this behavior as resistant and oppositional because it departs from the child's previously compliant behavior. Parents often respond to the lack of compliance with increased pressure for compliance. In this situation, expectations that were stabilized during a period of relatively slow developmental change are lagging behind the behavior of the adolescent in the period of rapid pubertal change.

What dimensions of the adolescent's social world contribute to parent-adolescent relationships? Adolescence brings with it new definitions of socially appropriate behavior. In our society, these definitions are associated with changes in schooling. As they make the transition to middle or junior high school, adolescents are required to function in a more anonymous, larger environment with multiple and varying teachers. More work is required, and students must show more initiative and responsibility to adapt successfully. The school is not the only social arena that contributes to parent-adolescent relationships. Adolescents spend more time with peers than when they were children, and they develop more sophisticated friendships than in childhood. Adolescents also begin to push more strongly for independence. In sum, parents are called on to adapt to the changing world of the adolescent's schooling, peer relations, and push for autonomy (Grotevant, 1998).

Parental Changes   Parental changes that contribute to parent-adolescent relationships involve marital satisfaction, economic burdens, career reevaluation and time perspective, and health and body concerns (Collins & Laursen, 2004; MacDermid & Crouter, 1995; Silverberg & Steinberg, 1990). A longitudinal study of almost 7,000 spouses found that marital dissatisfaction was greater when the offspring was an adolescent than when the offspring was a child or an adult (Benin, 1997). In addition,

Expectancy violations on the part of parents and adolescents are especially likely during the transition to adolescence.

—W. Andrew Collins
Contemporary Psychologist,
University of Minnesota

Parents' and Adolescents' Expectations

parents feel a greater economic burden during the rearing of adolescents. During this time, parents may reevaluate their occupational achievement, deciding whether they have met their youthful aspirations of success (Collins & Laursen, 2004). They may look to the future and think about how much time they have remaining to accomplish their life goals. Adolescents, meanwhile, look to the future with unbounded optimism, sensing that they have an unlimited amount of time to accomplish what they desire. Parents of adolescents may become preoccupied with concerns about their own health, body integrity, and sexual attractiveness. Even when their body and sexual attractiveness are not deteriorating, many parents of adolescents perceive that they are. By contrast, adolescents have reached or are beginning to reach the peak of their physical attractiveness, strength, and health. Although both adolescents and their parents show a heightened preoccupation with their bodies, adolescents' outcome probably is more positive.

In one study of middle-aged parents and their adolescents, the relation between parents' midlife concerns and their adolescents' pubertal development could not be characterized simply as positive, negative, or nil (MacDermid & Crouter, 1995). Parents reported less intense midlife concerns when their adolescents were further along in puberty. Spousal support in midlife emerged as an important factor in helping parents meet the challenges of pubertal changes in their adolescents.

The changes in adolescents' parents we have just described are typical of development in middle adulthood. Most adolescents' parents either are in middle adulthood or are rapidly approaching this period of life. However, in the last two decades, the timing of parenthood in the United States has undergone some dramatic shifts (Parke, 2001, 2002; Parke & Buriel, 1998). Parenthood is taking place earlier for some, and later for others, than in previous decades. First, the number of adolescent pregnancies substantially increased during the 1980s. Second, the number of women who postpone childbearing until their thirties and early forties simultaneously increased. We discussed adolescents as parents in chapter 7, "Sexuality." Here we focus on sociohistorical changes related to postponement of childbearing until the thirties or forties.

There are many contrasts between becoming a parent in adolescence and becoming a parent 15 to 30 years later. Delayed childbearing allows for considerable progress in occupational and educational domains. For both males and females, education usually has been completed, and career development is well established.

The marital relationship varies with the timing of parenthood onset. In one investigation, couples who began childbearing in their early twenties were compared with those who began in their early thirties (Walter, 1986). The late-starting couples had more egalitarian relationships, with men participating in child care and household tasks more often.

Is parent-child interaction different for families in which parents delay having children until their thirties or forties? Investigators have found that older fathers are warmer, communicate better, encourage more achievement, place fewer demands on their children, are more lax in enforcing rules, and show less rejection with their children than younger fathers. However, older fathers also are less likely to engage in physical play or sports with their children (MacDonald, 1987). These findings suggest that sociohistorical changes are resulting in different developmental trajectories for many families, trajectories that involve changes in the way marital partners and parents and adolescents interact.

> *The generations of living things pass in a short time, and like runners hand on the torch of life.*
>
> —LUCRETIUS
> *Roman Poet, 1st Century B.C.*

Parenting Adolescents

Sociocultural and Historical Changes

Family development does not occur in a social vacuum. Important sociocultural and historical influences affect family processes (Day, 2002; Goldscheider, 1997; McHale & Grolnick, 2001). Family changes might be due to great upheavals in a nation, such as war, famine, or mass immigration. The Great Depression in the early 1930s had some negative effects on families. During its height, the depression produced economic deprivation, adult discontent, depression about living conditions, marital conflict, inconsistent child rearing, and unhealthy lifestyles—heavy drinking, demoralized attitudes, and health disabilities—especially in the father (Elder, 1998). But family changes can also be due to less dramatic transitions in society. Subtle changes in a culture that have significant influences on the family were described by the famous anthropologist Margaret Mead (1978). The changes Mead observed focus on the longevity of the older adults and the role of older adults in the family, the urban and suburban orientation of families and their mobility, the advent of television, and a general sense of dissatisfaction and restlessness.

Fifty years ago, the older people who survived were usually hearty and still closely linked to the family, often helping to maintain the family's existence. Today, older people live longer, which means that their middle-aged children are often pressed to decide whether to assume a caretaking role for their parents or to place an older parent in a nursing home. Many older parents have lost some of their socializing role in the family during the twentieth century as their children moved great distances away.

In the middle of the twentieth century, many of these family moves were away from farms and small towns to urban and suburban settings. In the small towns and farms, individuals were surrounded by lifelong neighbors, relatives, and friends. Today, neighborhood and extended-family support systems are not nearly as prevalent. Families now move all over the country, often uprooting adolescents from school and peer groups they have known for a considerable length of time. And for many families, this type of move occurs every few years, as one or both parents are transferred from job to job.

Television and computers also play a major role in the changing family. Many children who watch television and work or play on computers find that parents are too busy working to share this experience with them. Children thus increasingly experience a world their parents are not a part of. Instead of participating in neighborhood peer groups, children come home after school and plop down in front of the television set or a computer screen. These electronic devices allow children and their families to see new ways of life. Lower-SES families can look into the family lives of higher-SES families by simply pushing a button or surfing the Internet.

Another dramatic change in families is the increasing number of adolescents who grow up in a hodgepodge of family structures, with far greater numbers of single-parent and stepparent families than ever before in history (Hetherington & Kelly, 2002). Later in the chapter, we discuss such aspects of the changing social world of the adolescent and the family in greater detail.

Review and reflect Learning goal 1

1 **Discuss the nature of family processes in adolescence**

REVIEW
- What is reciprocal socialization? How can the family be described as a system?
- How does the developmental construction of relationships take place?
- What roles do maturation of the adolescent and maturation of parents play in understanding parent-adolescent relationships?
- What sociocultural and historical changes characterize the families of adolescents?

REFLECT
- What do you predict will be some major changes in the families of adolescents in the twenty-first century?

2 PARENT-ADOLESCENT RELATIONSHIPS

Parents as Managers	**Gender, Parenting, and Coparenting**	**Autonomy and Attachment**
	Parenting Styles	**Parent-Adolescent Conflict**

We have seen how the expectations of adolescents and their parents often seem violated as adolescents change dramatically during the course of puberty. Many parents see their child changing from a compliant being into someone who is noncompliant, oppositional, and resistant to parental standards. Parents often clamp down and put more pressure on the adolescent to conform to parental standards. Many parents often deal with the young adolescent as if they expect him or her to become a mature being within the next 10 to 15 minutes. But the transition from childhood to adulthood is a long journey with many hills and valleys. Adolescents are not going to conform to adult standards immediately. Parents who recognize that adolescents take a long time "to get it right" usually deal more competently and calmly with adolescent transgressions than do parents who demand immediate conformity to parental standards. Yet other parents, rather than placing heavy demands on their adolescents for compliance, do virtually the opposite, letting them do as they please in a very permissive manner.

As we discuss parent-adolescent relationships, we will discover that neither high-intensity demands for compliance nor an unwillingness to monitor and be involved in the adolescent's development is likely to be a wise parenting strategy. Further, we will explore another misperception that parents of adolescents sometimes entertain. Parents may perceive that virtually all conflict with their adolescent is bad. We will discover that a moderate degree of conflict with parents in adolescence is not only inevitable but may also serve a positive developmental function.

Parents as Managers

Parents can play important roles as managers of adolescents' opportunities, as monitors of adolescents' social relationships, and as social initiators and arrangers (Parke & Buriel, 1998). An important developmental task in adolescence is to develop the ability to make competent decisions in an increasingly independent manner (Mortimer & Larson, 2002). To help adolescents reach their full potential, an important parental role is to be an effective manager, one who finds information, makes contacts, helps structure choices, and provides guidance (Youniss & Ruth, 2002). Parents who fulfill this important managerial role help adolescents to avoid pitfalls and to work their way through a myriad of choices and decisions they face (Furstenberg & others, 1999).

Parents can serve as regulators of opportunities for their adolescents' social contact with peers, friends, and adults. From infancy through adolescence, mothers are more likely than fathers to have a managerial role in parenting. In infancy, this might involve taking a child to a doctor and arranging for child care; in early childhood, it might involve a decision about which preschool the child should attend; in middle and late childhood, it might include directing the child to take a bath, to match their clothes and wear clean clothes, and to put away toys; in adolescence, it could involve

Through the Eyes of Adolescents

Needing Parents as Guides

Stacey Christensen, age 16: "I am lucky enough to have open communication with my parents. Whenever I am in need or just need to talk, my parents are there for me. My advice to parents is to let your teens grow at their own pace, be open with them so that you can be there for them. We need guidance; our parents need to help but not be too overwhelming."

Stacey Christensen

authoritarian parenting This is a restrictive, punitive style in which the parent exhorts the adolescent to follow the parent's directions and to respect work and effort. Firm limits and controls are placed on the adolescent, and little verbal exchange is allowed. This style is associated with adolescents' socially incompetent behavior.

authoritative parenting This style encourages adolescents to be independent but still places limits and controls on their actions. Extensive verbal give-and-take is allowed, and parents are warm and nurturant toward the adolescent. This style is associated with adolescents' socially competent behavior.

neglectful parenting A style in which the parent is very uninvolved in the adolescent's life. It is associated with adolescents' social incompetence, especially a lack of self-control.

participating in a parent-teacher conference and subsequently managing the adolescent's homework activity.

A key aspect of the managerial role of parenting is effective monitoring of the adolescent. This is especially important as children move into the adolescent years. Monitoring includes supervising an adolescent's choice of social settings, activities, and friends. As we will see in chapter 14, "Adolescent Problems," a lack of adequate parental monitoring is the parental factor that is related to juvenile delinquency more than any other (Patterson & Stouthamer-Loeber, 1984).

Parenting Styles

Parents want their adolescents to grow into socially mature individuals, and they often feel a great deal of frustration in their role as parents. Psychologists have long searched for parenting ingredients that promote competent social development in adolescents. For example, in the 1930s, behaviorist John Watson urged parents not to be too affectionate with their children. Early research focused on a distinction between physical and psychological discipline, or between controlling and permissive parenting. More recently, there has been greater precision in unraveling the dimensions of competent parenting.

Especially widespread is the view of Diana Baumrind (1971, 1991), who believes that parents should be neither punitive nor aloof from their adolescents, but rather should develop rules and be affectionate with them. She emphasizes four styles of parenting that are associated with different aspects of the adolescent's social behavior: authoritarian, authoritative, neglectful, and indulgent:

- **Authoritarian parenting** is a restrictive, punitive style in which the parent exhorts the adolescent to follow directions and to respect work and effort. The authoritarian parent places firm limits and controls on the adolescent and allows little verbal exchange. For example, an authoritarian parent might say, "You do it my way or else. There will be no discussion!" Authoritarian parenting is associated with adolescents' socially incompetent behavior. Adolescents of authoritarian parents often are anxious about social comparison, fail to initiate activity, and have poor communication skills.

- **Authoritative parenting** encourages adolescents to be independent but still places limits and controls on their actions. Extensive verbal give-and-take is allowed, and parents are warm and nurturant toward the adolescent. An authoritative father, for example, might put his arm around the adolescent in a comforting way and say, "You know you should not have done that. Let's talk about how you can handle the situation better next time." Authoritative parenting is associated with adolescents' socially competent behavior. The adolescents of authoritative parents are self-reliant and socially responsible.

- **Neglectful parenting** is a style in which the parent is very uninvolved in the adolescent's life. The neglectful parent cannot answer the question, "It is 10:00 P.M. Do you know where your adolescent is?" Neglectful parenting is associated with adolescents' socially incompetent behavior, especially a lack of self-control. Adolescents have a strong need for their parents to care about them; adolescents whose parents are neglectful develop the sense that other aspects of the parents' lives are more important than they are. Adolescents whose parents are neglectful are socially incompetent: They show poor self-control and do not handle independence well.

© Michael Fry. Reprinted with permission.

Closely related to the concept of neglectful parenting is a lack of parental monitoring. In one recent study, parental monitoring of adolescents was linked with higher grades, lower sexual activity, and less depression in adolescents (Jacobson & Crockett, 2000).

- **Indulgent parenting** is a style in which parents are highly involved with their adolescents but place few demands or controls on them. Indulgent parents allow their adolescents to do what they want, and the result is that the adolescents never learn to control their own behavior and always expect to get their way. Some parents deliberately rear their adolescents in this way because they mistakenly believe that the combination of warm involvement with few restraints will produce a creative, confident adolescent. Indulgent parenting is associated with adolescents' social incompetence, especially a lack of self-control. In one family with indulgent parents, the 14-year-old son moved his parents out of their master bedroom suite and claimed it—along with their expensive stereo system and color television—as his. The boy is an excellent tennis player but behaves in the manner of John McEnroe in his younger days, raving and ranting around the tennis court. He has few friends, is self-indulgent, and has never learned to abide by rules and regulations. Why should he? His parents never made him follow any.

In our discussion of parenting styles, we have talked about parents who vary along the dimensions of acceptance, responsiveness, demand, and control. As shown in figure 9.2 , the four parenting styles—authoritarian, authoritative, neglectful, and indulgent—can be described in terms of these dimensions (Maccoby & Martin, 1983).

In one investigation, Diana Baumrind (1991) analyzed parenting styles and social competence in adolescence. The comprehensive assessment involved observations and interviews with 139 boys and girls 14 years of age and their parents. More than any other factor, the responsiveness (considerateness and supportiveness, for example) of the parents was related to the adolescents' social competence. And when parents had problem behaviors themselves (alcohol problems and marital conflict, for example), adolescents were more likely to have problems and show decreased social competence. Other researchers continue to find support for the belief that authoritarian and permissive parenting are less effective strategies than authoritative parenting (Durbin & others, 1993).

Why is authoritative parenting likely to be the most effective style? These reasons have been given (Steinberg & Silk, 2002): (1) Authoritative parents establish an appropriate balance between control and autonomy, giving adolescents opportunities to develop independence while providing the standards, limits, and guidance that adolescents need (Rueter & Conger, 1995). (2) Authoritative parents are more likely to

indulgent parenting A style in which parents are highly involved with their adolescents but place few demands or controls on them. This is associated with adolescents' social incompetence, especially a lack of self-control.

Accepting, responsive, child-centered	Rejecting, unresponsive, parent-centered
Demanding, controlling Authoritative reciprocal, high in bidirectional communication	Authoritarian, power assertive
Undemanding, low in control attempts Indulgent	Neglectful, ignoring, indifferent, uninvolved

FIGURE 9.2 A Fourfold Scheme of Parenting Styles

*I*t is clear that most American children suffer too . . . little father.

—GLORIA STEINEM
American Feminist and Author, 20th Century

engage adolescents in verbal give-and-take and allow adolescents to express their views (Kuczynski & Lollis, 2002). This type of family discussion is likely to help adolescents to understand social relationships and what is required for being a socially competent person. (3) The warmth and parental involvement provided by authoritative parents make the adolescent more receptive to parental influence (Sim, 2000).

Do the benefits of authoritative parenting transcend the boundaries of ethnicity, socioeconomic status, and household composition? Although occasional exceptions to patterns have been found, the evidence linking authoritative parenting with competence on the part of the adolescent has been found in research across a wide range of ethnic groups, social strata, cultures, and family structures (Steinberg & Silk, 2002).

Several caveats about parenting styles are in order. First, the parenting styles do not capture the important themes of reciprocal socialization and synchrony (Collins & Laursen, 2004). Keep in mind that adolescents socialize parents, just as parents socialize adolescents. Second, many parents use a combination of techniques rather than a single technique, although one technique may be dominant. Although consistent parenting is usually recommended, the wise parent may sense the importance of being more permissive in certain situations, more authoritarian in others, and yet more authoritative in others.

Gender, Parenting, and Coparenting

What is the mother's role in the family? The father's role? What is coparenting and how effective is it?

The Mother's Role   What do you think of when you hear the word *motherhood?* If you are like most people, you associate motherhood with a number of positive qualities, such as being warm, selfless, dutiful, and tolerant (Matlin, 1993). And while most women expect that motherhood will be happy and fulfilling, the reality is that motherhood has been accorded relatively low prestige in our society. When stacked up against money, power, and achievement, motherhood unfortunately doesn't fare too well and mothers rarely receive the appreciation they warrant. When children and adolescents don't succeed or they develop problems, our society has had a tendency to attribute the lack of success or the development of problems to a single source—mothers. One of psychology's most important lessons is that behavior is multiply determined. So it is with adolescent development—when development goes awry, mothers are not the single cause of the problems even though our society may stereotype them in this way.

The reality of motherhood today is that while fathers have increased their child-rearing responsibilities somewhat, the main responsibility for children and adolescents still falls on the mother's shoulders (Barnard & Solchany, 2002; Brooks & Bronstein, 1996). In one study, adolescents said that their mothers were more involved in parenting than fathers in both the ninth and twelfth grades (Sputa & Paulson, 1995).

In sum, the mother's role brings with it benefits as well as limitations. Although most women do not devote their entire lives to motherhood, for most mothers, it is one of the most meaningful experiences of their lives.

The Father's Role   The father's role has undergone major changes (Day & Lamb, 2004; Lamb, 1997; Parke, 2001, 2002, 2004; Parke & others, 2002). During the colonial period in America, fathers were primarily responsible for moral teaching. Fathers provided guidance and values, especially through religion. With the Industrial Revolution, the father's role changed; he gained the responsibility as the breadwinner, a role that continued through the Great Depression. By the end of World War II, another role for fathers emerged, that of a gender role model. Although being a bread winner and a moral guardian continued to be important father roles, attention shifted to his role as a male, especially for sons. Then, in the 1970s, the current interest in the father as an active, nurturant, caregiving parent emerged. Rather than being responsible only for the discipline and control of older children and for providing the family's economic base, the father now is being evaluated in terms of his active, nurturant involvement with his children.

How actively are today's fathers involved with their children and adolescents? One longitudinal study of adolescents in fifth to twelfth grade found that fathers spend only a small portion of their time with adolescents (Larson & others, 1996). Studies reveal that fathers spend from one-third to three-fourths as much time with children and adolescents as mothers do (Biller, 1993; Pleck, 1997; Yeung & others, 1999). In one study, fathers of more than 1,700 children up to 12 years old were spending an increasing amount of time with their children, compared with their counterparts in the early 1990s, but still less time than mothers were (Yeung & others, 1999). Though some fathers are exceptionally committed parents, others are virtual strangers to their adolescents even though they reside in the same household (Burton & Synder, 1997; Day & Acock, 2004).

Adolescents' social development can significantly benefit from interaction with a caring, accessible, and dependable father who fosters a sense of trust and confidence (Carlson & McLanahan, 2002; Parke, 2002). In one investigation, Frank Furstenberg and Kathleen Harris (1992) documented how nurturant fathering can overcome children's difficult life circumstances. In low-income African American families, children who reported close attachments and feelings of identification with their fathers during adolescence were twice as likely as young adults to have found a stable job or to have entered college and were 75 percent less likely to have become unwed parents, 80 percent less likely to have been in jail, and 50 percent less likely to have developed depression. Unfortunately, however, only 10 percent of the economically disadvantaged children they studied experienced a stable, close relationship with their father during childhood and adolescence. In two other studies, college females and males reported better personal and social adjustment when they had grown up in a home with a nurturant, involved father rather than a negligent or rejecting father (Fish & Biller, 1973; Reuter & Biller, 1973). And in another study, fathers characterized by positive affect had adolescents who were less likely to be depressed (Duckett & Richards, 1996).

Coparenting: Partners in Parenting A dramatic increase in research on coparenting has occurred in the last two decades. The organizing theme of this research is that poor coordination, active undermining and disparagement of the other parent, lack of cooperation and warmth, and disconnection by one parenting partner—either alone or in combination with overinvolvement by the other—are conditions that place children and adolescents at developmental risk (McHale & others, 2002). By contrast, parental solidarity, cooperation, and warmth show clear ties to children's and adolescents' prosocial behavior and competence in peer relations.

When parents show cooperation, mutual respect, balanced communication, and attunement to each other's needs, this helps children and adolescents to develop positive attitudes toward both males and females (Biller, 1993; Tamis-LeMonda & Cabrera, 2002). It is much easier for working parents to cope with changing family circumstances when the mother and the father cooperate and equitably share child-rearing responsibilities. Mothers feel less stress and have more positive attitudes toward their husbands when the husband is a supportive partner.

Parent-Adolescent Conflict

A common belief is that there is a huge gulf that separates parent and adolescents in the form of a so-called *generation gap*—that is, that during adolescence the values and attitudes of adolescents become increasingly distanced from those of their parents. For

**Fathering
The Fatherhood Project**

Conflict with parents increases in early adolescence. *What is the nature of this conflict in a majority of American families?*

the most part, the generation gap is a stereotype. For example, most adolescents and their parents have similar beliefs about the value of hard work, achievement, and career aspirations (Gecas & Seff, 1990). They also often have similar religious and political beliefs. As we will see in our discussion of research on parent-adolescent conflict, a minority of adolescents (perhaps 20 to 25 percent) have a high degree of conflict with their parents, but for a substantial majority the conflict is moderate or low.

That said, the fact remains that early adolescence is a time when parent-adolescent conflict escalates beyond parent-child conflict (Laursen & Collins, 2004; Montemayor, 1982; Weng & Montemayor, 1997). This increase may be due to a number of factors already discussed involving the maturation of the adolescent and the maturation of parents: the biological changes of puberty, cognitive changes involving increased idealism and logical reasoning, social changes focused on independence and identity, violated expectations, and physical, cognitive, and social changes in parents associated with middle adulthood. In an analysis of a number of studies, it was concluded that parent-adolescent conflict decreases from early adolescence through late adolescence (Laursen, Coy, & Collins, 1998).

Although conflict with parents does increase in early adolescence, it does not reach the tumultuous proportions envisioned by G. Stanley Hall at the beginning of the twentieth century (Holmbeck, 1996; Steinberg & Silk, 2002). Rather, much of the conflict involves the everyday events of family life, such as keeping a bedroom clean, dressing neatly, getting home by a certain time, not talking on the phone forever, and so on. The conflicts rarely involve major dilemmas like drugs and delinquency. In one recent study of middle-socioeconomic-status African American families, parent-adolescent conflict was common but low in intensity and focused on everyday living issues such as the adolescent's room, chores, choice of activities, and homework (Smetana & Gaines, 1999). Nearly all conflicts were resolved by adolescents giving in to parents, but adolescent concession declined with age.

In one study of conflict in a number of social relationships, adolescents reported having more disagreements with their mother than with anyone else—followed in order by friends, romantic partners, siblings, fathers, other adults, and peers (Laursen, 1995). In another study of 64 high school sophomores, interviews were conducted in their homes on three randomly selected evenings during a three-week period (Montemayor, 1982). The adolescents were asked to tell about the events of the previous day, including any conflicts they had with their parents. Conflict was defined as "either you teased your parent or your parent teased you; you and your parent had a difference of opinion; one of you got mad at the other; you and your parent had a quarrel or an argument; or one of you hit the other." During a period of 192 days of tracking the 64 adolescents, an average of 68 arguments with parents was reported. This represents a rate of 0.35 arguments with parents per day or about 1 argument every 3 days. The average length of the arguments was 11 minutes. Most conflicts were with mothers, and the majority were between mothers and daughters.

Still, a high degree of conflict characterizes some parent-adolescent relationships. It has been estimated that in about 20 percent of families, parents and adolescents engage in prolonged, intense, repeated, unhealthy conflict (Montemayor, 1982). Although this figure represents a minority of adolescents, it indicates that 4 to 5 million American families encounter serious, highly stressful parent-adolescent conflict. And this prolonged, intense conflict is associated with a number of adolescent problems—moving away from home, juvenile delinquency, school dropout rates, pregnancy and early marriage, membership in religious cults, and drug abuse (Brook & others, 1990).

Although in some cases these problems may be caused by intense, prolonged parent-adolescent conflict, in others the problems might have originated before the onset of adolescence. Simply because children are physically much smaller than parents, parents might be able to suppress oppositional behavior. But by adolescence, increased size and strength—especially in boys—can result in an indifference to or confrontation with parental dictates. At the same time, some psychologists have argued that conflict is a normative part of adolescent development (watch the video "Adolescent–Parent Conflict" to learn more about this line of reasoning).

Judith Smetana (1988) believes that parent-adolescent conflict can be better understood by considering the adolescent's changing social cognitive abilities. In her research, she has found that parent-adolescent conflict is related to the different approaches parents and adolescents take when addressing various points of contention. For example, consider parents who are displeased with the way the adolescent dresses. The adolescent often defines the issue as a personal one ("It's my body and I can do what I want to with it"), whereas parents usually define such issues in broader terms ("Look, we are a family and you are part of it. You have a responsibility to us to present yourself in a better fashion"). Many such issues punctuate the lives of parents and adolescents (keeping a room clean, curfew, choice of friends, and so on). As adolescents grow older, they are more likely to see their parents' perspective and look at issues in broader terms.

It should be pointed out that there is less conflict in some cultures than in others. American psychologist Reed Larson (1999) spent six months in India studying middle-SES adolescents and their families. He observed that in India there seems to be little parent-adolescent conflict and that many families likely would be described as "authoritarian" in Baumrind's categorization. Larson also observed that in India adolescents do not go through a process of breaking away from their parents and that parents choose their youths' marital partners. Conflict between parents and adolescents in Japan has also been observed as lower than in the United States (Rothbaum & others, 2000).

Next, we explore autonomy and attachment. As with most topics in this chapter, this discussion focuses on mainstream U.S. families. Keep in mind that there can be cultural variations in autonomy and attachment in adolescence, just as there are in parent-adolescent conflict.

Careers in Adolescent Development

Martha Chan
Marriage and Family Therapist

Martha Chan is a marriage and family therapist who works for Adolescent Counseling Services in Palo Alto, California. She has been the program director of adolescent counseling services for more than a decade.

Among her activities, Martha counsels parents and adolescents about family issues, conducts workshops for parents at middle schools, and writes a monthly column that addresses such topics as "I'm a single mom; How do I talk with my son about sex?," "My daughter wants to dye her hair purple," and "My son is being bullied."

LifeMAP

Autonomy and Attachment

It has been said that there are only two lasting bequests that we can leave our children—one is roots, the other wings. These words reflect the importance of attachment and autonomy in the adolescent's successful adaptation to the world. Historically, developmentalists have shown far more interest in autonomy than in attachment during the adolescent period. Recently, however, interest has heightened in attachment's role in healthy adolescent development. Adolescents and their parents live in a coordinated social world, one involving both autonomy and attachment. In keeping with the historical interest in these processes, we discuss autonomy first.

Autonomy   The increased independence that typifies adolescence is interpreted as rebellion by some parents, but in many instances adolescents' push for autonomy has little to do with their feelings toward the parents. Psychologically healthy families adjust to adolescents' push for independence by treating the adolescents in more adult ways and including them more in family decision making. Psychologically unhealthy families often remain locked into power-oriented parent control, and parents move even more heavily toward an authoritarian posture in their relationships with their adolescents.

However, it is important to recognize that parental control comes in different forms (Zimmer-Gembeck & Collins, 2003). In one study, adolescent adjustment depended on the type of parental control exerted (Keener & Boykin, 1996). Control characterized by psychological manipulation and the imposition of guilt was linked with lower levels of adolescent adjustment; control characterized by parental awareness of the adolescent's activities, efforts to control the adolescent's deviance, and low harshness was associated with better adjustment.

The adolescent's quest for autonomy and sense of responsibility creates puzzlement and conflict for many parents. Parents begin to see their teenagers slipping away from their grasp. As we have seen, the urge is to take stronger control as the adolescent seeks autonomy and personal responsibility. Heated, emotional exchanges might ensue, with either side calling names, making threats, and doing whatever seems necessary to gain control. Parents can become frustrated because they expected their teenager to heed their advice, to want to spend time with the family, and to grow up to do what is right. To be sure, they anticipated that their teenager would have some difficulty adjusting to the changes adolescence brings, but few parents are able to imagine and predict the strength of adolescents' determination to spend time with their peers and to show that it is they, not the parents, who are responsible for their success or failure.

A number of investigators have studied the relation between parental attitudes and adolescent autonomy. In general, authoritarian parenting is associated with low adolescent autonomy (Hill & Steinberg, 1976). Democratic parenting (much like authoritative parenting) is usually associated with increased adolescent autonomy (Kandel & Lesser, 1969), although findings in this regard are less consistent.

The Complexity of Adolescent Autonomy   Defining adolescent autonomy is more complex and elusive than it might at first seem (Zimmer-Gembeck & Collins, 2003). The term *autonomy* generally connotes self-direction and independence. But what does it really mean? Is it an internal personality trait that consistently characterizes the adolescent's immunity from parental influence? Is it the ability to make responsible decisions for oneself? Does autonomy imply consistent behavior in all areas of adolescent life, including school, finances, dating, and peer relations? What are the relative contributions of peers and other adults to the development of an adolescent's autonomy?

Adolescent autonomy is not a unitary personality dimension displayed consistently in all behaviors (Hill & Holmbeck, 1986). For example, in one investigation, high school students were asked 25 questions about their independence from their families (Psathas, 1957). Four distinct patterns of adolescent autonomy emerged from analyses of the high school students' responses. One dimension was labeled "permissiveness in outside activities" and was represented by such questions as "Do you have to account to parents for the way you spend your money?" A second dimension was called "permissiveness in age-related activities" and was reflected in such questions as "Do your parents help you buy your clothes?" A third independent aspect of adolescent autonomy was referred to as "parental regard for judgment," indicated by responses to items like "In family discussions, do your parents encourage you to give your opinion?" And a fourth dimension was characterized as "activities with status implications" and was indexed by parental influence on the adolescent's intended choice of occupation.

One aspect of autonomy that is especially important is **emotional autonomy,** the capacity to relinquish childlike dependencies on parents. In developing emotional autonomy, adolescents increasingly de-idealize their parents, perceive them as people rather than simply as parenting figures, and become less dependent on them for immediate emotional support.

Gender and Culture   Gender differences characterize autonomy granting in adolescence with boys usually being given more independence than girls. In one recent study, this gender difference was especially present in families with a traditional gender-role orientation (Bumpus, Crouter, & McHale, 2001).

Expectations about the appropriate timing of adolescent autonomy often vary across cultures, parents, and adolescents. For example, expectations for early autonomy on the part of adolescents are more prevalent in Whites, single parents, and adolescents themselves than they are in Asian Americans or Latinos, married parents, and parents themselves (Feldman & Rosenthal, 1999).

In one recent cross-cultural analysis, it was concluded that adolescents in the United States strive for autonomy from parents earlier than adolescents in Japan (Rothbaum & others, 2000). Even Asian adolescents raised in the United States do not usually seek autonomy as early as their Anglo-American peers (Greenberger & Chu, 1996). In the transition to adulthood, many Japanese are surprised by U.S. parents' practice of taking out loans to pay for their children's education, a practice they believe implies a distance between family members that is uncomfortable (Lebra, 1994). Also in the transition to adulthood, Japanese are less likely to live outside the home than Americans (Hendry, 1999).

Developmental Transition in Autonomy Involved in Going Away to College   Many youth experience a transition in the development of autonomy when they leave home and go away to college (Bleeker & others, 2002; Silver & others, 2002). The transition from high school to college involves increased autonomy for most individuals. For some, homesickness sets in; for others, sampling the privileges of life without parents hovering around is marvelous. For the growing number of students whose families have been torn by separation and divorce, though, moving away can be especially painful. Adolescents in such families may find themselves in the roles of comforter, confidant, and even caretaker of their parents as well as their siblings. In the words of one college freshman, "I feel responsible for my parents. I guess I shouldn't, but I can't help it. It makes my separation from them, my desire to be free of others' problems, my motivation to pursue my own identity more difficult." For yet other students, the independence of being a college freshman is not always as stressful. According to 18-year-old Brian, "Becoming an adult is kind of hard. I'm having to learn to balance my own checkbook, make my own plane reservations, do my own laundry, and the hardest thing of all is waking up in the morning. I don't have my mother there banging on the door."

In one investigation, the psychological separation and adjustment of 130 college freshmen and 123 college upperclassmen were studied (Lapsley, Rice, & Shadid, 1989). As expected, freshmen showed more psychological dependency on their parents and poorer social and personal adjustment than upperclassmen. Female students

emotional autonomy The capacity to relinquish childlike dependencies on parents.

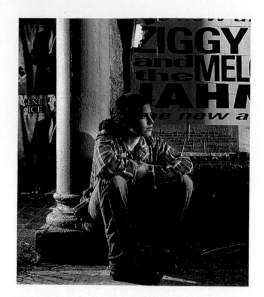

This adolescent has run away from home. *What is it about family relationships that causes adolescents to run away from home? Are there ways society could better serve runaways?*

also showed more psychological dependency on their parents than male students did. In another recent study, parent-child relationships were less satisfactory prior to the transition from high school to college (Silver, 1995). And in another recent study, students who went away to college reported feeling closer to their mother, less conflict with parents, and more decision-making control and autonomy than did college students who lived at home (Holmbeck, Durbin, & Kung, 1995).

Adolescent Runaways   Why do adolescents run away from their homes? Generally, runaways are desperately unhappy at home. The reasons many of them leave seem legitimate by almost anyone's standards. When they run away, they usually do not leave a clue as to their whereabouts—they just disappear.

Many runaways are from families in which a parent or another adult beats them or sexually exploits them. Their lives may be in danger daily. Their parents may be drug addicts or alcoholics. In some cases, the family may be so impoverished that the parents are unable to feed and clothe their teenagers adequately. The parents may be so overburdened by their own emotional and/or material inadequacies that they fail to give their adolescents the attention and understanding they need. So teenagers hit the streets in search of the emotional and material rewards they are not getting at home.

But runaways are not all from our society's lower-SES tier. Teenage lovers, confronted by parental hostility toward their relationship, might decide to elope and make it on their own. Or the middle-SES teenager might decide that he has seen enough of his hypocritical parents—people who try to make him live by an unrealistically high set of moral standards, while they live by a loose, false set of ideals. Another teen might live with parents who constantly bicker. Any of these adolescents might decide that they would be happier away from home. In one study, homeless adolescents reported having experienced more parental maltreatment, been scolded more often, and felt less loved by their parents than did housed adolescents (Wolfe, Toro, & McCaskill, 1999).

Running away often is a gradual process, as adolescents begin to spend less time at home and more time on the streets or with a peer group. The parents might be telling them that they really want to see them, to understand them; but runaways often feel that they are not understood at home and that the parents care much more about themselves.

Adolescent runaways are especially susceptible to drug abuse. In one investigation, as part of the National Longitudinal Study of Youth Survey, runaway status at ages 14 to 15 was associated with drug abuse and alcohol problems four years later at ages 18 to 19 (Windle, 1989). Repeat runaways were more likely to be drug abusers than one-time runaways were. Both one-time and repeat runaways were more likely to be school dropouts when this was assessed four years later.

Some provision must be made for runaways' physical and psychological well-being. In recent years, nationwide hotlines and temporary shelters for runaways have been established. However, there are still too few of these shelters, and there is often a noted lack of professional psychological help for the runaways at such shelters.

One exception is the temporary shelter in Dallas, Texas, called Casa de los Amigos (house of friends). At the Casa, there is room for 20 runaways, who are provided with the necessities of life as well as medical and legal assistance. In addition, a professional staff of 13 includes counselors and case managers, assisted by VISTA volunteers and high school and college interns. Each runaway is assigned a counselor, and daily group discussion sessions expose the youth to one another's feelings. Whenever possible, the counselors explore the possibility of working with the runaways' families to see if all of the family members can learn to help one another in more competent ways than in the past. It is hoped that more centers like Casa de los Amigos will appear in cities in the United States.

Conclusions   In sum, the ability to attain autonomy and gain control over one's behavior in adolescence is acquired through appropriate adult reactions to the adolescent's desire for control. An individual at the onset of adolescence does not have the knowledge to make appropriate or mature decisions in all areas of life. As the adolescent pushes for autonomy, the wise adult relinquishes control in those areas in which the adolescent can make reasonable decisions and continues to guide the adolescent in areas where the adolescent's knowledge is more limited. Gradually, adolescents improve their ability to make mature decisions on their own. The discussion that follows reveals in greater detail how important it is to view the development of autonomy in relation to connectedness to parents.

Attachment and Connectedness   Adolescents do not simply move away from parental influence into a decision-making world all their own. As they become more autonomous, it is psychologically healthy for them to be attached to their parents.

Secure and Insecure Attachment   Attachment theorists such as British psychiatrist John Bowlby (1989) and American developmental psychologist Mary Ainsworth (1979) argue that secure attachment in infancy is central to the development of social competence. In **secure attachment,** infants use the caregiver, usually the mother, as a secure base from which to explore the environment. Secure attachment is theorized to be an important foundation for psychological development later in childhood, adolescence, and adulthood. In **insecure attachment,** infants either avoid the caregiver or show considerable resistance or ambivalence toward the caregiver. Insecure attachment is theorized to be related to difficulties in relationships and problems in later development.

In the last decade, developmentalists have begun to explore the role of secure attachment and related concepts, such as connectedness to parents, in adolescence (Allen, Hauser, & Borman-Spurrell, 1996; Allen & others, 2003; Easterbrooks & Biesecker, 2002; Kobak, 1999). They believe that secure attachment to parents in adolescence can facilitate the adolescent's social competence and well-being, as reflected in such characteristics as self-esteem, emotional adjustment, and physical health (Cooper, Shaver, & Collins, 1998; Egeland & Carlson, 2004; Hilburn-Cobb, 2004). In the research of Joseph Allen and his colleagues (Allen & others, 1994), securely attached adolescents have somewhat lower probabilities of engaging in problem behaviors. In one recent study, secure attachment to both the mother and the father was related positively to adolescents' peer and friendship relations (Lieberman, Doyle, & Markiewicz, 1999).

Many studies that assess secure and insecure attachment in adolescence use the Adult Attachment Interview (AAI) (George, Main, & Kaplan, 1984). This measure examines an individual's memories of significant attachment relationships. Based on the responses to questions on the AAI, individuals are classified as secure-autonomous (which corresponds to secure attachment in infancy) or as being in one of three insecure categories:

- **Dismissing/avoidant attachment** is an insecure category in which individuals de-emphasize the importance of attachment. This category is associated with consistent experiences of rejection of attachment needs by caregivers. One possible outcome of dismissing/avoidant attachment is that parents and adolescents mutually distance themselves from each other, which lessens parents' influence. In one study, dismissing/avoidant attachment was related to violent and aggressive behavior on the part of the adolescent.
- **Preoccupied/ambivalent attachment** is an insecure category in which adolescents are hypertuned to attachment experiences. This is thought to mainly occur because parents are inconsistently available to the adolescent. This can result in a high degree of attachment-seeking behavior, mixed with angry feelings. Conflict between parents and adolescents in this type of attachment classification can be too high for healthy development.
- **Unresolved/disorganized attachment** is an insecure category in which the adolescent has an unusually high level of fear and might be disoriented. This can result from such traumatic experiences as a parent's death or abuse by parents.

Joseph Allen's Attachment Research

secure attachment In this attachment pattern, infants use their primary caregiver, usually the mother, as a secure base from which to explore the environment. Secure attachment is theorized to be an important foundation for psychological development later in childhood, adolescence, and adulthood.

insecure attachment In this attachment pattern, infants either avoid the caregiver or show considerable resistance or ambivalence toward the caregiver. This pattern is theorized to be related to difficulties in relationships and problems in later development.

dismissing/avoidant attachment An insecure attachment category in which individuals de-emphasize the importance of attachment. This category is associated with consistent experiences of rejection of attachment needs by caregivers.

preoccupied/ambivalent attachment An insecure attachment category in which adolescents are hypertuned to attachment experiences. This is thought to mainly occur because parents are inconsistently available to the adolescents.

unresolved/disorganized attachment An insecure category in which the adolescent has an unusually high level of fear and is disoriented. This can result from such traumatic experiences as a parent's death or abuse by parents.

Old Model

Autonomy, detachment from parents; parent and peer worlds are isolated

Intense, stressful conflict throughout adolescence; parent-adolescent relationships are filled with storm and stress on virtually a daily basis

New Model

Attachment and autonomy; parents are important support systems and attachment figures; adolescent-parent and adolescent-peer worlds have some important connections

Moderate parent-adolescent conflict common and can serve a positive developmental function; conflict greater in early adolescence, especially during the apex of puberty

FIGURE 9.3 The Old and New Models of Parent-Adolescent Relationships

Developmental Transformations Transformations characterize adolescents' autonomy and connectedness with their families. In one study by Reed Larson and his colleagues (1996), 220 White middle-SES adolescents from 10 to 18 years of age carried beepers and, when beeped at random times, reported whom they were with, what they were doing, and how they were feeling. The amount of time adolescents spent with their families decreased from 35 percent for 10-year-olds to 14 percent for 18-year-olds, suggesting increased autonomy with age. However, increased family connectedness was evident with increased age, with more family conversation about interpersonal issues, especially for girls. As adolescents got older, they were more likely to perceive themselves as leading the interactions. Also, after a decrease in early adolescence, older teenagers reported more favorable affect with others during family interactions.

Conclusions In sum, the old model of parent-adolescent relationships suggested that, as adolescents mature, they detach themselves from parents and move into a world of autonomy apart from parents. The old model also suggested that parent-adolescent conflict is intense and stressful throughout adolescence. The new model emphasizes that parents serve as important attachment figures, resources, and support systems as adolescents explore a wider, more complex social world. The new model also emphasizes that, in the majority of families, parent-adolescent conflict is moderate rather than severe and that everyday negotiations and minor disputes are normal, serving the positive developmental function of promoting independence and identity (see figure 9.3).

Review and reflect Learning goal 1

2 **Describe parent-adolescent relationships**

REVIEW

- How can parents be effective managers of adolescents?
- What are four important parenting styles and how are they linked with adolescent development?
- What roles do mothers and fathers play in adolescent development? How effective is coparenting?
- How can parent-adolescent conflict be accurately described?
- What roles do autonomy and attachment play in adolescent development?

REFLECT

- What are some ways that parents can reduce parent-adolescent conflict? Consider such things as curfews, choice of friends, keeping a room clean, respect for adults, and rules for dating.

So far in this chapter we have examined the nature of family processes and parent-adolescent relationships. In addition to parent-adolescent relationships, there is another aspect to the family worlds of most adolescents—sibling relationships—which we discuss next.

3 SIBLING RELATIONSHIPS

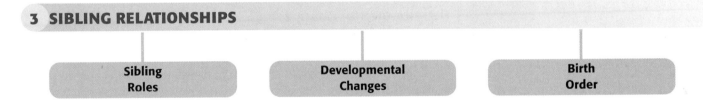

| Sibling Roles | Developmental Changes | Birth Order |

Sandra describes to her mother what happened in a conflict with her sister:

> We had just come home from the ball game. I sat down in the chair next to the light so I could read. Sally (the sister) said, "Get up. I was sitting there first. I just got up for a second to get a drink." I told her I was not going to get up and that I didn't see her name on the chair. I got mad and started pushing her—her drink spilled all over her. Then she got really mad; she shoved me against the wall, hitting and clawing at me. I managed to grab a handful of hair.

At this point, Sally comes into the room and begins to tell her side of the story. Sandra interrupts, "Mother, you always take her side." Sound familiar? How much does conflict characterize sibling relations? As we examine the roles siblings play in social development, you will discover that conflict is a common dimension of sibling relationships but that siblings also play many other roles in social development.

Sibling Roles

More than 80 percent of American adolescents have one or more siblings—that is, sisters and brothers. As anyone who has had a sibling knows, the conflict experienced by Sally and Sandra in their relationship with each other is a common interaction style of siblings. However, conflict is only one of the many dimensions of sibling relations. Adolescent sibling relations include helping, sharing, teaching, fighting, and playing, and adolescent siblings can act as emotional supports, rivals, and communication

More than 80 percent of us have one or more siblings. *What are some developmental changes in siblings?*

partners (Zukow-Goldring, 2002). One recent study found that adolescent siblings spent an average of 10 hours a week together with an average of 12 percent of that time spent in constructive time (creative activities such as art, music, and hobbies; sports; religious activities; and games) and 25 percent in nonconstructive time (watching TV and hanging out) (Tucker, McHale, & Crouter, 2003). Also, in one study, positive sibling relationships in adolescence contributed to a sense of emotional and school-related support (Seginer, 1998).

In some instances, siblings can be stronger socializing influences on the adolescent than parents are (Teti, 2002). Someone close in age to the adolescent—such as a sibling—might be able to understand the adolescent's problems and communicate more effectively than parents can. In dealing with peers, coping with difficult teachers, and discussing taboo subjects (such as sex), siblings can be more influential in socializing adolescents than parents are. In one recent study, both younger and older adolescent siblings viewed older siblings as sources of support for social and scholastic activities (Tucker, McHale, & Crouter, 2001). Furthermore, in one study, children showed more consistent behavior when interacting with siblings and more varied behavior when interacting with parents (Baskett & Johnson, 1982). In this study, children interacted in much more aggressive ways with their siblings than with their parents. In another study, adolescents reported a higher degree of conflict with their siblings than with anyone else (Buhrmester & Furman, 1990).

Developmental Changes

Although adolescent sibling relations reveal a high level of conflict in comparison to adolescents' relationships with other social agents (parents, peers, teachers, and romantic partners, for example), there is evidence that sibling conflict is actually lower in adolescence than in childhood. In one study, the lessened sibling conflict during adolescence was due partly to a dropoff in the amount of time siblings spent playing and talking with each other (Buhrmester & Furman, 1990). The decline also reflected a basic transformation in the power structure of sibling relationships that seems to occur in adolescence. In childhood, there is an asymmetry of power, with older siblings frequently playing the role of "boss" or caregiver. This asymmetry of power often produces conflicts when one sibling tries to force the other to comply with his or her demands. As younger siblings grow older and their maturity level "catches up" to older siblings', the power asymmetry decreases. As siblings move through adolescence, most learn how to relate to each other on a more equal footing and, in doing so, come to resolve more of their differences than in childhood. Nonetheless, as we said earlier, sibling conflict in adolescence is still relatively high.

Birth Order

Birth order has been of special interest to sibling researchers, who want to identify the characteristics associated with being born into a particular slot in a family. Firstborns have been described as more adult oriented, helpful, conforming, anxious, and self-controlled, and less aggressive than their siblings. Parental demands and high standards established for firstborns may result in firstborns realizing higher academic and professional achievements than their siblings (Furman & Lanthier, 2002). For example, firstborns are overrepresented in *Who's Who* and among Rhodes scholars. However, some of the same pressures placed on firstborns for high achievement can be the reason firstborns also have more guilt, anxiety, difficulty in coping with stressful situations, and higher admission to guidance clinics.

Birth order also plays a role in siblings' relationships with each other (Vandell, Minnett, & Santrock, 1987). Older siblings invariably take on the dominant role in sibling interaction, and older siblings report feeling more resentful that parents give preferential treatment to younger siblings.

What are later-borns like? Characterizing later-borns is difficult because they can occupy so many different sibling positions. For example, a later-born might be the second-born male in a family of two siblings or a third-born female in a family of four siblings. In two-child families, the profile of the later-born child is related to the sex of his or her sibling. For example, a boy with an older sister is more likely to develop "feminine" interests than a boy with an older brother. Overall, later-borns usually enjoy better relations with peers than firstborns. Last-borns, who are often described as the "baby" in the family even after they have outgrown infancy, run the risk of becoming overly dependent. Middle-borns tend to be more diplomatic, often performing the role of negotiator in times of dispute (Sutton-Smith, 1982).

The popular conception of the only child is of a "spoiled brat" with such undesirable characteristics as dependency, lack of self-control, and self-centered behavior. But research presents a more positive portrayal of the only child, who often is achievement oriented and displays a desirable personality, especially in comparison to later-borns and children from large families (Thomas, Coffman, & Kipp, 1993).

So far our consideration of birth-order effects suggests that birth order might be a strong predictor of adolescent behavior. However, an increasing number of family researchers believe that birth order has been overdramatized and overemphasized. The critics argue that, when all of the factors that influence adolescent behavior are considered, birth order itself shows limited ability to predict adolescent behavior. Consider just sibling relationships alone. They vary not only in birth order, but also in number of siblings, age of siblings, age spacing of siblings, and sex of siblings. For example, in one recent study male sibling pairs had a less positive relationship (less caring, less intimate, and lower conflict resolution) than male/female or female/female sibling pairs (Cole & Kerns, 2001).

Consider also the temperament of siblings. Researchers have found that siblings' temperamental traits (such as "easy" and "difficult"), as well as differential treatment of siblings by parents, influence how siblings get along (Brody, Stoneman, & Burke, 1987). Siblings with "easy" temperaments who are treated in relatively equal ways by parents tend to get along with each other the best, whereas siblings with "difficult" temperaments, or siblings whose parents gave one sibling preferential treatment, get along the worst.

Beyond temperament and differential treatment of siblings by parents, think about some of the other important factors in adolescents' lives that influence their behavior beyond birth order. They include heredity, models of competency or incompetency that parents present to adolescents on a daily basis, peer influences, school influences, socioeconomic factors, sociohistorical factors, cultural variations, and so on. Although birth order itself may not be a good predictor of adolescent behavior, sibling relationships and interaction are important dimensions of family processes in adolescence (Conger & Bryant, 2004).

Through the Eyes of Adolescents

Dealing with My Sister

"Like a lot of brothers and sisters, my sister and I have our fights. Sometimes when I talk to her, it is like talking to a brick! Her favorite thing to do is to storm off and slam the door when she gets mad at me. After a while, I cool off. When I calm down, I realize fighting with your sister is crazy. I go to my sister and apologize. It's a lot better to cool off and apologize than to keep on fighting and make things worse."

—*Cynthia, Age 11*

Big sisters are the crab grass in the lawn of life.

—CHARLES SCHULTZ
*American Cartoonist,
20th Century*

Review and reflect Learning goal 3

3 Characterize sibling relationships in adolescence

REVIEW

• What is the nature of sibling roles?
• What developmental changes characterize sibling relationships?
• How strongly is birth order linked to adolescent development?

REFLECT

• If you grew up with a sibling, you likely showed some jealousy of your sibling and vice versa. How can parents help children reduce their jealousy toward a sibling?

4 THE CHANGING FAMILY IN A CHANGING SOCIETY

| Divorced Families | Working Parents | Culture and Ethnicity |

| Stepfamilies | Gay and Lesbian Parents |

More adolescents are growing up in a greater variety of family structures than ever before in history (Hernandez, 1997). Many mothers spend the greater part of their day away from their children. More than one of every two mothers with a child under the age of 5, and more than two of every three with a child from 6 to 17 years of age, is in the labor force. The number of adolescents growing up in single-parent families is staggering. The United States has the highest percentage of single-parent families, compared with virtually all other countries (see figure 9.4). And, by age 18, approximately one-fourth of all American children will have lived a portion of their lives in a stepfamily.

Divorced Families

The U.S. divorce rate increased dramatically in the 1960s and 1970s but has declined since the 1980s. Many other countries around the world have also experienced significant changes in their divorce rate. For example, Japan saw an increase in its divorce rate in the 1990s (Ministry of Health, Education, and Welfare, 2002). However, the

FIGURE 9.4 Single-Parent Families in Different Countries

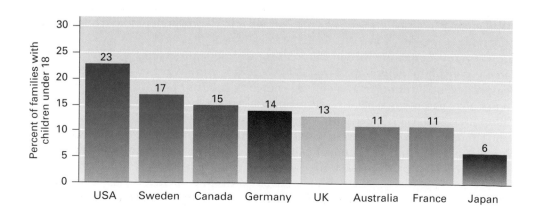

divorce rate in the United States is still much higher than in Japan and higher than in most other countries as well. It is estimated that 40 percent of children born to married parents will experience their parents' divorce (Hetherington & Stanley-Hagan, 2002).

These are the questions that we will now explore regarding the effects of divorce: Are adolescents better adjusted in intact, never-divorced families than in divorced families? Should parents stay together for the sake of their children and adolescents? How much do parenting skills matter in divorced families? What factors affect the adolescent's individual risk and vulnerability in a divorced family? What role does socioeconomic status play in the lives of adolescents in divorced families? (Hetherington, 2000; Hetherington and Kelly, 2002; Hetherington & Stanley-Hagan, 2002).

Adolescents' Adjustment in Divorced Families   Most researchers agree that children and adolescents from divorced families show poorer adjustment than their counterparts in nondivorced families (Amato & Keith, 1991; Harvey & Fine, 2004; Hetherington & Stanley-Hagan, 2002) (see figure 9.5). Those who have experienced multiple divorces are at greater risk. Adolescents in divorced families are more likely than adolescents from nondivorced families to have academic problems, to show externalized problems (such as acting out and delinquency) and internalized problems (such as anxiety and depression), to be less socially responsible, to have less-competent intimate relationships, to drop out of school, to become sexually active at an earlier age, to take drugs, to associate with antisocial peers, and to have lower self-esteem (Conger & Chao, 1996). Nonetheless, the majority of adolescents in divorced families do not have these problems (Emery, 1999). The weight of the research evidence underscores that most adolescents competently cope with their parents' divorce.

Should Parents Stay Together for the Sake of the Children and Adolescents?
Whether parents should stay in an unhappy or conflicted marriage for the sake of their children and adolescents is one of the most commonly asked questions about divorce (Hetherington, 2000). If the stresses and disruptions in family relationships associated with an unhappy, conflicted marriage that erode the well-being of the children are reduced by the move to a divorced, single-parent family, divorce might be advantageous. However, if the diminished resources and increased risks associated with divorce also are accompanied by inept parenting and sustained or increased conflict, not only between the divorced couple but also between parents, children, and siblings, the best choice for the children would be for an unhappy marriage to be retained (Hetherington & Stanley-Hagan, 2002). These are "ifs," and it is difficult to determine how these will play out when parents either remain together in an acrimonious marriage or become divorced. Note that marital conflict may have negative consequences for children in the context of marriage or divorce (Cummings, Braungart-Rieker, & Du Rocher-Schudlich, 2003; Cummings & Davies, 2002; Hetherington & Kelly, 2002).

How Much Do Family Processes Matter in Divorced Families?   In divorced families, family processes matter a great deal (Wallerstein & Johnson-Reitz, 2004). When the divorced parents have a harmonious relationship and use authoritative parenting, the adjustment of adolescents is improved (Hetherington, 2000; Hetherington, Bridges, & Insabella, 1998; Hetherington & Stanley-Hagan, 2002). A number of researchers have shown that a disequilibrium, including diminished parenting skills, occurs in the year following the divorce but that by two years after the divorce restabilization has occurred and parenting skills have improved (Hetherington, 1989). About one-fourth to one-third of adolescents in divorced families, compared with 10 percent in nondivorced families, become disengaged from their families, spending as little time as possible at home and in interaction with family members (Hetherington & Kelly, 2002). This disengagement is higher for boys than for girls in divorced families. However, if there is a caring adult outside the home, such as a mentor, the disengagement can be a positive solution to a disrupted, conflicted family circumstance.

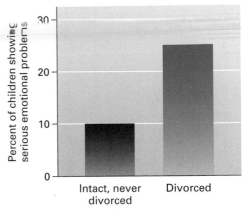

FIGURE 9.5 Divorce and Children's Emotional Problems

In Hetherington's research, 25 percent of children from divorced families showed serious emotional problems compared with only 10 percent of children from intact, never-divorced families. However, keep in mind that a substantial majority (75 percent) of the children from divorced families did not show serious emotional problems.

What roles do noncustodial parents play in the lives of children and adolescents in divorced families? Most nonresidential fathers have a friendly, companionable relationship with their children and adolescents rather than a traditional parental relationship (Munsch, Woodward, & Darling, 1995). They want their visits to be pleasant and entertaining, so they are reluctant to assume the role of a disciplinarian or teacher. They are less likely than nondivorced fathers to criticize, control, and monitor the child's or adolescent's behavior or to help them with such tasks as homework (Bray & Berger, 1993). Frequency of contact with noncustodial fathers and adjustment of children and adolescents are usually found to be unrelated (Amato & Keith, 1991). The quality of the contact matters more. Under conditions of low conflict, when noncustodial fathers participate in a variety of activities with their offspring and engage in authoritative parenting, children and adolescents, especially boys, benefit (Lindner-Gunnoe, 1993). We know less about noncustodial mothers than fathers, but research suggests that these mothers are less adept than custodial mothers at controlling and monitoring their child's or adolescent's behavior (Furstenberg & Nord, 1987). Noncustodial mothers' warmth, support, and monitoring can improve children's and adolescents' adjustment (Lindner-Gunnoe, 1993).

What Factors Are Involved in the Adolescent's Individual Risk Vulnerability in a Divorced Family?

Among the factors involved in individual risk vulnerability are the adolescent's adjustment prior to the divorce, personality and temperament, developmental status, gender, and custody. Children and adolescents whose parents later divorce show poorer adjustment before the breakup (Amato & Booth, 1996). When antecedent levels of problem behaviors are controlled, differences in the adjustment of children and adolescents in divorced and nondivorced families are reduced (Cherlin & others, 1991).

Personality and temperament also play a role in adolescent adjustment in divorced families. Adolescents who are socially mature and responsible, who show few behavioral problems, and who have an easy temperament are better able to cope with their parents' divorce. Children and adolescents with a difficult temperament often have problems coping with their parents' divorce (Hetherington & Stanley-Hagan, 2002).

Focusing on the developmental status of the child or adolescent involves taking into account the age of onset of the divorce and the time when the child's or adolescent's adjustment is assessed. In most studies, these factors are confounded with length of time since the divorce occurred. Some researchers have found that preschool children whose parents divorce are at greater risk for long-term problems than are older children (Zill, Morrison, & Coiro, 1993). The explanation for this focuses on their inability to realistically appraise the causes and consequences of divorce, their anxiety about the possibility of abandonment, their self-blame for the divorce, and their inability to use extrafamilial protective resources. However, problems in adjustment can emerge or increase during adolescence, even if the divorce occurred much earlier.

Earlier studies reported gender differences in response to divorce, with divorce being more negative for boys than for girls in mother-custody families. However, more-recent studies have shown that gender differences are less pronounced and consistent than was previously believed. Some of the inconsistency could be due to the increase in father-custody and joint-custody families and increased involvement of noncustodial fathers, especially in their sons' lives. Female adolescents in divorced families are more likely to drop out of high school and college than are their male counterparts. Male and female adolescents from divorced families are similarly affected in the likelihood of becoming teenage parents, but single parenthood affects girls more adversely (McLanahan & Sandefur, 1994).

In recent decades, an increasing number of children and adolescents have lived in father-custody and joint-custody families. What is their adjustment like, compared with the adjustment of children and adolescents in mother-custody families?

As marriage has become a more optional, less permanent institution in contemporary America, children and adolescents are encountering stresses and adaptive challenges associated with their parents' marital transitions.

—E. MAVIS HETHERINGTON
Contemporary Psychologist,
University of Virginia

www.mhhe.com/santrocka10

For Adolescents: Dealing with Parents' Divorce
Divorce Resources
Single Fathers

Although there have been few thorough studies of the topic, a recent review of studies concluded that children benefit from joint custody because it facilitates ongoing positive involvement with both parents (Bauserman, 2003). Some studies have shown that boys adjust better in father-custody families and that girls adjust better in mother-custody families, but other studies have not. In one study, adolescents in father-custody families had higher rates of delinquency, believed to be due to less-competent monitoring by the fathers (Buchanan, Maccoby, & Dornbusch, 1992).

Another factor involved in an adolescent's adjustment in a divorced family is relocation (Kelly & Lamb, 2003). One recent study found that when children and adolescents whose parents have divorced experience a move away of either of their parents, they show less effective adjustment (Braver, Ellman, & Fabricus, 2003).

What Role Does Socioeconomic Status Play in the Lives of Adolescents in Divorced Families? On the average, custodial mothers lose about 25 to 50 percent of their predivorce income, in comparison to an income loss of only 10 percent for custodial fathers (Emery, 1999). This income loss for divorced mothers is typically accompanied by increased workloads, high rates of job instability, and residential moves to less desirable neighborhoods with inferior schools.

Stepfamilies

Although parents are divorcing in greater numbers than ever before, many of them remarry (Dunn & others, 2001; White & Gilbreth, 2001). It takes time for couples to marry, have children, get divorced, and then remarry. Consequently, there are far more elementary and secondary school children than infant or preschool children in stepfamilies.

The number of remarriages involving children has grown steadily in recent years. As a result of their parents' successive marital transitions, about half of all children whose parents divorce will have a stepfather within four years of parental separation. Furthermore, divorces occur at a 10 percent higher rate in remarriages than in first marriages (Cherlin & Furstenberg, 1994).

Types of Stepfamilies There are different types of stepfamilies. Some types are based on family structure, others on relationships.

Family Structure Types In some, the stepfamily may have been preceded by a circumstance in which a spouse died. However, a large majority of stepfamilies are preceded by a divorce rather than a death.

Three common types of stepfamily structure are (1) stepfather, (2) stepmother, and (3) blended or complex. In stepfather families, the mother typically had custody of the children and became remarried, introducing a stepfather into her children's lives. In stepmother families, the father usually had custody and became remarried, introducing a stepmother into his children's lives. And in a blended or complex stepfamily, both parents bring children from previous marriages to live in the newly formed stepfamily.

Researchers have found that children's relationships with custodial parents (mother in stepfather families, father in stepmother families) are often better than with stepparents (Santrock, Sitterle, & Warshak, 1998). However, when adolescents have a positive relationship with their stepfather, it is related to fewer adolescent problems (White & Gilbreth, 2001). Also, children in simple stepfamilies (stepfather, stepmother) often show better adjustment than their counterparts in complex (blended) families (Anderson & others, 1999).

Relationship Types In addition to their structure (stepfather, stepmother, or blended), stepfamilies also develop certain patterns of relationships. In a study of 200 stepfamilies, James Bray and his colleagues (Bray, Berger, & Boethel, 1999; Bray

& Kelly, 1998) found that over time stepfamilies often fall into three types based on their relationships: neotraditional, matriarchal, and romantic.

- *Neotraditional.* Both adults want a family and are able to successfully cope with the challenges of new stepfamily. After three to five years, these families often look like intact, never-divorced families with positive relationships often characterizing the stepfamily members.
- *Matriarchal.* In this type of stepfamily, the mother has custody and is accustomed to managing the family herself. The stepfather did not marry her because he especially wanted to be a father. She runs the family and the stepfather is kind of a bystander, often ignoring the children or occasionally engaging in some enjoyable activities with them. This type of stepfamily may function adequately except when the mother wants help and the stepfather doesn't want to give it. This type of stepfamily also may not function well if the husband decides to become very involved (which typically occurs after they have a baby of their own) and she feels that her turf has been invaded.
- *Romantic.* These adults married with very high, unrealistic expectations for their stepfamily. They try to create an instant, very happy family and can't understand why it doesn't happen immediately. This type of stepfamily is the one that is most likely to end in a divorce.

**Stepfamily Resources
Working Mothers**

How does living in a stepfamily influence an adolescent's development?

boundary ambiguity The uncertainty in stepfamilies about who is in or out of the family and who is performing or responsible for certain tasks in the family system.

Adjustment As in divorced families, children in stepfamilies have more adjustment problems than their counterparts in nondivorced families (Hetherington, Bridges, & Insabella, 1998; Hetherington & Kelly, 2002). The adjustment problems of children are much like those of children in divorced families: academic problems, externalizing and internalizing problems, lower self-esteem, early sexual activity, delinquency, and so on (Anderson & others, 1999). Adjustment for parents and children may take longer in stepfamilies (up to five years or more) than in divorced families, in which a restabilization is more likely to occur within two years (Anderson & others, 1999). One aspect of a stepfamily that makes adjustment difficult is **boundary ambiguity,** the uncertainty in stepfamilies about who is in or out of the family and who is performing or responsible for certain tasks in the family system.

There is an increase in adjustment problems of children in newly remarried families (Hetherington & Clingempeel, 1992). In research conducted by Bray and his colleagues (Bray, Berger, & Boethel, 1999; Bray & Kelly, 1998), the formation of a stepfamily often meant that children had to move, which involved changing schools and friends. It took time for the stepparent to get to know the stepchildren. The new spouses had to learn how to cope with the challenges of their relationship and parenting together. In Bray's view, the formation of a stepfamily was like merging two cultures.

Bray and his colleagues also found that it was not unusual for the following problems to develop early in the stepfamily's existence. When the stepparent tried to discipline the stepchild, this often did not work well. Most experts recommend that in the early period of a stepfamily the biological parent should be the parent doing any disciplining of the child that is needed. The stepparent-stepchild relationship develops best when the stepparent spends time with the stepchild in activities that the child enjoys.

A newly formed stepfamily sometimes has difficulty coping with changes that they cannot control. For example, the husband and wife may be looking forward to going away for a weekend without the children. At the last minute, the other biological parent calls and cancels taking the children. This is bound to cause some angry feelings. Unfortunately, both parents may take their frustration out on the children. Successful stepfamilies adjust to such unexpected circumstances and have backup plans (Coleman, Ganong, & Fine, 2004).

In terms of the age of the child, researchers have found that early adolescence is an especially difficult time for the formation of a stepfamily (Bray & Kelly, 1998; Hetherington & others, 1999). This may occur because the stepfamily circumstances exacerbate normal adolescent concerns about identity, sexuality, and autonomy.

Now that we have considered the changing social worlds of adolescents when their parents divorce and remarry, we turn our attention to another aspect of the changing family worlds of adolescents—the situation when both parents work.

Working Parents

Interest in the effects of parental work on the development of children and adolescents has increased in recent years (Gottfried, Gottfried, & Bathurst, 2002; Hoffman, 2000). Our examination of parental work focuses on the following issues: the role of working mothers in adolescents' development, the adjustment of latchkey adolescents, the effects of relocation on adolescent development, and the influence of unemployment on adolescents' lives.

Working Mothers   Most of the research on parental work has focused on young children. Little attention has been given to early adolescence, even though it is during this period that many mothers return to full-time work, in part due to presumed independence of their young adolescents. In one study, 10- to 13-year olds carried electronic pagers for one week and completed self-report forms in response to random signals sent to them every other hour (Richards & Duckett, 1994). The most striking aspect of the study was the absence of significant differences associated with maternal employment. There were few differences in the quantity and quality of time associated with maternal employment. Other researchers have arrived at similar conclusions (Lerner, Jacobson, & del Gaudio, 1992). As a leading authority on maternal employment, Lois Hoffman (1989), stated, maternal employment is a fact of modern life. It is not an aberrant aspect of it, but a response to other social changes. It meets the needs not met by the traditional family ideal of a full-time mother and homemaker. Not only does it meet the parents' needs, but in many ways, it may be a pattern better suited to socializing children for the adult roles they will occupy. This is especially true for daughters, but it is true for sons, too. The broader range of emotions and skills that each parent presents is more consistent with this adult role. Just as the father shares the breadwinning role and the child-rearing role with the mother, so the son, too, will be more likely to share these roles. The rigid gender-role stereotyping perpetuated by the divisions of labor in the traditional family is not appropriate for the demands children of both sexes will have made on them as adults. The needs of the growing child require the mother to loosen her hold on the child, and this task may be easier for the working woman whose job is an additional source of identity and self-esteem.

Gender differences have sometimes been associated with parental work patterns. In some studies, no gender differences are found, but in others, maternal employment has greater benefits for adolescent daughters than for sons (Law, 1992), and in yet others, adolescent sons benefit academically and emotionally when they identify with the work patterns of their fathers more than with those of their mothers (Orthner, Giddings, & Quinn, 1987).

In one study, Nancy Galambos and her colleagues (1995) studied the effects of parents' work overload on their relationships with their adolescent and on the adolescent's development. They found some evidence for the impact of work overload, but the effects differed for mothers and fathers. The mother's warmth and acceptance shown toward the adolescent helped to reduce the negative impact of her work overload on the adolescent's development. The key factor for fathers was parent-adolescent conflict—when it was lower, the negative impact of the father's work overload on the adolescent's development was reduced. Also, when both parents were stressed, parent-adolescent conflict was highest.

Latchkey Adolescents Although the mother's working is not necessarily associated with negative outcomes for adolescents, a certain set of adolescents from working-mother families bears further scrutiny—those called latchkey adolescents. Latchkey adolescents typically do not see their parents from the time they leave for school in the morning until about 6:00 or 7:00 P.M. They are called "latchkey" children or adolescents because they carry a key to their home and let themselves into the home while their parents are still at work. Many latchkey adolescents are largely unsupervised for two to four hours a day during each school week, or for entire days, five days a week, during the summer months.

Thomas and Lynette Long (1983) interviewed more than 1,500 latchkey children. They concluded that a slight majority of these children had negative latchkey experiences. Some latchkey children grow up too fast, hurried by the responsibility placed on them. How do latchkey children handle the lack of limits and structure during the latchkey hours? Without limits and parental supervision, it becomes easier for latchkey children and adolescents to find their way into trouble—possibly abusing a sibling, stealing, or vandalizing. The Longs found that 90 percent of the adjudicated juvenile delinquents in Montgomery County, Maryland, were from latchkey families. In another investigation of more than 4,900 eighth-graders in Los Angeles and San Diego, those who cared for themselves 11 hours a week or more were twice as likely to have abused alcohol and other drugs than were their counterparts who did not care for themselves at all before or after school (Richardson & others, 1989). Adolescence expert Joan Lipsitz (1983), testifying before the Select Committee on Children, Youth, and Families, called the lack of adult supervision of children and adolescents in the after-school hours one of the nation's major problems. Lipsitz called it the "3:00 to 6:00 P.M. problem" because it was during this time frame that the Center for Early Adolescence in North Carolina, where she was director, experienced a peak of adolescent referrals for clinical help.

Although latchkey adolescents can be vulnerable to problems, keep in mind that the experiences of latchkey adolescents vary enormously, just as do the experiences of all children with working mothers. Parents need to give special attention to the ways their latchkey adolescents' lives can be monitored effectively. Variations in latchkey experiences suggest that parental monitoring and authoritative parenting help the adolescent to cope more effectively with latchkey experiences, especially in resisting peer pressure (Galambos & Maggs, 1991; Steinberg, 1986). The degree to which latchkey adolescents are at developmental risk remains unsettled. A positive sign is that researchers are beginning to conduct more precise analyses of adolescents' latchkey experiences in an effort to determine which aspects of latchkey circumstances are the most detrimental and which aspects foster better adaptation. In one study that focused on the after-school hours, unsupervised peer contact, lack of neighborhood safety, and low monitoring were linked with externalizing problems (such as acting-out and delinquency) in young adolescents (Pettit & others, 1999).

Relocation Geographical moves or relocations are a fact of life for many American families. Each year, about 17 percent of the population changes residences. This figure does not include multiple moves within the same year, so it may even underestimate the mobility of the U.S. population. The majority of these moves are made because of job demands. Moving can be especially stressful for adolescents, disrupting friendship ties and school activities. The sources of support to which adolescents and their parents turn, such as extended-family members and friends, are often unavailable to recently moved families.

Although relocations are often stressful for all individuals involved, they may be especially stressful for adolescents because of their developing sense of identity and the importance of peer relations in their lives. In one study, geographical relocation was detrimental to the well-being of 12- to 14-year-old females but not of their male counterparts (Brown & Orthner, 1990). The adolescent girls' life satisfaction was negatively related both to recent moves and to a high number of moves in their history, and a history of frequent moves was also associated with the girls' depression. However, the immediate negative effects on the girls disappeared over time. The researchers concluded that female adolescents might require more time to adapt to family relocations. Male adolescents might use sports and other activities in their new locale to ease the effects of relocation.

Unemployment What effects does unemployment have on families and on adolescents' development? During the Great Depression, unemployment dramatically increased parental stress and undermined the school achievement and health of children and adolescents (Elder, 2000). More recently, a study in the 1990s examined the effects of changes in parental work status on young adolescents' school adjustment (Flanagan & Eccles, 1993). Four groups were compared. *Deprived* families reported a layoff or demotion at time 1 but no recovery two years later. *Declining* families experienced a layoff or demotion between times 1 and 2. *Recovery* families reported similar losses at time 1 but reemployment two years later. *Stable* families reported no layoffs or demotion between times 1 and 2. Adolescents in deprived and declining families showed less competent peer interaction, and adolescents in deprived families were the most disruptive in school. The transition to adolescence was especially difficult for children whose parents were coping with changes in their work status. Other researchers have also found that economic downturn and joblessness can have negative effects on the adolescent's development (Gomel, Tinsley, & Clark, 1995; Lord, 1995). Parent-adolescent relationships in families experiencing a sudden economic loss are often characterized by less engagement, higher conflict, and more negative emotions (Collins & Laursen, 2004).

Gay and Lesbian Parents

Another aspect of the changing family in a changing society focuses on adolescents raised by gay and lesbian parents (Patterson, 2002; Savin-Williams, 2001). Increasingly, gay and lesbian couples are creating families that include children. This is controversial to many heterosexual individuals who view gay or lesbian couples as unacceptable role models for children. Approximately 20 percent of lesbians and 10 percent of gay men are parents, most of whom have children from a heterosexual marriage that ended in a divorce (Patterson, 2002). There may be more than one million gay and lesbian parents in the United States today.

Diversity Among Lesbian Mothers, Gay Fathers, and Their Adolescents An important aspect of lesbian and gay families with adolescents is the sexual identity of parents at the time of a child's birth or adoption (Patterson, 2002).The largest group of adolescents with lesbian and gay parents are likely those who were born in the context of heterosexual relationships with one or both parents only later identifying themselves as gay or lesbian. Gay and lesbian parents may be single or they may have same-gender partners. In addition, lesbians and gay men are increasingly choosing parenthood through donor insemination or adoption. Custodial arrangements also may vary.

Another issue focuses on custody arrangements for adolescents. Many lesbian mothers and gay fathers have lost custody of their adolescents to heterosexual spouses following divorce. For this reason, many lesbian mothers and gay fathers are noncustodial parents.

Effects on Adolescents of Having Lesbian Mothers and Gay Fathers
Researchers have found few differences in children and adolescents growing up with lesbian mothers or gay fathers and children and adolescents growing up with

heterosexual parents (Patterson, 2002). For example, adolescents growing up in gay or lesbian families are just as popular with their peers and there are no differences in the adjustment and mental health of adolescents living in these families when they are compared with adolescents in heterosexual families (Hyde & DeLamater, 2003). Also, the overwhelming majority of adolescents growing up in a gay or lesbian family have a heterosexual orientation (Tasker & Golombok, 1997).

Culture and Ethnicity

Family Diversity

What are some variations in families across different cultures? How do families vary across different ethnic groups?

Cross-Cultural Comparisons   Cultures vary on a number of issues involving families, such as what the father's role in the family should be, the extent to which support systems are available to families, and how children should be disciplined (Harkness & Super, 2002). Although there are cross-cultural variations in parenting, in one study of parenting behavior in 186 cultures around the world, the most common pattern was a warm and controlling style, one that was neither permissive nor restrictive (Rohner & Rohner, 1981). The investigators commented that the majority of cultures have discovered, over many centuries, a "truth" that only recently emerged in the Western world—namely, that children's and adolescents' healthy social development is most effectively promoted by love and at least some moderate parental control.

Nonetheless, in some countries, authoritarian parenting continues to be widely practiced. In the Arab world, families today are still very authoritarian and dominated by the father's rule (Booth, 2002). In Arab countries, adolescents are taught strict codes of conduct and family loyalty.

In many countries around the world, there are trends toward greater family mobility, migration to urban areas, family members working in distant cities or countries, smaller families, fewer extended-family households, and increases in the mother' employment (Brown & Larson, 2002). These trends can change the resources that are available to adolescents. For example, many families have fewer extended family members nearby, resulting in a decrease in support and guidance for adolescents. Also, smaller families may produce more openness and communication between parents and adolescents. We will have much more to say about culture and parenting in chapter 13, "Culture."

Ethnicity and Parenting   Ethnic minority families differ from White American families in their size, structure and composition, reliance on kinship networks, and level of income and education (Coll & Pachter, 2002). Large and extended families are more common among ethnic minority groups than among White Americans. For example, more than 30 percent of Latino families consist of five or more individuals. African American and Latino children interact more with grandparents, aunts, uncles, cousins, and more distant relatives than do White American children (Lyendecker & others, 2002; McAdoo, 2002).

Ethnic minority adolescents are more likely to come from low-income families than White American adolescents are (Magnuson & Duncan, 2002; McLoyd, 2000; Parke, 2004). Single-parent families are more common among African Americans and Latinos than among White Americans. In comparison with two-parent households, single-parent households often have more-limited resources of time, money, and energy. This shortage of resources can prompt parents to encourage autonomy among their adolescents prematurely. Ethnic minority parents, on average, are less well educated and engage in less joint decision making than White American parents.

The family reunion of the Limon family in Austin, Texas. Mexican American children often grow up in families with a network of relatives that runs into scores of individuals.

A 14-year-old adolescent, his 6-year-old sister, and their grandmother. The African American cultural tradition of an extended family household has helped many African American parents cope with adverse social conditions.

Although impoverished families often raise competent youth, poor parents can have a diminished capacity for supportive and involved parenting (McLoyd, 1990).

Some aspects of home life can help to protect ethnic minority youth from social patterns of injustice. The community and family can filter out destructive racist messages, parents can provide alternate frames of reference than those presented by the majority, and parents can also provide competent role models and encouragement. And the extended-family system in many ethnic minority families provides an important buffer to stress.

A sense of family duty and obligation also varies across ethnic groups (Fulgini, 2001). Asian American and Latino families place a greater emphasis on family duty and obligation than do non-Latino White families. Researchers have found that Asian American and Latino adolescents believe that they should spend more time taking care of their siblings, helping around the house, assisting their parents at work, and being with their family than adolescents with a European heritage (Fulgini, Tseng, & Lamb, 1999). Researchers also find that this sense of obligation does not diminish when Asian American and Latino adolescents become adults (Fulgini, 2001). In one recent study of 745 Americans from the twelfth grade into emerging adulthood three years later, a sense of family obligation increased for all Asian American, Latino American, and non-Latino White groups as they got older (Fulgini & Pedersen, 2002) (see figure 9.6). However, emerging adults from Filipino and Latin American families reported the strongest sense of familial duty during emerging adulthood, which provided an explanation of their tendency to live with and contribute financially to their families.

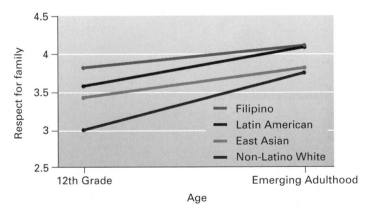

FIGURE 9.6 Changes in Attitudes Regarding Respect for Family from the Twelfth Grade into Emerging Adulthood for Individuals from Different Ethnic Groups

Note: The scale for respect for family ranged from 1 (not important at all) to 5 (very important). The scale is derived from the scores on 7 items, such as "makes sacrifices for your family," "follow your parents' advice about choosing a job or major in college," and "do well for the sake of your family." The graph shows the mean scores across the 7 items.

Review and reflect Learning goal 4

4 **Describe the changing family in a changing society**

REVIEW

- What are the effects of divorce on adolescents?
- How does growing up in a stepfamily influence adolescents' development?
- How do working parents influence adolescent development?
- What are the effects on adolescents of having gay or lesbian parents?
- What roles do culture and ethnicity play in families with adolescents?

REFLECT

- You have studied many aspects of families and adolescents in this chapter. Imagine that you have decided to write a book on adolescents and families. What would the title of the book be? What would be the main theme of the book?

5 SOCIAL POLICY, ADOLESCENTS, AND FAMILIES

We have seen in this chapter that parents play very important roles in adolescent development. Although adolescents are moving toward independence, they are still connected with their families, which are far more important to them than is commonly believed. We know that competent adolescent development is most likely to happen when adolescents have parents who (Small, 1990)

- Show them warmth and respect,
- Demonstrate sustained interest in their lives,
- Recognize and adapt to their changing cognitive and socioemotional development,
- Communicate expectations for high standards of conduct and achievement, and
- Display authoritative, constructive ways of dealing with problems and conflict.

Families as Asset Builders

However, compared with families with young children, families with adolescents have been neglected in community programs and public policies. The Carnegie Council on Adolescent Development (1995) identified some key opportunities for improving social policy regarding families with adolescents. These are some of the council's recommendations:

- School, cultural arts, religious and youth organizations, and health-care agencies should examine the extent to which they involve parents in activities with adolescents and should develop ways to engage parents and adolescents in activities they both enjoy.
- Professionals such as teachers, psychologists, nurses, physicians, youth specialists, and others who have contact with adolescents need not only to work with the individual adolescent but also to increase the time they spend interacting with the adolescent's family.
- Employers should extend to the parents of young adolescents the workplace policies now reserved only for the parents of young children. These policies include flexible work schedules, job sharing, telecommuting, and part-time work with benefits. This change in work/family policy would free parents to spend more time with their teenagers.
- Community institutions such as businesses, schools, and youth organizations should become more involved in providing after-school programs. After-school

programs for elementary school children are increasing, but such programs for adolescents are rare. More high-quality, community-based programs for adolescents are needed in the after-school, weekend, and vacation time periods.

Review and reflect   Learning goal 5

5   **Explain what is needed for improved social policy involving adolescents and their families**

REVIEW

- What is needed for improved social policy regarding adolescents and their families?

REFLECT

- If you were a U.S. senator, what would you seek to do to improve social policy involving the families of adolescents? What would be your number one priority?

REACH YOUR LEARNING GOALS

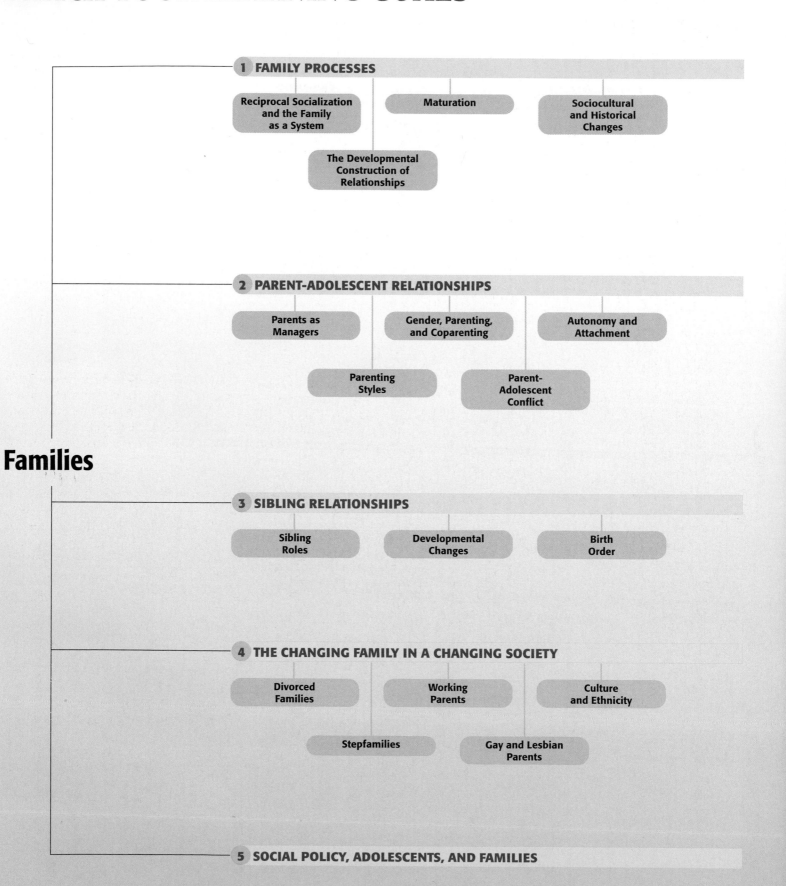

Families

1 FAMILY PROCESSES

- Reciprocal Socialization and the Family as a System
- Maturation
- Sociocultural and Historical Changes
- The Developmental Construction of Relationships

2 PARENT-ADOLESCENT RELATIONSHIPS

- Parents as Managers
- Gender, Parenting, and Coparenting
- Autonomy and Attachment
- Parenting Styles
- Parent-Adolescent Conflict

3 SIBLING RELATIONSHIPS

- Sibling Roles
- Developmental Changes
- Birth Order

4 THE CHANGING FAMILY IN A CHANGING SOCIETY

- Divorced Families
- Working Parents
- Culture and Ethnicity
- Stepfamilies
- Gay and Lesbian Parents

5 SOCIAL POLICY, ADOLESCENTS, AND FAMILIES

Summary

1 Discuss the nature of family processes in adolescence

- Adolescents socialize parents just as parents socialize adolescents. Synchrony involves the carefully coordinated interaction between parent and adolescent, in which, often unknowingly, they are attuned to each other's behavior. The family is a system of interacting individuals with different subsystems—some dyadic, some polyadic.
- The developmental construction views share the belief that as individuals develop they acquire modes of relating to others. There are two main variations within this view, one that emphasizes continuity and one that stresses discontinuity and change in relationships.
- Relationships are influenced by the maturation of the adolescent and the maturation of parents. Adolescent changes include puberty, expanded logical reasoning, increased idealistic and egocentric thought, violated expectations, changes in schooling, peers, friendships, dating, and movement toward independence. Changes in parents might include marital dissatisfaction, economic burdens, career reevaluation, time perspective, and health/body concerns.

2 Describe parent-adolescent relationships

- An increasing trend is to conceptualize parents as managers of adolescents' lives. This involves being a parent who finds information, makes contacts, helps structure choices, and provides guidance. Parents also can serve as regulators of their adolescents' social contacts with peers, friends, and adults.
- Authoritarian, authoritative, neglectful, and indulgent are four main parenting styles. Authoritative parenting is associated with socially competent adolescent behavior more than the other styles.
- Most people associate motherhood with a number of positive images, but the reality is that motherhood is accorded a relatively low status in American society. Over time, the father's role in the child's development has changed. Fathers are less involved in child rearing than mothers are, but fathers are increasing the time they spend with children. Coparenting, father-mother cooperation, and mutual respect help the adolescent to develop positive attitudes toward males and females.
- Conflict with parents does increase in early adolescence, but such conflict is usually moderate and can serve a positive developmental function of increasing independence and identity exploration. The generation gap is exaggerated, although in as many as 20 percent of families parent-adolescent conflict is too high and is linked with adolescent problems.
- Many parents have a difficult time handling the adolescent's push for autonomy. Autonomy is a complex concept with many referents. Developmental transitions in autonomy include the onset of early adolescence and the time when individuals leave home and go to college. A special concern about autonomy involves runaways. The wise parent relinquishes control in areas where the adolescent makes mature decisions and retains more control in areas where the adolescent makes immature decisions. Adolescents do not simply move away into a world isolated from parents. Attachment to parents in adolescence increases the probability that an adolescent will be socially competent and explore a widening social world in a healthy way. Increasingly, researchers classify attachment in adolescence into one secure category (secure-autonomous) and three insecure categories (dismissing/avoidant, preoccupied/ambivalent, and unresolved/disorganized).

3 Characterize sibling relationships in adolescence

- Sibling relationships often involve more conflict than relationships with other individuals. However, adolescents also share many positive moments with siblings through emotional support and social communication.
- Although sibling conflict in adolescence is reasonably high, it is usually less than in childhood.
- Birth order has been of special interest and differences between firstborns and later-borns have been reported. The only child often is more socially competent than the stereotype "spoiled child" suggests. An increasing number of family researchers believe that birth-order effects have been overdramatized and that other factors are more important in predicting the adolescent's behavior.

4 Describe the changing family in a changing society

- Adolescents in divorced families have more adjustment problems than their counterparts in non-divorced families, although the size of the effects is debated. Whether parents should stay together for the sake of the adolescent is difficult to determine, although conflict has a negative effect on the adolescent. Adolescents are better adjusted in divorced families when their parents have a harmonious relationship with each other and use authoritative parenting. Among other factors to be considered in adolescent adjustment are adjustment prior to the divorce, personality and temperament, developmental status, gender, and custody. Income loss for divorced mothers is linked to a number of other stresses that can affect adolescent adjustment.
- An increasing number of adolescents are growing up in stepfamilies. Stepfamilies involve different types of structure (stepfather, stepmother, blended) and relationships (neotraditional, matriarchal, and romantic). Adolescents in stepfamilies have more adjustment problems than children in nondivorced homes. Adjustment is especially difficult in the first several years of a stepfamily's existence and is difficult for young adolescents.
- Overall, the mother's working outside the home does not have an adverse effect on the adolescent. Latchkey experiences do not have a uniformly negative effect on adolescents. Parental monitoring and structured activities in the

345

after-school hours benefit latchkey adolescents. Relocation can have a more adverse effect on adolescents than children, although research on this issue is sparse. Unemployment of parents has detrimental effects on adolescents.

- Approximately 20 percent of lesbians and 10 percent of gays are parents. There is considerable diversity among lesbian mothers, gay fathers, and their adolescents. Researchers have found few differences in adolescents growing up in gay or lesbian families and adolescents growing up in heterosexual families.
- Authoritative parenting is the most common form of parenting around the world. Ethnic minority families differ from non-Latino White families in their size, structure, and composition, their reliance on kinship networks, and their levels of income and education.

5 Explain what is needed for improved social policy involving adolescents and their families

- Families with adolescents have been neglected in social policy. A number of recommendations for improving social policy for families include the extent parents are involved in schools, youth organizations, and health-care agencies; the degree teachers and other professionals invite and encourage parents to be involved in schools and other settings that adolescents frequent; the extent to which policies are developed to allow employers to provide more flexible scheduling for parents; and greater funding by institutions such as businesses, schools, and youth organizations for involving parents in after-school youth programs.

Key Terms

reciprocal socialization 309
synchrony 310
developmental construction views 311
continuity view 311

discontinuity view 313
authoritarian parenting 318
authoritative parenting 318
neglectful parenting 318
indulgent parenting 319

emotional autonomy 325
secure attachment 327
insecure attachment 327
dismissing/avoidant attachment 327

preoccupied/ambivalent attachment 327
unresolved/disorganized attachment 327
boundary ambiguity 336

Key People

Andrew Collins 313
Diana Baumrind 318

John Bowlby and Mary Ainsworth 327

Joseph Allen 327
E. Mavis Hetherington 334

Lois Hoffman 337

Resources for Improving the Lives of Adolescents

Between Parent and Teenager

(1969) by Haim Ginott
New York: Avon

Despite the fact that *Between Parent and Teenager* is well past its own adolescence (it was published in 1969), it continues to be one of the most widely read and recommended books for parents who want to communicate more effectively with their teenagers.

Big Brothers/Big Sisters of America

17 South 17th Street, Suite 1200
Philadelphia, PA 19103
215–567–2748

Single mothers and single fathers who are having problems with a son or daughter might want to get a responsible adult to spend at least one afternoon every other week with the son or daughter.

Raising Black Children

(1992) by James P. Comer and Alvin E. Poussaint
New York: Plume

This excellent book includes many wise suggestions for raising African American children.

Stepfamily Association of America

602 East Joppa Road
Baltimore, MD 21204
410–823–7570

This organization provides a support network for stepparents, remarried parents, and their children.

You and Your Adolescent

(1997, 2nd ed.) by Laurence Steinberg and Ann Levine
New York: Harper Perennial

You and Your Adolescent provides a broad, developmental overview of adolescence, with parental advice mixed in along the way.

E-Learning Tools

To help you master the material in this chapter, you will find a number of valuable study tools on the student CD-ROM that accompanies this book. In addition, visit the Online Learning Center for *Adolescence, 10th Edition,* where you will find helpful resources for chapter 9, "Families."

Taking It to the Net

http://www.mhhe.com/santrocka10

1. Parents are a valuable resource for adolescents who need to cope with extreme stress, such as that which often is felt when parents divorce, when the adolescent must deal with the death of a friend or family member, or when a disaster occurs. What tips would you include in a list that parents could use to help their adolescents cope with extreme stress?

2. All parents must determine how to discipline their children. Discipline techniques used during childhood may have important implications for adolescent development and behavior. What would you advise parents about spanking their children? Does it have important consequences for later adolescent behavior?

3. Some evidence suggests that the way we parent is influenced by how our parents parented us. How did your parents rear you? What was their style? Will yours be the same?

Connect to **http://www.mhhe.com/santrocka10** to research the answers and complete these exercises. In some cases, you'll also find further instructions on this site.

Self-Assessment

To evaluate yourself regarding family and parenting issues and ideas, complete the self-assessment: How Much Did My Parents Monitor My Behavior During Adolescence?

Health and Well-Being, Parenting, and Education

To practice your decision-making skills, complete the health and well-being, parenting, and education scenarios.

CHAPTER
10

A man's growth is seen in the successive choirs of his friends.
—RALPH WALDO EMERSON, 1841
American Poet and Essayist, 19th Century

Peers

Images of Adolescent Development

Young Adolescent Girls' Friends and Relational Worlds

Lynn Brown and Carol Gilligan (1992) conducted in-depth interviews of 100 girls 10 to 13 years of age who were making the transition to the relational worlds of adolescence. They listened to what these girls were saying about how important friends were to them. The girls were very curious about the world they lived in and kept track of what was happening to the peers and friends in their world. The girls spoke about the pleasure they derived from the intimacy and fun of human connection, and about the potential for hurt in relationships. They especially highlighted the importance of clique formation in their lives.

One girl, Noura, says that she learned about what it feels like to be the person that everyone doesn't like and that it was very painful. Another girl, Gail, reflected on her life over the last year and says that she is now getting along better with people, probably because she is better at understanding how they think and at accepting them. A number of the girls talked about "whitewashing" in the adolescent relational world. That is, many girls say nice and kind things to be polite but often don't really mean them. They know the benefits of being perceived as the perfect, happy girl, at least on the surface. Suspecting that people prefer the "perfect girl," they experiment with her image and the happiness she might bring. The perfectly nice girl seems to gain popularity with other girls, and as many girls strive to become her, jealousies and rivalries break out. Cliques can provide emotional support for girls who are striving to be perfect but know they are not. One girl, Victoria, commented that some girls like her, who weren't very popular, nonetheless were accepted into a "club" with three other girls. She now feels that when she is sad or depressed she can count on the "club" for support. Though they were "leftovers" and did not get into the most popular cliques, these girls say they know they are liked and it feels great.

Another girl, Judy, at age 13, spoke about her interest in romantic relationships. She says that although she and her girlfriends are only 13, they want to have romantic relationships. She covers her bodily desires and sexual feelings with romantic ideals. She describes a girl who goes out with guys and goes farther than most girls would and says the girl's behavior is "disgusting." Rather than sex, Judy says she is looking for a really good relationship with a guy.

W hen you think back to your adolescent years, you may recall many of your most enjoyable moments as being spent with peers—on the telephone, in school activities, in the neighborhood, on dates, at dances, or just hanging out. In this chapter we will explore many aspects of peer relations, especially focusing on the developmental changes that they undergo. Adolescents have a larger number of acquaintances in their peer network than children do. Beginning in early adolescence, teenagers also typically prefer a smaller number of friendships that are more intense and intimate than those of children. Cliques and crowds take on more importance as adolescents "hang out" together. And dating and romantic relationships become part of most adolescents' lives.

1   EXPLORING PEER RELATIONS

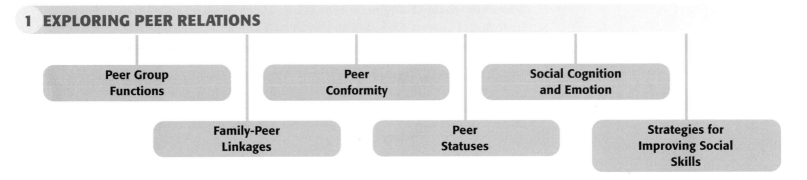

Peers play very important roles in the lives of adolescents. Let's explore what these roles are.

Peer Group Functions

Adolescents have strong needs to be liked and accepted by friends and the larger peer group, which can result in pleasurable feelings when accepted or extreme stress and anxiety when excluded and disparaged by peers. To many adolescents, how they are seen by peers is the most important aspect of their lives. Contrast Bob, who has no close friends, with Steve, who has three close buddies he pals around with all of the time. Sally was turned down by the group at school that she was working for six months to get into, in contrast to Sandra, who is a member of the group and who frequently is told by her peers how "super" her personality is.

Some friends of mine have a 13-year-old daughter. Last year, she had a number of girlfriends—she spent a lot of time on the phone talking with them, and they frequently visited each other's homes. Then her family moved, which meant that she was transferred to a school with a lower socioeconomic mix of students than at her previous school. Many of the girls at the new school feel that my friend's daughter is "too good" for them, and because of this she is having difficulty making friends this year. One of her most frequent complaints is, "I don't have any friends. . . . None of the kids at school ever call me. And none of them ever ask me over to their houses. What can I do?"

Peers are children or adolescents who are about the same age or maturity level. Same-age peer interaction serves a unique role in U.S. culture. Age grading would occur even if schools were not age graded and adolescents were left alone to determine the composition of their own societies. After all, one can learn to be a good fighter only among age-mates: The bigger guys will kill you, and the little ones are no challenge. One of the most important functions of the peer group is to provide a source of information about the world outside the family. From the peer group, adolescents receive feedback about their abilities. Adolescents learn whether what they do is better than, as good as, or worse than what other adolescents do. Learning this at home is difficult because siblings are usually older or younger.

peers Children or adolescents who are about the same age or maturity level.

Adolescent Peer Relations

As you read about peers, also keep in mind that although peer experiences have important influences on children's development, those influences vary according to the way peer experience is measured, the outcomes specified, and the developmental trajectories traversed (Hartup, 1999). "Peers" and "peer group" are global concepts. These can be beneficial concepts in understanding peer influences as long as they are considered as "setting conditions," and the specific type of setting in which the child participates, such as "acquaintance," "clique," "neighborhood associates," "friendship network," and "activity group," is taken into account. For example, one analysis of the peer groups describes these aspects of the youth culture: membership crowd, neighborhood crowd, reference crowd, church crowd, sports team, friendship group, and friend (Brown, 1999).

Developmental Changes in Peer Time   Children spend an increasing amount of time in peer interaction during middle and late childhood and adolescence. In one investigation, children interacted with peers 10 percent of their day at age 2, 20 percent at age 4, and more than 40 percent between the ages of 7 and 11 (Barker & Wright, 1951). In a typical school day, there were 299 episodes with peers per day. By adolescence, peer relations occupy large chunks of an individual's life. In one investigation, over the course of one weekend, young adolescent boys and girls spent more than twice as much time with peers as with parents (Condry, Simon, & Bronfenbrenn 1968).

What do adolescents do when they are with their peers? In one study, sixth-graders were asked what they do when they are with their friends (Medrich & others, 1982). Team sports accounted for 45 percent of boys' activities but only 26 percent of girls'. General play, going places, and socializing were common listings for both sexes. Most peer interactions occur outside the home (although close to home), occur more often in private than public places, and occur more between children of the same sex than of the opposite sex.

Are Peers Necessary for Development?   When peer monkeys who have been reared together are separated from one another, they become depressed and less advanced socially (Suomi, Harlow, & Domek, 1970). The human development literature contains a classic example of the importance of peers in social development. Anna Freud (Freud & Dann, 1951) studied six children from different families who banded together after their parents were killed in World War II. Intensive peer attachment was observed; the children were a tightly knit group, dependent on one another and aloof with outsiders. Even though deprived of parental care, they became neither delinquent nor psychotic.

Good peer relations might be necessary for normal social development in adolescence. Social isolation, or the inability to "plug in" to a social network, is linked with many different forms of problems and disorders, ranging from delinquency and problem drinking to depression (Kupersmidt & Coie, 1990). In one study of adolescents, positive peer relationships were associated with positive social adjustment (Ryan & Patrick, 1996). Peer relations in childhood and adolescence are also related to later development. In one study, poor peer relations in childhood were associated with dropping out of school and delinquency in late adolescence (Roff, Sells, & Golden, 1972). In another study, harmonious peer relations during adolescence were linked with positive mental health at midlife (Hightower, 1990).

And in another study, children who had a stable best friend in fifth grade and their fifth-grade counterparts who were friendless were assessed 12 years later as adults (Bagwell, Newcomb, & Bukowski, 1998). Children who had a stable best friend in fifth grade had a more positive sense of self-worth as adults than their counterparts who had been friendless in fifth grade.

Positive and Negative Peer Relations   As you might have detected from our discussion of peer relations thus far, peer influences can be both positive and negative

(Brown, 2004; Rubin, Bukowski & Parker, 1998). Both Jean Piaget (1932) and Harry Stack Sullivan (1953) were influential theorists who stressed that it is through peer interaction that children and adolescents learn the symmetrical reciprocity mode of relationships discussed in chapter 5. Children explore the principles of fairness and justice by working through disagreements with peers. They also learn to be keen observers of peers' interests and perspectives in order to smoothly integrate themselves into ongoing peer activities. In addition, Sullivan argued that adolescents learn to be skilled and sensitive partners in intimate relationships by forging close friendships with selected peers. These intimacy skills are carried forward to help form the foundation of later dating and marital relationships, according to Sullivan.

In contrast, some theorists have emphasized the negative influences of peers on children's and adolescents' development. Being rejected or overlooked by peers leads some adolescents to feel lonely or hostile. Further, such rejection and neglect by peers are related to an individual's subsequent mental health and criminal problems. Some theorists have also described the adolescent peer culture as a corrupt influence that undermines parental values and control. Further, peers can introduce adolescents to alcohol, drugs, delinquency, and other forms of behavior that adults view as maladaptive.

Family-Peer Linkages

Some researchers have found that parents and adolescents perceive that parents have little authority over adolescents' choices in some areas but more authority of choices in other areas. For example, Judith Smetana's research has revealed that both parents and adolescents view peer relations as an arena in which parents have little authority to dictate adolescents' choices, in contrast to moral, religious, and educational arenas in which parents are perceived as having more authority (Smetana, 2002; Smetana & Turiel, 2003).

Adolescents do show a strong motivation to be with their peers and become independent. However, it is incorrect to assume that movement toward peer involvement and autonomy are unrelated to parent-adolescent relationships. Recent studies have provided persuasive evidence that adolescents live in a connected world with parents and peers, not a disconnected one (Ladd & Le Sieur, 1995; Ladd & Pettit, 2002; Scharf & Schulman, 2000; Tilton-Weaver & Leighter, 2002).

What are some of the ways the worlds of parents and peers are connected? Parents' choices of neighborhoods, churches, schools, and their own friends influence the pool from which their adolescents select possible friends (Cooper & Ayers-Lopez, 1985). For example, parents can choose to live in a neighborhood with playgrounds, parks, and youth organizations or in a neighborhood where houses are far apart, few adolescents live, and youth organizations are not well developed.

Parents can model or coach their adolescents in ways of relating to peers. In one study, parents acknowledged that they recommended specific strategies to their adolescents to help them develop more positive peer relations (Rubin & Solman, 1984). For example, parents discussed with their adolescents ways that disputes could be mediated and how to become less shy. They also encouraged them to be tolerant and to resist peer pressure. And in one study, young adolescents talked more frequently about peer-related problems with their mothers than with their fathers (Gauze, 1994).

In addition, as we discussed in chapter 9, an increasing number of researchers have found that secure attachment to parents is related to the adolescent's positive peer relations (Allen & others, 2003). In one study, adolescents who were securely attached to parents were also securely attached to their peers; adolescents who were insecurely attached to their parents were likewise insecurely attached to their peers (Armsden & Greenberg, 1984). And in another study, older adolescents who had an ambivalent attachment history with their parents reported less satisfaction in their relationship with their best friend than did their securely attached counterparts (Fisher, 1990).

What are some links between parent-adolescent and adolescent-peer relations?

However, whereas adolescent-parent attachments are correlated with adolescent outcomes, the correlations are moderate, indicating that the success or failure of parent-adolescent attachments does not necessarily guarantee success or failure in peer relationships. Clearly, secure attachment with parents can be an asset for the adolescent, fostering the trust to engage in close relationships with others and lay down the foundation for close relationship skills. But a significant minority of adolescents from strong, supportive families, nonetheless, struggle in peer relations for a variety of reasons, such as being physically unattractive, maturing late, and experiencing cultural and SES discrepancies. On the other hand, some adolescents from troubled families find a positive, fresh start with peer relations that can compensate for their problematic family backgrounds. For a personal account of the kinds of relationships teenagers form with their peers and with their parents, watch the video segment entitled "Views on Family and Peers at Age 15."

Peer Conformity

Conformity comes in many forms and affects many aspects of adolescents' lives. Do adolescents take up jogging because everyone else is doing it? Do adolescents let their hair grow long one year and cut it short the next because of fashion? Do adolescents take cocaine if pressured by others, or do they resist the pressure? **Conformity** occurs when individuals adopt the attitudes or behavior of others because of real or imagined pressure from them. The pressure to conform to peers becomes very strong during the adolescent years. Consider the comments of Kevin, an eighth-grader:

> I feel a lot of pressure from my friends to smoke and steal and things like that. My parents do not allow me to smoke, but my best friends are really pushing me to do it. They call me a pansy and a momma's boy if I don't. I really don't like the idea of smoking, but my good friend Steve told me in front of some of our friends, "Kevin, you are an idiot and a chicken wrapped up in one little body." I couldn't stand it any more, so I smoked with them. I was coughing and humped over, but I still said, "This is really fun—yeah, I like it." I felt like I was part of the group.

conformity This occurs when individuals adopt the attitudes or behaviors of others because of real or imagined pressure from them.

Also, think about the statement by 14-year-old Andrea:

> Peer pressure is extremely influential in my life. I have never had very many friends, and I spend quite a bit of time alone. The friends I have are older. . . . The closest friend I have had is a lot like me in that we are both sad and depressed a lot. I began to act even more depressed than before when I was with her. I would call her up and try to act even more depressed than I was because that is what I thought she liked. In that relationship, I felt pressure to be like her.

Conformity to peer pressure in adolescence can be positive or negative. Teenagers engage in all sorts of negative conformity behavior—using seedy language, stealing, vandalizing, and making fun of parents and teachers. However, a great deal of peer conformity is not negative and consists of the desire to be involved in the peer world, such as dressing like friends and wanting to spend huge chunks of time with members of a clique. Such circumstances may involve prosocial activities as well, as when clubs raise money for worthy causes.

In a study focused on negative, neutral, and positive aspects of peer conformity, Thomas Berndt (1979) studied 273 third-grade through twelfth-grade students. Hypothetical dilemmas that were presented to the students required the students to make choices about conformity with friends on prosocial and antisocial behavior and about conformity with parents on neutral and prosocial behaviors. For example, one prosocial item questioned whether students relied on their parents' advice in such situations as deciding about helping at the library or instructing another child to swim. An antisocial question asked a boy what he would do if one of his peers wanted him to help steal some candy. A neutral question asked a girl if she would follow peer suggestions to engage in an activity she wasn't interested in, such as going to a movie she did not want to see.

Some interesting developmental patterns were found in this investigation (see figure 10.1). In the third grade, parent and peer influences often directly contradicted each other. Since parent conformity is much greater for third-grade children, children of this age are probably still closely tied to and dependent on their parents. However, by the sixth grade, parent and peer influences were found to be no longer in direct opposition. Peer conformity had increased, but parent and peer influences were operating in different situations—parents had more impact in some situations, while peers had more clout in others.

By the ninth grade, parent and peer influences were once again in strong opposition to each other, probably because the conformity of adolescents to the social behavior of peers is much stronger at this grade level than at any other. At this time, adolescent adoption of antisocial standards endorsed by the peer group inevitably leads to conflict between adolescents and parents. Researchers have also found that the adolescent's attempt to gain independence meets with more parental opposition around the ninth grade than at any other time (Douvan & Adelson, 1966).

A stereotypical view of parent-child relationships suggests that parent-peer opposition continues through high school into the college-age years. But Berndt (1979) found that adolescent conformity to antisocial, peer-endorsed behavior decreases in the late high school years, and agreement between parents and peers begins to increase in some areas. In addition, by the eleventh and twelfth grades, students show signs of developing a decision-making style more independent of peer and parental influence.

In sum, peer pressure is a pervasive theme of adolescents' lives. Its power can be observed in almost every dimension of adolescents' behavior—their choice of dress, music, language, values, leisure activities, and so on. Parents, teachers, and other adults can help adolescents to deal with peer pressure (Clasen & Brown, 1987). Adolescents need many opportunities to talk with both peers and adults about their social worlds and the pressures involved. The developmental changes of adolescence often bring forth a sense of insecurity. Young adolescents may be especially vulnerable

> *Teenagers are people who express a burning desire to be different by dressing exactly alike.*
> —ANONYMOUS

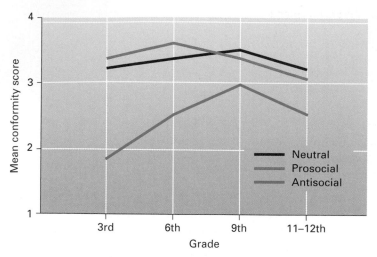

FIGURE 10.1 Developmental Changes in Conformity to Peer Standards
The conformity scale ranged from 1 to 7 with higher scores indicating greater conformity.

because of this insecurity and the many developmental changes taking place in their lives. To counter this stress, young adolescents need to experience opportunities for success, both in and out of school, that increase their sense of being in control. Adolescents can learn that their social world is reciprocally controlled. Others might try to control them, but they can exert personal control over their actions and influence others in turn. Next, in our discussion of peer popularity, neglect, and rejection, we discuss further the powerful role that peer relations play in adolescent development.

Peer Statuses

Most adolescents want to be popular—you probably thought about popularity a lot when you were in junior and senior high school. Teenagers commonly think, "What can I do to have all of the kids at school like me?" "How can I be popular with both girls and guys?" "What's wrong with me? There must be something wrong, or I would be more popular." Sometimes, adolescents go to great lengths to be popular; and in some cases, parents go to even greater lengths to try to insulate their adolescents from rejection and to increase the likelihood that they will be popular. Students show off and cut up because it gets attention and makes their peers laugh. Parents set up elaborate parties, buy cars and clothes for their teens, and drive adolescents and their friends all over in the hope that their sons or daughters will be popular.

Popular children are frequently nominated as a best friend and rarely are disliked by their peers. Researchers have discovered that popular children and adolescents give out reinforcements, listen carefully, maintain open lines of communication with peers, are happy, act like themselves, show enthusiasm and concern for others, and are self-confident without being conceited (Hartup, 1983). In one study, popular youth were more likely than unpopular youth to communicate clearly with their peers, elicit their peers' attention, and maintain conversation with peers (Kennedy, 1990).

Certain physical and cultural factors also affect adolescents' popularity. Adolescents who are physically attractive are more popular than those who are not (Kennedy, 1990) and, contrary to what some believe, brighter adolescents are more popular than less intelligent ones. Adolescents growing up in middle-SES surroundings tend to be more popular than those growing up in lower-SES surroundings, presumably in part because they are more in control of establishing standards for popularity (Hollingshead, 1975). But remember that findings such as these reflect group averages—there are many physically attractive teenagers who are unpopular, and some physically unattractive ones who are very well liked. Sociologist James Coleman (1980) points out that, for adolescents in the average range, there is little or no relation between physical attractiveness and popularity. It is only in the extremes (very attractive and very unattractive) that a link between popularity and attractiveness holds.

Developmentalists distinguish three types of children who have a different status than popular children: those who are (1) neglected, (2) rejected, or (3) controversial (Wentzel & Asher, 1995):

- **Neglected children** are infrequently nominated as a best friend but are not disliked by their peers.
- **Rejected children** are infrequently nominated as someone's best friend and are actively disliked by their peers.
- **Controversial children** are frequently nominated both as someone's best friend and as being disliked.

popular children Children who are frequently nominated as a best friend and are rarely disliked by their peers.

neglected children Children who are infrequently nominated as a best friend but are not disliked by their peers.

rejected children Children who are infrequently nominated as a best friend and are actively disliked by their peers.

controversial children Children who are frequently nominated both as a best friend and as being disliked.

Rejected children and adolescents often have more serious adjustment problems later in life than those who are neglected. For example, in one study, 112 fifth-grade boys were evaluated over a period of 7 years until the end of high school (Kupersmidt & Coie, 1990). The key factor in predicting whether rejected children would engage in delinquent behavior or drop out of school later during adolescence was their aggression toward peers in elementary school.

Not all rejected children and adolescents are aggressive. Although aggression and its related characteristics of impulsiveness and disruptiveness underlie rejection about half the time, approximately 10 to 20 percent of rejected children and adolescents are shy (Cillessen & others, 1992). Later in the chapter, we will discuss strategies for improving the social skills of adolescents, including ways to improve the peer relations of neglected and rejected children.

Social Cognition and Emotion

The social cognitive skills and social knowledge of adolescents are important aspects of successful peer relations. So is the ability to manage and regulate one's emotions.

Social Cognition   A distinction can be made between knowledge and process in cognition. In studying cognitive aspects of peer relations, this distinction can be made. Learning about the social knowledge adolescents bring with them to peer relations is important, as is studying how adolescents process information during peer interaction.

As children move into adolescence, they acquire more social knowledge, and there is considerable individual variation in how much one adolescent knows about what it takes to make friends, to get peers to like him or her, and so forth. For example, does the adolescent know that giving out reinforcements will increase the likelihood that he or she will be popular? That is, does Mary consciously know that, by telling Barbara such things as "I really like that sweater you have on today" and "Gosh, you sure are popular with the guys," she will enhance the likelihood Barbara will want her to be her friend? Does the adolescent know that, when others perceive that he or she is similar to them, he or she will be liked better by the others? Does the adolescent know that friendship involves sharing intimate conversations and that a friendship likely is improved when the adolescent shares private, confidential information with another adolescent? To what extent does the adolescent know that comforting and listening skills will improve friendship relations? To what extent does the adolescent know what it takes to become a leader? Think back to your adolescent years. How sophisticated were you in knowing about such social matters? Were you aware of the role of nice statements and perceived similarity in determining popularity and friendship? While you may not have been aware of these factors, those of you who were popular and maintained close friendships likely were competent at using these strategies.

From a social cognitive perspective, children and adolescents may have difficulty in peer relations because they lack appropriate social cognitive skills (Coie & Dodge, 1998; Crick & Dodge, 1994; Dodge, 1993; Lochman & Dodge, 1998). One investigation explored the possibility that social cognitive skill deficits characterize children who have peer-related difficulties (Asarnow & Callan, 1985). Boys with and without peer adjustment difficulties were identified, and then a number of social cognitive processes or skills were assessed. These included the boys' ability to generate alternative solutions to hypothetical problems, to evaluate these solutions in terms of their effectiveness, and to describe self-statements. It was found that boys without peer adjustment problems generated more alternative solutions, proposed more assertive and mature solutions, gave less intense aggressive solutions, showed more adaptive planning, and evaluated physically aggressive responses less positively than the boys with peer adjustment problems. For example, as shown in figure 10.2, negative-peer-status sixth-grade boys were not as likely to generate alternative solutions and were much less likely to adaptively plan ahead than their positive-peer-status counterparts.

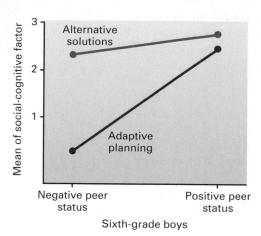

FIGURE 10.2 Generation of Alternative Solutions and Adaptive Planning by Negative- and Positive-Peer-Status Boys

Notice that negative-peer-status boys were less likely to generate alternative solutions and plan ahead than were their positive-peer-status counterparts.

Now let's examine how social information processing might be involved in peer relations. For example, consider the situation when a peer accidentally trips and knocks a boy's soft drink out of his hand. The boy misinterprets the encounter as hostile, which leads him to retaliate aggressively against the peer. Through repeated encounters of this kind, peers come to perceive the boy as having a habit of acting inappropriately. Kenneth Dodge (1993) argues that children go through five steps in processing information about their social world: decoding of social cues, interpretation, response search, selecting an optimal response, and enactment. Dodge has found that aggressive boys are more likely to perceive another child's actions as hostile when the peer's intention is ambiguous. And when aggressive boys search for cues to determine a peer's intention, they respond more rapidly, less efficiently, and less reflectively than nonaggressive children. These are among the social cognitive factors believed to be involved in children's and adolescents' conflicts with each other.

Emotion   Not only does cognition play an important role in peer relations, so does emotion. For example, the ability to regulate emotion is linked to successful peer relations (Rubin, 2000; Underwood, 2003; Underwood & Hurley, 2000). Moody and emotionally negative individuals experience greater rejection by peers, whereas emotionally positive individuals are more popular (Saarni, 1999). Adolescents who have effective self-regulatory skills can modulate their emotional expressiveness in contexts that evoke intense emotions, as when a peer says something negative. In one study, rejected children were more likely than popular children to use negative gestures in a provoking situation (Underwood & Hurley, 1997).

Strategies for Improving Social Skills

A number of strategies have been proposed for improving social skills that can lead to better peer relations (Ladd, Buhs, & Troop, 2002). **Conglomerate strategies,** also referred to as coaching, involve the use of a combination of techniques, rather than a single approach, to improve adolescents' social skills. A conglomerate strategy might consist of demonstration or modeling of appropriate social skills, discussion, and reasoning about the social skills, as well as the use of reinforcement for their enactment in actual social situations. In one coaching study, students with few friends were selected and trained in ways to have fun with peers. The "unpopular" students were encouraged to participate fully, to show interest in others, to cooperate, and to maintain communication. A control group of students (who also had few friends) was directed in peer experiences but was not coached specifically in terms of improved peer

conglomerate strategies The use of a combination of techniques, rather than a single approach, to improve adolescents' social skills; also called coaching.

strategies. Subsequent assessment revealed that the coaching was effective, with the coached group members showing more sociability when observed in peer relationships than their noncoached counterparts.

Other efforts to teach social skills also have used conglomerate strategies (Merrell & Gimpel, 1997). In one study, middle school adolescents were instructed in ways to improve their self-control, stress management, and social problem solving (Weissberg & Caplan, 1989). For example, as problem situations arose, teachers modeled and students practiced six sequential steps: (1) stop, calm down, and think before you act; (2) go over the problem and state how you feel; (3) set a positive goal; (4) think of lots of solutions; (5) plan ahead for the consequences; (6) go ahead and try the best plan. The 240 adolescents who participated in the program improved their ability to devise cooperative solutions to problem situations, and their teachers reported that the students showed improved social relations in the classroom following the program. In another study, boys and girls in a low-income area of New Jersey were given instruction in social decision making, self-control, and group awareness (Clabby & Elias, 1988). When compared with boys and girls who did not receive the training, the program participants were more sensitive to the feelings of others, more mindful of the consequences of their actions, and better able to analyze problem situations and act appropriately.

More specifically, how can neglected children and adolescents be trained to interact more effectively with their peers? The goal of training programs with neglected children and adolescents is often to help them attract attention from their peers in positive ways and to hold their attention by asking questions, by listening in a warm and friendly way, and by saying things about themselves that relate to the peers' interests. They also are taught to enter groups more effectively.

The goal of training programs with rejected children and adolescents is often to help them listen to peers and "hear what they say" instead of trying to dominate peer interactions. Rejected children and adolescents are trained to join peers without trying to change what is taking place in the peer group.

One issue that has been raised about improving the peer relations of rejected children and adolescents is whether the focus should be on improving their prosocial skills (better empathy, careful listening, improved communication skills, and so on) or on reducing their aggressive, disruptive behavior and improving their self-control (Coie & Koeppl, 1990). In one study, socially rejected young adolescents were coached on the importance of showing behaviors that would improve their chance of being liked by others (Murphy & Schneider, 1994). The intervention was successful in improving the friendships of the socially rejected youth.

Despite the positive outcomes of some programs that attempt to improve the social skills of adolescents, researchers have often found it difficult to improve the social skills of adolescents who are actively disliked and rejected. Many of these adolescents are rejected because they are aggressive or impulsive and lack the self-control to keep these behaviors in check. Still, some intervention programs have been successful in reducing the aggressive and impulsive behaviors of these adolescents (Ladd, Buhs, & Troop, 2002).

Social skills training programs have generally been more successful with children 10 years of age or younger than with adolescents (Malik & Furman, 1993). Peer reputations become more fixed as cliques and peer groups become more salient in adolescence. Once an adolescent gains a negative reputation among peers as being "mean," "weird," or a "loner," the peer group's attitude is often slow to change, even after the adolescent's problem behavior has been corrected. Thus, researchers have found that skills interventions may need to be supplemented by efforts to change the minds of peers. One such intervention strategy involves cooperative group training (Slavin, Hurley, & Chamberlin, 2003). In this approach, children or adolescents work toward a common goal that holds promise for changing reputations. Most cooperative group programs have been conducted in academic settings, but other contexts might be used. For example, participation in cooperative games and sports increases sharing and feelings of happiness. And some video games require cooperative efforts by the players.

Review and reflect Learning goal 1

1 **Discuss the role of peer relations in adolescent development**

REVIEW

- What functions does the peer group serve in adolescence?
- How are families and peers linked?
- How extensively do adolescents conform to peers?
- What are four peer statuses? How are they related to adolescent development?
- What roles do social cognition and emotion play in adolescent development?
- What are some strategies for improving adolescent social skills?

REFLECT

- Think back to when you were in middle/junior high school and high school. What was your relationship with your parents like? Were you securely or insecurely attached to them? How do you think your relationship with your parents affected your peer relations and friendships in adolescence?

2 FRIENDSHIP

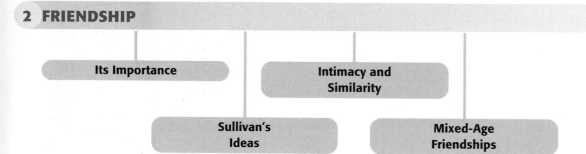

Earlier we indicated that peers are individuals who are about the same age or maturity level. **Friends** are a subset of peers who engage in mutual companionship, support, and intimacy. Thus, relationships with friends are much closer and more involved than is the case with the peer group. Some adolescents have several close friends, others one, and yet others none. The important role of friendships in adolescent development is exemplified in this description of her best friend by a 13-year-old girl:

> My best friend is nice. She's honest, and I can trust her. I can tell her my innermost secrets and know that nobody else will find out about them. I have other friends, too, but she is my best friend. We consider each other's feelings and don't want to hurt each other. We help each other out when we have problems. We make up funny names for people and laugh ourselves silly. We make lists of which boys are the sexiest and which are the ugliest, which are the biggest jerks, and so on. Some of these things we share with other friends; some we don't.

Its Importance

The functions that adolescents' friendships serve can be categorized in six ways (Gottman & Parker, 1987) (see figure 10.3):

1. *Companionship.* Friendship provides adolescents with a familiar partner, someone who is willing to spend time with them and join in collaborative activities.
2. *Stimulation.* Friendship provides adolescents with interesting information, excitement, and amusement.
3. *Physical support.* Friendship provides resources and assistance.

friends A subset of peers who engage in mutual companionship, support, and intimacy.

4. *Ego support.* Friendship provides the expectation of support, encouragement, and feedback that helps adolescents to maintain an impression of themselves as competent, attractive, and worthwhile individuals.

5. *Social comparison.* Friendship provides information about where adolescents stand vis-à-vis others and whether adolescents are doing okay.

6. *Intimacy/affection.* Friendship provides adolescents with a warm, close, trusting relationship with another individual, a relationship that involves self-disclosure.

However, the quality of friendship varies. Some friendships are deeply intimate and long-lasting, others more shallow and short-lived. Some friendships run smoothly, others can be conflicted. One recent study focused on conflict with parents and friends (Adams & Laursen, 2001). Parent-adolescent conflicts were more likely to be characterized by a combination of daily hassle topics, neutral or angry affect afterward, power-assertive outcomes, and win-lose outcomes. Friend conflicts were more likely to involve a combination of relationship topics, friendly affect afterward, disengaged resolutions, and equal or no outcomes.

Not only does the quality of friendships have important influences on adolescents, but the friend's character, interests, and attitudes also matter (Brown, 2004). For example, researchers have found that delinquent adolescents often have delinquent friends, and they reinforce each other's delinquent behavior (Dishion, Andrews, & Crosby, 1995). Other research has indicated that nonsmoking adolescents who become friends with smoking adolescents are more likely to start smoking themselves (Urberg, 1992). By the same token, having friends who are into school, sports, or religion is likely to have a positive influence on the adolescent.

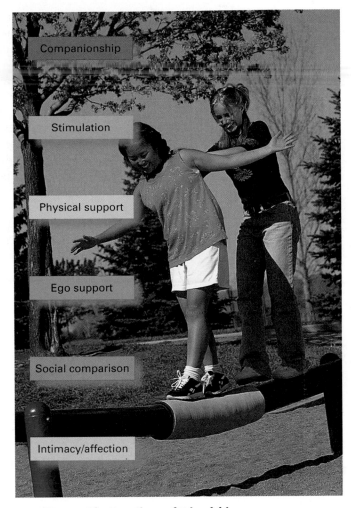

FIGURE 10.3 The Functions of Friendships

Sullivan's Ideas

Harry Stack Sullivan (1953) was the most influential theorist to discuss the importance of adolescent friendships. He argued that there is a dramatic increase in the psychological importance and intimacy of close friends during early adolescence. In contrast to other psychoanalytic theorists' narrow emphasis on the importance of parent-child relationships, Sullivan contended that friends also play important roles in shaping children's and adolescents' well-being and development. In terms of well-being, he argued that all people have a number of basic social needs, including the need for tenderness (secure attachment), playful companionship, social acceptance, intimacy, and sexual relations. Whether or not these needs are fulfilled largely determines our emotional well-being. For example, if the need for playful companionship goes unmet, then we become bored and depressed; if the need for social acceptance is not met, we suffer a lowered sense of self-worth. Developmentally, friends become increasingly depended on to satisfy these needs during adolescence, and thus the ups-and-downs of experiences with friends increasingly shape adolescents' state of well-being. In particular, Sullivan believed that the need for intimacy intensifies during early adolescence, motivating teenagers to seek out close friends. He felt that, if adolescents failed to forge such close friendships, they would experience painful feelings of loneliness coupled with a reduced sense of self-worth.

Although Sullivan formulated his ideas more than half a century ago, more recent research findings support many of Sullivan's ideas. For example, adolescents report more often disclosing intimate and personal information to their friends than do younger children (Buhrmester & Furman, 1987) (see figure 10.4). Adolescents also

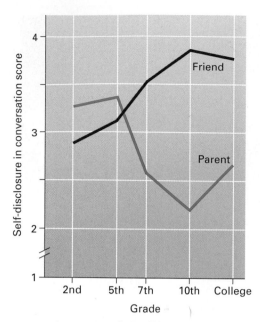

Friendships

FIGURE 10.4 Developmental Changes in Self-Disclosing Conversations

Self-disclosing conversations with friends increased dramatically in adolescence while declining in an equally dramatic fashion with parents. However, self-disclosing conversations with parents began to pick up somewhat during the college years. The measure of self-disclosure involved a 5-point rating scale completed by the children and youth with a higher score representing greater self-disclosure. The data shown represent the means for each age group.

say they depend more on friends than parents to satisfy needs for companionship, reassurance of worth, and intimacy (Furman & Buhrmester, 1992). In one study, researchers conducted daily interviews with 13- to 16-year-old adolescents over a five-day period to find out how much time they spent engaged in meaningful interactions with friends and parents (Buhrmester & Carbery, 1992). Adolescents spent an average of 103 minutes per day in meaningful interactions with friends, compared with just 28 minutes per day with parents. In addition, the quality of friendship is more strongly linked to feelings of well-being during adolescence than during childhood. Teenagers with superficial friendships, or no close friendships at all, report feeling lonelier and more depressed, and they have a lower sense of self-esteem than teenagers with intimate friendships (Buhrmester, 1990; Yin, Buhrmester, & Hibbard, 1996). And in another study, friendship in early adolescence was a significant predictor of self-worth in early adulthood (Bagwell, Newcomb, & Bukowski, 1994).

Adolescents also regard loyalty or faithfulness as more critical in friendships than children do (Rotenberg, 1993). When talking about their best friend, adolescents frequently refer to the friend's willingness to stand up for them when around other people. Typical comments are: "Bob will stick up for me in a fight," "Sally won't talk about me behind my back," or "Jennifer wouldn't leave me for somebody else." In these descriptions, adolescents underscore the obligations of a friend in the larger peer group.

In one study of adolescent peer networks in the sixth grade through the twelfth grade, adolescents were more selective in naming friends (Urberg & others, 1995). In the twelfth grade, they made and received fewer friendship choices and had fewer mutual friends. This increased selectivity might be due to increased social cognitive skills that allow older adolescents to make more accurate inferences about who likes them.

The increased closeness and importance of friendship challenges adolescents to master evermore sophisticated social competencies. Viewed from the developmental constructionist perspective described in chapter 9, adolescent friendship represents a new mode of relating to others that is best described as a *symmetrical intimate mode*. During childhood, being a good friend involves being a good playmate: Children must know how to play cooperatively and must be skilled at smoothly entering ongoing games on the playground. By contrast, the greater intimacy of adolescent friendships demands that teenagers learn a number of close relationship competencies, including knowing how to self-disclose appropriately, being able to provide emotional support to friends, and managing disagreements in ways that do not undermine the intimacy of the friendship. These competencies require more sophisticated skills in perspective taking, empathy, and social problem solving than were involved in childhood playmate competencies.

In addition to the role they play in the socialization of social competence, friendship relationships are often important sources of support (Berndt, 1999; Hartup & Collins, 2000). Sullivan described how adolescent friends support one another's sense of personal worth. When close friends disclose their mutual insecurities and fears about themselves, they discover that they are not "abnormal" and that they have nothing to be ashamed of. Friends also act as important confidants that help adolescents work through upsetting problems (such as difficulties with parents or the breakup of romance) by providing both emotional support and informational advice. Friends can also protect "at-risk" adolescents from victimization by peers. In addition, friends can become active partners in building a sense of identity. During countless hours of conversation, friends act as sounding boards as teenagers explore issues ranging from future plans to stances on religious and moral issues.

Willard Hartup (1996), who has studied peer relations across four decades, concluded that children and adolescents use friends as cognitive and social resources on a regular basis. Hartup also commented that normative transitions, such as moving from elementary to middle school, are negotiated more competently by children who have friends than by those who don't. The quality of friendship is also important to consider. Supportive friendships between socially skilled individuals are developmentally advantageous, whereas coercive and conflict-ridden friendships are not. Friendship and its developmental significance can vary from one adolescent to another. Adolescents' characteristics, such as temperament ("easy" versus "difficult," for example), likely influence the nature of friendships.

Intimacy and Similarity

Two important characteristics of friendship are intimacy and similarity.

Intimacy In the context of friendship, *intimacy* has been defined in different ways. For example, it has been defined broadly to include everything in a relationship that makes the relationship seem close or intense. In most research studies, though, **intimacy in friendship** is defined narrowly as self-disclosure or sharing of private thoughts. Private or personal knowledge about a friend also has been used as an index of intimacy (Selman, 1980; Sullivan, 1953).

The most consistent finding in the last two decades of research on adolescent friendships is that intimacy is an important feature of friendship (Berndt & Perry, 1990; Bukowski, Newcomb, & Hoza, 1987). When young adolescents are asked what they want from a friend, or how they can tell if someone is their best friend, they frequently say that a best friend will share problems with them, understand them, and listen when they talk about their own thoughts or feelings. When young children talk about their friendships, comments about intimate self-disclosure or mutual understanding are rare. In one investigation, friendship intimacy was more prominent in 13- to 16-year-olds than in 10- to 13-year-olds (Buhrmester, 1990).

Similarity Another predominant characteristic of friendship is that, throughout the childhood and adolescent years, friends are generally similar—in terms of age, sex, ethnicity, and many other factors. Friends often have similar attitudes toward school, similar educational aspirations, and closely aligned achievement orientations. Friends enjoy the same music, wear the same style of clothes, and prefer the same leisure activities (Berndt, 1982). If friends have different attitudes about school, one of them may want to play basketball or go shopping rather than do homework. If one friend insists on completing homework while the other insists on playing basketball, the conflict may weaken the friendship and the two may drift apart.

In one recent study of young adolescents, students usually selected friends who had achievement levels similar to their own (Ryan & Patrick, in press). Of course, not all adolescents associate with friends whose characteristics are all similar to their own, and this can make a difference in attitudes toward school. For example, in the study just mentioned, students who "hung out" with a group of friends who disliked school showed a greater decrease in their own enjoyment of school over the course of the school year compared with students who spent time with friends who liked school (Ryan & Patrick, in press).

Mixed-Age Friendships

Although most adolescents develop friendships with individuals who are close to their own age, some adolescents become best friends with younger or older individuals.

Through the Eyes of Adolescents

We Defined Each Other with Adjectives

"I was funky. Dana was sophisticated. Liz was crazy. We walked to school together, went for bike rides, cut school, got stoned, talked on the phone, smoked cigarettes, slept over, discussed boys and sex, went to church together, and got angry at each other. We defined each other with adjectives and each other's presence. As high school friends, we simultaneously resisted and anticipated adulthood and womanhood.

"What was possible when I was 15 and 16? We still had to tell our parents where we were going! We wanted to do excitedly forbidden activities like going out to dance clubs and drinking whiskey sours. Liz, Dana, and I wanted to do these forbidden things in order to feel; to have intense emotional and sensual experiences that removed us from the suburban sameness we shared with each other and everyone else we knew. We were tired of the repetitive experiences that our town, our siblings, our parents, and our school offered to us. . . .

"The friendship between Dana, Liz, and myself was born out of another emotional need: the need for trust. The three of us had reached a point in our lives when we realized how unstable relationships can be, and we all craved safety and acceptance. Friendships all around us were often uncertain. We wanted and needed to be able to like and trust each other."

---

intimacy in friendship In most research, this is defined narrowly as self-disclosure or sharing of private thoughts.

A common fear, especially among parents, is that adolescents who have older friends will be encouraged to engage in delinquent behavior or early sexual behavior. Researchers have found that adolescents who interact with older youths do engage in these behaviors more frequently, but it is not known whether the older youths guide younger adolescents toward deviant behavior or whether the younger adolescents were already prone to deviant behavior before they developed the friendship with the older youths (Billy, Rodgers, & Udry, 1984).

In a longitudinal study of eighth-grade girls, early-maturing girls developed friendships with girls who were chronologically older but biologically similar to them (Magnusson, 1988). Because of their associations with older friends, the early-maturing girls were more likely than their peers to engage in a number of deviant behaviors, such as being truant from school, getting drunk, and stealing. Also, as adults (26 years of age), the early-maturing girls were more likely to have had a child and were less likely to be vocationally and educationally oriented than their later-maturing counterparts. Thus, parents do seem to have reason to be concerned when their adolescents become close friends with individuals who are considerably older than they are.

Review and reflect Learning goal 2

2 **Explain how friendship contributes to adolescent development**

REVIEW

- Why is friendship important in adolescence?
- What is Sullivan's view of adolescent friendship?
- What roles do intimacy and similarity play in adolescent friendship?
- What characterizes mixed-age adolescent friendships?

REFLECT

- How much time did you spend in adolescence with friends and what activities did you engage in? What were your friends like? Were they similar to you or different? Has the nature of your friendships changed since adolescence? Explain.

3 ADOLESCENT GROUPS

Group Function and Formation

Cliques and Crowds

Groups in Childhood and Adolescence

Youth Organizations

During your adolescent years, you probably were a member of both formal and informal groups. Examples of formal groups include the basketball team or drill team, the Girl Scouts or Boy Scouts, the student council, and so on. A more informal group could be a group of peers, such as a clique. Our study of adolescent groups focuses on the functions of groups and how groups are formed, differences between children groups and adolescent groups, cultural variations, cliques, and youth organizations.

Group Function and Formation

Why does an adolescent join a study group? A church? An athletic team? A clique? Groups satisfy adolescents' personal needs, reward them, provide information, raise their self-esteem, and give them an identity. Adolescents might join a group because they think that group membership will be enjoyable and exciting and satisfy their need for affiliation and companionship. They might join a group because they will have the opportunity to receive rewards, either material or psychological. For example, an adolescent may reap prestige and recognition from membership on the school's student council. Groups also are an important source of information. As adolescents participate in a study group, they learn effective study strategies and valuable information about how to take tests. The groups in which adolescents are members—their family, their school, a club, a team—often make them feel good, raise their self-esteem, and provide them with an identity.

Any group to which adolescents belong has two things in common with all other groups: norms and roles. **Norms** are rules that apply to all members of a group. An honor society, for example, might require all members to have a 3.5 grade point average. A school might require its male students to keep their hair cut so that it does not touch their shirt. A football team might require its members to work on weight lifting in the off-season. **Roles** are certain positions in a group that are governed by rules and expectations. Roles define how adolescents should behave in those positions. In a family, parents have certain roles, siblings have other roles, and grandparents have still other roles. On a basketball team, many different roles must be filled: center, forward, guard, rebounder, defensive specialist, and so on.

Groups in Childhood and Adolescence

Childhood groups differ from adolescent groups in several important ways. The members of childhood groups often are friends or neighborhood acquaintances, and the groups usually are not as formalized as many adolescent groups. During the adolescent years, groups tend to include a broader array of members; in other words, adolescents other than friends or neighborhood acquaintances often are members of adolescent groups. Try to recall the student council, honor society, or football team at your junior high school. If you were a member of any of these organizations, you probably remember that they were made up of many individuals you had not met before and that they were a more heterogeneous group than your childhood peer groups. Rules and regulations were probably well defined, and captains or leaders were formally elected or appointed in the adolescent groups.

A well-known observational study by Dexter Dunphy (1963) indicates that opposite-sex participation in social groups increases during adolescence. In late childhood, boys and girls tend to form small, same-sex groups. As they move into the early adolescent years, the same-sex groups begin to interact with each other. Gradually, the leaders and high-status members form further groups based on mixed-sex relationships. Eventually, the newly created mixed-sex groups replace the same-sex groups. The mixed-sex groups also interact with each other in large crowd activities, too—at dances and athletic events, for example. In late adolescence, the crowd begins to dissolve as couples develop more serious relationships and make long-range plans that may include engagement and marriage. A summary of Dunphy's ideas is presented in figure 10.5.

Cliques and Crowds

In our discussion of Dunphy's work, the importance of heterosexual relationships in the evolution of adolescent crowds was noted. Let's now examine adolescent cliques and crowds in greater detail.

Cliques   **Cliques** are small groups that range from two to about twelve individuals and average about five to six individuals. These clique members are usually of the same sex and are similar in age.

Cliques can form because adolescents engage in similar activities, such as being in a club together or on a sports team. Some cliques also form purely because of friendship. Several adolescents may form a clique because they have spent time with

norms Rules that apply to all members of a group.

roles Certain positions in a group that are governed by rules and expectations. Roles define how adolescents should behave in those positions.

cliques Small groups that range from two to about twelve individuals and average about five to six individuals.

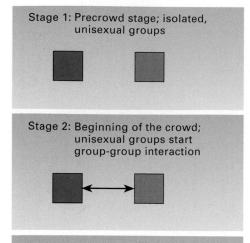

Stage 1: Precrowd stage; isolated, unisexual groups

Stage 2: Beginning of the crowd; unisexual groups start group-group interaction

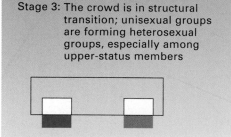

Stage 3: The crowd is in structural transition; unisexual groups are forming heterosexual groups, especially among upper-status members

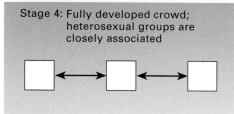

Stage 4: Fully developed crowd; heterosexual groups are closely associated

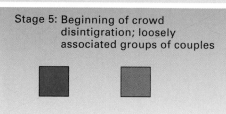

Stage 5: Beginning of crowd disintigration; loosely associated groups of couples

Boys   Girls   Boys and girls

FIGURE 10.5 Dunphy's Progression of Peer Group Relations in Adolescence

crowds A larger group structure than cliques. Adolescents are usually members of a crowd based on reputation and may or may not spend much time together.

each other and enjoy each other's company. Not necessarily friends before forming the clique, they often develop a friendship if they stay in the clique.

What do adolescents do in cliques? They share ideas, hang out together, and often develop an in-group identity in which they believe their clique is better than other cliques. In the video clip entitled "Talking about Cliques at 15 Years of Age," observe how three teenage girls discuss the various dynamics of personality and popularity within the high school cliques.

Crowds   **Crowds** are a larger group structure than cliques. Adolescents are usually members of a crowd based on reputation and may or may not spend much time with other crowd members (Brown, 2003, 2004). Crowds are less personal than cliques. Many crowds are defined by the activities adolescents engage in (such as "jocks" who are good at sports or "druggies" who take drugs), although some crowds are defined more by the nature of their interaction. For example, in Dexter Dunphy's developmental sequence that was described earlier in the chapter, the crowds were interactional-based crowds, not reputation-based crowds.

In one study, Bradford Brown and Jane Lohr (1987) examined the self-esteem of 221 seventh- through twelfth-graders. The adolescents were either associated with one of the five major school crowds or were relatively unknown by classmates and not associated with any school crowd. Crowds included the following: jocks (athletically oriented), populars (well-known students who lead social activities), normals (middle-of-the-road students who make up the masses), druggies/toughs (known for illicit drug use or other delinquent activities), and nobodies (low in social skills or intellectual abilities). The self-esteem of the jocks and the populars was highest, that of the nobodies was lowest. But one group of adolescents not in a crowd had self-esteem equivalent to the jocks and the populars. This group was the independents, who indicated that crowd membership was not important to them. Keep in mind that these data are correlational—self-esteem could increase an adolescent's probability of becoming a crowd member just as clique membership could increase the adolescent's self-esteem.

One of the main factors that distinguish crowds is group norms regarding school orientation (Brown, 2003, 2004; Brown & Theobald, 1998). In one study of adolescents in nine midwestern and West Coast high schools, grade-point differences of almost two full letter grades were found between the highest achievers ("brains") and lowest achievers ("druggies") (Brown & others, 1993). The norms of particular crowds can place adolescents on a trajectory for school failure. Members of deviantly oriented crowds are more likely to drop out of school early (Cairns & Cairns, 1994).

Crowd membership is also associated with drug use and sexual behavior. In one study, five adolescent crowds were identified: jocks (athletes), brains (students who enjoy academics), burnouts (adolescents who get into trouble), populars (social, student leaders), nonconformists (adolescents who go against the norm), as well as a none/average group (Prinstein, Fetter, & La Greca, 1996). Burnouts and nonconformists were the most likely to smoke cigarettes, drink alcohol, and use marijuana; brains were the least likely. Jocks were the most sexually active clique.

Bradford Brown made these conclusions about adolescent crowds (Brown, 2003; Brown, Mory, & Kinney, 1994):

1. *The influence of crowds is not entirely negative.* Crowds emerge in adolescence to provide youth with provisional identities they can adopt, at least temporarily, on their way to a more integrated identity later in development. In Brown's research with 1,000 midwestern middle school and high school students, peer pressure was strongest regarding getting good grades, finishing high school, and spending time with friends. The students reported little pressure to engage in drinking, drug use, sexual intercourse, and other potentially health-compromising behaviors.

2. *The influence of crowds is not uniform for all adolescents.* Crowds vary not only in terms of dress, grooming styles, musical tastes, and hangouts at school, but also in terms of more-consequential activities such as effort in school or deviant behavior (Youniss, McLellan, & Strouse, 1994). Thus, whether crowds are "friend" or

"foe" depends largely on the particular crowd with which the adolescent is associated. Furthermore, in Brown's research, one-third of the student body floated among several crowds; some students isolates—were totally detached from crowds.

3. *Developmental changes occur in crowds.* In Brown's research, barriers against moving from one crowd to another were much stronger in the ninth grade than in the twelfth grade. It was easier for high school seniors than for freshmen to shift affiliations among crowds or forge friendships across crowd lines.

Youth Organizations

Youth organizations can have an important influence on the adolescent's development (Brown, 2004; Mahoney, Larson, & Eccles, 2004; Roth & Brooks-Gunn, 2003). More than 400 national youth organizations currently operate in the United States (Erickson, 1996). The organizations include career groups, such as Junior Achievement; groups aimed at building character, such as Girl Scouts and Boy Scouts; political groups, such as Young Republicans and Young Democrats; and ethnic groups, such as Indian Youth of America (Price & others, 1990). They serve approximately 30 million young people each year. The largest youth organization is 4-H, with nearly 5 million participants. Among the smallest are ASPIRA, a Latino youth organization that provides intensive educational enrichment programs for about 13,000 adolescents each year; and WAVE, a dropout-prevention program that serves about 8,000 adolescents each year.

Adolescents who join such groups are more likely to participate in community activities in adulthood and have higher self-esteem, are better educated, and come from families with higher incomes than their counterparts who do not participate in youth groups (Erickson, 1982). Participation in youth groups can help adolescents practice the interpersonal and organizational skills that are important for success in adult roles.

The Search Institute (1995) conducted a study that sheds light on both the potential for and barriers to participation in youth programs. The study focused on Minneapolis, which faces many of the same challenges regarding youth as other major U.S. cities. The after-school hours and summer vacations are important time slots during which adolescents could form positive relationships with adults and peers. Yet this study found that more than 50 percent of the youth said they don't participate in any type of after-school youth program in a typical week. More than 40 percent reported no participation in youth programs during the summer months.

About 350 youth programs were identified in Minneapolis, about one program for every 87 adolescents. However, about one-half of the youth and their parents agree that there are not enough youth programs. Parents with the lowest incomes were the least satisfied with program availability.

Some of the reasons given by middle school adolescents for not participating in youth programs were a lack of interest in available activities, a lack of transportation, and lack of awareness about what is available. Here are several adolescents' comments about why they don't participate in youth programs:

"Some things I don't like, like sports stuff because I'm not good at it."
"Nobody is going to take a bus across town just to get to a program."
"I have enough time but my parents don't. I need them to take me there."

Parents see similar barriers, especially transportation and costs.

Adolescents express an interest in activities that would foster their peer relations. They want more informal programs or places where their time is not highly structured—places where they can drop by, hang out, and spontaneously choose what

www.mhhe.com/santrocka10

Youth Programs
Boys and Girls Clubs

These adolescents are participating in Girls Club and Boys Club activities. *What effects do youth organizations have on adolescents?*

they want to do. However, many adolescents also reported having an interest in participating more in structured activities such as taking lessons, playing sports, dances, youth-led programs, and youth service.

To increase the participation of low-income and ethnic minority adolescents in youth groups, Girls Clubs and Boys Clubs are being established in locations where young adolescents are at high risk for dropping out of school, becoming delinquents, and developing substance-abuse problems. The locations include 15 housing projects in different American cities. The club programs are designed to provide individual, small-group, and drop-in supportive services that enhance educational and personal development. Preliminary results suggest that the Boys and Girls Clubs help to reduce vandalism, drug abuse, and delinquency (Boys and Girls Clubs of America, 1989).

According to Reed Larson (2000; Larson, Hansen, & Walker, 2004), structured voluntary youth activities are especially well suited for the development of initiative. One study of structured youth activities that led to increased initiative involved adolescents in low-income areas who began participating in art and drama groups, sports teams, Boys and Girls Clubs, YMCA gang intervention programs, and other community organizations (Heath, 1999; Heath & McLaughlin, 1993). When the adolescents first joined these organizations, they seemed bored. Within three to four weeks, though, they reported greater confidence in their ability to affect their world and adjusted their behavior in pursuit of a goal.

In sum, youth activities and organizations provide excellent developmental contexts in which to provide adolescents opportunities to develop many positive qualities. Participation in these contexts can help to increase achievement and decrease delinquency (Dworkin & others, 2001; Hughes, Alfano, & Harkness, 2002; Larson, 2000).

Review and reflect Learning goal 3

3 Summarize what takes place in adolescent groups

REVIEW

- What functions do adolescent groups serve? How are groups formed in adolescence?
- How are childhood groups different from adolescent groups?
- What are cliques and crowds? What roles do they play in adolescent development?
- How can youth organizations be characterized?

REFLECT

- What do you think would have been the ideal youth organization to support your needs when you were an adolescent?

4 GENDER AND CULTURE

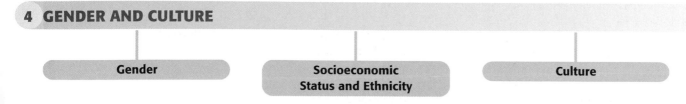

Gender	Socioeconomic Status and Ethnicity	Culture

The social worlds of adolescent peer groups and friendships are linked to gender and culture. In chapter 6, we indicated that during the elementary school years children spend a large majority of their free time with children of their own sex. Preadolescents spend an hour or less a week interacting with the other sex (Furman & Shaeffer, 2003). With puberty, though, more time is spent in heterosexual peer groups, which was reflected in Dunphy's developmental view that we just described. And by the twelfth grade, boys spend an average of 5 hours a week with the other sex, girls 10 hours a week (Furman, 2002). Nonetheless, there are some significant differences between adolescent peer groups comprised of males and those made up of females.

Gender

There is increasing evidence that gender plays an important role in the peer group and friendships. The evidence related to the peer group focuses on group size and interaction in same-sex groups (Maccoby, 2002):

- *Group size.* From about 5 years of age forward, boys are more likely than girls to associate in larger clusters than girls are. Boys are more likely to participate in organized games and sports than girls are.
- *Interaction in same-sex groups.* Boys are more often likely than girls to engage in competition, conflict, ego displays, risk taking, and seek dominance. By contrast, girls are more likely to engage in "collaborative discourse," in which they talk and act in a more reciprocal manner.

With regard to friendship, the interest in gender especially focuses on intimacy. When asked to describe their best friends, girls refer to intimate conversations and faithfulness more than boys do. For example, girls are more likely to describe their best friend as "sensitive just like me" or "trustworthy just like me" (Duck, 1975). The assumption behind this gender difference is that girls are more oriented toward interpersonal relationships. Boys may discourage one another from openly disclosing their problems, as part of their masculine, competitive nature.

In one study of adolescent peer networks, the most robust finding was that female students were more integrated into school social networks than males were (Urberg & others, 1995). Girls were also more likely than boys to have a best friend and to be a clique member. We will have more to say about gender and romantic relationships later in this chapter and about the role of gender in bullying in chapter 11, "Schools."

Socioeconomic Status and Ethnicity

Whether adolescents grow up as part of the peer culture in a ghetto or in a middle-SES suburban area influences the nature of the groups to which they belong. For example, in a comparison of middle- and lower-SES adolescent groups, lower-SES adolescents displayed more aggression toward the low-status members of the group but showed less aggression toward the president of the class or group than their middle-SES counterparts (Maas, 1954).

In many schools, peer groups are strongly segregated according to socioeconomic status and ethnicity. In schools with large numbers of middle- and lower-SES students, middle-SES students often assume the leadership roles in formal organizations, such as student council, the honor society, fraternity-sorority groups, and so on. Athletic teams are one type of adolescent group in which African American adolescents and adolescents from low-income families have been able to gain parity or even surpass adolescents from middle- and upper-SES families in achieving status.

Ethnic minority adolescents, especially immigrants, may rely on peer groups more than White adolescents (Spencer & Dornbusch, 1990). This is especially true when ethnic minority adolescents' parents have not been very successful in their careers. The desire to be accepted by the peer group is especially strong among refugee adolescents, whose greatest threat is not the stress of belonging to two cultures but the stress of belonging to none.

For many ethnic minority youth, especially immigrants, peers from their own ethnic group provide a crucial sense of brotherhood or sisterhood within the majority culture. Peer groups may form to oppose those of the majority group and to provide adaptive supports that reduce feelings of isolation.

Culture

So far, we have considered adolescents' peer relations in regard to gender, socioeconomic status, and ethnicity. Are there also some foreign cultures in which the peer group plays a different role than in the United States?

In some countries, adults restrict adolescents' access to peers. For example, in many areas of rural India and in Arab countries, opportunities for peer relations in adolescence are severely restricted, especially for girls (Brown & Larson, 2002). If girls attend school in these regions of the world, it is usually in sex-segregated schools. In these countries, interaction with the other sex or opportunities for romantic relationships are restricted (Booth, 2002).

In chapter 9, we indicated that Japanese adolescents seek autonomy from their parents later and have less conflict with them than American adolescents do. In a recent cross-cultural analysis, the peer group was more important to U.S. adolescents than to Japanese adolescents (Rothbaum & others, 2000). Japanese adolescents spend less time outside the home, have less recreational leisure time, and engage in fewer extracurricular activities with peers than U.S. adolescents (White, 1993). Also, U.S. adolescents are more likely to put pressure on their peers to resist parental influence than Japanese adolescents are (Rothbaum & others, 2000).

A trend, though, is that in societies in which adolescents' access to peers has been restricted, adolescents are engaging in more peer interaction during school and in shared leisure activities, especially in middle-SES contexts (Brown & Larson, 2002). For example, in Southeast Asia and some Arab regions, adolescents are starting to rely more on peers for advice and share interests with them (Booth, 2002; Santa Maria, 2002).

In many countries and regions, though, peers play more prominent roles in adolescents' lives (Brown & Larson, 2002). For example, in sub-Saharan Africa, the peer group is a pervasive aspect of adolescents' lives (Nsamenang, 2002); similar results have been observed throughout Europe and North America (Arnett, 2002).

In some cultures, children are placed in peer groups for much greater lengths of time at an earlier age than they are in the United States. For example, in the Murian culture of eastern India, both male and female children live in a dormitory from the age of 6 until they get married (Barnouw, 1975). The dormitory is a religious haven where members are devoted to work and spiritual harmony. Children work for their parents, and the parents arrange the children's marriages. The children continue to live in the dormitory through adolescence, until they marry.

In some cultural settings, peers even assume responsibilities usually assumed by parents. For example, street youth in South America rely on networks of peers to help them negotiate survival in urban environments (Welti, 2002).

Review and reflect Learning goal 4

4   Describe the roles of gender and culture in adolescent peer groups and friendships

REVIEW

- What role does gender play in adolescent peer groups and friendships?
- How are socioeconomic status and ethnicity linked to adolescent peer relations?
- How is culture involved in adolescent peer relations?

REFLECT

- Do you think the peer group has too strong of an influence on adolescents in the United States? Explain.

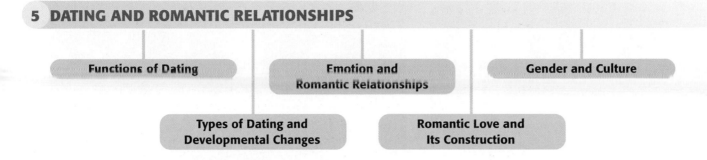

5 DATING AND ROMANTIC RELATIONSHIPS

Functions of Dating

Emotion and
Romantic Relationships

Gender and Culture

Types of Dating and
Developmental Changes

Romantic Love and
Its Construction

Though many adolescent boys and girls have social interchanges through formal and informal peer groups, it is through dating that more serious contacts between the sexes occur (Bouchey & Furman, 2003; Carver, Joyner, & Udry, 2003; Collins, 2003; Florsheim, 2003; Furman, 2002; Furman & Shaeffer, 2003). Young male adolescents spend many agonizing moments worrying about whether they should call a certain girl and ask her out: "Will she turn me down?" "What if she says yes, what do I say next?" "How am I going to get her to the dance? I don't want my mother to take us!" "I want to kiss her, but what if she pushes me away?" "How can I get to be alone with her?" And, on the other side of the coin, young adolescent girls wonder: "What if no one asks me to the dance?" "What do I do if he tries to kiss me?" Or, "I really don't want to go out with him. Maybe I should wait two more days before I give him an answer and see if Bill will call me."

Functions of Dating

Dating is a relatively recent phenomenon. It wasn't until the 1920s that dating as we know it became a reality, and even then, its primary role was for the purpose of selecting and winning a mate. Prior to this period, mate selection was the sole purpose of dating, and "dates" were carefully monitored by parents, who completely controlled the nature of any heterosexual companionship. Often, parents bargained with each other about the merits of their adolescents as potential marriage partners and even chose mates for their children. In recent times, of course, adolescents have gained much more control over the dating process and whom they go out with. Furthermore, dating has evolved into something more than just courtship for marriage.

Dating today can serve at least eight functions (Paul & White, 1990):

1. Dating can be a form of recreation. Adolescents who date seem to have fun and see dating as a source of enjoyment and recreation.
2. Dating is a source of status and achievement. Part of the social comparison process in adolescence involves evaluating the status of the people one dates: Are they the best looking, the most popular, and so forth?
3. Dating is part of the socialization process in adolescence: It helps the adolescent to learn how to get along with others and assists in learning manners and sociable behavior.
4. Dating involves learning about intimacy and serves as an opportunity to establish a unique, meaningful relationship with a person of the opposite sex.
5. Dating can be a context for sexual experimentation and exploration.
6. Dating can provide companionship through interaction and shared activities in an opposite-sex relationship.
7. Dating experiences contribute to identity formation and development; dating helps adolescents to clarify their identity and to separate from their families of origin.
8. Dating can be a means of mate sorting and selection, thereby retaining its original courtship function.

Exploring Dating

In the first half of the twentieth century, dating served mainly as a courtship for marriage.

Today the functions of dating include courtship but also many others. *What are some of these other functions of dating?*

Types of Dating and Developmental Changes

A number of dating variations and developmental changes characterize dating and romantic relationships. First, we examine heterosexual romantic relationships and then turn to romantic relationships in sexual minority youth (gay and lesbian adolescents).

Heterosexual Romantic Relationships   In one recent study, announcing that "I like someone" occurred by the sixth grade for 40 percent of the individuals sampled (Buhrmester, 2001) (see figure 10.6). However, it was not until the tenth grade that 50 percent of the adolescents had a sustained romantic relationship that lasted 2 months or longer. By their senior year, 25 percent still had not engaged in this type of sustained romantic relationship. Also, in this study, girls' early romantic involvement was linked with lower grades, less active participation in class discussion, and school-related problems. A rather large portion of adolescents in a steady dating relationship said that their steady relationship had persisted 11 months or longer: 20 percent of adolescents 14 or younger, 35 percent of 15- to16-year-olds, and almost 60 percent of 17- and 18-year-olds (Carver, Joyner, & Udry, 2003).

In their early romantic relationships, many adolescents are not motivated to fulfill attachment or even sexual needs. Rather, early romantic relationships serve as a context for adolescents to explore how attractive they are, how to interact romantically, and how all of this looks to the peer group. Only after adolescents acquire some basic competencies in interacting with romantic partners does the fulfillment of attachment and sexual needs become a central function of these relationships (Furman & Wehner, 1998). Watch the video segment entitled "15-Year-Old Girls' Relationships with Boys" to learn more about how attitudes toward dating can change between middle school and high school.

In their early exploration of romantic relationships, today's adolescents often find comfort in numbers and begin hanging out together in heterosexual groups. Sometimes they just hang out at someone's house or get organized enough to ask an adult to drive them to a mall or a movie. A special concern is early dating and "going with" someone, which is associated with adolescent pregnancy and problems at home and school.

One study had fifth- to eighth-grade adolescents carry electronic pagers for one week and complete self-report forms in response to signals sent to them at random times (Richards & others, 1998). Four years later the participants underwent the same

LifeMAP

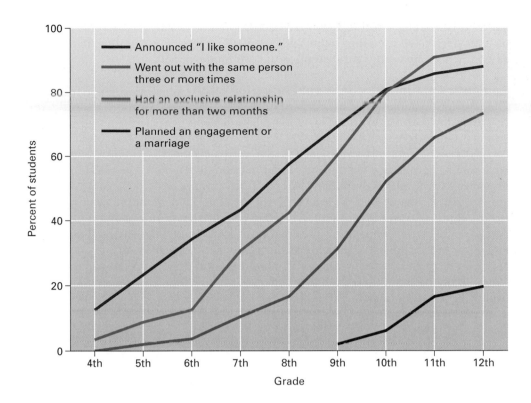

FIGURE 10.6 Age of Onset of Romantic Activity
In this study, announcing that "I like someone" occurred earliest, followed by going out with the same person three or more times, having an exclusive relationship for over two months, and finally planning an engagement or marriage (which characterized only a very small percentage of participants by the twelfth grade) (Buhrmester, 2001).

procedure. Time with, and thoughts about, the opposite sex occupied more of the adolescents' week in high school than in fifth and sixth grades. Fifth- and sixth-grade girls spent approximately 1 hour a week in the presence of a boy, and their male counterparts spent even less time in the presence of a girl. Although more time was spent thinking about an individual of the opposite sex, it still added up to less than 2 hours a week for girls, and less than 1 hour per week for boys, in fifth and sixth grades. By eleventh and twelfth grade, girls were spending about 10 hours a week with a boy, boys about half that time with a girl. Frequency of thoughts had increased as well. The high school girls spent about 8 hours a week thinking about a boy, the high school boys about 5 or 6 hours thinking about a girl.

In sum, during early adolescence, individuals spent more time thinking about the opposite sex than they actually spent with them. In seventh and eighth grade, they spent 4 to 6 hours thinking about them but only about 1 hour actually with them. By eleventh and twelfth grade, this had shifted to more time spent in their actual presence than thinking about them.

A new form of dating has recently emerged. *Cyberdating* is dating over the Internet (Thomas, 1998). One 10-year-old girl posted this ad on the Net:

> Hi! I'm looking for a Cyber Boyfriend! I'm 10. I have brown hair and brown eyes. I love swimming, playing basketball, and think kittens are adorable!!!

Cyberdating is especially becoming popular among middle school students. By the time they reach high school and are

Through the Eyes of Adolescents

They Were Thinking About Having Sex with Girls from Budweiser Ads

"During ninth and tenth grade, I constantly fell in love with older boys I knew only slightly and shy boys my own age I knew well. I never went out on any dates with these boys; I just thought about them a lot. I knew some older guys from school government and committees. They were nice to me. Some flirted quite a bit with me. But I never went on dates with the older guys because they never asked me out. They usually had girlfriends who were seniors. The shy boys my own age were not quite ready for dating. While I was thinking about true love and romantic walks through the park, they were thinking about videogames, rock music, and having sex with girls from Budweiser ads. I never quite felt much like 'dating material.' I was tall and like school and talked a lot in class. I wore weird clothes and wrote articles for the school newspaper and about local political candidates. Sometimes bizarre boys who wanted to be comic strip heroes or felt as stifled as I did by our relatively small town would confess their true love for me. These incidents never led to sexual relationships with these boys. I would tell them I knew how they felt, seeing that I had a few unfruitful crushes of my own. I never liked any of the boys who liked me."

able to drive, dating usually has evolved into a more traditional real-life venture. Adolescents need to be cautioned about the potential hazards of cyberdating and not really knowing who is on the other end of the computer connection.

Romantic Relationships in Sexual Minority Youth   Most research on romantic relationships in adolescence has focused on heterosexual relationships. Recently, researchers have begun to study romantic relationships in gay, lesbian, and bisexual youth (Diamond & Savin-Williams, 2003; Savin-Williams & Diamond, 2004).

Most sexual minority youth have same-sex sexual experience, but relatively few have same-sex romantic relationships because of limited opportunities and the social disapproval such relationships may generate from families or heterosexual peers (Diamond, 2003; Diamond, Savin-Williams, & Dube, 1999). The importance of romance to sexual minority youth was underscored in a study that found that they rated the breakup of a current romance as their second most stressful problem, second only to disclosure of their sexual orientation to their parents (D'Augelli, 1991).

What romantic pathways do sexual minority youth follow? Let's examine three common myths about these pathways and explore how they are more variable than usually believed (Diamond, 2003):

- *Myth 1: All sexual minority youth quietly struggle with same-sex attractions in childhood, shun heterosexual dating, and gradually sense that they are gay in mid to late adolescence.* Many youth do follow this pathway, but others deviate from it. For example, many adolescents have no memories of same-sex attractions during their childhood and experience more abrupt realization of their same-sex sexual attraction during late adolescence (Diamond & Savin-Williams, 2003). Also, many sexual minority youth date other sex peers, which may help them to clarify their sexual orientation or to disguise it from others (Furman, 2002).
- *Myth 2: All gay and lesbian youth only have same-sex attractions.* Researchers have found that, like sexual minority adults, many gay and lesbian youth experience some degree of other-sex attractions (Garofalo & others, 1999).
- *Myth 3: Adolescents who sexually desire the same sex always fall in love with the same sex.* Some youths say that their same-sex attractions are purely physical, whereas others claim they have more to do with emotional attachment (Savin-Williams, 1998).

In sum, there is a great deal of complexity in the romantic possibilities of sexual minority youth (Diamond, 2003; Savin-Williams & Diamond, 2004). To adequately address the relational interests of sexual minority youth, we can't simply generalize from heterosexual youth and simply switch the labels. Instead, the full range of variation in sexual minority youths' sexual desires and romantic relationships for same- and other-sex partners need to be considered.

So far, we have examined various types of dating and romantic relationships, as well as their developmental trajectories. As we see next, emotion plays an important role in understanding adolescent romance.

Emotion and Romantic Relationships

Romantic emotions can envelop adolescents' lives (Barber & Eccles, 2003; Harper, Welsh, & Woody, 2002; Larson, Clore, & Wood, 1999). A 14-year-old reports being in love and unable to think about anything else. A 15-year-old is distressed that "everyone else has a boyfriend but me." As we just saw, adolescents spend a lot of time thinking about romantic involvement. Some of this thought can involve positive emotions of compassion and joy, but it also can include negative emotions such as worry, disappointment, and jealousy.

Romantic relationships often are involved in an adolescent's emotional experiences. In one study of ninth- to twelfth-graders, girls gave real and fantasized heterosexual relationships as the explanation for more than one-third of their strong

How is emotion involved in adolescent romantic relationships?

emotions, and boys gave this reason for 25 percent of their strong emotions (Wilson-Shockley, 1995). Strong emotions were attached far less to school (13 percent), family (9 percent), and same-sex peer relations (8 percent). The majority of the emotions were reported as positive, but a substantial minority (42 percent), were reported as negative, including feelings of anxiety, anger, jealousy, and depression.

Adolescents who have a boyfriend or girlfriend reported wider daily emotional swings than their counterparts who did not (Richards & Larson, 1990). In a period of three days, one eleventh-grade girl went from feeling "happy because I'm with Dan," to upset because they had a "huge fight" and "he won't listen to me and keeps hanging up on me," to feeling "suicidal because of the fight," to feeling "happy because everything between me and Dan is fine."

In one recent study of more than 8,000 adolescents, those in love had a slightly higher risk for depression than their counterparts who did not get romantically involved (Joyner & Udry, 2000). Young adolescent girls who were in love were especially at risk for depression. Other researchers have also found that depression may result, especially in girls, following a romantic breakup (Welsh, Grello, & Harper, 2003).

Romantic Love and Its Construction

Romantic love is also called passionate love or eros; it has strong sexual and infatuation components, and it often predominates in the early part of a love relationship. The fires of passion burn hot in romantic love. It is the type of love Juliet had in mind when she cried, "O Romeo, Romeo, wherefore art thou Romeo?" It is the type of love portrayed in new songs that hit the charts virtually every week.

Romantic love characterizes most adolescent love, and romantic love is also extremely important among college students. In one investigation, unmarried college males and females were asked to identify their closest relationship (Berscheid, Snyder, & Omoto, 1989). More than half named a romantic partner, rather than a parent, sibling, or friend.

Another type of love is **affectionate love,** also called companionate love, which occurs when individuals desire to have another person near and have a deep, caring

romantic love Also called passionate love or eros, this love has strong sexual and infatuation components, and it often predominates in the early part of a love relationship.

affectionate love Also called companionate love, this love occurs when an individual desires to have another person near and has a deep, caring affection for that person.

Through the Eyes of Adolescents

Where Is He?

Where is he?

I thought I was his bumble bee

I cried and cried

Like someone just died

My love from him is so strong

Cause I had him for so long

I love him with all my heart

And when I see him he

makes

me tremble in that spot

But where is he?

Please, please tell me

I cannot see

I looked and looked all the

way around

But I saw nothing

And my heart hit the ground

I love him with all my heart and soul

But the way he left me

Was so, so cold

Please, please tell me

I cannot see

WHERE IS HE?

—*Kelly Excellus, Age 13*
East Boston, Massachusetts

$\mathcal{L}$ove is a canvas furnished by nature and embroidered by imagination.

—VOLTAIRE
French Philosopher, 18th Century

affection for that person. There is a strong belief that affectionate love is more characteristic of adult love than adolescent love and that the early stages of love have more romantic ingredients than the later stages (Berscheid & Reis, 1998).

Similarity, physical attractiveness, and sexuality are important ingredients of dating relationships (Metts, 2004). So is intimacy, which we discussed in greater detail in chapter 9. But to fully understand dating relationships in adolescence, we need to know how experiences with family members and peers contribute to the way adolescents construct their dating relationships, as first discussed in chapter 9 with regard to the developmental construction view of relationships (Day & others, 2001).

In the continuity version of the developmental construction view, relationships with parents are carried forward to influence the construction of other relationships, such as dating (Fang & Bryant, 2000). Thus, adolescents' relationships with opposite-sex parents, as well as same-sex parents, contribute to adolescents' dating. For example, the adolescent male whose mother has been nurturant but not smothering probably feels that relationships with females will be rewarding. By contrast, the adolescent male whose mother has been cold and unloving toward him likely feels that relationships with females will be unrewarding.

In chapter 9, "Families," we saw that attachment history and early child care were precursors to forming positive couple relationships in adolescence (Sroufe, Egeland, & Carlson, 1999). For example, infants who had an anxious attachment with their caregiver in infancy were less likely to develop positive couple relationships in adolescence than were their securely attached counterparts. It might be that adolescents with a history of secure attachment are better able to control their emotions and more comfortable self-disclosing in romantic relationships.

Wyndol Furman and Elizabeth Wehner (1998) discussed how specific insecure attachment styles might be related to adolescents' romantic relationships. Adolescents with a secure attachment to parents are likely to approach romantic relationships expecting closeness, warmth, and intimacy. Thus, they are likely to feel comfortable developing close, intimate romantic relationships. Adolescents with a dismissing/avoidant attachment to parents are likely to expect romantic partners to be unresponsive and unavailable. Thus, they might tend to behave in ways that distance themselves from romantic relationships. Adolescents with a preoccupied/ambivalent attachment to parents are likely to be disappointed and frustrated with intimacy and closeness in romantic relationships.

According to Peter Blos (1962, 1989), at the beginning of adolescence, boys and girls try to separate themselves from the opposite-sex parent as a love object. As adolescents separate themselves, they often are self-centered. Blos believes that this narcissism gives adolescents a sense of strength. Especially in early adolescence, this narcissistic self-orientation is likely to produce self-serving, highly idealized, and superficial dating relationships.

Adolescents' observations of their parents' marital relationship also contribute to their own construction of dating relationships. Consider an adolescent girl from a divorced family who grew up watching her parents fight on many occasions. Her dating relationships may take one of two turns: She may immerse herself in dating relationships to insulate herself from the stress she has experienced, or she may become aloof and untrusting with males and not wish to become involved heavily in dating relationships. Even when she does become involved in dating, she may find it difficult to develop a trusting relationship with males because she has seen promises broken by her parents.

Mavis Hetherington (1972, 1977) found that divorce was associated with a stronger heterosexual orientation of adolescent daughters than was the death of a parent or living in an intact family. Further, the daughters of divorced parents had a more negative opinion of males than did the girls from other family structures. And girls from divorced and widowed families were more likely to marry images of their fathers than were girls from intact families. Hetherington believes that females from intact families likely have had a greater opportunity to work through relationships with their fathers and therefore are more psychologically free to date and marry someone different from their fathers. Parents are also likely to be more involved or interested in their daughters' dating patterns and relationships than their sons'. For example, in one investigation, college females were much more likely than their male counterparts to say that their parents tried to influence whom they dated during adolescence (Knox & Wilson, 1981). They also indicated that it was not unusual for their parents to try to interfere with their dating choices and relationships.

So far we have been discussing the continuity version of the developmental construction view. In contrast, in the discontinuity version peer relations and friendships provide the opportunity to learn modes of relating that are carried over into romantic relationships (Furman & Wehner, 1998; Sullivan, 1953). Remember that in chapter 9, "Families," we described longitudinal research in which friendship in middle childhood was linked with security in dating, as well as intimacy in dating at age 16 (Collins, Henninghausen, & Sroufe, 1998). Other researchers also have found links between adolescents' friendships and romantic relationships (Furman, 2002).

Harry Stack Sullivan (1953) believed that it is through intimate friendships that adolescents learn a mature form of love he referred to as "collaboration." Sullivan felt that it was this collaborative orientation, coupled with sensitivity to the needs of the friend, that forms the basis of satisfying dating and marital relationships. He also pointed out that dating and romantic relationships give rise to new interpersonal issues that youths had not encountered in prior relationships with parents and friends. Not only must teenagers learn tactics for asking partners for dates (and gracefully turning down requests), but they must also learn to integrate sexual desires with psychological intimacy desires. These tactics and integration are not easy tasks and it is not unusual for them to give rise to powerful feelings of frustration, guilt, and insecurity.

In addition to past relationships with parents and friends influencing an adolescent's dating relationships, family members and peers can directly influence dating experiences (Niederjohn, Welsh, & Scheussler, 2000). For example, sibling relationships can serve as important resources for dating. In one study, adolescents said that they got more support for dating from siblings than from their mothers (O'Brien, 1990). In late adolescence, siblings were viewed as more important advisers and confidants than mothers when concerns about dating were involved. Adolescents sometimes use siblings to their advantage when dealing with parents. In one study, younger siblings pointed to how their older siblings were given dating privileges that they had been denied (Place, 1975). In this investigation, an adolescent would sometimes side with a sibling when the sibling was having an argument with parents in the hope that the sibling would reciprocate when the adolescent needed dating privileges the parents were denying.

Peer relations are also involved in adolescent dating (Morales & Roberts, 2002). In Dunphy's research, discussed earlier in the chapter, all large peer crowds in adolescence were mixed-sex, and males in these crowds were consistently older than females (Dunphy, 1963). In this research, group leaders also played an important role. Both the leaders of large crowds and smaller cliques were highly involved with the

Romance and Attraction

opposite sex. Leaders dated more frequently, were more likely to go steady, and achieved these dating patterns earlier than nonleaders in the cliques. Leaders also were ascribed the task of maintaining a certain level of mixed-sex involvement in the group. Peer leaders functioned as dating confidants and advisers, even putting partners together in the case of "slow learners."

Research by Jennifer Connolly and her colleagues (Connolly, Furman, & Konarksi, 1995, 2000; Connolly & Goldberg, 1999; Connolly & Stevens, 1999) documents the role of peers in the emergence of romantic involvement in adolescence. In one study, adolescents who were part of mixed-sex peer groups moved more readily into romantic relationships than their counterparts whose mixed-sex peer groups were more limited (Connolly, Furman, & Konarksi, 2000). In another study, there was a similar degree of romantic involvement described by adolescents and their friends (Connolly & Stevens, 1999).

Gender and Culture

Dating and romantic relationships may vary according to gender and culture. Think back to your middle school/junior high and high school years and consider how gender likely influenced your romantic relationships.

Gender Do male and female adolescents bring different motivations to the dating experience? Candice Feiring (1996) found that they did. Fifteen-year-old girls were more likely to describe romance in terms of interpersonal qualities, boys in terms of physical attraction. For young adolescents, the affiliative qualities of companionship, intimacy, and support were frequently mentioned as positive dimensions of romantic relationships, but love and security were not. Also, the young adolescents described physical attraction more in terms of being cute, pretty, or handsome than in terms of sexuality (such as being a good kisser). Possibly, however, the failure to discuss sexual interests was due to the adolescents' discomfort in talking about such personal feelings with an unfamiliar adult.

Dating scripts are the cognitive models that adolescents and adults use to guide and evaluate dating interactions. In one recent study, first dates were highly scripted along gender lines (Rose & Frieze, 1993). Males followed a proactive dating script, females a reactive one. The male's script involved initiating the date (asking for and planning it), controlling the public domain (driving and opening doors), and initiating sexual interaction (making physical contact, making out, and kissing). The female's script focused on the private domain (concern about appearance, enjoying the date), participating in the structure of the date provided by the male (being picked up, having doors opened), and responding to his sexual gestures. These gender differences give males more power in the initial stage of a relationship.

Ethnicity and Culture The sociocultural context exerts a powerful influence on adolescent dating patterns and on mate selection (Booth, 2002; Stevenson & Zusho, 2002). Values and religious beliefs of people in various cultures often dictate the age at which dating begins, how much freedom in dating is allowed, the extent to which dates are chaperoned by parents or other adults, and the respective roles of males and females in dating. In the Arab world, Asian countries, and South America, adults are typically highly restrictive of adolescent girls' romantic relationships.

Immigrants to the United States have brought these restrictive standards with them. For example, in the United States, Latino and Asian American families typically have more conservative standards regarding adolescent dating than the Anglo-American culture. Especially when an immigrant adolescent wants to date outside of his or her ethnic group, dating can be a source of cultural conflict for families who come from cultures in which dating begins at a late age, little freedom in dating is allowed, dates are chaperoned, and adolescent girls' dating is especially restricted.

dating scripts The cognitive models that adolescents and adults use to guide and evaluate dating interactions.

In one recent study, Latino young adults living in the midwestern region of the United States reflected on their socialization for dating and sexuality (Raffaelli & Ontai, 2001). Because most of their parents viewed U.S. style dating as a violation of traditional courtship styles, strict boundaries were imposed on youths' romantic involvements. As a result, many of the Latinos described their adolescent dating experiences as filled with tension and conflict. The average age at which the girls began dating was 15.7 years, with early dating experiences usually occurring without parental knowledge or permission. Over half of the girls engaged in "sneak dating."

Review and reflect　Learning goal 5

5　Characterize adolescent dating and romantic relationships

REVIEW

- What functions does dating serve?
- What are some different types of dating? How does dating change developmentally during adolescence?
- What roles does emotion play in romantic relationships?
- What is romantic love and how is it constructed?
- How are gender and culture involved in dating and romantic relationships?

REFLECT

- Think back to your middle school/junior high and high school years. How much time did you spend thinking about dating? If you dated, what were your dating experiences like? What would you do over again the same way? What would you do differently? What characteristics did you seek in the people you wanted to date? Were you too idealistic? What advice would you give today's adolescents about dating and romantic relationships?

In this chapter, we have studied many aspects of peers. In the next chapter, "Schools," we will explore peer relations in the school setting, including bullying.

Reach Your Learning Goals

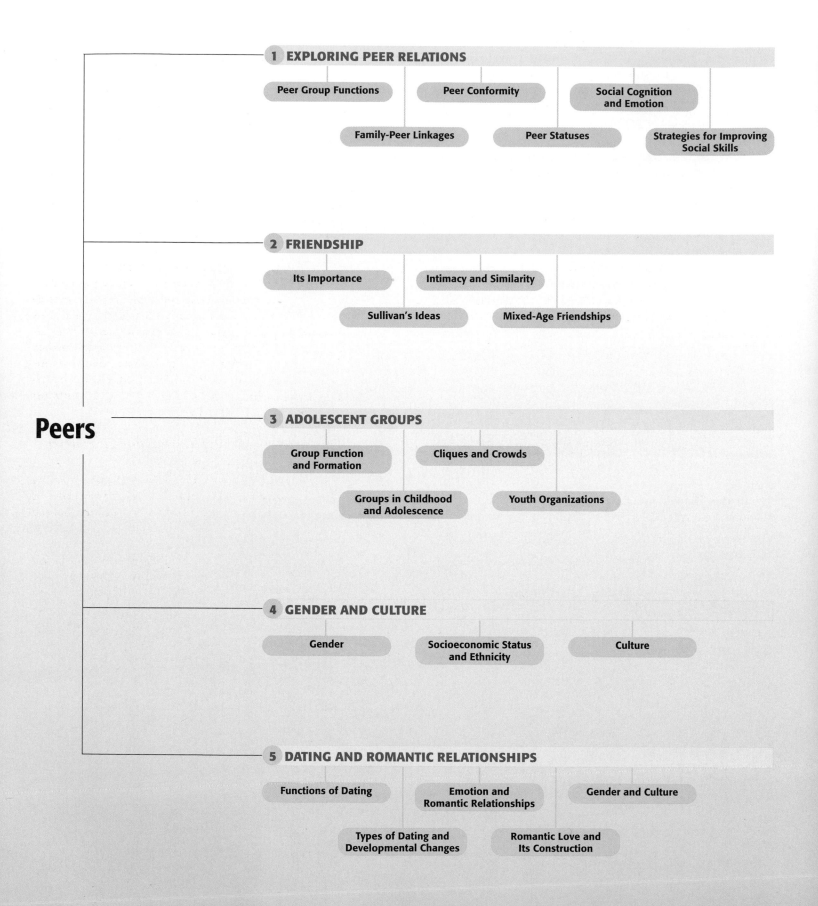

Peers

1 EXPLORING PEER RELATIONS

Peer Group Functions

Peer Conformity

Social Cognition and Emotion

Family-Peer Linkages

Peer Statuses

Strategies for Improving Social Skills

2 FRIENDSHIP

Its Importance

Intimacy and Similarity

Sullivan's Ideas

Mixed-Age Friendships

3 ADOLESCENT GROUPS

Group Function and Formation

Cliques and Crowds

Groups in Childhood and Adolescence

Youth Organizations

4 GENDER AND CULTURE

Gender

Socioeconomic Status and Ethnicity

Culture

5 DATING AND ROMANTIC RELATIONSHIPS

Functions of Dating

Emotion and Romantic Relationships

Gender and Culture

Types of Dating and Developmental Changes

Romantic Love and Its Construction

Summary

1 Discuss the role of peer relations in adolescent development

- Peers are individuals who are about the same age or maturity level. Peers provide a means of social comparison and a source of information beyond the family. Good peer relations may be necessary for normal social development. The inability to "plug in" to a social network is associated with a number of problems. Peer relations can be negative or positive. Piaget and Sullivan each stressed that peer relations provide the context for learning the symmetrical reciprocity mode of relationships. Hartup states that peer relations are complex and may vary according to the way they are measured, the outcomes specified, and the developmental trajectories traversed.
- Healthy family relations usually promote healthy peer relations. Parents can model or coach their child in ways of relating to peers. Parents' choice of neighborhoods, churches, schools, and their own friends influence the pool from which their children select possible friends.
- Conformity occurs when individuals adopt the attitudes or behavior of others because of real or imagined pressure to do so. Conformity to antisocial peer standards peaks around the eighth or ninth grade, then diminishes by the twelfth grade.
- Popular children are frequently nominated as a best friend and are rarely disliked by their friends. Neglected children are infrequently nominated as a best friend but are not disliked by their peers. Rejected children are rarely nominated as a best friend and are disliked by their peers. Controversial children are frequently nominated both as a best friend and as being disliked by peers.
- Social knowledge and social information-processing skills are associated with improved peer relations. Self-regulation of emotion is associated with positive peer relations.
- Conglomerate strategies, also referred to as coaching, involve the use of a combination of techniques, rather than a single strategy, to improve adolescents' social skills.

2 Explain how friendship contributes to adolescent development

- Friends are a subset of peers who engage in mutual companionship, support, and intimacy. The functions of friendship include companionship, stimulation, physical support, ego support, social comparison, and intimacy/affection.
- Sullivan argued that the psychological importance and intimacy of close friends increases dramatically in adolescence. Research supports this view.
- Intimacy and similarity are two of the most important characteristics of friendships.
- Children and adolescents who become close friends with older individuals engage in more deviant behaviors than their counterparts with same-age friends. Early-maturing girls are more likely than late-maturing girls to have older friends, which can contribute to problem behaviors.

3 Summarize what takes place in adolescent groups

- Groups satisfy adolescents' personal needs, reward them, provide information, can raise their self-esteem, and contribute to their identity. Norms are the rules that apply to all members of a group. Roles are rules and expectations that govern certain positions in the group.
- Childhood groups are less formal, less heterogeneous, and less mixed-sex than adolescent groups. Dunphy's study found that adolescent group development proceeds through five stages.
- Cliques are small groups that range from two to about twelve individuals and average about five to six individuals. Crowds are a larger group structure than cliques. Adolescents are members of crowds usually based on reputation and may or may not spend much time together.
- Youth organizations can have important influences on adolescent development. More than 400 national youth organizations currently exist in the United States. Boys and Girls Clubs are examples of youth organizations designed to increase membership in youth organizations in low-income neighborhoods. Participation in youth organizations may increase achievement and decrease delinquency. Youth activities and organizations also may provide opportunities for adolescents to develop initiative.

4 Describe the roles of gender and culture in adolescent peer groups and friendships

- The social world of adolescent peer groups varies according to gender, socioeconomic status, ethnicity, and culture. In terms of gender, boys are more likely than girls to associate in larger clusters and organized games than girls are. Boys also are more likely than girls to engage in competition, conflict, ego displays, risk taking, and seek dominance. By contrast, girls are more likely to engage in collaborative discourse. Girls engage in more intimacy in their friendships than boys do.
- In many cases, peer groups are segregated according to socioeconomic status. In some cases, ethnic minority adolescents rely on peers more than non-Latino White adolescents in the United States.
- In some countries, such as rural India, Arab countries, and Japan, adults restrict access to the peer group. In North America and Europe, the peer group is a pervasive aspect of adolescents' lives.

5 Characterize adolescent dating and romantic relationships

- Dating can be a form of recreation, a source of social status and achievement, an aspect of socialization, a context for learning about intimacy and sexual experimentation, a source of companionship, and a means of mate sorting.
- Younger adolescents often begin to hang out together in mixed-sex groups. Hooking up, seeing each other, and going

out represent different forms of commitment. A special concern is early dating, which is associated with a number of problems. In early adolescence, individuals spend more time thinking about the opposite sex than actually being with them, but this tends to reverse in the high school years. Recently, cyberdating has begun to take place. Most sexual minority youth have same-sex sexual experience but relatively few have same-sex romantic relationships. Many sexual minority youth date other sex peers, which can help them to clarify their sexual orientation or disguise it from others.

• The emotions of romantic relationships can envelop adolescents' lives. Sometimes these emotions are positive, sometimes negative, and can change very quickly.

• Romantic love, also called passionate love, involves sexuality more than affectionate love. Romantic love is especially prominent among adolescents and traditional-aged college students. Affectionate love is more common in middle and late adulthood, characterizing love that endures over time. The developmental construction view emphasizes how relationships with parents, siblings, and peers influence how adolescents construct their romantic relationships. Dunphy's study found that group leaders play a role in dating and Connolly's research revealed the importance of peers and friends in adolescent romantic relationships.

• Culture can exert a powerful influence on dating. Many adolescents from immigrant families face conflicts with their parents about dating.

Key Terms

peers 351
conformity 354
popular children 356
neglected children 356

rejected children 356
controversial children 356
conglomerate strategies 358
friends 360

intimacy in friendship 363
norms 365
roles 365
cliques 365

crowds 366
romantic love 375
affectionate love 375
dating scripts 378

Key People

Thomas Berndt 355
Kenneth Dodge 358
Harry Stack Sullivan 361

Willard Hartup 362
Dexter Dunphy 365
Bradford Brown 366

Reed Larson 368
Wyndol Furman 376
Jennifer Connolly 378

Candice Feiring 378

Resources for Improving the Lives of Adolescents

Adolescent Relationships with Peers

(2004) by Bradford Brown. In R. Lerner & L. Steinberg (Eds.), *Handbook of adolescent psychology.* New York: Wiley.

A leading researcher provides a number of ideas about the current state of knowledge in the field of adolescent peer relations and describes some key areas where more research is needed.

Adolescent Romantic Relations and Sexual Behavior

(2003) by Paul Florsheim
Mahwah, NJ: Erlbaum

A number of experts address the much-neglected topic of romantic relationships in adolescence.

Boys and Girls Clubs of America

771 First Avenue
New York, NY 10017
213–351–5900

The Boys and Girls Clubs of America is a national, nonprofit youth organization that provides support services to almost 1,500 Boys and Girls Club facilities.

Boys and Girls Clubs of Canada/Clubs des Garons et Filles du Canada

7030 Woodbine Avenue, Suite 703
Markham, Ontario L3R 6G2
416–477–7272

Boys and Girls Clubs, with families and other adults, offer children and youth opportunities to develop skills, knowledge, and values to become fulfilled individuals.

Just Friends

(1985) by Lillian Rubin
New York: HarperCollins

Just Friends explores the nature of friendship and intimacy.

National Peer Helpers Association

818–240–2926

This association has publications and information on peer programs across the United States.

Youth-Reaching-Youth Project

202–783–7949

The Youth-Reaching-Youth Project offers a model peer program that involves young people and students in preventing and reducing alcohol use among high-risk youth.

E-Learning Tools

To help you master the material in this chapter, you will find a number of valuable study tools on the student CD-ROM that accompanies this book. In addition, visit the Online Learning Center for *Adolescence, 10th Edition,* where you will find helpful resources for chapter 10, "Peers."

Taking It to the Net

http://www.mhhe.com/santrocka10

1. Media portrayals of adolescents' peer interactions often involve negative instances of peer pressure, including drinking and smoking, delinquency, and drug use. What would you and your friends say to a reporter from the campus newspaper to illustrate the positive side of peer pressure and influence?
2. Having stressed the importance of adolescence as a period of transition from childhood to adult forms of behavior, your psychology of adolescent instructor assigns as a paper topic the emergence of romantic relationships. How would you describe adolescence as a transition from immature to adult forms of romantic relationships?

3. Cyberdating is increasing in popularity, particularly among older children and younger adolescents. What would you advise your younger sibling who is dabbling in cyberdating about important cautions?

Connect to **http://www.mhhe.com/santrocka10** to research the answers and complete these exercises. In some cases, you'll also find further instructions on this site.

Self-Assessment

To evaluate your experiences, complete these self-assessments: (1) My Romantic and Sexual Involvement in Adolescence, (2) Am I Ready for a Committed Relationship?, (3) How Well Do I Know My Partner?, and (4) The Characteristics I Desire in a Potential Mate.

Health and Well-Being, Parenting, and Education

To practice your decision-making skills, complete the health and well-being, parenting, and education scenarios.

CHAPTER

11

The whole art of teaching is only the art of awakening the natural curiosity of young minds.
—Anatole France,
French Novelist, 20th Century

Schools

Chapter Outline		*Learning Goals*
APPROACHES TO EDUCATING STUDENTS	**1**	Describe approaches to educating students
Historical Aspects		
Contemporary Approaches		
APA Learner-Centered Principles		
Social Policy		
TRANSITIONS IN SCHOOLING	**2**	Discuss transitions in schooling from early adolescence to emerging adulthood
Transition to Middle or Junior High School		
What Makes a Successful Middle School?		
The American High School		
High School Dropouts and Noncollege Youth		
Transition from High School to College		
Transition from College to Work		
THE SOCIAL CONTEXTS OF SCHOOLS	**3**	Explain how the social contexts of schools influence adolescent development
Changing Social Developmental Contexts		
Size and Climate of Schools		
Person-Environment Fit		
Teachers and Parents		
Peers		
Culture		
ADOLESCENTS WHO ARE EXCEPTIONAL	**4**	Characterize adolescents who are exceptional and their education
Who Are Adolescents with Disabilities?		
Learning Disabilities		
Attention Deficit Hyperactivity Disorder		
Educational Issues Involving Adolescents with Disabilities		
Adolescents Who Are Gifted		

Images Of Adolescent Development

From No More "What If" Questions to Authors' Week

Some schools for adolescents are ineffective, others effective, as revealed in these excerpts (Lipsitz, 1984):

A teacher in a social studies class squelches several imaginative questions, exclaiming, "You're always asking 'what if' questions. Stop asking 'what if.'" When a visitor asks who will become president if the president-elect dies before the electoral college meets, the teacher explodes, "You're as bad as they are! That's another 'what if' question!"

A teacher drills students for a seemingly endless amount of time on prime numbers. After the lesson, not one student can say why it is important to learn prime numbers.

A visitor asks a teacher if hers is an eighth-grade class. "It's called eighth grade," the teacher answers harshly, "but we know it's really kindergarten, right, class?"

In a predominantly Latino school, only the one adult hired as a bilingual teacher speaks Spanish.

In a biracial school, the principal and the guidance counselor cite test scores with pride. They are asked if the difference between the test scores of African American and White students is narrowing: "Oh, that's an interesting question!" says the guidance counselor with surprise. The principal agrees. It has never been asked by or of them before.

The preceding vignettes are from middle schools where life seems to be difficult and unhappy for students. By contrast, consider these circumstances in effective middle schools (Lipsitz, 1984):

Everything is peaceful. There are open cubbies instead of locked lockers. There is no theft. Students walk quietly in the corridors. "Why?" they are asked. "So as not to disturb the media center," they answer, which is self-evident to them, but not the visitor. . . . When asked, "Do you like this school?" [they] answer, "No, we don't like it. We love it!"

When asked how the school feels, one student answered, "It feels smart. We're smart. Look at our test scores." Comments from one of the parents of a student at the school are revealing: "My child would have been a dropout. In elementary school, his teacher said to me, 'That child isn't going to give you anything but heartaches.' He had perfect attendance here. He didn't want to miss a day. Summer vacation was too long and boring. He got here and someone cared for him."

The humane environment that encourages teachers' growth is translated by the teachers into a humane environment that encourages students' growth. The school feels cold when one first enters. It has the institutional feeling of any large school building with metal lockers and impersonal halls. Then one opens the door to a team area, and it is filled with energy, movement, productivity, doing. There is a lot of informal relating among students and between students and teachers. Visible from one vantage point are students working on written projects, putting the last touches on posters, watching a film, and working independently from reading kits. . . . Most know what they are doing, can say why it is important, and go back to work immediately after being interrupted.

Authors' Week is a special activity built into the school's curriculum that entices students to consider themselves in relation to the rich variety of making and doing in peoples' lives. Based on student interest, availability, and diversity, authors are invited to discuss their craft. Students sign up to meet with individual authors. They must have read one individual book by the author. Students prepare questions for their sessions with the authors. Sometimes, an author stays several days to work with a group of students on his or her manuscript.

In youth, we learn. An important context for that learning is school. Schools not only foster adolescents' academic learning, they also provide a social arena where peers, friends, and cliques can have a powerful influence on their development. Our exploration of schools in this chapter focuses on approaches to educating students, transitions in schooling, the social contexts of schools, and educating adolescents who are exceptional.

1 APPROACHES TO EDUCATING STUDENTS

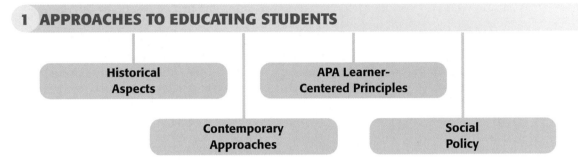

Today, virtually all American adolescents under the age of 16, and most 16- to 17-year-olds, are in school. More than half of all high school graduates continue their education by attending technical schools, colleges, or universities. Schools for adolescents are varied settings with many functions and diverse makeups offering an array of approaches to educating students. Let's begin our exploration of approaches to educating students by examining how U.S. adolescents have been educated at different points in history.

Historical Aspects

During the twentieth century, American schools assumed a more prominent role in the lives of adolescents. Between 1890 and 1920, virtually every state enacted laws that excluded youth from work and required them to attend school. In this time frame, the number of high school graduates increased by 600 percent. By making secondary education compulsory, the adult power structure placed adolescents in a submissive position and made their move into the adult world of work more manageable. In the nineteenth century, high schools had mainly been for the elite, with educational emphasis on classical, liberal arts courses. By the 1920s, educators perceived that this type of curriculum was no longer appropriate. Schools for the masses, it was thought, should involve not just intellectual training but also training for work and citizenship. Accordingly, the curriculum of secondary schools became more comprehensive and grew to include general education, college preparatory, and vocational education courses. As the twentieth century unfolded, secondary schools continued to expand their orientation, adding courses in music, art, health, physical education, and other subjects. By the middle of the twentieth century, schools had moved further toward preparing students for comprehensive roles in life (Conant, 1959). Today, secondary schools have retained their comprehensive orientation, designed to train adolescents not only intellectually but vocationally and socially as well.

Although school attendance has consistently increased for more than 150 years, in the 1960s distress over alienated and rebellious youth raised the issue of how well secondary schools served the needs of adolescents. In the 1970s, three independent panels agreed that high schools contributed to adolescent alienation and actually impeded the transition to adulthood (Brown, 1973; Coleman & others, 1974; Martin, 1976). The argument was that high schools segregate adolescents into "teenage warehouses," isolating them in their own self-contained world with their own values away from adult society. The prestigious panels stressed that adolescents should be given educational alternatives to the comprehensive high school, such as on-the-job community work, to increase their exposure to adult roles and to decrease their isolation from adults. Partially in response to these reports, a number of states lowered the age at which adolescents could leave school from 16 to 14.

Another development in the 1970s was the trend toward open education. The open-education approach, which was based on the British educational system, allowed adolescents to learn and develop at their own pace within a highly structured classroom. However, too many school systems that implemented open education in the United States thought it meant tearing down classroom walls and letting adolescents do whatever they wanted. Incorrect application of open education in American schools resulted in a strong backlash against it.

In the 1980s, partly as a backlash against open education, the back-to-basics movement gained momentum. The **back-to-basics movement** stresses that the function of schools should be the rigorous training of intellectual skills through such subjects as English, mathematics, and science. Back-to-basics advocates seek to eliminate "fluff" in secondary school curricula—alternative subjects that do not give students a basic education in intellectual subjects. They also believe that schools should be in the business of imparting knowledge to adolescents and should not be concerned about adolescents' social and emotional lives. They sometimes argue that the school day should be longer and that the school year should be extended into the summer months. Back-to-basics advocates want students to have more homework, more tests, and more discipline. They usually believe that adolescents should be behind their desks and not roaming around the room, while teachers should be at the head of the classroom, drilling knowledge into adolescents' minds.

In 1985, adolescent educators Arthur Powell, Eleanor Farrar, and David Cohen conducted an in-depth examination of fifteen diverse high schools across the United States by interviewing students, teachers, and school personnel, as well as by observing and interpreting what was happening in the schools. The metaphor of the "shopping mall" high school emerged as the authors tried to make sense of the data they had collected.

Variety, choice, and neutrality are important dimensions of the "shopping mall" high school. Variety appears in the wide range of courses offered (one school has 480 courses in its curriculum!), with something for apparently every student. Variety usually stimulates choice. Choice is often cited as a positive aspect of curricula, but the choice often rests in the hands of students, who, in too many instances, make choices based on ignorance rather than information. The investigators found that the diversity of individuals, multiple values, and wide range of course offerings combined to produce neutrality. Because they try to accommodate the needs of different student populations, high schools may become neutral institutions that take few stands on the products and services they offer. The shopping mall is an intriguing metaphor for America's high schools and provides insight into some general characteristics that have emerged.

Should the main and perhaps only major goal of schooling for adolescents be the development of an intellectually mature individual? Or should schools also focus on the adolescent's maturity in social and emotional development? Should schools be comprehensive and provide a multifaceted curriculum that includes many electives and alternative subjects to a basic core? These provocative questions continue to be heatedly debated in educational and community circles (Alexander, 2000; Sadker & Sadker, 2003).

Researchers have studied the role of extracurricular activities in adolescents' school success (Valentine & others, 2002). One longitudinal study followed approximately 400 students from seventh through twelfth grades (Mahoney & Cairns, 1997). Participation in extracurricular activities was linked with decreased likelihood of dropping out of school, especially for high-risk students. Also, in one recent study, participation on school teams was linked with a lower sense of social isolation (Stone, Barber, & Eccles, 2001). Participation in academic clubs (debate, foreign language, math club, chess club, science fair, or tutoring) and in school band, drama, and/or

*N*o one can be given an education. All you can give is the opportunity to learn.

—Carolyn Warner
American Author, 20th Century

back-to-basics movement This philosophy stresses that the function of schools should be the rigorous training of intellectual skills through such subjects as English, mathematics, and science.

dance was related to higher self-esteem in adolescents. In sum, there appear to be academic and social benefits to participating in extracurricular activities for some students, although studies have not adequately focused on the relation of such activities to many aspects of schooling and achievement. Yet another recent study found positive benefits for participation in extracurricular activities over an eight-year period (Mahoney, Cairns, & Farmer, in press). The positive benefits included increased likelihood of college attendance and enhanced interpersonal competence.

Why might participating in extracurricular activities contribute to long-term educational success? The fact that extracurricular activities are structured, challenging, and voluntary make them an ideal context for developing initiative (Larson, 2000; Larson, Hansen, & Walker, 2004). Further, participation in extracurricular activities reflects school engagement and the opportunity to interact with other students outside of the classroom in meaningful activities.

The debate about the function of schools produces shifts of emphases, much like a swinging pendulum, moving toward basic skills at one point in time, toward options, frills, or comprehensive training for life at another, and so on back and forth. What we should strive for, though, is not a swinging pendulum but something like a spiral staircase; that is, we should continually be developing more sophisticated ways of fulfilling the varied and changing functions of schools (Duffy & Kirkley, 2004; Reynolds, 2000; Reynolds & Miller, 2003).

Contemporary Approaches

What do educators today believe should be the approach to student learning? This is a controversial topic. The back-to-basics movement still has strong advocates who believe that children should mainly be taught in a **direct instruction approach,** a teacher-centered approach that is characterized by teacher direction and control, mastery of academic skills, high expectations for students' progress, and maximum time spent on learning tasks. This approach has much in common with the behavioral approach we discussed in chapter 2, "The Science of Adolescent Development."

In the 1990s, a wave of interest in constructivist approaches to school reform appeared; that interest has continued in the early part of the twenty-first century (Reynolds & Miller, 2003; Santrock, 2004). Two main types of constructivist approaches are (1) cognitive constructivist and (2) social constructivist:

- **Cognitive constructivist approaches** emphasize the adolescent's active, cognitive construction of knowledge and understanding. Piaget's theory (discussed in chapters 2 and 4) is an example of a cognitive constructivist approach. A central implication of Piaget's theory is that teachers should provide support for students to explore their world and develop understanding.
- **Social constructivist approaches** focus on collaboration with others to produce knowledge and understanding. Vygotsky's theory (also discussed in chapters 2 and 4) is an example of a social constructivist approach. A central implication of Vygtosky's theory is that teachers should create many opportunities for students to learn with the teacher and the peers in coconstructing understanding (Bearison & Dorval, 2002; Rogoff, 2003).

Advocates of the cognitive and social constructivist approaches argue that the direct instruction approach turns adolescents into passive learners and does not adequately challenge them to think in critical and creative ways. The direct instruction advocates, on the other hand, argue that the constructivist approaches often do not give enough attention to the content of a discipline, such as history or science. They also point out that many constructivist approaches are too relativistic and vague. Debate about which approach—direct instruction or constructivist—is the best one continues. An increasing number of experts, though, suggest that the best instruction may include both direct and constructivist aspects (Pressley & others, 2003).

www.mhhe.com/santrocka10

AskERIC and the Educator's Reference Desk Phi Delta Kappan

direct instruction approach A teacher-centered approach characterized by teacher direction and control, mastery of academic skills, high expectations for students' progress, and maximum time spent on learning tasks.

cognitive constructivist approaches Approaches that emphasize the adolescent's active, cognitive construction of knowledge and understanding; an example is Piaget's theory.

social constructivist approaches Approaches that focus on collaboration with others to produce knowledge and understanding; an example is Vygotsky's theory.

APA Learner-Centered Principles

Learner-centered principles move instruction away from the teacher and toward the student. The increased interest in learner-centered principles has resulted in the publication by the APA of *Learner-Centered Psychological Principles: A Framework for School Reform and Redesign* (Learner-Centered Principles Work Group, 1997; Presidential Task Force on Psychology and Education, 1992; Work Group of the American Psychological Association's Board of Educational Affairs, 1995). These principles were constructed, and are periodically revised, by a prestigious group of scientists and educators from a wide range of disciplines and interests. The principles have important implications for the way teachers instruct students.

The 14 learner-centered principles involve cognitive and metacognitive factors, motivational and affective factors, developmental and social factors, and individual difference factors. To read further about the learner-centered principles, see figure 11.1.

Social Policy

In *Turning Points,* the Carnegie Council on Adolescent Development (1989) issued a set of eight principles for transforming adolescents' education. These principles can inform social policy initiatives for improving the education of adolescents, especially young adolescents. The eight principles are:

**National Education Research Centers
Pathways to School Improvement
APA's Education Directorate
Constructivist Teaching and Learning
APA's Learner-Centered
Psychological Principles**

- *Create communities for learning.* Many American middle and high schools are large, impersonal institutions. Teachers have few opportunities to develop the stable relationships with students that are essential to teaching them effectively. Unacceptably large schools should be brought to a human scale by creating "schools-within-schools," or "houses" within the school, and then dividing these subunits into smaller "teams" of teachers and students. Such smaller groupings can enable each student to receive increased individual attention in a supportive context.
- *Teach a core of common knowledge.* An important task for educators is to identify the most important principles and concepts within each academic discipline and concentrate their efforts on integrating these ideas into a connected, interdisciplinary curriculum. Depth and quality of information should be emphasized rather than coverage of a large quantity of information. *Turning Points* also considers community service to be an integral part of the curriculum. Community service can stimulate adolescents to think critically about real-world problems.
- *Provide an opportunity for all students to succeed.* A troubling dimension of schools is the inequitable distribution of opportunities to learn among youth. Educators can do a great deal more to teach students of diverse abilities. One strategy is to expand cooperative learning. Researchers have found that cooperative learning in mixed-ability learning groups helps high achievers deepen their understanding of material by explaining it to lower achievers, who in turn benefit by receiving help as needed from their peers. Cooperative learning can also help students to become acquainted with classmates from different ethnic and cultural backgrounds.
- *Strengthen teachers and principals.* States and school districts need to give teachers and principals more authority in transforming their schools. The teachers and principals know more about what will work effectively in their schools than do administrators and government officials, who are often far removed from the classrooms. The creation of governance committees composed of teachers, principals, support staff, parents, and community representatives can make schools more effective.
- *Prepare teachers for the middle grades.* Most teachers in middle schools are not specifically educated to teach young adolescents. Teacher education programs need to develop curricula that train middle school teachers to work with the special needs of young adolescents.

Cognitive and Metacognitive Factors

1. Nature of the Learning Process
   The learning of complex subject matter is most effective when it is an intentional process of constructing meaning and experience.

2. Goals of the Learning Process
   Successful learners, over time and with support and instructional guidance, can create meaningful, coherent representations of knowledge.

3. Construction of Knowledge
   Successful learners can link new information with existing knowledge in meaningful ways.

4. Strategic Thinking
   Successful learners can create a repertoire of thinking and reasoning strategies to achieve complex goals.

5. Thinking about Thinking
   Higher order strategies for selecting and monitoring mental operations facilitate creative and critical thinking.

6. Context of Learning
   Learning is influenced by environmental factors, including culture, technology, and instructional practices.

Motivational and Instructional Factors

7. Motivational and Emotional Influences on Learning
   What and how much is learned is influenced by the learner's motivation. Motivation to learn, in turn, is influenced by the learner's emotional states, beliefs, interests, goals, and habits of thinking.

8. Intrinsic Motivation to Learn
   The learner's creativity, higher-order thinking, and natural curiosity all contribute to motivation to learn. Intrinsic (internal, self-generated) motivation is stimulated by tasks of optimal novelty and difficulty, tasks that are relevant to personal interests, and when learners are provided personal choice and control.

9. Effects of Motivation on Effort
   Acquiring complex knowledge and skills requires extended learner effort and guided practice. Without learner's motivation to learn, the willingness to exert this effort is unlikely without coercion.

Developmental and Social Factors

10. Developmental Influences on Learning
    As individuals develop, there are different opportunities and constraints for learning. Learning is most effective when development within and across physical, cognitive, and socioemotional domains is taken into account.

11. Social Influences on Learning
    Learning is influenced by social interactions, interpersonal relations, and communication with others.

Individual Difference Factors

12. Individual Differences in Learning
    Learners have different strategies, approaches, and capabilities for learning that are a function of prior experience and heredity.

13. Learning and Diversity
    Learning is most effective when differences in learners' linguistic, cultural, and social backgrounds are considered.

14. Standards and Assessment
    Setting appropriately high and challenging standards and assessing the learner as well as learning progress are integral aspects of the learning experience.

FIGURE 11.1 Learner-Centered Psychological Principles

- *Improve academic performance through better health and fitness.* Schools for adolescents often lack the support of health and social service agencies to address adolescents' physical and mental health needs. Developmentally appropriate health facilities, based in or near schools, need to be established.
- *Engage families in the education of adolescents.* Despite the clearly documented positive effects of parental involvement in education, parental involvement of all types declines considerably in adolescence, often to the point where it is nonexistent. An important social policy recommendation is to involve parents in decision making in significant ways, especially in low-income and ethnic minority neighborhoods (Epstein & Sanders, 2002). Parents who are involved in planning the school's work feel useful, develop confidence in their relations with the school staff, and are more likely to attend school functions, which signals to their adolescents that education is important.
- *Connect schools with communities.* "Full-service schools," those that represent a variety of school-based efforts to assist students and their families, should be considered in many locations. These efforts include comprehensive youth-service programs, community schools, and family resource centers. Strengthening the academic environment in conjunction with supporting students and the basic needs of their families is the common core of all such efforts.

In *Turning Points 2000* (Jackson & Davis, 2000), there was continued reliance on the eight recommendations set forth in *Turning Points 1989*. However, seven new recommendations that reflect what has been learned since the original report appeared in *Turning Points 2000:*

- Teach a curriculum grounded in rigorous academic standards for what students should know and be able to do. These efforts should be relevant to the concerns of adolescents and based on how students learn best.
- Use instructional methods designed to prepare all students to achieve higher standards and become lifelong learners.
- Staff middle schools with teachers who are experts on teaching young adolescents. Also, engage teachers in ongoing professional activities.
- Organize relationships for learning to create a climate of intellectual development and a caring community of shared educational purpose. Large schools should be divided into small learning communities with teams of teachers and students.
- Govern democratically through direct participation by all school staff members.
- Provide a safe and healthy school environment.
- Involve parents and communities in supporting student learning and healthy development.

Review and reflect Learning goal 1

1 Describe approaches to educating students

REVIEW
- How have U.S. adolescents been educated through history?
- What are the main contemporary approaches to educating adolescents?
- What are APA's learner-centered principles?
- What are the social policy recommendations for educating adolescents based on *Turning Points*?

REFLECT
- Which approach to educating adolescents do you think should most often be used: direct approach or constructivist approach? Explain.

2 TRANSITIONS IN SCHOOLING

Transition to Middle or Junior High School	The American High School	Transition from High School to College

What Makes a Successful Middle School?	High School Dropouts and Noncollege Youth	Transitions from College to Work

As children become adolescents and as adolescents develop and then become adults, they experience transitions in schooling (Seidman, 2000). We have just seen how the social setting changes from preschools through secondary schools. Additional important considerations involve transitions from elementary school to middle school or junior high school, from school to work for noncollege youth, from high school to college, and from college to work. To preview how psychological research can affect our understanding of the educational process, watch the video segment entitled "Schools and Public Policy," in which Dr. Eccles of the University of Michigan describes her research on gender and school transitions.

LifeMAP

Transition to Middle or Junior High School

The emergence of junior high schools in the 1920s and 1930s was justified on the basis of physical, cognitive, and social changes that characterize early adolescence, as well as on the need for more schools in response to the growing student population. Old high schools became junior high schools, and new, regional high schools were built. In most systems, the ninth grade remained a part of the high school in content, although physically separated from it in a 6-3-3 system (a system whereby students are grouped as follows: first through sixth grade, seventh through ninth grade, and tenth through twelfth grade). Gradually, the ninth grade has been restored to the high school, as many school systems have developed middle schools that include the seventh and eighth grades, or sixth, seventh, and eighth grades. The creation of middle schools has been influenced by the earlier onset of puberty in recent decades. Figure 11.2 reveals the dramatic increase in sixth- through eighth-grade middle schools and the corresponding decrease in seventh- through ninth-grade junior high schools.

One worry of educators and psychologists is that junior highs and middle schools have become simply watered-down versions of high schools, mimicking high schools' curricular and extracurricular schedules. The critics argue that unique curricular and extracurricular activities reflecting a wide range of individual differences in biological and psychological development in early adolescence should be incorporated into junior high and middle schools. The critics also stress that too many high schools foster passivity rather than autonomy and that schools should create a variety of pathways for students to achieve an identity.

The transition to middle school or junior high school from elementary school is a normative experience for virtually all children. However, the transition can be stressful because it occurs simultaneously with many other changes—in the individual, in the family, and in school (Eccles & Wigfield, 2000; Hawkins & Berndt, 1985; Seidman, 2000). These changes include puberty and related concerns about body image; the emergence of at least some aspects of formal operational thought, including accompanying changes in social cognition; increased responsibility and independence in adolescents' dealings with their parents; change from a small, contained classroom structure to a larger, more impersonal school structure; change from one teacher to many teachers and a small, homogeneous set of peers to a larger, more heterogeneous set of peers; and increased focus on

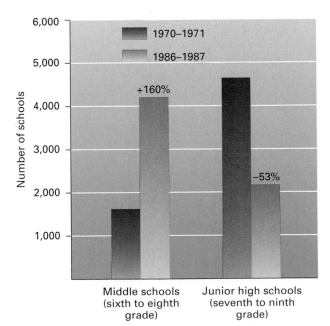

FIGURE 11.2 The Middle School Movement

Through the Eyes of Adolescents

Hoping a Pill Will Be Invented to Get You Through School

"I do good in school, but I don't want to do it. I want to get a good job and a good education and stuff, but I wish there was a pill or something that you could take to get you through school.

"I try to stay away from fights at school. I try to settle things just by talking, but if somebody pushes me too far I'll take them on.

"I wish everybody would pay more attention to kids. Sometimes grown-ups pay attention, but not a lot. They are kind of wrapped up in their jobs and don't pay attention to us kids. I don't think kids would get into as much trouble if people spent more time with kids."

—*Howard, Age 11*

www.mhhe.com/santrocka10

Educating Young Adolescents for a Changing World
First Days of Middle School
Middle School Reform
Middle School Programs

top-dog phenomenon The circumstance of moving from the top position (in elementary school, the oldest, biggest, and most powerful students) to the lowest position (in middle or junior high school, the youngest, smallest, and least powerful).

achievement and performance, and their assessment. This list includes a number of negative, stressful features, but aspects of the transition can also be positive. Students are more likely to feel grown up, have more subjects from which to select, have more opportunities to spend time with peers and to locate compatible friends, enjoy increased independence from direct parental monitoring, and be more challenged intellectually by academic work.

When students make the transition from elementary school to middle or junior high school, they experience the **top-dog phenomenon,** the circumstance of moving from the top position (in elementary school, the oldest, biggest, and most powerful students in the school) to the lowest position (in middle or junior high school, the youngest, smallest, and least powerful students in the school). Researchers who have charted the transition from elementary to middle or junior high school find that the first year of middle or junior high school can be difficult for many students. For example, in one investigation of the transition from sixth grade in an elementary school to the seventh grade in a junior high school, adolescents' perceptions of the quality of their school life plunged in the seventh grade (Hirsch & Rapkin, 1987). In the seventh grade, the students were less satisfied with school, were less committed to school, and liked their teachers less. The drop in school satisfaction occurred regardless of how academically successful the students were.

Is the transition to sixth- through eighth-grade middle schools easier for students than the transition to seventh- through ninth-grade junior high schools? It is hard to say. The middle school transition does guarantee that more girls will experience pubertal change when they are in the large, impersonal context of the middle school, but middle schools do not reduce the number of times adolescents are "bottom dogs." And with another arrangement, in which the middle school consists of the fifth, sixth, and seventh grades, boys may be subjected to more stress than in the past because their pubertal change coincides with school change.

Schools that provide more support, less anonymity, more stability, and less complexity improve student adjustment during the transition from elementary to middle or junior high school (Fenzel, Blyth, & Simmons, 1991). In one investigation, 101 students were studied at three points in time: spring of the sixth grade (pretransition), fall of the seventh grade (early transition), and spring of the seventh grade (late transition) (Hawkins & Berndt, 1985). Two different schools were sampled—one a traditional junior high school, the other a junior high in which the students were grouped into small teams (100 students, four teachers). Students' adjustment was assessed through self-reports, peer ratings, and teacher ratings. Adjustment dropped during the posttransition—for example, seventh-grade students' self-esteem was lower than that of sixth-grade students. Students in the team-oriented junior high reported that they received more support from teachers. Friendship patterns also influenced the students' adjustment. Students who reported more contact with their friends and higher-quality friendships had more positive perceptions of themselves and of their junior high school than their low-friendship counterparts.

Two studies further highlight the factors that mediate school transition during early adolescence. In the first study, when parents were attuned to their young adolescents' developmental needs and supported their autonomy in decision-making situations, the young adolescents showed better adjustment and higher self-esteem across the transition from elementary school to junior high school (Eccles, Lord, & Buchanan, 1996). In the second study, support from parents and friends was associated with better adjustment of young adolescents following the school transition of both sixth- and ninth-graders (Costin & Jones, 1994).

The transition from elementary to middle or junior high school occurs at the same time as a number of other developmental changes. *What are some of these other developmental changes?*

What Makes a Successful Middle School?

Joan Lipsitz (1984) searched the nation for the best middle schools. Extensive contacts and observations were made. Based on the recommendations of education experts and observations in schools in different parts of the United States, four middle schools were chosen for their outstanding ability to educate young adolescents. The most striking feature of these middle schools was their willingness and ability to adapt all school practices to the individual differences in physical, cognitive, and social development of their students. The schools took seriously the knowledge investigators have developed about young adolescents. This seriousness was reflected in decisions about different aspects of school life. For example, one middle school fought to keep its schedule of minicourses on Friday so that every student could be with friends and pursue personal interests. Two other middle schools expended considerable energy on a complex school organization so that small groups of students worked with small groups of teachers who could vary the tone and pace of the school day, depending on students' needs. Another middle school developed an advisory scheme so that each student had daily contact with an adult who was willing to listen, explain, comfort, and prod the adolescent. Such school policies reflect thoughtfulness and personal concern about individuals whose developmental needs are compelling. Another aspect observed was that, early in their existence—the first year in three of the schools and the second year in the fourth school—these effective middle schools emphasized the importance of creating an environment that was positive for the adolescent's social and emotional development. This goal was established not only because such environments contribute to academic excellence but also because social and emotional development are intrinsically valued as important in themselves in adolescents' schooling.

Recognizing that the vast majority of middle schools do not approach the excellent schools described by Joan Lipsitz (1984), in 1989 the Carnegie Council on Adolescent Development issued an extremely negative evaluation of U.S. middle schools. In the report—*Turning Points: Preparing American Youth for the Twenty-First*

Century—the conclusion was reached that most young adolescents attend massive, impersonal schools; learn from seemingly irrelevant curricula; trust few adults in school; and lack access to health care and counseling. The Carnegie report recommended the following:

- Developing smaller "communities" or "houses" to lessen the impersonal nature of large middle schools
- Lowering student-to-counselor ratios from several hundred to 1 to 10 to 1
- Involving parents and community leaders in schools
- Developing curricula that produce students who are literate, understand the sciences, and have a sense of health, ethics, and citizenship
- Having teachers team-teach in more flexibly designed curriculum blocks that integrate several disciplines, instead of presenting students with disconnected, rigidly separated 50-minute segments
- Boosting students' health and fitness with more in-school programs and helping students who need public health care to get it

Through its Middle Grade School State Policy Initiative, the Carnegie Foundation of New York is implementing the *Turning Points* recommendations in nearly 100 schools and 15 states nationwide. A national evaluation of this initiative is currently under way. Data from the state of Illinois already show that in 42 schools participating in at least one year of the study since 1991, enactment of the *Turning Points* recommendations is associated with significant improvements in students' reading, math, and language arts achievement. In 31 schools with several years of data, the same pattern of positive results has been found *within* schools over time. That is, as schools continue to implement the *Turning Points* recommendations, students' achievement continues to improve (Carnegie Council on Adolescent Development, 1995).

The American High School

Many high school graduates not only are poorly prepared for college, they also are poorly prepared for the demands of the modern, high-performance workplace. In a review of hiring practices at major companies, it was concluded that many companies now have sets of basic skills they want the individuals they hire to have. These include the ability to read at relatively high levels, do at least elementary algebra, use personal computers for straightforward tasks such as word processing, solve semistructured problems in which hypotheses must be formed and tested, communicate effectively (orally and in writing), and work effectively in groups with persons of various backgrounds (Murnane & Levy, 1996).

An increasing number of educators believe that the nation's high schools need a new mission for the twenty-first century, which addresses the following problems (National Commission on the High School Senior Year, 2001):

High Schools

1. More support is needed to enable all students to graduate from high school with the knowledge and skills needed to succeed in postsecondary education and careers. Many parents and students, especially those in low-income and minority communities, are unaware of the knowledge and level of skills required to succeed to postsecondary education and careers. A recent survey found that only 32 percent of high school seniors in 2001 in the United States met three criteria believed to be important markers for success in college (Greene & Forster, 2003). The three criteria consisted of how many students took basic courses in high school, passed a 12th grade reading test, and graduated on time. African American, Latino, and Native American students fared worse than non-Latino Whites and Asian American high school seniors in meeting all three criteria: African American (20 percent), Latino (16 percent), Native American (14 percent), non-Latino White (37 percent), and Asian American (38 percent).

2. High schools need to have higher expectations for student achievement. A special concern is the senior year of high school, which has become too much of a "party time" rather than a time to prepare for one of life's most important transitions. Some students who have been accepted to college routinely ignore the academic demands of their senior year. Low academic expectations harm students from all backgrounds.

3. U.S. high school students spend too much time working in low-level service jobs. Researchers have found that when tenth-graders work more than 14 hours a week and when eleventh-graders work 20 or more hours a week, their grades drop (Greenberger & Steinberg,1986). At the same time, shorter, higher-quality work experiences, including community service and internships, have been shown to benefit high school students. We will further explore the role of work in adolescent development in chapter 12, "Achievement, Careers, and Work."

4. There has been too little coordination and communication across the different levels of the K–12 schools, as well as between K–12 schools and institutions of higher education.

At the middle and secondary school levels, every student needs strong, positive connections with adults, preferably many of them, as they explore options for school, postsecondary education, and work (Hemmings, 2004).

High School Dropouts and Noncollege Youth

Dropping out of high school has been viewed as a serious educational and societal problem for many decades. By leaving high school before graduating, adolescents approach adult life with educational deficiencies that severely curtail their economic and social well-being. In this section, we study the scope of the problem, the causes of dropping out, and ways to reduce dropout rates.

High School Dropout Rates   In the last half of the twentieth century, high school dropout rates declined overall (National Center for Education Statistics, 2001). For example, in the 1940s, more than half of 15- to 24-year-olds had dropped out of school, but in 2000 this figure had decreased to about 11 percent. Figure 11.3 shows the trends in high school dropout rates from 1972 through 2000. Notice that the dropout rate of Latino adolescents remains precariously high (27.8 percent of 16- to 24-year old Latino adolescents had dropped out of school in 2000). The highest dropout rate in the United States, though, occurs for Native American youth—only about 10 percent finish their high school education.

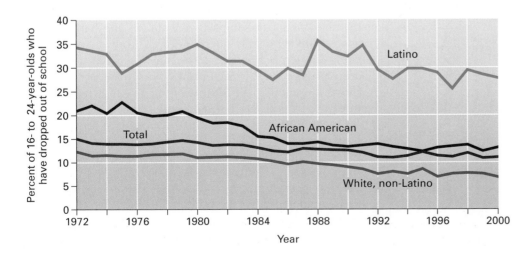

FIGURE 11.3 Trends in High School Dropout Rates

From 1972 through 2000, the school dropout rate for Latinos remained very high (27.8 percent of 16- to 24-year-olds in 2000). The African American dropout rate was still higher (13.1 percent) than the White non-Latino rate (6.9 percent) in 2000. The overall dropout rate declined considerably from the 1940s through the 1960s but has declined only slightly since 1972.

**Issues in Dropping Out of School
Raising Achievement and Reducing
Dropout Rates**

The Causes of Dropping Out Students drop out of school for school-related, economic, family-related, peer-related, and personal reasons. School-related problems are consistently associated with dropping out of school (Ianni & Orr, 1996; Sewell, 2000). In one investigation, almost 50 percent of the dropouts cited school-related reasons for leaving school, such as not liking school, being suspended, or being expelled (Rumberger, 1983). Twenty percent of the dropouts (but 40 percent of the Latino students) cited economic reasons for dropping out. Many of these students quit school and go to work to help support their families. Socioeconomic status is the main factor in family background that is strongly related to dropping out of school: Students from low-income families are more likely to drop out than those from middle-income families. Many school dropouts have friends who also are school dropouts. Approximately one-third of the girls who drop out of school do so for personal reasons, such as pregnancy or marriage. Overall, however, males are more likely than females to drop out.

One recent study found that students in high schools with fewer than 1,500 students were less likely to drop out of school (Lee & Burkam, 2001). Also in this study, students were less likely to drop out when they had consistently positive relationships with teachers.

Most research on dropouts has focused on high school students. An examination of middle school dropouts (Rumberger, 1995) found that observed differences in dropout rates among ethnic groups were related to differences in family background—especially socioeconomic status. Lack of parental academic support, low parental supervision, and low parental educational expectations for their adolescents were also related to dropping out of middle school.

Many of the factors just mentioned were related to dropping out of school in one large-scale investigation called *The High School and Beyond Study,* in which 30,000 high school sophomores were followed through graduation (Goertz, Ekstrom, & Rock, 1991). High school dropouts were more likely to come from low-income families, be in vocational programs, be males, be an ethnic minority (but not Asian American), and be in an urban school district (compared with rural or suburban). In addition, high school dropouts had lower grades in school (especially in reading), more disciplinary problems, lower rates of homework completion, lower self-esteem, lower educational expectations, and a more externalized sense of control. In one longitudinal study, high school dropouts had less language stimulation early in their development, compared with students who graduated from high school in a normal time frame (Cohen, 1994). And in another longitudinal study, very high, cumulative, early family stress had an impact on about one-half of the adolescents who subsequently dropped out of school (Jacobs, Garnier, & Weisner, 1996). In this same study, children at risk for dropping out of school who subsequently showed resilience and did not drop out of school had a more positive relational system within the family.

A number of research studies suggest that it is important to view dropping out of school as a long-term process of disengagement that begins in the earliest grades (Finn, Gerber, & Boyd-Zaharias, 2002). Early school failure may begin a process that causes children to question their competence, weaken their attachment to school, and eventually lead them to drop out. For example, one study examined the first- to ninth-grade records of Baltimore

Through the Eyes of Adolescents

Adolescents Who Hate School

For some adolescents, school is a miserable place. Here are four of them:

- I'm 16 years old and I hate school. How do I get out of school? I'm in the eleventh grade. I don't like my teachers. They are jerks. How do I get through all of this?

- I'm 15 and I have one teacher who really hacks me off. He makes me want to hit him sometimes. One of these days I'm going to hit him. I don't care about school, anyway. My dad hits me. I steal from stores.

- I'm thinking about dropping out of school. I just don't want to put my time in on it. It's not what I want. What's going to happen to me if I do drop out? What are my parents going to do to me? I know they could kick me out of the house.

- I'm 14 and I hate school!!! It's too much pressure and I can't deal with it. What am I supposed to do? I don't even have time for myself. I need time to exercise, to sing, and to organize my life. I wish I liked school but I doubt if I ever will.

schoolchildren and found that low test scores and poor report cards from as early as the first grade forecast dropout risk with considerable accuracy (Alexander, Entwisle, & Kabbani, 2000). In another study of 611 inner-city children, behavior problems in kindergarten through grade three were linked with misconduct in the classroom at 14 to 15 years of age and subsequent higher dropout rates (Finn, 1989).

Reducing the Dropout Rate and Improving the Lives of Noncollege Youth   Clearly, then, early detection of children's school-related difficulties and getting children engaged with school in positive ways are important strategies for reducing the dropout rate. One innovative program is the "I Have a Dream" (IHAD) Program, a comprehensive, long-term dropout prevention program administered by the National "I Have a Dream" Foundation in New York. Local IHAD projects around the country "adopt" entire grades (usually the third or fourth) from public elementary schools, or corresponding age cohorts from public housing developments. These children—"Dreamers"—are then provided with a program of academic, social, cultural, and recreational activities throughout their elementary, middle school, and high school years. An important part of this program is that it is personal rather than institutional: IHAD sponsors and staff develop close long-term relationships with the children. When participants complete high school, IHAD provides the tuition assistance necessary for them to attend a state or local college or vocational school.

These adolescents participate in the "I Have a Dream" (IHAD) Program, a comprehensive, long-term dropout prevention program that has been very successful. *What are some other strategies for reducing high school dropout rates?*

The IHAD Program was created in 1981, when philanthropist Eugene Lang made an impromptu offer of college tuition to a class of graduating sixth-graders at P.S. 121 in East Harlem. Statistically, 75 percent of the students should have dropped out of school; instead, 90 percent graduated and 60 percent went on to college. Since the National IHAD Foundation was created in 1986, it has grown to number over 150 projects in 57 cities and 28 states, serving some 12,000 children.

Community institutions, especially schools, need to break down the barriers between work and school. Many youth step off the education ladder long before reaching the level of a professional career, often with nowhere to step next, left to their own devices to search for work. These youth need more assistance than they are now receiving. Among the approaches worth considering are these:

- Monitored work experiences, such as through cooperative education, apprenticeships, internships, preemployment training, and youth-operated enterprises
- Community and neighborhood services, including voluntary service and youth-guided services
- Redirected vocational education, the principal thrust of which should not be preparation for specific jobs but acquisition of basic skills needed in a wide range of work
- Guarantees of continuing education, employment, or training, especially in conjunction with mentoring programs
- Career information and counseling to expose youth to job opportunities and career options as well as to successful role models
- School volunteer programs, not only for tutoring but to provide access to adult friends and mentors

Some countries provide a much better transition from school to work than the United States (Kerckhoff, 2002). These include the apprenticeship systems in Germany, Austria, and Switzerland that provide youth with marketable educational credentials and clear bridges into the labor market. In the United States, Canada, and many other countries, students who leave school early must find their way into the full-time labor force mainly on their own (Mortimer & Larson, 2002).

Transition from High School to College

Just as the transition from elementary school to middle or junior high school involves change and possible stress, so does the transition from high school to college (Johnson, 2002; Rog, Hunsberger & Alisat, 2002). In many ways, the two transitions involve parallel changes. Going from being a senior in high school to a freshman in college replays the top-dog phenomenon of going from the oldest and most powerful group of students to the youngest and least powerful group of students. For many of you, the transition from high school to college was not too long ago. You may vividly remember the feeling of your first days, weeks, and months on campus. You were called a freshman. Dictionary definitions of *freshmen* describe them not only as being in the first year of high school or college, but also as novices or beginners. *Senior* not only designates the fourth year of high school or college, but also implies being above others in decision-making power. The transition from high school to college involves a move to a larger, more impersonal school structure, interaction with peers from more diverse geographical and sometimes more diverse ethnic backgrounds, and increased focus on achievement and performance, and their assessment.

However, as with the transition from elementary school to middle or junior high school, the transition from high school to college can have positive aspects. Students are more likely to feel grown up, have more subjects from which to select, have more time to spend with peers, have more opportunities to explore different lifestyles and values, enjoy greater independence from parental monitoring, and may be more challenged intellectually by academic work.

In one study, the transition from high school to college or full-time work was characterized as a time of growth rather than hardship (Aseltine & Gore, 1993). During this transition, the individuals showed lower levels of depression and delinquency than when they were in the last two years of high school. The improvement was related to better relationships with their parents.

(a)

(b)

(*a*) The transition from high school to college has a number of parallels with the transition from elementary school to middle or junior high school, including the "top-dog" phenomenon. (*b*) An especially important aspect of the transition to college is reduced interaction with parents.

For many individuals, a major change from high school to college is reduced contact with parents. One investigation revealed that going away to college might not only benefit the individual's independence but also improve relationships with parents (Sullivan & Sullivan, 1980). Two groups of parents and their sons were studied. One group of sons left home to board at college; the other group remained home and commuted daily to college. The students were evaluated both before they had completed high school and after they were in college. Those who boarded at college were more affectionate toward their parents, communicated better with them, and were more independent from them than their counterparts who lived at home while attending college. In another study, preestablished affective relationships were related to college adjustment (Takahashi & Majima, 1994). Peer-oriented students adjusted better to the high school/college transition than family-dominant students did. However, in one recent study, secure attachment with parents was linked with positive socioemotional adjustment in the transition to the first year of college (Larose & Boivin, 1998).

The large number of individuals who go directly to college after completing high school delay formal entry into the adult world of work. You might remember from chapter 1 the description of *youth,* a post–high-school age period involving a sense of economic and personal "temporariness" (Kenniston, 1970). For many individuals, going to college postpones career or marriage/family decisions. The major shift to college attendance occurred in the post–World War II years, as the GI Bill opened up a college education for large numbers of veterans who might not have otherwise considered college to be an option. Since the 1960s college attendance has steadily increased.

Students often go to college expecting something special. As one high school student said, "My main concern is that, without a college education, I won't have much chance in today's world. I want a better life, which to me, means going to college." Though high school students usually approach college with high expectations, their transition from high school to college may be less than ideal. In a study of undergraduate education in the United States, the Carnegie Foundation for the Advancement of Teaching pointed out the disturbing discontinuity between public high schools and institutions of higher learning (Boyer, 1986). Almost half of the prospective college students surveyed said that trying to select a college is confusing because there is no sound basis for making a decision. Many high school seniors choose a college almost blindfolded. Once enrolled, they might not be satisfied with their choice and might transfer or drop out, sometimes for the wrong reasons. The transition from high school to college needs to become smoother (Stevenson, Kochanek, & Schneider, 1998). As a first step, public schools should take far more responsibility for assisting students in the transition from high schools to college. Public high schools could learn considerably from the best private schools, which have always taken this transition seriously, according to the Carnegie Foundation report. Colleges also need to provide more helpful guidance to prospective students, going beyond glossy brochures and becoming more personalized in their interaction with high school students. Figure 11.4 suggests that college representatives, high school counselors, comparative guides, and college publications have a long way to go.

Today's college freshmen appear to be experiencing more stress and depression than in the past, according to a UCLA survey of more than 300,000 freshmen at more than 500 colleges and universities (Sax & others, 2002). In 1985, 18 percent of college freshmen said they frequently felt overwhelmed; in 2001 that figure had risen to 27 percent. Fear of failing in a success-oriented world is frequently given as a reason for stress and depression among college students. The pressure to succeed in college, get an outstanding job, and make lots of money is pervasive, according to many of the students.

Transition from College to Work

Having a college degree is a strong asset. College graduates can enter careers that will earn them considerably more money in their lifetimes than those who do not go to

		Students %	Parents %
College representatives at "College Nights"	Relevant	62	65
	Accurate	73	68
High school counselors	Relevant	57	49
	Accurate	70	62
Comparative guides	Relevant	53	50
	Accurate	65	59
College publications	Relevant	32	34
	Accurate	59	49

FIGURE 11.4 Evaluation of Major Sources of College Information by College-Bound High School Seniors and Their Parents (percentage agreeing)

college, and income differences between college graduates and high school graduates continue to grow (*Occupational Outlook Handbook,* 2004–2005). In the United States, individuals with a bachelor's degree make over $1,000 a month more on the average than those with only a high school degree. Over a lifetime, a college graduate will make approximately $600,000 more on average than a high school graduate will.

Nonetheless, in North American countries, the transition from college to work is often a difficult one (Kerckhoff, 2002; Mortimer & Larson, 2002). U.S. colleges train many students to develop general skills rather than vocationally specific skills, with the result that many college graduates are poorly prepared for specific jobs or occupations. After finishing college, many individuals have difficulty obtaining the type of job they desire, or any job. Bouncing from one job to another after college is also not unusual.

Accelerated technical and occupational change in the future may make it even more difficult for colleges to provide training that keeps up with a fluid and shifting job market. Thus, it is important for colleges and employers to become better connected with each other to provide improved training for changing job opportunities (Mortimer & Larson, 2002).

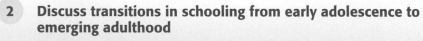

Review and reflect Learning goal 2

2 Discuss transitions in schooling from early adolescence to emerging adulthood

REVIEW

- How can the transition to middle or junior high school be characterized?
- What makes a successful middle school?
- What is the American high school like? How can it be improved?
- How can the transition from high school to college be described?
- What are some difficulties that high school dropouts and noncollege youth face?

REFLECT

- What was your own middle or junior high school like? How did it measure up to Lipsitz's criteria for effective schools and the recommendations made by the Carnegie Foundation?

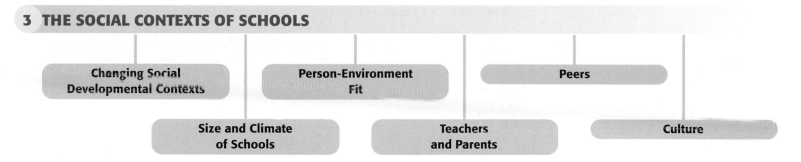

Schools and classrooms vary along many dimensions, including size of school or class and school or class atmosphere. Adolescents' school life also involves thousands of hours of interactions with teachers. A special concern is parent involvement in the adolescent's schooling. Also, as we see next, the social context of schools changes with the developmental level of students.

Changing Social Developmental Contexts

The social context differs at the preschool, elementary, and secondary level. The preschool setting is a protected environment, whose boundary is the classroom. In this limited social setting, preschool children interact with one or two teachers, almost always female, who are powerful motherlike figures in the young child's life. The preschool child also interacts with peers in a dyadic relationship or in small groups. Preschool children have little concept of the classroom as an organized social system, although they are learning how to make and maintain social contacts and communicate their needs. The preschool serves to modify some patterns of behavior developed through family experiences. Greater self-control may be required in the preschool years than earlier in development.

The classroom is still the major context for the elementary school child, although it is more likely to be experienced as a social unit than in the preschool. The network of social expression also is more complex now. Teachers and peers have a prominent influence on children during the elementary school years. The teacher symbolizes authority, which establishes the climate of the classroom, conditions of social interaction, and the nature of group functioning. The peer group becomes more salient, with increased interest in friendship, belonging, and status. And the peer group also becomes a learning community in which social roles and standards related to work and achievement are formed.

As children move into middle or junior high schools, the school environment increases in scope and complexity. The social field is the school as a whole rather than the classroom. Adolescents socially interact with many different teachers and peers from a range of social and ethnic backgrounds. Students are often exposed to a greater mix of male and female teachers. And social behavior is heavily weighted toward peers, extracurricular activities, clubs, and the community. The student in secondary schools is usually aware of the school as a social system and may be motivated to conform and adapt to the system or to challenge it (Minuchin & Shapiro, 1983).

Size and Climate of Schools

What size were the schools you went to as an adolescent? Do you think they were too big? too small? Let's explore the effects of school size, as well as classroom size, on adolescent development.

School Size and Classroom Size A number of factors led to the increased size of secondary schools in the United States: increasing urban enrollments, decreasing budgets, and an educational rationale of increased academic stimulation in consolidated institutions. But is bigger really better? No systematic relation between school size and academic achievement has been found, but more prosocial and possibly less antisocial behavior occur in small schools (Rutter & others, 1979). Large schools, especially those with more than 500 to 600 students, may not provide a personalized climate that allows for an effective system of social control. Students may feel alienated and not take responsibility for their conduct. This might be especially true for unsuccessful students who do not identify with their school and who become members of oppositional peer groups. The responsiveness of the school can mediate the impact of school size on adolescent behavior. For example, in one investigation, low-responsive schools (which offered few rewards for desirable behavior) had higher crime rates than high-responsive schools (McPartland & McDill, 1976). Although school responsiveness, regardless of size, may mediate adolescent conduct, small schools may be more flexible in their responsiveness than larger schools.

Two common beliefs are that smaller schools provide adolescents with a better education, and that smaller classes are better than larger classes. Traditional schools in the United States have 30 to 35 students per classroom. The balance of the evidence suggests that substantial reductions in class size do improve student achievement (Blatchford & Mortimore, 1994; Finn, 2002). The effects are strongest for students in the early primary grades, for low-achieving students, and for students from low-SES backgrounds. The greatest gains in achievement occur when the class size is 20 or fewer students.

Classroom Climate It is important for classrooms to present a positive environment for learning. Two effective general strategies for creating positive classroom environments are using an authoritative strategy and effectively managing the group's activities.

The idea of an authoritative classroom management strategy is derived from Diana Baumrind's (1971) typology of parenting styles, which was discussed in chapter 9, "Families." Like authoritative parents, authoritative teachers have students who tend to be self-reliant, delay gratification, get along well with their peers, and show high self-esteem. An **authoritative strategy of classroom management** encourages students to be independent thinkers and doers but still involves effective monitoring. Authoritative teachers engage students in considerable verbal give-and-take and show a caring attitude toward them. However, they still declare limits when necessary. Teachers clarify rules and regulations, establishing these standards with input from students.

The authoritative strategy contrasts with two ineffective strategies: authoritarian and permissive. The **authoritarian strategy of classroom management** is restrictive and punitive. The focus is mainly on keeping order in the classroom rather than on instruction and learning. Authoritarian teachers place firm limits and controls on students and have little verbal exchange with them. Students in authoritarian classrooms tend to be passive learners, fail to initiate activities, express anxiety about social comparison, and have poor communication skills.

The **permissive strategy of classroom management** offers students considerable autonomy but provides them with little support for developing learning skills or managing their behavior. Not surprisingly, students in permissive classrooms tend to have inadequate academic skills and low self-control.

Researchers recently have found continuing support for the importance of an authoritative teaching style in adolescent development (Paulson, Marchant, & Rothlisberg, 1998; Wentzel, 2002). Thus, overall, an authoritative strategy will benefit students more than authoritarian or permissive strategies. An authoritative strategy will help students become active, self-regulated learners (Evertson, Emmer, & Worsham, 2003).

authoritative strategy of classroom management This teaching strategy encourages students to be independent thinkers and doers but still involves effective monitoring. Authoritative teachers engage students in considerable verbal give-and-take and show a caring attitude toward them. However, they still declare limits when necessary.

authoritarian strategy of classroom management This teaching strategy is restrictive and punitive. The focus is mainly on keeping order in the classroom rather than on instruction and learning.

permissive strategy of classroom management This strategy offers students considerable autonomy but provides them with little support for developing learning skills or managing their behavior.

In Jacob Kounin's (1970) classic research on classroom management, effective teachers did not differ from ineffective ones in the way they responded to students' misbehaviors; where they differed was in how competently they managed the group's activities. The effective teachers closely monitored students on a regular basis, which allowed them to detect problem behavior before it got out of hand. Effective teachers also kept the flow of a lesson moving smoothly, maintaining students' interest and refraining from giving them opportunities to be easily distracted. And effective teachers engaged students in a variety of challenging, but not impossible, classroom activities.

To function smoothly, classrooms need clearly defined rules and routines (Emmer, Evertson, & Worsham, 2003). Students need to know how they are expected to behave. Without clearly defined classroom rules and routines, misunderstandings that can breed chaos are inevitable. Rules should be reasonable and necessary, clear and comprehensible, and consistent with instructional and learning goals (Weinstein, 1997, 2003). Teachers can improve the likelihood that students will cooperate with them if they develop a positive relationship with students, get students to share and assume responsibility, and reward appropriate behavior.

The effectiveness of classroom climate is often linked to a teacher's beliefs and practices (Eccles, Wigfield, & Schiefele, 1998). For example, student satisfaction, personal growth, and achievement are maximized only when teacher warmth and support are accompanied by efficient organization, an emphasis on academics, and provision of goal-oriented activities (Trickett & Moos, 1974).

Researchers have examined the climate not only of the classroom but also of the entire school. Schools with a climate of self-efficacy and positive expectations for students' success serve to benefit student learning and achievement (Bandura, 1997; Bryk, Lee, & Holland, 1993). Other investigators argue that an emphasis on ability tracking, comparative performance evaluations, and ego, rather than a mastery focus, undermines the motivation of both students and teachers (Maehr & Midgley, 1996). Later, in chapter 12, "Achievement, Careers, and Work," we will further explore aspects of achievement that are important in understanding classroom and school climate.

Person-Environment Fit

Some of the negative psychological changes associated with adolescent development might result from a mismatch between the needs of developing adolescents and the opportunities afforded them by the schools they attend. Adolescent expert Jacquelynne Eccles and her colleagues (Eccles & Wigfield, 2000; Eccles & others, 1993) described ways in which developmentally appropriate school environments can be created that match up better with adolescents' needs. Their recommendations are based on a large-scale study of 1,500 young adolescents in middle-income communities in Michigan. These adolescents were studied as they made the change from the sixth grade in an elementary school to the seventh grade in a junior high school.

Both the early adolescents and their teachers reported less opportunity for adolescent participation in classroom decision making in the seventh grade than in the sixth grade. By contrast, the students wanted to participate more in classroom decision making in the seventh grade than in the sixth grade. According to Eccles (2004), such findings represent a person-environment mismatch that harms adolescent development.

Teachers and Parents

Adolescents' development is influenced by teachers. In addition, an increasingly important issue is parent involvement in schooling.

Interactions with Teachers   Virtually everyone's life is affected in one way or another by teachers (Oakes & Lipton, 2003; Newman, 2002). You probably were

www.mhhe.com/santrocka10

Managing Today's Classroom

"My mom told me to tell you that I am the educational challenge you were told about in college."
Reprinted by permission of Heisertoons.

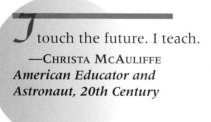

I touch the future. I teach.
—CHRISTA MCAULIFFE
American Educator and Astronaut, 20th Century

Teaching Resources

influenced by teachers as you grew up. One day you may have, or perhaps you already have, children and adolescents whose lives will be guided by many different teachers. You likely can remember several of your teachers vividly. Perhaps one never smiled, another required you to memorize everything in sight, and yet another always appeared vibrant and encouraged students to ask questions. Psychologists and educators have tried to compile a profile of a good teacher's personality traits, but the complexity of personality, education, learning, and individuals makes this a difficult task. Nonetheless, some teacher traits are associated with positive student outcomes more than others—enthusiasm, ability to plan, poise, adaptability, warmth, flexibility, and awareness of individual differences, for example. And in one study, positive teacher expectations were linked with higher student achievement (Jussim & Eccles, 1993).

Erik Erikson (1968) proposed that good teachers produce a sense of industry, rather than inferiority, in their students. Good teachers are trusted and respected by the community and know how to alternate work and play, study and games, says Erikson. They know how to recognize special efforts and to encourage special abilities. They also know how to create a setting in which adolescents feel good about themselves, and they know how to handle those adolescents to whom school is not important. In Erikson's (1968) own words, adolescents should be "mildly but firmly coerced into the adventure of finding out that one can learn to accomplish things which one would never have thought of by oneself."

Other recommendations for successful teaching with young adolescents have been offered by adolescent educator Stephanie Feeney (1980). She believes that meaningful learning takes place when the developmental characteristics of the age group are understood, when trust has been established, and when adolescents feel free to explore, to experiment, and to make mistakes. The variability and change that characterize young adolescents make them a difficult age group to instruct. The student who leans on the teacher one day for help may be strutting around independently the next day. Teachers who work successfully with young adolescents probably have vivid memories of their own adolescence and are likely to have mastered the developmental tasks of those years. Able to recall their youthful vulnerability, they understand and respect their students' sensitivity to criticism, desire for group acceptance, and feelings of being acutely conspicuous. Successful teachers of adolescents are secure in their own identity and comfortable with their sexuality. Possessing clear values, they use power and authority wisely and are sensitive to their students' feelings. Young adolescents respond best to teachers who exercise natural authority—based on greater age, experience, and wisdom—rather than either arbitrary authority or abdication of authority by being pals with the adolescent. Young adolescents need teachers who are fair and consistent, who set reasonable limits, and who realize that adolescents need someone to push against while testing those limits.

In the study of adolescents and schooling by Jacquelynne Eccles and her colleagues (1993), some characteristics of the teachers in the seventh grade have implications for the quality of adolescent education. Seventh-grade teachers had less confidence in their teaching efficacy than their sixth-grade counterparts did. Moreover, students who moved from high-efficacy teachers in the sixth grade to low-efficacy teachers in the seventh grade had lower expectations for themselves and said school was more difficult at the end of the seventh grade than did adolescents who experienced no change in teacher efficacy or who moved from low-efficacy to high-efficacy teachers.

Student-teacher relationships began to deteriorate after the transition to junior high school. Also, students who moved from elementary school teachers they perceived to be supportive to junior high school teachers they perceived to be unsupportive showed a decline in the value they attached to an important school subject—math. Low-achieving students were especially at risk when they moved to less facilitative classroom environments after the junior high transition.

Parents and Schools   It is commonly believed that parent involvement is important in schooling during childhood, but that during adolescence parents play a much smaller role in schooling. Increasingly, though, researchers are finding that parents can be key factors in schooling at all grade levels (Connors & Epstein, 1995). Research suggests that parents are not as involved in their adolescents' schooling as they or the schools would like (Comer, 1988; Epstein & Sanders, 2002). Even though parental involvement is minimal in elementary school, it is even less in secondary school (Eccles & Harold, 1993). In one study, teachers listed parental involvement as the number one priority in improving education (Chira, 1993). In an analysis of 16,000 students, the students were more likely to get A's and less likely to repeat a grade or be expelled if both parents were highly involved in their schooling (National Center for Education Statistics, 1997).

One example of a successful school-family partnership involves the New York City School System and the Children's Aid Society, which provide school-based programs for 1,200 adolescents and their families (Carnegie Council on Adolescent Development, 1995). The participating school's family resource center is open from 8:30 A.M. to 8:30 P.M. Staffed by social workers, parents, and other volunteers, the center houses adult education, drug-abuse prevention, and other activities. Because many of the families who send adolescents to the school are Spanish speakers (of Dominican origin), the school offers English-as-a-second-language classes for parents, 400 of whom were enrolled at the time of this study.

Joyce Epstein (1990, 1996; Epstein & Sanders, 2002) has provided a framework for understanding how parental involvement in adolescents' schooling can be improved. First, *families have a basic obligation to provide for the safety and health of their adolescents.* Many parents are not knowledgeable about the normal age-appropriate changes that characterize adolescents. School-family programs can help to educate parents about the normal course of adolescent development. Schools also can offer programs about health issues in adolescence, including sexually transmitted infections, depression, drugs, delinquency, and eating disorders. Schools also can help parents find safe places for their adolescents to spend time away from home. Schools are community buildings that could be used as program sites by youth organizations and social service agencies.

Second, *schools have a basic obligation to communicate with families about school programs and the individual progress of their adolescents.* Teachers and parents rarely get to know each other in the secondary school years. Programs are needed to facilitate more direct and personalized parent-teacher communication. Parents also need to receive better information about how curricular choices can lead to eventual career choices. This is especially important with regard to females and ethnic minority students enrolling in science and math courses.

Third, *parents' involvement at school needs to be increased.* Parents and other family members may be able to assist teachers in the classroom in a variety of ways, such as tutoring, teaching special skills, and providing clerical or supervisory assistance. Such involvement is especially important in inner-city schools.

Fourth, *parent involvement in the adolescent's learning activities at home needs to be encouraged.* Secondary schools often raise a concern about parents' expertise and ability

Careers in Adolescent Development

Jimmy Furlow
Secondary School Teacher

Ninth-grade history teacher Jimmy Furlow believes that students learn best when they have to teach others. He has groups of students summarize textbook sections and put them on transparencies to help the entire class prepare for a test. Furlow lost both legs in Vietnam but he rarely stays in one place, moving his wheelchair around the room, communicating with students at eye level. When the class completes their discussion of all the points on the overhead, Furlow edits their work to demonstrate concise, clear writing and helps students zero in on an important point (Marklein, 1998).

Ninth-grade history teacher Jimmy Furlow converses with a student in his class.

www.mhhe.com/santrocka10

Parent Involvement in Schools

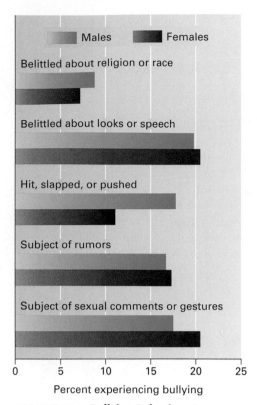

FIGURE 11.5 Bullying Behaviors Among U.S. Youth

This graph shows the type of bullying most often experienced by U.S. youth. The percentages reflect the extent to which bullied students said that they had experienced a particular type of bullying. In terms of gender, note that when they were bullied, boys were more likely to be hit, slapped, or pushed than girls were.

in helping their adolescents with homework. Given this concern, schools could provide parents with supplementary educational training so that parents can be more helpful and confident in their ability. "Family Math" and "Family Computers" are examples of programs that have been developed by some secondary schools to increase parent involvement in adolescent learning.

Fifth, *parents need to be increasingly involved in decision making at school.* Parent-teacher associations are the most common way for parents to be involved in school decision making. In some school districts, school improvement teams consisting of school staff and parents have been formed to address specific concerns.

Sixth, *collaboration and exchange with community organizations need to be encouraged.* Agencies and businesses can join with schools to improve adolescents' educational experiences. Business personnel can especially provide insights into careers and the world of work. Some schools have formed partnerships with businesses, which provide some financial backing for special projects.

In summary, the collaborative relationship between parents and schools has usually decreased as children move into the adolescent years. Yet parent involvement might be just as important in the adolescent's schooling as in the child's schooling. For example, Epstein (1996) created a program designed to increase parents' involvement in the education of their middle school students and it had positive effects on the students' school performance. It is hoped that the future will bring much greater family/school/community collaboration in the adolescent years (Eccles & Harold, 1993).

Peers

We examined many aspects of adolescent peer relations in chapter 10, "Peers." Here we explore peer relations in school contexts.

Structure of Middle Schools The way middle schools are structured encourages students to interact with larger numbers of peers on a daily basis (Wentzel, 2003). The relative uncertainty and ambiguity of multiple classroom environments and more complex class schedules may result in middle school students turning to each other for information, social support, and strategies for coping.

Peer Statuses Peer statuses have been studied in relation to school success. Being popular or accepted by peers is usually associated with academic success, whereas being rejected by peers is related to more negative academic outcomes (Wentzel, 2003).

Bullying A special concern regarding peer relations in schools involves bullying (Garbarino, 2004). Significant numbers of children and adolescents are victimized by bullies (Card, 2003; Espelage & Swearer, 2004; Parker, 2002; Pellegrini, 2002; Swearer & Espelage, 2004). In one recent national survey of more than 15,000 sixth- through tenth-graders, 20 percent said they had been involved in moderate or frequent bullying (Nansel & others, 2001) (see figure 11.5). Middle school students and boys were more likely to be involved in bullying than high school boys or girls. In another recent study of more than 4,000 middle school students in Maryland, 31 percent reported being victimized three or more times in the past year (Haynie & others, 2001).

Victims of bullying have been found to have certain characteristics (Card, Isaacs & Hodges, 2000; Ladd & Kochenderfer-Ladd, 2002; Swearer & others, 2004). One study found that victims of bullies had parents who were intrusive, demanding, and unresponsive with their children (Ladd & Kochenderfer, 1998). Also in this study, parent-child relationships characterized by intense closeness were linked with higher levels of peer victimization in boys. Overly close and emotionally intense relationships between parents and sons might not foster assertiveness and independence. Rather, they might foster self-doubts and worries that are perceived as weaknesses when expressed in male peer groups. Another study (Olweus, 1980) found that for both bullies and

How are peer relations linked to adolescents' academic success?

victims, the parenting they experienced was linked with their peer interaction. Bullies' parents were more likely to be rejecting, authoritarian, or permissive about their son's aggression, whereas victims' parents were more likely to be anxious and overprotective.

In another study, third- and sixth-grade boys and girls who internalized problems (for instance, were anxious and withdrawn) were physically weak and were rejected by peers (Hodges & Perry, 1999). Yet another study found that the relation between internalizing problems and increased victimization was reduced for children with a protective friendship (Hodges & others, 1999).

Victims of bullies can suffer both short-term and long-term effects (Limber, 1997). Short-term, they can become depressed, lose interest in schoolwork, or even avoid going to school. The effects of bullying can persist into adulthood. One longitudinal study of male victims who were bullied during childhood found that in their twenties they were more depressed and had lower self-esteem than their counterparts who had not been bullied in childhood (Olweus, 1993).

Bullying also can indicate a serious problem for the bully as well as the victim. In the study just mentioned, about 60 percent of the boys who were identified as bullies in middle school had at least one criminal conviction (and about one-third had three or more convictions) in their twenties, rates that are far higher than the rates for nonbullies. Some strategies that teachers can use to reduce bullying are (Limber, 1997, 2004; Olweus, 1994; Stevens, DeBourdeaudhuij, & Van Oost, 2001) as follows:

- Get older peers to serve as monitors for bullying and intervene when they see it taking place.
- Develop schoolwide rules and sanctions against bullying and post them throughout the school.
- Form friendship groups for adolescents who are regularly bullied by peers.
- Incorporate the message of the antibullying program into church, school, and other community activities where adolescents are involved.

Friendship Another aspect of peer relations that is linked with school success involves friendship. Having friends is related to higher grades and test scores in adolescents (Berndt & Keefe, 1996). One longitudinal study found that having at least one friend was related to academic success over a two-year period (Wentzel & Caldwell, 1997).

Crowds Also recall from chapter 10, "Peers," that being a member of a particular crowd is related to academic success (Brown, 2003, 2004). In one analysis, the highest academic success was achieved by the "brains," the lowest by the "druggies" (Brown, Mory, & Kinney, 1994).

Culture

As we saw in chapter 10, "Peers," in some cultures—such as Arab countries and rural India—adults often restrict access to peers, especially for girls. The peer restriction includes the social setting of schools, where girls are educated separately from boys.

Indeed, culture can have a powerful effect on the nature and quality of schools that adolescents experience. First, we explore the roles of socioeconomic status and ethnicity in U.S. schools for adolescents; we then examine schools for adolescents in different countries around the world.

Socioeconomic Status and Ethnicity Adolescents from low-income, ethnic minority backgrounds often have more difficulties in school than their middle-socioeconomic-status, White counterparts (Books, 2004). Why? Critics argue that schools have not done a good job of educating low-income, ethnic minority students to overcome the barriers to their achievement (Scott-Jones, 1995). Let's examine the roles of socioeconomic status (SES) and ethnicity in schools.

Socioeconomic Status Adolescents in poverty often face problems at home and at school that present barriers to their learning (McLoyd, 2000; Spring, 2002). At home, they might have parents who don't set high educational standards for them, who are incapable of helping them read, who don't have the skills to help them with their homework, and who don't have enough money to pay for educational materials and experiences such as books, music lessons, and trips to zoos and museums. They might experience malnutrition and live in areas where crime and violence are a way of life.

Schools in low-SES areas are more likely to have a higher percentage of students with lower achievement test scores, lower graduation rates, and fewer students going to college. These schools often have fewer resources than schools in higher-SES neighborhoods (Shade, Kelly, & Oberg, 1997). They also are more likely to have young teachers with less experience than those in schools in higher-SES neighborhoods. Schools in low-SES areas are more likely to encourage rote learning, whereas schools in higher-SES areas are more likely to work with adolescents to improve their thinking skills (Spring, 2002). In sum, far too many schools in low-SES neighborhoods provide students with environments that are not conducive to effective learning and the schools' buildings and classrooms often are old, crumbling, and poorly maintained.

Jonathan Kozol (1991) vividly described some of these problems adolescents in poverty face in their neighborhood and at school in *Savage Inequalities.* Following are some of his observations in East St. Louis, Illinois, an inner-city area that is 98 percent African American and has no obstetric services, no regular trash collection, and few jobs. Nearly one-third of the families live on less than $7,500 a year, and 75 percent of the population lives on some form of welfare. Blocks upon blocks of housing consist of dilapidated, skeletal buildings. Residents breathe in chemical pollution from the nearby Monsanto Chemical Company plant. Raw sewage repeatedly backs up into homes. Lead from nearby smelters poisons the soil. Malnutrition is common. Fear of violence is real.

The problems of the streets spill over into the East St. Louis schools, where sewage also backs up from time to time. Classrooms and hallways are old and unattractive, athletic facilities inadequate. Teachers run out of chalk and paper, the science labs are 30 to 50 years out of date, and the school's heating system never has worked right. A history teacher has 110 students but only 26 books.

Kozol says that anyone who visits places like East St. Louis, even for a brief time, comes away profoundly shaken. Kozol's interest was in describing what life is like in

**Poverty and Learning
Interview with Jonathan Kozol**

the nation's inner-city neighborhoods and schools, which are predominantly African American and Latino. However, there are many non-Latino White adolescents who also live in poverty, mainly in suburban and rural areas. Kozol asserts that many inner-city schools are racially segregated, are grossly underfunded, and do not provide anywhere near adequate opportunities for students to learn effectively.

Ethnicity   Despite decades of desegregation mandates, school segregation is still a fact of life in the education of children and adolescents of color in the United States (Simons, Finlay, & Yang, 1991). Almost one-third of African American and Latino students attend schools in which 90 percent or more of the students are from ethnic minority groups.

The school experiences of students from different ethnic groups vary considerably (Cooper & others, 2002; Jackson & Rodriquez, 2002; Meece & Kurtz-Costes, 2001; Yeakey & Henderson, 2002). African American and Latino students are much less likely than non-Latino White or Asian American students to be enrolled in college preparatory academic programs, and much more likely to be enrolled in remedial and special education programs. Asian American students are far more likely than other ethnic minority groups to take advanced math and science courses in high school. African American students are twice as likely as Latinos, Native Americans, or Whites to be suspended from school. Ethnic minorities of color constitute the majority in 23 of the 25 largest school districts in the United States, a trend that is increasing (Banks, 2002). However, 90 percent of the teachers in America's schools are non-Latino White, and the percentage of minority teachers is projected to decrease even further in coming years.

In one recent study, African American adolescents were more likely to have U.S.-born, college-educated parents whereas Latino adolescents were more likely to have immigrant parents with a high school education or less (Cooper & others, 2001). In this study, resources and challenges across social worlds (parents' and teachers' help and siblings' challenges) were positively linked with adolescents' higher grade point average, eligibility, and admission to more prestigious colleges.

In another recent study, it was concluded that U.S. schools are doing an especially poor job of meeting the needs of America's fastest-growing minority population—Latinas (the term used for Latino females) (Ginorio & Huston, 2001). The study focuses on how Latinas' futures—or "possible selves"—are influenced by their families, culture, peers, teachers, and media. The report indicates that many high school counselors view success as "going away to college," yet some Latinas, because of family responsibilities, believe it is important to stay close to home. The high school graduation rate for Latinas lags behind that for girls of any other ethnic minority group. Latinas also are less likely to take the SAT exam than other non-Latino White and other ethnic group females. Thus, a better effort needs to be made at encouraging Latinas' academic success and involving their families more fully in the process of college preparation.

American anthropologist John Ogbu (1989; Ogbu & Stern, 2001) argues that students of color, especially African American and Latino students, have inferior educational opportunities, have teachers and school administrators who have low academic expectations for them, and encounter negative stereotypes of ethnic minority groups. In one study of middle schools in predominantly Latino areas of Miami, Latino and non-Latino White teachers rated African American students as having more behavior problems than African American teachers rated the same students as having (Zimmerman & others, 1995).

Like Ogbu, Margaret Beale Spencer (Spencer & Dornbusch, 1990) says that a form of institutional racism permeates many American schools. That is, well-meaning

Dr. Henry Gaskins began an after-school tutorial program for ethnic minority students in 1983 in Washington, D.C. For four hours every weeknight and all day Saturday, 80 students receive one-on-one assistance from Gaskins and his wife, two adult volunteers, and academically talented peers. Those who can afford it contribute five dollars to cover the cost of school supplies. In addition to tutoring in specific subjects, Gaskins' home-based academy helps students to set personal goals and to commit to a desire to succeed. Many of his students come from families in which the parents are high school dropouts and either cannot or are not motivated to help their adolescents achieve in school. In addition, the academy prepares students to qualify for scholarships and college entrance exams. Gaskins was recently awarded the President's Volunteer Action Award at the White House.

teachers, acting out of misguided liberalism, fail to challenge students of color to achieve. Such teachers prematurely accept a low level of performance from these students, substituting warmth and affection for high standards of academic success.

Strategies for improving relations between ethnically diverse students include (Santrock, 2004):

- *Turn the class into a jigsaw.* When social psychologist Elliot Aronson was a professor at the University of Texas at Austin, the Austin School system asked him for ideas on how to reduce the increasing racial tension in the classrooms. Aronson (1986) developed the concept of the **jigsaw classroom,** where students from different cultural backgrounds are placed in a cooperative group in which they have to construct different parts of a project to reach a common goal. Aronson used the term "jigsaw" because he envisioned the technique as being like a group of students cooperating to put together different pieces of a jigsaw puzzle.

  How might this work? Consider a class of students, some White, some African American, some Latino, and some Asian American. The lesson to be learned by the groups focuses on the life of Joseph Pulitzer. The class might be broken up into groups of six students each, with the groups being as equal as possible in terms of ethnic composition and achievement level. The lesson about Pulitzer's life is divided into six parts, with each part given to a member of each six-person group. The parts might be paragraphs from Pulitzer's biography, such as how the Pulitzer family came to the United States, Pulitzer's childhood, his early work, and so on. All students in each group are given an allotted time to study their parts. Then group members teach their parts to the group. Learning depends on the students' interdependence and cooperation in reaching the same goal.

**Exploring Multicultural Education
Multicultural Pavilion**

- *Encourage students to have positive personal contact with diverse other students.* Contact alone does not do the job of improving relationships with diverse others. For example, busing ethnic minority students to predominantly White schools, or vice versa, has not reduced prejudice or improved interethnic relations. What matters is what happens after children and adolescents get to school. Especially beneficial in improving interethnic relations is for people of different ethnicities to share with one another their worries, successes, failures, coping strategies, interests, and other personal information. This helps them see other people more as individuals than as members of a stereotyped cultural group.
- *Encourage students to engage in perspective taking.* Exercises and activities that help students see others' perspectives can improve interethnic relations. This helps students "step into the shoes" of students who are culturally different and feel what it is like to be treated in fair or unfair ways (Cushner, McClelland, & Safford, 2003).
- *Help students to think critically and be emotionally intelligent when cultural issues are involved.* Students who learn to think critically and deeply about interethnic relations are likely to decrease their prejudice (Bennett, 2003; Diaz, 2003). Students who think in narrow ways are more likely to be prejudiced. Becoming emotionally intelligent includes understanding the causes of one's feelings, managing anger, listening to what others are saying, and being motivated to share and cooperate.
- *View the school and community as a team to help support teaching efforts.* James Comer (1988; Comer & others, 1996) believes that a community, team approach is the best way to educate students. Three important aspects of the Comer Project for Change are (1) a governance and management team that develops a comprehensive school plan, assessment strategy, and staff development plan; (2) a mental health or school support team; and (3) a parents' program. Comer believes the entire school community should have a cooperative rather than an

jigsaw classroom A strategy in which students from different cultural backgrounds are placed in a cooperative group in which, together, they have to construct different parts of a project to reach a common goal.

adversarial attitude. The Comer program is currently operating in more than 600 schools in 26 states.

Evaluation of the effectiveness of the Comer School Development program has been mixed. However, in one recent evaluation with fifth- through eighth-grade students in 10 inner-city Chicago schools over four years, students in the Comer schools did slightly better on reading and math, engaged in less acting-out behavior, and showed greater ability to control their anger than comparable students in non-Comer schools (Cook, Hunt, & Murphy, 2001).

- *Be a competent cultural mediator.* Teachers can play a powerful role as cultural mediators (Banks, 2002). This includes being sensitive to racist content in materials and classroom interactions, learning more about different ethnic groups, being sensitive to students' ethnic attitudes, viewing students of color positively, and thinking of positive ways to get parents of color more involved as partners with teachers in educating students.

Cross-Cultural Comparisons Many countries recognize that quality, universal education of children and youth is critical for the success of any country. However, countries vary considerably in their ability to attain this mission.

Secondary Schools Secondary schools in different countries share a number of similar features, but differ on others (Cameron & others, 1983). Let's explore the similarities and differences in secondary schools in six countries: Australia, Brazil, Germany, Japan, Russia, and the United States.

Most of these countries mandate that children begin school at 6 to 7 years of age and stay in school until they are 14 to 17 years of age. Brazil requires students to go to school only until they are 14 years of age, while Russia mandates that students stay in school until they are 17. Germany, Japan, Australia, and the United States require school attendance until 15 to 16 years of age.

Most secondary schools in these countries, as elsewhere around the world, are divided into two or more levels, such as middle school (or junior high school) and high school. However, Germany's schools are divided according to three educational ability tracks: (1) the main school provides a basic level of education, (2) the middle school gives students a more advanced education, and (3) the academic school prepares students for entrance to a university. German schools, like most European schools, offer a classical education, which includes courses in Latin and Greek.

To what extent do countries have entrance exams for secondary school? Japanese secondary schools have an entrance exam, but secondary schools in the other five countries do not. Only Australia and Germany have comprehensive exit exams. Recently, as part of a movement toward more accountability in schools, many states in the

Careers in Adolescent Development

James Comer
Psychiatrist

James Comer grew up in a low-income neighborhood in East Chicago, Indiana, and credits his parents with leaving no doubt about the importance of education. He obtained a BA degree from Indiana University. He went on to obtain a medical degree from Howard University College of Medicine, a Master of Public Health degree from the University of Michigan School of Public Health, and psychiatry training at the Yale University School of Medicine's Child Study Center. He currently is the Maurice Falk Professor of Child Psychiatry at the Yale University Child Study Center and an associate dean at the Yale University Medical School. During his years at Yale, Comer has concentrated his career on promoting a focus on child development as a way of improving schools. His efforts in support of healthy development of young people are known internationally.

Dr. Comer, perhaps, is best known for the founding of the School Development Program in 1968, which promotes the collaboration of parents, educators, and community to improve social, emotional, and academic outcomes for children. His concept of teamwork is currently improving the educational environment in more than 600 schools throughout America.

James Comer (*left*) is shown with some of the inner-city African American children who attend a school that became a better learning environment because of Comer's intervention. Comer is convinced that a strong, familylike atmosphere is a key to improving the quality of inner-city schools.

The juku or "cramming school," is available to Japanese adolescents in the summertime and after school. It provides coaching to help them improve their grades and their entrance exam scores for high schools and universities. The Japanese practice of requiring an entrance exam for high school is a rarity among the nations of the world.

United States have introduced competency exams that must be passed before going on to the next grade. A number of states have also recently instituted high school exit exams and are examining whether to require passing them as a precondition for graduation.

How extensively are sports teams a part of schools in countries around the world? The United States is the only country in the world in which sports teams are an integral part of the public school system. Only a few private schools in other countries have their own sports teams, sports facilities, and highly organized sports events. Some critics have recently argued that community groups, clubs, and businesses should finance and run adolescents' sports programs so that schools can concentrate on core academics (Kralovec, 2003).

How does coursework vary in different countries? In Brazil, students are required to take Portuguese (the native language) and four foreign languages (Latin, French, English, and Spanish). Brazil requires these languages because of the country's international character and emphasis on trade and commerce. Seventh-grade students in Australia take courses in sheep husbandry and weaving, two areas of economic and cultural interest in the country. In Japan, students take a number of Western courses in addition to their basic Japanese courses; these courses include Western literature and languages (in addition to Japanese literature and language), Western physical education (in addition to Japanese martial arts classes), and Western sculpture and handicrafts (in addition to Japanese calligraphy). The Japanese school year is also much longer than that of other countries.

A special concern is the low quality of education and low percentage of students receiving education in many developing countries (Brown & Larson, 2002). Many countries in Africa, South Asia, and Latin America have a long way to go even to achieve universal elementary education.

Colleges What is college attendance like around the world? Canada has the largest percentage of 18- to 21-year-olds enrolled in college (41 percent) followed by Belgium (40 percent), France (36 percent), the United States (35 percent), Ireland (31 percent), and New Zealand (25 percent) (U.S. Department of Education, 1996). The greatest percentage increase in college attendance is taking place in Africa—128 percent from 1980 through 1996. In many developing countries, the relatively few students who graduate from high school cannot usually afford to pursue higher education (Welti, 2002).

In chapter 12, "Achievement, Careers, and Work," we will further explore the role of culture in education and achievement. In that chapter, we will examine how the United States fares against other countries in literacy, math, and science achievement.

Review and reflect   Learning goal 3

3   Explain how the social contexts of schools influence adolescent development

REVIEW

- How do the social contexts of schools change as children and adolescents get older?
- How do the size and climate of schools and classrooms influence adolescent development?
- How is person-environment fit involved in understanding the education of adolescents?
- How do teachers and parents influence the education adolescents experience?
- How are peers involved in adolescents' schooling?
- What roles do socioeconomic status and ethnicity have in adolescent education? How do schools vary across different countries?

REFLECT

- What are the three characteristics of the best teachers you have had? What are the three characteristics of the worst teachers you have ever had?

So far in this chapter, we have studied approaches to educating students, transitions in schooling, and the social contexts of schools. Another important topic in schools for adolescents involves the education of adolescents who are exceptional.

4   ADOLESCENTS WHO ARE EXCEPTIONAL

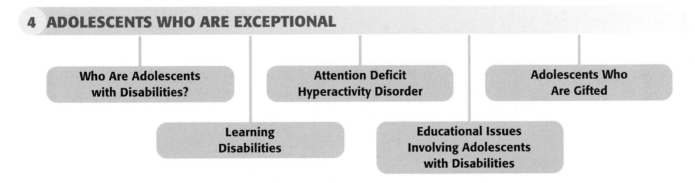

| Who Are Adolescents with Disabilities? | Attention Deficit Hyperactivity Disorder | Adolescents Who Are Gifted |
| Learning Disabilities | Educational Issues Involving Adolescents with Disabilities | |

For many years, public schools did little to educate adolescents with disabilities. However, in the last several decades, federal legislation has mandated that all children and adolescents with disabilities receive a free, appropriate education. And increasingly, these students are being educated in the regular classroom (Hardman, Drew, & Egan, 2002). We examine these aspects of adolescents who are exceptional: who adolescents with disabilities are, learning disabilities, attention deficit hyperactivity disorder, educational issues involving adolescents with disabilities, and adolescents who are gifted.

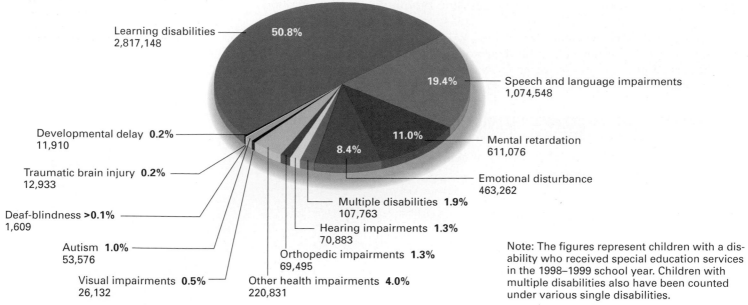

FIGURE 11.6 The Diversity of Children and Adolescents Who Have a Disability

Who Are Adolescents with Disabilities?

Approximately 10 percent of all students receive special education or related services (Reschly, 1996). Figure 11.6 shows the approximate percentages, of all who receive special education services, of children and adolescents who have various disabilities (U.S. Department of Education, 1996). Slightly more than half have a learning disability. Substantial percentages also have speech or language impairments (19.4 percent of those with disabilities), mental retardation (11 percent), and serious emotional disturbance (8.4 percent). Educators prefer to speak of "adolescents with disabilities" rather than "disabled adolescents," to emphasize the person rather than the disability. Also, the term *disability* is now preferred over *handicap*—the current view being that a handicap is a limitation imposed by society or institutions in response to an individual's disability.

Learning Disabilities

Children and adolescents with a **learning disability** are of normal intelligence or above and have difficulties in at least one academic area and usually several, and their difficulty cannot be attributed to any other diagnosed problem or disorder, such as mental retardation. The global concept of learning disabilities includes problems in listening, concentrating, speaking, and thinking (Raymond, 2004).

About three times as many boys as girls are classified as having a learning disability (U.S. Department of Education, 1996). Explanations for this gender difference include a greater biological vulnerability of boys as well as referral bias (boys are more likely to be referred by teachers because of their disruptive, hyperactive behavior).

By definition, adolescents do not have a learning disability unless they have an academic problem. The academic areas in which adolescents with a learning disability most commonly have problems are reading, written language, and math (Hallahan & Kaufman, 2003). About 5 percent of all school-age children receive special education or related services because of a learning disability. In the federal classification of children receiving special education and services, attention deficit hyperactivity disorder (ADHD) is included in the learning disability category. Because of the significant increase in ADHD today, we will discuss it by itself in the next section.

learning disability Individuals with a learning disability are of normal intelligence or above, have difficulties in at least one academic area and usually several, and their difficulties cannot be attributed to any other diagnosed problem or disorder, such as mental retardation.

Many children and adolescents show impulsive behavior, such as this boy who is jumping out of his seat and throwing a paper airplane at classmates. *What is the best way for teachers to handle such situations?*

Adolescents with a learning disability most commonly have problems with reading (Ho & others, 2004; Kamphaus, 2000). They especially show problems with phonological skills, which involve understanding how sounds and letters match up to make words. They often have difficulties with handwriting, spelling, or composition.

Many interventions have focused on improving the child's reading ability (Bender, 2004; Lyon & Moats, 1997; Siegel, 2003). Most children whose reading disability is not diagnosed until third grade or later and receive standard instruction fail to show noticeable improvement (Lyon, 1996). However, intensive instruction over a period of time by a competent teacher can remediate the deficient reading skills of many children and adolescents. The success of even the best-designed reading intervention depends on the training and skills of the teacher.

Improving outcomes for adolescents with a learning disability is a challenging task and generally has required intensive intervention for even modest improvement in outcomes. No model program has proven to be effective for all adolescents with learning disabilities (Terman & others, 1996).

Attention Deficit Hyperactivity Disorder

Attention deficit hyperactivity disorder (ADHD) is a disability in which children and adolescents show one or more of the following characteristics over a period of time: inattention, hyperactivity, and impulsivity. Adolescents who are inattentive have difficulty focusing on any one thing and might become bored with a task after only a few minutes. Adolescents who are hyperactive show high levels of physical activity, seeming to almost always be in motion. Adolescents who are impulsive have difficulty curbing their reactions and don't do a good job of thinking before they act.

The U.S. Department of Education statistics shown in figure 11.6 include children and adolescents with ADHD in the category of children with specific learning disabilities, an overall category that comprises slightly more than one-half of all children and adolescents who receive special education or related services. The number of children and adolescents with ADHD has increased substantially, by some estimates doubling in the 1990s. The disorder occurs as much as 4 to 9 times more in boys than in girls. There is controversy about the increased diagnosis of ADHD (Guyer, 2000; Terman & others, 1996). Some experts attribute the increase mainly to heightened awareness of the disorder. Others are concerned that many children and adolescents are being misdiagnosed without undergoing extensive professional evaluation based on input from multiple sources (Timimi & Taylor, 2004; Whalen, 2000). Indeed, some critics argue

www.mhhe.com/santrocka10

**Learning Disabilities Association
Learning Disabilities Resources
ADHD Resources**

attention deficit hyperactivity disorder (ADHD) Children and adolescents with ADHD show one or more of the following characteristics over a period of time: inattention, hyperactivity, and impulsivity.

that too often what is just typical masculine behavior—inattention and high activity level—is considered to be pathological and labeled as ADHD (Pollock, 1998).

It used to be thought that ADHD decreased in adolescence, but it now is believed that it often does not. Estimates suggest that ADHD decreases in only about one-third of adolescents with this disorder. Increasingly it is recognized that these problems can continue into adulthood (Faraone & others, 2004).

Definitive causes of ADHD have not been found. For example, scientists have not been able to identify causal sites in the brain. However, a number of causes have been proposed, such as low levels of certain neurotransmitters (chemical messengers in the brain), prenatal and postnatal abnormalities, and environmental toxins such as lead. Heredity might play a role; 30 to 50 percent of children and adolescents with ADHD have a sibling or parent who has the disorder (Woodrich, 1994).

It is estimated that about 85 to 90 percent of students with ADHD are taking prescription medication such as Ritalin to control their behavior (Whalen, 2001). A child or adolescent should be given medication only after a complete assessment that includes a physical examination (Whalen, 2000). The problem behaviors of many students with ADHD can be controlled by these prescriptive stimulants. However, not all students with ADHD respond positively to prescription stimulants, and some critics argue that physicians are too quick to prescribe stimulants for students with milder forms of ADHD (Clay, 1997; Mash & Wolfe, 2003). Many experts recommend a combination of academic, behavioral, and medical interventions to help students with ADHD learn and adapt more effectively. For example, in one recent study, a combination of Ritalin and behavioral intervention (such as note-taking instruction and social skills training) increased the likelihood by 17 percent that adolescents with ADHD did their homework and increased their test scores (Evans & others, 2001).

Educational Issues Involving Adolescents with Disabilities

The legal requirement that schools serve all children and adolescents with a disability is a fairly recent one. Beginning in the mid-1960s to mid-1970s, legislatures, the federal courts, and the U.S. Congress established special educational rights for children and adolescents with disabilities. Prior to that time, most children and adolescents with a disability were either refused enrollment or inadequately served by schools. In 1975, Congress enacted **Public Law 94-142,** the Education for All Handicapped Children Act, which requires that all students with disabilities be given a free, appropriate public education. It also provides funding to help implement this education.

In 1990, Public Law 94-142 was renamed the **Individuals with Disabilities Education Act (IDEA).** The IDEA spells out broad mandates for services to all children and adolescents with disabilities. These include evaluation and eligibility determination, appropriate education, the individualized education program (IEP), and a least restrictive environment.

The IDEA has many specific provisions, such as requiring schools to send notices to parents of proposed actions, attendance of parents at meetings regarding the adolescent's placement, and the right to appeal school decisions to an impartial evaluator. The IDEA, including its 1997 amendments, requires that technology devices and services be provided to students when these are necessary to ensure a free, appropriate education (Bryant & Seay, 1998; Male, 2003).

Under the IDEA, the child or adolescent with a disability must be educated in the **least restrictive environment,** a setting that is as similar as possible to the one in which the children or adolescents without a disability are educated. This has given a legal basis to make an effort to educate children and adolescents with a disability in the regular classroom. The term for educating children and adolescents with a disability in the regular classroom used to be *mainstreaming.* However, that term has been replaced by the term **inclusion,** which means educating a child or adolescent with special education needs full-time in a general school program (Choate, 2004; Friend & Bursuck, 2002; Idol, 1997).

**Special Education Resources
The Council for Exceptional Children
Inclusion
Legal Issues and Disabilities**

Public Law 94-142 The Education for All Handicapped Children Act, which requires all students with disabilities to be given a free, appropriate education and provides the funding to help implement this education.

Individuals with Disabilities Education Act (IDEA) This spells out broad mandates for services to all children and adolescents with disabilities. These include evaluation and eligibility determination, appropriate education and the individualized education program (IEP), and a least restrictive environment.

least restrictive environment A setting that is as similar as possible to the one in which the children or adolescents without a disability are educated; under the Individuals with Disabilities Education Act, the child or adolescent must be educated in this setting.

inclusion Educating a child or adolescent with special education needs full-time in a general school program.

The principle of "least restrictive environment" compels schools to examine possible modifications of the regular classroom before moving the child or adolescent with a disability to a more restrictive placement (Hallahan & Kaufmann, 2003; Heward, 2000; Smith & others, 2004). Also, regular classroom teachers often need specialized training to help some children and adolescents with a disability, and state educational agencies are required to provide that training (Sitlington, Clark, & Kolstoe, 2000). For many children and adolescents, inclusion in the regular classroom, with modifications or supplemental services, is appropriate (Choate, 2000; Coleman & Webber, 2002). However, some experts believe that separate programs can be more effective and appropriate for other children and adolescents with disabilities (Martin, Martin, & Terman, 1996).

Adolescents Who Are Gifted

The final type of exceptionality we discuss is quite different from the disabilities we have described so far. **Adolescents who are gifted** have above-average intelligence (usually defined as an IQ of 130 or higher) and/or superior talent in some domain, such as art, music, or mathematics. Programs for gifted adolescents in schools typically base admission to the programs on intelligence and academic aptitude, although experts increasingly advocate widening the criteria to include such factors as creativity and commitment (Davidson, 2000; Olszewski-Kubilius, 2003).

Eighteen-year-old Chandra "Peaches" Allen was born without arms. Despite this disability, she has learned to write, eat, type, paint, and draw with her feet. She can even put on earrings. She is well-known for her artistic skills. She has won three grand-prize awards for her art in various shows. She is getting ready to enter college and plans to pursue a career in art and physical therapy. Chandra Allen's accomplishments reflect remarkable adaptation and coping. She is an excellent example of how adolescents can conquer a disability and pursue meaningful goals.

Some critics argue that too many adolescents in gifted programs really aren't gifted in a particular area but are just somewhat bright (there can be a substantial difference in giftedness between adolescents with IQs in the 130s and their counterparts with IQs of 150+), usually cooperative, and usually White. They believe the mantle of brilliance is cast on many adolescents who are not that far from simply being "smart normal." General intelligence as defined by an overall IQ score still remains a key component of many states' criteria for placing an adolescent in a gifted program. But as changing conceptions of intelligence increasingly include ideas such as Gardner's theory of multiple intelligences, there is likely to be movement away from a specific IQ score as a criterion for giftedness (Castellano & Diaz, 2002).

Ellen Winner (1996), an expert on giftedness, describes three characteristics of adolescents who are gifted:

1. *Precocity.* Adolescents who are gifted are precocious when given the opportunity to use their gift or talent. They begin to master an area earlier than their peers do. Learning in their domain is more effortless for them than for adolescents who are not gifted. Most adolescents who are gifted are precocious because they have an inborn high ability in a particular domain or domains, although this inborn precocity has to be identified and nourished.
2. *Marching to their own drummer.* Adolescents who are gifted learn in a qualitatively different way than their nongifted counterparts do. One way they march to a different drummer is that they require less support, or scaffolding, from adults to learn than their nongifted peers do. Often, in fact, they resist explicit instruction. They also make discoveries on their own and find unique solutions to problems within their area of giftedness.
3. *A passion to master.* Adolescents who are gifted are driven to understand the domain in which they have high ability. They display an intense, obsessive interest and an ability to focus. They do not need to be pushed by their parents. They frequently have a high degree of internal motivation.

At 10 years of age, Alexandra Nechita burst onto the child prodigy scene. She paints quickly and impulsively on large canvases, some as large as 5 feet by 9 feet. It is not unusual for her to complete several of these large paintings in a week. Her

adolescents who are gifted Adolescents who have above-average intelligence (usually defined as an IQ of 130 or higher) and/or superior talent in some domain, such as art, music, or mathematics.

Youth Who Are Gifted Speak

James Delisle (1984) interviewed hundreds of students who are gifted. Here are some of their comments.

In response to: Describe Your "Typical School Day"
"I sit there pretending to be reading along when I'm actually six pages ahead. When I understand something and half the class doesn't, I have to sit there and listen."

—*Girl, Age 11*
New York

In response to: Describe a Perfect Day
". . . if I learned to understand something new in most subjects."

—*Boy, Age 12*
New York

In response to: What Makes a Teacher a "Gifted" Teacher?
". . . opens your mind to help you with your life."

—*Boy, Age 11*
New Jersey

". . . will challenge you and let the sky be your limit."

—*Boy, Age 11*
Michigan

Gifted Education

modernist paintings sell for up to $80,000 apiece. When she was only 2 years old, Alexandra colored in coloring books for hours. She never has had an interest in dolls or friends. Once she started going to school, she couldn't wait to get home to paint. And she continues to paint, relentlessly and passionately. It is, she says, what she loves to do.

In addition to the three characteristics of giftedness that we just mentioned (precocity, marching to the tune of a different drummer, and a passion to master), a fourth area in which gifted adolescents excel is *information-processing skills.* Researchers have found that adolescents who are gifted learn at a faster pace, process information more rapidly, are better at reasoning, use better strategies, and monitor their understanding better than their nongifted peers (Jackson & Butterfield, 1996).

When adolescents who are gifted are underchallenged, they can become disruptive, skip classes, and lose interest in achieving (Olszewski-Kubilius, 2003). Sometimes these adolescents just disappear into the woodwork, becoming passive and apathetic toward school. Four program options for adolescents who are gifted are (Hertzog, 1998):

- Special classes. Historically, this has been the common way to educate adolescents who are gifted. The special classes during the regular school day are called "pull-out" programs. Some special classes also are arranged after school, on Saturdays, or in the summer.
- Acceleration and enrichment in the regular classroom setting.
- Mentor and apprenticeship programs. Some experts believe these are important, underutilized ways to motivate, challenge, and effectively educate adolescents who are gifted.
- Work/study and community service programs.

The wave of educational reform has brought into the regular classroom many strategies that once were the domain of separate gifted programs. These include an emphasis on problem-based learning, projects, learning portfolios, and critical thinking. Combined with the increasing emphasis on educating all adolescents in the regular classroom, many schools now try to challenge and motivate adolescents who are gifted in the regular classroom (Hertzog, 1998). Some schools include after-school or Saturday programs or develop mentor/apprenticeship, work/study, or community service programs. In this way, an array of in-school and out-of-school opportunities can be provided.

Ellen Winner (1996) says that too often adolescents who are gifted are socially isolated and underchallenged in the classroom. It is not unusual for them to be ostracized and labeled "nerds" or "geeks." An adolescent who is the only gifted student in the room does not have the opportunity to learn with students of like ability. Many eminent adults report that for them school was a negative experience, that they were bored and sometimes knew more than their teachers (Bloom, 1985). Winner believes that American education will benefit when standards are raised for all adolescents. For adolescents who are still underchallenged, she recommends that they be allowed to attend advanced classes in their domain of exceptional ability. For example, some especially precocious middle school students are allowed to take college classes in their area of expertise.

It also is important for teachers to understand that while students who are gifted often require less support from teachers than their nongifted peers, teachers still need to closely monitor and guide their learning (Olszewski-Kubilius, 2003). Too many teachers assume that students who are gifted will do fine without their attention and guidance. Like other students, students who are gifted need instruction from teachers and need to be challenged to learn.

According to Winner (2000), many children who are gifted do not turn out to be gifted adults. One reason for this is that some of them are pushed so hard by overzealous parents and teachers that they lose their intrinsic (internal) motivation. As adolescents, they may ask themselves, "Who am I doing this for?" If the answer is not for one's self, they may not want to do it anymore.

Review and reflect Learning goal 4

4 Characterize adolescents who are exceptional and their education

REVIEW

- Who are adolescents with disabilities?
- How can learning disabilities be characterized?
- What is known about attention deficit hyperactivity disorder?
- What educational issues are involved in educating adolescents with disabilities?
- How can adolescents who are gifted be described?

REFLECT

- Think back on your own schooling and how students with learning disabilities either were or were not diagnosed. Were you aware of such individuals in your classes? Were they helped by teachers and/or specialists? You might know one or more people with a learning disability. Interview them about their school experiences and what could have been better to help them learn more effectively.

Careers in Adolescent Development

Sterling Jones
Supervisor of Gifted and Talented Education

Sterling Jones is program supervisor for gifted and talented children in the Detroit Public School system. Sterling has been working for more than three decades with children who are gifted. He believes that students' mastery of skills mainly depends on the amount of time devoted to instruction and the length of time allowed for learning. Thus, he believes that many basic strategies for challenging children who are gifted to develop their skills can be applied to a wider range of students than once believed. He has written several pamphlets for use by teachers and parents, including *How to Help Your Child Succeed* and *Gifted and Talented Education for Everyone.*

Sterling has undergraduate and graduate degrees from Wayne State University and taught English for a number of years before becoming involved in the program for gifted children. He also has written materials on African Americans, such as *Voices from the Black Experience,* that are used in the Detroit schools.

Sterling Jones with students in the gifted program in the Detroit Public Schools.

In this chapter, we have examined many aspects of schools for adolescents. An important aspect of the education of adolescents involves achievement. In the next chapter, "Achievement, Careers, and Work," we will examine the development of achievement in adolescents.

Reach Your Learning Goals

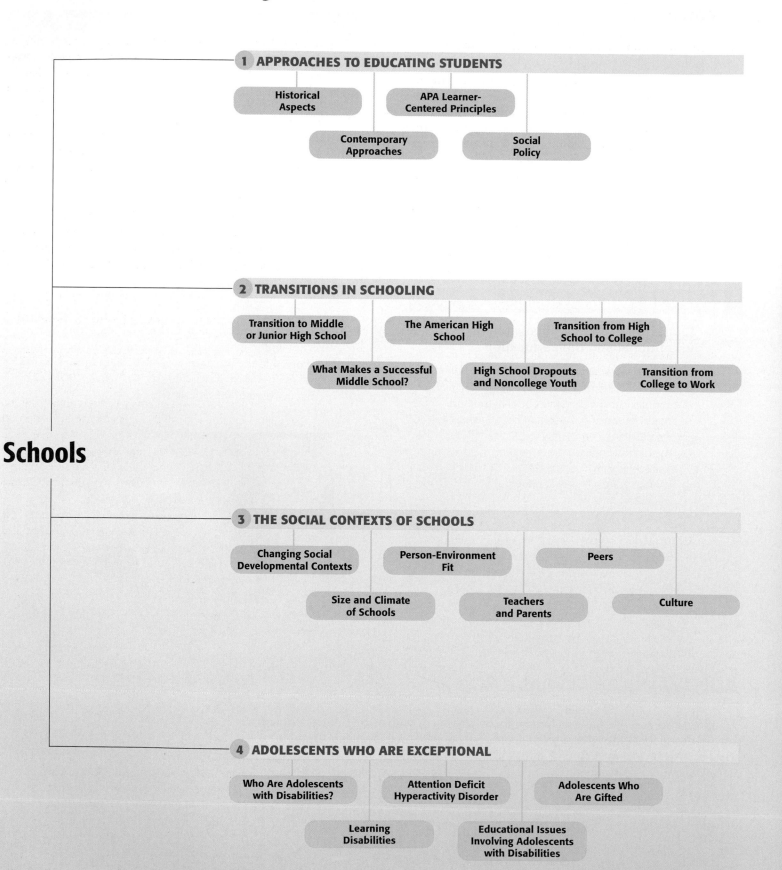

Schools

1 APPROACHES TO EDUCATING STUDENTS

- Historical Aspects
- APA Learner-Centered Principles
- Contemporary Approaches
- Social Policy

2 TRANSITIONS IN SCHOOLING

- Transition to Middle or Junior High School
- The American High School
- Transition from High School to College
- What Makes a Successful Middle School?
- High School Dropouts and Noncollege Youth
- Transition from College to Work

3 THE SOCIAL CONTEXTS OF SCHOOLS

- Changing Social Developmental Contexts
- Person-Environment Fit
- Peers
- Size and Climate of Schools
- Teachers and Parents
- Culture

4 ADOLESCENTS WHO ARE EXCEPTIONAL

- Who Are Adolescents with Disabilities?
- Attention Deficit Hyperactivity Disorder
- Adolescents Who Are Gifted
- Learning Disabilities
- Educational Issues Involving Adolescents with Disabilities

Summary

1 Describe approaches to educating students

- In the nineteenth century, secondary schools were for the elite. By the 1920s, they had become more comprehensive and trained adolescents not only for intellect, but also for work and citizenship. The comprehensive high school remains today, but the functions of schools continue to be debated.
- Contemporary approaches to student learning include the direct instruction and constructivist approaches.
- The American Psychological Association has proposed 14 learner-centered psychological principles to guide education. These principles focus on cognitive and metacognitive factors, motivational and instructional factors, developmental and social factors, and individual difference factors.
- Social policy recommendations initially proposed by *Turning Points 1989* included creating communities for learning, teaching a core of common knowledge, providing an opportunity for students to succeed, and strengthening teachers and principals. *Turning Points 2000* recommendations focused on teaching a curriculum grounded in rigorous academic standards, instructional methods that prepare all students to achieve higher standards, staffing middle schools with teachers who are experts on teaching young adolescents, organizing relationships for learning, governing democratically, providing a safe and healthy school environment, and involving parents and communities in students' schooling.

2 Discuss transitions in schooling from early adolescence to emerging adulthood

- The emergence of junior high schools in the 1920s and 1930s was justified on the basis of the developmental changes of early adolescence and meeting the needs of a growing student population. Middle schools have become more popular and their appearance coincided with earlier pubertal development. The transition to middle/junior high school is often stressful because it occurs at the same time as a number of physical, cognitive, and socioemotional changes. This transition involves going from the "top-dog" to the "bottom-dog" position. Lipsitz concluded that successful middle schools take individual differences seriously, show a deep concern for what is known about early adolescence, and emphasize socioemotional development at least as much as cognitive development. In 1989, the Carnegie Foundation recommended a major redesign of American middle schools.
- An increasing number of educators believe that U.S. high schools need a new mission for the twenty-first century, one that involves more support for graduating with the knowledge and skills to succeed in college and a career, higher expectations for achievement, less time spent working in low-level service jobs, and better coordination of the K–12 curriculum.
- Many school dropouts have educational deficiencies that limit their economic and social well-being for much of their adult lives. Progress has been made in lowering the dropout rate for African American youth, but the dropout rate for Native American and Latino youth remains very high. Dropping out of school is associated with demographic, family-related, peer-related, school-related, economic, and personal factors. The dropout rate could be reduced by strengthening schools and bridging the gap between school and work.
- In many ways, the transition to college parallels the transition from elementary to middle/junior high school. Reduced interaction with parents is usually involved in this transition. A special problem today is the discontinuity between high schools and colleges.
- Having a college degree is highly beneficial for increasing one's income. However, the transition from college to work is often a difficult one. One reason is that colleges train many students to develop general skills rather than job-specific skills.

3 Explain how the social contexts of schools influence adolescent development

- The social context differs at the preschool, elementary school, and secondary school levels, increasing in complexity and scope for adolescents.
- In terms of school size and class size, smaller is usually better. Large schools might not provide a personalized climate that allows for effective social control. Most class sizes are 25 to 35 but a class size of 15 or fewer benefits learning. A positive classroom climate, which is promoted by an authoritative management strategy and effective management of group activities, improves student learning and achievement. The effectiveness of classroom climate is often linked to the teacher's beliefs and practices. Researchers also have studied the effects of the entire school's climate on achievement.
- Person-environment fit involves the concept that some of the negative psychological changes associated with adolescent development might result from a mismatch between adolescents' developing needs and the lack of opportunities afforded by schools.
- Teacher characteristics involve many different dimensions and compiling a profile of the competent teacher's characteristics has been difficult. Parent involvement usually decreases as the child moves into adolescence. Epstein argues that greater collaboration between schools, families, and communities is needed.
- The way middle schools are structured encourages students to interact with larger numbers of peers on a daily basis. A popular or accepted peer status is linked with academic success; a rejected status is related to less academic success. An increasing concern in schools is bullying. Victims of bullying can experience both short-term and long-term negative effects. Friendship is also related to school success, as is being a member of certain crowds.
- At home, in their neighborhoods, and at school, adolescents in poverty face problems that present barriers to effective

learning. Schools in low-SES neighborhoods have fewer resources, have less experienced teachers, and encourage rote learning more than thinking skills than schools in higher-SES neighborhoods. The school experiences of students from different ethnic groups vary considerably. It is important for teachers to have positive expectations and challenge students of color to achieve. Strategies that teachers can use to improve relations among ethnically diverse students include turning the classroom into a "jigsaw," encouraging positive personal contact, stimulating perspective taking, viewing the school and community as a team, and being a competent cultural mediator. Schools vary across cultures. For example, U.S. schools have by far the strongest emphasis on athletics.

4 **Characterize adolescents who are exceptional and their education**

- An estimated 10 percent of U.S. students receive special education services. Slightly more than 50 percent of these students are classified as having a learning disability.
- Students with a learning disability are of normal intelligence or above and have difficulties in at least one academic area

and usually several, and their difficulty cannot be traced to another diagnosed problem. Reading difficulties represent the most common problem of students with a learning disability.

- Attention deficit hyperactivity disorder (ADHD) involves problems in one or more of these areas: inattention, hyperactivity, and impulsivity. Most experts recommend a combination of interventions for ADHD—medical (stimulants such as Ritalin), behavioral, and academic.
- Public Law 94-142 requires that all children and youth be given a free, appropriate education. IDEA spells out broad mandates for services to all children and youth with disabilities. The concept of least restrictive environment (LRE) also has been set forth. Inclusion means educating students with disabilities in the regular classroom.
- Adolescents who are gifted have above-average intelligence (usually defined by an IQ of 130 or higher) and/or superior talent in some domain, such as art, music, or math. Characteristics of adolescents who are gifted include precocity, marching to their own drummer, a passion to master, and superior information-processing skills.

Key Terms

back-to-basics movement 388
direct instruction
    approach 389
cognitive constructivist
    approaches 389
social constructivist
    approaches 389

top-dog phenomenon 394
authoritative strategy of
    classroom management 404
authoritarian strategy of
    classroom management 404
permissive strategy of
    classroom management 404

jigsaw classroom 412
learning disability 416
attention deficit hyperactivity
    disorder (ADHD) 417
Public Law 94-142 418
Individuals with Disabilities
    Education Act (IDEA) 418

least restrictive
    environment 418
inclusion 418
adolescents who are
    gifted 419

Key People

Joan Lipsitz 395
Jacquelynne Eccles 405
Erik Erikson 406

Joyce Epstein 407
Jonathan Kozol 410
John Ogbu 411

Elliot Aronson 412
James Comer 412
Ellen Winner 419

Resources for Improving the Lives of Adolescents

Adolescence in the 1990s

(1993) edited by Ruby Takanishi
New York: Teachers College Press

A number of experts on adolescence discuss the risk and opportunity for adolescents in today's world. Many chapters focus on improving the quality of schooling for adolescents.

Council for Exceptional Children (CEC)

1920 Association Drive
Reston, VA 22091
703–620–3660

The CEC maintains an information center on the education of children and adolescents who are exceptional and publishes materials on a wide variety of topics.

Handbook of Psychology, Vol. 7: Educational Psychology

Edited by William A. Reynolds and Gloria E. Miller (2003)
New York: Wiley

This up-to-date volume examines a number of topics in educational psychology related to the chapter you have just read, such as learning disabilities, adolescents who are gifted, teaching processes, and social adjustment and peer relations in schools.

National Dropout Prevention Center

205 Martin Street
Clemson University
Clemson, SC 29634
803–656–2599

The center operates as a clearinghouse for information about dropout prevention and at-risk youth and publishes the National Dropout Prevention Newsletter.
School-Based Youth Services Program

New Jersey Department of Human Services

222 South Warren Street
Trenton, NJ 08625-0700
609–292–1617

E-Learning Tools

To help you master the material in this chapter, you will find a number of valuable study tools on the student CD-ROM that accompanies this book. In addition, visit the Online Learning Center for *Adolescence, 10th Edition,* where you will find helpful resources for chapter 11, "Schools."

Taking It to the Net

http://www.mhhe.com/santrocka10

1. The dramatic increase in the number of prescriptions for Ritalin due to the large increase in the diagnosis of ADD and ADHD has sparked considerable controversy, particularly among parents. What are the pros and cons surrounding the use of Ritalin?
2. Much has been made of altering curricula, lowering student/teacher ratios, and providing special programs for varying groups of students as means of enhancing the high school experience. As a future parent, what types of educational experiences and career-planning opportunities would you want to see if you had a gifted child?

This program operates in 37 sites in or near schools. The sites are open during and after school, on weekends, and all summer. They offer a core set of services, all of which require parental consent. Services include primary and preventive health care, individual and family counseling, drug- and alcohol-abuse counseling, recreation, and summer and part-time job development.

Turning Points 2000: Educating Adolescents in the 21st Century

(2000) by Anthony Jackson and Gayle Davis
New York: Teachers College Press

This follow-up to earlier *Turning Points* recommendations includes a number of strategies for meeting the educational needs of adolescents.

3. Some have argued that larger schools are better because they offer greater curricular and extracurricular opportunities to students. Others have noted that smaller schools provide a more personalized instructional atmosphere that benefits students. What are the major issues that a school board should address when considering concerns over school size?

Connect to **http://www.mhhe.com/santrocka10** to research the answers and complete these exercises. In some cases, you'll also find further instructions on this site.

Self-Assessment

To evaluate your school experiences, complete this self-assessment: (1) The Best and Worst Characteristics of My Teachers.

Health and Well-Being, Parenting, and Education

To practice your decision-making skills, complete the health and well-being, parenting, and education scenarios.

CHAPTER
12

*They can because they
think they can.*
—Virgil
Roman Poet, 1st Century B.C.

Achievement, Work, and Careers

Images of Adolescent Development

Kim-Chi and Thuy

Kim-Chi Trinh was only 9 years old in Vietnam when her father used his savings to buy passage for her on a fishing boat. It was a costly and risky sacrifice for the family, who placed Kim-Chi on the small boat, among strangers, in the hope that she eventually would reach the United States, where she would get a good education and enjoy a better life.

Kim made it to the United States and coped with a succession of three foster families. When she graduated from high school in San Diego in 1988, she had a straight-A average and a number of college scholarship offers. When asked why she excels in school, Kim-Chi says that she has to do well because she owes it to her parents, who are still in Vietnam.

Kim-Chi is one of a wave of bright, highly motivated Asians who are immigrating to America. Asian Americans are the fastest-growing ethnic minority group in the United States—two out of five immigrants are now Asian. Although Asian Americans make up only 2.4 percent of the U.S. population, they constitute 17 percent of the undergraduates at Harvard, 18 percent at MIT, 27 percent at the University of California at Berkeley, and a staggering 35 percent at the University of California at Irvine.

Not all Asian American youth do this well, however. Poorly educated Vietnamese, Cambodian, and Hmong refugee youth are especially at risk for school-related problems. Many refugee children's histories are replete with losses and trauma. Thuy, a 12-year-old Vietnamese girl, has been in the United States for two years and resides with her father in a small apartment with a cousin's family of five in the inner city of a West Coast metropolitan area (Huang, 1989). While trying to escape from Saigon, the family became separated, and the wife and two younger children remained in Vietnam. Thuy's father has had an especially difficult time adjusting to the United States, struggling with English classes and being unable to maintain several jobs as a waiter. When Thuy received a letter from her mother saying that her 5-year-old brother had died, Thuy's schoolwork began to deteriorate, and she showed marked signs of depression—lack of energy, loss of appetite, withdrawal from peer relations, and a general feeling of hopelessness. At the insistence of the school, she and her father went to the child and adolescent unit of a community mental health center. It took the therapist a long time to establish credibility with Thuy and her father, but eventually they began to trust the therapist as a good listener who had competent advice about how to handle different experiences in the new country. The therapist also contacted Thuy's teacher, who said that Thuy had been involved in several interethnic skirmishes at school. With the assistance of the mental health clinic, the school initiated interethnic student panels to address cultural differences and discuss reasons for ethnic hostility. Thuy was selected to participate in these panels. Her father became involved in the community mutual assistance association, and Thuy's academic performance began to improve.

This chapter focuses on achievement, work, and careers. As adolescence and emerging adulthood unfold, achievement takes on a more central role in development, work becomes a major aspect of life, and a stronger interest in careers emerges. The chapter begins by examining the role that achievement plays in adolescent development. Next, we explore the ways in which work is involved in the lives of high school and college students. In the final section, we evaluate the major theories of career development and the contexts that influence adolescents' career choices.

1 ACHIEVEMENT

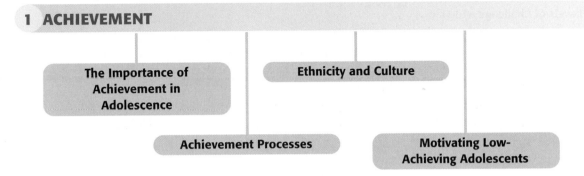

Some developmentalists worry that the United States is rapidly becoming a nation of hurried, wired people who are raising their youth to become the same way—too uptight about success and failure, and far too preoccupied with how personal accomplishments compare with those of others (Elkind, 1981). Others worry that our achievement expectations for youth are too low and that adolescents are not adequately challenged to achieve (Stevenson, Hofer, & Randell, 2000).

The Importance of Achievement in Adolescence

Adolescence is a critical juncture in achievement (Eccles & Wigfield, 2000; Henderson & Dweck, 1990). New social and academic pressures force adolescents toward different roles, roles that often involve more responsibility. Achievement becomes a more serious business in adolescence, and adolescents begin to sense that the game of life is now being played for real. They even may begin to perceive current successes and failures as predictors of future outcomes in the adult world. And as demands on adolescents intensify, different areas of their lives may come into conflict. Adolescents' social interests may cut into the time they need to pursue academic matters, or ambitions in one area may undermine the attainment of goals in another, as when academic achievement leads to social disapproval.

How effectively adolescents adapt to these new academic and social pressures is determined, in part, by psychological, motivational, and contextual factors (Pintrich, 2003; Stipek, 2002; Wigfield & Eccles, 2001). Indeed, adolescents' achievement is due to much more than their intellectual ability. Students who are less bright than others often show an adaptive motivational pattern—persistent at tasks and confident about their ability to solve problems, for example—and turn out to be high achievers. In contrast, some of the brightest students show maladaptive achievement patterns—give up easily and do not have confidence in their academic skills, for example—and turn out to be low achievers.

Achievement Processes

A number of motivational processes are involved in achievement. We explore these processes next, beginning with the distinction between intrinsic and extrinsic motivation.

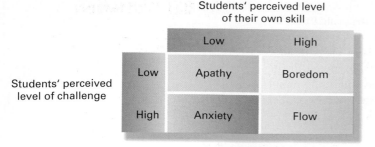

Students' perceived level
of their own skill

	Low	High
Low	Apathy	Boredom
High	Anxiety	Flow

Students' perceived
level of challenge

FIGURE 12.1 Outcomes of Perceived Levels of Challenge and Skill

www.mhhe.com/santrocka10

Intrinsic Motivation

intrinsic motivation Internal motivational factors such as self-determination, curiosity, challenge, and effort.

extrinsic motivation External motivational factors such as rewards and punishments.

flow Csikszentmihalyi's concept of optimal life experiences, which he believes occur most often when people develop a sense of mastery and are absorbed in a state of concentration when they're engaged in an activity.

attribution theory The concept that individuals are motivated to discover the underlying causes of their own behavior or performance in their effort to make sense of it.

Intrinsic and Extrinsic Motivation **Intrinsic motivation** is based on internal factors such as self-determination, curiosity, challenge, and effort. **Extrinsic motivation** involves external incentives such as rewards and punishments. The humanistic and cognitive approaches stress the importance of intrinsic motivation in achievement. Some adolescents study hard because they are internally motivated to achieve high standards in their work (intrinsic motivation). Other adolescents study hard because they want to make good grades or avoid parental disapproval (extrinsic motivation).

Self-Determination and Personal Choice One view of intrinsic motivation emphasizes self-determination (Deci, Koestner, & Ryan, 2001; Deci & Ryan, 1994). In this view, adolescents want to believe that they are doing something because of their own will, not because of external success or rewards.

Researchers have found that giving adolescents some choice and providing opportunities for personal responsibility increases their internal motivation and intrinsic interest in school tasks (Alderman, 2004; Covington & Mueller, 2001; Stipek, 2002). For example, one study found that high school science students who were encouraged to organize their own experiments demonstrated more care and interest in laboratory work than their counterparts who were given detailed instructions and directions (Rainey, 1965). In another study that included mainly African American students from low-SES backgrounds, teachers were encouraged to give them more responsibility for their school program (deCharms, 1984). This consisted of opportunities to set their own goals, plan how to reach the goals, and monitor their progress toward the goals. Students were given some choice in the activities they wanted to engage in and when they would do them. They also were encouraged to take personal responsibility for their behavior, including reaching the goals they had set. Compared with a control group, students in the intrinsic motivation/self-determination group had higher achievement gains and were more likely to graduate from high school.

Optimal Experiences and Flow Mihaly Csikszentmihalyi (1990, 1993; Nakamaura & Csikszentmihalyi, 2002), whose work on creativity was discussed in chapter 4, also has developed ideas that are relevant to understanding motivation. He has studied the optimal experiences of people for more than two decades. These optimal experiences occur when people report feelings of deep enjoyment and happiness. Csikszentmihalyi uses the term **flow** to describe optimal experiences in life. Flow occurs most often when people develop a sense of mastery and are absorbed in a state of concentration while they engage in an activity. He argues that flow occurs when individuals are engaged in challenges they find neither too difficult nor too easy.

Perceived levels of challenge and skill can result in different outcomes (see figure 12.1) (Brophy, 1998). Flow is most likely to occur in areas in which adolescents are challenged and perceive themselves as having a high degree of skill. When adolescents' skills are high but the activity provides little challenge, the result is boredom. When both challenge and skill levels are low, apathy occurs. And when adolescents perceive themselves as not having adequate skills to master a challenging task they face, they experience anxiety.

Attribution **Attribution theory** states that in their effort to make sense out of their own behavior or performance, individuals are motivated to discover its underlying causes. Attributions are perceived causes of outcomes. Attribution theorists say that adolescents are like scientists, seeking to explain the cause behind what happens. For example, an adolescent asks "Why am I not doing well in this class?" "Did I get a good grade because I studied hard or the teacher made up an easy test, or both?" The search for a cause or an explanation is most likely to be initiated when unexpected and important events end in failure, such as when a good student gets a low grade

Calvin and Hobbes

by **Bill Watterson**

WHO WOULD LIKE TO SUMMARIZE WHAT WE JUST READ? CALVIN, HOW ABOUT YOU?

SORRY! I'M HERE AGAINST MY WILL. I REFUSE TO COOPERATE.

THEY CAN TRANSPORT MY *BODY* TO SCHOOL, BUT THEY CAN'T CHAIN MY *SPIRIT!* MY SPIRIT ROAMS FREE! WALLS CAN'T CONFINE IT! LAWS CAN'T RESTRAIN IT! AUTHORITY HAS NO POWER OVER IT!

CALVIN, IF YOU'D PUT HALF THE ENERGY OF YOUR PROTESTS INTO YOUR SCHOOLWORK...

YOU CAN TRY TO LEAVE A MESSAGE, BUT MY SPIRIT SCREENS ITS CALLS.

(Graham & Weiner, 1996). Some of the most frequently inferred causes of success and failure are ability, effort, task ease or difficulty, luck, mood, and help or hindrance from others.

Bernard Weiner (1986, 1992, 2000) identified three dimensions of causal attributions: (1) *locus* refers to whether the cause is internal or external, (2) *stability* focuses on the extent to which the cause remains the same or changes, and (3) *controllability* is the extent to which the individual can control the cause. For example, an adolescent might consider his or her aptitude to be internally located, stable, and uncontrollable. The adolescent also might consider chance or luck as external to himself, variable, and uncontrollable. Figure 12.2 lists eight possible combinations of locus, stability, and controllability and how they match up with various common explanations of failure.

An adolescent's perception of success or failure as due to internal or external factors influences the adolescent's self-esteem. Adolescents who perceive their success as due to internal reasons, such as effort, are more likely to increase their self-esteem following success than are adolescents who believe that their success was due to external reasons, such as luck.

An adolescent's perception of the stability of a cause influences her expectation of success. If she ascribes a positive outcome to a stable cause, such as aptitude, she expects future success. Similarly, if she ascribes a negative outcome to a stable cause, she expects future failure. When adolescents attribute failure to unstable causes such as bad luck or lack of effort, they can develop expectations that they will be able to succeed in the future, because they perceive the cause of their failure as changeable.

An adolescent's perception of the controllability of a cause is related to a number of emotional outcomes such as anger, guilt, pity, and shame (Graham & Weiner, 1996). When adolescents perceive themselves as prevented from succeeding because of external factors that other people could have controlled (such as noise or bias), they often become angry. When adolescents perceive themselves as not having done well because of internally controllable causes (such as not making enough effort or being negligent), they often feel guilty. When students perceive others as not achieving their goals because of uncontrollable causes (such as lack of ability or a physical handicap), they feel pity or sympathy. And when adolescents perceive themselves as failing because of internally uncontrollable factors (such as low ability), they feel shame, humiliation, and embarrassment.

To see how attributions affect subsequent achievement strivings, consider these two adolescents (Graham & Weiner, 1996):

1. Jane flunks her math test. She subsequently seeks tutoring and increases her study time.
2. Susan also fails her math test but decides to drop out of school.

www.mhhe.com/santrocka10

Attribution

Combination of causal attributions	Reason students give for failure
Internal-Stable-Uncontrollable	Low aptitude
Internal-Stable-Controllable	Never study
Internal-Unstable-Uncontrollable	Sick the day of the test
Internal-Unstable-Controllable	Did not study for this particular test
External-Stable-Uncontrollable	School has tough requirements
External-Stable-Controllable	The instructor is biased
External-Unstable-Uncontrollable	Bad luck
External-Unstable-Controllable	Friends failed to help

FIGURE 12.2 Combinations of Causal Attributions and Explanations for Failure

When students fail or do poorly on a test or assignment, they attribute the outcome to certain causes. The explanations reflect eight combinations of Weiner's three main categories of attributions: locus (internal-external), stability (stable-unstable), and controllability (controllable-uncontrollable).

Jane's negative outcome (failing the test) motivated her to search for the reasons behind her low grade. She attributes the failure to herself, not blaming her teacher or bad luck. She also attributes the failure to an unstable factor—lack of preparation and study time. Thus, she perceives that her failure is due to internal, unstable, and controllable factors. Because the factors are unstable, Jane has a reasonable expectation that she can still succeed in the future. And because the factors are controllable, she also feels guilty. Her expectations for success enable her to overcome her deflated sense of self-esteem. Her hope for the future results in renewed goal-setting and increased motivation to do well on the next test.

Susan's negative outcome (also failing the test) led her to drop out of school rather than resolve to study harder. Her failure also stimulates her to make causal attributions. Susan ascribes failure to herself and attributes her poor performance to lack of ability, which is internal, stable, and uncontrollable. Because the cause is internal, her self-esteem suffers. Because it is stable, she sees failure in her future and has a helpless feeling that she can't do anything about it. And because it is uncontrollable, she feels ashamed and humiliated. In addition, her parents and teacher express concern for her poor performance but don't provide any recommendations or strategies for success, furthering her belief that she is incompetent. With low expectations for success, low self-esteem, and a depressed mood, Susan decides to drop out of school.

What are the best strategies for teachers to use in helping students like Susan change their attributions? Educational psychologists often recommend providing students with a planned series of experiences in achievement contexts in which modeling, information about strategies, practice, and feedback are used to help them (1) concentrate on the task at hand rather than worry about failing; (2) cope with failures by retracing their steps to discover their mistake or analyzing the problem to discover another approach; and (3) attribute their failures to a lack of effort rather than a lack of ability (Brophy, 2004; Dweck & Elliott, 1983).

The current strategy is that rather than exposing adolescents to models who handle tasks with ease and demonstrate success, they should be presented with models who struggle to overcome mistakes before finally succeeding (Brophy, 1998). In this way, adolescents learn how to deal with frustration, persist in the face of difficulties, and cope constructively with failure.

Mastery Motivation Closely related to intrinsic motivation and attribution is mastery motivation. Researchers have identified mastery as one of three types of achievement orientation: mastery, helpless, and performance.

Carol Dweck and her colleagues (Dweck, 2002; Henderson & Dweck, 1990; Dweck & Leggett, 1988) have found that adolescents show one of two distinct responses to challenging or difficult circumstances: a mastery orientation or a helpless orientation. Adolescents with a **mastery orientation** focus on the task rather than on their ability, have positive affect (suggesting they enjoy the challenge), and generate solution-oriented strategies that improve performance. Mastery-oriented students often instruct themselves to pay attention, to think carefully, and to remember strategies that worked for them in the past (Anderman, Maehr, & Midgley, 1996). In contrast, adolescents with a **helpless orientation** focus on their personal inadequacies, often attribute their difficulty to a lack of ability, and display negative affect (including boredom and anxiety). This orientation undermines their performance. Figure 12.3 describes some behaviors that might reflect helplessness (Stipek, 2002).

mastery orientation An outlook in which individuals focus on the task rather than on their ability, have positive affect, and generate solution-oriented strategies that improve their performance.

helpless orientation An outlook in which individuals focus on their personal inadequacies, often attribute their difficulty to a lack of ability, and display negative affect (including boredom and anxiety). This orientation undermines performance.

Mastery- and helpless-oriented adolescents do not differ in general ability. However, they have different theories about their abilities. Mastery-oriented adolescents believe their ability can be changed and improved. They endorse such statements as "Smartness is something you can increase as much as you want to." Helpless-oriented adolescents believe that ability is basically fixed and cannot be changed. They endorse such statements as "You can learn new things, but how smart you are pretty much stays the same." The mastery orientation is much like the attributional combination of internal locus, unstable, and controllable cause. The helpless orientation is much like the attributional combination of external locus, stable, and uncontrollable cause.

Researchers recently conducted two studies to examine various aspects of motivation in young adolescents' mathematics achievement (Blackwell, Trzesniewski, & Dweck, 2003). In the first study, thinking that intelligence is malleable, setting learning goals, having positive beliefs about the importance of effort, and demonstrating mastery-oriented attributions were linked with higher math grades in the seventh grade. In the second study, low-achieving seventh-grade math students were taught to think of intelligence as malleable, which resulted in improved math performance.

A mastery orientation also can be contrasted with a **performance orientation,** which involves being concerned with outcome rather than process. For performance-oriented adolescents, winning is what matters and happiness is thought to be a result of winning. For mastery-oriented adolescents, what matters is the sense that they are effectively interacting with their environment. Mastery-oriented adolescents do like to win, but winning isn't as important to them as it is to performance-oriented adolescents. Developing their skills is more important.

Mastery motivation has much in common with Csikszentmihalyi's concept of flow, which occurs when adolescents become absorbed in a state of concentration during an activity. Mastery-oriented adolescents immerse themselves in a task and focus their concentration on developing their skills rather than on worrying about whether they are going to outperform others. In a state of flow, adolescents become so attuned to what they are doing that they are oblivious to distractions.

Performance-oriented adolescents who are not confident of their success face a special problem (Stipek, 2002). If they try but fail, they often take their failure as evidence of low ability. This problem leads some students to engage in behavior that protects them from an image of incompetence in the short run but interferes with their learning and achievement in the long run (Covington, 2002): To avoid the attribution of low ability, some of these adolescents simply don't try, or they cheat, or they resort to more subtle image-protecting strategies such as procrastinating, making excuses, working halfheartedly, or setting unrealistic goals. By not trying at all, they can maintain an alternative, personally more acceptable explanation for their failure.

Self-Efficacy

Self-efficacy is the belief that one can master a situation and produce favorable outcomes. Albert Bandura (1997, 2000), whose social cognitive theory we described in chapter 2, "The Science of Adolescent Development," believes that self-efficacy is a critical factor in whether or not adolescents achieve. Self-efficacy has much in common with mastery motivation and intrinsic motivation. Self-efficacy is the belief that "I can"; helplessness is the belief that "I cannot" (Stipek, 2002). Adolescents with high self-efficacy endorse such statements as "I know that I will be able to learn the material in this class" and "I expect to be able to do well at this activity."

Dale Schunk (1991, 2001, 2004; Schunk & Zimmerman, 2003; Zimmerman & Schunk, 2004) has applied the concept of self-efficacy to many aspects of students' achievement. In his view, self-efficacy influences a student's choice of activities.

The student:

- Says "I can't"
- Doesn't pay attention to teacher's instructions
- Doesn't ask for help, even when it is needed
- Does nothing (for example, stares out the window)
- Guesses or answers randomly without really trying
- Doesn't show pride in successes
- Appears bored, uninterested
- Is unresponsive to teacher's exhortations to try
- Is easily discouraged
- Doesn't volunteer answers to teacher's questions
- Maneuvers to get out of or to avoid work (for example, has to go to the nurse's office)

FIGURE 12.3 Behaviors That Suggest Helplessness

performance orientation An outlook in which individuals are concerned with performance outcome rather than performance process. For performance-oriented students, winning is what matters.

self-efficacy The belief that one can master a situation and produce positive outcomes.

Students with low self-efficacy for learning might avoid many learning tasks, especially those that are challenging. In contrast, their high-self-efficacy counterparts eagerly work at learning tasks. High-self-efficacy students are more likely to expend effort and persist longer at a learning task than low-self-efficacy students.

A teacher's self-efficacy will have a major impact on the quality of learning that students experience (Pintrich & Schunk, 2002). Teachers with a low sense of self-efficacy often become mired in classroom problems. Low-self-efficacy teachers don't have confidence in their ability to manage their classrooms, become stressed and angered at students' misbehavior, are pessimistic about students' ability to improve, take a custodial view of their job, often resort to restrictive and punitive modes of discipline, and say that if they had it to do all over again they would not choose teaching as a profession (Melby, 1995).

**Mastery Motivation
Self-Efficacy Resources**

In one study, teachers' instructional self-efficacy was linked with their students' mathematical and language achievement over the course of an academic year (Ashton & Webb, 1986). Students learned much more from teachers with a sense of efficacy than from those beset by self-doubts. Teachers with high self-efficacy tend to view difficult students as reachable and teachable. They regard learning problems as surmountable with extra effort and ingenious strategies to help struggling students. Low-self-efficacy teachers are inclined to say that low student ability is the reason that their students are not learning.

Bandura (1997) also addressed the characteristics of efficacious schools. School leaders seek ways to improve instruction. They figure out ways to work around stifling policies and regulations that impede academic innovations. Masterful academic leadership by the principal builds teachers' sense of instructional efficacy. In low-achieving schools, principals function more as administrators and disciplinarians.

High expectations and standards for achievement pervade efficacious schools. Teachers regard their students as capable of high academic achievement, set challenging academic standards for them, and provide support to help them reach these high standards. In contrast, in low-achieving schools not much is expected academically of students; teachers spend less time actively teaching and monitoring students' academic progress, and they tend to write off a high percentage of students as unteachable (Brookover & others, 1979). Not surprisingly, students in such schools have low self-efficacy and a sense of academic futility.

Goal-Setting, Planning, and Self-Monitoring   Goal-setting, planning, and self-monitoring are important aspects of adolescent achievement (Maehr, 2001; Midgley, 2002; Pintrich, 2003). Researchers have found that self-efficacy and achievement improve when adolescents set goals that are specific, proximal, and challenging (Bandura, 1997). A nonspecific, fuzzy goal is "I want to be successful." A more concrete, specific goal is "I want to make the honor roll at the end of this semester."

Adolescents can set both long-term (distal) and short-term (proximal) goals. It is okay to let adolescents set some long-term goals, such as "I want to graduate from high school" or "I want to go to college," but they also need to create short-term goals, which are steps along the way. "Getting an A on the next math test" is an example of a short-term, proximal goal. So is "Doing all of my homework by 4 P.M. Sunday." David McNally, author of *Even Eagles Need a Push* (1990), advises that when adolescents set goals and make plans, they should be reminded to live their lives one day at a time and make their commitments in bite-size chunks. A house is built one brick at a time, a cathedral one stone at a time. The artist paints one stroke at a time. The student should also work in small increments.

Another good strategy is for adolescents to set challenging goals (Elliot & Thrash, 2001; Kaplan & others, 2002). A challenging goal is a commitment to self-improvement. Strong interest and involvement in activities is sparked by challenges. Goals that are easy to reach generate little interest or effort. However, goals should be optimally matched to the adolescent's skill level. If goals are unrealistically high, the result will be repeated failures that lower the adolescent's self-efficacy.

Carol Dweck (2002; Dweck & Leggett, 1988) and John Nicholls (1979) define goals in terms of immediate achievement-related focus and definition of success. For example, Nicholls distinguishes between ego-involved goals, task-involved goals, and work-avoidant goals. Adolescents who have ego-involved goals strive to maximize favorable evaluations and minimize unfavorable ones. For example, ego-involved adolescents focus on how smart they will look and how effectively they can outperform other adolescents. In contrast, adolescents who have task-involved goals focus on mastering tasks. They concentrate on how they can do the task and what they will learn. Adolescents with work-avoidant goals try to exert as little effort as possible when faced with a task.

It is not enough for adolescents to simply set goals. They also need to learn to plan how they will reach their goals (Pintrich, 2003). Being a good planner means managing time effectively, setting priorities, and being organized.

In the short term, adolescents not only should plan their next week's activities but also monitor how well they are sticking to their plan. Once adolescents engage in a task, they need to monitor their progress, judge how well they are doing on the task, and evaluate the outcomes to regulate what they do in the future (Eccles, Wigfield, & Schiefele, 1998). Researchers have found that high-achieving adolescents often are self-regulatory learners (Schunk & Zimmerman, 2003). For example, high-achieving adolescents self-monitor their learning more and systematically evaluate their progress toward a goal more than low-achieving students do. When parents and teachers encourage adolescents to self-monitor their learning, they give them the message that they are responsible for their own behavior and that learning requires their active, dedicated participation (Zimmerman, Bonner, & Kovach, 1996).

Expectations Adolescents' motivation, and likely their performance, are influenced by the expectations that their parents, teachers, and other adults have for their achievement. Adolescents benefit when both parents and teachers have high expectations for them and provide the necessary support for them to meet those expectations.

Researchers have found that parents' expectations are linked with children's and adolescents' academic achievement (Burchinal & others, 2002; Fan & Chen, 2001). One longitudinal study found that the mother's expectations for the child's educational attainment when assessed in the first grade was linked with the child's eventual educational attainment at age 23 (Englund, Luckner, & Whaley, 2003). Children whose mothers had higher academic expectations for them in the first grade were more likely to reach a higher level of educational attainment in emerging adulthood than children whose mothers had lower expectations for them in the first grade.

Too often parents and teachers attempt to protect adolescents' self-esteem by setting low standards (Stipek, 2002). In reality, it is more beneficial to set standards that challenge adolescents and expect performance at the highest levels they are capable of achieving. Adolescents who are not challenged may develop low standards for themselves and the fragile self-confidence they develop from reaching these low expectations can be shattered the first time they encounter more challenging work and are held to higher standards.

Teachers often have higher expectations for high-ability than low-ability students. For example, researchers have found that teachers require high-ability students to work harder, wait longer for them to respond to questions, respond to them with more information and in a more elaborate manner, criticize them less often, are more friendly to them, and are more likely to give them the benefit of the doubt on close calls in grading than they are students with low ability (Brophy, 2004).

Anxiety Anxiety is a vague, highly unpleasant feeling of fear and apprehension. It is normal for students to be concerned or worried when they face school challenges, such as doing well on a test. Indeed, researchers have found that many successful students have moderate levels of anxiety (Bandura, 1997). However, some students have

*L*ife is a gift . . . Accept it.
Life is an adventure . . . Dare it.
Life is a mystery . . . Unfold it.
Life is a struggle . . . Face it.
Life is a puzzle . . . Solve it.
Life is an opportunity . . . Take it.
Life is a mission . . . Fulfill it.
Life is a goal . . . Achieve it.
—AUTHOR UNKNOWN

www.mhhe.com/santrocka10

**Goal-Setting
Anxiety**

anxiety A vague, highly unpleasant feeling of fear and apprehension.

high levels of anxiety and worry constantly, which can significantly impair their ability to achieve.

Some adolescents' high anxiety levels are the result of parents' unrealistic achievement expectations and pressure. For many individuals, anxiety increases across the school years as they face more frequent evaluation, social comparison, and, for some, experiences of failure (Eccles, Wigfield, & Schiefele, 1998). When schools create such circumstances, they likely increase students' anxiety.

A number of intervention programs have been created to reduce high anxiety levels (Wigfield & Eccles, 1989). Some intervention programs emphasize relaxation techniques. These programs often are effective at reducing anxiety but do not always lead to improved achievement. Anxiety intervention programs linked to the worry aspect of anxiety emphasize changing the negative, self-damaging thoughts of anxious students and replacing them with positive, task-focused thoughts (Meichenbaum & Butler, 1980). These programs have been more effective than the relaxation programs in improving students' achievement.

Ethnicity and Culture

What is the nature of achievement in adolescents from various ethnic groups? How does culture influence children's achievement?

Ethnicity   The diversity that exists among ethnic minority adolescents is evident in their achievement. For example, many Asian American students have a strong academic achievement orientation, but some do not.

In addition to recognizing the diversity that exists within every cultural group in terms of their achievement, it also is important to distinguish between difference and deficiency. Too often the achievement of ethnic minority students—especially African American, Latino, and Native American students—has been interpreted as *deficits* by middle-socioeconomic-status White standards, when they simply are *culturally different and distinct* (Jones, 1994).

At the same time, many investigations overlook the socioeconomic status (SES) of ethnic minority students (Graham & Taylor, 2001). In many instances, when ethnicity *and* SES are investigated in the same study, SES predicts achievement better than ethnicity. Students from middle- and upper-SES families fare better than their counterparts from low-SES backgrounds in a host of achievement situations—expectations for success, achievement aspirations, and recognition of the importance of effort, for example (Gibbs, 1989).

Sandra Graham (1986, 1990) has conducted a number of studies that reveal not only stronger differences in SES than in ethnicity in achievement, but also the importance of studying ethnic minority student motivation in the context of general motivational theory. Her inquiries fall within the framework of attribution theory and focus on the causes African American students cite for their achievement orientation, such as why they succeed or fail. She has found that middle-SES African American students do not fit the stereotype of being unmotivated. Like their White middle-SES counterparts, they have high achievement expectations and understand that failure is usually due to a lack of effort rather than bad luck.

A special challenge for many ethnic minority students, especially those living in poverty, is dealing with racial prejudice, conflict between the values of their group and the majority group, and a lack of high-achieving adults in their cultural group who can serve as positive role models (McLoyd, 1998, 2000; Spencer & Dornbusch, 1990).

It also is important to consider the nature of the schools that primarily serve ethnic minority students (Eccles, Wigfield, & Schiefele, 1998). More than one-third of African American and almost one-third of Latino students attend schools in the 47 largest city school districts in the United States, compared with only 5 percent of White and 22 percent of Asian American students. Many of these ethnic minority students come from low-SES families (more than one-half are eligible for free or reduced-cost lunches). These inner-city schools are less likely than other schools to

Careers in Adolescent Development

Jaime Escalante
Secondary School Math Teacher

An immigrant from Bolivia, Jaime Escalante became a math teacher at Garfield High School in East Los Angeles in the 1970s. When he began teaching at Garfield, many of the students had little confidence in their math abilities and most of the teachers had low expectations for the students' success. Escalante took it as a special challenge to improve the students' math skills and even get them to the point where they could perform well on the Educational Testing Service Advance Placement (AP) calculus exam.

The first year was difficult. Escalante's calculus class began at 8 A.M. He told the students the doors would be open at 7 A.M. and that instruction would begin at 7:30 A.M. He also worked with them after school and on weekends. He put together lots of handouts, told the students to take extensive notes, and required them to keep a folder. He gave them a five-minute quiz each morning and a test every Friday. He started with fourteen students but within two weeks only half remained. Only five students lasted through the spring. One of the boys who quit said, "I don't want to come at 7 o'clock. Why should I?"

Due to Escalante's persistent, challenging, and inspiring teaching, Garfield High—a school plagued by poor funding, violence, and inferior working conditions—became ranked seventh in the United States in calculus. Escalante's commitment and motiva-

tion were transferred to his students, many of whom no one believed in before Escalante came along. Escalante's contributions were portrayed in the film *Stand and Deliver*. Escalante, his students, and celebrity guests also introduce basic math concepts for sixth- to twelfth-grade students on the *Futures with Jaime Escalante* PBS series. Now retired from teaching, Escalante continues to work in a consulting role to help improve students' motivation to do well in math and improve their math skills. Escalante's story is testimony to how *one* teacher can make a major difference in students' motivation and achievement.

Jaime Escalante in a classroom teaching math.

serve more advantaged populations or to offer high-quality academic support services, advanced courses, and courses that challenge students' active thinking skills. Even students who are motivated to learn and achieve can find it difficult to perform effectively in such contexts.

Culture Since the early 1990s the poor performance of American children in math and science has become well publicized (Peak, 1996). For example, in a recent cross-national comparison of the math and science achievement of 14- and 15-year-olds in the world's 24 wealthiest countries, the United States finished near the bottom in 18th place. Korea was first, followed by Japan and Finland (see figure 12.4).

Harold Stevenson's research (Stevenson, 1992, 1995; Stevenson, Hofer, & Randell, 2000) explores reasons for the poor performance of American students. Stevenson and his colleagues have completed five cross-cultural comparisons of students in the United States, China, Taiwan, and Japan. Students in these Asian countries consistently outperform American students. And the longer they are in school, the wider the gap between Asian and American students becomes—the lowest difference is in first grade, the highest is in the eleventh grade (the highest grade studied).

To learn more about the reasons for these large cross-cultural differences, Stevenson and his colleagues spent thousands of hours observing in classrooms, as well as interviewing and surveying teachers, students, and parents. They found that Asian teachers spent more of their time teaching math than American teachers did. For example, in Japan more than one-fourth of total classroom time in first grade was

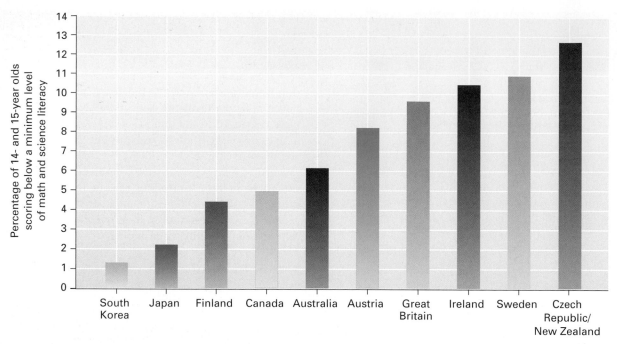

FIGURE 12.4 **A Comparison of the Math and Science Literacy of 14- and 15-year-olds in the World's Wealthiest Nations**

Rankings indicate the percentage of 14- and 15-year-olds scoring below a minimum level of math and science literacy. In this analysis, the United States finished near the bottom, in 18th place, among the world's wealthiest countries. This analysis is based on five different tests given in the Program for International Student Assessment (PISA) and the Trends in International Math and Science Study (TIMMS) (UNICEF, 2002).

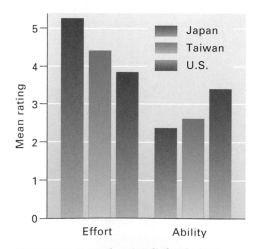

FIGURE 12.5 **Mothers' Beliefs About the Factors Responsible for Children's Math Achievement in Three Countries**

In one study, mothers in Japan and Taiwan were more likely to believe that their children's math achievement was due to effort rather than innate ability, while U.S. mothers were more likely to believe their children's math achievement was due to innate ability (Stevenson, Lee, & Stigler, 1986). If parents believe that their children's math achievement is due to innate ability and their children are not doing well in math, the implication is that they are less likely to think their children will benefit from putting forth more effort.

spent on math instruction, compared with only one-tenth of the time in U.S. first-grade classrooms. Also, Asian students were in school an average of 240 days a year compared with 178 days in the United States.

In addition to the substantially greater time spent on math instruction in Asian schools than in American schools, differences were found between Asian and American parents. American parents had much lower expectations for their children's education and achievement than the Asian parents did. Also, American parents were more likely to attribute their children's math achievement to innate ability, whereas Asian parents were more likely to say that their children's math achievement is the consequence of effort and training (see figure 12.5). Asian students were more likely than American students to do math homework, and Asian parents were far more likely to help their children with their math homework than American parents were (Chen & Stevenson, 1989).

Critics of the cross-national comparisons argue that in many comparisons virtually all U.S. students are being compared with a "select" group of students from other countries, especially in the secondary school comparisons. Therefore, they conclude, it is no wonder that American students don't fare so well. That criticism holds for some international comparisons. However, when the top 25 percent of students in different countries were recently compared, U.S. students did not rank much better (Mullis & others, 1998).

Motivating Low-Achieving Adolescents

Jere Brophy (2004) described strategies for improving the motivation of hard-to-reach, low-achieving adolescents. These adolescents include (1) low achievers with low ability who have difficulty keeping up and have developed low achievement expectations, (2) adolescents with failure syndrome, and (3) adolescents obsessed with protecting their self-worth by avoiding failure.

Low Achievers with Low Ability   Adolescents with low ability need to be consistently reassured that they can meet goals and challenges and that they will be given the help and support that they need to succeed. However, they need to be reminded that they will make progress only as long as they make a real effort. They might require individualized instruction materials or activities to provide an optimal challenge for their skill level. They need to be guided in setting learning goals and provided with support for reaching these goals. These students need to be required to put forth their best effort and make progress, even though they might not have the ability to perform at the level of many other adolescents.

Adolescents with Failure Syndrome   **Failure syndrome** involves having low expectations for success and giving up at the first sign of difficulty. Adolescents with failure syndrome are different from low-achieving adolescents who fail despite putting forth their best effort. Adolescents with failure syndrome don't put forth enough effort, often beginning tasks in a halfhearted manner and giving up quickly at the first hint of a challenge. They often have low self-efficacy or attribution problems, ascribing failure to internal, stable, and uncontrollable causes, such as low ability.

A number of strategies can be used to increase the motivation of adolescents who display failure syndrome. Especially beneficial are cognitive retraining methods, such as efficacy retraining, attribution retraining, and strategy retraining, which are described in figure 12.6.

Adolescents Motivated to Protect Their Self-Worth by Avoiding Failure   Some adolescents are so interested in protecting their self-worth and avoiding failure that they become distracted from pursuing learning goals and engage in ineffective learning strategies. These self-esteem and failure-avoiding strategies include (Covington, 2002; Covington & Teel, 1996):

Harold Stevenson and his colleagues have found that Asian schools embrace many of the ideals Americans have for their own schools, but are more successful in implementing them in interesting and productive ways that make learning more enjoyable for children and adolescents.

- *Nonperformance.* The most obvious strategy for avoiding failure is to not try. Adolescents' nonperformance tactics include appearing eager to answer a teacher's question but hoping the teacher will call on another student, sliding down in the seat to avoid being seen by the teacher, and avoiding eye contact. These can seem like minor deceptions, but they might portend other, more chronic forms of noninvolvement such as dropping out and excessive absences.
- *Sham effort.* To avoid being criticized for not trying, some adolescents appear to participate but do so more to avoid punishment than to succeed. Adolescent behaviors that reflect a sham effort include asking a question even though they already know the answer, adopting a pensive, quizzical expression, and feigning focused attention during a class discussion.
- *Procrastination.* Adolescents who postpone studying for a test until the last minute can blame failure on poor time management, thus deflecting attention away from the possibility that they are incompetent. A variation on this theme involves students who take on so many activities and responsibilities that they have an excuse for not doing any one of them in a highly competent manner.
- *Setting unreachable goals.* By setting goals so high that success is virtually impossible, adolescents can avoid the implication that they are incompetent, because virtually all adolescents would fail to reach this goal.
- *The academic wooden leg.* This strategy involves admitting to a minor personal weakness in order to avoid acknowledging the greater, feared weakness of being incompetent. One example is to blame a failing test score on anxiety. Having test anxiety is not as devastating to a personal sense of self-worth as lack of ability.

failure syndrome Having low expectations for success and giving up at the first sign of difficulty.

TRAINING METHOD	PRIMARY EMPHASIS	MAIN GOALS
Efficacy Retraining	Improve Students' Self-efficacy Perceptions	Teach students to set, and strive to reach, specific, proximal, and challenging goals. Monitor students' progress and frequently support students by saying things like "I know you can do it." Use adult and peer modeling effectively. Individualize instruction and tailor it to the student's knowledge and skills. Keep social comparison to a minimum. Be an efficacious teacher who has confidence in your abilities. View students with failure syndrome as challenges rather than losers.
Attribution and Achievement Orientation Retraining	Change Students' Attributions and Achievement Orientation	Teach students to attribute failures to factors that can be changed, such as insufficient knowledge or effort and ineffective strategies. Work with students to develop a mastery orientation rather than a performance orientation by helping them focus on the achievement process (learning the task) rather than the achievement product (winning or losing).
Strategy Retraining	Improve Students' Domain- and Task-Specific Skills and Strategies	Help students acquire, and self-regulate their use of, effective learning and problem-solving strategies. Teach students what to do, how to do it, when to do it, and why to do it.

FIGURE 12.6 Cognitive Retraining Methods for Increasing the Motivation of Students Who Display Failure Syndrome

The efforts of adolescents to avoid failure have been grouped as **self-handicapping strategies** (Urdan & Midgley, 2001; Urdan, Midgley, & Anderman, 1998). That is, some adolescents deliberately do not try in school, put off studying until the last minute, fool around the night before a test, and use other self-handicapping strategies so that if their subsequent performance is at a low level, these circumstances, rather than lack of ability, will be seen as the cause.

In contrast to attributions, self-handicapping strategies precede success or failure. They are proactive efforts to protect oneself and to manipulate others' perceptions of causes of performance outcomes. For example, saying that you did not perform well on a test because you were tired is an attribution, whereas deliberately staying up late to use lack of sleep as an excuse in case you do poorly is a self-handicapping strategy.

What are some predictors of self-handicapping? Boys are more likely than girls to use self-handicapping strategies (Midgley & Urdan, 1995). Students with good grades and perceptions of academic competence are less likely to use self-handicapping than students with low grades and perceptions of academic incompetence (Urdan, Midgley, & Anderman, 1998).

Martin Covington and his colleagues (Covington, 2002; Covington & Teel, 1996; Covington, Teel, & Parecki, 1994) proposed a number of strategies teachers can use to help all adolescents, not just low achievers, reduce their preoccupation with protecting their self-worth and avoiding failure:

- Give adolescents assignments that are inherently interesting and stimulate their curiosity. The assignments should challenge, but not overwhelm, their skills. Allow them some choice of which learning activities they pursue. As their expertise increases, increase the level of challenge correspondingly.
- Establish a reward system so that all adolescents, not just the brightest, highest-achieving adolescents, can attain rewards if they put forth enough effort. Make sure that rewards reinforce students for setting meaningful goals. Also, try to make the act of learning itself a desirable goal.
- Help adolescents set challenging but realistic goals, and provide them with the academic and emotional support to reach those goals.
- Strengthen adolescents' association between effort and self-worth. Encourage adolescents to take pride in their effort and minimize social comparison.
- Encourage adolescents to have positive beliefs about their abilities.

self-handicapping strategies Some adolescents deliberately do not try in school, put off studying until the last minute, and use other self-handicapping strategies so that if their subsequent performance is at a low level, these circumstances, rather than lack of ability, will be seen as the cause.

- Improve teacher-adolescent relationships by emphasizing your role as a resource person who will guide and support learning efforts rather than an authority figure who controls student behavior.

Review and reflect Learning goal 1

1 Discuss achievement in the lives of adolescents

REVIEW

- Why is achievement so important in adolescence?
- What are some important achievement processes?
- How can low-achieving adolescents be motivated?
- What roles do ethnicity and culture play in the development of achievement in adolescence?

REFLECT

- Would you consider yourself highly motivated to achieve? Or do you have trouble becoming motivated to achieve? Has your motivation to achieve changed since you were in middle or junior high school and high school? If so, how?

2 WORK

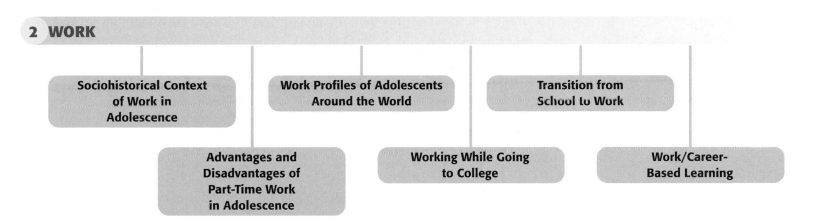

Achievement and motivation not only show up in school but also in work. One of the greatest changes in adolescents' lives in recent years has been the increased likelihood that they will work in some part-time capacity and still attend school on a regular basis. Our discussion of work focuses on the sociohistorical context of work in adolescents' lives, the advantages and disadvantages of part-time work, work-based learning, and the transition from school to work.

Sociohistorical Context of Work in Adolescence

Over the past century, the percentage of youth in the United States who work full-time as opposed to those who are in school has decreased dramatically. In the late 1800s, 1 of every 20 high school age adolescents were in school. Today 9 of every 10 adolescents receive high school diplomas. In the nineteenth century, most adolescent males learned a trade from their father or some other adult member of the community rather than being trained for a career in school.

Even though prolonged education has kept many of today's youth in the United States from holding full-time jobs, it has not prevented them from working on a part-time basis while going to school. In 1940, only 1 of 25 tenth-grade males attended school and simultaneously worked part-time. In the 1970s, the number had increased to 1 in 4. Today, 3 of 4 combine school and part-time work. The typical part-time job

What are the effects of working and going to school on adolescents' grades and integration into school activities?

The Working Adolescent

for high school seniors involves 16 to 20 hours of work per week, although 10 percent work 30 hours or more. A similar increase has occurred for younger adolescents.

What kinds of jobs are U.S. adolescents working at today? About 17 percent who work do so in fast-food restaurants waiting on customers and cleaning up. Other adolescents work in retail stores as cashiers or salespeople (about 20 percent), in offices as clerical assistants (about 10 percent), or as unskilled laborers (about 10 percent). In one recent study, boys reported higher self-esteem and well-being when they perceived that their jobs were providing skills that would be useful to them in the future (Mortimer & others, 1992).

Do male and female adolescents take the same types of jobs, and are they paid equally? Some jobs (such as busboy, gardener, manual laborer, newspaper carrier) are held almost exclusively by male adolescents, while other jobs (such as baby-sitter, maid) are held almost exclusively by female adolescents. Male adolescents work longer hours and are paid more per hour than female adolescents (Helson, Elliot, & Leigh, 1989).

Advantages and Disadvantages of Part-Time Work in Adolescence

Does the increase in work have benefits for adolescents? In some cases, yes; in others, no. Ellen Greenberger and Laurence Steinberg (1981, 1986) examined the work experiences of students in four California high schools. Their findings disproved some common myths. For example, generally it is assumed that adolescents get extensive on-the-job training when they are hired for work. The reality is that they get little training at all. Also, it is assumed that youths—through work experiences—learn to get along better with adults. However, in Greenberger and Steinberg's studies, adolescents reported that they rarely felt close to the adults with whom they worked. The work experiences of the adolescents did help them to understand how the business world works, how to get and how to keep a job, and how to manage money. Working also helped adolescents to learn to budget their time, to take pride in their accomplishments, and to evaluate their goals. But working adolescents often have to give up sports, social affairs with peers, and sometimes sleep. And they have to balance the demands of work, school, family, and peers.

Greenberger and Steinberg asked students about their grade point averages, school attendance, satisfaction from school, and the number of hours spent studying and participating in extracurricular activities since they began working. They found that the working adolescents had lower grade point averages than nonworking adolescents. More than 1 of 4 students reported that their grades dropped when they began working; only 1 of 9 said that their grades improved. But it was not just working that affected adolescents' grades—more important was how long they worked. Tenth-graders who worked more than 14 hours a week suffered a drop in grades. Eleventh-graders worked up to 20 hours a week before their grades dropped. When adolescents spend more than 20 hours per week working, there is little time to study for tests and to complete homework assignments.

In addition to work's affecting grades, working adolescents felt less involved in school, were absent more, and said that they did not enjoy school as much as their nonworking counterparts did. Adolescents who worked also spent less time with their families—but just as much time with their peers—as their nonworking counterparts. Adolescents who worked long hours also were more frequent users of alcohol and marijuana.

More-recent research confirms the link between part-time work during adolescence and problem behaviors. In one large-scale study, the role of part-time work in the adjustment of more than 70,000 high school seniors was investigated (Bachman & Schulenberg, 1993). Consistent with other research, part-time work in high school was associated with a number of problem behaviors: insufficient sleep, not eating breakfast, not exercising, not having enough leisure time, and using drugs. For the most part, the results occurred even when students worked 1 to 5 hours per week, but they became more pronounced after 20 hours of work per week. And in another study, taking on a job for more than 20 hours per week was associated with increasing disengagement from school, increased delinquency and drug use, increased autonomy from parents, and self-reliance (Steinberg, Fegley, & Dornbusch, 1993). In sum, the overwhelming evidence is that working part-time while going to high school is associated with a number of problem behaviors when the work consumes 20 or more hours of the adolescent's week.

Some states have responded to these findings by limiting the number of hours adolescents can work while they are attending secondary school. In 1986, in Pinellas County, Florida, a new law placed a cap on the previously unregulated hours that adolescents could work while school is in session. The allowable limit was set at 30 hours, which—based on research evidence—is still too high.

Although working too many hours may be detrimental to adolescent development, work may especially benefit adolescents in low-income, urban contexts by providing them with economic benefits and adult monitoring. This may increase school engagement and decrease delinquency. In one recent study, low-income, urban adolescents who never worked had more school-related difficulties than those who did work (Leventhal, Graber, & Brooks-Gunn, 2001). Stable work increased the likelihood that the adolescent males in low-income, urban contexts would go to college more so than for the adolescent females.

Several investigations have focused on the important question of how the costs and benefits of working in adolescence might vary as a function of the quality of the job (Larson & Verma, 1999). In one longitudinal study, adolescents in jobs with opportunities for advancement showed increases in mastery motivation, heightened work values, and reduced depression (Mortimer & others, 1996). Jobs that youth described as extrinsically rather than intrinsically rewarding appear to detract from schoolwork (Mortimer, Harley, & Johnson, 1998). In another study, positive effects of working were found (Marsh, 1991). Adolescents reported that their jobs encouraged good work habits and that they were using their earnings for high school or college costs. Negative effects occurred when adolescents perceived their job as more important than school and used their income for nonschool purposes.

Work Profiles of Adolescents Around the World

So far, our exploration of work during adolescence has primarily focused on U.S. adolescents. How does work in adolescence vary in different countries around the world?

In many developing countries where it is common for adolescents to not attend school on a regular basis, boys often spend more time in income-generating labor than girls do (Larson & Verma, 1999). In these developing countries, adolescent girls often engage in unpaid household labor. For example, in one study, at 13–15 years of age, boys in rural Bangladesh spent an average of 2.7 hours per day in wage work as compared with 1.1 hours by girls (Cain, 1980). For boys in the lowest socioeconomic status, the figure was 5.9 hours per day for boys and 3.5 hours for girls.

Income-generating labor outside the home is less prevalent in schooled, developed countries, and enforcement of child labor laws restricts it to the mid- to late-adolescent years. In the high school years, employment is more common for U.S. adolescents than in many developed countries, such as those in Europe and East Asia. As we saw earlier, many U.S. high school students work 10 or even 20 hours or more per week. One study found that U.S. high school students spent an average of 50 minutes per day working at a job while North European adolescents spent an average of only 15 minutes per day working at a job (Alsaker & Flammer, 1999). In this study, employment of adolescents was virtually nonexistent in France and Russia. In another study, 80 percent of Minneapolis eleventh-graders had part-time jobs compared with only 27 percent of Japanese eleventh-graders and 26 percent of Taiwanese eleventh-graders (Fulgini & Stevenson, 1995).

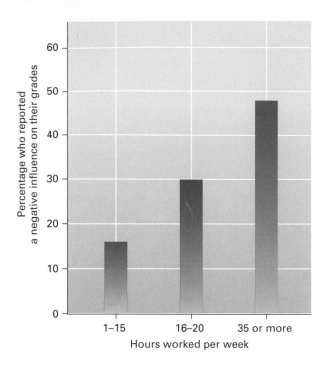

FIGURE 12.7 The Relation of Hours Worked Per Week in College to Grades
Among students working to pay for school expenses, 16 percent of those working 1 to 15 hours per week reported that working negatively influenced their grades. Thirty percent of college students who worked 16 to 20 hours a week said the same, as did 48 percent who worked 35 hours or more per week.

**Improving School-Work Transitions
School-to-Work Transitions in Canada**

Overall, the weight of the evidence suggests that spending large amounts of time in paid labor has limited developmental benefits for youth, and for some it is associated with risk behavior and costs to physical health (Larson & Verma, 1999). Some youth, though, are engaged in challenging work activities, are provided constructive supervision by adults, and experience favorable work conditions. However, in general, given the repetitive nature of most labor carried out by adolescents around the world, it is difficult to argue that working 15 to 25 hours per week in such labor provides developmental gains (Larson & Verma, 1999).

Working While Going to College

Eighty percent of U.S. undergraduate students worked during the 1999–2000 academic year (National Center for Education Statistics, 2002). Forty-eight percent of undergraduates identified themselves mainly as students working to meet school expenses and 32 percent as employees who decided to enroll in school. Undergraduate students who identified themselves as working to meet expenses worked an average of 26 hours per week while those who considered themselves to be employees worked an average of 40 hours per week.

Working can pay or help offset some costs of schooling, but working can also restrict students' opportunities to learn and negatively influence grades. One recent national study found that as the number of hours worked per week increased for those who identified themselves primarily as students, their grades suffered and the number of classes, class choice, and library access became more limited (National Center for Education Statistics, 2002) (see figure 12.7).

Other research has found that as the number of hours college students work increases, the more likely they are to drop out of college (National Center for Education Statistics, 1998). Thus, college students need to carefully examine the number of hours they work and the extent the work is having a negative impact on their college success. Although borrowing to pay for education can leave students with considerable debt, working long hours reduces the amount of time students have for studying and can decrease the likelihood that these students will complete their college degree. Indeed, it would seem that setting priorities is crucial, to being successful in both work and school — as one young college couple would certainly agree (watch the video segment entitled "Balancing Work and School" to learn more).

Transition from School to Work

In some cases, the media have exaggerated the degree of adolescent unemployment. For example, based on data collected by the U.S. Department of Labor, 9 of 10 adolescents are either in school, working at a job, or both. Only 5 percent are out of school, without a job, and looking for full-time employment. Most adolescents who are unemployed are not unemployed for long. Only 10 percent are without a job for six months or longer. Most unemployed adolescents are high school dropouts.

Certain segments of the adolescent population, however, are more likely than others to be unemployed. For example, a disproportionate percentage of unemployed adolescents are African American. The unemployment situation is especially acute for African American and Latino youth between the ages of 16 and 19. The job situation, however, has improved somewhat for African American adolescents: In 1969, 44 percent of African American 16- to 19-year-olds were unemployed; today, that figure is approximately 32 percent.

How can adolescents be helped to bridge the gap between school and work? For adolescents bound for higher education and a professional degree, the educational system provides ladders from college to career. Most youth, though, step off the educational ladder before reaching the level of a professional career. Often, they are on their own in their search for work. Recommendations for bridging the gap from school to work were described briefly in chapter 11 on schools but are expanded on here (William T. Grant Foundation Commission on Work, Family, and Citizenship, 1988):

1. Monitored work experiences, including cooperative education, internships, apprenticeships, preemployment training, and youth-operated enterprises, should be implemented. These experiences provide opportunities for youth to gain work experience, to be exposed to adult supervisors and models in the workplace, and to relate their academic training to the workplace.

2. Community and neighborhood services, including individual voluntary service and youth-guided services, should be expanded. Youth need experiences not only as workers but as citizens. Service programs not only expose youth to the adult world, but provide them with a sense of the obligations of citizenship in building a more caring and competent society.

3. Vocational education should be redirected. With few exceptions, today's vocational education does not prepare youth adequately for specific jobs. However, its hands-on methods can provide students with valuable and effective ways of acquiring skills they will need to be successful in a number of jobs. One promising approach is the career academy, which originated in Philadelphia and was replicated extensively in California (Glover & Marshall, 1993). At the end of the ninth grade, students at risk for failure are identified and invited to volunteer for a program based on a school-within-a-school format. The students and teachers remain together for three years. Students spend the tenth grade catching up on academic course work; computers and field trips are integrated into the curriculum. In the eleventh grade, every student has a mentor from industry who introduces the student to his or her workplace and joins the student for recreational activities at least once a month. By the end of the eleventh grade, the student obtains a summer job with one of the business partners. Students who stay in the program are promised a job when they graduate from high school.

4. Incentives need to be introduced. Low motivation and low expectations for success in the workplace often restrict adolescents' educational achievement. Recent efforts to guarantee postsecondary and continuing education and to provide guaranteed employment and guaranteed work-related training for students who do well show promise of encouraging adolescents to work harder and be more successful in school.

5. Career information and counseling need to be improved. A variety of information and counseling approaches can be implemented to expose adolescents to job opportunities and career options. These services can be offered both in school and in community settings. They include setting up career information centers, developing the capacity of parents as career educators, and expanding the work of community-based organizations.

6. More school volunteers should be used. Tutoring is the most common form of school volunteer activity. However, adults are needed even more generally—as friends, as mentors for opening up career opportunities, and for assisting youth in mastering the dilemmas of living in a stressful time.

Improving education, elevating skill levels, and providing "hands-on" experience will help adolescents to bridge the gap between school and work. We need to address the needs of youth if we are to retain the confidence of youth who have been brought up to believe in the promise of the American Dream.

Work/Career-Based Learning

In our discussion of schools in chapter 11, we indicated that a number of experts believe that a better connection between school and work needs to be forged. One way to improve this connection is through work/career-based learning experiences.

National Center for Research in Vocational Education

High School   Work/career-based learning increasingly has become part of the effort to help youth make the transition from school to employment (Moore, 1998). Each year, approximately 500,000 high school students participate in cooperative education or other arrangements where learning objectives are met through part-time employment in office occupations, retailing, and other vocational fields. Vocational classes also involve large numbers of adolescents in school-based enterprises, through which they build houses, run restaurants, repair cars, operate retail stores, staff child care centers, and provide other services.

As we begin the twenty-first century, some important changes are taking place in vocational education (Stern & Rahn, 1998). Today's high school diploma provides access to fewer and fewer stable, high-paying jobs. Thus, more of the training for specific occupations is occurring in two-year colleges and postsecondary technical institutes.

In high schools, new forms of career-related education are creating options for many students, ranging from students with disabilities to students who are gifted. Among the new models are career academies, youth apprenticeships, and tech prep and career major programs. These models rely on work-related themes to focus the curriculum and prepare students for postsecondary education, including four-year colleges and universities. These new options are supported by the 1990 Perkins Act and the 1994 School-to-Work-Opportunities Act.

Three new types of high schools exemplify a college-and-career approach: single-theme schools; schools-within-schools; and majors, clusters, or pathways (Stern & Hallinan, 1997).

Most often found in large cities where the high population density allows more specialization, the *single-theme school* has a curriculum that is organized around a theme such as agriculture, aviation, fashion, or finance. Some of these schools have a strong college preparation orientation. Several examples of the single-theme school are the High School for Agricultural Sciences in Chicago and the High School of Economics and Finance in New York City.

The single-theme schools connect classroom learning with practical contexts through work-based learning, community service, and research projects. For example, at the High School for Agricultural Sciences, some class assignments are based on student internships at the Chicago Board of Trade or the Quaker Oats company. At the High School of Economics and Finance, students are required to spend time in paid internships at Wall Street firms and participate in unpaid community service.

A second variation of the college-and-career approach divides an entire high school into several *schools-within-schools*. These smaller groupings are referred to as "academies" or "houses." Their size can range from 80 to 300 students with 4 to 10 teachers each. The curriculum is organized around a career theme in an academy or house. A core academic curriculum is maintained but applied to broad occupational themes such as health careers, business and finance, natural resources, manufacturing sciences, communications media, law and government, graphic arts, and environmental studies. Some academies cover four years of schooling, others only the last two or three years.

A third version of the college-and-career approach divides high schools into *majors, clusters,* or *pathways.* In these schools, technical and vocational courses are organized according to broad themes, similar to academies, but academic classes usually are not composed of students who all major in the same field. Students in a career pathway, major, or cluster take academic classes in grades 9 through 12 with students from several other majors, but also take a sequence of electives specific to the pathway.

These different forms of high school organization also can be combined. For example, in a single-theme school, the range of student career interests can lead to the development of pathways or majors within the single theme. Gateway Institute of Technology in St. Louis uses this approach. The entire school is focused on preparing students for careers in high-tech science and engineering fields, but students can major in such areas as agriculture, biology, and health; engineering technology; applied physical sciences; or math and computer science.

College   College students can participate in cooperative education programs, or part-time or summer work relevant to their field of study. This experience can be critical in helping students obtain the job they want when they graduate. Many employers expect job candidates to have this type of experience. One survey found that almost 60 percent of employers said their entry-level college hires had co-op or internship experience (Collins, 1996).

More than 1,000 colleges offer co-op (cooperative education) programs. A co-op is a paid apprenticeship in a career that a college student is interested in pursuing. Many college students are not allowed to participate in co-op programs until their junior year.

Review and reflect Learning goal 2

2   **Describe the role of work in adolescence and college**

REVIEW

- What is the sociohistorical context of adolescent work?
- What are the advantages and disadvantages of part-time work in secondary school and college?
- What is the profile of adolescent work around the world?
- How does work during college influence students' academic success?
- How can the transition from school to work be characterized?
- What is work/career-based learning?

REFLECT

- Did you work during high school? What were some of the pluses and minuses of the experience if you did work? Are you working part-time now while you are going to college? If so, what effect does the work experience have on your academic success?

3 CAREER DEVELOPMENT

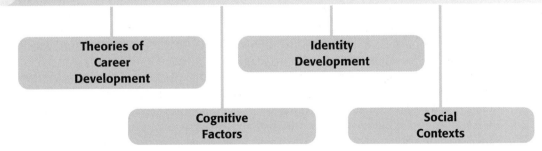

What theories have been developed to direct our understanding of adolescents' career choices? What roles do exploration, decision making, and planning play in career development? How do sociocultural factors affect career development?

Theories of Career Development

Three main theories describe the manner in which adolescents make choices about career development: Ginzberg's developmental theory, Super's self-concept theory, and Holland's personality type theory.

Parents play an important role in the adolescent's achievement. It is important for parents to neither pressure the adolescent too much nor challenge the adolescent too little.

developmental career choice theory
Ginzberg's theory that children and adolescents go through three career choice stages: fantasy, tentative, and realistic.

career self-concept theory Super's theory that an individual's self-concepts play a central role in his or her career choices and that in adolescence individuals first construct their career self-concept.

personality type theory Holland believes that an effort should be made to match an individual's career choice with his or her personality.

Ginzberg's Developmental Theory **Developmental career choice theory** is Eli Ginzberg's theory that children and adolescents go through three career choice stages: fantasy, tentative, and realistic (Ginzberg, 1972; Ginzberg & others, 1951). When asked what they want to be when they grow up, young children may answer "a doctor," "a superhero," "a teacher," "a movie star," "a sports star," or any number of other occupations. In childhood, the future seems to hold almost unlimited opportunities. Ginzberg argues that, until about the age of 11, children are in the fantasy stage of career choice. From the ages of 11 to 17, adolescents are in the tentative stage of career development, a transition from the fantasy stage of childhood to the realistic decision making of young adulthood. Ginzberg believes that adolescents progress from evaluating their interests (11 to 12 years of age) to evaluating their capacities (13 to 14 years of age) to evaluating their values (15 to 16 years of age). Thinking shifts from less subjective to more realistic career choices at around 17 to 18 years of age. Ginzberg calls the period from 17 to 18 years of age through the early twenties the realistic stage of career choice. During this time, the individual extensively explores available careers, then focuses on a particular career, and finally selects a specific job within the career (such as family practitioner or orthopedic surgeon, within the career of doctor).

Critics have attacked Ginzberg's theory on a number of grounds. For one, the initial data were collected from middle-SES youth, who probably had more career options than low-SES youth. As with other developmental theories (such as Piaget), the time frames are too rigid. Moreover, Ginzberg's theory does not take into account individual differences—some adolescents make mature decisions about careers (and stick with them) at much earlier ages than specified by Ginzberg, and some 30-year-olds have still not reached a realistic stage of career choice. Not all children engage in career fantasies, either.

In a revision of his theory, Ginzberg (1972) conceded that lower-SES individuals do not have as many options available as middle-SES individuals do. Still, Ginzberg's general point—that at some point during late adolescence or early adulthood more realistic career choices are made—probably is correct.

Super's Self-Concept Theory **Career self-concept theory** is Donald Super's theory that an individual's self-concept plays a central role in his or her career choice. Super believes that it is during adolescence that individuals first construct a career self-concept (Super, 1967, 1976). He emphasizes that career development consists of five different phases. First, at about 14 to 18 years of age, adolescents develop ideas about work that mesh with their already existing global self-concept—this phase is called *crystallization*. Between 18 and 22 years of age, they narrow their career choices and initiate behavior that enables them to enter some type of career—this phase is called *specification*. Between 21 and 24 years of age, young adults complete their education or training and enter the world of work—this phase is called *implementation*. The decision on a specific, appropriate career is made between 25 and 35 years of age—this phase is called *stabilization*. Finally, after the age of 35, individuals seek to advance their careers and to reach higher-status positions—this phase is called *consolidation*. The age ranges should be thought of as approximate rather than rigid. Super believes that career exploration in adolescence is a key ingredient of adolescents' career self-concept. He constructed the Career Development Inventory to assist counselors in promoting adolescents' career exploration.

Holland's Personality Type Theory **Personality type theory** is John Holland's theory that an effort should be made to match an individual's career choice with his or her personality (Holland, 1973, 1987). According to Holland, once individuals find a career that fits their personality, they are more likely to enjoy that particular career and to stay in a job for a longer period of time than individuals who work at jobs not suited to their personality. Holland believes that six basic personality types need to be considered when matching the individual's psychological makeup to a career (see figure 12.8):

1. *Realistic.* These individuals are physically strong, deal in practical ways with problems, and have very little social know-how. They are best oriented toward practical careers, such as labor, farming, truck driving, and construction.
2. *Investigative.* These individuals are conceptually and theoretically oriented. They are thinkers rather than doers. They often avoid interpersonal relations and are best suited to careers in math and science.
3. *Social.* These individuals often have good verbal skills and interpersonal relations. They are likely to be best equipped to enter "people" professions, such as teaching, social work, counseling, and the like.
4. *Conventional.* These individuals show a distaste for unstructured activities. They are best suited for jobs as subordinates, such as bank tellers, secretaries, and file clerks.
5. *Enterprising.* These individuals energize their verbal abilities toward leading others, dominating individuals, and selling people on issues or products. They are best counseled to enter careers such as sales, politics, and management.
6. *Artistic.* These individuals prefer to interact with their world through artistic expression, avoiding conventional and interpersonal situations in many instances. These youth should be oriented toward such careers as art and writing.

FIGURE 12.8 Holland's Model of Personality Types and Career Choices

If all individuals fell conveniently into Holland's personality types, career counselors would have an easy job. But individuals are more varied and complex than Holland's theory suggests. Even Holland (1987) later admitted that most individuals are not pure types. Still, the basic idea of matching the abilities and attitudes of individuals to particular careers is an important contribution to the career field (Lent & others, 2003; Vondracek, 1991). Holland's personality types are incorporated into the Strong-Campbell Vocational Interest Inventory, a widely used measure in career guidance.

Criticism of Career Choice Theories Career choice theories have been criticized on a number of fronts. Some critics argue that they are too simple. Others stress that there is little data to support them. Also, theories such as Holland's assume that interests and abilities are fixed during adolescence and early adulthood; critics emphasize that individuals can continue to change and develop as they grow older (Mortimer & Lorence, 1979). Further, career choice is influenced by many factors other than personality; such factors include individual preferences, the influences of parents, peers, and teachers, and sociocultural dimensions.

Holland's Personality Types
Career Development Quarterly
Journal of Counseling Psychology

Cognitive Factors

Exploration, decision making, and planning play important roles in adolescents' career choices (Germeijs & DeBoeck, 2003; Millar & Shevlin, 2003; Spokane, 2000). In countries where equal employment opportunities have emerged—such as the United States, Canada, Great Britain, and France—exploration of various career paths is critical in adolescents' career development. Adolescents often approach career exploration and decision making with considerable ambiguity, uncertainty, and stress. Many of the career decisions made by youth involve floundering and unplanned changes. Many adolescents do not adequately explore careers on their own and also receive little direction from guidance counselors at their schools. On the average, high school students spend less than three hours per year with guidance counselors, and in some schools the average is even less (National Assessment of Educational Progress, 1976). In many schools, students not only do not know what information to seek about careers, they do not know how to seek it.

One of the crucial aspects of planning in career development is awareness of the educational requirements for a particular career. In one investigation of a sample of 6,029 high school seniors from 57 different school districts in Texas, students lacked accurate information about two aspects of careers: (1) the educational requirements of careers they desired and (2) the vocational interests predominantly associated with their career choices (Grotevant & Durrett, 1980).

In a large-scale longitudinal investigation, Mihaly Csikszentmihalyi and Barbara Schneider (2000) studied how U.S. adolescents develop attitudes and acquire skills to achieve their career goals and expectations. They assessed the progress of more than 1,000 students from 13 school districts across the United States. Students recorded at random moments their thoughts and feelings about what they did, and they filled out questionnaires regarding school, family, peers, and career aspirations. The researchers also interviewed the adolescents, as well as their friends, parents, and teachers. Among the findings of the study:

- Girls anticipated the same lifestyles as boys in terms of education and income.
- Lower-income minority students were more positive about school than more affluent students were.
- Students who got the most out of school—and had the highest future expectations—were those who perceived school to be more playlike than worklike.
- Clear vocational goals and good work experiences did not guarantee a smooth transition to adult work. Engaging activities—with intensive involvement regardless of content—were essential to building the optimism and resilience that are important for achieving a satisfying work life. This finding fits with Csikszentmihalyi's concept of flow, which we explored earlier in the chapter.

In another study, adolescents were more ambitious in the 1990s than reports from adolescents in other studies conducted in the 1970s and 1980s (Schneider & Stevensen, 1999). The rising ambitions of adolescents were not confined to those from White middle-income families but also characterized adolescents from low-income and ethnic minority families.

Today, more than 90 percent of high school seniors expect to attend college and more than 70 percent anticipate working in professional jobs. Four decades ago the picture was substantially different with only 55 percent expecting to go college and 42 percent anticipating working in professional jobs. In the study on adolescent ambitions in the 1990s, parents shared their adolescents' ambitious visions (Schneider & Stevenson, 1999). However, both adolescents and their parents often failed to make meaningful connections between educational credentials and future work opportunities. Parents can improve this by becoming more knowledgeable about which courses their adolescents are taking in school, developing a better understanding of the college admissions process, providing adolescents with better information about various careers, and realistically evaluating their adolescents' abilities and interests in relation to these careers.

Identity Development

Career development is related to identity development in adolescence. Career decidedness and planning are positively related to identity achievement, whereas career planning and decidedness are negatively related to identity moratorium and identity diffusion statuses (Wallace-Broscious, Serafica, & Osipow, 1994). Adolescents farther along in the process of identity formation are better able to articulate their occupational choices and their next steps in obtaining short-term and long-term goals (Raskin, 1985). By contrast, adolescents in the moratorium and diffusion statuses of identity are more likely to struggle with making occupational plans and decisions.

One study focused on vocational identity development in relation to other identity domains (Skorikov & Vondracek, 1998). A cross-sectional study of 1,099 high school students in grades 7 through 12 revealed a developmental progression in adolescent vocational identity characterized by an increase in the proportion of students classified as diffused and foreclosed. Statuses in general ideological, religious, lifestyle, and political identity domains lagged behind identity status development in the domain of vocation (see figure 12.9). Thus, in line with the developmental tasks outlined in Erikson's (1968) theory, vocational identity development plays a leading role in identity development.

Social Contexts

Not every individual born into the world can grow up to become a nuclear physicist or a doctor—there is a genetic limitation that keeps some adolescents from performing at the high intellectual levels necessary to enter such careers: Similarly, there are genetic limitations that restrict some adolescents from becoming professional football players or professional dancers. But there are many careers available to most of us, careers that provide a reasonable match with our abilities. Our sociocultural experiences exert strong influences on career choices from among the wide range available. Among the important social contexts that influence career development are socioeconomic status, parents and peers, schools, and gender.

Socioeconomic Status The channels of upward mobility open to lower-SES youth are largely educational in nature. The school hierarchy from grade school through high school, as well as through college and graduate school, is programmed to orient individuals toward some type of career. Less than 100 years ago, it was believed that only eight years of education were necessary for vocational competence, and anything beyond that qualified the individual for advanced placement in higher-status occupations. By the middle of the twentieth century, the high school diploma had already lost ground as a ticket to career success, and in today's workplace college is a prerequisite for entering a higher-status occupation.

Parents and Peers Parents and peers also are strong influences on adolescents' career choices (Vondracek & Porfeli, 2003). Some experts argue that American parents have achievement expectations that are too low, while others believe that some parents put too much pressure on adolescents to achieve beyond their capabilities. Let's look at a situation in which parents oriented an adolescent toward marriage and away from academic achievement. A 25-year-old woman vividly describes the details of her adolescence that prevented her from seeking a competent career. From early in adolescence, both of her parents encouraged her to finish high school, but at the same time they emphasized that she needed to get a job to help them pay the family's bills. She was never told that she could not go to college, but both parents encouraged her to find someone to marry who could support her financially, which she did. This very bright young woman is now divorced and feels intellectually cheated by her parents, who socialized her in the direction of marriage and away from a college education.

From an early age, children see and hear about the jobs their parents have. In some cases, parents even take their children to work with them on jobs. Recently, when we were building our house, the bricklayer brought his two sons to help with the work. They were only 14 years old, yet they were already engaging in apprenticeship work with their father.

Many factors influence parents' roles in adolescents' career development (Young, 1994). For one, mothers who work regularly outside the home and show effort and pride in their work probably have strong influences on their adolescents' career choices. A reasonable conclusion is that when both parents work and enjoy their work, adolescents learn work values from both parents.

Domain/Identity Status	Grade 8	Grade 10	Grade 12
Vocational Moratorium	33.5	38.0	42.1
Achievement	13.5	13.5	19.6
General Ideological Moratorium	25.5	27.8	36.4
Achievement	5.1	11.2	5.6
Religious Moratorium	14.6	15.6	20.0
Achievement	5.6	7.8	5.4
Lifestyle Moratorium	14.0	18.9	15.6
Achievement	3.6	6.5	4.6
Political Moratorium	11.3	13.8	11.2
Achievement	3.1	4.8	6.5

FIGURE 12.9 Identity Status Development in Different Domains.
Note: Numbers represent percentages.

Some researchers argue that the development of work values is transmitted more strongly in same-sex parent adolescent relationships than in opposite-sex parent adolescent relationships. They also believe that the transmission of work values is more likely to occur in father-son than mother-daughter relationships (Ryu & Mortimer, 1996).

Anna Roe (1956) argued that parent-child relationships play an important role in occupation selection. For example, she said that individuals who have warm and accepting parents are likely to choose careers that include work with people, such as sales positions and public relations jobs. By contrast, she stated, individuals who have rejecting or neglectful parents are more likely to choose careers that do not require a good "personality" or strong social skills, such as accounting and engineering. Critics argue that Roe's ideas are speculative, might not hold in today's world, and are too simple (Grotevant, 1996).

Parents can potentially influence adolescents' occupational choices through the way they present information about occupations and values, as well as through the experiences they provide adolescents (Hargrove, Creagh, & Burgess, 2003). For example, parents can communicate to their children and adolescents that they value the importance of going to college and attaining a professional degree as a means to attaining a career in medicine, law, or business. Other parents might communicate that college is not as important and place a higher value on being a sports or movie star.

In terms of the experiences they provide children, parents who read to their children, take them to the library on a regular basis, and make sure they go to the museums in the area send a more positive message about the value of academic pursuits compared with parents who use their spare time to coach their children's Little League team. In this manner, parenting behaviors can influence adolescents' activity preferences and ultimately their educational and occupational choices. Of course, some parents try to develop both academic and sports orientations in their children, but many parents spend more time with their children in one area or the other.

In one recent research study, parents' roles in shaping early adolescents' occupational aspirations in two domains—academics (such as doctor, lawyer, architect) and sports (such as professional football or baseball player)—were examined (Jodl & others, 2001). In terms of the adolescent's interest in a career that requires a strong academic background, parents' values (which included their belief in positive outcomes for their youth, their educational aspirations for their youth, and their perception of their youths' academic ability) were closely related to their young adolescents' values (which included self-concept of academic ability, value of education in the future, and educational aspirations). However, in terms of the adolescent's interest in a sports career, the father's behavior (which included sports activity involvement, support of the adolescent's sports talent, and involvement as a coach) played a more important role.

Peers also can influence adolescents' career development. Adolescents often choose peers from within the school setting at an achievement level similar to their own (Vondracek & Porfeli, 2003). In one investigation, when adolescents had friends and parents with high career standards, they were more likely to seek higher-status careers, even if they came from low-income families (Simpson, 1962).

School Influences Schools, teachers, and counselors can exert a powerful influence on adolescents' career development. School is the primary setting where individuals first encounter the world of work. School provides an atmosphere for continuing self-development in relation to achievement and work. And school is the only institution in society that is presently capable of providing the delivery systems necessary for career education—instruction, guidance, placement, and community connections.

A national survey revealed the nature of career information available to adolescents (Chapman & Katz, 1983). The most common single resource was the *Occupational Outlook Handbook (OOH)*, with 92 percent of the schools having one or more copies. The second major source was the *Dictionary of Occupational Titles (DOT)*, with 82 percent having this book available for students. Fewer than 30 percent had no established committee to review career information resources. When students talked to counselors, it

Career Planning
National Career
Occupational Outlook Handbook

was more often about high school courses than about career guidance.

School counseling has been criticized heavily, both inside and outside the educational establishment (Heppner & Heppner, 2003). Insiders complain about the large number of students per school counselor and the weight of non-counseling administrative duties. Outsiders complain that school counseling is ineffective, biased, and a waste of money. Short of a new profession, several options are possible (William T. Grant Foundation Commission on Work, Family, and Citizenship, 1988). First, twice the number of counselors are needed to meet all students' needs. Second, there could be a redefinition of teachers' roles, accompanied by retraining and reduction in teaching loads, so that classroom teachers could assume a stronger role in handling the counseling needs of adolescents. The professional counselor's role in this plan would be to train and assist teachers in their counseling and to provide direct counseling in situations the teacher could not handle. Third, the whole idea of school counselors would be abandoned, and counselors would be located elsewhere—such as in neighborhood social service centers or labor offices. (Germany forbids teachers to give career counseling, reserving this task for officials in well-developed networks of labor offices.)

The College Board Commission on Precollege Guidance and Counseling (1986) recommends other alternatives. It believes that local school districts should develop broad-based planning that actively involves the home, school, and community. Advocating better-trained counselors, the commission supports stronger partnerships between home and school to increase two-way communication about student progress and better collaboration among schools, community agencies, colleges, businesses, and other community resources.

Gender   Because many females have been socialized to adopt nurturing roles rather than career or achieving roles, they traditionally have not planned seriously for careers, have not explored career options extensively, and have restricted their career choices to careers that are gender-stereotyped (Betz, 2002; Gates, 2001). The motivation for work is the same for both sexes. However, females and males make different choices because of their socialization experiences and the ways that social forces structure the opportunities available to them.

As growing numbers of young women pursue careers, they are faced with questions involving career and family: Should they delay marriage and childbearing and establish their career first? Or should they combine their career, marriage, and childbearing in their twenties? Some females in the last decade have embraced the domestic patterns of an earlier historical period. They have married, borne children, and committed themselves to full-time mothering. These "traditional" females have worked outside the home only intermittently, if at all, and have subordinated the work role to the family role.

Many other females, though, have veered from this time-honored path and developed committed, permanent ties to the workplace that resemble the pattern once reserved only for males. When they have had children, it has been after their careers are well established, and rather than leaving the workforce to raise children, they have made efforts to combine a career and motherhood. Although there have always been "career" females, who pursued work instead of marrying, today's women are more likely to try to "have it all."

Careers in Adolescent Development

Grace Leaf
College/Career Counselor

Grace Leaf is a counselor at Spokane Community College in Washington. She has a master's degree in educational leadership and is working toward a doctoral degree in educational leadership at Gonzaga University in Washington. Her job involves teaching, orientation for international students, conducting individual and group advising, and doing individual and group career planning. Grace tries to connect students with goals and values and helps them design an educational program that fits their needs and visions.

Grace Leaf (standing) advising college students about potential careers.

Yes, I am wise but it is wisdom for the pain.
Yes, I've paid the price but look how much I've gained.
If I have to I can do anything.
I am strong, I am invincible,
I am woman . . .

—HELEN REDDY
American Singer, 20th Century

Thinking About Barriers

At 15, Monica Moffitt already has spent quite a bit of time thinking about the terrible "toos": too tall, according to some, to dance ballet, too black and female to aim for a career in neurosurgery, say others.

Monica's reply: "Too bad. I want to be a pioneer. If I'm the first one, that's even better."

Eighteen-year-old Trude Goodman says that the glass ceiling is still pretty powerful, but she thinks her generation of females has a lot more going for it than the generations that came before. Her classmate Kerri Geller agrees: "We have more confidence so we can achieve whatever we want to." However, another 18-year-old, Alison Fisher, says "I'm sometimes a little taken aback . . . shocked, really, at the prejudice I see in the workplace and academics. I hope we will be able to step above that but getting to college and work will definitely be a reality check."

Trude Goodman

For women to succeed in careers, they need to be competent in using modern technology equipment, such as computers and telecommunications equipment. Concerns about developing these competencies are magnified further for many ethnic minority girls who attend schools in impoverished neighborhoods, because they often show less interest in technology than their male counterparts do.

In one effort to improve the interest of such girls in pursuing careers in the sciences and computer technology, the Young Women Scholars' Early Alert Initiative Program was created by Wayne State University, school districts in southeastern Michigan, and industry (Gipson, 1997). They surveyed elementary, middle school, and high school teachers from 18 school districts. Almost 40 percent of the teachers had no computer equipment in their classrooms, and even more lacked adequate computer training to fully utilize the computers they had.

Forty seventh-grade girls, primarily from low-SES ethnic minority families, were selected for the program. The girls were brought to Wayne State University on a number of occasions to participate in math, computer, and science workshops. The girls also were taken on field trips to the Medical School and the Information Technology Center, where they interacted with female scientists. These scientists described how they became interested in their specialty area, personal hardships, career paths, and current lives. Two field trips to industrial sites and three field trips to museums occurred during the five-month program. At each site, the girls met and spoke with scientists and museum staff. In addition, parents participated in some of the programs and assisted on at least one field trip.

Ethnic Minority Adolescents African Americans, Asian Americans, Latinos, and Native Americans are four distinct subgroups of the American culture that share a history of exclusion from mainstream American society. This exclusion has occurred in history books, the educational system, the socioeconomic structure, and the labor force (Osipow & Littlejohn, 1995).

Math and science awareness interventions also are needed (Spokane, Fouad, & Swanson, 2003). One such intervention is a career-linking program that has been effectively used with inner-city middle school students (Fouad, 1995). The intervention combined printed career information, speakers and role models, field trips, and integration of career awareness into the curriculum. The intervention increased students' knowledge of careers, and the students performed better in math and science than a control group of students who did not get the career intervention experience. Two years after the intervention, the students also had chosen more difficult math courses than the control group students.

To intervene effectively in the career development of ethnic minority youth, counselors need to increase their knowledge of communication styles, values regarding the importance of the family, the impact of language fluency, and achievement expectations in various ethnic minority groups. Counselors need to be aware of and respect the cultural values of ethnic minority youth, but such values need to be

Careers in Adolescent Development

Armando Ronquillo
High School Counselor/College Adviser

Armando Ronquillo is a high school counselor and college adviser at Pueblo High School, which is in a low-socioeconomic-status area in Tucson, Arizona. More than 85 percent of the students have a Latino background. Armando was named top high school counselor in the state of Arizona for the year 2000. He has especially helped to increase the number of Pueblo High School students who go to college.

Armando has an undergraduate degree in elementary and special education, and a master's degree in counseling. He counsels the students on the merits of staying in school and on the lifelong opportunities provided by a college education. Armando guides students in obtaining the academic preparation that will enable them to go to college, including how to apply for financial aid and scholarships. He also works with parents to help them understand that their child going to college is not only doable but also affordable.

Armando works with students on setting goals and planning. He has students plan for the future in terms of 1-year (short-term), 5-year (midrange), and 10-plus-year (long-term) time periods. Armando says he does this "to help students visualize how the educational plans and decisions they make today will affect them in the future." He also organizes a number of college campus visitations for students from Pueblo High School each year.

Armando Ronquillo, counseling a Latina high school student about college.

discussed within the context of the realities of the educational and occupational world (Leong, 1995, 2000). For example, assertiveness training might be called for when Asian youth are following a cultural tradition of nonassertiveness. The counselor can emphasize to these youth that they can choose when and where to follow the more assertive style.

Review and reflect   Learning goal 3

3 **Characterize career development in adolescence**

REVIEW

- What are the three main theories of career development and how have they been criticized?
- How are cognitive factors involved in adolescents' career development?
- How is identity development linked with career development in adolescence?
- What roles do social contexts play in adolescents' career development?

REFLECT

- What are your career goals? Write down some of the specific work, job, and career goals that you have for the next 20, 10, and 5 years. Be as concrete and specific as possible. In creating your career goals, start from the farthest point—20 years from now—and work backward. If you start from a near point, you run the risk of adopting goals that are not precisely and clearly connected to your long-term career goals.

In this chapter, we have explored many aspects of achievement, careers, and work. One topic we examined was the influence of culture and ethnicity on achievement. We devote the next chapter entirely to culture and adolescent development.

Reach Your Learning Goals

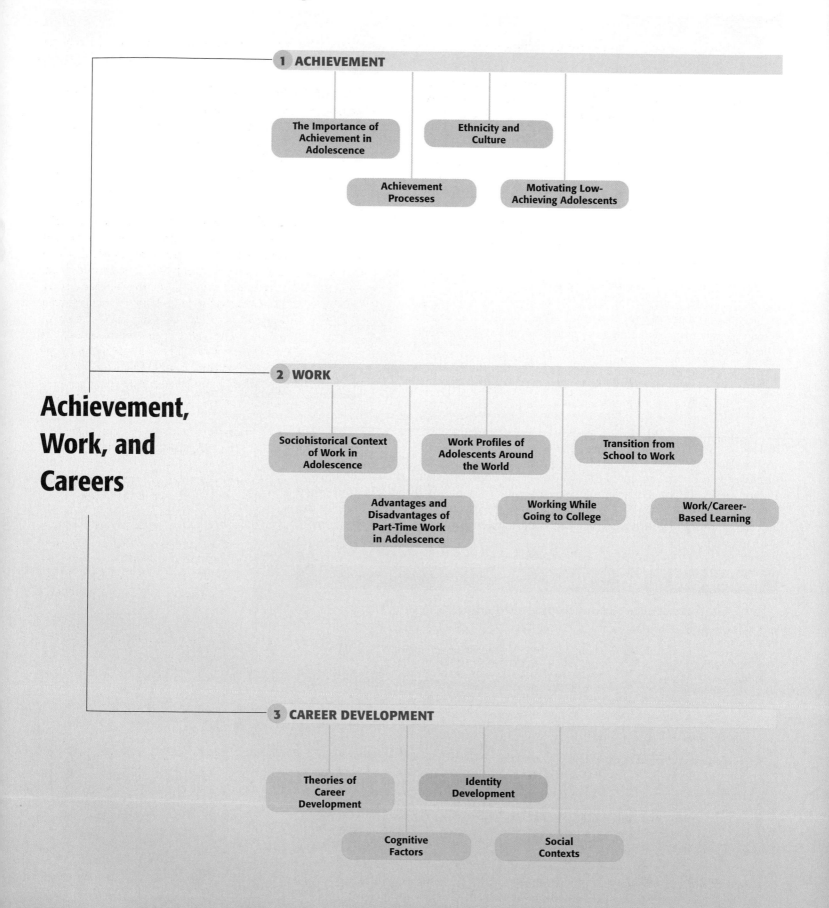

CHAPTER 12

Achievement, Work, and Careers

1 ACHIEVEMENT

- The Importance of Achievement in Adolescence
- Achievement Processes
- Ethnicity and Culture
- Motivating Low-Achieving Adolescents

2 WORK

- Sociohistorical Context of Work in Adolescence
- Advantages and Disadvantages of Part-Time Work in Adolescence
- Work Profiles of Adolescents Around the World
- Working While Going to College
- Transition from School to Work
- Work/Career-Based Learning

3 CAREER DEVELOPMENT

- Theories of Career Development
- Cognitive Factors
- Identity Development
- Social Contexts

Summary

1 Discuss achievement in the lives of adolescents

- Social and academic pressures force adolescents to cope with achievement in new ways. Achievement expectations increase in secondary schools. Whether adolescents effectively adapt to these new pressures is determined in part by psychological and motivational factors.
- Intrinsic motivation is based on internal factors such as self-determination, curiosity, challenge, and effort. Extrinsic motivation involves external incentives such as rewards and punishment. One view is that giving students some choice and providing opportunities for personal responsibility increase intrinsic motivation. Flow is most likely to occur in areas in which adolescents are challenged and perceive themselves as having a high degree of skill. Attribution theory states that individuals are motivated to discover the underlying causes of behavior in an effort to make sense out of the behavior. Weiner identified three dimensions of causal attributions: locus, stability, and controllability. A mastery orientation is preferred over helpless or performance orientations in achievement situations. Self-efficacy is the belief that one can master a situation and attain positive outcomes. Self-efficacy has been shown to be an important process in achievement. Goal-setting, planning, and self-monitoring are important aspects of achievement. Adolescents benefit when their parents, teachers, and other adults have high expectations for their achievement. A special concern is when adolescents have too much anxiety in achievement situations, which sometimes is linked to unrealistic parental expectations.
- Too often research has failed to tease apart effects of ethnicity and socioeconomic status. It is always important to consider diversity of achievement within an ethnic group. American adolescents are more achievement oriented than their counterparts in many countries, but in recent years Asian adolescents have outperformed American adolescents in math and science achievement.
- One main type of low-achieving student is the discouraged student who lacks confidence and motivation to learn. This might be an adolescent with low ability and low expectations for success who needs reassurance and support, but who also needs to be reminded that progress only can be made when considerable effort is put forth. Adolescents with failure syndrome (having low expectations for success and giving up easily) likely will benefit from cognitive training methods. An adolescent who is motivated to protect self-worth by avoiding failure will likely benefit from inherently interesting activities, setting challenging but achievable goals, and other positive strategies. Self-handicapping is a strategy that some adolescents use to avoid the perception that their low performance is due to a lack of ability.

2 Describe the role of work in adolescence and college

- Adolescents are not as likely to hold full-time jobs today as their counterparts from the nineteenth century were. The number of adolescents who work part-time, though, has increased dramatically.
- Advantages of part-time work in adolescence include learning how the business world works, how to get and keep a job, how to manage money, how to budget time, how to take pride in accomplishments, and how to evaluate goals. Disadvantages include giving up extracurricular activities at school, social affairs with peers, and sometimes sleep; as well as balancing the demands of school, family, peers, and work.
- Profiles of adolescent work vary around the world. In many developing countries, boys engage in considerably more paid labor than girls, who participate in more unpaid labor at home. U.S. adolescents engage in more work than their counterparts in many other developed countries. There appears to be little developmental advantage for most adolescents when they work 15 to 25 hours per week.
- Working while going to college can also have a negative impact on students' grades.
- Rates of adolescent unemployment are sometimes exaggerated, but some adolescents—especially ethnic minority adolescents from low-SES backgrounds—face unemployment problems. To bridge the gap between school and work, better monitoring of adolescents' work experiences and better career counseling need to be accomplished.
- Interest in work-based learning in high school is increasing. Three new types of high schools exemplify a college-and-career approach: (1) single-theme schools; (2) schools-within-schools; and (3) majors, clusters, or pathways. Many successful college students engage in cooperative learning or internship programs.

3 Characterize career development in adolescence

- Three theories of career development are Ginzberg's developmental theory, Super's self-concept theory, and Holland's personality type theory. Criticisms of each of these theories have been made.
- Exploration, decision making, and planning are important cognitive dimensions of career development in adolescence. Career development is linked to identity development in adolescence. Among the most important social contexts that influence career development in adolescence are socioeconomic status, parents and peers, schools, gender, and ethnicity.

Key Terms

intrinsic motivation 430
extrinsic motivation 430
flow 430
attribution theory 430

mastery orientation 432
helpless orientation 432
performance orientation 433
self-efficacy 433

anxiety 435
failure syndrome 439
self-handicapping
    strategies 440

developmental career choice
    theory 448
career self-concept theory 448
personality type theory 448

Key People

Mihaly Csikszentmihalyi 430
Bernard Weiner 431
Carol Dweck 432
Albert Bandura 433

Dale Schunk 433
Sandra Graham 436
Harold Stevenson 437
Martin Covington 440

Ellen Greenberger and
    Laurence Steinberg 442
Eli Ginzberg 448
Donald Super 448

John Holland 448
Anna Roe 452

Resources for Improving the Lives of Adolescents

Becoming Adult

(2000) by Mihaly Csikszentmihalyi and Barbara Schneider
New York: Basic Books

This report of a longitudinal study provides valuable information about the ways that work during adolescence influences developmental pathways into adulthood.

Motivation to Learn (4th ed.)

(2002) by Deborah Stipek
New York: McGraw-Hill

This is an excellent book on motivating students in the classroom.

National Youth Employment Coalition

1501 Broadway, Room 111
New York, NY 10036
212–840–1801

This organization promotes youth employment.

Through Mentors

202–393–0512

Mentors are recruited from corporations, government agencies, universities, and professional firms. Their goal is to provide every youth in the District of Columbia with a mentor through high school. To learn how to become involved in a mentoring program or to start such a program, call the number listed here. Also, the National One-to-One Partnership Kit guides businesses in establishing mentoring programs (call 202–338–3844).

What Color Is Your Parachute?

(2004) by Richard Bolles
Berkeley, CA: Ten Speed Press

This is an extremely popular book on job hunting.

What Kids Need to Succeed

(2003) by Peter Benson, Judy Galbraith, and Pamela Espeland
Minneapolis: Search Institute

This easy-to-read book presents commonsense ideas for parents, educators, and youth workers that can help youth succeed.

E-Learning Tools

To help you master the material in this chapter, you will find a number of valuable study tools on the student CD-ROM that accompanies this book. In addition, visit the Online Learning Center for *Adolescence, 10th Edition,* where you will find helpful resources for chapter 12, "Achievement, Work, and Careers."

Taking It to the Net

http://www.mhhe.com/santrocka10

1. A number of career tests can be used as an aid in helping people select potential careers. If you took several, would you get the same recommendations? How well did they do for you? What cautions would you advise friends taking such tests to keep in mind?
2. One of your concerns as an undergraduate member of the College Curriculum Committee is making education relevant to the world of work that you and the other students will be entering. How would you suggest the curriculum be structured to maximize its relevance to the world of work?
3. The study of motivation is an important component of explaining human behavior. How might the study of needs, attribution theory, and other aspects of motivation be important to the study of personality?

Connect to **http://www.mhhe.com/santrocka10** to research the answers and complete these exercises. In some cases, you'll also find further instructions on this site.

Self-Assessment

To evaluate yourself, complete these self-assessments: (1) Evaluating My Career Interests and (2) How Assertive Will I Be in Hunting for a Job?

Health and Well-Being, Parenting, and Education

To practice your decision-making skills, complete the health and well-being, parenting, and education scenarios.

CHAPTER

13

Consider the flowers of a garden: Though differing in kind, color, form, and shape, yet, inasmuch as they are refreshed by the waters of one spring, revived by the breath of one wind, invigorated by the rays of one sun, this diversity increases their charm and adds to their beauty. . . . How unpleasing to the eye if all the flowers and plants, the leaves and blossoms, the fruits, the branches, and the trees of that garden were all of the same shape and color! Diversity of hues, form, and shape enriches and adorns the garden and heightens its effect.

—'ABDU'L BAHA
*Persian Baha'i Religious Leader,
19th/20th Century*

Culture

Learning Goals

1 Discuss the role of culture in adolescent development

2 Summarize how ethnicity is involved in adolescent development

3 Describe how socioeconomic status and poverty are related to adolescent development

4 Characterize the roles of the media and technology in adolescent development

Images of Adolescent Development

Dilemmas of a 16-Year-Old Japanese American Girl and a 17-Year-Old Chinese American Boy

Sonya, a 16-year-old Japanese American girl, was upset over her family's reaction to her White American boyfriend. Her parents refused to meet him and more than once threatened to disown her. Her older brothers also reacted angrily to Sonya's dating a White American, warning that they were going to beat him up. Her parents were also disturbed that Sonya's grades, above average in middle school, were beginning to drop.

Generational issues contributed to the conflict between Sonya and her family (Nagata, 1989). Her parents had experienced strong sanctions against dating Whites when they were growing up and were legally prevented from marrying anyone but a Japanese. As Sonya's older brothers were growing up, they valued ethnic pride and solidarity. The brothers saw her dating a White as "selling out" her own ethnic group. Sonya's and her family members' cultural values obviously differ.

Michael, a 17-year-old Chinese American high school student, was referred to an outpatient adolescent crisis center by the school counselor for depression and suicidal tendencies (Huang & Ying, 1989). Michael was failing several subjects and was repeatedly absent or late for school. Michael's parents were successful professionals who told the therapist that there was nothing wrong with them or with Michael's younger brother and sister, so they wondered what was wrong with Michael! What was wrong was that the parents expected all of their children to become doctors. They were frustrated and angered by Michael's school failures, especially since he was the firstborn son, who in Chinese families is expected to achieve the highest standards of all siblings.

The therapist underscored the importance of the parents' putting less pressure for achievement on Michael and gradually introduced more realistic expectations for Michael (who was not interested in becoming a doctor and did not have the necessary academic record). The therapist supported Michael's desire not to become a doctor and empathized with the pressure he had experienced from his parents. As Michael's school attendance improved, his parents noted his improved attitude toward school and supported a continuation of therapy. Michael's case illustrates how expectations for Asian American youth to be "whiz kids" can become destructive.

Sonya's and Michael's circumstances underscore the importance of culture in understanding adolescent development.

lthough we have much in common with all humans who inhabit the earth, we also vary according to our cultural and ethnic backgrounds. The sociocultural worlds of adolescents are a recurrent theme throughout this book. And because culture is such a pervasive dimension of adolescence, we devote this chapter to exploring it in greater depth. We will describe cross-cultural comparisons of adolescents, study ethnicity and socioeconomic status as major aspects of culture, and examine ways in which the dramatic growth of mass media and technology affect the lives of adolescents.

1 CULTURE AND ADOLESCENCE

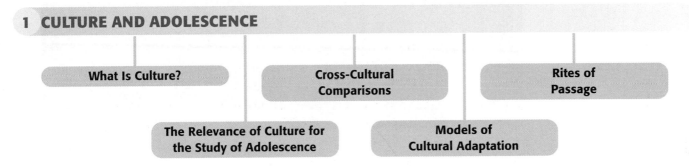

What is culture, and why is it relevant to the study of adolescence? What is the importance of cross-cultural comparisons? How does change take place within and across cultures? What are rites of passage?

What Is Culture?

Culture is the behavior, patterns, beliefs, and all other products of a particular group of people that are passed on from generation to generation. The products result from the interaction between groups of people and their environment over many years (Kottak, 2002; Triandis, 2000). For example, in the section at the beginning of this chapter, we read about how the cultural values of Sonya's parents and brothers conflicted with her dating interests. We also read how the Chinese American cultural tradition of Michael's parents led to Michael's school-related problems.

Culture is a broad concept—it includes many components and can be analyzed in many ways. We already have analyzed the effects of four important cultural settings on adolescent development—the family, peers, school, and work. Later in this chapter, we will examine how much time adolescents spend in these and other settings.

Cross-cultural expert Richard Brislin (1993) described a number of features of culture, including these:

- Culture is made up of ideals, values, and assumptions about life that guide people's behaviors.
- Culture is made by people.
- Culture is transmitted from generation to generation, with the responsibility for transmission resting on the shoulders of parents, teachers, and community leaders.
- Culture's influence often becomes noticed the most in well-meaning clashes between people from very different cultural backgrounds.
- Despite compromises, cultural values endure.
- When their cultural values are violated or when their cultural expectations are ignored, people react emotionally.
- It is not unusual for people to accept a cultural value at one point in their lives and reject it at another point. For example, rebellious individuals might accept a culture's values and expectations after having children of their own.

culture The behavior, patterns, beliefs, and all other products of a particular group of people that are passed on from generation to generation.

Culture has a powerful impact on people's lives. In Xinjian, China, a woman prepares for horseback courtship. Her suitor must chase her, kiss her, and evade her riding crop—all on the gallop. A new marriage law took effect in China in 1981. The law sets a minimum age for marriage—22 years for males, 20 years for females. Late marriage and late childbirth are critical aspects of China's effort to control population growth.

Two additional important dimensions of culture in adolescents' lives are socioeconomic status and ethnicity:

- **Socioeconomic status (SES)** refers to a grouping of people with similar occupational, educational, and economic characteristics. Individuals with different SES have varying levels of power, influence, and prestige. In this chapter, for example, we will evaluate what it is like for an adolescent to grow up in poverty.
- **Ethnicity** is based on cultural heritage, nationality characteristics, race, religion, and language. A striking feature of the United States today is the increasing ethnic diversity of America's adolescents. In this chapter, we study African American adolescents, Latino adolescents, Asian American adolescents, and Native American adolescents, and the sociocultural issues involved in their development. This chapter concludes with an overview of how an important dimension of culture—television and other media—affects adolescent development.

The Relevance of Culture for the Study of Adolescence

If the study of adolescence is to be a relevant discipline in the twenty-first century, increased attention will have to be focused on culture and ethnicity (Cooper & Denner, 1998; Eccles, 2002; Matsumoto 2000, 2004). Extensive contact between people from varied cultural and ethnic backgrounds is rapidly becoming the norm. Schools and neighborhoods are no longer the fortresses of a privileged group whose agenda is the exclusion of those with a different skin color or different customs. Immigrants, refugees, and ethnic minority individuals increasingly decline to become part of a homogeneous melting pot, instead requesting that schools, employers, and governments honor many of their cultural customs. Adult refugees and immigrants might find more opportunities and better-paying jobs here, but they are concerned that their children and adolescents might learn attitudes in school that challenge traditional authority patterns at home (Brislin, 1993).

In the twentieth century, the study of adolescents was primarily ethnocentric, emphasizing American values, especially middle-SES, White, male values (Spencer, 2000). Cross-cultural psychologists point out that many of the assumptions about contemporary ideas in fields like adolescence were developed in Western cultures

socioeconomic status (SES) A grouping of people with similar occupational, educational, and economic characteristics.

ethnicity A dimension of culture based on cultural heritage, nationality, race, religion, and language.

(Triandis, 1994). One example of **ethnocentrism**—the tendency to favor one's own group over other groups—is the American emphasis on the individual or self. Many Eastern countries, such as Japan, China, and India, are group oriented. So is the Mexican culture. The pendulum may have swung too far in the individualistic direction in many Western cultures.

People in all cultures have a tendency to (Brewer & Campbell, 1976):

- Believe that what happens in their culture is "natural" and "correct" and that what happens in other cultures is "unnatural" and "incorrect"
- Perceive their cultural customs as universally valid; that is, what is good for us is good for everyone
- Behave in ways that favor their cultural group
- Feel proud of their cultural group
- Feel hostile toward other cultural groups

In fact, many cultures define being human by reference to their own cultural group. The ancient Greeks distinguished between those who spoke Greek and those whose language was incomprehensible and sounded like "bar-bar" (a repetitive chatter), so they called them *barbarians.* The ancient Chinese labeled themselves "the central kingdom." In many languages, the word for *human* is the same as the name of the tribe, implying that people from other cultures are not perceived as fully human (Triandis, 1994).

Over the past few centuries and at an increasing rate in recent decades, technological advances in transportation, communication, and commerce have made these ways of thinking obsolete. Global interdependence is no longer a matter of belief or choice. It is an inescapable reality (Miller & Schaberg, 2003; Saraswathi & Mistry, 2003). Adolescents are not just citizens of the United States or Canada. They are citizens of the world, a world that has become increasingly interactive (Mortimer & Larson, 2002). By understanding the behavior and values of cultures around the world, we can interact more effectively with each other and make this planet a more hospitable, peaceful place to live (Brislin, 2000; Brown, Larson, & Saraswathi, 2002; Matsumoto, 2004; Sternberg & Grigorenko, 2004).

Cross-Cultural Comparisons

In the early twentieth century, inspired by the view of G. Stanley Hall (1904), it was widely believed that adolescents everywhere went through a period of "storm and stress" characterized by self-doubt and conflict. However, as we saw in chapter 1, when Margaret Mead visited the island of Samoa, she found that the adolescents of the Samoan culture were not experiencing much stress.

Cross-cultural studies involve the comparison of a culture with one or more other cultures, which provides information about the degree to which adolescent development is similar, or universal, across cultures, or the degree to which it is culture-specific (Saraswathi, 2003). The study of adolescence has emerged in the context of Western industrialized society, with the practical needs and social norms of this culture dominating thinking about adolescents. Consequently, the development of adolescents in Western cultures has evolved as the norm for all adolescents of the human species, regardless of economic and cultural circumstances. This narrow viewpoint can produce erroneous conclusions about the nature of adolescents (Berry, 2000; Miller & Schaberg, 2003). To develop a more global, cosmopolitan perspective on adolescents, we next consider how adolescents around the world spend their time as well as how achievement behavior and sexuality vary in different cultures.

How Adolescents Around the World Spend Their Time
Do adolescents around the world spend their time in ways similar to U.S. adolescents? In chapter 12, "Achievement, Work, and Careers," we saw that there is considerable variation in the number of hours adolescents spend in paid work across different countries.

ethnocentrism A tendency to favor one's own group over other groups.

cross-cultural studies Studies that compare a culture with one or more other cultures. Such studies provide information about the degree to which adolescent development is similar, or universal, across cultures or about the degree to which it is culture-specific.

Activity	Nonindustrial, unschooled populations	Postindustrial, schooled populations		
		United States	Europe	East Asia
Household labor	5 to 9 hours	20 to 40 minutes	20 to 40 minutes	10 to 20 minutes
Paid labor	0.5 to 8 hours	40 to 60 minutes	10 to 20 minutes	0 to 10 minutes
Schoolwork	—	3.0 to 4.5 hours	4.0 to 5.5 hours	5.5 to 7.5 hours
Total work time	6 to 9 hours	4 to 6 hours	4.5 to 6.5 hours	6 to 8 hours
TV viewing	insufficient data	1.5 to 2.5 hours	1.5 to 2.5 hours	1.5 to 2.5 hours
Talking	insufficient data	2 to 3 hours	insufficient data	45 to 60 minutes
Sports	insufficient data	30 to 60 minutes	20 to 80 minutes	0 to 20 minutes
Structured voluntary activities	insufficient data	10 to 20 minutes	1.0 to 20 minutes	0 to 10 minutes
Total free time	4 to 7 hours	6.5 to 8.0 hours	5.5 to 7.5 hours	4.0 to 5.5 hours

Note. The estimates in the table are averaged across a 7-day week, including weekdays and weekends. Time spent in maintenance activities like eating, personal care, and sleeping is not included. The data for nonindustrial, unschooled populations come primarily from rural peasant populations in developing countries.

FIGURE 13.1 Average Daily Time Use of Adolescents in Different Regions of the World

The Web of Culture
Worldwide Classroom
Cross-Cultural Comparisons

Reed Larson and Suman Verma (Larson, 2001; Larson & Verma, 1999) have examined how adolescents spend their time in work, play, and developmental activities such as school. As we saw in chapter 12, U.S. adolescents spend more time in paid work than their counterparts in most developed countries. We also saw that adolescent males in developing countries often spend more time in paid work than adolescent females, who spend more time in unpaid household labor.

Figure 13.1 summarizes the average daily time use by adolescents in different regions of the world (Larson & Verma, 1999). U.S. adolescents spend about 60 percent as much time on schoolwork as East Asian adolescents do, which is mainly due to U.S. adolescents doing less homework.

What U.S. adolescents have in greater quantities than adolescents in other industrialized countries is discretionary time. About 40 to 50 percent of U.S. adolescents' waking hours (not counting summer vacations) is spent in discretionary activities, compared with 25 to 35 percent in East Asia and 35 to 45 percent in Europe. Whether this additional discretionary time is a liability or an asset for U.S. adolescents, of course, depends on how they use it.

The largest amounts of U.S. adolescents' free time are spent using the media and engaging in unstructured leisure activities, often with friends. We will further explore adolescents' media use later in the chapter. U.S. adolescents spend more time in voluntary structured activities—such as sports, hobbies, and organizations—than East Asian adolescents.

According to Reed Larson (2001), U.S. adolescents may have too much unstructured time for optimal development. When adolescents are allowed to choose what they do with their time, they typically engage in unchallenging activities such as hanging out and watching TV. Although relaxation and social interaction are important aspects of adolescence, it seems unlikely that spending large numbers of hours per week in unchallenging activities fosters development. Structured voluntary activities may provide more promise for adolescent development than unstructured time, especially if adults give responsibility to adolescents, challenge them, and provide competent guidance in these activities (Larson, 2001; Larson & Seepersad, 2003).

Achievement The United States is an achievement-oriented culture, and U.S. adolescents are more achievement oriented than the adolescents in many other countries, but less so than East Asians, as we saw in the comparison of time spent on school and work. Many U.S. parents socialize their adolescents to be achievement oriented and independent. In one investigation of 104 societies, parents in industrialized countries like the United States placed a higher value on socializing adolescents for achievement and independence than did parents in nonindustrialized countries like Kenya, who placed a higher value on obedience and responsibility (Bacon, Child, & Barry, 1963).

Anglo-American adolescents are more achievement oriented than Mexican and Mexican American adolescents are. For example, in one study, Anglo-American adolescents were more competitive and less cooperative than their Mexican and Mexican American counterparts (Kagan & Madsen, 1972). In this study, Anglo-Americans were more likely to discount the gains of other students when they could not reach the goals themselves. In other investigations, Anglo-American youth were more individual centered, while Mexican youth were more family centered (Holtzmann, 1982). Some developmentalists believe that the American culture is too achievement oriented for rearing mentally healthy adolescents (Elkind, 1981).

Although non-Latino White American adolescents are more achievement oriented than adolescents in many other cultures, as we saw in chapter 12, "Achievement, Work, and Careers," they are not as achievement oriented as many Chinese and Japanese adolescents. When they have immigrated to the United States, many Asian families have brought their strong emphasis on academic achievement with them. For example, as a group, Asian adolescents demonstrate exceptional achievement patterns (Stevenson, 1995; Stevenson & Zusko, 2002). Asian American adolescents exceed the national average for high school and college graduates. Eighty-six percent of Asian Americans, compared with 64 percent of White Americans, are in some higher-education program two years after high school graduation. Clearly, education and achievement are highly valued by many Asian American youth.

Sexuality   Culture also plays a prominent role in adolescent sexuality. Some cultures consider adolescent sexual activity normal; others forbid it. Consider the extremes illustrated by the Ines Beag and Mangaian cultures: Ines Beag is a small island off the coast of Ireland. Its inhabitants are among the most sexually inhibited in the world. They know nothing about French kissing or hand stimulation of the penis. Sex education does not exist. They believe that, after marriage, nature will take its course. The men think that intercourse is bad for their health. Individuals in this culture detest nudity. Only babies are allowed to bathe nude, and adults wash only the parts of their body that extend beyond their clothing. Premarital sex is out of the question. After marriage, sexual partners keep their underwear on during intercourse. It is not difficult to understand why females in the Ines Beag culture rarely, if ever, achieve orgasm (Messinger, 1971).

By contrast, consider the Mangaian culture in the South Pacific. Boys learn about masturbation as early as age 6 or 7. At age 13, boys undergo a ritual that introduces them to manhood in which a long incision is made in the penis. The individual who conducts the ritual instructs the boy in sexual strategies, such as how to help his partner achieve orgasm before he does. Two weeks after the incision ceremony, the 13-year-old boy has intercourse with an experienced woman. She helps him to hold back his ejaculation so she can achieve orgasm with him. Soon after, the boy searches for girls to further his sexual experience, or they seek him, knowing that he now is a "man." By the end of adolescence, Mangaians have sex virtually every night.

Adolescents in the United States experience a culture far more liberal than that of the Ines Beag but that does not come close to matching the liberal sexual behavior of the Mangaians. The cultural diversity in the sexual behavior of adolescents is testimony to the power of environmental experiences in determining sexuality. As we move up in the animal kingdom, experience seems to take on more power as a determinant of sexuality. Although human beings cannot mate in midair like bees or display their plumage as magnificently as peacocks, adolescents can—and do—talk about

HUNTER-GATHERERS, NORTH AMERICA, LATE 20TH CENTURY

Copyright © 1994 Sidney Harris. Reprinted with permission.

sex with one another, read about it in magazines, and watch it on television and at the movies.

Models of Cultural Adaptation

The models that have been used to understand the process of adaptation within and between cultures are (1) assimilation, (2) acculturation, (3) alternation, and (4) multiculturalism.

Assimilation occurs when individuals relinquish their cultural identity and move into the larger society. The nondominant group might be absorbed into an established "mainstream," or many groups might merge to form a new society (often called a "melting pot"). Individuals often suffer from a sense of alienation and isolation until they have been accepted into, and perceive their acceptance in, the new culture. However, some non-Latino White Americans whose ancestors for several generations were U.S. citizens do not know what countries or cultures their earlier ancestors came from.

Acculturation is cultural change that results from continuous, firsthand contact between two distinctive cultural groups. In contrast to assimilation (which emphasizes that people will eventually become full members of the majority group's culture and lose their identification with their culture of origin), the acculturation model stresses that people can become competent participants in the majority culture while still being identified as members of a minority culture (Hurtado, 1997; Marin & Gamba, 2003). For example, many Hasidic Jews in New York City preserve the Yiddish language and traditions of dress and religious observances while interacting with business associates from a myriad of other cultures.

The **alternation model** assumes that it is possible for an individual to know and understand two different cultures. It also assumes that individuals can alter their behavior to fit a particular social context. The alternation model differs from the assimilation and acculturation models in the following way: In the alternation model, it is possible to maintain a positive relationship with both cultures (LaFromboise, Coleman, & Gerton, 1993). For example, an African American teacher might use standard English in the classroom but Black English at home and at church.

The **multicultural model** promotes a pluralistic approach to understanding two or more cultures. This model is a way for people to maintain their distinct identities while working with others from different cultures to meet common national or economic needs. Cross-cultural psychologist John Berry (1990, 2003) believes that a multicultural society encourages all groups to (a) maintain and/or develop their group identity, (b) develop other-group acceptance and tolerance, (c) engage in intergroup contact and sharing, and (d) learn each other's language. In the multicultural model, people can maintain a positive identity as members of their culture of origin while simultaneously developing a positive identity with another culture (Berry, 2003).

Depending on the situation and person, any of these models might explain people's experiences as they acquire competency in a new culture. For example, consider an African American family that has moved from the rural South to live in a city. One member of the family might assimilate into the dominant Anglo culture, another might follow the path of acculturation, a third member might choose to actively alternate between the two cultures, and yet a fourth member might choose to live in a context in which the two cultures exist side by side as described in the multicultural model. Teresa LaFromboise and her colleagues (1993) argue that the more people are able to maintain active and effective relationships through alternation between the cultures, the less difficulty they will have in acquiring and maintaining competency in both cultures.

assimilation The absorption of ethnic minority groups into the dominant group, which often means the loss of some or virtually all of the behavior and values of the ethnic minority group.

acculturation Cultural change that results from continuous, firsthand contact between two distinctive cultural groups.

alternation model This model assumes that it is possible for an individual to know and understand two different cultures. It also assumes that individuals can alter their behavior to fit a particular social context.

multicultural model This model promotes a pluralistic approach to understanding two or more cultures. It argues that people can maintain their distinctive identities while working with others from different cultures to meet common national or economic needs.

So far, we have discussed the nature of culture, cross-cultural comparisons, and models of cultural adaptation. Next, we turn our attention to an aspect of adolescent life that is more pronounced in some cultures than others.

Rites of Passage

Rites of passage are ceremonies or rituals that mark an individual's transition from one status to another, such as the entry into adulthood. Some societies have elaborate rites of passage that signal the adolescent's transition to adulthood; others do not. In many primitive cultures, rites of passage are the avenue through which adolescents gain access to sacred adult practices, responsibilities, knowledge, and sexuality (Sommer, 1978). These rites often involve dramatic ceremonies intended to facilitate the adolescent's separation from the immediate family, especially boys from the mother. The transformation usually is characterized by some form of ritual death and rebirth, or by means of contact with the spiritual world. Bonds are forged between the adolescent and the adult instructors through shared rituals, hazards, and secrets to allow the adolescent to enter the adult world. This kind of ritual provides a forceful and discontinuous entry into the adult world at a time when the adolescent is perceived to be ready for the change.

These Congolese Kota boys painted their faces as part of a rite of passage to adulthood. *What rites of passage do American adolescents have?*

Africa, especially sub-Saharan Africa, has been the location of many rites of passage for adolescents. Under the influence of Western culture, many of these rites are disappearing today, although some vestiges remain. In locations where formal education is not readily available, rites of passage are still prevalent.

Western industrialized countries are notable for their lack of formal rites of passage that mark the transition from adolescence to adulthood. Some religious and social groups, however, have initiation ceremonies that indicate an advance in maturity—the Jewish bar mitzvah, Catholic and Protestant confirmations, and social debuts, for example. School graduation ceremonies come the closest to being culturewide rites of passage in the United States. The high school graduation ceremony has become nearly universal for middle-SES adolescents and increasing numbers of adolescents from low-income backgrounds (Fasick, 1994). Nonetheless, high school graduation does not result in universal changes—many high school graduates continue to live with their parents, to be economically dependent on them, and to be undecided about questions of career and lifestyle. Another rite of passage for increasing numbers of American adolescents is sexual intercourse (Halonen & Santrock, 1999). By the end of adolescence, more than 70 percent of American adolescents have had sexual intercourse.

The absence of clear-cut rites of passage makes the attainment of adult status so ambiguous that many individuals are unsure whether they have reached it or not. In Texas, for example, the age for beginning employment is 15, but many younger adolescents and even children are employed, especially Mexican immigrants. The age for driving is 16, but when emergency need is demonstrated, a driver's license can be obtained at age 15, and some parents might not allow their son or daughter to obtain a driver's license even at age 16, believing that they are too young for this responsibility. The age for voting is 18, and the age for drinking recently has been raised to 21. In sum, exactly when adolescents become adults in the United States has not been clearly delineated as it has in primitive cultures where rites of passage are universal.

rites of passage Ceremonies or rituals that mark an individual's transition from one status to another, such as the entry into adulthood.

Review and reflect Learning goal 1

1 **Discuss the role of culture in adolescent development**

REVIEW

- What is culture?
- What is the relevance of culture in the study of adolescent development?
- What are cross-cultural comparisons? How do cultures vary in the time adolescents spend in various activities, as well as the achievement and sexuality of adolescents?
- What are some models of cultural change?
- What are rites of passage? How do cultures vary in terms of rites of passage?

REFLECT

- Have you experienced a rite of passage in your life? If so, what was it? Was it a positive or negative influence on your development? Is there a rite of passage you did not experience that you wished you had?

2 ETHNICITY

| Immigration | Ethnicity Issues | The United States and Canada: Nations with Many Cultures |

| Adolescence: A Special Juncture for Ethnic Minority Individuals | Ethnic Minority Adolescents |

Adolescents live in a world that has been made smaller and more interactive by dramatic improvements in travel and communication. U.S. adolescents also live in a world that is far more diverse in its ethnic makeup than it was in past decades: Ninety-three languages are spoken in Los Angeles alone!

As mentioned earlier in the chapter, *ethnicity* refers to the cultural heritage, national characteristics, race, religion, and language of individuals. The waves of ethnic animosity around the world today are an indication of how badly we need better understanding across ethnic groups.

Immigration

Relatively high rates of immigration are contributing to the growth in the proportion of ethnic minorities in the U.S. population (Chun & Akutsu, 2003; McLoyd, 1998, 2000; Phinney, 2003). Immigrants often experience stressors uncommon to or less prominent among longtime residents such as language barriers, dislocations and separations from support networks, the dual struggle to preserve identity and to acculturate, and changes in SES status. Consequently, adaptations in intervention programs can be required to achieve optimal cultural sensitivity when working with adolescents and their immigrant families (Suarez-Orozco, 1999, 2002).

The Apache Indians of the American Southwest celebrate a girl's entrance into puberty with a four-day ritual that includes special dress, day-long activities, and solemn spiritual ceremonies.

Though the United States has always included significant immigrant populations, psychologists have been slow to study these families. One recent study looked at the cultural values and intergenerational value discrepancies in immigrant (Vietnamese, Armenian, and Mexican) and nonimmigrant (African American and European American) families (Phinney, Madden, & Ong, 2000). Although family obligations were endorsed more by parents than adolescents in all groups, the intergenerational value discrepancy generally increased with time in the United States.

Recent research increasingly shows links between acculturation and adolescent problems (Gonzales & others, 2002). For example, more-acculturated Latino youths in the United States experience higher rates of conduct problems, substance abuse, and risky sexual behavior than their less-acculturated counterparts (Brook & others, 1998; Epstein, Botvin, & Diaz, 1998).

Margaret Beale Spencer, shown here talking with adolescents, believes that adolescence is a critical juncture in the identity development of ethnic minority individuals. Most ethnic minority individuals consciously confront their ethnicity for the first time in adolescence.

Adolescence: A Special Juncture for Ethnic Minority Individuals

As we indicated in chapter 5, "The Self, Identity, Emotions, and Personality," for ethnic minority individuals, adolescence is often a special juncture in their development (Phinney, 2003; Rodriquez & Quinlan, 2002; Spencer & Dornbusch, 1990). Although children are aware of some ethnic and cultural differences, most ethnic minority individuals first consciously confront their ethnicity in adolescence. In contrast to children, adolescents have the ability to interpret ethnic and cultural information, to reflect on the past, and to speculate about the future. As they mature cognitively, ethnic minority adolescents become acutely aware of how the majority White culture evaluates their ethnic group (Comer, 1993). One researcher commented that the young African American child may learn that Black is beautiful but conclude as an adolescent that White is powerful (Semaj, 1985).

Ethnic minority youths' awareness of negative appraisals, conflicting values, and restricted occupational opportunities can influence their life choices and plans for the future (Spencer & Dornbusch, 1990). As one ethnic minority youth stated, "The future seems shut off, closed. Why dream? You can't reach your dreams. Why set goals? At least if you don't set any goals, you don't fail."

For many ethnic minority youth, a special concern is the lack of successful ethnic minority role models (Blash & Unger, 1992). The problem is especially acute for inner-city youth. Because of the lack of adult ethnic minority role models, some ethnic minority youth may conform to middle-SES White values and identify with successful White role models. However, for many ethnic minority adolescents, their ethnicity and skin color limit their acceptance within the White culture. Thus, they face the difficult task of negotiating two values systems—that of their own ethnic group and that of the White society. Some adolescents reject the mainstream, forgoing the rewards controlled by White Americans; others adopt the values and standards of the majority White culture; and still others take the path of biculturality.

Ethnicity Issues

A number of ethnicity issues are involved in adolescent development. First, we explore the importance of considering SES when drawing conclusions about the role of ethnicity in adolescent development.

Ethnicity and Socioeconomic Status   Much of the research on ethnic minority adolescents has failed to identify distinctions between the dual influences of ethnicity and SES. Ethnicity and SES can interact in ways that exaggerate the influence of ethnicity because ethnic minority individuals are overrepresented in the lower socioeconomic levels of American society (Spencer & Dornbusch, 1990). Consequently, too

www.mhhe.com/santrocka10

Migration and Ethnic Relations
Exploring Diversity
Diversity Resources
Ethnic Groups

Careers in Adolescent Development

Carola Suárez-Orozco
Lecturer, Researcher, and Codirector of Immigration Projects

Carola Suárez-Orozco is a researcher and lecturer in the Human Development and Psychology area at Harvard University. She also is codirector of the Harvard Immigration Projects. She obtained her undergraduate degree (development studies) and graduate (clinical psychology) degree from the University of California at Berkeley.

Carola has worked both in clinical and public school settings in California and Massachusetts. She currently is codirecting a five-year longitudinal study of immigrant adolescents' (coming from Central America, China, and the Dominican Republic) adaptation to schools and society. One of the courses she teaches at Harvard is on the psychology of immigrant youth. She especially believes that more research needs to be conducted on the intersection of cultural and psychological factors in the adaptation of immigrant and ethnic minority youth (Suárez-Orozco, 2002; Suárez-Orozco & Suárez-Orozco, 2002).

Carola Suárez-Orozco, with her husband Marcelo, who also studies the adaptation of immigrants.

often researchers have given ethnic explanations of adolescent development that were in reality based on SES rather than ethnicity. For example, decades of research on group differences in self-esteem failed to consider the SES of African American and White American children and adolescents (Hare & Castenell, 1985). When the self-esteem of African American adolescents from low-income backgrounds is compared with that of White American adolescents from middle-SES backgrounds, the differences are often large but not informative because of the confounding of ethnicity and social class (Scott-Jones, 1995).

Some ethnic minority youth are from middle-SES backgrounds, but economic advantage does not entirely enable them to escape their ethnic minority status. Middle-SES ethnic minority youth are still subject to much of the prejudice, discrimination, and bias associated with being a member of an ethnic minority group. Often characterized as a "model minority" because of their strong achievement orientation and family cohesiveness, Japanese Americans still experience stress associated with ethnic minority status (Sue, 1990). Although middle-SES ethnic minority adolescents have more resources available to counter the destructive influences of prejudice and discrimination, they still cannot completely avoid the pervasive influences of negative stereotypes about ethnic minority groups.

That being said, the fact remains that many ethnic minority families are poor and poverty contributes to the stressful life experiences of many ethnic minority adolescents (Fuligni & Yoshikawa, 2003). Vonnie McLoyd (1990) concluded that ethnic minority youth experience a disproportionate share of the adverse effects of poverty and unemployment in America today. Thus, many ethnic minority adolescents experience a double disadvantage: (1) prejudice, discrimination, and bias because of their ethnic minority status; and (2) the stressful effects of poverty.

Differences and Diversity Historical, economic, and social experiences produce legitimate differences between various ethnic minority groups, and between ethnic minority groups and the majority White group (Halonen & Santrock, 1999). Individuals belonging to a particular ethnic or cultural group conform to the values, attitudes, and stresses of that culture. Their behavior, while possibly different from our own, is, nonetheless, often functional for them. Recognizing and respecting these differences is an important aspect of getting along with others in a diverse, multicultural world (Leong, 2000). Every adolescent and adult needs to take the perspective of individuals from ethnic and cultural groups that are different from theirs and think, "If I were in their shoes, what kind of experiences might I have had?" "How would I feel if I were a member of their ethnic or cultural group?" "How would I think and behave if I had grown up in their world?" Such perspective taking is a valuable way to increase our empathy and understanding of individuals from other ethnic and cultural groups. For example, watch the Discovery video clip entitled "In Group-Out Group Bias and Racism" and see for yourself how subjective—and yet seductive—power can be when a group of brown-eyed people are encouraged to subjugate a group of blue-eyed people.

Unfortunately, the emphasis often placed by society on the differences between ethnic minority groups and the White majority has been damaging to ethnic minority individuals. Ethnicity has defined who will enjoy the privileges of citizenship and to what degree and in what ways (Jones, 1994). An individual's ethnic background has determined whether the individual will be alienated, oppressed, or disadvantaged.

The current emphasis on differences between ethnic groups underscores the strengths of various ethnic minority groups and is long overdue (Cushner, McClelland, & Safford, 2003). For example, the extended-family support system that characterizes many ethnic minority groups is now recognized as an important factor in coping. And researchers are finding that African American males are better than Anglo males at nonverbal cues, multilingual/multicultural expression, improvised problem solving, and using body language in communication (Evans & Whitfield, 1988).

For most of the twentieth century, the ways ethnic minority groups differed from Whites were conceptualized as *deficits* or inferior characteristics on the part of the ethnic minority group. Indeed, research on ethnic minority groups often focused only on a group's negative, stressful aspects. For example, research on African American adolescent females invariably examined such topics as poverty, unwed motherhood, and dropping out of school. These topics continue to be important research areas of adolescent development, but research on the positive aspects of African American adolescent females in a pluralistic society is also much needed and sorely neglected. The self-esteem, achievement, motivation, and self-control of adolescents from different ethnic minority groups deserve considerable study.

Another important dimension of ethnic minority adolescents is their diversity (Spring, 2000; Wilson, 2000). Ethnic minority groups are not homogeneous; the individuals within them have different social, historical, and economic backgrounds (Stevenson, 1998). For example, Mexican, Cuban, and Puerto Rican immigrants are Latinos, but they had different reasons for migrating, came from varying socioeconomic backgrounds in their native countries, and experience different rates and types of employment in the United States (Ramirez, 1989). The U.S. federal government now recognizes the existence of 511 different Native American tribes, each having a unique ancestral background with differing values and characteristics. Asian Americans include the Chinese, Japanese, Filipinos, Koreans, and Southeast Asians, each group having distinct ancestries and languages. The diversity of Asian Americans is reflected in their educational attainment: Some achieve a high level of education, while many others do not. For example, 90 percent of Korean American males graduate from high school, but only 71 percent of Vietnamese American males do.

Well-meaning individuals sometimes fail to recognize the diversity within an ethnic group (Sue, 1990). For example, a sixth-grade teacher went to a human relations workshop and was exposed to the necessity of incorporating more ethnicity into her instructional planning. She had two Mexican American adolescents in her class, and she asked them to be prepared to demonstrate to the class on the following Monday how they danced at home. The teacher expected both of them to perform Mexican folk dances, reflecting their ethnic heritage. The first boy got up in front of the class and began dancing in a typical American fashion. The teacher said, "No, I want you to dance like you and your family do at home, like you do when you have Mexican American celebrations." The boy informed the teacher that his family did not dance that way. The second boy demonstrated a Mexican folk dance to the class. The first boy was highly assimilated into the American culture and did not know how to dance Mexican folk dances. The second boy was less assimilated and came from a Mexican American family that had retained more of its Mexican heritage.

This example illustrates the diversity and individual differences that exist within any ethnic minority group. Failure to recognize diversity and individual variations results in the stereotyping of an ethnic minority group.

Prejudice, Discrimination, and Bias   **Prejudice** is an unjustified negative attitude toward an individual because of the individual's membership in a group. The group toward which the prejudice is directed can be made up of people of a particular

prejudice An unjustified negative attitude toward an individual because of her or his membership in a group.

www.mhhe.com/santrocka10

Prejudice

*P*rejudice narrows understanding by biasing our judgments and predetermining what will be discovered from exploring our environment.

—JAMES JONES,
Contemporary Psychologist,
University of Delaware

ethnic group, sex, age, religion, or other detectable difference. Our concern here is prejudice against ethnic minority groups.

In a Gallup poll, a majority of Americans stated that they believe that the United States is ethnically tolerant and that overt racism is basically unacceptable ("Poll Finds Racial Tension Decreasing," 1990). However, many ethnic minority individuals continue to experience persistent forms of prejudice, discrimination, and bias (Dion, 2003; Monteith, 2000; Sue, 1990). Ethnic minority adolescents are taught in schools that often have a middle-SES, White bias, and in classroom contexts that are not adapted to ethnic minority adolescents' learning styles. They are assessed by tests that are often culturally biased and are evaluated by teachers whose appreciation of their abilities may be hindered by negative stereotypes about ethnic minorities (Spencer & Dornbusch, 1990). Discrimination and prejudice continue to be present in the media, interpersonal interactions, and daily conversations. Crimes, strangeness, poverty, mistakes, and deterioration are often mistakenly attributed to ethnic minority individuals or foreigners (van Dijk, 1987). One recent study found that African American and Latino adolescents experienced discrimination at school and in shopping malls (Fajardo & others, 2003). In another recent study, African American adolescents' connection to their ethnic group served as a buffer against threats of discrimination (Wong, Eccles, & Sameroff, 2001).

Stanley Sue (1990) points out that people frequently have opposing views about discrimination and prejudice. On one side are individuals who value and praise the significant strides made in civil rights in recent years, pointing to affirmative action programs as proof of these civil rights advances. On the other side are individuals who criticize American institutions, such as education, because they believe that many forms of discrimination and prejudice still characterize these institutions.

For several reasons, the "browning" of America portends heightened racial/ethnic prejudice and conflict, or at least sharper racial and ethnic divisions (Jenkins & others, 2003; McLoyd, 2000). First, it is occurring against a backdrop of long-standing White privilege and an ingrained sense of entitlement and superiority among non-Latino Whites. Second, the youth of today's immigrants are less likely than their counterparts in the early twentieth century to believe that rejection of the values and ways of their parents' homeland is needed to succeed in American society. Many espouse economic, but not cultural, assimilation into mainstream society. Third, today's immigrants often settle in inner-city neighborhoods where assimilation often means joining a world that is antagonistic to the American mainstream because of its experience of racism and economic barriers.

Progress has been made in ethnic minority relations, but discrimination and prejudice still exist, and equality has not been achieved. Much remains to be accomplished (Pederson, 2004; Scott, 2003).

Ethnic Minority Adolescents

Now that we have considered a number of ideas about ethnic minority adolescents in general, we turn our attention to specific ethnic minority groups in America, beginning with African American adolescents.

African American Adolescents   African Americans make up the largest easily visible ethnic minority group in the United States. African American adolescents and their parents are distributed throughout the socioeconomic structure, although they constitute a larger proportion of poor and lower-SES individuals than does the majority non-Latino White group (Books, 2004; McLoyd, 2000). No cultural characteristic is common to all or nearly all African Americans and absent in Whites, unless it is the experience of being African American and the ideology that develops from that experience (Havighurst, 1987).

The majority of African American youth stay in school, do not take drugs, do not prematurely get married and become parents, are employed and eager to work, are not involved in crime, and grow up to lead productive lives in spite of social and economic disadvantage. While much of the writing and research about African American adolescents has focused on low-SES youth from families mainly residing in inner cities, the majority of African American youth do not reside in the ghettos of inner cities. At the heart of the new model of studying African American youth is recognition of the growing diversity in African American communities in the United States (McHale, 1995; Stevenson, 1998).

Prejudice against African Americans in some occupations persists, but the proportion of African American males and females in middle-SES occupations has been increasing since 1940. A substantial and increasing proportion of African American adolescents are growing up in middle-SES families and share middle-class values and attitudes with White middle SES adolescents. Nonetheless, large numbers of African American adolescents still live in poverty-enshrouded ghettos.

In one investigation of African Americans, a mixture of factors was related to the problems of adolescents in the inner city (Wilson, 1987). Increased social isolation in concentrated areas of poverty and little interaction with the mainstream society were related to the difficulties experienced by inner-city African American youth. Unattractive jobs and a lack of community standards to reinforce work increased the likelihood that inner-city African American youth would turn to either underground illegal activity, idleness, or both.

In the inner city, African American youth often have difficulty in finding legitimate employment, among other reasons because of the lack of even low-paying jobs (Spencer & Dornbusch, 1990). The exodus of middle-SES African Americans from the cities to the suburbs has removed leadership, reduced the tax base, decreased the educated political constituency, and diminished the support of churches and other organizations.

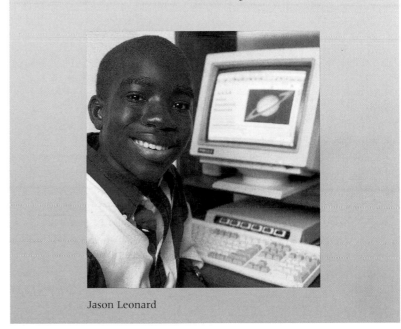

Through the Eyes of Adolescents

Seeking a Positive Image for African American Youth

"I want America to know that most of us black teens are not troubled people from broken homes and headed to jail. . . . In my relationships with my parents, we show respect for each other and we have values in our house. We have traditions we celebrate together, including Christmas and Kwanza."
—*Jason Leonard, Age 15*

Jason Leonard

In many ethnic minority communities, religious institutions play an important role. Many African Americans report that their religious beliefs help them to get along with others and to accept the realities of the American workplace (Spencer & Dornbusch, 1990). In one research study of successful African American students, a strong religious faith was common (Lee, 1985). Regular church attendance characterized the lives of the successful African American students, many of whom mentioned Jesus Christ, Martin Luther King, Jr., and their own church deacons as important influences in their lives. For many African American families, the church has served as an important resource and support system, not only in spiritual matters, but in the development of a social network as well. In other research, Howard Stevenson (1998) found that the more African American adolescents were aware of the need for cultural pride and society's racism struggles, the angrier they were. Their anger was controlled or inhibited if they received communication about spirituality or religion connected to cultural pride.

As mentioned earlier, there is a high percentage of single-parent African American families, many of whom are in low-SES categories. Low SES taxes the coping ability of single parents and can in turn have negative effects on children and adolescents (Wilson, Cook, & Arrington, 1997). However, a characteristic of many African American families that helps to offset the high percentage of single-parent households is the extended-family household—in which one or several grandparents, uncles, aunts, siblings, or cousins either live together or provide support. The extended-family system has helped many African American parents to cope with adverse social conditions and

www.mhhe.com/santrocka10

African Americans

*P*overty and stress are common in the lives of many ethnic minority women who are single parents, and too often this translates into stressful lives for their children.

—VONNIE McLOYD,
Contemporary Psychologist,
University of Michigan

economic impoverishment. The African American extended family can be traced to the African heritage of many African Americans; in many African cultures, a newly married couple does not move away from relatives. Instead, the extended family assists its members with basic family functions. Researchers have found that the extended family helps to reduce the stress of poverty and single parenting through emotional support, sharing of income and economic responsibility, and surrogate parenting (McAdoo, 2002). The presence of grandmothers in the households of many African American adolescents and their infants has also been an important support system for the teenage mother and the infant (Stevens, 1984).

Latino Adolescents In the year 2000, the number of Latino Americans in the United States swelled to 30 million people, 15 percent of the total U.S. population. Most trace their roots to Mexico (almost two-thirds), Puerto Rico (12 percent), and Cuba (5 percent), the rest to Central and South American countries and the Caribbean. About one-third of all Latino Americans marry non-Latinos, promising a day when the Latino culture will be even more intertwined with other cultures in the United States.

By far the largest group of Latino adolescents consists of those who identify themselves as having a Mexican origin, although many of them were born in the United States (Ramirez, 2004). Their largest concentration is in the U.S. Southwest. They represent more than 50 percent of the student population in the schools of San Antonio and close to that percentage in the schools of Los Angeles. Mexican Americans have a variety of lifestyles and come from a range of socioeconomic statuses—from affluent professional and managerial status to migrant farm worker and welfare recipient in big-city barrios. Even though they come from families with diverse backgrounds, Latino adolescents on average have one of the lowest educational levels of any ethnic minority group in the United States. Social support from parents and school personnel may be especially helpful in developing stronger academic achievement in Latino youth (Adamson, 2004; Romo, 2000).

Many of today's Latino adolescents have developed a new political consciousness and pride in their cultural heritage (Comas-Díaz, 2001). Some have fused strong cultural links to Mexican and Indian cultures with the economic limitations and restricted opportunities in the barrio. **Chicano** is the name politically conscious Mexican American adolescents give themselves to reflect the combination of their Spanish-Mexican-Indian heritage and Anglo influences (Cuéllar, Siles, & Bracamontes, 2004; Quintana, 2004; Velásquez, Arellano, & McNeil, 2004).

As we saw with African American adolescents, the church and family play important roles in Latino adolescents' lives. Many, but not all, Latino families are Catholic. And a basic value in Mexico is represented by saying, "As long as our family stays together, we are strong." Mexican children are brought up to stay geographically and socially close to their family, a tradition continued by Mexican Americans. Unlike the father in many Anglo-American families, the Mexican father is the undisputed authority on all family matters and is usually obeyed without question. The mother is revered as the primary source of affection and care. This emphasis on family attachment leads the Mexican to say, "I will achieve mainly because of my family, and for my family, rather than myself." By contrast, the self-reliant non-Latino White American would say, "I will achieve mainly because of my ability and initiative, and for myself, rather than for my family." Unlike most American families, Mexican families tend to stretch out in a network of relatives that often runs to scores of individuals (Harwood & others, 2002).

Chicano The name politically conscious Mexican American adolescents give themselves, reflecting the combination of their Spanish-Mexican-Indian heritage and Anglo influence.

Asian American Adolescents Asian American adolescents are the fastest-growing segment of the American adolescent population, and they, too, show considerable diversity. In the 1970 census, only three Asian American groups were prominent—Japanese, Chinese, and Filipino. But in the last two decades, there has been rapid growth in three other groups—Koreans, Pacific Islanders (Guam and Samoa), and Vietnamese.

Immigrant adolescents of Japanese or Chinese origin can be found in virtually every large city. For many, their grasp of the English language is good and they have been raised in a subculture in which family loyalty and family influence are powerful. This has tended to maintain their separate subcultures. The Japanese American adolescents are somewhat more integrated into the Anglo lifestyle than are the Chinese American adolescents. However, both groups have been very successful in school. They tend to take considerable advantage of educational opportunities.

Asian families and practices, such as high expectations for success, induction of guilt about parental sacrifices and the need to fulfill obligations, parental control of after-school time, and respect for education, are among the reasons identified to explain the high achievement of Asian adolescents (Sue & Okazaki, 1990).

As we saw in chapter 12, "Achievement, Work, and Careers," many Asian adolescents have a very strong motivation for academic success. This motivation has been carried to the United States by Asian immigrants. For example, one study compared the achievement experiences of Asian American and non-Latino White American adolescents (Asakawa & Csikszentmihalyi, 1998). Asian American students saw studying as more connected to their future goals than their non-Latino White American counterparts did.

Native American Adolescents   Approximately 100,000 Native American (American Indian) adolescents are scattered across many tribal groups in about 20 states. About 90 percent are enrolled in school. About 15,000 are in boarding schools, many of which are maintained by the federal government's Bureau of Indian Affairs.

The tapestry of American society is rapidly changing with an increasing number of ethnic minority youth. *What issues are involved in the development of African American, Latino, Asian American, and Native American youth in America?*

Another 45,000 are in public schools on or near Indian reservations. In these schools, Native American adolescents make up more than 50 percent of the students. The remaining 30,000 are in public schools where they are an ethnic minority. A growing proportion of Native American families with adolescents have moved to large cities.

Historically, Native Americans have experienced an inordinate amount of discrimination. While virtually any minority group experiences some discrimination in being a member of a larger, majority-group culture, in the early years of the United States, Native Americans were the victims of terrible physical abuse and punishment. Injustices that the ancestors of these 800,000 individuals experienced are reflected in their having the lowest standard of living, the highest teenage pregnancy rate, the highest suicide rate, and the highest school dropout rate of any ethnic group in the United States (Chandler, 2002; LaFromboise & Low, 1989).

**Latinos
Asian Americans**

The United States and Canada: Nations with Many Cultures

The United States has been and continues to be a great receiver of ethnic groups (Glazer, 1997). It has embraced new ingredients from many cultures. The cultures often collide and cross-pollinate, mixing their ideologies and identities. Some of the culture of origin is retained, some of it lost, some of it mixed with the American culture (Chun, Organista, and Marin, 2003). One after another, immigrants have come to the United States and been exposed to new channels of awareness and, in turn, exposed Americans to new channels of awareness. African American, Latino, Asian American, Native American, and other cultural heritages mix with the mainstream, receiving a new content and giving a new content.

Not only is there considerable diversity in the United States, but the United States' northern American neighbor, Canada, also is a country with diverse ethnic groups. Although Canada shares many similarities with the United States, there are some important differences (Majhanovich, 1998; Siegel & Wiener, 1993). Canada comprises a mixture of cultures that are loosely organized along the lines of economic power. The Canadian cultures include these:

- Native peoples, or First Nations, who were Canada's original inhabitants
- Descendants of French settlers who came to Canada during the seventeenth and eighteenth centuries
- Descendants of British settlers who came to Canada during and after the seventeenth century, or from the United States after the American Revolution in the latter part of the eighteenth century

The late nineteenth century brought three more waves of immigrants:

- From Asia, mainly China, immigrants came to the west coast of Canada in the latter part of the nineteenth and early twentieth centuries.
- From various European countries, immigrants came to central Canada and the prairie provinces.
- From countries in economic and political turmoil (in Latin America, the Caribbean, Asia, Africa, the Indian subcontinent, the former Soviet Union, and the Middle East), immigrants have come to many different parts of Canada.

Canada has two official languages—English and French. Primarily French-speaking individuals reside mainly in the province of Quebec; primarily English-speaking individuals reside mainly in other Canadian provinces. In addition to its English- and French-speaking populations, Canada has a large multicultural community. In three large Canadian cities—Toronto, Montreal, and Vancouver—more than 50 percent of the children and adolescents come from homes in which neither English nor French is the native language (Siegel & Wiener, 1993).

2 Summarize how ethnicity is involved in adolescent development

REVIEW

- How has immigration affected ethnic minority adolescents?
- Why is adolescence a special juncture in the development of ethnic minority individuals?
- What are some important ethnic issues involved in adolescence?
- How can various groups of ethnic minority adolescents be characterized?
- How can the United States and Canada be described in terms of their ethnic makeup?

REFLECT

- No matter how well intentioned adolescents are, their life circumstances likely have given them some prejudices, such as prejudice against people with cultural and ethnic backgrounds different from their own. Psychologist William James once observed that one function of education is to rearrange prejudices. How could adolescents' education rearrange prejudices? In answering this question, you might want to review the discussion of improving interethnic relations in chapter 11, "Schools."

We just described the importance of teasing apart socioeconomic status from ethnicity when examining the influences of ethnicity on adolescent development. Let's now explore socioeconomic status in greater depth.

3 SOCIOECONOMIC STATUS AND POVERTY

What Is Socioeconomic Status?	Socioeconomic Variations in Families, Neighborhoods, and Schools	Poverty

Many subcultures exist within countries. For example, the values and attitudes of adolescents growing up in an urban ghetto or rural Appalachia may differ from those of adolescents growing up in a wealthy suburb. A key difference between such subcultures is socioeconomic status.

What Is Socioeconomic Status?

Earlier in this chapter, we defined *socioeconomic status (SES)* as the grouping of people with similar occupational, educational, and economic characteristics. Socioeconomic status carries with it certain inequalities. Generally, members of a society have (1) occupations that vary in prestige with some individuals having more access than others to higher-status occupations; (2) different levels of educational attainment with some individuals having more access than others to better education; (3) different economic resources; and (4) different levels of power to influence a community's institutions. These differences in the ability to control resources and to participate in society's rewards produce unequal opportunities for adolescents (Bornstein & Bradley, 2003).

The number of visibly different socioeconomic statuses depends on the community's size and complexity. In most investigators' descriptions of SES, two categories, low and middle, are used, although as many as five categories have been delineated. Sometimes low SES is described as low income, working class, or blue collar; sometimes the middle category is described as middle income, managerial, or white collar. Examples of low-SES occupations are factory worker, manual laborer, welfare recipient, and maintenance worker. Examples of middle-SES occupations include salesperson, manager, and professional (doctor, lawyer, teacher, accountant, and so on). Professionals at the pinnacle of their field, high-level corporate executives, political leaders, and wealthy individuals are among those in the upper-SES category.

Socioeconomic Variations in Families, Neighborhoods, and Schools

The families, schools, and neighborhoods of adolescents have socioeconomic characteristics (Bornstein & Bradley, 2003; Leventhal & Brooks-Gunn, 2000, 2003). Some adolescents have parents who have a great deal of money, and who work in prestigious occupations. These adolescents live in attractive houses and neighborhoods, enjoy vacations abroad and at high-quality camps, and attend schools where the mix of students is primarily from middle- and upper-SES backgrounds. Other adolescents have parents who do not have very much money and who work in less prestigious occupations. These adolescents do not live in very attractive houses and neighborhoods, rarely go on vacations, and attend schools where the mix of students is mainly from lower-SES backgrounds. Such variations in neighborhood settings can influence adolescents' adjustment (Blyth, 2000; Booth & Crouter, 2000; Fuligni & Yoshikawa, 2003).

In America and most Western cultures, differences have been found in child rearing among different SES groups (Hoff, Laursen, & Tardif, 2002):

Research on Poverty

- Lower-SES parents (1) are more concerned that their children and adolescents conform to society's expectations, (2) create a home atmosphere in which it is clear that parents have authority over children and adolescents, (3) use physical punishment more in disciplining their children and adolescents, and (4) are more directive and less conversational with their children and adolescents.
- Higher-SES parents (1) are more concerned with developing children's and adolescents' initiative and delay of gratification, (2) create a home atmosphere in which children and adolescents are more nearly equal participants and in which rules are discussed rather than being laid out in an authoritarian manner, (3) are less likely to use physical punishment, and (4) are less directive and more conversational with their children and adolescents.

There also are socioeconomic differences in the way that parents think about education (Hoff, Laursen, & Tardif, 2002; Magnuson & Duncan, 2002). Middle- and upper-income parents more often think of education as something that should be mutually encouraged by parents and teachers. By contrast, low-income parents are more likely to view education as the teacher's job. Thus, increased school-family linkages can especially benefit children and adolescents from low-income families.

SES differences also are involved in an important aspect of adolescents' intellectual orientation. Most school tasks require adolescents to use and process language. As a part of developing language skills, students must learn to read efficiently, write effectively, and give competent oral reports. Although variations exist within SES students, in one study students from low-SES families read less and watched television more than their middle-SES counterparts (see figure 13.2) (Erlick & Starry, 1973).

In one study, SES, parenting, and skill-building activities were examined in divorced families (DeGarmo, Forgatch, & Martinez, 1998). Each of three indicators of SES—education, occupation, and income—were studied independently to determine their effects on achievement in elementary school boys. Each indicator was associated

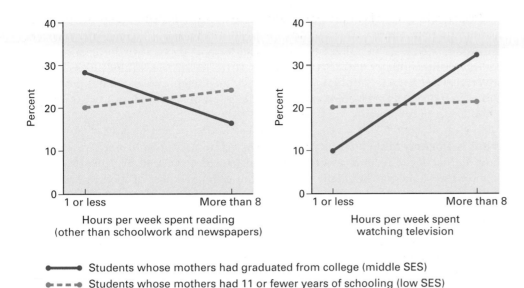

FIGURE 13.2 **The Reading and Television Habits of High School Students from Low- and Middle-SES Families**

with better parenting in the divorced families in the direction expected. Especially noteworthy was the finding that the effects of maternal education on boys' achievement was mediated by skill-building activities in the home that included time spent reading and engaging in other skill-building activities and time not spent watching television.

Like their parents, children and adolescents from low-SES backgrounds are at high risk for experiencing mental health problems (Magnuson & Duncan, 2002; McLoyd, 1998, 2000). Social maladaptation and psychological problems, such as depression, low self-confidence, peer conflict, and juvenile delinquency, are more prevalent among poor adolescents than among economically advantaged adolescents (Gibbs & Huang, 1989). Although psychological problems are more prevalent among adolescents from low-SES backgrounds, these adolescents vary considerably in intellectual and psychological functioning. For example, a sizable portion of adolescents from low-SES backgrounds perform well in school; some perform better than many middle-SES students. When adolescents from low-SES backgrounds are achieving well in school, it is not unusual to find a parent or parents making special sacrifices to provide the necessary living conditions and support to contribute to school success.

In one study, although positive times occurred in the lives of ethnically diverse young adolescents growing up in poverty, many of their negative experiences were worse than those of their middle-SES counterparts (Richards & others, 1994). These adversities involved (1) physical punishment and lack of structure at home, (2) violence in the neighborhood, and (3) domestic violence in their buildings.

In chapter 11, "Schools," we read about schools in low-SES neighborhoods having fewer resources than schools in higher-SES neighborhoods. The schools in the low-SES areas also are more likely to have more students with lower achievement test scores, lower rates of graduation, and smaller percentages of students going to college (Garbarino & Asp, 1981). In some instances, however, federal aid to schools has provided a context for enhanced learning in low-income areas.

Poverty

In a report on the state of America's children and adolescents, the Children's Defense Fund (1992) described what life is like for all too many youth. When sixth-graders in a poverty-stricken area of St. Louis were asked to describe a perfect day, one boy said he would erase the world, then he would sit and think. Asked if he wouldn't rather go outside and play, the boy responded, "Are you kidding, out there?"

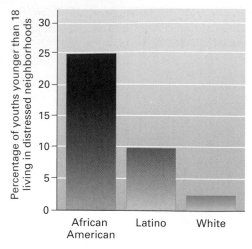

Note: A distressed neighborhood is defined by high levels (at least one standard deviation above the mean) of (1) poverty; (2) female-headed families; (3) high school dropouts; (4) unemployment; and (5) reliance on welfare.

FIGURE 13.3 Living in Distressed Neighborhoods

The world is a dangerous and unwelcoming place for too many of America's youth, especially those whose families, neighborhoods, and schools are low-income (Edelman, 1997). Some adolescents are resilient and cope with the challenges of poverty without major setbacks, but many struggle unsuccessfully. Each child of poverty who reaches adulthood unhealthy, unskilled, or alienated keeps our nation from being as competent and productive as it can be (Children's Defense Fund, 1992).

What Is Poverty Like? Poverty is defined by economic hardship, and its most common marker is the federal poverty threshold (Huston, McLoyd, & Coll, 1994). The poverty threshold was originally based on the estimated cost of food (a basic diet) multiplied by 3. This federal poverty marker is adjusted annually for family size and inflation.

Based on the U.S. government's criteria for poverty, the proportion of children under the age of 18 living in families below the poverty threshold has increased from approximately 15 percent in the 1970s to 17 percent in the late 1990s (National Center for Health Statistics, 2001).

The U.S. figure of 17 percent of adolescents living in poverty is much higher than other industrialized nations. For example, Canada has a child/youth poverty rate of 9 percent, and Sweden has a rate of 2 percent. Poverty in the United States has demarcated along ethnic lines. Almost 40 percent of African American and Latino adolescents live in poverty (National Center for Health Statistics, 2001). Compared with White adolescents, ethnic minority adolescents are more likely to experience persistent poverty over many years and live in isolated poor neighborhoods where social supports are minimal and threats to positive development are abundant (Jarrett, 1995) (see figure 13.3).

Why is poverty among American youth so high? Three reasons are apparent (Huston, McLoyd, & Coll, 1994): (1) Economic changes have eliminated many blue-collar jobs that paid reasonably well, (2) the percentage of youth living in single-parent families headed by the mother has increased, and (3) government benefits were reduced during the 1970s and 1980s.

Poor children and their families are often exposed to poor health conditions, inadequate housing and homelessness, environmental toxins, and violent or unsupportive neighborhoods (Bolland, 2003). Unemployment, unstable work history, and income loss may, but do not always, push families into poverty. Unlike income loss or unemployment due to job loss, poverty is not a homogeneous variable or distinct event.

Let's further consider some of the psychological ramifications of living in poverty. First, the poor are often powerless. In occupations, they are rarely the decision makers. Rules are handed down to them in an authoritarian manner. Second, the poor are often vulnerable to disaster. They are not likely to be given notice when they are laid off from work and usually do not have financial resources to fall back on when problems arise. Third, their range of alternatives is often restricted. Only a limited number of jobs are open to them. Even when alternatives are available, the poor might not know about them or be prepared to make a wise decision, because of inadequate education and inability to read well. Fourth, being poor means having less prestige. This lack of prestige is transmitted to children early in their lives. Children in poverty might observe, for example, that many other children are treated more positively than they are and surmise that this is because they wear nicer clothes and live in more attractive houses.

When poverty is persistent and long-standing, it can have especially damaging effects on children. In one study, the longer children lived in families with income below the poverty line, the lower was the quality of their home environments (Garrett, Ng'andu, & Ferron, 1994). Also in this study, improvements in family income had their strongest effects on the home environments of chronically poor children. In another study, children in families experiencing both persistent and occasional poverty had lower IQs and more internalized behavior problems than never-poor children, but persistent poverty had a much stronger negative effect on these outcomes than occasional poverty did (Duncan, Brooks-Gunn, & Klebanov, 1994).

A special concern is the high percentage of single mothers, more than one-third of whom are in poverty, compared with only 10 percent of single fathers. Vonnie McLoyd (1998, 2000) concludes that because poor, single mothers are more distressed than their middle-class counterparts are, they often show low support, nurturance, and involvement with their children. Among the reasons for the high poverty rate of single mothers are women's low pay, infrequent awarding of alimony payments, and poorly enforced child support by fathers (Graham & Beller, 2002). The term **feminization of poverty** refers to the fact that far more women than men live in poverty. Women's low income, divorce, and the resolution of divorce cases by the judicial system, which leaves women with less money than they and their children need to adequately function, are the likely causes of the feminization of poverty.

Antipoverty Programs   One recent trend in antipoverty programs is to conduct two-generation interventions (McLoyd, 1998). This involves providing both services for children (such as educational day care or preschool education) and services for parents (such as adult education, literacy training, and job skill training). Recent evaluations of the two-generation programs suggest that they have more positive effects on parents than they do on children (St. Pierre, Layzer, & Barnes, 1996). Also discouraging, regarding children, is the finding that when the two-generational programs show benefits, they are more likely to be in health benefits than in cognitive gains.

A downward trajectory is not inevitable for youth living in poverty (Carnegie Council on Adolescent Development, 1995). One potential positive path for such youth is to become involved with a caring mentor. The Quantum Opportunities Program, funded by the Ford Foundation, was a four-year, year-round mentoring effort. The students were entering the ninth grade at a high school with high rates of poverty, were minorities, and came from families that received public assistance. Each day for four years, mentors provided sustained support, guidance, and concrete assistance to their students.

The Quantum program required students to participate in (1) academic-related activities outside school hours, including reading, writing, math, science, and social studies, peer tutoring, and computer skills training; (2) community service projects, including tutoring elementary school students, cleaning up the neighborhood, and volunteering in hospitals, nursing homes, and libraries; and (3) cultural enrichment and personal development activities, including life skills training, and college and job planning. In exchange for their commitment to the program, students were offered financial incentives that encouraged participation, completion, and long-range planning. A stipend of $1.33 was given to students for each hour they participated in these activities. For every 100 hours of education, service, or development activities, students received a bonus of $100. The average cost per participant was $10,600 for the four years, which is one-half the cost of one year in prison.

An evaluation of the Quantum project compared the mentored students with a nonmentored control group. Sixty-three percent of the mentored students graduated from high school but only 42 percent of the control group did; 42 percent of the

Through the Eyes of Adolescents

Being Poor Was Awful

"Kids were mean there, not physically, but with their words, 'Who does your shopping for you? You've *never* been to the Calhoun Club? *Where* do you get your clothes from? You mean you *haven't* been out of the U.S.? You *rent* your home? You mean you don't get an *allowance?*' I couldn't have what they had or really understand the importance of it all, and I felt it acutely. There were the times when I would be talking with someone, and instead of listening to whatever it was I was saying, they'd be staring at my clothes.

". . . Being poor was awful, the bills were too many and too much. It didn't help me in dealing with the daily questionings or scornful looks from my peers. When they did that, I just looked away or down, shoulders slumped, because I felt self-conscious."
—*Native American Adolescent Girl*

feminization of poverty The fact that far more women than men live in poverty. Women's low income, divorce, and the resolution of divorce cases by the judicial system, which leaves women with less money than they and their children need to adequately function, are the likely causes.

These adolescents participate in the programs of El Puente, located in a predominantly low-SES Latino neighborhood in Brooklyn, New York. The El Puente program stresses five areas of youth development: health, education, achievement, personal growth, and social growth.

mentored students are currently enrolled in college but only 16 percent of the control group are. Furthermore, control-group students were twice as likely as the mentored students to receive food stamps or welfare, and they had more arrests. Such programs clearly have the potential to overcome the intergenerational transmission of poverty and its negative outcomes.

Another effort to improve the lives of adolescents living in poverty is the El Puente program, which is primarily aimed at Latino adolescents living in low-SES areas. El Puente ("the bridge") was opened in New York City in 1983 because of community dissatisfaction with the health, education, and social services youth were receiving (Simons, Finlay, & Yang, 1991). El Puente emphasizes five areas of youth development: health, education, achievement, personal growth, and social growth.

El Puente is located in a former Roman Catholic church on the south side of Williamsburg in Brooklyn, a neighborhood made up primarily of low-income Latino families, many of which are far below the poverty line. Sixty-five percent of the residents receive some form of public assistance. The neighborhood has the highest school dropout rate for Latinos in New York City and the highest felony rate for adolescents in Brooklyn.

When the youths, aged 12 through 21, first enroll in El Puente, they meet with counselors and develop a four-month plan that includes the programs they are interested in joining. At the end of four months, youth and staff develop a plan for continued participation. Twenty-six bilingual classes are offered in such subjects as music, theater, photography, and dance. In addition, a medical and fitness center, GED night school, and mental health and social services centers are also a part of El Puente.

El Puente is funded through state, city, and private organizations and serves about 300 youth. The program has been replicated in Chelsea and Holyoke, Massachusetts, and two other sites in New York are being developed.

Review and reflect Learning goal 3

3 Describe how socioeconomic status and poverty are related to adolescent development

REVIEW

- What is socioeconomic status?
- How is poverty related to adolescent development?
- What are some socioeconomic variations in families, neighborhoods, and schools?

REFLECT

- What was the socioeconomic status of your family as you were growing up? How did it impact your development?

So far in this chapter, we have examined the role of culture and cross-cultural comparisons of adolescents, ethnicity, and socioeconomic status. In the next section, you will see that there are substantial variations across countries, ethnic groups, and socioeconomic groups in the use of media and technology.

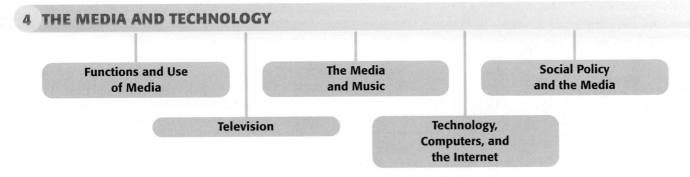

4 THE MEDIA AND TECHNOLOGY

Functions and Use of Media

The Media and Music

Social Policy and the Media

Television

Technology, Computers, and the Internet

Few developments in society over the last 40 years have had a greater impact on adolescents than television (Calvert, 1999; Roberts, Henriksen, & Foehr, 2004; Strasburger & Wilson, 2002). The persuasion capabilities of television are staggering. Many of today's adolescents have spent more time since infancy in front of a television set than with their parents or in the classroom. In addition to television, radio, CDs, and music video are other media that are especially important influences in the lives of many adolescents.

Functions and Use of Media

The functions of media for adolescents include these (Arnett, 1991):

1. *Entertainment.* Adolescents, like adults, often use media simply for entertainment and an enjoyable diversion from everyday concerns.
2. *Information.* Adolescents use media to obtain information, especially about topics that their parents may be reluctant to discuss in the home, such as sexuality.
3. *Sensation.* Adolescents tend to be higher in sensation seeking than adults are; certain media provide intense and novel stimulation that appeals to adolescents.
4. *Coping.* Adolescents use media to relieve anxiety and unhappiness. Two of the most frequently endorsed coping responses of adolescents are "listen to music" and "watch TV."
5. *Gender-role modeling.* Media present models of female and male gender roles; these media images of females and males can influence adolescents' gender attitudes and behavior.
6. *Youth culture identification.* Media use gives many adolescents a sense of being connected to a larger peer network and culture, which is united by the kinds of values and interests conveyed through adolescent-oriented media.

If the amount of time spent in an activity is any indication of its importance, then there is no doubt that the mass media play important roles in adolescents' lives. A national study took an in-depth look at the media habits of children and adolescents (Roberts & others, 1999). Surveying more than 3,000 children and adolescents from 2 through 18 years of age, the study confirmed that youth today are surrounded by the media. The average adolescent in the United States lives in a home that has three TVs, three tape players, three radios, two VCRs, two CD players, one video game player, and one computer. The survey found that the bedrooms of adolescents are inundated with media. Two-thirds of 8- to 18-year-olds in the United States had a television and about one-fifth had a computer there.

In terms of exposure, the average 8- to 18-year-old in the United States spends more than 7 hours a day—more than 49 hours a week—using media (Roberts & Foehr, 2003). Yet, despite all of the newly developed technologies available, the most time is spent watching television except for 15- to 18-year-olds' use of audio media

	Age group		
	8–10 years	11–14 years	15–18 years
Television	3:19	3:30	2:23
Videos (rented & self-recorded)	:46	:43	:37
Movies in theaters	:26	:19	:09
Audio media (radios, CDs, tapes)	:55	1:43	2:38
Print media	:54	:42	:37
Videogames	:31	:26	:21
Computer	:23	:31	:26
Total leisure media	7:13	7:55	7:11

FIGURE 13.4 Average Daily Adolescent Leisure-time Media Use by Age

Note: Entries are means for daily time use.

(radio, tapes, CDs) (Roberts & Foehr, 2003) (see figure 13.4). However, later in our discussion, you will see that adolescents are rapidly increasing the amount of time they spend online.

In the national survey just described, the average 2- to 18-year-old watched television for 2 hours and 46 minutes per day. Other surveys have found that adolescents watch television for 1½ to 3 hours a day (Kaiser Family Foundation, 2002a; Larson & Verma, 1999). Somewhat similar numbers of hours spent in TV watching by adolescents have been found in European and East Asian adolescents (Larson, 2001).

Television viewing often peaks in early adolescence and then begins to decline at some point in late adolescence in response to competing media and the demands of school and social activities (Huston & Alvarez, 1990; Roberts, Henriksen, & Foehr, 2004). As television viewing declines, the use of music media—radio, CDs, tapes, and music video—increases dramatically. In a recent national survey, music exposure increased from less than 1 hour per day among 8- to 10-year-olds to more than 2½ hours daily by late adolescence (Roberts & Foehr, 2003) (see figure 13.4). As adolescents get older, movie attendance increases—more than 50 percent of 12- to 17-year-olds report at least monthly attendance.

U.S. adolescents also use the print media more than children do (Anderson & others, 2001). Newspaper reading often begins at about 11 to 12 years of age and gradually increases until 60 to 80 percent of late adolescents report at least some newspaper reading. In similar fashion, magazine and book reading gradually increase during adolescence. Approximately one-third of high school juniors and seniors say that they read magazines daily, while 20 percent say that they read nonschool books daily, reports that are substantiated by the sales of teen-oriented books and magazines. However, comic book reading declines steeply between the ages of 10 and 18.

Large, individual differences characterize all forms of adolescent media use. In addition to the age differences just described, gender, ethnicity, socioeconomic status, and intelligence are all related to which media are used, to what extent, and for what purposes. For example, a national survey found that 8- to 18-year-old boys spend more time watching television than girls do but girls spent considerably more time listening to music (Roberts & Foehr, 2003). Boys use computers and video games more than girls (Roberts & others, 1999).

African American and Latino adolescents spend significantly more time using media—especially television—than non-Latino White children do (Roberts, Henriksen, & Foehr, 2004; Roberts & others, 1999). Media exposure among African American 8- to 18-year-olds averages just over 9 hours daily, among Latino youths more than 8 hours, and among non-Latino White youth about 7 hours (Roberts, Henriksen, & Foehr, 2004). Brighter adolescents and adolescents from middle-SES families are more likely to read the newspaper and news magazines, and also are more likely to watch television news, than are less intelligent adolescents and adolescents from low-income backgrounds (Chafee & Yang, 1990).

In sum, as youth progress through adolescence, television viewing decreases, music listening and computer use increase, and media use is more likely to take place in adolescents' bedrooms (Roberts, Henriksen, & Foehr, 2004). As adolescents become older, they are more likely to use media alone or with friends or siblings, indicating increasing independence from parents and the importance of peers.

Television

The messages of television are powerful. What are those messages? What are television's functions? How extensively does television affect adolescents? What is MTV's role in adolescents' lives?

Television's Functions   Television has been called a lot of things, not all of them good. Depending on one's point of view, it is a "window to the world," the "one-eyed monster," the "boob tube," or a "vast wasteland." Scores on national achievement tests in reading and mathematics, while showing a small improvement recently, have generally been lower than in the past decades—and television has been attacked as one of the reasons. Television may take adolescents away from the printed media and books. One study found that children who read books and the printed media watched television less than those who did not (Huston, Siegle, & Bremer, 1983). It is argued that television trains individuals to become passive learners. Rarely, if ever, does television require active responses from the observer. Heavy television use may produce not only a passive learner, but a passive lifestyle. In one investigation of 406 adolescent males, those who watched little television were more physically fit and physically active than those who watched a lot (Tucker, 1987). In a recent study, heavy TV viewing was correlated with obesity in adolescent girls (Anderson & others, 2001).

Television also can deceive. It can teach adolescents that problems are easily resolved and that everything turns out all right in the end. For example, it takes only about 30 to 60 minutes for detectives to sort through a complex array of clues and discover the killer—and they always find the killer. Violence is pictured as a way of life in many shows, and police are shown to use violence and break moral codes in their fight against evildoers. The lasting results of violence are rarely brought home to the viewer. An individual who is injured in a TV show suffers for only a few seconds. In real life, the individual might take months or even years to recover, or perhaps remain permanently disabled.

A special concern is how ethnic minority groups are portrayed on television. Ethnic minorities have historically been underrepresented and misrepresented on television (Schiff & Truglio, 1995; Williams & Cox, 1995). Ethnic minority characters—whether African American, Asian, Latino, or Native American—have often been presented as more stereotyped, less dignified, and less positive than White characters.

But there are some positive aspects to television's influence on adolescents (Clifford, Gunter, & McAleer, 1995; Fisch, 2004). For one thing, television presents adolescents with a world that is different from the one in which they live. This means that, through television, adolescents are exposed to a wider variety of views and knowledge than when they are informed only by their parents, teachers, and peers. Before television's advent, adolescents' identification models came in the form of parents, relatives, older siblings, and neighborhood peers, as well as more distant famous individuals heard about in conversation or on the radio and read about in newspapers or magazines, and the film stars seen in movies. Because many of these identification figures were family or peers, adolescents learned attitudes, clothing styles, and occupational objectives that were relatively homogeneous. The imagery and pervasiveness of television have exposed children and adolescents to hundreds of different neighborhoods, cultures, clothing fashions, career possibilities, and patterns of intimate relationships.

Television and Violence   How strongly does televised violence influence a person's behavior? In one longitudinal study, the amount of violence viewed on television at age 8 was significantly related to the seriousness of criminal acts performed as an adult (Huesmann, 1986). In a second longitudinal study, childhood exposure to TV violence was linked with aggressive behavior on the part of young adult males and females (Huesmann & others, 2003). In another investigation, long-term exposure to television violence was significantly related to the likelihood of aggression in 1,565 12- to 17-year-old boys (Belson, 1978). Boys who watched the most aggression on television were the most likely to commit a violent crime, swear, be aggressive in sports, threaten violence toward another boy, write graffiti, or break windows.

These investigations are *correlational*, so we cannot conclude from them that television violence causes individuals to be more aggressive, only that watching television

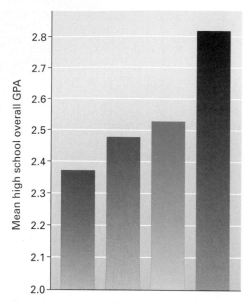

FIGURE 13.5 Educational TV Viewing in Early Childhood and High School Grade Point Average for Boys

When boys watched more educational television (especially *Sesame Street*) as preschoolers, they had higher grade point averages in high school. The graph displays the boys' early TV viewing patterns in quartiles and the means of their grade point averages. The bar on the left is for the lowest 25 percent of boys who viewed educational TV programs, the next bar the next 25 percent, and so on, with the bar on the right for the 25 percent of the boys who watched the most educational TV shows as preschoolers.

**Exploring Television Violence
Children, Youth, Media, and Violence**

violence is *associated with* aggressive behavior. However, experimental research does provide evidence that viewing television violence can increase aggression. In one experiment, children were randomly assigned to one of two groups: One group watched shows taken directly from violent Saturday morning cartoon offerings on 11 different days; the second group watched cartoon shows with all of the violence removed (Steur, Applefield, & Smith, 1971). The children then were observed during play. The children who saw the TV cartoon violence kicked, choked, and pushed their playmates more than the children who watched nonviolent TV cartoon shows did. Because the children were assigned randomly to the two conditions (TV cartoons with violence versus TV cartoons with no violence), we can conclude that exposure to TV violence caused the increased aggression in this study.

In an extensive study of television violence, a number of conclusions were reached (Federman, 1997). Television violence can have at least three types of harmful effects on viewers: A viewer can learn aggressive attitudes and behaviors from watching television violence, become sensitized to the seriousness of the violence, and feel frightened of becoming a victim of real-life violence. The effects are more likely to occur in certain types of violent portrayals. Contextual features of television violence like an attractive perpetrator, justification for violence, and violence that goes unpunished can increase the risk of harmful effects. Other features, such as showing the harmful consequences, may reduce the likelihood of violence.

An example of a high-risk portrayal of violence on television involves a hostile motorcycle gang that terrorizes a neighborhood. In their harassment, they kidnap a well-known rock singer. A former boyfriend of the singer then tries to rescue her. He sneaks up on the gang and shoots six of them, one at a time. Some of the gunfire causes the motorcycles to blow up. The scene ends with the former boyfriend rescuing the singer.

This violence contains all of the features that encourage aggression in adolescents. The ex-boyfriend, one of the perpetrators of violence, is young and good looking and cast as a rugged hero. His attack on the gang is depicted as justified—the gang members are ruthless and uncontrollable and have kidnapped an innocent, beautiful woman. This "hero" is never punished or disciplined even though it appears that he has taken the law into his own hands. As the ultimate reward, the young woman proclaims her love for him after he rescues her. Also, in spite of the extensive violence in this movie, no one is shown as being seriously hurt. The focus quickly shifts away from the gang members after they have been shot, so we don't see them suffer or die.

The television that young children watch may influence their behavior as adolescents. If so, then this supports the continuity view of adolescence discussed in chapter 1. In one recently completed longitudinal study, girls who were more frequent preschool viewers of violent TV programs had lower grades than those who were infrequent viewers of such violence in preschool (Anderson & others, 2001). Also, viewing educational TV programs as preschoolers was associated with higher grades, reading more books, and less aggression, especially for boys, in adolescence (see figure 13.5).

In addition to television violence, there is increased concern about adolescents who play violent video games, especially those that are highly realistic (Anderson, 2003). Electronic games share some characteristics with other forms of audiovisual violence but differ from them in several important ways (Roberts, Henriksen, & Foehr, 2004). One difference is the electronic games' ability to immerse adolescents so deeply that they experience an altered state of consciousness in which rational thought is suspended and arousing aggressive scripts are learned. Another difference is the direct rewards that game players receive ("winning points") for their actions.

Correlational studies indicate that adolescents who extensively play violent electronic games are more aggressive than their counterparts who spend less time playing the games or do not play them at all (Cohen, 1995). Surveys have found that adolescents who frequently play violent electronic games are more likely to engage in delinquent behavior and are rated as more aggressive by their teachers than adolescents who are infrequent players (Anderson & Dill, 2000; Fling & others, 1992). One study also found that college males who spent the most time playing violent video games were more likely than other college students to acknowledge having hit or attacked someone else (Anderson & Dill, 2000). Experiments have not yet been conducted to demonstrate increased aggression subsequent to playing violent video games, although a recent analysis of research studies concluded that playing violent video games is linked to aggression in both males and females (Anderson & Bushman, 2001).

Television and Sex   Adolescents, not unlike adults, like to watch television programs with sexual content. In one study, the four TV programs preferred most by adolescents were the ones with the highest percentage of interactions containing sexual messages (Ward, 1995). Watching television sex can influence adolescents' sexual attitudes and behavior. One experiment found that 13- to 14-year-old boys and girls who watched 15 hours of prime-time TV shows that included sexual relations between unmarried partners rated sexual indiscretions as less objectionable than their counterparts who viewed sexual relations between married partners or saw nonsexual relationships (Bryant & Rockwell, 1994). Researchers also have shown that exposure to sexual content is related to more permissive attitudes about premarital and recreational sex (Ward, 2002).

These studies, along with a number of others, lead to the conclusion that television teaches children and adolescents about sex (Bence, 1991; Caruthers & Ward, 2002; Ward, Gorvine, & Cytron, 2002). One recent national study surveyed 15- to 17-year-olds in the United States and found that almost 3 of 4 believed that sexual content on TV influences adolescents their age "somewhat" (40 percent) or "a lot" (32 percent) (Kaiser Family Foundation, 2002b). On the positive side, in this survey, many adolescents said that they have learned something positive from sexual scenes on TV, such as how to say no to a sexual situation that makes them uncomfortable (60 percent) and how to talk with a partner about safer sex (43 percent). Nonetheless, the overall conclusion about adolescent exposure to sex in the entertainment media is very negative. One recent review concluded that, overall, evidence indicates that frequent and involved exposure to sexually oriented media such as soap operas and music videos is linked to adolescents' greater acceptance of stereotypical and casual attitudes about sex, as well as higher expectations about the prevalence of sexual activity and in some cases greater sexual experience (Ward, 2003).

In recent years, sexual content on television has increased and become more explicit. The consistent sexual messages adolescents learn from television's content are that sexual behaviors usually occur between unmarried couples, that contraception is rarely discussed, and that the negative consequences of sexuality (such as an unwanted pregnancy and sexually transmitted diseases) are rarely shown (Greenberg & others, 1986).

A special concern about adolescents and television sex is that while parents and teachers often feel comfortable discussing occupational and educational choices, independence, and consumer behavior with adolescents, they usually don't feel comfortable discussing sex with them (Roberts, 1993). The resulting absence of competing information (peers do talk about sex but often perpetuate misinformation) intensifies television's role in imparting information about sex. Nonetheless, as with television aggression, whether television sex influences the behavior of adolescents depends on a number of factors, including the adolescent's needs, interests, concerns, and maturity (Strasburger & Donnerstein, 1999).

How might playing violent video games be linked to adolescent aggression?

FIGURE 13.6 Percentage of Substance-Abuse References in Different Types of Music

Note: Based on 212 rap songs, 211 alternative rock songs, 212 hot-100 songs, 211 heavy metal songs, and 212 country-western songs popular in 1996–1997.

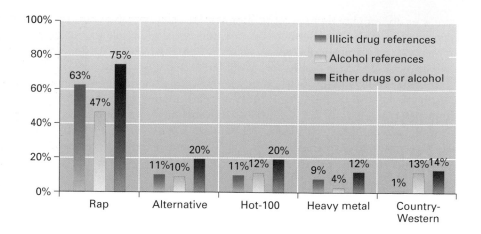

The Media and Music

Anyone who has been around adolescents very long knows that many of them spend huge amounts of time listening to music on the radio, playing CDs or tapes of their favorite music, and watching music videos on television. Approximately two-thirds of all records and tapes are purchased by the 10- to 24-year-old age group. And one-third of the nation's 8,200 radio stations aim their broadcast rock music at adolescent listeners.

Music tastes become more specific and differentiated from the beginning to the end of adolescence (Christenson & Roberts, 1991). In early adolescence, individuals often prefer middle-of-the-road, top 40 rock music. By high school, however, adolescents frequently identify with much narrower music types, such as heavy metal, new wave, rap, and so on. Boys typically prefer "harder" forms of rock, girls softer, more romantic forms of "pop."

Rap music has its roots in the Black culture and is characterized by talking to a musical beat. At times, it is angry and violent (as in "gangsta rap"). Rap lyrics, as well as heavy metal lyrics, are controversial (Strasburger & Wilson, 2002). Figure 13.6 shows that compared with other types of music, rap music contains more illicit drug and alcohol references (Roberts, Henriksen, & Christenson, 1999).

Music meets a number of personal and social needs for adolescents (Strasburger & Wilson, 2002). The most important personal needs are mood control and silence filling. Popular music's social functions range from providing a party atmosphere to expressing rebellion against authority. However, the latter function is not as common as popular stereotypes suggest. Somewhat surprisingly, relatively few adolescents say that popular music lyrics are very important to them. Few use music "to learn about the world," although African American adolescents are more likely than their White counterparts to say popular music fulfills this function for them.

The music adolescents enjoy on records, tapes, radio, and television is an important dimension of their culture. Rock music does not seem to be a passing fad, having been part of U.S. culture since the mid-1950s. However, it has had its share of controversy, almost continuously since its inception. Starting in 1983, MTV (the first music video television channel) and music videos in general were targets of debate in the media. About a year later, rock music lyrics were attacked by the Parents Music Resource Center (PMRC). This group charged in a congressional hearing that rock music lyrics were dangerously shaping the minds of adolescents in the areas of sexual morality, violence, drugs, and satanism. The national Parent Teacher Association agreed. And Tipper Gore (1987), a PMRC founder, voiced her views about the dangers of rock music lyrics in a book.

Connections have been found between a preference for heavy metal music and reckless or antisocial behavior. For example, researchers have found that heavy metal

© Zits Partnership. Reprinted with special permission of King Features Syndicate.

music is more popular among antisocial youth than among the general population (Wass, Miller, & Redditt, 1991). In one study, male fans of heavy metal music were more likely to engage in reckless driving and casual sex and to use drugs than were males who were not fans of heavy metal music (Arnett, 1991). In this same study, female heavy metal fans were more likely to engage in unprotected sex, marijuana use, shoplifting, and vandalism than were females who were not fans of heavy metal. In yet another study, heavy metal music was more popular among adolescents who used drugs than among those who did not (King, 1988). However, these studies are correlational in nature, so we cannot conclude that the music causes problem behaviors in adolescents—it is only related to the problem behaviors. That is, young people with particular views are attracted to a particular kind of music, such as punk. At the same time, it may be these particular young people who pay attention to, comprehend, and are vulnerable to the lyrics' influence.

One of the most frightening claims made by detractors of heavy metal music is that the music causes adolescents to attempt or commit suicide. This was exemplified in highly publicized cases in which parents charged that songs by Judas Priest and Ozzy Osbourne were related to their adolescents' suicides. However, no research data to date link depression or suicide to heavy metal or rap music.

Motivation, experience, and knowledge are factors in the interpretation of lyrics. In one investigation, preadolescents and adolescents often missed sexual themes in lyrics (Prinsky & Rosenbaum, 1987). Adult organizations such as the PMRC interpret rock music lyrics in terms of sex, violence, drugs, and satanism more than adolescents themselves do. In this investigation, it was found that, in contrast to these adult groups, adolescents interpreted their favorite songs in terms of love, friendship, growing up, life's struggles, having fun, cars, religion, and other topics in teenage life.

Despite rock 'n' roll now being middle-aged and with MTV turning 21 in 2001, research on popular music and music videos is in its infancy (Strasburger & Wilson, 2002). Little attention has been given to how the popular media might be used to provide prosocial or health-related messages for youth. To date, no cause-and-effect studies exist to link either music or videos to an increased risk of early drug use in adolescence (Strasburger & Wilson, 2002). For a small percentage of adolescents, certain music may provide a behavioral marker for psychological problems, although the precise connection between "which music" and "which adolescents" is not yet known.

Technology, Computers, and the Internet

Culture involves change, and nowhere is that change greater than in the technological revolution today's adolescents are experiencing with increased use of computers

Tips for Using the Internet
Webliography
Internet Pals
Critical Analysis of the Internet

Send e-mail	94%
Research schoolwork	94%
Get info on movies, music, or TV	85%
Play games	81%
Download music	80%
Get news	78%
Participate in chat room	71%
Check sports scores	50%
Buy something	36%

FIGURE 13.7 Percentage of U.S. 15- to 17-Year-Olds Engaging in Different Online Activities

Note: Study conducted by telephone Fall 2001, with a national random sample of 398 15- to 17-year-olds

Internet The core of computer-mediated communication. The Internet system is worldwide and connects thousands of computer networks, providing an incredible array of information adolescents can access.

and the Internet (Mortimer & Larson, 2002). If adolescents are to be adequately prepared for tomorrow's jobs, technology needs to become an integral part of their lives (Bereiter, 2002; Sharp, 1999). In a poll of seventh- to twelfth-graders jointly conducted by CNN and the National Science Foundation (1997), 82 percent predicted that they would not be able to make a good living unless they have computer skills and understand other technology, indicating a healthy awareness that the technology revolution is part of the information society in which we now live.

The increasing importance of computers in adolescents' lives was underscored in a national survey (Roberts & others, 1999). When forced to choose which medium to bring to a desert island, 33 percent of 8- to 18-year-olds selected a computer with Internet access, 24 percent CDs, tapes, or radio, and only 13 percent said a television.

Today's adolescents are using computers to communicate the way their parents used pens, postage stamps, and telephones. The new information society still relies on some basic nontechnological competencies that adolescents need to develop: good communication skills, the ability to solve problems, thinking deeply, thinking creatively, and having positive attitudes. However, how young people pursue these competencies is being challenged and extended in ways and at a speed unknown to previous generations.

The Internet The **Internet** is the core of computer-mediated communication. The Internet system is worldwide and connects millions of computer networks, providing an incredible array of information adolescents can access (Donnerstein, 2002). Because of its fluid capabilities, the Internet has more current, up-to-date information than books.

Youth throughout the world are increasingly using the Internet, despite substantial variation in use in different countries around the world and in socioeconomic groups. Between 1998 and 2001, the percentage of U.S. 14- to 17-year-olds using the Internet increased from 51 percent to 75 percent and the percentage of U.S. 10- to 13-year-olds increased from 39 percent to 65 percent (Kaiser Family Foundation, 2002a). Most U.S. adolescents say that they teach themselves how to use the Internet (40 percent), while others learn from their parents (30 percent), friends (23 percent), and siblings (10 percent) (Kaiser Family Foundation, 2002a). Only 5 percent said they learned how to use the Internet at school. Studies have found that almost 50 percent of adolescents go online every day (Kaiser Family Foundation, 2001). Among 15- to 17-year-olds, one-third use the Internet for 6 hours a week or more, 24 percent use it for 3 to 5 hours a week, and 20 percent use it for 1 hour a week or less (Woodard, 2000).

What do adolescents do when they are online? As shown in figure 13.7, e-mail is the most frequent activity they engage in, and more than 70 percent of the adolescents who go online connect with a chat room (Kaiser Family Foundation, 2001).

E-mail (electronic mail) is another valuable way that the Internet can be used. Messages can be sent to and received from individuals as well as large numbers of people.

Special concerns have emerged about children's and adolescents' access to information on the Internet, which has been largely unregulated. Adolescents can access adult sexual material, instructions for making bombs, and other information that is inappropriate for them. Information on the Internet is not well organized or regulated, indicating a critical need for adolescents to develop the navigational and evaluative skills to sort through complex information.

With as many as 11 million American adolescents now online, more and more of adolescent life is taking place in a landscape that is inaccessible to many parents (Roberts, 2003). Popular music's social functions range from providing a party atmosphere to expressing rebellion against authority. However, the latter function is not as common as popular stereotypes suggest. Many adolescents have a computer in their bedroom, and most parents don't have any idea what information their adolescents are obtaining online. Some psychologists recommend putting the computer in the family room, where adults and adolescents have more opportunities to discuss what information is being accessed online. Every Web browser records what sites users visit. With very rudimentary computer know-how, parents can monitor their adolescents' computer activities.

In one study, about half of parents said that being online is more enjoyable than watching TV for adolescents (Tarpley, 2001). However, an analysis of content suggests they might be wise to be more concerned about their adolescents' use of the Internet (Donnerstein, 2002; Tarpley, 2001):

- Of the 1,000 most visited sites, 10 percent are adult sex oriented.
- Forty-four percent of adolescents have viewed an adult Internet site.
- Twenty-five percent of adolescents have visited an Internet site that promotes hate groups.
- Twelve percent have visited an Internet site where they can obtain information about how to purchase a gun.

In sum, the Internet holds a great deal of potential for increasing adolescents' educational opportunities. However, the Internet also has limitations and dangers. The Internet is a technology that needs parents to monitor and regulate adolescents' use of it (Donnerstein, 2002).

Technology and Sociocultural Diversity   Technology brings with it certain social issues. A special concern is whether increased use of technology (especially computers) in homes and schools will widen the learning gap between rich and poor and male and female students (Kaiser Family Foundation, 2002a; Roblyer & Edwards, 2000). One national survey found that children and adolescents who go to school in lower-income communities spend more time with most types of media than their counterparts in wealthier neighborhoods, but they were significantly less likely to use computers (Roberts & others, 1999) (see figure 13.8). There are gaps in computer availability across ethnic groups as well. A recent study found that approximately half of all African American and Latino adolescents do not use the Internet, compared with just one-fifth of non-Latino White or Asian American adolescents (U.S. Department of Commerce, 2002).

Technology and Education   The number of computers in schools has increased dramatically. Yet despite the potential of computers to improve student learning, schools continue to lag behind other segments of society, such as businesses, in the use of technology. Computers are still used too often for drill-and-practice activities rather than constructive learning.

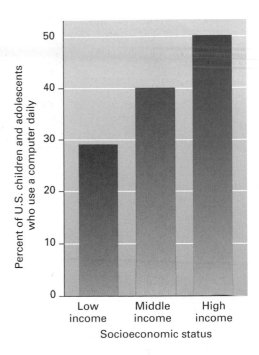

FIGURE 13.8 Daily Computer Use by Children and Adolescents in Different Socioeconomic Groups

Technology and Education
Educational Technology Journal
Critical Issues in Technology and Education
Technology Standards in Education
Mediascope

e-mail Electronic mail, a valuable way the Internet can be used. Messages can be sent to and received by individuals as well as large numbers of people.

"I see what's wrong with your calculator—it's the remote control to your T.V."

John Shanks/*Phi Delta Kappan,* June 1997. Reprinted with permission.

Many teachers do not have adequate training in using computers, and school districts have been slow to provide much-needed technology workshops. Also, with rapidly changing technology, the computers that many schools purchase quickly become outdated. Other computers break and sit in need of repair.

Such realities mean that in most schools, learning has not yet been technologically revolutionized. Only when schools have technologically trained teachers and current, workable technologies will classrooms have the opportunity to be truly transformed by the technology revolution (Newby & others, 2000). National Educational Technology Standards (NETS) are being established by the International Society for Technology in Education (2000, 2001).

It is important to keep in mind that technology itself does not improve an adolescent's ability to learn (Male, 2003). Several essential conditions are necessary to create learning environments that adequately support students' learning. These include vision and support from educational leaders, educators who are skilled in the use of technology for learning, access to contemporary technologies, and an emphasis on the adolescent as an active, constructivist learner.

Social Policy and the Media

Adolescents are exposed to an expanding array of media that carry messages that shape adolescents' judgments and behavior (Nichols & Good, 2004). The social policy initiatives listed here were recommended by the Carnegie Council on Adolescent Development (1995):

- *Encourage socially responsible programming.* There is good evidence of a link between media violence and adolescent aggression. The media also shape many other dimensions of adolescents' development—gender, ethnic, and occupational roles, as well as standards of beauty, family life, and sexuality. Writers, producers, and media executives need to recognize how powerful their messages are to adolescents and work with experts on adolescent development to provide more positive images to youth.
- *Support public efforts to make the media more adolescent friendly.* Essentially, the U.S. media regulate themselves in regard to their influence on adolescents. All other Western nations have stronger regulations than the United States to foster appropriate educational programming.
- *Encourage media literacy programs as part of school curricula, youth and community organizations, and family life.* Many adolescents do not have the knowledge and skills to critically analyze media messages. Media literacy programs should focus not only on television, but also on the Internet, newspapers, magazines, radio, videos, music, and electronic games.
- *Increase media presentations of health promotions.* Community-wide campaigns using public service announcements in the media have been successful in reducing smoking and increasing physical fitness in adolescents. Use of the media to promote adolescent health and well-being should be increased.
- *Expand opportunities for adolescents' views to appear in the media.* The media should increase the number of adolescent voices in their presentations by featuring editorial opinions, news stories, and videos authored by adolescents. Some schools have shown that this strategy of media inclusion of adolescents can be an effective dimension of education.

One organization that is trying to do something about the media's impact on adolescents is Mediascope, which is developing an ethics curriculum on violence to be used in courses that train the thousands of film students who hope to become moviemakers. Mediascope is also monitoring the entire television industry to assess such issues as the gratuitous use of violence.

Review and reflect Learning goal 4

4 **Characterize the roles of the media and technology in adolescent development**

REVIEW

- What are the functions of the media? How does adolescents' use of media vary across different types of media?
- How is watching television related to adolescent development?
- What roles do music and the music media play in adolescents' lives?
- How are technology, computers, and the Internet linked to adolescent development?
- What are some social policy recommendations regarding media use by adolescents?

REFLECT

- What was your use of various media in middle/junior and high school like? Did your use of the media in adolescence influence your development in positive or negative ways? Explain.

Reach Your Learning Goals

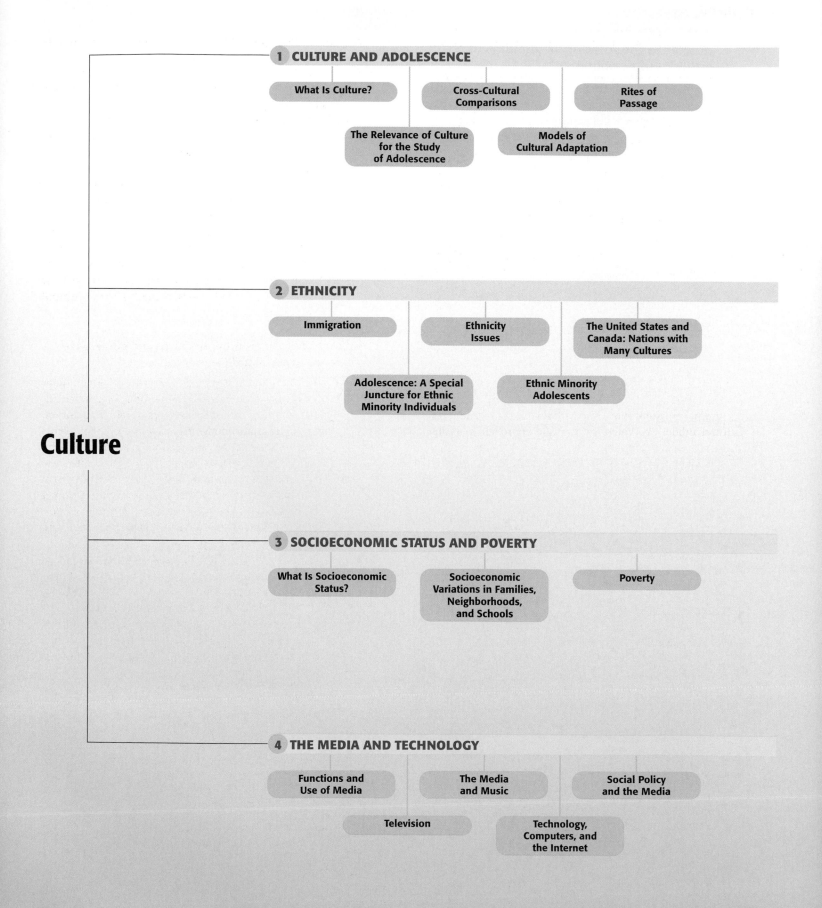

Culture

1 CULTURE AND ADOLESCENCE

- What Is Culture?
- Cross-Cultural Comparisons
- Rites of Passage
- The Relevance of Culture for the Study of Adolescence
- Models of Cultural Adaptation

2 ETHNICITY

- Immigration
- Ethnicity Issues
- The United States and Canada: Nations with Many Cultures
- Adolescence: A Special Juncture for Ethnic Minority Individuals
- Ethnic Minority Adolescents

3 SOCIOECONOMIC STATUS AND POVERTY

- What Is Socioeconomic Status?
- Socioeconomic Variations in Families, Neighborhoods, and Schools
- Poverty

4 THE MEDIA AND TECHNOLOGY

- Functions and Use of Media
- The Media and Music
- Social Policy and the Media
- Television
- Technology, Computers, and the Internet

Summary

1 Discuss the role of culture in adolescent development

- Culture is the behavior, patterns, beliefs, and all other products of a particular group of people that are passed on from generation to generation.
- If the study of adolescence is to be a relevant discipline in the twenty-first century, increased attention will need to be focused on culture and ethnicity because there will be increased contact between people from varied cultural and ethnic backgrounds. For too long, the study of adolescence has been ethnocentric in the sense that the main participants in research studies have been middle-socioeconomic-status adolescents from the United States.
- Cross-cultural studies involve the comparison of a culture with one or more other cultures, which provides information about the degree to which information about adolescent development is culture-specific. The study of adolescence emerged in the context of Western industrialized society. Cross-cultural comparisons reveal variations in the time adolescents spend in different activities, in achievement, and in sexuality. U.S. adolescents have more discretionary time than adolescents in other countries.
- The models that have been used to understand cultural changes within and across cultures include assimilation, acculturation, alternation, and multiculturalism. The multicultural model promotes a pluralistic approach to understanding two or more cultures.
  - Rites of passage are ceremonies that mark an individual's transition from one status to another, especially into adult status.

2 Summarize how ethnicity is involved in adolescent development

- Relatively high rates of immigration among minorities are contributing to the growth in the population of ethnic minority adolescents in the United States. Immigrants often experience stressors uncommon to or less prominent among longtime residents (such as language barriers, dislocations, and separations from support networks).
- Adolescence often is a critical juncture in the development of ethnic minority individuals. Most ethnic minority consciously confront their ethnicity in adolescence. As they cognitively mature, ethnic minority adolescents become acutely aware of how the non-Latino White culture evaluates their ethnic group.
- Too often researchers do not adequately tease apart SES and ethnicity when they study ethnic minority groups, with the result that conclusions about ethnicity are sometimes made that are not warranted. Historical, economic, and social experiences produce many legitimate differences among ethnic minority groups, and between ethnic minority groups and the White majority. Too often differences have been interpreted as deficits in ethnic minority groups. Failure to recognize the diversity within an ethnic minority group can lead to stereotyping. Many ethnic minority adolescents continue to experience prejudice, discrimination, and bias.
- African American adolescents make up the largest visible ethnic minority group. The church and extended family have helped many African American adolescents cope with stressful circumstances. Latino adolescents trace their roots to many countries, including Mexico, Cuba, Puerto Rico, and Central America. Asian American adolescents are a diverse group and the fastest-growing ethnic minority group in the United States. Native American adolescents have faced painful discrimination and have the highest school dropout rate of any ethnic group.
- The United States has been and continues to be a great receiver of ethnic groups. The cultures mix their ideologies and identities. Adolescents in Canada are exposed to some cultural dimensions that are similar and different to their counterparts in the United States. Canada's main cultural ties are British and French.

3 Describe how socioeconomic status and poverty are related to adolescent development

- Socioeconomic status (SES) is the grouping of people with similar occupational, educational, and economic characteristics. Socioeconomic status often involves certain inequalities.
- The families, neighborhoods, and schools of adolescents have socioeconomic characteristics that are related to the adolescent's development. Parents in low-SES families are more concerned that their children and adolescents conform to society's expectations, have an authoritarian parenting style, use physical punishment more in disciplining, and are more directive and conversational with their children and adolescents than higher-SES parents are.
- Poverty is defined by economic hardship, and its most common marker is the federal poverty threshold (based on the estimated cost of food multiplied by 3). Based on this threshold, the percentage of children in poverty increased from 15 percent in the 1970s to 17 percent in the late 1990s. The subculture of the poor often is characterized not only by economic hardship, but also by social and psychological difficulties. When poverty is persistent and long-standing, it especially can have devastating effects on adolescent development.

4 Characterize the roles of the media and technology in adolescent development

- The functions of the media include entertainment, information, sensation, coping, gender-role modeling, and youth culture identification. In terms of exposure, the average U.S. 8- to 18-year-old spends almost 7 hours a day using media with the most time spent watching television. However, adolescents are rapidly increasing the time they spend online. One recent study found that the average 2- to 18-year-old spends almost 3 hours a day watching television, although television viewing often declines in adolescence while the use of music media increases. Adolescents also use the print media more than children do. There are large individual variations in adolescent media use.

- The functions of television include providing information and entertainment, as well as a portrait of the world beyond the immediate context in which they live. One negative aspect of television is that it involves passive learning. Special concerns are the ways ethnic minorities, sex, and aggression are portrayed on television.
- Adolescents are heavy consumers of CDs, tapes, and rock music. Music meets a number of personal and social needs of adolescents.

- Today's adolescents are experiencing a technology revolution through computers and the Internet. In one national survey, adolescents said that if they had to live on a desert island, they would rather have a computer with Internet access than a television. Between 1998 and 2001, the percentage of U.S. 14- to 17-year-olds who said they are using the Internet increased from 51 to 75 percent.
- Social policy recommendations regarding the media include encouraging socially responsible programming, supporting public efforts to make the media more adolescent friendly, and encouraging media literacy campaigns.

Key Terms

culture 463	ethnocentrism 465	alternation model 468	Chicano 476
socioeconomic status (SES) 464	cross-cultural studies 465	multicultural model 468	feminization of poverty 483
	assimilation 468	rites of passage 469	Internet 492
ethnicity 464	acculturation 468	prejudice 473	e-mail 493

Key People

Richard Brislin 463	Carola Suárez-Orozco 472	Stanley Sue 474	Vonnie McLoyd 483

Resources for Improving the Lives of Adolescents

The Adolescent and Young Adult Fact Book

(1991) by Janet Simons, Belva Finlay, and Alice Yang
Washington, DC: Children's Defense Fund

This book is filled with valuable charts that describe the roles that poverty and ethnicity play in adolescent development.

Advocates for Youth Media Project

3733 Motor Avenue, Suite 204
Los Angeles, CA 90034
310–559–5700

This project promotes responsible portrayals of sexuality in the entertainment media. The project members work with media professionals by sponsoring informational events and offering free consultation services to writers, producers, and other media personnel.

Canadian Ethnocultural Council/Conseil Ethnoculturel du Canada

251 Laurier Avenue West, Suite 110
Ottawa, Ontario K1P 5J6
613–230–3867

CEC's objective is to secure equality of opportunity, of rights, and of dignity for ethnocultural minorities and all other Canadians.

Children, Adolescents, and the Media

(2002) by Victor Strasburger and Barbara Wilson
Newbury Park, CA: Sage

This is an excellent, contemporary treatment of many dimensions of the information age, such as television and computers.

Cybereducator

(1999) by Joan Bissell, Anna Manring, and Veronica Roland
A guide to using the Internet for K–12 education.

Quantum Opportunity Program

1415 North Broad Street
Philadelphia, PA 19122
215–236–4500

This is a year-round youth development program funded by the Ford Foundation. It has demonstrated that intervening in the lives of 13-year-old African Americans from poverty backgrounds can significantly improve their prospects.

Studying Ethnic Minority Adolescents

(1998) edited by Vonnie McLoyd and Laurence Steinberg
Mahwah, NJ: Erlbaum

An excellent resource book for learning about the best methods for studying ethnic minority adolescents.

The World's Youth

(2002) edited by Bradford Brown, Reed Larson, and T.S. Saraswathi
Fort Worth, TX: Harcourt Brace

This is an excellent book on adolescent development in eight regions of the world.

E-Learning Tools

To help you master the material in this chapter, you will find a number of valuable study tools on the student CD-ROM that accompanies this book. In addition, visit the Online Learning Center for *Adolescence, 10th Edition*, where you will find helpful resources for chapter 13, "Culture."

Taking It to the Net

http://www.mhhe.com/santrocka10

1. Adolescents who come from severe poverty, who experience parental divorce, who are the subjects of discrimination, and who attend very poor schools are at risk for various psychological and behavioral disorders. Yet, it is not at all inevitable that those who are at risk will experience poor development. How do they develop the resilience that insulates them from the negative environmental conditions?

2. Rites of passage mark important developmental milestones. Some are more formal, for example, a religious ceremony, and others are less formal, for example, entrance into sexual behavior. How might you use the concept of rites of passage to explain various aspects of adolescent behavior (for example, body piercing, tattooing) to high school teachers?

3. The multicultural model of cultural change promotes a pluralistic approach to meeting common needs. As a student in higher education, how would you explain the role of education, and particularly multicultural education, in achieving this form of cultural change?

Connect to **http://www.mhhe.com/santrocka10** to research the answers and complete these exercises. In some cases, you'll also find further instructions on this site.

Self-Assessment

To evaluate yourself, complete this self-assessment:
(1) Stereotyping.

Health and Well-Being, Parenting, and Education

To practice your decision-making skills, complete the health and well-being, parenting, and education scenarios.

Adolescent Problems

SECTION

5

There is no easy path leaving out of life, and few are the easy ones that lie within it.
WALTER SAVAGE LANDOR
English Poet, 19th Century

Modern life is stressful and leaves its psychological scars on too many adolescents, who, unable to cope effectively, never reach their human potential. The need is not only to find better treatments for adolescents with problems, but to find ways to encourage adolescents to adopt healthier lifestyles, which can prevent problems from occurring in the first place. This sections consists of one chapter (14), "Adolescent Problems."

They cannot scare me with their empty spaces. Between stars—on stars where no human race is. I have it in me so much nearer home. To scare myself with my own desert places.
—ROBERT FROST
American Poet, 20th Century

Adolescent Problems

Learning Goals

1 Discuss two main approaches to understanding adolescent problems and the characteristics of these problems

2 Describe some main problems that characterize adolescents

3 Summarize the interrelation of adolescent problems and ways to prevent or intervene in problems

Images of Adolescent Development

Annie and Arnie

Annie, a 15-year-old cheerleader, was tall, blonde, and good-looking. No one who sold liquor to her questioned her age. She got her money from babysitting and what her mother gave her to buy lunch. Annie was kicked off the cheerleading squad for missing practice so often, but that didn't stop her drinking. Soon she and several of her peers were drinking almost every day. Sometimes they skipped school and went to the woods to drink. Annie's whole life began to revolve around her drinking. After a while, her parents began to detect Annie's problem. But their attempts to get her to stop drinking by punishing her were unsuccessful. It went on for two years, and, during the last summer, anytime she saw anybody, she was drunk. Not long ago Annie started dating a boy she really liked and who refused to put up with her drinking. She agreed to go to Alcoholics Anonymous and has just successfully completed treatment. She has stopped drinking for four consecutive months now, and her goal is continued abstinence.

Arnie is 13 years old. He has a history of committing thefts and physical assaults. The first theft occurred when Arnie was 8—he stole a cassette player from an electronics store. The first physical assault took place a year later, when he shoved his 7-year-old brother up against the wall, bloodied his face, and then threatened to kill him with a butcher knife. Recently, the thefts and physical assaults have increased. In just the past week, he stole a television set, struck his mother repeatedly and threatened to kill her, broke some neighborhood streetlights, and threatened youths with a wrench and a hammer. Arnie's father left home when Arnie was 3 years old. Until the father left, his parents argued extensively, and his father often beat up his mother. Arnie's mother indicates that, when Arnie was younger, she was able to control him, but in the last several years she has lost that control. Arnie's volatility and dangerous behavior have resulted in the recommendation that he be placed in a group home with other juvenile delinquents.

A t various points in this book, we have described adolescent problems. For example, we discussed sexual problems in chapter 7, "Sexuality;" explored school-related problems in chapter 11, "Schools;" and examined achievement-related problems in chapter 12, "Achievement, Work, and Careers." We devote this chapter exclusively to adolescent problems, covering different approaches to understanding these problems, some main problems we have not yet discussed, and ways to prevent and intervene in problems.

1 EXPLORING ADOLESCENT PROBLEMS

The Biopsychosocial Approach	**Characteristics of Adolescent Problems**
The Developmental Psychopathology Approach	**Resilience**

What causes adolescents like Annie and Arnie to have problems? What are some characteristics of the problems adolescents develop?

The Biopsychosocial Approach

The **biopsychosocial approach** emphasizes that biological, psychological, and social factors interact to produce the problems that adolescents and people of other ages develop. Thus, if an adolescent engages in substance abuse it may be due to a combination of biological (heredity or brain processes), psychological (emotional turmoil or relationship difficulties), and social (poverty) factors. Let's further explore each of these factors.

Biological Factors   In the biological approach, adolescent problems are believed to be caused by a malfunctioning of the adolescent's body. Scientists who adopt a biological approach usually focus on the brain and genetic factors as causes of adolescent problems. In the biological approach, drug therapy is frequently used to treat problems. For example, if an adolescent is depressed, an antidepressant drug might be prescribed.

Psychological Factors   Among the psychological factors that have been proposed as causing adolescent problems are distorted thoughts, emotional turmoil, inappropriate learning, and troubled relationships. Two of the theoretical perspectives that we discussed in chapter 2, "The Science of Adolescent Development," address why adolescents might develop problems. Recall that psychoanalytic theorists attribute problems to stressful early experiences with parents and that behavioral and social cognitive theorists see adolescent problems as a consequence of social experiences with others.

Family and peer influences are especially believed to be important contributors to adolescent problems. For example, when we discuss substance abuse as well as juvenile delinquency, you will see that relationships with parents and peers are linked with these adolescent problems.

Social Factors   The psychological problems that adolescents develop appear in most cultures. However, the frequency and intensity of the problems vary across cultures with the variations being linked to social, economic, technological, and religious aspects of the cultures (Draguns, 1990; Tanaka-Matsumi, 2001).

www.mhhe.com/santrocka10

American Psychiatric Association Mental Health Net

biopsychosocial approach Emphasizes that problems develop through an interaction of biological, psychological, and social factors.

Social factors that influence the development of adolescent problems include socioeconomic status and neighborhood quality (Brown & Adler, 1998). For example, poverty is a factor in the occurrence of delinquency.

The Developmental Psychopathology Approach

The field of **developmental psychopathology** focuses on describing and exploring the developmental pathways of problems. Many researchers in this field seek to establish links between early precursors of a problem (such as risk factors and early experiences) and outcomes (such as delinquency or depression) (Egeland, Warren, & Aquilar, 2001; Harper, 2000). A developmental pathway describes continuities and transformations in factors that influence outcomes (Chang & Gjerde, 2000).

Adolescent problems can be categorized as internalizing or externalizing:

- **Internalizing problems** occur when individuals turn their problems inward. Examples of internalizing disorders include anxiety and depression.
- **Externalizing problems** occur when problems are turned outward. An example of an externalizing problem is juvenile delinquency.

Links have been established between patterns of problems in childhood and outcomes in adulthood. In one study, males with internalizing patterns (such as anxiety and depression) in the elementary school years were likely to have similar forms of problems at age 21, but they did not have an increased risk of externalizing problems as young adults (Quinton, Rutter, & Gulliver, 1990). Similarly, the presence of an externalizing pattern (such as aggression or antisocial behavior) in childhood elevated risk for antisocial problems at age 21. For females in the same study, early internalizing and externalizing patterns both predicted internalizing problems at age 21.

Alan Sroufe and his colleagues (Sroufe, 2002; Sroufe, Egeland, & Carlson, 1999) have found that anxiety problems in adolescence are linked with anxious/resistant attachment in infancy, and that conduct problems in adolescence are related to avoidant attachment in infancy. Sroufe believes that a combination of early supportive care (attachment security) and early peer competence help to buffer adolescents from developing problems. In another recent developmental psychopathology study, Ann Masten (2001; Masten & Reed, 2002) followed 205 children for 10 years from childhood into adolescence. She found that good intellectual functioning and parenting served protective roles in keeping adolescents from engaging in antisocial behaviors. Later in this chapter, we will further explore such factors in our discussion of resilient adolescents.

Characteristics of Adolescent Problems

The spectrum of adolescent problems is wide. The problems vary in their severity and in how common they are for girls versus boys and for different socioeconomic groups. Some adolescent problems are short-lived; others can persist over many years. One 13-year-old might show a pattern of acting-out behavior that is disruptive to his classroom. As a 14-year-old, he might be assertive and aggressive, but no longer disruptive. Another 13-year-old might show a similar pattern of acting-out behavior. At age 16, she might still be a disruptive influence in the classroom and have been arrested for numerous juvenile offenses.

Some problems are more likely to appear at one developmental level than at another. For example, fears are more common in early childhood, many school-related problems surface for the first time in middle and late childhood, and drug-related problems become more common in adolescence (Achenbach & Edelbrock, 1981). In one study, depression, truancy, and drug abuse were more common among older adolescents, while arguing, fighting, and being too loud were more common among younger adolescents (Edelbrock, 1989).

The term "developmental pathways" is central to discussions of developmental psychopathology as a way of conceptualizing the relations between early and later adaptation.

—BYRON EGELAND,
*Contemporary Psychologist,
University of Minnesota*

developmental psychopathology The area of psychology that focuses on describing and exploring the developmental pathways of problems.

internalizing problems Occur when individuals turn problems inward. Examples include anxiety and depression.

externalizing problems Occur when individuals turn problems outward. An example is juvenile delinquency.

In the large-scale investigation by Thomas Achenbach and Craig Edel-brock (1981), adolescents from a lower-SES background were more likely to have problems than those from a middle-SES background. Most of the problems reported for adolescents from a lower-SES background were undercontrolled, externalizing behaviors—destroying others' belongings and fighting, for example. These behaviors also were more characteristic of boys than girls. The problems of middle-SES adolescents and girls were more likely to be overcontrolled and internalizing—anxiety or depression, for example.

The behavioral problems most likely to cause adolescents to be referred to a clinic for mental health treatment were feelings of unhappiness, sadness, or depression, and poor school performance (see figure 14.1). Difficulties in school achievement, whether secondary to other kinds of problems or primary problems in themselves, account for many referrals of adolescents.

In another investigation, Achenbach and his colleagues (1991) compared the problems and competencies of 2,600 children and adolescents 4 to 16 years old assessed at intake into mental health services with those of 2,600 demographically matched nonreferred children and adolescents. Lower-SES children and adolescents had more problems and fewer competencies than did their higher-SES counterparts. Children and adolescents had more problems when they had fewer related adults in their homes, had biological parents who were unmarried in their homes, had parents who were separated or divorced, lived in families who received public assistance, and lived in households in which family members had received mental health services. Children and adolescents who had more externalized problems came from families in which parents were unmarried, separated, or divorced, as well as from families receiving public assistance.

Many studies have shown that factors such as poverty, ineffective parenting, and mental disorders in parents *predict* adolescent problems. Predictors of problems are called *risk factors*. Risk factor means that there is an elevated probability of a problem outcome in groups of people who have that factor. Children with many risk factors are said to have a "high risk" for problems in childhood and adolescence, but not every one of these children will develop problems.

The Search Institute in Minneapolis has prescribed 40 developmental assets that they believe adolescents need to achieve positive outcomes in their lives (Benson, 1997). Half of these assets are external, half internal. The 20 *external* assets include support (such as family and neighborhood), empowerment (such as adults in the community valuing youth and youth being given useful community roles), boundaries and expectations (such as the family setting clear rules and consequences and monitoring the adolescent's whereabouts as well as positive peer influence), and constructive use of time (such as engaging in creative activities three or more times a week and participating three or more hours a week in organized youth programs). The 20 *internal* assets include commitment to learning (such as motivation to achieve in school and doing at least one hour of homework on school days), positive values (such as helping others and demonstrating integrity), social competencies (such as knowing how to plan and make decisions, and having interpersonal competencies like empathy and friendship skills), and positive identity (such as having a sense of control over life and high self-esteem). In research conducted by the Search Institute, adolescents with more assets reported engaging in fewer risk-taking behaviors, such as alcohol and tobacco use, sexual intercourse, and violence. For example, in one survey of more than 12,000 ninth- to twelfth-graders, 53 percent of the students with 0 to 10 assets reported using alcohol three or more times in the past month or getting drunk more than once in the past two weeks, compared with only 16 percent of the students with 21 to 30 assets or 4 percent of the students with 31 to 40 assets.

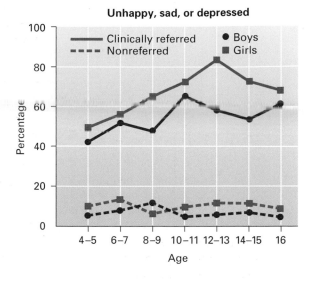

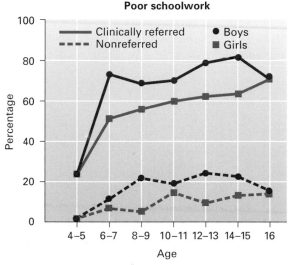

FIGURE 14.1 **The Two Items Most Likely to Differentiate Clinically Referred and Nonreferred Children and Adolescents**

Source	Characteristic
Individual	Good intellectual functioning
	Appealing, sociable, easygoing disposition
	Self-confidence, high self-esteem
	Talents
	Faith
Family	Close relationship to caring parent figure
	Authoritative parenting: warmth, structure, high expectations
	Socioeconomic advantages
	Connections to extended supportive family networks
Extrafamilial Context	Bonds to caring adults outside the family
	Connections to positive organizations
	Attending effective schools

FIGURE 14.2 Characteristics of Resilient Children and Adolescents

www.mhhe.com/santrocka10

**Developmental Assets
Developing Resilience in Urban Youth**

Resilience

Even when children and adolescents are faced with adverse conditions, such as poverty, are there characteristics that help buffer and make them resilient to developmental outcomes? Some children and adolescents do triumph over life's adversities (Compas, 2004; Olsson & others, 2003; Taylor & Wang, 2000). Ann Masten (2001; Masten & Coatsworth, 1998; Masten & Reed, 2002) analyzed the research literature on resilience and concluded that a number of individual factors (such as good intellectual functioning), family factors (close relationship to a caring parent figure), and extrafamilial factors (bonds to prosocial adults outside the family) characterize resilient children and adolescents (see figure 14.2).

Norman Garmezy (1993) described a setting in a Harlem neighborhood of New York City to illustrate resilience: In the foyer of the walkup apartment building is a large frame on a wall in the entranceway. It displays the photographs of children who live in the apartment building, with a written request that if anyone sees any of the children endangered on the street, they bring them back to the apartment house. Garmezy commented that this is an excellent example of adult competence and concern for the safety and well-being of children.

Review and reflect Learning goal 1

1 Discuss two main approaches to understanding adolescent problems and the characteristics of these problems

REVIEW

- How can the biopsychosocial approach be characterized?
- What is the developmental psychopathology approach like?
- What are some general characteristics of adolescent problems?
- How can the resilience of some adolescents be explained?

REFLECT

- Why do you think adolescent males are more likely to develop externalizing problems and adolescent females internalizing problems?

---

2 PROBLEMS AND DISORDERS

Drug Use

Depression and Suicide

Juvenile Delinquency

Eating Disorders

What are some of the major problems and disorders in adolescence? They include drugs and alcohol, juvenile delinquency, school-related problems, high-risk sexual behavior, depression and suicide, and eating disorders. We discussed school-related and sexual problems in earlier chapters. Here we will examine the other problems, beginning with drugs and alcohol.

Drug Use

Why do adolescents use drugs? How pervasive is adolescent drug use in the United States? What are the nature and effects of various drugs taken by adolescents? What factors contribute to adolescent drug use? These are among the questions we now evaluate.

Why Do Adolescents Take Drugs?
Since the beginning of history humans have searched for substances that would sustain and protect them and also act on the nervous system to produce pleasurable sensations. Individuals are attracted to drugs because drugs help them to adapt to an ever-changing environment. Smoking, drinking, and taking drugs reduce tension and frustration, relieve boredom and fatigue, and in some cases help adolescents to escape the harsh realities of their world. Drugs provide pleasure by giving inner peace, joy, relaxation, kaleidoscopic perceptions, surges of exhilaration, or prolonged heightened sensation. They may help some adolescents to get along better in their world. For example, amphetamines might help the adolescent to stay awake to study for an exam. Drugs also satisfy adolescents' curiosity—some adolescents take drugs because they are intrigued by sensational accounts of drugs in the media, while others may listen to a popular song and wonder if the drugs described can provide them with unique, profound experiences. Drugs are also taken for social reasons, allowing adolescents to feel more comfortable and to enjoy the company of others.

But the use of drugs for personal gratification and temporary adaptation carries a very high price tag: drug dependence, personal and social disorganization, and a predisposition to serious and sometimes fatal diseases (Gullotta, Adams, & Montemayor, 1995; Ksir, 2000). Thus, what is intended as adaptive behavior is maladaptive in the long run. For example, prolonged cigarette smoking, in which the active drug is nicotine, is one of the most serious yet preventable health problems. Smoking has been described by some experts as "suicide in slow motion."

As adolescents continue to take a drug, their bodies develop **tolerance,** which means that a greater amount of the drug is needed to produce the same effect. The first time someone takes 5 milligrams of Valium, for example, the drug will make them feel very relaxed. But after taking the pill every day for six months, the same person might need 10 milligrams to achieve the same calming effect.

Physical dependence is the physical need for a drug that is accompanied by unpleasant withdrawal symptoms when the drug is discontinued. **Psychological dependence** is the strong desire and craving to repeat the use of a drug because of various emotional reasons, such as a feeling of well-being and reduction of stress. Both physical and psychological dependence mean that the drug is playing a powerful role in the adolescent's life.

Trends in Overall Drug Use
The 1960s and 1970s were a time of marked increases in the use of illicit drugs. During the social and political unrest of those years, many youth turned to marijuana, stimulants, and hallucinogens. Increases in adolescent alcohol consumption during this period also were noted (Robinson & Greene, 1988). More precise data about drug use by adolescents have been collected in recent years.

Each year since 1975 Lloyd Johnston, Patrick O'Malley, and Gerald Bachman, working at the Institute of Social Research at the University of Michigan, have carefully monitored the drug use of America's high school seniors in a wide range of public and private high schools. Since 1991 they also have surveyed drug use by eighth- and tenth-graders. The University of Michigan study is called the Monitoring the Future Study. In 2003, the study surveyed nearly 50,000 students in 392 secondary schools.

The use of drugs among U.S. secondary school students declined in the 1980s but began to increase in the early 1990s (Johnston, O'Malley, & Bachman, 2001). In the

tolerance The condition in which a greater amount of a drug is needed to produce the same effect as a smaller amount used to produce the effect.

physical dependence Physical need for a drug that is accompanied by unpleasant withdrawal symptoms when the drug is discontinued.

psychological dependence Strong desire and craving to repeat the use of a drug for various emotional reasons, such as a feeling of well-being and reduction of distress.

FIGURE 14.3 Trends in Drug Use by U.S. Eighth-, Tenth-, and Twelfth-Grade Students

This graph shows the percentage of U.S. eighth-, tenth-, and twelfth-grade students who reported having taken an illicit drug in the last 12 months from 1991 to 2003 for eighth- and tenth-graders, and from 1975 to 2003 for twelfth-graders (Johnston, O'Malley, & Bachman, 2003).

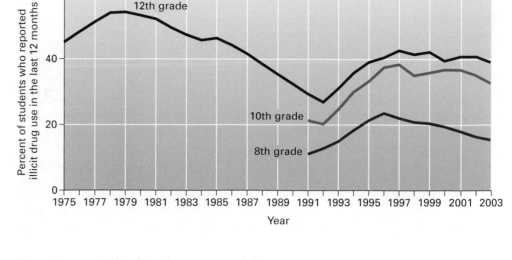

National Clearinghouse for Alcohol and Drug Information
National Institute of Drug Abuse
Drug Abuse and Adolescents
Monitoring the Future Study

late 1990s and the first three years of the twenty-first century, the proportions of tenth- and twelfth-grade students reporting the use of any illicit drug had been holding fairly steady or declining in use (Johnston, O'Malley, & Bachman, 2003). In 2003, the proportion of students reporting the use of any illicit drug in the past 30 days declined at all three grade levels, significantly so in grades 8 and 10. Figure 14.3 shows the overall trends in drug use by U.S. high school seniors since 1975 and by U.S. eighth- and tenth-graders since 1991.

Nonetheless, even with the recent leveling off in use, the United States still has the highest rate of adolescent drug use of any industrialized nation. Moreover, the University of Michigan survey likely underestimates the percentage of adolescents who take drugs because it does not include high school dropouts, who have a higher rate of drug use than do students who are still in school. Johnston, O'Malley, and Bachman (1999) believe that "generational forgetting" contributed to the rise of adolescent drug use in the 1990s, with adolescents' beliefs about the dangers of drugs eroding considerably. The recent downturn in drug use by U.S. adolescents has been attributed to such factors as an increase in the perceived dangers of drug use and the tragedy of the terrorist attacks of September 11, 2001, having a sobering effect on youth (Johnston, O'Malley, & Bachman, 2003). Let's now consider separately a number of drugs that are used by some adolescents.

Alcohol   To learn more about the role of alcohol in adolescents' lives, we examine how alcohol influences behavior and brain activity, the use and abuse of alcohol by adolescents, and risk factors in adolescents' alcohol abuse.

Effects of Alcohol on Adolescents' Behavior and Brain Activity   Alcohol is an extremely potent drug. It acts on the body as a depressant and slows down the brain's activities. If used in sufficient quantities, it will damage or even kill biological tissues, including muscle and brain cells. The mental and behavioral effects of alcohol include reduced inhibition and impaired judgment. Initially, adolescents feel more talkative and more confident when they use alcohol. However, skilled performances, such as driving, become impaired, and as more alcohol is ingested, intellectual functioning, behavioral control, and judgment become less efficient. Eventually, the drinker becomes drowsy and falls asleep. With extreme intoxication, the drinker may lapse into a coma. Each of these behavioral effects varies according to how the adolescent's body metabolizes alcohol, the individual's body weight, the amount of alcohol ingested, and whether previous drinking has led to tolerance.

Alcohol is the drug most widely used by U.S. adolescents. It has produced many enjoyable moments and many sad ones as well. Alcoholism is the third-leading killer

One issue in juvenile justice is whether an adolescent who commits a crime should be tried as an adult (Cassell & Bernstein, 2001). One study found that trying adolescent offenders as adults increased rather than reduced their crime rate (Myers, 1999). The study evaluated more than 500 violent youths in Pennsylvania, which has adopted a "get tough" policy. Although these 500 offenders had been given harsher punishment than a comparison group retained in juvenile court, they were more likely to be rearrested—and rearrested more quickly—for new offenses once they were returned to the community. This suggests that the price of short-term public safety attained by prosecuting juveniles as adults might increase long-term criminal offenses.

Some psychologists have proposed that individuals 12 and under should not be evaluated under adult criminal laws and that those 17 and older should be (Steinberg & Cauffman, 1999, 2001). They also recommended that individuals 13 to 16 years of age be given some type of individualized assessment in terms of whether to be tried in a juvenile court or an adult criminal court. This framework argues strongly against court placement based solely on the nature of an offense and takes into account the offender's developmental maturity.

In addition to the legal classifications of index offenses and status offenses, many of the behaviors considered delinquent are included in widely used classifications of abnormal behavior (Capaldi & Shortt, 2003). **Conduct disorder** is the psychiatric diagnostic category used when multiple behaviors occur over a six-month period. These behaviors include truancy, running away, fire setting, cruelty to animals, breaking and entering, excessive fighting, and others. When three or more of these behaviors co-occur before the age of 15 and the child or adolescent is considered unmanageable or out of control, the clinical diagnosis is conduct disorder.

In sum, most children or adolescents at one time or another act out or do things that are destructive or troublesome for themselves or others. If these behaviors occur often in childhood or early adolescence, psychiatrists diagnose them as conduct disorders. If these behaviors result in illegal acts by juveniles, society labels them as *delinquents*.

How many adolescents are arrested each year for committing juvenile delinquency offenses? In 1997, law enforcement agencies made an estimated 2.8 million arrests of individuals under the age of 18 in the United States (Office of Juvenile Justice and Prevention, 1998). This represents about 10 percent of adolescents 10 to 18 years of age in the United States. Note that this figure reflects only adolescents who have been arrested and does not include those who committed offenses but were not apprehended.

Recent U.S. government statistics reveal that 8 of 10 cases of juvenile delinquency involve males (Snyder & Sickmund, 1999) and that although males are still far more likely to engage in juvenile delinquency, there has been a greater percentage increase in female than male juvenile delinquents in the last two decades (Hoyt & Scherer, 1998; Quinsey & others, 2004). For both male and female delinquents, rates for property offenses are higher than rates for other offenses (such as toward persons, drug offenses, and public order offenses).

Antecedents of Juvenile Delinquency Predictors of delinquency include conflict with authority, minor covert acts that are followed by property damage and other more serious acts, minor aggression followed by fighting and violence, identity (negative identity), self-control (low degree), cognitive distortions (egocentric bias), age (early initiation), sex (male), expectations for education (low expectations, little commitment), school achievement (low achievement in early grades), peer influence (heavy influence, low resistance), socioeconomic status (low), parental role (lack of monitoring, low support, and ineffective discipline), siblings (having an older sibling who is a delinquent), and neighborhood quality (urban, high crime, high mobility). A summary of these antecedents of delinquency is presented in figure 14.9.

www.mhhe.com/santrocka10

Office of Juvenile Justice and Delinquency Prevention
Justice Information Center
National Youth Gang Center

conduct disorder The psychiatric diagnostic category for the occurrence of multiple delinquent activities over a six-month period. These behaviors include truancy, running away, fire setting, cruelty to animals, breaking and entering, and excessive fighting.

Antecedent	Association with delinquency	Description
Authority conflict	High degree	Youth show stubborness prior to age 12, then become defiant of authority.
Covert acts	Frequent	Minor covert acts, such as lying, are followed by property damage and moderately serious delinquency, then serious delinquency.
Overt acts of aggression	Frequent	Minor aggression is followed by fighting and violence.
Identity	Negative identity	Erikson believes delinquency occurs because the adolescent fails to resolve a role identity.
Cognitive distortions	High degree	The thinking of delinquents is frequently characterized by a variety of cognitive distortions (such as egocentric bias, externalizing of blame, and mislabeling) that contribute to inappropriate behavior and lack of self-control.
Self-control	Low degree	Some children and adolescents fail to acquire the essential controls that others have acquired during the process of growing up.
Age	Early initiation	Early appearance of antisocial behavior is associated with serious offenses later in adolescence. However, not every child who acts out becomes a delinquent.
Sex	Male	Boys engage in more antisocial behavior than girls do, although girls are more likely to run away. Boys engage in more violent acts.
Expectations for education and school grades	Low expectations and low grades	Adolescents who become delinquents often have low educational expectations and low grades. Their verbal abilities are often weak.
Parental influences	Monitoring (low), support (low), discipline (ineffective)	Delinquents often come from families in which parents rarely monitor their adolescents, provide them with little support, and ineffectively discipline them.
Sibling relations	Older delinquent sibling	Individuals with an older delinquent sibling are more likely to become delinquent.
Peer influences	Heavy influence, low resistance	Having delinquent peers greatly increases the risk of becoming delinquent.
Socioeconomic status	Low	Serious offenses are committed more frequently by low socioeconomic status males
Neighborhood quality	Urban, high crime, high mobility	Communities often breed crime. Living in a high-crime area, which also is characterized by poverty and dense living conditions, increases the probability that a child will become a delinquent. These communities often have grossly inadequate schools.

FIGURE 14.9 The Antecedents of Juvenile Delinquency

In the Pittsburgh Youth Study, a longitudinal study focused on more than 1,500 inner-city boys, three developmental pathways to delinquency were identified (Loeber & Farrington, 2001; Loeber & others, 1998; Stouthamer-Loeber & others, 2002):

- *Authority conflict.* Youth on this pathway showed stubbornness prior to age 12, then moved on to defiance and avoidance of authority.
- *Covert.* This pathway included minor covert acts, such as lying, followed by property damage and moderately serious delinquency, then serious delinquency.
- *Overt.* This pathway included minor aggression followed by fighting and violence.

Another recent study examined the developmental trajectories of childhood disruptive behaviors and adolescent delinquency (Broidy & others, 2003). For boys, early problem behavior involving aggression was linked with delinquency in adolescence.

One issue in juvenile justice is whether an adolescent who commits a crime should be tried as an adult (Cassell & Bernstein, 2001). One study found that trying adolescent offenders as adults increased rather than reduced their crime rate (Myers, 1999). The study evaluated more than 500 violent youths in Pennsylvania, which has adopted a "get tough" policy. Although these 500 offenders had been given harsher punishment than a comparison group retained in juvenile court, they were more likely to be rearrested—and rearrested more quickly—for new offenses once they were returned to the community. This suggests that the price of short-term public safety attained by prosecuting juveniles as adults might increase long-term criminal offenses.

Some psychologists have proposed that individuals 12 and under should not be evaluated under adult criminal laws and that those 17 and older should be (Steinberg & Cauffman, 1999, 2001). They also recommended that individuals 13 to 16 years of age be given some type of individualized assessment in terms of whether to be tried in a juvenile court or an adult criminal court. This framework argues strongly against court placement based solely on the nature of an offense and takes into account the offender's developmental maturity.

In addition to the legal classifications of index offenses and status offenses, many of the behaviors considered delinquent are included in widely used classifications of abnormal behavior (Capaldi & Shortt, 2003). **Conduct disorder** is the psychiatric diagnostic category used when multiple behaviors occur over a six-month period. These behaviors include truancy, running away, fire setting, cruelty to animals, breaking and entering, excessive fighting, and others. When three or more of these behaviors co-occur before the age of 15 and the child or adolescent is considered unmanageable or out of control, the clinical diagnosis is conduct disorder.

In sum, most children or adolescents at one time or another act out or do things that are destructive or troublesome for themselves or others. If these behaviors occur often in childhood or early adolescence, psychiatrists diagnose them as conduct disorders. If these behaviors result in illegal acts by juveniles, society labels them as *delinquents.*

How many adolescents are arrested each year for committing juvenile delinquency offenses? In 1997, law enforcement agencies made an estimated 2.8 million arrests of individuals under the age of 18 in the United States (Office of Juvenile Justice and Prevention, 1998). This represents about 10 percent of adolescents 10 to 18 years of age in the United States. Note that this figure reflects only adolescents who have been arrested and does not include those who committed offenses but were not apprehended.

Recent U.S. government statistics reveal that 8 of 10 cases of juvenile delinquency involve males (Snyder & Sickmund, 1999) and that although males are still far more likely to engage in juvenile delinquency, there has been a greater percentage increase in female than male juvenile delinquents in the last two decades (Hoyt & Scherer, 1998; Quinsey & others, 2004). For both male and female delinquents, rates for property offenses are higher than rates for other offenses (such as toward persons, drug offenses, and public order offenses).

Antecedents of Juvenile Delinquency   Predictors of delinquency include conflict with authority, minor covert acts that are followed by property damage and other more serious acts, minor aggression followed by fighting and violence, identity (negative identity), self-control (low degree), cognitive distortions (egocentric bias), age (early initiation), sex (male), expectations for education (low expectations, little commitment), school achievement (low achievement in early grades), peer influence (heavy influence, low resistance), socioeconomic status (low), parental role (lack of monitoring, low support, and ineffective discipline), siblings (having an older sibling who is a delinquent), and neighborhood quality (urban, high crime, high mobility). A summary of these antecedents of delinquency is presented in figure 14.9.

**Office of Juvenile Justice and
Delinquency Prevention
Justice Information Center
National Youth Gang Center**

conduct disorder The psychiatric diagnostic category for the occurrence of multiple delinquent activities over a six-month period. These behaviors include truancy, running away, fire setting, cruelty to animals, breaking and entering, and excessive fighting.

Antecedent	Association with delinquency	Description
Authority conflict	High degree	Youth show stubborness prior to age 12, then become defiant of authority.
Covert acts	Frequent	Minor covert acts, such as lying, are followed by property damage and moderately serious delinquency, then serious delinquency.
Overt acts of aggression	Frequent	Minor aggression is followed by fighting and violence.
Identity	Negative identity	Erikson believes delinquency occurs because the adolescent fails to resolve a role identity.
Cognitive distortions	High degree	The thinking of delinquents is frequently characterized by a variety of cognitive distortions (such as egocentric bias, externalizing of blame, and mislabeling) that contribute to inappropriate behavior and lack of self-control.
Self-control	Low degree	Some children and adolescents fail to acquire the essential controls that others have acquired during the process of growing up.
Age	Early initiation	Early appearance of antisocial behavior is associated with serious offenses later in adolescence. However, not every child who acts out becomes a delinquent.
Sex	Male	Boys engage in more antisocial behavior than girls do, although girls are more likely to run away. Boys engage in more violent acts.
Expectations for education and school grades	Low expectations and low grades	Adolescents who become delinquents often have low educational expectations and low grades. Their verbal abilities are often weak.
Parental influences	Monitoring (low), support (low), discipline (ineffective)	Delinquents often come from families in which parents rarely monitor their adolescents, provide them with little support, and ineffectively discipline them.
Sibling relations	Older delinquent sibling	Individuals with an older delinquent sibling are more likely to become delinquent.
Peer influences	Heavy influence, low resistance	Having delinquent peers greatly increases the risk of becoming delinquent.
Socioeconomic status	Low	Serious offenses are committed more frequently by low socioeconomic status males
Neighborhood quality	Urban, high crime, high mobility	Communities often breed crime. Living in a high-crime area, which also is characterized by poverty and dense living conditions, increases the probability that a child will become a delinquent. These communities often have grossly inadequate schools.

FIGURE 14.9 The Antecedents of Juvenile Delinquency

In the Pittsburgh Youth Study, a longitudinal study focused on more than 1,500 inner-city boys, three developmental pathways to delinquency were identified (Loeber & Farrington, 2001; Loeber & others, 1998; Stouthamer-Loeber & others, 2002):

- *Authority conflict.* Youth on this pathway showed stubbornness prior to age 12, then moved on to defiance and avoidance of authority.
- *Covert.* This pathway included minor covert acts, such as lying, followed by property damage and moderately serious delinquency, then serious delinquency.
- *Overt.* This pathway included minor aggression followed by fighting and violence.

Another recent study examined the developmental trajectories of childhood disruptive behaviors and adolescent delinquency (Broidy & others, 2003). For boys, early problem behavior involving aggression was linked with delinquency in adolescence.

However, no connection between early aggression problems and later delinquency was found for girls.

Let's look in more detail at several other factors that are related to delinquency. Erik Erikson (1968) believes that adolescents whose development has restricted their access to acceptable social roles or made them feel that they cannot measure up to the demands placed on them may choose a negative identity. Adolescents with a negative identity may find support for their delinquent image among peers, reinforcing the negative identity. For Erikson, delinquency is an attempt to establish an identity, although it is a negative identity.

Family support systems are also associated with delinquency (Capaldi & Shortt, 2003; Quincey & others, 2004). Parents of delinquents are less skilled in discouraging antisocial behavior and in encouraging skilled behavior than are parents of nondelinquents. Parental monitoring of adolescents is especially important in determining whether an adolescent becomes a delinquent (Patterson, DeBaryshe, & Ramsey, 1989). One recent longitudinal study found that the less parents knew about their adolescents' whereabouts, activities, and peers, the more likely they were to engage in delinquent behavior (Laird & others, 2003). Family discord and inconsistent and inappropriate discipline are also associated with delinquency (Capaldi & Shortt, 2003). An increasing number of studies have found that siblings can have a strong influence on delinquency (Conger & Reuter, 1996). In one recent study, high levels of hostile sibling relationships and older sibling delinquency were linked with younger sibling delinquency in both brother pairs and sister pairs (Slomkowski & others, 2001).

Peer relations also play an important role in delinquency. Having delinquent peers increases the risk of becoming delinquent (Henry, Tolan, & Gorman-Smith, 2001).

Although delinquency is less exclusively a lower-SES phenomenon than it was in the past, some characteristics of lower-SES culture can promote delinquency. The norms of many low-SES peer groups and gangs are antisocial, or counterproductive, to the goals and norms of society at large. Getting into and staying out of trouble are prominent features of life for some adolescents in low-income neighborhoods. Adolescents from low-income backgrounds may sense that they can gain attention and status by performing antisocial actions. Being "tough" and "masculine" are high-status traits for low-SES boys, and these traits are often measured by the adolescent's success in performing and getting away with delinquent acts. A community with a high crime rate also lets the adolescent observe many models who engage in criminal activities. These communities may be characterized by poverty, unemployment, and feelings of alienation toward higher-SES individuals. Quality schooling, educational funding, and organized neighborhood activities may be lacking in these communities.

The nature of a community can contribute to delinquency (Farrington, 2000; Tolan, Guerra, & Kendall, 1995). A community with a high crime rate allows adolescents to observe many models who engage in criminal activities and might be rewarded for their criminal accomplishments. Such communities often are characterized by poverty, unemployment, and feelings of alienation. The quality of schools, funding for education, and organized neighborhood activities are other community factors that might be related to delinquency. Are there caring adults in the schools and neighborhood who can convince adolescents with delinquent tendencies that education is the best route to success? When family support becomes inadequate, then such community supports take on added importance in preventing delinquency.

Violence and Youth   An increasing concern is the high rate of adolescent violence (Dodge & Pettit, 2003; Flannery & others, 2003; Tolan, 2001). In one school year, 57 percent of elementary and secondary school principals reported that one or more incidents of crime or violence occurred in their school and were reported to law enforcement officials (National Center for Education Statistics, 1998). Ten percent of all public schools experience one or more serious violent crimes (murder, rape, physical attack or fight with a weapon, robbery) each year (National Center for Education

A current special concern in low-income areas is escalating gang violence.

Statistics, 1998). Physical attacks or fights with a weapon lead the list of reported crimes. Each year more than 6,000 students are expelled for bringing firearms or explosives to school.

In one study, 17 percent of high school students reported carrying a gun or other weapon in the past 30 days (National Center for Health Statistics, 2000). In this same study, a smaller percentage (7 percent) reported bringing a gun or other weapon onto school property. Not all violence-related behaviors involve weapons. In this study 44 percent of male and 27 percent of female high school students said that they were involved in one or more physical fights.

In the late 1990s, a series of school shootings gained national attention. In April 1999, two Columbine High School (in Littleton, Colorado) students, Eric Harris (18) and Dylan Klebold (17), shot and killed 12 students and a teacher, wounded 23 others, and then killed themselves. In May 1998, slightly built Kip Kinkel strode into a cafeteria at Thurston High School in Springfield, Oregon, and opened fire on his fellow students, murdering two and injuring many others. Later that day, police went to Kip's home and found his parents lying dead on the floor, also victims of Kip's violence. In 2001, 15-year-old Charles Andrew "Andy" Williams fired shots at Santana High School in Santee, California, that killed 2 classmates and injured 13 others. According to students at the school, Andy was a victim of bullying at the school and had joked the previous weekend of his violent plans, but no one took him seriously after he later said he was just kidding.

Is there any way that psychologists can predict whether a youth will turn violent? It's a complex task, but they have pieced together some clues (Cowley, 1998). The violent youth are overwhelmingly male and many are driven by feelings of powerlessness. Violence seems to infuse these youth with a sense of power.

Suburban and small-town shooting sprees attract attention, but youth violence is far greater in poverty-infested areas of inner cities. Urban poverty fosters powerlessness and the rage that goes with it. Living in poverty is frustrating, and many inner-city neighborhoods provide almost daily opportunities to observe violence. Many urban youth who live in poverty also lack adequate parent involvement and supervision.

James Garbarino (1999, 2001) says there is a lot of ignoring that goes on in these kinds of situations. Parents often don't want to acknowledge what might be a very upsetting reality. Harris and Klebold were members of the Trenchcoat Mafia clique of Columbine outcasts. The two even had made a video for a school video class the previous fall that depicted them walking down the halls at the school and shooting other students. Allegations were made that a year earlier the Sheriff's Department had been given information that Harris had bragged openly on the Internet that he and Klebold had built four bombs. Kip Kinkel had an obsession with guns and explosives, a history of abusing animals, and a nasty temper when crossed. When police examined his room, they found two pipe bombs, three larger bombs, and bomb-making recipes that Kip had downloaded from the Internet. Clearly, some signs were present in these students' lives to suggest some serious problems, but it is still very difficult to predict whether youth like these will actually act on their anger and sense of powerlessness to commit murder.

Garbarino (1999, 2001) has interviewed a number of youth killers. He concludes that nobody really knows precisely why a tiny minority of youth kill but that it might be a lack of a spiritual center. In the youth killers he interviewed, Garbarino often found a spiritual or emotional emptiness in which the youth sought meaning in the dark side of life.

The following factors often are present in at-risk youths and seem to propel them toward violent acts (Walker, 1998):

- Early involvement with drugs and alcohol
- Easy access to weapons, especially handguns
- Association with antisocial, deviant peer groups
- Pervasive exposure to violence in the media

Many at-risk youths are also easily provoked to rage, reacting aggressively to real or imagined slights and acting on them, sometimes with tragic consequences. They might misjudge the motives and intentions of others toward them because of the hostility and agitation they carry (Coie & Dodge, 1998). Consequently, they frequently engage in hostile confrontations with peers and teachers. It is not unusual to find the anger-prone youth issuing threats of bodily harm to others.

In one recent study based on data collected in the National Longitudinal Study of Adolescent Health, secure attachment to parents, living in an intact family, and attending church services with parents were linked with lower incidences of engaging in violent behavior in seventh- through twelfth-graders (Franke, 2000).

These are some of the Oregon Social Learning Center's recommendations for reducing youth violence (Walker, 1998):

- *Recommit to raising children safely and effectively.* This includes engaging in parenting practices that have been shown to produce healthy, well-adjusted children. Such practices include consistent, fair discipline that is not harsh or severely punitive, careful monitoring and supervision, positive family management techniques, involvement in the child's daily life, daily debriefings about the child's experiences, and teaching problem-solving strategies.
- *Make prevention a reality.* Too often lip service is given to prevention strategies without investing in them at the necessary levels to make them effective.
- *Give more support to schools, which are struggling to educate a population that includes many at-risk children.*
- *Forge effective partnerships among families, schools, social service systems, churches, and other agencies to create the socializing experiences that will provide all youth with the opportunity to develop in positive ways.*

David and Roger Johnson (1995, 2003) believe it is important to go beyond violence prevention to include conflict resolution training in schools. Violence does need to be prevented in schools, but many violence prevention programs haven't worked because they are poorly targeted (too general and not focused on the relatively small

Andrew "Andy" Williams, escorted by police after being arrested for killing 2 classmates and injuring 13 others at Santana High School. *What factors might contribute to youth murders?*

www.mhhe.com/santrocka10

**Oregon Social Learning Center
A Guide for Safe Schools
Youth Violence Prevention**

Careers in Adolescent Development

Rodney Hammond
Health Psychologist

When Rodney Hammond went to college at the University of Illinois in Champaign-Urbana, he had not decided on a major. To help finance his education, he took a part-time job in a child development research program sponsored by the psychology department. In this job, he observed inner-city children in contexts designed to improve their learning. He saw firsthand the contributions psychology can make and knew then that he wanted to be a psychologist.

Rodney Hammond went on to obtain a doctorate in school and community psychology with a focus on children's development. Today, he is Director of Violence Prevention at the National Center for Injury Prevention and Control in Atlanta. Rodney calls himself a "health psychologist," although when he went to graduate school, training for that profession did not exist as it does now. He and his associates teach at-risk youth how to use social skills to manage conflict effectively and to recognize situations that could become violent. They have shown in their research that with this intervention many youth are less likely to become juvenile delinquents. Hammond's message to undergraduates: "If you are interested in people and problem solving, psychology is a great way to combine the two."

Rodney Hammond, talking with an adolescent about strategies for coping with stress and avoiding risk-taking behaviors.

group of students who need them the most), provide materials but don't focus on program implementation (too often they assume that a few hours will "fix" students who engage in violent behavior), and are unrealistic about the strength of social factors that produce violent behavior (schools alone can't solve all of our nation's social problems, such as decaying neighborhoods, lack of parental support, and so on).

Two approaches to conflict resolution programs are the cadre approach and the total student body approach. In the *cadre approach,* a small number of students are trained to serve as peer mediators for the entire school. Johnson and Johnson do not believe this approach is as effective as the *total student body approach,* in which every student learns how to manage conflicts constructively by negotiating agreements and mediating schoolmates' conflicts. A disadvantage of the total student body approach is the time and commitment required from school personnel to implement it. However, the more students there are who are trained in conflict resolution, the more likely it is that conflicts will be constructively managed.

One example of the total student body approach was developed by Johnson and Johnson (1995, 2003). Their Teaching Students to Be Peacemakers program involves both negotiation and mediation strategies. The steps students learn in negotiation are to (1) define what they want, (2) describe their feelings, (3) explain the reasons underlying the wants and feelings, (4) take the perspective of the other student to see the conflict from both sides, (5) generate at least three optional agreements that benefit both parties, and (6) come to an agreement about the best course of action.

The steps students learn in mediation are to (1) stop the hostilities, (2) ensure that the disputants are committed to the mediation, (3) facilitate negotiations between the disputants, and (4) formalize the agreement.

When students have completed negotiation and mediation training, the school or teacher implements the Peacemakers program by choosing two student mediators for each day. Being a mediator helps students learn how to negotiate and resolve conflicts. Evaluations of the Peacemakers program have been positive, with participants showing more constructive conflict resolution than nonparticipants (Johnson & Johnson, 1995).

Depression and Suicide

As mentioned earlier in the chapter, one of the most frequent characteristics of adolescents referred for psychological treatment is sadness or depression, especially among girls. In this section, we discuss the nature of adolescent depression and adolescent suicide.

Depression   An adolescent who says "I'm depressed" or "I'm so down" may be describing a mood that lasts only a few hours or a much longer lasting mental disorder. In **major depressive disorder,** an individual experiences a major depressive episode and depressed characteristics, such as lethargy and hopelessness, for at least two weeks or longer and daily functioning becomes impaired. According to the *DSM-IV* classification of mental disorders (American Psychiatric Association, 1994), nine symptoms define a major depressive episode, and to be classified as having major depressive disorder, at least five of these must be present during a two-week period:

1. Depressed mood most of the day
2. Reduced interest or pleasure in all or most activities
3. Significant weight loss or gain, or significant decrease or increase in appetite
4. Trouble sleeping or sleeping too much
5. Psychomotor agitation or retardation
6. Fatigue or loss of energy
7. Feeling worthless or guilty in an excessive or inappropriate manner
8. Problems in thinking, concentrating, or making decisions
9. Recurrent thoughts of death and suicide

In adolescence, pervasive depressive symptoms might be manifested in such ways as tending to dress in black clothes, writing poetry with morbid themes, or a preoccupation with music that has depressive themes. Sleep problems can appear as all-night television watching, difficulty in getting up for school, or sleeping during the day. Lack of interest in usually pleasurable activities may show up as withdrawal from friends or staying alone in the bedroom most of the time. A lack of motivation and energy level can show up in missed classes. Boredom might be a result of feeling depressed. Adolescent depression also can occur in conjunction with conduct disorder, substance abuse, or an eating disorder.

How serious a problem is depression in adolescence? Surveys have found that approximately one-third of adolescents who go to a mental health clinic suffer from depression (Fleming, Boyle, & Offord, 1993). Depression is more common in the adolescent years than the elementary school years (Compas & Grant, 1993). By about age 15, adolescent females have a rate of depression that is twice that of adolescent males. Some of the reasons for this sex difference that have been proposed are these:

- Females tend to ruminate in their depressed mood and amplify it.
- Females' self-images, especially their body images, are more negative than males.
- Females face more discrimination than males do.
- Hormonal changes alter vulnerability to depression in adolescence, especially among girls.

Mental health professionals believe that depression often goes undiagnosed in adolescence. Why is this so? According to conventional wisdom, normal adolescents often show mood swings, ruminate in introspective ways, express boredom with life,

major depressive disorder The diagnosis when an individual experiences a major depressive episode and depressed characteristics, such as lethargy and depression, for two weeks or longer and daily functioning becomes impaired.

Depression is more likely to occur in adolescence than in childhood and more likely to characterize female adolescents than male adolescents. *Why might female adolescents be more likely to develop depression than adolescent males?*

www.mhhe.com/santrocka10

**Exploring Adolescent Depression
Depression Research**

and indicate a sense of hopelessness. Thus, parents, teachers, and other observers may see these behaviors as simply transitory and not reflecting a mental disorder but rather normal adolescent behaviors and thoughts.

Follow-up studies of depressed adolescents indicate that the symptoms of depression experienced in adolescence predict similar problems in adulthood (Garber & others, 1988). This means that adolescent depression needs to be taken seriously. It does not just automatically go away. Rather, adolescents who are diagnosed as having depression are more likely to experience the problem on a continuing basis in adulthood than are adolescents not diagnosed as having depression. In one recent longitudinal study, transient problems in adolescence were related to situation-specific factors (such as negative peer events), whereas chronic problems were defined by individual characteristics, such as internalizing behaviors (Brooks-Gunn & Graber, 1995).

Other family factors are involved in adolescent depression (Graber, 2004; Seroczynski, Jacquez, & Cole, 2003; Sheeber, Hops, & Davis, 2001). Having a depressed parent is a risk factor for depression in childhood and adolescence (Windle & Dumenci, 1998). Parents who are emotionally unavailable, immersed in marital conflict, or who have economic problems may set the stage for the emergence of depression in their adolescent children (Marmorstein & Shiner, 1996; Sheeber, Hops, & Davis, 2001).

Poor peer relationships also are associated with adolescent depression. Not having a close relationship with a best friend, having less contact with friends, and peer rejection increase depressive tendencies in adolescents (Vernberg, 1990).

The experience of difficult changes or challenges is associated with depressive symptoms in adolescence (Compas, 2004; Compas & Grant, 1993). Parental divorce increases depressive symptoms in adolescents. Also, when adolescents go through puberty at the same time as they move from elementary school to middle or junior high school, they report being depressed more than do adolescents who go through puberty after the school transition (Petersen, Sarigiani, & Kennedy, 1991).

Depression has been treated with drug therapy and psychotherapy techniques (Beckham, 2000; Blatt, 2004). Antidepressant drugs reduce the symptoms of depression in about 60 to 70 percent of cases, often taking about two to four weeks to improve mood. Cognitive therapy also has been effective in treating depression (Beck, 1993).

Suicide Suicide behavior is rare in childhood but escalates in adolescence. Suicide is the third-leading cause of death in 10- to 19-year-olds today in the United States (National Center for Health Statistics, 2002a). Although the incidence of suicide in adolescence has increased in recent years, it is still a relatively rare event. In 2000, 1,921 U.S. individuals from 10 to 19 years of age committed suicide (National Center for Health Statistics, 2002a).

Although a suicide threat should always be taken seriously, far more adolescents contemplate or attempt it unsuccessfully than actually commit it (Borowsky, Ireland, & Resnick, 2001; Seroczynski, Jacquez, & Cole, 2003). In a national study, 19 percent of U.S. high school students said that they had seriously considered or attempted suicide in the last 12 months (National Center for Health Statistics, 2002a). Less than 3 percent reported a suicide attempt that resulted in an injury, poisoning, or drug overdose that had been treated by a doctor. Females were more likely to attempt suicide than males, but males were more likely to succeed in committing suicide. Males use more lethal means, such as guns, in their suicide attempts, whereas adolescent females are more likely to cut their wrists or take an overdose of sleeping pills—methods less likely to result in death.

What to do	What not to do
1. Ask direct, straightforward questions in a calm manner: "Are you thinking about hurting yourself?"	1. Do not ignore the warning signs.
2. Assess the seriousness of the suicidal intent by asking questions about feelings, important relationships, who else the person has talked with, and the amount of thought given to the means to be used. If a gun, pills, a rope, or other means has been obtained and a precise plan developed, clearly the situation is dangerous. Stay with the person until help arrives.	2. Do not refuse to talk about suicide if a person approaches you about it. 3. Do not react with humor, disapproval, or repulsion. 4. Do not give false reassurances by saying such things as "Everything is going to be OK." Also do not give out simple answers or platitudes, such as "You have everything to be thankful for."
3. Be a good listener and be very supportive without being falsely reassuring.	5. Do not abandon the individual after the crisis has passed or after professional help has commenced.
4. Try to persuade the person to obtain professional help and assist him or her in getting this help.	

FIGURE 14.10 What to Do and What Not to Do When You Suspect Someone Is Likely to Attempt Suicide

Some researchers argue that homosexual adolescents may be vulnerable to suicide. For example, in one study of 12,000 adolescents, approximately 15 percent of gay and lesbian youth said that they had attempted suicide compared with 7 percent of heterosexual youth (Russell & Joyner, 2001). However, in another study, gay and lesbian adolescents were only slightly more likely than heterosexual adolescents to attempt suicide (Savin-Williams, 2001). According to a leading researcher on gay youth, Richard Savin-Williams (2001), the earlier studies likely exaggerated the suicide rates for gay adolescents because they only surveyed the most disturbed youth who were attending support groups or hanging out at shelters for gay youth.

Distal, or earlier, experiences often are involved in suicide attempts as well (Gould, 2003). The adolescent might have a long-standing history of family instability and unhappiness. Just as a lack of affection and emotional support, high control, and pressure for achievement by parents during childhood are related to adolescent depression, such combinations of family experiences are also likely to show up as distal factors in suicide attempts. The adolescent might also lack supportive friendships.

Just as genetic factors are associated with depression, they are also associated with suicide. The closer a person's genetic relationship to someone who has committed suicide, the more likely that person is to also commit suicide. Another factor is previous attempts, with the risk of actual suicide increasing with each prior attempt.

What is the psychological profile of the suicidal adolescent? Suicidal adolescents often have depressive symptoms (American Academy of Pediatrics, 2000; Mean & others, 2004). Although not all depressed adolescents are suicidal, depression is the most frequently cited factor associated with adolescent suicide. A sense of hopelessness, low self-esteem, and high self-blame are also associated with adolescent suicide (Harter & Marold, 1992; Seroczynski, Jacquez, & Cole, 2003).

In some instances, suicides in adolescence occur in clusters. That is, when one adolescent commits suicide, other adolescents who find out about this also commit suicide. Such "copycat" suicides raise the issue of whether or not suicides should be reported in the media; a news report might plant the idea of committing suicide in other adolescents' minds.

Figure 14.10 provides valuable information about what to do and what not to do when you suspect someone is likely to commit suicide.

Suicide Facts
What Do You Know about Suicide?
Suicide and Homicide
Research on Suicidal Behavior

Eating Disorders

Eating Disorders

Eating disorders have become increasing problems in adolescence. Here are some research findings regarding adolescent eating disorders:

- Girls who felt negatively about their bodies in early adolescence were more likely to develop eating disorders two years later than their counterparts who did not feel negatively about their bodies (Attie & Brooks-Gunn, 1989).
- Girls who had positive relationships with both parents had healthier eating habits than girls who had negative relationships with one or both parents (Swarr & Richards, 1996). Negative parent-adolescent relationships were linked with increased dieting in adolescent girls over a one-year period (Archibald, Graber, & Brooks-Gunn, 1999).
- Girls who were both sexually active with their boyfriends and in pubertal transition were the most likely to be dieting or engaging in disordered eating patterns (Cauffmann, 1994).
- Girls who were making a lot of effort to look like same-sex figures in the media were more likely than their peers to become very concerned with their weight (Field & others, 2001).
- Many adolescent girls have a strong desire to weigh less (Graber & Brooks-Gunn, 2001; Jacobi & others, 2004).

Let's now examine different types of eating disorders in adolescence, beginning with obesity.

Obesity   In a national survey, 14 percent of 12- to 19-year-olds in the United States were overweight (National Center for Health Statistics, 2000). Being overweight was determined by body mass index (BMI), which is computed by a formula that takes into account height and weight. Only adolescents at or above the 95th percentile of BMI were included in the overweight category. This represents a significant increase in obesity over past years (see figure 14.11).

Are there ethnic variations in being overweight during adolescence in the United States? A recent survey by the National Center for Health Statistics (2002b) found that African American girls and Latino boys have especially high risks of being overweight during adolescence (see figure 14.12). Another recent study of 2,379 girls from 9 to 19 years of age found that the prevalence of being overweight was considerably higher for African American girls than non-Latino White girls (Kimm & others, 2002).

Eating patterns established in childhood and adolescence are highly associated with obesity in adulthood (Engeland & others, 2004). For example, 80 percent of obese adolescents become obese adults. Many obese adolescents feel that everything would be great in their lives if they only could lose weight. A typical example is Debby, who at 17 has been obese since she was 12. She came from a middle-SES family and her parents pressured her to lose weight, repeatedly sending her to weight reduction centers and physicians. One summer Debby was sent to a diet camp, where she went from 200 to 150 pounds. On returning home, she was terribly disappointed when her parents pressured her to lose more. With increased tension and parental preoccupation with her weight, she gave up her dieting efforts and her weight rose rapidly. Debby isolated herself and continued her preoccupation with food. Later, clinical help was sought and fortunately Debby was able to work through her hostility toward her parents and understand her self-destructive behavior. Eventually she gained a sense of self-control and became willing to reduce her weight for herself, not for her peers or her parents.

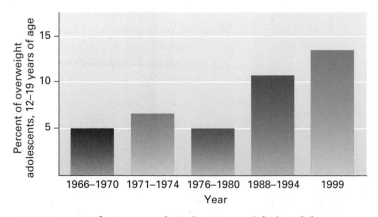

FIGURE 14.11 The Increase in Being Overweight in Adolescence from 1968 to 1999 in the United States

In this study, being overweight was determined by body mass index (BMI), which is computed by a formula that takes into account height and weight (National Center for Health Statistics, 2000). Only adolescents above the 95th percentile in the overweight category were included in the study. There was a substantial increase in the percentage of adolescents who were overweight from 1966 to 1999.

There have been few cross-cultural comparisons of obesity in childhood and adolescence. However, researchers have found that U.S. children and adolescents (6 to 18 years of age) were four times more likely to be classified as obese than their counterparts in China and almost three times as likely to be classified as obese than their counterparts in Russia (Wang & Dietz, 2002).

One recent study examined the extent to which adolescents in the United States, China, Brazil, and Russia have been overweight in the last two to three decades (Wang, Monteiro, & Popkin, 2002). In the last two to three decades, adolescent overweight increased 7.7 percent in China, 13.9 percent in Brazil, and 25.6 percent in the United States.

In a recent U.S. study, adolescents who had an overweight mother or father were more likely to be overweight than their counterparts without an overweight parent (Dowda & others, 2001). Also in this study, adolescent girls who watched four or more hours of television a day were more likely to be overweight than those who watched less than four hours a day. Adolescent boys who participated in sports teams and exercise programs were less likely to be overweight than those who did not participate in these programs.

Both heredity and environmental factors are involved in obesity (Corrado, Patashnick, & Rich, 2004; Stunkard, 2000). Some individuals inherit a tendency to be overweight. Only 10 percent of children who do not have obese parents become obese themselves, whereas 40 percent of children who become obese have one obese parent and 70 percent of children who become obese have two obese parents. Identical twins, even when they are reared apart, have similar weights.

Strong evidence of the environment's role in obesity is the doubling of the rate of obesity in the United States since 1900, as well as the significant increase in adolescent obesity since the 1960s, which was described earlier. This dramatic increase in obesity likely is due to greater availability of food (especially food high in fat), energy-saving devices, and declining physical activity. American adolescents also are more obese than European adolescents and adolescents in many other parts of the world.

Anorexia Nervosa and Bulimia Nervosa

Two eating disorders that may appear in adolescence are anorexia nervosa and bulimia nervosa.

Anorexia Nervosa **Anorexia nervosa** is an eating disorder that involves the relentless pursuit of thinness through starvation. Anorexia nervosa is a serious disorder that can lead to death. Three main characteristics of anorexia nervosa are as follows (Davison & Neale, 2001):

- Weighing less than 85 percent of what is considered normal for the individual's age and height.
- Having an intense fear of gaining weight. The fear does not decrease with weight loss.
- Having a distorted image of body shape (Polivy & others, 2003; Stice, 2002). Even when individuals with anorexia are extremely thin, they see themselves as too fat. They never think they are thin enough, especially in the abdomen, buttocks, and thighs. They usually weigh themselves frequently, often take their body measurements, and gaze critically at themselves in mirrors.

Anorexia nervosa typically begins in the early to middle teenage years, often following an episode of dieting and the occurrence of some type of life stress. It is about 10 times more likely to characterize females than males. Although most U.S. adolescent girls have been on a diet at some point, slightly less than 1 percent ever develop anorexia nervosa (Walters & Kendler, 1994). When anorexia nervosa does occur in males, the symptoms and other characteristics (such as family conflict) are usually similar to those reported by females who have the disorder (Olivardia & others, 1995).

Most anorexics are White adolescent or young adult females from well-educated, middle- and upper-income families that are competitive and high-achieving. They set

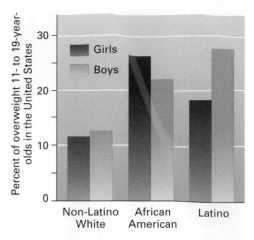

FIGURE 14.12 Percentage of Overweight U.S. Adolescent Boys and Girls in Different Ethnic Groups

anorexia nervosa An eating disorder that involves the relentless pursuit of thinness through starvation.

Anorexia nervosa has become an increasing problem for adolescent girls and young adult women. *What are some possible causes of anorexia nervosa?*

LifeMAP

www.mhhe.com/santrocka10

Anorexia Nervosa and Other Eating Disorders
Anorexia Nervosa

bulimia nervosa In this eating disorder, the individual consistently follows a binge-and-purge eating pattern.

Through the Eyes of Adolescents

The Struggles of an Anorexic Adolescent

Like her mother, Melinda Montovani is petite and small-boned. She always has been known as "the skinny one" in her family, an image she likes. When her body started to change in puberty, Melinda began to worry that she no longer would be thin. When she was a sophomore in high school, she decided to lose weight. Melinda said, "My goal was to reach 75 pounds. I figured that if I could do that, I was a success and in control. I remember when I stepped on the scale and saw that 75—I was really proud of myself."

That was the beginning of a 10-year battle with anorexia nervosa. To outsiders, Melinda looked like she had it all—good grades, captain of the track team. Yet she felt that no one liked her. "The only thing I was good at was losing weight and no matter what weight I got to, it wasn't enough. I hated myself."

high standards, become stressed about not being able to reach the standards, and are intensely concerned about how others perceive them (Streigel-Moore, Silberstein, & Rodin, 1993). Unable to meet these high expectations, they turn to something they can control: their weight. (For an in-depth discussion about this particular claim, watch the video segment entitled "Eating Disorders.")

The fashion image in the American culture, which emphasizes that "thin is beautiful," contributes to the incidence of anorexia nervosa (Polivy & others, 2003). This image is reflected in the saying, "You never can be too rich or too thin." The media portray thin as beautiful in their choice of fashion models, which many adolescent girls want to emulate.

About 70 percent of patients with anorexia nervosa eventually recover. Recovery often takes six to seven years and relapses are common before a stable pattern of eating and healthy weight maintenance is achieved (Strober, Freeman, & Morrel, 1997). In a longitudinal study of individuals diagnosed with anorexia nervosa in adolescence, 10 years later, approximately two-thirds were fully recovered, 3 percent still had anorexia nervosa, and none of them had died (Herpertz-Dahlmann & others, 2001). However, in another longitudinal study, 21 years after being diagnosed with anorexia nervosa, 16 percent of the individuals had died because of factors related to anorexia nervosa (Lowe & others, 2001).

Bulimia Nervosa Whereas anorexics control their eating by restricting it, most bulimics cannot. **Bulimia nervosa** is an eating disorder in which the individual consistently follows a binge-and-purge eating pattern. The bulimic goes on an eating binge and then purges by self-induced vomiting or by using a laxative. Although many people binge and purge occasionally and some experiment with it, for a person to be considered to have a serious bulimic disorder, the episodes must occur at least twice a week for 3 months.

As with anorexics, most bulimics are preoccupied with food, have a strong fear of becoming overweight, and are depressed or anxious (Davison & Neale, 2001). Unlike anorexia nervosa, the binge-and-purging of bulimia nervosa occurs within a normal

weight range, which means that it often is difficult to detect, although telltale signs may include prematurely brittle bones, tooth decay, and bad breath (Mizes & Miller, 2000).

Bulimia nervosa typically begins in late adolescence or early adulthood. About 90 percent of the cases are women. Approximately 1 to 2 percent of women are esti mated to develop bulimia nervosa (Gotesdam & Agras, 1995). Many women who de velop bulimia nervosa were somewhat overweight before the onset of the disorder and the binge eating often began during an episode of dieting. One recent study of adolescent girls found that increased dieting, pressure to be thin, exaggerated impor tance of appearance, body dissatisfaction, depression symptoms, low self-esteem, and low social support predicted binge eating two years later (Stice, Presnell, & Spangler, 2002). As with anorexia nervosa, about 70 percent of individuals who develop bulimia nervosa eventually recover from the disorder (Keel & others, 1999).

Review and reflect   Learning goal 2

2   Describe some main problems that characterize adolescents

REVIEW

- Why do adolescents take drugs? What are some trends in adolescent drug use? What are some characteristics of the use of alcohol, hallucinogens, stimulants, depressants, and anabolic steroids by adolescents? What are the main factors that are related to adolescent drug use?
- What is juvenile delinquency? What are the antecedents of juvenile delin- quency? What characterizes violence in youth?
- What characterizes adolescent depression? How common is suicide in adoles- cence? What are some possible causes of suicide in adolescence?
- How can obesity, anorexia nervosa, and bulimia nervosa be described?

REFLECT

- Imagine that you have just been appointed to head the U.S. President's Commission on Adolescent Drug Abuse. What would be the first program you would try to put in place? What would its components be?

3 INTERRELATION OF ADOLESCENT PROBLEMS AND PREVENTION/INTERVENTION

| Adolescents with Multiple Problems | Prevention and Intervention |

What characterizes at-risk adolescents? What are the best strategies for preventing or intervening in adolescent problems?

Adolescents with Multiple Problems

The four problems that affect the most adolescents are (1) drug abuse, (2) juvenile delinquency, (3) sexual problems, and (4) school-related problems (Dryfoos, 1990; 1997; Ohene, Ireland, & Blum, 2004). The adolescents most at risk have more than one of these problems. Researchers are increasingly finding that problem behaviors in adolescence are interrelated (Santelli & others, 2001; Tubman, Windle, & Windle, 1996). For example, heavy substance abuse is related to early sexual activity, lower grades, dropping out of school, and delinquency. Early initiation of sexual activity is associated with the use of cigarettes and alcohol, use of marijuana and other illicit drugs, lower grades, dropping out of school, and delinquency. Delinquency is related to early sexual activity, early pregnancy, substance abuse, and dropping out of school. As many as 10 percent of the adolescent population in the United States have serious multiple-problem behaviors (adolescents who have dropped out of school, or are behind in their grade level, are users of heavy drugs, regularly use cigarettes and marijuana, and are sexually active but do not use contraception). Many, but not all, of these very high-risk youth "do it all." Another 15 percent of adolescents participate in many of these same behaviors but with slightly lower frequency and less deleterious consequences. These high-risk youth often engage in two- or three-problem behaviors (Dryfoos, 1990).

Prevention and Intervention

In addition to understanding that many adolescents engage in multiple-problem behaviors, it also is important to develop programs that reduce adolescent problems (Weissberg, Kumpfer, & Seligman, 2003). We described a number of prevention and intervention strategies for specific adolescent problems, such as drug abuse and juvenile delinquency, earlier in the chapter. Here we focus on some general strategies for preventing and intervening in adolescent problems. In a review of the programs that have been successful in preventing or reducing adolescent problems, adolescent researcher Joy Dryfoos (1990; 1997) described the common components of these successful programs. The common components include these:

1. *Intensive individualized attention.* In successful programs, high-risk youth are attached to a responsible adult who gives the youth attention and deals with the child's specific needs (Nation & others, 2003). This theme occurred in a number of different programs. In a successful substance-abuse program, a student assistance counselor was available full-time for individual counseling and referral for treatment.
2. *Community-wide multiagency collaborative approaches.* The basic philosophy of community-wide programs is that a number of different programs and services have to be in place. In one successful substance-abuse program, a community-wide health promotion campaign was implemented that used local media and community education in concert with a substance-abuse curriculum in the schools. Community programs that include policy changes and media campaigns are more effective when they are coordinated with family, peer, and school components (Wandersman & Florin, 2003).
3. *Early identification and intervention.* Reaching children and their families before children develop problems, or at the beginning of their problems, is a successful strategy (Botvin, 1999; Ripple & Zigler, 2003). Here are three prevention programs/research studies that merit attention:

Prevention Research

- *High Scope.* One preschool program serves as an excellent model for the prevention of delinquency, pregnancy, substance abuse, and dropping out of school. Operated by the High Scope Foundation in Ypsilanti, Michigan, the Perry Preschool has had a long-term positive impact on its students. This enrichment program, directed by David Weikart, services disadvantaged African American children. They attend a high-quality two-year preschool program and receive weekly home visits from program personnel. Based on official police records, by age 19 individuals who had attended the Perry Preschool program were less likely to have been arrested and reported fewer adult offenses than a control group. The Perry Preschool students also were less likely to drop out of school, and teachers rated their social behavior as more competent than that of a control group who did not receive the enriched preschool experience.

- *Fast Track.* Another program that seeks to prevent adolescent problems is called *Fast Track* (Dodge, 2001; The Conduct Problems Prevention Research Group, 2002). High-risk children who show conduct problems at home and at kindergarten were identified. Then, during the elementary school years, the at risk children and their families are given support and training in parenting, problem-solving and coping skills, peer relations, classroom atmosphere and curriculum, academic achievement, and home-school relations. Ten project interventionists work with the children, their families, and schools to increase the protective factors and decrease the risk factors in these areas. Thus far, results show that the intervention effectively improved parenting practices and children's problem-solving and coping skills, peer relations, reading achievement, and problem behavior at home and school during the elementary school years compared with a control group of high-risk children who did not experience the intervention.
- *National Longitudinal Study on Adolescent Health.* This study is based on interviews with 12,118 adolescents and has implications for the prevention of adolescent problems (Resnick & others, 1997). Perceived adolescent connectedness to a parent and to a teacher were the main factors that were linked with preventing these adolescent problems: emotional distress, suicidal thoughts and behavior, violence, use of cigarettes, use of alcohol, use of marijuana, and early sexual intercourse. This study also provides support for the first component of successful prevention/intervention programs described under the preceding number 1, intensive individualized attention, which is especially important when coming from important people in the adolescent's life like parents and teachers (Greenberg & others, 2003; Kumpfer & Alvarado, 2003).

Review and reflect Learning goal 3

3 Summarize the interrelation of adolescent problems and ways to prevent or intervene in problems

REVIEW
- How are adolescent problems interrelated?
- What are the three main ways to prevent or intervene in adolescent problems?

REFLECT
- Why might risk taking in adolescence have more serious consequences than in the past?

In this, the final chapter in the book, we have examined a number of ideas about adolescent problems. To conclude the book, following this chapter is an epilogue that is designed to encourage you to think about some of the main themes we have discussed throughout the book and to consider what adolescents' lives will be like in the future.

Reach Your Learning Goals

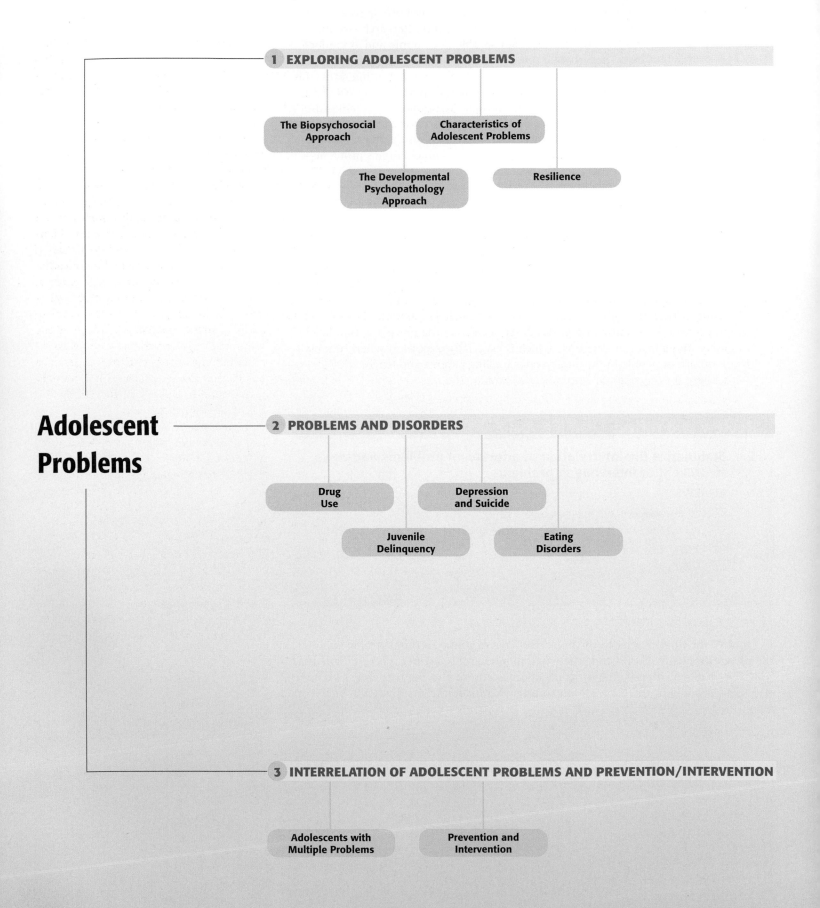

Adolescent Problems

1 EXPLORING ADOLESCENT PROBLEMS

- The Biopsychosocial Approach
- Characteristics of Adolescent Problems
- The Developmental Psychopathology Approach
- Resilience

2 PROBLEMS AND DISORDERS

- Drug Use
- Depression and Suicide
- Juvenile Delinquency
- Eating Disorders

3 INTERRELATION OF ADOLESCENT PROBLEMS AND PREVENTION/INTERVENTION

- Adolescents with Multiple Problems
- Prevention and Intervention

Summary

1 Discuss two main approaches to understanding adolescent problems and the characteristics of these problems

- Biological, psychological, and social factors have been proposed as causes of adolescent problems. In the biopsychosocial approach, all three factors—biological, psychological, and sociocultural—are emphasized.
- In the developmental psychopathology approach, the emphasis is on describing and exploring developmental pathways of problems.
- The spectrum of adolescent problems is wide, varying in severity, developmental level, sex, and socioeconomic status. One way of classifying problems is as internalizing or externalizing. Middle-SES adolescents and females have more internalizing problems; low-SES adolescents and males have more externalizing problems. Adolescents who have a number of external and internal assets have fewer problems than their counterparts with few external and internal assets.
- Three sets of characteristics are reflected in the lives of children and adolescents who show resilience in the face of adversity and disadvantage: (1) cognitive skills and positive responsiveness from others; (2) families marked by warmth, cohesion, and the presence of a caring adult; and (3) some source of external support.

2 Describe some main problems that characterize adolescents

- Drugs have been used since the beginning of human existence for pleasure, utility, curiosity, and social reasons. Understanding drugs requires an understanding of addiction and psychological dependence. The 1960s and 1970s were a time of marked increase in the use of illicit drugs. Drug use began to decline in the 1980s but increased again in the 1990s. Since the mid-1990s there has been a decline in the overall use of illicit drugs by U.S. adolescents. Still, the United States has the highest adolescent drug-use rate of any industrialized nation. Alcohol is a depressant and is the drug most widely used by adolescents. Alcohol abuse is a major adolescent problem although its use by secondary school students has begun to decline. There is an increase in alcohol use and binge drinking during emerging adulthood. Binge drinking by college students is very high. This binge drinking typically declines by the midtwenties. Risk factors for alcohol use include heredity, negative family and peer influences, and certain personality factors. Other drugs that can be harmful to adolescents include hallucinogens (LSD and marijuana—their use increased in the 1990s), stimulants (such as nicotine, cocaine, and amphetamines), and depressants (such as barbiturates, tranquilizers, and alcohol). A special concern is cigarette use by adolescents, although the good news is that it has been declining in recent years. Anabolic steroid use by adolescents has increased since the early 1990s and remains at peak levels. Drug use in childhood and early adolescence has more negative long-term effects than when it first occurs in late adolescence. Parents and peers can provide important supportive roles in preventing adolescent drug use. Early intervention, a K–12 approach, teacher training, social skills training, and other strategies can be used in school-based efforts to reduce adolescent drug use.
- Juvenile delinquency consists of a broad range of behaviors, from socially undesirable behavior to status offenses. For legal purposes, a distinction is made between index and status offenses. Conduct disorder is a psychiatric category often used to describe delinquent-type behaviors. Predictors of juvenile delinquency include authority conflict, minor covert acts such as lying, overt acts of aggression, a negative identity, cognitive distortions, low self-control, early initiation of delinquency, being a male, low expectations for education and school grades, low parental monitoring, low parental support and ineffective discipline, having an older delinquent sibling, heavy peer influence and low resistance to peers, low socioeconomic status, and living in a high-crime, urban area. The high rate of violence among youth is an increasing concern. Ten percent of public schools experience one or more serious violent incidents each year. A number of strategies have been proposed for reducing youth violence, including conflict resolution training.
- Adolescents have a higher rate of depression than children do. Female adolescents are far more likely to develop depression than adolescent males are. Adolescents who develop depression are more likely than nondepressed adolescents to have depression as adults. Treatment of depression has involved both drug therapy and psychotherapy. The U.S. adolescent suicide rate has tripled since the 1950s. Both proximal and distal factors likely are involved in suicide.
- Studies suggest an increasing percentage of U.S. adolescents are obese. Both hereditary and environmental factors are involved in obesity. Anorexia nervosa is an eating disorder that involves the relentless pursuit of thinness through starvation. Anorexia nervosa primarily afflicts non-Latino White, middle- and upper-SES females. Bulimia nervosa is an eating disorder in which the individual consistently follows a binge-and-purge pattern.

3 Summarize the interrelation of adolescent problems and ways to prevent or intervene in problems

- The four problems that affect the most adolescents are (1) drug abuse, (2) juvenile delinquency, (3) sexual problems, and (4) school-related problems. Researchers are finding that adolescents who are the most at risk often have more than one problem and that the highest-risk adolescents often have all four of these problems.
- In Dryfoos' analysis, these were the common components of successful prevention/intervention programs: (1) extensive individual attention, (2) community-wide intervention, and (3) early identification.

Key Terms

biopsychosocial approach 505
developmental
   psychopathology 506
internalizing problems 506
externalizing problems 506

tolerance 509
physical dependence 509
psychological dependence 509
hallucinogens 514
stimulants 515

depressants 518
anabolic steroids 519
juvenile delinquency 522
index offenses 522
status offenses 522

conduct disorder 523
major depressive disorder 529
anorexia nervosa 533
bulimia nervosa 534

Key People

Thomas Achenbach and Craig
   Edelbrock 507
Norman Garmezy 508

Lloyd Johnston, Patrick
   O'Malley, and Gerald
   Bachman 509

Joy Dryfoos 521
James Garbarino 527
David and Roger Johnson 527

Resources for Improving the Lives of Adolescents

American Anorexia/Bulimia Association

133 Cedar Lane
Teaneck, NJ 07666
201–836–1800

This organization provides information, referrals, and publications related to anorexia nervosa and bulimia.

Developmental Psychopathology

(1999) edited by Suniya Luthar, Jacob Burack, Dante Cicchetti, and John Weisz
New York: Cambridge University Press

This volume presents many aspects of developmental psychopathology by leading experts.

Lost Boys

(1999) by James Garbarino
New York: Free Press

This book explores why some youth are violent and kill.

National Adolescent Suicide Hotline

800–621–4000

This hotline can be used 24 hours a day by teenagers contemplating suicide, as well as by their parents.

National Clearinghouse for Alcohol Information

P.O. Box 2345
1776 East Jefferson Street
Rockville, MD 20852
301–468–2600

This clearinghouse provides information about a wide variety of issues related to drinking problems, including adolescent drinking.

Reducing Adolescent Risk

(2003) edited by Daniel Romer.
Thousand Oaks, CA: Sage.

A number of experts analyze ways to reduce adolescent risk in a number of problem areas.

E-Learning Tools

To help you master the material in this chapter, you will find a number of valuable study tools on the student CD-ROM that accompanies this book. In addition, visit the Online Learning Center for *Adolescence, 10th Edition,* where you will find helpful resources for chapter 14, "Adolescent Problems."

Taking It to the Net

http://www.mhhe.com/santrocka10

1. Depression is one example of a mood disorder. How common are mood disorders in adolescents? What are other examples of mood disorders, and how do the symptoms differ from "normal" behavior?
2. Obesity is the major eating disorder. A common stereotype is that obese people simply eat too much and that they easily could achieve normal weight if they just watched how and what they ate. If one of your friends expressed this view, how would you counter it?

3. Think of an important stressful event or situation in which you found yourself sometime during the past three months. What did you do; how did you deal with the stressor? Is that how you generally cope? Take the coping test and find out.

Connect to **http://www.mhhe.com/santrocka10** to research the answers and complete these exercises. In some cases, you'll also find further instructions on this site.

Self-Assessment

To evaluate yourself, complete the self-assessment: Am I Depressed?

Health and Well-Being, Parenting, and Education

To practice your decision-making skills, complete the health and well-being, parenting, and education scenarios.

Epilogue
Adolescents: The Future of Society

In the end the power behind development is life.
—ERIK ERIKSON, *AMERICAN PSYCHOANALYST, 20TH CENTURY*

At the beginning of the twenty-first century, the well-being of adolescents is one of our most important concerns. We all cherish the future of adolescents, for they are the future of any society. Adolescents who do not reach their full potential, who are destined to make fewer contributions to society than society needs, and who do not take their place as productive adults diminish that society's future. In this epilogue, we revisit a number of important themes and issues in adolescent development and then present a montage of thoughts that convey the beauty, power, and complexity of adolescents' development.

Our journey through adolescence has been long and complex, and you have read about many facets of adolescents' lives. This is a good time to stand back and ask yourself what you have learned. What theories, studies, and ideas struck you as more important than others? What did you learn about your own development as an adolescent? Did anything you learned stimulate you to rethink how adolescents develop? How did you develop into the person you are today?

THEMES AND ISSUES IN ADOLESCENT DEVELOPMENT

As we look back across the chapters of *Adolescence,* some common themes and issues emerge. Let's explore what some of the most important themes and issues are.

The Storm-and-Stress View of Adolescence Has Been Overdramatized

Growing up has never been easy. However, adolescence is not best viewed as a time of rebellion, crisis, pathology, and deviance. A far more accurate vision of adolescence describes it as a time of evaluation, of decision making, of commitment, and of carving out a place in the world. Most problems of today's youth are not with the youth themselves. What adolescents need is access to a range of legitimate opportunities and long-term support from adults who care deeply about them.

In matters of taste and manners, the youth of every generation have seemed radical, unnerving, and different from adults—different in how they look, how they behave, the music they enjoy, their hairstyles, and the clothing they choose. But it is an enormous error to confuse the adolescent's enthusiasm for trying on new identities and enjoying moderate amounts of outrageous behavior with hostility toward parental and societal standards. Acting out and boundary testing are time-honored ways in which adolescents move toward accepting, rather than rejecting, parental values.

Although adolescence has been portrayed too negatively for too long, many adolescents today are at risk for not reaching their full potential. These at-risk youth do experience far too much storm and stress. This discussion underscores an important point about adolescents: They are not a homogeneous group. Different portrayals of adolescence emerge, depending on the particular group of adolescents being described.

We Need to Dramatically Reduce the Number of Adolescents at Risk for Not Reaching Their Potential

Although we emphasized that the majority of adolescents navigate the long journey of adolescence successfully, far too many adolescents in America are not reaching their potential because they are not being adequately reared by caregivers, not being adequately instructed in school, and not being adequately supported by society. Adolescents who do not reach their full potential and do not grow up to make competent contributions to their world invariably have not been given adequate individual attention and support as they were growing up. Adolescents need parents who love them; monitor their development; are sensitive to their needs; have a sound understanding of their own, as well as their adolescents', development; and help to steer them away from health-compromising behaviors.

We also need schools that place a greater emphasis on a curriculum that is developmentally appropriate and pays closer attention to adolescent health and well-being. This needs to be accomplished at all levels of education, but especially in the middle school and junior high school years. And we need to give more attention to our nation's social policy, especially in terms of ways to break the poverty cycle that enshrouds nearly 20 percent of adolescents in the United States. Our nation's political values need to reflect greater concern for the inadequate conditions in which far too many adolescents live. To reduce the number of adolescents at risk for not reaching their full potential, community-wide agency cooperation and integration, as well as early prevention or early intervention, need to be given special attention.

Knowledge About Adolescent Development Has Benefited from a Diversity of Theories and an Extensive Research Enterprise

A number of theories have made important contributions to our understanding of adolescent development. From the social theories of Erikson and Bronfenbrenner to the cognitive theory of Piaget, each has contributed an important piece of the developmental puzzle. However, no single theory is capable of predicting, explaining, and organizing the rich, complex, multifaceted landscape of the adolescent's developmental journey. The inability of a single theory to explain all of adolescent development should not be viewed as a shortcoming of the theory. Any theory that attempts to explain all of adolescent development is too general. The field of adolescent development has been moved forward by theories that are precise and zero in on key aspects of one or two dimensions of adolescents' lives rather than by theories that try to do everything.

Knowledge about adolescent development has also benefited from a research effort that has greatly expanded over the last two decades. The science of adolescent development is rapidly becoming a highly sophisticated field in which collecting evidence about adolescent development is based on well-defined rules, exemplary practices, mathematical procedures for handling the evidence, and drawing inferences from what has been found.

Adolescents Benefit from Both Basic and Applied Research

Across the fourteen chapters of *Adolescence*, we have discussed both basic research and applied research. Basic research, sometimes called pure research, is the study of issues to obtain knowledge for its own sake rather than for practical application. In contrast, applied research is the study of issues that have direct practical significance, often with the intent of changing human behavior. Social policy research is applied research, not basic research.

A developmentalist who conducts basic research might ask: How is the cognitive development of adolescents different from that of children? In contrast, a developmentalist who conducts applied research might ask: How can knowledge about adolescents' and children's cognitive development be used to educate them more effectively or help them cope more effectively with stress?

Most developmentalists believe that both basic and applied research contributes to improving adolescents' lives. Although basic research sometimes produces information that can be applied to improve the well-being of adolescents, it does not guarantee this application. But insisting that research always be relevant is like trying to grow flowers by focusing only on the blossoms and not tending to the roots.

Adolescent Development Is Influenced by an Interaction of Heredity and Environment

Both heredity and environment are necessary for adolescents to even exist. Heredity and environment operate together—or cooperate—to produce an adolescent's height and weight, ability to shoot a basketball, intelligence, reading skills, temperament, and all other dimensions of the adolescent's development.

We discussed the nature-nurture controversy, the debate about whether development is primarily influenced by heredity and maturation (nature) or by environment and experience (nurture). The debate shows no signs of subsiding, but for now virtually all developmentalists are interactionists, accepting that adolescent development is determined by both heredity and environment. Behavior geneticists continue to specify more precisely the nature of heredity-environment interaction through concepts such as those of passive, evocative, and active genotype/environment interactions and shared and nonshared environmental influences.

Adolescent Development Involves Both Continuity and Discontinuity

Some developmentalists emphasize the continuity of development, the view that development involves gradual, cumulative change from conception to death. Others stress the discontinuity of development, the view that development consists of distinct stages in the life span.

Development involves both continuity and discontinuity. For example, although Piaget's stages reflect discontinuity, in the sense that adolescents change from being concrete to formal operational thinkers, researchers have found that children's and adolescents' intelligence shows more continuity than once was believed. Who is right? Probably both. As Piaget envisioned, most concrete operational children do not think hypothetically and don't solve problems in a scientific manner. In this aspect, development is stagelike, as Piaget proposed. However, as information-processing psychologists believe, adolescents' thinking is not as stagelike as Piaget believed.

Adolescent Development Is Determined by Both Early and Later Experiences

Adolescents' development is determined by both early and later experiences. However, developmentalists still debate how strong the contributions of each type of experience are. The early-experience advocates argue that early experiences, especially in infancy, are more important than later experiences are. They believe, for example, that warm, nurturant, sensitive parenting in the first year of life is necessary for optimal later development, even in adolescence or adulthood. Later experiences in childhood and adolescence are not as important in shaping the individual's developmental path, they say.

By contrast, other developmentalists stress that later experiences are just as important as early experiences in adolescent development. That is, warm, nurturant, sensitive parenting is just as important in the elementary school years and adolescence in shaping development as it is in infancy. People in Western cultures are stronger advocates of early experience, those in Eastern cultures of later experiences. The debate continues.

Adolescent Development Is Determined by an Interaction of Biological, Cognitive, and Socioemotional Processes

Biological processes involve changes in the adolescent's physical nature, such as genes inherited from parents and the hormonal changes of puberty. Cognitive processes involve changes in the adolescent's thought and intelligence, such as memorizing a poem or solving a math problem. Socioemotional processes involve changes in the adolescent's relationships with other people, emotions, and personality, such as the intimate conversation of two friends, an adolescent girl's sadness and depression, and a shy, introverted adolescent boy.

In many parts of the book, you read about how biological, cognitive, and socioemotional processes are intricately interwoven. For example, biology plays a role in adolescents' temperament, especially influencing how shy or gregarious they are. Inadequate parenting and schooling can harm the adolescent's intelligence. Cognitive changes substantially alter how adolescents think about their parents and peers. Both theory and research focused on adolescent development are becoming more integrated and less compartmentalized as links across different domains are sought.

Adolescent Development Involves Both Commonalities with Other Adolescents and Individual Variation

Most every adolescent develops like all other adolescents, in certain ways. Most every adolescent is reared by one or more adult caregivers who have more power than the adolescent does; most every adolescent engages in peer relations, goes to school, and becomes more independent and searches for an identity.

But adolescents are not always like collections of geese; they are unique, each adolescent writing an individual history. One adolescent may grow up in the well-manicured lawns of suburbia, another in the ghetto confines of an inner city. One adolescent may be tall, another short. One adolescent may be a genius, another might have mental retardation. One adolescent may have been abused as a child, another lavished with love. And while one adolescent may be highly motivated to learn, another couldn't care less.

Adolescent Development Is Embedded in Sociocultural, Historical Contexts

Throughout this book we have emphasized the importance of considering the contexts in which the adolescent develops. *Context* refers to the setting in which development occurs, a setting that is influenced by historical, economic, social, and cultural factors. These contexts or settings include homes, schools, peer groups, churches, neighborhoods, communities, cities, the United States, Canada, Russia, France, Japan, Egypt, and many others—each with meaningful historical, economic, social, and cultural legacies.

In the twentieth century alone in the United States, successive waves of adolescents witnessed dramatic historical changes, including two world wars and their violence, the Great Depression and its economic woes, the advent of television and computers, increased levels of education, and altered gender roles. And as new generations appear, they increasingly have had an ethnic minority heritage.

Global interdependence is no longer a matter of belief or preference. It is an inescapable reality. By increasing our knowledge of the behavior, values, and nature of adolescent development in cultures around the world, we can learn about the universal aspects of adolescent development, cultural variations on their development, and how to interact with adolescents more effectively to make this planet a more hospitable, peaceful place to live.

Understanding our own culture better also can improve adolescents' lives. There is a special sense of urgency in addressing the nature of ethnicity and how it affects adolescent development because of the dramatic changes in the ethnic composition of

America's population. The Asian, Latino, and African American populations are expected to increase at a much faster pace than the Anglo-American population in the foreseeable future. At a point early in the twenty-first century, one-third of the population in the United States will be members of ethnic minority groups.

To help adolescents of any ethnic heritage reach their full potential, we need to do the following:

- Recognize the diversity within every cultural and ethnic group. Not recognizing this diversity leads to unfortunate, harmful stereotyping.
- Understand that there are legitimate differences among cultural and ethnic groups. Recognizing and accepting these differences are important dimensions of getting along with others in a diverse, multicultural world. For too long, differences between ethnic minority individuals and Anglo-Americans were characterized as deficits on the part of ethnic minority individuals.
- Recognize and accept similarities among cultural and ethnic groups when differences have been incorrectly assumed. Through much of its history, America has had a White, middle-SES bias. The search for legitimate similarities among White Americans and ethnic minority Americans is important because incorrectly assumed differences involve stereotyping and can lead to prejudice.
- Reduce discrimination and prejudice. Discrimination and prejudice continue to haunt too many adolescent lives—in interpersonal relations, in the media, and in daily conversations. Crimes, strangeness, poverty, mistakes, and deterioration too often are attributed to ethnic minority individuals without full consideration of the circumstances.
- Consider different sides of sensitive cultural and ethnic issues. We need to see things from different points of view and encourage adolescents to do likewise. If we don't seek alternative explanations and interpretations of problems and issues, our conclusions, and those of adolescents, may be based solely on expectations, prejudices, stereotypes, and personal experiences.

Adolescents Deserve to Live and Develop in a More Equitable Gender World

Another important dimension of adolescents' lives that needs to be addressed in helping them reach their full potential is gender. Throughout *Adolescence* we emphasized how the world of adolescents and adults has not been a very fair gender world. Not only have ethnic minority adolescents grown up in a world that has confronted them with bias and discrimination, so have adolescent girls.

An important goal of this book has been to extensively evaluate the gender worlds of adolescents and to promote gender equity in adolescent development. I (your author) have two daughters who are now adults. As Tracy and Jennifer were growing up, there were many instances when I felt they experienced bias and discrimination because they were females—in school, in athletics, and in many other contexts of their lives. My wife and I wanted them to have the opportunities to reach their full potential and not be limited by a gender-biased society and authority figures. Our hope was that they would not only develop strengths in traditional feminine domains, such as relationship skills, but also acquire a sense of self-assertiveness, a traditionally masculine domain, that would serve them well in their quest to become competent persons. I hope that all adolescents have this opportunity, and that Tracy's and Jennifer's children will have fewer gender barriers to break through as adolescents than their mothers did.

The Family Plays an Important Role in Adolescent Development

At a point not too long ago, we heard rumblings about the decreasing influence of the family in adolescents' lives and how the family as we had come to know it was breaking down. Although the structure of many families has changed as a result of increasing numbers of divorced, working-mother, and stepparent families, the family is still a powerful socializing influence on adolescent development. Regardless of the type of culture and family structure in which adolescents grow up, they benefit enormously when one or both parents are highly involved in their upbringing, provide them with warmth and nurturance, help them to develop self-control, and provide them with an environment that promotes their health and well-being.

Competent parents are knowledgeable about the nature of adolescent development, effectively monitor their adolescent's life, and adapt their behavior as the adolescent grows and matures.

A special concern is that too many of America's adolescents grow up in low-SES families and suffer the stressful and burdensome perils of poverty. In a number of places in *Adolescence* we called attention to programs that will benefit adolescents who live in low-SES settings. These programs currently are improving the lives of thousands of adolescents but need to be expanded to help far more adolescents than currently are being served by them.

For those of you who will become parents someday, or are already parents, I underscore how important it is for each of you to take seriously the rearing of your children and adolescents. Remember that good parenting takes an incredible amount of time—so if you become a parent, you should be willing to commit yourself, day after day, week after week, month after month, and year after year, to providing your children and adolescents with a warm, supportive, safe, and stimulating environment that will make them feel secure and allow them to reach their full potential as human beings. This is true for fathers as well as mothers. Although there has been an increase in the amount of time fathers spend with their adolescents, far too many fathers still do not develop adequate relationships with their adolescent daughters and sons.

Adolescents Deserve a Better Education

The importance of education in adolescent development was highlighted throughout *Adolescence*. There is a widespread agreement that something needs to be done about our nation's schools. We need schools that place a stronger emphasis on education that is developmentally appropriate. This needs to be accomplished at all levels of education, but especially in the middle school and junior high school grades.

The information and thinking society of the twenty-first century will not be content with products of education who have been trained to merely take in and recycle information handed out by teachers and other authority figures. Today's adolescents, who will become tomorrow's adults, need to experience an education that teaches them to think for themselves and to generate new information. This transformation is occurring in some, but not nearly enough, schools.

Schools and classrooms for adolescents also need to be smaller, place more emphasis on health and well-being, involve parents and community leaders, provide better counseling services, and be more sensitive to individual variations in adolescent development. In short, our nation's secondary schools need a major overhaul if we are to truly be sensitive to how adolescents develop.

Adolescent Development Is Determined by Internal/External and Self/Other Influences

Controversy still surrounds whether adolescents are architects of their own development (internal, self-determined) or whether their development primarily is orchestrated by the external forces of others. However, most experts on adolescence recognize that development is not entirely external and other-determined and, likewise, not entirely internal and self-generated. Trying to tease apart internal/external and self/other influences is extraordinarily difficult because the adolescent is always embedded in a social context with others. To be certain, adolescents are not helplessly buffeted about by their environment. Adolescents bring certain developmental capacities to any situation and act on the situation. At the same time, however, they interact with others who offer their own versions of the world, which adolescents sometimes learn from and adopt for themselves. At times, adolescents are like solitary scientists, crafting their own books of dreams and reality as Piaget envisioned; at other times, they are socially intertwined with skilled teachers and peers, as Vygotsky conceived.

America, especially male America, has had a history of underscoring the importance of self-determination and individualism. Recently, however, females have challenged the status of self-determination as a more important human value than being connected to others and competent at relationships. And as psychologists have become more interested in cultures around the world, they have begun to recognize that many cultures, especially Eastern cultures, promote values that emphasize concern for others, interdependence, and harmonious relationships. It is important for us to raise a nation of adolescents who not only value a separate "I," uniqueness, and self-determination, but who also value connectedness with others, concern for others, and harmony in relationships.

Adolescents' Behavior Is Multiply Determined

An important aspect of thinking about the behavior of any adolescent is that the adolescent's behavior is multiply determined. When we think about what causes an adolescent's behavior, we often lean toward explaining it in terms of a single cause. Consider a 12-year-old adolescent boy named Josh. His teachers say that he is having trouble in school because he is from a father-absent home. The implication is that not having a father present in the home causes Josh's poor academic performance. Not having a father may be one factor in Josh's poor performance in school, but many others also influence his behavior. These factors include his genetic heritage and a host of environmental and sociocultural experiences, both in the past and in the present. On closer inspection of Josh's circumstances, we learn that not only has his father been absent all of Josh's life, but that his extended-family support system also has been weak. We also learn that he lives in a low-SES area with little community support for recreation, libraries, and families. The school system in which Josh is enrolled has a poor record of helping low-achieving adolescents and has little interest in developing programs for adolescents from disadvantaged circumstances. We could find other reasons that help explain Josh's poor school achievement, but these examples illustrate the importance of going beyond accepting a single cause as the reason for an adolescent's behavior. As with each of us, Josh's behavior is multiply determined.

Adolescents Will Benefit from an Interdisciplinary Approach to Their Development

Some of you taking this class on adolescence are being taught by a developmental psychologist, others by someone who specializes in human development or family relationships, others by an educational psychologist or professor in an education department, others by a nurse or pediatrician, and yet others by professors from different disciplines. The field of adolescent development has become more interdisciplinary. Our knowledge about adolescents, and how to improve adolescents' lives, has benefited, and will continue to benefit, from the contributions of scholars and professionals in a number of disciplines, including developmental psychology, education and educational psychology, pediatrics and nursing, clinical psychology, counseling, psychiatry, sociology, anthropology, and law. The collaboration between developmental psychologists and pediatricians, nurses, and psychiatrists is one example of this interdisciplinary cooperation; the emerging area of how development influences adolescents' health reflects this cross-disciplinary trend.

The Journey of Adolescence

We have come to the end of this book. I hope you can now look back and say that you learned a lot about adolescents, not only other adolescents but yourself as an adolescent and how your adolescent years contributed to who you are today. The insightful words of philosopher Søren Kierkegaard capture the importance of looking backward to understand ourselves: "Life is lived forward, but understood backwards." I also hope that those of you who become the parents of adolescents or work with adolescents in some capacity—whether as teacher, counselor, or community leader—feel that you now have a better grasp of what adolescence is all about. I leave you with the following montage of thoughts and images that convey the power, complexity, and beauty of adolescence in the human life span:

In no order of things is adolescence the time of simple life. Adolescents feel like they can last forever, think they know everything, and are quite sure about it. They clothe themselves with rainbows and go brave as the zodiac, flashing from one end of the world to the other both in mind and body. In many ways, today's adolescents are privileged, wielding unprecedented economic power. At the same time, they move through a seemingly endless preparation for life. They try on one face after another, seeking to find a face of their own. In their most pimply and awkward moments, they become acquainted with sex. They play furiously at "adult games" but are confined to a society of their own peers. They want their parents to understand them and hope that their parents will accord them the privilege of understanding them. Their generation of young people is the fragile cable by which the best and the worst of their parents' generation is transmitted to the present. In the end, there are only two lasting gifts parents can leave youth—one is roots, the other is wings.

John W. Santrock

Glossary

accommodation an adjustment to new information. 121

acculturation cultural change that results from continuous, firsthand contact between two distinctive cultural groups. 468

active (niche-picking) genotype-environment correlations correlations that occur when children seek out environments that they find compatible and stimulating. 111

adolescence the developmental period of transition from childhood to early adulthood; it involves biological, cognitive, and socio-emotional changes. 21

adolescent egocentrism the heightened self-consciousness of adolescents, which is reflected in their belief that others are as interested in them as they themselves are, and in their sense of personal uniqueness. 156

adolescent generalization gap Adelson's concept of generalizations about adolescents based on information about a limited, highly visible group of adolescents. 12

adolescents who are gifted adolescents who have above-average intelligence (usually defined as an IQ of 130 or higher) and/or superior talent in some domain, such as art, music, or mathematics. 419

adoption study a study in which investigators seek to discover whether the behavior and psychological characteristics of adopted children are more like their adoptive parents, who have provided a home environment, or more like those of their biological parents, who have contributed their heredity. Another form of adoption study involves comparing adoptive and biological siblings. 110

affectionate love also called companionate love, this love occurs when an individual desires to have another person near and has a deep, caring affection for that person. 375

AIDS acquired immune deficiency syndrome, a primarily sexually transmitted infection caused by the HIV virus, which destroys the body's immune system. 252

alternation model this model assumes that it is possible for an individual to know and understand two different cultures. It also assumes that individuals can alter their behavior to fit a particular social context. 468

altruism unselfish interest in helping another person. 284

anabolic steroids drugs derived from the male sex hormone, testosterone. They promote muscle growth and lean body mass. 519

androgens the main class of male sex hormones. 84

androgyny the presence of a high degree of desirable feminine and masculine characteristics in the same individual. 216

anorexia nervosa an eating disorder that involves the relentless pursuit of thinness through starvation. 533

anxiety a vague, highly unpleasant feeling of fear and apprehension. 435

assimilation the absorption of ethnic minority groups into the dominant group, which often means the loss of some or virtually all of the behavior and values of the ethnic minority group. 121

assimilation the incorporation of new information into existing knowledge. 468

attention deficit hyperactivity disorder (ADHD) children and adolescents with ADHD show one or more of the following characteristics over a period of time: inattention, hyperactivity, and impulsivity. 417

attribution theory the concept that individuals are motivated to discover the underlying causes of their own behavior or performance in their effort to make sense of it. 430

authoritarian parenting this is a restrictive, punitive style in which the parent exhorts the adolescent to follow the parent's directions and to respect work and effort. Firm limits and controls are placed on the adolescent, and little verbal exchange is allowed. This style is associated with adolescents' socially incompetent behavior. 318

authoritarian strategy of classroom management this teaching strategy is restrictive and punitive. The focus is mainly on keeping order in the classroom rather than on instruction and learning. 404

authoritative parenting this style encourages adolescents to be independent but still places limits and controls on their actions. Extensive verbal give-and-take is allowed, and parents are warm and nurturant toward the adolescent. This style is associated with adolescents' socially competent behavior. 318

authoritative strategy of classroom management this teaching strategy encourages students to be independent thinkers and doers but still involves effective monitoring. Authoritative teachers engage students in considerable verbal give-and-take and show a caring attitude toward them. However, they still declare limits when necessary. 404

autonomous morality the second stage of moral development in Piaget's theory, displayed by older children (about 10 years of age and older). The child becomes aware that rules and laws are created by people and that, in judging an action, one should consider the actor's intentions as well as the consequences. 274

back-to-basics movement this philosophy stresses that the function of schools should be the rigorous training of intellectual skills through such subjects as English, mathematics, and science. 388

basal metabolism rate (BMR) the minimum amount of energy an individual uses in a resting state. 99

behavior genetics the field that seeks to discover the influence of heredity and environment on individual differences in human traits and development. 109

big five factors of personality five core traits of personality: openness to experience, conscientiousness, extraversion, agreeableness, and neuroticism (emotional instability). 191

biological processes physical changes in an individual's body. 20

biopsychosocial approach emphasizes that problems develop through an interaction of biological, psychological, and social factors. 505

bisexual a person who is attracted to people of both sexes. 238

boundary ambiguity the uncertainty in stepfamilies about who is in or out of the family and who is performing or responsible for certain tasks in the family system. 336

bulimia nervosa in this eating disorder, the individual consistently follows a binge-and-purge eating pattern. 534

care perspective the moral perspective of Carol Gilligan, which views people in terms of their connectedness with others and emphasizes interpersonal communication, relationships with others, and concern for others. 280

career self-concept theory Super's theory that an individual's self-concepts play a central role in his or her career choices and that in adolescence individuals first construct their career self-concept. 448

case study an in-depth look at a single individual. 62

character education a direct moral education approach that involves teaching students a basic moral literacy to prevent them from engaging in immoral behavior or doing harm to themselves or others. 289

Chicano the name politically conscious Mexican American adolescents give themselves, reflecting the combination of their Spanish-Mexican-Indian heritage and Anglo influence. 176

chlamydia one of most common sexually transmitted infections, named for *Chlamydia trachomatis,* an organism that spreads by sexual contact and infects the genital organs of both sexes. 256

chromosomes threadlike structures that contain deoxyribonucleic acid or DNA. 107

cliques small groups that range from two to about twelve individuals and average about five to six individuals. 365

cognitive constructivist approaches approaches that emphasize the adolescent's active, cognitive construction of knowledge and understanding; an example is Piaget's theory. 389

cognitive developmental theory of gender in this view, children's gender-typing occurs after they have developed a concept of gender. Once they begin to consistently conceive of themselves as male or female, children often organize their world on the basis of gender. 208

cognitive disequilibrium theory Hoffman's theory that adolescence is an important period in moral development, in which, because of broader experiences associated with the move to high school or college, individuals recognize that their set of beliefs is but one of many and that there is considerable debate about what is right and wrong. 274

cognitive moral education an approach based on the belief that students should learn to value things like democracy and justice as their moral reasoning develops; Kohlberg's theory has been the basis for many of the cognitive moral education approaches. 290

cognitive processes changes in an individual's thinking and intelligence. 20

commitment the part of identity development in which adolescents show a personal investment in what they are going to do. 180

concrete operational stage Piaget's third stage, which lasts approximately from 7 to 11 years of age. In this stage, children can perform operations. Logical reasoning replaces intuitive thought as long as the reasoning can be applied to specific or concrete examples. 122

conduct disorder the psychiatric diagnostic category for the occurrence of multiple delinquent activities over a six-month period. These behaviors include truancy, running away, fire setting, cruelty to animals, breaking and entering, and excessive fighting. 523

conformity this occurs when individuals adopt the attitudes or behaviors of others because of real or imagined pressure from them. 354

conglomerate strategies the use of a combination of techniques, rather than a single approach, to improve adolescents' social skills; also called coaching. 358

connectedness an important element in adolescent identity development. It consists of two dimensions: mutuality, or sensitivity to and respect for others' views; and permeability, openness to others' views. 182

conscience the component of the superego that involves behaviors disapproved of by parents. 285

contexts the settings in which development occurs. These settings are influenced by historical, economic, social, and cultural factors. 14

continuity-discontinuity issue the issue regarding whether development involves gradual, cumulative change (continuity) or distinct stages (discontinuity). 26

continuity view a developmental view that emphasizes the role of early parent-child relationships in constructing a basic way of relating to people throughout the life span. 311

controversial children children who are frequently nominated both as a best friend and as being disliked. 356

conventional reasoning the second, or intermediate, level in Kohlberg's theory of moral development. Internalization is intermediate. Individuals abide by certain standards (internal), but they are the standards of others (external), such as parents or the laws of society. 276

convergent thinking a pattern of thinking in which individuals produce one correct answer; characteristic of the items on conventional intelligence tests; coined by Guilford. 140

correlational research the goal is to describe the strength of the relationship between two or more events or characteristics. 63

creativity the ability to think in novel and unusual ways and discover unique solutions to problems. 140

crisis a period of identity development during which the adolescent is choosing among meaningful alternatives. 180

critical thinking thinking reflectively and productively and evaluating the evidence. 139

cross-cultural studies studies that compare a culture with one or more other cultures. Such studies provide information about the degree to which adolescent development is similar, or universal, across cultures or about the degree to which it is culture-specific. 465

cross-sectional research a research strategy in which individuals of different ages are compared at one time. 65

crowds a larger group structure than cliques. Adolescents are usually members of a crowd based on reputation and may or may not spend much time together. 366

culture the behavior, patterns, beliefs, and all other products of a particular group of people that are passed on from generation to generation. 463

culture-fair tests tests of intelligence that are intended to be free of cultural bias. 154

date, or acquaintance, rape coercive sexual activity directed at someone whom the perpetrator knows. 257

dating scripts the cognitive models that adolescents and adults use to guide and evaluate dating interactions. 378

dependent variable the factor that is measured in experimental research. 64

depressants drugs that slow the central nervous system, bodily functions, and behavior. 518

descriptive research has the purpose of observing and recording behavior. 59

development the pattern of change that begins at conception and continues throughout the life span. Most development involves growth, although it also includes decay (as in death and dying). 20

developmental career choice theory Ginzberg's theory that children and adolescents go through three career choice stages: fantasy, tentative, and realistic. 448

developmental construction views views sharing the belief that as individuals grow up, they acquire modes of relating to others. There are two main variations of this view. One emphasizes continuity and stability in relationships throughout the life span; the other emphasizes discontinuity and changes in relationships throughout the life span. 311

developmental psychopathology the area of psychology that focuses on describing and exploring the developmental pathways of problems. 506

difficult child this child reacts negatively to many situations and is slow to accept new experiences. 193

direct instruction approach a teacher-centered approach characterized by teacher direction and control, mastery of academic skills, high expectations for students' progress, and maximum time spent on learning tasks. 389

discontinuity view a developmental view that emphasizes change and growth in relationships over time. 313

dismissing/avoidant attachment an insecure attachment category in which individu-als de-emphasize the importance of attachment. This category is associated with consistent experiences of rejection of attachment needs by caregivers. 327

divergent thinking a pattern of thinking in which individuals produce many answers to the same question; more characteristic of creativity than convergent thinking; coined by Guilford. 140

DNA a complex molecule that contains genetic information. 107

e-mail electronic mail, a valuable way the Internet can be used. Messages can be sent to and received by individuals as well as large numbers of people. 493

early adolescence the developmental period that corresponds roughly to the middle school or junior high school years and includes most pubertal change. 21

early adulthood the developmental period beginning in the late teens or early twenties and lasting into the thirties. 21

early childhood the developmental period extending from the end of infancy to about 5 or 6 years of age; sometimes called the preschool years. 20

early-later experience issue this issue focuses on the degree to which early experiences (especially early in childhood) or later experiences are the key determinants of development. 27

easy child this child is generally in a positive mood, quickly establishes regular routines, and adapts easily to new experiences. 193

eclectic theoretical orientation an orientation that does not follow any one theoretical approach, but rather, selects from each theory whatever is considered the best in it. 58

ecological, contextual theory Bronfenbrenner's environmental systems theory that focuses on five environmental systems: microsystem, mesosystem, exosystem, macrosystem, and chronosystem. 57

ego ideal the component of the superego that involves ideal standards approved by parents. 285

emerging adulthood occurring from approximately 18 to 25 years of age, this transitional period between adolescence and adulthood is characterized by experimentation and exploration. 24

emotion feeling or affect that involves physiological arousal, behavioral expression, and sometimes conscious experience. 188

emotional autonomy the capacity to relinquish childlike dependencies on parents. 325

emotional intelligence the ability to perceive and express emotion accurately and adaptively, to understand emotion and emotional knowledge, to use feelings to facilitate thought, and to manage emotions in oneself and others. 150

emotional isolation a type of loneliness that arises when a person lacks an intimate attachment relationship; single, divorced, and widowed adults often experience this type of loneliness. 187

empathy reacting to another's feelings with an emotional response that is similar to the other's response. 286

epigenetic view emphasizes that development is the result of an ongoing bidirectional interchange between heredity and environment. 112

equilibration a mechanism in Piaget's theory that explains how children or adolescents shift from one state of thought to the next. The shift occurs as they experience cognitive conflict or a disequilibrium in trying to understand the world. Eventually, the child or adolescent resolves the conflict and reaches a balance, or equilibrium. 122

Erikson's theory includes eight stages of human development. Each stage consists of a unique developmental task that confronts individuals with a crisis that must be faced. 50

estrogens the main class of female sex hormones. 84

ethnic gloss using an ethnic label such as African American or Latino in a superficial way that portrays an ethnic group as being more homogeneous than it really is. 70

ethnic identity an enduring, basic aspect of the self that includes a sense of membership in an ethnic group and the attitudes and feelings related to that membership. 183

ethnicity a dimension of culture based on cultural heritage, nationality, race, religion, and language. 464

ethnocentrism a tendency to favor one's own group over other groups. 465

evocative genotype-environment correlations correlations that occur when an adolescent's genetically shaped characteristics elicit certain types of physical and social environments. 110

evolutionary psychology an approach that emphasizes the importance of adaptation, reproduction, and "survival of the fittest" in explaining behavior. 105

experience sampling method (ESM) involves providing participants with electronic pagers and then beeping them at random times, at which time they are asked to report on various aspects of their lives. 62

experimental research research that involves an experiment, a carefully regulated procedure in which one or more of the factors believed to influence the behavior being studied are manipulated while all other factors are held constant. 64

externalizing problems occur when individuals turn problems outward. An example is juvenile delinquency. 506

extrinsic motivation external motivational factors such as rewards and punishments. 430

failure syndrome having low expectations for success and giving up at the first sign of difficulty. 439

feminization of poverty the fact that far more women than men live in poverty. Women's low income, divorce, and the resolution of divorce cases by the judicial system, which leaves women with less money than they and their children need to adequately function, are the likely causes. 483

flow Csikszentmihalyi's concept of optimal life experiences, which he believes occur most often when people develop a sense of mastery and are absorbed in a state of concentration when they're engaged in an activity. 430

forgiveness this is an aspect of prosocial behavior that occurs when an injured person releases the injurer from possible behavioral retaliation. 284

formal operational stage Piaget's fourth and final stage of cognitive development, which he believed emerges at 11 to 15 years of age. It is characterized by abstract, idealistic, and logical thought. 123

friends a subset of peers who engage in mutual companionship, support, and intimacy. 360

gender the sociocultural and psychological dimensions of being male or female. 202

gender intensification hypothesis this hypothesis states that psychological and behavioral differences between boys and girls become greater during early adolescence because of increased socialization pressures to conform to masculine and feminine gender roles. 220

gender role a set of expectations that prescribes how females and males should think, act, and feel. 202

gender-role transcendence the belief that, when an individual's competence is at issue, it should be conceptualized not on the basis of masculinity, femininity, or androgyny but, rather, on a person basis. 219

gender schema a cognitive structure that organizes the world in terms of male and female. 209

gender schema theory according to this theory, an individual's attention and behavior are guided by an internal motivation to conform to gender-based sociocultural standards and stereotypes. 209

gender stereotypes broad categories that reflect our impressions and beliefs about females and males. 210

generational inequity the unfair treatment of younger members of an aging society in which older adults pile up advantages by receiving inequitably large allocations of resources, such as Social Security and Medicare. 15

genes the units of hereditary information, which are short segments composed of DNA. 107

genital herpes a sexually transmitted infection caused by a large family of viruses of different strains. These strains produce other, non-sexually transmitted diseases such as chicken pox and mononucleosis. 255

genital warts caused by the human papillomavirus, and the most common STI in the United States, genital warts are very contagious. 255

genotype a person's genetic heritage; the actual genetic material. 109

gonorrhea reported to be one of the most common STIs in the United States, this sexually transmitted infection is caused by a bacterium called *Neisseria gonorrhoeae*, which thrives in the moist mucous membranes lining the mouth, throat, vagina, cervix, urethra, and anal tract. This disease is commonly called the "drip" or the "clap." 255

goodness of fit the match between an individual's temperament style and the

environmental demands the individual must cope with. 194

hallucinogens also called psychedelic (mind-altering) drugs, these drugs alter an individual's perceptual experiences and produce hallucinations. 514

helpless orientation an outlook in which individuals focus on their personal inadequacies, often attribute their difficulty to a lack of ability, and display negative affect (including boredom and anxiety). This orientation undermines performance. 432

heritability the fraction of the variance in a population that is attributed to genetics. 152

heteronomous morality the first stage of moral development in Piaget's theory, occurring at 4 to 7 years of age. Justice and rules are conceived of as unchangeable properties of the world, removed from the control of people. 274

hidden curriculum the pervasive moral atmosphere that characterizes schools. 289

hormones powerful chemicals secreted by the endocrine glands and carried through the body by the bloodstream. 83

hostile environment sexual harassment sexual harassment in which students are subjected to unwelcome sexual conduct that is so severe, persistent, or pervasive that it limits the students' ability to benefit from their education. 258

hypotheses specific assumptions and predictions that can be tested to determine their accuracy. 47

hypothetical-deductive reasoning Piaget's term for adolescents' ability, in the formal operational stage, to develop hypotheses, or best guesses, about ways to solve problems; they then systematically deduce, or conclude, the best path to follow in solving the problem. 124

identity achievement Marcia's term for an adolescent who has undergone a crisis and made a commitment. 181

identity diffusion Marcia's term for the state adolescents are in when they have not yet experienced a crisis or made any commitments. 180

identity foreclosure Marcia's term for the state adolescents are in when they have made a commitment but have not experienced a crisis. 181

identity moratorium Marcia's term for the state of adolescents who are in the midst of a crisis but who have not made a clear commitment to an identity. 181

identity versus identity confusion Erikson's fifth developmental stage, which occurs during adolescence. At this time, individuals are faced with deciding who they are, what they are all about, and where they are going in life. 178

immanent justice Piaget's concept that if a rule is broken, punishment will be meted out immediately. 274

implicit personality theory the layperson's conception of personality. 158

inclusion educating a child or adolescent with special education needs full-time in a general school program. 418

independent variable the factor that is manipulated in experimental research. 64

index offenses whether they are committed by juveniles or adults, these are criminal acts, such as robbery, rape, and homicide. 522

individuality an important element in adolescent identity development. It consists of two dimensions: self-assertion, the ability to have and communicate a point of view; and separateness, the use of communication patterns to express how one is different from others. 182

Individuals with Disabilities Education Act (IDEA) this spells out broad mandates for services to all children and adolescents with disabilities. These include evaluation and eligibility determination, appropriate education and the individualized education program (IEP), and a least restrictive environment. 418

induction a discipline technique in which a parent uses reason and explanation of the consequences for others of a child's actions. 288

indulgent parenting a style in which parents are highly involved with their adolescents but place few demands or controls on them. This is associated with adolescents' social incompetence, especially a lack of self-control. 319

infancy the developmental period that extends from birth to 18 or 24 months. 20

information-processing theory emphasizes that individuals manipulate information, monitor it, and strategize about it. Central to

this approach are the processes of memory and thinking. 54

insecure attachment in this attachment pattern, infants either avoid the caregiver or show considerable resistance or ambivalence toward the caregiver. This pattern is theorized to be related to difficulties in relationships and problems in later development. 327

intelligence the ability to solve problems and to adapt to and learn from everyday experiences; not everyone agrees on what constitutes intelligence. 145

intelligence quotient (IQ) a person's tested mental age divided by chronological age, multiplied by 100. 145

internalization the developmental change from behavior that is externally controlled to behavior that is controlled by internal standards and principles. 275

internalizing problems occur when individuals turn problems inward. Examples include anxiety and depression. 506

Internet the core of computer-mediated communication. The Internet system is worldwide and connects thousands of computer networks, providing an incredible array of information adolescents can access. 492

intimacy in friendship in most research, this is defined narrowly as self-disclosure or sharing of private thoughts. 363

intimacy versus isolation Erikson's sixth developmental stage, which individuals experience during the early adulthood years. At this time, individuals face the developmental task of forming intimate relationships with others. 186

intimate style the individual forms and maintains one or more deep and long-lasting love relationships. 186

intrinsic motivation internal motivational factors such as self-determination, curiosity, challenge, and effort. 430

inventionist view the view that adolescence is a sociohistorical creation. Especially important in this view are the sociohistorical circumstances at the beginning of the twentieth century, a time when legislation was enacted that ensured the dependency of youth and made their move into the economic sphere more manageable. 9

isolated style the individual withdraws from social encounters and has little or no attachment to same- or opposite-sex individuals. 186

jigsaw classroom a strategy in which students from different cultural backgrounds are placed in a cooperative group in which, together, they have to construct different parts of a project to reach a common goal. 412

justice perspective a moral perspective that focuses on the rights of the individual; individuals independently make moral decisions. 280

juvenile delinquency a broad range of child and adolescent behaviors, including socially unacceptable behavior, status offenses, and criminal acts. 522

laboratory a controlled setting in which many of the complex factors of the "real world" are removed. 60

late adolescence approximately the latter half of the second decade of life. Career interests, dating, and identity exploration are often more pronounced in late adolescence than in early adolescence. 21

late adulthood the developmental period that lasts from about 60 to 70 years of age until death. 22

learning disability individuals with a learning disability are of normal intelligence or above, have difficulties in at least one academic area and usually several, and their difficulties cannot be attributed to any other diagnosed problem or disorder, such as mental retardation. 416

least restrictive environment a setting that is as similar as possible to the one in which the children or adolescents without a disability are educated; under the Individuals with Disabilities Education Act, the child or adolescent must be educated in this setting. 418

longitudinal research a research strategy in which the same individuals are studied over a period of time, usually several years or more. 65

love withdrawal a discipline technique in which a parent removes attention or love from a child. 288

major depressive disorder the diagnosis when an individual experiences a major depressive episode and depressed characteristics, such as lethargy and depression, for two weeks or longer and daily functioning becomes impaired. 529

mastery orientation an outlook in which individuals focus on the task rather than on their ability, have positive affect, and generate solution-oriented strategies that improve their performance. 432

menarche a girl's first menstrual period. 86

mental age (MA) an individual's level of mental development relative to others; a concept developed by Binet. 145

metacognition cognition about cognition, or "knowing about knowing." 142

middle adulthood the developmental period that is entered at about 35 to 45 years and exited at about 55 to 65 years of age. 21

middle and late childhood the developmental period extending from about 6 to about 10 or 11 years of age; sometimes called the elementary school years. 20

moral development thoughts, behaviors, and feelings regarding standards of right and wrong. 273

multicultural model this model promotes a pluralistic approach to understanding two or more cultures. It argues that people can maintain their distinctive identities while working with others from different cultures to meet common national or economic needs. 468

naturalistic observation observing behavior in real-world settings. 60

nature-nurture issue involves the debate about whether development is primarily influenced by nature or nurture. Nature refers to an organism's biological inheritance, nurture to its environmental experiences. 26

neglected children children who are infrequently nominated as a best friend but are not disliked by their peers. 356

neglectful parenting a style in which the parent is very uninvolved in the adolescent's life. It is associated with adolescents' social incompetence, especially a lack of self-control. 318

neo-Piagetians theorists who argue that Piaget got some things right but that his theory needs considerable revision. In their revision, they give more emphasis to information processing that involves attention, memory, and strategies; they also seek to provide more precise explanations of cognitive changes. 129

neurons nerve cells, which are the nervous system's basic units. 94

nonshared environmental experiences the adolescent's own unique experiences, both within a family and outside the family, that are not shared by another sibling. 111

normal distribution a symmetrical distribution of values or scores, with a majority of scores falling in the middle of the possible range of scores and few scores appearing toward the extremes of the range; a distribution that yields what is called a "bell-shaped curve." 146

norms rules that apply to all members of a group. 365

passive genotype-environment correlations correlations that occur because biological parents, who are genetically related to the child, provide a rearing environment for the child. 110

peers children or adolescents who are about the same age or maturity level. 351

performance orientation an outlook in which individuals are concerned with performance outcome rather than performance process. For performance-oriented students, winning is what matters. 433

permissive strategy of classroom management this strategy offers students considerable autonomy but provides them with little support for developing learning skills or managing their behavior. 404

personality type theory Holland believes that an effort should be made to match an individual's career choice with his or her personality. 448

phenotype the way an individual's genotype is expressed in observed and measurable characteristics. 109

physical dependence physical need for a drug that is accompanied by unpleasant withdrawal symptoms when the drug is discontinued. 509

Piaget's theory states that children actively construct their understanding of the world and go through four stages of cognitive development. 53

popular children children who are frequently nominated as a best friend and are rarely disliked by their peers. 356

possible self what individuals might become, what they would like to become, and what they are afraid of becoming. 170

postconventional reasoning the highest level in Kohlberg's theory of moral development. Morality is completely internalized. 276

postformal thought thought that is reflective, relativistic, and provisional; realistic; and open to emotions and subjective. 129

power assertion a discipline technique in which a parent attempts to gain control over a child or a child's resources. 288

preconventional reasoning the lowest level in Kohlberg's theory of moral development. The individual shows no internalization of moral values—moral reasoning is controlled by external rewards and punishment. 275

preintimate style the individual shows mixed emotions about commitment, an ambivalence reflected in the strategy of offering love without obligations. 186

prejudice an unjustified negative attitude toward an individual because of her or his membership in a group. 473

prenatal period the time from conception to birth. 20

preoccupied/ambivalent attachment an insecure attachment category in which adolescents are hypertuned to attachment experiences. This is thought to mainly occur because parents are inconsistently available to the adolescents. 327

preoperational stage Piaget's second stage, which lasts approximately from 2 to 7 years of age. In this stage, children begin to represent their world with words, images, and drawings. 122

pseudointimate style the individual maintains a long-lasting sexual attachment with little or no depth or closeness. 186

psychoanalytic theory describes development as primarily unconscious and heavily colored by emotion. Behavior is merely a surface characteristic and the symbolic workings of the mind have to be analyzed to understand behavior. Early experiences with parents are emphasized. 48

psychological dependence strong desire and craving to repeat the use of a drug for various emotional reasons, such as a feeling of well-being and reduction of distress. 509

psychometric/intelligence view a view that emphasizes the importance of individual differences in intelligence; many advocates of this view also argue that intelligence should be assessed with intelligence tests. 144

psychosocial moratorium Erikson's term for the gap between childhood security and adult autonomy that adolescents experience as part of their identity exploration. 178

puberty a period of rapid physical maturation involving hormonal and bodily changes that take place primarily in early adolescence. 83

Public Law 94-142 The Education for All Handicapped Children Act, which requires all students with disabilities to be given a free, appropriate education and provides the funding to help implement this education. 418

quid pro quo sexual harassment sexual harassment in which a school employee threatens to base an educational decision (such as a grade) on a student's submission to unwelcome conduct. 258

rape forcible sexual intercourse with a person who does not give consent. 257

rapport talk the language of conversation, establishing connections, and negotiating relationships. 214

reciprocal socialization the process by which children and adolescents socialize parents, just as parents socialize them. 309

rejected children children who are infrequently nominated as a best friend and are actively disliked by their peers. 356

report talk talk that gives information; public speaking is an example. 214

rites of passage ceremonies or rituals that mark an individual's transition from one status to another, such as the entry into adulthood. 469

roles certain positions in a group that are governed by rules and expectations. Roles define how adolescents should behave in those positions. 365

romantic love also called passionate love or eros, this love has strong sexual and infatuation components, and it often predominates in the early part of a love relationship. 375

schema a concept or framework that exists in the individual's mind to organize and interpret information. 209

schema a mental concept or framework that is useful in organizing and interpreting information. 121

secure attachment in this attachment pattern, infants use their primary caregiver, usually the mother, as a secure base from which to explore the environment. Secure attachment is theorized to be an important foundation for psychological development later in childhood, adolescence, and adulthood. 327

self-concept domain-specific evaluations of the self. 173

self-efficacy the belief that one can master a situation and produce positive outcomes. 433

self-esteem the global evaluative dimension of the self; also referred to as self-worth or self-image. 173

self-handicapping strategies some adolescents deliberately do not try in school, put off studying until the last minute, and use other self-handicapping strategies so that if their subsequent performance is at a low level, these circumstances, rather than lack of ability, will be seen as the cause. 440

self-regulatory learning the self-generation and self-monitoring of one's thoughts, feelings, and behaviors in order to reach a goal. 143

self-understanding the adolescent's cognitive representation of the self; the substance and content of the adolescent's self-conceptions. 169

sensorimotor stage Piaget's first stage of development, lasting from birth to about 2 years of age. In this stage, infants construct an understanding of the world by coordinating sensory experiences with physical, motoric actions. 122

service learning a form of education that promotes social responsibility and service to the community. 290

sexism prejudice and discrimination against an individual because of her or his sex. 211

sexual script a stereotyped pattern of role prescriptions for how individuals should sexually behave. Females and males have been socialized to follow different sexual scripts. 236

sexually transmitted infections (STIs) diseases that are contracted primarily through sexual contact. This contact is not limited to vaginal intercourse but includes oral-genital contact and anal-genital contact as well. 252

shared environmental experiences siblings' common experiences such as their parents' personalities and intellectual orientation, the family's social class, and the neighborhood in which they live. 111

slow-to-warm-up child this child has a low activity level, is somewhat negative, and displays a low intensity of mood. 193

social cognitive theory the view of psychologists who emphasize behavior, environment, and cognition as the key factors in development. 56

social cognitive theory of gender this theory emphasizes that children's and adolescents' gender development occurs through observation and imitation of gender behavior, and through rewards and punishments they experience for gender-appropriate and -inappropriate behavior. 205

social cognitive theory of moral development the theory that distinguishes between moral competence (the ability to produce moral behaviors) and moral performance (performing those behaviors in specific situations). 283

social constructivist approach emphasizes the social contexts of learning and the construction of knowledge through social interaction. 132

social constructivist approaches approaches that focus on collaboration with others to produce knowledge and understanding; an example is Vygotsky's theory. 389

social isolation a type of loneliness that occurs when a person lacks a sense of integrated involvement. Being deprived of participation in a group or community involving companionship, shared interests, organized activities, and meaningful roles causes a person to feel alienated, bored, and uneasy. 187

social policy a national government's course of action designed to influence the welfare of its citizens. 15

social role theory states that gender differences result from the contrasting roles of females and males with females having less power and status than males have and they control fewer resources. 204

socioeconomic status (SES) a grouping of people with similar occupational, educational, and economic characteristics. 464

socioemotional processes changes in an individual's relationships with other people, emotions, personality, and social contexts. 20

spermarche a boy's first ejaculation of semen. 86

standardized test a test with uniform procedures for administration and scoring. Many standardized tests allow a person's performance to be compared with the performance of other individuals. 61

status offenses performed by youths under a specified age, these are juvenile offenses that are not as serious as index offenses. These offenses may include such acts as drinking under age, truancy, and sexual promiscuity. 522

stereotype a generalization that reflects our impressions and beliefs about a broad group of people. All stereotypes refer to an image of what the typical member of a particular group is like. 11

stereotyped style the individual has superficial relationships that tend to be dominated by friendship ties with same-sex rather than opposite-sex individuals. 186

stimulants drugs that increase the activity of the central nervous system. 515

storm-and-stress view G. Stanley Hall's concept that adolescence is a turbulent time charged with conflict and mood swings. 8

synchrony the carefully coordinated interaction between the parent and the child or adolescent in which, often unknowingly, they are attuned to each other's behavior. 310

syphilis a sexually transmitted infection caused by the bacterium *Treponema pallidum,* a spirochete. 255

temperament an individual's behavioral style and characteristic way of responding. 192

theory an interrelated, coherent set of ideas that helps to explain observations and make predictions. 47

tolerance the condition in which a greater amount of a drug is needed to produce the same effect as a smaller amount used to produce the effect. 509

top-dog phenomenon the circumstance of moving from the top position (in elementary school, the oldest, biggest, and most powerful students) to the lowest position (in middle or junior high school, the youngest, smallest, and least powerful). 394

triarchic theory of intelligence Sternberg's view that intelligence comes in three main forms: analytical, creative, and practical. 149

twin study a study in which the behavioral similarity of identical twins is compared with the behavioral similarity of fraternal twins. 109

unresolved/disorganized attachment an insecure category in which the adolescent has an unusually high level of fear and is disoriented. This can result from such traumatic experiences as a parent's death or abuse by parents. 327

values beliefs and attitudes about the way things should be. 292

values clarification an educational approach that focuses on helping people clarify what is important to them, what is worth working for, and what purpose their lives are to serve. Students are encouraged to define their own values and understand others' values. 289

Vygotsky's theory a sociocultural cognitive theory that emphasizes how culture and social interaction guide cognitive development. 54

youth Kenniston's term for the transitional period between adolescence and adulthood, which is a time of economic and personal temporariness. 24

zone of proximal development (ZPD) Vygotsky's concept that refers to the range of tasks that are too difficult for an individual to master alone, but that can be mastered with the guidance or assistance of adults or more-skilled peers. 130

References

Abrahamson, A.C., Baker, L.A., & Caspi, A. (2002). Rebellious teens? Genetic and environmental influences on the social attitudes of adolescents. *Journal of Social Psychology, 83,* 1392–1408.

Acebo, C., & Carskadon, M.A. (2002). Influence of irregular sleep patterns on waking behavior. In M.A. Carskadon (Ed.), *Adolescent sleep patterns.* New York: Cambridge University Press.

Achenbach, T.M., & Edelbrock, C.S. (1981). Behavioral problems and competencies reported by parents of normal and disturbed children aged four through sixteen. *Monographs of the Society for Research in Child Development, 46* (1, Serial No. 188).

Achenbach, T.M., Howell, C.T., Quay H.C., & Conners, C.K. (1991). National survey of problems and competencies among four- to sixteen-year-olds. *Monographs of the Society for Research in Child Development, 56* (3, Serial No. 225).

Adair, L.S. (2001). Size at birth predicts age at menarche. *Pediatrics, 107,* E59.

Adams, G.R., Abraham, K.G., & Markstrom, C.A. (2000). The relations among identity development, self-consciousness and self-focusing during middle and late adolescence. In G. Adams (Ed.), *Adolescent development: The essential readings.* Malden, MA: Blackwell.

Adams, G.R., Gulotta, T.P., & Montemayor, R. (Eds.). (1992). *Adolescent identity formation.* Newbury Park, CA: Sage.

Adams, H. (2000). Behavior therapy. In A. Kazdin (Ed.), *Encyclopedia of psychology.* Washington, DC, and New York: American Psychological Association and Oxford University Press.

Adams, R., & Laursen, B. (2001). The organization and dynamics of adolescent conflict with parents and friends. *Journal of Marriage and the Family, 63,* 97–110.

Adamson, H.D. (2004). *Language minority students in America.* Mahwah, NJ: Erlbaum.

Adelson, J. (1979, January). Adolescence and the generalization gap. *Psychology Today,* pp. 33–37.

Adler, N.E., Ozer, E.J., & Tschann, J. (2003). Abortion among adolescents. *American Psychologist, 58,* 211–217.

Aertgeerts, B., & Buntinx, F. (2002). The relation between alcohol abuse or dependence and academic performance in first-year college students. *Journal of Adolescent Health, 31,* 223–225.

Ahn, N. (1994). Teenage childbearing and high school completion: Accounting for individual heterogeneity. *Family Planning Perspectives, 26,* 17–21.

Aiken, L.R. (2003). *Psychological testing and assessment* (11th ed.). Boston: Allyn & Bacon.

Ainsworth, M.D.S. (1979). Infant-mother attachment. *American Psychologist, 34,* 932–937.

Alan Guttmacher Institute. (1995). *National survey of the American male's sexual habits.* New York: Author.

Alan Guttmacher Institute. (1998). *Teen sex and pregnancy.* New York: Author.

Alan Guttmacher Institute. (2002). Teen pregnancy: Trends and lessons learned. In *Policy analysis: Issues in brief.* New York: Alan Guttmacher Institute.

Alan Guttmacher Institute. (2003). *Sex education: Needs, programs, and policies.* New York: Author.

Alan Guttmacher Institute. (2003a). *U.S. teenage pregnancy statistics.* New York: Alan Guttmacher Institute.

Alan Guttmacher Institute. (2003b). *An overview of abortion in the United States.* New York: Alan Guttmacher Institute.

Alderman, M.K. (2004). *Motivation and achievement.* Mahwah, NJ: Erlbaum.

Alexander, C., Piazza, M., Mekos, D., & Valente, T. (2001). Peers, schools, and cigarette smoking. *Journal of Adolescent Health, 29,* 22–30.

Alexander, K., Entwisle, D., and Kabbani, N. (2000). *The dropout process in life course perspective: Part I, profiling risk factors at home and school.* Baltimore: Johns Hopkins University.

Alexander, P.A. (2000). Toward a model of academic development: Schooling and the acquisition of knowledge. *Educational Researcher, 29,* 28–33.

Allen, J.P., Hauser, S.T., & Borman-Spurrell, E. (1996). Attachment security and related sequelae of severe adolescent psychopathology: An eleven-year follow-up study. *Journal of Consulting and Clinical Psychology, 64,* 254–263.

Allen, J.P., Hauser, S., Eickholt, C., Bell, K., & O'Connor, T. (1994). Autonomy and relatedness in family interactions as predictors of expressions of negative adolescent affect. *Journal of Research on Adolescence, 4,* 535–552.

Allen, J.P., McElhaney, K.B., Land, D.J., Kuminc, G.P., Moore, C.W., O'Beirne-Kelly, H., & Kilmer, S.L. (2003). A secure base in adolescence: Markers of attachment security in the mother-adolescent relationship. *Child Development, 74,* 292–307.

Allen, J.P., Philliber, S., Herring, S., & Kuperminc, G.P. (1997). Preventing teen pregnancy and academic failure: Experimental evaluation of a developmentally-based approach. *Child Development, 68,* 729–742.

Almagor, M., Tellegen, A., & Waller, N.G. (1995). The big seven model: A cross-cultural replication and further exploration of the basic dimensions of natural language trait descriptors.

Alsaker, F.D., & Flammer, A. (1999). *The adolescent experience: European and American adolescents in the 1990s.* Mahwah, NJ: Erlbaum.

Amabile, T. (1993). (Commentary). In D. Goleman, P. Kafman, & M. Ray, (Eds.), *The creative spirit.* New York: Plume.

Amato, P.R., & Booth, A. (1996). A prospective study of divorce and parent-child relationships. *Journal of Marriage and the Family, 58,* 356–365.

Amato, P.R., & Keith, B. (1991). Parental divorce and the well-being of children: A meta-analysis. *Psychological Bulletin, 110,* 26–46.

Ambuel, B., & Rappaport, J. (1992). Developmental trends in adolescents' psychological and legal competence to consent to abortion. *Law and Human Behavior, 16,* 129–154.

American Academy of Pediatrics. (2000). Suicide and suicide attempts in adolescence. *Pediatrics, 105,* 871–874.

American Association of University Women. (1992). *How schools shortchange girls: A study of major findings on girls and education.* Washington, DC: Author.

American Association of University Women. (1993). *Hostile hallways.* Washington, DC: Author.

American Psychiatric Association. (1994). *Diagnostic and statistical manual of mental disorders* (4th ed.). Washington, DC: Author.

American Sports Data. (2001). *Superstudy of sports participation.* Hartsdale, NY: American Sports Data.

Anastasi, A., & Urbina, S. (1996). *Psychological testing* (7th ed.). Upper Saddle River, NJ: Prentice-Hall.

Anderman, E.M., Maehr, M.L., & Midgley, C. (1996). *Declining motivation after the transition to middle school: Schools can make a difference.* Unpublished manuscript, University of Kentucky, Lexington.

Anderson, C.A. (2003). Video games and aggressive behavior. In D. Ravitch & J.P. Viteritti (Eds.), *Kids stuff: Marketing sex and violence to America's children.* Baltimore, MD: Johns Hopkins University Press.

Anderson, C.A., & Bushman, B.J. (2001). Effects of violent video games on aggressive behavior, aggressive cognition, aggressive affect, physiological arousal, and prosocial behavior: A meta-analytic review of the scientific literature. *Psychological Science, 12,* 353–359.

Anderson, C.A., & Dill, K.E. (2000). Video games and aggressive thoughts, feelings, and behavior in the laboratory and in life. *Journal of Personality and Social Psychology, 78,* 772–790.

Anderson, D.R., Huston, A.C., Schmitt, K., Linebarger, D.L., & Wright, J.C. (2001). Early childhood viewing and adolescent behavior: The recontact study. *Monographs of the Society for Research in Child Development, 66* (1), Serial No. 264.

Anderson, E., Greene, S.M., Hetherington, E.M., & Clingempeel, W.G. (1999). The dynamics of parental remarriage. In E.M. Hetherington (Ed.), *Coping with divorce, single parenting, and remarriage.* Mahwah, NJ: Erlbaum.

Anderson, S.E., Dallal, G.E., & Must, A. (2003). Relative weight and race influence average age at menarche: Results from two nationally representative surveys of U.S. girls studied 25 years apart. *Pediatrics, 111,* 844–850.

Anderton, B.H. (2002). Aging of the brain. *Mechanisms of Aging and Development, 123,* 811–817.

Andre, T., Frevert, R.L., & Schuchmann, D. (1989). From whom have college students learned what about sex? *Youth and Society, 20,* 241–268.

Angold, A., Costello, E.J., & Worthman, C.M. (1999). Puberty and depression: The roles of age, pubertal status and pubertal timing. *Psychological Medicine, 28,* 51–61.

Apter, D., & Hermanson, E. (2002). Update on female pubertal development. *Current Opinions in Obstetrics and Gynecology, 14,* 475–481.

Archer, S.L. (1989). The status of identity: Reflections on the need for intervention. *Journal of Adolescence, 12,* 345–359.

Archer, S.L., & Waterman, A.S. (1994). Adolescent identity development: Contextual perspectives. In C.B. Fisher & R.M. Lerner (Eds.), *Applied developmental psychology.* New York: McGraw-Hill.

Archibald, A.B., Graber, J.A., & Brooks-Gunn, J. (1999). Associations among parent-adolescent relationships, pubertal growth, dieting, and body image in young adolescent girls: A short-term longitudinal study. *Journal of Research on Adolescence, 9,* 395–415.

Archibald, A.B., Graber, J.A., & Brooks-Gunn, J. (2003). Pubertal processes and physical growth in adolescence. In G. Adams & M. Berzonsky (Eds.), *Blackwell handbook of adolescence.* Malden, MA: Blackwell.

Ardila-Rey, A., & Killen, M. (in press). Middle-class Colombian children's evaluations of personal, moral, and social-conventional interactions in the classroom. *International Journal of Behavioral Development.*

Arehart, D.M., & Smith, P.H. (1990). Identity in adolescence: Influences on dys- function and psychosocial task issues. *Journal of Youth and Adolescence, 19,* 63–72.

Armsden, G., & Greenberg, M.T. (1984). *The inventory of parent and peer attachment: Individual differences and their relationship to psychological well-being in adolescence.* Unpublished manuscript, University of Washington.

Arnett, J.J. (1990). Contraceptive use, sensation seeking, and adolescent egocentrism. *Journal of Youth and Adolescence, 19,* 171–180.

Arnett, J.J. (1991). Heavy metal music and reckless behavior among adolescents. *Journal of Youth and Adolescence, 20,* 573–592.

Arnett, J.J. (1995, March). *Are college students adults?* Paper presented at the meeting of the Society for Research in Child Development, Indianapolis.

Arnett, J.J. (2000). Emerging adulthood. *American Psychologist, 55,* 469–480.

Arnett, J.J. (2002). Adolescents in Western countries in the 21st century: Vast opportunities—for all? In B.B. Brown, R.W. Larson, & T.S. Saraswathi (Eds.), *The world's youth.* New York: Cambridge University Press.

Arnold, M.L. (1989, April). *Moral cognition and conduct: A quantitative review of the literature.* Paper presented at the Society for Research in Child Development, Indianapolis.

Aronson, E. (1986, August). *Teaching students things they think they know all about: The case of prejudice and desegregation.* Paper presented at the meeting of the American Psychological Association, Washington, DC.

Aronson, J. (2002). Stereotype threat: Contending and coping with unnerving expectations. *Improving academic achievement.* San Diego: Academic Press.

Aronson, J.M., Fried, C.B., & Good, C. (2002). Reducing the effects of stereotype threat on African American college students by shaping theories of intelligence. *Journal of Experimental Social Psychology, 38,* 113–125.

Aronson, J.M., Lustina, M.J., Good, C., Keough, K., Steele, C.M., & Brown, J. (1999). When white men can't do math: Necessary and sufficient factors in stereotype threat. *Journal of Experimental Social Psychology, 35,* 29–46.

Asakawa, K., & Csikszentmihalyi, M. (1998). The quality of experience of Asian American adolescents in academic activities: An exploration of educational achievement. *Journal of Research on Adolescence, 8,* 241–262.

Asarnow, J.R., & Callan, J.W. (1985). Boys with peer adjustment problems: Social cognitive processes. *Journal of Consulting and Clinical Psychology, 53,* 80–87.

Aseltine, R.H., & Gore, S. (1993). Mental health and social adaptation following the transition from high school. *Journal of Research on Adolescence, 3,* 247–270.

Ashton, P.T., & Webb, R.B. (1986). *Making a difference: Teachers' sense of efficacy and student achievement.* White Plains, NY: Longman.

Attie, I., & Brooks-Gunn, J. (1989). Development of eating problems in adolescent girls: A longitudinal study. *Developmental Psychology, 25,* 70–79.

Best, D. (2001). Cross-cultural gender roles. In J. Worrell (Ed.), *Encyclopedia of women and gender.* San Diego: Academic Press.

Buss, D.M. (1995). Psychological sex differences: Origins through sexual selection. *American Psychologist, 50,* 164–168.

Buss, D.M. (2000). Evolutionary psychology. In A. Kazdin (Ed.), *Encyclopedia of psychology.* Washington, DC, & New York: American Psychological Association and Oxford U. Press.

Buss, D.M. (2004). *Evolutionary psychology* (2nd ed.). Boston, Allyn & Bacon.

Bachman, J.G., O'Malley, P.M., Schulenberg, J., Johnston, L.D., Bryant, A.L., & Merline, A.C. (2002). *The decline of substance abuse in young adulthood.* Mahwah, NJ: Erlbaum.

Bachman, J.G., & Schulenberg, J. (1993). How part-time work intensity relates to drug use, problem behavior, time use, and satisfaction among high school seniors: Are these consequences or just correlates? *Developmental Psychology, 29,* 220–235.

Bacon, M.K., Child, I.L., & Barry, H. (1963). A cross-cultural study of correlates of crime. *Journal of Abnormal and Social Psychology, 66,* 291–300.

Baddeley, A. (1992). Working Memory. *Science, 255,* 556–560.

Baddeley, A. (2000). Short-term and working memory. In E. Tulving & F.I.M. Craik (Eds.), *The Oxford handbook of memory.* New York: Oxford University Press.

Baer, R.A., Ballenger, J., Berry, D.T.R., & Wetter, M.W. (1997). Detection of random responding on the MMPI-A. *Journal of Personality Assessment, 68,* 139–151.

Bagwell, C.I., Newcomb, A.F., & Bukowski, W.M. (1998, February). *Early adolescent friendship as a predictor of adult adjust-ment: A twelve-year follow-up investigation.* Paper presented at the biennial meeting of the Society for Research on Adolescence, San Diego.

Baird, A.A., Gruber, S.A., Cohen, B.M., Renshaw, R.J., & Yureglun-Todd, D.A. (1999). FMRI of the amygdala in children and adolescents. *American Academy of Child and Adolescent Psychiatry, 38,* 195–199.

Baldwin, S., & Hoffman, J.P. (2002). The dynamics of self-esteem: A growth curve analysis. *Journal of Youth and Adolescence, 31,* 101–113.

Baltes, P.B. (1987). Theoretical propositions of life-span developmental psychology: On the dynamics between growth and decline. *Developmental Psychology, 23,* 611–626.

Baltes, P.B. (2000). Life-span developmental theory. In A. Kazdin (Ed.), *Encyclopedia of psychology.* Washington, DC, and New York: American Psychological Association and Oxford University Press.

Baltes, P.B., Lindenberger, U., & Staudinger, U.M. (1998). Life-span theory in developmental psychology. In W. Damon (Ed.), *Handbook of child psychology* (5th ed., Vol. 1). New York: Wiley.

Bandura, A. (1965). Influences of models' reinforcement contingencies on the acquisition of imitative responses. *Journal of Personality and Social Psychology, 1,* 589–596.

Bandura, A. (1986). *Social foundations of thought and action: A social cognitive theory.* Englewood Cliffs. NJ: Prentice-Hall.

Bandura, A. (1991). Social cognitive theory of moral thought and action. In W.M. Kurtines & J. Gewirtz (Eds.), *Handbook of moral behavior and development* (Vol. 1), Hillsdale, NJ: Erlbaum.

Bandura, A. (1997). *Self-efficacy.* New York: W.H. Freeman.

Bandura, A. (1998, August). *Swimming against the mainstream: Accentuating the positive aspects of humanity.* Paper presented at the meeting of the American Psychological Association, San Francisco.

Bandura, A. (1999). Moral disengagement in the perpetuation of inhumanities. *Personality and Social Psychology Review, 3,* 193–209.

Bandura, A. (2000). Self-efficacy. In A. Kazdin (Ed.), *Encyclopedia of psychology.* Washington, DC, and New York: American Psychological Association and Oxford University Press.

Bandura, A. (2000). Social cognitive theory. In A. Kazdin (Ed.), *Encyclopedia of psychology.*

Washington, DC, and New York: American Psychological Association and Oxford University Press.

Bandura, A. (2001). Social cognitive theory. *Annual Review of Psychology,* Vol. 52. Palo Alto, CA: Annual Reviews.

Bandura, A. (2002). Selective moral disengagement in the exercise of moral agency. *Journal of Moral Education, 31,* 101–119.

Banks, J.A. (2002). *Introduction to multicultural education.* Boston: Allyn & Bacon.

Barakat, L.P., Kunin-Batson, & Kazak, A.E. (2003). Child health psychology. In I.B. Weiner (Ed.), *Handbook of psychology* (Vol. 9). New York: Wiley.

Barber, B., & Eccles, J. (2003). The joy of romance: Healthy adolescent relationships as an educational agenda. In P. Florsheim (Ed.), *Adolescent romantic relations and sexual behavior.* Mahwah, NJ: Erlbaum.

Barber, B.L., Eccles, J.S., & Stone, M.R. (2001, April). *Whatever happened to the jock, the brain, and the princess? Young adult pathways linked to adolescent activity involvement and identity.* Paper presented at the meeting of the Society for Research in Child Development, Minneapolis.

Barenboim, C. (1981). The development of person perception in childhood and adolescence: From behavioral comparisons to psychological constructs to psychological comparisons. *Child Development, 52,* 129–144.

Barker, R., & Wright, H.F. (1951). *One boy's day.* New York: Harper.

Barnard, K.E., & Solchany, J.E. (2002). Mothering. In M.H. Bornstein (Ed.), *Handbook of parenting.* (2nd ed.). Mahwah, NJ: Erlbaum.

Barnes, G.M., Farrell, M.P., & Banerjee, S. (1995). Family influences on alcohol abuse and other problem behaviors among Black and White Americans. In G.M. Boyd, J. Howard, & R.A. Zucker (Eds.), *Alcohol problems among adolescents.* Hillsdale, NJ: Erlbaum.

Barnouw, V. (1975). *An introduction to anthropology: Vol. 2. Ethnology.* Homewood, IL: Dorsey Press.

Basen-Enquist, K., Coyle, K.K., Parcel, G.S., Kirby, D., Bnanspach, S.W., Carvajal, S.C., & Baumler, E. (2001). Schoolwide effects of a multicomponent HIV, STD, and pregnancy prevention program for high school students. *Health Education and Behavior, 28,* 166–185.

Baskett, L.M., & Johnston, S.M. (1982). The young child's interaction with parents versus siblings. *Child Development, 53,* 643–650.

Bat-Chava, Y., Allen, L., Aber, J.L., & Seidman, E. (1997, April). *Racial and ethnic identity and the contexts of development.* Paper presented at the meeting of the Society for Research in Child Development, Washington, DC.

Bauer, R.M., Bowers, D., & Leritz, E.C. (2003). Neuropsychology. In I.B. Weiner (Ed.), *Handbook of psychology* (Vol. 2). New York: Wiley.

Baumeister, R.E. (1991). Identity crisis. In R.M. Lerner, A.C. Petersen, & J. Brooks-Gunn (Eds.), *Encyclopedia of adolescence* (Vol. 1). New York: Garland.

Baumrind, D. (1971). Current patterns of parental authority. *Developmental Psychology Monographs, 4* (1, Pt. 2).

Baumrind, D. (1991). Effective parenting during the early adolescent transition. In P.A. Cowan & E.M. Hetherington (Eds.), *Advances in family research* (Vol. 2). Hillsdale, NJ: Erlbaum.

Baumrind, D. (1999, November). Unpublished review of J.W. Santrock's *Child Development,* 9th ed. New York: McGraw-Hill.

Bauserman, R. (2003). Child adjustment in joint-custody versus sole-custody arrangements: A meta-analytic review. *Journal of Family Psychology, 16,* 91–102.

Beal, C.R. (1994). *Boys and girls: The development of gender roles.* New York: McGraw-Hill.

Bearison, D.J., & Dorval, B. (2002). *Collaborative cognition.* Westport, CT: Ablex.

Beck, A.T. (1993). Cognitive therapy: Past, present, and future. *Journal of Consulting and Clinical Psychology, 61,* 194–198.

Beckham, E.E. (2000). Depression. In A. Kazdin (Ed.), *Encyclopedia of psychology.* Washington, DC, and New York: American Psychological Association and Oxford University Press.

Bednar, R.L., Wells, M.G., & Peterson, S.R. (1995). *Self-esteem* (2nd ed.). Washington, DC: American Psychological Association.

Beins, B. (2004). *Research methods.* Boston: Allyn & Bacon.

Belansky, E.S., & Clements, P. (1992, March). *Adolescence: A crossroads for gender-role transcendence or gender-role intensification.* Paper presented at the meeting of the Society for Research on Adolescence, Washington, DC.

Bell, A.P., Weinberg, M.S., & Mammersmith, S.K. (1981). *Sexual prefer-ence: Its development in men and women.* New York: Simon & Schuster.

Belsky, J. (1981). Early human experience: A family perspective. *Developmental Psychology, 17,* 3–23.

Belson, W. (1978). *Television violence and the adolescent boy.* London: Saxon House.

Bem, S.L. (1977). On the utility of alternative procedures for assessing psychological androgyny. *Journal of Consulting and Clinical Psychology, 45,* 196–205.

Bence, P. (1991). Television, adolescents and development. In R.M. Lerner, A.C. Petersen, & J. Brooks-Gunn (Eds.), *Encyclopedia of adolescence* (Vol. 2). New York: Garland.

Bender, W.N. (2004). *Learning disabilities* (5th ed.). Boston: Allyn & Bacon.

Benin, M. (1997, August). *A longitudinal study of marital satisfaction.* Paper presented at the meeting of the American Sociological Association, Toronto.

Bennett, C. (2003). *Comprehensive multicultural education* (5th ed.). Boston: Allyn & Bacon.

Bennett, W. (1993). *The book of virtues.* New York: Simon & Schuster.

Benson, E. (2003, February). Intelligence across cultures. *Monitor on Psychology, 34* (2), 56–58.

Benson, P. (1993). *The troubled journey.* Minneapolis: The Search Institute.

Benson, P.L. (1997). *All kids are our kids: What communities must do to raise caring and responsible children and adolescents.* Minneapolis: Search Institute.

Bereiter, C. (2002). *Education and the mind in the knowledge age.* Mahwah, NJ: Erlbaum.

Bergman, R. (2004). Identity as motivation: Toward a theory of the moral self. In D.K. Lapsley & D. Narvez (Eds.), *Moral development, self, and identity.* Mahwah, NJ: Erlbaum.

Berkowitz, M.W., & Gibbs, J.C. (1983). Measuring the developmental features of moral discussion. *Merrill-Palmer Quarterly, 29,* 399–410.

Berndt, T.J. (1979). Developmental changes in conformity to peers and parents. *Developmental Psychology, 15,* 608–616.

Berndt, T.J. (1982). The features and effects of friendship in early adolescence. *Child Development, 53,* 1447–1460.

Berndt, T.J. (1999). Friends' influence on children's adjustment. In W.A. Collins & B. Laursen (Eds.), *Relationships as developmental contexts.* Mahwah, NJ: Erlbaum.

Berndt, T.J., & Keefe, K. (1996). Friends' influence on school adjustment: A motivational analysis. In J. Juvonen & K. Wentzel (Eds.), *Social motivation: Understanding children's school adjustment.* New York: Cambridge.

Berndt, T.J., & Perry, T.B. (1990). Distinctive features and effects of early adolescent friendships. In R. Montemayor (Ed.), *Advances in adolescent research.* Greenwich, CT: JAI Press.

Berry, J.W. (1990). Psychology of acculturation: Understanding individuals moving between cultures. In R.W. Brislin (Ed.), *Applied cross-cultural psychology.* Thousand Oaks, CA: Sage.

Berry, J.W. (2000). Cultural foundations of human behavior. In A. Kazdin (Ed.), *Encyclopedia of Psychology.* Washington, DC, and New York: American Psychological Association and Oxford University Press.

Berry, J.W. (2003). Conceptual approaches to acculturation. In K.M. Chun, P.B. Organista, & G. Marn (Eds.), *Acculturation.* Washington, DC: American Psychological Association.

Berscheid, E., & Reis, H.T. (1998). Attraction and close relationships. In D.T. Gilbert, S.T. Fiske, & G. Lindzey (Eds.), *The handbook of social psychology* (4th ed.). New York: McGraw-Hill.

Berscheid, E., Snyder, M., & Omoto, A.M. (1989). Issues in studying close relationships. In C. Hendrick (Ed.), *Close relationships.* Newbury Park, CA: Sage.

Berzonsky, M.D., & Adams, G.R. (1999). Reevaluating the identity status paradigm: Still useful after 35 years. *Developmental Review, 19,* 557–590.

Best, J.W., & Kahn, J.V. (2003). *Research in education* (9th ed.). Boston: Allyn & Bacon.

Betz, N. (2002). Explicating an ecological approach to the career development of women. *Career Development Quarterly, 50,* 335–338.

Bhutta, A.T., & Anand, K.J. (2002). Vulnerability of the developing brain: Neuronal mechanisms. *Clinical Perinatology, 29,* 357–372.

Biller, H.B. (1993). *Fathers and families: Paternal factors in child development.* Westport, CT: Auburn House.

Billy, J.O.G., Rodgers, J.L., & Udry, J.R. (1984). Adolescent sexual behavior and friendship choice. *Social Forces, 62,* 653–678.

Bingham, C.R., & Crockett, L.J. (1996). Longitudinal adjustment patterns of boys and girls experiencing early, middle, and late sexual intercourse. *Developmental Psychology, 32,* 647–658.

Bissell, J., Manring, A., & Rowland, V. (1999). *Cybereducator.* New York: McGraw-Hill.

Bjorklund, D.F. (2000). *Children's thinking: Developmental function and individual differences* (3rd ed.). Belmont, CA: Wadsworth.

Bjorklund, D.F., & Pellegrini, A.D. (2002). *The origins of human nature.* Washington, DC: American Psychological Association.

Blackwell, L.S., Trzesniewski, K.H., & Dweck, C.S. (2003, April). *Academic achievement over the junior high school transition: A longitudinal study and an intervention.* Paper presented at the meeting of the Society for Research in Child Development, Tampa.

Blake, S.M., Ledsky, R., Goodenow, C., Sawyer, R., Lohrmann, D., & Windsor, R. (2003). Condom availability programs in Massachusetts high schools: Relationships with condom use and sexual behavior. *American Journal of Public Health, 93,* 955–962.

Blash, R., & Unger, D.G. (1992, March). *Cultural factors and the self-esteem and aspirations of African-American adolescent males.* Paper presented at the meeting of the Society for Research on Adolescence, Washington, DC.

Blasi, A. (1988). Identity and the development of the self. In D. Lapsley & F.C. Power (Eds.), *Self, ego, and identity: Integrative approaches.* New York: Springer-Verlag.

Blatchford, P., & Mortimore, P. (1994). The issue of class size for young children in school: What can we learn from research? *Oxford Review of Education 20,* (4), 411–428.

Blatt, S.J. (2004). *Experiences of depression.* Washington, DC: American Psychological Association.

Bleeker, M.M., Kohler, K., Verson, M.K., & Messersmith, E. (2002, April). *Adolescence into young adulthood: The perspectives of parents and as their children grow up.* Paper presented at the meeting of the Society for Research on Adolescence, New Orleans.

Block, J. (1993). Studying personality the long way. In D.C. Funder, R.D. Peake, C. Tomlinson-Keasey, & K. Widaman (Eds.), *Studying lives through time.* Washington, DC: American Psychological Association.

Block, J. (2002). *Personality as an affect processing system.* Mahwah, NJ: Erlbaum.

Block, J.H., & Block, J. (1980). The role of ego-control and ego-resiliency in the organization of behavior. In W.A. Collins (Ed.), *Minnesota symposium on child psychology* (Vol.

13). Minneapolis: University of Minnesota Press.

Bloom, B. (Ed.). (1985). *Developing talent in young people.* New York: Ballantine Books.

Blos, P. (1962). *On adolescence.* New York: Free Press.

Blos, P. (1989). The inner world of the adolescent. In A.H. Esman (Ed.), *International annals of adolescent psychiatry* (Vol. 1). Chicago: University of Chicago Press.

Blum, R.W. (2003). Positive youth development: A strategy for improving adolescent health. In R.M. Lerner, F. Jacobs, & D. Wertlieb (Eds.), *Handbook of applied developmental psychology* (Vol. 2). Thousand Oaks, CA: Sage.

Blum, R., & Nelson-Mmari, K. (2004). Adolescent health from an international perspective. In R. Lerner & L. Steinberg (Eds.), *Handbook of adolescent psychology.* New York: Wiley.

Blumenthal, J., Jeffries, N.O., Castellanos, F.X., Liu, H., Zidjdenbos, A., Paus, T., Evans, A.C., Rapoport, J.L., & Giedd, J.N. (1999). Brain development during childhood and adolescence: A longitudinal MRI study. *Nature Neuroscience 10,* 861–863.

Blyth, D.A. (2000). Community approaches to improving outcomes for urban children, youth, and families. In A. Booth & A.C. Crouter (Eds.), *Does it take a village?* Mahwah, NJ: Erlbaum.

Blyth, D.A., Durant, D., & Moosbrugger, L. (1985, April). *Perceived intimacy in the social relationships of drug- and nondrug-using adolescents.* Paper presented at the meeting of the Society for Research in Child Development, Toronto.

Bogenschneider, K. (2002). *Family policy matters.* Mahwah, NJ: Erlbaum.

Bolland, J.M. (2003). Hopelessness and risk behavior among adolescents living in high-poverty inner-city neighborhoods. *Journal of Adolescence, 26,* 145–158.

Bonner, J.T. (1988). *The evolution of culture in animals.* Princeton, NJ: Princeton University Press.

Books, S. (2004). *Poverty and schooling in the U.S.* Mahwah, NJ: Erlbaum.

Booth, A., & Crouter, A.C. (2000). *Does it take a village?* Mahwah, NJ: Erlbaum.

Booth, A., Johnson, D.R., Granger, D.A., Crouter, A.C., & McHale, S. (2003). Testosterone and child and adolescent adjustment: The moderating role of parent-child

relationships. *Developmental Psychology, 39,* 85–98.

Booth, M. (2002). Arab adolescents facing the future: Enduring ideals and pressures to change. In B.B. Brown, R.W. Larson, & T.S. Saraswathi (Eds.), *The world's youth.* New York: Cambridge University Press.

Borden, L.M., Donnermeyer, J.F., & Scheer, S.D. (2001). The influence of extracurricular activities and peer influence on substance use. *Adolescent and Family Health, 2,* 12–19.

Bornstein, M.H., & Bradley, R.H. (Eds.). (2003). *Socioeconomic status, parenting, and child development.* Mahwah, NJ: Erlbaum.

Bornstein, R.F. (2003). Psychodynamic models of personality. In I.B. Weiner (Ed.), *Handbook of psychology* (Vol. 5). New York: Wiley.

Borowsky, I.W., Ireland, M., & Resnick, M.D. (2001). Adolescent suicide attempts: Risks and protectors. *Pediatrics, 107,* 485–493.

Bosma, H.A., & Kunnen, E.S. (Eds.). (2001). *Identity and emotion.* New York: Cambridge University Press.

Botvin, G.J. (1999, June). *Impact of preventive interventions on protection for drug use, onset, and progression.* Paper presented at the meeting of the Society for Prevention Research, New Orleans.

Bouchey, H.A., & Furman, W. (2003). Dating and romantic relationships in adolescence. In G. Adams & M. Berzonsky (Eds.), *Blackwell handbook of adolescence.* Malden, MA: Blackwell.

Bowlby, J. (1989). *Secure attachment.* New York: Basic Books.

Boyer, E.L. (1986, December). Transition from school to college. *Phi Delta Kappan,* pp. 283–287.

Boyes, M.C., Giordano, R., & Galperyn, K. (1993, March). *Moral orientation and interpretive contexts of moral deliberation.* Paper presented at the biennial meeting of the Society for Research in Child Development, New Orleans.

Boys and Girls Clubs of America. (1989, May 12). *Boys and Girls Clubs in public housing projects: Interim report.* Minneapolis: Boys and Girls Clubs of America.

Brabeck, M.M. (2000). Kohlberg, Lawrence. In A. Kazdin (Ed.), *Encyclopedia of psychology.* Washington, DC, and New York: American Psychological Association and Oxford University Press.

Bradley, R., & Corwyn, R. (2004). "Family process" investments that matter for child well being. In A. Kalil & T. DeLeire (Eds.), *Family investments in children's potential.* Mahwah, NJ: Erlbaum.

Brainard, C.J. (2002). Jean Piaget, learning research, and American education. In B.J. Zimmerman & D.H. Schunk (Eds.), *Educational psychology.* Mahwah, NJ: Erlbaum.

Braver, S.L., Ellman, I.M., & Fabricus, W.V. (2003). Relocation of children after divorce and children's best interests: New evidence and legal considerations. *Journal of Family Psychology, 17,* 206–219.

Bray, J.H., & Berger, S.H. (1993). Developmental Issues in Stepfamilies Research Project: Family relationships and parent-child interactions. *Journal of Family Psychology, 7,* 76–90.

Bray, J.H., Berger, S.H., & Boethel, C.L. (1999). Marriage to remarriage and beyond. In E.M. Hetherington (Ed.), *Coping with divorce, single parenting, and remarriage.* Mahwah, NJ: Erlbaum.

Bray, J.H., & Kelly, J. (1998). *Stepfamilies.* New York: Broadway.

Bredemeier, B., & Shields, D. (1996). Moral development and children's sport. In F. Smoll & R. Smith (Eds.), *Children and youth in sport: A biopsychosocial perspective.* Chicago: Brown & Benchmark.

Breur, J.T. (1999). In search of . . . brain-based education. *Phi Delta Kappan, 80,* 648–655.

Brewer, M.B., & Campbell, D.T. (1976). *Ethnocentrism and intergroup attitudes.* New York: Wiley.

Brim, O.G., & Kagan, J. (1980). Constancy and change: A view of the issues. In O.G. Brim & J. Kagan (Eds.), *Constancy and change in human development.* Cambridge, MA: Harvard University Press.

Brislin, R. (1993). *Understanding culture's influence on behavior.* Fort Worth, TX: Harcourt Brace.

Brislin, R.W. (2000). Cross-cultural training. In A. Kazdin (Ed.), *Encyclopedia of psychology.* Washington, DC, and New York: American Psychological Association and Oxford University Press.

Brock, L.J., & Jennings, G.H. (1993). What daughters in their 30s wish their mothers had told them. *Family Relations, 42,* 61–65.

Brody, G.H., & Ge, X. (2001). Linking parenting processes and self-regulation to psychological functioning and alcohol use during early adolescence. *Journal of Family Psychology, 15,* 82–94.

Brody, G.H., & Shaffer, D.R. (1982). Contributions of parents and peers to children's moral socialization. *Developmental Review, 2,* 31–75.

Brody, G.H., Stoneman, Z., & Burke, M. (1987). Child temperaments, maternal differential behavior and sibling relationships. *Developmental Psychology, 23,* 354–362.

Brody, N. (2000). Intelligence. In A. Kazdin (Ed.), *Encyclopedia of psychology.* Washington, DC, and New York: American Psychological Association and Oxford University Press.

Broidy, L.M., Nagin, D.S., Tremblay, R.E., Bates, J.E., Dodge, K.A., Fegusson, D., Horwood, J.L., Loeber, R., Laird, R., Lynam, D.R., Moffitt, T.E., Pettit, G.S., & Vitaro, F. (2003). Developmental trajectories of childhood disruptive behaviors and adolescent delinquency: A six-site, cross-national study. *Developmental Psychology, 39,* 222–245.

Bronfenbrenner, U. (1986). Ecology of the family as a context for human development: Research perspectives. *Developmental psychology, 22,* 723–742.

Bronfenbrenner, U. (1995). Developmental ecology through space and time: A future perspective. In P. Moen, G.H. Elder, & K. Lüscher (Eds.), *Examining lives in context.* Washington, DC: American Psychological Association.

Bronfenbrenner, U. (2000). Ecological theory. In A. Kazdin (Ed.), *Encyclopedia of psychology.* Washington, DC, and New York: American Psychological Association and Oxford University Press.

Bronfenbrenner, U., & Morris, P. (1998). The ecology of developmental processes. In W. Damon (Ed.), *Handbook of child psychology* (5th ed., Vol. 1). New York: Wiley.

Bronner, G., Peretz, C., & Ehrenfeld, M. (2003). Sexual harassment of nurses and nursing students. *Journal of Advanced Nursing, 42,* 637–644.

Brook, J.S., Brook, D.W., Gordon, A.S., Whiteman, M., & Cohen, P. (1990). The psychological etiology of adolescent drug use: A family interactional approach. *Genetic Psychology Monographs, 116,* no. 2.

Brook, J.S., Whiteman, M., Balka, E.B., Win, P.T., & Gursen, M.D. (1998). Drug use among Puerto Ricans: Ethnic identity as a protective factor. *Hispanic Journal of Behavioral Sciences, 20,* 241–254.

Brookover, W.B., Beady, C., Flood, P., Schweitzer, U., & Wisenbaker, J. (1979). *School social systems and student achievement: Schools make a difference.* New York: Praeger.

Brooks, J.G., & Brooks, M.G. (1993). *The case for constuctivist classrooms.* Alexandria, VA: Association for Supervision and Curriculum Development.

Brooks, J.G., & Brooks, M.G. (2001). *The case for constructivist classrooms* (2nd ed.). Upper Saddle River, NJ: Erlbaum.

Brooks, T., & Bornstein, P. (1996, March). *Cross-cultural comparison of mothers' and fathers' behaviors toward girls and boys.* Paper presented at the Society for Research on Adolescence, Boston.

Brooks-Gunn, J. (1988). Antecedents and consequences of variations in girls' maturational timing. In M.D. Levine & E.R. McAnarney (Eds.), *Early adolescent transitions.* Lexington, MA: Lexington Books.

Brooks-Gunn, J. (1992, March). *Revisiting theories of "storm and stress": The role of biology.* Paper presented at the meeting of the Society for Research on Adolescence, Washington, DC.

Brooks-Gunn, J., & Chase-Landsdale, P.L. (1995). Adolescent parenthood. In M.H. Bornstein (Ed.), *Children and parenting* (Vol. 3). Hillsdale, NJ: Erlbaum.

Brooks-Gunn, J., Duncan, G., Glebanov, P.K., & Sealand, N. (1993). Do neighborhoods influence child and adolescent development? *American Journal of Sociology, 99,* 353–395.

Brooks-Gunn, J., & Graber, J.A. (1995, March). *Depressive affect versus positive adjustment: Patterns of resilience in adolescent girls.* Paper presented at the meeting of the Society for Research in Child Development, Indianapolis.

Brooks-Gunn, J., & Graber, J.A. (1999). *What's sex got to do with it? The development of health and sexual identities during adolescence.* Unpublished manuscript, Department of Psychology, Columbia University, New York City.

Brooks-Gunn, J., Graber, J.A., & Paikoff, R.L. (1994). Studying links between hormones and negative affect: Models and measures. *Journal of Research on Adolescence, 4,* 469–486.

Brooks-Gunn, J., & Paikoff, R.L. (1997). Sexuality and developmental transitions during adolescence. In J. Schulenberg, J. Maggs, & K. Hurrelmann (Eds.), *Health risks and developmental transitions during adolescence.* New York: Cambridge University Press.

Brooks-Gunn, J., & Ruble, D.N. (1982). The development of menstrual-related beliefs and behaviors during early adolescence. *Child Development, 53,* 1567–1577.

Brooks-Gunn, J., & Warren, M.P. (1989). The psychological significance of secondary sexual characteristics in 9- to 11-year-old girls. *Child Development, 59,* 161–169.

Brophy, J. (1998). *Motivating students to learn.* New York: McGraw-Hill.

Brophy, J. (2004). *Motivating students to learn* (2nd ed.). Mahwah, NJ: Erlbaum.

Broughton, J. (1983). The cognitive developmental theory of adolescent self and identity. In B. Lee & G. Noam (Eds.), *Developmental approaches to self.* New York: Plenum.

Brown, A.C., & Orthner, D.K. (1990). Relocation and personal well-being among early adolescents. *Journal of Early Adolescence, 10,* 366–381.

Brown, A.L., Metz, K.F., & Campione, J.C. (1996). Social interaction and individual understanding in a community of learners: The influence of Piaget and Vygotsky. In A. Tryphon & J. Voneche (Eds.), *Piaget-Vygotsky.* Mahwah, NJ: Erlbaum.

Brown, A.L., & Palincsar, A.M. (1984). Reciprocal teaching of comprehension-fostering and monitoring activities. *Cognition and Instruction, 1,* 175–177.

Brown, B.B. (1999). Measuring the peer environment of American adolescents. In S.L. Friedman & T.D. Wachs (Eds.), *Measuring environment across the life span.* Washington, DC: American Psychological Association.

Brown, B.B. (2002, April). *Changes and diversity in adolescents' social lives and interpersonal competence.* Paper presented at the meeting of the Society for Research on Adolescence, New Orleans.

Brown, B.B. (2003). Crowds, cliques, & friendships. In G. Adams & M. Berzonsky (Eds.), *Blackwell handbook of adolescence.* Malden, MA: Blackwell.

Brown, B.B. (2004). Adolescent relationships with peers. In R. Lerner & L. Steinberg (Eds.), *Handbook of adolescent psychology.* New York: Wiley.

Brown, B.B., Lambron, S.L., Mounts, N.S., & Steinberg, L. (1993). Parenting practices and peer group affiliation in adolescence. *Child Development, 64,* 467–482.

Brown, B.B., & Larson, R.W. (2002). The kaleidoscope of adolescence: Experiences of the world's youth at the beginning of the 21st century. In B.B. Brown, R.W. Larson, & T.S. Saraswathi (Eds.), *The world's youth.* New York: Cambridge University Press.

Brown, B.B., Larson, R.W., & Saraswathi, T.S. (Eds.). (2002). *The world's youth.* New York: Cambridge University Press.

Brown, B.B., & Lohr, M.J. (1987). Peer group affiliation and adolescent self-esteem: An integration of ego-identity and symbolic-interaction theories. *Journal of Personality and Social Psychology, 52,* 47–55.

Brown, B.B., Mory, M., & Kinney, D.A. (1994). Casting adolescent crowds in relational perspective: Caricature, channel, and context. In R. Montemayor, G.R. Adams, & T.P. Gullotta (Eds.), *Advances in adolescent development: Vol. 6. Personal relationships during adolescence.* Newbury Park, CA: Sage.

Brown, B.B., & Theobald, W. (1998). Learning contexts beyond the classroom: Extracurricular activities, community organizations, and peer groups. In K. Borman & B. Schneider (Eds.), *The adolescent years.* Chicago: University of Chicago Press.

Brown, F. (1973). *The reform of secondary education: Report of the national commission on the reform of secondary education.* New York: McGraw-Hill.

Brown, H.D., & Adler, N.E. (1998). Socioeconomic status. In H.S. Friedman (Ed.), *Encyclopedia of mental health* (Vol. 3). San Diego: Academic Press.

Brown, J.D., & Siegel, J.D. (1988). Exercise as a buffer of life stress: A prospective study of adolescent health. *Health Psychology, 7,* 341–353.

Brown, L.M., & Gilligan, C. (1992). *Meeting at the crossroads: Women's and girls' development.* Cambridge, MA: Harvard University Press.

Brown, L.M., Way, N., & Duff, J.L. (1999). The others in my I: Adolescent girls' friendships and peer relations. In N.G. Johnson, M.C. Roberts, & J. Worrell (Eds.), *Beyond appearance.* Washington, DC: American Psychological Association.

Brown, R. (1986). *Social psychology* (2nd ed.). New York: Macmillan.

Bruer, J.T. (1999). *The myth of the first three years.* New York: Free Press.

Bruess, C.E., & Richardson, G.E. (1992). *Decisions for health* (3rd ed.). Dubuque, IA: Brown & Benchmark.

Bryant, B.R., & Seay, P.C. (1998). The technology-related assistance to individuals with learning disabilities and their advocates. *Journal of Learning Disabilities, 31,* 4–15.

Bryant, J., & Rockwell, S.C. (1994). Effects of massive exposure to sexually oriented prime-time television programming on adolescents' moral judgment. In D. Zillman, J. Bryant, & A.C. Huston (Eds.), *Media, children, and the family: Social scientific, psychodynamic, and clinical perspectives.* Hillsdale, NJ: Erlbaum.

Bryk, A.S., Lee, V.E., & Holland, P.B. (1993). *Catholic schools and the common good.* Cambridge, MA: Harvard University Press.

Buchanan, C.M., Maccoby, E.E., & Dornsbusch, S. (1992). Adolescents and their families after divorce: Three residential arrangements compared. *Journal of Research on Adolescence, 2,* 261–291.

Buhrmester, D. (1990). Friendship, interpersonal competence, and adjustment in preadolescence and adolescence. *Child Development, 61,* 1101–1111.

Buhrmester, D. (2001, April). *Does age at which romantic involvement start matter?* Paper presented at the meeting of the Society for Research in Child Development, Minneapolis.

Buhrmester, D., Camparo, L., Christensen, A., Gonzalez, L.S., & Hinshaw, S.P. (in press). Mothers and fathers interacting in dyads and triads with normal and hyperactive sons. *Developmental Psychology.*

Buhrmester, D., & Carbery, J. (1992, March). *Daily patterns of self-disclosure and adolescent adjustment.* Paper presented at the biennial meeting of the Society for Research on Adolescence, Washington, DC.

Buhrmester, D., & Furman, W. (1987). The development of companionship and intimacy. *Child Development, 58,* 1101–1113.

Buhrmester, D., & Furman, W. (1990). Perceptions of sibling relationships during middle childhood and adolescence. *Child Development, 61,* 1387–1398.

Bukowski, W.M., Newcomb, A.F., & Hoza, B. (1987). Friendship conceptions among early adolescents: A longitudinal study of stability and change. *Journal of Early Adolescence, 7,* 143–152.

Bumpas, M.F., Crouter, A.C., & McHale, S.M. (2001). Parental autonomy granting during adolescence: Gender differences in context. *Developmental Psychology, 37,* 163–173.

Burchinal, M.R., Peisner-Feinberg, E., Pianta, R., & Howes, C. (2002). Development of academic skills from preschool through second grade: Family and classroom predictors of developmental trajectories. *Journal of School Psychology, 40* (5), 415–436.

Burton, L.M., & Snyder, A.R. (1997). The invisible man revisited. In A. Booth & A.C. Crouter (Eds.), *Men in families.* Mahwah, NJ: Erlbaum.

Burton, R.V. (1984). A paradox in theories and research in moral development. In W.M. Kurtines & J.L. Gewirtz (Eds.), *Morality, moral behavior, and moral development.* New York: Wiley.

Buss, D.M. (1995). Psychological sex differences: Origins through sexual selection. *American Psychologist, 50,* 164–168.

Buss, D.M. (1998). The psychology of human mate selection. In C.B. Crawford & D.L. Krebs (Eds.), *Handbook of evolutionary psychology.* Mahwah, NJ: Erlbaum.

Buss, D.M. (1999). *Evolutionary psychology: The new science of the mind.* Boston: Allyn & Bacon.

Buss, D.M. (2000). Evolutionary psychology. In A. Kazdin (Ed.), *Encyclopedia of psychology.* Washington, DC, and New York: American Psychological Association and Oxford University Press.

Buss, D.M. (2001). Human nature and culture: An evolutionary psychology perspective. *Journal of Personality, 69,* 955–978.

Buss, D.M. (2004). *Evolutionary psychology* (2nd ed.). Boston: Allyn & Bacon.

Buss, D.M., & Schmitt, D.P. (1993). Sexual strategies theory: An evolutionary perspective on human mating. *Psychological Review, 100,* 204–232.

Bussey, K., & Bandura, A. (1999). Social cognitive theory of gender development and differentiation. *Psychological Review, 106,* 676–713.

Butcher, J. (2000). Computerized assessment. In A. Kazdin (Ed.), *Encyclopedia of psychology.* Washington, DC, and New York: American Psychological Association and Oxford University Press.

Butcher, J.N., Williams C.L, Graham, J.R., Archer, R.P., Tellegen, A., Ben-Porath, Y.S., & Kaemmer, B. (1992). *MMPI-A (Minnesota Multiphasic Personality Inventory–Adolescent): Manual for administration, scoring, and interpretation.* Minneapolis: University of Minnesota Press.

Buzwell, S., & Rosenthal, D. (1996). Constructing a sexual self: Adolescents' sexual self-perceptions and sexual risk-taking. *Journal of Research on Adolescence, 6,* 489–513.

Byrnes, J.P. (1998). *The nature and development of decision making.* Mahwah, NJ: Erlbaum.

Byrnes, J.P. (2001). *Cognitive development and learning in instructional contexts* (2nd ed.). Boston: Allyn & Bacon.

Byrnes, J.P. (2003). Cognitive development during adolescence. In G. Adams &

M. Berzonsky (Eds.), *Blackwell handbook of adolescence.* Malden, MA: Blackwell.

Cain, M.T. (1980). The economic activities in a village in Bangladesh. In R.E. Evenson, C.A. Florencio, & F.B.N. White (Eds.), *Rural household studies in Asia.* Kent Ridge, Singapore: Singapore University Press.

Cairns, R.B., & Cairns, B.D. (1994). *Lifelines and risks: Pathways of youth in our time.* New York: Cambridge University Press.

Calabrese, R.L., & Schumer, H. (1986). The effects of service activities on adolescent alienation. *Adolescence, 21,* 675–687.

Call, K.A., Riedel, A., Hein, K., McLoyd, V., Kpke, M., & Petersen, P. (2002). Adolescent health and well-being in the 21st century: A global perspective. *Journal of Research on Adolescence, 12,* 69–98.

Calvert S. (1999). *Children's journeys through the information age.* New York: McGraw-Hill.

Cameron, J., Cowan, L., Holmes, B., Hurst, P., & McLean, M. (Eds.). (1983). *International handbook of educational systems.* New York: Wiley.

Campbell, C.Y. (1988, August 24). Group raps depiction of teenagers. *Boston Globe,* p. 44.

Campbell, L., Campbell B., & Dickinson, D. (2004). *Teaching and learning thorough multiple intelligences* (3rd ed.). Boston: Allyn & Bacon.

Capaldi, D.M., & Shortt, J.W. (2003). Understanding conduct problems in adolescence from a life-span perspective. In G. Adams & M. Berzonsky (Eds.), *Blackwell handbook of adolescence.* Malden, MA: Blackwell.

Caplan, P.J., & Caplan, J.B. (1999). *Thinking critically about research on sex and gender* (2nd ed.). New York: Longman.

Caporael, L.R. (2001). Evolutionary psychology. *Annual Review of Psychology* (Vol. 52). Palo Alto, CA: Annual Reviews.

Card, N.A. (2003, April). *Victims of peer aggression: A meta-analytic review.* Paper presented at the meeting of the Society for Research in Child Development, Tampa.

Card, N.A., Isaacs, J., & Hodges, E.V.E. (2000, April). *Dynamics of interpersonal aggression in the school context: Who aggresses against whom?* Paper presented at the meeting of the

Society for Research on Adolescence, Chicago.

Cardelle-Elawar, M. (1992). Effects of teaching metacognitive skills to students with low mathematics ability. *Teaching & Teacher Education, 8,* 109–121.

Carey, M.P., & Venable, P.A. (2003). AIDS/HIV. In I.B. Weiner (Ed.), *Handbook of psychology* (Vol. 9). New York: Wiley.

Carlson, C., Cooper, C., & Hsu, J. (1990, March). *Predicting school achievement in early adolescence: The role of family process.* Paper presented at the meeting of the Society for Research in Adolescence, Atlanta.

Carlson, M.J., & McLanahan, S.S. (2002). Fragile families, father involvement, and public policy. In C.S. Tamis-LeMonda & N. Cabrera (Eds.), *The handbook of father involvement.* Mahwah, NJ: Erlbaum.

Carnegie Council on Adolescent Development. (1989). *Turning points: Preparing American youth for the twenty-first century.* New York: Carnegie Foundation.

Carnegie Council on Adolescent Development. (1995). *Great transitions.* New York: Carnegie Foundation.

Carnegie Foundation. (1994). *Starting points: Meeting the needs of our youngest children.* New York: Author.

Carroll, J. (1993) *Human cognitive abilities.* Cambridge: Cambridge University Press.

Carskadson, M.A. (Ed.). (2002). *Adolescent sleep patterns.* New York: Cambridge University Press.

Carskadon, M.A., Acebo, C., & Seifer, R. (2001). Extended nights, sleep loss, and recovery sleep in adolescence. *Archives of Italian Biology, 139,* 301–312.

Carskadon, M.A., Labyak, S.E., Acebo, C., & Seifer, R. (1999). Intrinsic circadian period of adolescent humans measured in conditions of forced desynchrony. *Neuroscience Letters, 260,* 129–132.

Carskadon, M.A., Wolfson, A.R., Acebo, C., Tzischinsky, O., & Seifer, R. (1998). Adolescent sleep patterns, circadian timing, and sleepiness at a transition to early school days. *Sleep, 21,* 873–884.

Caruthers, A.S., & Ward, L.M. (2002, April). *Mixed messages: The divergent nature of sexual communication received from parents, peers, and the media.* Paper presented at the meeting of the Society for Research on Adolescence, New Orleans.

Carver, J., Joyner, K., & Udry, J.R. (2003). National estimates of romantic relationships. In P. Florsheim (Ed.), *Adolescent romantic rela-*

tions and sexual behavior. Mahwah, NJ: Erlbaum.

Case, R. (Ed.). (1992). *The mind's staircase: Exploring the conceptual underpinnings of children's thought and knowledge.* Hillsdale, NJ: Erlbaum.

Case, R. (1998). The development of conceptual structures. In W. Damon (Ed.), *Handbook of child psychology* (5th ed., Vol. 2). New York: Wiley.

Case, R. (2000). Conceptual development. In M. Bennett (Ed.), *Developmental psychology.* Philadelphia: Psychology Press.

Caspi, A. (1998). Personality development across the life course. In W. Damon (Series Ed.) & N. Eisenberg (Ed.), *Handbook of child psychology. Vol. 3. Social, emotional, and personality development* (5th ed., pp. 311–388). New York: Wiley.

Caspi, A., & Bem, D.J. (1990). Personality continuity and change across the life course. In L. Pervin (Ed.), *Handbook of personality.* New York: Guilford.

Cassell, E., & Bernstein, D.A. (2001). *Criminal behavior.* Boston: Allyn & Bacon.

Castellano, J.A., & Diaz, E. (Eds.). (2002). *Reaching new horizons: Gifted and talented education for culturally and linguistically diverse students.* Boston: Allyn & Bacon.

Cauffman, B.E. (1994, February). *The effects of puberty, dating, and sexual involvement on dieting and disordered eating in young adolescent girls.* Paper presented at the meeting of the Society for Research on Adolescence, San Diego.

Ceci, S.J. (2000). Bronfenbrenner, Urie. In A. Kazdin (Ed.), *Encyclopedia of psychology.* Washington, DC, and New York: American Psychological Association and Oxford University Press.

Centers for Disease Control and Prevention. (1997, August 8). Abortion surveillance—United States, 1993 and 1994. *Morbidity and Mortality Weekly Report, 46* (SS-4), 37–98.

Centers for Disease Control and Prevention. (2000). Youth risk behavior surveillance—United States, 1999. *MMWR, 49* (No. SS-5).

Centers for Disease Control and Prevention. (2001a). *Data and statistics: Adolescent pregnancy.* Atlanta: Author.

Centers for Disease Control and Prevention. (2001b). *Sexually transmitted diseases.* Atlanta: Author.

Centers for Disease Control and Prevention. (2002). *Sexually transmitted diseases.* Atlanta: Centers for Disease Control and Prevention.

Chafee, S.H., & Yang, S.M. (1990). Communication and political socialization. In O. Ichilov (Ed.), *Political socialization, citizen education, and democracy.* New York: Columbia University Press.

Chan, W.S. (1963). *A source book in Chinese philosophy.* Princeton, NJ: Princeton Books.

Chandler, M.J. (2002, April). *Suicide and the persistence of identity in the face of radical cultural and developmental change.* Paper presented at the meeting of the Society for Research on Adolescence, New Orleans.

Chang, R., & Gjerde, P.F. (2000, April). *Pathways toward and away from depression in young adult females: Person-centered analysis of longitudinal data.* Paper presented at the meeting of the Society for Research on Adolescence, Chicago.

Chapman, W., & Katz, M.R. (1983). Career information systems in secondary schools: A survey and assessment. *Vocational Guidance Quarterly, 31,* 165–177.

Chase-Lansdale, P.S., & Brooks-Gunn, J. (1994). Correlates of adolescent pregnancy. In C.B. Fisher & R.M. Lerner (Eds.), *Applied developmental psychology.* New York: McGraw-Hill.

Chassin, L., Pitts, S.C., & Prost, J. (2001, April). *Binge drinking trajectories from adolescence to emerging adulthood in a high risk sample: Predictors and substance abuse outcomes.* Paper presented at the meeting of the Society for Research in Child Development, Minneapolis.

Chen, C., & Stevenson, H.W. (1989). Homework: A cross-cultural examination. *Child Development, 60,* 551–561.

Cherlin, A.J., & Furstenberg, F.F. (1994). Stepfamilies in the United States: A reconsideration. In J. Blake & J. Hagen (Eds.), *Annual review of sociology.* Palo Alto, CA: Annual Reviews.

Cherlin, A.J., Furstenberg, F.F., Chase-Lansdale, P.L., Kiernan, K.E., Robins, P.K., Morrison, D.R., & Teitler, J.O. (1991). Longitudinal studies of effects of divorce in children in Great Britain and the United States. *Science, 252,* 1386–1389.

Chess, S., & Thomas, A. (1977). Temperamental individuality from childhood to adolescence. *Journal of Child Psychiatry, 16,* 218–226.

Child Trends. (2000). Trends in sexual activity and contraceptive use among teens. *Child trends research brief.* Washington, DC: Author.

Child Trends. (2001). *Trends among Hispanic children, youth, and families.* Washington, DC: Author.

Children's Defense Fund. (1992). *The state of America's children, 1992.* Washington, DC: Author.

Chilman, C. (1979). *Adolescent sexuality in a changing American society: Social and psychological perspectives.* Washington, DC: Public Health Service, National Institute of Mental Health.

Chira, S. (1993, June 23). What do teachers want most? Help from parents. *New York Times,* p. 17.

Chmielewski, C. (1997, September). Sexual harassment meet Title IX. *NEA Today, 16* (2), 24–25.

Choate, J.S. (2000). *Successful inclusive teaching* (3rd ed.). Boston: Allyn & Bacon.

Choate, J.S. (2004). *Successful inclusive teaching* (4th ed.). Boston: Allyn & Bacon.

Chodorow, N.J. (1978). *The reproduction of mothering.* Berkeley: University of California Press.

Chodorow, N.J. (1989). *Feminism and psychoanalytic theory.* New Haven, CT: Yale University Press.

Christensen, L.B. (2004). *Experimental methodology* (9th ed.). Boston: Allyn & Bacon.

Christenson, P.W., & Roberts, D.F. (1991, August). *Music media in adolescent health promotion: Problems and prospects.* Paper presented at the meeting of the American Psychological Association, San Francisco.

Christopher, F.S., & Kisler, T.S. (2004). Sexual aggression in romantic relationships. In J.H. Harvey, A. Wenzel, & S. Sprecher (Eds.), *The handbook of sexuality in close relationships.* Mahwah, NJ: Erlbaum.

Chun, K.M., & Akutsu, P.D. (2003). Acculturation among ethnic minority families. In K.M. Chun, P.B. Organista, & G. Marín (Eds.), *Acculturation.* Washington, DC: American Psychological Association.

Chun, K.M., Organista, P.B., & Marin, G. (Eds.) (2003). *Acculturation.* Washington, DC: American Psychological Association.

Churchill, J.D., Galvez, R., Colcombe, S., Swain, R.A., Kramer, A.F., & Greenough, W.T. (2002). Exercise, experience, and the aging brain. *Neurobiology of Aging, 23,* 941.

Cialdini, R., & Rhoad, K. (1999). *Cults: Questions and answers.* Retrieved from the World Wide Web: http://www.influenceatwork.com/cult.html.

Cillessen, A.H.N., Van Ijzendoorn, H.W., Van Lieshout, C.F.M., & Hartup, W.W.

(1992). Heterogeneity among peer-rejected boys: Subtypes and stabilities. *Child Development, 63,* 893–905.

Clabby, J.G., & Elias, M.J. (1988). Improving social problem-solving and awareness. *William T. Grant Foundation Annual Report,* p. 18.

Clark, K.B., & Clark, M.P. (1939). The development of the self and the emergence of racial identification in Negro preschool children. *Journal of Social Psychology, 10,* 591–599.

Clark, M.S., Powell, M.C., Ovellette, R., & Milberg, S. (1987). Recipient's mood, relationship type, and helping. *Journal of Personality and Social Psychology, 43,* 94–103.

Clark, R.D., & Hatfield, E. (1989). Gender differences in receptivity to sexual offers. *Journal of Psychology and Human Sexuality, 2,* 39–55.

Clark, S.D., Zabin, L.S., & Hardy, J.B. (1984). Sex, contraception, and parenthood: Experience and attitudes among urban black young men. *Family Planning Perspectives, 16,* 77–82.

Clasen, D.R., & Brown, B.B. (1987). Understanding peer pressure in the middle school. *Middle School Journal, 19,* 21–23.

Clay, R.A. (1997, December). Are children being overmedicated? *APA Monitor,* pp. 1, 27.

Clifford, B.R., Gunter, B., & McAleer, J.L. (1995). *Television and children.* Hillsdale, NJ: Erlbaum.

Cloninger, C.R. (1991, January). *Personality traits and alcoholic predisposition.* Paper presented at the conference of the National Institute on Drug Abuse, University of California at Los Angeles.

CNN and the National Science Foundation. (1997). *Poll on technology and education.* Washington, DC: National Science Foundation.

Cobb, P. (2000). Constructivism. In A. Kazdin (Ed.), *Encyclopedia of psychology.* Washington, DC, and New York: American Psychological Association and Oxford University Press.

Cochran, S.D., & Mays, V.M. (1990). Sex, lies, and HIV. *New England Journal of Medicine, 322* (11), 774–775.

Cognition and Technology Group at Vanderbilt. (1997). *The Jasper Project.* Mahwah, NJ: Erlbaum.

Cohen, L.B. (1995). Violent video games: Aggression, arousal, and desensitization in young adolescent boys. Doctoral dissertation, University of Southern California, 1995.

Dissertation Abstracts International, 57 (2-B), 1463. (University Microfilms No. 9616947)

Cohen, P., Kasen, S., Chen, H., Hartmark, C., & Gordon, K. (2003). Variations in patterns of developmental transitions in the emerging adulthood period. *Developmental Psychology, 39,* 657–669.

Cohen, R.J., & Swerdlik, M.E. (2002). *Psychological testing and assessment* (5th ed). New York: McGraw-Hill.

Cohen, S.E. (1994, February). *High school dropouts.* Paper presented at the meeting of the Society for Research on Adolescence, San Diego.

Coie, J.D., & Dodge, K.A. (1998). Aggression and antisocial behavior. In N. Eisenberg (Ed.), *Handbook of child psychology* (5th ed., Vol. 3). New York: Wiley.

Coie, J.D., & Koeppl, G.K. (1990). Adapting intervention to the problems of aggressive and disruptive rejected children. In S.R. Asher & J.D. Coie (Eds.), *Peer rejection in childhood.* New York: Cambridge University Press.

Colby, A., Kohlbeg, L., Gibbs, J., & Lieberman, M. (1983). A longitudinal study of moral judgment. *Monographs of the Society for Research in Child Development, 48* (21, Serial No. 201).

Cole, A.K., & Kerns, K.A. (2001). Perceptions of sibling qualities and activities of early adolescents. *Journal of Early Adolescence, 21,* 204–226.

Cole, M. (1997). *Cultural psychology.* Cambridge, MA: Harvard University Press.

Coleman, J.S. (1980). The peer group. In J. Adelson (Ed.), *Handbook of adolescent psychology.* New York: Wiley.

Coleman, J.S., & others. (1974). *Youth: Transition to adulthood.* Report of the Panel on Youth of the President's Science Advisory Committee. Chicago: University of Chicago Press.

Coleman, M., Ganong, L., & Fine, M. (2004). Communication in stepfamilies. In A.L. Vangelisti (Ed.), *Handbook of family communication.* Mahwah, NJ: Erlbaum.

Coleman, M.C., & Webber, J. (2002). *Emotional and behavioral disorders* (4th ed.). Boston: Allyn & Bacon.

Coleman, P.D. (1986, August). *Regulation of dendritic extent: Human aging brain and Alzheimer's disease.* Paper presented at the meeting of the American Psychological Association, Washington, DC.

Coley, R. (2001). *Differences in the gender gap: Comparisons across racial/ethnic groups in the United States.* Princeton, NJ: Educational Testing Service.

Coll, C.G., Bearer, E.L., & Lerner, R.M. (Eds.). (2004). *Nature and nurture.* Mahwah, NJ: Erlbaum.

Coll, C.T.G., & Pachter, L.M. (2002). Ethnic and minority parenting. In M. Bornstein (Ed.), *Handbook of parenting* (2nd ed., Vol. 4). Mahwah, NJ: Erlbaum.

College Board Commission on Precollege Guidance and Counseling. (1986). *Keeping the options open.* New York: College Entrance Examination Board.

Collins, M. (1996, Winter). The job outlook for '96 grads. *Journal of Career Planning,* pp. 51–54.

Collins, W.A. (2003). More than myth: The developmental significance of romantic relationships during adolescence. *Journal of Research on Adolescence, 13,* 1–24.

Collins, W.A., Hennighausen, K.H., & Sroufe, L.A. (1998, June). *Developmental precursors of intimacy in romantic relationships: A longitudinal analysis.* Paper presented at the International Conference on Personal Relationships, Saratoga Springs, NY.

Collins, W.A., & Laursen, B. (2004). Parent-adolescent relationships and influences. In R. Lerner & L. Steinberg (Eds.), *Handbook of adolescent psychology.* New York: Wiley.

Collins, W.A., & Luebker, C. (1994). Parent and adolescent expectancies: Individual and relational significance. In J.G. Smetana (Ed.), *New directions for child development: Beliefs about parenting.* San Francisco: Jossey-Bass.

Collins, W.A., Maccoby, E.E., Steinberg, L., Hetherington, E.M., & Bornstein, M.H. (2000). Contemporary research on parenting: The case for nature and nurture. *American psychologist, 55,* 218–232.

Collins, W.A., Maccoby, E.E., Steinberg, L., Hetherington, E.M., & Bornstein, M.H. (2001). Toward nature WITH nurture. *American Psychologist, 56,* 171–173.

Collins, W.A., & Madsen, S. (2002, April). *Relational roots of romance: Beyond "chumships."* Paper presented at the meeting of the Society for Research on Adolescence, New Orleans.

Comas Díaz, L. (2001). Hispanics, Latinos, or Americanos: The evolution of identity. *Cultural Diversity and Ethnic Minority Psychology, 7,* 115–120.

Comer, J.P. (1988). Educating poor minority children. *Scientific American, 259,* 42–48.

Comer, J.P. (1993). *African-American parents and child development: An agenda for school success.* Paper presented at the biennial meeting of the Society for Research on Child Development, New Orleans.

Comer, J.P., Haynes, N.M., Joyner, E.T., & Ben-Avie, M. (1996). *Rallying the whole village: The Comer process for reforming urban education.* New York: Teachers College Press.

Commoner, B. (2002). Unraveling the DNA myth: The spurious foundation of genetic engineering. *Harper's Magazine, 304,* 39–47.

Commons, M.L., & Richards, F.A. (2003). Four postformal stages. In J. Demick & C. Andreoletti (Eds.), *Handbook of adult development.* New York: Kluwer.

Commons, M.L., Sinnott, J.D., Richards, F.A., & Armon, C. (1989). *Adult development. Vol. 1: Comparisons and applications of developmental models.* New York: Praeger.

Compas, B.E. (2004). Processes of risk and resilience during adolescence: Linking contexts and individuals. In R. Lerner & L. Steinberg (Eds.), *Handbook of adolescent psychology.* New York: Wiley.

Compas, B.E., & Grant, K.E. (1993, March). *Stress and adolescent depressive symptoms: Underlying mechanisms and processes.* Paper presented at the biennial meeting of the Society for Research in Child Development, New Orleans.

Conant, J.B. (1959). *The American high school today.* New York: McGraw-Hill.

Condry, J.C., Simon, M.L., & Bronfenbrenner, U. (1968). *Characteristics of peer- and adult-oriented children.* Unpublished manuscript, Cornell University, Ithaca, NY.

Conger, J.J. (1981). Freedom and commitment: Families, youth, and social change. *American Psychologist, 36,* 1475–1484.

Conger, J.J. (1988). Hostages to the future: Youth, values, and the public interest. *American Psychologist, 43,* 291–300.

Conger, K.J., & Bryant, C.M. (2004). The changing nature of adolescent sibling relationships. In R.D. Conger, F.O. Lorenz, & K.A.S. Wickrama (Eds.), *Continuity and change in family relations.* Mahwah, NJ: Erlbaum.

Conger, R.D., & Chao, W. (1996). Adolescent depressed mood. In R.I. Simons (Ed.), *Understanding differences between divorced and intact families: Stress, interaction, and child outcome.* Thousand Oaks, CA: Sage.

Conger, R.D., Lorenz, F.O., & Wickrama, K.A.S. (2004). *Continuity and change in family relations.* Mahwah, NJ: Erlbaum.

Conger, R.D., & Reuter, M. (1996). Siblings, parents, and peers: A longitudinal study of social influences in adolescent risk for alcohol use and abuse. In G.H. Brody (Ed.), *Sibling relationships: Their causes and consequences.* Norwood, NJ: Ablex.

Connell, J.P., Halpern-Felsher, B.L., Clifford, E., Crichlow, W., & Usinger, P. (1995). Hanging in there: Behavioral, psychological, and contextual factors affecting whether African-American adolescents stay in high school. *Journal of Adolescent Research, 10,* 41–63.

Conner, J.P. (1988). Educating poor minority children. *Scientific American, 259,* 42–48.

Connolly, J., Furman, W., & Konarski, R. (1995, April). *The role of social networks in the emergence of romantic relationships in adolescence.* Paper presented at the meeting of the Society for Research in Child Development, Indianapolis.

Connolly, J., Furman, W., & Konarski, R. (2000). The role of peers in the emergence of heterosexual romantic relationships in adolescence. *Child Development, 71,* 1395–1408.

Connolly, J., & Goldberg, A. (1999). Romantic relationships in adolescence: The role of friends and peers in their emergence and development. In W. Furman, B.B. Brown, & C. Feiring (Eds.), *The development of romantic relationships in adolescence.* New York: Cambridge University Press.

Connolly, J., & Stevens, V. (1999, April). *Best friends, cliques, and young adolescents' romantic involvement.* Paper presented at the meeting of the Society for Research in Child Development, Albuquerque.

Connors, L.J., & Epstein, J.L. (1995). Parent and school partnerships. In M.H. Bornstein (Ed.), *Children and parenting* (Vol. 4). Hillsdale, NJ: Erlbaum.

Conti, K., & Amabile T. (1999). Motivation and creativity. In M.A. Runco & S. Pritzker (Eds.), *Encyclopedia of creativity.* San Diego: Academic Press.

Cook, T.D., Hunt, H.D., & Murphy, R.F. (2001, April). *Comer's school development program in Chicago: A theory-based evaluation.* Paper presented at the meeting of the Society for Research in Child Development, Minneapolis.

Cooper, C.R., & Ayers-Lopez, S. (1985). Family and peer systems in early adolescence: New models of the role of relationships in development. *Journal of Early Adolescence, 5,* 9–22.

Cooper, C.R., Baker, H., Polichar, D., & Welsh, M. (1993). Values and communication of Chinese, European, Filipino, Mexican, and Vietnamese American adolescents with their families and friends. *New Directions in Child Development, 62,* 73–89.

Cooper, C.R., Cooper, R.G., Azmitia, M., & Chavira, G. (2001). *Bridging multiple worlds: How African American and Latino youth in academic outreach programs navigate math pathways to college.* Unpublished manuscript, University of California at Santa Cruz.

Cooper, C.R., Cooper, R.G., Azmitia, M., Chavira, G., & Gullatt, Y. (2002). Bridging multiple worlds: How African American and Latino youth in academic outreach programs navigate math pathways to college. *Applied Developmental Science, 6,* 73–87.

Cooper, C.R., & Denner, J. (1998). Theories linking culture and psychology: Universal and community-specific processes. *Annual Review of Psychology, 49,* 559–584.

Cooper, C.R., & Grotevant, H.D. (1989, April). *Individuality and connectedness in the family and adolescent's self and relational competence.* Paper presented at the meeting of the Society for Research in Child Development, Kansas City.

Cooper, M.L., Shaver, P.R., & Collins, N.L. (1998). Attachment styles, emotional regulation, and adjustment in adolescence. *Journal of Personality and Social Psychology, 74,* 1380–1397.

Coopersmith, S. (1967). *The antecedents of self-esteem.* San Francisco: W.H. Freeman.

Copeland, H.L., Heim, A., & Rome, E.S. (2001, March). *Developing a relevant and effective smoking program.* Paper presented at the meeting of the Society for Adolescent Medicine, San Diego.

Cornock, B., Bowker, A., & Gadbois, S. (2001, April). *Sports participation and self-esteem: Examining the goodness of fit.* Paper presented at the meeting of the Society for Research in Child Development, Minneapolis.

Corrado, S.P., Patashnick, B.S., & Rich, M. (2004). Factors affecting change among obese adolescents. *Journal of Adolescent Health, 23,* 112.

Corsica, J.A., & Perri, M.G. (2003). Obesity. In I.B. Weiner (Ed.), *Handbook of psychology* (Vol. 9). New York: Wiley.

Cosmides, L., Tooby, J., Cronin, H., & Curry, O. (Eds.). (2003). *What is evolutionary psychology? Explaining the new science of the mind.* New Haven, CT: Yale University Press.

Costa, P.T., & McRae, R.R. (1998). Personality assessment. In H.S. Friedman

(Ed.), *Encyclopedia of mental health* (Vol. 3). San Diego: Academic Press.

Costin, S.E., & Jones, F. (1994, February). *The stress-protective role of parent and friend support for 6th and 9th graders following a school transition.* Paper presented at the meeting of the Society for Research on Adolescence, San Diego.

Cota-Robles, S., Neiss, M., & Hunt, C. (2000, April). *Future parent, future scholars: A longitudinal study of adolescent "possible selves" and adult outcomes.* Paper presented at the meeting of the Society for Research on Adolescence, Chicago.

Cote, J.E., & Levine, C. (1988). On critiquing the identity crisis paradigm: A rejoinder to Waterman. *Developmental Review, 8,* 209–218.

Cotman, C.W., & Berchtold, N.C. (2002). Exercise: A behavioral intervention to enhance brain health and plasticity. *Trends in Neuroscience, 25,* 295–301.

Covington, M.V. (2002). Patterns of adaptive learning study: Where do we go from here? In C. Midgley (Ed.), *Goals, goal structures, and patterns of adaptive learning.* Mahwah, NJ: Erlbaum.

Covington, M.V., & Mueller, K.J. (2001). Intrinsic and extrinsic motivation: An approach/avoidance reformulation. *Educational Psychology Review, 13,* 157–176.

Covington, M.V., & Teel, K.T. (1996). *Overcoming student failure.* Washington, DC: American Psychological Association.

Covington, M.V., Teel, K.T., & Parecki, A.D. (1994, April). *Motivation benefits of improved academic performance among middle-school African American students through an effort-based grading system.* Paper presented at the meeting of the American Educational Research Association, New Orleans.

Cowley, C. (1998, April 6). Why children turn violent. *Newsweek,* 24–25.

Crano, W., & Brewer, M. (2002). *Principles and methods of social research* (2nd ed.). Mahwah, NJ: Erlbaum.

Crawford, C., & Salmon, C. (Eds.). (2004). *Evolutionary psychology, public policy, and private decisions.* Mahwah, NJ: Erlbaum.

Crawford, M., & MacLeod, M. (1990). Gender in the college classroom: An assessment of the "chilly climate" for women. *Sex Roles, 23,* 101–122.

Creighton, S., & Miller, R. (2003). Unprotected sexual intercourse in teenagers—causes and consequences. *Journal of Research on Social Health, 123,* 7–8.

Crews, F. (2001, January 2). Commentary in "Brain growth gets blame for turbulent years." *USA Today,* p. 6D.

Crick, N.R., & Dodge, K.A. (1994). A review and reformulation of social information-processing mechanisms in children's social adjustment. *Psychological Bulletin, 115,* 74–101.

Crick, N.R., Nelson, D.A., Morales, J.R., Cullerton-Sen, C., Cases, J.F., & Hickman, S. (2001). Relational victimization in childhood and adolescence: I hurt you through the grapevine. In J. Juvonen & S. Graham (Eds.), *Peer harassment in school: The plight of the vulnerable and victimized.* New York: Guilford.

Crockett, L.J., Raffaelli, M., & Moilanen, K. (2003). Adolescent sexuality: Behavior and meaning. In G. Adams & M. Berzonsky (Eds.), *Blackwell handbook of adolescence.* Malden, MA: Blackwell.

Crooks, R., & Bauer, K. (2002). *Our sexuality* (8th ed.). Belmont, CA: Wadsworth.

Crouter, A.C., Manke, B.A., & McHale, S.M. (1995). The family context of gender intensification in early adolescence. *Child Development, 66,* 317–329.

Crowley, K., Callahan, M.A., Tenenbaum, H.R., & Allen, E. (2001). Parents explain more to boys than to girls during shared scientific thinking. *Psychological Science, 12,* 258–261.

Crump, A.D., Haynie, D., Aarons, S., & Adair, E. (1996, March). *African American teenagers' norms, expectations, and motivations regarding sex, contraception, and pregnancy.* Paper presented at the meeting of the Society for Research on Adolescence, Boston.

Csikszentmihalyi, M. (1990). *Flow.* New York: HarperCollins.

Csikszentmihalyi, M. (1993). *The evolving self.* New York: Harper & Row.

Csikszentmihalyi, M. (1995). *Creativity.* New York: HarperCollins.

Csikszentmihalyi, M. (2000). Creativity: An overview. In A. Kazdin (Ed.), *Encyclopedia of psychology.* Washington, DC, and New York: American Psychological Association and Oxford University Press.

Csikszentmihalyi, M., & Schmidt, J.A. (1998). Stress and resilience in adolescence: An evolutionary perspective. In K. Borman & B. Schneider (Eds.), *The adolescent years: Social influences and educational challenges.* Chicago: University of Chicago Press.

Csikszentmihalyi, M., & Schneider, B. (2000). *Becoming adult.* New York: Basic Books.

Cuéllar, I., Siles, R.I., & Bracamontes, E. (2004). Acculturation: A psychological construct of continued relevance for Chicana/o psychology. In R.J. Velasquez, B.W. McNeil, & L.M. Arellano (Eds.), *The handbook of Chicano psychology and mental health.* Mahwah, NJ: Erlbaum.

Cummings, E.M., Braungart-Rieker, J.M., & DuRocher-Schudlich, T. (2003). Emotion and personality development in childhood. In I.B. Weiner (Ed.), *Handbook of psychology* (Vol. 6). New York: Wiley.

Cummings, E.M., & Davies, P.T. (2002). Effects of marital conflict on children: Recent advances and emerging themes in process-oriented research. *Journal of Child Psychology and Psychiatry, 43,* 31–63.

Cushner, K.H., McClelland, A., & Safford, P. (2003). *Human diversity in education* (3rd ed.). Boston: Allyn & Bacon.

Cutrona, C.E. (1982). Transition to college: Loneliness and the process of social adjustment. In L.A. Peplau & D. Perlman (Eds.), *Loneliness: A sourcebook of current theory, research, and therapy.* New York: Wiley.

Dahl, R.E. (2001). Affect regulation, brain development, and behavioral/emotional health in adolescence. *CNS Spectrums, 6,* 60–72.

Dahl, R.E., & Lewin, D.S. (2002). Pathways to adolescent health sleep regulation and behavior. *Journal of Adolescent Health, 31* (6 Supplement), 175–184.

Damon, W. (1988). *The moral child.* New York: Free Press.

Damon, W. (1995). *Greater expectations.* New York: Free Press.

Damon, W. (2000). Moral development. In A. Kazdin (Ed.), *Encyclopedia of psychology.* Washington, DC, and New York: American Psychological Association and Oxford University Press.

Damon, W. (2003). Bringing in a new era in the field of youth development. In R.M. Lerner, F. Jacobs, & D. Wertlieb (Eds.), *Handbook of applied developmental science* (Vol. 3). Thousand Oaks, CA: Sage.

Damon, W., & Hart, D. (1988). *Self-understanding in childhood and adolescence.* New York: Cambridge University Press.

Danish, S. (2003). Sports and leisure. In G. Adams & M. Berzonsky (Eds.), *Blackwell* *handbook of adolescence.* Malden, MA: Blackwell.

Dannhausen-Brun, C.A., Shalowitz, M.U., & Berry, C.A. (1997, April). *Challenging the assumptions: Teen moms and public policy.* Paper presented at the meeting of the Society for Research in Child Development, Washington, DC.

Darling, C.A., Kallen, D.J., & VanDusen, J.E. (1984). Sex in transition, 1900–1984. *Journal of Youth and Adolescence, 13,* 385–399.

Darroch, J.E., Landry, D.J., & Singh, S. (2000). Changing emphases in sexuality education in U.S. public secondary schools, 1988–1999. *Family Planning Perspectives, 32,* 204–211, 265.

Darwin, C. (1859). *On the origin of species.* London: John Murray.

Dattilio, F.M. (Ed.). (2001). *Case studies in couple and family therapy.* New York: Guilford.

Davidson, J. (2000). Giftedness. In A. Kazdin (Ed.), *Encyclopedia of psychology.* Washington, DC, and New York: American Psychological Association and Oxford University Press.

Davis, S.S., & Davis, D.A. (1989). *Adolescence in a Moroccan town.* New Brunswick, NJ: Rutgers University Press.

Davison, G.C., & Neale, J.M. (2001). *Abnormal psychology* (8th ed.). New York: Wiley.

Day, R.D. (2002). *Introduction to family processes.* Mahwah, NJ: Erlbaum.

Day, R.D., & Acock, A. (2004). Youth ratings of family processes and father role performance of resident and nonresident fathers. In R.D. Day & M.E. Lamb (Eds.), *Conceptualizing and measuring father involvement.* Mahwah, NJ: Erlbaum.

Day, R.D., & Lamb, M.E. (2004). Conceptualizing and measuring father involvement. In R.D. Day & M.E. Lamb (Eds.), *Conceptualizing and measuring father involvement.* Mahwah, NJ: Erlbaum.

Day, S., Markiewitcz, D., Doyle, A.B., & Ducharme, J. (2001, April). *Attachment to mother, father, and best friend as predictors to the quality of adolescent romantic relationships.* Paper presented at the meeting of the Society for Research in Child Development, Minneapolis.

de Bellis, M.D., Clark, D.B., Beers, S.R., Soloff, P.H., Boring, A.M., Hall, J., Kersh, A., & Keshaan, M.S. (2000). Hippocampal volume in adolescent-onset alcohol use disorders. *American Journal of Psychiatry, 157,* 737–744.

de Bellis, M.D., Keshavan, M.S., Beers, S.R., Hall, J., Frustaci, K., Masalehdan, A., & Boring, N.J. (2001). Sex differences in brain maturation during childhood and adolescence *Cerebral Cortex, 11,* 552–557.

de Munich Keizer, S.M., & Mul, D. (2001). Trends in pubertal development in Europe. *Human Reproduction Update, 7,* 287–291.

de Charms, R. (1984). Motivation enhancement in educational settings. In R. Ames & C. Ames (Eds.), *Research on motivation in education* (Vol. 1). Orlando: Academic Press.

Deci, E.L., Koestner, R., & Ryan, R.M. (2001). Extrinsic rewards and intrinsic motivation in education: Reconsidered once again. *Review of Educational Research, 71,* 1–28.

Deci, E.L., & Ryan, R. (1994). Promoting self-determined education. *Scandinavian Journal of Educational Research, 38,* 3–14.

Dedikdes, C., & Brewer, M.B. (Eds.). (2001). *Individual self, relational self, and collective self.* Philadelphia: Psychology Press.

DeGarmo, D.S., Forgatch, M.S., & Martinez, C.R. (1998). *Parenting of divorced mothers as a link between social status and boys' academic outcomes: Unpacking the effects of SES.* Unpublished manuscript, Oregon Social Learning Center, University of Oregon, Eugene.

Delisle, J.R. (1984). *Gifted children speak out.* New York: Walker.

Demick, J., & Andreoletti, C. (Eds.). (2003). *Handbook of adult development.* New York: Kluwer.

Dempster, F.N. (1981). Memory span: Sources of individual and developmental differences. *Psychological Bulletin, 89,* 63–100.

Denmark, F. L., Russo, N.F., Frieze, I.H., & Eschuzur, J. (1988). Guidelines for avoiding sexism in psychological research: A report of the ad hoc committee on nonsexist research. *American Psychologist, 43,* 582–585.

Dewey, J. (1933). *How we think.* Lexington, MA: D.C. Heath.

DeZolt, D.M., & Hull, S.H. (2001). Classroom and school climate. In J. Worrell (Ed.), *Encyclopedia of women and gender.* San Diego: Academic Press.

Diamond, L.M. (2003). Love matters: Romantic relationships among sexual-minority adolescents. In P. Florsheim (Ed.), *Adolescent romantic relations and sexual behavior.* Mahwah, NJ: Erlbaum.

Diamond, L.M., & Savin-Williams, R.C. (2003). The intimate relationships of sexual-minority youths. In G. Adams & M.

Berzonsky (Eds.), *Blackwell handbook of adolescence.* Malden, MA: Blackwell.

Diamond, L.M., Savin-Williams, R.C., & Dubé, E.M. (1999). Sex, dating, passionate friendships, and romance: Intimate peer relations among lesbian, gay, and bisexual adolescents. In W. Furman, B.B. Brown & C. Feiring (Eds.), *The development of relationships during adolescence.* New York: Cambridge University Press.

Diaz, C. (2003). *Multicultural education in the 21st century.* Boston: Allyn & Bacon.

Dickens, W.T., & Flynn, J.R. (2001). Heritability estimates versus large environmental effects: The IQ paradox resolved. *Psychological Review 108,* 346–369.

Dickerscheid, J.D., Schwarz, P.M., Noir, S., & El-Taliawy, T. (1988). Gender concept development of preschool-aged children in the United States and Egypt. *Sex Roles, 18,* 669–677.

DiClemente, R.J., & Crosby, R.A. (2003). Sexually transmitted diseases among adolescents. In G. Adams & M. Berzonsky (Eds.), *Blackwell handbook of adolescence.* Malden, MA: Blackwell.

Dielman, T.E., Schulenberg, J., Leech, S., & Shope, J.T. (1992, March). *Reduction of susceptibility to peer pressure and alcohol use/misuse through a school-based prevention program.* Paper presented at the meeting of the Society for Research on Adolescence, Washington, DC.

Dielman, T.E., Shope, J.T., & Butchart, A.T. (1990, March). *Peer, family, and intrapersonal predictors of adolescent alcohol use and misuse.* Paper presented at the meeting of the Society for Research in Adolescence, Atlanta.

Dion, K.L. (2003). Prejudice, racism, and discrimination. In I.B. Weiner (Ed.), *Handbook of psychology* (Vol. 5). New York: Wiley.

Dishion, T. (2002, April). *Understanding and preventing adolescent drug abuse.* Paper presented at the meeting of the Society for Research on Adolescence, New Orleans.

Dishion, T.J., Andrews, D.W., & Crosby, L. (1995). Antisocial boys and their friends in early adolescence: Relationship characteristics, quality, and interactional process. *Child Development, 66,* 139–151.

Dittman, M. (2003, April). Sex: Worth the risk? *Monitor on Psychology, 34,* 58–60.

D'Augelli, A.R. (1991). Gay men in college: Identity processes and adaptations. *Journal of College Student Development, 32,* 140–146.

D'Augelli, A.R. (2000). Sexual orientation. In A. Kazdin (Ed.), *Encyclopedia of psychology.*

Washington, DC, and New York: American Psychological Association and Oxford University Press.

Dodge, K.A. (1993). Social cognitive mechanisms in the development of conduct disorder and depression. *Annual Review of Psychology, 44,* 559–584.

Dodge, K.A. (2001). The science of youth violence prevention: Progressing from developmental psychopathology to efficacy to effectiveness in public policy. *American Journal of Preventive Medicine, 20,* 63–70.

Dodge, K.A., & Pettit, G.S. (2003). A biopsychosocial model of the development of chronic conduct problems in adolescence. *Developmental Psychology, 39,* 349–371.

Dolcini, M.M., Coh, L.D., Adler, N.E., Millstein, S.G., Irwin, C.E., Kegeles, S.M., & Stone, G.C. (1989). Adolescent egocentrism and feelings of invulnerability: Are they related? *Journal of Early Adolescence, 9,* 409–418.

Donnerstein, E. (2002). The Internet. In Wilson, B.J., & Strasburger, V.C. *Children, adolescents, and the media.* Newbury Park, CA: Sage.

Dorn, L.D., Williamson, D.E., & Ryan, N.D. (2002, April). *Maturational hormone differences in adolescents with depression and risk for depression.* Paper presented at the meeting of the Society for Research on Adolescence, New Orleans.

Dornbusch, S.M., Petersen, A.C., & Hetherington, E.M. (1991). Projecting the future of research on adolescence. *Journal of Research on Adolescence, 1,* 7–17.

Douvan, E., & Adelson, J. (1966). *The adolescent experience.* New York: Wiley.

Dowda, M., Ainsworth, B.E., Addy, C.L., Saunders, R., & Riner, W. (2001). Environmental influences, physical activity, and weight status in 8- to 16-year-olds. *Archives of Pediatric and Adolescent Medicine, 155,* 711–717.

Downs, J. (2003). *Interactive video DVD intervention.* Pittsburgh: Carnegie Mellon Department of Social and Decision Making Sciences.

Draguns, J.G. (1990). Applications of cross-cultural psychology in the field of mental health. In R.W. Brislin (Ed.), *Applied cross-cultural psychology.* Newbury Park, CA: Sage.

Drotar, D. (2000). *Promoting adherence to medical treatment in chronic childhood illness.* Mahwah, NJ: Erlbaum.

Dryfoos, J.G. (1990). *Adolescents at risk: Prevalence and prevention.* New York: Oxford University Press.

Dryfoos, J.G. (1995). Full service schools: Revolution or fad? *Journal of Research on Adolescence, 5,* 147–172.

Dryfoos, J.G. (1997). The prevalence of problem behaviors: Implications for programs. In R.P. Weissberg, T.P. Gullotta, R.L. Hampton, B.A. Ryan, & G.R. Adams (Eds.), *Healthy children 2010: Enhancing children's wellness.* Thousand Oaks, CA: Sage.

Duck, S.W. (1975). Personality similarity and friendship choices by adolescents. *European Journal of Social Psychology, 5,* 351–365.

Duckett, E., & Richards, M.H. (1996, March). *Fathers' time in child care and the father-child relationship.* Paper presented at the meeting of the Society for Research on Adolescence, Boston.

Duckett, R.H. (1997, July). *Strengthening families/building communities.* Paper presented at the conference on Working with America's Youth, Pittsburgh.

Duffy, T.M., & Kirkley, J.R. (Eds.). *Learner-centered theory and practice in distance education.* Mahwah, NJ: Erlbaum.

Duncan, G.J., Brooks-Gunn, J., & Klebanov, P.K. (1994). Economic deprivation and early childhood development. *Child Development, 65,* 296–318.

Dunn, J., Davies, L.C., O'Connor, T.G., & Sturgess, W. (2001). Family lives and friendships: The perspectives of children in step-, single-parent, and nonstep families. *Journal of Family Psychology, 15,* 272–287.

Dunphy, D.C. (1963). The social structure of urban adolescent peer groups. *Society, 26,* 230–246.

Durbin, D.L., Darling, N., Steinberg, L., & Brown, B.B. (1993). Parenting style and peer group membership among European-American adolescents. *Journal of Research on Early Adolescence, 3,* 87–100.

Durkin, K., & Hutchins, G. (1984). Challenging traditional sex role stereotypes via career education broadcasts: The reactions of young secondary school pupils. *Journal of Educational Television, 10,* 25–33.

Dusek, J.B., & McIntyre, J.G. (2003). Self-concept and self-esteem development. In G. Adams & M. Berzonsky (Eds.), *Blackwell handbook of adolescence.* Malden, MA: Blackwell.

Dweck, C.S. (2002). The development of ability conceptions. In A. Wigfield & J.S.

Eccles (Eds.), *Development of achievement motivation.* San Diego: Academic Press.

Dweck, C.S., & Elliott, E. (1983). Achievement motivation. In P. Mussen (Ed.), *Handbook of child psychology* (4th ed., Vol. 4). New York: Wiley.

Dweck, C.S., & Leggett, E. (1988). A social cognitive approach to motivation and personality. *Psychological Review, 95,* 256–273.

Dworkin, J.B., Larson, R., & Hansen, D. (2003). Adolescents' accounts of growth experiences in youth activities. *Journal of Youth and Adolescence, 32,* 17–26.

Dworkin, J.B., Larson, R., Hansen, D., Jones, J., & Midle, T. (2001, April). *Adolescents' accounts of their growth experiences in youth activities.* Paper presented at the meeting of the Society for Research in Child Development, Minneapolis.

Eagly, A.H. (2000). Gender roles. In A. Kazdin (Ed.), *Encyclopedia of psychology.* Washington, DC, and New York: American Psychological Association and Oxford University Press.

Eagly, A.H. (2001). Social role theory of sex differences and similarities. In J. Worrel (Ed.), *Encyclopedia of women and gender.* San Diego: Academic Press.

Eagly, A.H., & Crowley, M. (1986). Gender and helping behavior: A meta-analytic review of the social psychological literature. *Psychological Bulletin, 100,* 283–308.

Eagly, A.H., & Diekman, A.B. (2003). The malleability of sex differences in response to social roles. In L.G. Aspinwall & V.M. Staudinger (Eds.), *A psychology of human strengths.* Washington, DC: American Psychological Association.

Eagly, A.H., & Steffen, V.J. (1986). Gender and aggressive behavior: A meta-analytic review of the social psychological literature. *Psychological Bulletin, 111,* 3–22.

East, P., & Adams, J. (2002). Sexual assertiveness and adolescents' sexual rights. *Perspectives on Sexual and Reproductive Health, 34,* 198–202.

Easterbrooks, M.A., & Giesecker, G. (2002, April). *Attachments to mothers, fathers, and peers: Connections with emotion regulation and working models of self and world.* Paper presented at the meeting of the Society for Research on Adolescence, New Orleans.

Eberly, M.B., & Montemayor, R. (1996, March). *Adolescent prosocial behavior toward mothers and fathers: A reflection of parent-adolescent relationships.* Paper presented at the meeting of the Society for Research on Adolescence, Boston.

Eccles, J.S. (1987). Gender roles and achievement patterns: An expectancy value perspective. In J.M. Reinisch, L.A. Rosenblum, & S.A. Sanders (Eds.), *Masculinity/femininity.* New York: Oxford University Press.

Eccles, J.S. (2002, April). *Ethnicity as a context for development.* Paper presented at the meeting of the Society for Research on Adolescence, New Orleans.

Eccles, J.S. (2004). Schools, academic motivation, and stage-environment fit. In R. Lerner & L. Steinberg (Eds.), *Handbook of adolescent psychology.* New York: Wiley.

Eccles, J.S., & Goodman, J. (Eds). (2002). *Community programs to promote youth development.* Washington, DC: National Academy Press.

Eccles, J.S., & Harold, R.D. (1993). Parent-school involvement during the adolescent years. In R. Takanishi (Ed.), *Adolescence in the 1990s.* New York: Columbia University Press.

Eccles, J.S., Lord, S., & Buchanan, C.M. (1996). School transitions in early adolescence: What are we doing to our young people? In J.A. Graber, J. Brooks-Gunn, & A.C. Petersen (Eds.), *Transitions in adolescence.* Mahwah, NJ: Erlbaum.

Eccles, J.S., Midgley, C., Wigfield, A., Buchanan, C.M., Reuman, D., Flanagan, C., & Mac Iver, D. (1993). Development during adolescence: The impact of stage-environment fit on young adolescents' experiences in schools and families. *American Psychologist, 48,* 90–101.

Eccles, J.S., Templeton, J., Barber, B., & Stone, M. (2003). Adolescence and emerging adulthood. In M.H. Bornstein, L. Davidson, C.L.M. Keyes, & K.A. Moore (Eds.), *Well-being: Positive development across the life course.* Mahwah, NJ: Erlbaum.

Eccles, J.S., & Wigfield, A. (2000). Social patterns, achievements, and problems. In A. Kazdin (Ed.), *Encyclopedia of psychology.* Washington, DC, and New York: American Psychological Association and Oxford University Press.

Eccles, J., Wigfield, A., & Byrnes, J. (2003). Cognitive development in adolescence. In I.B. Weiner (Ed.), *Handbook of psychology* (Vol. 6). New York: Wiley.

Eccles, J.S., Wigfield, A., & Schiefele, U. (1998). Motivation to succeed. In W. Damon (Ed.), *Handbook of child psychology* (5th ed., Vol. 3). New York: Wiley.

Edelbrock, C.S. (1989, April). *Self-reported internalizing and externalizing problems in a community sample of adolescents.* Paper presented at the meeting of the Society for Research in Child Development, Kansas City.

Edelman, M.W. (1996). *The state of America's children.* Washington, DC: Children's Defense Fund.

Edelman, M.W. (1997, April). *Children, families, and social policy.* Paper presented at the meeting of the Society for Research in Child Development, Washington, DC.

Egeland, B., & Carlson, B. (2004). Attachment and psychopathology. In L. Atkinson & S. Goldberg (Eds.), *Attachment issues in psychopathology and intervention.* Mahwah, NJ: Erlbaum.

Egeland, B., Warren, S., & Aguilar, B. (2001, April). *Perspectives on the development of psychopathology from the Minnesota Longitudinal Study.* Paper presented at the meeting of the Society for Research in Child Development, Minneapolis.

Eisenberg, N., Cumberland, A., Spinrad, T.L., Fabes, R.A., Shepard, S.A., Reiser, M., Murphy, B.C., Losoya, S.H., & Guthrie, I.K. (2001). The relations of regulation and emotionality to children's externalizing and internalizing problem behavior. *Child Development, 72,* 1112–1134.

Eisenberg, N., & Fabes, R.A. (1998). Prosocial development. In N. Eisenberg (Ed.), *Handbook of child psychology* (5th ed., Vol. 3). New York: Wiley.

Eisenberg, N., Fabes, R.A., Guthrie, I.K., & Reiser, M. (2002). The role of emotionality and regulation in children's social competence and adjustment. In L. Pulkkinen & A. Caspi (Eds.), *Paths to successful development.* New York: Cambridge University Press.

Eisenberg, N., Gutherie, I.K., Murphy, B.C., Shepard, S.A., Cumberland, A., & Carlo, G. (1999). Consistency and development of prosocial dispositions: A longitudinal study. *Child Development, 70,* 1360–1372.

Eisenberg, N., & Morris, A. (2004). Moral cognitions and prosocial responding in adolescence. In R. Lerner & L. Steinberg (Eds.), *Handbook of adolescent psychology.* New York: Wiley.

Eisenberg, N., & Murphy, B. (1995). Parenting and children's moral development. In M.H. Bornstein (Ed.), *Children and parenting* (Vol. 4). Hillsdale, NJ: Erlbaum.

Eisenberg, N., & Valiente, C. (2002). Parenting and children's prosocial and moral development. In M.H. Bornstein (Ed.), *Handbook of parenting* (2nd ed.). Mahwah, NJ: Erlbaum.

Eisenberg, N., Valiente, C., Morris, A.S., Fabes, R.A., Cumberland, A., Reiser, M., Gershoff, E.T., Shepard, S.A., & Losoya, S. (2003). Longitudinal relations among parental emotional expressivity, children's regulation, and quality of socioemotional functioning. *Developmental Psychology, 39,* 2–19.

Eisenberg, N., & Wang, V.O. (2003). Toward a positive psychology: Social developmental and cultural contributions. In L.G. Aspinwall & U. Staudinger (Eds.), *A psychology of human strengths.* Washington, DC: American Psychological Association.

Eisenberg, N., Zhou, Q., & Koller, S. (2001). Brazilian adolescents' prosocial moral judgment and behavior: Relations to sympathy, perspective taking, gender-role orientation, and demographic characteristics. *Child Development, 72,* 518–534.

Elder, G.H. (1975). Adolescence in the life cycle. In S.E. Dragastin & G.H. Elder (Eds.), *Adolescence in the life cycle: Psychological change and social context.* New York: Wiley.

Elder, G.H. (1998). The life course and human development. In W. Damon (Ed.), *Handbook of child psychology* (5th ed., Vol. 1). New York: Wiley.

Elder, G.H. (2000). Life course theory. In A. Kazdin (Ed.), *Encyclopedia of psychology.* Washington, DC, and New York: American Psychological Association and Oxford University Press.

Elkind, D. (1961). Quantity conceptions in junior and senior high school students. *Child Development, 32,* 531–560.

Elkind, D. (1976). *Child development and education. A Piagetian perspective.* New York: Oxford University Press.

Elkind, D. (1981). *The hurried child.* Reading, MA: Addison-Wesley.

Elkind, D. (1985). Reply to D. Lapsley and M. Murphy's *Developmental Review* paper. *Developmental Review, 5,* 218–226.

Elliot, A.J., & McGregor, H.A. (2001). A 2 × 2 achievement goal framework. *Journal of Personality and Social Psychology 80,* 501–519.

Elliot, A.J., & Thrash, T.M. (2001). Achievement goals and the hierarchical model of achievement motivation. *Educational Psychology Review, 13,* 139–156.

Ellis, L., & Ames, M.A. (1987). Neurohormonal functioning and sexual orientation: A theory of homosexuality-heterosexuality. *Psychological Bulletin, 101,* 233–258.

Elmes, D.G., Kantowitz, B.H., & Roedinger, H.L. (2003). *Research methods in psychology* (7th ed.). Belmont, CA: Wadsworth.

Embretson, S.E., & McCollam, K.M.S. (2000). Psychometric approaches to understanding and measuring intelligence. In R.J. Sternberg (Ed.), *Handbook of intelligence.* New York: Cambridge University Press.

Emery, R.E. (1999). *Renegotiating family relationships* (2nd ed.). New York: Guilford Press.

Emery, R.E., & Tuer, M. (1993). Parenting and the marital relationship. In T. Luster & L. Okagaki (Eds.), *Parenting: An Ecological perspective.* Hillsdale, NJ: Erlbaum.

Emmer, E.T., Evertson, C.M., & Worsham, M.E. (2003). *Classroom management for secondary teachers* (6th ed.). Boston: Allyn & Bacon.

Engeland, A., Bjorge, T., Tverdal, A., & Sogaard, A.J. (2004). Obesity in adolescence and adulthood and the risk of adult mortality. *Epidemiology, 15,* 79–85.

Englund, M.M., Luckner, A.E., & Whaley, G. (2003, April). *The importance of early parenting for children's long-term educational attainment.* Paper presented at the meeting of the Society for Research in Child Development, Tampa.

Enright, R.D., Lapsley, D.K., Dricas, A.S., & Fehr, L.A. (1980). Parental influence on the development of adolescent autonomy and identity. *Journal of Youth and Adolescence, 9,* 529–546.

Enright, R.D., Levy, V.M., Harris, D., & Lapsley, D.K. (1987). Do economic conditions influence how theorists view adolescents? *Journal of Youth and Adolescence, 16,* 541–559.

Enright, R.D., Santos, M.J.D., & Al-Mabuk, R. (1989). The adolescent as forgiver. *Journal of Adolescence, 12,* 95–110.

Epstein, J.A., Botvin, G.J., & Diaz, T. (1998). Linguistic acculturation and gender effects on smoking among Hispanic youth. *Preventive Medicine, 27,* 538–589.

Epstein, J.L. (1990). School and family connections: Theory, research, and implications for integrating sociologies of education and family. In D.G. Unger & M.B. Sussman (Eds.), *Families in community settings: Interdisciplinary responses.* New York: Haworth Press.

Epstein, J.L. (1996). Perspectives and previews on research and policy for school, family, and community partnerships. In A. Booth & J.F. Dunn (Eds.), *Family-school links.* Mahwah, NJ: Erlbaum.

Epstein, J.L., & Sanders, M.G. (2002). Family, school, and community partnerships. In M. Bornstein (Ed.), *Handbook of parenting* (2nd ed., Vol. 5). Mahwah, NJ: Erlbaum.

Epstein, S. (2003). Cognitive-experiential self-theory of personality. In I.B. Weiner (Ed.), *Handbook of psychology* (Vol. 5). New York: Wiley.

Erickson, J.B. (1982). *A profile of community youth organization members, 1980.* Boys Town, NE: Boys Town Center for the Study of Youth Development.

Erickson, J.B. (1996). Directory of American youth organizations (2nd rev. ed.). Boys Town, NE: Boys Town Communication and Public Services Division.

Erikson, E.H. (1950). *Childhood and society.* New York: W.W. Norton.

Erikson, E.H. (1962). *Young man Luther.* New York: W.W. Norton.

Erikson, E.H. (1968). *Identity: Youth and crisis.* New York: W.W. Norton.

Erikson, E.H. (1969). *Gandhi's truth.* New York: W.W. Norton.

Erikson, E.H. (1970). Reflections on the dissent of contemporary youth. *Internationl Journal of Psychoanalysis, 51,* 11–22.

Erlick, A.C., & Starry, A.R. (1973, June). *Sources of information for career decisions.* Report of Poll No. 98, Purdue Opinion Panel.

Erlick Robinson, G. (2003). Violence against women in North America. *Archives of Women's Mental Health, 6,* 185–191.

Escobedo, L.G., Marcus, S.E., Holtzman, D., & Giovino, G.A. (1993). Sports participation, age at smoking initiation, and risk of smoking among U.S. high school students. *Journal of the American Medical Association, 269,* 1391–1395.

Espelage, D., & Swearer, S. (Eds.). (2004). *Bullying in American schools.* Mahwah, NJ: Erlbaum.

Etaugh, C., & Bridges, J.S. (2001). *Psychology of women: A life-span perspective.* Boston: Allyn & Bacon.

Ethier, K., & Deaux, K. (1990). Hispanics in ivy: Assessing identity and perceived threat. *Sex Roles, 20,* 59–70.

Evans, B.J., & Whitfield, J.R. (Eds.). (1988). *Black males in the United States: An annotated bibliography from 1967 to 1987.*

Washington, DC: American Psychological Association.

Evans, S.W., Pelham, W.E., Smith, B.H., Bukstein, O., Gnagy, E.M., Greiner, A.R., Altenderfer, L., & Baron-Myak, C. (2001). Dose-response effects of methylphenidate on ecologically valid measures of academic performance and classroom behavior in adolescents with ADHD. *Experimental and Clinical Psychopharmacology, 9,* 163–175.

Evertson, C.M., Emmer, E.T., & Worsham, M.E. (2003). *Classroom management for elementary teachers* (6th ed.). Boston: Allyn & Bacon.

Fajardo, G., Wakefield, W.D., Godinez, M., & Simental, J.F. (2003, April). *Latino and African American adolescents' experiences with discrimination.* Paper presented at the meeting of the Society for Research in Child Development, Tampa.

Fan, X., & Chen, M. (2001). Parental involvement and students' academic achievement: A meta-analysis. *Educational Psychology Review, 13* (1), 1–22.

Fang, S., & Bryant, C.M. (2000, April). *Influences of parents on young adults' romantic relationships: A prospective analysis of parents' impact on attitudes and behavior.* Paper presented at the meeting of the Society for Research on Adolescence, Chicago.

Faraone, S.V., Spencer, T., Aleardi, M., Pagano, C., & Biederman, J. (2004). Meta-analysis of the efficacy of methylpendiate for treating adult attention deficit hyperactivity disorder. *Journal of Clinical Psychopharmacology, 24,* 24–29.

Farrington, D.P. (2000). Delinquency. In A. Kazdin (Ed.), *Encyclopedia of psychology.* Washington, DC, and New York: American Psychological Association and Oxford University Press.

Farrington, D.P. (2004). Conduct disorder, aggression, and delinquency. In R. Lerner & L. Steinberg (Eds.), *Handbook of adolescent psychology.* New York: Wiley.

Fasick, F.A. (1994). On the "invention" of adolescence. *Journal of Early Adolescence, 14,* 6–23.

Federman, J. (Ed.). (1997). *National television violence study* (Vol. 2). Santa Barbara: University of California.

Feeney, S. (1980). *Schools for young adolescents: Adapting the early childhood model.* Carrboro, NC: Center for Early Adolescence.

Fehring, R.J., Cheever, K.H., German, K., & Philpot, C. (1998). Religiosity and sexual activity among older adolescents. *Journal of Religion and Health, 37,* 229–239.

Feinberg, M.,& Hetherington, E.M. (2001). Differential parenting as a within-family variable. *Journal of Family Psychology, 15,* 22–37.

Feiring, C. (1996). Concepts of romance in 15-year-old adolescents. *Journal of Research on Adolescence, 6,* 181–200.

Feiring, C. (1999). Gender identity and the development of romantic relationships in adolescence. In W. Furman, B.B. Brown, & C. Feiring (Eds.), *Heartaches and heartthrobs: Adolescent romantic relationships.* Cambridge, UK: Cambridge University Press.

Feist, J., & Brannon, L. (1989). *An introduction to behavior and health.* Belmont, CA: Wadsworth.

Feldman, D.H. (2003). Cognitive development in childhood. In I.B. Weiner (Ed.), *Handbook of psychology* (Vol. 6). New York: Wiley.

Feldman, S.S. (1999). Unpublished review of J.W. Santrock's *Adolescence,* 8th ed. (New York: McGraw-Hill).

Feldman, S.S., & Elliott, G.R. (1990). Progress and promise of research on normal adolescent development. In S.S. Feldman & G. Elliott (Eds.), *At the threshold: The developing adolescent.* Cambridge, MA: Harvard University Press.

Feldman, S.S., & Rosenthal, D.A. (1999). *Factors influencing parents' and adolescents' evaluations of parents as sex communicators.* Unpublished manuscript, Stanford Center on Adolescence, Stanford University.

Feldman, S.S., & Rosenthal, D.A. (Eds.). (2002). *Talking sexually: Parent-adolescent communication.* San Francisco: Jossey-Bass.

Feldman, S.S., Turner, R., & Araujo, K. (1999). Interpersonal context as an influence on sexual timetables of youths: Gender and ethnic effects. *Journal of Research on Adolescence, 9,* 25–52.

Fenzel, L.M. (1994, February). *A prospective study of the effects of chronic strains on early adolescent self-worth and school adjustment.* Paper presented at the meeting of the Society for Research on Adolescence, San Diego.

Fenzel, L.M., Blyth, D.A., & Simmons, R.G. (1991). School transitions, secondary. In R.M. Lerner, A.C. Petersen, & J. Brooks-Gunn (Eds.), *Encyclopedia of adolescence* (Vol. 2). New York: Garland.

Ferber, T. (2002, April). *Social policy recommendations of adolescence in the 21st century.* Paper presented at the meeting of the Society for Research on Adolescence, New Orleans.

Ferguson, A. (1999, July 12). Inside the crazy culture of kids' sports. *Time,* pp. 52–60.

Fessler, K.B. (2003). Social outcomes of early childbearing. *Journal of Midwifery and Women's Health, 48,* 178–185.

Field, A.E., Cambargo, C.A., Taylor, C.B., Berkey, C.S., Roberts, S.B., & Colditz, G.A. (2001). Peer, parent, and media influences on the development of weight concerns and frequent dieting among preadolescent and adolescent girls and boys. *Pediatrics, 107,* 54–60.

Field, T., Diego, M., & Sanders, C.E. (2001). Exercise is positively related to adolescents' relationships and academics. *Adolescence, 36,* 105–110.

Fine, M. (1988). Sexuality, schooling, and adolescent females: The missing discourse of desire. *Harvard Educational Review, 58* (1), 29–53.

Finkelstein, J.W., Susman, E.J., Chinchilli, V., Kunselman, S.J., D'Arcangelo, M.R., Schwab, J., Demers, L.M., Liben, L., Lookingbill, M.S., & Kulin, H.E. (1997). Estrogen or testosterone increases self-reported aggressive behavior in hypogonadal adolescents. *Journal of Clinical Endocrinology and Metabolism, 82,* 2433–2438.

Finn, J.D. (1989). Withdrawing from school. *Review of Educational Research, 59,* 131.

Finn, J.D. (2002). Class size reduction in grades K–3. In A. Molnar (Ed.), *School reform proposals: The research evidence.* Greenwich, CT: Information Age Publishing.

Finn, J.D., Gerber, S.B., & Boyd-Zaharias, J. (2002). *Early school experiences and dropping out.* Unpublished manuscript, Graduate School of Education, The University at Buffalo-SUNY, Buffalo, NY.

Firpo-Triplett, R. (1997, July). *Is it flirting or sexual harassment?* Paper presented at the conference on Working with America's Youth, Pittsburgh.

Fisch, S.M. (2004). *Children's learning from educational television.* Mahwah, NJ: Erlbaum.

Fischer, K.W., & Pruyne, E. (2003). Reflective thinking in adulthood: Emergence, development, and variation. In J. Demick & C. Andreoletti (Eds.), *Handbook of adult development.* New York: Kluwer.

Fish, K.D., & Biller, H.B. (1973). Perceived childhood paternal relationships and college females' personal adjustment. *Adolescence, 8,* 415–420.

Fisher, B.S., Cullen, F.T., & Turner, M.G. (2000). *The sexual victimization of college women.* Washington, DC: National Institute of Justice.

Fisher, D. (1990, March) *Effects of attachment on adolescents' friendships.* Paper presented at the meeting of the Society for Research in Adolescence, Atlanta.

Fisher, T.D. (1987). Family communication and the sexual behavior and attitudes of college students. *Journal of Youth and Adolescence, 16,* 481–495.

Fiske, S.T., Bersoff, D.N., Borgida, E., Deaux, K., & Heilman, M.E. (1991). Social science research on trial: Use of sex stereotyping research in *Price Waterhouse v. Hopkins. American Psychologist, 23,* 399–427.

Fitzgerald, L. (2000). Sexual harassment. In A. Kazdin (Ed.), *Encyclopedia of psychology.* Washington, DC, and New York: American Psychological Association and Oxford University Press.

Flanagan, A.S. (1996, March). *Romantic behavior of sexually victimized and nonvictimized women.* Paper presented at the meeting of the Society for Research on Adolescence, Boston.

Flanagan, C.A. (2002, April). *Inclusion and reciprocity: Developmental sources of social trust and civic hope.* Paper presented at the meeting of the Society for Research on Adolescence, New Orleans.

Flanagan, C.A. (2004). Volunteerism, leadership, political socialization, and civic engagement. In R. Lerner & L. Steinberg (Eds.), *Handbook of adolescent psychology.* New York: Wiley.

Flanagan, C.A., & Eccles, J.S. (1993). Changes in parents' work status and adolescents' adjustment at school. *Child Development, 64,* 246–257.

Flanagan, C.A., & Faison, N. (2001). Youth civic development: Implications for social policy and programs. *SRCD Social Policy Report, 15* (1), 1–14.

Flanagan, C.A., Gill, S., & Gallay, L. (1998, November). *Intergroup understanding, social justice, and the "social contract" in diverse communities of youth.* Project report prepared for the workshop on research to improve intergroup relations among youth, Forum on Adolescence, National Research Council, Washington, DC.

Flannery, D.J., Hussey, D., Biebelhausen, L., & Weser, K. (2003). Crime, delinquency, and youth gangs. In G. Adams & M. Berzonsky (Eds.), *Blackwell handbook of adolescence.* Malden, MA: Blackwell.

Flannery, D.J., Rowe D.C., & Gulley B.L. (1993). Impact of pubertal status, timing, and age on adolescent sexual experience and delinquency. *Journal of Adolescent Research, 8,* 21–40

Flavell, J.H. (1999). Cognitive development: Children's knowledge about the mind. *Annual Review of Psychology,* Vol. 50. Palo Alto, CA: Annual Reviews.

Flavell, J.H., Miller, P.H., & Miller, S.A. (2002). *Cognitive development* (4th ed). Upper Saddle River, NJ: Prentice-Hall.

Flay, B. (2003). Positive youth is necessary and possible. In D. Romer (Ed.), *Reducing adolescent risk.* Newbury Park, CA: Sage.

Fleming, J.E., Boyle, M., & Offord, D.R. (1993). The outcome of adolescent depression in the Ontario child health study follow-up. *Journal of the American Academy of Child and Adolescent Psychiatry, 32,* 28–29.

Fling, S., Smith, L., Rodriguez, T., Thornton, D., Atkins, E., & Nixon, K. (1992). Videogames, aggression, and self-esteem: A survey. *Social Behavior and Personality, 20,* 39–46.

Florsheim, P. (Ed.). (2003). *Adolescent romantic relations and sexual behavior.* Mahwah, NJ: Erlbaum.

Flowers, P., & Buston, K. (2001). "I was terrified of being different," Exploring gay men's accounts of growing up in a heterosexist society. *Journal of Adolescence, 24,* 51–66.

Flynn, J.R. (1999). Searching for justice: The discovery of IQ gains over time. *American Psychologist, 54,* 5–20.

Ford, C.A., Bearman, P.S., & Moody, J. (1999). Foregone health care among adolescents. *Journal of the American Medical Association, 282* (No. 23), 2227–2234.

Ford, K., Sohn, W., & Lepkowski, J. (2001). Characteristics of adolescents' sexual partners and their association with use of condoms and other contraceptive methods. *Family Planning Perspectives, 33,* 100–105, 132.

Ford, N., Odallo, D., & Chorlton, R. (2003). Communication from a human rights perspective: Responding to the HIV/AIDS pandemic in Eastern and Southern Africa. *Journal of Health Communication, 8,* 599–602.

Forrest, J.D., & Singh, S. (1990). The sexual and reproductive behavior of American women, 1982–1988. *Family Planning Perspectives, 22,* 206–214.

Fouad, N.A. (1995). Career behavior of Hispanics: Assessment and career intervention. In F.T.L. Leong (Ed.), *Career development and vocational behavior of racial and ethnic minorities.* Hillsdale, NJ: Erlbaum.

Fowler, J.W. (1981). *Stages of faith: The psychology of human development and the quest for faith.* New York: HarperCollins.

Fowler, J.W. (1996). *Faithful change.* Nashville, TN: Abingdon Press.

Fox, B.A. (1993). *The Human Tutorial Dialogue Project.* Mahwah, NJ: Erlbaum.

Fox, K., Page, A., Armstrong, N., & Kirby, B. (1994). Dietary restraint and self-esteem in early adolescence. *Personality and Individual Differences, 17,* 87–96.

Francis, J., Fraser, G., & Marcia, J.E. (1989). *Cognitive and experimental factors in moratorium-achievement (MAMA) cycles.* Unpublished manuscript, Department of Psychology, Simon Fraser University, Burnaby, British Columbia.

Franke, T.M. (2000, Winter). The role of attachment as a protective factor in adolescent violent behavior. *Adolescent and Family Health, 1,* 29–39.

Franz, C.E. (1996). The implications of preschool tempo and motoric activity level for personality decades later. Reported in Caspi, A. (1998). Personality development across the life course. In W. Damon (Ed.), *Handbook of child psychology* (Vol. 3). New York: Wiley, p. 337.

Fraser, S. (Ed.). (1995). *The bell curve wars: Race, intelligence, and the future of Amercia.* New York: Basic Books.

Frazier, P.A. (2003). Perceived control and distress following sexual assault: A longitudinal test of a new model. *Journal of Personality and Social Psychology, 84,* 1257–1269.

Frederikse, M., Lu, A., Aylward, E., Barta, P., Sharma, T., & Pearlson, G. (2000). Sex differences in inferior lobule volume in schizophrenia. *American Journal of Psychiatry, 157,* 422–427.

Freeman, D. (1983). *Margaret Mead and Samoa.* Cambridge, MA: Harvard University Press.

Frenn, M., Malin, S., Bansal, N., Delgado, M., Greer, Y., Havice, M., Ho, M., & Schweizer, H. (2003). Addressing health disparities in middle school students' nutrition and exercise. *Journal of Community Health Nursing, 20,* 1–14.

Freud, A. (1966). Instinctual anxiety during puberty. In *The writings of Anna Freud: The ego and the mechanisms of defense.* New York: International Universities Press.

Freud, A., & Dann, S. (1951). Instinctual anxiety during puberty. In A. Freud (Ed.), *The ego and its mechanisms of defense.* New York: International Universities Press.

Freud, S. (1917/1958). *A general introduction to psychoanalysis.* New York: Washington Square Press.

Fridrich, A.H., & Flannery, D.J. (1995). The effects of ethnicity and acculturation on early adolescent delinquency. *Journal of Child and Family Studies, 4*(1), 69–87.

Friend, M., & Bursuck, W.D. (2002). *Including students with special needs* (3rd ed.). Boston: Allyn & Bacon.

Friesch, R.E. (1984). Body fat, puberty and fertility, *Biological Review, 59,* 161–188.

Fujii, K., & Demura, S. (2003). Relationship between change in BMI with age and delayed menarche in female athletes. *Journal of Physiological Anthropology and Applied Human Science, 22,* 97–104.

Fukuda, K., & Ishihara, K. (2001). Age-related changes in sleeping patterns in adolescence. *Psychiatry and Clinical Neuroscience, 55,* 231–232.

Fuligini, A.J. (2001). Family obligation and the academic motivation of adolescents from Asian and Latin American, and European backgrounds. In A.J. Fuligini (Ed.), *Family obligation and assistance during adolescence: Contextual variations and developmental implications.* San Francisco: Jossey-Bass.

Fuligini, A.J., & Pedersen, S. (2002). Family obligation and the transition to young adulthood. *Developmental Psychology, 38,* 856–868.

Fulgini, A.J., & Stevenson, H.W. (1995). Time use and mathematics achievement among American, Chinese, and Japanese high school students. *Child Development, 66,* 830–842.

Fuligini, A.J., Tseng, V., & Lam, M. (1999). Attitudes toward family obligations among American adolescents from Asian, Latin American, and European backgrounds. *Child Development, 70,* 1030–1044.

Fuligini, A.J., & Yoshikawa, H. (2003). Socioeconomic resources, poverty, and child development among immigrant families. In M.H. Bornstein & R.H. Bradley (Eds.), *Socioeconomic status, parenting, and child development.* Mahwah, NJ: Erlbaum.

Furman, W. (2002). The emerging field of adolescent romantic relationships. *Current Directions in Psychological Science, 11,* 177–180.

Furman, W., & Buhrmester, D. (1992). Age and sex differences in perceptions of networks of personal relationships. *Child Development, 63,* 103–115.

Furman, W., & Lanthier, R. (2002). Parenting siblings. In M. Borstein (Ed.), *Handbook of parenting* (2nd ed., Vol. 1). Mahwah, NJ: Erlbaum.

Furman, W., & Shaeffer, L. (2003). The role of romantic relationships in adolescent development. In P. Florsheim (Ed.), *Adolescent romantic relations and sexual behavior.* Mahwah, NJ: Erlbaum.

Furman, W., & Wehner, E.A. (1997). Adolescent romantic relationships: A developmental perspective. In S. Shulman & W.A. Collins (Eds.), *New directions for child development: Adolescent romantic relationships.* San Francisco: Jossey-Bass.

Furr-Holden, C.D., Ialongo, N.S., Anthony, J.C., Petras, H., & Kellam, S.G. (2004). Developmentally inspired drug prevention: Middle school outcomes in a school-based randomized prevention trial. *Drug and Alcohol Dependency, 73,* 149–173.

Furstenberg, F.F., Cook, T.D., Eccles, J., Elder, G.H., & Sameroff, A. (1999). *Managing to make it: Urban families and adolescent success.* Chicago: The University of Chicago Press.

Furstenberg, F.F., & Harris, K.Y. (1992). When fathers matter/where fathers matter. In R. Lerman and T. Oooms (Eds.), *Young unwed fathers.* Philadelphia: Temple University Press.

Furstenberg, F.F., Jr., & Nord, C.W. (1987). Parenting apart: Patterns of childrearing after marital disruption. *Journal of Marriage and the Family, 47,* 893–904.

Fussell, E., & Greene, M.E. (2002). Demographic trends affecting youth around the world. In B.B. Brown, R.W. Larson, & T.S. Saraswathi (Eds.), *The world's youth.* New York: Cambridge University Press.

Galambos, N.L. (2004). Gender and gender-role development in adolescence. In R. Lerner & L. Steinberg (Eds.), *Handbook of adolescent psychology.* New York: Wiley.

Galambos, N.L., & Costigan, C.L. (2003). Emotional and personality development in adolescence. In I.B. Weiner (Ed.), *Handbook of psychology* (Vol. 6). New York: Wiley.

Galambos, N.L., & Maggs, J.L. (1991). Out-of-school care of young adolescents and self-reported behavior. *Developmental Psychology, 27,* 644–655.

Galambos, N.L., Petersen, A.C., Richards, M., & Gitleson, I.B. (1985). The Attitudes toward Women Scale for Adolescents (AWSA): A study of reliability and validity. *Sex Roles, 13,* 343–356.

Galambos, N.L., Sears, H.A., Almeida, D.M., & Kolaric, G.C. (1995). Parents' work overload and problem behavior in young adolescents. *Journal of Research on Adolescence, 5,* 201–224.

Galambos, N.L., & Turner, P.K. (1999). Parent and adolescent temperaments and the quality of parent-adolescent relations. *Merrill-Palmer Quarterly, 45,* 493–511.

Galanter, M. (1999). *Cults.* New York: Oxford University Press.

Galanter, M. (2000). Cults. In A. Kazdin (Ed.), *Encyclopedia of psychology.* Washington, DC, and New York: American Psychological Association and Oxford University Press.

Galliano, G. (2003). *Gender: Crossing boundaries.* Belmont, CA: Wadsworth.

Gallup, G. (1987). *The Gallup poll: Public opinion 1986.* Wilmington, DE: Scholarly Resources.

Gallup, G.W., & Bezilla, R. (1992). *The religious life of young Americans.* Princeton, NJ: Gallup Institute.

Galotti, K.M., & Kozberg, S.F. (1996). Adolescents' experience of a life-framing decision. *Journal of Youth and Adolescence, 25,* 3–16.

Garbarino, J. (1999). *Lost boys: Why our sons turn violent and how we can save them.* New York: Free Press.

Garbarino, J. (2001). Violent children. *Archives of Pediatrics and Adolescent Medicine, 155,* 1–2.

Garbarino, J. (2004). Forward. In D. Espelage & S. Swearer (Eds.), *Bullying in American Schools.* Mahwah, NJ: Erlbaum.

Garbarino, J., & Asp, C.E. (1981). *Successful schools and competent students.* Lexington, MA: Lexington Books.

Garber, J., Kriss, M.R., Koch, M., & Lindholm, L. (1988). Recurrent depression in adolescents: A follow up study. *Journal of the American Academy of Child and Adolescent Psychiatry, 27,* 49–54.

Gardner, H. (1983). *Frames of mind.* New York: Basic Books.

Gardner, H. (1993). *Multiple intelligences.* New York: Basic Books.

Gardner, H. (2001, March 13). *An education for the future.* Paper presented to the Royal Symposium, Amsterdam.

Gardner, H. (2002). The pursuit of excellence through education. In M. Ferrari (Ed.), *Learning from extraordinary minds.* Mahwah, NJ: Erlbaum.

Garmezy, N. (1993). Children in poverty: Resilience despite risk. *Psychiatry, 56,* 127–136.

Garofalo, R., Wolf, R.C., Wissow, L.S., Woods, E.R., & Goodman, E. (1999). Sexual orientation and risk of suicide attempts among a representative sample of youth. *Archives of Pediatrics and Adolescent Medicine, 153,* 487–493.

Garrett, P., Ng'andu, N., & Ferron, J. (1994). Poverty experiences of young children and the quality of their home environments. *Child Development, 65,* 331–345.

Gates, G.J., & Sonnenstein, F.L. (2000). Heterosexual genital activity among adolescent males: 1988 and 1995. *Family Planning Perspectives, 32,* 295–297, 304.

Gates, J.L. (2001, April). *Women's career choices in math and science-related fields.* Paper presented at the meeting of the Society for Research in Child Development, Minneapolis.

Gauze, C.M. (1994, February). *Talking to Mom about friendship: What do mothers know?* Paper presented at the meeting of the Society for Research on Adolescence, San Diego.

Ge, X., & Brody, G.H. (2002, April). *The role of puberty, neighborhood, and life events in the development of internalizing problems.* Paper presented at the meeting of the Society for Research on Adolescence, New Orleans.

Ge, X., Brody, G.H., Conger, R.D., Simons, R.L., & Murry, V. (2002). Contextual amplification of pubertal transitional effect on African American children's problem behaviors. *Developmental Psychology, 38,* 42–54.

Ge, X., Conger, R.D., & Elder, G.H. (2001). The relation between puberty and psychological distress in adolescent boys. *Journal of Research on Adolescence, 11,* 49–70.

Gecas, V., & Seff, M. (1990). Families and adolescents: A review of the 1980s. *Journal of Marriage and the Family, 52,* 941–958.

Gelman, R., & Williams, E.M. (1998). Enabling constraints for cognitive development and learning. In W. Damon (Ed.), *Handbook of child psychology* (5th ed., Vol. 4). New York: Wiley.

George, C., Main, M., & Kaplan, N. (1984). *Attachment interview with adults.* Unpublished manuscript, University of California, Berkeley.

Germeijs, V., & DeBoeck, P. (2003). Career indecision: Three factors from decision theory. *Journal of Vocational Behavior, 62,* 11–25.

Giannotti, F., Cortesi, F., Sebastiani, T., & Ottaviano, S. (2002). Circadian preference, sleep, and daytime behavior in adolescence. *Journal of Sleep Research, 11,* 191–199.

Gibbons, J.L. (2000). Gender development in cross-cultural perspective. In T. Eckes & H.M. Trautner (Eds.), *The developmental social psychology of gender.* Mahwah, NJ: Erlbaum.

Gibbs, J.C. (2003). *Moral development & reality.* Thousand Oaks, CA: Sage.

Gibbs, J.T. (1989). Black American adolescents. In J.T. Gibbs & L.N. Huang (Eds.), *Children of color.* San Francisco: Jossey-Bass.

Gibbs, J.T., & Huang, L.N. (1989). A conceptual framework for assessing and treating minority youth. In J.T. Gibbs & L.N. Huang (Eds.), *Children of color.* San Francisco: Jossey-Bass.

Giedd, J.N. (1998). Normal brain development ages 4–18. In K.R.R. Krishman & P.M. Doraiswamy (Eds.), *Brain imaging in clinical psychiatry.* NewYork: Marcel Dekker.

Giedd, J.N, Jeffries. N., Blumenthal, J., Castellanos, F., Vaituzis, A., Fernandez, T., Hamburger, S., Liu, H., Nelson, J., Bedwell, J., Tran, L., Lenane, M., Nicolson, R., & Rapoport, J. (1999). Childhood-onset schizophrenia: Progressive brain changes during adolescence. *Biological Psychiatry, 46,* 892–898.

Gilliam, F.D., & Bales, S.N. (2001). Strategic frame analysis: Refraining America's youth. *Social Policy Report, Society for Research in Child Development, 15,* no. 3, 1–14.

Gilligan, C. (1982). *In a different voice.* Cambridge, MA: Harvard University Press.

Gilligan, C. (1992, May). *Joining the resistance: Girls' development in adolescence.* Paper presented at the symposium on development and vulnerability in close relationships, Montreal, Quebec.

Gilligan, C. (1996). *Minding women: Reshaping the education realm.* Cambridge, MA: Harvard University Press.

Gilligan, C., Brown, L.M., & Rogers, A.G. (1990). Psyche embedded: A place for body, relationships, and culture in personality theory. In A.I. Rabin, R.A. Zuker, R.A. Emmons, & S. Frank (Eds.), *Studying persons and lives.* New York: Springer.

Gilligan, C., Spencer, R., Weinberg, M.K., & Bertsch, T. (2003). On the listening guide: A voice-centered relational model. In P.M. Carnic & J.E. Rhodes (Eds.), *Qualitative research in psychology.* Washington, DC: American Psychological Association.

Ginorio, A.B., & Huston, M. (2001). *Si! Se Puede! Yes, we can: Latinas in school.* Washington, DC: AAUW.

Ginzberg, E. (1972). Toward a theory of occupational choice: A restatement. *Vocational Guidance Quarterly, 20,* 169–176.

Ginzberg, E., Ginzberg, S.W., Axelrad, S., & Herman, J.L. (1951). *Occupational choice.* New York: Columbia University.

Gipson, J. (1997, March/April). Girls and computer technology: Barrier or key? *Educational Technology,* pp. 41–43.

Girls, Inc. (1991). *It's my party: Girls choose to be substance free.* Indianapolis: Author.

Girls, Inc. (1991). *Truth, trusting, and technology: New research on preventing adolescent pregnancy.* Indianapolis: Author.

Gjerde, P.F. (1986). The interpersonal structure of family interaction settings: Parent-adolescents relations in dyads and triads. *Developmental Psychology, 22,* 297–304.

Gjerde, P.F., Block, J., & Block, J.H. (1991). The preschool family context of 18-year-olds with depressive symptoms: A prospective study. *Journal of Research on Adolescence, 1,* 63–92.

Glassman, M.J. (1997, April). *Moral action in the context of social activity.* Paper presented at the meeting of the Society for Research in Child Development, Washington, DC.

Glassman, M.J. (2001). Dewey and Vygotsky: Society, experience, and inquiry in educational practice. *Educational Researcher 30,* 3–14.

Glazer, N. (1997). *We are all multiculturalists now.* Cambridge, MA: Harvard University Press.

Glover, R.W., & Marshall, R. (1993). Improving the school-to-work transition of American adolescents. In R. Takanishi (Ed.), *Adolescence in the 1990s.* New York: Teachers College Record.

Goertz, M.E., Ekstrom, R.B., & Rock, D. (1991). Dropouts, high school: Issues of race and sex. In R.M. Lerner, A.C. Petersen, & J. Brooks-Gunn (Eds.), *Encyclopedia of adolescence* (Vol. 1). New York: Garland.

Goldman, R. (1967). *Religious thinking from childhood to adolescence.* London: Routledge & Kegan Paul.

Goldman-Rakic, P. (1996). *Bridging the gap.* Presentation at the workshop sponsored by the Education Commission of the States and the Charles A. Dana Foundation, Denver.

Goldscheider, F.C. (1997). Family relationships and life course strategies for the 21st century. In S. Dreman (Ed.), *The family on the threshold of the 21st century.* Mahwah, NJ: Erlbaum.

Goldscheider, F., & Goldscheider, C. (1999). *The changing transition to adulthood: Leaving and returning home.* Thousand Oaks, CA: Sage.

Goldstein, J.M., Seidman, L.J., Horton, N.J., Makris, N., Kennedy, D.N., Caviness, V.S., Faraone, S.V., & Tsuang, M.T. (2001). Normal sexual dimorphism of the adult human brain assessed by in vivo magnetic resonance imaging. *Cerebral Cortex, 11,* 490–497.

Goleman, D. (1995). *Emotional intelligence.* New York: Basic Books.

Goleman, D., Kaufman, P., & Ray, M. (1993). *The creative spirit.* New York: Plume.

Gomel, J.N., Tinsley, B.J., & Clark, K. (1995, March). *Family stress and coping during times of economic hardship: A multi-ethnic perspective.* Paper presented at the meeting of the Society for Research in Child Development, Indianapolis.

Gonzales, N.A., Knight, G.P., Morgan Lopez, A., Saenz, D., & Sirolli, A. (2002). Acculturation and the mental health of Latino youths: An integration and critique of the literature. In J.M. Contreras, K.A. Kerns, & A.M. Neal-Barnett (Eds.), *Latino children and families in the United States.* Westport, CT: Greenwood.

Goodchilds, J.D., & Zellman, G.L. (1984). Sexual signaling and sexual aggression in adolescent relationships. In N.M. Malamuth & E.D. Donnerstein (Eds.), *Pornography and sexual aggression.* New York: Academic Press.

Goodman, E., & Capitman, J. (2000). Depressive symptoms and cigarette smoking among teens. *Pediatrics, 106,* 748–755.

Goodman, R.A. (2001). Improving adolescent preventative care in community health centers. *Pediatrics, 107,* 318–327.

Goodman, R.A., Mercy, J.A., Loya, F., Rosenberg, M.L., Smith, J.C., Allen, N.H., Vargas, L., & Kolts, R. (1986). Alcohol use and interpersonal violence: Alcohol detected in homicide victims. *American Journal of Public Health, 76,* 144–149.

Goosens, L. (1995). Identity status development and students' perception of the university environment: A cohort-sequential study. In A. Oosterwegel & R. Wicklund (Eds.), *The self in European and North American culture: Development and processes.* Dordrecht: Kluwer.

Gordon-Larson, P., McMurray, R.G., & Popkin, B.M. (2000). Determinants of adolescent physical activity patterns. *Pediatrics, 105*, E83–E84.

Gore, T. (1987). *Raising PG kids in an X-rated society.* Nashville, TN: Abingdon Press.

Gotesdam, K.G., & Agras, W.S. (1995). General population-based epidemiological survey of eating disorders in Norway. *International Journal of Eating Disorders, 18*, 119–126.

Gottfried, A.E., Gottfried, A.W., & Bathurst, K. (2002). Maternal and dual-earner employment status and parenting. In M. Bornstein (Ed.), *Handbook of parenting* (2nd ed., Vol. 2). Mahwah, NJ: Erlbaum.

Gottlieb, G. (1998). Normally occurring environmental and behavioral influences on gene activity: From central dogma to probabilistic epigenesis. *Psychological Review, 105*, 792–802.

Gottlieb, G. (2002). Origin of the species: The potential significance of early experience for evolution. In W.W. Hartup & R.A. Weinberg (Eds.), *Child psychology in retrospect and prospect.* Mahwah, NJ: Erlbaum.

Gottlieb, G. (2004). Normally occurring environmental influences on gene activity. In C.G. Coll, E.L. Bearer, & R.M. Lerner (Eds.), *Nature and nurture.* Mahwah, NJ: Erlbaum.

Gottlieb, G., Wahlsten, D., & Lickliter, R. (1998). The significance of biology for human development: A developmental psychobiological systems view. In W. Damon (Ed.), *Handbook of child psychology* (5th ed., Vol. 1). New York: Wiley.

Gottman, J.M., & Parker, J.G. (Eds.). (1987). *Conversations of friends.* New York: Cambridge University Press.

Gould, E., Reeves, A.J., Graziano, M.S., & Gross, C.G. (1999). Neurogenesis in the neocortex of adult primates. *Science, 286*, 548–552.

Gould, M. (2003). Suicide risk among adolescents. In D. Romer (Ed.), *Reducing adolescent risk.* Thousand Oaks, CA: Sage.

Gould, S.J. (1981). *The mismeasure of man.* New York: W.W. Norton.

Graber, J.A. (2004). Internalizing problems during adolescence. In R. Lerner & L. Steinberg (Eds.), *Handbook of adolescent psychology.* New York: Wiley.

Graber, J.A., Britto, P.R., & Brooks-Gunn, J. (1999). What's love got to do with it? Adolescents' and young adults' beliefs about sexual and romantic relationships. In W. Furman, C. Feiring, & B.B. Brown (Eds.), *Contemporary perspectives on adolescent relationships.* New York: Cambridge University Press.

Graber, J.A., & Brooks-Gunn, J. (1996). Expectations for and precursors of leaving home in young women. In J.A. Graber & J.S. Dubas (Eds.), *Leaving home.* San Francisco: Jossey-Bass.

Graber, J.A., & Brooks-Gunn, J. (2001). *Co-occurring eating and depressive problems: An 8-year study of adolescent girls.* Unpublished manuscript, Center for Children and Families, Columbia University.

Graber, J.A., & Brooks-Gunn, J. (2002). Adolescent girls' sexual development. In G.M. Wingood & R.J. DiClemente (Eds.), *Handbook of women's sexual and reproductive health.* New York: Kluwer Academic/Plenum.

Graber, J.A., Brooks-Gunn, J., & Galen, B.R. (1999). Betwixt and between: Sexuality in the context of adolescent transitions. In R. Jessor (Ed.), *New perspectives on adolescent risk behavior.* New York: Cambridge University Press.

Graber, J.A., Brooks-Gunn, J., & Warren, M.P. (in press). Pubertal effects on adjustment in girls: Moving from demonstrating effects to identifying pathways. *Journal of Youth and Adolescence.*

Graham, J.H., & Beller, A.H. (2002). Nonresident fathers and their children: Child support and visitation from an economic perspective. In C.S. Tamis-LeMonda & N. Cabrera (Eds.), *The handbook of father involvement.* Mahwah, NJ: Erlbaum.

Graham, S. (1986, August). *Can attribution theory tell us something about motivation in blacks?* Paper presented at the meeting of the American Psychological Association, Washington, DC.

Graham, S. (1990). Motivation in Afro-Americans. In G.L. Berry & J.K. Asamen (Eds.), *Black students: Psychosocial issues and academic achievement.* Newbury Park, CA: Sage.

Graham, S. (1992). Most of the subjects were white and middle class. *American Psychologist, 47*, 629–637.

Graham, S. & Taylor, A.Z. (2001). Ethnicity, gender, and the development of achievement values. In A. Wigfield, & J.S. Eccles (Eds.), *Development of achievement motivation.* San Diego: Academic Press.

Graham, S., & Weiner, B. (1996). Theories and principles of motivation. In D.C. Berliner & R.C. Calfee (Eds.), *Handbook of educational psychology.* New York: Macmillan.

Granic, I., & Dishion, T.J. (2003). The family ecology of adolescence. In G. Adams & M. Berzonsky (Eds.), *Blackwell handbook of adolescence.* Malden, MA: Blackwell.

Greenberg, B.S., Stanley, C., Siemicki, M., Heeter, C., Soderman, A., & Linsangan, R. (1986). *Sex content on soaps and prime-time television series most viewed by adolescents.* Project CAST Report /ns/2. East Lansing: Michigan State Department of Telecommunication.

Greenberg, M.T., Weissberg. R.P., O'Brien, M.U., Zins, J.E., Fredericks, L., Resnik, H., & Elias, M.J. (2003). Enhancing school-based prevention and youth development through coordinated social, emotional, and academic learning. *American Psychologist, 58*, 466–474.

Greenberger, E., & Chu, C. (1996). Perceived family relationships and depressed mood in early adolescence: A comparison of European and Asian Americans. *Developmental Psychology, 32*, 707–716.

Greenberger, E., & Steinberg, L. (1981). *Project for the study of adolescent work: Final report.* Report prepared for the National Institute of Education, U.S. Department of Education, Washington, DC.

Greenberger, E., & Steinberg, L. (1986). *When teenagers work: The psychological social costs of adolescent employment.* New York: Basic Books.

Greene, B. (1988, May). The children's hour. *Esquire Magazine*, pp. 47–49.

Greene, J.P., & Forster, G. (2003). *Public high school graduation and college readiness rates in the United States.* New York: The Manhattan Institute.

Greenfield, P.M. (2000). Culture and development. In A. Kazdin (Ed.), *Encyclopedia of psychology.* Washington, DC, and New York: American Psychological Association and Oxford University Press.

Greenfield, P.M. (2002, April). *The role of cultural values in adolescent peer conflict.* Paper presented at the meeting of the Society for Research on Adolescence, New Orleans.

Greenfield, P.M. (2003, February). Commentary. *Monitor on Psychology, 34* (2), 58.

Greenfield, P.M., Keller, H., Fulgini, A., & Maynard, A. (2003). Cultural pathways through universal development. *Annual Review of Psychology, 54*, 461–490.

Greeno, J.G., Collins, A.M., & Resnick, L.B. (1996). Cognition and learning. In D.C. Berliner & R.C. Chafee (Eds.), *Handbook of educational psychology.* New York: Macmillan.

Greenough, W.T. (1997, April 21). Commentary in article, "Politics of biology." *U.S. News & World Report*, p. 79.

Greenough, W.T. (1999, April). *Experience, brain development, and links to mental retardation.* Paper presented at the meeting of the Society for Research in Child Development, Albuquerque.

Greenough, W.T. (2000). Brain development. In A. Kazdin (Ed.), *Encyclopedia of psychology.* Washington, DC, and New York: American Psychological Association and Oxford University Press.

Greenough, W.T., & Black, J.R. (1992). Induction of brain structure by experience: Substrates for cognitive development. In M.R. Gunnar & C.A. Nelson (Eds.), *Minnesota Symposia on Child Psychology: Vol 24. Developmental behavioral neuroscience* (pp. 155–200). Hillsdale, NJ: Erlbaum.

Greenough, W.T., Klintsova, A.Y., Irvan, S.A., Galvez, R., Bates, K.E., & Weiler, I.J. (2001). Synaptic regulation of protein synthesis and the fragile X protein. *Proceedings of the National Academy of Science, USA, 98,* 7101–7106.

Grigorenko, E.L. (2001). The relationship between academic and practical intelligence: A case study in Kenya. *Intelligence, 29,* 401–418.

Grigorenko, E.L., Geissler, P., Prince, R., Okatcha, F., Nokes, C., Kenney, D.A., Bundy, D.A., & Sternberg, R.J. (2001). The organization of Luo conceptions of intelligence: A study of implicit theories in a Kenyan village. *International Journal of behavioral development, 25,* 367–378.

Grimes, B., & Mattimore, K. (1989, April). *The effects of stress and exercise on identity formation in adolescence.* Paper presented at the biennial meeting of the Society for Research in Child Development, Kansas City.

Grotevant, H.D. (1996). Unpublished review of J.W. Santrock's *Adolescence,* 7th ed. (Dubuque, IA: Brown & Benchmark).

Grotevant, H.D. (1998). Adolescent development in family contexts. In W. Damon (Ed.), *Handbook of child psychology* (5th ed., Vol. 3). New York: Wiley.

Grotevant, H.D., & Cooper, C.R. (1985). Patterns of interaction in family relationships and the development of identity exploration in adolescence. *Child Development, 56,* 415–428.

Grotevant, H.D., & Cooper, C.R. (1998). Individuality and connectedness in adolescent development: Review and prospects for research on identity, relationships, and context. In E. Skoe & A. von der Lippe (Eds.), *Personality development in adolescence: A cross-national and life-span perspective.* London: Routledge.

Grotevant, H.D., & Durrett, M.E. (1980). Occupational knowledge and career development in adolescence. *Journal of Vocational Behavior, 17,* 171–182.

Grumbach, M.M., & Styne, D.M. (1992). Puberty: Ontogeny, neuroendocrinology, physiology, and disorders. In J.D. Wilson & P.W. Foster (Eds.),*Williams textbook of endocrinology.* Philadelphia: W.B. Saunders.

Grych, J.H. (2002). Marital relationships and parenting. In M.H. Bornstein (Ed.), *Handbook of parenting* (2nd ed.). Mahwah, NJ: Erlbaum.

Guercio, G., Rivarola, M.A., Chaler, E., Maceiras, M., & Belgorosky, A. (2003). Relationship between the growth hormone/insulin-like growth factor-I axis, insulin sensitivity, and adrenal androgens in normal prepubertal and pubertal girls. *Journal of Clinical Endocrinology and Metabolism, 88,* 1389–1393.

Guerin, D.W., Gottfried, A.W., Oliver, P.H., & Thomas, C.W. (2003). *Temperament: Infancy through adolescence.* New York: Kluwer.

Guilford, J.P. (1967). *The structure of intellect.* New York: McGraw-Hill.

Gullotta, T.P., Adams, G.R., & Montemayor, R. (Eds.). (1995). *Substance misuse in adolescence.* Newbury Park, CA: Sage.

Gur, R.C., Mozley, L.H., Mozley, P.D., Resnick, S.M., Karp, J.S., Alavi, A., Arnold, S.E., & Gur, R.E. (1995). Sex differences in regional cerebral glucose metabolism during a resting state. *Science, 267,* 528–531.

Gutman, L.M. (2002, April). *The role of stage-environment fit from early adolescence to young adulthood.* Paper presented at the meeting of the Society for Research on Adolescence, New Orleans.

Guttentag, M., & Bray, H. (1976). *Undoing sex stereotypes: Research and resources for educators.* New York: McGraw-Hill.

Guyer, B. (2000). *ADHD.* Boston: Allyn & Bacon.

Hair, E.C., & Graziano, W.G. (2003). Self-esteem, personality, and achievement in high school: A prospective longitudinal study in Texas. *Journal of Personality, 71,* 971–994.

Hall, G.S. (1904). *Adolescence* (Vols. 1 & 2). Englewood Cliffs, NJ: Prentice Hall.

Hallahan, D.P., & Kaufman, J.M. (2003). *Exceptional learners* (9th ed.). Boston: Allyn & Bacon.

Halonen, J. (1995). Demystifying critical thinking. *Teaching of Psychology, 22,* 75–81.

Halonen, J.A., & Santrock, J.W. (1999). *Psychology: Contexts and applications* (3rd ed.). New York: McGraw-Hill.

Halpern, D.F. (1996). *Thinking critically about critical thinking.* Mahwah, NJ: Erlbaum.

Halpern, D.F. (2001). Sex difference research: Cognitive abilities. In J. Worrell (Ed.), *Encyclopedia of women and gender.* San Diego: Academic Press.

Halpern, D.F., Loehlin, J.C., Perloff, R.J., Sternberg, R., & Urbina, S. (1996). Intelligence: Knowns and unknowns. *American Psychologist, 51,* 77–101.

Hambleton, R.K., Merenda, P.F., & Spielberger, C.D. (Eds.). (2004). *Adapting educational and psychological tests for cross-cultural assessment.* Mahwah, NJ: Erlbaum.

Hamburg, D.A. (1997). Meeting the essential requirements for healthy adolescent development in a transforming world. In R. Takanishi & D. Hamburg (Eds.), *Preparing adolescents for the 21st century.* New York: Cambridge University Press.

Hardman, M.L., Drew, C.J., & Egan, M.W. (2002). *Human exceptionality* (7th ed.). Boston: Allyn & Bacon.

Hargrove, B.K., Creagh, M.G., & Burgess, B.L. (2003). Family interaction patterns as predictors of vocational identity and career decision-making self-efficacy. *Journal of Vocational Behavior, 61,* 185–201.

Harkness, S., & Super, C.M. (2002). Culture and parenting. In M.H. Bornstein (Ed.), *Handbook of parenting* (2nd ed., Vol. 2). Mahwah, NJ: Erlbaum.

Harper, D.C. (2000). Developmental disorders. In A. Kazdin (Ed.), *Encyclopedia of psychology.* Washington, DC, and New York: American Psychological Association and Oxford University Press.

Harper, M.S., Welsch, D., & Woody, T. (2002, April). *Silencing the self: Depressive symptoms and loss of self in adolescent romantic relationships.* Paper presented at the meeting of the Society for Research on Adolescence, New Orleans.

Harre, R. (2004). The social construction of persons. In C. Lightfoot, C. Lalonde, & M. Chandler (Eds.), *Changing conceptions of psychological life.* Mahwah, NJ: Erlbaum.

Harris, J.R. (1998). *The nurture assumption: Why children turn out the way they do: Parents* *matter less than you think and peers matter more.* New York: Free Press.

Hart, D. (1996). Unpublished review of J.W. Santrock's *Child development,* 8th ed. (Dubuque, IA: Brown & Benchmark).

Hart, D., & Fegley, S. (1995). Prosocial behavior and caring in adolescence: Relations to self-understanding and social judgment. *Child Development, 66,* 1346–1359.

Harter, S. (1986). Processes underlying the construction, maintenance, and enhancement of the self-concept of children. In J. Suls & A. Greenwald (Eds.), *Psychological perspective on the self* (Vol. 3). Hillsdale, NJ: Erlbaum.

Harter, S. (1989). *Self-perception profile for adolescents.* Denver: University of Denver, Department of Psychology.

Harter, S. (1990a). Processes underlying adolescent self-concept formation. In R. Montemayer, G.R. Adams, & T.P. Gullotta (Eds.), *From childhood to adolescence: A transitional period?* Newbury Park, CA: Sage.

Harter, S. (1990b). Self and identity development. In S.S. Feldman & G.R. Elliott (Eds.), *At the threshold: The developing adolescent.* Cambridge, MA: Harvard University Press.

Harter, S. (1998). The development of self-representations. In W. Damon (Ed.), *Handbook of child psychology* (5th ed., Vol. 3). New York: Wiley.

Harter, S. (1999). *The construction of the self.* New York: Guilford.

Harter, S. (2002). Unpublished review of Santrock, *Child development,* 10th ed. (New York: McGraw-Hill).

Harter, S., & Lee, L. (1989). *Manifestations of true and false selves in adolescence.* Paper presented at the meeting of the Society for Research in Child Development, Kansas City.

Harter, S., & Marold, D.B. (1992). Psychosocial risk factors contributing to adolescent suicide ideation. In G. Noam & S. Borst (Eds.), *Child and adolescent suicide.* San Francisco: Jossey-Bass.

Harter, S., & Monsour, A. (1992). Developmental analysis of conflict caused by opposing attributes in the adolescent self-portrait. *Developmental Psychology, 28,* 251–260.

Harter, S., Stocker, C., & Robinson, N.S. (1996). The perceived directionality of the link between approval and self-worth: The liabilities of a looking glass self orientation among young adolescents. *Journal of Research on Adolescence, 6,* 285–308.

Harter, S., Waters, P., & Whitesell, N. (1996, March). *False self behavior and lack of voice among adolescent males and females.* Paper presented at the meeting of the Society for Research on Adolescence, Boston.

Harter, S., & Whitesell, N. (2002, April). *Global and relational features of the fluctuating and stable self among adolescents.* Paper presented at the meeting of the Society for Research on Adolescence, New Orleans.

Hartshorne, H., & May, M.S. (1928–1930). *Moral studies in the nature of character: Studies in deceit* (Vol. 1); *Studies in self-control* (Vol. 2); *Studies in the organization of character* (Vol. 3). New York: Macmillan.

Hartup, W.W. (1983). The peer system. In P.H. Mussen (Ed.), *Handbook of child psychology* (4th ed., Vol. 4). New York: Wiley.

Hartup, W.W. (1996). The company they keep: Friendships and their developmental significance. *Child Development, 67,* 1–13.

Hartup, W.W. (1999, April). *Peer relations and the growth of the individual child.* Paper presented at the meeting of the Society for Research in Child Development, Albuquerque.

Hartup, W.W., & Collins, A. (2000). Middle childhood: Socialization and social contexts. In A. Kazdin (Ed.), *Encyclopedia of psychology.* Washington, DC, and New York: American Psychological Association and Oxford University Press.

Hartwell, L., Hutchison, F., Hood, L., Goldberg, M.L., Reynolds, A.F., Silver, L.M., & Veres, R. (2004). *Genetics* (2nd ed.). New York: McGraw-Hill.

Harvey, J.H., & Fine, M.A. (2004). *Children of divorce.* Mahwah, NJ: Erlbaum.

Harwood, R., Leyendecker, B., Carlson, V., Asencio, M., & Miller, A. (2002). Parenting among Latino families in the U.S. In M.H. Bornstein (Ed.), *Handbook of parenting* (2nd ed.). Mahwah, NJ: Erlbaum.

Hauser, S.T., & Bowlds, M.K. (1990). Stress, coping, and adaptation. In S.S. Feldman & G.R. Elliott (Eds.), *At the threshold: The developing adolescent.* Cambridge, MA: Harvard University Press.

Hauser, S.T., Powers, S.I., Noam, G.G., Jacobson, A.M., Weisse, B., & Follansbee, D.J. (1984). Familial contexts of adolescent ego development. *Child Development, 55,* 195–213.

Havighurst, R.J. (1987). Adolescent culture and subculture. In V.B. Van Hasselt & M. Hersen (Eds.), *Handbook of adolescent psychology.* New York: Pergamon.

Haviland, J.M., Davidson, R.B., Ruetsch, C., & Gebelt, J.L. (1994). The place of emotion in identity. *Journal of Research on Adolescence, 4,* 503–518.

Hawkins, J.A., & Berndt, T.J. (1985, April). *Adjustment following the transition to junior high school.* Paper presented at the biennial meeting of the Society for Research in Child Development, Toronto.

Hayes, C. (Ed.). (1987). *Risking the future: Adolescent sexuality, pregnancy, and childbearing* (Vol. 1). Washington, DC: National Academy Press.

Haynie, D.L., Nansel, T., Eitel, P., Crump, A.D., Saylor, K., Yu, K., & Simons-Morton, B. (2001). Bullies, victims, and bully/victims: Distinct groups of at-risk youth. *Journal of Early Adolescence, 21,* 29–49.

Heath, S.B. (1999). Dimensions of language development: Lessons from older children. In A.S. Masten (Ed.), *Cultural processes in child development: The Minnesota symposium on child psychology* (Vol. 29). Mahwah, NJ: Erlbaum.

Heath, S.B., & McLaughlin, M.W. (Eds.). (1993). *Identity and inner-city youth: Beyond ethnicity and gender.* New York: Teachers College Press.

Hechinger, J. (1992). *Fateful choices.* New York: Hill & Wang.

Hecht, M.L., Jackson, R.L., & Ribeau, S.A. (2002). *African American communication* (2nd ed.). Mahwah, NJ: Erlbaum.

Hellmich, N. (2000, November 7). Kids' bodies break down at play. *USA Today,* p. 1D.

Helms, J.E. (Ed.). (1990). *Black and white racial identity: Theory, research, and practice.* Westport, CT: Greenwood Press.

Helms, J.E. (1996). *Where do we go from here? Affirmative action: Who benefits?* Washington, DC: American Psychological Association.

Helson, R., Elliot, T., & Leigh, J. (1989). Adolescent antecedents of women's work patterns. In D. Stern & D. Eichorn (Eds.), *Adolescence and work.* Hillsdale, NJ: Erlbaum.

Hemmings, A. (2004). *Coming of age in U.S. high schools.* Mahwah, NJ: Erlbaum.

Henderson, K.A., & Zivian, M.T. (1995, March). *The development of gender differences in adolescent body image.* Paper presented at the meeting of the Society for Research in Child Development, Indianapolis.

Henderson, V.L., & Dweck, C.S. (1990). Motivation and achievement. In S.S. Feldman & G.R. Elliott (Eds.), *At the threshold: The developing adolescent.* Cambridge, MA: Harvard University Press.

Hendry, J. (1999). *Social anthropology.* New York: Macmillan.

Henry, D.B., Tolan, P.H., & Gorman-Smith, D. (2001). Longitudinal family and peer group effects on violence and nonviolent delinquency. *Journal of Clinical Child Psychology, 30,* 172–186.

Heppner, M.J., & Heppner, P.P. (2003). Identifying process variables in career counseling: A research agenda. *Journal of Vocational Behavior, 62,* 429–452.

Herek, G. (2000). Homosexuality. In A. Kazdin (Ed.), *Encyclopedia of psychology.* Washington, DC, and New York: American Psychological Association and Oxford University Press.

Hernandez, D.J. (1997). Child development and the social demography of childhood. *Child Development, 68,* 149–169.

Herpertz-Dahlmann, B., Muller, B., Herpertz, S., Heussen, N., Hebebrand, J., & Remschmidt, H. (2001). Prospective 10-year follow up in adolescent anorexia nervosa—course, outcome, psychiatric comorbidity, and psychosocial adaptation. *Journal of Child Psychology and Psychiatry, 42,* 603–612.

Herrnstein, R.J., & Murray, C. (1994). *The bell curve: Intelligence and class structure in American life.* New York: Macmillan.

Hertzog, N.B. (1998, Jan/Feb). Gifted education specialist. *Teaching Exceptional Children,* pp. 39–43.

Hess, L., Lonky, E., & Roodin, P.A. (1985, April). *The relationship of moral reasoning and ego strength to cheating behavior.* Paper presented at the meeting of the Society for Research in Child Development, Toronto.

Hetherington, E.M. (1972). Effects of father-absence on personality development in adolescent daughters. *Developmental Psychology, 7,* 313–326.

Hetherington, E.M. (1977). *My heart belongs to daddy: A study of the remarriages of daughters of divorces and widows.* Unpublished manuscript, University of Virginia.

Hetherington, E.M. (1989). Coping with family transitions: Winners, losers, and survivors. *Child Development, 60,* 1–14.

Hetherington, E.M. (1993). An overview of the Virginia Longitudinal Study of Divorce and Remarriage with a focus on early adolescence. *Journal of Family Psychology, 7,* 39–56.

Hetherington, E.M. (2000). Divorce. In A. Kazdin (Ed.), *Encyclopedia of psychology.* Washington, DC, and New York: American Psychological Association and Oxford University Press.

Hetherington, E.M., Bridges, M., & Insabella, G.M. (1998). What matters? What does not? Five perspectives on the association between marital transitions and children's adjustment. *American Psychologist, 53,* 167–184.

Hetherington, E.M., & Clingempeel, W.G. (1992). Coping with marital transitions: A family systems perspective. *Monographs of the Society for Research in Child Development, 57,* (2–3, Serial No. 227).

Hetherington, E.M., Henderson, S.H., Reiss, D., & others. (1999). Adolescent siblings in stepfamilies: Family functioning and adolescent adjustment. *Monographs of the Society for Research in Child Development, 64* (No. 4).

Hetherington, E.M., & Kelly, J. (2002). *For better or worse: Divorce reconsidered.* New York: Norton.

Hetherington, E.M., Reiss, D., & Plomin, R. (Eds.). (1994). *Separate social worlds of siblings: The impact of nonshared environment on development.* Hillsdale, NJ: Erlbaum.

Hetherington, E.M., & Stanley-Hagan, M. (2002). Parenting in divorced and remarried families. In M. Bornstein (Ed.), *Handbook of parenting* (2nd ed., Vol. 3). Mahwah, NJ: Erlbaum.

Heward, W.L. (2000). *Exceptional children* (6th ed.). Upper Saddle River, NJ: Merrill.

Hicks, R., & Connolly, J.A. (1995, March). *Peer relations and loneliness in adolescence: The interactive effects of social self-concept, close friends, and peer networks.* Paper presented at the meeting of the Society for Research in Child Development, Indianapolis.

Higgins, A., Power, C., & Kohlberg, L. (1983, April). *Moral atmosphere and moral judgment.* Paper presented at the biennial meeting of the Society for Research in Child Development, Detroit.

Hightower, E. (1990). Adolescent interpersonal and familial precursors of positive mental health at midlife. *Journal of Youth and Adolescence, 19,* 257–275.

Hilburn-Cobb, C. (2004). Adolescent psychopathology in terms of multiple behavior systems. In L. Atkinson & S. Goldberg (Eds.), *Attachment issues in psychopathology and intervention.* Mahwah, NJ: Erlbaum.

Hill, J.P., & Holmbeck, G.N. (1986). Attachment and autonomy during adolescence. *Annals of Child Development, 3,* 145–189.

Hill, J.P., Holmbeck, G.N., Marlow, L., Green, T.M., & Lynch, M.E. (1985). Pubertal status and parent-child relations in families of seventh-grade boys. *Journal of Early Adolescence, 5,* 31–44.

Hill, J.P., & Lynch, M.E. (1983). The intensification of gender-related role expectations during early adolescence. In J. Brooks-Gunn & A.C. Petersen (Eds.), *Girls at puberty: Biological and psychosocial perspectives.* New York: Plenum.

Hill, J.P., & Steinberg, L.D. (1976, April). *The development of autonomy in adolescence.* Paper presented at the Symposium on Research on Youth Problems, Fundacion Orbegoza Eizaquirre, Madrid, Spain.

Hiort, O. (2002). Androgens and puberty. *Best Practice and Research: Clinical Endocrinology and Metabolism, 16,* 31–41.

Hirsch, B.J., & Rapkin, B.D. (1987). The transition to junior high school: A longitudinal study of self-esteem, psychological symptomatology, school life, and social support. *Child Development, 58,* 1235–1243.

Ho, C.S., Chan, D.W., Lee, S.H., Tsang, S.M., & Luan, V.H. (2004). Cognitive profiling and preliminary subtyping in Chinese developmental dyslexia. *Cognition, 91,* 43–75.

Hodges, E.V.E., Boivin, M., Vitaro, F., & Bukowski, W.M. (1999). The power of friendship: Protection against an escalating cycle of peer victimization. *Developmental Psychology, 35,* 94–101.

Hodges, E.V.E., & Perry, D.G. (1999). Personal and interpersonal antecedents and consequences of victimization by peers. *Journal of Personality and Social Psychology, 76,* 677–685.

Hoff, E., Laursen, B., & Tardif, T. (2002). Socioeconomic status and parenting. In M.H. Bornstein (Ed.), *Handbook of parenting* (2nd ed.). Mahwah, NJ: Erlbaum.

Hofferth, S.L. (1990). Trends in adolescent sexual activity, contraception, and pregnancy in the United States. In J. Bancroft & J.M. Reinisch (Eds.), *Adolescence and puberty.* New York: Oxford University Press.

Hofferth, S.L., & Reid, L. (2002). Early childbearing and children's achievement and behavior over time. *Perspectives on Sexual and Reproductive Health, 34,* 41–49.

Hoffman, L.W. (1989). Effects of maternal employment in the two-parent family. *American Psychologist, 44,* 283–292.

Hoffman, L.W. (2000). Maternal employment: Effects of social context. In R.D. Taylor & M.C. Wang (Eds.), *Resilience across contexts.* Mahwah, NJ: Erlbaum.

Hoffman, M.L. (1970). Moral development. In P.H. Mussen (Ed.), *Manual of child psychology* (3rd ed., Vol. 2). New York: Wiley.

Hoffman, M.L. (1980). Moral development in adolescence. In J. Adelson (Ed.), *Handbook of adolescent psychology*. New York: Wiley.

Hoffman, M.L. (1988). Moral development. In M.H. Bornstein & E. Lamb (Eds.), *Developmental psychology: An advanced textbook* (2nd ed.). Hillsdale, NJ: Erlbaum.

Hoffman, S., Foster, E., & Furstenberg, F. (1993). Reevaluating the costs of teenage childbearing. *Demography, 30,* 1–13.

Hogan, D.M., & Tudge, J. (1999). Implications of Vygotsky's theory for peer learning. In A.M. O'Donnell & A. King (Eds.), *Cognitive perspectives on peer learning.* Mahwah, NJ: Erlbaum.

Holditch, P., Broomfield, K., Foster, J., Emshoff, J., & Adamczak, J. (2002, April). *Cool Girls, Inc.: Evaluating a developmentally sensitive intervention for at-risk girls.* Paper presented at the meeting of the Society for Research on Adolescence, New Orleans.

Holland, J.L. (1973). *Making vocational choices: A theory of careers.* Englewood Cliffs, NJ: Prentice Hall.

Holland, J.L. (1987). Current status of Holland's theory of careers: Another perspective. *Career Development Quarterly, 36,* 24–30.

Hollingshead, A.B. (1975). *Elmtown's youth and Elmtown revisited.* New York: Wiley.

Hollingworth, L.S. (1914). *Functional periodicity: An experimental study of the mental and motor abilities of women during menstruation.* New York: Columbia University, Teachers College.

Hollingworth, L.S. (1916). Sex differences in mental tests. *Psychological Bulletin 13,* 377–383.

Holmbeck, G.N. (1996). A model of family relational transformations during the transition to adolescence: Parent-adolescent conflict and adaptation. In J.A. Graber, J. Brooks-Gunn, & A.C. Petersen (Eds.), *Transitions in adolescence.* Mahwah, NJ: Erlbaum.

Holmbeck, G.N., Durbin, D., & Kung, E. (1995, March). *Attachment, autonomy, and adjustment before and after leaving home: Sullivan and Sullivan revisited.* Paper presented at the meeting of the Society for Research in Child Development, Indianapolis.

Holmbeck, G.N., & Shapera, W. (1999). Research methods with adolescents. In P. Kendall, J. Butcher, & G. Holmbeck (Eds.),

Handbook of research methods in clinical psychology. New York: Wiley.

Holmes, L.D. (1987). *Quest for the real Samoa: The Mead-Freeman controversy and beyond.* South Hadley, MA: Bergin & Garvey.

Holtzmann, W. (1982). Cross-cultural comparisons of personality development in Mexico and the United States. In D. Wagner & H.W. Stevenson (Eds.), *Cultural perspectives on child development.* San Francisco: W.H. Freeman.

Hopkins, J.R. (2000). Erikson, E.H. In A. Kazdin (Ed.), *Encyclopedia of psychology.* Washington, DC, and New York: American Psychological Association and Oxford University Press.

Hops, H. (2002, April). *Multiple pathways to adolescent drug use and abuse.* Paper presented at the meeting of the Society for Research on Adolescence, New Orleans.

Horney, K. (1967). *Feminine psychology.* New York: W.W. Norton.

Horth, M.M., & Benson, J.B. (1998). Infant cognition. In W. Damon (Ed.), *Handbook of child psychology* (5th ed., Vol. 2). New York: Wiley.

Howard, R.W. (2001). Searching the real world for signs of rising population intelligence. *Personality and Individual Differences, 30,* 1039–1058.

Howe, N., & Strauss, W. (2000). *Millenials rising: The next great generation.* New York: Vintage.

Hoyle, R.H., & Judd, C.M. (2002). *Research methods in social psychology* (7th ed.). Belmont, CA: Wadsworth.

Hoyt, S., & Scherer, D.G. (1998). Female juvenile delinquency. *Law and Human Behavior, 22,* 81–107.

Huang, L.N. (1989). Southeast Asian refugee children and adolescents. In J.T. Gibbs & L.N. Huang (Eds.), *Children of color.* San Francisco: Jossey-Bass.

Huang, L.N., and Ying, Y. (1989). Chinese American children and adolescents. In J.T. Gibbs and L.N. Huang, (Eds.), *Children of color.* San Francisco: Jossey-Bass.

Huebner, A.J., & Howell, L.W. (2003). Examining the relationship between adolescent sexual risk-taking and perceptions of monitoring, communication, and parenting styles. *Journal of Adolescent Health, 33,* 71–78.

Huebner, A.M., & Garrod, A.C. (1993). Moral reasoning among Tibetan monks: A study of Buddhist adolescents and young adults in Nepal. *Journal of Cross-Cultural Psychology, 24,* 167–185.

Huesmann, L.R. (1986). Psychological processes promoting the relation between exposure to media violence and aggressive behavior by the viewer. *Journal of Social Issues, 42,* 125–139.

Huesmann, L.R., Moise-Titus, Podolski, C., & Eron, L.D. (2003). Longitudinal relations between children's exposure to TV violence and their aggressive and violent behavior in young adulthood: 1977–1992. *Developmental Psychology, 39,* 201–221.

Hughes, M., Alfano, M., & Harkness, S. (2002, April). *The GEAR UP Project: Strengthening academic transitions and attainment through relationship building.* Paper presented at the meeting of the Society for Research on Adolescence, New Orleans.

Hunt, E. (1995). *Will we be smart enough? A cognitive analysis of the coming work force.* New York: Russell Sage.

Hunter, J.P., & Csikszentmihalyi, M. (2003). The positive psychology of interested adolescents. *Journal of Youth and Adolescence, 32,* 27–35.

Hurtado, M.T. (1997, April). *Acculturation and planning among adolescents.* Paper presented at the meeting of the Society for Research in Child Development, Washington DC.

Huston, A.C., & Alvarez, M. (1990). The socialization context of gender-role development in early adolescence. In R. Montemayor, G.R. Adams, & T.P. Gulotta (Eds.), *From childhood to adolescence: A transitional period?* Newbury Park, CA: Sage.

Huston, A.C., McLoyd, V.C., & Coll, C.G. (1994). Children and poverty: Issues in contemporary research. *Child Development, 65,* 275–282.

Huston, A.C., Siegle, J., & Bremer, M. (1983, April). *Family environment television use by preschool children.* Paper presented at the biennial meeting of the Society for Research in Child Development, Detroit.

Huttenlocher, J., Haight, W., Bruk, A., Seltzer, M., & Lyons, T. (1991). Early vocabulary growth: Relation to language input and gender. *Developmental Psychology, 27,* 236–248.

Huttenlocher, P.R., & Dabholkar, A.S. (1997). Regional differences in synaptogenesis in human cerebral cortex. *Journal of Comparative Neurology, 37 (2),* 167–178.

Hyde, J.S. (1993). Meta-analysis and the psychology of women. In F.L. Denmark & M.A. Paludi (Eds.), *Handbook on the psychology of women.* Westport, CT: Greenwood.

Hyde, J.S. (2004). *Half the human experience* (6th ed.). Boston: Houghton Mifflin.

Hyde, J.S., & DeLamater, J.D. (2003). *Understanding human sexuality* (8th ed.). New York: McGraw-Hill.

Hyde, J.S., & Mezulis, A.H. (2001). Gender difference research: Issues and critique. In J. Worrell (Ed.), *Encyclopedia of women and gender.* San Diego: Academic Press.

Hyde, J.S., & Plant, E.A. (1995). Magnitude of psychological gender differences: Another side of the story. *American Psychologist, 50,* 159–161.

Ianni, F.A.J., & Orr, M.T. (1996). Dropping out. In J.A. Graber, J. Brooks-Gunn, & A.C. Petersen (Eds.), *Transitions in adolescence.* Mahwah, NJ: Erlbaum.

Idol, L. (1997). Key questions related to building collaborative and inclusive schools. *Journal of Learning Disabilities, 30,* 384–394.

International Society for Technology in Education. (2000). *National educational technology standards for students: Connecting curriculum and technology.* Eugene, OR: Author.

International Society for Technology in Education. (2001). *National educational technology standards for teachers—preparing teachers to use technology.* Eugene, OR: Author.

Irwin, C.E. (1993). The adolescent, health, and society: From the perspective of the physician. In S.G. Millstein, A.C. Petersen, & E.O. Nightingale (Eds.), *Promoting the health of adolescents.* New York: Oxford University Press.

Jaccard, J., Dodge, T., & Dittus, P. (2002). Parental-adolescent communication about sex and birth control. In S.S. Feldeman & D.A. Rosenthal (Eds.), *Talking sexually: Parent-adolescent communication.* San Francisco: Jossey-Bass.

Jackson, A., & Davis, G. (2000). *Turning points 2000.* New York: Teachers College Press.

Jackson, L.R., & Rodriguez, J.L. (Eds.). (2002). *School matters.* Mahwah, NJ: Erlbaum.

Jackson, N., & Butterfield, E. (1996). A conception of giftedness designed to promote research. In R.J. Sternberg & J.E. Davidson

(Eds.), *Conceptions of giftedness.* New York: Cambridge University Press.

Jacob, N., Van Gestel, S., Derom, C., Theiry, E., Vernon, P., Derom, R., & Vlietinck, R. (2001). Heritability estimates of intelligence in twins: Effect of chorion type. *Behavior Genetics, 31,* 209–217.

Jacobi, C., Hayward, C., DeZwann, M., Kraemer, H.C., & Agras, W.S. (2004). Coming to terms with risk factors for eating disorders: Application of risk terminology and suggestions for a general taxonomy. *Psychological Bulletin, 130,* 19–65.

Jacobs, J.E., & Kalczynski, P.A. (2002). The development of judgment and decision making during childhood and adolescence. *Current Directions in Psychological Science, 11,* 145–149.

Jacobs, J.E., & Potenza, M. (1990, March). *The use of decision-making strategies in late adolescence.* Paper presented at the meeting of the Society for Research in Adolescence, Atlanta.

Jacobs, J.K., Garnier, H.E., & Weisner, T. (1996, March). *The impact of family life on the process of dropping out of high school.* Paper presented at the meeting of the Society for Research on Adolescence, Boston.

Jacobson, K.C., & Crockett, L.J. (2000). Parental monitoring and adolescent adjustment: An ecological perspective. *Journal of Research on Adolescence, 10,* 65–97.

Jaffe, S., & Hyde, J.S. (2000). Gender differences in moral orientation: A meta-analysis. *Psychological Bulletin, 126,* 703–726.

Janz, N.K., Zimmerman, M.A., Wren, P.A., Israel, B.A., Freudenberg, N., & Carter, R.J. (1996). Evaluation of 37 AIDS prevention projects: Successful approaches and barriers to program effectiveness. *Health Education Quarterly, 23,* 80–97.

Jarrett, R.L. (1995). Growing up poor: The family experiences of socially mobile youth in low-income African-American neighborhoods. *Journal of Adolescent Research, 10,* 111–135.

Jenkins, A.M., Albee, G.W., Paster, V.S., Sue, S., Aker, D.B., Comaz-Diaz, L., Puente, A., Suinn, R.M., Caldwell-Colbert, A.T., Williams, V.M., & Root, M.P.P. (2003). Ethnic minorities. In I.B. Weiner (Ed.), *Handbook of psychology.* New York: Wiley.

Jhally, S. (1990). *Dreamworlds: Desire/sex/power in rock video* (Video). Amherst: University of Massachusetts at Amherst, Department of Communications.

Jodl, K.M., Michael, A., Malanchuk, O., Eccles, J.S., & Sameroff, A. (2001). Parents' roles in shaping early adolescents' occupational aspirations. *Child Development, 72,* 1247–1265.

John, O.P., Caspi, A., Robins, R.W., Moffitt, T.E., & Stouthamer-Loeber, M. (1994). The "little five:" Exploring the nomological network of the five-factor model of personality in adolescent boys. *Child Development, 65,* 160–178.

Johnson, D.W. (1990). *Teaching out: Interpersonal effectiveness and self-actualization.* Upper Saddle River, NJ: Prentice Hall.

Johnson, D.W., & Johnson, R.T. (1995). (2003). Why violence prevention programs don't work—and what does. *Educational Leadership,* pp. 63–68.

Johnson, D.W., & Johnson, R.T. (2003). *Joining together: Group theory and group skills.* (7th ed.). Boston: Allyn & Bacon.

Johnson, J.G., Cohen, P., Pine, D.S., Klein, D.F., Kasen, S., & Brook, J.S. (2000). Association between cigarette smoking and anxiety disorders during adolescence and adulthood. *Journal of the American Medical Association, 284,* 348–351.

Johnson, M.K., Beebe, T., Mortimer, J.T., & Snyder, M. (1998). Volunteerism in adolescence: A process perspective. *Journal of Research on Adolescence, 8,* 309–332.

Johnson, V.K. (2002). *Managing the transition to college: The role of families and adolescents' coping strategies.* Paper presented at the meeting of the Society for Research on Adolescence, New Orleans.

John-Steiner, V., & Mahn, H. (2003). Sociocultural contexts for teaching and learning. In I.B. Weiner (Ed.), *Handbook of psychology* (Vol. 7). New York: Wiley.

Johnston, B.T., Carey, M.P., Marsh, K.L., Levin, K.D., & Scott-Sheldon, L.A. (2003). Intervention to reduce sexual risk for the human immunodeficiency virus in adolescents, 1985–2000: A research synthesis. *Archives of Pediatric and Adolescent Medicine, 157,* 381–388.

Johnston, J., Etteman, J., & Davidson, T. (1980). *An evaluation of "Freestyle": A television series to reduce sex-role stereotypes.* Ann Arbor: University of Michigan, Institute for Social Research.

Johnston, L.D., O'Malley, P.M., & Bachman, J.G. (1999, December 17). *Drug trends in the United States are mixed* (press release). Ann Arbor, MI: Institute of Social Research, University of Michigan.

Johnston, L.D., O'Malley, P.M., & Bachman, J.G. (2001, December 19). *Monitoring the Future: 2001.* Ann Arbor, MI: Institute for Social Research, University of Michigan.

Johnston, L.D., O'Malley, P.M., & Bachman, J.G. (2003). *Monitoring the Future national results on adolescent drug use. Overview of key findings, 2002.* Bethesda, MD: National Institute on Drug Abuse.

Jones, B.F., Rasmussen, C.M., & Moffit, M.C. (1997). *Real-life problem solving.* Washington, DC: American Psychological Association.

Jones, J.M. (1994). The African American: A duality dilemma? In W.J. Lonner & R. Malpass (Eds.), *Psychology and culture.* Needham Heights, MA: Allyn & Bacon.

Jones, M.C. (1965). Psychological correlates of somatic development. *Child Development, 36,* 899–911.

Joyner, K., & Udry, J.R. (2000). "You don't bring me anything but down: Adolescent romance and depression. *Journal of Health and Social Behavior, 41,* 369–391.

Jozefowicz, D.M.H. (2002, April). *Quantitative and qualitative perspectives on the transition to adulthood.* Paper presented at the meeting of the Society for Research on Adolescence, New Orleans.

Jussim, L., & Eccles, J.S. (1993). Teacher expectations II: Construction and reflection of student achievement. *Journal of Personality and Social Psychology, 63,* 947–961.

Kagan, J. (1992). Yesterday's premises, tomorrow's promises. *Developmental Psychology 28,* 990–997.

Kagan, J. (2000). Temperament. In A. Kazdin (Ed.), *Encyclopedia of psychology.* Washington, DC, and New York: American Psychological Association and Oxford University Press.

Kagan, J. (2002). Behavioral inhibition as a temperamental category. In R.J. Davidson, K.R. Scherer, & H.H. Goldsmith (Eds.), *Handbook of affective sciences.* New York: Oxford University Press.

Kagan, J., & Snidman, N. (1991). Infant predictors of inhibited and uninhibited behavioral profiles. *Psychological Science, 2,* 40–44.

Kagan, S., & Madsen, M.C. (1972). Experimental analysis of cooperation and competition of Anglo-American and Mexican children. *Developmental Psychology, 6,* 49–59.

Kahn, J.A., Kaplowitz, R.A., Goodman, E., & Emans, J. (2002). The association between impulsiveness and sexual risk behaviors in adolescent and young adult women. *Journal of Adolescent Health, 30,* 229–232.

Kaiser Family Foundation. (1996). *Kaiser Family Foundation survey of 1,500 teenagers ages 12–18.* San Francisco: Kaiser Foundation.

Kaiser Family Foundation. (2001). *Generation Rx.com: How young people use the Internet for health information.* Menlo Park, CA: Henry J. Kaiser Family Foundation.

Kaiser Family Foundation. (2002a). *Key facts: Teens online.* Menlo Park, CA: Henry J. Kaiser Family Foundation.

Kaiser Family Foundation. (2002b). *Teens say sex on TV influences behavior of peers.* Menlo Park, CA: Henry J. Kaiser Family Foundation.

Kalil, A., & Kunz, J. (2000, April). *Psychological outcomes of adolescent mothers in young adulthood.* Paper presented at the meeting of the Society for Research on Adolescence, Chicago.

Kamphaus, R.W. (2000). Learning disabilities. In A. Kazdin (Ed.), *Encyclopedia of psychology.* Washington, DC, and New York: American Psychological Association and Oxford University Press.

Kamphaus, R.W., & Kroncke, A.P. (2004). "Back to the future" of the Stanford-Binet Intelligence Scales. In M. Hersen (Ed.), *Comprehensive handbook of psychological assessment* (Vol. 1). New York: Wiley.

Kandel, D.B., & Lesser, G.S. (1969). Parent-adolescent relationships and adolescence independence in the United States and Denmark. *Journal of Marriage and the Family, 31,* 348–358.

Kandel, D.B., & Wu, P. (1995). The contributions of mothers and fathers to the intergenerational transmission of cigarette smoking. *Journal of Research on Adolescence, 5,* 225–252.

Kaplan, M.J., Middleton, T., Urdan, C., & Midgley, C. (2002). Achievement goals and goal structures. In C. Midgley (Ed.), *Goals, goal structures, and patterns of adaptive learning.* Mahwah, NJ: Erlbaum.

Kaplow, J.B., Curran, P.J., Dodge, K.A., & The Conduct Problems Prevention Research Group. (2002). Child, parent, and peer predictors of early-onset substance use: A multisite longitudinal study. *Journal of Abnormal Child Psychology, 30,* 199–216.

Kaplowitz, P.B., Slora, E.J., Wasserman, R.C., Pedlow, S.E., & Herman-Giddens, M.E. (2001). Earlier onset of puberty in girls: Relation to increased body mass index and race. *Pediatrics, 108,* 347–353.

Karniol, R., Gabay, R., Ochioin, Y., & Harari, Y. (1998). Is gender or gender-role orientation a better predictor of empathy in adolescence? *Sex Roles, 39,* 45–59.

Kaufman, A.S. (2000a). Tests of intelligence. In R.J. Sternberg (Ed.), *Handbook of intelligence.* New York: Cambridge University Press.

Kaufmann, A.S. (2000b). Wechsler, David. In A. Kazdin (Ed.), *Encyclopedia of psychology.* Washington, DC, and New York: American Psychological Association and Oxford University Press.

Keating, D.P. (1990). Adolescent thinking. In S.S. Feldman & G.R. Elliott (Eds.), *At the threshold: The developing adolescent.* Cambridge, MA: Harvard University Press.

Keating, D.P. (2004). Cognitive and brain development. In R. Lerner & L. Steinberg (Eds.), *Handbook of adolescent psychology.* New York: Wiley.

Keel, P.K., Mitchell, J.E., Miller, K.B., Davis, T.L., & Crowe, S.J. (1999). Long-term outcome of bulimia nervosa. *Archives of General Psychiatry 56,* 63–69.

Keener, D.C., & Boykin, K.A. (1996, March). *Parental control, autonomy, and ego development.* Paper presented at the meeting of the Society for Research on Adolescence, Boston.

Kelly, G.F. (2004). *Sexuality today* (7th ed. Updated). New York: McGraw-Hill.

Kelly, J. (2000). Sexually transmitted diseases. In A. Kazdin (Ed.), *Encyclopedia of psychology.* Washington, DC, and New York: American Psychological Association and Oxford University Press.

Kelly, J.B., & Lamb, M.E. (2003). Developmental issues in relocation cases involving young children: When, whether, and how? *Journal of Family Psychology, 17,* 193–205.

Kennedy, J.H. (1990). Determinants of peer social status: Contributions of physical appearance, reputation, and behavior. *Journal of Youth and Adolescence, 19,* 233–244.

Kenney, A.M. (1987, June). Teen pregnancy: An issue for schools. *Phi Delta Kappan,* pp. 728–736.

Kenniston, K. (1970). Youth: A "new" stage of life. *American Scholar, 39,* 631–654.

Kerckhoff, A.C. (2002). The transition from school to work. In J.T. Mortimer & R.W.

Larson (Eds.), *The changing adolescent experience*. New York: Cambridge University Press.

Kern, S.I., & Alessi, D.J. (2003). Sexual harassment complaints: Mandate from the board of medical examiners. *New Jersey Medicine, 100,* 23–25.

Kiess, W., Reich, A., Meyer, K., Glasow, A., Deutscher, J., Klammt, J., Yang, Y., Muller, G., & Kratzsch, J. (1999). A role for leptin in sexual maturation and puberty? *Hormone Research, 51,* 55–53.

Killen, M. (1991). Social and moral development in early childhood. In W.M. Kurtines & J.L. Gewirtz (Eds.), *Handbook of moral behavior and development* (Vol. 2). Mahwah, NJ: Erlbaum.

Killen, M., McGlothlin, H., & Lee-Kim, J. (in press). Between individuals and culture: Individuals' evaluations of exclusion from groups. In H. Keller, Y. Poortinga, & A. Schoelmerich (Eds.), *Between biology and culture: Perspectives on ontogenetic development*. Cambridge, UK: Cambridge University Press.

Kim, J. (2002, April). *"Cosmo chicks": The impact of contemporary women's magazines on readers' sexual attitudes and self perceptions.* Paper presented at the meeting of the Society for Research on Adolescence, New Orleans.

Kimm, S.Y., Barton, B.A., Obarzanek, E., McMahon, R.P., Kronsberg, S.S., Waclawiw, M.A., Morrison, J.A., Schreiber, G.G., Sabry, Z.I., & Daniels, S.R. (2002). Obesity development during adolescence in a biracial cohort: The NHLBI Growth and Health Study. *Pediatrics, 110,* e54.

Kimm, S.Y., Glynn, N.W., Kriska, A.M., Barton, B.A., Kronsberg, S.S., Daniels, S.R., Crawford, P.B., Sabry, Z.I., & Liu, K. (2002). Decline in physical activity in black girls and white girls during adolescence. *New England Journal of Medicine, 347,* 709–715.

Kimm, S.Y., & Obarzanek, E. (2002). Childhood obesity: A new pandemic of the new millennium. *Pediatrics, 110,* 1003–1007.

Kimura, D. (2000). *Sex and cognition.* Cambridge, MA: MIT Press.

Kindlundh, A.M.S., Isacson, D.G.L., Berlund, L., & Nyberg, F. (1999). Factors associated with adolescence use of doping agents: Anabolic-androgenic steroids. *Addiction, 94,* 543–553.

King, P. (1988). Heavy metal music and drug use in adolescents. *Postgraduate Medicine, 83,* 295–304.

Kinsey, A.C., Pomeroy, W.B., & Martin, C.E. (1948). *Sexual behavior in the human male.* Philadelphia: Saunders.

Kirby, D., & Miller, B.C. (2002). Interventions designed to promote parent-teen communication about sexuality. In S.S. Feldman & D.A. Rosenthal (Eds.), *Talking sexually: Parent-adolescent communication.* San Francisco: Jossey-Bass.

Kirby, D., Resnick, M.D., Downes, B., Kocher, T., Gunderson, P., Pothoff, S., Zelterman, D., & Blum, R.W. (1993). The effects of school-based health clinics in St. Paul on school-wide birthrates. *Family Planning Perspectives, 25,* 12–16.

Kirkman, M., Rosenthal, D.A., & Feldman, S.S. (2002). Talking to a tiger: Fathers reveal their difficulties in communicating sexually with adolescents. In S.S. Feldman & D.A. Rosenthal (Eds.), *Talking sexually: Parent-adolescent communication.* San Francisco: Jossey-Bass.

Kitchener, K.S., & King, P.M. (1981). Reflective judgment: Concepts of justification and their relationship to age and education. *Journal of Applied Developmental Psychology, 2,* 89–111.

Kite, M. (2001). Gender stereotypes. In J. Worrell (Ed.), *Encyclopedia of women and gender.* San Diego: Academic Press.

Klaczynski, P.A. (1997). Bias in adolescents' everyday reasoning and its relationship with intellectual ability, personal theories, and self-serving motivation. *Developmental Psychology, 33,* 273–283.

Klaczynski, P.A., Byrnes, J.P., & Jacobs, J.E. (2001). Introduction to the special issue The development of decision making. *Applied Developmental Psychology, 22,* 225–236.

Klaczynski, P.A., & Narasimham, G. (1998). Development of scientific reasoning biases: Cognitive versus ego-protective explanations. *Developmental Psychology, 34,* 175–187.

Klaw, E., & Saunders, N. (1994). *An ecological model of career planning in pregnant African American teens.* Paper presented at the biennial meeting of the Society for Research on Adolescence, San Diego.

Klein, J.D., Allan, M.J., Elster, A.B., Stevens, D., Cox, C., Hedberg, V.A., & Goodman, R.A. (2001). Improving adolescent preventative care in community health centers. *Pediatrics, 107,* 318–327.

Klein, J.D., Allan, M.J., Elster, A.B., Stevens, D., Cox, C., Hedberg, V.A., Marcell, A.V., & Milstein, S.G. (2001, March). *Quality of adolescent preventive services: The role of physician attitudes and self-efficacy.*

Paper presented at the meeting of the Society for Adolescent Medicine, San Diego.

Kling, K.C., Hyde, J.S., Showers, C.J., & Buswell, B.N. (1999). Gender differences in self-esteem: A meta-analysis. *Psychological Bulletin, 125,* 470–500.

Knox, D., & Wilson, K. (1981). Dating behaviors of university students. *Family Relations, 30,* 255–258.

Kobak, R. (1999). The emotional dynamics of disruptions in attachment relationships: Implications for theory, research, and clinical intervention. In J. Cassidy & P. Shaver (Eds.), *Handbook of attachment.* New York: Guilford.

Koch, J. (2003). Gender issues in the classroom. In I.B. Weiner (Ed.), *Handbook of psychology* (Vol. 7). New York: Wiley.

Koenig, L.J., & Faigeles, R. (1995, March). *Gender differences in adolescent loneliness and maladjustment.* Paper presented at the meeting of the Society for Research in Child Development, Indianapolis.

Kohlberg, L. (1958). *The development of modes of moral thinking and choice in the years 10 to 16.* Unpublished doctoral dissertation, University of Chicago.

Kohlberg, L. (1966). A cognitive-developmental analysis of children's sex-role concepts and attitudes. In E.E. Maccoby (Ed.), *The development of sex differences.* Palo Alto, CA: Stanford University Press.

Kohlberg, L. (1969). Stage and sequence: The cognitive-developmental approach to socialization. In D.A. Goslin (Ed.), *Handbook of socialization theory and research.* Chicago: Rand McNally.

Kohlberg, L. (1976). Moral stages and moralization: The cognitive-developmental approach. In T. Lickona (Ed.), *Moral development and behavior.* New York: Holt, Rinehart, & Winston.

Kohlberg, L. (1986). A current statement on some theoretical issues. In S. Modgil & C. Modgil (Eds.), *Lawrence Kohlberg.* Philadelphia: Falmer.

Kohlberg, L., & Candee, D. (1979). *Relationships between moral judgment and moral action.* Unpublished manuscript, Harvard University.

Kohn, M.L. (1977). *Class and conformity: A study in values* (2nd ed.). Chicago: University of Chicago Press.

Koss, M.P. (1993). Rape: Scope, impact, interventions, and public policy responses. *American Psychologist, 48,* 1062–1069.

Koss-Chiono, J.D., & Vargas, L.A. (Eds.). (1999). *Working with Latino youth.* San Francisco: Jossey-Bass.

Kottak, C.P. (2002). *Cultural anthropology* (9th ed.). New York: McGraw-Hill.

Kounin, J.S. (1970). *Discipline and management in classrooms.* New York: Holt, Rinehart & Winston.

Kozol, J. (1991). *Savage inequalities.* New York: Crown.

Kozulin, A. (2000). Vygotsky. In A. Kazdin (Ed.). *Encyclopedia of psychology.* Washington, DC, and New York: American Psychological Association and Oxford University Press.

Kralovec, E. (2003). *Schools that do too much.* Boston: Beacon Press.

Kramer, D., Kahlbaugh, P.E., & Goldston, R.B. (1992). A measure of paradigm beliefs about the social world. *Journal of Gerontology: Psychological Sciences, 47,* P180–P189.

Kroger, J. (2003). Identity development during adolescence. In G. Adams & M. Berzonsky (Eds.), *Blackwell handbook of adolescence.* Malden, MA: Blackwell.

Krupnik, C.G. (1985). Women and men in the classroom: Inequality and its remedies. *On Teaching and Learning: The Journal of the Harvard University Derek Bok Center, 10,* 18–25.

Ksir, C. (2000). Drugs. In A. Kazdin (Ed.), *Encyclopedia of psychology.* Washington, DC and New York: American Psychological Association and Oxford University Press.

Kuchenbecker, S. (2000). *Raising winners.* New York: Times Books/Random House.

Kucynski, L., & Lollis, S. (2002). Four foundations for a dynamic model of parenting. In J.R.M. Gerris (Eds.), *Dynamics of parenting.* Hillsdale, NJ: Erlbaum.

Kuhn, D. (1998). Afterword to Volume 2: Cognition, perception, and language. In W. Damon (Ed.), *Handbook of child psychology* (5th ed., Vol. 2). New York: Wiley.

Kuhn, D. (2000). Adolescence: Adolescent thought processes. In A. Kazdin (Ed.), *Encyclopedia of psychology.* Washington, DC, and New York: American Psychological Association and Oxford University Press.

Kulig, J.W., Mandel, L., Ruthazer, R., & Stone, D. (2001, March). *School-based substance use prevention for female students.* Paper presented at the meeting of the Society for Adolescent Medicine, San Diego.

Kumpfer, K.L., & Alvarado, R. (2003). Family-strengthening approaches for the prevention of youth problem behaviors. *American Psychologist, 58,* 457–465.

Kuperminc, G., Jurkovic, G., Perilla, J., Murphy, A., Casey, S., Ibanez, G., Parker, J., & Urruzmendi, A. (2002, April). *Latino self, American self: Mexican and immigrant Latino adolescents' bicultural identity constructions.* Paper presented at the meeting of the Society for Research on Adolescence, New Orleans.

Kupersmidt, J.B., & Coile, J.D. (1990). Preadolescent peer status, aggression, and school adjustment as predictors of externalizing problems in adolescence. *Child Development, 61,* 1350–1363.

Kurdek, L.A., & Krile, D. (1982). A developmental analysis of the relation between peer acceptance and both interpersonal understanding and perceived social self-competence. *Child Development, 53,* 1485–1491.

Kurtz, D.A., Cantu, C.L., & Phinney, J.S. (1996, March). *Group identities as predictors of self-esteem among African American, Latino, and White adolescents.* Paper presented at the meeting of the Society for Research on Adolescence, Boston.

L

Labouvie-Vief, G. (1986, August). *Modes of knowing and life-span cognition.* Paper presented at the meeting of the American Psychological Association, Washington, DC.

Labouvie-Vief, G. (1996). Knowledge and the construction of women's development. In P.B. Baltes & U. Staudinger (Eds.), *Interactive minds: Life-span perspectives on the social foundations of cognition.* New York: Cambridge University Press.

Ladd, G., Buhs, E., & Troop, W. (2002). School adjustment and social skills training. In P.K. Smith & C.H. Hart (Eds.), *Blackwell handbook of childhood social development.* Malden, MA: Blackwell.

Ladd, G.W., & Kochenderfer-Ladd, B. (1998). Parenting behaviors and parent-child relationships: Correlates of peer victimization in kindergarten. *Developmental Psychology, 34,* 1450–1458.

Ladd, G.W., & Kochenderfer-Ladd, B. (2002). Identifying victims of peer aggression from early to middle childhood: Analysis of cross-informant data for concordance, incidence of victimization, characteristics of identified victims, and estimation of relational adjustment. *Psychological Assessment, 14,* 74–96.

Ladd, G.W., & Le Sieur, K.D. (1995). Parents and children's peer relationships. In M.H. Bornstein (Ed.), *Children and parenting* (Vol. 4). Hillsdale, NJ: Erlbaum.

Ladd, G.W., & Pettit, G. (2002). Parents and children's peer relationships. In M. Bornstein (Ed.), *Handbook of parenting* (2nd ed., Vol. 5). Mahwah, NJ: Erlbaum.

LaFromboise, T., Coleman, H.L.K., & Gerton, J. (1993). Psychological impact of biculturalism: Evidence and theory. *Psychological Bulletin, 114,* 393–412.

LaFromboise, T., & Low, K.G. (1989). American Indian children and adolescents. In J.T. Gibbs & L.N. Huang (Eds.), *Children of color.* San Francisco: Jossey-Bass.

Laird, R.D., Pettit, G.S., Bates, J.E., & Dodge, K.A. (2003). Parents' monitoring-relevant knowledge and adolescents' delinquent behavior: Evidence of correlated developmental changes and reciprocal influences. *Child Development, 74,* 752–768.

Lalonde, C., & Chandler, M. (2004). Culture, selves, and time. In C. Lightfoot, C. Lalonde, & M. Chandler (Eds.), *Changing conceptions of psychological life.* Mahwah, NJ: Erlbaum.

Lamb, M.E. (1997). Fatherhood then and now. In A. Booth & A.C. Crouter (Eds.), *Men in families.* Mahwah, NJ: Erlbaum.

Landry, D.J., Singh, S., & Darroch, J.E. (2000). Sexuality education in fifth and sixth grades in U.S. public schools, 1999. *Family Planning Perspectives, 32,* 212–219.

Lapsley, D.K. (1990). Continuity and discontinuity in adolescent social cognitive development. In R. Montemayor, G. Adams, & T. Gulotta (Eds.), *From childhood to adolescence: A transitional period?* Newbury Park, CA: Sage.

Lapsley, D.K. (1996). *Moral psychology.* Boulder, CO: Westview Press.

Lapsley, D.K., Enright, R.D., & Serlin, R.C. (1985). Toward a theoretical perspective on the legislation of adolescence. *Journal of Early Adolescence, 5,* 441–466.

Lapsley, D.K., & Murphy, M.N. (1985). Another look at the theoretical assumptions of adolescent egocentrism. *Developmental Review, 5,* 201–217.

Lapsley, D.K., & Narvaez, D. (Eds.). (2004). *Moral development, self, and identity.* Mahwah, NJ: Erlbaum.

Lapsley, D.K., & Power, F.C. (Eds.). (1988). *Self, ego, and identity.* New York: Springer-Verlag.

Lapsley, D.K., Rice, K.G., & Shadid, G.E. (1989). Psychological separation and adjustment to college. *Journal of Counseling Psychology, 36,* 286–294.

Larose, S., & Boivin, M. (1998). Attachment to parents, social support expectations, and socioemotional adjustment during the high school–college transition. *Journal of Research on Adolescence, 8,* 1–28.

Larsen, R.J., & Buss, D.M. (2002). *Personality psychology: Domains of knowledge about human nature.* New York: McGraw-Hill.

Larson, R.W. (1999, September). Unpublished review of J.W. Santrock's *Adolescence,* 8th ed. (New York: McGraw-Hill).

Larson, R.W. (2000). Toward a psychology of positive youth development. *American Psychologist, 55,* 170–183.

Larson, R.W. (2001). How U.S. children and adolescents spend time: What it does (and doesn't) tell us about their development. *Current Directions in Psychological Science, 10,* 160–164.

Larson, R.W., Brown, B.B., & Mortimer, J. (2003). Introduction: Globalization, societal change, and new technologies: What they mean for the future of adolescence. In R. Larson, B. Brown, & J. Mortimer (Eds.), *Adolescents' preparation for the future: Perils and promise.* Malden, MA: Blackwell.

Larson, R.W., Clore, G.L., & Wood, G.A. (1999). The emotions of romantic relationships. In W. Furman, B.B. Brown, & C. Feiring (Eds.), *Contemporary perspectives on romantic relationships.* New York: Cambridge University Press.

Larson, R.W., Hansen, D., & Walker, K. (2004). Everybody's gotta give adolescents' development of initiative within a youth program. In J.L. Mahoney, R.W. Larson, & J.S. Eccles (Eds.), *Organized activities as contexts of development.* Mahwah, NJ: Erlbaum.

Larson, R.W., & Lampman-Petraitis, C. (1989). Daily emotional states as reported by children and adolescents. *Child Development, 60,* 1250–1260.

Larson, R.W., & Richards, M.H. (1994). *Divergent realities.* New York: Basic Books.

Larson, R.W., Richards, M.H., Moneta, G., Holmbeck, G., & Duckett, E. (1996). Changes in adolescents' daily interactions with their families from 10 to 18: Disengagement and transformation. *Developmental Psychology, 32,* 744–754.

Larson, R.W., & Seepersad, S. (2003). Adolescents' leisure time in the U.S.: Partying, sports, and the American

Experiment. In S. Verma & R. Larson (Eds.), *Examining adolescent leisure time across cultures.* San Francisco: Jossey-Bass.

Larson, R.W., & Verma, S. (1999). How children and adolescents spend time across the world: Work, play, and developmental opportunities. *Psychological Bulletin, 125,* 701–736.

Larson, R.W., & Wilson, S. (2004). Adolescence across place and time: Globalization and the changing pathways to adulthood. In R. Lerner & L. Steinberg (Eds.), *Handbook of adolescent psychology.* New York: Wiley.

Larson, R.W., Wilson, S., Brown, B.B., Furstenberg, F.F., & Verma, S. (2002). Changes in adolescents' interpersonal experiences: Are they being prepared for adult relationships in the 21st century? *Journal of Research on Adolescence, 12,* 31–68.

Laursen, B. (1995). Conflict and social interaction in adolescent relationships. *Journal of Research on Adolescence, 5,* 55–70.

Laursen, B., & Collins, W.A. (2004). Parent-child communication during adolescence. In A.L. Vangelisti (Ed.), *Handbook of family communication.* Mahwah, NJ: Erlbaum.

Laursen, B., Coy, K.C., & Collins, W.A. (1998). Reconsidering changes in parent-child conflict across adolescence: A meta-analysis. *Child Development, 69,* 817–832.

LaVoie, J. (1976). Ego identity formation in middle adolescence. *Journal of Youth and Adolescence, 5,* 371–385.

Law, T.C. (1992, March). *The relationship between mothers' employment status and perception of child behavior.* Paper presented at the meeting of the Society for Research on Adolescence, Washington, DC.

Lazarus, R.S. (1991). *Emotion and adaptation.* New York: Oxford University Press.

Le Vay, S. (1994). *The sexual brain.* Cambridge, MA: MIT Press.

Leadbetter, B.J. (1994, February). *Reconceptualizing social supports for adolescent mothers: Grandmothers, babies, fathers, and beyond.* Paper presented at the meeting of the Society for Research on Adolescence, San Diego.

Leadbetter, B.J., & Way, N. (2000). *Growing up fast.* Mahwah, NJ: Erlbaum.

Leadbetter, B.J., Way, N., & Raden, A. (1994, February). *Barriers to involvement of fathers of the children of adolescent mothers.* Paper presented at the meeting of the Society for Research on Adolescence, San Diego.

Learner-Centered Principles Work Group (1997). *Learner-centered psychological principles: A framework for school reform and redesign.* Washington, DC: American Psychological Association.

Leary, M.R. (2004). *Introduction to behavioral research methods* (4th ed.). Boston: Allyn & Bacon.

Lebra, T.S. (1994). Mother and child in Japanese socialization: A Japan-U.S. comparison. In P. Greenfield & R. Cocking (Eds.), *Cross-cultural roots of minority child development* (pp. 259–274). Hillsdale, NJ: Erlbaum.

Lee, C.C. (1985). Successful rural black adolescents: A psychological profile. *Adolescence, 20,* 129–142.

Lee, M.M. (2003). Is treatment with luteinizing hormone-releasing hormone agonist justified in short adolescents? *New England Journal of Medicine, 348,* 942–945.

Lee, V.E., & Burkam, D.T. (2001, January 13). *Dropping out of high school: The role of school organization and structure.* Paper presented at the conference Dropouts in America: How Severe Is the Problem? Cambridge, MA, Harvard Graduate School of Education.

Lee, V.E., Croninger, R.G., Linn, E., & Chen, X. (1995, March). *The culture of sexual harassment in secondary schools.* Paper presented at the meeting of the Society for Research in Child Development, Indianapolis.

Lefkowitz, E.S., Afifi, T.L., Sigman, M., & Au, T.K. (1999, April). *He said, she said: Gender differences in mother-adolescent conversations about sexuality.* Paper presented at the meeting of the Society for Research in Child Development, Albuquerque.

Leitenberg, H., Detzer, M.J., & Srebnik, D. (1993). Gender differences in masturbation and the relation of masturbation experience in preadolescence and/or early adolescence to sexual behavior and adjustment in young adulthood. *Archives of Sexual Behavior, 22,* 87–98.

Lent, R.W., Brown, S.D., Nota, L., & Soresi, S. (2003). Testing social cognitive interest and choice hypotheses across Holland types in Italian high school students. *Journal of Vocational Behavior, 62,* 101–118.

Leong, F.T.L. (1995). Introduction and overview. In F.T.L. Leong (Ed.), *Career development and vocational behavior of racial and ethnic minorities.* Hillsdale, NJ: Erlbaum.

Leong, F.T.L. (2000). Cultural pluralism. In A. Kazdin (Ed.), *Encyclopedia of psychology.* Washington, DC, and New York: American Psychological Association and Oxford University Press.

Lerner, J.V., Jacobson, L., & del Gaudio, A. (1992, March). *Maternal role satisfaction and family variables as predictors of adolescent adjustment.* Paper presented at the meeting of the Society for Research on Adolescence, Washington, DC.

Lerner, R.M. (2000). Developmental psychology: Theories. In A. Kazdin (Ed.), *Encyclopedia of psychology.* Washington, DC, and New York: American Psychological Association and Oxford University Press.

Lerner, R.M., Jacobs, F., & Wertlieb, D. (Eds.). (2003). *Handbook of applied developmental science* (Vols. 1–4). Newbury Park, CA: Sage.

Lerner, R.M., & Olson, C.K. (1995, February). "My body is so ugly." *Parents,* pp. 87–88.

Lerner, R.M., & Steinberg, L. (2004). The scientific study of adolescent development: past, present, and future. In R. Lerner & L. Steinberg (Eds.), *Handbook of adolescent psychology.* New York: Wiley.

Levant, R.F. (1999, August). *Boys in crisis.* Paper presented at the meeting of the American Psychological Association, Boston.

LeVay, S. (1991). A difference in hypothalamic structure between heterosexual and homosexual men. *Science, 253,* 1034–1037.

Leventhal, T., & Brooks-Gunn, J. (2000). The neighborhoods they live in: The effects of neighborhood residence on child and adolescent outcomes. *Psychological Bulletin, 126,* 309–337.

Leventhal, T., & Brooks-Gunn, J. (2003). Moving up: Neighborhood effects on children and families. In M.H. Bornstein & R.H. Bradley (Eds.), *Socioeconomic status, parenting, and child development.* Mahwah, NJ: Erlbaum.

Leventhal, T., Graber, J.A., & Brooks-Gunn, J. (2001). *Adolescent transitions into young adulthood.* Unpublished manuscript, Center for Children and Families, Columbia University, New York.

Levesque, J., & Prosser, T. (1996). Service learning connections. *Journal of Teacher Education, 47,* 325–334.

Lewis, C.G. (1981). How adolescents approach decisions: Changes over grades seven to twelve and policy implications. *Child Developments, 52,* 538–554.

Lewis, D.A. (1997). Development of the prefrontal cortex during adolescence: Insights into vulnerable neural circuits in schizophrenia. *Neuropsychopharmacology, 16,* 385–398.

Lewis, R. (1997). With a marble and telescope: Searching for play. *Childhood Education, 36,* 346.

Lewis, R. (2003). *Human genetics* (5th ed.). New York: McGraw-Hill.

Lewis, R., Gaffin, D., Hoefnagels, M., & Parker, B. (2004). *Life* (5th ed.). New York: McGraw-Hill.

Lewis, V.G., Money, J., & Bobrow, N.A. (1977). Idiopathic pubertal delay beyond the age of 15: Psychological study of 12 boys. *Adolescence, 12,* 1–11.

Liben, L.S., Susman, E.J., Finkelstein, J.W., Chinchilli, V.M., Kunselman, S., Schwab, J., Dubas, J.S., Demers, L.M., Lookingfill, G., Dariangelo, M.R., Krogh, H.R., & Kulin, H.E. (2002). The effects of sex steroids on spatial performance: A review and an experimental clinical investigation. *Developmental Psychology, 38* (2), 236–256.

Lieberman, M., Doyle, A., & Markiewicz, D. (1999). Developmental patterns in security of attachment to mother and father in late childhood and early adolescence: Associations with peer relations. *Child Development, 70,* 202–213.

Limber, S.P. (1997). Preventing violence among school children. *Family Futures, 1,* 27–28.

Limber, S.P. (2004). Implementation of the Olweus bullying prevention program in schools: Lessons learned from the field. In D. Espelage & S. Swearer (Eds.), *Bullying in American Schools.* Mahwah, NJ: Erlbaum.

Lindberg, C.E. (2003). Emergency contraception for prevention of adolescent pregnancy. *American Journal of Maternal Child Nursing, 28,* 199–204.

Lindner-Gunnoe, M. (1993). *Noncustodial mothers' and fathers' contributions to the adjustment of adolescent stepchildren.* Unpublished doctoral dissertation. University of Virginia.

Linn, M.C. (1991). Scientific reasoning, adolescent. In R.M. Lerner, A.C. Petersen, & J. Brooks-Gunn (Eds.), *Encyclopedia of adolescence* (Vol. 2). New York: Garland.

Liprie, M.L. (1993). Adolescents' contributions to family decision making. In B.H. Settles, R.S. Hanks, & M.B. Sussman (Eds.), *American families and the future: Analyses of possible destinies.* New York: Haworth Press.

Lipsitz, J. (1980, March). *Sexual development in young adolescents.* Invited speech given at the American Association of Sex Educators, Counselors, and Therapists, New York City.

Lipsitz, J. (1983, October). *Making it the hard way: Adolescents in the 1980s.* Testimony presented at the Crisis Intervention Task Force, House Select Committee on Children, Youth, and Families, Washington, DC.

Lipsitz, J. (1984). *Successful schools for young adolescents.* New Brunswick, NJ: Transaction Books.

Lissau, I., Overpeck, M.D., Ruan, W.J., Due, P., Holstein, B.E., & Hediger, M.L. (2004). Body mass index and overweight in adolescents in 13 European countries, Israel, and the United States. *Archives of Pediatrics & Adolescent Medicine, 158,* 27–33.

Livesley, W.J., & Bromley, D.B. (1973). *Person perception in childhood and adolescence.* New York: Wiley.

Lochman, J.E., & Dodge, K.A. (1998). Distorted perceptions in dyadic interactions of aggressive and nonaggressive boys: Effects of prior expectations, context, and boys' age. *Development and Psychopathology, 10,* 495–512.

Loeber, R., & Farrington, D.P. (Eds.). (2001). *Child delinquents: Development, intervention and service needs.* Thousand Oaks, CA: Sage.

Loeber, R., DeLamatre, M., Keenan, K., & Zhang, Q. (1998). A prospective replication of developmental pathways in disruptive and delinquent behavior. In R. Cairns, L. Bergman, & J. Kagan (Eds.), *Methods and models for studying the individual.* Thousand Oaks, CA: Sage.

Loehlin, J. (1995, August). *Heritability of intelligence.* Paper presented at the meeting of the American Psychological Association, New York City.

Loehlin, J.C. (2000). Group differences in intelligence. In R.J. Sternberg (Ed.), *Handbook of intelligence.* New York Cambridge University Press.

Loewen, I.R., & Leigh, G.K. (1986). *Timing of transition to sexual intercourse: A multivariate analysis of white adolescent females ages 15–17.* Paper presented at the meeting of the Society for the Scientific Study of Sex, St. Louis.

Logan, G. (2000). Information processing theories. In A. Kazdin (Ed.), *Encyclopedia of psychology.* Washington, DC, and New York: American Psychological Association and Oxford University Press.

Long, T., & Long, L. (1983). *Latchkey children.* New York: Penguin.

Lord, S. (1995, March). *Parent psychological experiences as mediators of the influence of economic conditions on parenting in low income urban contexts.* Paper presented at the meeting of the Society for Research in Child Development, Indianapolis.

Lord, S.E., & Eccles, J.S. (1994, February). *James revisited: The relationship of domain self-concepts and values to Black and White adolescents' self-esteem.* Paper presented at the meeting of the Society for Research on Adolescence, San Diego.

Lowe, B., Zipfel, S., Buchholz, C., Dupont, Y., Reas, D.L., & Herzog, W. (2001). Long-term outcome of anorexia nervosa in a prospective 21-year follow-up study. *Psychology and Medicine, 31,* 881–890.

Lubart, T.I. (2003). In search of creative intelligence. In R.J. Sternberg, J. Lautrey, & T.I. Lubert (Eds.), *Models of intelligence: International perspectives.* Washington, DC: American Psychological Association.

Lubinski, D. (2000). Measures of intelligence: Intelligence tests. In A. Kazdin (Ed.), *Encyclopedia of psychology.* Washington, DC, and New York: American Psychological Association and Oxford University Press.

Luborsky, L.B. (2000). Psychoanalysis: Psychoanalytic psychotherapies. In A. Kazdin (Ed.), *Encyclopedia of psychology.* Washington, DC, and New York: American Psychological Association and Oxford University Press.

Luria, A., & Herzog, E. (1985, April). *Gender segregation across and within settings.* Paper presented at the biennial meeting of the Society for Research in Child Development, Toronto.

Luster, T.J., Perlstadt, J., McKinney, M.H., & Sims, K.E. (1995, March). *Factors related to the quality of the home environment adolescents provide for their infants.* Paper presented at the meeting of the Society for Research in Child Development, Indianapolis.

Lyendecker, B., Carlson, V., Ascencio, M., & Miller, A. (2002). Parenting among Latino families in the United States. In M. Bornstein (Ed.), *Handbook of parenting* (2nd ed., Vol. 4). Mahwah, NJ: Erlbaum.

Lynch, M.E. (1991). Gender intensification. In R.M. Lerner, A.C. Petersen, & J. Brooks-Gunn (Eds.), *Encyclopedia of adolescence* (Vol. 1). New York: Garland.

Lynn, R. (1996). Racial and ethnic differences in intelligence in the U.S. on the Differential Ability Scale. *Personality and Individual Differences, 26,* 271–273.

Lyon, G.R. (1996). Learning disabilities. In *Special education for students with disabilities.* Los Altos, CA: Packard Foundation.

Lyon, G.R., & Moats, L.C. (1997). Critical conceptual and methodological considerations in reading intervention research. *Journal of Learning Disabilities, 30,* 578–588.

Maas, H.S. (1954). The role of members in clubs of lower-class and middle-class adolescents. *Child Development, 25,* 241–251.

Maccoby, E.E. (1984). Middle childhood in the context of the family. In W.A. Collins (Ed.), *Development during middle childhood.* Washington, DC: National Academy Press.

Maccoby, E.E. (1987, November). Interview with Elizabeth Hall: All in the family. *Psychology Today,* pp. 54–60.

Maccoby, E.E. (1996). Peer conflict and intrafamily conflict: Are there conceptual bridges? *Merrill-Palmer Quarterly, 42,* 165–176.

Maccoby, E.E. (1998). *The two sexes.* Cambridge, MA: Harvard University Press.

Maccoby, E.E. (2002). Gender and group process: A developmental perspective. *Current Directions in Psychological Science, 11,* 54–57.

Maccoby, E.E. (2002). Parenting effects: Issues and controversies. In J.G. Borkowski, S.I. Ramey, & M. Bristol-Power (Eds.), *Parenting and the child's world.* Mahwah, NJ: Erlbaum.

Maccoby, E.E. (2003). The gender of child and parent as factors in family dynamics. In A.C. Crouter & A. Booth (Eds.), *Children's influence on family dynamics.* Mahwah, NJ: Erlbaum.

Maccoby, E.E., & Jacklin, C.N. (1974). *The psychology of sex differences.* Palo Alto, CA: Stanford University Press.

Maccoby, E.E., & Martin, J.A. (1983). Socialization in the context of the family. In E.M. Hetherington (Ed.), *Handbook of child psychology: Vol. 4. Socialization, personality, and social development.* New York: Wiley.

MacDermid, S., & Crouter, A.C. (1995). Midlife, adolescence, and parental employment in family systems. *Journal of Youth and Adolescence, 24,* 29–54.

MacDonald, K. (1987). Parent-child physical play with rejected, neglected, and popular boys. *Developmental Psychology, 23,* 705–711.

Mader, S.S. (2004). *Human biology* (8th ed.). New York: McGraw-Hill.

Madison, B.E., & Foster-Clark, F.S. (1996, March). *Pathways to identity and intimacy: Effects of gender and personality.* Paper presented at the meeting of the Society for Research on Adolescence, Boston.

Maeda, K. (1999). *The Self-Perception Profile for Children administered to a Japanese sample.* Unpublished data, Ibaraki Prefectural University of Health Sciences, Ibaraki, Japan.

Maehr, M.L. (2001). Goal theory is *not* dead—not yet, anyway: A reflection on the special issue. *Educational Psychology Review, 13,* 177–186.

Maehr, M.L., & Midgley, C. (1996). *Transforming school cultures.* Boulder, CO: Westview Press.

Maggs, J.L., Schulenberg, J., & Hurrelmann, K. (1997). Developmental transitions in adolescence: Health promotion implications. In J. Schulenberg, J.L. Maggs, & K. Hurrelmann (Eds.), *Health risks and developmental transitions during adolescence.* New York: Cambridge University Press.

Magnuson, K.A., & Duncan, G.J. (2002). Poverty and parenting. In M.H. Bornstein (Ed.), *Handbook of parenting.* Mahwah, NJ: Erlbaum.

Magnusson, D. (1988). *Individual development from an interactional perspective: A longitudinal study.* Hillsdale, NJ: Erlbaum.

Maguin, E., Zucker, R.A., & Fitzgerald, H.E. (1995). The path to alcohol problems through conduct problems: A family-based approach to very early intervention with risk. In G.M. Boyd, J. Howard, & R.A. Zucker (Eds.), *Alcohol problems among adolescents.* Hillsdale, NJ: Erlbaum.

Mahoney, J.L., & Cairns, R.B. (1997). Do extracurricular activities protect against early school dropout? *Developmental Psychology, 33,* 241–253.

Mahoney, J.L., Cairns, B.D., & Farmer, T. (in press). Promoting interpersonal competence and educational success through extracurricular activity participation. *Journal of Educational Psychology.*

Mahoney, J.L., Larson, R.W., & Eccles, J.S. (Eds.). (2004). *Organized activities as contexts of development.* Mahwah, NJ: Erlbaum.

Main, M. (2000). Attachment theory. In A. Kazdin (Ed.). *Encyclopedia of psychology.* Washington, DC, and New York: American Psychological Association and Oxford University Press.

Majhanovich, S. (1998, April). *Unscrambling the semantics of Canadian multiculturalism.* Paper presented at the meeting of the American Educational Research Association, San Diego.

Male, M. (2003). *Technology for inclusion* (3rd ed.). Boston: Allyn & Bacon.

Malik, N.M., & Furman, W. (1993). Practitioner review: Problems in children's peer relations: What can the clinician do? *Journal of Child Psychology and Psychiatry, 34,* 1303–1326.

Malina, R.M. (2001). Physical activity and fitness: Pathways from childhood to adulthood. *American Journal of Human Biology, 13,* 162–172.

Manis, F.R., Keating, D.P., & Morrison, F.J. (1980). Developmental differences in the allocation of processing capacity. *Journal of Experimental Child Psychology, 29,* 156–169.

Mantzoros, C.S. (2000). Role of leptin in reproduction. *Annals of the New York Academy of Sciences, 900,* 174–183.

Maradiegue, A. (2003). Minors' rights versus parental rights: Review of legal issues in adolescent health care. *Journal of Midwifery and Women's Health, 48,* 170–177.

Marcell, A.V., Klein, J.D., Fischer, I., Allan, M.J., & Kokotailo, P.K. (2002). Male adolescent use of health care services: Where are the boys? *Journal of Adolescent Health Care, 30,* 35–43.

Marcell, A.V., & Millstein, S.G. (2001, March). *Quality of adolescent preventive services: The role of physician attitudes and self-efficacy.* Paper presented at the meeting of the Society for Adolescent Medicine, San Diego.

Marcia, J.E. (1980). Ego identity development. In J. Adelson (Ed.), *Handbook of adolescent psychology.* New York: Wiley.

Marcia, J.E. (1987). The identity status approach to the study of ego identity development. In T. Honess & K. Yardley (Eds.), *Self and identity: Perspectives across the lifespan.* London: Routledge & Kegan Paul.

Marcia, J.E. (1989). Identity in adolescence. *Journal of Adolescence, 12,* 401–410.

Marcia, J.E. (1994). The empirical study of ego identity. In H.A. Bosma, T.L.G. Graafsma, H.D. Grotevant, & D.J. De Levita (Eds.), *Identity and development.* Newbury Park, CA: Sage.

Marcia, J.E. (1996). Unpublished review of J.W. Santrock's *Adolescence,* 7th ed. (Dubuque, IA: Brown & Benchmark).

Marcia, J.E., & Carpendale, J. (2004). Identity: Does thinking make it so? In C. Lightfoot, C. Lalonde, & M. Chandler (Eds.), *Changing conceptions of psychological life.* Mahwah, NJ: Erlbaum.

Marín, G., & Gamba, R.J. (2003). Acculturation and changes in cultural values. In K.M. Chun, P.B. Organista, & G. Marín (Eds.), *Acculturation.* Washington, DC: American Psychological Association.

Marklein, M.B. (1998, November 24). An eye-level meeting of the minds. *USA Today,* p. 9D.

Markus, H.R., & Kitayama, S. (1994). The cultural construction of self and emotion: Implications for social behavior. In S. Kitayama & H.R. Markus (Eds.), *Emotion and culture.* Washington, DC: American Psychological Association.

Markus, H.R., Mullally, P.R., & Kitayama, S. (1999). *Selfways: Diversity in modes of cultural participation.* Unpublished manuscript, Department of Psychology, University of Michigan.

Markus, H.R., & Nurius, P. (1986). Possible selves. *American Psychologist, 41,* 954–969.

Marmorstein, N.R., & Shiner, R.L. (1996, March). *The family environments of depressed adolescents.* Paper presented at the meeting of the Society for Research on Adolescence, Boston.

Marsh, H.W. (1991). Employment during high school: Character building or a subversion of academic goals? *Sociology of Education, 64,* 172–189.

Martin, C.L., & Dinella, L. (2001). Gender development: Gender schema theory. In J. Worrell (Ed.), *Encyclopedia of women and gender.* San Diego: Academic Press.

Martin, C.L., & Halverson, C.F. (1981). A schematic processing model of sex typing and stereotyping in children. *Child Development, 52,* 1119–1134.

Martin, C.L., Ruble, D.N., & Szkrybalo, J. (2002). Cognitive theories of early gender development. *Psychological Bulletin, 128,* 903–933.

Martin, E.W., Martin, R., & Terman, D.L. (1996). The legislative and litigation history of special education. *Future of Children, 6* (1), 25–53.

Martin, J. (1976). *The education of adolescents.* Washington, DC: U.S. Department of Education.

Martin, N.C. (1997, April). *Adolescents' possible selves and the transition to adulthood.* Paper presented at the meeting of the Society for Research in Child Development, Washington, DC.

Mash, E.J., & Wolfe, D.A. (2003). Disorders of childhood and adolescence. In I.B. Weiner (Ed.), *Handbook of psychology* (Vol. 7). New York: Wiley.

Masten, A.S. (2001). Ordinary magic: Resilience processes in development. *American Psychologist, 56,* 227–238.

Masten, A.S., & Coatsworth, J.D. (1998). The development of competence in favorable and unfavorable environments: Lessons from research on successful children. *American Psychologist, 53,* 205–220.

Masten, A.S., & Reed, M.G. (2002). Resilience in development. In C.R. Snyder & S.J. Lopez (Eds.), *The handbook of positive psychology.* Oxford University Press.

Matheny, A.P., & Phillips, K. (2001). Temperament and context: Correlates of home environment with temperament continuity and change. In T.D. Wachs & G.A. Kohnstamm (Eds.), *Temperament in context.* Mahwah, NJ: Erlbaum.

Mathes, P.G., Howard, J.K., Mien, S.H., & Fuchs, D. (1998). Peer-assisted learning strategies for first-grade readers: Responding to the needs of diverse learners. *Reading Research Quarterly, 33,* 62–94.

Matlin, M.W. (1993). *The psychology of women* (2nd ed.). San Diego: Harcourt Brace Jovanovich.

Matlin, M.W. (2004). *The psychology of women* (5th ed.). Belmont, CA: Wadsworth. In C.B. Crawford & C.A. Salmon (Eds.), *Evolutionary psychology, public policy, and personal decisions.* Mahwah, NJ: Erlbaum.

Matsumoto, D. (2000). Cross-cultural communication. In A. Kazdin (Ed.), *Encyclopedia of psychology.* Washington, DC, and New York: American Psychological Association and Oxford University Press.

Matsumoto, D. (2004). *Culture and psychology* (3rd ed.). Belmont, CA: Wadsworth.

Mauro, V.P., Wood, I.C., Krushel, L., Crossin, K.L., & Edelman, G.M. (1994). Cell adhesion alters gene transcription in chicken embryo brain cells and mouse embryonal carcinoma cells. *Proceedings of the National Academy of Sciences USA, 91,* 2868–2872.

Maxson, S. (2003). Behavioral genetics. In I.B. Weiner (Ed.), *Handbook of psychology* (Vol. 3). New York: Wiley.

Mayer, J.D., Salovey, P., & Caruso, D.R. (2002). *Mayer-Salovey-Caruso Emotional Intelligence Test (MSCEIT): User's Manual.* Toronto, Ontario, Canada: Multi-Health Systems.

Mayer, R.E. (2003). Memory and information processes. In I.B. Weiner (Ed.), *Handbook of psychology* (Vol. 7). New York: Wiley.

McAdoo, H.P. (2002). African-American parenting. In M. Bornstein (Ed.), *Handbook of parenting* (2nd ed., Vol. 4). Mahwah, NJ: Erlbaum.

McAdoo, H.P., & Martin, A. (2003). Families and ethnicity. In R.M. Lerner, F. Jacobs, & D. Wertlieb (Eds.), *Handbook of* *applied developmental psychology* (Vol. 1). Thousand Oaks, CA: Sage.

McAlister, A., Perry, C., Killen, J., Slinkard, L.A., & Maccoby, N. (1980). Pilot study of smoking, alcohol, and drug abuse prevention. *American Journal of Public Health, 70,* 719–721.

McCabe, M.P., & Ricciardelli, L.A. (2003). Sociocultural influences on body image and body changes among adolescent boys and girls. *Journal of Social Psychology, 143,* 5–26.

McCormick, C.B. (2003). Metacognition and classroom learning. In I.B. Weiner (Ed.), *Handbook of psychology* (Vol. 7). New York: Wiley.

McCormick, C.B., & Pressley, M. (1997). *Educational psychology.* New York: Longman.

McCrae, R.R., & Costa, P.T. (2003). *Personality in adulthood* (2nd ed.). New York: Guilford.

McHale, J.P., & Grolnick, W.S. (Eds.). (2001). *Retrospect and prospect in the psychological study of families.* Mahwah, NJ: Erlbaum.

McHale, J.P., Khazan, I., Erera, P., Rotman, T., DeCourcey, W., & McConnell, M. (2002). Coparenting in diverse family systems. In M.H. Bornstein (Ed.), *Handbook of parenting* (2nd ed., Vol. 3). Mahwah, NJ: Erlbaum.

McHale, S.M. (1995). Lessons about adolescent development from the study of African-American youth. In L.J. Crockett & A.C. Crouter (Eds.), *Pathways through adolescence.* Hillsdale, NJ: Erlbaum.

McHale, S.M., Crouter, A.C., & Whiteman, S.D. (2003). The family contexts of gender development in childhood and adolescence. *Social Development, 12,* 125–152.

McHale, S.M., Updegraff, K.A., Helms-Erikson, H., & Crouter, A.C. (2001). Sibling influences on gender development in middle childhood and early adolescence: A longitudinal study. *Developmental Psychology, 37,* 115–125.

McLanahan, S., & Sandefur, G. (1994). *Growing up with a single parent: What hurts, what helps?* Cambridge, MA: Harvard University Press.

McLoyd, V.C. (1990). The impact of economic hardship on Black families and children: Psychological distress, parenting, and socioemotional development. *Child Development, 61,* 311–346.

McLoyd, V.C. (1998). Children in poverty. In I.E. Siegel & K.A. Renninger (Eds.), *Handbook of child psychology* (5th ed., Vol. 4). New York: Wiley.

McLoyd, V.C. (2000). Poverty. In A. Kazdin (Ed.), *Encyclopedia of psychology.* Washington, DC, and New York: American Psychological Association and Oxford University Press.

McMillan, J.H., & Wergin, J.F. (2002). *Understanding and evaluating educational research* (2nd ed.). Upper Saddle River, NJ: Prentice-Hall.

McNally, D. (1990). *Even eagles need a push.* New York: Dell.

McNulty, R.D., & Burnette, M.M. (2004). *Exploring human sexuality* (2nd ed.). Boston: Allyn & Bacon.

McPartland, J.M., & McDill, E.L. (1976). *The unique role of schools in the causes of youthful crime.* Baltimore: Johns Hopkins University Press.

McRee, J.N., & Gebelt, J.L. (2001, April). *Pubertal development, choice of friends, and adolescent male tobacco use.* Paper presented the meeting of the Society for Research in Child Development, Minneapolis.

Mead, M. (1928). *Coming of age in Samoa.* New York: Morrow.

Mead, M. (1978, Dec. 30–Jan. 5). The American family: An Endangered species. *TV Guide.*

Mean, M., Righini, N.C., Narring, F., Jeannin, A., & Michaud, P.A. (2004). Psychoactive substance use disorder and suicidal conducts in a prospective study of adolescents hospitalized for suicide attempt or suicidal ideation. *Journal of Adolescent Health, 34,* 139–140.

Medrich, E.A., Rosen, J., Rubin, V., & Buckley, S. (1982). *The serious business of growing up.* Berkeley: University of California Press.

Meece, J.L., & Kurtz-Costes, B. (2001). Introduction: The schooling of ethnic minority children. *Educational Psychologist, 36,* 1–8.

Meichenbaum, D., & Butler, L. (1980). Toward a conceptual model of the treatment of test anxiety: Implications for research and treatment. In I.G. Sarason (Ed.), *Test anxiety.* Mahwah, NJ: Erlbaum.

Mein, J.K., Palmer, C.M., Shand, M.C., Templeton, D.J., Parekh, V., Mobbs, M., Haig, K., Huffam, S.E., & Young, L. (2003). Management of acute sexual assault. *Medical Journal of Australia, 178,* 226–230.

Melby, L.C. (1995). *Teacher efficacy and classroom management: A study of teacher cognition, emotion, and strategy usage associated with externalizing student behavior.* Ph.D. dissertation, University of California at Los Angeles.

Merenda, P.F. (2004). Cross-cultural adaptation of educational and psychological testing. In R.K. Hambleton, P.F. Merenda, & C.D. Spielberger (Eds.), *Adapting educational tests for cross-cultural assessment.* Mahwah, NJ: Erlbaum.

Merrell, K.W., & Gimpel, G.A. (1997). *Social skills of children and adolescents.* Mahwah, NJ: Erlbaum.

Messinger, J.C. (1971). Sex and repression in an Irish folk community. In D.S. Marshal & R.C. Suggs (Eds.), *Human sexual behavior: Variations in the ethnographic spectrum* (pp. 3–37). New York: Basic Books.

Metts, S. (2004). First sexual involvement in romantic relationships. In J.H. Harvey & A. Wentzel (Eds.), *The handbook of sexuality in close relationships.* Mahwah, NJ: Erlbaum.

Meyer, I.H. (2003). Prejudice, social stress, and mental health in gay, lesbian, and bisexual populations: conceptual issues and research evidence. *Psychological Bulletin, 129,* 674–697.

Meyer-Bahlburg, H.F., Ehrhart, A.A., Rosen, L.R., Gruen, R.S., Veridiano, N.P., Vann, F.H., & Neuwalder, H.F. (1995). Prenatal estrogens and the development of homosexual orientation. *Developmental Psychology, 31,* 12–21.

Michael, R.T., Gagnon, J.H., Laumann, E.O., & Kolata, G. (1994). *Sex in America.* Boston: Little, Brown.

Midgley, C. (Ed.). (2002). *Goals, goal structures, and patterns of adaptive learning.* Mahwah, NJ: Erlbaum.

Midgley, C., & Urdan, T. (1995). Predictors of middle school students' use of self-handicapping strategies. *Journal of Early Adolescence, 15,* 389–411.

Millar, R., & Shevlin, M. (2003). Predicting career information-seeking behavior of school pupils using the theory of planned behavior. *Journal of Vocational Behavior, 62,* 26–42.

Miller, B.C., Benson, B., & Galbraith, K.A. (2001). Family relationships and adolescent pregnancy risk: A research synthesis. *Developmental Review, 21,* 1–38.

Miller, J.G. (1995, March). *Culture, context, and personal agency: The cultural grounding of self and morality.* Paper presented at the meeting of the Society for Research in Child Development, Indianapolis.

Miller, J.G., & Schaberg, L. (2003). Cultural perspectives on personality and social psychology. In I.B. Weiner (Ed.),

Handbook of psychology (Vol. 5). New York: Wiley.

Miller, L., & Gur, M. (2002). Religiousness and sexual responsibility in adolescent girls. *Journal of Adolescent Health, 31,* 401–406.

Miller, S.K., & Slap, G.G. (1989). Adolescent smoking: A review of prevalence and prevention. *Journal of Adolescent Health Care, 10,* 129–135.

Miller-Jones, D. (1989). Culture and testing. *American Psychologist, 44,* 360–366.

Ministry of Health, Education, and Welfare. (2002). *Divorce trends in Japan.* Tokyo: Author.

Minuchin, P. (2002). Looking toward the horizon: Present and future in the study of family systems. In J.P. McHale & W.S. Grolnick (Eds.), *Retrospect and prospect in the study of families.* Mahwah, NJ: Erlbaum.

Minuchin, P.P., & Shapiro, E.K. (1983). The school as a context for social development. In P.H. Mussen (Ed.), *Handbook of child psychology* (4th ed., Vol. 4). New York: Wiley.

Mischel, W. (1968). *Personality and assessment.* New York: Wiley.

Mischel, W. (1973). Toward a cognitive social learning reconceptualization of personality. *Psychological Review, 80,* 252–283.

Mischel, W. (1995, August). *Cognitive-affective theory of person-environment psychology.* Paper presented at the meeting of the American Psychological Association, New York City.

Mischel, W. (2004). Toward an integrative science of the person. *Annual Review of Psychology,* Vol. 55. Palo Alto, CA: Annual Reviews.

Mischel, W., & Mischel, H. (1975, April). *A cognitive social-learning analysis of moral development.* Paper presented at the meeting of the Society for Research in Child Development, Denver.

Mischel, W., Shoda, Y., & Mendoza-Denton, R. (2002). Situation-behavior profiles as a locus of consistency in personality. *Current Directions in Psychological Science, 11,* 50–53.

Mizes, J.S., & Miller, K.J. (2000). Eating disorders. In M. Herson & R.T. Ammerman (Eds.), *Advanced abnormal child psychology* (2nd ed). Mahwah, NJ: Erlbaum.

Monteith, M. (2000). Prejudice. In A. Kazdin (Ed.), *Encyclopedia of psychology.* Washington, DC, and New York: American Psychological Association and Oxford University Press.

Montemayor, R. (1982). The relationship between parent-adolescent conflict and the amount of time adolescents spend with parents, peers, and alone. *Child Development, 53,* 1512–1519.

Montemayor, R., Adams, G.R., & Gulotta, T.P. (Eds.). (1990). *From childhood to adolescence: A transitional period?* Newbury Park, CA: Sage.

Montemayor, R., & Flannery, D.J. (1991). Parent-adolescent relations in middle and late adolescence. In R.M. Lerner, A.C. Petersen, & J. Brooks-Gunn (Eds.), *Encyclopedia of adolescence* (Vol. 2). New York: Garland.

Montgomery, M.J., & Cote, J.E. (2003). College as a transition to adulthood. In G. Adams & M. Berzonsky (Eds.), *Blackwell handbook of adolescence.* Malden, MA: Blackwell.

Moore, D. (1998, Fall). Gleanings: Focus on work-based learning. *CenterWork Newsletter* (NCRVE, University of California, Berkeley), pp. 1–4.

Moore, D. (2001). *The dependent gene.* New York: W.H. Freeman.

Moos, R.H., Finney, J.W., & Cronkite, R.C. (1990). *Alcoholism treatment. Context, process, and outcome.* New York: Oxford University Press.

Morales, J., & Roberts, J. (2002, April). *Developmental pathways from peer competence to romantic relationships.* Paper presented at the meeting of the Society for Research on Adolescence, New Orleans.

Morgan, M. (1984). Reward-induced decrements and increments in intrinsic motivation. *Review of Educational Research, 54,* 5–30.

Morgan, M. (1987). Television, sex-role attitudes, and sex-role behavior. *Journal of Early Adolescence, 7,* 269–282.

Morrison, L.L., & L'Heureux, J. (2001). Suicide and gay/lesbian/bisexual youth: Implications for clinicians. *Journal of Adolescence, 24,* 39–50.

Morrow, L. (1988. August 8). Through the eyes of children. *Time,* pp. 32–33.

Mortimer, J.T., Finch, M., Ryu, S., Shanahan, M., & Call, K. (1996). The effects of work intensity on adolescent mental health, achievement, and behavioral adjustment: New evidence from a prospective study. *Child Development, 67,* 1243–1261.

Mortimer, J.T., Finch, M., Shanahan, M., & Ryu, S. (1992). Work experience, mental health, and behavioral adjustment in adolescence. *Journal of Research on Adolescence, 2,* 24–57.

Mortimer, J.T., Harley, C., & Johnson, M.K. (1998, February). *Adolescent work quality and the transition to adulthood.* Paper presented at the meeting of the Society for Research on Adolescence, San Diego, CA.

Mortimer, J.T., & Larson, R.W. (2002). Macrostructural trends and the reshaping of adolescence. In J.T. Mortimer & R.W. Larson (Eds.), *The changing adolescent experience.* New York: Cambridge University Press.

Mortimer, J.T., & Lorence, J. (1979). Work experience and occupational value socialization: A longitudinal study. *American Journal of Sociology, 84,* 1361–1385.

Mullis, I.V.S., Martin, M.O., Beaton, A.E., Gonzales, E.J., Kelly, D.L., & Smith, T.A. (1998). *Mathematics and science achievement in the final year of secondary school.* Chestnut Hill, MA: Boston College, TIMSS International Study Center.

Munsch, J., Woodward, J., & Darning, N. (1995). Children's perceptions of their relationships with coresiding and non-custodial fathers. *Journal of Divorce and Remarriage, 23,* 39–54.

Murnane, R.J., & Levy, F. (1996). *Teaching the new basic skills.* New York: Free Press.

Murphy, E.M. (2003). Being born female is dangerous for your health. *American Psychologist, 58,* 205–210.

Murphy, K., & Schneider, B. (1994). Coaching socially rejected early adolescents regarding behaviors used by peers to infer liking: A dyad-specific intervention. *Journal of Early Adolescence, 14,* 83–95.

Murray, J.P. (2000). Media effects. In A. Kazdin (Ed.), *Encyclopedia of psychology.* Washington, DC, and New York: American Psychological Association and Oxford University Press.

Mustanski, B.S., Chivers, M.L., & Bailey, J.M. (2003). A critical review of recent biological research on human sexual orientation. *Annual Review of Sex Research, 13,* 89–140.

Myers, D.L. (1999). *Excluding violent youths from juvenile court: The effectiveness of legislative waiver.* Doctoral dissertation, University of Maryland, College Park.

Myers, M.G., & MacPherson, L. (2004). Smoking cessation efforts among substance abusing adolescents. *Drug and Alcohol Dependency, 73,* 209–213.

Myerson, J., Rank, M.R., Raines, F.Q., & Schnitzler, M.A. (1998). Race and general cognitive ability: The myth of diminishing returns in education. *Psychological Science, 9,* 139–142.

Nadien, M.B., & Denmark, F.L. (Eds.). (1999). *Females and autonomy.* Boston: Allyn & Bacon.

Nagata, D.K. (1989). Japanese American children and adolescents. In J.T. Gibbs & L.N. Huang (Eds.), *Children of color.* San Francisco: Jossey-Bass.

Nakamura, J., & Csikszentmihalyi, M. (2002). The concept of flow. In C.R. Snyder & S.J. Lopez (Eds.), *Handbook of positive psychology.* New York: Oxford University Press.

Nansel, T.R., Overpeck, M., Pilla, R.S., Ruan, W.J., Simons-Morton, B., & Scheidt, P. (2001). Bullying behaviors among U.S. youth: Prevalence and association with psychosocial adjustment. *Journal of the American Medical Association, 285,* 2094–2100.

Nation, M., Crusto, C., Wandersman, A., Kumpfer, K.L., Seybolt, D., Morrissey-Kane, E., & Davino, K. (2003). What works in prevention: Principles of effective prevention programs. *American Psychologist, 58,* 449–456.

National Assessment of Educational Progress. (1976). *Adult work skills and knowledge* (Report No. 35-COD-01). Denver: National Assessment of Educational Progress.

National Center for Addiction and Substance Abuse. (2001). *2000 teen survey.* New York: Author.

National Center for Education Statistics. (1997). *School-family linkages* [Unpublished manuscript]. Washington, DC: U.S. Department of Education.

National Center for Education Statistics. (1998). *Postsecondary financing strategies: How undergraduates combine work, borrowing, and attendance.* Washington, DC: U.S. Office of Education.

National Center for Education Statistics. (1998). *Violence and discipline problems in U.S. public schools.* Washington, DC: Author.

National Center for Education Statistics. (2001). *Dropout rates in the United States: 2000.* Washington, DC: U.S. Department of Education.

National Center for Education Statistics. (2002). *Contexts of postsecondary education: Learning opportunities.* Washington, DC: U.S. Office of Education.

National Center for Health Statistics. (2000a). *Health United States, 2000, with adolescent health chartbook.* Bethesda, MD: U.S. Department of Health and Human Services.

National Center for Health Statistics. (2000b). *National Vital Statistics Reports, 50,* No. 15. Atlanta: National Center for Health Statistics.

National Center for Health Statistics. (2001). *Health, United States, socioeconomic status.* Atlanta, GA: Centers for Disease Control and Prevention.

National Center for Health Statistics. (2002a). Deaths, Tables 1 and 60. *National Vital Statistics Report, 50,* 13, 194.

National Center for Health Statistics. (2002b). Prevalence of overweight among children and adolescents: United States 1999–2000 (Table 71). *Health United States, 2002.* Atlanta, GA: Centers for Disease Control and Prevention.

National Clearinghouse for Alcohol and Drug Information. (1999). *Physical and psychological effects of anabolic steroids.* Washington, DC: Substance Abuse and Mental Health Services Administration.

National Commission on the High School Senior Year. (2001). *Youth at the crossroads: Facing high school and beyond.* Washington, DC: The Education Trust.

National Community Service Coalition. (1995). *Youth volunteerism.* Washington, DC: Author.

Neimark, E.D. (1982). Adolescent thought: Transition to formal operations. In B.B. Wolman (Ed.), *Handbook of developmental psychology.* Englewood Cliffs, NJ: Prentice Hall.

Neisser, U., Boodoo, G., Bouchard, T.J., Boykin, A.W., Brody, N., Ceci, S.J., Halpern, D.F., Loehlin, J.C., Perloff, R.J., Sternberg, R., & Urbina, S. (1996). Intelligence: Knowns and unknowns, *American Psychologist, 51,* 77–101.

Neisser, U., Boodoo, G., Bouchard, T.J., Boykin, A.W., Brody, N., Ceci, S.J., & Okagaki, L. (2000). Determinants of intelligence: Socialization of intelligence. In A. Kazdin (Ed.), *Encyclopedia of psychology.* Washington, DC, and New York: American Psychological Association and Oxford University Press.

Nell, V. (2004). Translation and test administration techniques to meet the assessment needs of ethnic minorities, immigrants, and refugees. In M. Hersen (Ed.), *Comprehensive handbook of psychological assessment* (Vol. 1). New York: Wiley.

Nelson, C.A. (2003). Neural development and lifelong plasticity. In R.M. Lerner, F. Jacobs, & D. Wertlieb (Eds.), *Handbook of applied developmental science* (Vol. 1). Thousand Oaks, CA: Sage.

Nelson, L.J., Badger, S., & Wu, B. (2004). The influence of culture in emerging adulthood: Perspectives of Chinese college students. *International Journal of Behavioral Development, 28,* 26–36.

Nester, E.W., Anderson, D.G., Roberts, C.E., Pearsall, N.N., & Nester, M.T. (2004). *Microbiology* (4th ed.). New York: McGraw-Hill.

Neugarten, B.L. (1988, August). *Policy issues for an aging society.* Paper presented at the meeting of the American Psychological Association, Atlanta.

Newby, T.J., Stepich, D.A., Lehman, J.D., & Russell, J.D. (2000). *Instructional technology for teaching and learning* (2nd ed.). Upper Saddle River, NJ: Prentice Hall.

Newcomb, M.D., & Bender, P.M. (1989). Substance use and abuse among children and teenagers. *American Psychologist, 44,* 242–248.

Newman, B.S., & Muzzonigro, P.G. (1993). The effects of traditional family values on the coming out process of gay male adolescents. *Adolescence, 28,* 213–226.

Newman, J.W. (2002). *America's teachers.* Boston: Allyn & Bacon.

Nicholls, J.G. (1979). Development of perception of own attainment and causal attribution for success and failure in reading. *Journal of Educational Psychology, 71,* 94–99.

Nichols, S., & Good, T.L. (2004). *America's teenagers—myths and realities.* Mahwah, NJ: Erlbaum.

Niederjohn, D.M., Welsh, D.P., & Scheussler, M. (2000, April). *Adolescent romantic relationships: Developmental influences of parents and peers.* Paper presented at the meeting of the Society for Research on Adolescence, Chicago.

Nisbett, R. (2003). *The geography of thought.* New York: Free Press.

Nolen-Hoeksema, S. (2004). *Abnormal psychology* (3rd ed.). New York: McGraw-Hill.

Nottebohm, F. (2002). Neuronal replacement in the aging brain. *Brain Research Bulletin, 57,* 737–750.

Nottelmann, E.D., Susman, E.J., Blue, J.H., Inoff-Germain, G., Dorn, L.D., Loriaux, D.L., Cutler, G.B., & Chrousos, G.P. (1987). Gonadal and adrenal hormone correlates of adjustment in early adolescence. In R.M. Lerner & T.T. Foch (Eds.), *Biological-psychological interactions in early adolescence.* Hillsdale, NJ: Erlbaum.

Nsamenang, A.B. (2002). Adolescence in sub-Saharan Africa: An image constructed from Africa's triple heritage. In B.B. Brown, R.W. Larson, & T.S. Saraswathi (Eds.), *The world's youth*. New York: Cambridge University Press.

Nucci, L. (1996). Morality and the personal sphere of actions. In E. Reed, E. Turiel, & T. Brown (Eds.), *Values and knowledge*. Mahwah, NJ: Erlbaum.

Nucci, L. (2001). *Education in the moral domain*. Cambridge, UK: Cambridge University Press.

Oakes, J., & Lipton, M. (2003). *Teaching to change the world* (2nd ed.). New York: McGraw-Hill.

Obregon, R. (2003). Communication from a human rights perspective: Responding to the HIV/AIDS pandemic in Eastern and Southern Africa. *Journal of Health Communication, 8,* 613–614.

Occupational outlook handbook (2004–2005). Washington, DC: U.S. Department of Labor.

Offer, D., Ostrov, E., Howard, K.I., & Atkinson, R. (1988). *The teenage world: Adolescents' self-image in ten countries.* New York: Plenum.

Office of Juvenile Justice and Prevention. (1998). *Arrests in the United States under age 18: 1997.* Washington, DC: Author.

Ogbu, J.U. (1989, April). *Academic socialization of black children: An inoculation against future failure?* Paper presented at the meeting of the Society for Research in Child Development, Kansas City.

Ogbu, J., & Stern, P. (2001). Caste status and intellectual development. In R.J. Sternberg & E.L. Grigorenko (Eds.), *Environmental effects on cognitive abilities.* Mahwah, NJ: Erlbaum.

Ohene, S-A., Ireland, M., & Blum, R. (2004). The clustering of risk behaviors among Caribbean youth. *Journal of Adolescent Health, 34,* 143.

Okagaki, L. (2000). Determinants of intelligence: Socialization of intelligence. In A. Kazdin (Ed.), *Encyclopedia of psychology,* Washington, DC, and New York: American Psychological Association and Oxford University Press.

Olivardia, R., Pope, H.G., Mangweth, B., & Hudson, J.I. (1995). Eating disorders in college men. *American Journal of Psychiatry, 152,* 1279–1284.

Olsson, C., Bond, L., Burns, J.M., Vella-Brodrick, D.A., & Sawyer, S.M. (2003). Adolescent resilience: A concept analysis. *Journal of Adolescence, 26,* 1–11.

Olszewski-Kubilius, P. (2003). Gifted education programs and procedures. In I.B. Weiner (Ed.), *Handbook of psychology* (Vol. 7). New York: Wiley.

Olweus, D. (1980). Bullying among schoolboys. In R. Barnen (Ed.), *Children and violence.* Stockholm: Acaemic Litteratur.

Olweus, D. (1993). *Bullying at school.* Cambridge, MA: Blackwell.

Olweus, D. (1994). Development of stable aggressive reaction patterns in males. *Advances in the study of aggression* (Vol. 1). Orlando: Academic Press.

Onwuegbuzi, A.J., & Daley, C.E. (2001). Racial differences in IQ revisited: A synthesis of nearly a century of research. *Journal of Black Psychology, 27,* 209–220.

O'Brien, R.W. (1990, March). *The use of family members and peers as resources during adolescence.* Paper presented at the meeting of the Society for Research in Adolescence, Atlanta.

O'Quin, K., & Dirks, P. (1999). Humor. In M.A. Runco & S. Pritzker (Eds.), *Encyclopedia of creativity.* San Diego: Academic Press.

Orlofsky, J. (1976). Intimacy status: Relationship to interpersonal perception. *Journal of Youth and Adolescence, 5,* 73–88.

Orlofsky, J., Marcia, J., & Lesser, I. (1973). Ego identity status and the intimacy vs. isolation crisis of young adulthood. *Journal of Personality and Social Psychology, 27,* 211–219.

Orthner, D.K., Giddings, M., & Quinn, W. (1987). *Youth in transition: A study of adolescents from Air Force and civilian families.* Washington, DC: U.S. Air Force.

Oser, F., & Gmünder, P. (1991). *Religious judgment: A developmental perspective.* Birmingham, AL: Religious Education Press.

Osipow, S.H., & Littlejohn, E.M. (1995). Toward a multicultural theory of career development: Prospects and dilemmas. In F.T.L. Leong (Ed.), *Career development and vocational behavior of racial and ethnic minorities.* Hillsdale, NJ: Erlbaum.

Osofsky, J.D. (1990, Winter). Risk and protective factors for teenage mothers and their infants. *SRCD Newsletter,* pp. 1–2.

Overton, W.F. (2003). Development across the lifespan. In I.B. Weiner (Ed.), *Handbook of psychology* (Vol. 6). New York: Wiley.

Overton, W.F. (2004). Embodied development: Biology, person, and culture in a relational context. In C.R. Coll, E.L. Bearer, & R.M. Lerner (Eds.), *Nature and nurture.* Mahwah, NJ: Erlbaum.

Overton, W.F., & Byrnes, J.P. (1991). Cognitive development. In R.M. Lerner, A.C. Petersen, & J. Brooks-Gunn (Eds.), *Encyclopedia of adolescence* (Vol. 1). New York: Garland.

Owens, T., Stryker, S., & Goodman, N. (Eds.). (2001). *Extending self-esteem theory and research.* New York: Cambridge University Press.

Paige, K.E., & Paige, J.M. (1985). *Politics and reproductive rituals.* Berkeley: University of California Press.

Paikoff, R.L., Parfenoff, S.H., Williams, S.A., McCormick, A., Greenwood, G.L., & Holmbeck, G.N. (1997). Parenting, parent-child relationships, and sexual possibility situations among urban African American preadolescents: Preliminary findings and implications for HIV prevention. *Journal of Family Psychology, 11,* 11–22.

Paloutzian, R.F. (2000). *Invitation to the psychology of religion* (3rd ed.). Needham Heights, MA: Allyn & Bacon.

Paloutzian, R.F., & Santrock, J.W. (2000). The psychology of religion. In J.W. Santrock, *Psychology* (6th ed.). New York: McGraw-Hill.

Pals, J.L. (1999). Identity consolidation in early adulthood: Relations with ego-resiliency, the context of marriage, and personality change. *Journal of Personality, 67,* 295–329.

Paludi, M.A. (2002). *The psychology of women* (2nd ed.). Upper Saddle River, NJ: Prentice-Hall.

Papini, D., & Sebby, R. (1988). Variations in conflictual family issues by adolescent pubertal status, gender, and family member. *Journal of Early Adolescence, 8,* 1–15.

Parcel, G.S., Simons-Morton, G.G., O'Hara, N.M., Baranowski, T., Kolbe, L.J., & Bee, D.E. (1987). School promotion of healthful diet and exercise behavior: An integration of organizational change and social learning theory interventions. *Journal of School Health, 57,* 150–156.

Paris, S.G., & Paris A.H. (2001). Classroom applications of research on self-regulated learning. *Educational Psychologist 36,* 89–102.

Park, Y.M., Matasumoto, K., Seo, Y.J., Kang, M.J., & Nagashima, H. (2002). Changes of sleep or waking habits by age and sex in Japanese. *Perceptual and Motor Skills, 94,* 1119–1213.

Parke, R.D. (2001). Parenting in the new millennium: Prospects, promises, and pitfalls. In J.P. McHale & W.S. Grolnick (Eds.), *Retrospect and prospect in the psychological study of families.* Mahwah, NJ: Erlbaum.

Parke, R.D. (2002). Fathers and families. In M. Bornstein (Ed.), *Handbook of parenting* (2nd ed., Vol. 3). Mahwah, NJ: Erlbaum.

Parke, R.D. (2004). Development in the family. *Annual Review of Psychology,* Vol. 55. Palo Alto, CA: Annual Reviews.

Parke, R.D., & Buriel, R. (1998). Socialization in the family. In N. Eisenberg (Ed.), *Handbook of child psychology* (5th ed., Vol. 3). New York: Wiley.

Parke, R.D., McDowell, D.J., Kim, M., Killian, C., Dennis, J., Flyr, M.L., & Wild, M.N. (2002). Fathers' contributions to children's peer relationships. In C.S. Tamis-LeMonda & N. Cabrera (Eds.), *The handbook of father involvement.* Mahwah, NJ: Erlbaum.

Parker, A., & Fischhoff, B. (2002, April). *Individual differences in decision-making competence.* Paper presented at the meeting of the Society for Research on Adolescence, New Orleans.

Parker, L. (2002, April). *A correlational analysis of factors associated with bullying.* Paper presented at the meeting of the Society for Research on Adolescence, New Orleans.

Pate, R.R., Trost, S.G., Levin, S., & Dowda, M. (2000). Sports participation and health-related behaviors of U.S. youth. *Archives of Pediatric and Adolescent Medicine, 154,* 904–911.

Patterson, C.J. (2000). Family relationships of lesbians and gay men. *Journal of Marriage and the Family, 62,* 1052–1069.

Patterson, C.J. (2002). Lesbian and gay parenthood. In M.H. Bornstein (Ed.), *Handbook of parenting* (2nd ed., Vol. 3). Mahwah, NJ: Erlbaum.

Patterson, G.R., DeBaryshe, B.D., & Ramsey, E. (1989). A developmental perspective on antisocial behavior. *American Psychologist, 44,* 329–335.

Patterson, G.R., & Fisher, P.A. (2002). Recent developments in our understanding of parenting: Bidirectional effects, causal models, and the search for parsimony. In M.H. Bornstein (Ed.), *Handbook of parenting* (2nd ed.). Mahwah, NJ: Erlbaum.

Patterson, G.R., & Stouthamer-Loeber, M. (1984). The correlation of family management practices and delinquency. *Child Development, 55,* 1299–1307.

Paukku, M., Quan, J., Darney, P., & Raine, T. (2003). Adolescents' contraceptive use and pregnancy history: Is there a pattern? *Obstetrics and Gynecology, 101,* 534–538.

Paul, E.L., & White, K.M. (1990). The development of intimate relationships in late adolescence. *Adolescence, 25,* 375–400.

Paulson, S.E., Marchant, G.J., & Rothlisberg, B.A. (1998). Early adolescents' perceptions of parenting, teaching, and school atmosphere: Implications for achievement. *Journal of Early Adolescence, 18,* 5–26.

Peak, L. (1996). *Pursuing excellence: A study of U.S. eighty-grade mathematics and science teaching, learning, curriculum, and achievement in international context.* Washington, DC: U.S. Department of Education, National Center for Educational Statistics.

Pederson, P.B. (2004). *110 experiences for multicultural learning.* Washington, DC: American Psychological Association.

Pellegrini, A.D. (2002). Bullying, victimization, and sexual harassment during the transition to middle school. *Educational Psychologist, 37,* 151–164.

Pentz, M.A. (1994). Primary prevention of adolescent drug abuse. In C. Fisher & R. Lerner (Eds.), *Applied developmental psychology.* New York: McGraw-Hill.

Peplau, L.A., & Perlman, D. (Eds.). (1982). *Loneliness: A sourcebook of current theory, research, and therapy.* New York: Wiley.

Perkins, D.F., & Borden, L.M. (2003). Positive behaviors, problem behaviors, and resiliency in adolescence. In I.B. Weiner (Ed.), *Handbook of psychology* (Vol. 6). New York: Wiley.

Perret-Clermont, A., Resnick, L.B., Pontecorvo, C., Zittoun, T., & Burge, B. (Eds.). (2004). *Joining society.* New York: Cambridge University Press.

Perry, C., Hearn, M., Murray, D., & Klepp, K. (1988). *The etiology and prevention of adolescent alcohol and drug abuse.* Unpublished manuscript, University of Minnesota.

Perry, C.L., Kelder, S.H., & Komro, K.A. (1993). The social world of adolescents: Families, peers, schools, and the community. In S.G. Millstein, A.C. Petersen, & E.O. Nightingale (Eds.), *Promoting the health of adolescents.* New York: Oxford University Press.

Perry, W.G. (1970). *Forms of intellectual and ethical development in the college years.* New York: Holt, Rinehart & Winston.

Peskin, H. (1967). Pubertal onset and ego functioning. *Journal of Abnormal Psychology, 72,* 1–15.

Petersen, A.C. (1979, January). Can puberty come any faster? *Psychology Today,* pp. 45–56.

Petersen, A.C. (1987, September). Those gangly years. *Psychology Today,* pp. 28–34.

Petersen, A.C. (1993). Creating adolescents: The role of context and process in developmental trajectories. *Journal of Research on Adolescence, 3,* 1–18.

Petersen, A.C., & Crockett, L. (1985). Pubertal timing and grade effects on adjustment. *Journal of Youth and Adolescence, 14,* 191–206.

Petersen, A.C., Sarigiani, P.A., & Kennedy, R.E. (1991). Coping with adolescence. In M.E. Colte & S. Gore (Eds.), *Adolescent stress: Causes and consequences.* New York: Aldine de Gruyter.

Peterson, P.L., Hawkins, J.D., Abbott, R.D., & Catalano, R.E. (1994). Disentangling the effects of parent drinking, family management, and parental alcohol norms on current drinking by Black and White adolescents. *Journal of Research on Adolescence, 4,* 203–228.

Petraitis, J., Flay, B.R., & Miller, T.Q. (1995). Reviewing theories of adolescent substance use: Organizing pieces of the puzzle. *Psychological Bulletin 17,* 67–86.

Petrill, S.A. (2003). The development of intelligence: Behavioral genetic approaches. In R.J. Sternberg, J. Lautrey, & T.I. Lubert (Eds.), *Models of intelligence: International perspectives.* Washington, DC: American Psychological Association.

Pettit, G.S., Bates, J.E., Dodge, K.A., & Meece, D.W. (1999). The impact of after-school peer contact on early adolescent externalizing problems is moderated by parental monitoring, perceived neighborhood safety, and prior adjustment. *Child Development, 70,* 768–778.

Pettit, R.B. (2003). Sexual teens, sexual media: Investigating media's influence on adolescent sexuality. *Journal of Social and Personal Relationships, 20,* 262–263.

Pfefferbaum, A., Mathalon, D.H., Sullivan, E.V., Rawles, J.M., Zipursky, R.B., & Lim, K.O. (1994). A quantitative magnetic resonance imaging study of changes in brain morphology from infancy to late adulthood. *Archives of Neurology, 51,* 874.

Phillips, S. (2003). Adolescent health. In I.B. Weiner (Ed.), *Handbook of psychology* (Vol. 9). New York: Wiley.

Phinney, J.S. (1989). Stages of ethnic identity development in minority group adolescents. *Journal of Early Adolescence, 9,* 34–49.

Phinney, J.S. (1996). When we talk about American ethnic groups, what do we mean? *American Psychologist, 51,* 918–927.

Phinney, J.S. (2000). Ethnic identity. In A. Kazdin (Ed.), *Encyclopedia of psychology.* Washington, DC, and New York: American Psychological Association and Oxford University Press.

Phinney, J.S. (2003). Ethnic identity and acculturation. In K.M. Chun, P.B. Organista, & G. Marín (Eds.), *Acculturation.* Washington, DC: American Psychological Association.

Phinney, J.S., & Alipuria, L.L. (1990). Ethnic identity in college students from four ethnic groups. *Journal of Adolescence, 13,* 171–183.

Phinney, J.S., Ferguson, D.L., & Tate, J.D. (1997). Intergroup attitudes among ethnic minority adolescents: A causal model. *Child Development, 68,* 955–969.

Phinney, J.S., Madden, T., & Ong, A. (2000). Cultural values and intergenerational discrepancies in immigrant and non-immigrant families. *Child Development, 71,* 528–539.

Piaget, J. (1932). *The moral judgment of the child.* New York: Harcourt Brace Jovanovich.

Piaget, J. (1952). *The origins of intelligence in children.* (M. Cook, Trans.). New York: International Universities Press.

Piaget, J. (1954). *The construction of reality in the child.* New York: Basic Books.

Piaget, J. (1972). Intellectual evolution from adolescence to adulthood. *Human Development, 15,* 1–12.

Pintrich, P.R. (2003). Motivation for classroom learning. In. I.B. Weiner (Ed.), *Handbook of psychology* (Vol. 7). New York: Wiley.

Pintrich, P.R., & Schunk, D.H. (2002). *Motivation in education* (2nd ed.). Boston: Allyn & Bacon.

Piotrowski, C.C. (1997, April). *Mother and sibling triads in conflict: Linking conflict style and the quality of sibling relationships.* Paper presented at the meeting of the Society for Research in Child Development, Washington, DC.

Pisani, E. (2001). AIDS in the 21st century: Some critical considerations. *Reproductive Health Matters, 8,* 63–76.

Pittman, K., & Diversi, M. (2003). Social policy for the 21st century. In R. Larson, B. Brown, & J. Mortimer (Eds.), *Adolescents' preparation for the future: Perils and promises.* Malden, MA: Blackwell.

Pittman, K., Diversi, M., Irby, M., & Fabber, T. (2003). Social policy implications. In R. Larson, B. Brown, & J. Mortimer (Eds.), *Adolescents' preparation for the future: Perils and promises.* Malden, MA: Blackwell.

Pittman, K.J., Yohalem, N., & Irby, M. (2003). Exploring youth policy in the United States: Options for progress. In R.M. Lerner, F. Jacobs, & D. Wertlieb (Eds.), *Handbook of applied developmental science* (Vol. 2). Thousand Oaks, CA: Sage.

Pittman, L.D. (2000, April). *Links to parenting practices of African American mothers in impoverished neighborhoods.* Paper presented at the meeting of the Society for Research on Adolescence, Chicago.

Place, D.M. (1975). The dating experience for adolescent girls. *Adolescence, 38,* 157–173.

Pleck, J.H. (1983). The theory of male sex role identity: Its rise and fall, 1936–present. In M. Levin (Ed.), *In the shadow of the past. Psychology portrays the sexes.* New York: Columbia University Press.

Pleck, J.H. (1995). The gender-role strain paradigm. In R.F. Levant & W.S. Pollack (Eds.), *A new psychology of men.* New York: Basic Books.

Pleck, J.H. (1997). Paternal involvement: Levels, sources, and consequences. In M.E. Lamb (Ed.), *The role of the father in child development.* New York: Wiley.

Pleck, J.H., Sonnenstein, F., & Ku, L. (1991). Adolescent males' condom use: Relationships between perceived cost benefits and consistency. *Journal of Marriage and the Family, 53,* 733–745.

Plomin, R. (1993, March). *Human behavioral genetics and development: An overview and update.* Paper presented at the biennial meeting of the Society for Research in Child Development, New Orleans.

Plomin, R., Asbury, K., & Dunn, J. (2001). Why are children in the same family so different? Nonshared environment a decade later. *Canadian Journal of Psychiatry, 46,* 225–233.

Plomin, R., DeFries, J.C., McClearn, G.E., & McGuffin, P. (2001). *Behavioral genetics* (4th ed.). New York: Worth.

Plomin, R., & McGuffin, P. (2002). Psychopathology in the postgenomic era. *Annual Review of Psychology, 52.* Palo Alto, CA: Annual Reviews.

Polce-Lynch, M., Myers, B.J., Kliewer, W., & Kilmartin, C. (2001). Adolescent self-esteem and gender: Exploring relations to sexual harassment, body image, media influence, and emotional expression. *Journal of Youth and Adolescence, 30,* 225–244.

Polivy, J., Herman, C.P., Mills, J., & Brock, H. (2003). Eating disorders in adolescence. In G. Adams & M. Berzonsky (Eds.), *Blackwell handbook of adolescence.* Malden, MA: Blackwell.

Poll finds racial tension decreasing. (1990, June 29). *Asian Week,* p. 4.

Pollack, W. (1999). *Real boys.* New York: Henry Holt.

Pollak, C.P., & Bright, D. (2003). Caffeine consumption and weekly sleep patterns in U.S. seventh-, eighth-, and ninth-graders. *Pediatrics, 111,* 42–46.

Pontecorvo, C. (2004). Thinking with others: The social dimension of learning in families and schools. In A. Perret-Clermont, L.B. Resnick, C. Pontecorvo, T. Zittoun, & B. Burge, (Eds.). *Joining society.* New York: Cambridge University Press.

Ponterotto, J.G., Casas, J.M., Suzuki, L.A., & Alexander, C.M. (Eds.). (2001). *Handbook of multicultural counseling.* Thousand Oaks, CA: Sage.

Pope, L.M., Adler, N.E., & Tschann, J.M. (2001). Post-abortion psychological adjustment: Are minors at increased risk? *Journal of Adolescent Health, 29,* 2–11.

Potvin, L., Champagne, F., & Laberge-Nadeau, C. (1988). Mandatory driver training and road safety: The Quebec experience. *American Journal of Public Health, 78,* 1206–1212.

Powell, A.G., Farrar, E., & Cohen, D.K. (1985). *The shopping mall high school: Winners and losers in the educational marketplace.* Boston: Houghton Mifflin.

Presidential Task Force on Psychology and Education (1992). *Lerner-centered psychological principles: Guidelines for school redesign and reform (draft).* Washington, DC: American Psychological Association.

Pressley, M. (1983). Making meaningful materials easier to learn. In M. Pressley & J.R. Levin (Eds.), *Cognitive strategy research: Educational applications* (pp. 239–266). New York: Springer-Verlag.

Pressley, M. (1995). More about the development of self-regulations: Complex, long-term, and thoroughly social. *Educational Psychologist, 30,* 207–212.

Pressley, M. (2003). Psychology of literacy and literacy instruction. In I.B. Weiner (Ed.), *Handbook of psychology* (Vol. 7). New York: Wiley.

Pressley, M., & Roehrig, A. (2002). Educational psychology in the modern period. In B.J. Zimmerman & D.H.. Schunk (Eds.), *Educational psychology.* Mahwah, NJ: Erlbaum.

Pressley, M., Roehrig, A., Raphael, L., Dolezal, S., Bohn, K., Mohna, L., Wharton-McDonald, R., Bogner, K., & Hogan, K. (2003). Teaching processes in elementary and secondary education. In I.B. Weiner (Ed.), *Handbook of psychology* (Vol. 7). New York: Wiley.

Pressley, M., & Schneider, W. (1997). *Introduction to memory development during childhood and adolescence.* Mahwah, NJ: Erlbaum.

Price, R.H., Cioci, M., Penner, W., & Trautlein, B. (1990). *School and community support programs that enhance adolescent health and education.* Washington, DC: Carnegie Council on Adolescent Development.

Prinsky, L.E., & Rosenbaum, J.L. (1987). Leerics or lyrics? *Youth and Society, 18,* 384–394.

Prinstein, M.J., Fetter, M.D., & La Greca, A.M. (1996, March). *Can you judge adolescents by the company they keep? Peer group membership, substance use, and risk-taking behaviors.* Paper presented at the meeting of the Society for Research on Adolescence, Boston.

Pritchard, F.F., & Whitehead, F.F. (2004). *Serve and learn.* Mahwah, NJ: Erlbaum.

Provenzo, E.F. (2002). *Teaching, learning, and schooling in American culture: A critical perspective.* Boston: Allyn & Bacon.

Psathas, G. (1957). Ethnicity, social class, and adolescent independence. *Sociological Review, 22,* 415–523.

Puka, B. (2004). Altruism and character. In D.K. Lapsley & D. Narvaez (Eds.), *Moral development, self, and identity.* Mahwah, NJ: Erlbaum.

Pulkkinen, L., & Kokko, K. (2000). Identity development in adulthood: A longitudinal study. *Journal of Research in Personality, 34,* 445–470.

Putnam, S.P., Sanson, A.V., & Rothbart, M.K. (2002). Child temperament and parenting. In M. Bornstein (Ed.), *Handbook of parenting* (2nd ed.). Mahwah, NJ: Erlbaum.

Quadrel, M.J., Fischhoff, B., & Davis, W. (1993). Adolescent (in)vulnerability. *American Psychologist, 48,* 102–116.

Quinsey, V.L. (2003). The etiology of anomalous sexual preferences in men. *Annals of the New York Academy of Science, 989,* 105–117.

Quinsey, V.L., Skilling, T.A., Lalumiére, M.L., & Craig, W.M. (2004). *Juvenile delinquency.* Washington, DC: American Psychological Association.

Quintana, S.M. (2004). Ethnic identity development in Chicana/o youth. In R.J. Velasquez, B.W. McNeil, & L.M. Arellano (Eds.), *The handbook of Chicano psychology and mental health.* Mahwah, NJ: Erlbaum.

Quinton, D., Rutter, M., & Gulliver, L. (1990). Continuities in psychiatric disorders from childhood to adulthood in the children of psychiatric patients. In L. Robins & M. Rutter (Eds.), *Straight and devious pathways from childhood to adulthood.* New York: Cambridge University Press.

Quinton, W., Major, B., & Richards, C. (2001). Adolescents and adjustment to abortion: Are minors at greater risk? *Psychology, Public Policy, and Law, 7,* 491–514.

Rafaelli, M., & Crockett, L.J. (2003). Sexual risk taking in adolescence: The role of self-regulation and attraction to risk. *Developmental Psychology, 39,* 1036–1046.

Raffaelli, M., & Ontai, L. (2001). "She's sixteen years old and there's boys calling over to the house": An exploratory study of sexual socialization in Latino families. *Culture, Health, and Sexuality, 3,* 295–310.

Rainey, R. (1965). The effects of directed vs. non-directed laboratory work on high school chemistry achievement. *Journal of Research in Science Teaching, 3,* 286–292.

Rajapakse, J.C., DeCarli, C., McLaughlin, A., Giedd, J.N., Krain, A.L., Hamburger, S.D., & Rapoport, J.L. (1996). Cerebral magnetic resonance image segmentation using data fusion. *Journal of Computer Assisted Tomography, 20,* 206.

Ramey, S.L., & Ramey, C.T. (2000). Early childhood experiences and developmental competence. In S. Danzinger & J. Waldfogel (Eds.), *Securing the future: Investing in children from birth to college.* New York: Russell Sage Foundation.

Ramirez, M. (2004). Mestiza/o and Chicana/o: General issues. In R.J. Velasquez, B.W. McNeil, & L.M. Arellano (Eds.), *The handbook of Chicano psychology and mental health.* Mahwah, NJ: Erlbaum.

Ramirez, O. (1989). Mexican American children and adolescents. In J.T. Gibbs & L.N. Huang (Eds.), *Children of color.* San Francisco: Jossey-Bass.

Raskin, P.M. (1985). Identity in vocational development. In A.S. Waterman (Ed.), *Identity in adolescence.* San Francisco: Jossey-Bass.

Raudenbush, S. (2001). Longitudinal data analysis. *Annual Review of Psychology* (Vol. 52). Palo Alto, CA: Annual Reviews.

Raven, P.H., Johnson, G.B., Singer, S., & Loso, J. (2002). *Biology* (6th ed.). New York: McGraw-Hill.

Raymond, E.B. (2004). *Learners with mild disabilities* (2nd ed.). Boston: Allyn & Bacon.

Raymore, L.A., Barber, B.L., & Eccles, J.S. (2001). Leaving home, attending college, partnership, and parenthood: The role of life transition events in leisure pattern stability from adolescence to early adulthood. *Journal of Youth and Adolescence, 30,* 197–223.

Ream, G.L., & Savin-Williams, R. (2003). Religious development in adolescence. In G. Adams & M. Berzonsky (Eds.), *Blackwell handbook of adolescence.* Malden, MA: Blackwell.

Regnerus, M.D. (2001). *Making the grade: The influence of religion upon the academic performance of youth in disadvantaged communities.* Report 01-04, Center for Research on Religion and Urban Civil Society, University of Pennsylvania.

Reinisch, J.M. (1990). *The Kinsey Institute new report on sex: What you must know to be sexually literate.* New York: St. Martin's Press.

Reis, S.D., Neiderhiser, J.M., Hetherington, E.M., & Plomin, R. (2000). *The relationship code.* Cambridge, MA: Harvard University Press.

Remez, L. (2000). Oral sex among adolescents: Is it sex or is it abstinence? *Family Planning Perspectives, 32,* 212–226.

Reschly, D. (1996). Identification and assessment of students with disabilities. *Future of children 6* (1), 40–53.

Resnick, L., & Nelson-Gall, S. (1997). Socializing intelligence. In L. Smith, J. Dockrell, & P. Tomlinson (Eds.), *Piaget, Vygotsky, and beyond.* London: Routledge Paul.

Resnick, M.D., Bearman, P.S., Blum, R.W., Auman, K.E., Harris, K.M., Jones, J., Tabor, J., Beuhring, T., Sieving, R.E., Shew, M., Ireland, M., Bearinger, L.II., & Udry, J.R. (1997). Protecting adolescents from harm: Findings from the National Longitudinal Study on Adolescent Health. *Journal of the American Medical Association, 278,* 823–832.

Resnick, M.D., Wattenberg, E., & Brewer, R. (1992, March). *Paternity avowal/disavowal among partners of low income mothers.* Paper presented at the meeting of the Society for Research on Adolescence, Washington, DC.

Rest, J.R. (1986). *Moral development: Advances in theory and research.* New York: Praeger.

Rest, J.R., Narvaez, D., Bebeau, M.J., & Thomas, S.J. (1999). *Postconventional moral thinking.* Mahwah, NJ: Erlbaum.

Reuter, M.W., & Biller, H.B. (1973). Perceived paternal nurturance-availability and personality adjustment among college males. *Journal of Consulting and Clinical Psychology, 40,* 339–342.

Reynolds, D. (2000). School effectiveness and improvement. In A. Kazdin (Ed.), *Encyclopedia of psychology.* Washington, DC, and New York: American Psychological Association and Oxford University Press.

Reynolds, W.M., & Miller, G.E. (2003). Current perspectives in educational psychology. In I.B. Weiner (Ed.), *Handbook of psychology* (Vol. 7). New York: Wiley.

Rich, G.J. (2003). The positive psychology of youth and adolescence. *Journal of Youth and Adolescence, 32,* 1–3.

Richards, M.H., Crowe, P.A., Larson, R., & Swarr, A. (1998). Developmental patterns and gender differences in the experience of peer companionship during adolescence. *Child Development, 69,* 154–163.

Richards, M.H., & Duckett, E. (1994). The relationship of maternal employment to early adolescent daily experiences with and without parents. *Child Development, 65,* 225–236.

Richards, M.H., & Larson, R. (1990, July). *Romantic relations in early adolescence.* Paper presented at the Fifth International Conference on Personal Relations, Oxford University, England.

Richards, M.H., Suleiman, L., Sims, B., & Sedeno, A. (1994, February). *Experiences of ethnically diverse young adolescents growing up in poverty.* Paper presented at the meeting of the Society for Research on Adolescence, San Diego.

Richardson, J.L., Dwyer, K., McGrugan, K., Hansen, W.B., Dent, C., Johnson, C.A., Sussman, S.Y., Brannon, B., & Glay, B. (1989). Substance use among eighth-grade students who take care of themselves after school. *Pediatrics, 84,* 556–566.

Rickert, V.I., Sanghvi, R., & Wiemann, C.M. (2002). Is lack of sexual assertiveness among adolescent women a cause for concern? *Perspectives on Sexual and Reproductive Health, 34,* 162–173.

Rimberg, H.M., & Lewis, R.J. (1994). Older adolescents and AIDS: Correlates of self-reported safer sex practices. *Journal of Research on Adolescence, 4,* 453–464.

Rimsza, M.E. (2003). Counseling the adolescent about contraception. *Pediatric Review, 24,* 162–170.

Ripple, C.H., & Zigler, E. (2003). Research, policy, and the federal role in prevention initiatives for children. *American Psychologist, 58,* 482–490.

Roberts, B.W., & Caspi, A. (2003). The cumulative model of personality development. In R.M. Staudinger & U. Lindenberger (Eds.), *Understanding human development.* Dordrecht: Kluwer.

Roberts, B.W., Caspi, A., & Moffitt, T.E. (2001). The kids are alright: Growth and stability in personality development from adolescence to adulthood. *Journal of Personality and Social Psychology, 81,* 670–683.

Roberts, B.W., & DelVecchio, W.F. (2000). The rank-order consistency of personality from childhood to old age: A quantitative review of longitudinal studies. *Psychological Bulletin, 126,* 3–25.

Roberts, B.W., & Robins, R.W. (2004). Person-environment fit and its implications for personality development: A longitudinal study. *Journal of Personality, 72,* 89–110.

Roberts, D.F. (1993). Adolescents and the mass media: From "Leave It to Beaver" to "Beverly Hills 90210." In R. Takanishi (Ed.), *Adolescence in the 1990s.* New York: Teachers College Press.

Roberts, D.F. (2003). From Plato's Republic to Hillary's village: Children and the changing media environment. In R. Weissberg, C. Kuster, H. Walbert, O. Reyes (Eds.), *Trends in the well-being of children and youth.* Washington, DC: Child Welfare League of America Press.

Roberts, D.F., & Foehr, U.G. (2003). *Kids and media in America: Patterns of use at the millennium.* New York: Cambridge University Press.

Roberts, D.F., Foehr, U.G., Rideout, V.J., & Brodie, M. (1999). *Kids and media at the new millennium: A Kaiser Family Foundation Report.* Menlo Park, CA: Henry J. Kaiser Family Foundation.

Roberts, D.F., Henriksen, L., & Christenson, P.G. (1999). *Substance use in popular movies and music.* Washington, DC: Office of National Drug Control Policy.

Roberts, D.F., Henriksen, L., & Foehr, U.G. (2004). Adolescents and the media. In R. Lerner & L. Steinberg (Eds.), *Handbook of adolescent psychology.* New York: Wiley.

Roberts, G.C., Treasure, D.C., & Kavussanu, M. (1997). Motivation in physical activity contexts: An achievement goal perspective. *Advances in Motivation and Achievement, 10,* 413–447.

Robertson, H. (2003). Rape among incarcerated men: Sex, coercion, and STDs. *17,* 423–430.

Robins, R.W., Trzesniewski, K.H., Tracey, J.L., Potter, J., & Gosling, S.D. (2002). Age differences in self-esteem from age 9 to 90. *Psychology and Aging, 17,* 423–434.

Robinson, D.P., & Greene, J.W. (1988). The adolescent alcohol and drug problem: A practical approach. *Pediatric Nursing, 14,* 305–310.

Robinson, N.S. (1995). Evaluating the nature of perceived support and its relation to perceived self-worth in adolescents. *Journal of Research on Adolescence, 5,* 253–280.

Roblyer, M.D., & Edwards, J. (2000). *Integrating educational psychology into teaching.* (2nd ed.). Upper Saddle River, NJ: Prentice Hall.

Rodgers, J.L., & Bard, D.E. (2003). Behavior genetics and adolescent development. In G. Adams & M. Berzonsky (Eds.), *Blackwell handbook of psychology.* Malden, MA: Blackwell.

Rodriguez, M.L., & Quinlan, S.L. (2002, April). *Searching for a meaningful identity: Self/ethnic representations and family beliefs in Latino youth.* Paper presented at the meeting of the Society for Research on Adolescence, New Orleans.

Roe, A. (1956). *The psychology of occupations.* New York: Wiley.

Roemmich, J.N., Clark, P.A., Berr, S.S., Mai V., Mantzoros, C.S., Flier, J.S., Weltman, A., & Rogol, A.D. (1999). Gender differences in leptin levels during puberty are related to the subcutaneous fat depot and sex steroids. *American Journal of Physiology, 275,* E543–551.

Roff, M., Sells, S.B., & Golden, M.W. (1972). *Social adjustment and personality development in children.* Minneapolis: University of Minnesota Press.

Rog, E., Hunsberger, B., & Alisat, S. (2002, April). *Bridging the gap between high-school and college through a social support intervention: A long-term evaluation.* Paper presented at the meeting of the Society for Research on Adolescence, New Orleans.

Rogers, C.R. (1950). The significance of the self regarding attitudes and perceptions. In M.L. Reymart (Ed.), *Feelings and emotions.* New York: McGraw-Hill.

Rogers, J.L., & Bard, D.E. (2003). Behavior genetics and adolescent development: A review of recent literature. In G. Adams & M. Berzonsky (Eds.), *Blackwell handbook of adolescence.* Malden, MA: Blackwell.

Rogoff, B. (1990). *Apprenticeship in thinking.* New York: Oxford University Press.

Rogoff, B. (1998). Cognition as a collaborative process. In W. Damon (Ed.), *Handbook of child psychology* (5th ed., Vol. 2). New York: Wiley.

Rogoff, B. (2001, April). *Examining cultural processes in developmental research.* Paper presented at the meeting of the Society for Research in Child Development, Minneapolis.

Rogoff, B. (2003). *The cultural nature of human development.* New York: Oxford University Press.

Rogol, A.D., Roemmich, J.N., & Clark, P.A. (1998, September). *Growth at puberty.* Paper presented at a workshop, Physical Development, Health Futures of Youth II: Pathways to Adolescent Health, Maternal and Child Health Bureau, Annapolis, MD.

Rogol, A.D., Roemmich, J.N., & Clark, P.A. (2002). Growth at puberty. *Journal of Adolescent Health, 31* (6 Supplement), 192–200.

Rohner, R.P., & Rohner, E.C. (1981). Parental acceptance-rejection and parental control: Cross-cultural codes. *Ethnology, 20,* 245–260.

Romo, H. (2000, April). *Keeping Latino youth in school.* Paper presented at the meeting of the Society for Research on Adolescence, Chicago.

Rose, H.A., & Rodgers, K.B. (2000, April). *Suicide ideation in adolescents who are confused about sexual orientation: A risk and resiliency approach.* Paper presented at the meeting of the Society for Research in Adolescence, Chicago.

Rose, L.C., & Gallup, A.M. (2000). The 32nd annual Phi Delta Kappa/Gallup Poll of the public's attitudes toward the public schools. *Phi Delta Kappan, 82* (No. 10), 41–58.

Rose, R.J., Koskenvuo, M., Kaprio, J., Sarna, S., & Langinvainio, H. (1988). Shared genes, shared experiences and similarity of personality: Data from 14,288 adult Finnish cotwins. *Journal of Personality and Social Psychology, 54,* 161–17l.

Rose, S., & Frieze, I.R. (1993). Young singles' contemporary dating scripts. *Sex Roles, 28,* 499–509.

Rosenbaum, E., & Kandel, D.B. (1990). Early onset of adolescent sexual behavior and drug involvement. *Journal of Marriage and the Family, 52,* 783–798.

Rosenberg, M. (1979). *Conceiving the self.* New York: Basic Books.

Rosenblum, G.D., & Lewis, M. (2003). Emotional development in adolescence. In G. Adams & M. Berzonsky (Eds.), *Blackwell Handbook of Adolescence.* Malden, MA: Blackwell.

Rosenthal, R. (2000). Expectancy effects. In A. Kazdin (Ed.), *Encyclopedia of psychology.* Washington, DC, and New York: American Psychological Association and Oxford University Press.

Rosenthal, R., & Jacobsen, I. (1968). *Pygmalion in the classroom.* Fort Worth: Harcourt Brace.

Rosenzweig, M.R. (1969). Effects of heredity and environment on brain chemistry, brain anatomy, and learning ability in the rat. In M. Monosevitz, G. Lindzey, & D.D. Thiessen (Eds.), *Behavioral genetics.* New York: Appleton-Century-Crofts.

Rosner, B.A., & Rierdan, J. (1994, February). *Adolescent girls' self-esteem: Variations in developmental trajectories.* Paper presented at the meeting of the Society for Research on Adolescence, San Diego.

Rosnow, R.L. (1995). Teaching research ethics through role-playing and discussion. In M.E. Ware & D.E. Johnson (Eds.), *Demonstrations and activities in teaching psychology* (Vol. 1). Mahwah, NJ: Erlbaum.

Rotenberg, K.T. (1993, March). *Development of restrictive disclosure to friends.* Paper presented at the biennial meeting of the Society for Research in Child Development, New Orleans.

Roth, J.L., & Brooks-Gunn, J. (2000). What do adolescents need for healthy development? Implications for youth policy. *Social Policy Report. Society for Research in Child Development, XIV* (No. 1), 1–19.

Roth, J.L., & Brooks-Gunn, J. (2003). What exactly is a youth development program? Answers from research and practice. *Applied Developmental Science, 7,* 94–111.

Roth, J.L., Brooks-Gunn, J., Murray, L., & Foster, W. (1998). Promoting healthy adolescents: Synthesis of youth development program evaluations. *Journal of Research on Adolescence, 8,* 423–459.

Rothbart, M.K., & Bates, J.E. (1998). Temperament. In W. Damon (Ed.), *Handbook of child psychology* (5th ed., Vol. 3). New York: Wiley.

Rothbart, M.K., & Putnam, S.P. (2002). Temperament and socialization. In L. Pulkkinen & A. Caspi (Eds.), *Paths to successful development.* New York: Cambridge University Press.

Rothbaum, F., Poll, M., Azuma, H., Miyake, K., & Weisz, J. (2000). The development of close relationships in Japan and the United States: Paths of symbiotic harmony and generative tension. *Child Development, 71,* 1121–1142.

Rowe, S.M., & Wertsch, J.V. (2002). Vygotsky's model of cognitive development. In U. Gowsami (Ed.), *Blackwell handbook of child development.* Malden, MA: Blackwell.

Rubin, K.H. (2000). Middle childhood: Social and emotional development. In A. Kazdin (Ed.), *Encyclopedia of psychology.* Washington, DC, and New York: American Psychological Association and Oxford University Press.

Rubin, K.H., Bukowski, W., & Parker, J.G. (1998). Peer interactions, relationships, and groups. In N. Eisenberg (Ed.), *Handbook of child psychology* (5th ed., Vol. 3). New York: Wiley.

Rubin, Z., & Mitchell, C. (1976). Couples research as couples counseling. *American Psychologist, 31,* 17–25.

Rubin, Z., & Solman, J. (1984). How parents influence their children's friendships. In M. Lewis (Ed.), *Beyond the dyad.* New York: Plenum.

Ruble, D.N. (2000). Gender constancy. In A. Kazdin (Ed.), *Encyclopedia of psychology.* Washington, DC, and New York: American Psychological Association and Oxford University Press.

Ruble, D.N., Boggiano, A.K., Feldman, N.S., & Loebl, J.H. (1980). Developmental analysis of the role of social comparison in self evaluation. *Developmental Psychology, 16,* 105–115.

Rudolph, K.D., Lambert, S.F., Clark, A.G., & Kurlakowsky, K.D. (2001). Negotiating the transition to middle school: The role of self-regulatory processes. *Child Development, 72,* 929–946.

Rueter, M., and Conger, R. (1995). Antecedents of parent-adolescent disagreements. *Journal of Marriage and the Family, 57,* 435–448.

Rumberger, R.W. (1983). Dropping out of high school: The influence of race, sex, and family background. *American Educational Research Journal, 20,* 199–220.

Rumberger, R.W. (1995). Dropping out of middle school: A multilevel analysis of students and schools. *American Education Research Journal, 3,* 583–625.

Runco, M. (2000). Creativity: Research on the processes of creativity. In A. Kazdin (Ed.), *Encyclopedia of psychology.* Washington, DC, and New York: American Psychological Association and Oxford University Press.

Runco, M. (2004). Creativity. *Annual Review of Psychology, 55.* Palo Alto, CA: Annual Reviews.

Rusak, B., Robertson, H.A., Wisden, W., & Hunt, S.P. (1990). Light pulses that shift rhythms induce gene expression in the suprachiasmatic nucleus. *Science, 248,* 1237–1240.

Russell, S.T., & Joyner, K. (2001). Adolescent sexual orientation and suicide risk: Evidence from a national study. *American Journal of Public Health, 91,* 1276–1281.

Russell, S.T., & Truong, N.L. (2002, April). *Adolescent sexual orientation, family relationships, and emotional health.* Paper presented at the meeting of the Society for Research on Adolescence, New Orleans.

Rutter, M. (2002). Family influences on behavior and development. In J.P. McHale & W.S. Grolnick (Eds.), *Retrospect and prospect in the study of families.* Mahwah, NJ: Erlbaum.

Rutter, M. Maughan, B., Mortimore, P., & Ouston, J. (1979). *Fifteen thousand hours: Secondary Schools and their effects on children.* Cambridge, MA: Harvard University Press.

Ryan, A.M., & Patrick H. (in press). The classroom social environment and adolescent achievement beliefs and behaviors. *American Educational Research Journal.*

Ryan-Finn, K.D., Cauce, A.M., & Grove, K. (1995, March). *Children and adolescents of color: Where are you? Selection, recruitment, and retention in developmental research.*

Paper presented at the meeting of the Society for Research in Child Development, Indianapolis.

Ryu, S., & Mortimer, J.T. (1996). The "occupational linkage hypothesis" applied to occupational value formation in adolescence. In J.T. Mortimer & M.D. Finch (Eds.), *Adolescents, work, and family: An intergenerational developmental analysis: Understanding Families,* Vol. 6. Thousand Oaks, CA: Sage.

Saarni, C. (1999). *The development of emotional competence.* New York: Guilford.

Sackett, P. (2003, February). Commentary in E. Benson, "Breaking new ground." *Monitor on Psychology, 34,* 52–56.

Sadeh, A., Raviv, A., & Gruber, R. (2000). Sleep patterns and sleep disruptions in school-age children. *Developmental Psychology, 36,* 291–301.

Sadker, M., & Sadker, D. (2003). *Teachers, schools, and society* (6th ed.). New York McGraw-Hill.

Sagan, C. (1977). *The dragons of Eden.* New York: Random House.

Saliba, J.A. (1996). *Understanding new religious movements.* Grand Rapids, MI: William B. Erdmans.

Salovey, P., & Mayer, J.D. (1990). Emotional intelligence. *Imagination, Cognition, and Personality, 9,* 185–211.

Salovey, P., & Pizarro, D.A. (2003). The value of emotional intelligence. In R.J. Sternberg, J. Lautrey, & T.I. Lubert (Eds.), *Models of intelligence: International perspectives.* Washington, DC: American Psychological Association.

Santa Maria, M. (2002). Youth in Southeast Asia: Living within the continuity of tradition and the turbulence of change. In B.B. Brown, R.W. Larson, & T.S. Saraswathi (Eds.), *The world's youth.* New York: Cambridge University Press.

Santelli, J.S., Rogin, L., Brener, N.D., & Lowry, R. (2001, March). *Timing of alcohol and other drug use and sexual risk behaviors among unmarried adolescents.* Paper presented at the meeting of the Society for Research on Adolescence, San Diego.

Santrock, J.W. (2003). *Psychology* (7th ed.). New York: McGraw-Hill.

Santrock, J.W. (2004). *Educational psychology* (2nd ed.). New York: McGraw-Hill.

Santrock, J.W. (2004). *Life-span development* (9th ed.). New York McGraw-Hill.

Santrock, J.W., Sitterle, K.A., & Warshak, R.A. (1988). Parent-child relationships in stepfather families. In P. Bronstein & C.P. Cowan (Eds.), *Fatherhood today: Men's changing roles in the family.* New York: Wiley.

Saraswathi, T.S. (Ed.). (2003). *Cross-cultural perspectives on human development.* Thousand Oaks, CA: Sage.

Saraswathi, T.S., & Mistry, J. (2003). The cultural context of child development. In I.B. Weiner (Ed.), *Handbook of psychology* (Vol. 6). New York: Wiley.

Sarigiani, P.A., & Petersen, A.C. (2000). Adolescence: Puberty and biological maturation. In A. Kazdin (Ed.), *Encyclopedia of psychology.* Washington, DC, and New York: American Psychological Association and Oxford University Press.

Sarrel, P., & Masters, W. (1982). Sexual molestation of men by women. *Archives of Human Sexuality, 11,* 117–131.

Savin-Williams, R.C. (1995). An exploratory study of pubertal maturation timing and self-esteem among gay and bisexual male youths. *Developmental Psychology, 31,* 56–64.

Savin-Williams, R.C. (1998). *". . . And then I became gay": Young men's stories.* New York: Routledge.

Savin-Williams, R.C. (2001a). *"Mom, dad, I'm gay."* Washington, DC: American Psychological Association.

Savin-Williams, R.C. (2001b). A critique of research on sexual minority youths. *Journal of Adolescence, 24,* 5–13.

Savin-Williams, R.C., & Demo, D.H. (1983). Conceiving or misconceiving the self: Issues in adolescent self-esteem. *Journal of Early Adolescence, 3,* 121–140.

Savin-Williams, R.C., & Diamond, L. (2004). Sex. In R. Lerner & L. Steinberg (Eds.), *Handbook of adolescent psychology.* New York: Wiley.

Savin-Williams, R.C., & Rodriguez, R.G. (1993). A developmental, clinical perspective on lesbian, gay male, and bisexual youths. In T.P. Gullotta, G.R. Adams, & R. Montemayor (Eds.), *Adolescent sexuality.* Newbury Park, CA: Sage.

Sax, L.J., Lindholm, J.A., Astin, A.W., Korn, W.S., & Mahoney, K.M. (2002). *The American Freshman: National norms for fall 2002.* Los Angeles: Higher Education Research Institute, UCLA.

Saxena, R., Borzekowski, D.L., & Rickert, V.I. (2002). Physical activity levels among urban adolescent females. *Journal of Pediatric and Adolescent Gynecology, 15*, 279–284.

Scales, P.C., & Leffert, N. (1999). *Developmental assets: A synthesis of the scientific research on adolescent development*. Minneapolis, MN: Search Institute.

Scaramella, L.V., & Conger, R.D. (2004). Continuity versus discontinuity in parent and adolescent negative affect. In R.D. Conger, F.O. Lorenz, & K.A.S. Wickrama (Eds.), *Continuity and change in family relations*. Mahwah, NJ: Erlbaum.

Scarr, S. (1984, May). Interview. *Psychology Today*, pp. 59–63.

Scarr, S. (1993). Biological and cultural diversity: The legacy of Darwin for development. *Child Development, 64*, 1333–1353.

Scarr, S., & Weinberg, R.A. (1983). The Minnesota adoption studies: Genetic differences and malleability. *Child Development, 54*, 182–259.

Schaie, K.W. (1977). Toward a stage theory of adult cognitive development. *Aging and Human Development, 8*, 129–138.

Schaie, K.W. (2000). Review of Santrock *Life-span development* (8th ed.). Boston: McGraw-Hill.

Scharf, M., & Shulman, S. (2000, April). *Adolescents' socio-emotional competence and parental representations of peer relationships in adolescence*. Paper presented at the meeting of the Society for Research on Adolescence, Chicago.

Scheer, S.D. (1996, March). *Adolescent to adult transitions: Social status and cognitive factors*. Paper presented at the meeting of the Society for Research on Adolescence, Boston.

Scheer, S.D., & Unger, D.G. (1994, February). *Adolescents becoming adults: Attributes for adulthood*. Paper presented at the meeting of the Society for Research on Adolescence, San Diego.

Schegel, A. (2000). The global spread of adolescent culture. In L.J. Crockett & R.K. Silbereisen (Eds.), *Negotiating adolescence in times of social change*. New York: Cambridge University Press.

Schiff, J.L., & Truglio, R.T. (1995, March). *In search of the ideal family: The use of television family portrayals during early adolescence*. Paper presented at the meeting of the Society for Research in Child Development, Indianapolis.

Schneider, B., & Stevensen, D. (1999). *The ambitious generation*. New Haven, CT: Yale University.

Schneider, W., & Bjorklund, D. (1998). Memory. In W. Damon (Ed.), *Handbook of child psychology* (5th ed., Vol. 2). New York: Wiley.

Schonert-Reichl, K.A. (1999). Relations of peer acceptance, friendship adjustment, and social behavior to moral reasoning during early adolescence. *Journal of Early Adolescence, 19*, 249–279.

Schorr, L.B. (1989, April). *Within our reach: Breaking the cycle of disadvantage*. Paper presented at the biennial meeting of the Society for Research in Child Development, Kansas City.

Schulenberg, J., Maggs, J.L., Steinman, K.J., & Zucker, R.A. (2001). Development matters: Taking the long view on substance abuse etiology and intervention during adolescence. In P.M. Monti, S.M. Colbyk, & T.A. O'Leary (Eds.), *Adolescents, alcohol, and substance abuse*. New York: Guilford.

Schunk, D.H. (1991). Self-efficacy and cognitive skill learning. In C. Ames & R. Ames (Eds.), *Research on motivation and education* (Vol. 3). Orlando: Academic Press.

Schunk, D.H. (2001). Social cognitive theory and self-regulated learning. In B.J. Zimmerman & D.H. Schunk (Eds.), *Self-regulated learning and academic achievement* (2nd ed.). Mahwah, NJ: Erlbaum.

Schunk, D.H. (2004). *Learning theories* (4th Ed.). Upper Saddle River, NJ: Prentice Hall.

Schunk, D.H., & Ertmer, P.A. (2000). Self-regulation and academic learning: Self-efficacy enhancing interventions. In M. Boekaerts, P.R. Pintrich, & M. Zeidner (Eds.), *Handbook of self-regulation*. San Diego: Academic Press.

Schunk, D.H., & Zimmerman, B.J. (2003). Self-regulation and learning. In I.B. Weiner (Ed.), *Handbook of psychology* (Vol. 7). New York: Wiley.

Schuster, M. (2000, November 16). Commentary on the increase in oral sex in adolescence. *USA Today*, p. 2D.

Schwimmer, J.B., Burwinkle, T.M., & Varni, J.W. (2003). Health-related quality of life of severely obese children and adolescents. *Journal of the American Medical Association, 289*, 1813–1819.

Scott, L.D. (2003). The relation of racial identity and racial socialization to coping with discrimination among African American adolescents. *Journal of Black Studies, 33*, 520–538.

Scott-Jones, D. (1995, March). *Incorporating ethnicity and socioeconomic status in research with children*. Paper presented at the meeting of the Society for Research in Child Development, Indianapolis.

Scrimsher, S., & Tudge, J. (2003). The teaching/learning relationship in the first years of school: Some revolutionary implications of Vygotsky's theory. *Early Education and Development, 14*, 293–312.

Search Institute. (1995). *Barriers to participation in youth programs*. Unpublished manuscript, the Search Institute, Minneapolis.

Seginer, R. (1998). Adolescents' perception of relationships with older sibling in the context of other close relationships. *Journal of Research on Adolescence, 8*, 287–308.

Seidman, E. (2000). School transitions. In A. Kazdin (Ed.), *Encyclopedia of psychology*. Washington, DC, and New York: American Psychological Association and Oxford University Press.

Seiffge-Krenke, I. (1998). *Adolescents' health: A developmental perspective*. Mahwah, NJ: Erlbaum.

Seligman, M.E.P., & Csikszentmihalyi M. (2000). Positive psychology. *American Psychologist, 55*, 5–14.

Selman, R.L. (1980). *The growth of interpersonal understanding: Developmental and clinical analysis*. New York: Academic Press.

Selman, R.L., & Adalbjarnardottir, S. (2000). Developmental method to analyze the personal meaning adolescents make of risk and relationship: The case of "drinking." *Applied Developmental Science, 4*, 47–65.

Selman, R.L., & Schultz, L.H. (1999, August). *The GSID approach to developmental evaluation of conflict resolution and violence prevention programs*. Paper presented at the meeting of the American Psychological Association, Boston.

Semaj, L.T. (1985). Afrikanity, cognition, and extended self-identity. In M.B. Spencer, G.K. Brookins, & W.R. Allen (Eds.), *Beginnings: The social and affective development of Black children*. Hillsdale, NJ: Erlbaum.

Senanayake, P., & Faulkner, K.M. (2003). Unplanned teenage pregnancy. *Best Practices in Research and Clinical Obstetrics and Gynecology, 17*, 117–129.

Seroczynski, A.D., Jacquez, F.M., & Cole, D. (2003). Depression and suicide in adolescence. In G. Adams & M. Berzonsky (Eds.), *Blackwell handbook of adolescence*. Malden, MA: Blackwell.

Serow, R.C., Ciechalski, J., & Daye, C. (1990). Students as volunteers. *Urban Education, 25*, 157–168.

Serpell, R. (1974). Aspects of intelligence in a developing country. *African Social Research, 17,* 576–596.

Serpell, R. (1982). Measures of perception, skills, and intelligence. In W.W. Hartup (Ed.), *Review of child development research* (Vol. 6, pp. 392–440). Chicago: University of Chicago Press.

Serpell, R. (2000). Culture and intelligence. In A. Kazdin (Ed.), *Encyclopedia of psychology.* Washington, DC, and New York: American Psychological Association and Oxford University Press.

Sewell, T.E. (2000). School dropouts. In A. Kazdin (Ed.), *Encyclopedia of psychology.* Washington, DC, and New York: American Psychological Association and Oxford University Press.

Shade, S.C., Kelly, C., & Oberg, M. (1997). *Creating culturally responsive schools.* Washington, DC: American Psychological Association.

Shanahan, M.J., Mortimer, J.T., & Kruger, H. (2003). Preparation for work in the 21st century. In G. Adams & M. Berzonsky (Eds.), *Blackwell handbook of adolescence.* Malden, MA: Blackwell.

Sharp, V. (1999). *Computer education for teachers* (3rd ed.). New York: McGraw-Hill.

Sheeber, L., Hops, H., & Davis, B. (2001). Family processes in adolescent depression. *Clinical Child and Family Psychology Review, 4,* 19–32.

Shields, S.A. (1991). Gender in the psychology of emotion: A selective research review. In K.T. Strongman (Ed.), *International review of studies on emotion.* New York: Wiley.

Shields, S.A., & Eyssell, K.M. (2000). History of the study of gender psychology. In J. Worrell (Ed.), *Encyclopedia of women and gender.* New York: Oxford University Press.

Shifren, K., Furnham, A., & Bauserman, R.L. (2003). Emerging adulthood in American and British samples: Individuals' personality and health risk behaviors. *Journal of Adult Development, 10,* 75–88.

Shin, H.S. (2001). A review of school-based drug prevention program evaluations in the 1990s. *American Journal of Health Education, 32,* 139–147.

Shrier, D.K. (2003). Psychosocial aspects of women's lives: work, family, and life cycle issues. *Psychiatric Clinics of North America, 26,* 741–757.

Shweder, R.A. (1991). *Thinking through cultures: Expeditions in cultural psychology.* Cambridge, MA: Harvard University Press.

Sidhu, K.K. (2000, April). *Identity formation among second generation Canadian Sikh adolescent males.* Paper presented at the meeting of the Society for Research in Adolescence, Chicago.

SIECUS. (1999). *Public support for sexuality education.* Washington, DC: Author.

Siegel, L.S. (1993). The cognitive basis of dyslexia. In R. Pasnak & M.L. Howe (Eds.), *Emerging themes in cognitive development* (Vol. 2). New York: Springer-Verlag.

Siegel, L.S. (2003). Learning disabilities. In I.B. Weiner (Ed.), *Handbook of psychology* (Vol. 7). New York: Wiley.

Siegel, L.S., & Ryan, E.B. (1989). The development of working memory in normally achieving and subtypes of learning disabled children. *Child Development, 60,* 973–980.

Siegel, L.S., & Wiener, J. (1993, Spring). Canadian special education policies: Children with learning disabilities in a bilingual and multicultural society. *Social Policy Report, Society for Research in Child Development, 7,* 1–16.

Siegler, R.S. (1996). Information processing. In J.W. Santrock, *Child development* (7th ed.). Dubuque, IA: Brown & Benchmark.

Siegler, R.S. (1998). *Children's thinking* (3rd ed.). Upper Saddle River, NJ: Prentice Hall.

Siegler, R.S. (2001). Children's discoveries and brain-damaged patients' rediscoveries. In J.L. McClelland & R.J. Siegler (Eds.), *Mechanisms of cognitive development.* Mahwah, NJ: Erlbaum.

Silver, M.E., Levitt, M.J., Santos, J., & Perdue, L. (2002, April). *Changes in family relationships as adolescents become young adults.* Paper presented at the meeting of the Society for Research on Adolescence, New Orleans.

Silver, S. (1988, August). *Behavior problems of children born into early-childbearing families.* Paper presented at the meeting of the American Psychological Association, Atlanta.

Silver, S. (1995, March). *Late adolescent-parent relations and the high school to college transition.* Paper presented at the meeting of the Society for Research in Child Development, Indianapolis.

Silverberg, S.B., & Steinberg, L. (1990). Psychological well-being of parents with early adolescent children. *Developmental Psychology, 26,* 658–666.

Silverman, J.G., Raj, A., Mucci, L.A., & Hathaway, J.E. (2001). Dating violence against adolescent girls and associated substance use, unhealthy weight control, sexual risk behavior, pregnancy, and suicidality. *Journal of the American Medical Association, 386,* 572–579.

Sim, T. (2000). Adolescent psychosocial competence: The importance and role of regard for parents. *Journal of Research on Adolescence, 10,* 49–64.

Simmons, A.M., & Avery, P.G. (in press). Civic life as conveyed in U.S. civics and history textbooks. *Journal of Social Education.*

Simmons, R.G., & Blyth, D.A. (1987). *Moving into adolescence.* Hawthorne, NY: Aldine.

Simons, J.M., Finlay, B., & Yang, A. (1991). *The adolescent and young adult fact book.* Washington, DC: Children's Defense Fund.

Simons, J.S., Walker-Barnes, C., & Mason, C.A. (2001, April). *Predicting increases in adolescent drug use: A longitudinal investigation.* Paper presented at the meeting of the Society for Research in Child Development, Minneapolis.

Simons-Morton, B., Haynie, D.L., Crump, A.D., Eitel, P., & Saylor, K.E. (2001). Peer and parent influences on smoking and drinking among early adolescents. *Health Education and Behavior, 28,* 95–107.

Simpson, R.L. (1962). Parental influence, anticipatory socialization, and social mobility. *American Sociological Review, 27,* 517–522.

Singh, S., Wulf, D., Samara, R., & Cuca, Y.P. (2000). Gender differences in the timing of first intercourse: Data from 14 countries. *International Family Planning Perspectives, 26,* 21–28, 43.

Sinnott, J.D. (2003). Postformal thought and adult development: Living in balance. In J. Demick & C. Andreoletti (Eds.), *Handbook of adult development.* New York: Kluwer.

Sireci, S.G. (2004). Using bilinguals to evaluate the comparability of different language versions of a test. In R.K. Hambleton, P.F. Merenda, & C.D. Spielberger (Eds.), *Adapting educational and psychological tests for cross-cultural assessment.* Mahwah, NJ: Erlbaum.

Sitlington, P.L., Clark, G.M., & Kolstoe, O.P. (2000). *Transition education and services for adolescents with disabilities* (3rd ed.). Boston: Allyn & Bacon.

Skinner, B.F. (1938). *The behavior of organism. An experimental analysis.* New York: Appleton-Century-Crofts.

Skoe, E.E., Cumberland, A., Eisenberg, N., Hansen, K., & Perry, J. (2002). The influences of sex and gender-role identity on moral cognition and prosocial personality traits. *Sex Roles, 46,* 295–309.

Skoe, E.E., Hansen, K.L., Morch, W-T., Bakke, I., Hoffmann, T., Larsen, B., & Aasheim, M. (1999). Care-based moral reasoning in Norwegian and Canadian early adolescents: A cross-national comparison. *Journal of Early Adolescence, 19,* 280–291.

Skoe, E.E., Pratt, M.W., Matthews, M., & Curror, S.E. (1996). The ethic of care: Stability over time, gender differences and correlates in mid to late adulthood. *Psychology and Aging, 11,* 202–280.

Skorikov, V., & Vondracek, F.W. (1998). Vocational identity development: Its relationship to other identity domains and to overall identity development. *Journal of Career Assessment, 6* (1), 13–35.

Slavin, R.E. (1995). *Cooperative learning: Theory, research, and practice* (2nd ed.). Boston: Allyn & Bacon.

Slavin, R.E., Hurley, E.A., & Chamberlin, A. (2003). Cooperative learning and achievement theory and research. In I.B. Weiner (Ed.), *Handbook of psychology,* (Vol. 7). New York: Wiley.

Slomine, B.S., Gerring, J.P., Grados, M.A., Vasa, R., Brady, K.D., Christensen, J.R., & Denckla, M.B. (2002). Performance on measures of executive function following pediatric traumatic brain injury. *Brain Injury, 16,* 759–772.

Slomkowski, C., Rende, R., Conger, K.J., Simons, R.L., & Conger, R.D. (2001). Sisters, brothers, and delinquency: Social influence during early and middle adolescence. *Child Development, 72,* 271–283.

Small, S.A. (1990). *Preventive programs that support families with adolescents.* Washington, DC: Carnegie Council on Adolescent Development.

Smetana, J. (1988). Concepts of self and social convention: Adolescents' and parents' reasoning about hypothetical and actual family conflicts. In M. Gunnar (Ed.), *21st Minnesota symposium on child psychology.* Hillsdale, NJ: Erlbaum.

Smetana, J.G. (2002). Culture, autonomy, and personal jurisdiction in adolescent-parent relationships. In H.W. Reese & R. Kail (Eds.), *Advances in child development and behavior* (Vol. 29). New York: Academic Press.

Smetana, J.G., Abernethy, A., & Harris, A. (2000). Adolescent-parent interactions in middle-class African-American families: Longitudinal change and contextual variations. *Journal of Family Psychology, 14,* 458–474.

Smetana, J.G. & Gaines, C. (1999). Adolescent-parent conflict in middle-class African-American families. *Child Development, 70,* 1447–1463.

Smetana, J.G., & Turiel, E. (2003). Moral development during adolescence. In G. Adams & M. Berzonsky (Eds.), *Blackwell handbook of adolescence.* Malden, MA: Blackwell.

Smith, R.E., & Smoll, F.L. (1997). Coaching the coaches: Youth sports as a scientific and applied behavioral setting. *Current Directions in Psychological Science, 6,* 16–21.

Smith, T.E.C., Polloway, E.A., Patton, J.R., & Dowdy, C.A. (2004). *Teaching students with special needs in inclusive settings* (4th ed.). Boston: Allyn & Bacon.

Snarey, J. (1987, June). A question of morality. *Psychology Today,* pp. 6–8.

Snyder, C.R., & Lopez, S.J. (Eds.). (2002). *Handbook of positive psychology.* New York: Oxford University Press.

Snyder, H.N., & Sickmund, M. (1999, October). *Juvenile offenders and victims: 1999 national report.* Washington, DC: National Center for Juvenile Justice.

Sommer, B.B. (1978). *Puberty and adolescence.* New York: Oxford University Press.

Sonenstein, F.L., Pleck, J.H., & Ku, L.C. (1989). Sexual activity, condom use, and AIDS awareness among adolescent males. *Family Planning Perspectives, 21* (4), 152–158.

Sousa, D.A. (1995). *How the brain learns: A classroom teacher's guide.* Reston, VA: National Association of Secondary School Principals.

Sowell, E.R., Delis, D., Stiles, J., & Jernigan, T.L. (2001). Improved memory functioning and frontal lobe maturation between childhood and adolescence: A structural MRI study. *Journal of the International Neuropsychological Society, 7,* 312–322.

Sowell, E.R., & Jernigan, T. (1998). Further MRI evidence of late brain maturation: Limbic volume increases and changing asymmetries during childhood and adolescence. *Developmental Neuropsychology, 14,* 599–617.

Sowell, E.R., Trauner, D.A., Gamst, A., & Jernigan, T.L. (2002). Development of cortical and subcortical brain structures in childhood and adolescence: A structural MRI study. *Developmental Medicine and Child Neurology, 44* (1), 4–16.

Spear, L.P. (2000). Neurobehavioral changes in adolescence. *Current Directions in Psychological Science, 4,* 111–114.

Spearman, C.E. (1927). *The abilities of man.* New York: Macmillan.

Spence, J.T., & Helmreich, R. (1978). *Masculinity and femininity: Their psychological dimensions.* Austin: University of Texas Press.

Spencer, M.B. (1999). Social and cultural influences on school adjustment: The application of an identity-focused cultural ecological perspective. *Educational Psychologist, 34,* 43–57.

Spencer, M.B. (2000). Ethnocentrism. In A. Kazdin (Ed.), *Encyclopedia of psychology.* Washington, DC, and New York: American Psychological Association and Oxford University Press.

Spencer, M.B., & Dornbusch, S.M. (1990). Challenges in studying minority youth. In S.S. Feldman & G.R. Elliott (Eds.), *At the threshold: The developing adolescent.* Cambridge, MA: Harvard University Press.

Spencer, M.B., Noll, E., Stoltzfuz, J., & Harpalani, V. (2001). Identity and school adjustment: Revisiting the "acting white" assumption. *Educational Psychologist, 36,* 21–30.

Spokane, A.R. (2000). Career choice. In A. Kazdin (Ed.), *Encyclopedia of psychology.* Washington, DC, and New York: American Psychological Association and Oxford University Press.

Spokane, A.R., Fouad, N.A., & Swanson, J.L. (2003). Culture-centered career interventions. *Journal of Vocational Behavior, 62,* 453–458.

Spring, J. (2000). *The intersection of cultures.* New York: McGraw-Hill.

Spring, J. (2002). *American education* (10th ed.). New York: McGraw-Hill.

Sputa, C.L., & Paulson, S.E. (1995, March). *A longitudinal study of changes in parenting across adolescence.* Paper presented at the meeting of the Society for Research in Child Development, Indianapolis.

Sroufe, L.A. (2001). From infant attachment to adolescent autonomy: Longitudinal data on the role of parents in development. In J. Borkowski, S. Ramey, & M. Bristol-Power (Eds.), *Parenting and your child's world.* Mahwah, NJ: Erlbaum.

Sroufe, L.A., Egeland, B., & Carlson, E.A. (1999). One social world: The integrated development of parent-child and peer relationships. In W.A. Collins & B. Laursen (Eds.), *Minnesota symposium on child psychology* (Vol. 31). Mahwah, NJ: Erlbaum.

St. Pierre, R., Layzer, J., & Barnes, H. (1996). *Regenerating two-generation programs.* Cambridge, MA: Abt Associates.

Staats, A.W. (2003). A psychological behaviorism theory of personality. In I.B. Weiner

(Ed.), *Handbook of psychology* (Vol. 6). New York: Wiley.

Stake, J.E. (2000). When situations call for instrumentality and expressiveness: Resource appraisal, coping strategy choice, and adjustment. *Sex Roles, 42,* 865–885.

Stattin, H., & Magnusson, D. (1990). *Pubertal maturation in female development: Paths through life* (Vol. 2). Hillsdale, NJ: Erlbaum.

Steele, C.M., & Aronson, J. (1995). Stereotype threat and the intellectual test performance of African-Americans. *Journal of Personality and Social Psychology, 69,* 797–811.

Steen, T.A., Kachorek, L.V., & Peterson, C. (2003). Character strengths among youth. *Journal of Youth and Adolescence, 32,* 5–16.

Steinberg, L.D. (1986). Latchkey children and susceptibility to peer pressure: An ecological analysis. *Developmental Psychology, 22,* 433–439.

Steinberg, L.D. (1988). Reciprocal relation between parent-child distance and pubertal maturation. *Developmental Psychology, 24,* 122–128.

Steinberg, L.D., & Cauffman, E. (1999). A developmental perspective on jurisdictional boundary. In J. Fagan & F. Zimring (Eds.), *A developmental perspective on jurisdictional boundary.* Chicago: University of Chicago Press.

Steinberg, L.D., & Cauffman, E. (2001). Adolescents as adults in court. *SRCD Social Policy Report, 15* (4), 1–13.

Steinberg, L.D., Fegley, S., & Dornbusch, S.M. (1993). Negative impact of part-time work on adolescent adjustment: Evidence from a longitudinal study. *Developmental Psychology, 29,* 171–180.

Steinberg, L.D., & Levine, A. (1997). *You and your adolescent* (2nd ed.). New York: Harper Perennial.

Steinberg, L.D., & Silk, J.S. (2002). Parenting adolescents. In M. Bornstein (Ed.), *Handbook of parenting* (2nd ed., Vol. 1). Mahwah, NJ: Erlbaum.

Steinberg, R.J., & Nigro, C. (1980). Developmental patterns in the solution of verbal analogies. *Child Development, 51,* 27–38.

Steinberg, R.J., & Rifkin, B. (1979). The development of analogical reasoning processes. *Journal of Experimental Child Psychology, 27,* 195–232.

Stengel, R. (1985, December 9). The missing-father myth. *Time,* p. 90.

Stepp, L.S. (2000). *Our last best shot: Guiding our children through early adolescence.* New York: Riverhead Books.

Stern, D., & Hallinan, M.T. (1997, Summer). The high schools, they are a-changin'. *CenterWork Newsletter* (NCRVE, University of California, Berkeley), pp. 4–7.

Stern, D., & Rahn, M. (1998, Fall). How health career academies provide work-based learning. *CenterWork Newsletter* (NCRVE, University of California, Berkeley), pp. 5–8.

Sternberg, R.J. (1977). *Intelligence information processing, and analogical reasoning: The componential analysis of human abilities.* Hillsdale, NJ: Erlbaum.

Sternberg, R.J. (1985, December). Teaching critical thinking, Part 2: Possible solutions. *Phi Delta Kappan,* pp. 277–280.

Sternberg, R.J. (1986). *Intelligence applied.* Fort Worth: Harcourt Brace.

Sternberg, R.J. (1993). *Sternberg Triarchic Abilities Test (STAT).* Unpublished test, Department of Psychology, Yale University, New Haven, CT.

Sternberg, R.J. (1997). Educating intelligence: Infusing the triarchic theory into instruction. In R.J. Sternberg & E. Grigorenko (Eds.), *Intelligence, heredity, and environment.* New York: Cambridge University Press.

Sternberg, R.J. (1999). Intelligence. In M.A. Runco & S. Pritzker (Eds.), *Encyclopedia of creativity.* San Diego: Academic Press.

Sternberg, R.J. (2002). Intelligence: The triarchic theory of intelligence. In J.W. Gutherie (Ed.), *Encyclopedia of education* (2nd ed). New York: Macmillan.

Sternberg, R.J. (2003). Contemporary theories of intelligence. In I.B. Weiner (Ed.), *Handbook of psychology* (Vol. 3). New York: Wiley.

Sternberg, R.J., Castejen, J.L., Prieto, M.D., Hautam, J., & Grigorenko, E.L. (2001). Confirmatory factor analysis of the Sternberg triarchic abilities test in three international samples: An empirical test of the triarchic theory of intelligence. *European Journal of Psychological Assessment, 17* (1), 1–16.

Sternberg, R.J., & Grigorenko, E.L. (Eds.). (2001). *Environmental effects on cognitive abilities.* Mahwah, NJ: Erlbaum.

Sternberg, R.J., & Grigorenko, E.L. (Eds.) (2004). *Culture and competence.* Washington, DC: American Psychological Association.

Sternberg, R.J., Nokes, K., Geissler, P.W., Prince, R., Okatcha, F., Bundy, D.A., & Grigorenko, E.L. (2001). The relationship between academic and practical intelligence: A case study in Kenya. *Intelligence, 29,* 401–418.

Sternberg, R.J., Nokes, K., Geissler, P.W., Prince, R., Okatcha, F., Bundy, D.A., & Watras, J. (2002). *The foundations of educational curriculum and diversity: 1565 to the present.* Boston: McGraw-Hill.

Stetsenko, A. (2002). Adolescents in Russia: Surviving the turmoil and creating a brighter future. In B.B. Brown, R.W. Larson, & T.S. Saraswathi (Eds.), *The world's youth.* New York: Cambridge University Press.

Steur, F.B., Applefield, J.M., & Smith, R. (1971). Televised aggression and the interpersonal aggression of preschool children. *Journal of Experimental Child Psychology, 11,* 442–447.

Stevens, J.H. (1984). Black grandmothers' and black adolescent mothers' knowledge about parenting. *Developmental Psychology, 20,* 1017–1025.

Stevens, V., DeBourdeaudhuij, & Van Oost, P. (2001). Anti-bullying interventions at school. *Health Promotion International, 16,* 155–167.

Stevenson, D.L., Kochanek, J., & Schneider, B. (1998). Making the transition from high school: Recent trends and policies. In K. Borman & B. Schneider (Eds.), *The adolescent years: Social influences and educational challenges.* Chicago: University of Chicago Press.

Stevenson, H.G. (1995, March). *Missing data: On the forgotten substance of race, ethnicity, and socioeconomic classifications.* Paper presented at the meeting of the Society for Research in Child Development, Indianapolis.

Stevenson, H.G. (1998). Raising safe villages: Cultural-ecological factors that influence the emotional adjustment of adolescents. *Journal of Black Psychology, 24,* 44–59.

Stevenson, H.W. (1992, December). Learning from Asian schools. *Scientific American,* pp. 6, 70–76.

Stevenson, H.W. (1995). Mathematics achievement of American students: First in the world by the year 2000? In C.A. Nelson (Ed.), *Basic and applied perspectives on learning, cognition, and development.* Minneapolis: University of Minnesota Press.

Stevenson, H.W., Hofer, B.K., & Randell, B. (2000). Middle childhood: Education and schooling. In W. Damon (Ed.), *Encyclopedia of psychology.* Washington, DC, and New York: American Psychological Association and Oxford University Press.

Stevenson, H.W., Lee, S., & Stigler, J.W. (1986). Mathematics achievement of

Chinese, Japanese, and American children. *Science, 231*, 693–699.

Stevenson, H.W., & Zusho, A. (2002). Adolescence in China and Japan: Adapting to a changing environment. In B.B. Brown, R.W. Larson, & T.S. Saraswathi (Eds.), *The world's youth.* New York: Cambridge University Press.

Stewart, A.J., Ostrove, J.M., & Helson, R. (2001). Middle aging in women: Patterns of personality change from the 30s to the 50s. *Journal of Adult Development, 8,* 23–37.

Stice, E. (2002). Risk and maintenance factors for eating pathology: A meta-analytic review. *Psychological Bulletin, 128,* 825–848.

Stice, E., Presnell, K., & Spangler, D. (2002). Risk factors for binge eating onset in adolescent girls: A 2-year prospective investigation. *Health Psychology, 21,* 131–138.

Stipek, D.J. (2002). *Motivation to learn* (4th ed.). Boston: Allyn & Bacon.

Stone, M.R., Barber, B.L., & Eccles, J.S. (2001, April). *How to succeed in high school by really trying: Does activity participation benefit students at all levels of social self-concept?* Paper presented at the meeting of the Society for Research in Child Development, Minneapolis.

Stouthamer-Loeber, M., Loeber, R., Wei, E., Farrington, D.P., & Wikstrom, P.H. (2002). Risk and promotive effects in the explanation of persistent serious delinquency in boys. *Journal of Consulting and Clinical Psychology, 70,* 111–123.

Strahan, D.B. (1983). The emergence of formal operations in adolescence. *Transcendence, 11,* 7–14.

Strasburger, V.C., & Donnerstein, E. (1999). Children, adolescents, and the media: Issues and solutions. *Pediatrics, 103,* 129–137.

Strasburger, V.C., & Wilson, B.J. (2002). *Children, adolescents, and the media.* Newbury Park, CA: Sage.

Streib, H. (1999). Off-road religion? A narrative approach to fundamentalist and occult orientations of adolescents. *Journal of Adolescence, 22,* 255–267.

Streigel-Moore, R.H., Silberstein, L.R., & Rodin, J. (1993). The social self in bulimia nervosa: Public self-consciousness, social anxiety, and perceived fraudulence. *Journal of Abnormal Psychology, 102,* 297–303.

Strickland, B.R. (1995). Research on sexual orientation and human development: A commentary. *Developmental Psychology, 31,* 137–140.

Strober, M., Freeman, R., & Morrell, W. (1997). The long-term course of severe

anorexia nervosa in adolescents: Survival analysis of recovery, relapse, and outcome predictors over 10–15 years in a prospective study. *International Journal of Eating Disorders, 22,* 339–360.

Stunkard, A.J. (2000). Obesity. In A. Kazdin (Ed.), *Encyclopedia of psychology.* Washington, DC, and New York: American Psychological Association and Oxford University Press.

Suárez-Orozco, C. (1999, August). *Conceptual considerations in our understanding of immigrant adolescent girls.* Paper presented at the meeting of the American Psychological Association, Boston.

Suárez-Orozco, C. (2002). Afterward: Understanding and serving the children of immigrants. *Harvard Educational Review 71,* 579–589.

Suárez-Orozco, M., & Suárez-Orozco, C. (2002, April). *Global engagement: Immigrant youth and the social process of schooling.* Paper presented at the meeting of the Society for Research on Adolescence, New Orleans.

Sue, S. (1990, August). *Ethnicity and culture in psychological research and practice.* Paper presented at the meeting of the American Psychological Association, Boston.

Sue, S., & Okazaki, S. (1990). Asian-American educational achievements: A phenomenon in search of an explanation. *American Psychologist, 45,* 913–920.

Sullivan, H.S. (1953). *The interpersonal theory of psychiatry.* New York: W.W. Norton.

Sullivan, K., & Sullivan, A. (1980). Adolescent-parent separation. *Developmental Psychology, 16,* 93–99.

Suomi, S.J., Harlow, H.F., & Domek, C.J. (1970). Effect of repetitive infant-infant separations of young monkeys. *Journal of Abnormal Psychology, 76,* 161–172.

Super, D.E. (1967). *The psychology of careers.* New York: Harper & Row.

Super, D.E. (1976). *Career education and the meanings of work.* Washington, DC: U.S. Office of Education.

Susman, E.J. (1997). Modeling developmental complexity in adolescence: Hormones and behavior in context. *Journal of Research on Adolescence, 7,* 283–306.

Susman, E.J. (2001). Review of Santrock's *Adolescence,* 9th ed. (New York: McGraw-Hill).

Susman, E., Dorn, L.D., & Schiefelbein, V.L. (2003). Puberty, sexuality, and health. In I.B. Weiner (Ed.), *Handbook of psychology* (Vol. 6). New York: Wiley.

Susman, E.J., Finkelstein, J.W., Chinchilli, V.M., Schwab, J., Liben, L.S., D'Arcangelo, M.R., Meinke, J., Demers, L.M., Lookingbill, G., & Kulin, H.E. (1998). The effect of sex hormone replacement therapy on behavior problems and moods in adolescents with delayed puberty. *Journal of Pediatrics, 133* (4), 521–525.

Susman, E.J., Murowchick, E., Worrall, B.K., & Murray, D.A. (1995, March). *Emotionality, adrenal hormones, and context interactions during puberty and pregnancy.* Paper presented at the meeting of the Society for Research in Child Development, Indianapolis.

Susman, E.J., & Rogol, A. (2004). Puberty and psychological development. In R. Lerner & L. Steinberg (Eds.), *Handbook of adolescent psychology.* New York: Wiley.

Susman, E.J., Schiefelbein, V., & Heaton, J.A. (2002, April). *Cortisol attentuations, puberty, and externalizing behavior: Family adjustment mediators.* Paper presented at the meeting of the Society for Research on Adolescence, New Orleans.

Sutton-Smith, B. (1982). Birth order and sibling status effects. In M.E. Lamb & B. Sutton-Smith (Eds.), *Sibling relationships: Their nature and significance across the life span.* Hillsdale, NJ: Erlbaum.

Swaab, D.F., Chung, W.C., Kruijver, F.P., Hofman, M.A., & Ishunina, T.A. (2001). Structural and functional sex differences in the human hypothalamus. *Hormones and Behavior, 40,* 93–98.

Swaab, D.F., Chung, W.C. Kruijver, F.P., Hofman, M.A., & Ishunina, T.A. (2002). Sexual differentiation of the human hypothalamus. *Advances in Experimental Medicine and Biology, 511,* 75–100.

Swanson, H.L. (1999). What develops in working memory? A life-span perspective. *Developmental Psychology, 35,* 986–1000.

Swarr, A.E., & Richards, M.H. (1996). Longitudinal effects of adolescent girls' pubertal development, perceptions of pubertal timing, and parental relations. *Developmental Psychology, 32,* 636–646.

Swearer, S.M., & Espelage, D.L. (2004). Introduction: A social-ecological framework of bullying among youth. In D.L. Espelage & S.M. Swearer (Eds.), *Bullying in American schools.* Mahwah, NJ: Erlbaum.

Swearer, S.M, Grills, A., Hay, K., & Cary, P. (2004). Internalizing problems in students involved in bullying and victimization: Implications for intervention. In D. Espelage & S. Swearer (Eds.), *Bullying in American schools.* Mahwah, NJ: Erlbaum.

Swim, J.K., Aikin, K.J., Hall, W.S., & Hunter, B.A. (1995). Sexism and racism: Old-fashioned and modern prejudices. *Journal of Personality and Social Psychology, 67,* 199–214.

Takahashi, K., & Majima, N. (1994). Transition from home to college dormitory: The role of preestablished affective relationships in adjustment to a new life. *Journal of Research on Adolescence, 4,* 367–384.

Tamis-LeMonda, C.S., & Cabrera, N. (Eds.). (2002). *The handbook of father involvement.* Mahwah, NJ: Erlbaum.

Tanaka-Matsumi, J. (2001). Abnormal psychology and culture. In D. Matsumoto (Ed.), *The handbook of culture and psychology.* New York: Oxford University Press.

Tannen, D. (1990). *You just don't understand!* New York: Ballantine.

Tapert, S., Brown, G.S., Kindermann, S.S., Cheung, E.H., Frank, L.R., & Brown, S.A. (2001). MRI measurement of brain dysfunction in alcohol-dependent young women. *Alcoholism: Clinical and Experimental Research, 25,* 236–245.

Tarpley, T. (2001). Children, the Internet, and other new technologies. In D. Singer & J. Singer (Eds.), *Handbook of children and the media.* Thousand Oaks, CA: Sage.

Tasker, F.L., & Golombok, S. (1997). *Growing up in a lesbian family: Effects on child development.* New York: Guilford.

Tauber, M., Berro, B., Delagnes, V., Lounis, N., Jouret, B., Pienkowski, C., Oliver, I., & Rochiccioli, P. (2003). Can some growth hormone (GHD)-deficient children benefit from combined therapy with gonadotropin-releasing hormone analogs and GH? Results of a retrospective study. *Journal of Clinical Endocrinology and Metabolism, 88,* 1179–1183.

Tavris, C., & Wade, C. (1984). *The longest war: Sex differences in perspective* (2nd ed.). Fort Worth: Harcourt Brace.

Taylor, J.H., & Walker, L.J. (1997). Moral climate and the development of moral reasoning: The effects of dyadic discussions between young offenders. *Journal of Moral Education, 26,* 21–43.

Taylor, R.D., & Wang, M.C. (2000). *Resilience across contexts.* Mahwah, NJ: Erlbaum.

Taylor, S.E. (2002). *The tending instinct.* New York: Times Books.

Tellegen, A. (1982). *Brief manual of the Multidimensional Personality Questionnaire.* Unpublished manuscript, University of Minnesota.

Tenenbaum, H.R., Callahan, M., Alba-Speyer, C., & Sandoval, L. (2002). Parent-child science conversations in Mexican descent families: Educational background, activity, and past experience as moderators. *Hispanic Journal of Behavioral Sciences, 24,* 225–248.

Terman, D.L., Larner, M.B., Stevenson, C.S., & Behrman, R.E. (1996). Special education for students with disabilities: Analysis and recommendations. *Future of Children, 6* (1), 4–24.

Tesser, A., Fleeson, R.B., & Suls, J.M. (2000). *Psychological perspectives on self and identity.* Washington, DC: American Psychological Association.

Teti, D. (2001). Retrospect and prospect in the psychological study of sibling relationships. In J.P. McHale & W.S. Grolnick (Eds.), *Retrospect and prospect in the psychological study of families.* Mahwah, NJ: Erlbaum.

Tetreault, M.K.T. (1997). Classrooms for diversity: Rethinking curriculum and pedagogy. In J.A. Banks & C.A. Banks (Eds.), *Multicultural education* (3rd ed.). Boston: Allyn & Bacon.

The Conduct Problems Prevention Research Group. (2002). Evaluation of the first 3 years of the Fast Track prevention trial with children at high risk for adolescent conduct problems. *Journal of Abnormal Child Psychology, 30,* 19–35.

Thomas, A., & Chess, S. (1991). Temperament in adolescence and its functional significance. In R.M. Lerner, A.C. Petersen, & J. Brooks-Gunn (Eds.), *Encyclopedia of adolescence* (Vol. 2). New York: Garland.

Thomas, C.W., Coffman, J.K., & Kipp, L.K. (1993, March). *Are only children different from children with siblings? A longitudinal study of behavioral and social functioning.* Paper presented at the biennial meeting of the Society for Research in Child Development, New Orleans.

Thomas, K. (1998, November 4). Teen cyberdating is a new wrinkle for parents, too. *USA Today,* p. 9D.

Thompson, K.M., Crosby, R.D., Wonderlich, S.A., Mitchell, J.E., Redlin, J., Demuth, G., Smyth, J., & Haseltine, B. (2003). Psychopathology and sexual trauma in childhood and adulthood. *Journal of Traumatic Stress, 16,* 35–38.

Thompson, P.M., Giedd, J.N., Woods, R.P., MacDonald, D., Evans, A.C., & Toga, A.W. (2000). Growth patterns in the developing brain detected by using continuum mechanical tensor maps. *Nature, 404,* 190–193.

Thornburg, H.D. (1981). Sources of sex education among early adolescents. *Journal of Early Adolescence, 1,* 171–184.

Thurstone, L.L. (1938). *Primary mental abilities.* Chicago: University of Chicago Press.

Tilton-Weaver, L., & Leighter, S. (2002, April). *Peer management behavior: Linkages to parents' beliefs about adolescents and adolescents' friends.* Paper presented at the meeting of the Society for Research on Adolescence, New Orleans.

Timimi, S., & Taylor, E. (2004). ADHD is best understood as a cultural construct. *British Journal of Psychiatry, 184,* 8–9.

Tinsley, B.J. (2003). *How children learn to be healthy.* New York: Cambridge University Press.

Tolan, P.H. (2001). Emerging themes and challenges in understanding youth violence. *Journal of Clinical Child Psychology, 30,* 233–239.

Tolan, P.H., Guerra, N.G., & Kendall, P.C. (1995). A developmental-ecological perspective on antisocial behavior in children and adolescents: Toward a unified risk and intervention framework. *Journal of Consulting and Clinical Psychology, 63,* 579–584.

Tomlinson-Keasey, C. (1972). Formal operations in females from 11 to 54 years of age. *Developmental Psychology, 6,* 364.

Torff, B. (2000). Multiple intelligences. In A. Kazdin (Ed.), *Encyclopedia of psychology.* Washington, DC, and New York: American Psychological Association and Oxford University Press.

Torney-Purta, J. (1993, August). *Cross-cultural examination of stages of faith development.* Paper presented at the meeting of the American Psychological Association, Toronto.

Tourangeau, R. (2004). Survey research and societal change. *Annual Review of Psychology,* Vol. 55. Palo Alto, CA: Annual Reviews.

Triandis, H.C. (1994). *Culture and social behavior.* New York: McGraw-Hill.

Triandis, H.C. (2000). Cross-cultural psychology. In A. Kazdin (Ed.), *Encyclopedia of psychology.* Washington, DC, and New York: American Psychological Association and Oxford University Press.

Trickett, E.J., & Moos, R.H. (1974). Personal correlates of contrasting environments: Student satisfaction in high school classrooms. *American Journal of Community Psychology, 2,* 1–12.

Trimble, J.E. (1989, August). *The enculturation of contemporary psychology.* Paper presented at the meeting of the American Psychological Association, New Orleans, LA.

Trinidad, D.R., & Johnson, C.A. (2002). The association between emotional intelligence and early adolescent tobacco and alcohol use. *Personality and Individual Differences, 32,* 95–105.

Trulear, H.D. (2000). *Faith-based institutions and high-risk youth: First report to the field.* Philadelphia, PA: Public/Private Ventures.

Tubman, J.G., Windle, M., & Windle, R.C. (1996). The onset and cross-temporal patterning of sexual intercourse in middle adolescence: Prospective relations with behavioral and emotional problems. *Child Development, 67,* 327–343.

Tucker, C.J., McHale, S.M., & Crouter, A.C. (2001). Conditions of sibling support in adolescence. *Journal of Family Psychology, 15,* 254–271.

Tucker, C.J., McHale, S.M., & Crouter, A.C. (2003, April). *Adolescent sibling involvement and sibling personal qualities matter.* Paper presented at the meeting of the Society for Research in Child Development, Tampa.

Tucker, L.A. (1987). Television, teenagers, and health. *Journal of Youth and Adolescence, 16,* 415–425.

Tuckman, B.W., & Hinkle, J.S. (1988). An experimental study of the physical and psychological effects of aerobic exercise on schoolchildren. In B.G. Melamed & others (Eds.), *Child health psychology.* Hillsdale, NJ: Erlbaum.

Tudge, J. (2004). Practice and discourse as the intersection of individual and social in human development. In A.-N. Perret-Clermont, L. Resnick, C. Pontecorvo, & B. Burge (Eds.), *Joining society: Social interactions and learning in adolescence and youth.* New York: Cambridge University Press.

Tudge, J., & Scrimsher, S. (2003). Lev S. Vygotsky on education: A cultural-historical, interpersonal, and individual approach to development. In B.J. Zimmerman & D.H. Schunk (Eds.), *Educational psychology: A century of contributions.* Mahwah, NJ: Lawrence Erlbaum Associates.

Turiel, E. (1998). The development of morality. In N. Eisenberg (Ed.), *Handbook of child psychology* (5th ed., Vol. 3). New York: Wiley.

Turiel, E. (2003). *The culture of morality.* New York: Cambridge University Press.

Twenge, J.M., & Campbell, W.K. (2001). Age and birth cohort differences in self-esteem: A cross-temporal meta-analysis. *Personality and Social Psychology Bulletin, 5,* 321–344.

U.S. Census Bureau. (2002). *National population projections I. Summary files.* Washington, DC: U.S. Bureau of the Census.

U.S. Department of Commerce (2002). *A nation online: How Americans are expanding their use of the Internet.* Washington, DC: U.S. Department of Commerce.

U.S. Department of Education. (1996). *Number and disabilities of children and youth served under IDEA.* Washington, DC: Office of Special Education Programs, Data Analysis System.

U.S. Department of Education. (2000). *Trends in educational equity for girls and women.* Washington, DC: Author.

U.S. Department of Energy. (2001). *The human genome project.* Washington, DC: Author.

Udry, J.R. (1990). Hormonal and social determinants of adolescent sexual initiation. In J. Bancroft & J.M. Reinisch (Eds.), *Adolescence and puberty.* New York: Oxford University Press.

Underwood, M. (2002). Sticks and stones and social exclusion: Aggression among boys and girls. In P.K. Smith & C.H. Hart (Eds.), *Blackwell handbook of childhood social development.* Malden, MA: Blackwell.

Underwood, M. (2003). *Social aggression among girls.* New York: Guilford Press.

Underwood, M.K., & Hurley, J.C. (1997, April). *Children's responses to angry provocation as a function of peer status and aggression.* Paper presented at the meeting of the Society for Research in Child Development, Washington, DC.

Underwood, M.K., & Hurley, J.C. (2000). Emotion regulation in peer relationships in middle childhood. In L. Balter & C.S. Tamis-LeMonda (Eds.), *Child psychology.* Philadelphia: Psychology Press.

Unger, R., & Crawford, M. (2004). *Women and gender* (4th ed.). New York: McGraw-Hill.

UNICEF. (2000). *Educating girls, transforming the future.* Geneva: UNICEF.

UNICEF. (2002). *A league table of educational disadvantage in rich nations.* Florence, Italy: UNICEF Innocenti Research Center.

UNICEF. (2002). *Annual report: 2002.* Geneva, SWIT: UNICEF.

Urberg, K. (1992). Locus of peer influence: Social crowd and best friend. *Journal of Youth and Adolescence, 21,* 439–450.

Urberg, K.A., Degirmencioglu, S.M., Tolson, J.M., & Halliday-Scher, K. (1995). The structure of adolescent peer networks. *Developmental Psychology, 31,* 540–547.

Urberg, K.A., Goldstein, M.S., & Toro, P. (2002, April). *Social moderators of the effects of parent and peer drinking on adolescent drinking.* Paper presented at the meeting of the Society for Research on Adolescence, New Orleans.

Urdan, T., & Midgley, C. (2001). Academic self-handicapping: What we know, what more is there to learn. *Educational Psychology Review, 13,* 115–138.

Urdan, T., Midgley, C., & Anderman, E.M. (1998). The role of classroom goal structure in students' use of self-handicapping strategies. *American Educational Research Journal, 35,* 101–122.

Usher, B., Zahn-Waxler, C., Finch, C., & Gunlicks, M. (2000, April). *The relation between global self-esteem, perceived competence, and risk for psychopathology in adolescence.* Paper presented at the meeting of the Society for Research on Adolescence, Chicago.

Valencia, R.R., & Suzuki, L.A. (2001). *Intelligence testing and minority students.* Thousand Oaks, GA: Sage.

Valentine, J.C., Cooper, H., Bettencourt, B.A., & Dubois, D.L. (2002). Out-of-school activities and academic achievement: The mediating role of self-beliefs. *Educational Psychologist, 37,* 245–256.

Van Buren, E., & Graham, S. (2003). *Redefining ethnic identity: Its relationship to positive and negative school adjustment outcomes for minority youth.* Paper presented at the meeting of the Society for Research in Child Development, Tampa.

van Dijk, T.A. (1987). *Communicating racism.* Newbury Park, CA: Sage.

Van Evra, J. (2004). *Television and child development* (3rd ed.). Mahwah, NJ: Erlbaum.

Van Goozen, S.H.M., Matthys, W., Cohen-Kettenis, P.T., Thisjssen, J.H.H., & van

Engeland, H. (1998). Adrenal androgens and aggression in conduct disorder prepubertal boys and normal control. *Biological Psychiatry 43,* 156–158.

Van Hoof, A. (1999). The identity status field re-reviewed: An update of unresolved and neglected issues with a view on some alternative approaches. *Developmental Review, 19,* 497–565.

Vandell, D.L., Minnett, A., & Santrock, J.W. (1987). Age differences in sibling relationships during middle childhood. *Applied Developmental Psychology, 8,* 247–257.

Velasquez, R.J., Arellano, L.M., & McNeill, B.W. (Eds.). (2004). *Handbook of Chicana/o psychology and mental health.* Mahwah, NJ: Erlbaum.

Venter, J.E. (2003). A part of the human genome sequence. *Science, 299,* 1183–1184.

Verma, S., & Saraswathi, T.S. (2002). Adolescence in India: Street urchins or Silicon Valley millionaires? In B.B. Brown, R.W. Larson, & T.S. Saraswathi (Eds.), *The world's youth.* New York: Cambridge University Press.

Vernberg, E.M. (1990). Psychological adjustment and experience with peers during early adolescence: Reciprocal, incidental, or unidirectional relationships? *Journal of Abnormal Child Psychology, 18,* 187–198.

Vernberg, E.M., Ewell, K.K., Beery, S.H., & Abwender, D.A. (1994). Sophistication of adolescents' interpersonal negotiation strategies and friendship formation after relocation: A naturally occurring experiment. *Journal of Research on Adolescence, 4,* 5–19.

Vidal, F. (2000). Piaget, Jean. In A. Kazdin (Ed.), *Encyclopedia of psychology.* Washington, DC, and New York: American Psychological Association and Oxford University Press.

Vondracek, F.W. (1991). Vocational development and choice in adolescence. In R.M. Lerner, A.C. Petersen, & J. Brooks-Gunn (Eds.), *Encyclopedia of adolescence* (Vol. 2). New York: Garland.

Vondracek, F.W., & Porfeli, E.J. (2003). The world of work and careers. In G. Adams & M. Berzonsky (Eds.), *Blackwell handbook of adolescence.* Malden, MA: Blackwell.

Vygotsky, L.S. (1962). *Thought and language.* Cambridge, MA: MIT Press.

Wachs, T.D. (1994). Fit, context and the transition between temperament and personality. In C. Halverson, G. Kohnstamm, & R. Martin (Eds.), *The developing structure of personality from infancy to adulthood.* Hillsdale, NJ: Erlbaum.

Wachs, T.D. (2000). *Necessary but not sufficient.* Washington, DC: American Psychological Association.

Wachs, T.D., & Kohnstamm, G.A. (Eds.). (2001). *Temperament in context.* Mahwah, NJ: Erlbaum.

Wadsworth, S.J., Corley, R.P., Hewitt, J.K., Plomin, R., & DeFries, J.C. (2003). Parent-offspring resemblance for reading performance at 7, 12, and 16 years of age in the Colorado Adoption Study. *Journal of Child Psychology and Psychiatry, 43,* 769–774.

Wagennar, A.C. (1983). *Alcohol, young drivers, and traffic accidents.* Lexington, MA: D.C. Heath.

Wagner, R.K. (1997). Intelligence, training, and employment. *American Psychologist, 52,* 1059–1069.

Wagner, R.K., & Sternberg, R.J. (1986). Tacit knowledge and intelligent functioning in the everyday world. In R.J. Sternberg & R.K. Wagner (Eds.), *Practical intelligence.* New York: Cambridge University Press.

Waldron, H.B., Brody, J.L., & Slesnick, N. (2001). Integrative behavioral and family therapy for adolescent substance abuse. In P.M. Monti, S.M. Colby, & T.A. O'Leary (Eds.), *Adolescents, alcohol, and substance abuse.* New York: Guilford.

Walker, E.F. (2002). Adolescent neurodevelopment and psychopathology. *Current Directions in Psychological Science, 1,* 24–28.

Walker, H. (1998, May 31). Youth violence: Society's problem. *Eugene Register Guard,* p. 1C.

Walker, L.J. (1996). Unpublished review of J.W. Santrock's *Child development,* 8th ed. (New York: McGraw-Hill).

Walker, L.J., deVries, B., & Trevethan, S.D. (1987). Moral stages and moral orientation in real-life and hypothetical dilemmas. *Child Development, 58,* 842–858.

Walker, L.J., Hennig, K.H., & Krettenauer, R. (2000). Parent and peer contexts for children's moral reasoning development. *Child Development, 71,* 1033–1048.

Walker, L.J., & Pitts, R.C. (1998). Naturalistic conceptions of moral maturity. *Developmental Psychology, 34,* 403–419.

Walker, L.J., Pitts, R.C., Hennig, K.H., & Matsuba, M.K. (1995). Reasoning about morality and real-life moral problems. In M. Killen & D. Hart (Eds.), *Morality in everyday life.* New York: Cambridge University Press.

Walker, L.J., & Taylor, J.H. (1991). Family interaction and the development of moral reasoning. *Child Development, 62,* 264–283.

Wallace-Broscious, A., Serafica, F.C., & Osipow, S.H. (1994). Adolescent career development: Relationships to self-concept and identity status. *Journal of Research on Adolescence, 4,* 127–150.

Wallerstein, J.S., & Johnson-Reitz, L. (2004). Communication in divorced and single parent families. In A.L. Vangelisti (Ed.), *Handbook of family communication.* Mahwah, NJ: Erlbaum.

Wallis, C. (1985, December 9). Children having children. *Time,* pp. 78–88.

Walter, C.A. (1986). *The timing of motherhood.* Lexington, MA: D.C. Heath.

Walters, E., & Kendler, K.S. (1994). Anorexia nervosa and anorexia-like symptoms in a population based twin sample. *American Journal of Psychiatry, 152,* 62–71.

Wandersman, A., & Florin, P. (2003). Community interventions and effective prevention. *American Psychologist, 58,* 441–448.

Wang, G., & Dietz, W.H. (2002). Economic burden of obesity in youths aged 6 to 17 years: 1979–1999. *Pediatrics, 109,* e81.

Wang, J.Q. (2000, November). *A comparison of two international standards to assess child and adolescent obesity in three populations.* Paper presented at the meeting of American Public Health Association, Boston.

Wang, Y., Monteiro, C., & Popkin, B.M. (2002). Trends in obesity and underweight in older children and adolescents in the United States, Brazil, China, and Russia. *American Journal of Clinical Nutrition, 75,* 971–977.

Ward, L.M. (1995). Talking about sex: Common themes about sexuality in the prime-time television programs children and adolescents view most. *Journal of Youth and Adolescence, 24,* 595–615.

Ward, L.M. (2002). Does television exposure affect emerging adults' attitudes and assumptions about sexual relationships? Correlational and experimental confirmation. *Journal of Youth and Adolescence, 31,* 1–15.

Ward, L.M. (2003). Understanding the role of entertainment media in the sexual socialization of American youth: A review of empirical research. *Developmental Review, 23,* 347–388.

Ward, L.M., Gorvine, B., & Cytron, A. (2002). Would that really happen? Adolescents' perceptions of sexual relationships according to prime-time television. In J.D. Brown, J.R. Steele, & K. Walsh-Childers

(Eds.), *Sexual teens, sexual media*. Mahwah, NJ: Erlbaum.

Wark, G.R., & Krebs, D.L. (1996). Gender and dilemma differences in real-life moral judgment. *Developmental Psychology, 32,* 220–230.

Wark, G.R., & Krebs, D.L. (in press). The construction of moral dilemmas in everyday life. *Journal of Moral Education.*

Wass, H., Miller, M.D., & Redditt, C.A. (1991). Adolescents and destructive themes in rock music: A follow-up. *Omega, 23,* 199–206.

Waterman, A.S. (1985). Identity in the context of adolescent psychology. In A.S. Waterman (Ed.), *Identity in adolescence: Processes and contents*. San Francisco: Jossey-Bass.

Waterman, A.S. (1989). Curricula interventions for identity change: Substantive and ethical considerations. *Journal of Adolescence, 12,* 389–400.

Waterman, A.S. (1992). Identity as an aspect of optimal psychological functioning. In G.R. Adams, T.P. Gullotta, & R. Montemayor (Eds.), *Adolescent identity formation*. Newbury Park, CA: Sage.

Waterman, A.S. (1997). An overview of service-learning and the role of research and evaluation in service-learning programs. In A.S. Waterman (Ed.), *Service learning.* Mahwah, NJ: Erlbaum.

Waterman, A.S. (1999). Identity, the identity statuses, and identity status development: A contemporary statement. *Developmental Review, 19,* 591–621.

Watras, J. (2002). *The foundations of educational curriculum and diversity: 1565 to the present.* Boston: McGraw-Hill.

Watts, C., & Zimmerman, C. (2002). Violence against women: Global scope and magnitude. *Lancet, 359,* 1232–1237.

Wechsler, D. (1939). *The measurement of adult intelligence*. Baltimore: Williams & Wilkins.

Wechsler, H., Davenport, A., Sowdall, G., Moetykens, B., & Castillo, S. (1994). Health and behavioral consequences of binge drinking in college. *Journal of the American Medical Association, 272,* 1672–1677.

Wechsler, H., Lee, J.E., Kuo, M., Seibring, M., Nelson, T.F., & Lee, H. (2002). Trends in college binge drinking during a period of increased prevention efforts: Findings from 4 Harvard School of Public Health college alcohol study surveys: 1993–2001. *Journal of American College Health, 50,* 203–217.

Weineke, J.K., Thurston, S.W., Kelsey, K.T., Varkonyi, A., Wain, J.C., Mark, E.J., & Christiani, D.C. (1999). Early age at smoking initiation and tobacco carcinogen DNA damage in the lung. *Journal of the National Cancer Institute, 91,* 614–619.

Weiner, B. (1986). *An attributional theory of motivation and emotion.* New York: Springer.

Weiner, B. (1992). *Human motivation: Metaphors, theories, and research.* Newbury Park, CA: Sage.

Weiner, B. (2000). Motivation: An overview. In A. Kazdin (Ed.), *Encyclopedia of psychology.* Washington, DC, and New York: American Psychological Association and Oxford University Press.

Weinstein, C.S. (2003). *Secondary classroom management,* 2nd ed. New York: McGraw-Hill.

Weise, M., Eisenhofer, G., & Merke, D.P. (2002). Pubertal and gender-related changes in the sympathoadrenal system in healthy children. *Clinical Endocrinology and Metabolism, 87,* 5038–5043.

Weiss, R.S. (1973). *Loneliness: The experience of emotional and social isolation.* Cambridge, MA: MIT Press.

Weissberg, R., & Caplan, M. (1989, April). *A follow-up study of a school-based social competence program for young adolescents.* Paper presented at the meeting of the Society for Research in Child Development, Kansas City.

Weissberg, R.P., & Greenberg, M.T. (1998). School and community competence—Enhancement and prevention interventions. In I.E. Siegel & K.A. Renninger (Eds.), *Handbook of child psychology* (5th ed., Vol. 4). New York: Wiley.

Weissberg, R.P., Kumpfer, K.L., & Seligman, M.E.P. (2003). Prevention that works for children and youth. *American Psychologist, 58,* 425–432.

Weisz, A.N., & Black, B.M. (2002). Gender and moral reasoning: African American youth respond to dating dilemmas. *Journal of Human Behavior in the Social Environment, 5,* 35–52.

Welsh, D.P., Grello, C.M., & Harper, M.S. (2003). When love hurts: Depression and adolescent romantic relations. In P. Florsheim (Ed.), *Adolescent romantic relations and sexual behavior.* Mahwah, NJ: Erlbaum.

Welt, C.K., Pagan, Y.L., Smith, P.C., Rado, K.B., & Hall, J.E. (2003). Control of follicle-stimulating hormone by estradiol and the inhibins: Critical role of estradiol at the hypothalamus during the luteal-follecar transition. *Journal of Endocrinology and Metabolism, 88,* l766–1771.

Welti, C. (2002). Adolescents in Latin America: Facing the future with skepticism. In B.B. Brown, R.W. Larson, & T.S. Saraswathi (Eds.), *The world's youth.* New York: Cambridge University Press.

Welti, C. (2002). Adolescents in South America: Facing the future with skepticism. In B.B. Brown, R.W. Larson, & T.S. Saraswathi (Eds.), *The world's youth.* New York: Cambridge University Press.

Weng, A., & Montemayor, R. (1997, April). *Conflict between mothers and adolescents.* Paper presented at the meeting of the Society for Research in Child Development, Washington, DC.

Wenter, D.L., Ennett, S.T., Ribsil, K.M., Vincus, A.A., Rohrbach, L., Ringwalt, C.L., & Jones, S.M. (2002). Comprehensiveness of substance use prevention programs in U.S. middle schools. *Journal of Adolescent Health, 30,* 445–462.

Wentzel, K.R. (2002). Are effective teachers like good parents? Teaching styles and student adjustment in early adolescence. *Child Development, 73,* 287–301.

Wentzel, K.R. (2003). School adjustment. In I.B. Weiner (Ed.), *Handbook of psychology* (Vol. 7). New York: Wiley.

Wentzel, K.R., & Ahser, S.R. (1995). The academic lives of neglected, rejected, popular, and controversial children. *Child Development, 66,* 754–763.

Wentzel, K.R., & Caldwell, K. (1997). Close friend and group influence on adolescent cigarette smoking and alcohol use. *Child Development, 31,* 540–547.

Werner, E.E., & Smith, R.S. (1982). *Vulnerable but invincible: A study of resilient children.* New York: McGraw-Hill

Wertlieb, D., Jacobs, F., & Lerner, R.M. (2003). Enhancing civil society through youth development: A view of the issues. In R.M. Lerner, F. Jacobs, & D. Wertlieb (Eds.), *Handbook of applied developmental science* (Vol. 3). Thousand Oaks, CA: Sage.

Wertsch, J. (2000). Cognitive development. In M. Bennett (Ed.), *Developmental psychology.* Philadelphia: Psychology Press.

Weyman, A. (2003). Promoting sexual health to young people. *Journal of Research on Social Health, 123,* 6–7.

Whalen, C.K. (2000). Attention deficit hyperactivity disorder. In A. Kazdin (Ed.), *Encyclopedia of psychology.* Washington, DC, and New York: American Psychological

Association and Oxford University Press.

Whalen, C.K. (2001). ADHD treatment in the 21st century: Pushing the envelope. *Journal of Clinical Child Psychology, 30,* 136–140.

White, J.W. (2001). Aggression and gender. In J. Worrell (Ed.), *Encyclopedia of women and gender.* San Diego: Academic Press.

White, L., & Gilbreth, J.G. (2001). When children have two fathers: Effects of relationships with stepfathers and noncustodial fathers on adolescent outcomes. *Journal of Marriage and the Family, 63,* 155–167.

White, M. (1993). *The material child: Coming of age in Japan and America.* New York: Free Press.

Whiting, B.B. (1989, April). *Culture and interpersonal behavior.* Paper presented at the meeting of the Society for Research in Child Development, Kansas City.

Whitley, B.E. (2002). *Principles of research in behavioral science* (2nd ed.). New York: McGraw-Hill.

Whitman, F.L., Diamond, M., & Martin, J. (1993). Homosexual orientation in twins: A report on 61 pairs and three triplet sets. *Archives of Sexual Behavior, 22,* 187–206.

Wiesner, M., & Ittel, A. (2002). Relations of pubertal timing and depressive symptoms to substance use in early adolescence. *Journal of Early Adolescence, 22* (1), 5–23.

Wigfield, A., & Eccles, J.S. (1989). Test anxiety in elementary and secondary school students. *Journal of Educational Psychology, 24,* 159–183.

Wigfield, A., & Eccles, J.S. (Eds.). (2001). *Development of achievement motivation.* San Diego: Academic Press.

William T. Grant Foundation Commission on Work, Family, and Citizenship. (1988, February). *The forgotten half: Noncollege-bound youth in America.* New York: William T. Grant Foundation.

Williams, C., & Bybee, J. (1994). What do children feel guilty about? Developmental and gender differences. *Developmental Psychology, 30,* 617–623.

Williams, D.D., Yancher, S.C., Jensen, L.C., & Lewis, C. (2003). Character education in a public high school: A multi-year inquiry into unified studies. *Journal of Moral Education, 32,* 3–33.

Williams, F., & Schmidt, M. (2003, April). *Parent and peer relationships predicting early adolescent sexual behavior.* Paper presented at the meeting of the Society for Research in Child Development, Tampa.

Williams, J.E., & Best, D.L. (1982). *Measuring sex stereotypes: A thirty-nation study.* Newbury Park, CA: Sage.

Williams, J.E., & Best, D.L. (1989). *Sex and psyche: Self-concept viewed cross-culturally.* Newbury Park, CA: Sage.

Williams, T.M., Baron, D., Phillips, S., David, L., & Jackson, D. (1986, August). *The portrayal of sex roles on Canadian and U.S. television.* Paper presented at the conference of the International Association for Mass Media Research, New Delhi, India.

Williams, T.M., & Cox, R. (1995, March). *Informative versus other children's TV programs: Portrayals of ethnic diversity, gender, and aggression.* Paper presented at the meeting of the Society for Research in Child Development, Indianapolis.

Wilson, B.J., & Gottman, J.M. (1995). Marital interaction and parenting. In M.H. Bornstein (Ed.), *Children and parenting* (Vol. 4). Hillsdale, NJ: Erlbaum.

Wilson, J.W. (1987). *The truly disadvantaged: The inner city, the underclass, and public policy.* Chicago: University of Chicago Press.

Wilson, M.N. (2000). Cultural diversity. In A. Kazdin (Ed.), *Encyclopedia of psychology.* Washington, DC, and New York: American Psychological Association and Oxford University Press.

Wilson, M.N., Cook, D.Y., & Arrington, E.G. (1997). African-American adolescents and academic achievement: Family and peer influences. In R.D. Taylor & M.C. Wang (Eds.), *Social and emotional adjustment and relations in ethnic minority families.* Mahwah, NJ: Erlbaum.

Wilson-Shockley, S. (1995). *Gender differences in adolescent depression: The contribution of negative affect.* M.S. thesis, University of Illinois at Urbana-Champaign.

Windle, M. (1989). Substance use and abuse among adolescent runaways: A four-year follow-up study. *Journal of Youth and Adolescence, 18,* 331–341.

Windle, M., & Dumenci, L. (1998). An investigation of maternal and adolescent depressed mood using a latent trait-state model. *Journal of Research on Adolescence, 8,* 461–484.

Windle, M., & Windle, R.C. (2003). Alcohol and other substance use and abuse. In G. Adams & M. Berzonsky (Eds.), *Blackwell handbook of adolescence.* Malden, MA: Blackwell.

Winne, P.H. (1995). Inherent details in self-regulated learning. *Educational Psychologist, 30,* 173–187.

Winne, P.H. (1997). Experimenting to boot strap self-regulated learning. *Journal of Educational Psychology 89,* 397–410.

Winne, P.H., & Perry, N.E. (2000). Measuring self-regulated learning. In M. Boekaerts, P.R. Pintrich, & M. Zeidner (Eds.), *Handbook of self-regulation.* San Diego: Academic Press.

Winner, E. (1996). *Gifted children: Myths and realities.* New York: Basic Books.

Winner, E. (2000). The origins and ends of giftedness. *American Psychologist, 55,* 159–169.

Wodarski, J.S., & Hoffman, S.D. (1984). Alcohol education for adolescents. *Social Work in Education, 6,* 69–92.

Wolfe, S.M., Toro, P.A., & McCaskill, P.A. (1999). A comparison of homeless and matched housed adolescents on family environment variables. *Journal of Research on Adolescence, 9,* 53–66.

Wong, C.A. (1997, April). *What does it mean to be an African-American or European-American growing up in a multi-ethnic community?* Paper presented at the meeting of the Society for Research in Child Development, Washington, DC.

Wong, C.A., Eccles, J.S., & Sameroff, A. (2001, April). *Ethnic discrimination and ethnic identification: The influence of African Americans' and Whites' school and socioemotional development.* Paper presented at the meeting of the Society for Research in Child Development, Minneapolis.

Wong, CA., & Rowley, S.J. (2001). The schooling of ethnic minority children: A commentary. *Educational Psychologist, 36,* 57–66.

Wood, J.T. (2001). *Gendered lives.* Belmont, CA: Wadsworth.

Woodard, E. (2000). *Media in the home 2000: The fifth annual survey of parents and children.* Philadelphia: The Annenberg Public Policy Center.

Woodrich, D.L. (1994). *Attention-deficit hyperactivity disorder: What every parent should know.* Baltimore: Paul H. Brookes.

Work Group of the American Psychological Association's Board of Educational Affairs. (1995). *Learner-centered psychological principles: A framework for school redesign and reform (draft).* Washington, DC: American Psychological Association.

World Health Organization. (2000). *The world health report.* Geneva: Author.

World Health Organization. (2002). *The world health report 2002.* Geneva, Switzerland: World Health Organization.

World Health Organization. (February 2, 2000). *Adolescent health behavior in 28 countries.* Geneva: Author.

Wylie, R. (1979). *The self concept. Vol. 2.: Theory and research on selected topics.* Lincoln: University of Nebraska Press.

Yang, S., & Sternberg, R.J. (1997). Taiwanese Chinese people's conceptions of intelligence. *Intelligence, 25,* 21–36.

Yanovski, J.A., Rose, S.R., Municchi, G., Pescovitz, O.H., Hill, S.C., Cassorla, F.G., & Cutler, G.B. (2003). Treatment with a luteinizing hormone-releasing hormone agonist in adolescents with short stature. *New England Journal of Medicine, 348,* 908–917.

Yates, M. (1995, March). *Community service and political-moral discussions among Black urban adolescents.* Paper presented at the meeting of the Society for Research in Child Development, Indianapolis.

Yeakey, C.C., & Henderson, R.D. (Eds.). (2002). *Surmounting the odds: Equalizing educational opportunity in the new millenium.* Greenwich, CT: IAP.

Yeung, W.J., Sandberg, J.F., Davis-Kearn, P.E., & Hofferth, S.L. (1999, April). *Children's time with fathers in intact families.* Paper presented at the meeting of the Society for Research in Child Development, Albuquerque.

Yin, Y., Buhrmester, D., & Hibbard, D. (1996, March). *Are there developmental changes in the influence of relationships with parents and friends on adjustment during early adolescence?* Paper presented at the meeting of the Society for Research on Adolescence, Boston.

Young, R.A. (1994). Helping adolescents with career development: The active role of parents. *Career Development Quarterly, 42,* 195–203.

Youniss, J. (1980). *Parents and peers in the social environment: A Sullivan Piaget perspective.* Chicago: University of Chicago Press.

Youniss, J. (2002, April). *Youth civic engagement in the 21st century.* Paper presented at the meeting of the Society for Research on Adolescence, New Orleans.

Youniss, J., McLellan, J.A., & Strouse, D. (1994). "We're popular but we're not snobs": Adolescents describe their crowds. In R.

Montemayor, G.R. Adams, & T.P. Gullotta (Eds.), *Advances in adolescent development: Vol. 6. Personal relationships during adolescence.* Newbury Park, CA: Sage.

Youniss, J., McLellan, J.A., & Yates, M. (1997). What we know about engendering civic identity. *American Behavioral Scientist, 40,* 620–631.

Youniss, J., McLellan, J.A., & Yates, M. (1999). Religion, community service, and identity in American youth. *Journal of Adolescence, 22,* 243–253.

Youniss, J., & Ruth, A.J. (2002). Approaching policy for adolescent development in the 21st century. In J.T. Mortimer & R.W. Larson (Eds.), *The changing adolescent experience.* New York: Cambridge University Press.

Youniss, J., & Silbereisen, R. (2003). Civic and community engagement of adolescents in the 21st century. In G. Adams & M. Berzonsky (Eds.), *Blackwell handbook of adolescence.* Malden, MA: Blackwell.

Youniss, J., Silbereisen, R., Christmas-Best, V., Bales, S., Diversi, M., & McLaughlin, M. (2003). Civic and community engagement of adolescents in the 21st century. In R. Larson, B. Brown, & J. Mortimer (Eds.), *Adolescents' preparation for the future: perils and promises.* Malden, MA: Blackwell.

Yussen, S.R. (1977). Characteristics of moral dilemmas written by adolescents. *Developmental Psychology, 13,* 162–163.

Zabin, L.S. (1986, May/June). Evaluation of a pregnancy prevention program for urban teenagers. *Family Planning Perspectives,* p. 119.

Zabin, L.S., Hirsch, M.B., & Emerson, M.R. (1989). When urban adolescents choose abortion: Effects on education, psychological status and subsequent pregnancy. *Family Planning Perspectives, 21,* 248–255.

Zager, K., & Rubenstein, A. (2002). *The inside story on teen girls.* Washington, DC: American Psychological Association.

Zelnik, M., & Kantner, J.F. (1977). Sexual and contraceptive experiences of young unmarried women in the United States, 1976 and 1971. *Family Planning Perspectives, 9,* 55–71.

Zhou, Q., Eisenberg, N., Losoya, S.H., Fabes, R.A., Reiser, M., Gutherie, I.K., Murphy, B.C., Cumberland, A.J., &

Shepard, S.A. (2002). The relations of parental warmth and expressiveness to children's empathy-related responding and social functioning: A longitudinal study. *Child Development, 73,* 893–915.

Zhu, J., Weiss, L.G., Prifitera, A., & Coalson, D. (2004). The Wechsler Intelligence Scale for children and adolescents. In M. Hersen (Ed.), *Comprehensive handbook of psychological assessment* (Vol. 1). New York: Wiley.

Zill, N., Morrison, D.R., & Coiro, M.J. (1993). Long-term effects of parental divorce on parent-child relationships, adjustment, and achievement in young adulthood. *Journal of Family Psychology, 7,* 91–103.

Zimbardo, P. (1997, May). What messages are behind today's cults? *APA Monitor,* p. 14.

Zimmer-Gembeck, M.J., & Collins, W.A. (2003). Autonomy development during adolescence. In G. Adams & M. Berzonsky (Eds.), *Blackwell handbook of adolescence.* Malden, MA: Blackwell.

Zimmer-Gembeck, M.J., Doyle, L., & Daniels, J.A. (2001). Contraceptive dispensing and selection in school-based health centers. *Journal of Adolescent Health, 29,* 177–185.

Zimmerman, B.J. (2000). Attaining self-regulation: A social cognitive perspective. In M. Boekaerts, P.R. Pintrich, & M. Zeidner (Eds.), *Handbook of self-regulation.* San Diego: Academic Press.

Zimmerman, B.J. (2002). Achieving academic excellence: A self-regulatory perspective. In M. Ferrari (Ed.), *The pursuit of excellence through education.* Mahwah, NJ: Erlbaum.

Zimmerman, B.J., Bonner, S., & Kovach, R. (1996). *Developing self-regulated learners.* Washington, DC: American Psychological Association.

Zimmerman, B.J., & Schunk, D.H. (2002). Albert Bandura: The scholar and his contributions to educational psychology. In B.J. Zimmerman & D.H. Schunk (Eds.), *Educational psychology.* Mahwah, NJ: Erlbaum.

Zimmerman, B.J., & Schunk, D.H. (2004). Self-regulating intellectual processes and outcomes. In D.Y. Dai & R.J. Sternberg (Eds.), *Motivation, emotion, and cognition.* Mahwah, NJ: Erlbaum.

Zimmerman, M.A., Copeland, L.A., & Shope, J.T. (1997, April). *A longitudinal study of self-esteem: Implications for adolescent development.* Paper presented at the meeting of the Society for Research in Child Development, Washington, DC.

Zimmerman, R.S., Khoury, E., Vega, W.A., Gil, A.G., & Warheit, G.J. (1995). Teacher and student perceptions of behavior problems among a sample of African American, Hispanic, and non-Hispanic White students. *American Journal of Community Psychology, 23,* 181–197.

Zucker, A.N., Ostrove, J.M., & Stewart, A.J. (2002). College educated women's personality development in adulthood: Perceptions and age differences. *Psychology and Aging, 17,* 236–244.

Zukow-Goldring, P. (2002). Sibling caregiving. In M.H. Bornstein (Ed.), *Handbook of parenting* (Vol. 3). Mahwah, NJ: Erlbaum.

Credits

LINE ART AND TEXT

Chapter 1

Figure 1.1: After data presented by the U.S. Census Bureau (2002). *National population projections I. Summary Files.* Washington, DC: U.S. Bureau of the Census. **Figure 1.2:** After data presented by the U.S. Census Bureau (2002). *National population projections I. Summary Files.* Washington, DC: U.S. Bureau of the Census. **Figure 1.3:** From John W. Santrock, *Life-Span Development*, 9e, Fig. 1.5, p. 19. Copyright © The McGraw-Hill Companies, Inc. Reprinted with permission. **Figure 1.4:** (Line art) From John W. Santrock, *Life-Span Development*, 9e, Fig. 1.6, p. 21. Copyright © The McGraw-Hill Companies, Inc. Reprinted with permission. **Figure 1.5:** From J. Arnett, "Emerging Adulthood," in *American Psychologist*, Vol. 55, pp. 469–480, Figure 2. Copyright © 2000 by the American Psychological Association. Reprinted with permission.

Chapter 2

Figure 2.1: From John W. Santrock, *Life-Span Development*, 9e, Fig. 2.1, p. 45. Copyright © The McGraw-Hill Companies, Inc. Reprinted with permission. **Figure 2.3:** From John W. Santrock, *Life-Span Development*, 9e, Fig. 2.2, p. 46. Copyright © The McGraw-Hill Companies, Inc. Reprinted with permission. **Figure 2.4:** From John W. Santrock, *Psychology*, 7e, Fig. 4.7, p. 129. Copyright © The McGraw-Hill Companies, Inc. Reprinted with permission. **Figure 2.5:** From John W. Santrock, *Psychology*, 7e, Fig. 12.6, p. 487. Copyright © The McGraw-Hill Companies, Inc. Reprinted with permission. **Figure 2.6:** From John W. Santrock, *Life-Span Development*, 9e, Fig. 2.5, p. 55. Copyright © The McGraw-Hill Companies, Inc. Reprinted with permission. **Figure 2.7:** From John W. Santrock, *Life-Span Development*, 9e, Fig. 2.8, p. 60. Copyright © The McGraw-Hill Companies, Inc. Reprinted with permission. **Figure 2.10:** From John W. Santrock, *Psychology*, 7e, Fig. 2.4. Copyright © The McGraw-Hill Companies, Inc. Reprinted with permission. **Figure 2.11:** From John W. Santrock, *Psychology*, 7e, Fig. 2.5. Copyright © The McGraw-Hill Companies, Inc. Reprinted with permission. **Figure 2.12:** From John W. Santrock, *Life-Span Development*, 9e, Fig. 2.11, p. 64. Copyright © The McGraw-Hill Companies, Inc. Reprinted with permission.

Chapter 3

Figure 3.1: From John W. Santrock, *Adolescence*, 8e, Fig. 13.4, p. 443. Copyright © The McGraw-Hill Companies, Inc. Reprinted with permission. **Figure 3.2:** From John W. Santrock, *Children*, Fig. 15.2, p. 445. Copyright © The McGraw-Hill Companies, Inc. Reprinted with permission. **Figure 3.3:** From M. Grumbach, J. Roth, S. Kaplan & R. Kelch, "Hypothalamic-Pituitary Regulation of Puberty in Man," in Grumbach et al. *Control of the Onset of Puberty*, 1974. © 1974. Reprinted by permission of the publisher, Lippincott Williams & Wilkins. **Figure 3.4:** From J. M. Tanner, R. H. Whitehouse, and M. Takaishi, "Standards from Birth to Maturity for Height, Weight, Height Velocity, and Weight Velocity: British Children 1965," *Archives of Diseases in Childhood*, 1966, v. 41, pp. 613–633. Copyright ©1966. With permission from the BMJ Publishing Group. **Figure 3.6:** From John W. Santrock, *Children*, Fig. 15.5, p. 447. Copyright © The McGraw-Hill Companies, Inc. Reprinted with permission. **Figure 3.7:** From A. F. Roache, "Secular Trends in Stature, Weight and Maturation," *Monographs of the Society for Research in Child Development*, n. 179. (c) Society for Research in Child Development. Reprinted with permission of the Society for Research in Child Development. **Figure 3.8:** From Simmons, R.G.; Blyth, D.A.; & McKinney, K.L. (1983). "The Social and Psychological Effects of Puberty on White Females." In J. Brooks-Gunn & A.C. Petersen (Eds.), *Girls At Puberty: Biological and Psychological Perspectives* (pp. 229–272). NY: Plenum Press. Reprinted with permission. **Figure 3.9:** From John W. Santrock, *Child Development*, Fig. 5.1, p. 131. Copyright © The McGraw-Hill Companies Inc.. Reprinted with permission. **Figure 3.10:** From Arun Dabholkar, "Regional Differences in Synaptogenesis in Human Cerebral Cortex," *Journal of Comparative Neurology*, 39(2), 1997, pp. 169–178. Copyright © 1997. Reprinted by permission of Wiley-Liss, Inc., a subsidiary of John Wiley & Sons, Inc. **Figure 3.11:** From *Child Development*, John W. Santrock, Fig. 5.4, p. 133. Copyright © McGraw-Hill Companies Inc. Reprinted with permission. **Figure 3.13:** From John W. Santrock, *Adolescence*, 9e, Fig. 3.11, p. 91. Copyright © The McGraw-Hill Companies, Inc. Reprinted with permission. **Figure 3.14:** After data presented by the National Center for Health Statistics (2000). *National Vital Statistics Reports*, Vol. 50, No. 15, Table 11, "Death Rates for 113 Selected Causes by Age in the United States, 2000." **Figure 3.15:** After Bonner, J.T. (1988). Th*e Evolution of Culture in Animals*. Copyright © 1980 by Princeton University Press. Reprinted by permission of Princeton University Press. **Figure 3.16:** From John W. Santrock, *Psychology*, 7e. Copyright © The McGraw-Hill Companies, Inc. Reprinted with permission. **Figure 3.17:** From John W. Santrock, *Children*, 7e, Fig. 3.14. Copyright © The McGraw-Hill Companies, Inc. Reprinted with permission.

Chapter 4

Figure 4.6: From John W. Santrock, *Life-Span Development*, 9e, Fig. 8.11, p. 248. Copyright © The McGraw-Hill Companies, Inc. Reprinted with permission. **Figure 4.7:** After data from Dempster, 1981, "Memory Span: Sources of Individual Variation and Developmental Differences," *Psychological Bulletin*, 89, pp. 63–100. **Figure 4.8:** From John W. Santrock, *Psychology*, 7e, Fig. 8.8, p. 314. Copyright © The McGraw-Hill Companies, Inc. Reprinted with permission. **Figure 4.9:** From John W. Santrock , *Child Development*, 10e. Copyright © The McGraw-Hill Companies Inc. Reprinted with permission. **Figure 4.10:** From H. Lee Swanson, "What Develops in Working Memory? A Life Span Perspective" in *Developmental Psychology*, July 1999, 35, 4, 986–1000. Copyright © 1999 by the American Psychological Association. Reprinted with permission. **Figure 4.12:** From Zimmerman, Bonner & Kovach, *Developing Self-Regulated Learners: Beyond Achievement to Self-Efficacy (Psychology in the Classroom)*, 1996, p. 11, figure 1. Copyright © 1996 by the American Psychological Association. Reprinted with permission. **Figure 4.13:** From John W. Santrock, *Children*, 5e. Copyright © The McGraw-Hill Companies, Inc. Reprinted with permission. **Figure 4.15:** From John W. Santrock, *Psychology*, 7e, Fig. 10.5, p. 405. Copyright © The McGraw-Hill Companies, Inc. Reprinted with permission. **Figure 4.16:** From "The Increase in IQ Scores from 1932 to 1997" by Dr. Ulric Neisser. Reprinted with permission. **Figure 4.17:** "Raven Standard Progressive Matrices," F-A5. Reprinted by permission of J. C. Raven Ltd.

Chapter 5

Figure 5.2: From John W. Santrock, *Psychology*, 7e, Fig. 12.9, p. 494. Copyright © The McGraw-Hill Companies, Inc. Reprinted with permission.

Figure 5.3: From Harter, S. (1999). *The Construction of The Self*, Table 6.1. New York: The Guilford Press. Reprinted with permission. **Figure 5.5:** From John W. Santrock, *Educational Psychology*, 2e, Fig. 3.7. Copyright © The McGraw-Hill Companies, Inc. Reprinted with permission. **Figure 5.6:** From John W. Santrock, *Psychology*, 7e, Fig. 12.11, p. 499. Copyright © The McGraw-Hill Companies, Inc. Reprinted with permission. **Figure 5.7:** From Wachs, T.D. (1994). "Fit, Context and the Transition Between Temperament and Personality." In C. Halverson, G. Kohnstamm, & R. Martin (Eds.), *The Developing Structure of Personality from Infancy to Adulthood*, pp. 209–222. Hillsdale, N.J.: L. Erlbaum Associates, 1994.

Chapter 6

Figure 6.2: Based on data from Janet S. Hyde et al, "Gender Differences in Mathematics Performance: A Meta-Analysis," *Psychological Bulletin*, 107: 139, 155, 1990. Copyright © 1990 by the American Psychological Association. **Figure 6.5:** L.J. Sax, A.W. Astin, W.S. Korn, K.M. Mahony, 1999. *The American Freshman: National Norms for Fall 1999*. Higher Education Research Institute, UCLA. Reprinted with permission.

Chapter 7

Figure 7.4: From John W. Santrock, *Psychology*, 7e, Fig. 11.9, p. 444. Copyright © The McGraw-Hill Companies, Inc. Reprinted with permission. **Figure 7.6:** Reproduced with permission of The Alan Guttmacher Institute from Darroch JE et al., "Teenage Sexual and Reproductive Behavior in Developed Countries: Can More Progress Be Made?" *Occasional Report*, New York: The Alan Guttmacher Institute, 2001. **Figure 7.7:** National Center for Health Statistics, "Birth to Teenagers in the United States, 1940–2000, *National Vital Statistics Report*, Vol. 49, No. 10. **Figure 7.9:** Fisher, B.S., Cullen, F.T., & Turner, M.G. (2000). *The Sexual Victimization of College Women*. Washington, DC: National Institute of Justice, Exhibit 8, p. 19.

Chapter 8

Figure 8.1: From R.S. Selman, "Social-Cognitive Understanding," in Thomas Lickona (Ed.) *Moral Development and Behavior*, 1976. Reprinted with permission. **Figure 8.2:** From L. Kohlberg, 1969, "Stage and Sequence: The Cognitive-Developmental Approach to Socialization," in D.A. Goslin (Ed.), *Handbook of Socialization Theory and Research*. Chicago: Rand McNally. Reprinted with permission from David Goslin. **Figure 8.3:** From Colby, et al., 1983, "A Longitudinal Study of Moral Judgment," *Monographs for the Society for Research in Child Development*, Serial #201. Copyright © Society for Research in Child Development. Reprinted with permission of the Society for Research in Child Development. **Figure 8.4:** From Yussen, S. "Characteristics of Moral Dilemmas Written by Adolescents," *Developmental Psychology*, 13, pp. 162–163, 1977.

Copyright © 1977 by the American Psychological Association. Reprinted with permission. **Figure 8.5:** Data from Dey, et al. *The American Freshman: National Norms for Fall 1992*; A. W. Astin, et al. *The American Freshman: National Norms for Fall 1993*; A. W. Astin, et al. *The American Freshman: Norms for Fall 1994*. All works © Higher Education Research Institute, UCLA. Reprinted with permission. **Figure 8.6:** From John W. Santrock, *Adolescence*, 8e. Copyright © The McGraw-Hill Companies, Inc. Reprinted with permission.

Chapter 9

Figure 9.1: (art) From Belsky, J. (1981). "Early Human Experience: A Family Perspective." *Developmental Psychology*, 17, 3–23. Copyright © 1981 by the American Psychological Association. Reprinted with permission. **Figure 9.4:** From John W. Santrock, *Children*, Fig. 11.5, p. 306. Copyright © The McGraw-Hill Companies, Inc. Reprinted with permission. **Figure 9.5:** From John W. Santrock, *Child Development*, 10e, Fig. 15.6, p. 495. Copyright © The McGraw-Hill Companies Inc. Reprinted with permission. **Figure 9.6:** After data presented by Fuligni & Pedersen (2002), Figure 1. "Family Obligation and the Transition to Young Adulthood." *Developmental Psychology*, 38, 856–868. Copyright © 2002 by the American Psychological Association. Adapted with permission.

Chapter 10

Figure 10.1: After data presented by Berndt, T. (1979) "Developmental Changes In Conformity To Peers and Parents." *Developmental Psychology*, 15, 608–616. **Figure 10.2:** Based on data from Asarnow, J. & Callan, J. (1985). "Boys With Peer Adjustment Problems: Social Cognitive Processes." *Journal of Consulting and Clinical Psychology*, 53, 80–87. Copyright © 1985 by the American Psychological Association. **Figure 10.4:** From John W. Santrock, *Life-Span Development*, 9e, Fig. 13.4, p. 414. Copyright © The McGraw-Hill Companies, Inc. Reprinted with permission. **Figure 10.5:** From Dexter C. Dunphy, "The Social Structure of Urban Adolescent Peer Groups," *Sociometry*, Vol. 26, 1963. American Sociological Association, Washington, DC. **Figure 10.6:** From "Romantic Development: Does Age at Which Romantic Involvement Starts Matter?" by Duane Burhmester, April 2001. Paper presented at the meeting of the Society for Research in Child Development, Minneapolis, MN. Reprinted with permission.

Chapter 11

Figure 11.2: From Alexander, W. M. & McEwin, C. K. (1989). *Schools In the Middle: Status and Progress*. Columbus, OH: National Middle School Association. Used with permission of National Middle School Association. **Figure 11.3:** From John W. Santrock, *Life-Span Development*, 9e, Fig. 12.9. Copyright © The McGraw-Hill Companies,

Inc. Reprinted with permission. **Figure 11.4:** Copyright The Carnegie Foundation for the Advancement of Teaching. Reprinted by permission. **Figure 11.5:** From Nansel, et al., 2001, "Bullying Behaviors Among U.S. Youth," *Journal of the American Medical Association*, Vol. 285, pp. 2094–2100. **Figure 11.6:** From "To Assure the Free Appropriate Public Education of All Children With Disabilities," U.S. Department of Education, 2000.

Chapter 12

Figure 12.1: From J. Brophy, *Motivating Students to Learn*. Copyright © 1998 by McGraw-Hill College Division. Reprinted with permission. **Figure 12.2:** From B. Weiner in *Human Motivation: Metaphors, Theories and Research*. Copyright © 1992 by Sage Publications, Inc. Reprinted by permission of Sage Publications, Inc. **Figure 12.3:** From Deborah Stipek, *Motivation to Learn: Integrating Theory and Practice*, 4e. Copyright © 2002. Published by Allyn & Bacon, Boston, MA. Reprinted by permission of the publisher. **Figure 12.4:** After data presented by UNICEF Innocenti Research Center, Florence, Italy (2002). **Figure 12.5:** Reprinted with permission from Stevenson, Lee & Stigler, 1986, Figure 6, "Mathematics Achievement of Chinese, Japanese and American Children," *Science*, Vol. 231, pp. 693–699. Copyright © 1986 AAAS. **Figure 12.6:** From J. Brophy, *Motivating Students to Learn*. Copyright © 1998 by McGraw-Hill College Division. Reprinted with permission. **Figure 12.7:** After data presented by the National Center for Educational Statistics (2002), *Contexts of Postsecondary Education: Learning Opportunities*. Washington, DC: U.S. Department of Education. **Figure 12.8:** Reproduced by special permission of the publisher, Psychological Assessment Resources, Inc. from *Making Vocational Choices*. Copyright 1973, 1985 by Psychological Assessment Resource, Inc. All rights reserved. **Figure 12.9:** After data presented by Skorikov, V., & Vondracek, F. (1998). Table 3 from "Vocational Identity Development," in *Journal of Career Assessment*, 6 (No. 1) Winter. p. 453 "I Am Woman" by Helen Reddy and Ray Burton. © Copyright 1971 by Irving Music, Inc. on behalf of itself and Buggerlugs Music Co./BMI. Used by Permission. International Copyright Secured. All Rights Reserved.

Chapter 13

Figure 13.1: Larson, R.W. (2001), Table 1. "How U.S. Children and Adolescents Spend Time: What It Does (and Doesn't) Tell Us About Their Development. Current Directions" In *Psychological Science*, 10e, 160–164. Blackwell Publishing. Reprinted with permission. **Figure 13.4:** Adapted from Roberts, D.F. & Foehr, U.G. (2003, in press). *Kids and Media in America: Patterns of Use At the Millennium*. New York: Cambridge University Press. Reprinted with the permission of Cambridge University Press. **Figure 13.5:** From John W. Santrock, *Child Development*, 10e, Fig. 18.7, p. 598. Copyright

© The McGraw-Hill Companies Inc. Reprinted with permission. **Figure 13.6:** Roberts, D.F., Henriksen, L., & Christenson, P.G. (1999). *Substance Use in Popular Movies and Music*. Washington, DC: Office of National Drug Control Policy. **Figure 13.7:** After data presented by the Kaiser Family Foundation (2001). *Generation Rx.com: How Young People Use the Internet for Health Information*. Menlo Park, CA: The Henry J. Kaiser Family Foundation. **Figure 13.8:** From Roberts, D.F. & Foehr, U.G. (2003). *Kids and Media in America: Patterns of Use At the Millennium*, p. 39. New York: Cambridge University Press.

Chapter 14

p. 502 "Desert Places" from *The Poetry of Robert Frost* edited by Edward Connery Lathem. Copyright 1936 by Robert Frost, © 1964 by Lesley Frost Ballantine, © 1969 by Henry Holt and Company. Reprinted by permission of Henry Holt and Company, LLC. **Figure 14.1:** From Edelbrock, "Behavioral Problems and Parents of Normal and Disturbed Children Aged Four Through Sixteen," *Monographs for the Society for Research in Child Development*, #188. Copyright © Society for Research in Child Development. Reprinted with permission of the Society for Research in Child Development. **Figure 14.2:** Masten, A. S. & Coatsworth, J. D. (1998) "The Development of Competence In Favorable and Unfavorable Environments: A Tale of Resources, Risk and Resilience." *American Psychologist*, 53, 205–220. Copyright © 1998 by the American Psychological Association. Reprinted with permission. **Figure 14.3:** From Johnson, L.D., O'Malley, P.M., & Bachman, J.G., 2001, "The Monitoring of the Future: National Results on Adolescent Drug Use," Washington, DC: National Institute on Drug Abuse. **Figures 14.5, 14.6:** Johnston, L., O'Malley & Bachman, G. (2003). *Monitoring the Future National Results on Adolescent Drug Use: Overview of Key Findings 2002*. Bethesda, MD: National Institute on Drug Use. **Figure 14.7:** from John W. Santrock, *Psychology 7e*. Copyright © The McGraw-Hill Companies, Inc. Reprinted with permission. **Figure 14.8:** After data presented by Bachman et al. (1996). "Transitions In Drug Use During Late Adolescence and Young Adulthood," in J.A. Graber, J. Brooks-Gunn, & A.C. Peterson (Eds.) *Transitions Through Adolescence*. Mahwah, NJ: Erlbaum. **Figure 14.9:** From John W. Santrock, *Child Development 9e*. Copyright © The McGraw-Hill Companies, Inc. Reprinted with permission. **Figure 14.10:** From John W. Santrock, *Children 7e*. Copyright © The McGraw-Hill Companies, Inc. Reprinted with permission. **Figure 14.11:** Data from Center for Disease Control & Prevention, *Adolescent Chartbook 2000*, U.S. Department of Health and Human Statistics. **Figure 14.12:** After data presented by the National Center for Health Statistics (2002). "Prevalence of Overweight Among Children and Adolescents: United States 1999–2000." Table 71 from *Health, United States*, 2002.

PHOTO CREDITS

Section Openers

1: © David Young-Wolff/Stone/Getty Images; **2:** © Steve Prezant/CORBIS/The Stock Market; **3:** © Richard Hutchings/Photo Edit; **4:** © Butch Martin/The Image Bank/Getty Images; **5:** © Penny Tweedie/Stone/Getty Images

Chapter 1

Opener: © George Disario/CORBIS/The Stock Market; **p. 6 (top & bottom):** © AP/Wide World Photos; **p. 8 (top):** © Archives of the History of American Psychology, University of Akron, Akron, Ohio; **p. 8 (bottom):** Courtesy of the Institute for Intercultural Studies, Inc., New York; **p. 10a:** © Stock Montage; **p. 10b:** © Syndicated Features Limited/The Image Works; **p. 10c:** © Joe Monroe/Photo Researchers; **p. 10d:** © Jean-Claude Lejeune; **p. 10e:** © Roger Dollarhide; **p. 11:** © Archives of the History of American Psychology, University of Akron, OH; **p. 12:** © PhotoDisc website; **p. 16:** Courtesy of Peter Benson, Search Institute; **p. 18 (left):** © AFP/CORBIS; **p. 18 (middle):** © Dain Gair Photographic/Index Stock; **p. 18 (right):** © AP/Wide World Photos; **p. 22 (left to right):** Courtesy of Landrum Shettles; John Santrock; © Joe Sohm/Chromosohm Media/The Image Works; © CORBIS website; © James L. Shaffer; © Vol. 155/CORBIS; © CORBIS website; © CORBIS website; **p. 23 (left):** © Bill Aron/Photo Edit; **p. 23 (right):** © Marleen Ferguson/Photo Edit; **p. 25:** © Chuck Savage/Corbis/The Stock Market; **p. 31:** © M. Regine/The Image Bank/Getty Images; **p. 32:** Courtesy of Luis Vargas

Chapter 2

Opener: © PhotoDisc web site; **p. 48:** © Bettmann/CORBIS; **p. 49:** © Barton Silverman/NYT Pictures; **p. 50 (left):** © Bettmann/CORBIS; **p. 50 (right):** Courtesy of Nancy Chodorow, photo by Jean Margolis; **p. 52** © Sarah Putnam/Index Stock Imagery; **p. 53** © Yves Debraine/Black Star/Stock Photo; **p. 54:** © A.R. Lauria/Dr. Michael Cole, Laboratory of Human Cognition; **p. 56:** © Nita Winter; **p. 57:** Courtesy of Cornell University, Dept. of Human Development and Family Services; **p. 61:** © Michael Newman/Photo Edit; **p. 63a:** © David Grubin Productions, Inc. Reprinted by permission; **p. 63b:** Image courtesy of Dana Boatman, Ph.D., Department of Neurology, John Hopkins University. Reprinted with permission from *The Secret Life of the Brain*, © 2001 by the National Academy of Sciences. Courtesy of the National Academies Press, Washington, D.C.; **p. 67:** © McGraw-Hill Higher Education/photographer, John Thoeming; **p. 70:** Courtesy of Pamela Trotman Reid; **p. 71 (left):** © Syndicated Features Limited/The Image Works; **p. 71 (right):** © Thomas Craig/Index Stock

Chapter 3

Opener: © Ariel Skelley/CORBIS/The Stock Market; **p. 86:** © David Young-Wolff/Photo Edit; **p. 91:** © Jon Feingerssh/CORBIS/The Stock Market; **p. 93:** Courtesy of Anne Peterson, W K Kellogg Foundation; **p. 97:** Courtesy of Dr. Harry Chugani, Children's Hospital of Michigan; **p. 101:** © Tom Stewart/CORBIS/Stock Market; **p. 102:** © Rob Lewine Photography/CORBIS/The Stock Market; **p. 109:** © Tony Freeman/Photo Edit

Chapter 4

Opener: © Mug Shots/CORBIS/The Stock Market; **p. 123:** © Paul Fusco/Magnum Photos; **p. 124:** © Richard Hutchings/Photo Researchers; **p. 125:** © David Young-Wolff/Photo Edit; **p. 126:** © Paul Conklin; **p. 128:** © Yves deBraine/Black Star/Stock Photo; **p. 130:** © Elizabeth Crews/The Image Works; **p. 131:** © David Young-Wolff/Photo Edit; **p. 133 (left):** © A.R. Lauria/Dr. Michael Cole, Laboratory of Human Cognition; **p. 133 (right):** © Bettmann/CORBIS; **p. 135:** © Mug Shots/CORBIS/The Stock Market; **p. 140:** Courtesy of Laura Bickford; **p. 141:** © Cognition & Technology Group, LTC, Peabody College, Vanderbilt University; **p. 157 (top):** Stewart Cohen/Stone/Getty Images; **p. 157 (bottom):** © Mary Kate Denny/Photo Edit

Chapter 5

Opener: © Dominic Rouse/The Image Bank/Getty Images; **p. 177:** © CORBIS website; **p. 179:** © Bettmann/CORBIS; **p. 184:** © USA Today Library, photo by Robert Deutsch

Chapter 6

Opener: © David Young-Wolff/Photo Edit; **p. 207 (top):** © Vol. DV379 Digital Vision/Getty Images; **p. 207 (bottom):** © David Young Wolff/Photo Edit; **p. 218:** © Reuters NewMedia Inc./CORBIS; **p. 220:** © Tony Freeman/Photo Edit; **p. 222:** © Keith Carter Photography

Chapter 7

Opener: © SuperStock; **p. 232:** © Joel Gordon 1995; **p. 234:** © Lawrence Migdale/Stock Boston; **p. 237:** © Peter Correz/Stone/Getty Images; **p. 241:** © Marilyn Humphries; **p. 243:** © Bernard Gotfryd/Woodfin Camp & Associates; **p. 244:** © Michael Ray; **p. 249:** © Dana Fineman; **p. 251:** Courtesy of Lynn Blankinship; **p. 252:** © 1998 Frank Fournier; **p. 261:** © James D. Wilson/Woodfin Camp & Associates; **p. 262:** © SuperStock; **p. 264 (top):** © Steve Skjold/Photo Edit; **p. 264 (bottom):** © Michael Newman/Photo Edit

Chapter 8

Opener: © Mark Richards/Photo Edit; **p. 272:** © David R. Frazier Photolibrary; **p. 279:** © Reuters/New Media, Inc./CORBIS; **p. 281:** © Raghu-Rai/Magnum Photos; **p. 291:** © Ronald Cortes; **p. 292:** © Penney Tweedie/Stone/Getty Images; **p. 293:** Courtesy

Name Index

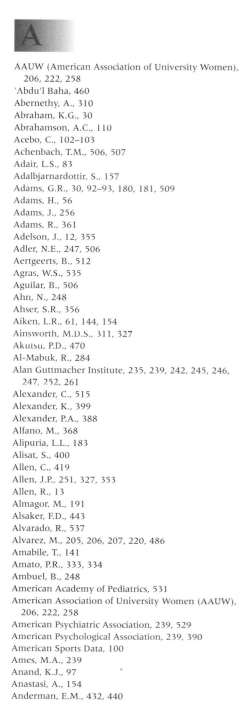

Subject Index